STANWAY:

AN ÉLITE BURIAL SITE AT CAMULODUNUM

BRITANNIA MONOGRAPH SERIES NO. 24

Published by the Society for the Promotion of Roman Studies
Senate House, Malet Street, London WC1E 7HU

This monograph was published with the aid of a grant from
English Heritage

Copies may be obtained from the Secretary of the Roman Society

© Copyright Society for the Promotion of Roman Studies 2007

British Library Catalogue in Publication Data
A catalogue record for this book is available from the British Library

ISBN 978 0 907764 35 9

Front cover illustration: Doctor's burial CF47: Lisa Hepi excavating the game board
Back cover illustration: the game board as uncovered (apart from the corner-piece in the top
                                                    right-hand corner, which had been removed for conservation and
                                                    then temporarily replaced for the photograph)

Printed by 4Word Ltd, Bristol BS13 7TT

Printed in England

CONTENTS

	Page
List of Figures	viii
List of Tables	xiii
Acknowledgements	xvi
List of Contributors	xvii
Summary	xviii

CHAPTER 1: INTRODUCTION AND BACKGROUND

The Stanway site	1
History of the excavations	1
Simplified chronology and key features	7
Explanation of the site codes and small find numbers	14
Introduction to the Late Iron Age and Roman pottery in this report	14
Definition of terms used in the report	15

CHAPTER 2: FEATURES AND FINDS PRE-DATING THE MIDDLE IRON AGE FARMSTEAD

The earliest occupation	16
The earlier prehistoric pottery (Nigel Brown)	17
The scatter of heat-affected stone across the site	18
The worked flint (Hazel Martingell)	21

CHAPTER 3: THE MIDDLE IRON AGE FARMSTEAD

The farmstead enclosure (Enclosure 2)	26
The currency bars (Richard Hingley)	33
The structural clay	36
The loomweights	38
The other objects from Enclosures 1 and 2	45
The latest material from Enclosure 2	47
The Early and Middle Iron Age pottery (Paul R. Sealey)	48
Palaeochannel CF52 and its finds	66

CHAPTER 4: THE FUNERARY SITE

The funerary enclosures	69
Funerary Enclosure 1	69
Funerary Enclosure 3	71
Funerary Enclosure 4	74
Funerary Enclosure 5	81
The pyre-site and ?mortuary enclosures	85
Pyre-site BF1/BF16	85
?Mortuary enclosure BF32	90
?Mortuary enclosure CF43–46	97
The chambers	101
Chamber AF25	101

Chamber BF6	104
Chamber BF24	127
Chamber CF42	142

Pits with pyre debris — 157

Pit BF17	157
Pit CF7	160

Pit with broken funerary goods — 162

Pit AF48	162

The cremation burials — 167

Cremation burial AF18	167
Examination of a bag of ?verdigris from AF18 (S. La Niece and C.R. Cartwright)	169
The Warrior's burial BF64	170
The Inkwell burial BF67	197
The Doctor's burial CF47	201
The Brooches burial CF72	254
The Mirror burial CF115	260
Cremation burial CF403	262
The shaft or pit CF23	265
The slot or trench CF96	266

CHAPTER 5: THE SPECIALISTS' REPORTS AND DISCUSSIONS

The Late Iron Age and Roman pottery fabrics (Stephen Benfield)	268
The pots from funerary contexts and pyre debris in pits (Valery Rigby)	271
The Late Iron Age and Roman pottery from the enclosure ditches and the mortuary enclosures BF32 and CF43–6 (Stephen Benfield)	274
The potters' stamps on *terra rubra*, *terra nigra* and *terra nigra*-type wares (Valery Rigby)	289
The amphoras (Paul R. Sealey)	297
The samian (G.B. Dannell)	305
The graffiti from the chamber BF6 (Paul R. Sealey)	307
The brooches (Nina Crummy)	314
The metal vessels (Nina Crummy)	320
Analysis of the currency bars, grave goods and pyre debris (Sarah Paynter)	327
The Iron Age and Roman coins (John A. Davies)	338
The glass vessels (H.E.M. Cool)	340
Textiles (John Peter Wild)	347
A scientific examination of the textile impressions in iron corrosion products on surgical instruments CF47.30 and CF47.35 (N.D. Meeks and C.R. Cartwright)	350
The gaming board in CF47: the remains as found, possible reconstructions, and post-depositional movements (Philip Crummy)	352
The Doctor's game – new light on the history of ancient board games (Ulrich Schädler)	359
The salt briquetage (Nina Crummy)	375

The environmental and faunal remains

The cremated human remains (S.A. Mays)	377
The faunal remains (Alec Wade and A.J. Legge)	382
The plant macrofossils (Peter Murphy and Val Fryer)	384
The wood and leather remains (Anne-Maria Bojko and Nina Crummy)	388
Palynological analysis of the organic material lodged in the spout of the strainer bowl (Patricia E.J. Wiltshire)	394
The palynological analysis of the palaeoturf forming the collapsed mound in the chamber CF42 (Patricia E.J. Wiltshire)	398

CHAPTER 6: EXCAVATIONS ON SITE D IN 2002–3

Introduction 400
The excavation 400
The cremation burials 402
Pits with pyre-related debris 410
Pits with charcoal-rich fill but no cremated bone, pottery or other artefacts 413
Other features 416

Specialists' reports
**Discussion of the Late Iron Age and Roman pottery from
 Site D** (Stephen Benfield and Valery Rigby) 418
The cremated bone from Site D (S.A. Mays) 418
The charred plant macrofossils and other remains from Site D (Val Fryer) 420
The worked flint from Site D (Hazel Martingell) 422

CHAPTER 7: ASPECTS OF THE STANWAY CEMETERY

Introduction 423
Aspects of the physical remains 424
    Symmetry and organisation of the funerary enclosures 424
    Chambers: structure, mounds and broken grave goods 424
    Pyres and pits with pyre debris 426
    ?Mortuary enclosures 427
    Cremation burials: covers, depths, character and presence or absence of a service 427
    Grave goods: social status and function 428
    Broken funerary goods as indicators of ritual 430
    Weights of the cremated human bone 433
    Cremated animal bone: horse and other remains 434
    Residual pottery: indicator of early episodes of pot-breaking? 434
Sequence and chronology 435
    The Middle Iron Age farmstead 435
    The funerary enclosures and associated contexts 436
    Refined sequence and dating for Enclosures 3, 4 and 5 438
Stanway in local and wider contexts 444
    Familial relationships between the dead 444
    The identities of the 'Doctor' and the 'Warrior' (Nina Crummy) 444
    Similar funerary sites 447
    Continuity and the Catuvellauni 455

BIBLIOGRAPHY 457

INDEX (Nina Crummy) 485

LIST OF FIGURES

		Page
Frontispiece	Impression of the graveside ceremony for the Warrior's burial. Image © Peter Froste and Colchester Archaeological Trust.	
Fig. 1	The Stanway site in relation to Camulodunum and the Roman town and its regional location.	2
Fig. 2	Overall site plan.	between 2–3
Fig. 3	The Stanway site in relation to the Iron Age and Roman archaeology at Gosbecks.	3
Fig. 4	Site areas (A–E) and areas of excavation.	4
Fig. 5	Phase 1 and earlier.	8
Fig. 6	Phase 2: second half of the 1st century B.C.	9
Fig. 7	Phase 3: mid 1st century A.D.	10
Fig. 8	Phase 4: mid 1st century A.D.	11
Fig. 9	Stanway: aerial view of cropmarks.	12
Fig. 10	Features pre-dating Enclosure 2: sections and profiles.	16
Fig. 11	Neolithic and Bronze Age pottery.	18
Fig. 12	Distribution of burnt stones by weight.	19
Fig. 13	?Iron Age worked flints.	22
Fig. 14	Enclosure 2 ditch: sections and plan showing location of currency bar hoard and pit CF415.	27
Fig. 15	Boundary ditch CF137/AF59: sections; Enclosure 2 ditch AF32: section; Enclosure 2 pits: sections.	28
Fig. 16	Enclosure 2 pits: sections and profiles.	29
Fig. 17	Interpretative plan of the layout of Enclosure 2.	31
Fig. 18	Pits outside Enclosure 2: sections and profiles.	32
Fig. 19	Iron currency bars from the Enclosure 2 ditch.	34
Fig. 20	Enclosure 2 ditch CF6: iron currency bars *in situ*.	35
Fig. 21	Loomweights from pit CF21.	39
Fig. 22	Loomweights from pit CF21.	41
Fig. 23	Loomweights from pits AF22 and AF38 and structural clay from pit CF21.	42
Fig. 24	Finds of stone (CF171.1) and iron (CF250.1–2) from Enclosure 2.	46
Fig. 25	Early and Middle Iron Age pottery: numbers 1–26.	64
Fig. 26	Middle Iron Age pottery: numbers 27–55.	65
Fig. 27	Iron spearheads from the palaeochannel.	67
Fig. 28	Enclosure 1 ditch: sections.	70
Fig. 29	Enclosure 1: copper-alloy brooch spring fragments from the ploughsoil.	71
Fig. 30	Enclosure 3 entrance: plan, ditch sections with fragment of glass vessel BF4.1 from the ditch and pit profiles.	72
Fig. 31	Enclosure 4 ditch: sections, pit profiles and pottery counter from the enclosure ditch.	74
Fig. 32	Enclosure 5 ditch: sections and objects of copper alloy and iron from the enclosure ditches.	84

LIST OF FIGURES

Fig. 33	Pyre-site BF1/BF16: objects of copper alloy (BF1.1–4 and BL.1–2) and iron (BF1.5).	89
Fig. 34	Enclosure 4 ?mortuary enclosure BF32, viewed from the south.	91
Fig. 35	?Mortuary enclosure BF32: plan, ditch sections, pit profiles, and copper-alloy objects and briquetage (BF30.2).	96
Fig. 36	?Mortuary enclosure CF43–46: plan, ditch and pit sections, and briquetage sherd.	99
Fig. 37	Enclosure 5 ?mortuary enclosure CF43–6, viewed from the north.	99
Fig. 38	Chamber AF25, half-section, viewed from the south-east.	101
Fig. 39	Chamber AF25: plan and section.	102
Fig. 40	Chamber AF25: pottery vessels and copper-alloy find.	103
Fig. 41	Chamber BF6, half-section, viewed from the south.	105
Fig. 42	Chamber BF6, fully excavated, viewed from the south.	105
Fig. 43	Chamber BF6 and pyre site BF1/BF16: plan.	106
Fig. 44	Chamber BF6: sections and profiles.	107
Fig. 45	Chamber BF6 and pyre site: BF1/BF16: plan showing location of small finds and decayed wooden planks.	108
Fig. 46	Chamber BF6: plan showing extent of collapsed mound and location of finds in mound material.	109
Fig. 47	Chamber BF6: plan showing location of cremated bone, decayed wood, and small finds on the chamber floor.	111
Fig. 48	Chamber BF6: plan showing location of sherds from pottery vessels BF6.1–5.	112
Fig. 49	Chamber BF6: plan showing location of sherds from pottery vessels BF6.6–12 and BF6.20–21.	113
Fig. 50	Chamber BF6: plan showing location of sherds from pottery vessels BF6.13–19.	114
Fig. 51	Chamber BF6: plan showing location of sherds from amphoras BF6.22–3.	115
Fig. 52	Chamber BF6: plan showing location of cremated bone, decayed wood, and small finds from above the chamber floor.	116
Fig. 53	Chamber BF6: detail plan of roof timbers.	118
Fig. 54	Chamber BF6: pottery vessels and amphoras.	124
Fig. 55	Chamber BF6: objects of copper alloy (BF6.24–29 and BF6.31–33) and iron (BF6.30).	125
Fig. 56	Chamber BF24: plan and section.	128
Fig. 57	Chamber BF24: isometric plan of chamber pit with traces of wood plank lining and nails.	129
Fig. 58	Chamber BF24: vertical finds distributions plotted against section for bone and pottery.	130
Fig. 59	Chamber BF24, fully excavated, viewed from the north.	131
Fig. 60	Chamber BF24: plan showing location of sherds from pottery vessels BF24.1–4 and BF24.5–7.	132
Fig. 61	Chamber BF24: plan showing location of sherds from pottery vessels BF24.8–11 and BF24.12–16.	133
Fig. 62	Chamber BF24: plan showing location of sherds from pottery vessels BF24.17–18 and BF24.19–21.	134
Fig. 63	Chamber BF24: pottery vessels BF24.1–22 and glass vessel BF24.23.	138
Fig. 64	Chamber BF24: glass beads (BF24.24a, BF24.24c–d), silver collars (BF24.25) and horn plaques (BF24.26a–c).	141
Fig. 65	Chamber CF42: plan of chamber pit after excavation.	143
Fig. 66	Chamber CF42: plan showing remains of wooden chamber and nails.	144
Fig. 67	Chamber CF42: isometric plan of the chamber pit showing the positions of the nails and the traces of decayed wood.	144

Fig. 68	Chamber CF42: sections.	145
Fig. 69	Chamber CF42: plan showing remains of wooden chamber and nails.	146
Fig. 70	CF42: plans showing location of sherds from pottery vessels CF42.1–9.	147
Fig. 71	Chamber CF42: plans showing location of residual sherds from pottery vessels 42.a–g and location of sherds from glass vessels CF42.11–13.	148
Fig. 72	Chamber CF42: plan showing location of small finds CF42.14–17.	149
Fig. 73	Chamber CF42: pottery vessels CF42.1 and CF42.6–9, glass vessels CF42.11–12, glass gaming counter (CF42.14), copper-alloy spoon (CF42.15), studs with glass head and metal shank (CF42.16a–c), and iron object (CF42.17).	155
Fig. 74	Pit with pyre debris BF17: finds of iron (BF17.1 and BF17.3) and copper alloy (BF17.2).	159
Fig. 75	Pit with pyre debris CF7: plan showing location of finds and section, pottery vessel, copper-alloy brooch (CF7.2), and iron object (CF7.3).	161
Fig. 76	Pit with broken funerary goods AF48: plan showing location of finds.	163
Fig. 77	Pit with broken funerary goods AF48: pottery vessel AF48.2, and objects of iron (AF48.3a–d), and copper alloy (AF48.4).	164
Fig. 78	Pit with broken funerary goods AF48: detailed illustration of remains of ?box AF48.3.	166
Fig. 79	Cremation burial AF18: plan showing location of finds, pottery vessel, and find of bag of ?verdigris.	168
Fig. 80	Warrior's burial BF64: plan showing location of finds.	between 171–2
Fig. 81	Warrior's burial: BF64 pottery vessels BF64.1–14, and amphora (BF64.15).	174
Fig. 82	Detail of crane pot BF64.14.	175
Fig. 83	Warrior's burial BF64: glass vessels BF64.16–18, copper-alloy brooches BF64.19–20, maker's name stamp on the Nertomarus brooch (BF64.19).	177
Fig. 84	Warrior's burial BF64: copper armlet BF64.21 and glass bead BF64.22.	179
Fig. 85	Warrior's burial BF64: shield boss BF64.23a.	182
Fig. 86	Warrior's burial BF64: ?part of shield boss BF64.23b, iron spearhead BF64.24a, and iron bands with fragments of wooden shaft BF64.24b.	183
Fig. 87	Warrior's burial BF64: copper-alloy jug BF64.25 and handled basin BF64.26.	185
Fig. 88	Warrior's burial BF64: fragment probably from a copper-alloy vessel BF64.27.	186
Fig. 89	Warrior's burial BF64: glass gaming counters BF64.28.	187
Fig. 90	Warrior's burial BF64: copper-alloy drop handles BF64.29a–b and handle attachments BF24.29c–d from the gaming board with part of the wooden board itself.	188
Fig. 91	Warrior's burial BF64: copper-alloy junction bindings BF64.29e–f and corner binding BF64.29g from the gaming board with part of the wooden board itself.	189
Fig. 92	Warrior's burial BF64: iron fittings from box (north-west area of burial pit) BF64.30a–d and 30g.	192
Fig. 93	Warrior's burial BF64: iron fittings from box (south-west area of burial pit) BF64.31a–b.	194
Fig. 94	Warrior's burial BF64: iron fittings from box (south-west area of burial pit) BF64.31c–d.	195
Fig. 95	Warrior's burial BF64: miscellaneous metal objects of copper alloy BF64.32–34 and iron BF64.35.	196
Fig. 96	Inkwell burial BF67: plan and profile.	198
Fig. 97	Inkwell burial BF67: pottery vessels BF67.1–2, copper-alloy brooch BF67.3, and selected decorated copper-alloy studs and sheet BF67.4a, c and f.	200
Fig. 98	Doctor's burial CF47: plan showing location of finds.	203

LIST OF FIGURES

Fig. 99	Doctor's burial CF47: plan showing burial pit after excavation with location of profiles 1–4, and plan locating detail Figs 100–1.	204
Fig. 100	Doctor's burial CF47: detail plan of finds at west end of grave.	205
Fig. 101	Doctor's burial CF47: detail plan of objects stacked on north side of grave, copper-alloy saucepan (CF47.21), samian bowl (CF47.1) and copper-alloy strainer bowl (CF47.22), showing remains of oak cover (CF47.41) (above), and pottery flagon (CF47.12) and remains of decorated wooden ?tray (CF47.25) (below).	206
Fig. 102	Doctor's burial CF47: plan showing the locations of the organic remains on the upper surfaces of objects at the west end of the grave.	between 206–7
Fig. 103	Doctor's burial CF47: plan showing the locations of the organic remains on the lower surfaces of objects at the west end of the grave.	between 206–7
Fig. 104	Doctor's burial CF47: profiles 1–4 through grave.	208
Fig. 105	Doctor's burial CF47: stages 3–4 in the deposition of the medical implements and rods on and around the gaming board.	209
Fig. 106	Doctor's burial CF47: stages 5–6 in the deposition of the medical implements and rods on and around the gaming board.	210
Fig. 107	Doctor's burial CF47: reconstruction of grave and the subsequent collapse of the wooden cover and grave goods.	211
Fig. 108	Doctor's burial CF47: samian bowl CF47.1 and potter's stamp, pottery vessels CF47.2–13, and amphora CF47.14.	214
Fig. 109	Doctor's burial CF47: copper-alloy brooches CF47.15 and 17, ring fragment CF47.16, and jet bead CF47.18.	216
Fig. 110	Doctor's burial CF47: glass gaming counters CF47.19b.	218
Fig. 111	Doctor's burial CF47: copper-alloy corner CF47.20a and hinges CF47.20b–c from the gaming board.	219
Fig. 112	Doctor's burial CF47: copper-alloy saucepan CF47.21.	221
Fig. 113	Doctor's burial CF47: copper-alloy strainer bowl CF47.22.	222
Fig. 114	Doctor's burial CF47: the copper-alloy strainer bowl *in situ*.	223
Fig. 115	Doctor's burial CF47: iron rods CF47.23a–c.	225
Fig. 116	Doctor's burial CF47: iron rod CF47.23d and copper-alloy rods CF47.23e–f.	226
Fig. 117	Doctor's burial CF47: copper-alloy rods CF47.23g–h.	227
Fig. 118	Doctor's burial CF47: the rods and rings *in situ*.	228
Fig. 119	Doctor's burial CF47: copper-alloy rings CF47.24a–h, and selection of decorated copper-alloy studs CF47.25a-f from the ?tray.	230
Fig. 120	Doctor's burial CF47: selection of decorated copper-alloy sheet fragments CF47.25g–i from the ?tray.	234
Fig. 121	Doctor's burial CF47: iron scalpels CF47.26 and 27, iron saw with composite handle CF47.28, and iron knife CF47.39.	237
Fig. 122	Doctor's burial CF47: copper-alloy combined sharp and blunt hook (double-ended retractor) CF47.29, iron combined sharp and blunt hook (double-ended retractor) CF47.30.	239
Fig. 123	Doctor's burial CF47: copper-alloy ?retractor CF47.31, copper-alloy smooth-jawed fixation forceps CF47.32, and iron forceps/ tweezers CF47.33.	241
Fig. 124	Doctor's burial CF47: iron handled needle CF47.34–36, copper-alloy scoop probe CF47.37, and copper-alloy handle CF47.38.	243
Fig. 125	Doctor's burial CF47.	246
Fig. 126	Doctor's burial CF47: vertical view of the gaming board and counters, with some of the surgical instruments, *in situ*.	247
Fig. 127	Doctor's burial CF47: the surgical instruments.	248
Fig. 128	Brooches burial CF72: plan and profile.	255

Fig. 129	Brooches burial CF72: pottery vessels CF72.1–3, glass pyxis CF72.4, copper-alloy brooches F72.5–10, glass bead CF72.11, iron shank with glass bead CF72.12, iron knife blade CF72.13, and iron ?nail shank CF72.14.	256
Fig. 130	Brooches burial CF72: annotated photograph showing shattered edge of flagon and line of possible subsoiler damage.	259
Fig. 131	Brooches burial CF72.	259
Fig. 132	Mirror burial CF115: pottery vessels CF115.1–2 and mirror fragment CF115.4.	261
Fig. 133	Cremation burial CF403: plan and profile, pottery vessels CF403.1–2, and interpretative plan showing presumed movement of a section of broken platter.	263
Fig. 134	Cremation burial CF403.	264
Fig. 135	Shaft or pit CF23: section and plan.	265
Fig. 136	Slot or trench CF96: section and rim from pottery flagon.	266
Fig. 137	Slot or trench CF96, viewed from the north.	267
Fig. 138	Distribution of pottery vessels in the ditches.	
Fig. 139	Pottery vessels from the ditches of Enclosure 1 and Enclosures 3–4: Pots 2–58.	278
Fig. 140	Pottery vessels from the ditches of Enclosure 4: Pots 59–78.	282
Fig. 141	Pottery vessels from the ditches of Enclosure 4: Pots 79–101.	284
Fig. 142	Pottery vessels from the ditches of Enclosure 4: Pots 102–110.	285
Fig. 143	Pottery vessels from the ditches of Enclosure 4: Pots 111–115 and amphora Pot 128.	286
Fig. 144	Pottery vessels from the ditches of Enclosure 5: Pots 132–143 and amphora Pot 146.	287
Fig. 145	Potters' stamps on *terra rubra*, *terra nigra* and *terra nigra*-type wares.	292
Fig. 146	Graffiti on pottery vessels from the chamber BF6: Pots BF6.1, 4, 6 and 8 (upper surface).	308
Fig. 147	Graffiti on pottery vessels from the chamber BF6: Pots BF6.8 (base), 13, 15 and 23.	309
Fig. 148	Coins: AF17.1, CF5.1, BF39.2, BF30.3, CF96.1–2.	339
Fig. 149	The amber glass bowl BF64.16 from the Warrior's burial.	342
Fig. 150	SEM images showing textile remains on the instruments CF47.30 and CF47.35 from the Doctor's burial CF47.	351
Fig. 151	Above: The counters and the remains of the gaming board in relation to a hypothetical 8 × 12 grid of 13/4 unciae squares. Below: The layout of the counters in relation to the same grid after allowing for a slight gap between the two halves of the board when folded out.	353
Fig. 152	Four possible arrangements of the counters on an 8 × 12 grid of squares before any post-depositional movements had taken place.	354
Fig. 153	Above: The counters and the remains of the gaming board in relation to a hypothetical 13 × 9 grid of squares whose width is equal to the width of the hypothetical 8 × 12 grid shown in FIG. 151. Below: The remains of the gaming board as found in relation to a hypothetical 9 × 13 grid of lines exactly 15/8 *unciae* apart.	355
Fig. 154	Two possible arrangements of the counters on an 9 × 13 grid of squares before any post-depositional movements had taken place.	359
Fig. 155	Doctor's burial CF47 strainer bowl: the proportions of artemisia to 'bee flower' pollen and that of probable adventive pollen from the plug of organic debris.	394
Fig. 156	Doctor's burial CF47 strainer bowl: the proportions of various bee flower pollens from the plug of organic debris.	394
Fig. 157	Chamber CF42: proportions of various palynological taxa present in the turf (turf 1) from the mound.	397

Fig. 158	Site D: plan.	401
Fig. 159	Cremation burial DF1: plan and section and pottery vessel DF1.1.	403
Fig. 160	Cremation burial DF26: plan and section and pottery vessels DF26.1–3.	404
Fig. 161	Cremation burial DF28: plan and profile.	406
Fig. 162	Cremation burial DF28.	407
Fig. 163	Cremation burial DF28: pottery vessels DF28.1–4, copper-alloy brooches DF28.5–7, and moulded sheet DF28.8.	408
Fig. 164	Pit with pyre debris DF3: plan and section.	410
Fig. 165	Pit with pyre debris DF7: copper-alloy brooch DF7.1.	412
Fig. 166	Area D: pit sections and profiles.	414
Fig. 167	Area D: ditch DF29 section and pit sections and profiles.	417
Fig. 168	Area D: early Mesolithic microlith.	422
Fig. 169	Conjectural reconstruction of chamber BF6.	425
Fig. 170	Speculative sequence and dates for the development of Enclosures 3–5.	442
Fig. 171	The funerary enclosures at Stanway in comparison with sites in Colchester and Verulamium.	447
Fig. 172	The Gosbecks temple site.	449
Fig. 173	King Harry Lane cemetery. Above: plan. Below: detailed plan of grave 41 from the same cemetery.	451
Fig. 174	Above: distribution of the Middle and Late La Tène chariot burials in northern Gaul. Below: distribution of Late La Tène burials in northern Gaul which contained Italian imports.	452
Fig. 175	Plans and locations of the aristocratic cemeteries at Avaux and Avançon in the Champagne region of France.	453
Fig. 176	Grave 3 at Vieux-les-Asfeld in the Champagne region of France.	454

LIST OF TABLES

		Page
Table 1	Fabric codes and names for the Roman, Gallo-Belgic and Gaulish wares.	15
Table 2	List of illustrated Neolithic pottery.	18
Table 3	Heat-affected stones and the dating evidence for them.	20
Table 4	Weights and approximate percentage of stone types from pits AF24, AF76, and CF175.	20
Table 5	Worked flint catalogue.	22
Table 6	Totals of worked flint types.	25
Table 7	Distribution of structural clay.	36
Table 8	The Middle Iron Age loomweights.	40
Table 9	Summary of other loomweight fragments.	40
Table 10	Incidence of Early and Middle Iron Age pottery by sherd count and sherd weight by phase.	49
Table 11	Phase 1 sherd count and sherd weight in grammes by fabric.	50
Table 12	Phase 2 sherd count and sherd weight by fabric.	51
Table 13	Phase 3 sherd count and sherd weight by fabric.	53
Table 14	Summary of the stratified pottery from the Enclosure 1 ditch by type.	53
Table 15	Details of the broken Late Iron Age pots in chamber AF25.	53

Table 16	Vertical distribution of Middle Iron Age pottery sherds in chamber AF25.	53
Table 17	Stratified and unstratified Middle Iron Age pottery from Enclosures 3–5.	54
Table 18	Stratified sherd count and sherd weight by fabric from Enclosures 3–5.	54
Table 19	Decorated rim sherds.	57
Table 20	Decorated body sherds.	58
Table 21	Details of sherds with black residues.	60
Table 22	Fragments of iron nails from the ditch of Enclosure 4.	75
Table 23	Iron nails from the enclosure ditch of Enclosure 5.	82
Table 24	Heat-affected copper alloy and amorphous slaggy iron with traces of copper-alloy from the pyre-site BF1/BF16 and the surrounding area.	86
Table 25	Small fragments of copper-alloy, the majority heat-affected, from the ditch of the ?mortuary enclosure BF32.	92
Table 26	Iron nail fragments from the ditch of the ?mortuary enclosure BF32.	92
Table 27	Small fragments of copper-alloy, the majority heat-affected, from the pits BF42 and BF62 inside the ditch of the ?mortuary enclosure BF32.	94
Table 28	Iron nails from the ditch of the ?mortuary enclosure CF43–6.	98
Table 29	Heat-affected copper alloy from BF6.	121
Table 30	Iron nails from BF6.	121
Table 31	Nails from the chamber BF24.	136
Table 32	Nails from the chamber CF42.	152
Table 33	Heat-affected and resolidified copper alloy from BF17.	159
Table 34	Fragments of iron nails from BF67.	199
Table 35	Typological groupings of the rods in CF47.	224
Table 36	The nails in the oak grave cover (CF47.41).	253
Table 37	Stanway pottery other than amphoras from the enclosure ditches and pyre-sites.	276
Table 38	Minimum number of broken pots represented in the enclosure ditches and ditches of the ?mortuary enclosures.	277
Table 39	Approximate number of identified examples of vessel types from the ?mortuary enclosures and enclosure ditches at Stanway.	277
Table 40	The incidence of pottery forms (other than amphoras) from the ?mortuary enclosures and enclosure ditches at Stanway and Sheepen, Colchester.	280
Table 41	Estimated vessel equivalence (eve) as a percentage of identified vessels.	283
Table 42	Comparison of selected pottery forms from Stanway ?mortuary enclosure and ditch assemblages, and Roman assemblages from the Colchester fortress and the early *colonia*.	288
Table 43	Amphoras from Stanway by minimum vessel number count.	297
Table 44	Plain samian.	306
Table 45	The graffiti at Stanway	307
Table 46	Iron Age graffiti by vessel type (Stanway excluded).	311
Table 47	Brooches from Enclosures 1–5.	314
Table 48	Analytical results for the slag inclusions in the fragmented currency bar CF6.2, as determined by EDS, normalised wt%.	327
Table 49	Results summary for glass objects.	330
Table 50	Results summary of the metal objects and glass brooch settings from BF64, BF67, CF7, CF42, CF47, CF72 and CF115.	332
Table 51	Results summary of the metal objects from Enclosure 3 chamber BF6, the pyre-site BF1/F16 and pit BF17.	337
Table 52	Results summary of the metal objects from the contexts associated with the ?mortuary enclosure BF32 in Enclosure 4.	337
Table 53	Summary of the rim diameters of pillar-moulded and tubular-rimmed bowls from Colchester.	341

LIST OF TABLES

Table 54	A comparison of the colours of the Stanway unguent bottles with those of tubular unguent bottles at various mid 1st-century sites in Britain.	345
Table 55	Sets of gaming counters associated with cremation and inhumation burials in Britain.	366
Table 56	Sets/groups of gaming counters from non-funerary contexts.	367
Table 57	The salt briquetage – summary of the evidence.	376
Table 58	Average sherd weight of salt briquetage from some Essex sites.	376
Table 59	Faunal remains.	383
Table 60	Plant macrofossils and other remains from Late Neolithic and ?Early Iron Age contexts.	385
Table 61	Charred plant macrofossils and other remains from Middle Iron Age to Late Iron Age/Early Roman contexts.	386
Table 62	Charcoal from Enclosure 2.	389
Table 63	Wood from burials and chambers in Enclosures 3 and 5.	391
Table 64	Charcoal from Enclosures 1, 3 and 4.	391
Table 65	Charcoal from the ditches of Enclosure 5.	392
Table 66	Charcoal from the ?mortuary enclosure CF43–6 in Enclosure 5.	393
Table 67	Charcoal from other features in Enclosure 5.	393
Table 68	The percentages of total land pollen and spores (tlp/s) of all the palynological taxa found in the plug.	395
Table 69	The proportions of the various taxa represented in the plug, excluding artemisia.	396
Table 70	The chemical compounds extracted from *Artemisia absinthium* and *A. vulgaris*.	396
Table 71	Percentage values for taxa found in the turf in chamber CF42.	399
Table 72	Plant macrofossils from from cremation burials DF1, DF26 and DF28.	421
Table 73	Plant macrofossils from pits DF3, DF7, DF20, DF21, DF30 and DF41.	421
Table 74	The worked flint from Site D.	
Table 75	Types of cremation burials.	428
Table 76	Vessels related to food and drink.	429
Table 77	Pots and sherds almost certainly burnt or scorched post-firing.	431
Table 78	Weights of cremated human bone in the chambers, pits with pyre debris, cremation burials, ?mortuary enclosures, and shaft/barrels in Enclosures 3–5.	433
Table 79	Refined chronologies for Enclosures 3–5.	440
Table 80	The most refined chronology with many links assumed and the Warrior's burial taken to be no later than A.D. 43.	441
Table 81	Dimensions of the chambers at Stanway and Folly Lane and possible chambers elsewhere.	448

ACKNOWLEDGEMENTS

As always, a report such as this is the result of the hard work and dedication of a great many people. As a starting point, we are grateful to Carl Crossan, who directed part of Site B, particularly for his work on Chamber BF24. The site supervisors and planners who were such important members of the team were Terry Cook, Robin Ellis, Simon Garrod, Andy Letch, Chris Lister, Mike Napthan, Kate Orr, Joe Partridge, Laura Pooley, Nigel Rayner, Rob Smith, and Rob Wardill. Geoff Carter directed the 1987 trial excavation. Photographic work, notably on Sites A and B, was carried out by Alison Colchester. Particular thanks are due to the very many people who worked so hard with the digging, especially Lisa Hepi and David Burnand for their careful excavation of the Doctor's burial.

Help in preparing the illustrations for publication was provided by Joseph Chittenden, Terry Cook, Stephen Crummy, Maureen MacDonald, Bob Moyes, David Ross, Emma Spurgeon, and Jason Walker. Editorial assistance was given by Gillian Adams.

Our work at Stanway was made much easier by the staff at Tarmac who were always extremely helpful, supportive, and interested in our progress. We are especially indebted to the estate managers (sequentially) Tim Slaven, Ian Findlater, David Marsh, and Alan Everard, and on site to the site managers Reg Hilton and Fred Mitchell for their considerable practical help. In particular Ian Findlater gave invaluable encouragement and support in the mid 1990s when we were excavating the Doctor's burial.

We are most appreciative of the voluntary work provided on site by James Fawn and Dennis Tripp and indoors on the sorting of the coarse pottery by Dan Biglin. Especial thanks go to Tim Dennis of the University of Essex who helped set up what was an early example of a live webcam broadcast from an archaeological site. This was done with the aid of a telephone line kindly installed and provided by British Telecom. We are grateful to Alec Livingstone for his help with this matter. Thanks are also due to Peter Cott for the geophysical survey carried out on Site C and to David and Aline Black for that on Site D. Archive reports were kindly provided on the Roman tile by Ernest Black and on post-Roman finds by Howard Brooks. Bernard Lambot generously gave permission for the reproduction of some of his illustrations. The interest and advice of Dr Ian Stead during the earlier phase of the excavations was much appreciated.

The contributors would also like to thank Justine Bayley, Dragan Božič, Olivier Caumont, S. Corson, Jon Cotton, S. Davis, U. Eckardt, Michel Feugère, Kordula Gostenčnik, Janet Lang, Hilary Major, Nicholas Moore, Rosalind Niblett, Nodge Nolan, Paola Pugsley, and Dave Webb for their help in various aspects of the project, and to acknowledge the benefit they received from all those people, too numerous to list, with whom they discussed the site and its finds.

Conservation was undertaken at Colchester Museums and metallurgical analysis at English Heritage's Centre for Archaeology, Fort Cumberland. Other specialist services were kindly provided by the following: SEM (British Museum), pigment analysis (Ashok Roy, National Gallery), real-time X-radiography (Vic Galert, Seifert X-Ray Ltd). Chris Salter cut and mounted one of the currency bars for Sarah Paynter and shared his expertise on this subject with her.

The excavations were funded mainly by English Heritage and Tarmac Ltd. Tarmac also provided the machinery needed for topsoil-stripping. The post-excavation programme and report publication was funded by English Heritage and monitored by Sarah Jennings, to whom we are indebted for her support. English Heritage inspectors were Philip Walker, Mike Parker Pearson, Caroline Malone, and Deborah Priddy. The consultant on Site D was Andrew Josephs. Additional funds for the excavation were kindly provided on several occasions by Essex County Council with the backing of the county archaeologist David Buckley. The Essex History Fair and the Essex Heritage Trust also generously provided funds for some additional excavations. Tarmac kindly funded the provision of various facilities for public visits to the site. Our thanks are also due to Lynn Pitts and John Peter Wild of the Society for the Promotion of Roman Studies, and to Val Kinsler of 100% Proof for her copy-editing and page make-up.

Philip Crummy, Stephen Benfield, Nina Crummy, Valery Rigby, and Donald Shimmin

Site direction and authorship of the report

The site directors were Donald Shimmin, Carl Crossan, and Stephen Benfield (consecutively) under the general direction of Philip Crummy. The unattributed parts of the report were the responsibility of Philip Crummy who incorporated or included in them adapted versions of texts written by Donald Shimmin (Sites A and most of B) and Stephen Benfield (Site C). They also take into account notes provided by Carl Crossan (part of Site B) and include sections of text and catalogue prepared by Nina Crummy (material culture) and Valery Rigby (Roman pottery from the burials). Other contributions by individuals are credited. Philip Crummy compiled the report and acted as general editor.

LIST OF CONTRIBUTORS

P. Crummy	Director, Colchester Archaeological Trust
S. Benfield	Colchester Archaeological Trust
D. Shimmin	Colchester Archaeological Trust
A-M. Bojko	Aberdeen Art Gallery and Museums; formerly Colchester and Ipswich Museums
N.D. Brown	Essex County Council
C.R. Cartwright	Materials Scientist, British Museum
H.E.M. Cool	Barbican Research Associates
N. Crummy	Small finds specialist
G. Dannell	Archaeological consultant
J. A. Davies	Norfolk Museums and Archaeology Service
B. Dickinson	University of Leeds
V. Fryer	Environmental Archaeologist
R. Hingley	University of Durham
R. Jackson	Curator of Romano-British Collections, British Museum
A.J. Legge	University of Cambridge
H. Martingell	Flint specialist
S.A. Mays	Centre for Archaeology, English Heritage
N.D. Meeks	Materials Scientist, British Museum
P. Murphy	English Heritage
S. La Niece	Materials Scientist, British Museum
K. Oak	Havering Sixth Form College
S. Paynter	Centre for Archaeology, English Heritage
V. Rigby	Gallo-Belgic pottery specialist
U. Schädler	Director, Musée Suisse du Jeu
P.R. Sealey	Colchester and Ipswich Museums
A. Wade	Animal bone specialist
J.P. Wild	Manchester Ancient Textile Unit, University of Manchester
P.E.J. Wiltshire	Forensic Ecologist and Palynologist, University of Aberdeen

SUMMARY

The Stanway site was excavated in intermittent stages between 1987 and 2003 in advance of its destruction for sand and gravel extraction. It lay on the outskirts of the modern town of Colchester in what had been Stanway Hall Farm. The Stanway site was on the fringe of the Late Iron Age and Roman oppidum of Camulodunum. It appears to have been the burial place of members of a high-status Catuvellaunian family. The characteristics of the site and the rites practised there reveal links with the Folly Lane and King Harry Lane sites in Verulamium and sites in northern Gaul. Stanway provides support for the possibility that Camulodunum may have existed as early as the time of Caesar's invasions of Britain.

Of the five enclosures which characterised Stanway, the smallest and earliest was the core of an Iron Age farmstead which had been abandoned by the mid 1st century B.C. A pair of currency bars was placed in the ditch of its enclosure. Four funerary enclosures followed, each of which incorporated a single wooden chamber in a central or axial position. The earliest of the enclosures (Enclosure 1) was the largest. As well as a wooden chamber, it included an unaccompanied urned cremation burial and a pit with broken funerary goods. All three features dated to the second half of the 1st century B.C. A single contemporary pit found some distance away contained pyre debris and was probably datable to between *c*. 60 and 1 B.C. (CF7). The other three enclosures (Enclosures 3–5) were laid out in a continuous row in two stages, one in *c*. A.D. 35–45 (Enclosure 3) and the other two (Enclosures 4 and 5) as a conjoined pair in c A.D. 40–50. Parts of deliberately broken pots and other objects were placed in the chambers as part of the funerary rite. The minimum number of vessels represented in the chambers ranges from two in the earliest of them (AF25) to 24 in the largest of them (BF6). Six cremation burials inside Enclosures 3–5 date probably to *c*. A.D. 40–60/75 with most in the range *c*. A.D. 40-60. The numbers of grave goods in those burials varies from none at all to the many in the well-endowed 'Warrior's burial' (BF64) and the 'Doctor's burial' (CF47). The former was distinguished by the inclusion of a shield and lance or spear and the latter by a set of surgical instruments, a gaming board with counters in place, and a copper-alloy strainer which had been used to prepare an infusion of artemisia. The only certain pyre-site was in the centre of one of the enclosures (Enclosure 3) and had apparently been used at least twice. Two small square ditched areas in the latest two enclosures (Enclosures 4 and 5) may have been the sites of pyres or structures for excarnation.

A small, probably unrelated, cemetery containing at least three cremation burials and five pyre-debris pits was situated about 200 m south-east of the enclosures. Its period of use, as far as can be judged, approximated to that of the enclosures but with a slightly later end date (*i.e.* from the early 1st century A.D. to the early Flavian period). However, the grave goods they contained are comparatively modest in nature and number.

RÉSUMÉ

Le site de Stanway a été fouillé de manière intermittente entre 1987 et 2003, date de sa destruction du fait de l'extraction de sable et de graviers. Il était situé à proximité de la ville moderne de Colchester, où se trouve Stanway Hall Farm et, à la fin de l'Âge du Fer et à la période romaine, était proche de l'*oppidum* de Camulodunum. Il semble avoir été le lieu de sépulture des membres d'une famille de rang élevé au sein des Catuvellauni. Les caractéristiques du site et les rites funéraires révèlent des liens avec les sites de Folly Lane et King Harry Lane à Verulamium, ainsi qu'avec des sites du Nord de la Gaule. Stanway vient étayer l'hypothèse selon laquelle Camulodunum a existé dès l'époque des invasions de la Bretagne par César.

Des cinq enclos de Stanway, le plus petit et le plus ancien constituait le cœur d'une ferme de l'Âge du Fer, abandonnée au milieu du Ier s. avant J.-C. Deux lingots en fer ont été recueillis dans son fossé. Quatre enclos funéraires ont suivi, chacun étant pourvu d'une unique chambre en bois, en position centrale ou axiale. Le premier de ces enclos (Enclos 1) est aussi le plus grand. Outre une chambre en bois, il contenait une incinération en urne mais sans mobilier, ainsi qu'un puits avec des dépôts funéraires brisés; ces trois structures datent à la deuxième moitié du Ier s. avant J.-C. Un seul puits contemporain, mais à quelque distance de l'enclos, contenait les restes d'un bûcher qui a pu être daté approximativement vers 60–1 av. J.-C. (CF7). Les trois autres enclos (Enclos 3–5) ont été disposés en deux étapes sur une ligne continue, l'un d'eux vers 35–45 ap. J.-C. (Enclos 3) et les deux autres (Enclos 4 et 5) en même temps, vers 40–50. Des fragments de vases volontairement brisés et d'autres objets ont été déposés dans les chambres funéraires au cours des funérailles. Le nombre minimum de vases représentés dans les tombes va de 2, pour la première (AF25), à 24 dans la plus grande (BF6). Six incinérations (Enclos 3–5) datent probablement de *c.* 40–60/75 ap. J.-C., sans doute pour la plupart de *c.* 40–60. Le mobilier funéraire dans ces sépultures va de l'absence totale à *c.* 30-40 objets, dans le cas de la sépulture du Guerrier (BF64) et celle du Médecin (CF47), toutes deux abondamment pourvues. L'une se distingue par la présence d'un bouclier et d'une lance ou javelot, l'autre par une série d'instruments chirurgicaux, une table de jeu avec des pions en place, et un bassin à bec verseur qui a servi à préparer une tisane à l'armoise. Le seul site de bûcher bien individualisé a été trouvé au centre de l'un des enclos (Enclos 3): de toute évidence, il a servi au moins deux fois. Deux petites fosses carrées dans les deux derniers enclos (Enclos 4 et 5) signalent peut-être des bûchers funéraires ou des structures d'excarnation.

Un petit cimetière, situé à env. 200 m au sud-est des ces enclos, n'a probablement pas de rapport direct avec eux. Il a livré trois incinérations et au moins cinq puits avec des restes de bûchers. Son utilisation semble contemporaine de celle des enclos mais aussi un peu plus tardive (soit du début du Ier siècle ap. J.-C. jusqu'au début des Flaviens). Du reste, les dépôts funéraires de ces sépultures sont relativement modestes, tant par leur caractère que par leur nombre.

Traduction: N. Crummy et M. Feugère

ZUSAMMENFASSUNG

Die Stanway Fundstätte wurde zwischen 1987 und 2003 in mehreren Kampagnen vor ihrer Zerstörung im Zuge der Sand- und Kiesgewinnung ergraben. Die Grabung befindet sich an der Peripherie der heutigen Stadt Colchester in der ehemaligen Stanway Hall Farm. Ursprünglich lag Stanway am Rande des späteisenzeitlichen und römischen oppidums Camulodunum und war wahrscheinlich der Begräbnisplatz einer hochrangigen Familie. Die charakteristischen Merkmale der Fundstätte und der Grabriten zeigen Verbindungen mit Folly Lane und King Harry Lane in Verulamium und dem nördlichen Gallien auf. Die Befunde von Stanway stützen die Hypothese, dass Camulodunum vielleicht schon zur Zeit von Caesars Britannienzügen existierte.

Die Anlage in Stanway besteht aus fünf Einfriedungen; die kleinste und zugleich älteste bildete das Zentrum eines eisenzeitlichen Gehöfts, das in der Mitte des 1. Jahrhunderts v. Chr. aufgegeben worden war. Zwei stabförmige Eisenbarren sind in den Graben dieser Einfriedung gelegt worden. Vier Grabanlagen schlossen sich an, jede mit einer hölzernen Grabkammer entweder im Zentrum oder längsachsig zur Umfassung. Die älteste Grabumfassung (Einfriedung 1) war auch die größte. Sie umschloss sowohl die Grabkammer als auch ein Urnengrab ohne Beigaben und eine Grube mit zerstörten und zerbrochenen Beigaben. Alle drei Befunde können in die zweite Hälfte des 1. Jahrhunderts v. Chr. datiert werden. Eine weitere zeitgleiche Grube, die in einigem Abstand gefunden wurde, enthielt die Reste eines Scheiterhaufens und stammt aus der Zeit von ca. 60 bis 1 v. Chr. Die drei anderen Einfriedigungen (Einfriedung 3 bis 5) sind in einer Linie, aber zu unterschiedlichen Zeiten angelegt worden: Enclosure 3 um ca. 35 bis 45 n. Chr. und die anderen zwei (Einfriedungen 4 und 5) als zusammengehörendes Paar um ca. 40 bis 50 n. Chr. Teile der zerbrochenen Keramik und die anderen Grabbeigaben wurden während des Begräbnisritus in die Kammern gelegt. Die Zahl der Gefäße in den Grabkammern reicht von zwei in der ältesten (AF25) bis zu vierundzwanzig in der größten Kammer (BF6). Sechs Brandgräber in den Einfriedungen 3 bis 5 können wahrscheinlich in die Jahre 40 bis 60/75 n. Chr. datiert werden, die meisten davon in die Jahre 40 bis 50 n. Chr. Die Ausstattung der Gräber ist sehr unterschiedlich. Der Bogen spannt sich von Gräbern ohne Beigabe bis hin zu dem Kriegergrab (BF64) und dem Arztgrab (CF47), die reich ausgestattet sind. Das Kriegergrab enthielt einen Schild und eine Lanze oder Speer. In dem Arztgrab wurden ein Satz chirurgischer Instrumente, ein Spiel, dessen Steine sich auf dem Brett noch in ihrer Position befanden, und ein bronzenes Siebgefäß, das zur Herstellung eines Kräuteraufgusses (mit Artemisia) diente, gefunden. Die einzige sicher identifizierte Scheiterhaufen-Stelle befindet sich in der Mitte einer der Einfriedungen (Einfriedung 3) und wurde vermutlich wenigstens zweimal benutzt. Zwei kleine quadratische, mit Gräben umgebene Gebiete in den zwei spätesten Einfriedungen (Einfriedungen 4 und 5) sind vielleicht die Stellen für Scheiterhaufen oder für die Vornahme von Dekarnationen (Entfleischungen).

Ein kleines und wahrscheinlich unabhängiges Gräberfeld mit mindestens drei Brandgräbern und fünf Gruben, die Scheiterhaufenreste enthielten, wurde ca. 200 m südöstlich der Einfriedungen gefunden. Dieser kleine Friedhof wurde, soweit datierbar, zur selben Zeit wie die Einfriedungen benutzt, aber er blieb ein wenig länger als diese in Gebrauch, mit einem Enddatum von dem frühen 1. Jahrhundert n. Chr. bis in die frühe flavische Zeit. Die Grabbeigaben sind jedoch relativ bescheiden in Anzahl und Qualität.

Übersetzung: U. Eckardt und D. Božič

CHAPTER 1

INTRODUCTION AND BACKGROUND

THE STANWAY SITE (FIGS 1–3, 9)

The subject of this report has come to be known simply as the 'Stanway site' after the wider area in which it lay. However, it could more accurately have been termed the 'Colchester Quarry site' after the quarry in which the site was situated until its gradual destruction during sand and gravel extraction between *c.* 1987 and 2005.

The site was located in the parish of Stanway at NGR TL 955 226, on a flat plateau to the south-west of modern Colchester (FIGS 1–2). It lay only 0.25 km west of Gryme's Dyke, the westernmost element of the system of dykes which protected the Late Iron Age and Roman *oppidum* of Camulodunum. The complex of dykes evolved over many decades. Some of the earthworks appear to have been of post-conquest date, the latest being Gryme's Dyke itself which is now dated to just after the Boudican revolt (*CAR* **11**, 107–14). The royal farmstead at Gosbecks (*CAR* **11**, 97–8) lay about 1.5 km to the east of the Stanway site, with the industrial site of Sheepen (Hawkes and Hull 1947; Niblett 1985; *CAR* **11**, 70–84) some 4 km further to the north-east. Various Late Iron Age burials have been found to the south-west of Sheepen at Lexden. These include the famous Lexden Tumulus, a rich grave dated to *c.* 15–10 B.C. and believed to be that of a British king (Foster 1986; *CAR* **11**, 85–94). Gosbecks continued to be an important place in the Roman period as is shown by the presence there of a Roman theatre and a Romano-Celtic temple within a monumental portico (*CAR* **11**, 95–105). Although not falling within the defended area provided by the dyke system, the high-status nature of the Stanway site suggests that it must nevertheless have been intimately linked with Camulodunum (FIG. 3).

The existence of archaeological remains on the Stanway site was first revealed by aerial photography in the 1930s. This showed clear cropmarks of five ditched enclosures, the largest being over 100 m across (FIGS 2 and 9). The enclosures were arranged in two north–south rows, with two end to end to the west and the rest conjoined in a line to the east. Until the 1990s, the function and date of the enclosures were uncertain, but the favoured view was that they were concerned with the management of stock. Archaeological excavation changed all that and revealed a remarkable funerary site with some extraordinary finds.

HISTORY OF THE EXCAVATIONS (FIG. 4)

The quarry has had a life of over thirty years, and the quarry face did not reach the enclosures until 1987 because they were near the south side of the site. The archaeological excavations were carried out in two stages, each just in front of the slowly advancing quarry face. The first stage took place yearly between 1987 and 1992, the second in 1996 and 1997.

The history of the excavation needs to be explained in some detail to make clear how and why the excavation strategy changed as the project progressed. Today for a site such as the Stanway pit, the quarry company would probably have been required to fund any archaeological work made necessary by their workings. This would have been achieved by making the initial planning consent subject to archaeological investigations that the quarry company would need to fund. But planning consent for the Stanway pit was granted in the 1960s, some considerable time before such conditions became the norm, and the result was that there was no financial provision to cover any archaeological work that might prove necessary.

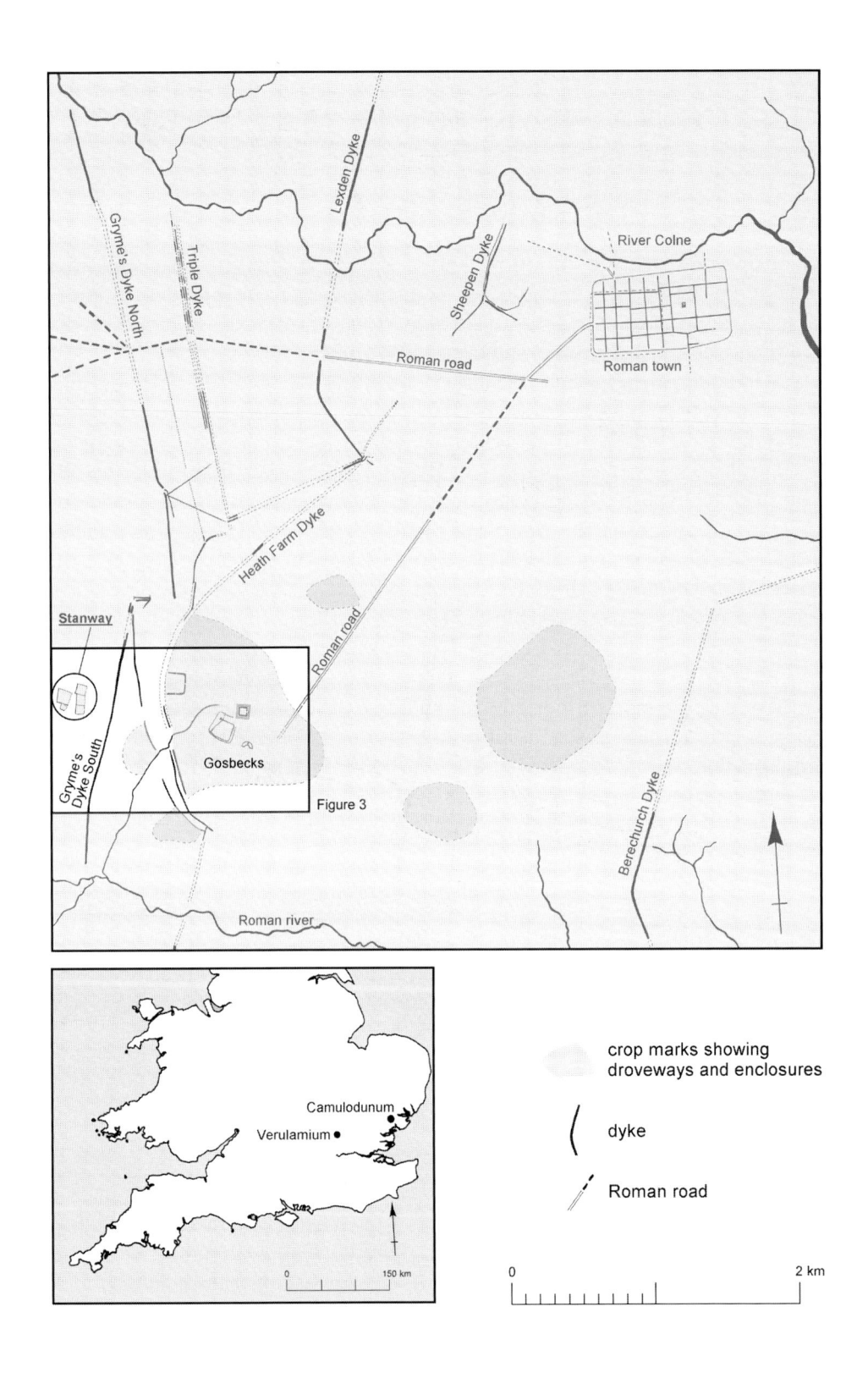

FIG. 1. The Stanway site in relation to Camulodunum and the Roman town and its regional location

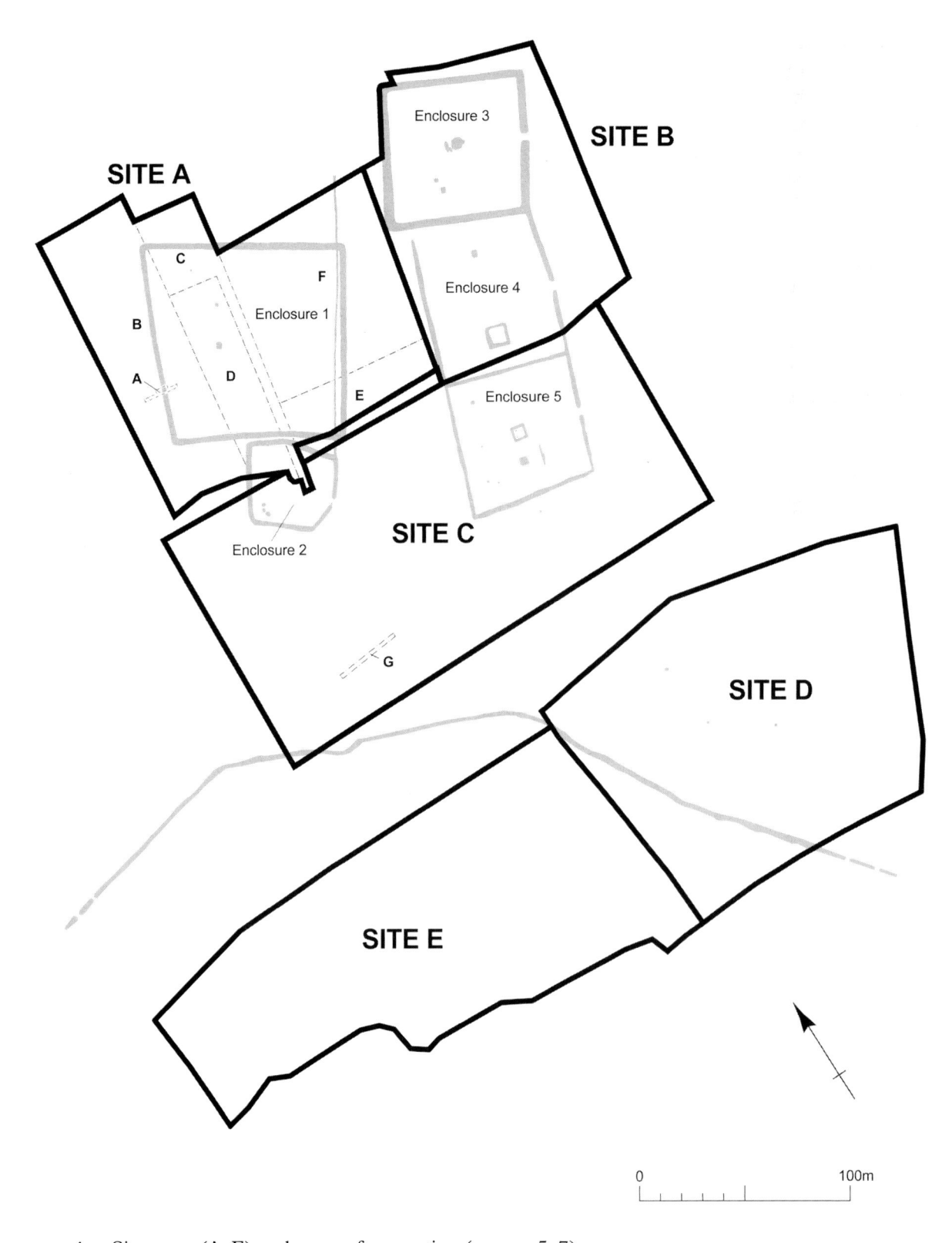

FIG. 4. Site areas (A–E) and areas of excavation (see pp. 5–7)

At the outset of the project, English Heritage and Tarmac both recognised that there was a problem and both kindly agreed to a jointly funded package which was to allow sampling of the ditches and interiors of the enclosures. Tarmac were under no obligation to do this, and English Heritage generously offered to support the project as a willing partner for Tarmac. Nobody at this point could have guessed the true extent of the work which would be needed to do the site justice.

The enclosures had never been highlighted as being of unusual interest or of exceptional archaeological potential. This only changed with the discovery of BF6 which, as it happened, coincided with the discovery of a similar but richer chamber at Folly Lane, Verulamium, St Albans, Herts. Recognition of the chamber meant that simply sampling ditches and the interiors of the enclosures was not going to be enough. This was because it became apparent that the enclosures represented the remains of a hitherto unrecognised kind of monument in Britain where it was not possible to predict what they might contain or what form such remains might take. Subsequent investigations did indeed confirm that the interiors and the ditch fills all merited total excavation.

With a gradually improving understanding of what the remains represented, the interiors of the enclosures were subject to greater examination as the excavation progressed, and, by the time Enclosure 5 was being excavated, the investigations were as thorough and comprehensive as could be managed within the limits of what resources could be mustered.

In retrospect, although the earliest work was not as exhaustive as the later investigations, it is doubtful if anything of great significance was missed. It would have been good if much more of the ditch fills could have been excavated on Site A, but, from the little that was done, it seems very likely that there were no great scatters of broken pottery as observed in Enclosures 4 and 5. And although all of the interior of Enclosure 1 was not subjected to methodical investigation, observations during machine-stripping, coupled with the careful hand-cleaning of some areas, suggest that few, if any, important features are likely to have been overlooked. This is not to say that total excavation would not have been worthwhile. Such an approach would have been helpful because it would have given confidence to our belief that little of significance was missed and it would have provided more data to map the distribution of the smashed pottery in the ditches. The main problems of the under-resourcing were the consequences of having to machine-excavate the ditches of Enclosures 3 and 4 and having to excavate the Warrior's burial in its entirety on the day on which it was discovered. The experience of the latter in particular made us determined to avoid a similar situation arising again. As it turned out, a similar grave did indeed subsequently emerge (*i.e.* the Doctor's burial), and this time it was excavated and recorded as carefully and as painstakingly as possible.

The sequence of excavation, the areas concerned, and the methodology employed are as summarised below. The thick lines on FIGURE 4 show the limits of the sites (*i.e.* Sites A, B, C, D and E). 'Hand-cleaning' usually involved hoeing with some surface trowelling.

May–June 1987
FIG. 4, Site A, Area A

A small trench was hand-dug to locate the western side of Enclosure 1. The enclosures were known from oblique aerial photographs, and fixing their position successfully in the field had to be the starting point of the investigation. The enclosure ditch was located and sectioned as a result.

March 1988
FIG. 4, Site A, Area B

Following unsupervised machine-stripping, limited areas were cleaned by hand and a few features of minor significance were excavated on the western side of Enclosure 1.

May–August 1988
FIG. 4, Site C, Area C

An area at the north end of Enclosure 1 was machine-stripped under archaeological supervision and then the surface was cleaned by hand. An evaluation trench was cut by machine through the unstripped area of Enclosures 1 and 2. The trench was parallel to the quarry face which at that time was a short distance to the west. All the finds were plotted in plan, and there was limited excavation of features, including the first of the cremation burials (*i.e.* AF18).

March–April 1989
FIG. 4, *Site A, Areas B, C and D*

Part of Enclosure 1 and the north end of Enclosure 2 were machine-stripped under archaeological supervision. Area excavation followed. This included the excavation of chamber AF25 and a pit with broken funerary goods, AF48.

1990
FIG. 4, *Site A, Area E*

The south-east corner of Enclosure 1 was stripped without archaeological supervision.

November–December 1990
FIG. 4, *Site A, Area F*

Most of the eastern half of Enclosure 1 was stripped under archaeological supervision. This was followed by limited area excavation which revealed various small pits and stake-holes of relatively early date.

February–July 1991
FIG. 4, *Site B*

Enclosures 3 and 4 were machine-stripped under archaeological supervision and large areas hand-cleaned. The funding package kindly provided by English Heritage and Tarmac was based on the examination of a 25 per cent sample of the stripped area, but the unexpected discovery of two chambers (BF6 and BF24), each requiring detailed recording, meant that much less could be achieved. In the event, the interiors of Enclosures 3 and 4 were not exhaustively examined, but instead work was focused on key locations and places where features were evident either during the mechanical stripping or the subsequent cleaning. Thus, in addition to the chambers, most of the work was concentrated on the entrances of Enclosures 3 and 4, and the pyre-sites BF16/BF1 and the ?mortuary enclosure BF32.

January–February 1992
FIG. 4, *Site B*

Funds were now exhausted, but the quarry face had reached the west side of Site B and the loss of that part of the site was imminent. With the aid of a small but invaluable grant from Essex County Council, unexcavated parts of the ditches of Enclosures 3 and 4 were excavated by machine to check for the presence of burials or other substantial remains. All of the ditch forming Enclosure 3 and the northern half of Enclosure 4 was dug out, except for a length on the west side of Enclosure 3, which was under the temporary roadway along the top of the quarry face. No burials were found and there was only sparse evidence for smashed pots such as subsequently discovered in much larger numbers in the ditch forming Enclosure 5 and the rest of Enclosure 4.

March–April 1992
FIG. 4, *Site B*

The excavations on-going at this time at Folly Lane, Verulamium, St Albans, had shown that grave goods (in this case chain mail and a horse bit) associated with chambers such as that in Site B could be buried in a secondary pit inside the funerary enclosure. It thus became apparent that it was important to check that nothing similar existed inside Enclosure 3 at Stanway. There was also a need to investigate the interior of the enclosure thoroughly for burials. With the aid of a grant of £500 from the Essex History Fair, the surface of Site B was again stripped and cleaned by machine at almost the very last minute before being destroyed by the advancing quarry face. All features (certain and dubious) were 'tested' by hand or, failing this, by machine. The work could only last a day and resulted in the discovery and hasty excavation of the Warrior's burial (BF64) and the Inkwell burial (BF67). No secondary pits like that at Folly Lane were found.

July–September 1996
FIG. 4, Site C

The whole of Site C was stripped by machine under archaeological supervision. All of Enclosure 5 was then hand-cleaned and excavated. Features investigated included the chamber CF42, the ?mortuary enclosure CF43–6, the slot CF96, the Doctor's burial CF47, the Brooches burial CF72, and the pit CF7. About 60 per cent of the ditch of Enclosure 5 was fully excavated. Little work was undertaken in Enclosure 2 that year except for a few sections across its enclosure ditch. Also at that time, the whole of Site C was metal-detected. This resulted in the discovery of a pair of currency bars in the enclosure ditch of Enclosure 2 and two Iron Age spearheads south of Enclosure 2.

July–August 1996
FIG. 4, Site C, Area G

An exploratory trench was cut by machine through a palaeochannel (CF52) south of Enclosure 2.

July–September 1997
FIG. 4, Site C

The uninvestigated part of Enclosure 2 was cleaned by hand. All internal features were then excavated, plus about 35 per cent of the enclosure ditch. At the same time, the interior of Enclosure 5 was re-cleaned by hand to make sure that no archaeological features had been mistaken for natural ones the previous year. Around 150 features were investigated that year. All but one of them (cremation burial CF403) appeared to be natural. Excavation of the chamber CF42 and the ?ritual shaft CF23 was completed.

November–December 2002
FIG. 4, Site D

The south-east corner of the field was machine-stripped without archaeological supervision in readiness for sand and gravel extraction. As a result, various dark patches were revealed that a preliminary investigation showed to include at least one cremation burial and a number of pits with charcoal and pyre debris. A geophysical survey of the site was carried out in March–April 2003 by Aileen Black and David Black.

December 2003
FIG. 4, Site D

Tarmac provided additional funds for a more thorough investigation of the stripped area. Just over 50 per cent of it was very lightly cleaned with a mini-digger fitted with a toothless bucket. This had to be done, because the surface was obscured by vegetation and lenses of redeposited material left behind during the site-stripping. Subsequently, excavation of the features uncovered in 2002 was completed and a further two cremation burials and more pits with charcoal and pyre debris were investigated.

August 2004
FIG. 4, Site E

The south-west corner of the field was machine-stripped under archaeological supervision in readiness for mineral extraction. The archaeological monitoring was funded by Tarmac. Little of archaeological significance was recorded.

SIMPLIFIED CHRONOLOGY AND KEY FEATURES (FIGS 5–9)

NEOLITHIC AND LATE BRONZE AGE/EARLY IRON AGE (FIG. 5)

The earliest occupation in the area is indicated by a limited scatter of flints, a small quantity of pottery and a number of pits, of which one was Late Neolithic, one was Early Bronze Age, and three were Late Bronze Age or Early Iron Age (FIG. 5).

MIDDLE IRON AGE (*c.* 200–50 B.C.) *(*FIGS 5, 9)

The core of a Middle Iron Age farmstead is represented by Enclosure 2 and a ?secondary boundary ditch (CF137/AF59) to the north (FIGS 5 and 9). There was a scatter of pits inside the enclosure and west of the boundary ditch. The largest of these were inside Enclosure 2. The spatial relationships between the pits inside Enclosure 2 and the presumed bank along the inner edge of its ditch allow the site of a single round-house to be tentatively identified.

There was a substantial scatter of Middle Iron Age pottery over the sites of Enclosures 1 and 2. Most of it fell within Enclosure 2, and much of it was residual in later contexts. Enclosure 2 contained many fragments of loomweights, which is consistent with a domestic/agricultural use

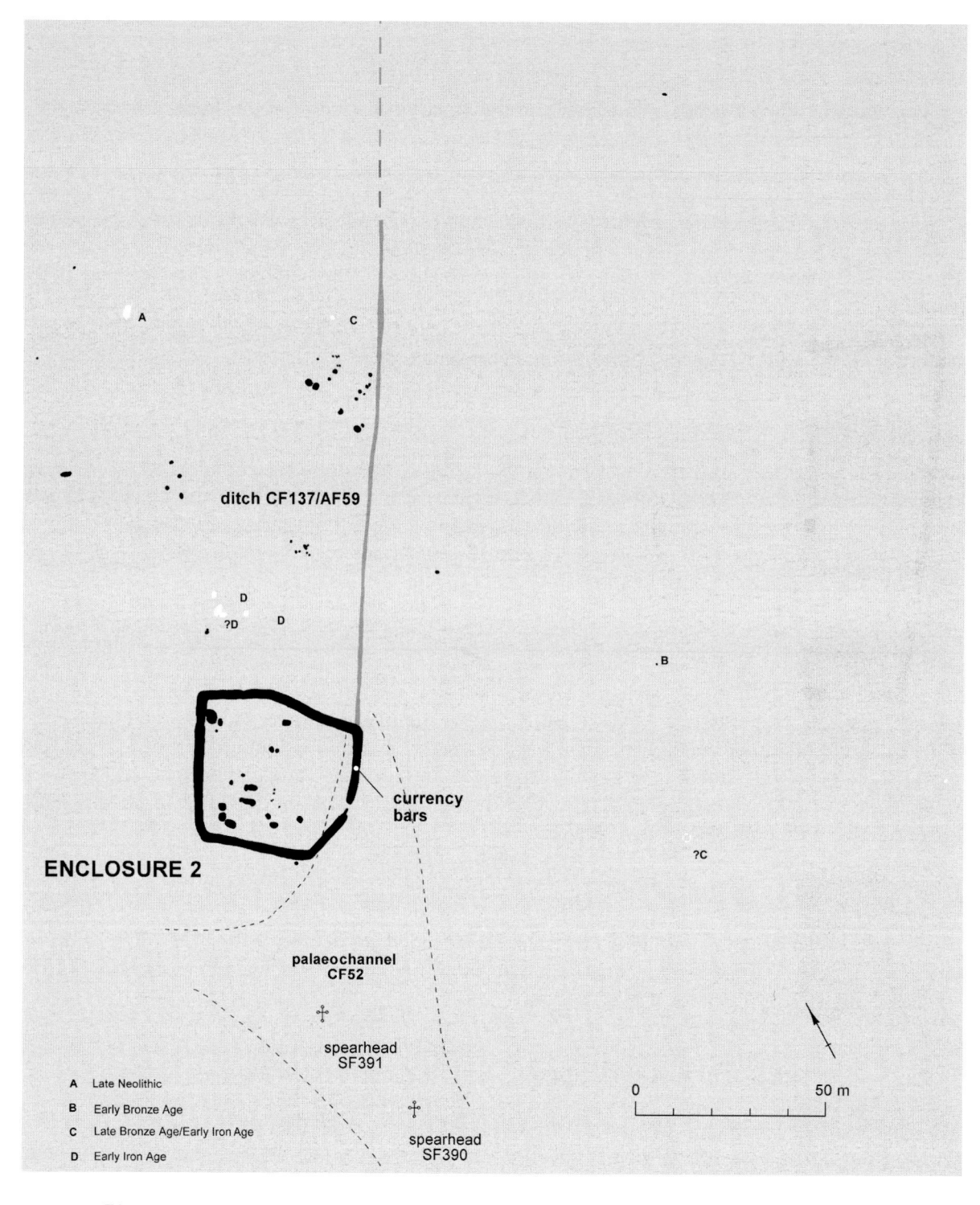

FIG. 5. Phase 1 and earlier

for the enclosure as opposed to a funerary one. Some flint tools and waste from the site also seem to be Iron Age.

A hoard of two currency bars was 'placed' in the enclosure ditch of the farmstead. Dating of the bars is not precise on stratigraphic grounds. However, they do seem to pre-date the earliest of the Late Iron Age burials, because they appear to have been deposited relatively early in the life of the farmstead (p. 26).

Spearheads found during a metal-detector survey to the south of the farmstead enclosure appear to be of Late Iron Age or early Roman date. In view of the nearby currency bars, they may have been ritually deposited.

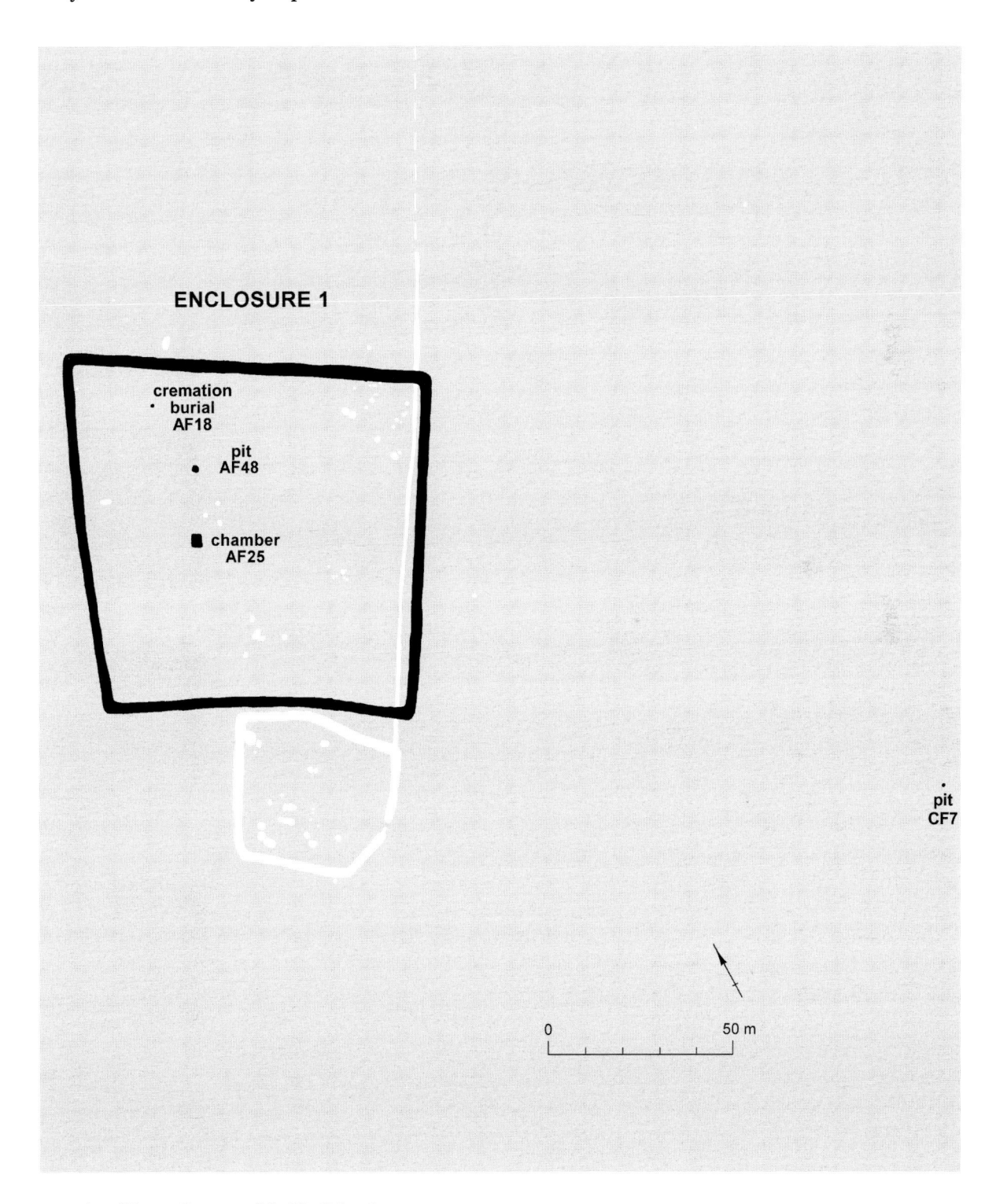

FIG. 6. Phase 2: second half of the 1st century B.C.

SECOND HALF OF THE 1ST CENTURY B.C. (FIGS 6 and 9)

Enclosure 1 was laid out during the second half of the 1st century B.C. and a small wooden burial chamber inserted into it (FIGS 6 and 9). A cremation in a single pot was later interred in the enclosure, and a large pit dug in which were buried the broken remains of a ?wooden box with decorative iron and copper-alloy bands and a pair of earrings or a finger-ring.

Some distance to the east of Enclosure 2, beyond the area later occupied by Enclosure 5, was a pit with pyre debris. The interred remains included a pot containing a brooch datable to *c.* 50–10 B.C.

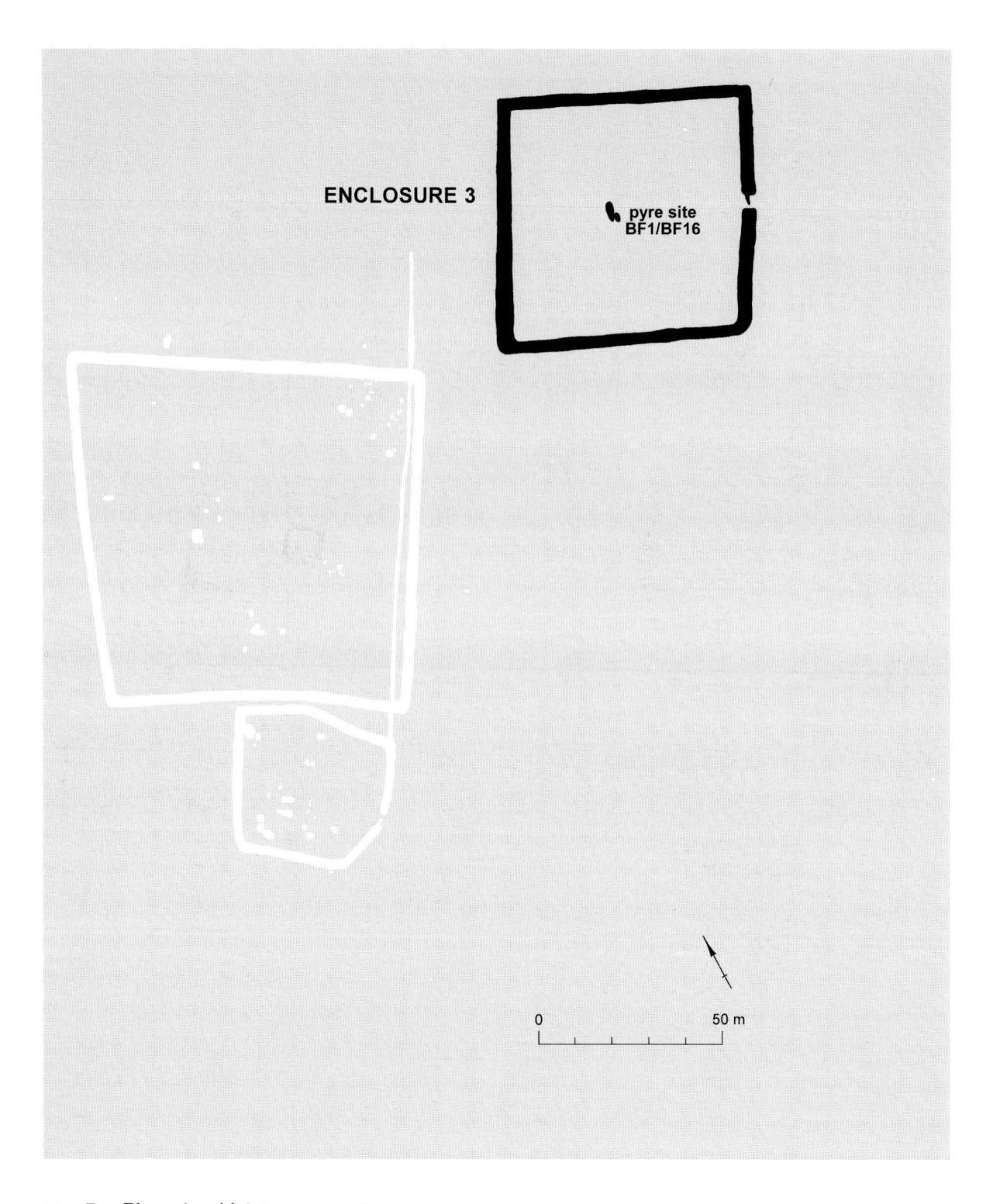

FIG. 7. Phase 3: mid 1st century A.D.

MID 1ST CENTURY A.D. (*c.* A.D. 40–60) (FIGS 7–9)

Enclosures 3 to 5 were laid out around the middle of the 1st century A.D. (FIGS 7–9). Burnt patches in the centre of Enclosure 3 indicate the probable sites of two sequential pyres (FIG. 7). Two small ditched areas in the other two enclosures are each likely to represent the site of a pyre-site and/or the remains of a platform or other above-ground structure for excarnation. Each of the enclosures contained a single wooden burial chamber (FIG. 8). The grave goods in the chambers had been smashed prior to deposition and only small samples of the resultant debris deposited in the chambers. Some of the vessels from at least one of the chambers appear to have been burnt on a pyre after having been broken.

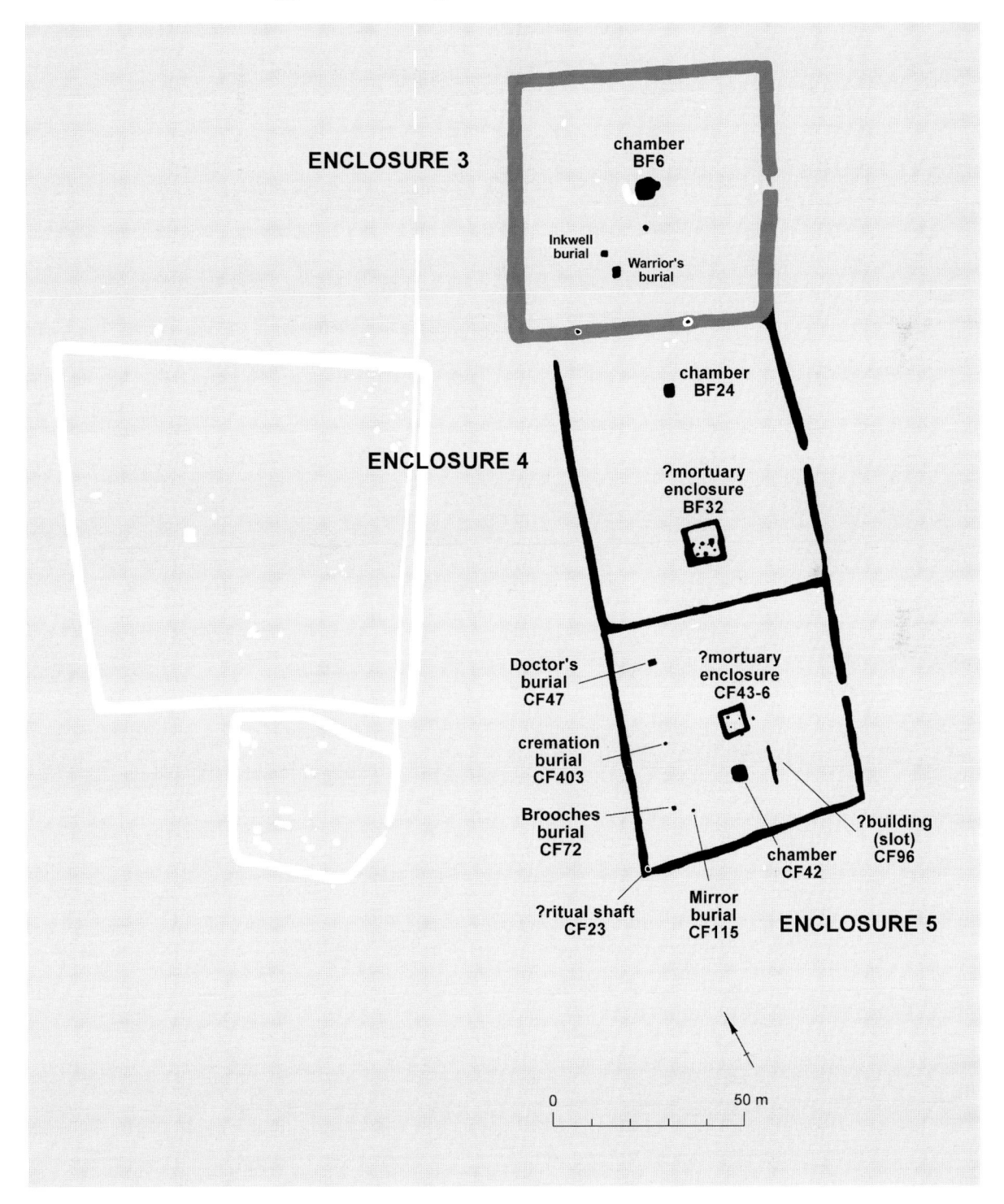

FIG. 8.   Phase 4: mid 1st century A.D.

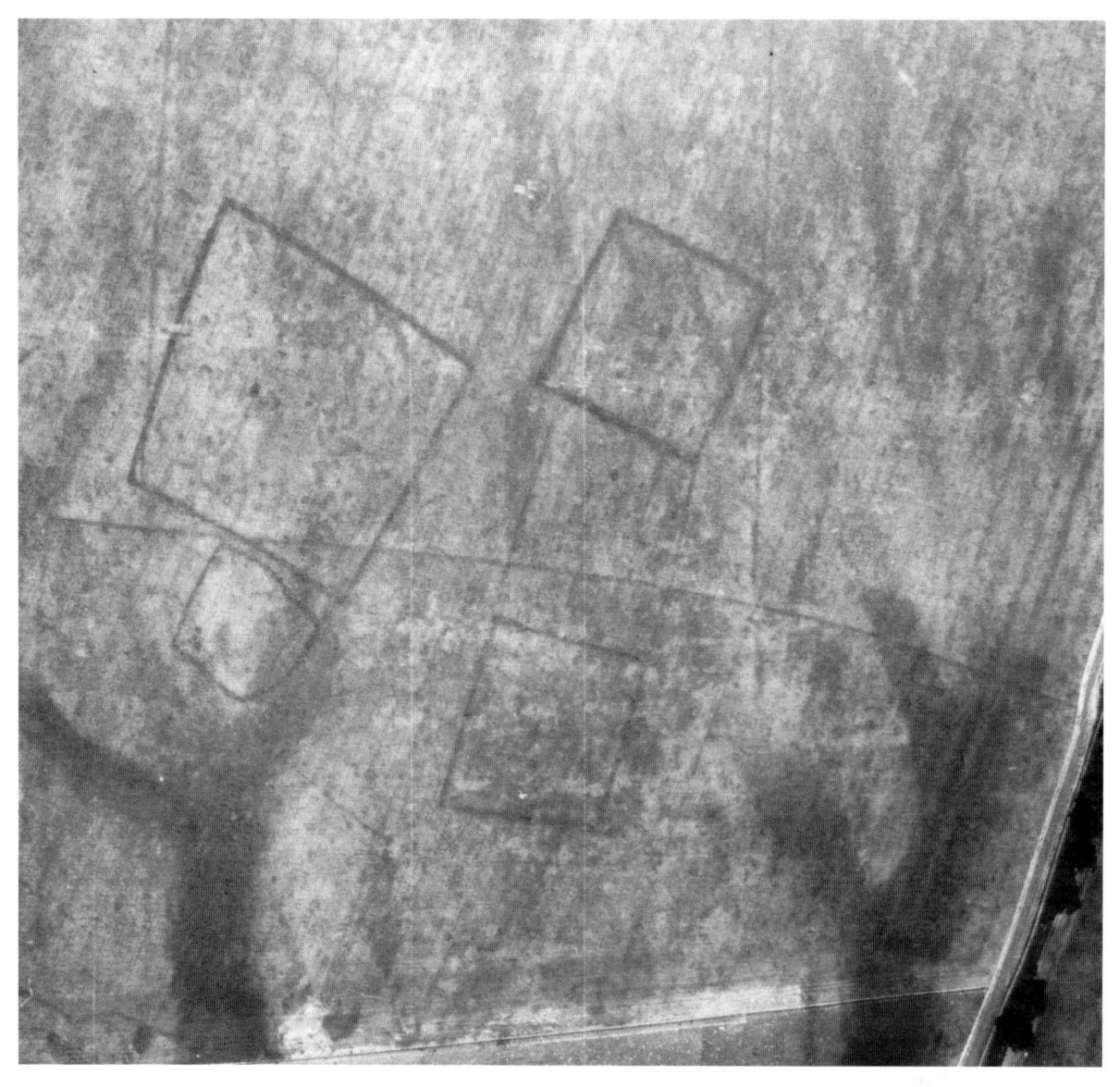

FIG. 9. Stanway: aerial view of cropmarks (Crown Copyright NMR)

In addition to the chambers, there were six secondary burials in this phase. Three are of exceptional interest, because their grave goods signify something about the occupation of the dead person: a 'doctor' (with surgical instruments), a presumed 'warrior' (with spear and shield), and a literate person (with an inkwell).

Ritual activity is indicated by hundreds of sherds of smashed pottery in the enclosure ditches especially along the east side of the enclosures and perhaps also by a 'shaft' in the south-west corner of Enclosure 5.

The possibility of an above-ground structure in the south-east corner of Enclosure 5 is indicated by a single north–south slot (CF96). A temple or excarnation platform are two possible explanations for this feature.

The relationships between the enclosure ditches suggest that Enclosures 4 and 5 were laid out as one, as an addition to Enclosure 3. Sequencing and dating closely not only the enclosures themselves but the various features and activities represented in them is difficult. No clear unequivocal solution can be offered, but the issues are discussed in detail on pages 438–43 where a possible scheme is tentatively outlined. At a simple level, it seems very likely that all three enclosures and the features in them were laid out between c. A.D. 40 and 60. The only definite exception is the slot CF96, the fill of which, because it contained a copper-alloy Neronian coin, must post-date A.D. 64.

The small number of burials (three) and pits with pyre-related debris (four, possibly five) in the south-east corner of the site (*i.e.* Site D) formed the remains of an apparently unenclosed cemetery area, which presumably was not directly related to Enclosures 1 and 3–5. The range of dates of these burials and pits equated with those of the funerary enclosures with, as in the latter, the emphasis on the Claudio-Neronian period, although the presence of a coin of Vespasian in one of the pits with pyre-related debris shows that the closing date of this group may have been a decade or so later.

POST-ROMAN FEATURES

A few sherds of medieval and later pottery have been found in the ploughsoil in the part of the site immediately south of the funerary enclosures. This material should probably be associated with medieval and later occupation along the street frontage forming the southern boundary of the quarry field. The frontage is opposite All Saints' church and the site of Stanway Hall, although the number of sherds seems too low to justify supposing that they belong to a now-deserted or shrunken village of Stanway.

The site of the enclosures was crossed by three post-Roman field boundaries. The archaeological remains were badly damaged by ploughing (as typically happens in Essex and East Anglia). Sand and gravel extraction started in the 1960s.

SUMMARY OF DATES

Middle Iron Age farmstead *c.* 200–50 B.C.

Enclosure 2 (the core of a Middle Iron Age farmstead)

Pits within Enclosure 2, some containing fragments of loomweights
Pits to the north on the site of the later Enclosure 1
Substantial scatter of Middle Iron Age pottery over sites of Enclosures 1 and 2, probably extending throughout Period 2
Ditch CF137/AF59 added on north side of Enclosure 2

Funerary enclosures and their associated funerary contexts

Late Iron Age: c. 50–1 B.C.

AF25: chamber in Enclosure 1 (contains fragments of two vessels)
AF18: cremation burial in Enclosure 1 (a single pot containing cremated bone)
AF48: pit with broken funerary goods (contained fragments of a ?box with decorative iron and copper-alloy bands and also a small amount of cremated human bone)

Late Iron Age/early Roman

Enclosure 3: laid out *c.* A.D. 35–45
BF1 and BF16: pyre-sites *c.* A.D. 35–45 (BF16 post-dates BF1)
Enclosures 4 and 5: laid out as one unit *c.* A.D. 40–50
BF32 and CF43–6: ?sites of pyres or (less likely) structures for the display of bodies *c.* A.D. 40–50, presumably laid out at the same time as their enclosures
BF6: chamber constructed *c.* A.D. 35–45
BF64: 'Warrior's burial' *c.* A.D. 40–50
BF67: 'Inkwell burial' *c.* A.D. 40–50
BF24: chamber *c.* A.D. 40–50
CF42: chamber *c.* A.D. 45–55
CF47: 'Doctor's burial' *c.* A.D. 40–50
CF72: 'Brooches burial' *c.* A.D. 43–50
CF115: 'Mirror burial' *c.* A.D. 50–60
CF403: cremation burial *c.* A.D. 50–60
CF23: ?shaft *c.* A.D. 40–50
CF96: slot *c.* A.D. 65–75 (part of an above-ground structure?)

Unenclosed funerary contexts
CF7: pit with pyre debris c. 50–10 B.C.

Site D
DF1: cremation burial c. A.D. 10–43/60
DF26: cremation burial early 1st century A.D.
DF28: cremation burial A.D. 43–70
DF2: pit with pyre debris c. A.D. 70–80/90
DF3: pit with pyre debris c. A.D. 43–70
DF7: pit with pyre debris c. A.D. 70–80/90
DF13/14: pit with pyre debris c. A.D. 43–?80/90
DF25: ?pit with pyre debris ?1st century A.D.

EXPLANATION OF THE SITE CODES AND SMALL FIND NUMBERS

The recording system used at Stanway was similar to that used at other sites in Colchester (*CAR* 3, 3–4; *CAR* 6, 3–5). Stanway was dug as a series of sub-sites which are referred to by a single-letter code (sub-sites A–E). These codes are used to prefix the context numbers (*e.g.* A509, BL25, CF68). An exception to this is the small trial-trench dug by hand in 1987. A few context numbers from this trench are referred to in the report and are prefixed by the Colchester Museums accession number 1987.16.

There are three separate sets of small find numbers and these can be distinguished by the prefix to the context number:
1) a short series for the 1987 trial-trench prefixed by 1987.16,
2) a series for sub-sites A and B (Colchester Museums accession number 1988.4) prefixed by A or B,
3) a series for sub-sites C and D (Colchester Museums accession numbers 1996.34 for C and 2002.247 for D) prefixed by C or D.

INTRODUCTION TO THE LATE IRON AGE AND ROMAN POTTERY IN THIS REPORT

The Late Iron Age and Roman pottery, including the samian and amphoras, is listed and catalogued by archaeological context where appropriate. The pottery assemblage is dominated by whole and broken pots (referred to here as 'partial pots') and divides naturally into two separate assemblages that are almost mutually exclusive, *i.e.* pots or broken pots from the burials and chambers, and broken pots from the enclosure ditches and ditches of the ?mortuary enclosures. Vessels from the latter, where individual pots could be identified, have been assigned a unique number (*e.g.* Pot 59). Elsewhere, they are referenced according to context (*e.g.* BF6.6). Reports and discussion about specific categories or groups of pottery appear as free-standing contributions in the second half of the report. These are amphoras (Paul R. Sealey), Gallo-Belgic wares (V. Rigby), stamps on the Gallo-Belgic wares (V. Rigby), samian (G. Dannell), and the pottery assemblages from the enclosure ditches and ?mortuary enclosures (Stephen Benfield). The fabric codes used in the report are listed in TABLE 1, and descriptions of them are given in Chapter 5 on pages 268–71. Where possible, pottery forms for the Gallo-Belgic, Gaulish, and coarsewares follow those of the Camulodunum pottery type series (Hawkes and Hull 1947, 202–7, 215–75; Hull 1958, 280–92).

A pot is regarded as 'partial' if, from joining sherds and other indications, it is apparent that parts of it had been deposited in the ditches after the pot had been broken. No doubt many more of the pots given pot numbers must have been partial than we have managed to identify. This is because similarities of forms and fabrics make the recognition of individual partial pots difficult unless they are distinctive in some way. It would appear that at least 20 per cent or so of any one vessel categorised as partial was present in the ditches, but this figure is likely to be meaningless because partial pots represented by a relatively small number of sherds will be harder to identify.

TABLE 1: FABRIC CODES AND NAMES FOR THE ROMAN, GALLO-BELGIC AND GAULISH WARES

Fabric code	Fabric name
BPW/NOG WH3	Butt-beaker parchment ware/North Gaulish (Gallo-Belgic) white ware 3
CAD AM	Cadiz amphora
CAM AM 1	Campanian (Black sand) amphora 1
CAM AM 2	(Northern) Campanian amphora 2
CAT AM	Catalan amphora
CG CC1 CC2	Central Gaulish colour-coated wares, 'Lyons' ware/Central Gaulish (white and cream) colour-coated wares
CNG GL1 GL2	Central Gaulish lead-glazed ware/Central Gaulish (white and cream) glazed wares 1 and 2
CSOW	Coarse sandy oxidised ware
DJ	Roman oxidised wares
FJ	Brockley Hill/Verulamium region oxidised ware
FMW	Fumed micaceous ware
FSOW	Fine sandy oxidised ware
FSW	Fine sandy ware/early grey ware
GBW	Glossy burnished ware
GFW	Gaulish flagon ware
GTW	Late Iron Age wares, commonly grog-tempered
GX	Other coarsewares, principally locally produced grey wares
HD	Shell-tempered and calcite-gritted wares
HZ	Large storage jars and other vessels in heavily tempered grey wares
MVW	Mixed vesicular ware
PW	'Pimply' ware
RCVW	Romanising coarse vesicular ware
RCW	Romanising coarseware
ROW	Romanising oxidised ware
SW	Sandy ware
TN/GAB TN1(A)	*Terra nigra*/Gallo-Belgic *terra nigra* 1
TR1(C)/GAB TR1(C)	*Terra-rubra* 1(C)/Gallo-Belgic *terra-rubra* 1(C)
TR3/GAB TR3	*Terra-rubra* 3/Gallo-Belgic *terra-rubra* 3
WPW/NOG WH1	White pipe clay ware/North Gaulish (Gallo-Belgic) white ware 1

DEFINITION OF TERMS USED IN THE REPORT

Funerary goods

A selection of objects that has been assembled for a funeral and would in most cases have been interred intact in a grave.

Grave goods

Funerary goods that have been interred in a grave.

Pyre debris

Debris from a funeral pyre characterised by the presence of charcoal and sometimes cremated bone and containing whole or broken funerary goods that have been placed on or very close to a pyre, including objects worn on the body.

CHAPTER 2

FEATURES AND FINDS PRE-DATING THE MIDDLE IRON AGE FARMSTEAD

THE EARLIEST OCCUPATION (FIGS 2, 5, 10)

The evidence for occupation pre-dating the enclosures is sparse and consists of at least five pits and a scatter of residual pottery sherds and flints, dating variously from the Late Neolithic to the Early Iron Age. A Neolithic component is particularly evident in the flint assemblage (p. 21).

To the north of where Enclosure 1 was later to lie, a single sherd of Peterborough Ware was recovered from AF16, while a quantity of probable Late Bronze Age/Early Iron Age pottery was found in AF71 (FIG. 5, A, C; FIG. 10). Further south, two pits (FIG. 2, AF28 and AF46) contained 61 sherds (872 g) of Early Iron Age pottery (FIG. 5, D; FIG. 10). Pit CF81 in the north-west part of the later Enclosure 5 contained a small quantity of Early Bronze Age pottery (FIG. 5, B; FIG. 10). Sherds (C66) from a heavily flint-tempered vessel of Late Bronze Age/Early Iron Age date were found in a small scatter about 1 m south of Enclosure 5 (FIG. 5, ?C). They probably derived from a shallow feature removed during machine stripping. The residual material includes a rim sherd from a Late Neolithic Peterborough Ware bowl from the ditch of Enclosure 2 (FIG. 2, CF6).

Near the Early Iron Age pits AF28 and AF46 were some undatable pits (AF30, AF34–5, AF42) containing charcoal, traces of burning and other indications of prehistoric occupation in the vicinity (FIG. 2). Pits AF28 and AF34 contained some fragments of burnt stones. These

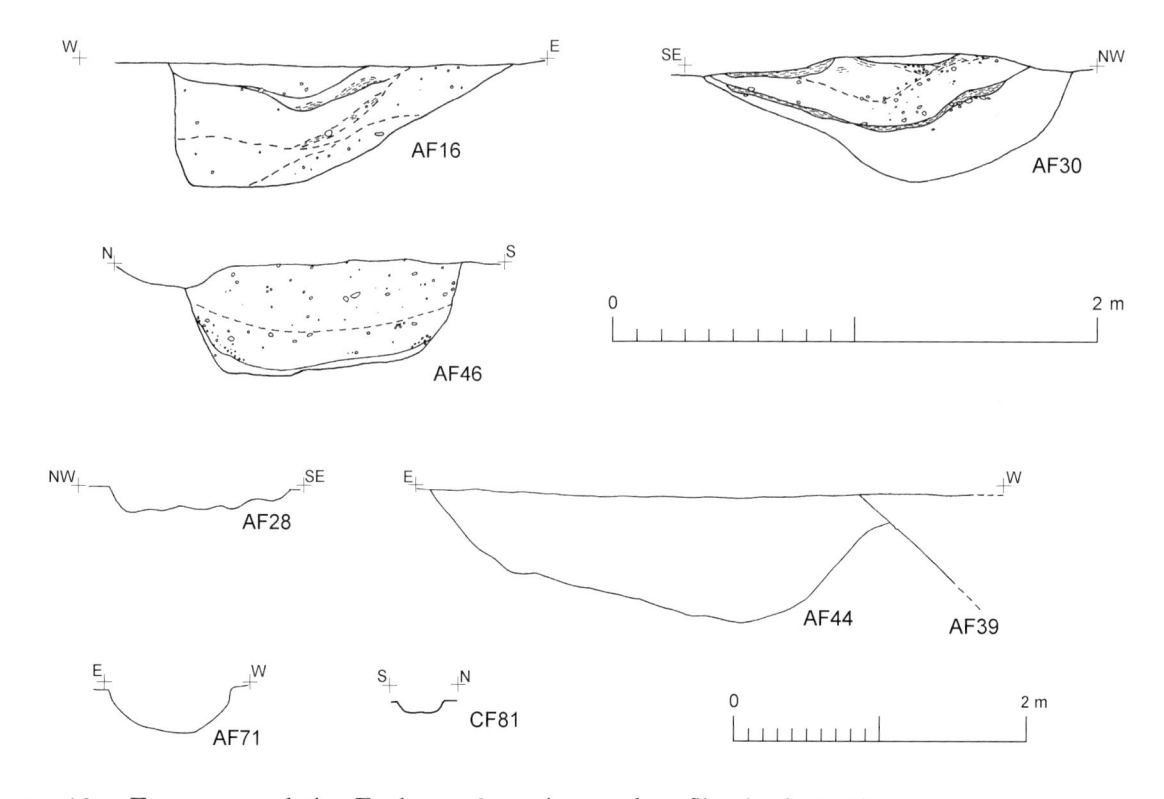

FIG. 10.   Features pre-dating Enclosure 2: sections and profiles (scale 1:50)

were part of the substantial scatter of such material across the western part of the site, apparently made up of burnt flint pebbles and sandstone/quartzite 'pot-boilers'. Neither group of burnt stone is datable, although a Middle Iron Age date for both seems the most likely (p. 20), in which case AF28, AF34 and the others in the undated group of pits are probably of this date or later. But the dating of these pits is problematic. The proximity of AF30 to AF28 and AF46 hints that the pits belong to the Early Iron Age, and plant remains in AF30 characteristic of Late Neolithic assemblages in Essex (p. 384) suggest that this pit and AF42, which was cut by it, may be even earlier. Another pit, AF44, was cut by the ditch of Enclosure 2 and is presumed to be part of the clearance of the site before the enclosure was laid out (p. 26).

THE EARLIER PREHISTORIC POTTERY (FIG. 11)

By Nigel Brown

The excavations produced a small amount of pottery (341 sherds weighing 1.855 kg), which has been recorded (details in archive) using a system devised for prehistoric pottery in Essex (Brown 1988). All decorated and rim sherds (with the exception of the rim fragments from AF71 and CF81) are illustrated (FIG. 11, TABLE 2). Fabrics present in the assemblage are:

Fabric
A, flint, S, 2 well sorted
B, flint, S–M, 2
C, flint, S–M with some L, 2
D, flint, S–L, 3
F, sand, S–M, 2–3 with addition of occasional large flint
J, sand, S 2 with veg. voids particularly on surfaces
M, grog, may have some sand or flint and occasional voids
L, quartz sometimes with sand, S–L 2
O, quartz and flint, S–L, 2
P, largely temperless, may have sparse very fine sand occasional flint or sparse irregular voids.

Size of inclusions: S = less than 1 mm diameter; M = 1–2 mm diameter; L = more than 2 mm diameter. Density of inclusions: 1 = less than 6 per cm^2; 2 = 6–10 per cm^2; 3 = more than 10 per cm^2.

The earliest pottery present is Peterborough Ware (FIG. 11, 1–3, TABLE 2), traditionally regarded as of Late Neolithic date, although recent reconsideration of the dating evidence (Gibson and Kinnes 1997) has suggested an earlier origin. This is supported locally by the stratigraphic sequence at the Springfield Cursus (Buckley *et al.* 2001). Body sherds and ?base sherds with cord-impressed decoration (FIG. 11, 1), and rim sherds, probably from Mortlake Style bowls (FIG. 11, 2–3), are present among the Stanway pottery. The material was derived from one of the enclosure ditches (CF6) and from a small pit (AF16). A small sherd of a flat base in Fabric F included with the Peterborough Ware from CF6 might be contemporary, but Fabric F commonly occurs in Middle Iron Age assemblages and consequently this sherd may well be of Iron Age date.

Early Bronze Age material is represented by a small fragment of the rim of a Collared Urn decorated with cord impressions on the exterior, together with a few other sherds from CF81, all in a grog-tempered fabric and possibly from the same pot.

Much of the earlier prehistoric pottery derived from AF71, and comprised body sherds probably derived from large jars. A small fragment of a plain rounded rim was present, but there were no decorated or otherwise diagnostic sherds. Dating is therefore problematic. The fabric and joining sherds of what appears to be the neck of a large round-shouldered jar might, by comparison with assemblages from elsewhere in Essex (*e.g.* Brown 1988; Wymer and Brown 1995), suggest a date within the first half of the 1st millennium B.C.

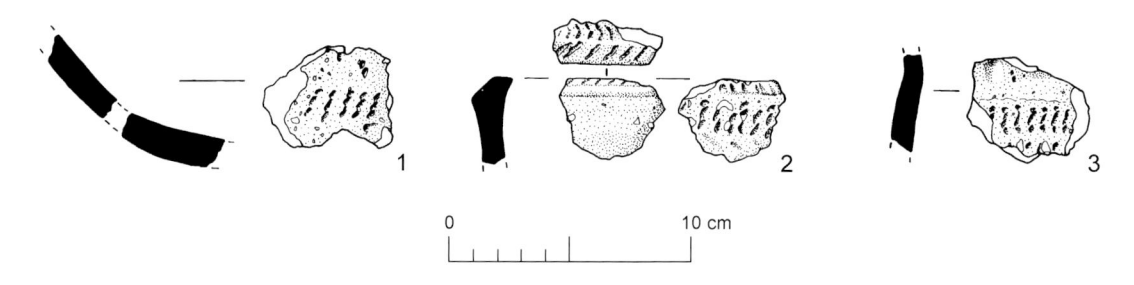

FIG. 11. Neolithic and Bronze Age pottery (scale 1:3)

TABLE 2: LIST OF ILLUSTRATED NEOLITHIC POTTERY

FIG. 11	Context	Description	Fabric
1	CF6	Peterborough Ware ?Mortlake bowl. Body and round base sherd. Rows of cord impressions arranged in herringbone pattern.	O
2	CF6	Peterborough Ware rim of Mortlake bowl. Row of cord impressions inside rim, and arranged in herringbone pattern on top of rim. Inside edge of rim also impressed. Part of two finger impressions survive on exterior of neck.	O
3	AF16	Peterborough Ware, neck/shoulder sherd of Mortlake bowl. Finger impressions on neck. Row of cord impressions on shoulder.	L

DISCUSSION

The Peterborough Ware from Stanway is decorated with a combination of impressed cord and finger impressions. These forms of decoration are common in Peterborough Ware assemblages and occur at the Springfield Cursus (Brown 2001). However, in most local groups cord decoration is less common than finger-tip and finger-nail impression (*e.g. ibid.*; Brown 2003). The use of quartz as a tempering agent for Peterborough pottery is frequent and widespread, and may well have had ritual or symbolic implications (Gibson 1995). One sherd from CF6 has a burnt deposit/residue adhering to the surface, presumably the result of use as a cooking pot. The material from both CF6 and AF16 is largely unabraded; this is of some interest, since the Peterborough Ware from CF6 was residual in an Iron Age ditch. It may be that the material was accidentally incorporated from an earlier feature cut by the ditch. Alternatively it may have been deliberately deposited in the ditch during the Iron Age, presumably having been uncovered during the creation of the Iron Age enclosures; apparent reverence for earlier artefacts, particularly Bronze Age metalwork, is quite well known in the Iron Age.

The sherds from AF71, which probably belong to the earlier 1st millennium B.C.,+ lack diagnostic features but are unabraded and appear to have been deposited soon after breakage. Such material commonly occurs on settlement sites of the period which are quite common in east Essex (*e.g.* Brown 1996).

THE SCATTER OF HEAT-AFFECTED STONE ACROSS THE SITE
(FIG. 12; TABLES 3–4)
(incorporating a note and TABLE 3 by Keith Oak)

The weight of heat-affected stones from the excavations is around 80–100 kg. Almost all of them came from the west side of the site, especially the features inside Enclosure 1, although precise numbers are not available for every context (FIG. 12, TABLE 3). The stones are mainly small and rounded, some having split in the heat. The whole ones are mostly naturally rounded (fluvio-glacial) small cobbles, commonly described as 'potboilers'. On average these stones are between about 50–70 mm, measured on the longest dimension. They are predominantly of two

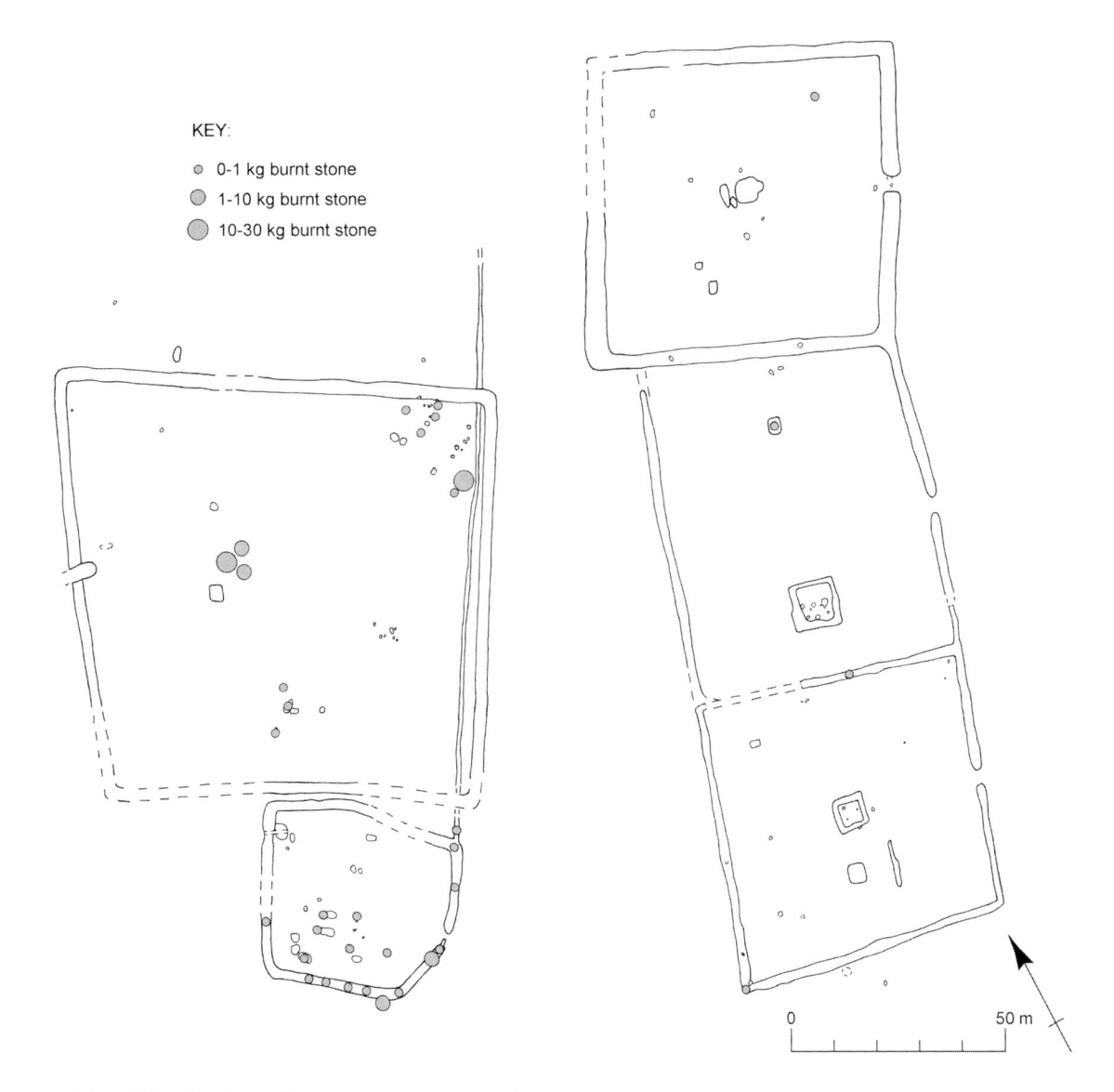

FIG. 12. Distribution of burnt stones by weight

stone types, *i.e.* sandstones/quartzite and flint. They are bigger than the stones which occur naturally in the underlying sand and gravels, which suggests that the largest ones, and hence presumably others, had been individually selected and had not been scorched accidentally by fires on the ground as might otherwise have been the case.

The pits AF24, AF76 and CF174 account for around half (about 41.2 kg) the total weight of the heat-affected stones. The groups of stones from these three pits (TABLE 4) consist of approximately 90% sandstones/quartzites and 10% flint. The composition of the remainder of the burnt stones from the site is almost exactly the reverse, being approximately 85% flint and 15% sandstones/quartzites. Flint makes up at least 95% of the local gravel deposits yet, in the three pit deposits, the equivalent figures are 2%, 8% and 12% respectively. Thus the stone from the pits reveals a deliberate policy of collecting well- or moderately cemented sandstones. Such stone types (quartzites) are mechanically strong and have survived being transported by glaciers and deposited by fluvio-glacial rivers. They were carefully selected because their thermal properties made them more suitable for pot-boilers than the ubiquitous flint pebble. The quartzites tend to be homogeneous and thus, when heated and rapidly cooled, generally expand and contract evenly and do not crack. Glacially derived flint, on the other hand, tends to have micro-fractures that are exploited by the expansion and contraction and so flint tends to shatter when heated in a fire, which makes such pebbles unsuitable for use as pot-boilers. Sandstone

TABLE 3: HEAT-AFFECTED STONES AND THE DATING EVIDENCE FOR THEM

Feature	Context	Date of latest pottery	Weight (kg)
Enclosure 1			
AF24	pit	–	29.20
AF26	pit	Middle Iron Age	<1
AF27	pit	Middle Iron Age	<1
AF28	pit	Early to Middle Iron Age	?<1
AF30	pit	–	?<1
AF34	pit	–	?<1
AF54	small pit	Middle Iron Age	<1
AF57	small pit	Middle Iron Age	<1
AF58	small pit	Middle Iron Age	<1
AF65	small pit	–	<1
AF76	small pit	–	approx. 10
AF80	pit	Middle Iron Age	?<1
ploughsoil	unstratified	n/a	0.03
Enclosure 2 and immediately south of it			
CF6	enclosure ditch	Middle Iron Age	2.51
CF21	pit	Middle Iron Age	0.45
CF137/AF59	boundary ditch	Middle Iron Age	0.03
CF168	pit	Middle Iron Age	0.09
CF169	pit	Middle Iron Age	0.02
CF170	pit	Middle Iron Age	0.16
CF172	pit	–	0.21
CF173	pit	Middle Iron Age	–
CF174	pit	–	approx. 2
CF183	small pit or post-/stake-hole	Middle Iron Age	0.03
CF415	pit with pyre debris	–	0.35
Enclosures 3–5			
BF13	pit	–	0.50
BF24	chamber	1st century A.D.	0.02
BF41/CF1	enclosure ditch	1st century A.D.	<1.00
CF4	enclosure ditch	1st century A.D.	0.01

TABLE 4: WEIGHTS AND APPROXIMATE PERCENTAGE OF STONE TYPES FROM PITS AF24, AF76, AND CF174

Feature	Weight (kg)	Well-cemented sandstones/ quartzites	Sandstones (less well cemented)	Micaceous sandstone	Vein quartz	Flint	Red sandstone (?Old Red Sandstone)	Unidentified
AF24	29.2	75%	12%	4%	4%	2%	2%	3%
AF76	10	65%	12%	2%	5%	12%	2%	2%
CF174	2	85%		3%	2%	8%	2%	

with laminations or thin beds is liable to fracture along the layers, and vein quartz would also tend to break, which is presumably why they too were rejected as pot-boilers. It would have been readily apparent which stone types worked best. They are easily identified and could have been collected with ease from surface deposits or stream/river banks.

Almost all the burnt stones were probably burnt in the prehistoric period. Their distribution on the site supports this view since most were found in Enclosures 1 and 2, and there is no apparent correlation between the heat-affected stone and the Late Iron Age and early Roman enclosures. In all probability most of the burnt flint pebbles occurred by chance, as a result of fires associated with prehistoric occupation or later funerary pyres. Others may have been deliberately burnt in the Middle Iron Age, because tiny flakes of burnt flint appear in pots as a temper (p. 48). The large numbers of burnt stones in the three pits AF24, AF76 and CF174 are different because they are a result of a careful selection process. They are likely to have been deliberately exposed to heat and are thus best interpreted as pot-boilers. However, their date is uncertain since none of the three pits contained any useful dating evidence. Curiously, these pits were not located inside Enclosure 2, as might be expected if the pot-boilers they contained were Middle Iron Age. Either the fires in which the stones were burnt were deliberately sited away from Enclosure 2 or the quartzite pot-boilers belong to an earlier phase of occupation, most probably the Late Bronze Age or Early Iron Age (p. 16) judging by the quantities of other prehistoric pottery from the site (limited as that is).

THE WORKED FLINT (FIG. 13; TABLES 5–6)

By Hazel Martingell

In total, 105 worked flints were studied from the excavations of 1987 (accession code 1987.16), 1988–92 (accession code 1988.4) and 1996–7 (accession code 1996.34) (TABLES 5–6). They came primarily from the excavated features, and it could be expected that the unexcavated areas would also contain a similar distribution of flint artefacts. A few worked flint fragments were also noted among the burnt stone.

The earliest piece is a good microdenticulated blade (SF327, not illustrated). These tools were used for cutting and reaping and were hafted into a wooden sheath along one long edge. They are associated with the Early Neolithic and the beginning of agriculture; they are not so evident in the Middle or Later Neolithic. It was recovered from ditch CF1 in Enclosure 5. The three scrapers (SF335, SF351, and SF375, not illustrated) are all good standard Neolithic types of the Middle or Later Neolithic periods. Scraper SF335 was recovered from ditch CF2 in Enclosure 5, scraper SF351 was from chamber CF42 in Enclosure 5, and scraper SF375 was also from Enclosure 5 but unstratified.

The bifacially worked fragment (SF384) is most likely to be a small part of a single-piece sickle of Late Neolithic date. It came from the Enclosure 5 area.

The remaining retouched and/or modified artefacts are those with minimal edge retouch or are on irregular 'blanks'. These pieces may occur in all periods and are not diagnostic of any one. With this in mind, we can look at the evidence for occupation on the site. The sequence of five enclosures covers the Middle to Late Iron Age, so there is a possibility that most of the worked flint recovered might belong to this time. In the past, it was thought that with the arrival of metal tools, flint tools ceased to be used. This was largely due to the recognition during the 19th and 20th centuries of distinct tool types that could be assigned to specific prehistoric periods — until the Iron Age. By the time metal had become the material for special items such as axes and swords, the importance of knapped flint had been reduced to basic sharp cutting edge pieces and strike-a-lights, with some natural flints modified by area of retouch called 'tools of convenience' made for specific tasks, for example SF381 and SF17. So, technically, there is no Iron Age flint tool typology in the traditional sense. However, over time and particularly from excavations of Iron Age sites (Young and Humphrey 1999), one particular artefact tends to dominate the collections and has become an acceptable Iron Age flint artefact. The criteria are:

1 A flint flake that may be described as 'squat', *i.e.* shorter than its width.
2 The platform is the widest part, which is usually unfaceted.
3 The positive and negative bulbs tend to be deep and rounded and lie one behind the other as though the flakes have been removed one after another from a split cobble without any core preparation.
4 The angle of the platform to the ventral/bulbar surface tends to be obtuse due to the angle of the blows removing the flakes, which tend to undercut the core, producing a thick butt end tapering to a sharp edge.
5 Occasionally this sharp edge may be modified by slight irregular retouch and sometimes the platform edge on the dorsal surface may have fine continuous retouch.

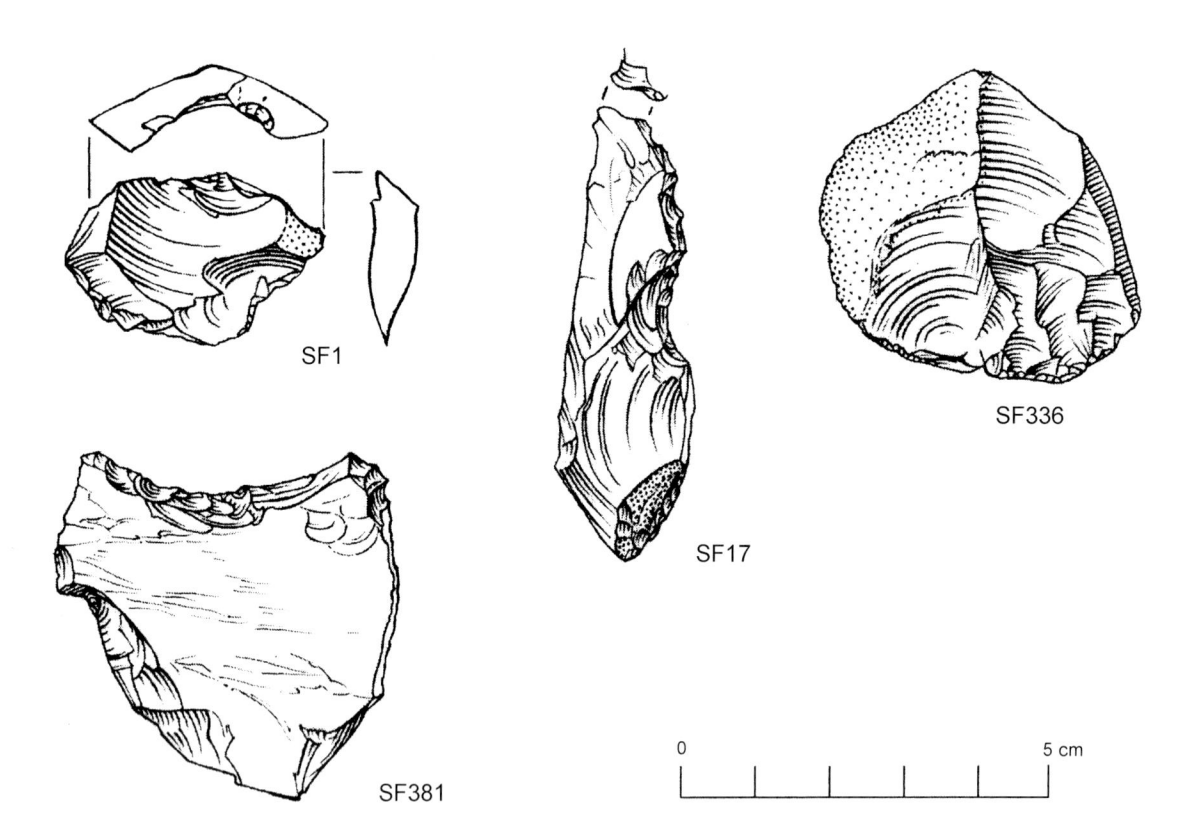

FIG. 13. ?Iron Age worked flints. SF1: typical Iron Age squat flake. SF17: flint rod with areas of retouch, ridges worn smooth. SF336: flake with two cones of percussion and fine retouch along platform edge. SF381: naturally split flint piece with sharp concave edge and areas of retouch. (Scale 1:1)

Of the illustrated artefacts, SF1 is typical of the basic squat flake and SF336 has fine continuous retouch along the platform edge (FIG. 13).

There are seven retouched pieces that could be Iron Age in date, four of which are illustrated (FIG. 13, SF1, SF17, SF336, SF381). The three that are not illustrated are either fragmentary or with little significant retouch. SF50 is a possible arrowhead. This is a naturally converging flake, with the butt end opposite the pointed end, thinned on both surfaces by invasive retouch; this may have been for hafting. The piece is now broken and its original shape may not have been a regular triangle and therefore it would not have been an arrowhead. SF18 and SF337 are both edge-retouched pieces of irregular form. SF1 and SF17 came from Enclosure 1. SF17 came from the floor of chamber AF25 in Enclosure 1. It is a flaked and retouched natural piece of flint, a multi-purpose 'tool of convenience', either buried as a funerary deposit in the chamber or residual. SF18 was found 140 m south-west of Enclosure 2. SF50, SF336, SF337 and SF381 came from the Enclosure 5 area.

TABLE 5: WORKED FLINT CATALOGUE

Middle Iron Age ditch CF137/AF59
1988.4 SF49	A549, AF59	Core, burnt, one flake removing core surface	

Enclosure 1 1987 trial-trench
1987.16 SF7	45, L1	Flake, converging, thick triangular section, retouch on ventral surface	?IA
1987.16 SF2	54, L1	Scraper, broken tertiary flake; fine retouch half-way round circumference, broken edge retouched	
1987.16 SF4	61, L1	Flake, small, trimming, secondary	
1987.16 SF10	102, L1	Flake, rough, two cones, good prepared platform, light grey flint	?IA

1987.16 SF5	103, L1	Blade, punch struck, fine butt, incurved profile, secondary, 63 mml	
1987.16 SF8	143, L2	Notch spall	
1987.16 SF3	167, L2	Flake, core preparation platform, secondary	

Enclosure 1
1988.4 SF17	A469, floor of chamber AF25	Retouched irregular converging flint piece, worn	?IA FIG. 13
1988.4 SF25	A503, mound of chamber AF25	Retouched small flake, tertiary	
1988.4 SF30	A504, mound of chamber AF25	Flake fragment, tertiary, thin section	
1988.4 SF16	A525, ?pit with cremation-related debris AF48	Flake fragment, tertiary, thinning flake	
1988.4 SF45	A615, pit AF80	Core, blade, three platforms: one and two opposing, three adjacent	
1988.4 SF15	A94, AL4	Flake, trimming, tertiary	
1988.4 SF1	A234, u/s	Flake, secondary, wide platform, deep bulb	?IA FIG. 13
1988.4 SF2	A234, u/s	Core, flake	

Enclosure 2 enclosure ditch (CF6)
1996.34 SF309	C20, CL13	Flakelet, tertiary	
1996.34 SF310	C55, CL29	Flake, thick, secondary	
1996.34 SF311	C55, CL29	Flake, tertiary, slight rolling	
1996.34 SF312	C55, CL29	Flake, secondary, slight rolling	
1996.34 SF313	C1210, CL86	Flake, thin section, straight, primary	
1996.34 SF314	C1211, CL81	Core, small, single platform	
1996.34 SF314	C1211, CL81	Flake, small, wide platform, tertiary	?IA
1996.34 SF315	C1219, CL89	Flake, primary, slight rolling	
1996.34 SF316	C1220, CL94	Flake, thinning, primary	
1996.34 SF317	C1221	Flake, primary, slight patination	
1996.34 SF318	C1279, CL126	Flake, butt removed, primary	
1996.34 SF319	C1292, CL114	Flake, trimming, secondary	
1996.34 SF320	C1299, CL142	Retouched blade, tertiary	
1996.34 SF321	C1299, CL142	Blade, thin section, tertiary	
1996.34 SF322	C1302, CL135	Flake, trimming, secondary	
1996.34 SF323	C1308, CL144	Notch spall, tertiary, good	
1996.34 SF324	C1326, CL142	Flake, thinning, tertiary	
1996.34 SF325	C1373	Flake, thinning, tertiary, good	

Enclosure 2
| 1996.34 SF326 | pit CF173, CL164, C1330 | Flakelet, thinning, secondary | |

Enclosure 2 (unstratified, topsoil)
1996.34 SF353	C1, CL1	Blade-flake, secondary	
1996.34 SF354	C1, CL1	Flake, tertiary, slight patination	
1996.34 SF355	C1, CL1	Flake, tertiary	
1996.34 SF356	C1, CL1	Flake, tertiary	

Outside Enclosures 1 and 2
1988.4 SF7	A164, AL4	Retouched blade fragment, tertiary	
1988.4 SF20	A420, u/s	Core, blade, good	
1988.4 SF22	A440, u/s	Retouched fragment, secondary, worn	
1988.4 SF18	A467, u/s	Retouched and obliquely truncated blade, tertiary	?IA
1988.4 SF46	A540, u/s	Retouched blade fragment	
1988.4 SF47	B59, u/s	Flake, secondary, axe thinning?	
1996.34 SF385	C1363, u/s	Flake, irregular, tertiary	
1996.34 SF386	C1376, u/s	Retouched blade, tertiary	

Enclosure 3
1988.4 SF294	B282, BL22 enclosure ditch BF27	Flake, faceted butt, tertiary	
1988.4 SF48	B22, u/s	Retouched and worn flake, retouch on ventral surface, tertiary	
1988.4 SF51	B23, u/s	Blade, tertiary, 57 mm, treacly white with black inclusions flint, good	

Enclosure 5 enclosure ditch (CF1)
| 1996.34 SF327 | C3, CL3 | Microdenticulate/saw on blade; fine retouch along both lateral edges – very good straight blade, tertiary | Early Neolithic |
| 1996.34 SF328 | C87, CL37 | Flake, sharpening/trimming; ochre stained patination | |

TABLE 5: WORKED FLINT CATALOGUE (CONT'D)

1996.34 SF329	C1349, CL170	Flake, trimming, notch spall type	
1996.34 SF330	C1387	Blade, irregular, converging, sharp, utilised, tertiary	

Enclosure 5 enclosure ditch (CF2)

1996.34 SF331	C72, CL40	Blade fragment, converging, thin section, straight section – tertiary, good	
1996.34 SF332	C72, CL40	Flake, waste, core/tool trimming, secondary	
1996.34 SF333	C72, CL40	Flake, waste, core/tool trimming, secondary	
1996.34 SF334	C72, CL40	Blade fragment, secondary	
1996.34 SF335	C72, CL40	Denticulate scraper on secondary flake; flake removals across distal end and down both lateral edges (ventral flaking on left edge)	Middle or Late Neolithic
1996.34 SF336	C146	Retouched flake, two cones of percussion removed by two ventral flakes; fine retouch along platform edge	?IA FIG. 13
1996.34 SF337	C1392	Microdenticulate on converging flake, retouch along right edge	
1996.34 SF338	C1399	Flake, secondary	
1996.34 SF339	C1399	Flake, secondary	

Enclosure 5 enclosure ditch (CF4)

1996.34 SF342	C15, CL11	Retouched converging flake; fine retouch along both lateral edges, glossy, slight patination	
1996.34 SF343	C68, CL27	Flake, trimming, tertiary	

Enclosure 5 Chamber (CF42)

1996.34 SF344	C501, CL49	Flake, gravel, secondary	
1996.34 SF345	C502, CL49	Flake, tertiary, tip of retouched piece	
1996.34 SF346	C511, CL55	Blade, thinning, tertiary, good	
1996.34 SF348	C594, CL59	Blade, converging, tertiary	
1996.34 SF349	C600	Blade, tertiary, good, tip missing (45 × 9 × 4mm)	
1996.34 SF350	C676	Flake, thinning, tertiary	
1996.34 SF351	C718	Scraper on long secondary flake, retouch around distal end, good	Middle or Late Neolithic
1996.34 SF352	C730, CL78	Flake, thinning, tertiary, good	

Other Enclosure 5 features

1996.34 SF340	C1284, shaft CF23	Flake, trimming, slight patination, secondary	Middle Palaeolithic?
1996.34 SF341	C98, pit CF53	Flake, trimming, core/artefact, tertiary	
1996.34 SF341	C98, pit CF53	Flake, trimming, core/artefact, tertiary	

Enclosure 5 (unstratified)

1988.4 SF50	B60, u/s	?Arrowhead, simple, broken, tertiary	?IA
1996.34 SF387	C1396, u/s	Core, small, small blade removals	

Site of Enclosures 2 and 5 (ploughsoil: unstratified)

1996.34 SF357	C2, CL1	Flake, secondary, shattered	
1996.34 SF358	C2, CL1	Flake, tertiary	trimming
1996.34 SF359	C2, CL1	Flake, secondary	pieces
1996.34 SF360	C2, CL1	Flake fragment, tertiary	
1996.34 SF361	C2, CL1	Flake, tertiary	
1996.34 SF362	C2, CL1	Flake, secondary	
1996.34 SF363	C2, CL1	Flake, secondary	
1996.34 SF364	C2, CL1	Flake, secondary	
1996.34 SF365	C2, CL1	Flake, secondary	
1996.34 SF366	C2, CL1	Flake, secondary, irregular	
1996.34 SF367	C2, CL1	Flake, secondary	
1996.34 SF368	C2, CL1	Flake from core trim, base part	
1996.34 SF369	C2, CL1	Flake, small, secondary	
1996.34 SF370	C2, CL1	Flake, small, tertiary	
1996.34 SF371	C2, CL1	Chipping	
1996.34 SF372	C2, CL1	Blade, secondary, irregular, 43 mm	
1996.34 SF373	C2, CL1	Retouched flake fragment, retouch at platform end	

1996.34 SF374	C2, CL1	Flake, secondary, irregular	
1996.34 SF375	C2, CL1	Retouched flake fragment, secondary, patinated ventral surface (scraper)	
1996.34 SF376	C2, CL1	Blade, triangular section, 57 × 17 × 10 mm	
1996.34 SF377	C2, CL1	Flake, secondary	
1996.34 SF378	C2, CL1	Flake, tertiary	
1996.34 SF379	C2, CL1	Gunflint, large, used	Modern
1996.34 SF380	C2, CL1	Flake fragment, secondary	
1996.34 SF381	C2, CL1	Retouched naturally fractured piece, retouched wide concave edge	?IA FIG. 13
1996.34 SF382	C2, CL1	Retouched flake, secondary, worn edges	
1996.34 SF384	C2, CL1	Bifacial fragment, notched broken edge, slight patination	Neolithic

TABLE 6: TOTALS OF WORKED FLINT TYPES

Flakes	60
Blades	11
Blade-flake	1
Cores	6
Notch spalls	2
Bifacial fragment	1
Retouched flakes	10
Retouched blades	4
Scrapers	3
Microdenticulates 'saws'	2
Retouched natural pieces – IA?	2
Retouched and obliquely truncated blade	1
?Arrowhead (atypical of any type)	1
Gunflint	1
Total of pieces	105

CHAPTER 3

THE MIDDLE IRON AGE FARMSTEAD

THE FARMSTEAD ENCLOSURE (ENCLOSURE 2) (FIGS 2, 5, 14–20)

The farmstead enclosure occupied a gravel area with a slight slope from west to east between the northern arms of a silt-filled palaeochannel (FIGS 2 and 5, CF52; p. 66). The enclosure ditch (AF39, CF6) was V-shaped in profile and must have been around 1.4–1.5 m in depth after allowing for the 0.4 m or so that had to be stripped off prior to excavation (FIGS 14–15). No remains survived of any bank, although the way in which the pits inside the enclosure were set back from the inner edge of the ditch points to the previous existence of an internal bank about 2.0 m wide at its base. The ditch and bank were substantial enough to secure any animals kept in the enclosure and protect them from predators (human as well as animal). However, it is dubious if they were large enough to provide anything more than this. A narrow ditch (FIG. 14, CF132) cut across the southern half of the entrance points to the entrance being blocked for a time, or to its having incorporated posts set in a construction trench. (A similar ditch was found across the entrance to Enclosure 3.) The uppermost surviving fills of the ditch of the farmstead enclosure contained a small quantity of later Iron Age pottery (44 g) indicating that it must still have been an earthwork in the funerary phase of the site.

Two currency bars had been carefully placed flat on their faces near the side of the enclosure ditch of Enclosure 2 (FIGS 14 and 20). They lay side by side with the socketed ends to the north. They appeared to have been placed on the surface of the ditch as opposed to buried in a pit. There were no indications of a pit, although detecting such a feature is likely to be difficult if, as is likely, its fill would have been very similar to the silt in the ditch. However, the relationship of the currency bars to the ditch and its fill gave the strong impression that they had simply been laid on the side of the ditch after about 0.4 m of silt had accumulated in the bottom of it (FIG. 14).

Close to the area where the currency bars had been placed, a pit (CF415) had been dug into the upper part of the ditch fill and part of the cremated remains of a human adult, together with some charcoal, put into it. The pit was not visible at the level of the excavation surface, but appeared to be sealed by the further accumulation of material into the ditch. Despite its proximity to the currency bars, the pit was stratigraphically much later than them (FIGS 2 and 14). The pit certainly relates to the funerary phase of the site, but the currency bars are more likely to be associated with the farmstead, because their deposition seems to be relatively early in terms of the ditch fill. (It should be borne in mind that the ditch is likely to have been about 400 mm deeper than shown in FIGURES 14–15.)

There were various other pits inside the enclosure. They can be divided into three groups based on size, shape, and fill. The first group may be the result of clearing the site of bushes and trees prior to the laying out of the farmstead. The second group seems to have been associated with a round-house, while the third may have been for storage. The groups are as follows.

Group 1) ?Clearance features (FIGS 2, 10, 15–16)

Several pit features (AF40, AF44, CF172, CF175, CF176, CF194, CF195; FIGS 15–16) have similar fills of slightly loamy stony sand. Most of them contained some charcoal, but with few or no datable finds. Three pits (CF172, CF175, CF194) are long shallow oval features orientated north-west/south-east and appear to form a distinct sub-group. Two of them (CF175 and CF194) are cut by pits datable to the Middle Iron Age within the ?round-house, and may be associated with them. AF44 (FIG. 10) was cut by the enclosure ditch (AF32/AF39/CF6).

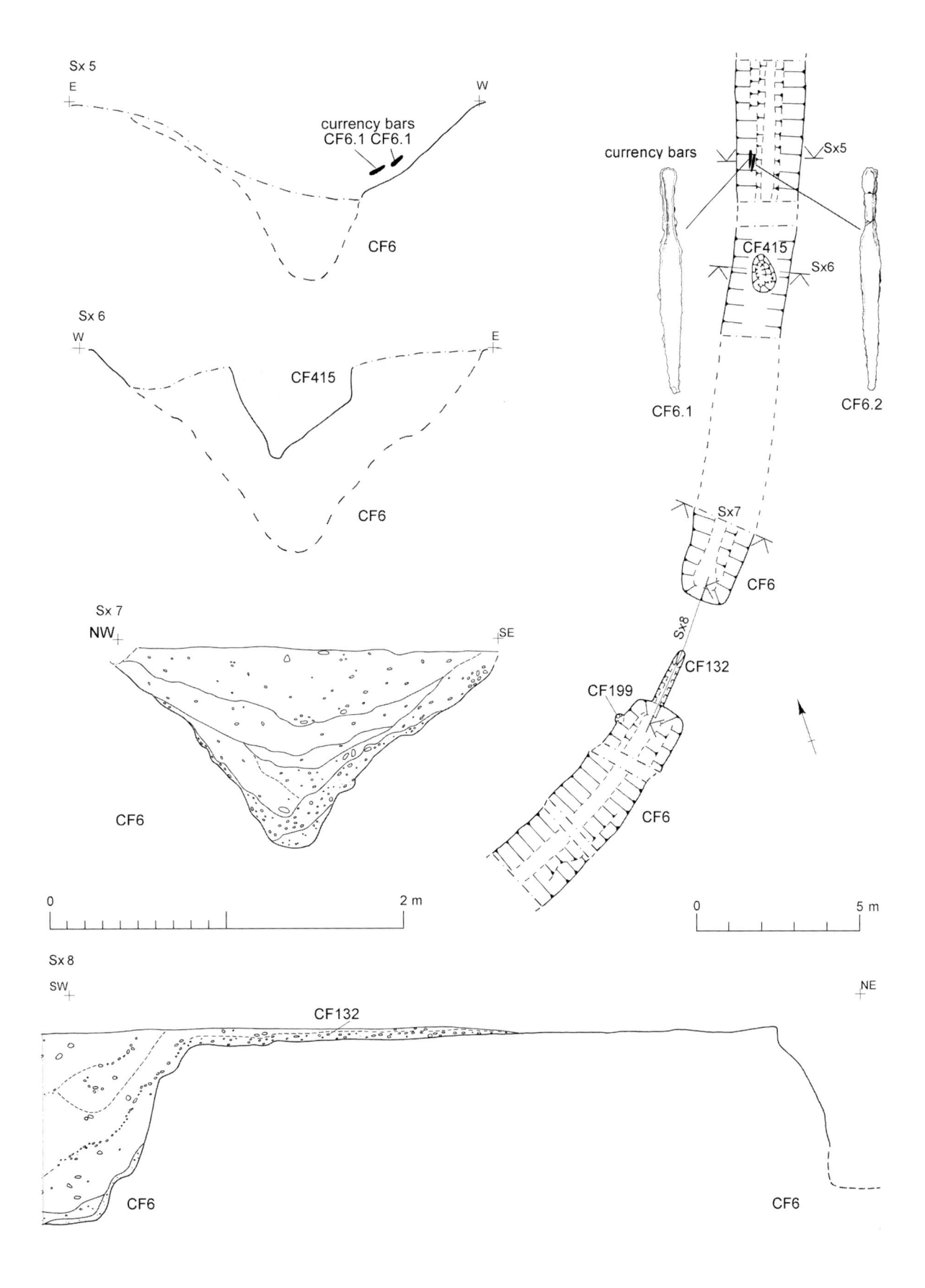

FIG. 14. Enclosure 2 ditch: sections (scale 1:30) and plan showing location of currency bar hoard and pit CF415

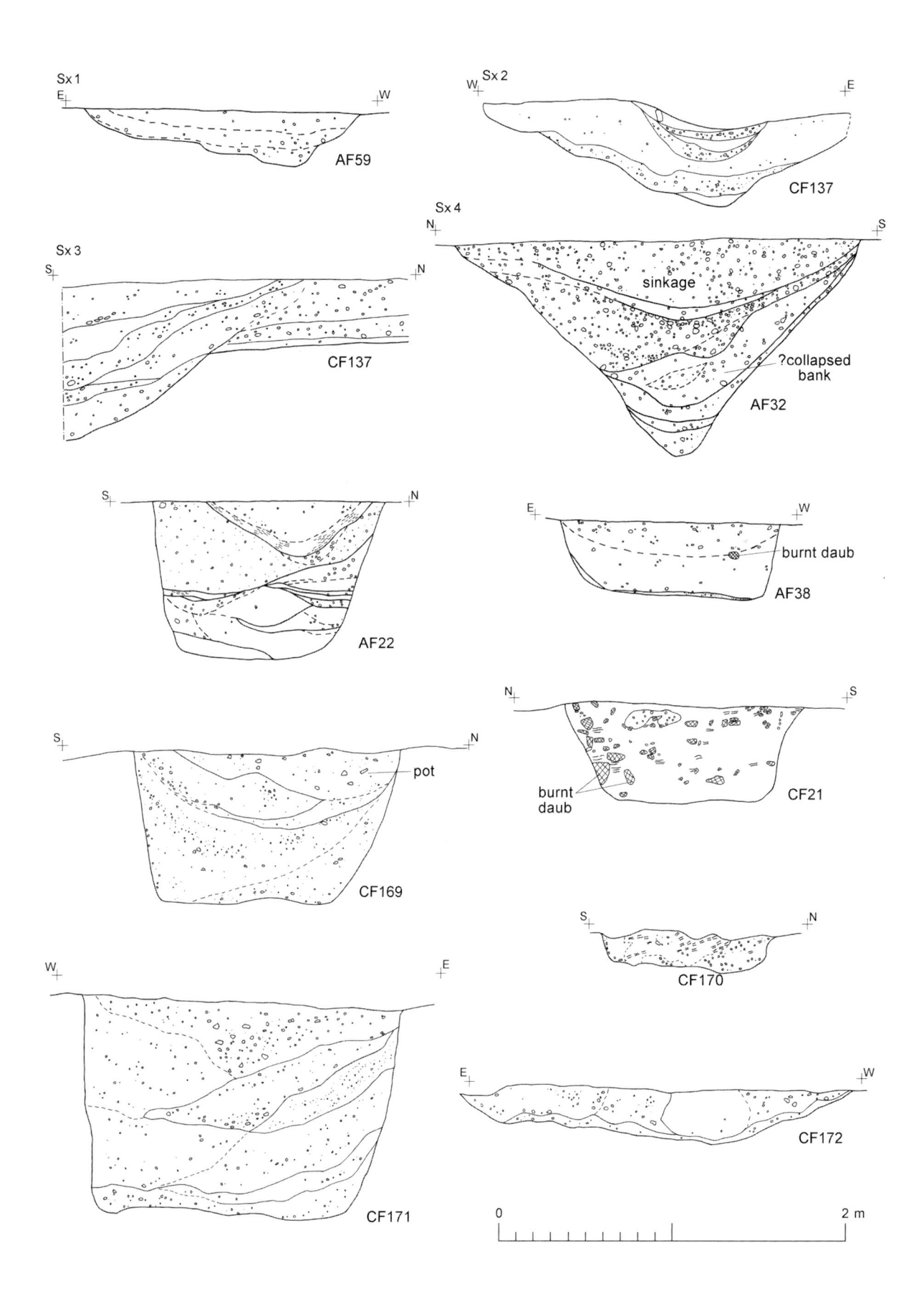

FIG. 15. Boundary ditch CF137/AF59: sections; Enclosure 2 ditch AF32: section; Enclosure 2 pits: sections (scale 1:30)

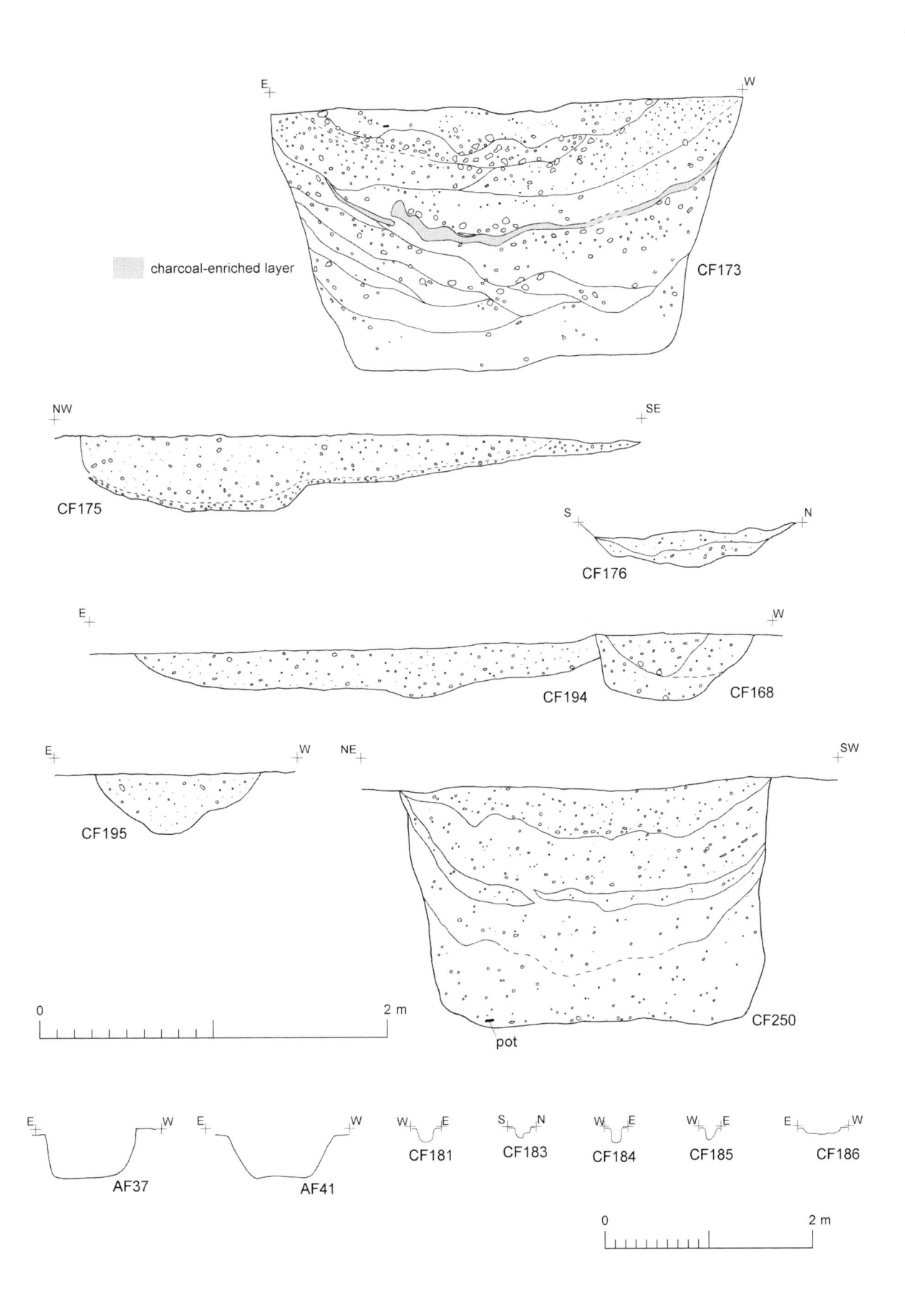

FIG. 16. Enclosure 2 pits: sections (scale 1:30) and profiles (scale 1:50)

Group 2) Pits associated with a possible round-house (FIGS 2, 16, 17)

A small group of features can tentatively be interpreted as the remains of a round-house (FIG. 17). The evidence is slender but the diameter (about 15 m) is consistent with such an interpretation, as is the position of the porch (facing the entrance to the enclosure) and the footprint of the building in relation to the distribution of pits (the two being mutually exclusive).

The wall and porch of the putative round-house are represented by five possible stake- or post-holes (FIG. 2, CF181 and CF183–6; FIG. 16). Four of them were in an arc which seemed to correspond to part of the circumference of the round-house. The fifth one was to the south-east of the other four, in a position compatible with one of two post-holes needed to form a porch.

The pits could be distinguished from the surrounding natural sand and gravel by their darker silty fills. Four of them (CF181 and CF183–5) were similar in size (about 100–150 mm in width and depth). CF186 was different from the others, being broad and shallow (about 350 mm across and 50 mm deep) and filled with stony clay.

There were two unusual smaller pits (FIG. 2, CF168 and CF170) about 7 m to the west of these features. CF168 contained a complete, intact Middle Iron Age pot (C1468) lying upright but tilted to one side, as if it had been knocked over when the pit was backfilled. Also within the fill at the south end of the pit was a patch of sandy clay containing fragments of fired daub. The fill of the other pit (CF170) included diffuse bands of charcoal. Both pits had rounded profiles, and both cut the west ends of earlier pits (CF175 and CF194). The latter are assumed to be clearance features, although their elongated shape, shallow profile, and relationships to CF168 and CF170 raise another possibility, *i.e.* that they were secondary features which were dug to allow the insertion of vertical posts into the round-house. This would mean that CF168 and CF170 were post-pits backfilled after the removal of the posts.

The group of five stake or post-holes would have probably been regarded as natural features or root holes had it not been for the presence of the pot in CF168 (FIG. 25, 20). This complete vessel, buried in the centre of a round-house, was clearly a deliberately placed deposit for which there is an identical parallel from elsewhere in Colchester. In 2003 on Area 2 of the Garrison redevelopment, a Middle Iron Age round-house was discovered with a pit in the centre containing a complete pot just as at Stanway (Brooks and Masefield 2005, figs 7–8; p. 61).

Group 3) ?Storage pits (FIGS 2, 15–16, 17)

In the south-west angle of the enclosure were three large deep pits (CF171, CF173, CF250; FIGS 2, 15–16, 17) dug so that they were almost touching without intercutting. The northern two (CF171 and CF250) were sub-circular features approximately 2.0 m in diameter and about 1.0 m deep, while the third (CF173) was sub-rectangular and just under 3.0 m long, 2.0 m wide and 1.5 m deep. All three had flat bases and vertical sides with no signs of a weathered profile, as if they had not been left open for any length of time. They all contained Middle Iron Age pottery but relatively few other finds. The latter included an iron disc and a fragment of an iron saw (CF250.1 and CF250.2), both from the middle of the fill of CF250, and a piece of worked sandstone (CF171.1) from pit CF171. The three pits are of the sort usually interpreted as having been used for storage.

To the north and east of these were six other pits (AF22, AF37, AF38, AF41, CF21, CF169; FIGS 2, 15–16) which may also have been used for storage. They all contained Middle Iron Age pottery, and had near-vertical sides and flat bases. They ranged in size from AF37, which was 1.1 m long and 0.45 m deep, to AF22, which was 2.3 m long and 0.9 m deep. Most of them were smaller than CF171, CF173 and CF250.

THE POSSIBLE DROVEWAY (FIGS 2, 5, 15, 17)

A shallow, linear ditch (CF137/AF59) up to 2.0 m wide and 0.5 m deep (as measured after stripping) extended in a north-eastwards direction from the north-east corner of Enclosure 2 (FIGS 2, 5, 15, 17). Its course is traceable as cropmarks on aerial photographs for a distance of

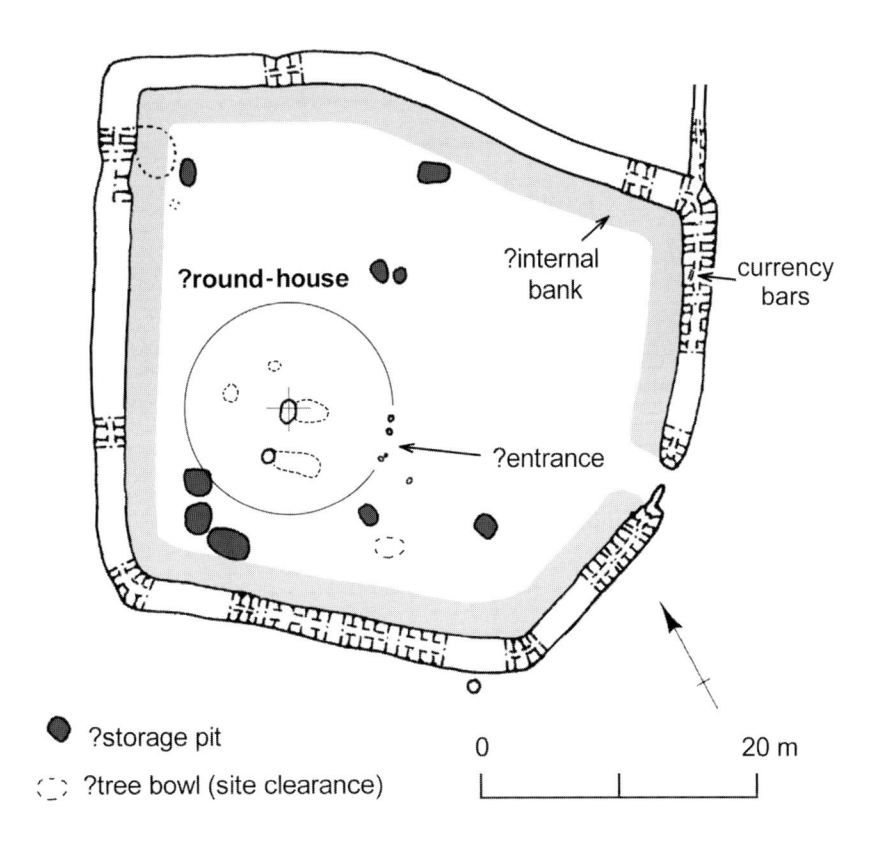

FIG. 17. ?Interpretative plan of the layout of Enclosure 2

about 450 m as far as a modern orchard where cropmarks would not show. A small quantity of Middle Iron Age pottery from AF59 shows that the feature represents a pre-existing boundary ditch which was respected during the construction of Enclosure 1.

Several enclosures similar to the farmstead at Stanway have been recognised in Essex and elsewhere (Buckley *et al.* 1987, 74–5), at Orsett 'Cock' (Carter 1998), Gosbecks (*CAR* 11, 96–8), and the Airport Catering Site, Stansted (Havis and Brooks 2004, 79–188). These indicate that the example at Stanway would have been integrated with a droveway or a system of droveways leading to fields and areas of pasture. At Gosbecks and elsewhere in Camulodunum, the droveways have been sufficiently well traced to indicate that they did not simply relate to individual homesteads, but formed a single system that must have facilitated the free movement of people and animals throughout the whole settlement. No such droveway can be recognised at Stanway, although the ditch CF137/AF59 might represent the west side of one, since Enclosure 3 is parallel to this ditch but offset by about 24 m, which is more than enough to accommodate a droveway.

THE PITS NORTH OF ENCLOSURE 2 (FIGS 2, 5, 18)

The features north of Enclosure 2 consisted mainly of isolated Middle Iron Age or undatable pits (FIG. 2). With only one minor exception (BF10 in Enclosure 3, see p. 71), all of them were to the west of the ?boundary ditch CF137/AF59 (FIG. 5). They can be described in terms of two groups plus two or three isolated examples. In the absence of vertical stratigraphy or dated finds their relationship to Enclosure 2 and the later Enclosure 1 was often uncertain.

The first group (AF24, AF26–27, AF47) was near the centre of what was to become Enclosure 1 (FIGS 2, 5, 18). Of all the pits, these seem to relate most clearly to Middle Iron Age occupation. Three contained small, burnt stones or 'pot-boilers' and charcoal. Burnt stones were found widely over the whole site, but the bulk of them (29.2 kg) were recovered from AF24. AF24 and AF27 had similar linings of thin sandy clay. Middle Iron Age pottery was recovered from AF26, AF27 and AF47 with some burnt daub from AF27. The general

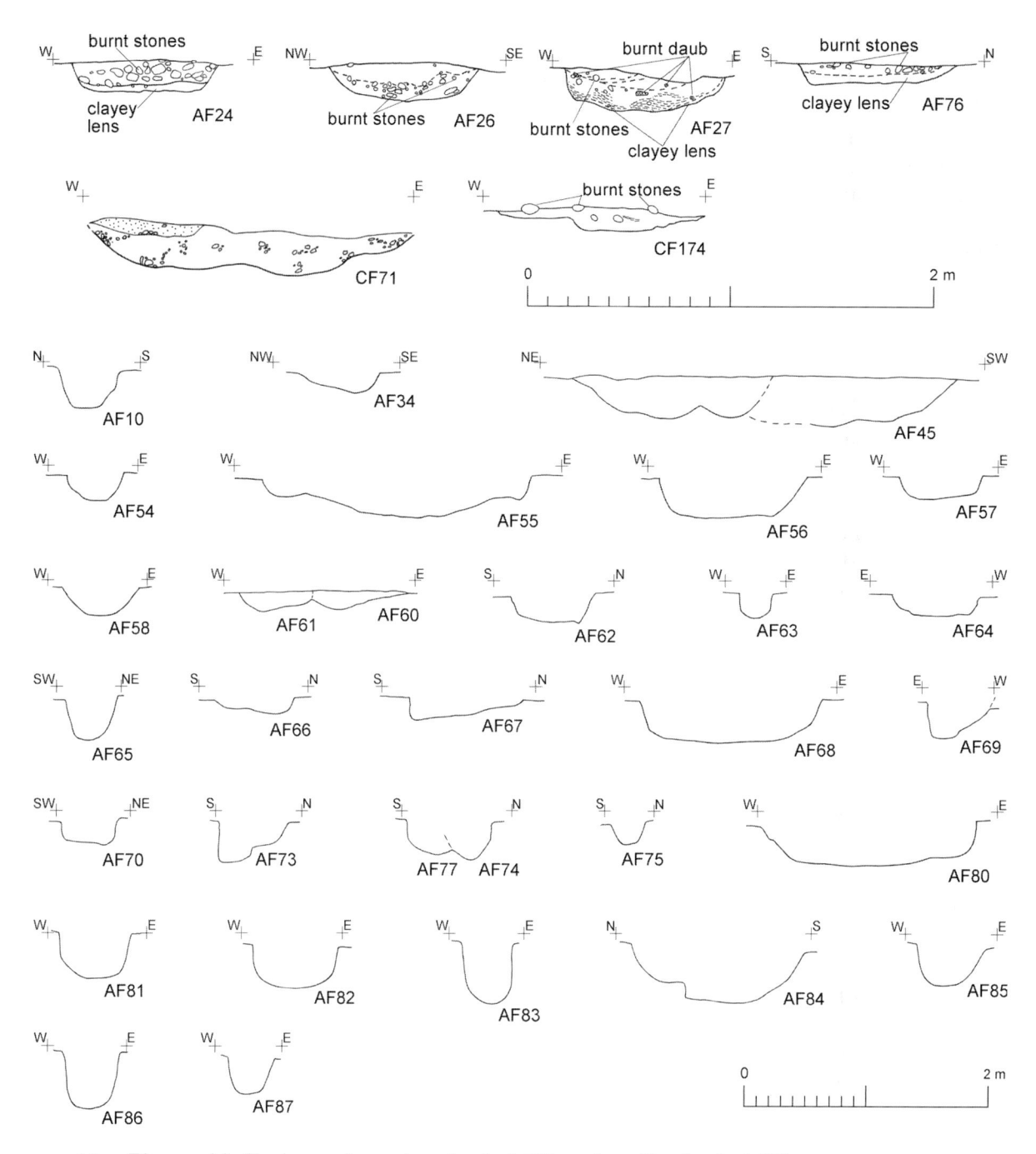

FIG. 18.   Pits outside Enclosure 2: sections (scale 1:30) and profiles (scale 1:50)

similarity of the features in the group suggests a common function, such as the parching of grain (Cunliffe and Poole 1991, 374–5), as well as a similarity in date.

The other group (AF54–58, AF60–62, AF64, AF68, AF73–F74, AF80) was situated near the north-east corner of Enclosure 1 (FIGS 2, 5, 17). They all contained Middle Iron Age pottery. Some nearby undated features (AF63, AF65–67, AF69–70, AF75–78) seemed to be associated with them. Burnt daub from AF69 (3.2 g) and AF77 (2.6 kg) included fragments with wattle voids that may have derived from an oven or kiln. Pit AF76 also contained burnt stones.

Other undated features in this area included a pit (AF45) with a layer of charcoal-rich fill on the bottom of the feature, and a group of small pits or post-holes (AF81–7; FIG. 18). A ?post-hole/pit (AF7) in the north-west corner of the enclosure contained Middle Iron Age pottery. An unstratified piece of worked flint from Enclosure 1 could have been of Iron Age date (FIG. 13, SF1).

If Enclosure 1 had had an internal bank, it would have sealed several of the Middle Iron Age features (*e.g.* AF54, AF58, AF73, AF74), which would therefore have pre-dated the Enclosure 1 ditch. Despite the relative shallowness of these pits (mostly 0.3 m or less), their position on plan suggests that some could have been post-holes from a structure, although the rectilinear alignment of the ?post-holes is perhaps unlikely in a structure of this date. It is possible that the apparent alignment of the pits is due to chance, and some or all could have pre-dated the Enclosure 1 ditch and ?bank while others could have been contemporary with them or post-dated them.

THE CURRENCY BARS

By Richard Hingley

DEFINITION AND DESCRIPTION (FIGS 5, 14, 19–20)

Two deliberately placed currency bars were located within the ditch on the eastern side of Enclosure 2 (FIGS 5, 14, 20). The two bars were positioned side by side on the inner side of the enclosure ditch, apparently early on in the history of the infilling of the ditch, but the context is open to some interpretation (p. 26). They may be comparable in form to the leaf-shaped currency bars discussed by Allen (1967, 314). This report considers the social context of the Stanway bars and their relationship to other currency bars that have been found in Britain and on the Continent.

The so-called currency bars of Britain are part of a widespread western and central European phenomenon. Crew has defined currency bars as: 'Refined bar iron, forged into a wide variety of blade shapes, usually with some form of socket. Density about 6.5 to 7. Used as trade iron.' (Crew 1995a, 277). Currency bars differ from other types of 'trade iron', including billets and hooked billets, in the distinctive range of forms that have been attributed to them (*ibid.*). The British examples have been discussed by a number of authors since their initial identification (*e.g.* Smith 1905; Allen 1967; Salter and Ehrenreich 1984; Hingley 1990; 1997; Crew 1994; 1995a; 1995b). Bars occur on at least 55 sites in Britain. A minimum number of 1,574 bars is represented, and these are made up of 67 distinct finds (Hingley 2005, appendix 1). Broadly similar bars have been found across France and in Belgium, Germany and Switzerland (Doswald 1994; Martin and Ruffat 1998, especially distribution map fig. 4; Serneels 1998, fig. 33, a typology of the various iron bars that occur in Western Europe; Feugère 2000).

The dating of currency bars in Britain is a problematic issue since few have been found in directly datable contexts (Crew 1994, 348). Allen argued that they are broadly of Middle Iron Age date as they pre-date the appearance of Belgic pottery and metalwork (Allen 1967, 322). Evidence from more recent excavations supports this suggestion in that, when dating evidence is found at all, the bars are usually associated with Middle Iron Age pottery, although no examples have been absolutely dated. The Stanway bars are particularly important in this respect, as Enclosure 2 is Middle Iron Age (with pottery), and pre-dates the Late Iron Age/early Roman burial enclosures. Currency bars in general may, however, have continued in use rather later than the Middle Iron Age. A hoard from Camerton, Somerset, contained three currency bars that appear to have been associated with an axe that, on typological grounds, should be of Roman date (Jackson 1990a, 20). Nevertheless, a Middle Iron Age date seems likely for the Stanway examples.

Crew has argued that a wide variety of bar forms occurred. The consistency of each type arises from the fact that each distinct group was made in single workshops, and that this is the reason for the regional distribution of the various types (Crew 1995a, 277–8). As a result, the four main kinds of currency bar that have been distinguished in past accounts, *i.e.* sword-shaped, spit-shaped, plough-share and leaf-shaped bars (Allen 1967; Hingley 1990), no longer constitute a viable classification. At least 20 distinct types of bar can now be distinguished (Crew 1994, 346; 1995a, 278). It still appears true, however, that the 'sword' and the 'plough' formed a basis for many of the regionally defined types of currency bar that Crew has defined (Hingley 2005, 197).

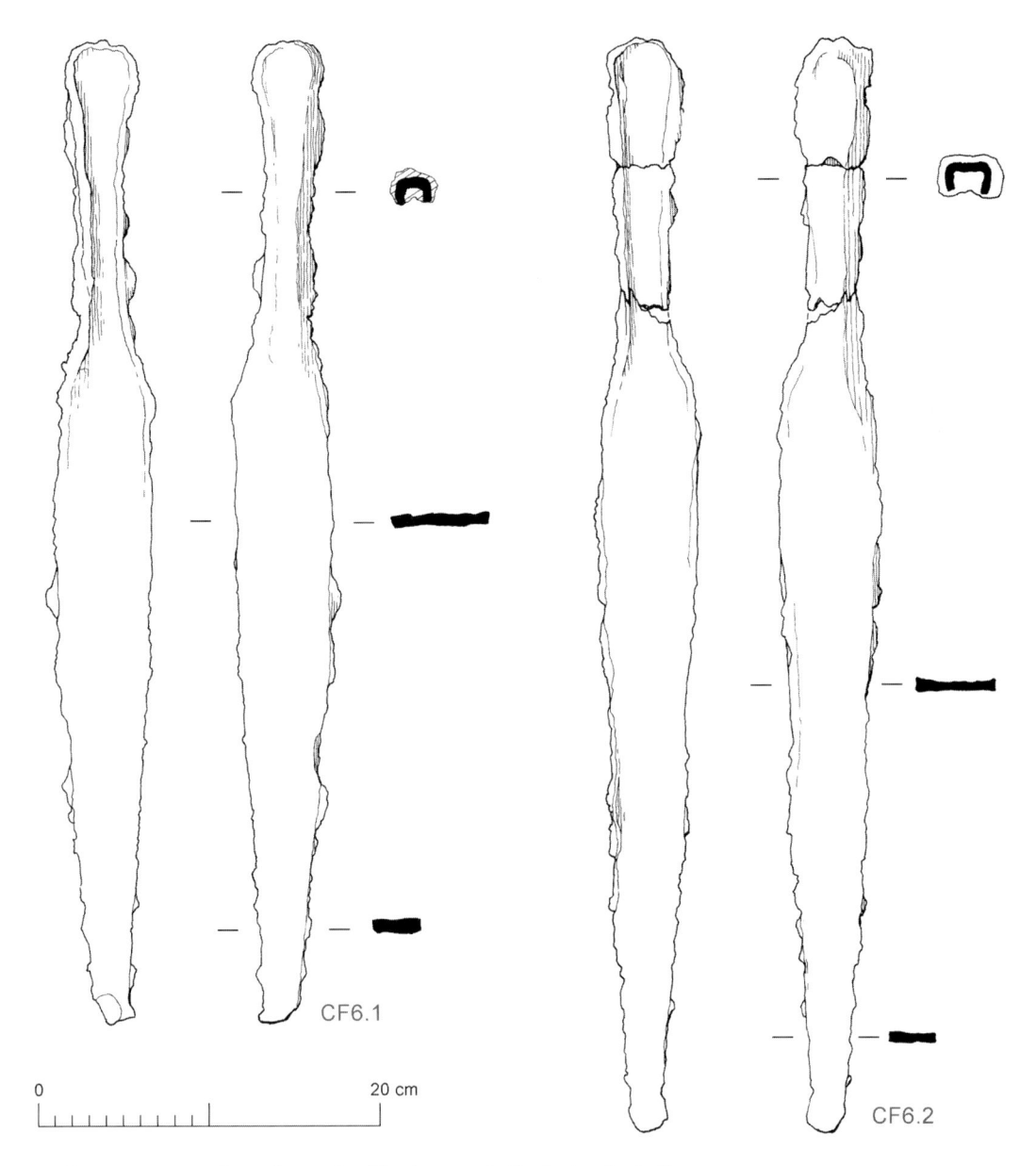

FIG. 19. Iron currency bars from the Enclosure 2 ditch (scale 1:4)

The Stanway bars would usually be identified as leaf-shaped (FIG. 19; catalogue descriptions pp. 46–7) and are most similar to examples from two findspots in Cambridgeshire, at Ely and Barrington. (For these bars, see Allen 1967, plate 32 and Crew 1995b.) These leaf-shaped bars may be based in symbolic terms on the spear-head (Allen 1967, 314). The two bars from Stanway and those from the other two sites in East Anglia may indicate a distinctive subgroup that emanated from a single workshop, as suggested by Crew. Further discoveries will be required if this supposed group is to be defined in any greater detail.

Crew has suggested that the wide variety of forms and weights militates against the idea that the bars operated as part of a standard currency system and that instead they represented trade iron (Crew 1994; 1995a). Currency bars appear to form one aspect of the increased evidence for exploitation of iron stock from the 3rd–2nd century B.C. onward, and they may have operated within a political system in which industrial production was becoming increasingly centralised within particular regions of southern Britain (Sharples 1990). They constitute one of a number of types of trade iron that occur across Britain at this time, including the billet and hooked billets (Crew 1995a). The forms adopted for currency bars, the thin blades and curved sockets, perhaps demonstrated their character as more fully refined than the other types of trade iron (Crew 1991).

FIG. 20.   Enclosure 2 ditch CF6: iron currency bars *in situ*

The idea that currency bars represented trade iron stresses the economic and practical value of the objects, interpreting them as having a primarily functional rôle in the manufacture of iron objects. The production and circulation of these items becomes part of the practical industry of iron production. The idea that the production and circulation of currency bars reflected the value of the objects in terms of the iron that they contained suggests that they were buried with the intention of retrieval and use. Were currency bars hoarded as items of material value, as many past studies have suggested, or were they deposited as a ritual activity, or a combination of both?

SYMBOLIC AND RITUAL ASPECTS

It is unlikely that the hoards in which these objects occur had a utilitarian function in the production of iron objects (Hingley 1990; Martin and Ruffat 1998). Most surviving bars, including the Stanway examples, were carefully buried and not subsequently disturbed. It is also evident that the currency bars themselves had more than a practical function (Doswald 1994, 335; Hingley 1997). The symbolic aspect of the bars is indicated by the use of symbols connected with the taking of life, the sword and perhaps the spear, and an item connected with agricultural production, the plough, as a basis for the form of some of these bars (Hingley 1990; 1997). The currency bar formed a stage in the production cycle of iron artefacts and at the same time had symbolic associations both with the agricultural cycle and human life cycles (*ibid.*, 13).

The bars occur in a range of contexts that indicate acts of ritual deposition both in Britain and on the Continent (Brunaux 1988, 44; Doswald 1994, 335; Hingley 1990; Martin and Ruffat 1998, 110; Muller 1990, 94). Three types of context of deposition have been defined within Britain (Hingley 1990): those that are closely related to settlement boundaries; those that can be termed 'natural'; and other contexts which do not fall into either of these categories. It appeared from the information that was available in 1990 that these three different types of context defined at least two distinct regional practices of deposition. They included a core zone in Dorset, Wessex and the West Midlands, in which hoards occur within settlement boundaries, and a peripheral area in which they were positioned in natural and other contexts (Hingley 1990). Discoveries since 1990, including the Stanway hoard, suggest that the distinction between the core and the peripheral zones is breaking down (Hingley 2005, 190). The Stanway examples come from the peripheral area but were deposited in a settlement boundary, in keeping with many of the hoards in the core zone. A second, recently discovered, hoard of two currency bars from Hinchingbrooke Park Road, Cambridgeshire, also came from a settlement boundary context (Hinman 2003, 8, 11, fig. 5).

Most finds of currency bars are single or occur in small groups. Some very large hoards have, however, been found, and it often appears that the bars were deliberately buried as a group (Hingley 2005, 185). Even a single object probably formed a deliberate deposit, for it is unlikely that a complete bar would be accidentally lost or discarded. In some cases, the small groups are buried together in a way that emphasises their significance as a group. This is the case for the two Stanway examples, which were placed side by side.

It is likely that currency bars had a practical function as trade iron, but at the same time the hoards do not make sense as stores of iron to be retrieved. Currency bars in general occur on a range of significant Middle Iron Age settlements. Some of the large hoards have been found on hillfort sites, and hoards from enclosed settlement sites tend to be smaller in size (Hingley 1990; 2005, 191). The exchange of trade iron may have formed one of the methods by which individual communities in later prehistoric Britain attempted to create domination over others. Iron was a very powerful material that was valuable in producing state-of-the-art weapons and vitally important agricultural tools. The acts of control over the process of production, circulation and deposition may have been used to create new forms of power (Hingley 1997). These forms of power, however, were not distinct from the symbolic context of the production, use and hoarding of these items. The deposition of currency bars at Stanway suggests that the occupants of Enclosure 2 in the Middle Iron Age had access to these valuable and powerful objects and were able to deposit them in a significant context.

THE STRUCTURAL CLAY (FIG. 23; TABLE 7)

The site produced nearly 52 kg of structural clay, much of it burnt, with most coming from Enclosure 2, where it was concentrated in pit CF21, and from Enclosure 1, where it was concentrated in two small pits in the north-east corner of the site, AF69 and AF77 (TABLE 7). As such a high proportion of the whole assemblage comes from the Middle Iron Age enclosure, with comparatively little coming from the line of enclosures to the east (just over 1 kg), it seems unlikely that any of the latter derives from the burial rite. Most of the clay from Enclosure 1 is probably also of Middle Iron Age origin, with that from AF69 and AF77 possibly indicating the site of one or more ovens or kilns. The Middle Iron Age material from CF21 in Enclosure 2 is examined in detail below.

TABLE 7: DISTRIBUTION OF STRUCTURAL CLAY

Enclosure	Total (kg)	Percentage of site assemblage	Concentration within enclosure	Percentage of enclosure assemblage
1	8.755	17%	Pits AF69, AF77: 5.6 kg	64%
2	42.050	81%	Pit CF21: 39.7 kg	94%
3	0.032	0.06%	–	–
4	0.635	1.22%	–	–
5	0.495	0.95%	–	–
total	**51.967**	–	–	–

ENCLOSURE 2: PIT CF21 (FIG. 23)

Pit CF21 in Enclosure 2, the Middle Iron Age farmstead, produced 39.7 kg of clay fragments, most with scorch marks or other evidence of burning, from one or more structures. A number of loomweight fragments were also found in the pit (p. 38), but two of the three fabrics from which they were made were quite distinctive, enabling even small pieces lacking any form or original surfaces to be separated from the main bulk of the clay assemblage. The third loomweight fabric closely resembles structural daub, and it is possible that some small featureless fragments in this fabric may be included in the material discussed below.

The assemblage can be broken down into three groups.

Group A. Large pieces with an outer surface and wattle marks, or one of these features. Made in a sandy clay, the fragments are usually orange to orange-brown in colour, although patches of reduction are present beneath the surface of some fragments, and on the surface of others. The wattle marks run in one direction only, often set very close together. On only one piece is there evidence of both vertical and horizontal wattling. The surfaces of these pieces were in general flat or nearly so, although some are slightly convex and some slightly concave. Others have been carefully shaped and a very few have edges as well as surfaces. FIGURE 23, CF21.9, appears to be from an entrance, with the edge set to one side of a wattle 20 mm in diameter and just covering one 14 mm in diameter. The former is noticeably stouter than the majority of the wattles. FIGURE 23, CF21.10, is similar, although the edge has not been dragged completely over the outer wattle. Most of the surface of this piece is reduced, including the wattle voids.

Group B. Fragments with a convex outer surface and no wattle marks. Occasionally a concave inner surface survives. The fabric is in general harder, denser and less sandy, and has many patches of greenish-yellow, as well as red streaks from naturally occurring iron deposits.

Group C. Fragments, both small and medium-sized, in the same fabric as Group A, but with no distinctive features, although some with small patches of sharp grit exposed may be from a floor.

The material breaks down by weight thus:

Group A (large fragments with a flat outer surface and/or wattles): 16.6 kg,
Group B (convex fragments with no wattles): 2.2 kg,
Group C (fragments in a similar fabric to Group A but with no distinctive features): 20.9 kg.

Groups A and C are structural daub, originally air-dried, but now scorched and 'fired'. The heat applied must have been prolonged, but does not seem to have been very intense, as no vitrification is present as it was on burnt daub fragments from the burnt hut C11 at Little Waltham, Essex (Drury 1978, 114). While patches of reduction are present both within the fabric and on the surface of some pieces, the surfaces of the voids left by the wattles are rarely blackened. The surviving wattle marks are rounded, most are about 10 mm in diameter but range from 6 to 20 mm, and show that small branches must have been used. The limited range of diameters and the concentration around 10 mm might be evidence for the use of coppiced wood.

At Little Waltham, the upright voids in the structural daub came from branches or saplings ranging from 20 to 40 mm in diameter as well as some riven timber, and there was clear evidence of horizontal wattling incorporated into the framework (*ibid.*). The Stanway material differs markedly from the Little Waltham assemblage in the use of smaller uprights, and the evidence for the use of horizontal pieces is extremely slight. In this respect it resembles elements of the assemblage of fired clay from a Late Iron Age to early Roman ditch at Woodham Walter, Essex. Among this material were some large fragments of daub with vertical wattling but little evidence for the use of horizontal timber (Major 1987, 39). The structure from which this daub derived was not positively identified, but may have been an oven rather than a hut.

The quantity of material recovered from pit CF21 is very small compared to that used in the construction of a hut, and the small size of the vertical wattles together with the lack of horizontal wattles suggests that these pieces come from a much smaller structure. Where the wattles are close together, in some cases touching each other, there was clearly no room for branches to be woven in horizontally. The internal reduction of the clay might argue for the daub deriving from a structure subjected to prolonged periods of heat, such as an oven, and something of that size would also be in keeping with the use of small close-set wattles, although the straight wattles and more or less flat outer surface show that the structure had a vertical wall.

Group B from pit CF21, with convex outer and concave inner surfaces, is almost certainly from the rounded top of an oven. The iron-rich clay is very distinctive, and its plasticity is shown in places by lines of torsion similar to those seen in some of the loomweights (see below). The pieces appear to have been subjected to more heat than those of Groups A and C, although this could be caused by a different response to the same heat by a different fabric.

If Group B derived from the same structure as Groups A and C, it would be expected that the hard and distinctively coloured fabric of the former would co-exist on some pieces with the softer sandy fabric of the latter, and that the convex outer surface of the former would give way to the flat surface of the latter. There are two small fragments in Group B which may provide this evidence, one with a flat outer surface, although only measuring 42 by 35 mm, and one only slightly convex piece, quite sandy on one side but with Group B fabric on the other, and some of the Group A fragments are slightly convex. This is not sufficient proof that all the fired clay from CF21 came from one structure, but does raise the possibility of only one source for this assemblage. Similarly, the mixture of structural clay and loomweights from this pit suggests that the oven might have been used as a kiln to fire the weights.

THE LOOMWEIGHTS

DESCRIPTION (FIGS 21–3; TABLES 8–9)

Four more or less complete loomweights and fragments of several others, totalling nearly 8 kg in weight, were recovered from pit CF21 in Enclosure 2, the Middle Iron Age farmstead. Isolated fragments came from other pits in Enclosure 2, the ditches of Enclosures 1, 2 and 5, the fill of the chambers in Enclosures 1 and 4, and the ditches of the ?mortuary enclosures in Enclosures 4 and 5 (FIGS 21–3; TABLES 8–9). With the possible exception of a few fragments from the north ditch of Enclosure 5, all are Middle Iron Age in date.

Four fabrics are distinguishable. Fabric A is a dull orange-brown and hard, with very rare small grits and pebbles, and the core, where exposed, clearly shows the lines of torsion caused during manufacture. The surface shows little abrasion. Fabric B is similar, but with a large number of pebbles included, and is in consequence very brittle. The core of both examples of this fabric has shattered rather than simply fractured. The surfaces of the weights in both these fabrics show many grass or straw marks from material that must have adhered to the surface during drying. Baked clay blocks from Willington, Derbyshire, were similarly marked (Elsdon 1979, 199). Fabric C is a pale orange-brown, soft, with a high sand content. The core shows comparatively few stress lines. The examples in this fabric, which is only slightly harder than structural daub, are more abraded than those of the other two. A fragment of a loomweight in a similar fabric came from a Middle Iron Age context at Birchanger, Essex (Major 1994, 43). Fabric D is orange-brown, and pale orange to buff in some places on the surfaces, which are smooth but have some voids from contact with vegetable matter. It is hard, with well-formed angles between surface and edge. This fabric occurs only in the northern ditch of Enclosure 5, and so may be Late, rather than Middle, Iron Age in date. Given the absence of Late Iron Age domestic occupation on the site, if the Fabric D fragments are contemporary with the burials, they may be associated in some way with the funerary rites.

Several of the faces of weights of Fabric A show some sinkage towards the centre, a feature that is most marked on one side of CF21.2 (FIG. 21), where the form of the depression echoes the triangular shape of the face, the points extended in sunken channels to the corners. The other side has also sagged in a similar way, but not as markedly, while on CF21.1 (FIG. 21), the

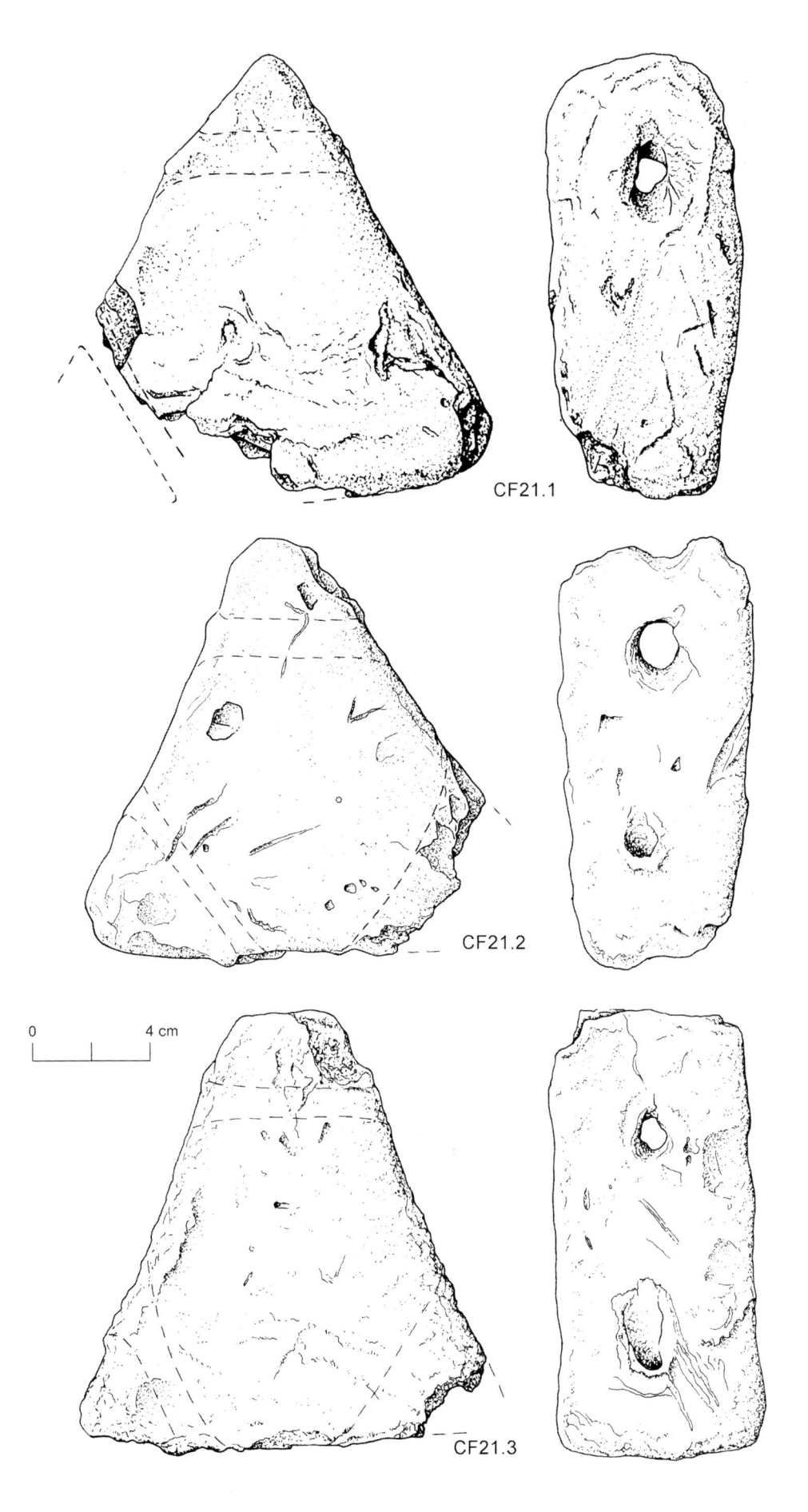

FIG. 21. Loomweights from pit CF21 (scale 1:2)

TABLE 8: THE MIDDLE IRON AGE LOOMWEIGHTS: SUMMARY OF THE MORPHOLOGICAL EVIDENCE

	Context	Fabric	Length	Width	Wt (g)	Angle form	Holes	Notes
CF21.1	Enclosure 2, pit	A	149	66	869	plain	2	
CF21.2	Enclosure 2, pit	A	144	66	997	saddle	3	
CF21.3	Enclosure 2, pit	A	137/145	69	1189	2 plain, 1 truncated	3	
CF21.4	Enclosure 2, pit	C	145	80	567	plain	2	
CF21.5	Enclosure 2, pit	A	148	72	1217	saddle	3	
CF21.6	Enclosure 2, pit	A	77	66	198	saddle	1	small corner fragment only
CF21.7	Enclosure 2, pit	B	135	64	528	saddle	1	other 2 corners missing; possibly same weight as CF21.8
CF21.8	Enclosure 2, pit	B	133	–	637	saddle	1	other 2 corners missing; possibly same weight as CF21.7
AF22.1	Enclosure 2, pit	A	87	–	215	flat sloping area, fingertip depression	1	other 2 corners missing
AF38.1	Enclosure 2, pit	A	122	–	373	saddle	2	3rd corner missing

TABLE 9: SUMMARY OF OTHER LOOMWEIGHT FRAGMENTS

Context or feature no.	Context	Fabric	No. of fragments	Total weight (g)
AF25	Enclosure 1, chamber	C	1	71
AF56	Enclosure 1, pit	A	1	111
AF17	Enclosure 1, north enclosure ditch	A	4	84
CF6	Enclosure 2, enclosure ditch	A	3	109
CF21	Enclosure 2, pit	A	21	1,784
CF250	Enclosure 2, pit	A	1	175
BF24	Enclosure 4, chamber	A	1	7
BF30	Enclosure 4, east ditch of ?mortuary encl.	A	10	79
BF30, BL23	Enclosure 4, east ditch of ?mortuary encl.	A	7	107
CF1	Enclosure 5, north enclosure ditch	A	9	154
CF1	Enclosure 5, north enclosure ditch	D	7	200
CF46	Enclosure 5, west ditch of ?mortuary encl.	A	3	82
C –	unstratified	A	4	102

feature shows only as stress marks in the centre of one face. This pattern is probably the result of laying the weights flat to dry before firing. While the edges dried quite quickly and kept the clay there taut, the weight of the wet clay could cause the upper face to sag downwards. When the weights were turned to allow the base to dry, the same effect occurred but was less marked.

Three of the weights were perforated at all three corners (FIG. 21, CF21.2, CF21.3, FIG. 22, CF21.5), and two were definitely perforated twice (FIG. 21, CF21.1, FIG. 22, CF21.4). Another with only two perforations is lacking its third corner (FIG. 23, AF38.1). Similarly, where only one perforation is recorded it should be viewed as a minimum, rather than evidence that some weights only had a single perforation. The perforations appear to have been made by pushing a stick completely through the clay, as there is clearly an entry hole and an exit hole for each perforation,

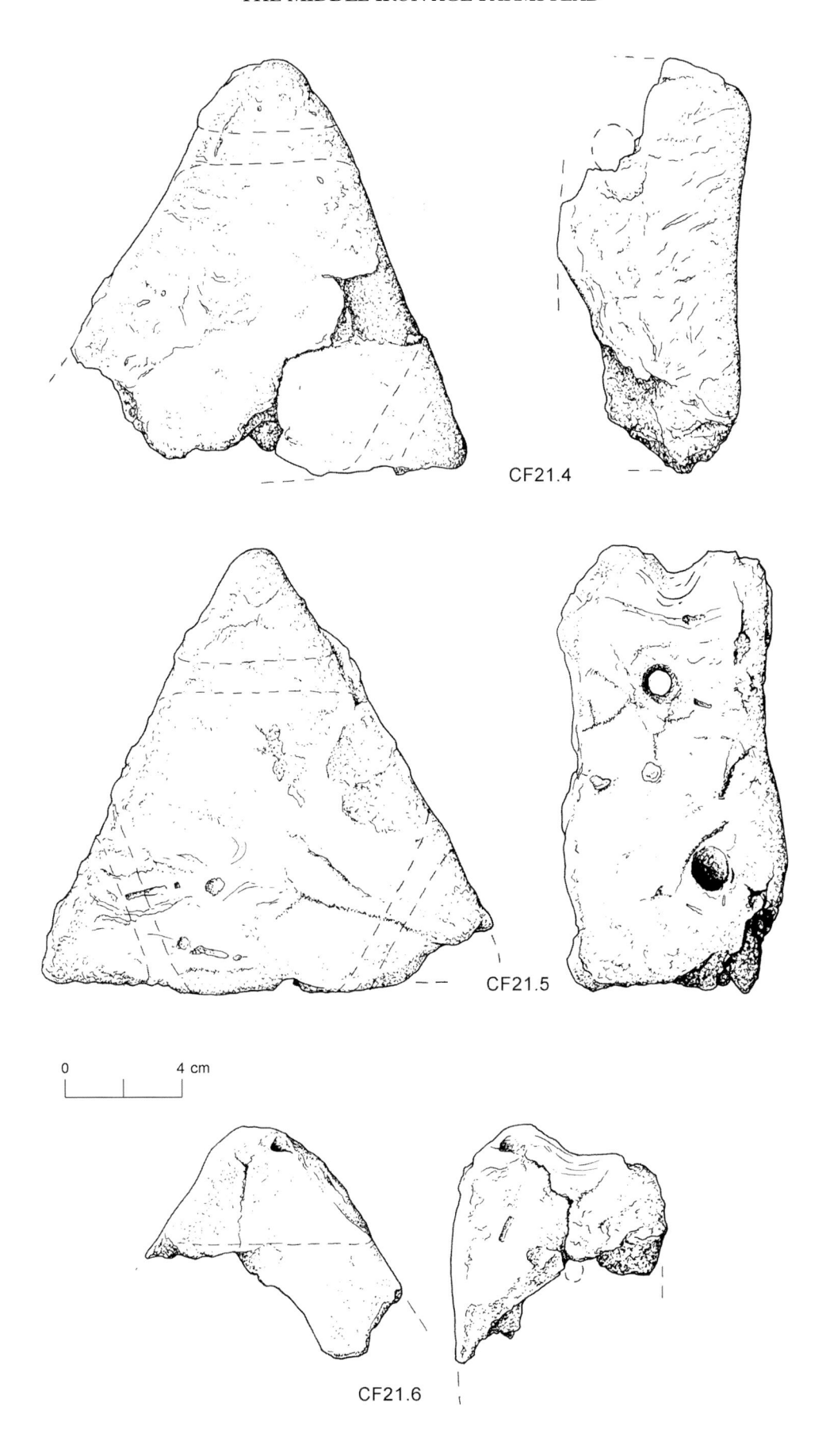

FIG. 22. Loomweights from pit CF21 (scale 1:2)

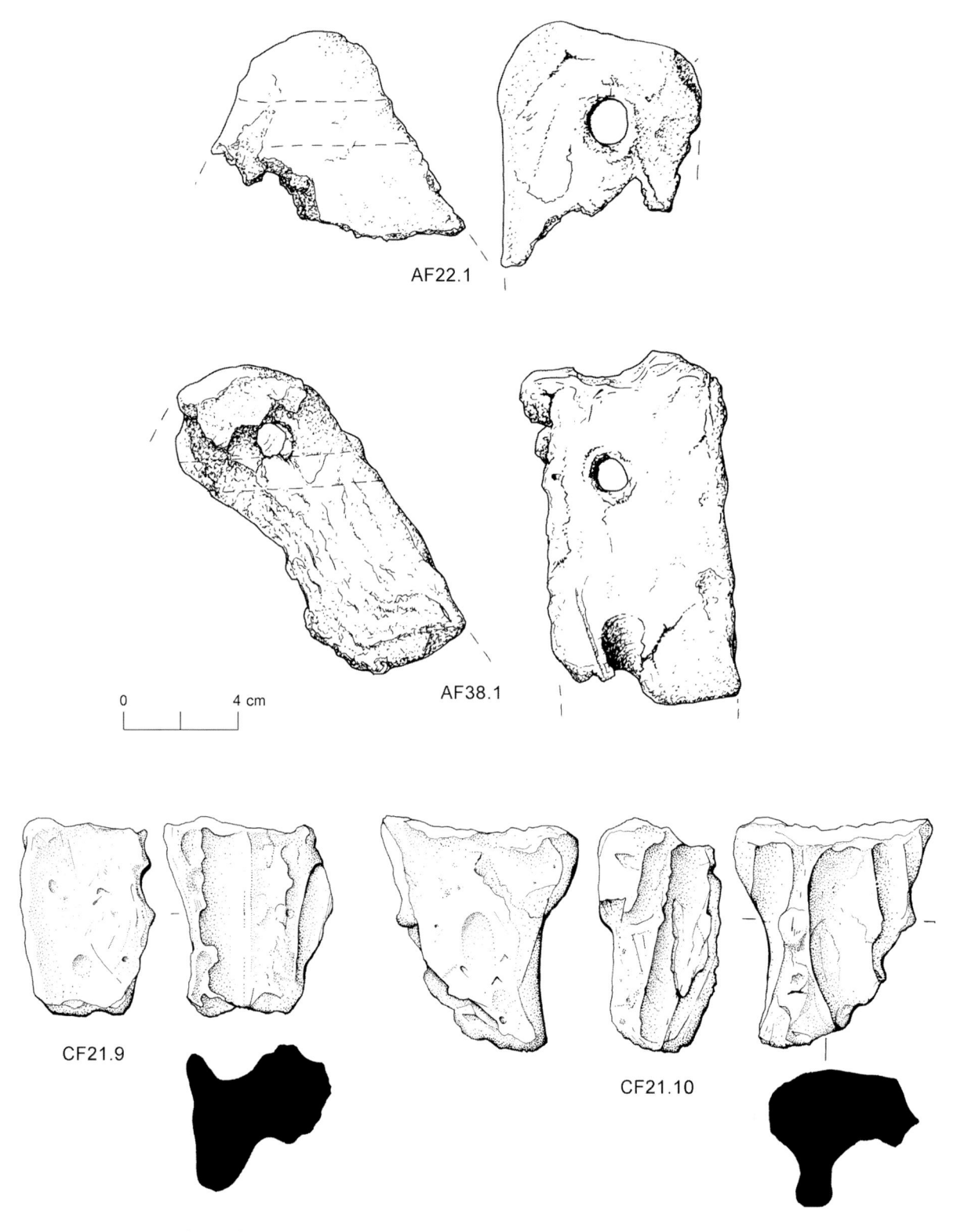

FIG. 23. Loomweights from pits AF22 and AF38 (1:2) and structural clay from pit CF21 (scale 1:1)

with clay dragged into the former and pushed outwards around the latter. The size of the perforations varies considerably; some are very narrow, the smallest only 6 mm, while others are much larger, up to 14 mm or more. Most of the weights are at their thickest across the position of a hole, the clay having been forced outwards when the hole was made.

Some weights have additional features on the corners: CF21.3 (FIG. 21) has one corner truncated to form a small platform; AF22.1 (FIG. 23) has a flattened sloping area, in the centre of which is a slight finger-tip depression marked with an incised X; and many have a groove or saddle set across the angle (*e.g.* FIG. 21, CF21.2, FIG. 22, CF21.5, CF21.6, FIG. 23, AF38.1). On some the groove is only about a finger's width across and has a smooth surface, but on CF21.6 it is wide and has an irregular surface. The narrow smooth grooves may have been made simply by pressing the side of a stick or finger into the clay, the larger rougher ones by both pressing and rolling. Grooves or saddles (wide grooves) have been noted on several weights dating to the Early, Middle, and Late Iron Age at a range of sites, such as Gussage All Saints, Dorset (Wainwright 1979, fig. 76, 4020), Winnall Down, Hampshire (Bates and Winham 1985, fig. 70, 4, 8), Maxey, Cambridgeshire (Crowther 1985, 174–9), West Stow, Suffolk (West 1990, fig. 51, 144c), and in Essex at North Shoebury (Wymer and Brown 1995, fig. 84, 8), Ardale (Major 1988, fig. 81, 4), Slough House Farm (Major 1998a, 162), Orsett 'Cock' (Major 1998b, 106, fig. 69, 1, 4), and Ardleigh (Major 1999, 158).

Wear around the holes of loomweights from Burgh, Suffolk, and Orsett 'Cock', Essex, suggest that they were hung with one point downwards (Martin 1988, 63; Major 1998b, 106). The purpose of the grooves noted on some weights may have been to anchor the warp thread firmly in place. Experimental work has shown that a triply perforated loomweight could have been used with the weight hung point downwards so that the warp threads passed through two holes, enabling the weight to ride freely up or down the threads. A string in the third hole was used either to move the weight backwards or forwards or to attach it to a frame (Wilhelmi 1977, 180–4).

The most complete examples suggest that loomweights in Fabrics A and B weighed approximately 1.2–1.3 kg when complete and had sides measuring between 145 and 150 mm. This is slightly smaller and lighter than many other triangular loomweights, but places them at the bottom of a range rather than defines them as specifically small. For example, Middle Iron Age loomweight Types B and C from Winnall Down, Hampshire, averaged about 1.7–1.8 and 1.9–2 kg respectively, with Type B having a minimum side length of 150 mm (Bates and Winham 1985, fig. 71). At Danebury, Hampshire, the weight of Type 1 loomweights was concentrated between 1.2–1.5 kg (Cunliffe and Poole 1991, 375). At North Shoebury, Essex, the side length was about 150 mm (Wymer and Brown 1995, 125), and at Maxey, Cambridgeshire, about 170 mm (Crowther 1985, fig. 120, 7). Gregory estimated a complete weight of 2 kg for examples from Thetford, Norfolk (1992, 148). Major gives an average of 2.5 kg for triangular loomweights from Essex (1983, 117), but this figure is affected by the inclusion of a group of large weights, some as heavy as 3.5 kg, which may be thatch rather than loomweights (Jones and Jones 1973, 33; Wymer and Brown 1995, 125), and is further complicated by the wide date range and the many types of fabrics from which these objects were made.

DISCUSSION

The triangular form of loomweight originated in the Middle Iron Age and did not die out until after the Roman conquest of Britain, when it is usually assumed that the form was replaced by the Roman pyramidal weight, though the latter are very rarely found (Wild 1970, 63; Lambrick and Robinson 1979, 57). The evidence for domestic weaving in Roman Britain is very slight compared to that of the immediately preceding Late Iron Age, and of the succeeding pagan Anglo-Saxon period, though spindlewhorls are comparatively frequent finds. Two factors are undoubtedly responsible: economic change, as increasingly urbanised communities ceased weaving their own textiles and bought commercially made, perhaps imported, fabrics instead, and technological change, as the paucity of loomweights of any form argues strongly for the warp-weighted loom having been replaced by the vertical two-beam loom.

In practical terms the presence of loomweights is indicative of the use of an upright warp-weighted loom for weaving textiles, and it is most likely that the fibre used was wool, though vegetable fibres may also have been produced. Wool implies the herding of a flock of sheep or goats, and permitting many of the animals to achieve maturity rather than slaughtering most within their first or second year, as would occur in a herd kept for the production of milk or meat (Payne 1973, 282–4). Unfortunately, the lack of animal bone resulting from the acidic soil conditions at Stanway means that this idea cannot be tested.

In many periods loomweights occur in clusters, and, again in practical terms, this is often taken to imply that they are from the same loom. From Bronze Age Sussex, for example, ten weights in association with part of a burnt loom frame were found in a pit at Cock Hill (Ratcliffe-Densham and Ratcliffe-Densham 1961, 86, 100–1, pl. XIb), and thirteen weights were found together at Itford Hill (Burstow and Holleyman 1957, 200). Early Iron Age pits at Winnall Down, Winchester, contained clusters of weights interpreted as coming from a single loom (Bates and Winham 1985, 92). Very large numbers of loomweights came from many of the huts of the Anglo-Saxon village at West Stow, Suffolk, and in Huts 15 and 21 lay in rows as they fell from burning looms (West 1985, 138). In this light, it is possible to see the group of loomweights from Enclosure 2 CF21 as deriving from one loom, though the presence in the same pit of a quantity of structural daub from an oven or kiln might imply that they are wasters (p. 37).

It has been argued that deposits of loomweights and other artefacts may have a ritual aspect, for example, at the Caburn, East Sussex, nearly all the loomweights (35 out of 38) were found only in the bottom 'third' of pits, as were many other types of finds, and it has been argued that this recurring pattern is evidence that the infilling of the pits was a ritual act, possibly a public one (Hamilton 1998, 29, 38, fig. 5). This does not seem to be the case at Stanway, where many of the weights are represented by small fragments only, recovered from features, mainly ditches, dating to the mid 1st century A.D. Similarly, in CF21 they were not deliberately positioned within the feature, but scattered throughout the fill and mixed with structural daub (p. 37).

In Essex a clear example of loomweights being used in a ritual feature dates to the Early Iron Age at Burnham-on-Crouch, though in a very different situation to the 'ritual' disposal in pits mentioned above. Broken loomweight fragments and baked clay slabs were used to construct a platform about a metre across for the votive placing of a Late Bronze Age omphalos pot (Couchman 1977, 75). Although many other loomweights have been recovered from excavations within the county (Major 1983), none has been recognised as a ritual deposit.

Catalogue of the largest fragments

CF21.1 FIG. 21. MIA pit. Enclosure 2. Fabric A. Perforated on two corners, though only a short part of the inner wall of one perforation remains at the broken corner. Diameter of complete hole 11 mm. Some sinkage on both faces. The angles are plain. Maximum length 149 mm. Maximum thickness 66 mm. Weight 869 g.

CF21.2. FIG. 21. MIA pit. Enclosure 2. Fabric A. Perforated on all three corners. The two surviving angles have a groove across the centre. Hole diameters vary from 6 mm to 14 mm. One face is markedly sunken, the other less so. Surviving width 144 mm. Maximum thickness 66 mm. Weight 997 g. Part of the damaged corner may be among the fragments from CF21 listed in TABLE 9.

CF21.3. FIG. 21. MIA pit. Enclosure 2. Fabric A. The apex is slightly truncated, the other angles plain. Perforated on all three corners. Stress marks rather than sinkage on one face. Height 137 mm, longest side about 145 mm. Maximum thickness 69 mm. Weight 1189 g.

CF21.4. FIG. 22. MIA pit. Enclosure 2. Fabric C. Slightly abraded. Perforated across two corners, but neither hole retains its full diameter as the weight has split in two lengthwise. No sign of sinkage on the surviving face. Maximum length, incomplete but with the break close to a corner, 145 mm. Assuming the holes to be set close to the middle of the edges, maximum thickness approximately 80 mm. Weight 567 g.

CF21.5. FIG. 22. MIA pit. Enclosure 2. Fabric A. Perforated on all three corners. The two surviving angles have a groove. Hole diameters 7 to 10 mm. Markedly sunk on one face. Complete side 148 mm. Maximum thickness 72.5 mm. Weight 1,217 g.

CF21.6. FIG. 22. MIA pit. Enclosure 2. Fabric A. Only one perforated corner remains. There is a wide irregular groove on the angle. Maximum length 77 mm. Maximum thickness 66 mm. Weight 198 g.

CF21.7. Not illustrated. MIA pit. Enclosure 2. Fabric B. Only one perforated corner survives. It has a groove across the angle. Length of longest incomplete edge 135 mm. Maximum thickness 64 mm. Weight 528 g. Possibly the same weight as CF21.8.

CF21.8. Not illustrated. MIA pit. Enclosure 2. Fabric B. Only one perforated corner remains, in many fragments. There is a wide irregular groove on the angle. One face is concave due to sinkage. The other is more or less flat. Maximum length 133 mm. Maximum thickness 68 mm. Weight 637 g. Possibly the same weight as CF21.7.

AF22.1. FIG. 23. SF13. A363. MIA pit. Enclosure 2. Fabric A. Perforated corner fragment, with part of the angle flattened, sloping, and with a finger-tip indent. The base of this small depression is marked by two crossing incised lines. There is a possibility that these are natural, as the surface of the weight is covered with grass or straw marks, but the positioning of the mark within the indent is quite precise. Maximum length 87 mm. Weight 215 g.

AF38.1. FIG. 23. SF34. A496. MIA pit. Enclosure 2. Fabric A. Fragment consisting of most of one edge and one corner. Two perforations, diameters 9–10 mm. The surviving corner has a groove across the angle. Maximum length 122 mm. Weight 373 g.

THE OTHER OBJECTS FROM ENCLOSURES 1 AND 2 (FIGS 24, 29)

ENCLOSURE 1

The fragments of Middle Iron Age loomweights residual in the features of Enclosure 1 (TABLE 9) suggest that some of the metalwork from the enclosure may also be Middle Iron Age. This is particularly likely in respect of the fragments of iron-working slag (SF44) from the southern ditch of Enclosure 1, especially as the north-western section of the Enclosure 2 ditch also produced a small fragment of iron-working slag. The identifications of these fragments are by Sarah Paynter (CfA).

Two brooch spring fragments (FIG. 29, AL4.1–AL4.2, SF9, SF8) came from the subsoil (AL4) immediately below the ploughsoil at the northern end of Enclosure 1 and may be contemporary with either enclosure.

The enclosure ditch of Enclosure 1

AF31: SF44. A490. South side of enclosure ditch. Fragments of iron-working slag. Three fragments are part of one piece (total weight 29 g), porous with quartz grains adhered to the surface. A fourth fragment is also porous, weight 11 g. These fragments are likely to be smithing debris. A fifth fragment is undiagnostic, weight 12 g. Probably residual from the Middle Iron Age activity in Enclosure 2.

AF31: A481. South side of enclosure ditch. Fragments of what may be an iron strip, now largely consisting of shattered corrosion bubbles. a) SF404 (from soil block). Maximum length 48 mm, width 10–23 mm. b) Bulk find. Maximum length 43 mm, width 9–14 mm.

AF53: A607. East side of enclosure ditch. Upper half of an iron nail with sub-circular head. Length 37 mm.

AF53: A616. East side of enclosure ditch. Iron ?nail shank fragment. Length 38 mm.

Pit

AF61: SF126. A565. Pit. Eight pieces of iron, including five nail shank fragments, two possible nail heads, and an amorphous fragment. Longest shank fragment 30 mm.

ENCLOSURE 2 (FIGS 19, 24)

Very little metal was recovered from Enclosure 2, but important items are fragments of slag from the enclosure ditch, AF39 and CF6. Further fragments of iron-working slag came from AF31, the south enclosure ditch of Enclosure 1, not far from AF39, and these, too, almost certainly relate to the occupation of Enclosure 2. The occupants of Enclosure 2 clearly worked iron on the site, and did not necessarily have to acquire manufactured metal goods from elsewhere.

Iron-working on the site is also implied by the deposition of two currency bars (FIG. 19, CF6.1–2) in CF6, the eastern arm of the ditch close to the entrance, although interpretation of these objects is bound up with their symbolic aspect as well as their utilitarian one (pp. 26, 33–6).

The other items from the enclosure include an iron saw (FIG. 24, CF250.1), which is evidence for woodworking within the enclosure, and a highly idiosyncratic sandstone artefact (FIG. 24, CF171.1). Almost every surface of this object appears to have been used either to sharpen or smooth metal items, probably blades, producing a very unusual shape, superficially similar to a large astragalus. While the form the stone has acquired may not have initially been intended, it appears ultimately to be deliberate, and therefore a ritual interpretation is tempting, although difficult to support.

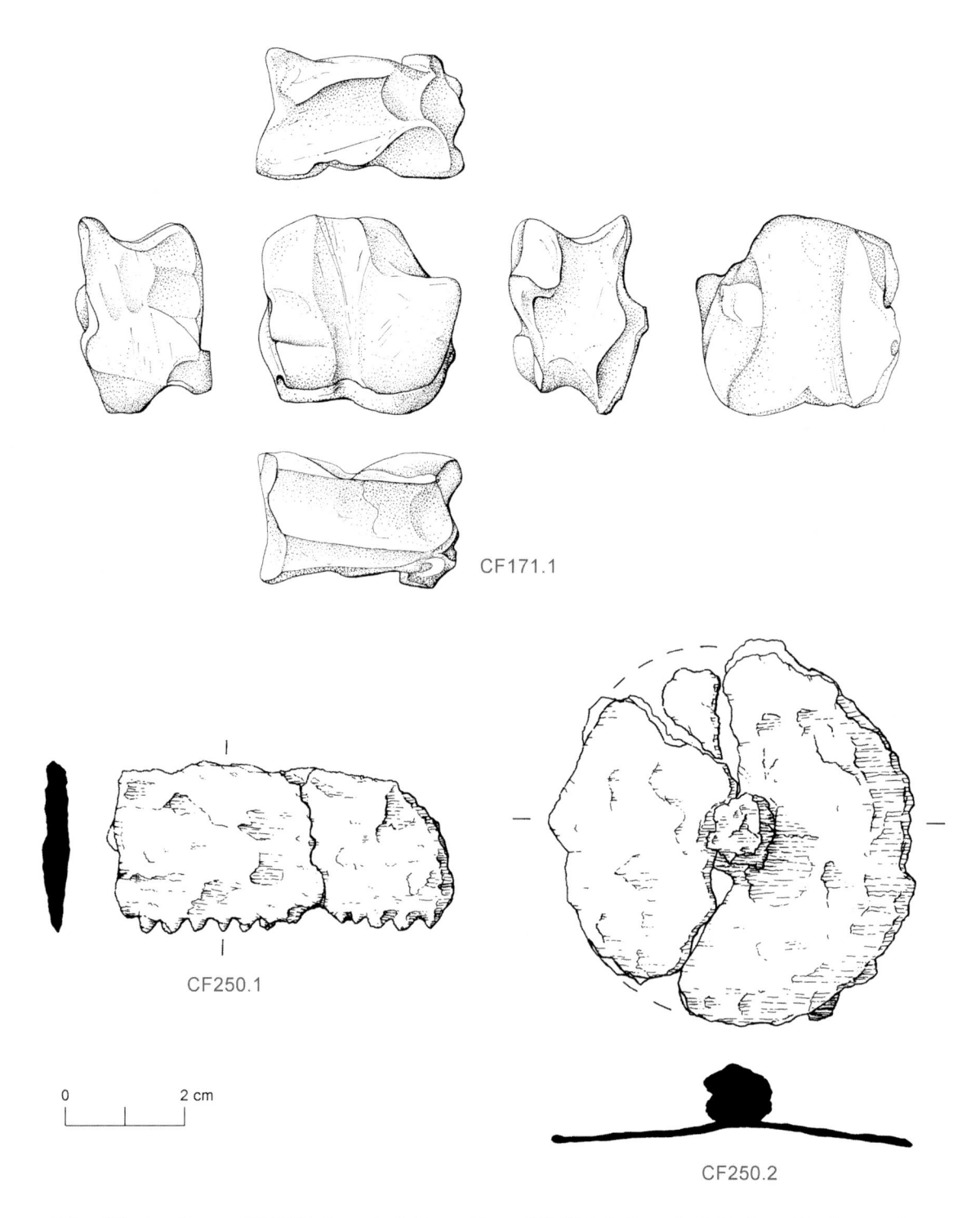

FIG. 24. Finds of stone (CF171.1; scale 1:2) and iron (CF250.1–2; scale 1:1) from Enclosure 2

The end of the occupation of this enclosure appears to have been marked by the deposition of the two currency bars in the boundary ditch, close to the entrance. They are briefly catalogued below and discussed above by R. Hingley (pp. 33–6). A report on the metallurgical analysis of the iron is given on pages 327–8.

Enclosure 2 ditch

AF39: A471. Small fragment of burnt cinder-like material. Weight 2 g.
AF39: SF43. A486. Fragment of undiagnostic iron-working slag. Weight 14.31 g.
CF6.1 FIG. 19. SF388. C201. Iron currency bar with leaf-shaped blade, rounded tip, long U-shaped socket, and rounded terminal. Length 542 mm, maximum width 52 mm.

CF6.2 FIG. 19. SF389. C202. Iron currency bar with tapering blade with rounded tip. The shoulders are much less marked than on SF388. The socket is long and U-shaped close to the blade, but flat-bottomed at the upper end. The terminal is missing. Length (incomplete) 564 mm, maximum width 62 mm.
CF6: C1333. Fragment of iron-working slag, probably from the bottom of a hearth as vitrified clay is incorporated on one side. Weight 289 g.
CF6: SF300. C1478. Tiny tapering strip of iron. Possibly from the tip of a knife. Length 18 mm, width 10 mm.
CL142/CF6: C1342. Fragment of undiagnostic iron-working slag. Weight 29 g.
CL26/CF6: C57. Iron nail with damaged circular head and square-section shank. Length 30 mm, tip missing.
CL114/CF6: SF305. C1340. Iron ring of circular section, in two fragments. Probably penannular, the ends appear to be plain and tapering. Internal diameter of 20 mm, 4 mm thick.

Enclosure pits

AF37: SF23. A493. Pit. About 40 small fragments of copper-alloy sheet. Most measuring at the greatest approximately 1–2 by 1–2 mm. The largest is 7 by 10 mm, and convex.
AF37: SF408. A448. Pit. Iron nail shank fragment. Shaft square in section. Length 75 mm.
AF38: A456. Pit. Iron nail shank with round-section shaft. Length 54 mm.
CF171.1 FIG. 24. SF307. C1329 CL159/CF171. Pit. Piece of sandstone abraded by use/wear into an unusual shape. Almost every surface appears to have been used either to sharpen or rub metal objects, in particular edged blades, and perhaps other materials. Rounded channels along two of the sides are particularly well worn. Maximum dimensions 60 by 65 by 41 mm. The highly idiosyncratic shape of this object tempts interpretation as a ritual item, although in the absence of a parallel, or of its recovery from an obviously structured deposit, this is difficult to prove.
CF250.1 FIG. 24. SF303. C1436. Pit. Fragment from the end of an iron saw, with rounded tip. The teeth are slightly irregularly spaced and set at varying angles, although in general they slope backwards. Length 55 mm, width 25 mm.
CF250.2 FIG. 24. SF304. C1444. Pit. Iron disc in three fragments, with a stud set in a central perforation. Diameter 60 mm. The precise function of discs such as this has yet to be determined (Sellwood 1984, 370).
SF299. CL173/CF173. C1443. Pit. Fragment of an iron square-section shank, almost certainly from a nail. Length 30 mm.

THE LATEST MATERIAL FROM ENCLOSURE 2

Cremated bone was recovered from various places in the enclosure ditch of Enclosure 2. Feature CF415 cut the upper fill of the eastern arm of the enclosure ditch of Enclosure 2. It contained a quantity of cremated human bone (30 g) mixed throughout its fill. Apart from CF415 and a few minute fragments, the remainder of the burnt bone (3.3 g) from CF6 came from its upper fill. Some 0.5 g of it came from the butt-end of the ditch forming the south side of the entrance where the bone was associated with a single grog-tempered ware sherd of Late Iron Age/early Roman date. Most of the bone (2.8 g) came from the fill of the ditch where it formed the south side of the enclosure, but was not closely associated with any sherds. The cremated human bone from CF6 seems likely therefore to have been intrusive or (more likely) to have belonged to a late phase in the silting up of the ditch and post-dated the use of the enclosure as part of a Middle Iron Age settlement.

There was no Late Iron Age–early Roman pottery from features inside the enclosure. A small number of sherds (14 sherds, 44 g) from the upper fill of CF6 indicate that the enclosure was almost certainly still an earthwork in the Late Iron Age/early Roman period. Two fabrics were present: fabric GTW (4 sherds although 1 sherd may be in fabric HZ), and fabric ROW (10 sherds). The sherds in fabric ROW are from the east side of the entrance ditch terminal and are probably from the same vessel. All of the Late Iron Age and early Roman pottery came from the surface or upper surviving ditch fill, although one sherd in Fabric ROW is recorded from the lower fill and is certainly an error or intrusive in that context.

Pottery from the upper fill of CF6: Fabric GTW, 3 sherds (C55, C1347, C147 — sherd crazed ?burnt). Fabric GTW or HZ, 1 sherd fragment (C60). Fabric ROW, 10 sherds possibly from a beaker (C19, C20, C26, C60, C62).

THE EARLY AND MIDDLE IRON AGE POTTERY (FIGS 25–6; TABLES 10–21)

By Paul R. Sealey

INTRODUCTION

Stanway produced 2,512 stratified sherds of Early and Middle Iron Age pottery weighing 17.476 kg. By far and away the majority is pottery of Middle Iron Age date or type, which is 95% by weight. Most of the Middle Iron Age pottery is abraded and the average sherd weight is 6.9 g, a low figure for assemblages of this date. Despite this, the site produced enough large sherds with diagnostic typological features to be able to attempt a characterisation of the pottery. This was possible because the assemblage had not been significantly contaminated with earlier pottery, and the abandonment of Stanway shortly after the Roman invasion meant that the Iron Age pottery has not been obscured by a complex depositional history. In Essex and neighbouring counties it can be difficult to distinguish Middle Iron Age from early Saxon pottery (Barton 1962, 95; Drury and Wickenden 1982, 12; Gregory 1995, 90; Woudhuysen 1998, 50–53; Brown 2004, 53), and so the absence of post-Roman activity on the site also allowed the Iron Age pottery to be kept in sharp focus.

The Early Iron Age pottery came from two adjacent pits in Enclosure 1. Most of the Middle Iron Age material came from pits inside Enclosure 2 and its ditch sections. More was retrieved from pits inside Enclosure 1 and its ditch. Some of the Enclosure 1 Middle Iron Age pottery was residual in two of the Late Iron Age burials. Very little Middle Iron Age pottery was retrieved from the three eastern enclosures, where it was residual. Very few contexts had large groups of material. The largest single group of Middle Iron Age pottery came from the Late Iron Age chamber in Enclosure 1.

EARLY AND MIDDLE IRON AGE POTTERY FABRICS

All the fabrics were fired in a reducing atmosphere to give pottery that is black, sometimes with darker or lighter brown and grey patches. Inclusions are described as temper whether or not there is reason to think they were deliberate additions to the clay by the potter. The only inclusions that might be described as temper in the technical sense are those which do not occur naturally, *i.e.* crushed burnt flint (which appears as angular white grains), chopped vegetable matter, and grog (crushed pottery). Even some of these might be accidental additions introduced by the conditions in which the potter worked (Woudhuysen 1998, 33).

To a greater or lesser degree, all the Stanway fabrics have inclusions of fine silver mica. Such mica is typical of much Iron Age and Roman pottery from Essex and East Anglia. It is quite distinct from the black or golden mica found in wares elsewhere in Britain. Indeed its presence in pottery from the Roman forts at Camelon in Scotland allows the detection of troop movements there when the last garrisons were withdrawn from East Anglia after the Boudican revolt (Swan and Bidwell 1998, 23–4).

The pottery was divided into fabric groups using a modified version of the scheme devised for Essex by Brown (1988, 263–4). Sand and flint inclusions were divided on the basis of size with a numeric code as follows: 1 = <0.25 mm, 2 = 0.25–1 mm, and 3 = 1–2 mm. Two more size categories were recognised with flint: 4 = 3–4 mm and 5 = >4 mm. Inclusions were divided on the basis of their frequency into three categories designated A, B and C as follows: A = <6 grains per cm^2, B = 6–10 grains per cm^2, and C = >10 grains per cm^2. Combinations of numbers and letters conveniently indicate inclusion size and frequency. When the pottery was processed, the many permutations of particle size and frequency led to the division of the material into 46 fabrics. Amalgamating related fabrics led to a more manageable set of 14 fabrics for the published report.

Fabric A   fine sand (1)
Fabric B   fine sand (1) with vegetable temper
Fabric C   sand (2A–2C)
Fabric D   sand (2A–2C) with vegetable temper
Fabric E   coarse sand (3A)
Fabric F   fine flint (1A–1B and 2A–2B)
Fabric G   fine flint and sand (flint 1A, with sand 1 and 2A)
Fabric H   flint and sand (flint 2A–2B, with sand 1 and 2A–2C)
Fabric I   coarse flint (flint 3A–3C and 4A)
Fabric J   coarse flint and sand (flint 3A–3B, with sand 1, 2A–2C and 3A)
Fabric K   coarser flint and sand (flint 4A, with sand 1, and 2A–2B)
Fabric L   very coarse flint (5A)
Fabric M   very coarse flint and sand (flint 5A, with sand 1, 2A–2C and 3A)
Fabric N   chalk and sand (chalk 3A, with sand 2A–2B)

PHASING OF THE EARLY AND MIDDLE IRON AGE POTTERY (TABLE 10)

Phasing features with Early and Middle Iron Age pottery was difficult because there was so little in the way of vertical stratigraphy on the site. None of the pits with such material actually cut each other, a circumstance that makes one wonder if pits were located with care so as to respect earlier pit activity. Despite these difficulties, it proved possible to arrange the material in three phases, details of which are given below; their absolute chronology is explained in a separate section (pp.55–6). It should be emphasised at the outset that Early and Middle Iron Age pottery is spread very unevenly throughout these phases: three-quarters come from IA Ceramic Phase 2, and the very modest amounts from some of the other phases means that comparisons between them can only be made with reservations (TABLE 10).

TABLE 10: INCIDENCE OF EARLY AND MIDDLE IRON AGE POTTERY BY SHERD COUNT AND SHERD WEIGHT BY PHASE

Phase	Date	Sherd count	Sherd wt (g)	Percentage count	Percentage weight	Average sherd weight (g)
Phase 1	600–300 B.C.	61	872	2.4	5	14.3
Phase 2	300–50 B.C.	1,755	13,467	69.9	77	7.7
Phase 3	50–25 B.C.	384	1,637	15.3	9.4	4.3
Enclosures 3–5	A.D. 35–60	113	717	4.5	4.1	6.3
unstratified		199	783	7.9	4.5	3.9
totals		2,512	17,476			6.9

IA CERAMIC PHASE 1 (FIG. 25; TABLE 11)

Phase 1 is Early Iron Age and is confined to two adjacent pits in the southern half of Enclosure 1, AF28 and AF46 dated c. 600–300 BC (TABLE 11). The latter had sherds from only two vessels, both of which had been burnt after breakage. None of the other pits in the immediate vicinity had any diagnostic finds at all (pits AF30, AF34, AF35 and AF42) and cannot be dated. Recognition of Early Iron Age material at Stanway turned on the high proportion of flint-tempered (as opposed to sand-tempered) pottery and on the typology of one of the two jars from AF46.

Typology of the Early Iron Age pottery (FIG. 25)

The AF46 jar (FIG. 25.1) has steep straight sides with a carinated high shoulder and a short neck with a flat-topped rim decorated by finger-tip impressions. There are oblique and vertical wipe marks on the exterior. It is in the coarse flint-tempered Fabric I. The antecedents of the form can be seen in the occasional smaller version from earlier, post-Deverel-Rimbury contexts (Brown 1988, fig. 15, no. 14). Larger vessels like the one from Stanway are later and typical of Early Iron Age assemblages in Essex, where they are associated with fineware carinated bowls of the Darmsden-Linton pottery style zone defined by Cunliffe (Cunliffe 1968, 178–81, figs 1–4; 1978, 42, 360). The Stanway jar exemplifies the coarseware component of Darmsden-Linton. A similar jar at Mucking (Essex) had been used for grain storage (Barford 2002, 125). Comparanda from elsewhere in the county include vessels from Linford, Lofts Farm, Maldon Beacon Green, and North Shoebury (Barton 1962, fig. 1, nos 1–3; Brown 1988, fig. 17, nos 72–5; 1992, fig. 6, no. 25; 1995, fig. 67, no. 123). Two more or less complete profiles of these large vessels have been published from Stansted airport (Brown 2004, figs 34–5).

Darmsden-Linton carinated bowls are found across Essex (Sealey 1996, 46) and, although none was present at Stanway, it seems reasonable to relate the Early Iron Age pottery at Stanway to this style zone. Further north the same linkage cannot be maintained. At Trowse (Norfolk), a large assemblage of Early Iron Age pottery had similar high-shouldered jars, but carinated fineware bowls of Darmsden-Linton type were conspicuous by their absence (Percival 2000, figs 138–42).

The declining incidence of flint tempers

As one moves from the Late Bronze Age into the Early and Middle Iron Age in Essex, there is a decline in the quantity of exclusively flint-tempered pottery and an increase in purely sand and sand-with-flint temper (Brown 1988, 269). The same is true of Cambridgeshire (Woudhuysen 1998, 36–7), Suffolk (Martin 1988, 34) and Norfolk (Gregory 1995, 90). Moreover, if Runnymede Bridge (Surrey) was typical, as flint temper receded in importance the flint grains tended to become smaller and sparser (Needham 1996a, 111). Although there was no uniform rate of progression, this trend from flint to sand is typical of much of southern Britain from the middle of the first millennium B.C. (Rigby 1988, 103).

It is significant that all the pottery from AF46 was in the flint-tempered Fabrics F and I (FIG. 25, 1–2). In the adjacent pit AF28, purely sand-tempered pottery sherds *are* present, but they amount to only 24% by weight. This is a far lower sand content than the other Enclosure 1 pits and so it seemed appropriate to place it in the same phase as AF46.

TABLE 11: PHASE 1 SHERD COUNT AND SHERD WEIGHT IN GRAMMES BY FABRIC

Fabric	Sherd count	Sherd weight (g)	Percentage by sherd count	Percentage by weight
A	4	5	6.6	0.6
C	2	8	3.3	0.9
F	22	231	36	26.5
H	1	4	1.6	0.5
I	24	586	39.3	67.2
J	7	33	11.5	3.8
K	1	5	1.6	0.6
totals	61	872		

IA CERAMIC PHASE 2 (FIGS 25–6; TABLE 12)

Phase 2 has most of the Middle Iron Age pottery from the site and has been assigned to the period *c.* 300–50 B.C. (TABLE 12). The Phase 2 features are the Enclosure 2 ditch sections with all the Enclosure 2 internal pits, the Enclosure 1 internal pits (apart from the two IA Ceramic Phase 1 pits and the IA Ceramic Phase 3 funerary features), and the ?droveway ditch AF59/CF137.

TABLE 12: PHASE 2 SHERD COUNT AND SHERD WEIGHT BY FABRIC

Fabric	Sherd count	Sherd weight (g)	Percentage by count	Percentage by weight
A	608	4,022	34.6	29.9
B	66	854	3.8	6.3
C	433	3,295	24.7	24.5
D	24	507	1.4	3.8
E	6	43	0.3	0.3
F	89	635	5.1	4.7
G	10	37	0.6	0.3
H	94	500	5.3	3.7
I	145	1,159	8.2	8.6
J	170	1,200	9.7	8.9
K	75	804	4.3	5.9
L	7	48	0.4	0.4
M	26	294	1.5	2.2
N	2	69	0.1	0.5
totals	**1,755**	**13,467**		

We saw above that as the Late Bronze Age gives way to the Early Iron Age in Essex, there is an increase in the amount of purely sand-tempered pottery and of pottery tempered with flint-with-sand. At the same time, the proportion of exclusively flint-tempered pottery declines. It is clear that this progression continues throughout the Iron Age at Stanway, because among the pottery of Middle Iron Age type from the c. 50–25 B.C. IA Ceramic Phase 3 Enclosure 1 ditch only about a quarter is flint- or flint-with-sand-tempered (28% by weight), compared to the 98% from the two Early Iron Age pits of Phase 1. Although it would be unrealistic to expect a uniform progression through time away from flint to sand temper, the proportions of the different fabrics in various features do hint at their relative dates. Some of the implications of this can be explored by looking at the fabrics in various of the Phase 2 features.

The Enclosure 2 ditch (FIG. 26)

The Enclosure 2 ditch produced 817 sherds of Middle Iron Age pottery weighing 5.454 kg. By sherd weight, the flint and flint-with-sand fabrics made up 62% of the total. Although the ditch included a few sherds of Neolithic Peterborough ware, there is no reason to think that the flint and flint-with-sand fabrics are seriously contaminated by earlier material because — apart from the pit CF174 (filled with burnt flints, but no pottery) just outside the ditch of Enclosure 2 — there are no earlier features on the site which could have contaminated the ditch fill. Moreover, the ditch fill included considerable quantities of the burnt flint pebbles that would have been the source of this temper. Even so, the proportion of Middle Iron Age pottery tempered with flint or with flint-and-sand looks high, certainly compared to the Iron Age village at Little Waltham (Essex) where tempers with flint never amounted to more than 8% of the illustrated vessels (Drury 1978, 55, 58). Little Waltham compares well with the Witham sites WH2 and WH3, where 91% by weight of the Middle Iron Age pottery was sand-tempered (Brown 1993, 108). But at Ivy Chimneys on the outskirts of Witham, only 11% by weight of a large Early and Middle Iron Age assemblage was tempered by sand without flint (Turner-Walker and Wallace 1999, 125), and at Orsett in south Essex no less than 49% of the Middle Iron Age pottery by sherd count was purely flint-tempered (Brown 1998b, 89). Clearly the composition of Middle Iron Age fabrics in Essex is a good deal more variable than has previously been allowed.

One assumed at the outset that study of the ditch sections in detail would have shown that most of the flint and flint-with-sand fabrics were in the lower levels, with exclusively sand-tempered fabrics dominating in the upper levels. In fact that was not the case. These fabrics were more or less evenly dispersed throughout the lower, middle and upper ditch fills. This was established by looking at the pottery from the most productive of the sections across the ditch. In their lower fills, flint and flint-with-sand fabrics accounted for 61% of all the pottery by sherd weight.

This is not far removed for the average figures for the ditch as a whole. Moreover, the material from the lower fills of these sections only amounted to 14% by sherd weight of the ditch fill. Most of the pottery came from the middle and upper fills. Study of the sections gives no reason to think the ditch was recut, although it could have been kept free of accumulations of infill by regular scouring. It would seem that the silting of the ditch took place quickly, at a time when exclusively sand-tempered fabrics made up rather less than half the pottery.

What this might mean in terms of absolute dates is little more than guesswork. But working backwards from the c. 50–25 B.C. IA Ceramic Phase 3 (when only about a fifth of the pottery was tempered with flint and flint-with-sand) towards the — less securely dated — beginning of Phase 2 c. 300 B.C., one can venture the suggestion that the Enclosure 2 ditch had silted up to the point where it was little more than a hollow by the end of the 2nd century B.C.

A very few Late Iron Age sherds (14 sherds weighing 43 g) were recovered from the Enclosure 2 ditch sections. Apart from an intrusive sherd in the lower fill and another sherd in the middle to upper fill, they all came from the upper fills. This is a trifling quantity compared to the Middle Iron Age pottery from the ditch, but it suggests the hollow which the Enclosure 2 ditch had by now become was still receiving pottery after the introduction of Late Iron Age pottery from c. 75 B.C., and it allows us to extend IA Ceramic Phase 2 towards the middle of the 1st century B.C.

The question immediately arises as to why it was thought necessary to have a ditch in the first place. If it had a utilitarian and purely functional role, it would presumably have been maintained. There are many Iron Age enclosures in southern Britain with ditches that were either deliberately backfilled or allowed to fill naturally soon after their excavation in antiquity, which raise important questions about their function (Bowden and McOmish 1987, 81–3), and Stanway Enclosure 2 may now be numbered among them.

Middle Iron Age pits in Enclosures 1 and 2 (FIGS 25–6)

The pits in the interior of Enclosure 2 produced 411 sherds of Middle Iron Age pottery weighing 3.476 kg. The incidence of pottery fabrics from these pits is very different to that of the ditch itself. By sherd weight, the flint and flint-with-sand fabrics made up only 17% of the total respectively. The corresponding figure for the ditch is 62%. Although the sample is small, the differences are striking and suggest that the interior pits were dug after the enclosure ditch had significantly silted up.

The pits inside Enclosure 1 have also been assigned to Phase 2. Although there is little direct stratigraphical evidence to support this, typologically their pottery is certainly Middle Iron Age. These pits produced 500 sherds weighing 4.406 kg. By sherd weight, the flint and flint-with-sand fabrics account for just 15% of the total, almost half the proportion coming from the Enclosure 1 ditch itself. It is interesting that the cluster of Middle Iron Age pits in the north-east corner lie within (and seem to respect) the ditch CF137/AF59. Some of them are close enough to the northern ditch of the enclosure to have been buried beneath an internal bank, and so pre-date the creation of the enclosure, in which case they can be assigned to Phase 2 rather than Phase 3.

IA CERAMIC PHASE 3 (FIGS 25–6, 39; TABLES 13–18)

Phase 3 sees the introduction of grog-tempered and wheel-thrown Late Iron Age pottery of 'Belgic' type (TABLE 13). Although such pottery starts to become significant in the funerary record in Essex and neighbouring counties from c. 75 B.C., it does not significantly impact on assemblages of pottery from other contexts in Essex until later, from c. 50 B.C. (p. 56).

Enclosure 1 (TABLE 14) was presumably cut at the time of the funeral represented by the chamber AF25 (p. 69). None of the funerary contexts in Enclosure 1 has any imported Roman pottery and this suggests a date for them — and for the Enclosure 1 ditch — before c. 25 B.C. By sherd weight, Middle Iron Age pottery constituted 32% of the pottery from the ditch fill. Its average sherd weight is far less than the Late Iron Age and early Roman pottery from the ditch, suggesting that at least some of it is residual, perhaps from Middle Iron Age pits destroyed when the ditch was cut. But such pits are only present in the north-east corner of Enclosure 1 and so

TABLE 13: PHASE 3 SHERD COUNT AND SHERD WEIGHT BY FABRIC

Fabric	Sherd count	Sherd weight (g)	Percentage by count	Percentage by weight
A	209	785	54.2	47.9
C	108	509	28.1	31.1
F	4	11	1	0.7
G	9	54	2.3	3.3
H	17	80	4.4	4.9
I	4	24	1	1.5
J	28	133	7.3	8.1
K	5	41	1.3	2.5
totals	**384**	**1,637**		

TABLE 14: SUMMARY OF THE STRATIFIED POTTERY FROM THE ENCLOSURE 1 DITCH BY TYPE

	Sherd count (g)	Sherd weight	Average sherd weight (g)
Middle Iron Age	77	392	5.1
Late Iron Age and Roman	63	848	13.5
totals 140		**1,240**	**8.9**

residuality cannot explain all the Middle Iron Age material in the ditch. The simplest explanation is to postulate that the ditch was cut when Middle and Late Iron Age wares were in contemporaneous use, and their relative proportions suggests the ditch was cut later — rather than earlier — in the transition period at *c.* 50–25 B.C.

Surprisingly, the major source of IA Ceramic Phase 3 Middle Iron Age pottery was AF25, the Late Iron Age chamber to the west of the centre of Enclosure 1. The chamber produced 295 sherds weighing 1.215 kg, 7% by sherd weight of the entire Early and Middle Iron Age pottery assemblage from Stanway (TABLE 16). Its early date raised the possibility that the funeral took place when Middle and Late Iron Age wares were in contemporary use. This raised the awkward possibility that the Middle Iron Age sherds were part of the funerary ritual, particularly as the two Late Iron Age pots from the floor of the grave were themselves represented by sherd material (FIG. 39, AF25.1–2). Details of the pottery from the chamber are given in TABLES 15–16.

The two Late Iron Age pots had been smashed before the chamber was backfilled and not all of the sherds from each vessel were present. Presumably both pots had been smashed outside the pit at the funeral and the missing sherds were not incorporated in the fill. AF25.1 is

TABLE 15: DETAILS OF THE BROKEN LATE IRON AGE POTS IN CHAMBER AF25

Pot	Sherd count (g)	Sherd weight	Average sherd weight (g)
AF25.1	61	377	6.2
AF25.2	69	314	4.6

TABLE 16: VERTICAL DISTRIBUTION OF MIDDLE IRON AGE POTTERY SHERDS IN CHAMBER AF25

Fill	Sherd count	Percentage by sherd count	Sherd weight (g)	Percentage by sherd weight
top	194	65.8	757	62.4
middle	62	21.0	262	21.6
floor	39	13.2	196	16.1
totals	**295**		**1,215**	

represented by a complete rim circuit and (very approximately) about 40% of the rest of the vessel. The second vessel (AF25.2) has about 60% of the rim circuit and some 30% of the remainder of the pot. Both lay on the floor of the chamber. As both pots were represented by sherd material and in neither case could the whole pot be restored, there was no logical difference between this Late Iron Age pottery and the Middle Iron Age sherds from the chamber. The similarities are reflected in the average sherd weights — 5.3 g for the Late and 4.1 g for the Middle Iron Age pottery. But the Middle Iron Age pottery was not confined to the floor of the chamber — indeed most of it came from the upper fill. Only eight joining sherds were found among the Middle Iron Age pottery, and the abraded condition of the sherds made it unlikely they represented funerary goods. There were seven fabrics present, and the rims show that at least fifteen vessels were represented. The impression given is of a disparate group of residual material that had no direct connection with the funeral.

The distribution by feature of the residual Middle Iron Age pottery from Enclosures 3–5 is shown in TABLE 17, where it was decided to include unstratified Middle Iron Age pottery to emphasise the fact of its presence. TABLE 18 gives the incidence by fabric for the stratified Middle Iron Age pottery.

There were no definite Middle Iron Age features in Enclosures 3–5 and it is worth asking how this pottery came to be there in the first place. The most plausible explanation is that they arrived as inadvertent inclusions in middens of organic material (food scraps, butchery waste, ash from fires, byre sweepings and the like) that had accumulated on settlements and subsequently been spread over fields as manure. Rhodes (1952, 13) was the first to suggest this to explain abraded sherds in ancient field systems, and his views have been widely endorsed (Taylor 1975, 30; Fowler 1981, 167, 202, 213–14; 2002, 138, 148, 156, 208–11, 311; Cunliffe 1995, 12). Manuring was of particular importance with arable fields because of the depletive effects of prolonged cultivation on the soil (White 1970, 124, 126). The potential of pottery scatters derived from manure to assess land use in the Roman period was fully developed in the Maddle Farm (Berkshire) project (Gaffney and Tingle 1989, 209–25). On this view, the area where Enclosures 3–5 were laid out had been cultivated farmland in the Middle Iron Age.

TABLE 17: STRATIFIED AND UNSTRATIFIED MIDDLE IRON AGE POTTERY FROM ENCLOSURES 3–5

Feature	Sherd count	Sherd weight (g)
Enclosure 3 pit BF10	2	2
Enclosure 3 pyre-site BF1/BF16	4	9
Enclosure 3 ditch	5	40
Enclosure 4 ditch	23	360
Enclosure 4 chamber BF24	58	245
Enclosure 4 ?mortuary enclosure	15	42
Enclosure 5 ditch	4	14
Enclosures 4–5 ditch	2	5
Enclosures 3–4 unstratified (Area B)	7	18
totals	**120**	**735**

TABLE 18: STRATIFIED SHERD COUNT AND SHERD WEIGHT BY FABRIC FROM ENCLOSURES 3–5

Fabric	Sherd count	Percentage by count	Sherd weight (g)	Percentage by weight
A	47	41.6	203	28.3
C	46	40.7	264	36.8
E	1	0.9	6	0.8
H	5	4.4	13	1.8
I	3	2.7	19	2.7
J	4	3.5	24	3.4
K	3	2.7	14	1.9
N	4	3.5	174	24.3
totals	**113**		**717**	

ABSOLUTE CHRONOLOGY OF THE EARLY AND MIDDLE IRON AGE POTTERY

Darmsden-Linton pottery: radiocarbon dates

The earliest Iron Age pottery at Stanway is a group of material whose affiliations are with the Darmsden-Linton pottery style zone. Stratigraphic evidence from the well at Lofts Farm (Essex) shows Darmsden-Linton pottery developed there after the Late Bronze Age wares on the site (Brown 1988, 271–2). A calibrated radiocarbon date for this Darmsden-Linton assemblage gives a date of cal. B.C. 905–805, but this is felt to be too early (Needham 1996b, 255, *pace* Martin 1993, 38 citing HAR-8514). One of the three calibrated radiocarbon dates from Stansted airport for Darmsden-Linton pottery also looks too early, at 1130–810 B.C. within the 95% confidence level range. Two others from Stansted within the 95% confidence level range look more reliable, at 518–384 B.C. and 760–520. The last date is from pit F2171, a group dominated by post-Deverel-Rimbury plain and decorated wares, but with a Darmsden-Linton pedestal base, evidently the start of the style (Brown 2004, 41). There are two uncalibrated radiocarbon dates for a large group of Early Iron Age pottery from Rectory Road at Orsett (Essex) of 160 ± 80 b.c. (HAR-4527) and 400 ± 70 b.c. (HAR-4635) (Hamilton 1988, 78). The pottery has typological features suggesting a date towards the end of Darmsden-Linton *c*. 300 B.C., and the radiocarbon dates are consistent with that chronology. Another (late) radiocarbon date from North Shoebury (Essex) for a similar jar to a Stanway Early Iron Age vessel from AF46 (FIG. 25, 1) has been calibrated to cal. B.C. 390–20 cal. A.D. (Brown 1995, 87 citing HAR-5104).

Although there is an understandable reluctance to resort to radiocarbon to refine chronologies for the Early Iron Age because of the relatively flat character of the Pearson and Stuiver calibration curve for the period *c*. 800–400 B.C. (Bowman 1990, 55, 57), the Essex radiocarbon dates for Darmsden-Linton pottery suggest a *floruit* somewhere between the 7th and 4th centuries B.C.

Darmsden-Linton typology and the links with Gaul

Another line of approach lies with Hawkes (1962), Hodson (1962, 142) and Barrett (1978, 286–7), who suggested that the pedestal bases of what we now call Darmsden-Linton (and indeed other wares in southern Britain) were modelled on continental prototypes of 6th-century B.C. and later date. There are apparently no groups of Darmsden-Linton bowls without such bases and so there is no need to put the start of the style back in the 7th century B.C. (*pace* Sealey 1996, 47). Subsequently, important evidence for the date of Darmsden-Linton pottery has come from the large assemblage excavated at Fordham (Cambridgeshire), kindly shown to me by Dr J.D. Hill. A series of luminescence dates for this material cluster in the 6th and 5th centuries B.C., with a pooled mean date for occupation of 520 B.C. ± 80 ± 180 (Barnett 2000, 441, 446–7, 454).

Similarities between the tripartite fineware bowls in Darmsden-Linton pottery and the La Tène I ceramics of the Marne confirm that it was still in vogue then (Bretz-Mahler 1971, pls 109 and 114). In absolute terms, this means *c*. 475–400 B.C. (Hatt and Roualet 1977, 11, 13, 17). Barrett suggests that pedestal bases may have lasted until the 4th century B.C. in Britain. This is borne out by the association of a La Tène Ib brooch associated with a Chinnor-Wandlebury pedestal-base bowl from Ravensburgh (Hertfordshire) (Dyer 1976, 157, 423; Hull and Hawkes 1987, 97, 103, pl. 30, no. 6932). The brooch was dated *c*. 350 B.C. by E.M. Jope (in Dyer 1976), and less specifically as 4th century B.C. by Hull and Hawkes. Evidence for the continued production of Darmsden-Linton pottery after the mid- to late 4th century B.C. is wanting, and it seems reasonable therefore to date the Early Iron Age pottery at Stanway *c*. 600–300 B.C.

Middle Iron Age pottery

The Middle Iron Age pottery from Stanway can be assigned to the following centuries, although there are very few radiocarbon dates for Essex Middle Iron Age pottery to confirm this. Four dates are available from the village at Little Waltham (Drury 1978), but two of them may have been contaminated by earlier, Neolithic charcoal. The other two are cal. B.C. 400–1 cal. A.D. at 2σ (HAR-1088) and cal. B.C. 370–50 cal. A.D. at 2σ (HAR-1120) suggesting that pottery of Middle Iron Age type was indeed current in the middle of the second half of the 1st millennium B.C. (Jordan *et al.* 1994, 93). A date of cal. B.C. 400–90 at 2σ (HAR-6701) from Asheldam Camp came from burnt grain associated with a Middle Iron Age pot with curvilinear decoration (Bedwin 1991, 24, 36). Two uncalibrated radiocarbon dates for Middle Iron Age pottery elsewhere in the county are consistent with this broad picture. One from Heybridge is 150 ± 80 b.c. (Wickenden 1987, 11) and another from Mucking, associated with a glauconite-tempered bowl of Little Waltham form 13, gave 140 ± 70 b.c. (Hamilton 1988, 80).

The start date of Late Iron Age wheel-thrown and grog-tempered pottery
The terminal date of the Middle Iron Age pottery at Stanway is best approached by considering when the wheel-thrown grog-tempered pottery of Late Iron Age type that displaced it made its first appearance. There is no consensus about when such Aylesford-Swarling 'Belgic' pottery developed in Britain. Thompson (1982, 16) saw it emerging late in the 1st century, after *c.* 30 B.C. On the other hand, the Baldock (Hertfordshire) report puts the earliest grog-tempered wheel-thrown material there in the early to mid-1st century B.C. (Rigby 1986, 273–7). Haselgrove (1997, 58) and Hill (2002, 146) have gone even further and claimed that 'Belgic' pottery was current in eastern England from as early as the late 2nd century B.C. The question of the start date of 'Belgic' pottery is discussed by the writer elsewhere (Sealey forthcoming a), but it may help to give a summary of the situation here.

A very few graves in Kent with 'Belgic' or Aylesford-Swarling pottery have Nauheim brooches. Such brooches were current from *c.* 125–50 B.C. and it is possible that these graves could be earlier rather than later in that time bracket. But the most common early brooch associated with Aylesford-Swarling pottery is the *c.* 75–25 B.C. *Knotenfibel* and it was in the lifetime of these brooches that 'Belgic' pottery first became significant (Stead 1976). Even so, in some areas there was a time lag between the first appearance of Aylesford-Swarling pottery in graves and its later adoption and use on settlement sites. This was the case at the *c.* 90–50 B.C. Westhampnett cemetery (Fitzpatrick 1997), although in West Sussex Aylesford-Swarling never became the dominant component of pottery assemblages in the prelude to the Roman invasion. North of the Thames, where it did become dominant, the timelag between the presence of 'Belgic' pottery in graves and settlements sites is most evident in parts of Essex and south Cambridgeshire (Thompson 1988; Thompson 1995, 90; Hill 1999b). In Hertfordshire, Aylesford-Swarling pottery had displaced earlier wares *c.* 75–50 B.C. at Foxholes Farm (Partridge 1989), although such an early date is not replicated on other settlements there or elsewhere north of the Thames. In Essex, Aylesford-Swarling pottery did not significantly impact on settlement pottery assemblages until at least *c.* 50–25 B.C. (Sealey 1996, 55).

Further north in Norfolk, Suffolk and Cambridgeshire, its adoption took place even later. Although some settlements on the periphery of East Anglia had developed a taste for this new pottery in the last decades B.C. and the start of the following century (Farrar *et al.* 2000), wheel-thrown grog-tempered wares did not reach most parts of East Anglia until after the Roman invasion (Gregory 1995, 93–4; Lyons and Percival 2000, 222).

The development of Aylesford-Swarling pottery was a protracted and piecemeal process that took place at different times in different parts of the country; the pace at which it displaced existing pottery styles also varied from region to region. We need to face up to the fact that contemporary pottery assemblages in parts of Essex and East Anglia can be quite different, even on sites not far apart: the awkward implications of this will need to be addressed more fully in the future.

TYPOLOGY OF THE MIDDLE IRON AGE POTTERY (FIGS 25–6; TABLES 19–20)
Typologically the earliest element in the Middle Iron Age pottery is a thin-walled and straight everted rim in the fine flint Fabric F from ditch AF59, which is quite unlike any other Iron Age rim from the site (FIG. 25, 4). Initially it was thought to be an Early Iron Age Darmsden-Linton

bowl, but the absence of horizontal grooving above the carination suggests the vessel is later than Phase 1. It is best explained by a very few bowls from the initial Essex Middle Iron Age that are transitional in form between Early Iron Age carinated bowls and their round-shouldered Middle Iron Age successors. There are parallels from the Ivy Chimneys site at Witham and from the Stansted Airport Social Club site (Turner-Walker and Wallace 1999, fig. 86, no. 13; Brown 2004, fig. 31, nos 16–18).

A limited range of forms is present in the developed Middle Iron Age pottery from Stanway. The typical Middle Iron Age vessel is a deep open bowl with a gently rounded or slack S-profile, often with a high shoulder and unemphatic neck (FIGS 25–6, 9, 20, 28, 33, 36). Sometimes the necks are deeper and more concave, with a more pronounced break in curve at the shoulder (FIGS 25–6, 10, and 40). Some vessels with this same general profile are narrow enough at the rim to be described as jars (FIGS 25–6, 11–12, 32, 39). Some profiles have no neck at all, and suggest a hemispherical bowl form (FIGS 25–6, 26, 31). Such pots offer a possible glimpse of some typological development in the Middle Iron Age pottery. One says this because they are confined to two vessels from pits in the interior of Enclosure 2 which had apparently been dug late in Phase 2, after the Enclosure 2 ditch had filled (there were none in the ditch itself). Another neckless vessel has steep straight sides descending from a rounded rim (FIG. 25, 22). Rims are usually round and plain, but some are pointed or tapered. Others are thickened, one by pinching between the thumb and forefinger. A few have neatly finished flat upper surfaces (FIGS 25–6, 3, 5, 7, 25, 33, 44–5, 55). Rim angle varies a great deal; a few even rise vertically from the shoulder (FIG. 26, 37, 49). Most bases are flat. Very occasionally they are slightly dished (FIGS 25–6, 18, 34). Usually the base is no thicker than the sides of the pot, with one exception (FIG. 25, 6); sometimes there is a protuberance at the junction of wall and base (FIG. 26, 46). A distinct novelty is the miniature pot, made by pushing the thumb into a ball of clay (FIG. 26, 50; *see* pp. 60–1 for its function).

Pottery transitional between the Middle and Late Iron Age (FIG. 26)

A very few sherds can be seen as transitional between Middle and Late Iron Age ceramics. The Enclosure 2 ditch had a rim in grog-tempered ware with a straight and flat top, more Middle than Late Iron Age (FIG. 26, 47). Another such rim was retrieved from the chamber BF24. The same context had a sand-tempered rim with corrugations or cordons typical of Aylesford-Swarling ceramics but here on a sand-tempered and handmade pot of Middle Iron Age technique (FIG. 26, 54 and 53 respectively). Another handmade pot with a flat rim of Middle Iron Age type in grog-temper from Enclosure 4 also looks transitional (FIG. 26, 55).

Decoration of the Middle Iron Age pottery (TABLES 19–20)

The only parts of the Early and Middle Iron Age pots that were at all regularly decorated were the tops of the rims (TABLE 19), but only twenty-five (17%) of the 149 rim sherds were decorated. The most common form of decoration was a line of finger-tip impressions; there was one example of finger-tip-with-nail impressions. The only other decoration consisted of straight incised lines neatly executed and cut obliquely across the rim at regular intervals (FIGS 25–6, 1, 5, 10, 16, 22, 44). In the Early Iron Age, finger-tip impressions are found on the bodies of vessels as well as on the rims. Eventually finger-tip impressions on the body pass out of fashion in the Essex and East Anglian Middle Iron Age and the technique becomes confined to the rim, as at Stanway (Percival 2000, 112).

TABLE 19: DECORATED RIM SHERDS

Type of decoration	Number of sherds	Sherd count by fabric
Finger-tip impressions	17	A (7), C (4), D (1), F (1), I (1) and J (3)
Finger-nail impressions	1	J (1)
Straight incised lines	7	A (6) and J (1)

TABLE 20: DECORATED BODY SHERDS

Type of decoration	Number of sherds	Sherd count by fabric
Incised lines	22	A (8), C (7), E (3), J (2) and K (2)
Wipe marks	6	B (1), H (1) and J (4)
Finger-nail impressions	1	C (1)

There is very little in the way of surface decoration on the Early and Middle Iron Age body sherds. Only 29 of the 2,512 sherds (1%) had some kind of decoration on parts of the vessel other than the top of the rim. One sherd had a row of three finger-nail impressions. A few others had shallow, generally parallel wipe marks. Incised decoration took the form of straight or occasionally curved and generally parallel lines. Sometimes a diagonal line might cut across one of these tramlines (TABLE 20). The tiny size of so many of the Stanway sherds means that it is impossible to judge how much of a vessel was decorated, but two vessels represented by larger sherds suggest that in their case at least much of their surface may have been (FIGS 25–6, 1, 32). Two other sherds decorated with incised lines are illustrated. One has two diverging straight lines, and the other two parallel horizontal lines below the rim (FIGS 25–6, 22, 54). So few of the Stanway Early and Middle Iron Age vessels have decorated bodies that one is left wondering why any were decorated at all. Although a few sherds have burnished or smoothed (wiped) surfaces, they are rare and the Stanway vessel population does divide itself convincingly into a fine- and coarseware component.

MANUFACTURE OF THE EARLY AND MIDDLE IRON AGE POTTERY

The Early and Middle Iron Age pottery was a handmade tradition. Interior surfaces often have the lumpy and uneven finish of handmade ceramics, and there were no signs of interior throw marks or the perfect symmetry of form found in competent wheel-thrown pottery. Vertical wipe marks on a few sherds may have been intended to disguise and consolidate the coil construction as well as make the vessel easier to handle (Percival 2000, 108).

SOURCES OF THE EARLY AND MIDDLE IRON AGE POTTERY

The contribution of ethnography

Ethnography suggests that most potters in pre-industrial societies obtained their clays and tempers from the immediate vicinity. Arnold (1985) showed that 33% of the potters in his research sample drew their clay from within 1 km of their workshops. No less than 84% secured clay from within a 7 km radius. Temper procurement revealed a similar pattern. Fifty-two per cent of the potters found suitable temper within 1 km, and 97% from within 6–9 km (Arnold 1985, 38–51). The relevance of this to the study of Iron Age pottery in Britain has been keenly advocated by E.L. Morris (1995; 1997). The implications are that most — in some cases all — of the pottery on an Iron Age site would have been made within 9 km and that wares made from materials only found further afield can be regarded as non-local.

Stanway and Abbotstone compared

Excavations at Abbotstone (Benfield and Brooks 1999), only 1.4 km west of Stanway, produced another assemblage of Middle Iron Age pottery (Sealey 2005). Phase 1a at Abbotstone was contemporary with Phase 2 at Stanway, but the proportions of fabrics are quite different. At Abbotstone, 93.4% by weight of the pottery was composed of fabrics tempered with sand (and some sporadic vegetable matter and chalk), but the comparable figure for Stanway is only 65.4%. Pottery tempered with only flint was rare at Abbotstone, whereas at Stanway it was significant: 1.9% and 13.5% respectively by weight. The same picture emerges from the fabrics tempered by sand-with-flint. At Abbotstone they were only 4.8% by weight, but at Stanway the proportion was 21.1%.

In antiquity, Abbotstone and Stanway are sites that could have been reached from each other on foot in only a few minutes. Although they used pottery that is indistinguishable typologically, there are sufficient differences in the incidence of pottery fabrics on both sites to suggest that they drew on different sources of supply. The simplest explanation is that both communities made their own pottery, in which case Abbotstone and Stanway confirm the findings of ethnography described above.

The nearest source of potting clay to Stanway lies 250 m away in two outcrops of London clay that lead south towards the Roman river. Another potential source is to be found 2.5 km to the east in the chalky boulder clay. Although this was never used in the Roman period (Rodwell 1983, 15), it was presumably the source of the very few chalk-tempered vessels in Fabric N. Sand and flint for use as temper were readily available at Stanway itself. The large deposits of burnt flints and stone on site (pp. 18–21) were presumably the source of the crushed burnt flint present in so much of the Early and Middle Iron Age pottery. Petrological analysis of the pottery was not attempted because there was no reason to think that any of the tempers were exotic.

Evidence for traded wares in the Middle Iron Age

Although the likelihood is that the Stanway pottery is essentially local, we should not exclude the possibility that some of it reached the site from elsewhere. The difficulty of sourcing Iron Age pottery in Essex and East Anglia on the basis of petrological investigation of tempers has hitherto tended to discourage attempts to identify imported products. But a few exotic pieces suggest that the movement of pots across quite long distances may have been more common than is generally allowed. A Glastonbury-ware bowl from Middle Iron Age Heybridge (Essex) had originated in the Shepton Mallet area of Somerset (Brown 1987, 31, fig. 15, no. 34, 32) and a fineware Early Iron Age bowl from Langwood Ridge (Cambridgeshire) had limestone inclusions showing it was made at least 20 km away (Hill 1999a, 25).

The homogeneity of so much of the Late Bronze Age and Early to Middle Iron Age pottery found in south-eastern England between the Thames and the Wash could not have come about without the movement of potters or their products across wide areas, even though it is unlikely that petrological analysis will be able to establish this for the bulk of the wares present. So one can only welcome signs that the identification of non-local pottery on the basis of its typology, decoration or general finish is now on the agenda. A bowl imported from the European mainland as early as the Late Bronze Age at Boreham (Essex) was recognised as such on the basis of its distinctive decoration and typology (Brown 1999, fig. 2.4, no. 21, 16). Hill (1999a, 25) has identified an exotic Early Iron Age Chinnor-Wandlebury fineware bowl from Wandlebury itself in Cambridgeshire. Another (unpublished) Chinnor-Wandlebury fineware bowl from Abbotstone quarry (Essex) — only 1.4 km west of Stanway — reached the site from the Cambridgeshire region (Sealey 2005). Another Early Iron Age vessel from Valley Belt at Trowse (Norfolk) has been identified as non-local on the basis of its decoration and form (Percival 2000, 175). At Late Iron Age Baldock (Hertfordshire), yet another pot was proposed as 'foreign' for much the same reasons (Rigby 1986, 260, 267, 270, fig. 106, no. 21). Other examples could be cited. Of course these ceramic items of exchange can only be recognised because they stand out from the milieu in which they were deposited. Exotic vessels of indistinguishable fabric and typology to that of the pottery at their ultimate destination may forever elude us.

BURNT RESIDUES ON MIDDLE IRON AGE POTTERY (TABLE 21)

Sixteen of the 2,512 Middle Iron Age sherds (0.6%) had black deposits adhering to the surfaces. They consist of thin patches of matter less than a millimetre or so thick, sometimes with a cracked surface. It is apparent these residues were formed in antiquity because they do not run over the edge of the break on the sherd. This matter gives every impression of being the remains of accidentally burnt or charred foodstuffs. Half were on the inside of the pot, half on the outside. Five of the sherds with exterior residues have them on the rim. To have consistently stuck to the outsides of pots on and below the rims, the foodstuff that caused the residues was presumably a thick and viscous fluid with a consistency like porridge.

TABLE 21: DETAILS OF SHERDS WITH BLACK RESIDUES

Feature	Sherd count	Date	Fabric	Position on sherd	Illustration
AF59	1	Phase 2	H	interior	not drawn
AF62	1	Phase 2	A	exterior	FIG. 25, 10
CF6	4	Phase 2	B	interior (1) exterior (3)	not drawn
CF6	1	Phase 2	N	exterior	FIG. 26, 36
CF6	1	Phase 2	C	interior	not drawn
CF6	1	Phase 2	A	exterior	not drawn
CF6	1	Phase 2	H	exterior	not drawn
CF6	1	Phase 2	H	interior	not drawn
CF6	1	Phase 2	A	interior	not drawn
CF6	1	Phase 2	A	interior	not drawn
Chamber AF25	2	Phase 3	C	interior	not drawn
Chamber BF24	1	early Roman	C	exterior	not drawn

The breakdown by fabric for sherds with burnt residues is as follows: Fabrics A, B and C (4 sherds each), Fabric H (3), and Fabric N (1). Details are given in TABLE 21. It is interesting that the residues are most common on the finer sandy fabrics. One might have expected them to have been more common on the coarser fabrics, where the larger size of the inclusions would have safeguarded the pot from thermal shock and stress during the cooking process. At Wardy Hill (Cambridgeshire), burnt residues were present in equal quantities on Middle and Late Iron Age fine- and coarsewares (Hill and Horne 2003, 181), reflecting the same apparent mismatch between fabric and function seen at Stanway. It is also puzzling that burnt residues are less common in south-east England on Late Iron Age grog-tempered and wheel-thrown pottery than they are on earlier wares. Eventually the tabulation of data from many different sites may elucidate the processes involved (Moorhouse 1986, 111).

Examination of a residue from the Middle Iron Age village at Little Waltham (Essex) showed it to be the remains of a vegetable gruel (Evans 1978). Four Middle Iron Age pots with burnt residues buried at a spring in Stock (Essex) had contained a starchy preparation derived in all likelihood from a cereal in water, to which salt had been added. The preparation had evidently been boiled until it burnt (Hedges 1977, 77). A cereal product has also been identified in a burnt deposit on a c. A.D. 40–60 sherd from another Essex site (Evans 1987a). Residues of this kind are seldom reported in Essex and East Anglia. The region has nothing comparable to Mount Farm (Oxfordshire), where burnt residues were found on 6% of the Iron Age sherds (Lambrick 1984, 169).

A recent review of the evidence for prehistoric food does not mention the topic of burnt food remains on pottery (Legge *et al.* 1998) and the work done by Evans is now felt to be less useful than analytical work addressed to organic residues actually lodged in the walls of the pot (Barclay 2001, 33–4). Even in those cases, reservations have been expressed on the grounds that a vessel might have been used for several different contents in the course of its life and that post-depositional contamination may distort the results (Barber and Ashmore 1990, 141).

Radiocarbon dating of burnt residues on Iron Age pottery from the Western Isles of Scotland by accelerator mass spectrometry has produced useful results (Haselgrove *et al.* 2001, 5). Eventually it may prove worthwhile to attempt the same elsewhere (Willis 2002, 13). In view of this, the recording of burnt residues in published reports should be undertaken as a matter of routine to signal this resource for future research.

MIDDLE IRON AGE POTTERY: FUNCTION AND RITUAL

Function

We may begin with the miniature pot from the Enclosure 2 ditch (FIG. 26, 50). Very similar miniatures were found at Middle Iron Age Heybridge in Essex (Brown 1987, fig. 15, no. 35,

33) and — with Early Iron Age Darmsden-Linton pottery — from Darmsden itself (Suffolk) (Cunliffe 1968, 184). It is too small to be a crucible of the kind found at Middle Iron Age Woodham Walter in Essex (Rodwell 1987, fig. 15, no. 13, 22; Evans 1987b), and, in any case, its clean surface has nothing that resembles industrial matter. A utilitarian function is not immediately obvious and it is worth considering the possibility that these were toys.

Ritual

No evidence has been adduced yet to show that Essex and East Anglia saw the regular structured filling of pits on a ritual basis in the Iron Age, as in Wessex and Sussex (Cunliffe 1992; 1995, 72–88; Hill 1995; Hamilton 1998). But a few instances are now known of deposits of pottery in the region that bear every appearance of intentional and even careful deposition (as opposed to the casual disposal of broken and unwanted sherd material).

Some examples will illustrate the range of practices involved. Two Middle Iron Age pots had been neatly stacked inside each other in a pit at Barley (Hertfordshire) to produce a *placed* deposit (Cra'ster 1965, 1). Rather different are two pit deposits from Essex. A small and steep-sided pit at Slough House Farm near Heybridge had Early Iron Age pottery of Darmsden-Linton type in the bottom fill. Sherds from at least eight fineware bowls and jars were present. Some were elaborately decorated with impressed circlets filled with a white mineral inlay. Vessels like this are rare, and the recovery of so many from the same context suggests selective and purposive deposition of material in a ritual act (Wallis 1998, 17; Brown 1998a, 132, 134–6, nos 41–7). Another unusual pit fill was SCS 2187 at Stansted airport, where another pit had been filled with Darmsden-Linton pottery in one operation. Many large and freshly broken sherds were present alongside tiny abraded sherds, suggesting that the pit had been filled with material from a surface midden as well as fresh domestic rubbish in a deliberate act (Brown 2004, 53). Every care was taken to identify pits with similarly anomalous fills at Stanway, but the exercise proved to be in vain.

The only possible instance of the ritual deposition of Iron Age pottery at Stanway involves the only full-size complete Middle Iron Age pot from the site (FIG. 25, 20). The vessel lay not quite upright but at an angle in the base of a small pit (CF168) in Enclosure 2. There were no other surviving finds. Apart from graves at the end of the period, complete pots are hardly ever found in pits in the region in the Iron Age. A prosaic explanation is possible of course: intact pots could have been discarded because their contents had turned rancid or the pot had been contaminated by mould (Rigby 1986, 259). Some other examples of complete non-funerary pots that come to mind are the vessel placed in the bottom of a bell-shaped pit at Late Iron Age Baldock in Hertfordshire (*ibid.*, 273, fig. 105, no. 1), a Darmsden-Linton bowl laid on its side in a pit at Stansted airport in Essex (Brown 2004, 53), and a complete Middle Iron Age jar buried in the primary silt of a ditch at the entrance to a small enclosure with round-house at Ardleigh (Essex). The excavators suggested the last example was a foundation deposit (Erith and Holbert 1970, 18, fig. 15, no. 36). A near-complete Middle Iron Age pot from Stansted airport buried with a cattle jaw bone was also described as an offering (Havis and Brooks 2004, 24; Brown 2004, 53). Complete pots were a component of the ritual fills of pits at Danebury hillfort in Hampshire (Poole 1995, 249, 261), and that alone should alert us to the possibility that these vessels from eastern England might also have a ritual dimension.

In the case of the Stanway pot, its credentials as a ritual deposit are enhanced by its position, central to the round-house postulated in Enclosure 2. Another Colchester round-house is relevant here. The structure was a Middle Iron Age house at Ypres Road on the Garrison site (Brooks and Masefield 2005, 20–1). In the centre of the house, a small pit contained large fresh sherds of a bowl with carefully wiped inner and outer surfaces to give a polished and smooth finish that suggests a pot made with particular care (Sealey in Brooks and Masefield). No other pottery was associated with the Ypres Road bowl. The position of both pots in identical positions can hardly be coincidental and we seem to be dealing here with a specific instance of placed deposition.

DISCUSSION

The Early and Middle Iron Age pottery from Stanway is an assemblage of significant size. Most of the entries on the register of later prehistoric pottery groups from England are smaller than 1,000 sherds (Morris and Champion 2001, 254), although Stanway is dwarfed by the very largest groups from Essex and East Anglia (Hill and Horne 2003, 146). Its interest is enhanced by the dearth of Middle Iron Age pottery from north-east Essex. The most important single group came from the Little Oakley villa in Tendring Hundred, 27.5 km east of Stanway (Barford 2002, 114–31). Closer to Stanway is an important group from Ardleigh, 7.5 km north-east of Colchester town centre (Erith and Holbert 1970, 18–24). But the usefulness of Ardleigh is undermined by a lack of information about the fabrics and their quantification, or indeed stratigraphy. Closer to Stanway, a few scraps of Early and Middle Iron Age pottery were found at Church Lane, 2 km to the north-east (Partridge 1993). A larger group than Church Lane — but still much smaller than Stanway — was excavated at Abbotstone 1.5 km to the west (Benfield and Brooks 1999; Sealey 2005). Otherwise there is little Early or Middle Iron Age pottery from the Colchester region at all. Stanway is the largest collection of Early and Middle Iron Age pottery from north-east Essex, and the first of significant size from the Colchester region. One needs to move further south-west in Essex to find groups of Early and Middle Iron Age pottery of comparable size. One of the closest is the 1,150 Early and Middle Iron Age sherds weighing 12.977 kg from Ivy Chimneys outside Witham, 17 km to the south-west of Stanway (Turner-Walker and Wallace 1999, 125).

The Middle Iron Age pottery from Stanway belongs to a distinctive pottery style zone found widely across Essex and East Anglia. For Norfolk and Suffolk, the tradition is described in two excellent surveys (Martin 1999, 74–81; Percival 1999). It is handmade in a range of sand, flint and flint-with-sand-tempered fabrics. Apart from finger-tip impressions on the tops of rims and the occasional decorated body sherd, it is a resolutely plain ware tradition. Vessel forms are limited and dominated by variations on the theme of bowls and jars with slack S-profiles. Bases are generally flat. Important assemblages have been published from Spong Hill (Gregory 1995) and Caistor St Edmund (Harford Farm) in Norfolk (Percival 2000, 108–14). To the north-west, this ceramic is flanked by the East Midlands scored ware so common beyond the Fens and the Wash (Elsdon 1992). In Suffolk there are key groups from West Stow (West 1990, 60–8) and Burgh-by-Woodbridge (Martin 1988, 37–9, 46–7). Cambridgeshire has two large assemblages, from Wardy Hill in the Fens and Little Paxton in the south-west of the county (Hill and Horne 2003; Hancocks 2003). It spills over into east Hertfordshire, where it is represented by the pottery from Barley (Ozanne 1961). In Essex the number of published sites with Middle Iron Age pottery is now considerable, far more than for neighbouring counties (Sealey 1996 for a survey). Since 1996 the major published groups from Essex are the sites at Witham (Rodwell 1993, 100–2; Brown 1993, 108–10; Turner-Walker and Wallace 1999, 123–7) as well as Slough House Farm and Howell's Farm, north of Heybridge (Brown 1998a, 134–6, 139–41).

Enough data are now available for regional groups to be distinguished within this pottery, particularly for Essex. A striking omission from the Stanway repertoire is the everted footring bowl, Little Waltham Form 13 (Drury 1978, 54–6). No base from Stanway has a footring. The closest approach is the faintly dished base found on only three vessels (FIGS 25–6, 18 and 34 for two of them). This is not the picture in central and south Essex, where Form 13 is common. Petrological analysis indicates the presence of glauconite in some of them, and an origin in the Mucking-Chadwell area has been claimed (Drury 1978, 128; Hamilton 1988, 76, with more details of the petrology). In fact, the source is the Maidstone region (Thompson 1982, 7, 11–12, her Medway zone; *see* also Pollard 1988, 31–2), and these pots represent a trade in vessels from Kent, north across the Thames (not the other way round). Local (Essex) copies are found in other fabrics. Along the Thames estuary, the composition of Middle Iron Age assemblages more closely resembles those of Kent than of districts further north. Both regions are further linked by the number of vessels decorated with stamped patterns and curvilinear decoration (Elsdon 1975; Brown 1991).

Stanway has nothing indicative of contact with the Thames estuary regions of south Essex. There are no Form 13 bowls or stamped and curvilinear pottery. Its Middle Iron Age pottery is plainer and more severe, in an idiom that has more in common with Suffolk than with central or south Essex. It is to be hoped that the differences between the Middle Iron Age pottery from the north and south of the county will be explored further in future research.

Catalogue of illustrated Early and Middle Iron Age pottery

FIGURE 25

1. Fabric F. Black core with light red-brown surfaces, burnt after breakage. Finger-tip-with-nail impressions on the rim, with oblique and vertical wipe marks on the exterior. Pit AF46 in Enclosure 1. Phase 1.
2. Fabric I. Black core with red surfaces, burnt after breakage. Pit AF46 in Enclosure 1. Phase 1.
3. Fabric J. Black core with a brown interior, and a mottled brown and dark brown exterior. Pit AF28 in Enclosure 1. Phase 1.
4. Fabric F. Brown core and surfaces; the exterior has been wiped smooth. Ditch AF59. Phase 2.
5. Fabric A. Black core and interior, brown exterior. Finger-tip impressions on the rim. Pit AF26 in Enclosure 1. Phase 2.
6. Fabric A. Black core with red surfaces. Pit AF55 in Enclosure 1. Phase 2.
7. Fabric C. Black core with mottled red-brown surfaces. Horizontal burnish marks on the outer surface. Pit AF55 in Enclosure 1. Phase 2.
8. Fabric D. Dark brown core and surfaces. Pit AF62 in Enclosure 1. Phase 2.
9. Fabric C. Grey core and brown surfaces. Burnished outer surface. Pit AF62 in Enclosure 1. Phase 2.
10. Fabric A. Black core with brown interior, light brown exterior. The rim is decorated with straight incised lines, and on the body below the shoulder there are incised straight lines cut obliquely across the surface. Burnt residues run down the exterior over the neck and shoulder. Pit AF62 in Enclosure 1. Phase 2.
11. Fabric C. Black core with light brown interior, dark brown exterior. Pit AF68 in Enclosure 1. Phase 2.
12. Fabric C. Black core with mottled brown and black surfaces. Pit AF80 in Enclosure 1. Phase 2.
13. Fabric A. Light brown core and black surfaces. Horizontal burnish marks on the outer surface. Pit AF80 in Enclosure 1. Phase 2.
14. Fabric G. Grey core and interior, brown exterior. Pit AF80 in Enclosure 1. Phase 2.
15. Fabric A. Grey core and red-brown interior, dark brown exterior. Pit AF80 in Enclosure 1. Phase 2.
16. Fabric C. Brown core and interior, dark grey-brown exterior. Finger-tip impressions on rim. Pit AF80 in Enclosure 1. Phase 2.
17. Fabric B. Black core with mottled brown and grey surfaces. Pit AF80 in Enclosure 1. Phase 2.
18. Fabric B. Black core and interior, brown exterior. Pit AF80 in Enclosure 1. Phase 2.
19. Fabric A. Black core with brown surfaces. Enclosure 1 ditch. Phase 3.
20. Fabric A. Black core and exterior, light brown interior. Pit CF168 in Enclosure 2. Phase 2.
21. Fabric E. Black core with light red-brown surfaces. Pit AF22 in Enclosure 2. Phase 2.
22. Fabric J. Brown core and surfaces. The rim is decorated with straight incisions cut obliquely across the top; below the rim there are two deep score lines. Pit AF22 in Enclosure 2. Phase 2.
23. Fabric A. Black core and interior, light red-brown exterior. Pit AF22 in Enclosure 2. Phase 2.
24. Fabric B. Black core with dark brown surfaces. Pit AF22 in Enclosure 2. Phase 2.
25. Fabric M with vegetable temper. Black core with a light brown interior, grey exterior. Pit AF22 in Enclosure 2. Phase 2.
26. Fabric B. Black core with light brown surfaces. Pit AF22 in Enclosure 2. Phase 2.

FIGURE 26

27. Fabric E. Brown core and surfaces. Pit CF159 in Enclosure 2. Phase 2.
28. Fabric C. Black core with grey interior, brown exterior. Pit CF168 in Enclosure 2. Phase 2.
29. Fabric C. Black core and surfaces. Pit CF168 in Enclosure 2. Phase 2.
30. Fabric K. Black core with grey interior, brown exterior. Pit CF250 in Enclosure 2. Phase 2.
31. Fabric A. Black core and exterior, light grey interior. Pit CF250 in Enclosure 2. Phase 2.
32. Fabric J. Dark grey core with red surfaces. Pit CF21 in Enclosure 2. Phase 2.

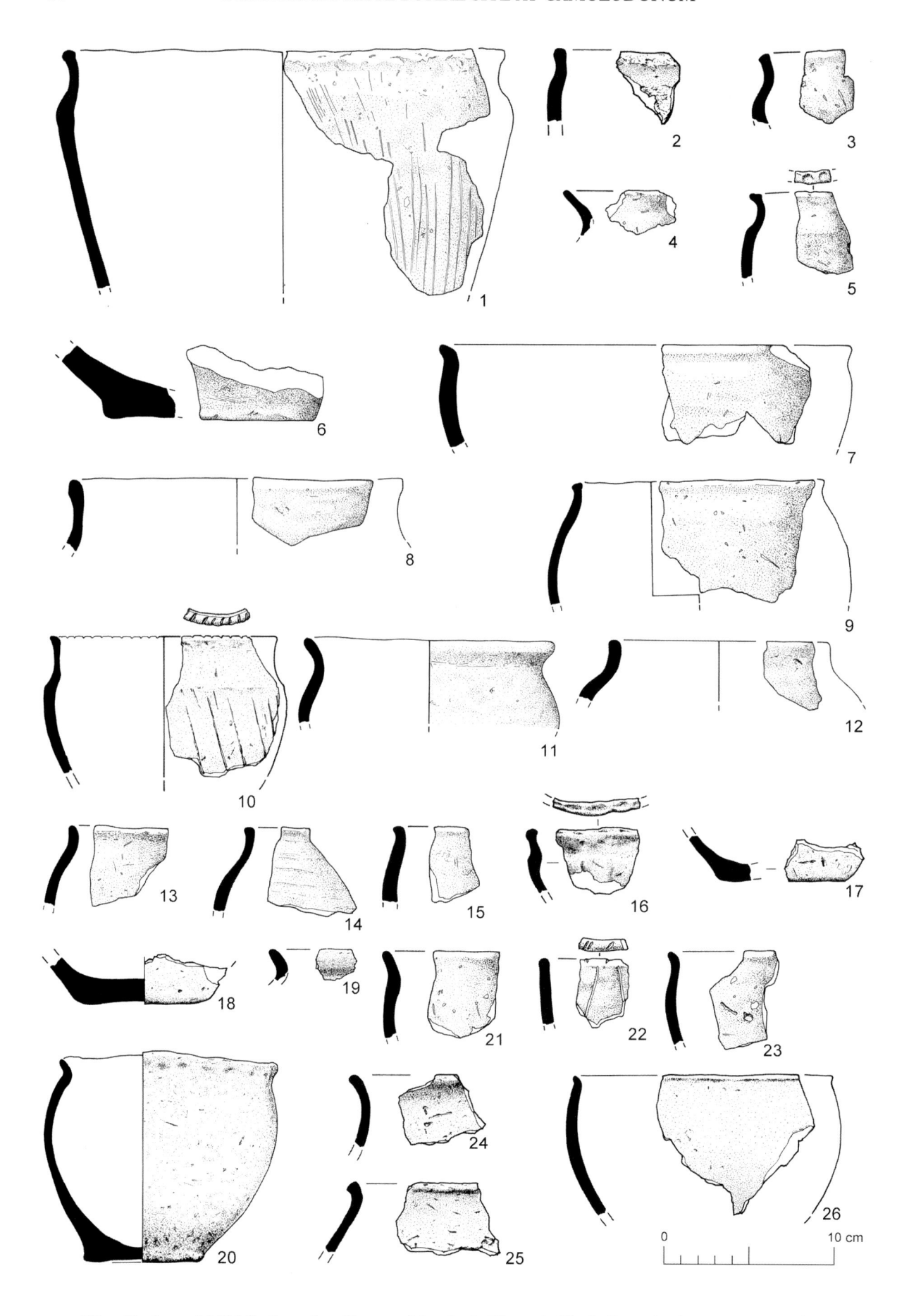

FIG. 25. Early and Middle Iron Age Pottery. Nos 1–3: Phase 1 (Early Iron Age); nos 4–18 and 20–28: Phase 2 (Middle Iron Age); no. 19: Phase 3 (transitional Middle to Late Iron Age)

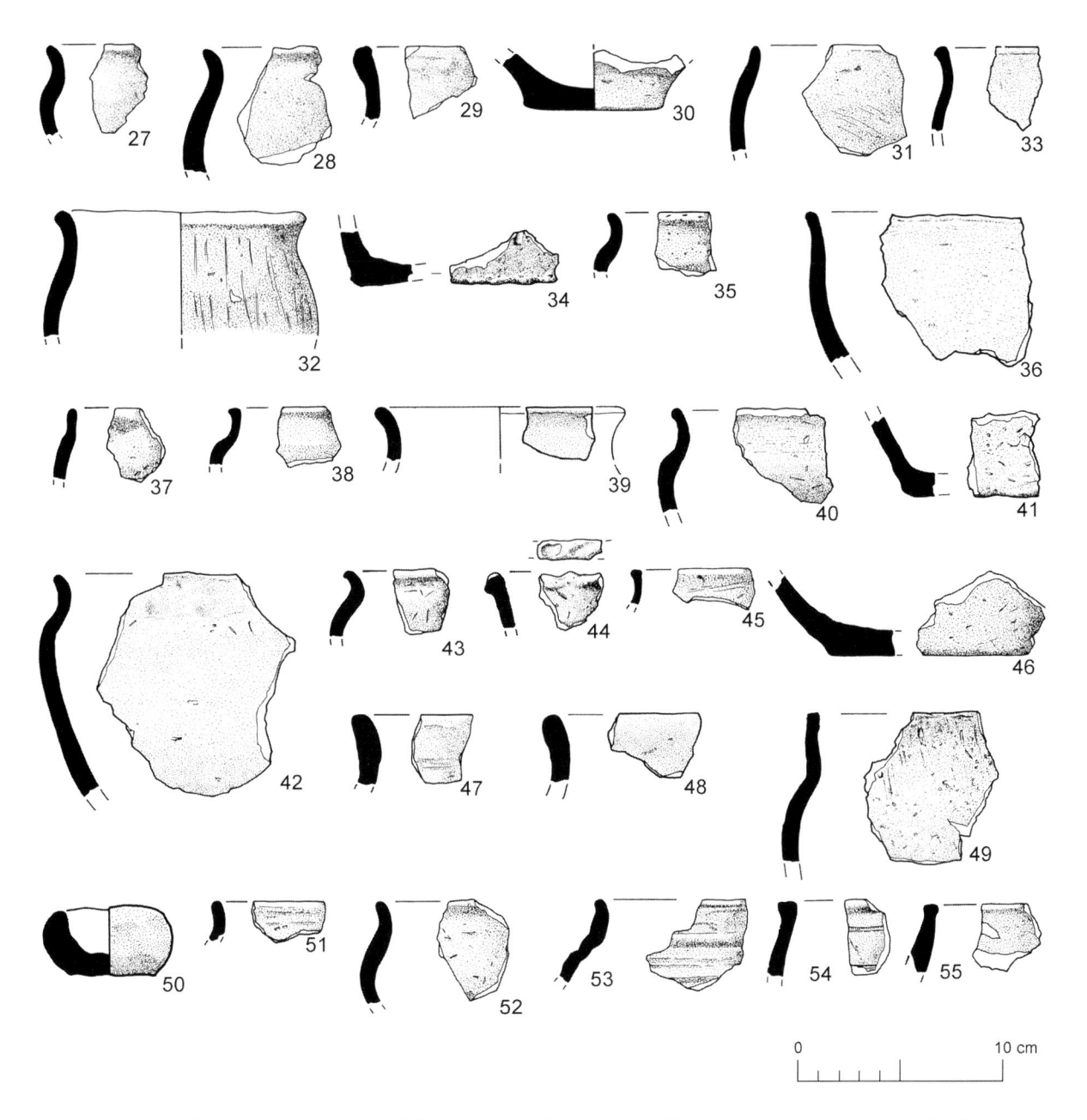

FIG. 26. Middle Iron Age Pottery. Nos 31–52: Phase 2 (Middle Iron Age); nos 53–5: Enclosure 4 (transitional Middle to Late Iron Age sherds in Late Iron Age/early Roman features)

33. Fabric B. Grey core with brown interior, black exterior. Burnt residues on the exterior. Enclosure 2 ditch, L15 (middle fill). Phase 2.
34. Fabric I. Dark grey to black core with brown surfaces. Enclosure 2 ditch, L15 (middle fill). Phase 2.
35. Fabric J. Grey core with brown surfaces. Enclosure 2 ditch, L15 (middle fill). Phase 2.
36. Fabric N. Black core with brown surfaces. Burnt residues run down the rim towards the shoulder. Enclosure 2 ditch, (middle fill, associated with the currency bar hoard). Phase 2.
37. Fabric B. Black core and surfaces. Enclosure 2 ditch, L126 (middle fill). Phase 2.
38. Fabric N. Black core with dark grey interior, brown exterior. Enclosure 2 ditch, L150 (lower fill). Phase 2.
39. Fabric C. Grey core with mottled brown and red-brown surfaces. Enclosure 2 ditch, L114 (upper fill). Phase 2.
40. Fabric C. Grey-brown core and interior, brown exterior. Enclosure 2 ditch, L114 (upper fill). Phase 2.

41. Fabric K. Dark grey core with mottled dark brown interior, mottled light brown exterior. Enclosure 2 ditch, L114 (upper fill). Phase 2.
42. Fabric D. Black core with light brown interior, mottled light red-brown to brown exterior. Enclosure 2 ditch, L114 (upper fill). Phase 2.
43. Fabric D. Black core with dark brown interior, brown exterior. Enclosure 2 ditch, L114 (upper fill). Phase 2.
44. Fabric D. Black core and inner surface, brown exterior. Finger-tip impressions on the rim. Enclosure 2 ditch, L114 (upper fill). Phase 2.
45. Fabric B. Grey core with light brown surfaces. Enclosure 2 ditch, L114 (upper fill). Phase 2
46. Fabric K. Black core with dark grey interior, mottled dark grey to dark brown exterior. Enclosure 2 ditch, L114 (upper fill). Phase 2.
47. Late Iron Age Fabric 3BA. Brown core and surfaces. The flat rim is Middle Iron Age in form, but the fabric is grog-tempered. Not enough survives to judge if it is hand- or wheel-made. Enclosure 2 ditch, L117 (upper fill). Phase 2.
48. Fabric A. Black core with brown surfaces. Enclosure 2 ditch, L116 (upper fill). Phase 2.
49. Fabric K. Black core with brown interior, dark brown exterior. Diagonal incised score marks on the exterior below the rim. Enclosure 2 ditch, L161 (middle fill). Phase 2.
50. Fabric J. Light brown surfaces (the core is not accessible for study). Complete miniature pot. Enclosure 2 ditch (middle to upper fill). Phase 2.
51. Fabric A. Brown core and interior, light brown exterior. Enclosure 2 ditch (middle to lower fill). Phase 2.
52. Fabric C. Dark grey-brown core and interior, brown to dark brown exterior. Enclosure 2 ditch, (middle to lower fill). Phase 2.
53. Fabric A. Black core and surfaces. Chamber BF24 in Enclosure 4. Early Roman.
54. Fabric A. Grey core with light brown interior, dark brown exterior. Two horizontal grooves on the exterior below the rim. Chamber BF24 in Enclosure 4. Early Roman.
55. Late Iron Age Fabric 3BA. Brown core and surfaces. The flat rim is Middle Iron Age in form, but the fabric is grog-tempered; hand-made. North ditch (BF31) of the ?mortuary enclosure BF32 in Enclosure 4. Late Iron Age/early Roman.

PALAEOCHANNEL CF52 AND ITS FINDS (FIGS 2, 5, 27)

Cremated bone   none
Objects   CF52.1   spearhead
                  CF52.2   spearhead
                  CF52.3   drip of lead
Residual finds none identified (context metal detected only)

On the west side of the 1996 excavation area was a broad palaeochannel (FIGS 2 and 5, CF52) which formed a shallow depression filled predominantly with pale silt. This ran at a gentle slope down from north–south. To the north the feature was formed from the merging of two smaller silt-filled channels. The main channel was between about 70 m across where the two smaller channels merged, and 30 m across at the south edge of the site area. This feature was cut by the Middle Iron Age enclosure (Enclosure 2). South of Enclosure 2, early Roman pottery sherds and two iron spearheads were found just below the excavation surface of the channel silt. A machine-excavated trench was cut across the main channel to its base and at that point the channel proved to be between about 0.8 m and 0.3 m deep, the deeper sections being on its eastern side. It was predominantly filled with pale brown sandy silt. In places in the lower part of the feature this overlay a thin gravel layer at the base and also divided pockets of gravels. These gravels were concentrated in the eastern, deeper half of the feature and merged into the sands and gravels at the channel base. The gravel pockets rising between broad areas of the silt fill gave the impression that the feature may have been formed from a number of smaller channels. There were no finds from the excavation section cut across the channel.

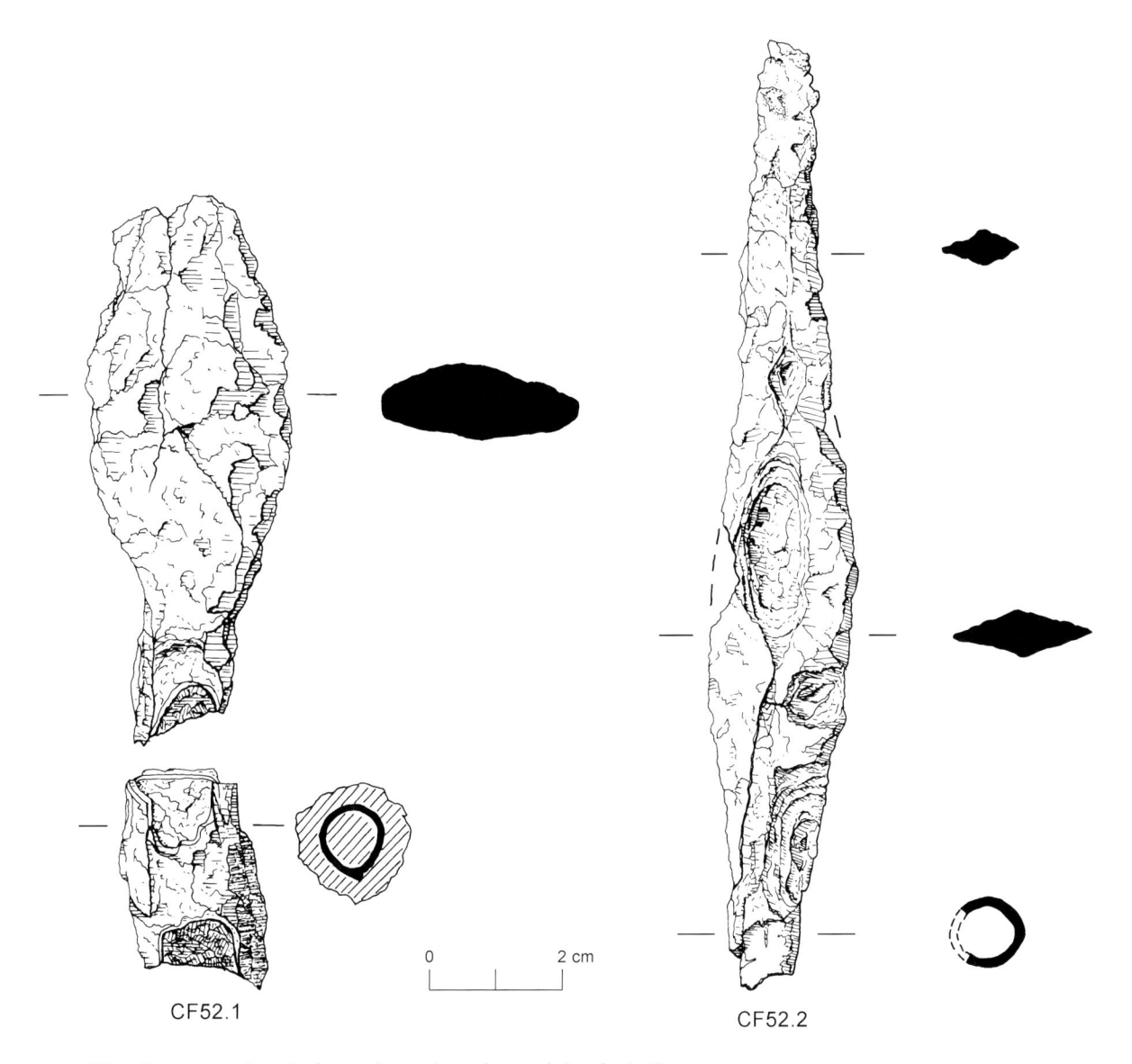

FIG. 27. Iron spearheads from the palaeochannel (scale 1:1)

Finds (FIG. 27)

The feature contained a small tapering resolidified drip of lead and two spearheads. The two spearheads were found some distance apart (FIG. 27), but probably form a small hoard or votive deposit; the lead drip is unlikely to belong with them. Three small body sherds (5 g) from a jar or bowl in fabric RCW were recovered from just below the level of the excavation surface when cleaning around spearhead CF52.1. The dating of spearheads is difficult, and usually depends upon associated material or stratigraphy (Feugère 2002a, 131). The location of this pair suggests that they relate to Enclosure 2, although they may well be later. A deposit of six spearheads found in the backfill of the inner ditch of a triple-ditched square enclosure at Orsett 'Cock', Essex, with a seventh found nearby in the central ditch, has been dated to about the time of the Roman invasion, supported by the retrieval of a possible Roman artillery bolt head from the inner ditch (Major 1998c, 83, figs 53–4; Carter 1998, 167–8, fig. 12). A major characteristic of the Orsett deposit was the range of shapes present, with no two spearheads being precisely the same, although the group can be divided broadly into leaf-shaped and narrow blades. That one example of each of these forms is present in the Stanway deposit suggests that the same rationale informed the selection of this group, but the evidence is slight and certainly not enough to prove that the two hoards were close in date or contemporary.

The lead drip, if deliberately deposited as part of the Stanway hoard, would support a date of after A.D. 43. However, similar resolidified drips of post-Roman date are often retrieved from ploughsoil, including from this site (listed in archive), and this piece may therefore be intrusive, perhaps the result of settlement, leaving open the question of the date of the hoard.

CF52.1 FIG. 27. SF390. C123 F52. Iron socketed spearhead in poor condition. The blade is leaf-shaped and smooth-edged and was probably of lenticular section with no obvious central rib, although the metal has delaminated and the original shape is therefore not certain. The tip of the blade is missing. Surviving length 110 mm, maximum width 28 mm.

CF52.2 FIG. 27. SF391. C204 F52. Iron socketed spearhead with most of the socket missing. The blade is narrow, with no angularity to the edges, and of lozenge-shaped section with a slightly flattened midrib. Surviving length 137 mm, maximum surviving width 23 mm.

CF52.3 SF204. C127 F52. Small tapering drip of lead, 24 mm long, maximum width 6 mm. Weight 1.24 g. Not illus.

CHAPTER 4

THE FUNERARY SITE

THE FUNERARY ENCLOSURES

FUNERARY ENCLOSURE 1 (FIGS 2, 6, 28–9, 139, 148)

Finds from the enclosure ditch
?Partial and other pots Pots 1–4   at least 2 partial vessels
Other finds   AF17.1   coin of Cunobelin A.D. 20–43, post-conquest sherds
                                             from upper fill
Residual finds   Early and Middle Iron Age pottery, loomweights and
                                             burnt daub

Enclosure 1 was set out on the north side of Enclosure 2 (FIGS 2 and 6). The new enclosure ditch cut the Middle Iron Age ditch CF137/AF59 in two places, showing that one post-dated the other. The juxtaposition of Enclosures 1 and 2 and the way in which both respected the ?boundary ditch (AF59) suggest that there must have been continuity of a sort between the two. However, the pottery from the earliest levels of the enclosure ditch included grog-tempered ware, unlike the internal features of Enclosure 2 where there was none. This disparity suggests that the farmstead represented by Enclosure 2 was no longer occupied when Enclosure 1 was laid out, and that the latter was created specifically for a funerary purpose. It will be suggested below (pp. 436–7) that the enclosure was created at the same time as the mortuary chamber (AF25) which it contained. In addition to the chamber, the enclosure contained a cremation burial (AF18) and a pit containing broken funerary goods (AF48).

Enclosure 1 approximated to a square in shape and measured externally about 92 m north–south and 84–98 m east–west. The ditch was roughly V-shaped, 2.5–3.0 m wide and up to 1.5 m deep (after stripping the site). The fill of the enclosure ditch was fairly homogeneous, although the lower fill tended to be sandier and to contain a higher proportion of gravels than the main fill so that, as in the other enclosure ditches, it could be divided into a 'lower', rapid fill and a 'main' fill which represented a much slower accumulation after the sides of the ditch had stabilised (FIG. 28). The tip-lines in the lower fill of the ditch (AF4 and AF31) were more marked on the inner slopes, perhaps providing evidence for an internal bank which was pushed into the ditch when it was levelled. There were no other indications of an inner bank except perhaps the near-absence of features close to the inner edge of the ditch. There was also no evidence that the ditch had been recut. A gap in the west ditch visible on aerial photographs was where the ditch had been cut through by a modern trench (AF23).

To judge by the other enclosures, the most likely position of an entrance is the middle of the eastern side. However, none can be identified. All of the ditch is clearly visible on cropmark photographs, but no break in it is apparent anywhere, and too little of the ditch could be excavated to solve the problem. One explanation is that there had been a wooden bridge over the ditch. Another is that the entrance was re-sited during the life of the enclosure. However, most likely of all is that the butt ends of the ditch forming the entrance were remodelled and altered to such an extent that the entrance became invisible as a cropmark.

Finds from the ditch sections were sparse, but included at least two deliberately broken pottery vessels (FIG. 139, Pots 2–3). Partial Pot 3 had been deposited in the lower fill of the enclosure ditch (AF53). It consisted of about 40% of a Late Iron Age Cam 229 ripple shouldered bowl. Pot 2, on the other hand, lay in the main fill of the ditch (AF17), and took the form of about 25% of a platter of Cam 14/28 in fabric FSW. This vessel is post-conquest and can be dated to c. A.D.

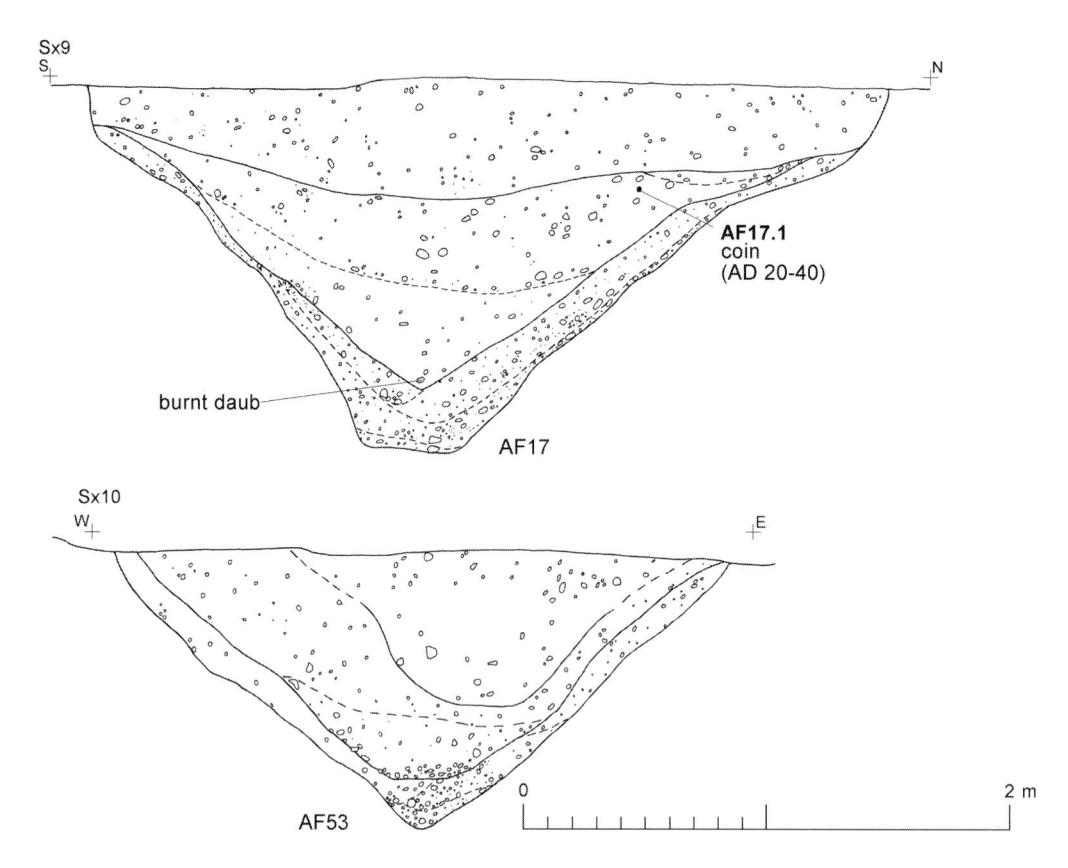

FIG. 28. Enclosure 1 ditch: sections (scale 1:30)

43–100 if not the Claudio–Neronian period (*CAR* 10, 468). The only other identifiable Late Iron Age piece from the ditches is a small abraded rim sherd of Cam 263 (Pot 4) from AF4. A sherd of Roman grey ware (fabric GX(H)), four sherds of fabric HZ, and a small number of RCW sherds from the ditch (AF17) all confim that the ditch was still open in the early Roman period.

Other finds from the ditch included a coin of Cunobelin (FIG. 148, AF17.1; *see* Sx 9; p. 340) dated A.D. 20–43, iron-working slag, an iron ?strip, and some possible nail fragments (for the iron objects and slag, which are probably residual Middle Iron Age, *see* p. 45). Two brooch spring fragments came from the base of the ploughsoil AL4 which covered the north-western area of Enclosure 2 and the adjacent eastern area of Enclosure 1 (FIG. 29, AL4.1–2). They may be contemporary with either enclosure.

Remains of ?deliberately broken pots from the enclosure ditch and other pots (FIG. 139)

Pot 1 Not illustrated. Ditch AF17 main fill. Flagon. Body sherd (A588). Fabric WPW.
Pot 2 Ditch AF17 main fill. Cam 14/28 platter (A592) (*CAR* 10 fabric group UR.LTC). Partial pot (approx. 25%), wall and base sherds. Burnished. Fabric FSW.
Pot 3 Ditch AF53 lower fill. Cam 229 ripple shouldered bowl (A616). Partial pot. Much of rim and shoulder with some body sherds, base missing. Partial vessel (approx 40%). Burnished over rim, neck and shoulder. Fabric GTW.
Pot 4 Ditch AF4 (1987.16 AF2 lower part of ditch fill). Cam 263 jar with stab decoration on shoulder. Single rim sherd only (1987.16 174), abraded. Burnished on neck and rim. Fabric GTW.

Other pottery sherds from the enclosure ditch (sherds of deliberately broken pots?)

AF17: Fabric GBW, sherd (B179); Fabric GX(H), single sherd (A580); Fabric HZ, 4 sherds (A580).
AF4: Fabric RCW, 20 sherds including 2 jar/bowl rims (1987.16 129, 165, 171, 172, 175, 177, 181).

Other finds from the enclosure ditch (FIG. 148)

AF17.1 SF106. A589. Middle fill of northern arm of ditch of Enclosure 1. Coin of Cunobelin A.D. 20–43 (see p. 340).

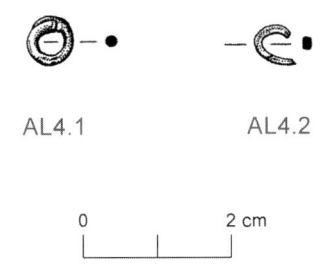

FIG. 29.   Enclosure 1: copper-alloy brooch spring fragments from the ploughsoil (scale 1:1)

Finds from the base of ploughsoil (AL4) in the north-western part of Enclosure 1
(FIG. 29)*

AL4.1 SF9. A231. Fragment, circular in section, from the spring of a copper-alloy brooch, representing just over one coil. Diameter 7 mm. It could derive from a brooch of La Tène I or II type, or a fairly small La Tène III brooch, perhaps of Nauheim or *Knotenfibel* form. It might therefore be contemporary with either Enclosure 1 or 2.

AL4.2 SF8. A278. U-shaped fragment from a small copper-alloy coil, almost certainly, as SF9 above, part of the spring from a brooch. Maximum diameter 7 mm.

* For finds from the internal features of Enclosure 1, *see* chamber AF25 (pp. 101–3), burial AF18 (pp. 167–70), and pit with broken funerary goods AF48 (pp. 162–7).

FUNERARY ENCLOSURE 3 (FIGS 2, 7–8, 30, 139)

Finds from the enclosure ditch
?Partial and other pots   Pots 5–13   parts of at least nine vessels
Glass vessel   BF4.1   sherd of polychrome glass vessel
Other finds   hobnails
                                              fragments of iron nails
Residual finds   Early and Middle Iron Age pottery, burnt daub

Enclosure 3 was laid out as a funerary enclosure around the middle of the 1st century A.D. (FIGS 2 and 7). Its alignment was similar to C137/AF59 and the eastern side of Enclosure 1 but differed from that of Enclosures 4 and 5 with which it was contiguous. The enclosure was square in shape. It was 70/74 m wide measured externally and was delineated by a substantial ditch (BF2, BF4, BF5, BF23, BF27) which was up to 4 m wide and approximately 1.1 m deep (after stripping) with a U-shaped profile (FIG. 30). The lower (*i.e.* 'rapid') fill consisted of a brownish-yellow loamy sand with moderate to abundant small and medium gravels. The main fill was typically a greyish-brown sandy clay loam with moderate small and medium gravels up to 1 m thick. No indications of a bank were found, although presumably there had been one. There was an entrance 3.4 m wide in the middle of the eastern side of the enclosure, where the butt-ends of the enclosure ditch (BF4 and BF27) were up to 1.0 m deep. No features were associated with the ditch apart from a gully (BF12), which possibly drained into BF4, and a shallow pit (BF14). The enclosure contained (FIGS 7–8) a pyre-site (BF1/BF16), a chamber (BF6) and two cremation burials (the 'Warrior's burial' (BF64) and the 'Inkwell burial' (BF67). Apart perhaps from a small pit (BF10), there was no convincing evidence for activity pre-dating the Late Iron Age. Few other features were found in the enclosure. These included several pits (FIG. 30, BF7–BF9, BF13, BF20), all of which are undatable.

With the exception of the ditch terminals, finds from the ditch sections were sparse. They consisted of the remains of at least nine deliberately broken pottery vessels, one fragment of polychrome glass (FIG. 30, BF4.1), an iron nail, fragments of three others, and three iron hobnails which presumably are post-conquest. A sherd of Roman grey ware (Fabric GX(H)) unstratified from ditch BF5 may relate to Enclosure 4 rather than Enclosure 3 since BF5 is common to both.

72   STANWAY: AN ÉLITE BURIAL SITE AT CAMULODUNUM

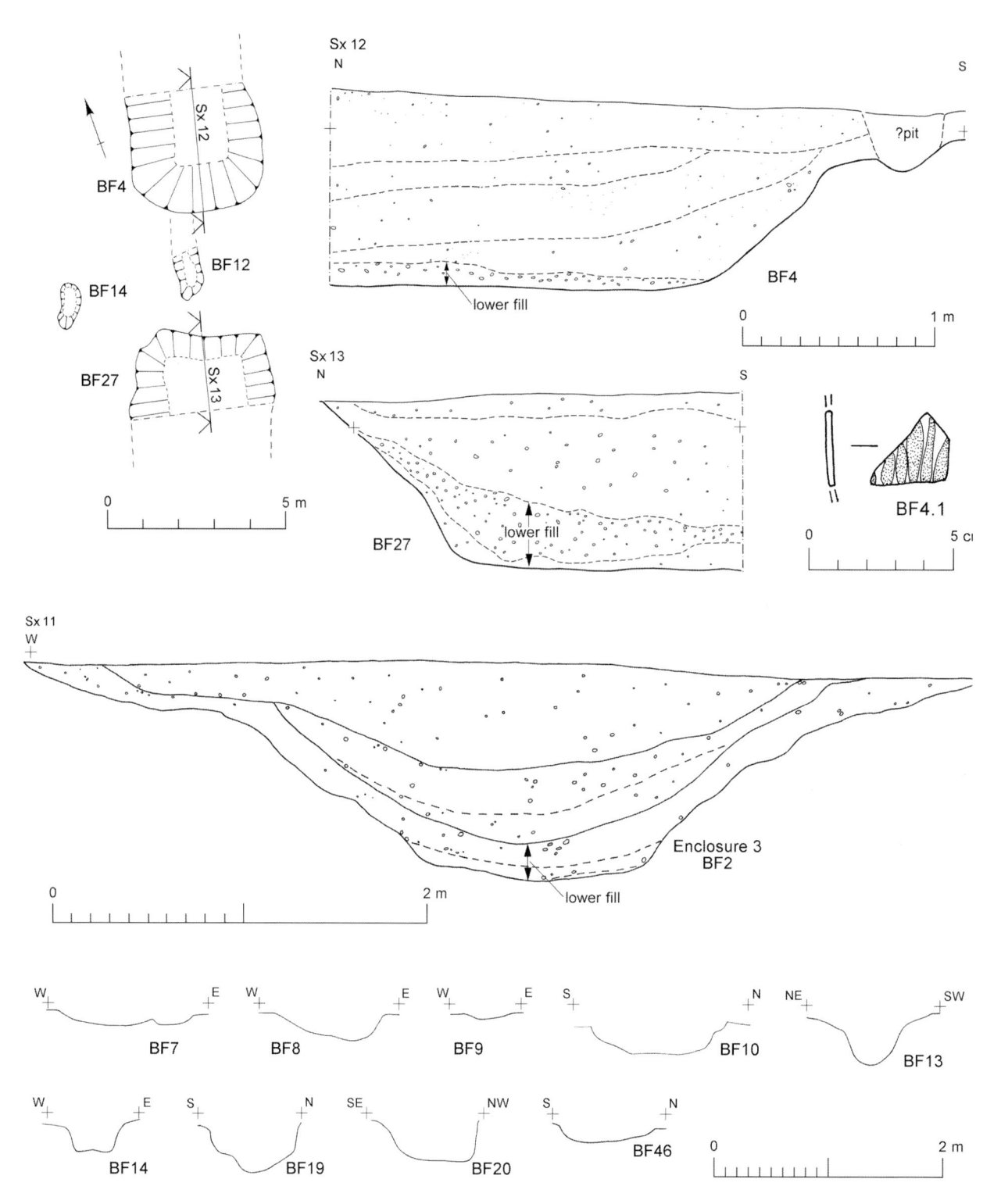

FIG. 30. Enclosure 3 entrance: plan, ditch sections (1:30) with fragment of glass vessel BF4.1 (1:2) from the ditch and pit profiles (scale 1:50)

The partial pots (Pots 5–13) and other vessels represented in the enclosure ditch include five or six imports, *i.e.* a Cam 113 butt-beaker (FIG. 139, Pot 6), two or possibly three flagons/*lagenae* (Pots 5, ?7, 8), and two amphoras (Pots 12–13). The coarsewares from the ditches (171 g) are dominated by the fabric RCW (120 g) in which two coarseware vessel forms can be identified. Almost all the partial pots lay on or close to the base of the ditch, showing that the breaking of those pots took place early in the life of the enclosure (p. 436). Most of the sherds (128 g) were found in the ditch terminal BF4; they include two jars of form Cam 266 (FIG. 139, 10–11).

The fragment of polychrome glass (FIG. 30, BF4.1) belongs to a yellow/brown vessel decorated with opaque white marvered spots. The sherd is too small to indicate the form of the vessel, but the type of decoration points to a date for it within the Tiberian to Flavian period. *See* further page 345.

The backfill of the southern enclosure ditch (BF5) was cut by a small pit (BF19) and also by a shallow charcoal-filled scoop (BF46) containing a small quantity of burnt bone (0.1 g).

?Partial and other pots from the enclosure ditch (FIG. 139)

Pot 5 Not illustrated. Ditch BF27 (lower fill 0.01 m above base of ditch) entrance south terminal. Flagon (form unknown). Partial pot. 40 small sherds — fragments, abraded (B292). 40+ body sherds, probably fewer larger sherds originally deposited and fragmented after deposition (B288, B292) 1 sherd only (B1184). Fabric WPW.

Pot 6 Ditch BF27 (lower fill 0.01 m above base of ditch) entrance south terminal. Cam 113 butt-beaker. Partial pot. Three joining rim sherds (B288, B292), rim sherd only (B1179) abraded, sherds (B288, B292) abraded surfaces but typical fabric and finish, blue-grey core. Fabric BPW.

Pot 7 Not illustrated. Ditch BF4 (at base of ditch fill and base of main fill) entrance north terminal. Flagon/*lagena* with four-ribbed handle (B1099, B1100). Joining sherds of handle only, abraded (?possibly part of Pot 5). Fabric WPW.

Pot 8 Not illustrated. Ditch BF4 (middle of main fill) entrance north terminal. Flagon/*lagena* (form unknown). Base sherd (B1110), abraded. Fragments (B213) probably from same vessel. Fabric ROW (possibly King Harry Lane 'silty ware', also found at Stansted Airport cemetery, source likely to be Hadham area).

Pot 9 Not illustrated. Ditch BF4 (at base of ditch fill) entrance north terminal. Cam 114 imitation butt-beaker (B1102). Vertical combed decoration. Fabric ROW.

Pot 10 Ditch BF4 (at base of ditch fill) entrance south terminal. Cam 266 jar. Partial pot. Rim sherd only (B1178). Burnished on top of rim. Fabric RCW.

Pot 11 Ditch BF4 (at base of ditch fill) entrance south terminal. Cam 266 jar. Joining sherds (B1180) from part of rim and shoulder (<5% of vessel), abraded. Burnished on neck. Fabric RCW.

Pot 12 Not illustrated. Ditch BF4 (middle of main fill) entrance south terminal. Dressel 2-4 amphora. sherd from neck of vessel (B1117) (5 g). Fine light pink (5YR 7/4) fabric of untempered clay.

Pot 13 Not illustrated. Ditch BF4, entrance south terminal. Amphora, Dressel 2-4, sherd from neck of vessel (B1101) (12 g). Italian amphora in a black sand fabric. Fabric CAM AM 1.

Other pottery sherds from the enclosure ditch

BF2: Fabric GTW, 2 sherds (B29, B33).
BF4: Fabric GTW, 4 sherds (B218, B677); Fabric RCW, 11 sherds (B250, B1099, B1139).
BF5: Fabric DJ(D), sherd fragment (B207); Fabric GX(H), sherd (B908).
BF23: Fabric GTW, 1 sherd (B916); Fabric RCW, 7 sherds (B247).
BF27: Fabric GTW, 1 sherd (B1185); Fabric HZ, 3 sherds (B287); Fabric RCW, 3 sherds (B292).

Glass vessel from the enclosure ditch (FIG. 30)

BF4.1 B249. Body fragment of glass. Light yellow/brown with opaque white spots marvered smooth. Straight side. Dimensions 13 × 11 mm, wall thickness 1 mm.

Other finds from the enclosure ditch

BF4: B1104. Two iron hobnails of Manning's Type 10 (1985, 136–7). Lengths 14 and 16 mm.
BF5: B207. Iron nail shank. Length 29 mm.
BF27/BL22: B281 Iron slag-like fragment, possibly pyre debris. Weight 7 g. SF175. B282. Iron square-section nail shank fragment, length 26 mm.
BF27/BL24: B289 Iron hobnail of Manning's Type 10 (1985, 136–7). Length 13 mm.

Finds from features inside Enclosure 3*

BF9: Shallow scoop. B27. Small fragment, either of iron slag or a burnt iron object. Weight 9 g.
BF10: Pit/post-hole SF88. B57. Small amorphous fragment of copper alloy. Weight 2.13 g.
B56. Two pottery sherd fragments only. MIA.

*For finds from the internal features of Enclosure 3, *see* pyre-site BF1/BF16 (pp. 85–90), chamber BF6 (pp. 104–27), and burials BF64 and BF67 (pp. 170–201).

upper fill of the pyre-site ditch (BF31) and the lower fill of the east enclosure ditch (BF40). Sherds from a large, decorated storage jar (FIG. 142, Pot 109) came from the ?mortuary enclosure BF32 (BF30) and the east enclosure ditch (BF40). This vessel's distinctive decoration points to the sherds almost certainly being parts of the same vessel despite the absence of diagnostic joins. Similarly, sherds from another jar (FIG. 141, Pot 80) from the ditch BF40 and pyre-site BF30 appear to be from the same pot.

Pieces of a few of the vessels were located in different parts of the enclosure ditch. Fragments of a jar (Pot 93, ?Cam 266) came from the east enclosure ditch (BF40) and the south-east ditch corner (CF1/CF2). Parts of a large storage jar (FIG. 143, Pot 111) came from several locations in the lower fill of the east enclosure ditch (BF40) and the north terminal of the entrance (BF39). Also sherds from a decorated beaker (FIG. 140, Pot 59) lay in the east enclosure ditch (BF40) as well as the lower fill in the ditch forming the south-east corner of the enclosure(CF1/CF2). Only one vessel appeared to have any scorching on the surface, *i.e.* a Cam 266 jar (FIG. 141, Pot 82) in fabric RCVW from the enclosure ditch BF40.

Other finds from the enclosure ditch include three Late Iron Age coins, two of Cunobelin datable to A.D. 20–43 (FIG. 148, BF39.2 and CF5.1) and one (BF39.3) which is undated. The ditch also contained a few iron nails or nail fragments (TABLE 22), a pottery counter (FIG. 31, BF39.1), some small copper-alloy fragments, one of which may be a belt-plate (BF39.4), and some weathered fragments of Mayen lava quern (BF39.5) from Germany. A small amount of residual Middle Iron Age sherds was also recovered from the Enclosure 4 ditches.

Querns made of Mayen lava were first brought into Britain by the Roman army in A.D. 43, and rapidly came to dominate quern assemblages in the Colchester area, both within the fortress and *colonia* (Buckley and Major 1983, 75–6) and on the rural site of Abbotstone, not far from the Stanway enclosures (Crummy 2005, 57), where Mayen lava fragments outnumber those of Hertfordshire puddingstone. Fragments as abraded as those from ditch BF39 were probably deposited some years after the conquest.

The pottery counter (FIG. 31, BF39.1) is made from a local coarseware. The function of these counters is far from clear. In Roman contexts they come in a wide range of sizes, which suggests a wide range of uses. Smaller examples could be used as game counters, while larger ones may serve as pot lids (*CAR* **2**, 93–4); that they were also used in groups as toys has been shown by a stacking set from Colchester (*Col. Archaeol.* **11**, 34).

All the nail fragments come from the eastern enclosure ditch, and most are from BF40, south of the enclosure entrance (TABLE 22). It is noticeable that several are heads which retain only a short length of the shank, rather than shanks missing the head, which suggests that they may derive from a single plank. One notable exception is a large shank that may be from a Manning Type 1a nail (1985, 134), examples of which exceeded about 150 mm in length. Like the holdfast from the central area of Enclosure 3 (p. 88), it implies the presence of a large wooden structure or object on the site and may also imply a post-conquest date.

?Partial and other pots from the enclosure ditch (FIGS 139–43)

Pot 25 FIG. 139. Ditch BF39 (machine spoil). Cam 91 globular beaker (B935). Rim sherd only, very abraded. Fabric TR3, red, fumed. (A.D. 40–65.)

Pot 26 Not illustrated. Ditch BF39 (probably main fill). Cam 113 butt-beaker (B934, B1192). 4 small sherds, very abraded (possibly part of Pot 35). Fabric BPW.

Pot 27 Not illustrated. Ditch BF39 (probably main fill). Cam 56 carinated cup copy (B648). Base sherd only, very abraded. Fabric sandy ware, probably a Colchester product. (A.D. 50–75.)

Pot 28 FIG. 139. Ditch BF40 (lower part of ditch fill) and pyre-site ditch BF30/BF31. Cam 8 small moulded platter (B965, B974). Partial pot. Cluster of sherds, 4 rim (eve 30%), 5 base, 1 other, no joins, abraded. Fabric TN, white powdery matrix, speckled blue-grey surfaces. (A.D. 25–65.)

Pot 29 Not illustrated. Ditch BF40. Large platter (B972). Base sherd only, very abraded. Fabric TN, sandy grey matrix, blue-black surfaces, no finish. (A.D. 15–50.)

Pot 30 Not illustrated. Ditch BF40. Cam 58 flanged cup (B944). 1 small sherd. Fabric TN, buff dense matrix, dark blue-grey polished surfaces, 1 incised circle. (A.D. 45–75.)

Pot 31 Not illustrated. Ditch BF40 (lower part of ditch fill). Cam 74 pedestal cup (B918). 2 rim sherds, 1 small carinated sherd, very abraded. Fabric TR1(C), orange ware, red slip. (A.D. 25–60.)

Pot 32 Not illustrated. Ditch BF40 (probably main fill). Cam 84 girth beaker (B1146). 1 small sherd, very abraded. Fabric TR3, red, fumed. (A.D. 25–50.)

Pot 33 Not illustrated. Ditch BF40. Cam 112Cb ovoid beaker (B919, B1197). Abraded. Fabric TR3, red, fumed. (A.D. 45–65.)

Pot 34 Not illustrated. Ditch BF40 (lower part of ditch fill). Beaker (B970). 2 small sherds, very abraded. Fabric TR3.

Pot 35 Not illustrated. Ditch BF40. Cam 113 butt-beaker (B979). Partial pot. Pot cluster of sherds, complete base circuit, abraded fractures. Fabric BPW. (A.D. 25–65.)

Pot 36 FIG. 139. Ditch BF40. Cam 113 butt-beaker (947). Rim sherd only, very abraded with abraded fractures (possibly same vessel as Pot 35, rim similar to Pot 40 although colours differ). Fabric BPW, pale cream, blue-grey core. (A.D. 25–65.)

Pot 37 Not illustrated. Ditch CF1 (lower part of main fill). Pedestal cup, probably Cam 74 (C1368, C139, C1370). Partial pot. Sherd cluster, complete pedestal circuit, partly burnt after time of fracture (possibly the same vessel as Pot 130). Fabric TR1(C) light orange, red slip.

Pot 38 FIG. 139. Ditch CF1 (lower part of main fill). Cam 112Cb beaker (C177, C189, C1354, C1355, C1388) decorated with chattered rouletting on one zone defined at top by a groove. Partial pot. Sherd cluster, 4 rim sherds (non-joining, making approximate eve 75%), 4 joining sherds forming base circuit although centre missing, 20+ other sherds. No join between upper and lower body circuits and fractures abraded. Fabric TR3, red, fumed. (A.D. 45–65.)

Pot 39 Not illustrated. Ditch CF1 (upper part of main fill). Beaker (C17). Sherd only, very abraded. Fabric TR3. (A.D. 25–60.)

Pot 40 FIG. 139. Ditch CF1 (main fill). Cam 113 butt-beaker (C177). Partial pot. ?Cluster of sherds, 1 rim sherd, abraded fractures (darker rim colour but rim shape similar to Pots 35 and 36). Fabric BPW. (A.D. 25–65.)

Pot 41 Not illustrated. Ditch CF1 (main fill). Cam 113 butt-beaker (C139, C146, C159, C1378). ?Partial pot. 9 small sherds, abraded (probably all same vessel, similar to Pots 35 and 36). Fabric BPW.

Pot 42 Not illustrated. Ditch CF1 (main fill). Cam 113 butt-beaker (C155). 1 small sherd, very abraded. Fabric BPW.

Pot 43 FIG. 139. Enclosure 5 ditch CF2 (lower part of main fill). Cam 140 collared flagon (C95). Sherd, part of rim only. Fabric DJ(D).

Pot 45 FIG. 139. Ditch BF40 (lower part of ditch fill). Cam 32 platter. Small part of vessel only (B910, B963). Burnished. Fabric GTW.

Pot 46 FIG. 139. Ditch BF39. Plain rounded platter Cam 30, no surviving indication of footring. Partial pot (B934). Burnished. Fabric RCW (*CAR* **10** fabric group UR.LTC).

Pot 47 FIG. 139. Ditch BF40. Cam 28 platter with in-curving wall. Partial pot (20%, B951). Burnished. Fabric GTW (*CAR* **10** fabric group UR.LTC).

Pot 48 FIG. 139. Ditch BF39 (possibly main fill). Cam 28C Platter. Part of vessel (B648). Burnished. Fabric GTW (*CAR* **10** fabric group UR.LTC).

Pot 49 FIG. 139. Enclosure 5 ditch CF1 (at the junction of the lower and main fills). Platter Cam 28C. Partial pot. Much of vessel (C139, C146). Burnished. Fabric GBW (*CAR* **10** fabric group UR.LTC).

Pot 51 FIG. 139. Ditch BF39 (lower part of ditch fill). Cam 92 globular beaker. Part of rim and shoulder (B927). Burnished. Fabric RCW.

Pot 52 FIG. 139. Ditch BF40 (lower part of ditch fill). Cam 119A beaker. Partial pot. Most of rim and neck (B964), abraded. Fabric RCW.

Pot 53 FIG. 139. Ditch BF40. Cam 119A beaker (B972, B973, B977). Partial pot. Most of rim and neck, post-firing hole through neck. Burnished externally extending over rim. Fabric RCW.

Pot 55 FIG. 139. Ditch CF1 (lower part of main fill). Cam 119A beaker (C1388). Partial pot. Most of rim and neck. Burnished, extending over rim. Fabric RCW.

Pot 56 FIG. 139. Ditch CF1 (main fill). Cam 119A beaker (C1355). Part of rim only. Fabric RCW.

Pot 57 Not illustrated. Ditch CF1 (lower part of main fill). Cam 119 beaker (C21, C18, C1388) with areas of stab decoration divided by girth cordon. Partial pot. Body sherds only, much of vessel present. Fabric RCW.

Pot 58 FIG. 139. Spoil machined from ditch BF39. Beaker with everted rim (B935). Small part of rim and shoulder, surfaces degraded. Fabric RCW.

Pot 59 FIG. 140. Ditch BF40 and CF2 (probably junction of lower and main fills). Beaker with slight neck and everted rim (B952, B955, B965, B980, C103). Decorated with wavy line and stab-dot decorated zones. Partial pot, profile reconstructed, abraded. Fabric ROW. (Numbered sherd clusters with joining sherds but with no joins between. However, all certainly part of a single individual vessel with matching decoration between sherd clusters.)

Pot 60 FIG. 140. Ditch BF40. Form is Cam 44A bowl with lid-seated rim (although this vessel might be a lid or could be used as one), and burnished lattice band around interior and around base. ?Partial pot. Single large sherd only (B976). Thick walled, slightly uneven, possibly hand built, with soapy surface feel. Traces of shiny black material (?coating) on exterior and interior, rim abraded. Burnished. Fabric RCW.

Pot 61 FIG. 140. Ditch BF40. Cam 68 carinated bowl with burnished lattice band around girth. Partial pot. Much of vessel although very broken up (B973). Burnished exterior and over rim. Fabric ROW.

Pot 62 FIG. 140. Ditch CF1 (main fill). Cam 222 bowl. Partial pot. Much of vessel (C3, C6, C10). Burnished, extending over rim. Fabric GBW.

Pot 63 FIG. 140. Ditch BF39 (lower part of ditch fill). Cam 222 carinated bowl, without shoulder cordon (B929). Central unburnished band on body, burnished over rim. Partial pot. Fabric RCW.

Pot 64 FIG. 140. Ditch CF2 (lower part of main fill). Cam 218 bowl (C103, C106, CL42). Partial pot. Much of upper half of vessel present. Burnished over upper half of body and extending over rim. Fabric RCW.

Pot 65 FIG. 140. Ditch BF40. Cam 218 bowl. Partial pot. Part of rim and shoulder, slightly degraded (?B955, B957). Burnished externally and over rim. Fabric RCW.

Pot 66 FIG. 140. Ditch BF40. Cam 218 bowl (B957). Partial pot. Part of rim, most of shoulder. Burnished, extending over rim. Surfaces dark grey, burnished. Fabric RCW.

Pot 67 FIG. 140. Ditch CF1 (main fill). Cam 228 bowl, part of rim and shoulder only (C1364). Burnished, extending over rim. Fabric RCW.

Pot 68 FIG. 140. Ditch BF40. Cam 221 bowl (B943). Part of rim and shoulder only. Burnished externally extending over rim. Fabric GBW.

Pot 69 FIG. 140. Ditch BF39. Jar/bowl. Single sherd (B937). Burnished, extending over rim. Fabric RCW.

Pot 70 FIG. 140. Spoil machined from ditch BF39. Rim, possibly from a pedestal jar (B935). Abraded. Fabric RCW.

Pot 71 FIG. 140. Spoil machined from ditch BF25. Jar rim. Single sherd only (B1121). Burnished. Fabric GTW.

Pot 73 FIG. 140. Ditch CF1 (main fill). Large jar ?Cam 271. Sherd only (C139). Fabric HZ.

Pot 74 FIG. 140. Ditch BF40. Cam 266 jar. Part of rim and shoulder (B956), slightly degraded. Fabric RCW.

Pot 75 FIG. 140. Enclosure 5 ditch CF1 (upper part of main fill). Cam 266 jar. Single sherd (C147), degraded. Fabric RCW.

Pot 76 FIG. 140. Ditch BF40 (lower part of ditch fill). Cam 266 jar. Partial pot. Most of upper part of vessel (B909, B950, B963), traces of carbonised matter on neck. Burnished on top of rim. Fabric RCW. (Numbered sherd clusters with joining sherds but with no joins between. Rims from pyre-site and enclosure ditch appear to be same rim. Probably parts of the same vessel.)

Pot 78 FIG. 140. Ditch BF40. Cam 266 jar. Sherd only (B950), traces of carbonised matter on shoulder and neck. Burnished. Fabric RCW.

Pot 79 FIG. 141. Ditch CF2 (lower part of main fill). Cam 266 jar. Partial pot. Part of rim and shoulder (C96, C106, CL42 base). Traces of carbonised matter on neck and shoulder. Fabric RCW.

Pot 80 FIG. 141. Ditch BF40 (lower part of ditch fill) and pyre-site ditch BF30 (main fill). Cam 266 jar (B283, B501, B910). Partial pot. Much of rim and shoulder with some body sherds, slightly abraded. Fabric RCVW. (Numbered sherd clusters with joining sherds, but with no joins between. Rims from pyre-site and enclosure ditch appear to be same rim. Probably parts of the same vessel.)

Pot 81 FIG. 141. Ditch BF40. Cam 266 jar (B941, B945). Partial pot. Much of rim and shoulder. Burnished on top of rim. Fabric RCW.

Pot 82 FIG. 141. Ditch BF40 (lower part of ditch fill). Cam 266 jar (B946, B963, B964, B950). Partial pot. Most of upper part of vessel, surfaces degraded. Fabric RCVW.

Pot 83 FIG. 141. Ditch BF40 (lower part of ditch fill). Cam 266 jar (B919). Partial pot. Most of vessel present, broken-up, degraded. Fabric RCVW.

Pot 85 FIG. 141. Ditch BF40 (lower part of ditch fill). Cam 266 jar (B922, B943). ?Partial pot. Much of upper part of vessel. Burnished externally extending over rim. Fabric RCW.

Pot 86 FIG. 141. Ditch CF1 (main fill). Cam 266 jar (C163). Partial pot. Most of upper part of vessel. Burnished on top of rim. Fabric RCW.

Pot 87 FIG. 141. Enclosure 5 ditch CF2 (lower part of main fill). Cam 266 jar (C106, CL42). Partial pot. Most if not all of vessel present. Fabric RCW.

Pot 88 FIG. 141. Ditch BF40. Cam 266 jar (B950, B951). Partial pot. Much of rim with shoulder with body sherds, traces of carbonised matter around shoulder. Burnished on neck and extending over rim. Fabric RCW.

Pot 89 FIG. 141. Ditch CF1 (lower part of main fill). Cam 266 jar (C150, CL71). Partial pot. Much of vessel present. Burnished on top of rim. Fabric RCW.

Pot 91 FIG. 141. Enclosure 5 ditch CF2 (lower part of main fill). Jar (C95, C103, C106, CL42). Part of rim only. Burnished, extending over rim. Fabric RCW.

Pot 92 FIG. 141. Enclosure 5 ditch CF1 (upper part of main fill). Jar (C6, CL2). Sherd only with post-firing hole through neck. Fabric RCW.

Pot 93 Not illustrated. Ditch BF40 and ?CF1/CF2 (lower part of main fill). Jar ?Cam 266 (C106, B574, B909, B942, B951, B955, B965, B972). Partial pot. Body sherds and shoulder. Fabric RCW.

Pot 96 FIG. 141. Enclosure 5 ditch CF1. Base of jar (C1367) with three post-firing holes through base and one hole unfinished. Burnished near base. Fabric RCW.

Pot 97 FIG. 141. Ditch BF40. Pedestal base (B979), abraded. Fabric RCW.

Pot 98 Not illustrated. Enclosure 4 ditch BF40 (lower part of ditch). Jar (B970, B971). Shoulder and body sherds. Traces of carbonised matter on body. Fabric RCW.

Pot 102 FIG. 142. Ditch CF1 (main fill). Cam 259 jar (C67, CL32). Partial pot. Most or all of vessel. Fabric HZ.

Pot 103 FIG. 142. Ditch BF39. Cam 259 jar with bead rim (B901). Partial pot. Part of rim and shoulder. Fabric HZ.

Pot 104 FIG. 142. Ditch BF40 (lower part of ditch fill). Cam 258C jar (B965), shoulder decorated with vertical strokes. Partial pot. Most of rim and shoulder, traces of carbonised matter on exterior. Burnished externally and over rim. Fabric HD(F). Pre-conquest to Claudian (*CAR* **10**, 478).

Pot 105 FIG. 142. Ditch BF40 (lower part of ditch fill). Cam 258C jar (B942, B963, B970). Burnished shoulder decorated with angled strokes. Part of rim and shoulder only, traces of black carbonised matter deposit on shoulder. Fabric HD (micaceous). Pre-conquest to Claudian (*CAR* **10**, 478).

Pot 107 FIG. 142. Ditch BF39 (main fill). Cam 270B (B648) large storage jar with hooked rim, line of stab decoration around shoulder. Part of rim and shoulder. Fabric HZ.

Pot 108 FIG. 142. Ditches BF40 (lower part of ditch fill) and BF30/BF31 (main fill; the ?mortuary enclosure in Enclosure 4). Cam 270B large storage jar with hook rim (B434, B524, B970, B1130). Partial pot. Rim sherds only positively identified as part of one vessel. Burnished on rim. Fabric HZ. (Rim sherds B434, B525 (pyre-site) and B970 (enclosure ditch) all join.)

Pot 109 FIG. 142. ?Mortuary enclosure ditch BF30 (main fill) and ditch BF40 (lower part of ditch fill). Cam 270B large hook-rim storage jar. Part of rim and shoulder only, two rows of circular indentations around shoulder (B586, B959, B963). Abraded. Fabric HZ. (No joins between sherds from different find numbers but almost certainly the same vessel as all have same circular indentations and matching shoulder bead.)

Pot 110 FIG. 142. Ditch BF40. Cam 270B/273 large storage jar (B959). Single sherd only. Burnished on neck. Fabric HZ.

Pot 111 FIG. 143. Ditches BF39 and BF40 (lower parts of ditch fills). Storage jar with bead rim (B909, B910, B922, B923, B925, B926, B928, B941, B950). Partial pot. Much of vessel present, traces of carbonised matter deposit on shoulder. Burnished over rim and neck. Fabric HZ. (Base from BF39 (B928) almost certainly part of same vessel, although no sherd join between features.)

Pot 112 FIG. 143. Ditch BF40. Cam 273 large storage jar (B971). Much of upper part of vessel present. Burnished, burnish extending over rim. Fabric HZ.

Pot 114 FIG. 143. Enclosure 5 ditch CF1 (main fill). Cam 273 large storage jar (C3). Part of rim only. Fabric HZ.

Pot 115 FIG. 143. Enclosure 5 ditch CF1 (main fill). Cam 273 large storage jar rim (C155). Burnished on neck, extending over rim. Part of vessel. Fabric HZ.

Pot 116 Not illustrated. Ditch CF2 (lower part of main fill). Large storage jar (C95, C96, C106). Partial pot. Fabric HZ.

Pot 117 Not illustrated. Ditch CF1 (lower part of main fill). Large jar with protruding footring (C6, C139, C146, C1331, C1365, C1371, C1377, C1384). Partial pot. Base and body sherds, burnished surface. Fabric GBW.

Pot 118 Not illustrated. Ditch CF2 (lower part of main fill). Jar (C103, C106). Base and body sherds with at least one post-firing hole through base. Fabric RCW.

Pot 119 Not illustrated. Ditch CF2 (lower part of main fill). Jar (C103, C106). Base and body sherds. Fabric RCW.

Pot 120 Not illustrated. Ditch CF1 (upper part of main fill). Large jar (C6, ?C139). Body sherds only. Fabric GBW.

Pot 122 Not illustrated. Ditch BF40. Samian cup, South Gaul, pre-Flavian (B950).

Pot 123 Not illustrated. Ditch BF40 (lower part of ditch fill). Samian platter, South Gaul, ?Claudian (B964).

Pot 124 Not illustrated. Ditch BF40 (main fill). Samian Drag 15/17, South Gaul, Claudian, 2 sherds probably from the same vessel (B1196, B1197).

Pot 125 Not illustrated. Ditch CF5 (BF40) (main fill). Samian Drag 17 (a small version), South Gaul, ?Claudian (C1380).

Pot 127 Not illustrated. Ditch BF39 (lower part of ditch fill). Amphora, Beltrán I *salazon*. Sherd from shoulder (B932). (104 g). Fine light yellow-green paste with powdery surfaces typical of Baetican *salazon* amphoras. Fabric CAD AM.

Pot 128 FIG. 143. Ditch BF40. Amphora, Dressel 2–4. Short terminal spike (B948) (287 g). Fabric light yellow (10YR 8/4) with common (6–10 per cm^2) sub-rounded and well-sorted white and grey inclusions <1mm across.

Other pottery sherds from the enclosure ditch

BF25: Fabric GTW, 1 sherd, rim fragment, (B1121); Fabric HZ, 2 sherds (B1123); Fabric RCW, 2 sherds (B1122).

BF39: Fabric GTW, 10 sherds (B901, B958, B1190); Fabric GTW (*CAR* 10 fabric group UR.LTC) rim sherd (B901); Fabric HZ1, 55 sherds, (B615, B897, B901, B911, B927, B930, B934, B936, B938, B939, B1190, B1192, B1194). RCVW, 18 sherds (B934, B1190); Fabric RCW, 275 sherds (B648, B897, B901, B924, B927, B932, B934, B935, B936, B937, B938, B939, B958, B1190, B1192, B1193, B1194).

BF40: Fabric GBW, 3 sherds (B910, B953); Fabric GTW, sherd, patter base, internal concentric grooves and part footring (B970). GX(H), 14 sherds (B951, B960, B965, B1198); Fabric HZ, 104 sherds (B909, B910, B918, B922, B940, B941, B942, B943, B950, B951, B955, B962, B964, B965, B970, B971, B972, B973, B974, B976, B977, B980, B1151, B1196); Fabric ROW, 33 sherds, (B973, B974, B976); Fabric RCW, 768 sherds, (B909, B910, B918, B919, B922, B940, B943, B945, B950, B951, B952, B953, B955, B960, B962 B963, B965, B970, B971, B972, B973, B974, B975, B976 B977, B979, B980, B1150, B1153, B1157, B1197, B1198); Fabric RVGW, 15 sherds (B910, B918, B919, B1197); Fabric SW (*CAR* 10 fabric group UR.LTC) 1 sherd part of ?platter base (B955).

CF5 (south end of BF40): Fabric HZ, 1 sherd (C9); Fabric RCW, 2 sherds (C1380).

CF1: Fabric GBW, 1 sherd (C11); Fabric HZ, 47 sherds (C6, C7, C8, C18, C139, C147, C155, C159, C163, C177, C1331, C1365, C1370, C1377, C1384, C1383); Fabric RCW, 381 sherds, includes sherds from tooth-comb decorated vessel ?Cam 108 or Cam 119 (C1349, C1354, C1356), other sherds (C7, C8, C10, C12, C18, C46, C71, C79, C86, C87, C139, C146, C151, C155, C157, C165, C177, C187, C189, C193, C194, C1331, C1349, C1354, C1356, C1357, C1362, C1364, C1365, C1369, C1370, C1377, C1378, C1379, C1381, C1382, C1383, C1384, C1388). Also 1 small sherd with red slip or colour coat (C1370).

North end of CF2: Fabric HZ, 5 sherds (C85, C106); Fabric RCW, 135 sherds (C95, C103, and C106 probably parts of same vessel), (C79, C85, C95, C96, C103, C106, C197, C1392, C1450).

Other finds from the enclosure ditch (FIGS 31, 148)

BF39.1 FIG. 31. B615. Unstratified, from the area of BF39. Pottery counter, made from a wall sherd of a local native coarseware jar or bowl. The edge is irregular but quite abraded, and the external surface is also slightly abraded. Maximum diameter 58 mm, thickness 9.5 mm.

BF39.2 FIG. 148. SF287, B931. Middle fill of northern part of eastern arm of enclosure ditch of Enclosure 4. Coin of Cunobelin A.D. 20–43 (see p. 340).

BF39.3 Not illustrated. SF384, B1165. Middle fill of northern part of eastern arm of enclosure ditch of Enclosure 4. Late Iron Age coin (see p. 340).

BF39.4 SF160. B650: main fill. Fragment of copper-alloy sheet with narrow triangular cut-out at one end. Probably from a belt-plate, as Feugère 1981, fig. 9, 20, from Villeneuve, Fréjus (Var). Length 17.5 mm, width 12 mm. Weight 0.7 g.

BF39.5 SF405. B1195: main fill. Ten weathered fragments of Mayen lava from a quernstone. No original surface survives. Weight 132 g.
CF5.1 FIG. 148. SF205, C5. CF5/CL6. Upper fill of southern part of eastern arm of enclosure ditch of Enclosure 4. Coin of Cunobelin A.D. 20–43 (see p. 340).
BF39: SF291. B933. Three small amorphous fragments of copper alloy. Total weight 0.25 g.
BF40: SF292. B946. Seven fragments of copper-alloy wire, 1.5 mm in diameter. All are slightly curved, one is half oval. Length of longest 9 mm. Total weight 0.4 g. Possibly from a chain.
CF5: C4. Fragment of hard cinder-like debris. Weight 1 g. Probably burnt organic material (Fryer 2003, 133).

For finds from the internal features of Enclosure 4, see ?mortuary enclosure BF32 (pp. 90–7) and chamber BF24 (pp. 127–41).

FUNERARY ENCLOSURE 5 (FIGS 2, 8, 32, 144; TABLE 23)

Finds from the enclosure ditch
?Partial and other pots	Nos 132–7, 142, 144, 148–9	parts of at least ten vessels
Other finds	CF1.1	fragments of a ?brooch
	CF2.1	fragment of nail-cleaner
	CF3.1	iron ring
		fragments of iron nails
Residual finds		Early and Middle Iron Age pottery, burnt daub

Enclosure 5 was approximately square being externally about 62 m west–east and 59–64 m north–south (FIGS 2 and 8). An entrance, 3.0 m wide, lay approximately halfway along the east ditch. The fill of the enclosure ditch could be divided into a lower fill and a main fill, just as in Enclosures 1, 3, and 4. The surviving parts of the ditch were generally broad, between 2.0 and 2.5 m across, flaring out toward the top, about 0.7–0.8 m deep (after stripping), with a flat base (FIG. 32). However, the ditch was slighter along much of the north ditch CF1 and towards the south-east, south-west and north-west corners. This reduction was especially marked in the south-east and north-west corners where the surviving part of the enclosure ditch was less than 1.0 m wide and only about 0.3 m deep. In most places, the lower part of the ditch was less flaring than the upper part and was filled with several layers of stony silty sand which had probably eroded from the ditch edges. Above this, the sides of the ditch raked back more sharply, and this upper part contained broader bands or layers of generally less stony silty sand. This material did not have the appearance of sands and gravels excavated from the ditch, for example from backfilling, using or including material from any enclosure bank, and probably represents a slower silting process once the ditch had become more stable. In the lower fill and around the boundary of the lower and upper fills, there were spreads and groups of pottery representing partial pots, mostly of early Claudio–Neronian date. These lay along the eastern end of the ditch CF1, the enclosure corner CF1/CF2, near the corner CF2/CF3, and the central part of CF3.

As in Enclosures 3 and 4, the remains of deliberately broken pots lay in the enclosure ditch. In all, approximately ten vessels could be identified (Pots 132–7, 142, 144, 148–9). Most of the pottery, *i.e.* just under 3 kg (2,750 g) of it, came from the ditches CF2, CF3, and the south end of CF4, with the bulk coming from several concentrated groups each representing the remains of one or more vessels in the ditches CF2 and CF3. No Gallo-Belgic or Gaulish imports were represented in the group, although there were two amphoras (Pot 148, Pot 149). Nearly all of a wide-mouth globular bowl (FIG. 144, Pot 136) and most of a pinch-mouth flagon (FIG. 144, Pot 132) lay in CF3. The body of the flagon had been smashed into very small pieces and the handle was missing. Two groups of sherds lay next to one another in the top of the lower ditch fill of CF2. Most of these sherds belonged to a broken Cam 251 bowl (FIG. 144, Pot 135), which had been heavily burnt on one side. An important aspect of the pots from the enclosure ditch which distinguishes it from the similar material from Enclosures 3 and 4 is the presence in it of vessel forms that were introduced after the conquest (FIG. 144, Pots 132, 133, 134 (not illustrated), 136, 137) .

TABLE 23: IRON NAILS FROM THE ENCLOSURE DITCH OF ENCLOSURE 5

Layer/Feat. no.	Find no.	Context	Head	Length (mm)	Description
CL32/CF1	C67	north ditch	sub-circular	62	in 2 pieces; clenched, giving wood thickness of about 48 mm
CL69/CF1	C132	north ditch		32	shank fragment
CF1	C146	north ditch	a) round	a) 30; b) 31	b) shank fragment
CL71/CF1	C152	north ditch	a) round	a) 18; b) 22; c) 19	b–c) shank fragments
CF1	C155	north ditch	a) round; b) sub-circular	a) 18; b) 31	
CL71/CF1	C157	north ditch	round	29	
CF1	C159	north ditch		33	shank fragment
CF1	C1377	north ditch	round	31	in 2 pieces
CF1	C1385	north ditch	sub-circular	93	
CF1	C1386 (SF302)	north ditch	round	41	tip of shaft coiled up and inwards
CF1	C1387	north ditch		25	shank fragment
CL41/CF2	C76	east ditch	round	27	
CL41/CF2	C91	east ditch	sub-circular	30	
CL42/CF2	C95	east ditch	sub-circular	29	
CL42/CF2	C103	east ditch		39	shank fragment
CF2	C154	east ditch		34	shank fragment
CL9/CF3	C14	south ditch		37	shank fragment, with a round head fixed vertically by corrosion onto lower part
CL31/CF4	C58	west ditch	round	23 (bent)	clenched, giving wood thickness of 13 mm
CF4	C198	west ditch	round	15	

The other finds in the main enclosure ditch of Enclosure 5 include an iron ring (FIG. 32, CF3.1), some fragments of copper-alloy wire (CF1.1) which may be parts of a small brooch, and a damaged bifid nail-cleaner (FIG. 32, CF2.1). Originating on the Continent (Miron 1989, 41–3), few bifid nail-cleaners are known from Iron Age Britain and their rarity suggests that their use was largely restricted to those of élite status. There is one from the Queen's Barrow at Arras, another from the rich grave at Welwyn Garden City, Herts, and one from Deal Grave II (Stead 1979, fig. 34; 1967, fig. 15; Birchall 1965, fig. 12, 101). From the 1st century A.D. the bifid nail-cleaner all but disappears from the archaeological record on the Continent, but in Britain after the Roman conquest they began to be produced in large numbers and so became available to all levels of society (Crummy 2001b, 3; Crummy and Eckardt 2004). The Stanway nail-cleaner is in an immediately post-conquest context and is likely therefore to be of pre-conquest origin and related to the high rank of the individuals buried on the site.

The enclosure ditches also produced a large number of nails, which are listed in TABLE 23. Most came from the north ditch, and so may be associated with activity in Enclosure 4 rather than in Enclosure 5. All are of Manning's Type 1b (1985, 134) and have square-section shanks. Most are small, with an approximate complete length of between 40 and 70 mm, but one (C1385) is incomplete at 93 mm long. None have wood grain present, but two are clenched giving a total wood thickness of 48 mm and 13 mm respectively. The latter was probably driven into a single board, rather than through two.

Two small pits (FIG. 2, CF17 and CF66) cut the upper fill of the enclosure ditch CF4. Neither feature contained any datable material. Pit CF17 was sub-rectangular in shape (about 0.6 m by 0.8 m across) and contained some charcoal which was more abundant in the upper fill. CF66 was a discrete area of burnt material in the uppermost surviving part of the ditch fill about 2 m long and 0.5 m wide aligned north–south along the ditch. It included an unusual mix of charred autumnal fruit and nuts matched only in the shaft or pit CF23 (pp. 266, 385).

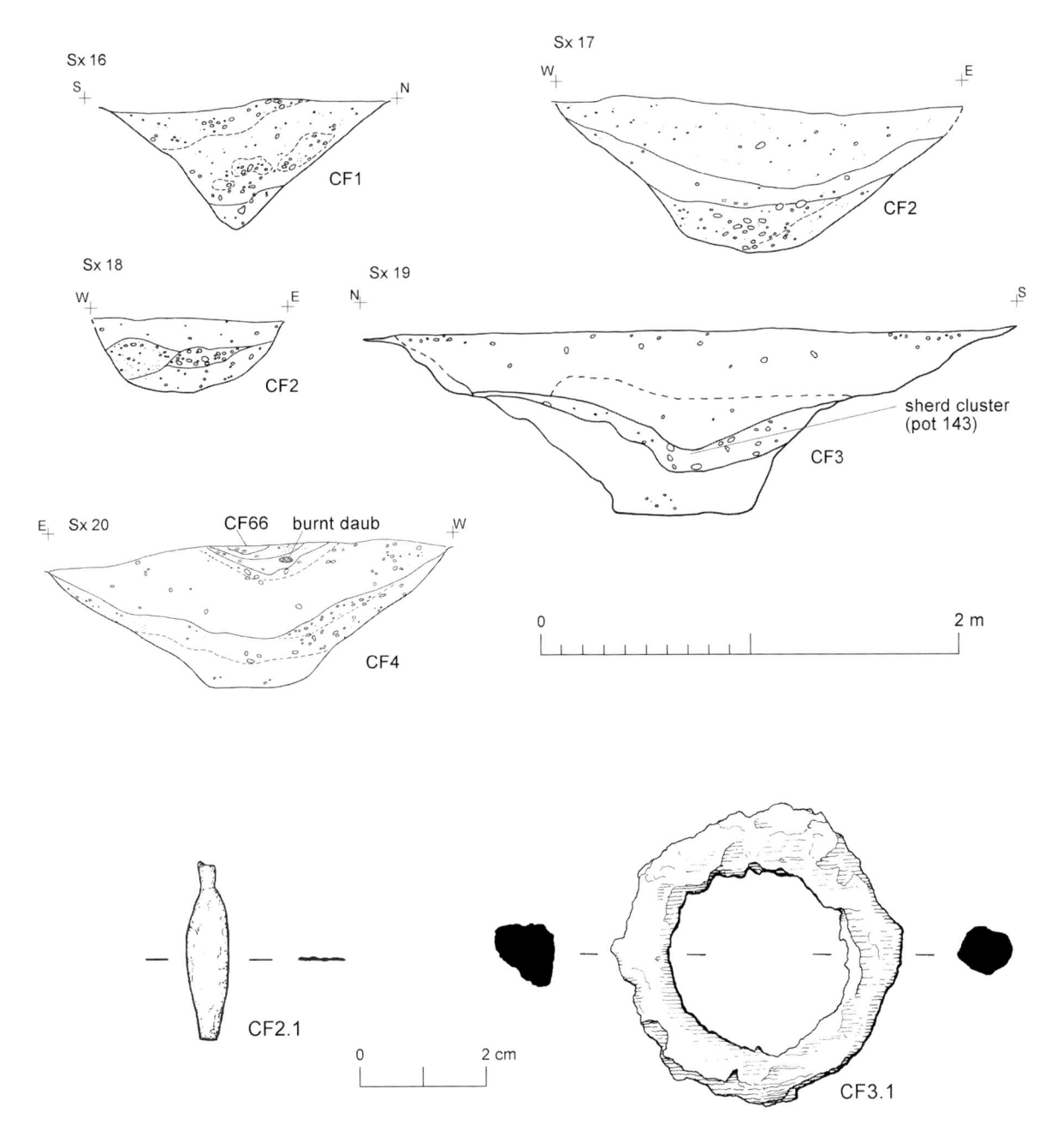

FIG. 32. Enclosure 5 ditch: sections (scale 1:30) and objects of copper alloy and iron from the enclosure ditches (scale 1:1)

The features inside Enclosure 5 were mainly funerary in nature (FIG. 2). The centre of the enclosure was occupied by a ditched ?mortuary enclosure (CF43–6, pp. 97–100), to the south of which was a chamber (CF42, pp. 142–57). Three cremation burials lay in the western half of the enclosure in a line 8.8–9.2 m from the edge of the west ditch. These were the Doctor's burial (CF47, pp. 201–53), the Brooches burial (BF72, pp. 254–60), and CF403. Another burial, the Mirror burial (CF115), lay in the south-west corner of the enclosure, not far from the Brooches burial. To the east of the chamber was a north–south slot or trench (CF96; pp. 266–7) which may be all that remains of a timber temple in the corner of the enclosure. A pit or shaft was located in the interior angle of the south-west corner of the enclosure ditch. There were only a few other features in the enclosure, namely a few small pits, a charcoal-filled stake-hole, and an area of subsoil possibly affected by heat.

There were two small features CF26 and CF50 in the north-east area of the enclosure which appear to represent the base of stake-holes or small post-holes. The fill of CF50 was very dark and was of sand mixed with charcoal. CF26 had a silty sand fill. Both were devoid of any dated finds.

CF62 and CF63 were two adjacent areas of slightly reddened stones and sand in the northern central area of the enclosure. CF63 was about 1.0 m long and 0.5 m wide while CF62 was a small patch about 0.3 m across. These may represent the scorched subsoil under one or more pyres. However, other reddish-coloured flint and sand was noted beneath unmodified sand and gravel in the same area, so that CF62 and CF63 may be natural in origin.

The site of a pyre may have been indicated by a small pit (CF71) approximately 6.5 m to the south of the enclosure. The pit contained charcoal and reddish-coloured sandy loam which had been scorched.

?Partial and other pots from the enclosure ditch (FIG. 144)

Pot 132 Ditch CF3 (main fill). Cam 158 pinched mouth flagon, with flat base (C13, CL10). Partial pot. Almost all of vessel except handle, very fragmented. Fabric CSOW.
Pot 133 Ditch CF3 (lower part of main fill). Cam 154 ring-necked flagon (C169). Part of rings and handle scar. Fabric DJ(D).
Pot 134 Not illustrated. Ditch CF4 (lower part of main fill). Handle, probably from a flagon (C114). Fabric FJ.
Pot 135 Ditch CF2 (junction of lower and main fiills). Cam 251 bowl (C77, C92, C102, C154). Partial pot. Most of vessel present, burnt on one side. Fabric GTW.
Pot 136 Ditch CF3 (junction of lower and upper fills). Wide-mouth bowl, with shallow incised wavy lines around girth (C148, C149, CL70). Partial pot. Much of vessel present. GX(H).
Pot 137 Ditch CF4 (lower part of main fill). Cam 243–244/246 reeded-rim bowl (C114, CL58). Fragment of rim only. GX(H).
Pot 142 Enclosure 5 ditch CF3 (main fill). Cam 271 large storage jar with combed shoulder (C109, CL56). Part of rim and shoulder. Burnished on neck, extending over rim. Fabric HZ.
Pot 144 Not illustrated. Ditch CF3 (main fill). Samian ?Drag 33, South Gaul (C1400). 1st century.
Pot 148 Not illustrated. Ditch CF4 (main fill). Amphora, Dressel 2-4. Body sherd (C53) (51 g). Italian. Fabric CAM AM 2.
Pot 149 Not illustrated. Ditch CF2 (lower part of main fill). Amphora. Dressel 2–4. Body sherd (C153) (43g). Fabric in a soft light brown fabric (7.5YR 7/6) with powdery surfaces. The inclusions are well-sorted sparse (<5 per cm^2) white and dark grey grains <0.5 mm across.

Other pottery sherds from the enclosure ditch

CF2: Fabric HZ, 4 sherds (C154); Fabric RCW, 21 sherds (C24, C32, C93, C94, C197, C1329, C1450).
CF3: Fabric GTW, 1 sherd (C1402); Fabric GX(H), 23 sherds (C1405, C1410, C1414); Fabric HZ, 3 sherds (C1397); Fabric RCW, 43 sherds (C16, C1394, C1398, C1404, C1405, C1406, C1407, C1408, C1409, C1451).
CF4: Fabric GX(H), 9 sherds (C84, C110, C122); Fabric HZ, 1 sherd, ?part of Pot 142 (C22); Fabric RCW, 1 sherd (C1359).

Other finds from the enclosure ditch

CF1.1 SF201. C156. Four small fragments of thin copper-alloy wire, two straight, two curved. Possibly from the pin and spring of a small brooch. The longest fragment measures 6 mm.
CF2.1 FIG. 32. SF208. C131. CF2/CL68. Fragment of a copper-alloy nail-cleaner. The points are missing. A thickening of the metal at the top suggests the suspension loop may have been at right-angles to the plane of the blade. Length 28 mm, maximum width 7 mm.
CF3.1 FIG. 32. SF196. C164. Iron ring of slightly flattened circular section. Internal diameter 30 mm, 6 mm thick.
CF1: SF209. C160. Iron strip, 37 mm long, 14 mm wide.
CF1/CL69. C139. Small fragment of vitrifed clay. Weight 4 g.

For finds from the internal features of Enclosure 4, *see* pyre-site CF43–6 (pp. 97–100), chamber CF42 (pp. 142–57), burials CF47, CF72, CF115, CF403 (pp. 201–53, 253–60, 260–2, and 262–4 respectively), slot CF96 (pp. 266–7), and shaft CF23 (pp. 265–6).

THE PYRE SITE AND ?MORTUARY ENCLOSURES

PYRE-SITE BF1/BF16 (FIGS 2, 7–8, 33, 43–5; TABLE 24)

Cremated bone	14.6 g	possibly including some unidentifiable animal bone, all from BF16
Pottery vessel	BF16.1	Dressel 2–4 amphora
Other finds	BF1.1	sheet fragments
	BF1.2	?brass fitting
	BF1.3	parts of five studs
	BF1.4	copper-alloy object
	BF1.5	iron holdfast
	BF16.2	part of a belt plate/stiffener
	BL6.1	probable strap-plate and stud
	BL6.2	possible stud
		many heat-affected fragments of objects of copper alloy and iron (including nails) from BF1, BF16, and BL6
Animal bone		a few fragments including a ?sheep carpal from BF1 and a fragment of ?dog mandible from BF16
Residual finds		2 Middle Iron Age sherds from BF1
		2 Middle Iron Age sherds from BF16

The pyre-site (BF1/BF16) lay immediately to the west of chamber BF6 in Enclosure 3 (FIGS 2, 7–8, 43–5). The site was hard to define clearly on the ground, but it seemed to resolve itself into two separate pits (BF1 and BF16) surrounded by amorphous patches of scorched natural and a thin charcoal-rich layer (BL6) which was similar, if not the same, as the thin layer of charcoal which sealed (very significantly) the top of the nearby roof of the chamber BF6 (p. 119). The complex (FIG. 45) was characterised by a scatter of cremated bone and distinctive fragments of iron and heat-affected copper alloy, which included broken studs and strap-plates such as those associated with Roman military equipment (TABLE 24).

The two pits BF1 and BF16 would have acted as flues to improve the passage of air through the burning fuel like those, for example, at Westhampnett (Fitzpatrick 1997, 18). They lay immediately below the modern ploughsoil and had been truncated by 0.3 m or more as a result of modern ploughing. The pits were separated by what appeared to be a shallow north–south plough-rut.

BF1 was a flat, intensely burnt area between chamber BF6 and the south end of the pit BF16. It measured 2.3 m (north–south) by 1.3 m (east–west), and was filled with the thin charcoal-rich layer BL6. The charcoal included large roundwood stems of oak but no large timbers. The feature must have formed the base of a shallow flat-bottomed pit but, when uncovered, protruded slightly above the surrounding area by about 0.15 m because of its fire-hardened nature. Its surface was impregnated with molten copper alloy, showing that this was where metal objects had been burnt. The western half of BF1 had been damaged by another north–south plough-rut. It also apparently included slight traces of unburnt mineral-replaced wood.

BF16 consisted of a long shallow pit, 0.2 m deep, which extended north–south for 5 m. It had a thin dark charcoal-rich upper fill (BL5) up to 0.05 m thick, while the lower fill (BL7) was a light clayey deposit 0.15 m thick with sparse charcoal flecks. The latter (BL7) was difficult in places to distinguish from natural, and may have represented disturbance of the subsoil resulting from raking over the base of the pyre. An environmental sample from BF16 (BL5, B72; p. 384) produced a diverse assemblage of seeds and other charred plant remains from grassland vegetation which probably derived from kindling and/or vegetation charred below the pyre.

Most of the cremated human bone was in the upper fill of BF16 (BL5, 13.4 g), although small quantities were found in the lower fill (BL7, 1.2 g) and when cleaning immediately east of BF16 (3.6 g). BF1 and BF16 both contained small sherds of amphora (BF16.1), most of which were burnt. BF1 contained seven sherds (111 g) and BF16 five sherds (32 g).

TABLE 24: HEAT-AFFECTED COPPER ALLOY AND AMORPHOUS SLAGGY IRON WITH TRACES OF COPPER ALLOY FROM THE PYRE-SITE BF1/BF16 AND THE SURROUNDING AREA

Obj. no.	Find no.	Small find no.	No. of pieces	Weight (g)	Notes
Pyre-pit BF1					
BF1.1	B13	66	8	56.16	
BF1.2	B75	95	6	6.34	
BF1.3	B81	100	58	86.54	1 heavy fragment may contain some iron; small studs, one illustrated
BF1.4	B81	102	1	47.80	
	B2	77	7	8.97	machining over BF1
	B14	79	5	77.95	layer of copper alloy over charcoal/ash layer
	B19	83	4	7.40	
	B34	71	5	3.20	
	B71	94	5	3.04	
	B76	–	7	30.00	mixed iron, copper alloy and clay
	B80	–	14	53.00	slaggy iron and clay, with slight traces of copper alloy
	B126	120	15	15.85	copper alloy
	B125	127	10	86.73	slaggy iron, with slight traces of copper alloy, unburnt mineral-replaced wood, and charcoal
	B130	130	8	130.00	burnt slaggy iron, with soil and charcoal adhering. Some of the iron is in the form of strips
totals			**153**	**612.98**	
Pyre-pit BF16					
BL5					
BF16.2	B83	103	5	6.90	includes small part of a belt-plate/stiffener similar to BF6.29 from BF6
	B65	92	3	2.02	
	B72	312	2	0.49	
	B74	96	2	3.26	
	B83	98	5	3.82	
	B89	99	12	6.95	
BL7					
	B94	104	2	1.71	
	B94	124	1	2.78	
totals			**32**	**27.93**	
BL6 around BF1 and BF16					
BL6.1a and b	B18	86	2	1.40	east of BF1
BL6.2	B87	101	3	1.27	north of BF1
	B18	70	2	5.00	incorporating ash; east of BF1
	B25	82	1	14.77	copper alloy; south-east of BF1
	B39	73	5	4.44	cleaning south-east of BF1
	B51	87	14	2.10	copper alloy; south-east of BF1
	B52	–	1	11.00	slaggy iron; south-east of BF1
	B467	165	1	0.48	copper alloy; north of BF1
	B733	166	2	0.73	copper alloy; west of BF16
totals			**31**	**41.19**	
Loosely stratified from surface cleaning in areas around BF1, BF16, and chamber BF6					
	B2	77	7	8.97	machining over BF1
	B3	84	4	7.47	machining east of BF1
	B5	75	1	21.96	cleaning north of BF1
	B6	65	1	2.60	cleaning north of BF1
	B7	61	7	20.62	cleaning north of BF1
	B10	76	1	11.43	cleaning north of BF1
	B12	67	2	1.71	cleaning north of BF1
	B16	58	1	0.34	cleaning north-east of BF1
	B17	80	2	4.51	cleaning over BF6

TABLE 24: (CONT'D)

Obj. no.	Find no.	Small find no.	No. of pieces	Weight (g)	Notes
	B21	64	4	1.48	cleaning south-east of BF6
	B25	82	1	14.77	cleaning charcoal patch south of F6
	B26	85	3	6.74	cleaning north-west of BF6
	B28	53	1	0.21	cleaning north-west of BF6
	B28	72	4	0.53	cleaning north-west of BF6
	B31	63	3	1.34	cleaning over plough-rut west of BF6
	B36	59	2	0.29	cleaning plough-rut north of BF1
	B36	68	4	4.93	cleaning plough-rut north of BF1
	B36	74	1	12.46	cleaning plough-rut north of BF1
	B39	73	5	4.44	cleaning south of BF6, probably BL6
	B40	56	3	0.56	cleaning west of BF6
	B41	52	3	0.8	cleaning west of BF1?
	B55	89	6	0.51	cleaning plough-rut south-west of BF6
	B190	148	1	1.51	possibly from BF6
totals			67	130.18	
Grand totals			283	812.28	

BF1 rather than BF16 must have been the source of the heat-affected copper-alloy fragments, because this is where the overwhelming majority of them were found. There were about twenty times as many by weight in BF1 as in BF16 (TABLE 24). Their concentration in BF1 also fits its baked and reddened character and its encrustation with resolidified metal which had melted and run in the intense heat of the pyre.

The same kind of objects (nearly all visibly heat-affected) as occurred on the pyre-site were also present in the pit BF17 immediately adjacent to chamber BF6 and, critically, in the packing material which had been placed between the outer faces of the walls of chamber BF6 and the pit in which the chamber had been constructed (FIG. 45). The material in the packing material is as follows (see pp. 126–7 for details): part of a ?brass fitting from Roman cavalry harness (BF6.27), a fragment of copper-alloy strap-plate (BF6.28), part of a ?brass strap-plate or stiffener (BF6.29), a short solid copper-alloy cylinder (BF6.32), a copper-alloy square-section rod or shaft (BF6.33), and 179 heat-affected copper-alloy fragments. The link between the finds from BF6 and BF1/BF16 is made more apparent by the occurrence of fragments of similar strap-plates in both, one (BF6.29) from BF6 and another (BF16.2) from BF16.

The configuration of pits and burnt patches is complicated and interpreting the complex is not easy. At first it was thought that BF1/BF16 represented the remains of a single pyre and that this pre-dated chamber BF6, as indicated by the heat-affected metal fragments in material relating to the chamber's construction. However, a less simplistic view fits the evidence better, namely that the complex represents the remains of two sequential pyres, and that BF1 and BF16 are the truncated remains of two separate flues, one for each of them. The distribution of the heat-affected metal fragments supports this view and provides information about relationships between BF1, BF16, and chamber BF6. The relatively low number of fragments from BF16 as compared with BF1 is consistent with their being residual in BF16 and having derived from BF1. Thus, if, as seems likely, BF1 and BF16 do indeed represent different pyres, then, crucially, BF1 must pre-date BF16. Moreover BF1, rather than BF1 and BF16 combined, must also pre-date chamber BF6, because the heat-affected metal fragments in BF6 must also be residual and derive from BF1, which of course explains why most of them occurred in its south-west corner where the chamber-pit must have cut it. (In plan the chamber pit does not appear to cut BF1, but, because of the need to strip the site, the plan shows the relationships well below ground-level, whereas BF6 would have cut BF1 at a higher level.)

The relationship between BF1, BF6 and BF16 indicated by the residual finds (*i.e.* that BF1 pre-dated the other two features) tells us nothing about the temporal relationship between

BF16 and BF6 other than that both are later than BF1. However, it seems that BF6 and pyre-pit BF16 may have been contemporary and that the roof of the chamber was exposed to the air when the pyre served by BF16 was in flames. The thin charcoal-rich layers in BF1 and BF16 (*i.e.* BL6 and BL5 respectively) were similar to the thin dark layer that overlay the roof of chamber BF6 (p. 119), opening up the possibility that they were all parts of the same deposit. To explain the presence of wind-blown charcoal on top of the roof, there must have been a period of time between the deposition of material from the pyre and subsequent replacement of the timbers and the raising of the mound. It might be objected that a pyre would not have been lit so close to a chamber because of the risk of setting the chamber alight, but of course the evidence suggests that it would have been the pyre over BF16 which was lit, not the one over BF1, in which case it would have been 2 m or so away from the edge of the chamber, far enough not to catch fire but close enough to be covered with ash and charcoal dust from the pyre. (An alternative interpretation of this layer, although one that we do not consider very likely, is that it was a ferromanganiferous deposit similar to others recorded in BF6 (p. 110).)

If BF6 and pyre-pit BF16 were indeed contemporary, then the obvious conclusion to draw from this relationship is that chamber BF6 was where a body and its associated grave goods had been kept prior to being burnt on a pyre over BF16. The implications of this conclusion are discussed below (pp. 439–40).

The heat-affected copper-alloy and iron fragments are summarised in TABLE 24 according to four groups relating to provenance, *i.e.* BF1, BF16, burnt and charcoal-rich patches around BF1/BF16, and 'loosely stratified'. The list of objects at the end of this section uses the same sub-headings, but is limited to those objects which are illustrated as well as the pieces of ironwork of meaningful form. Where no description is given and the objects are not illustrated, they consist of very small amorphous fragments of copper alloy. For completeness, this list also includes burnt bone and pottery. The copper-alloy objects in the catalogue have been incorporated in the table to provide the total weight of small metal fragments from each of the groups, but some of the larger and heavier pieces of ironwork have been omitted since they would distort the balance between the contextual groups. Although the number of fragments is great, the total weight of the metalwork is not. It is very noticeable, however, that there is no great distinction between any of the groups and the material from the fill of BF6. In particular, the strap-fitting from BL5 in BF16 (BF16.2) is very similar to one from BF6 (BF6.29).

Identifiable copper-alloy pieces are largely confined to studs and strap-fittings (FIG. 33, BF1.3, BL6.1 a–b; BL6.2), none of which can be closely dated, and all lack any decorative features, either of British Late Iron Age or Roman character. Some of the pieces have been identified as probably being brass, thus suggesting they are imports, although pre-conquest British-made Colchester brooches are also brass. The largest fragment is a piece of thick sheeting (FIG. 33, BF1.1), which is probably too thick to be part of a vessel (although its present form may not accurately reflect its original shape). One object consists of a tube with a strip passed around it and held in position by a two-piece stud; it retains its original shape, but its function is unknown (FIG. 33, BF1.4).

One iron object is, by contrast, quite distinctive and unusual in the context of this site, namely a large holdfast from BL6 (FIG. 33, BF1.5). Holdfasts are used to join two pieces of timber together, being essentially a nail with a large plate, or rove, fixed to the lower end, and this example may come from timber reused as pyre fuel. They more commonly have a square-section shank rather than a round one as here, although a bolt from Cadbury Castle has a round shank (Macdonald 2000, fig. 59, 3), and in many cases the nail head is much smaller than the rove. They occur chiefly in contexts of the Roman period, as at Fishbourne (Cunliffe 1971, 128, fig. 55, 6–7), Hengistbury Head (Cunliffe 1987, 159, Ill. 114, 104–5), Colchester town centre (*CAR* **6**, nos 1603–5), London, Borough Hill, and Hod Hill (Manning 1985, R74–83), but there was one among the pyre debris from the Late Iron Age cemetery at Westhampnett, West Sussex, and three from Danebury were found in association with pottery dated *c.* 300–100/50 B.C. (Montague 1997, table 20; Cunliffe and Poole 1991, 353, fig. 7.25, 2.347–349). Although the Stanway holdfast is therefore more likely to be post-conquest in date, it may be earlier.

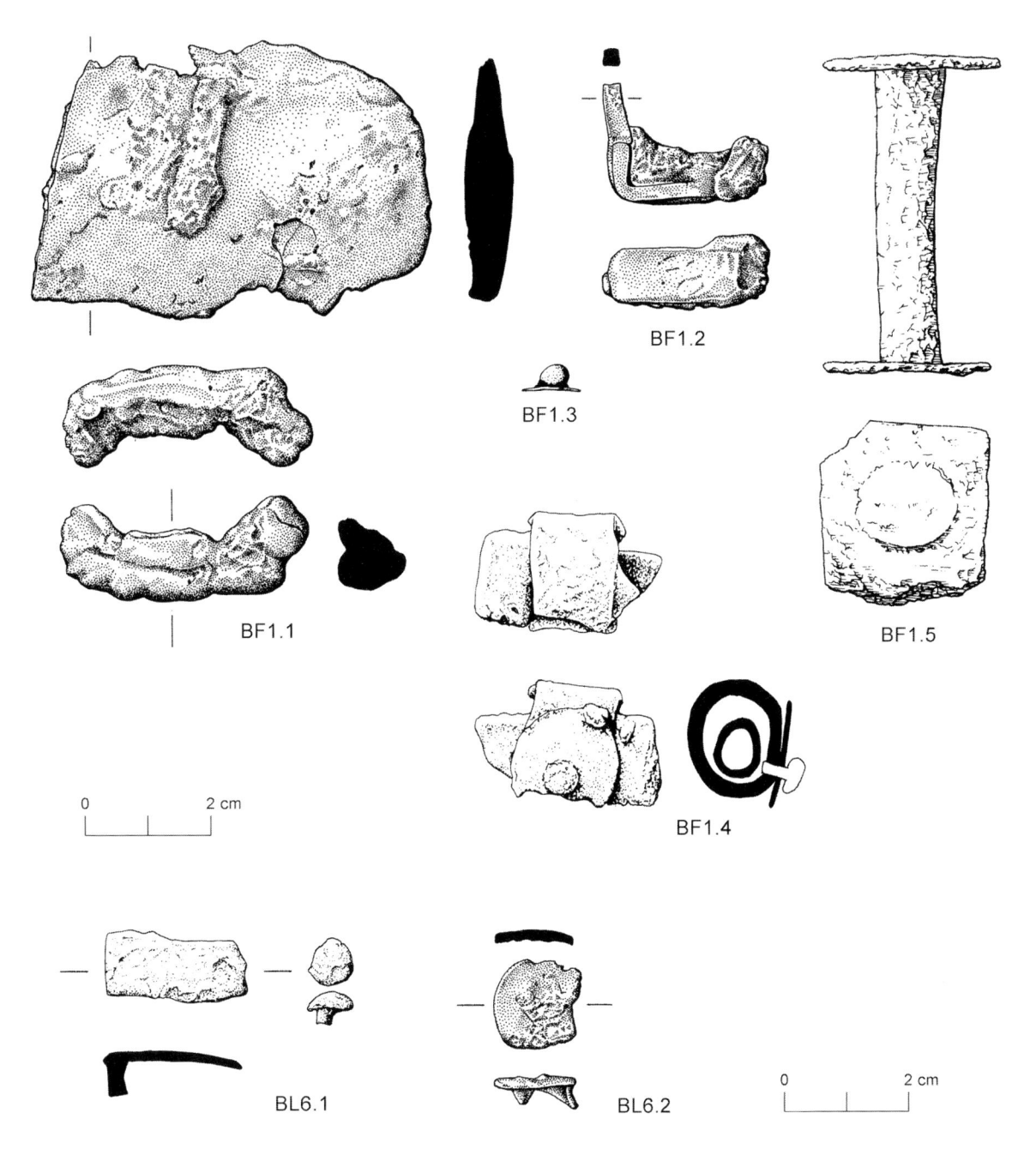

FIG. 33. Pyre-site BF1/BF16: objects of copper alloy (BF1.1–4 and BL6.1–2) and iron (BF1.5) (scale 1:1)

Pyre-pit BF1 (FIG. 33)

BF1.1 SF66. B13. Heat-affected copper-alloy sheet fragments of varying thickness, possibly from a vessel. Maximum dimensions 63 by 43.5 mm.

BF1.2 SF95. B75. Fragment of a brass(?) fitting (in two pieces), probably similar to a staple or dog. It appears to have consisted of a straight flat bar, measuring 21 mm externally, turned at right angles at each end and narrowing to two arms, only one of which now survives, 28 mm long. Weight 6.34 g. In the upper end are traces of organic material.

BF1.3 SF100. B81. The domed heads of four tiny studs of copper alloy and a probable shaft from a tack or small stud. One stud head only illustrated. It is fixed in a tiny fragment of sheet copper alloy. Diameter 5 mm, height 5 mm. Also many burnt fragments.

BF1.4 SF102. B81. Copper-alloy object consisting of a tube around which is passed a strip, to which in turn a circular disc is fixed by a dome-headed stud. Maximum dimensions 30 by 18 mm.

BF1.5 SF125. B125. Iron holdfast with large head, square rove, and round-section shank. Length 48 mm.

BF16.1 B70, B79 (burnt), B127.Dressel 2-4 amphora. See under pyre-site BF16 below.
SF62, B20. Iron fragment, roughly triangular, but no edge need be original. Maximum dimensions 38 by 17 mm, thickness varies from 7 to 1.5 mm, but at the thinnest part need not be original. Identification uncertain, unlikely to be from a blade.
B244. Four iron nail shank fragments, hollow from the action of corrosion. Length of longest 32 mm.
B79. A few fragments of burnt animal bone including a ?sheep carpal (none of the bone appears to be human).

Pyre-pit BF16

BF16.1 B82 (probably burnt), B88 (burnt), B204 (probably burnt). Dressel 2-4 amphora (144 g, average sherd weight of 12 g). Not illustrated. Burnt. Cream Catalan fabric (Williams 1981, 128; Williams 1995, 306). Many of the sherds have turned from cream to grey (5Y 7/1) in colour suggesting intense heat. Some sherds in BF1. *See* above.
BF16.2 SF 103 (part, see TABLE 24). B83. Part of a belt-plate/strap-fitting similar to an example (BF6.29) from the backfill in the south-west corner of BF6. Weight approx. 2 g.
BL5: B72–3, B88. Fragments of cremated human bone and some possible burnt animal bone (13.4 g).
BL7: B69, B204 Fragments of cremated human bone (1.2 g).
BL7: B204. A fragment of canid mandible (0.6 g).
BL5: B64. Distorted iron nail fragment. Length 23 mm.
BL5: B72. Iron nail with sub-circular head and round-section shank. Length 25 mm.

Burnt and charcoal-rich patches (BL6) in area around BF1 and BF16 (FIG. 33)

BL6.1 SF86. B18. From immediately to the east of BF1.
a) Fragment of copper-alloy sheet (in two pieces) with projecting rivet for attachment; probably a strap-plate. Length 22 mm, width 10 mm. Weight 1.12 g.
b) Small copper-alloy stud with slightly domed head. Diameter 7 mm, length 5 mm. Weight 0.28 g.
BL6.2. SF101. B87. From immediately north of BF1. Fragment of a heat-affected copper-alloy fitting with rounded end and straight edge at right angles to it. In the corner between is the stump of a projection for attachment. The other edges are not original. Possibly a stud. Length 14 mm, width 14 mm. Weight 1.24 g. Also two resolidified droplets.
SF82. B25. Cleaning charcoal patch south of BF6 and 3 m to the south-east of BF1. Copper-alloy stud with flat head and curved shank. Length 27 mm.
B30, B38. A small quantity of cremated bone (3.6 g).

Loosely stratified finds from surface cleaning areas around BF1, BF16 and BF6

SF55. B9. Unstratified: from cleaning north of BF1. Fragment of an iron narrow circular-section shaft, similar to one fitted with a glass bead head from CF72 in Enclosure 5. Length 14 mm. Weight 0.25 g.
SF78. B37. Unstratified: from cleaning ?plough rut north of BF1. Probably a severely corroded iron nail or stud with attached mineral-replaced wood. Maximum dimensions 12 by 12 by 10 mm.

?MORTUARY ENCLOSURE BF32 (FIGS 2, 8, 34–5, 139–43, 148; TABLES 25–7)

Cremated bone	0.1 g	indeterminate age and sex
?Partial and other pots	Nos 14–21, 23–4, 28, 44, 50, 54, 72, 77, 84, 90, 94–5, 99–101, 106, 108–9, 113, 121, 126	parts of at least 29 vessels
Other finds	BF28.1	?brass stud
	BF30.1	copper-alloy ring
	BF30.2	fragment of briquetage trough
	BF30.3	bronze coin of Cunobelin
	BF31.1	copper-alloy stud
	BF42.1	?brass strip
	BF42.2	?brass fitting/stud
		many nails and heat-affected fragments of copper alloy
Residual finds		Middle Iron Age sherds, loomweight fragments, burnt daub

The ?mortuary enclosure BF32 was neatly placed in the centre of the southern half of Enclosure 4 (FIGS 2, 8). It was in the form of a ditched enclosure externally measuring approximately 10.5 m square (FIGS 34–5). Its identification as a probable pyre-site stems from the presence in its fills of much charcoal and a considerable amount of heat-affected metalwork, a few pieces of cremated bone, and indications in one place of scorching of the natural.

The ditch (BF28–31) was rounded in profile and varied from 0.3 to 0.65 m in depth as measured after stripping (FIG. 35). Like the ditch of the enclosure in which it was located, the fill appeared to have consisted of two elements, a lower, rapid, fill and a main fill which had accumulated after the sides had stabilised. Ten small pits were distributed evenly across the central and southern parts of the interior. The presence of the pits is hard to explain. One possible interpretation is that they were post-holes or post-pits associated with vertical wooden posts used to stiffen and support the pyre. Another is that they represent the remains of an above-ground mortuary structure (*see* further p. 427). The only place where there was any sign of scorching was BF42, a small shallow pit with heavily burnt sides and many molten lumps and fragments of copper alloy in its fill (FIGS 2, 35). Pit BF62 included a thin scatter of charcoal flecks, and small lenses of charcoal were found in pits BF45 and BF69 (FIGS 2, 35). The ditch fills on all four sides of the enclosure also contained a few minute flecks and small lumps of charcoal. Copper-alloy drips and fragments were recovered from the north, east and west enclosure ditches. Crucially, two very small fragments of cremated bone were associated with the ?mortuary enclosure, one in the east ditch, and the other in pit BF42.

Approximately 29 partial pots and other vessels (Pots 14–21, 23–4, 28, 44, 50, 54, 72, 77, 84, 90, 94–5, 99–101, 106, 108–9, 113, 121, 126) can be identified from the pyre-site, including one Italian amphora (two sherds, Pot 126). As far as could be judged, most, if not all of the partial pots were in the main fill. None of them appeared to have been burnt. The presence of sherds from five to seven Gallo-Belgic imports (Pots 14–21, 23–24) in the ditches of the pyre-site contrasts with the pottery in the chamber BF24 where Gallo-Belgic imports are

FIG. 34.   Enclosure 4 ?mortuary enclosure BF32, viewed from the south

TABLE 25: SMALL FRAGMENTS OF COPPER ALLOY, THE MAJORITY HEAT AFFECTED, FROM THE DITCH OF THE ?MORTUARY ENCLOSURE BF32

	L/F no.	Find no.	Small find no.	No. pieces	Weight (g)
BF28.1	BF28	B531	153	1	0.80
BF30.1	BL23/BF30	B286	176	2	2.90
BF31.1	BF31	B1105	410	1	1.50
	BF28	B540	152	2	4.65
	BL18/BF28	B319	169	2	1.60
	BL18/BF28	B342	168	2	0.40
	BL18/BF28	B404	167	1	1.01
	BL19B/F28	B532	172	1	0.25
	BL19/BF28	B533	171	1	1.36
	BL19/BF28	B534	170	1	1.67
	BL30/BF30	B466	149	1	0.13
	BL31/BF31	B632	150	1	2.36
	BL44/BF32	B736	300	1	3.80
	BF32	B903	288	1	0.77
totals				**18**	**23.20**

TABLE 26: IRON NAIL FRAGMENTS FROM THE DITCH OF THE ?MORTUARY ENCLOSURE BF32

Feature/Layer no.	Find no.	Head	Length (mm)	Description
BF31	B526		38	shank fragment, clenched
BF31	B527		–	shank fragment
BF31	B528		–	shank fragment
BF31	B530		–	?shank fragment
BF31	B539		–	shank fragment
BF31	B581		–	?shank fragment
BF31	B582	sub-circular	36	in 2 fragments
BF31	B583		–	shank fragment
BF31	B584	sub-circular	36	in 3 fragments
BL21, junction of BF30 and BF31	B588 (SF174)	circular	58	in 5 fragments
BL21, junction of BF30 and BF31	B503	sub-rectangular	19	short part of shank only
BL23/BF30	B502	sub-circular	35	in 2 fragments
BL38/BF30	B589 (SF156)		26	shank fragment
BL37/BF30	B590 (SF157)	sub-circular	44	
BL38/BF30	B611 (SF155)	sub-circular	31	
BL28/BF29	B506	circular	27	in 2 fragments
BL18/BF28	B320 (SF409)		–	3 tiny fragments, perhaps from a nail head

absent. The Gallo-Belgic sherds from the pyre-site ditches are small, with the exception of the butt-beaker of Cam form 113 (Pot 18), which survived as a sherd 'cluster' (*i.e.* a clear example of a partial pot), although the vessel is far from complete. Of the local wares, there is approximately 11 kg from the pyre-site. Almost all of this material (approximately 10.5 kg) came from ditches BF30 and BF31 and was concentrated towards the north-east corner of the pyre. Sherds from the pyre-site could also be matched with sherds from vessels in the enclosure ditches (Pots 28 (FIG. 139) and 108 (FIG. 142), probably Pot 109 (FIG. 142) and possibly Pot 80 (FIG. 141)).

The ?mortuary enclosure contained a considerable amount of heat-affected metalwork similar to the material associated with the pyre-site BF1/BF16. However, its distribution was limited. Most of it (about 90%) derived from pit BF42, which seems appropriate given the pit's scorched sides (TABLE 27). The rest came from the pyre-enclosure ditch (TABLE 25), and most of that was found in its western arm. Much of the heat-affected metalwork was in the form of small pellets or resolidified droplets. The identifiable objects, apart from the iron nails, are mainly copper-alloy studs or strap-fittings.

The iron nails from the ditch are listed in TABLE 26. Unlike the heat-affected metalwork, most derived from the north and east sides of the enclosure. They are not well-preserved, with little or no traces of mineralised wood. Half were fragments of shanks.

The pyre-enclosure ditches also produced 11 sherds of salt briquetage (484 g, TABLE 57). Like the nails, they only occurred in the northern and eastern arms of the pyre-enclosure ditch. The largest piece (BF30.2) is part of a rim of a rectangular trough (*see* further pp. 375–6).

?Partial and other pots in the ditch of the ?mortuary enclosure (FIGS 139–43)

Pot 14 Not illustrated. ?Mortuary enclosure ditch BF30/BF31 (probably main fill) Cam 113 butt-beaker (B434). Abraded. Fabric BPW.

Pot 15 Not illustrated. ?Mortuary enclosure ditch BF29. Cam 113 butt-beaker. Fragment only (B1128). Fabric BPW.

Pot 16 Not illustrated. ?Mortuary enclosure ditch (main fill). Flagon (form unknown). Sherd only (B586), very abraded. Fabric WPW. (A.D. 15–60.)

Pot 17 FIG. 139. ?Mortuary enclosure ditch BF30 (main fill). Cam 5 platter (B586). 2 rim sherds, abraded. Fabric TN. (A.D. 15–60.)

Pot 18 Not illustrated. ?Mortuary enclosure ditch BF30 (main fill). Cam 113 butt-beaker (B283, B291, B586). Partial pot. 3 base sherds, abraded. Also 20+ small sherds (probably all part of same vessel). Fabric BPW.

Pot 19 Not illustrated. ?Mortuary enclosure ditch BF30 (main fill). Cam 84 girth beaker (B586). 3 small sherds, very abraded. Fabric TR3, red.

Pot 20 Not illustrated. ?Mortuary enclosure ditch BF30/BF31 (main fill). Cam 112 or 91 ovoid or globular beaker with chattered rouletting (B501 B524). 3 small sherds, very abraded (possibly part of 23). Fabric TR3, red.

Pot 21 Not illustrated. ?Mortuary enclosure ditch BF30/BF31 (main fill). Cam 113 butt-beaker (B524). 2 rim sherds plus 1 other, abraded (not part of 21). Fabric BPW.

Pot 23 Not illustrated. ?Mortuary enclosure ditch BF31 (main fill). Cam 113 butt-beaker (B297, B524, B633, B1130). Rim sherds, 1 small sherd, 10 fragments, abraded-very abraded. (Possibly same vessel as 21.) Fabric BPW. (A.D. 40–65.)

Pot 24 Not illustrated. ?Mortuary enclosure ditch BF31 (main fill). Beaker (form unknown). 1 sherd, very abraded (B299). Fabric TR3, red.

Pot 28 FIG. 139. ?Mortuary enclosure ditch BF30/BF31 (main fill) and ditch BF40. Cam 8 small platter (B524). 1 base sherd, abraded. Fabric TN.

Pot 44 FIG. 139. ?Mortuary enclosure ditch BF30/BF31 BF30 (probably main fill). Platter with flattened bead rim. Single sherd (B898). Burnished. Fabric RCW.

Pot 50 FIG. 139. ?Mortuary enclosure ditch BF30 (main fill). Cam 24 platter (*CAR* 10 fabric group UR.LTC). Single sherd (B283). Fabric RCW.

Pot 54 FIG. 139. ?Mortuary enclosure ditch BF30 (main fill). Cam 119b beaker. Rim sherd only (B501). Burnished, extending over rim. Fabric RCW.

Pot 72 FIG. 140. ?Mortuary enclosure ditch BF29. Jar, rim sherd (B1128). Burnished, extending over rim. Fabric RCW.

Pot 77 FIG. 140. Enclosure 4 ?Mortuary enclosure ditch BF30/31 BF30 (main fill). Cam 266 jar (B899). Partial pot. Part of rim and shoulder and upper body, traces of carbonised matter on exterior. Fabric RCW.

Pot 84 Not illustrated. ?Mortuary enclosure ditch BF30/31 (main fill). Cam 266 jar (B524, B283, B586, B501). Fabric RCVW.

Pot 90 FIG. 141. ?Mortuary enclosure ditch BF31. Jar (B614). Rim sherds only. Burnished extending over rim. Fabric GBW.

Pot 94 FIG. 141. ?Mortuary enclosure ditch BF30/31 (main fill). Small jar or beaker (B898). Rim sherd only. Fabric RCW.

Pot 95 FIG. 141. ?Mortuary enclosure ditch BF30. Jar (B521). Two post-firing holes through base. Partial pot. Most of lower half of vessel. Burnished. Fabric GBW.

Pot 99 Not illustrated. Enclosure 4 ?mortuary enclosure ditch corner BF30/BF31 (main fill). Cam 231/232 (B524, B586) large narrow necked jar, sherds from shoulder. Fabric RCW.

TABLE 27: SMALL FRAGMENTS OF COPPER ALLOY, THE MAJORITY HEAT AFFECTED, FROM THE PITS BF42 AND BF62 INSIDE THE DITCH OF THE ?MORTUARY ENCLOSURE BF32

	Layer/Feature no.	Find no.	Small find no.	No. of pieces	Weight (g)	Notes
Pit BF42						
BF42.1	BF42	B750	231	1	0.78	
BF42.2	BL41/BF42	B734	190	1	1.7	
	BL41/BF42	B619	180	3	0.32	2 × sheet
	BL41/BF42	B620	181	1	0.16	
	BL41/BF42	B634	179	1	0.11	
	BL41/BF42	B635	193	1	0.28	
	BL41/BF42	B636	195	1	0.38	
	BL41/BF42	B637	194	1	0.31	
	BL41/BF42	B638	182	1	0.1	
	BL41/BF42	B639	192	1	0.04	
	BL41/BF42	B640	183	2	0.05	
	BL41/BF42	B641	184	1	0.09	
	BL41/BF42	B642	185	1	0.04	
	BL41/BF42	B643	186	1	0.05	
	BL41/BF42	B644	187	1	0.12	
	BL41/BF42	B645	188	2	0.07	
	BL41/BF42	B646	177	8	0.67	
	BL41/BF42	B646	221	55	8.7	
	BL41/BF42	B647	178	2	0.25	
	BF42	B671	217	1	0.12	
	BF42	B672	244	2	0.12	
	BF42	B673	214	1	0.96	
	BF42	B674	247	specks	0	
	BF42	B675	237	6	0.62	
	BF42	B679	215	47	6.32	
	BF42	B679	246	6	0.76	
	BF42	B680	210	1	0.41	
	BF42	B701	219	10	1.69	1 may be a small stud
	BF42	B702	220	6	0.78	
	BF42	B703	209	1	0.93	
	BF42	B704	200	3	0.42	sheet
	BF42	B705	204	1	0.15	
	BF42	B706	201	1	0.18	
	BF42	B707	236	3	0.53	
	BF42	B708	202	1	0.15	
	BF42	B709	240	7	3.66	
	BF42	B710	206	6	5.18	
	BF42	B711	207	2	0.1	
	BF42	B712	218	1	0.21	
	BF42	B713	208	3	0.31	
	BF42	B714	227	1	0.24	
	BF42	B714	248	4	0.19	
	BF42	B715	249	4	0.33	2 may be from 1 small stud
	BF42	B716	228	specks	0	
	BF42	B718	229	1	0.22	
	BF42	B719	213	1	0.08	
	BF42	B720	205	specks	0	
	BF42	B720	250	2	1.04	
	BF42	B721	197	1	0.32	
	BF42	B722	198	2	0.4	sheet
	BF42	B723	199	2	0.27	1 × sheet
	BF42	B724	242	2	0	cindery flecks
	BF42	B725	233	2	1.95	
	BF42	B726	234	1	0.25	
	BF42	B727	235	5	0.33	1 × sheet
	BF42	B727	239	1	0.21	

TABLE 27: (CONT'D)

Layer/Feature no.	Find no.	Small find no.	No. of pieces	Weight (g)	Notes
BF42	B728	224	5	0.16	sheet
BF42	B728	243	specks	0	
BF42	B729	203	1	0.16	
BF42	B730	245	1	0.28	
BF42	B731	241	1	0.88	
BF42	B732	212	1	0.01	
BL41/BF42	B734	191	31	28.38	3 × sheet
BL41/BF42	B735	189	1	15.21	?globular-headed nail
BL41/BF42	B736	305	100+	20.98	3 × sheet
BF42	B742	211	1	0.07	
BF42	B742	230	1	0.13	
BL41/BF42	B743	225	1	0.13	probably a fragment of a small tack
BL41/BF42	B743	196	1	0.08	sheet
BF42	B745	226	1	0.98	possibly a small stud
BF42	B747	223	1	0.11	
BF42	B748	238	9	1.59	5 × sheet
BF42	B750	216	15	4.86	
BF42	B750	232	60	26.84	
BL41/BF42	B821	306	100+	40.17	1 × ?plaque
totals			554+	184.67+	
Pit BF62					
BF62	B982	385	8	3.2	crumpled sheet (not heat-affected?)

Pot 100 Not illustrated. Enclosure 4 ?mortuary enclosure ditch corner BF30/BF31 (main fill). Body sherds from large vessel with body cordon (B434, B524) partly burnished. Fabric RCW.

Pot 101 FIG. 141. ?Mortuary enclosure ditch BF31 (main fill). Cam 254 jar. Single sherd (B633), traces of carbonised matter on shoulder. Fabric HZ. Dated as mainly pre-conquest (*CAR* 10, 478).

Pot 106 FIG. 142. ?Mortuary enclosure ditch BF30/31 (main fill). Cam 109 jar (B898). Part of rim and upper body. Carbonised matter on neck and body. Burnished on neck and extending over rim. Fabric RCW.

Pot 108 FIG. 142. Ditches BF40 (lower part of ditch fill) and Enclosure 4 ?mortuary enclosure ditch BF30/BF31 (main fill). Cam 270B large storage jar with hook rim (B434, B524, B970, B1130). Rim sherds only positively identified as part of one vessel. Burnished on rim. Fabric HZ. (Rim sherds B434, B525 (pyre-site) and B970 (enclosure ditch) all join.)

Pot 109 FIG. 142. ?Mortuary enclosure ditch BF30 (main fill) and ditch BF40 (lower part of ditch fill). Cam 270B large hook-rim storage jar. Part of rim and shoulder only, two rows of circular indentations around shoulder (B586, B959, B963). Abraded. Fabric HZ. (No joins between sherds from different find numbers but almost certainly the same vessel as all have same circular indentations and matching shoulder bead.)

Pot 113 FIG. 143. ?Mortuary enclosure ditch BF30. Cam 273 large storage jar (B1129) rim sherd only. Burnished on neck and extending over rim. Fabric HZ.

Pot 121 Not illustrated. ?Mortuary enclosure ditch BF30 (main fill). Samian platter, Arezzo, Augustan-Tiberian (B586).

Pot 126 Not illustrated. ?Mortuary enclosure ditch BF31 (main fill). Amphora, Dressel 2-4. 2 body sherds (B386, B524) (79 g). Brick red fabric typical of much of Latium and Campania. Italian. Fabric CAM AM 2.

Other pottery sherds from the ?mortuary enclosure ditch

BF28: Fabric GTW, 9 sherds (B271, B587, B1126); Fabric RCW, 3 sherds (B1127).

BF29: Fabric HZ, 21 sherds (B341, B384, B433, B434, B470); Fabric RCW, 20 sherds and fragments, (B434, B464, B470).

BF30: Fabric GX(H), 1 sherd (B586). Fabric HZ, total 53 sherds, sherd decorated with small circular impressions (B1118, ?same vessel as Pot 109), jar rim Cam 254 (B586, ?same as Pot 101), Cam 271 rim

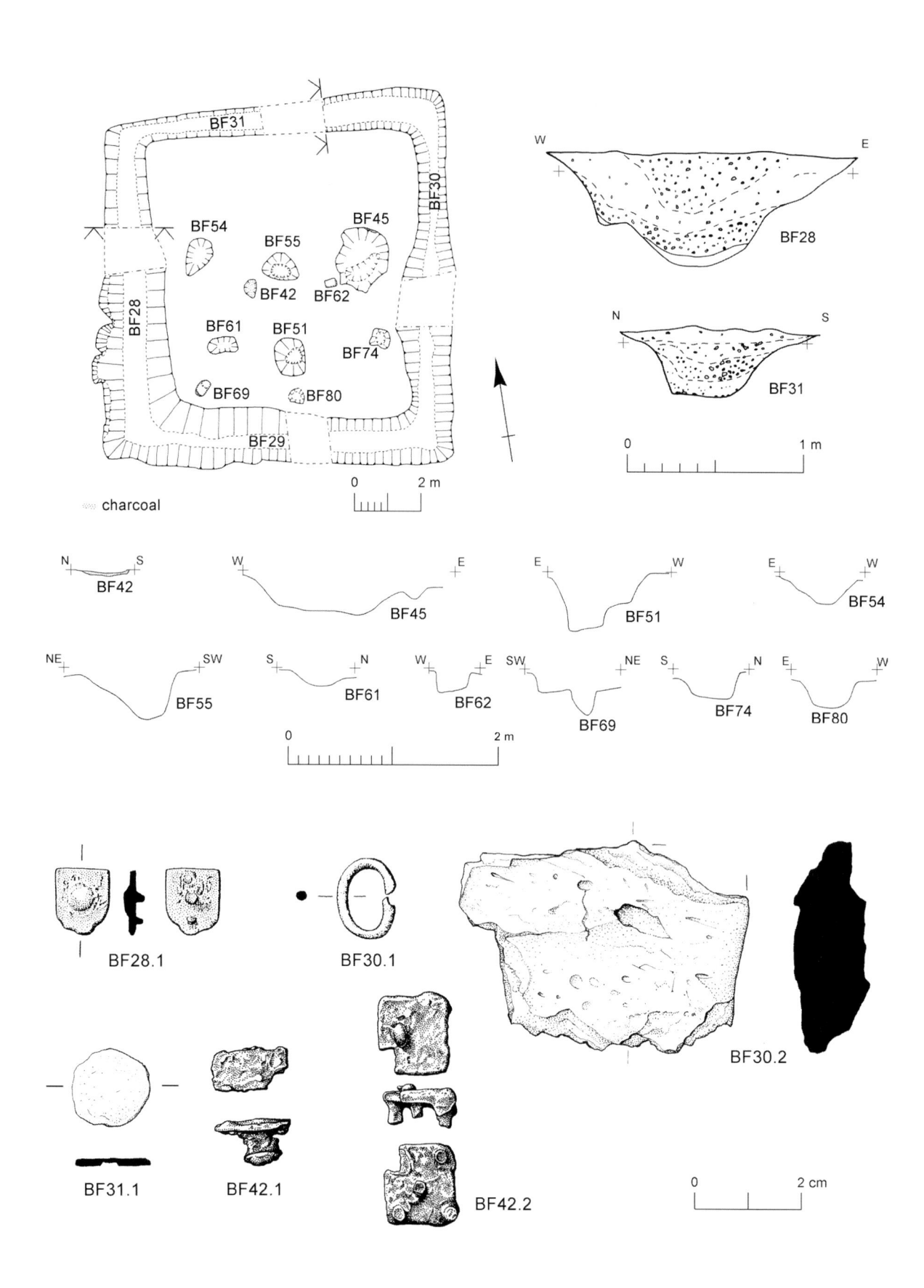

FIG. 35. ?Mortuary enclosure BF32: plan (scale 1:160), ditch sections (scale 1:30), pit profiles (scale 1:50), and copper-alloy objects and briquetage (BF30.2) (scale 1:1)

(B586), other sherds (B285, B291, B586, B1129); Fabric RCVW, total 24 sherds, jar rim, crazed and degraded (B291), jar/bowl rim(s) ?Cam 218 (B285), other sherds (B504, B586). Fabric ROW, 7 sherds (B285, B586). Fabric RCW, approximately 230 sherds and fragments, Cam 218 fragment (B1129), ?Cam 119 rim fragment (B586, ?same vessel as Pot 54), Cam 119 rim fragments (B285, ?same vessel as Pot 54), other sherds (B283, B291, B504, B505, B586).
BF30/31 corner area: Fabric GBW (*CAR* **10** fabric group UR.LTC), 2 sherds ?Cam 28 (524); Fabric GBW 1 sherd, rim (B524). Fabric GTW (*CAR* **10** fabric group UR.LTC), total 3 sherds (B524); Fabric HZ, 56 sherds (B272, B501, B524, B898); Fabric RCVW, 44 sherds (B272, B501, B524, B529, B898); Fabric ROW, rim sherd probably from a jar/bowl (B524); Fabric RCW, total 225 sherds and fragments, rim fragments including ?Cam 218 (B501), rim frag Cam 119 (B272, ?same vessel as Pot 54), other sherds (B296, B501, B52, B574, B898); Fabric RCW (*CAR* **10** fabric group UR.LTC) 2 rim sherds (join) Cam 30 rim, possibly part of vessel 61 (272, 524).
BF31: Fabric DJ(D), single sherd (B297); Fabric GBW, 5 sherds (B614); Fabric GTW, single sherd (B649); Fabric HZ, 93 sherds, rim Cam 254 (B297, B585, B633 ?same vessel as Pot 101), other sherds (B297, B299, B585, B612, B631, B633, B1130); Fabric RCVW total 95 sherds, rim ?Cam 266 (B1130) jar bowl rim frags (B297), other sherds (B299, B585, B612, B631, B633, B649); Fabric ROW, 9 sherds (B297); Fabric RCW total 272 sherds, jar/bowl rim fragments (B1130) (B297, B299, B385, B585, B612, B614, B633, B678).

Other finds in the ?mortuary enclosure ditch (FIGS 35, 148)

BF28.1 FIG. 35. SF153. B531. Brass(?) shield-shaped plaque with central stud for attachment. Two other slight projections on the rear appear to be original features rather than the effect of burning or corrosion. Length 12 mm, width 11 mm. Weight 0.8 g.
BF30.1 FIG. 35. SF176. B286. BL23/BF30, main fill.
a) An oval copper-alloy penannular ring (possibly annular originally), stained with iron. Length 15 mm, width 11 mm.
b) Not illustrated. The upper part of an iron nail, in two fragments, with the shank passing through a small fragment of copper-alloy sheet. a) and b) together weigh 2.9 g.
BF30.2 FIG. 35. B283. BL21, main fill. Large rim sherd of briquetage (see pp. 375–6).
BF30.3 FIG. 148. BF30/1. SF173. B538 BL21. Junction of northern and eastern arms of the ditch of ?mortuary enclosure BF32 in Enclosure 4. Coin of Cunobelin A.D. 10–20 (see p. 340).
BF31.1 FIG. 35. SF410. B1105. Plain flat head from a copper-alloy stud. There is a scar on the underside where the shank was attached. Diameter 14.5 mm. Weight 1.5 g.

Finds from pits inside the ?mortuary enclosure (FIG. 35)

BF42.1 FIG. 35. SF231. B750. Heat-damaged brass(?) strip with rivet on underside for attachment. Length 15 mm, width 7 mm. Weight 0.78 g.
BF42.2 FIG. 35. CF42/L41. SF190. B734. Square brass(?) fitting, one corner missing. Slightly heat-affected. There are short projections for attachment on the underside of the three surviving corners, and a dome-headed stud set slightly off-centre. Dimensions 14 by 15 mm, height at longest projection 7 mm. Weight 1.7 g.
BF45: SF402. B961. Fragment of an iron nail shank, square in section, and an oval convex piece of iron with part of a flat base. Both are heat-affected. The convex piece may be a corrosion bubble, or a shape created during heating and resolidifying. Length of shank 27.5 mm. Maximum length of ?bubble, 32 mm. B967. Iron nail shank fragment. Length (bent) 23 mm.
BF51: B966. Single pottery sherd, Fabric HZ.

?MORTUARY ENCLOSURE CF43–6 (FIGS 2, 8, 36–7, 144; TABLE 28)

Cremated bone	none	
?Partial and other pots	Pots 129–31, 138–41, 143, 145–7	parts of at least 11 vessels
Other finds	CF44.1	a fragment of a briquetage trough, many nail fragments, an iron stud, and two copper-alloy fragments
Residual finds	none identified	

In the centre of Enclosure 5 was a small, square, ditched enclosure with sides approximately 7 m long (FIGS 2, 8, 36–7). The ditch (CF43–6) after the ground strip was 0.8–1.0 m wide and

0.2–0.3 m deep (FIGS 36–7). It was filled with layers of stony sandy silt with patches of sandy gravel and a small amount of charcoal, a concentration of which (CF88) lay in the part of the ditch at the north-east corner of the pyre-site. The fill could not easily be split into the lower and main fills observed in pyre-site BF32.

Like the pyre-site BF32 in Enclosure 4, the enclosure ditch contained many fragments of broken pots (Pots 129–31, 138–41, 143, 145–7) and part of a salt briquetage trough (FIG. 36, CF44.1; pp. 375–6). The pots had been deliberately broken, but were much less fragmented than the material in the nearby chamber CF42. The absence of obvious lower and main fills means that it is now difficult to tell if the deposition of the burnt vessels took place as one episode and, if so, when such an event might have taken place in relation to the filling of the ditch. However, as far as we can judge, if there had been just one episode of deposition, this probably did not take place as soon as the ditch was dug but happened long enough afterwards for 100–200 mm of silt to accumulate rapidly in the bottom of the ditch.

In all, there were eleven identifiable vessels from the ditch, three of which were Gallo-Belgic imports (Pots 129–131) and two, or possibly three, were amphoras (Pots 145, 146 (FIG. 144), 147). Of the seven local vessels (which collectively weighed approximately 0.5 kg), the majority (approximately 0.4 kg) came from the south ditch CF45. Four of the vessels had been scorched. These are Pots 129, 130, 138 (FIG. 144), and 141 (FIG. 144). Pot 138 is a Cam 218 which had been distorted and discoloured either on the pyre (more likely) or in the kiln when made (FIG. 144). Pot 129 might be the same as Pot 37 from the enclosure ditch CF1.

Unlike the Enclosure 4 pyre-site, the ditch of CF43–6 produced very few metal finds, and only one of these (SF202) seems to have been heat-affected. Most of the metal finds are nails (TABLE 28). They are small, with an approximate complete length of between 40 and 70 mm, and, like those from BF32, they are all of Manning Type 1b. Most of the nail fragments were in the east arm of the pyre-enclosure ditch.

There were four possible features within the area of the enclosure, all of which are undated. These consist of a possible small pit (CF98) and three small possible stake-holes (CF97, CF99, and CF101) (FIG 36). They were poorly defined and all could be natural in origin. CF98 either sealed CF101 or was part of it. The features included charcoal but no finds. Two of them (CF98 and CF99) were discernible only as concentrations of charcoal, and may have been the result of animal burrows or root holes.

There was no evidence of any scorching either in or around the enclosure or the features associated with it. Nor was there the distinctive scatter of heat-affected copper-alloy metalwork which characterised the pyre-sites BF1, BF16, and BF32 in Enclosures 3 and 4. The identification of the complex as the remains of a pyre is tenuous and rests on the similarity of its plan with that of the ?mortuary enclosure BF32 in Enclosure 3, and the discovery of a tiny fragment of ?resolidified copper alloy (SF202) from the western arm of the pyre-enclosure ditch.

Immediately adjacent to the south of the southern arm of the pyre-enclosure was a small shallow pit (CF64) which may have been associated with it (FIGS 2, 36). The upper fill of the pit was a dark silty sand containing charcoal. There were very few finds in it, but one of two

TABLE 28: IRON NAILS FROM THE DITCH OF THE ?MORTUARY ENCLOSURE CF43–6

Feature no.	Find no.	Context	Head	Length (mm)	Description
CF44	C130	east ditch	sub-circular	44	shank curved
CF44	C137	east ditch	a) sub-circular	a) 40; b) 23	b) shank fragment
CF44	C145	east ditch		a) 34; b) 23	a–b) shank fragments
CF44	C181	east ditch	round	33	in 4 pieces
CF45	C125	south ditch	round	65	in 4 pieces
CF45	C142	south ditch	sub-circular	34	
CF46	C136	west ditch	round	29	in 2 pieces

THE FUNERARY SITE

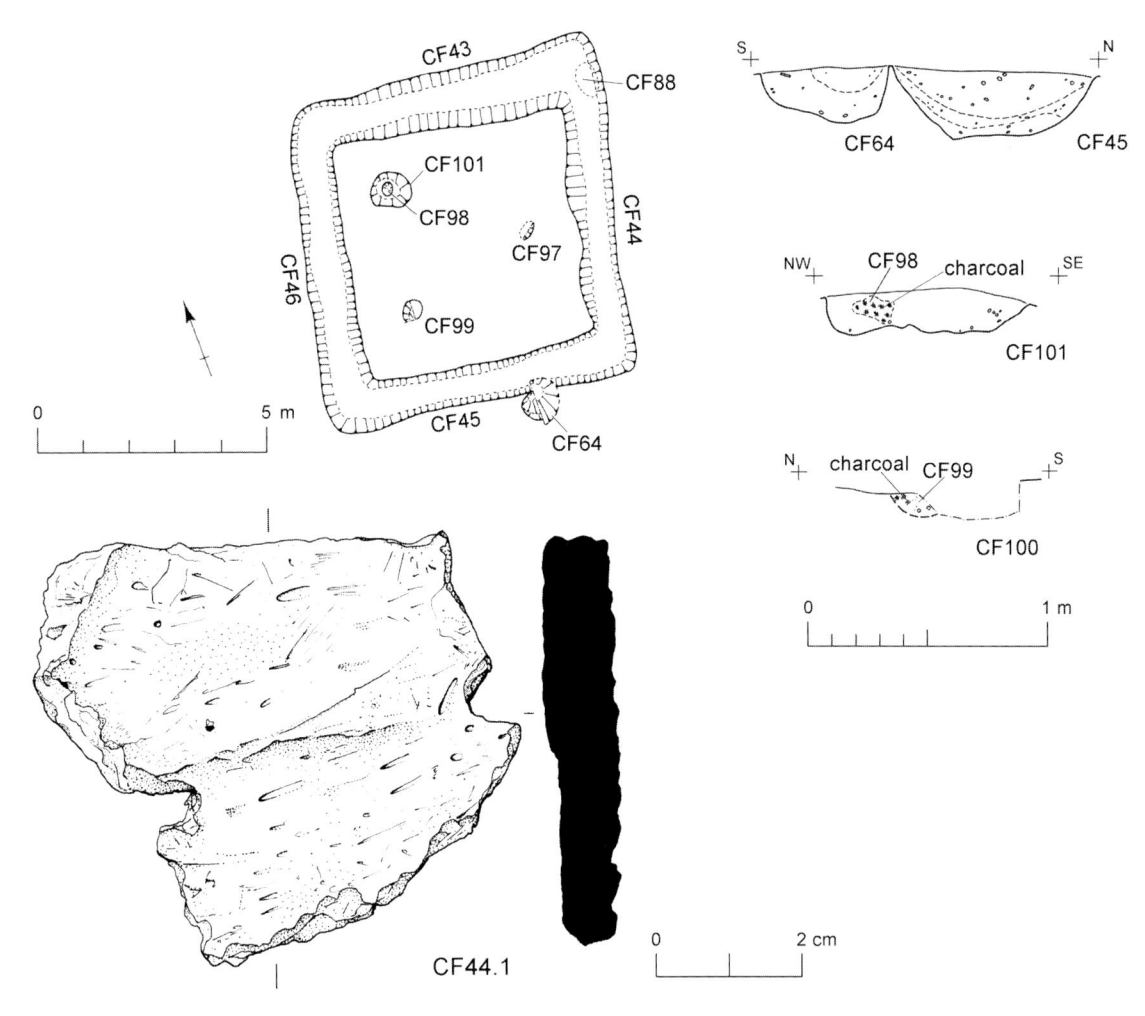

FIG. 36. ?Mortuary enclosure site CF43–6: plan, ditch and pit sections (scale 1:30), and briquetage sherd (scale 1:1)

FIG. 37. Enclosure 5 ?mortuary enclosure CF43–6, viewed from the north

Late Iron Age/Roman pottery sherds from its fill appeared to have been burnt. Just to the east of the pyre-enclosure was a small circular pit (CF53) about 0.6 m across (FIG. 2) which had a diffuse darker central fill containing charcoal. This feature produced a copper-alloy object (SF210; part of a large ring?) from within the darker central area of the fill.

?Partial and other pots from the ?mortuary enclosure ditch (FIG. 144)

Pot 129 Not illustrated. ?Mortuary enclosure ditch CF43. *Lagena* or flagon with 4-rib handle (C138). Handle sherd only (not part of any other vessel found at Stanway), burnt after or at time of fracture, abraded. Fabric WPW.

Pot 130 Not illustrated. ?Mortuary enclosure ditch CF43. Cam 74 Carinated pedestal cup (C180). 1 small sherd, burnt and abraded (possibly same vessel as Pot 37). Fabric TR1(C).

Pot 131 Not illustrated. ?Mortuary enclosure ditch CF45. Cam 113 butt-beaker (C142). 2 small sherds, abraded. Fabric BPW.

Pot 138 ?Mortuary enclosure ditch CF46. Cam 218 bowl (C136). Partial pot. Much of upper part of vessel, either a kiln waster or scorched on the pyre. Fabric RCW. Early Roman.

Pot 139 ?Mortuary enclosure ditch CF45. Cam 218 bowl (C142). Partial pot. Part of rim and shoulder only. Burnished, extending over rim. Fabric RCW. Early Roman.

Pot 140 ?Mortuary enclosure ditch CF43. Cam 212-217 bowl (C119). Part of rim only. Burnished, extending over rim. Fabric RCW.

Pot 141 ?Mortuary enclosure ditch CF44. Cam 266 jar (C134). Part of rim and neck only, burnt. Fabric RCW.

Pot 143 ?Mortuary enclosure ditch CF46. Lid with flanged rim (C138). ?Partial pot. Single sherd. Burnished exterior. Fabric GTW.

Pot 145 Not illustrated. ?Mortuary enclosure ditch CF44. Amphora, Dressel 2-4, Catalan. 3 sherds from shoulder and base (C112) (90 g). Fabric in the distinctive red paste with abundant white inclusions assigned to Catalonia. Fabric CAT AM.

Pot 146 ?Mortuary enclosure ditch CF45. Amphora, Dressel 2-4. Handle (C185) (202 g). Fabric light yellow (10YR 8/4) with common (6–10 per cm^2) sub-rounded and well-sorted white and grey inclusions <1mm across.

Pot 147 Not illustrated. ?Mortuary enclosure ditch CF45. Amphora, Dressel 2-4. 30 sherds (C185). (Too much attention should not be paid to the sherd counts because the crumbly and friable character of the vessel has led to disintegration since excavation.) (133 g). Fabric soft and powdery light yellow (10YR 8/6) fabric with sparse (less than 5 per cm^2) well-sorted rounded and sub-rounded white and light grey inclusions <1mm across.

Other pottery sherds from the ?mortuary enclosure ditch

CF43: Fabric GTW, 2 sherds (C113); Fabric RCW, 20 sherds including rim fragments and base (C113, C178, C180, C183).
CF44: Fabric DJ(D), 3 sherds (C186); Fabric HZ, 3 sherds, probabaly parts of same vessel as CF45 (C117, C179); Fabric RCW, 50 sherds and fragments, ?Cam 218 (C175), other sherds (C143, C145, C179, C181, C190) including fragments from probable lid (C117, C130, C134).
CF45: Fabric HZ, 1 sherd (C191); Fabric RCW, 1 sherd (C125).
CF46: Fabric HZ, 1 sherd (C136); Fabric RCW, 22 sherds (C124, C135, C138 C170, C184).

Other finds from the ?mortuary enclosure ditch (FIG. 36)

CF44.1 FIG. 36. C140. Large wall sherd of briquetage (see pp. 375–6).
CF44: SF206. C144. Convex iron stud in 4 fragments. The shank has broken off and only part remains attached by corrosion products to one edge of the head. Diameter 40 mm, height approximately 5 mm; SF212. C133. Flat iron disc, with part of the edge missing. Diameter 38 mm.
CF46: SF202. C176. Tiny fragment of copper alloy, about 4 mm in diameter. Possibly a tack head, resolidified droplet, or corrosion bubble.

Finds from immediately outside the ?mortuary enclosure ditch

CF53: Pit. SF210. C99. Curved copper-alloy fragment of circular section, probably part of a large ring. Length 18 mm, diameter 9 mm.
CF64: Pit. C118, C188. Two sherds, one burnt. Fabric RCW.

THE CHAMBERS

CHAMBER AF25 (FIGS 2, 6, 38–40)

Cremated bone	11.8 g	age and sex unknown
Pottery vessels	AF25.1	cordoned pedestal bowl (grog-tempered)
	AF25.2	corrugated constricted mug (grog-tempered)
Other finds	AF25.3	copper-alloy ?terminal
Animal bone		?burnt teeth (4 g) of a large mammal and a burnt pig molar (4 g)
Residual finds		Middle Iron Age sherds and burnt daub and a fragment of loomweight from the mound and the backfill of chamber

The remains of chamber AF25 lay a little to the west of centre of Enclosure 1 (FIGS 2, 6). It had been constructed in a large rectangular pit measuring 3.3 m north–south by 2.5 m east–west. The pit was 1.1 m deep as measured from the excavation surface, with a flat floor and vertical sides (FIGS 38–39).

A thin line of decayed wood extended for 2.5 m along the western side of the pit offset by 120–180 mm. The line extended vertically 0.3 m upwards from the floor. The decayed wood was probably the remains of a horizontal plank which had formed the base of the west side of the chamber. There were other traces of wood in the chamber including a lightly charred plank (FIG. 39) 1.1 m long and 0.3 m wide in the northern half of the pit, 0.15–0.40 m east of the line of decayed wood. The plank was only 0.05 m above the floor and appeared to lie at a haphazard angle at the base of the mound which had originally been constructed over the chamber but had subsequently collapsed into it. More decayed wood in the south-west corner of the pit (FIG. 39) was just above the vertical line of decayed wood, and there were small patches of charcoal in the northern half of the pit (not on plan), all 0.3 m above the floor. These appear to have been the remains of planks which had formed the sides of the chamber but which were trapped in the base of the mound when it collapsed following decay of the roof timbers. No nails were found in the pit.

The floor of the pit was sealed by a thin lens 5–10 mm thick of dark, charcoal-enriched soil incorporating a scatter of cremated human bone, parts of two Late Iron Age pots (FIG. 40, AF25.1–2), a burnt pig molar (A528), and an unidentifiable fragment of copper alloy (FIG. 40,

FIG. 38. Chamber AF25, half-section, viewed from the south-east

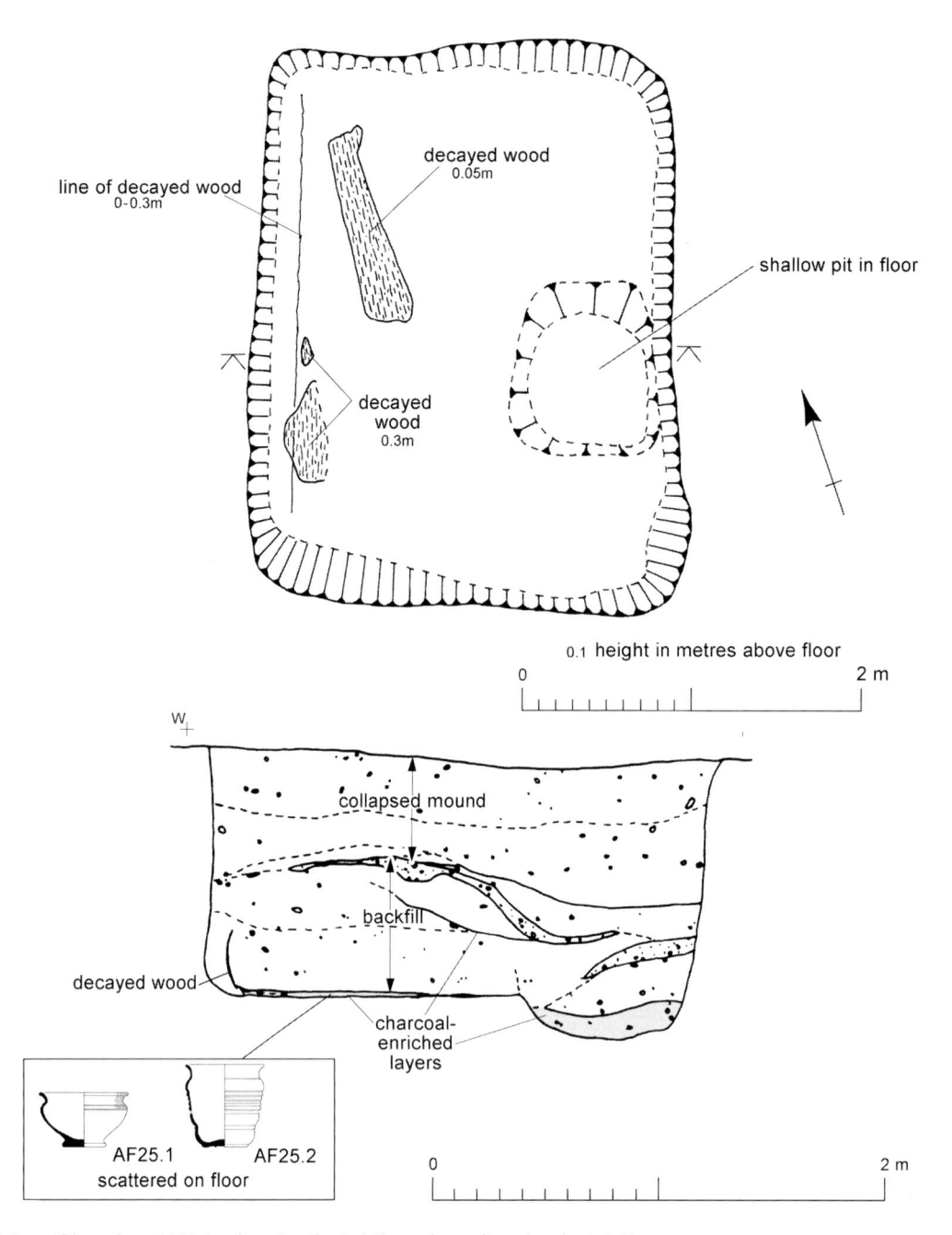

FIG. 39.   Chamber AF25: plan (scale 1:40) and section (scale 1:30)

AF25.3). The cremated human bone was concentrated in the central part of the floor with a bias towards the northern half of it (7.5 g). The pig molar also came from this area as did the copper-alloy fragment. A small quantity of cremated human bone (2.5 g) lay on the south-east corner of the floor. The pottery sherds were mainly around the centre of the northern part of the floor and covered a slightly wider area than the bone. The pots appear to have been deliberately broken prior to deposition. About 40% of one of the vessels (AF25.1) and 30% of the other (AF25.2) had been placed in the chamber; the latter may have been burnt. The corroded copper-alloy object (AF25.3) may perhaps be a solidified droplet of a metal object that had melted on the pyre, but it could simply be a fragment of something larger.

A shallow pit in the eastern part of the floor contained a darker deposit which was devoid of finds and was sealed by part of the presumed collapsed mound. The feature is hard to explain. However, the mound material directly above it showed some localised settlement as if the pit had originally contained something made of organic material which has decayed without trace. The contouring of the floor in this way is reminiscent of the treatment of the Doctor's burial (p. 202).

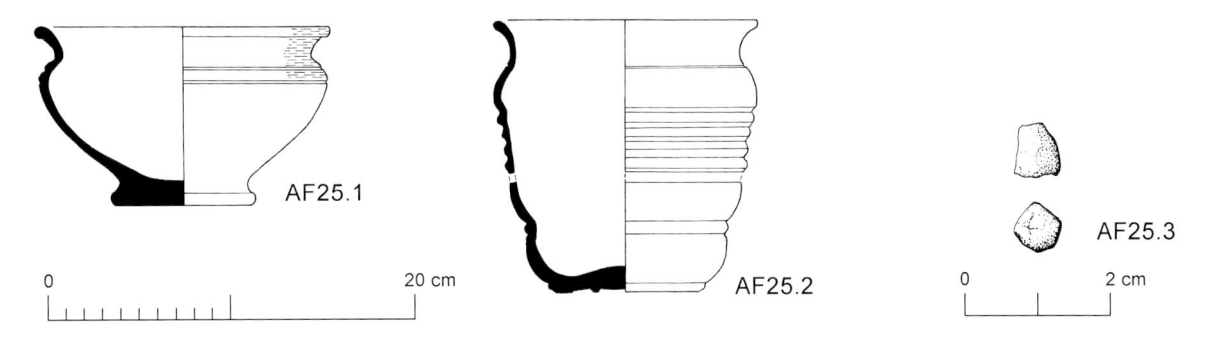

FIG. 40. Chamber AF25: pottery vessels (scale 1:4) and find of copper alloy (scale 1:1)

The base of the mound appeared to have been made up of at least two distinct deposits. The lower part consisted of a mixed brown sandy clay loam, 0.6 m thick, with occasional lenses of darker charcoal-enriched fill and of reddish-yellow sand and gravel. One of the sand lenses in this material contained a small quantity (1.7 g) of cremated human bone. Elsewhere there were tooth fragments of a large mammal (A512) apparently burnt, some ?human ?unburnt bone (p. 378), some residual sherds of pottery (largely from one vessel), and fragments of burnt daub, all of Middle Iron Age date. The upper part of the mound pit was a clean pale brown sandy silt loam 0.5–0.6 m thick. It contained similar residual material, namely a few small fragments of burnt bone (<0.1 g; A509), a large quantity of abraded Middle Iron Age sherds, a fragment of loomweight (SF27), some fragments of burnt daub and two flint flakes (SF25, SF30). With the probable exception of the bone, there was nothing in the mound which was of Late Iron Age date.

Although there were several thin lenses of sand in the lower part of the collapsed mound, clearly very little of the sand and gravel extracted during the digging of AF25 had found its way back into the pit. Instead the mound appeared to consist of soil and subsoil scraped up nearby or from the vicinity of the pyre, thereby incorporating some residual Middle Iron Age material.

The chamber was the earliest of the four at Stanway. The two broken pots on the floor of the chamber are typical Late Iron Age vessels, made any time within the range 75 B.C.–A.D. 65 but most probably deposited about the mid-1st century B.C. The absence of any Gallo-Belgic ware in the assemblage is in accordance with such a date.

Pottery vessels (FIG. 40)

AF25.1. Base: A452; rim: A468, A528; sherds: A452, A457, A468.
Cordoned pedestal bowl, wheel-thrown. Fabric GTW. Glossy burnished finish on the rim and cordon; burnished finish over the lower body; underside of base rilled.
Condition: in sherds, but restorable to complete circuit.

AF25.2. Base: A528; rims: A452, A468, A528; body: A452, A457, A468, A528.
Corrugated constricted mug, wheel-thrown. Fabric GTW; grey core, with black inclusions; unevenly oxidised surfaces, buff interior, exterior red shading to yellow ochre and brown. Abraded surfaces; unfinished interior, exterior has traces of a burnished finish.
Condition: in sherds, less than a complete pot; a complete base disc and about half of the rim circuit can be restored, but there are no joins between the base and the upper body and rim.
Condition at deposition: possibly burnt and discoloured by being near the pyre.

Other finds (FIG. 40)

AF25.3. SF35. A527, AF25. Copper-alloy ?terminal or droplet, circular in section, tapering slightly. Height 7 mm, maximum diameter 6 mm.

Residual Middle Iron Age sherds

In fill/mound (nos not listed), 194 sherds (757 g); on or near the floor of the chamber (nos not listed), 101 sherds (458 g).

CHAMBER BF6 (FIGS 2, 8, 41–55, 145–7, 170; TABLES 29–30)

Cremated bone	45.0 g	adult, sex unknown
Pottery vessels	BF6.1	samian carinated cup: Ritterling form 5
	BF6.2	samian carinated cup: Ritterling form 5
	BF6.3	samian platter: Dragendorff form 17
	BF6.4	samian platter: Ritterling form 1
	BF6.5	samian platter: Loeschcke form 1a
	BF6.6	TR1(C) moulded platter
	BF6.7	TR1(C) moulded platter
	BF6.8	TR1(C) moulded platter
	BF6.9	TR1(C) moulded platter
	BF6.10	TR1(C) moulded platter
	BF6.11	TR1(C) moulded platter
	BF6.12	TR1(C) moulded platter
	BF6.13	TN moulded platter
	BF6.14	TN moulded platter
	BF6.15	TN moulded platter
	BF6.16	TN moulded platter
	BF6.17	TN moulded platter
	BF6.18	TN moulded platter
	BF6.19	TN moulded platter
	BF6.20	TR1(C) carinated cup
	BF6.21	TR1(C) carinated cup
	BF6.22	Dressel 2-4 amphora
	BF6.23	Dressel 2-4 amphora
Other finds	BF6.24	bronze pedestal
	BF6.25	bronze vessel spout
	BF6.26	fragments of wooden game board with copper-alloy binding
	BF6.30	iron strap-slide
	BF6.31	copper-alloy strip fragments
	BF6.34	bone strip fragments plus three heat-affected copper-alloy fragments (may also be residual)
Animal bone		burnt horse teeth fragments (in mound)
Residual finds	BF6.27	copper-alloy harness fitting
	BF6.28	copper-alloy strap-plate
	BF6.29	copper-alloy strap-plate
	BF6.32	copper-alloy cylinder
	BF6.33	copper-alloy rod or shaft
	BF6.a–d	1 sherd from the backfill and 4 from the mound. All grog-tempered ware and similar to the pottery in the enclosure ditches. Also burnt daub in the mound plus 179 heat-affected copper-alloy fragments

The chamber BF6 was close to the centre of Enclosure 3 (FIGS 2, 8). Its remains were first noted on the surface during machining as a sub-rectangular patch of light brownish sandy silt loam. The patch measured 5.5 m × 5.0 m and was outlined by a ring of thin dark charcoal-rich soil. On excavation, the patch proved to be the base of a mound which had subsided into a large rectangular flat-bottomed pit aligned north–south, and the ring the edge of a sunken charcoal-rich layer (FIGS 41, 45–6, 53) which was contiguous with the remains of the chamber roof. The pit was 1.1–1.2 m deep and the sides defined a floor area of 4.2–4.3 m (north–south) by 3.4–3.6 m (east–west). The lower parts of the sides of the pit were vertical to a height of 0.4–0.7 m above the floor, above which level they splayed outwards in an inconsistent and irregular manner probably as a result of slumping and collapse (FIGS 42–4). A barrel had been set in a pit (FIGS 43–5, BF17) immediately adjacent to BF6, on the opposite side to the pyre-site BF1/BF16. The relationship of this feature to BF6 is discussed on pp. 157–8.

FIG. 41. Chamber BF6, half-section, viewed from the south

FIG. 42. Chamber BF6, fully excavated, viewed from the south

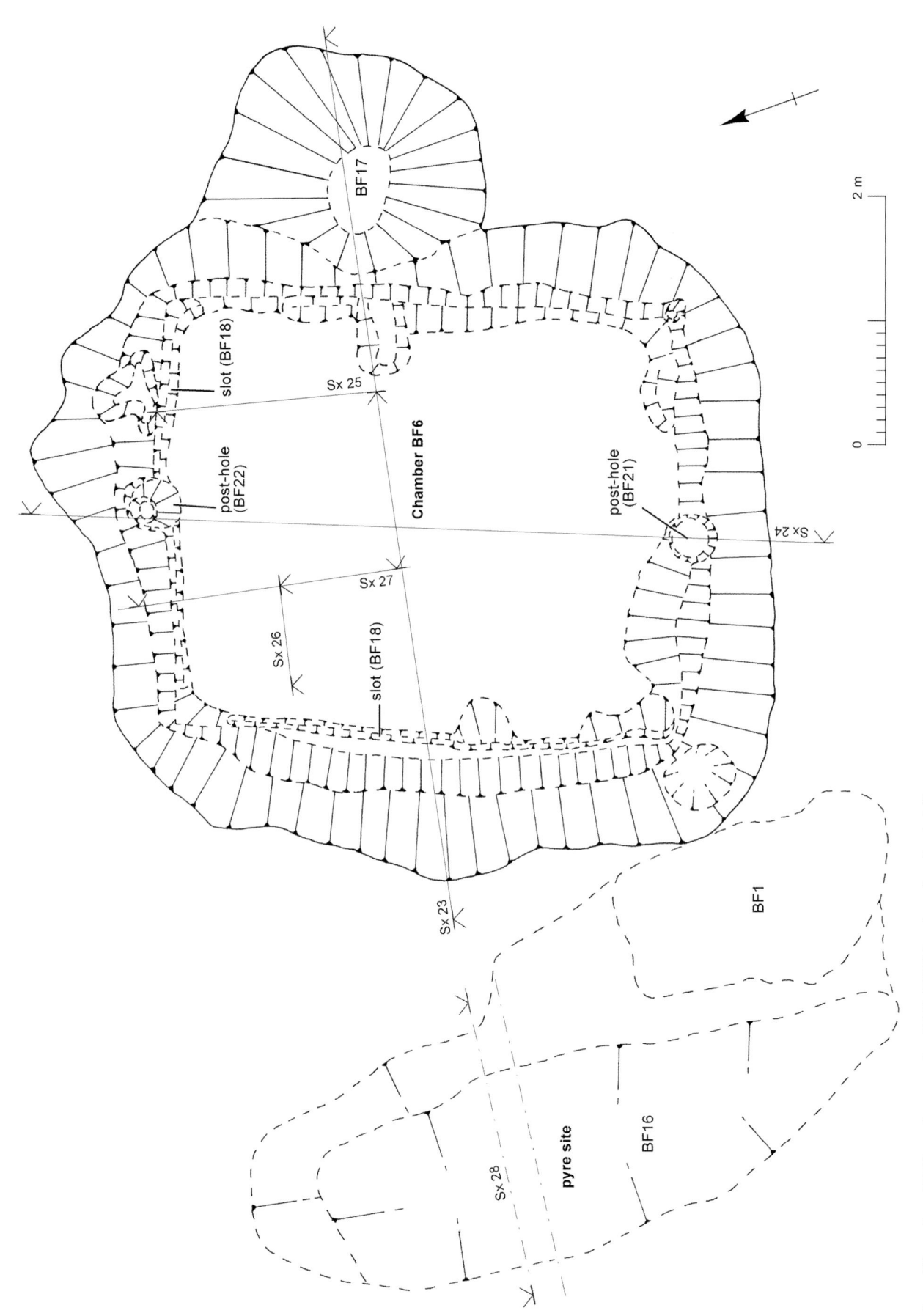

FIG. 43. Chamber BF6 and pyre site BF1/BF16: plan (scale 1:44)

THE FUNERARY SITE

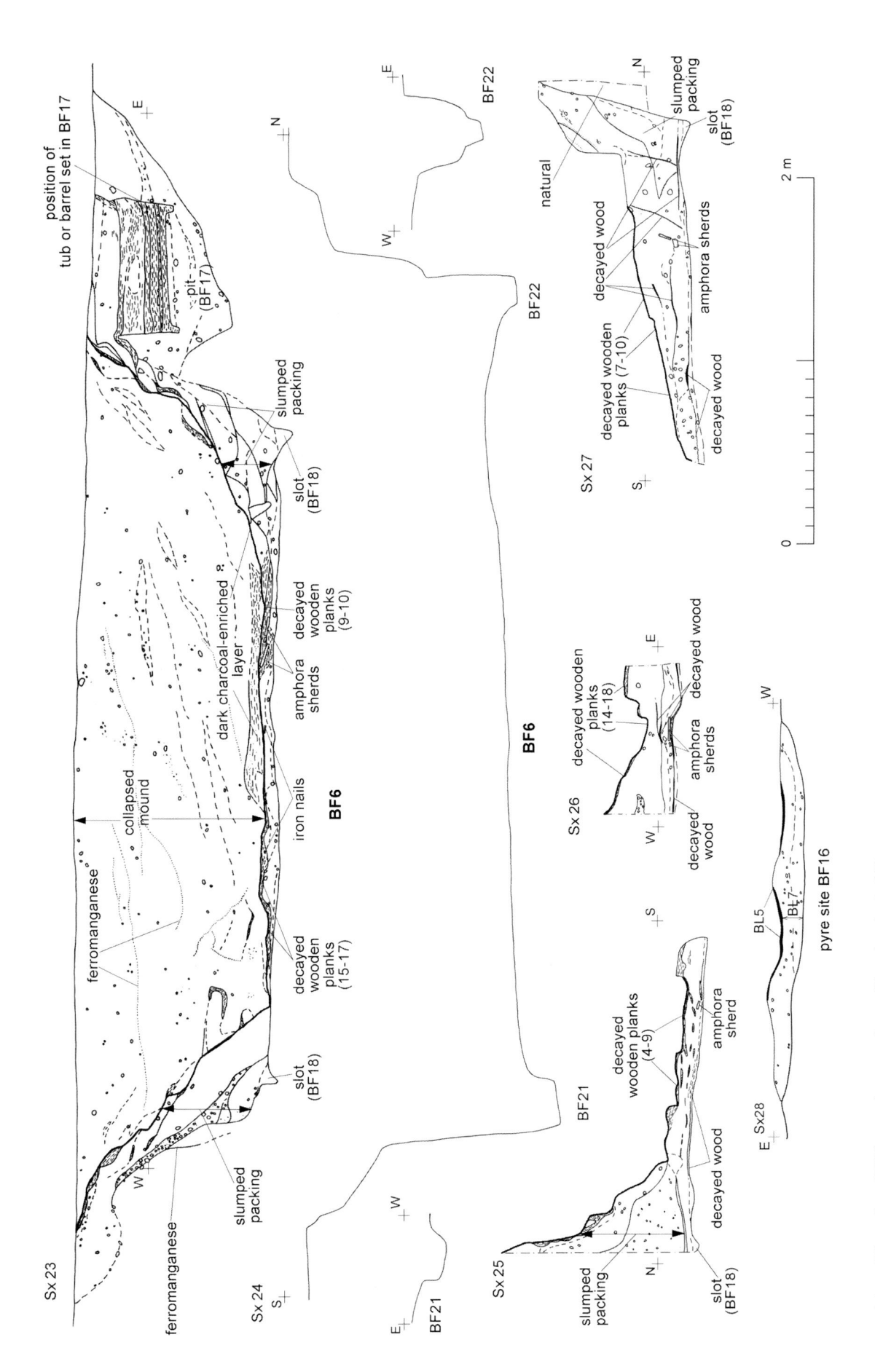

FIG. 44. Chamber BF6: sections and profiles (scale 1:30)

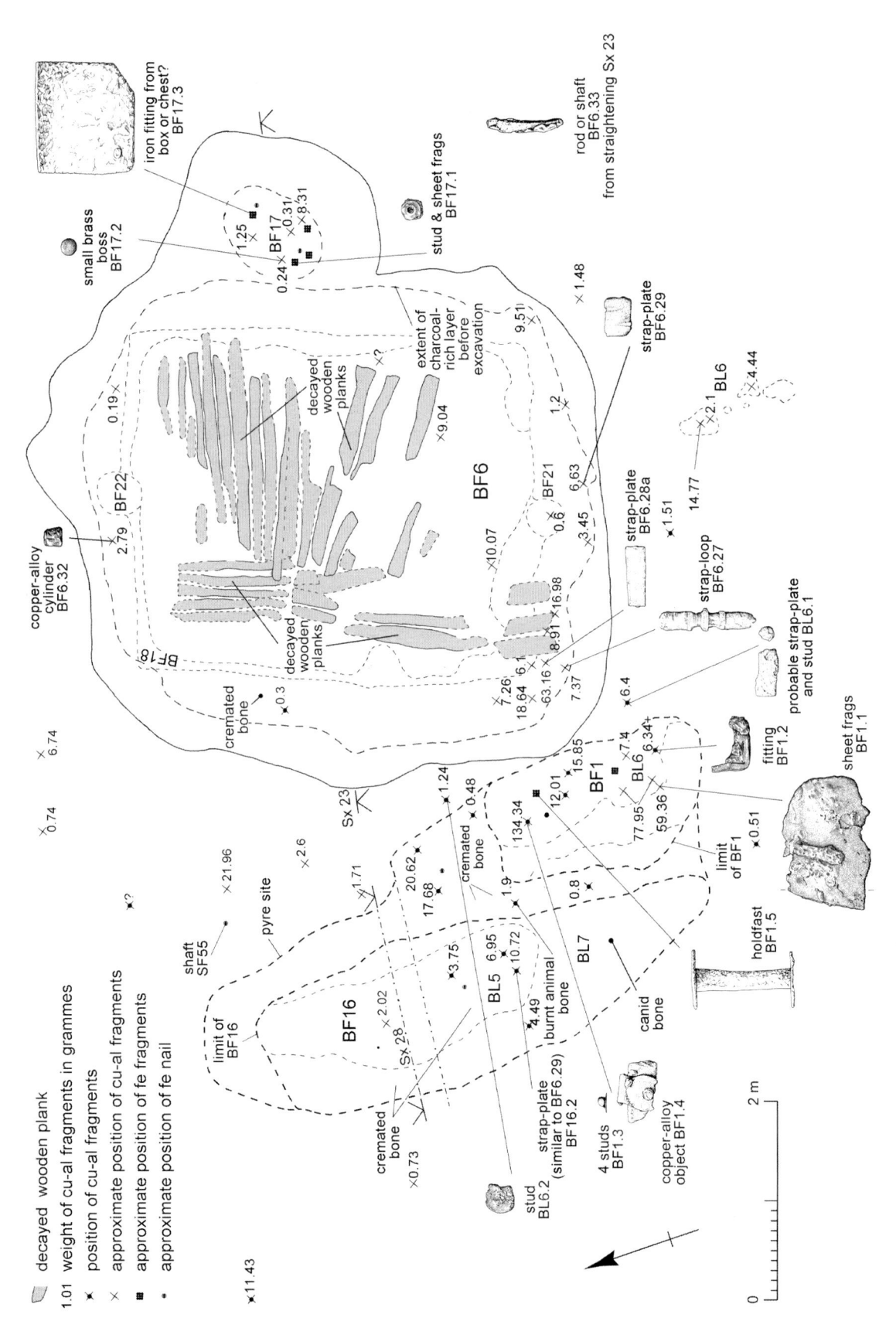

FIG. 45. Chamber BF6 and pyre site BF1/BF16: plan showing location of small finds and decayed wooden planks (scale 1:59)

A slot (BF18) around the perimeter of the floor of BF6 was 0.1–0.15 m wide and up to 0.15 m deep (FIGS 43–4). It was well defined in the northern half of the pit, although elsewhere the edges were less marked, especially along the south side. The slot indicates that the chamber would have had a floor measuring approximately 4.1 × 3.4 m, although it did not contain any decayed remains of the chamber walls as did the slots in chambers BF24 and CF42. The slot was not flush with the sides of the pit, thus pointing to the former presence of a gap all the way down between the walls of the chamber and the sides of the pit. However, it was not straight enough to be compatible with walls made of horizontal planks, especially on the north side of the pit where there was a distinct kink in it at the centre. The use of vertical rather than horizontal planks for the walls of the chamber is also indicated by the presence in the slot (notably along the northern side) of slight depressions about 0.2 m in width. These seem likely to represent the positions of the lower ends of vertical planks as in chambers BF24 and CF42. They were too faint to plan adequately. Some of the planks were also represented by very thin patches of decayed wood, *i.e.* an irregular horizontal strip 0.15 m above the floor in the collapsed packing at the eastern side of the chamber, and two vertical patches, one in the south-east corner and the other near the north side, extending to heights above the floor of 0.42 m and 0.3 m respectively (FIG. 44).

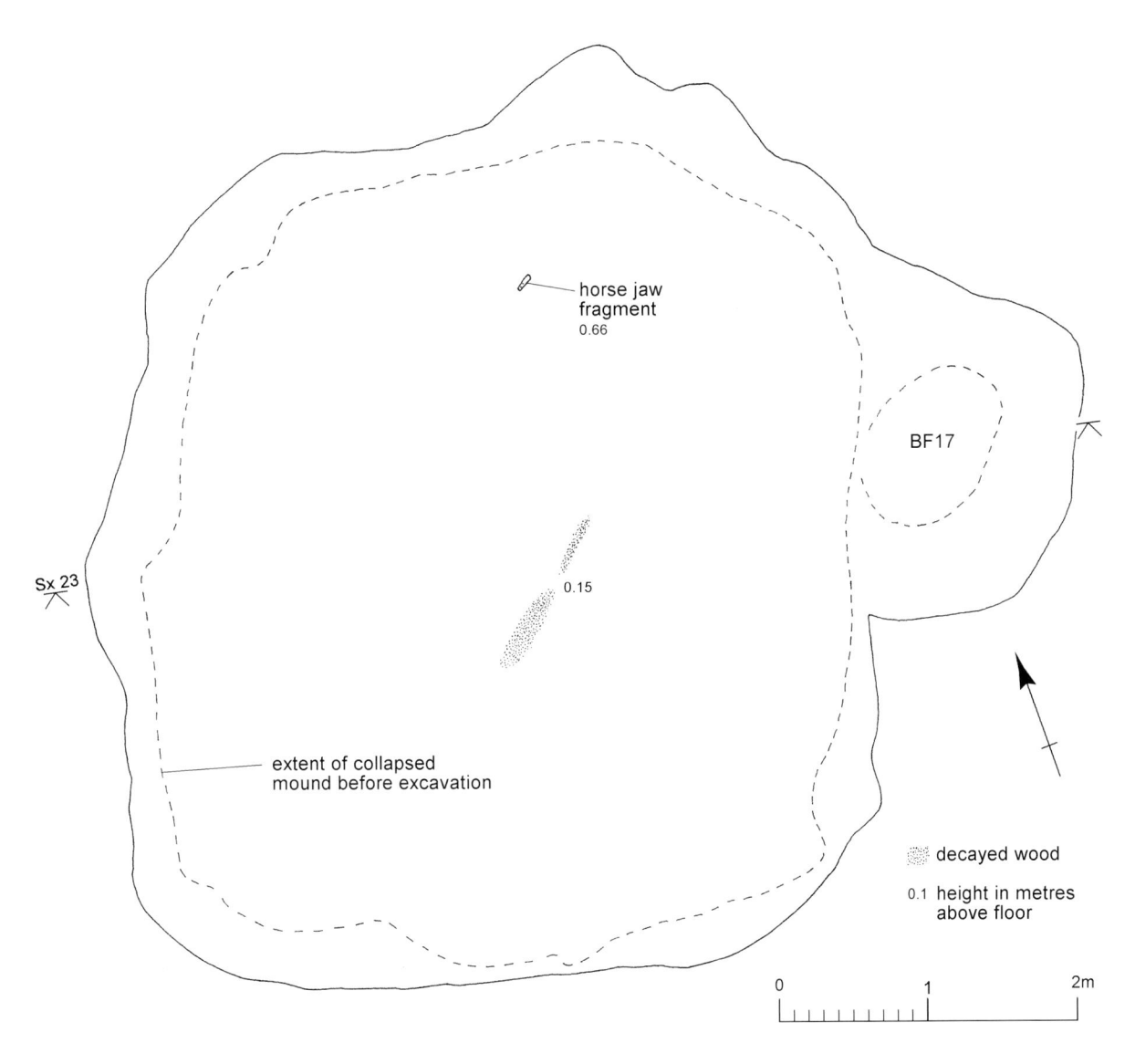

FIG. 46. Chamber BF6: plan showing extent of collapsed mound and location of finds in mound material (scale 1:44)

Two post-holes (BF21 and BF22) were recessed into the sides of the pit, one in the middle of each of the two shorter sides (FIG. 43). Both survived largely as a semi-circular hardening of the sandy subsoil, the edges highlighted by a coating of a thin dark ferromanganiferous deposit. The post-hole (BF21) on the south side was 0.30–0.35 m wide with a flat base some 0.2 m below the level of the pit floor. Its backfill was loose with no void. The well-defined recess survived to a height above the floor of approximately 1.0 m. The post-hole did not contain any iron nails or traces of decayed wood, although there was a small lump of heat-affected copper alloy (SF151) in the backfill which probably derived from the adjacent pyre-site BF1. The post-hole (BF22) on the north side was 0.4 m wide, and had a flat base 0.2 m below the level of the pit floor. Within it there was a small circular flat-bottomed depression, 0.18 m wide and 0.07 m deep. The semi-circular recessed edge survived to a height above the floor of 0.5 m. The lower part of the post-hole was a void, and there were traces of decayed wood in the bottom of the small depression.

The large size of the post-holes and the presence of the smaller depression within BF22 suggest that they were intended as post-pits for narrower posts. Their positions indicate that the posts were probably set behind the sides of the chamber so as not to be visible from inside it. A horizontal timber between the tops of the post presumably supported the planks which formed the chamber roof. Like the other chambers, there was no definite evidence for an entrance.

Several features, probably natural, were excavated in the sides of the pit, including a narrow post-hole-like feature 0.8 m deep in the south-east corner of BF6, and irregular pit-like features in the east side at the junction of BF6 and pit BF17 and in the north side east of BF22. These were all filled with loose fine sand.

In places on the sides of the slot BF18, there was a purplish-black coating about 1 mm thick of a naturally occurring ferromanganiferous deposit, also observed on the surface of the sand and gravel forming the lower sides of the pit and also much higher up in the fill of the chamber (FIG. 44). In some places, the deposit created two or more vertical lenses separated by thin layers of sand. The surface of the sides was also hardened probably due to iron induration. The deposit could not be confused with the effects of heat, because the small stones and gravels coated by it did not show any signs of heat-shattering, and there were only slight traces of charcoal flecks on the sides of the pit.

There appeared to be a very thin, dark lens in places on the floor, sealing the natural sand and gravel. This may have been the result of people walking or standing on the floor when the chamber was in use. Organic remains survived in mineral-replaced form in association with copper-alloy objects on the floor (*see* BF6.24 and BF6.25 on p. 126 and FIG. 47). This perhaps indicates that the floor had been strewn with hay or grass, as has also been suggested at the Lexden Tumulus and Folly Lane (Foster 1986, 144; Niblett 1999, 396). There were also traces of decayed wood on the floor which, because of their seemingly haphazard arrangement and stratigraphic relationships with later fills, are likely to have derived from furniture or other wooden items rather than planks from the walls or roof of the chamber (FIG. 47).

Various objects lay on the floor as if they had been thrown on to it before the first of the dumped material was deposited in the chamber (FIG. 47). Over the northern half of the floor these included an iron strap-slide (BF6.30) probably from harness, some fragments of a narrow ?bone strip (BF6.34), some copper-alloy fragments, probably heat-affected (BF6.31), and several iron nail fragments. Near the centre of the floor was a copper-alloy pedestal (BF6.24) and nearby part of the spout from a copper-alloy bowl (BF6.25). The pedestal was upright, as if it had been carefully placed on the floor in a standing position. However, this may have been accidental.

A substantial deposit of pale greyish-brown material had been dumped in the chamber so as to cover the northern half of the floor and the organic material on it. This deposit was up to 0.45 m thick at the north end, thinning out to almost nothing towards the middle of the chamber (FIG. 44, Sxs 25 and 27). The deposit had been placed in the chamber from the northern end of it, perhaps after part of the roof had been temporarily removed. It contained

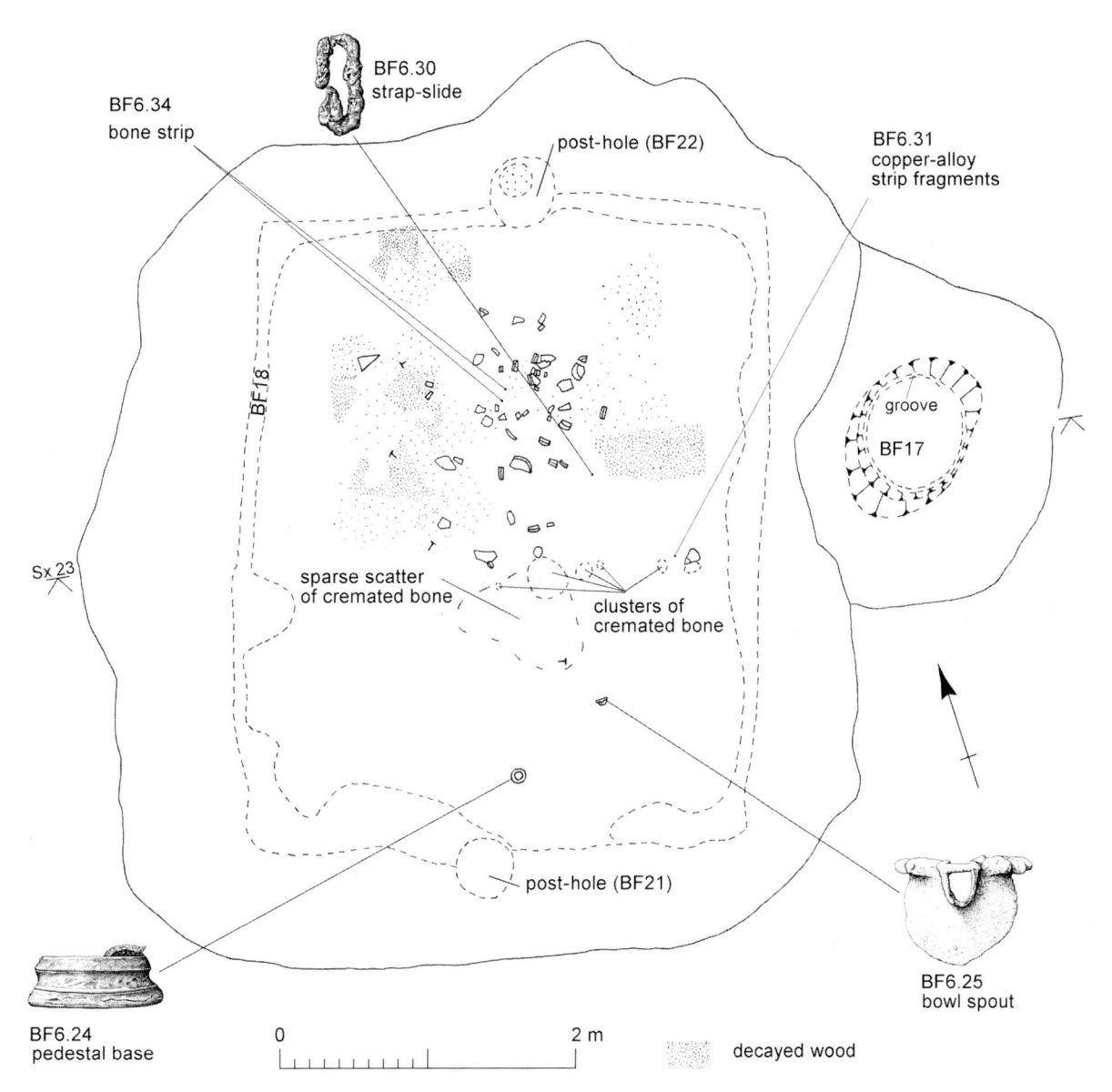

FIG. 47. Chamber BF6: plan showing location of cremated bone, decayed wood, and small finds on the chamber floor (scale 1:45)

fragments of cremated human bone, pottery sherds and parts of objects which appear to have been deliberately broken and placed in the chamber as it was being partly backfilled.

Twenty-three vessels (*i.e.* four cups, seventeen platters and two amphoras, FIG. 54, BF6.1–23) have been identified from the sherds in the dumped material in the chamber and the underlying thin charcoal-rich layer on the chamber floor. All of them seem to have been broken elsewhere, with only some sherds recovered for deposition in the chamber. There was further fragmentation *in situ* and so their condition was poor. Most of the sherds were scattered fairly evenly over the northern half of the chamber and a few were lightly burnt. They occurred at different levels throughout the dumped layer, most being concentrated in the lowest 0.1 m (FIGS 48–51). The assemblage included many large sherds from two amphoras (FIG. 54, BF6.22–3) as well as parts of vessels represented on the floor and two others found only in the dumped material. The sherds on the floor appeared to be more fragmented than in the overlying dumped material, and included proportionally fewer amphora sherds. At least four pots (FIG. 54, BF6.13, BF6.16, BF6.18 and BF6.19) had been scorched, presumably in the pyre.

All the vessels are imports and specialised functional types represented by complete examples in other funerary groups in the cemetery. Five were South Gaulish samian (FIG. 54, BF6.1–5),

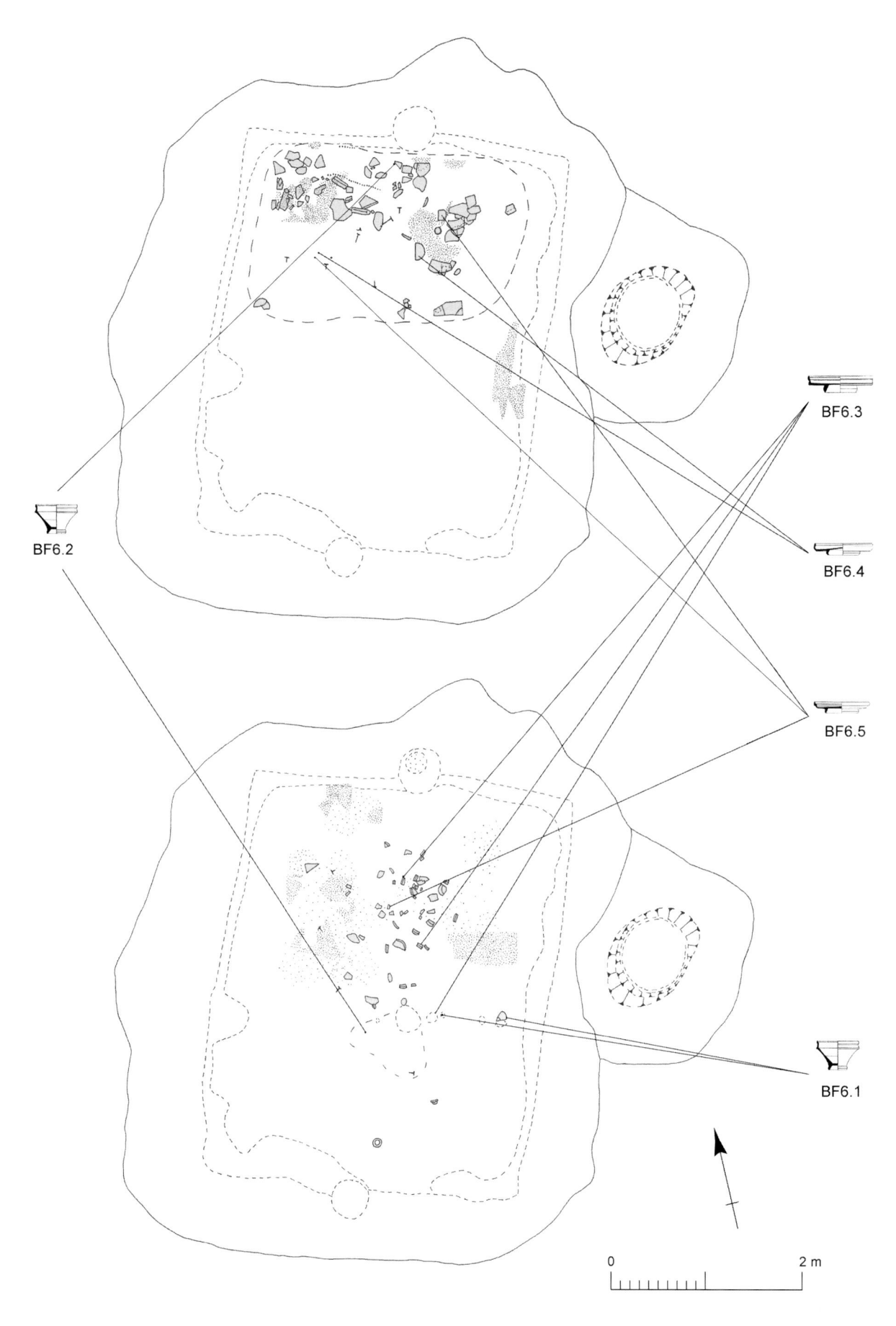

FIG. 48. Chamber BF6: plan showing location of sherds from pottery vessels BF6.1–5 (scale 1:55). Most of the lines point to groups of sherds rather than individual ones. Some small sherds are not plotted

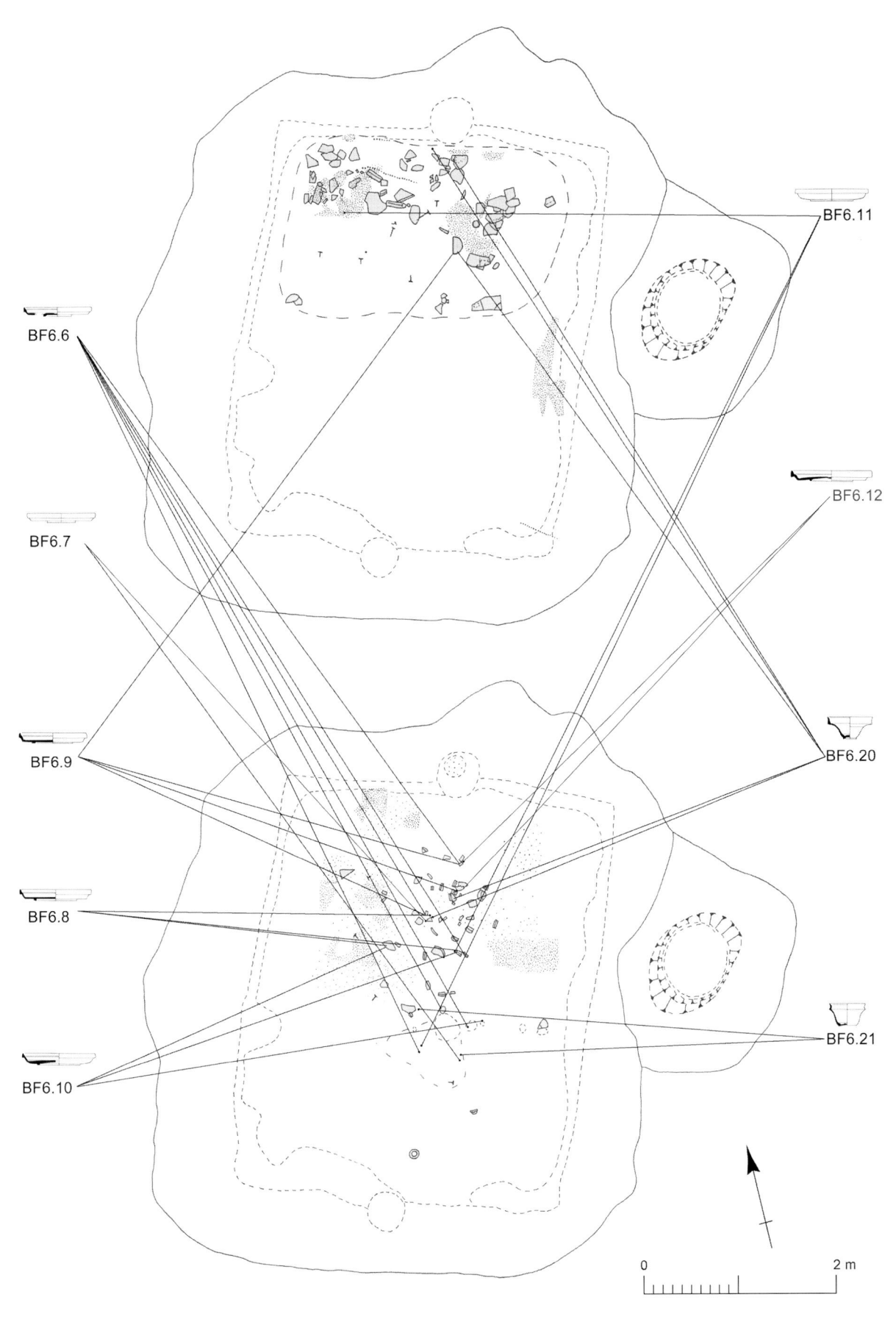

FIG. 49. Chamber BF6: plan showing location of sherds from pottery vessels BF6.6–12 and BF6.20–21 (scale 1:55). Most of the lines point to groups of sherds rather than individual ones. Some small sherds are not plotted

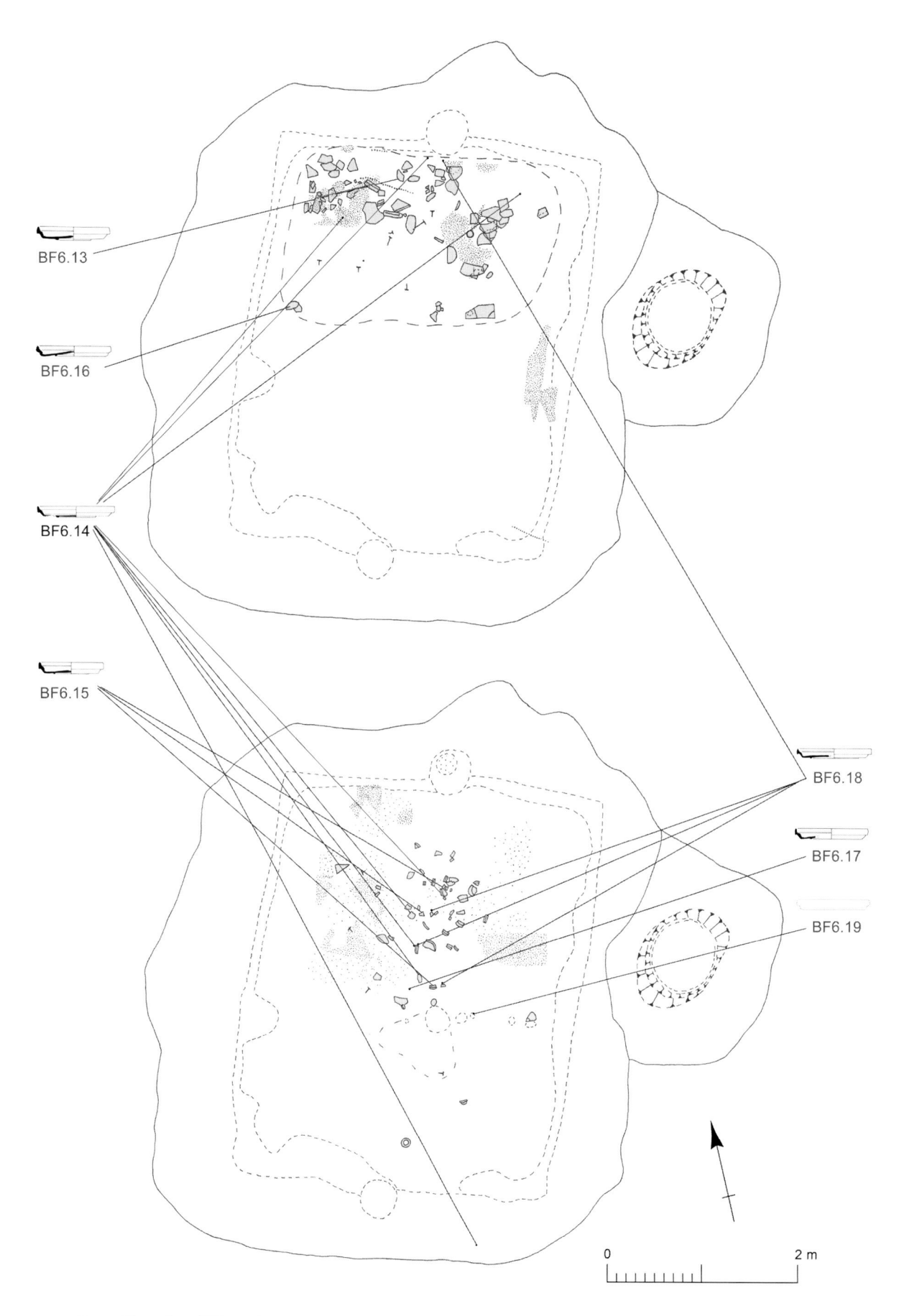

FIG. 50. Chamber BF6: plan showing location of sherds from pottery vessels BF6.13–19 (scale 1:55). Most of the lines point to groups of sherds rather than individual ones. Some small sherds are not plotted

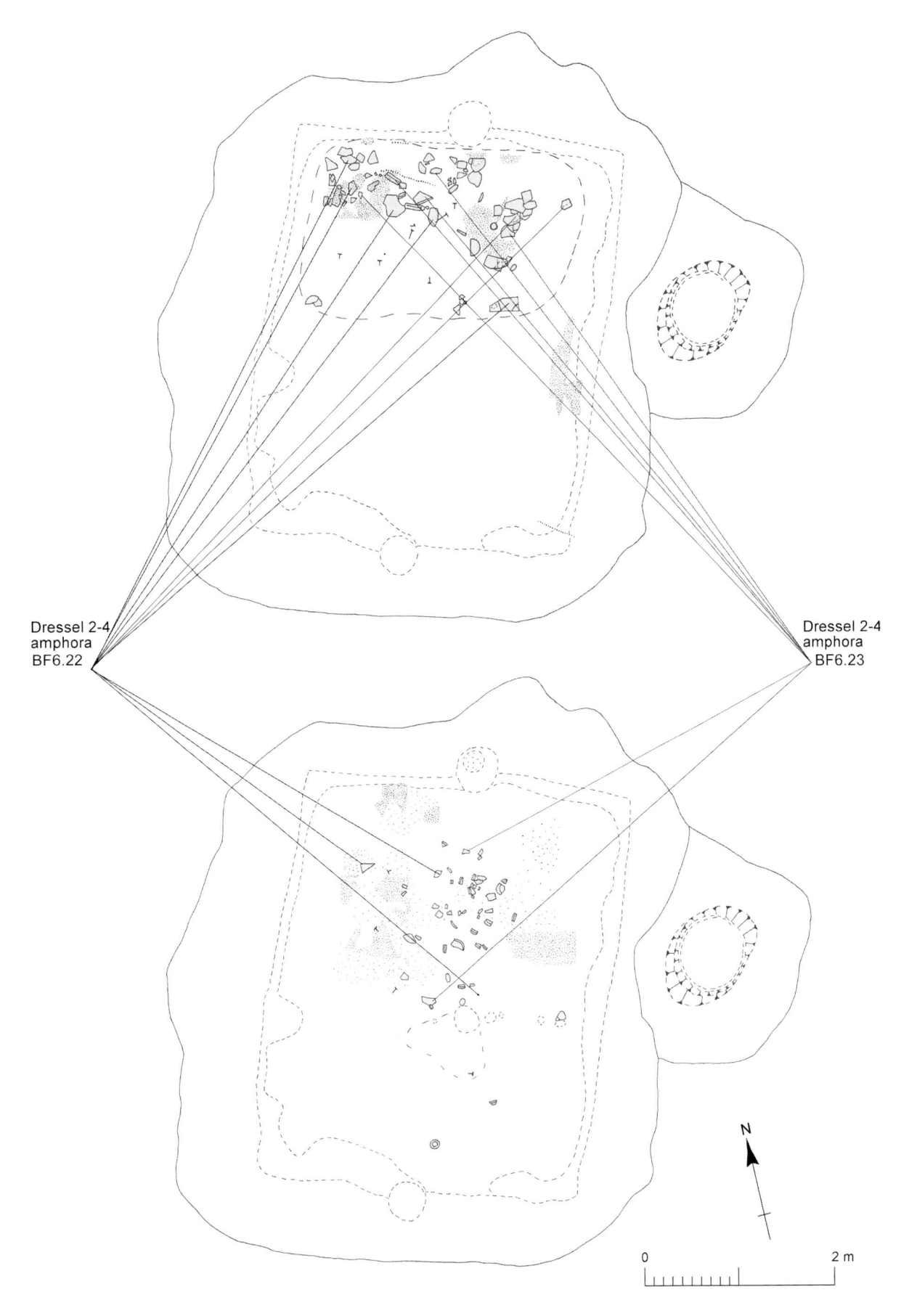

FIG. 51. Chamber BF6: plan showing location of sherds from amphoras BF6.22–3 (scale 1:55). Most of the lines point to groups of sherds rather than individual ones. Some small sherds are not plotted

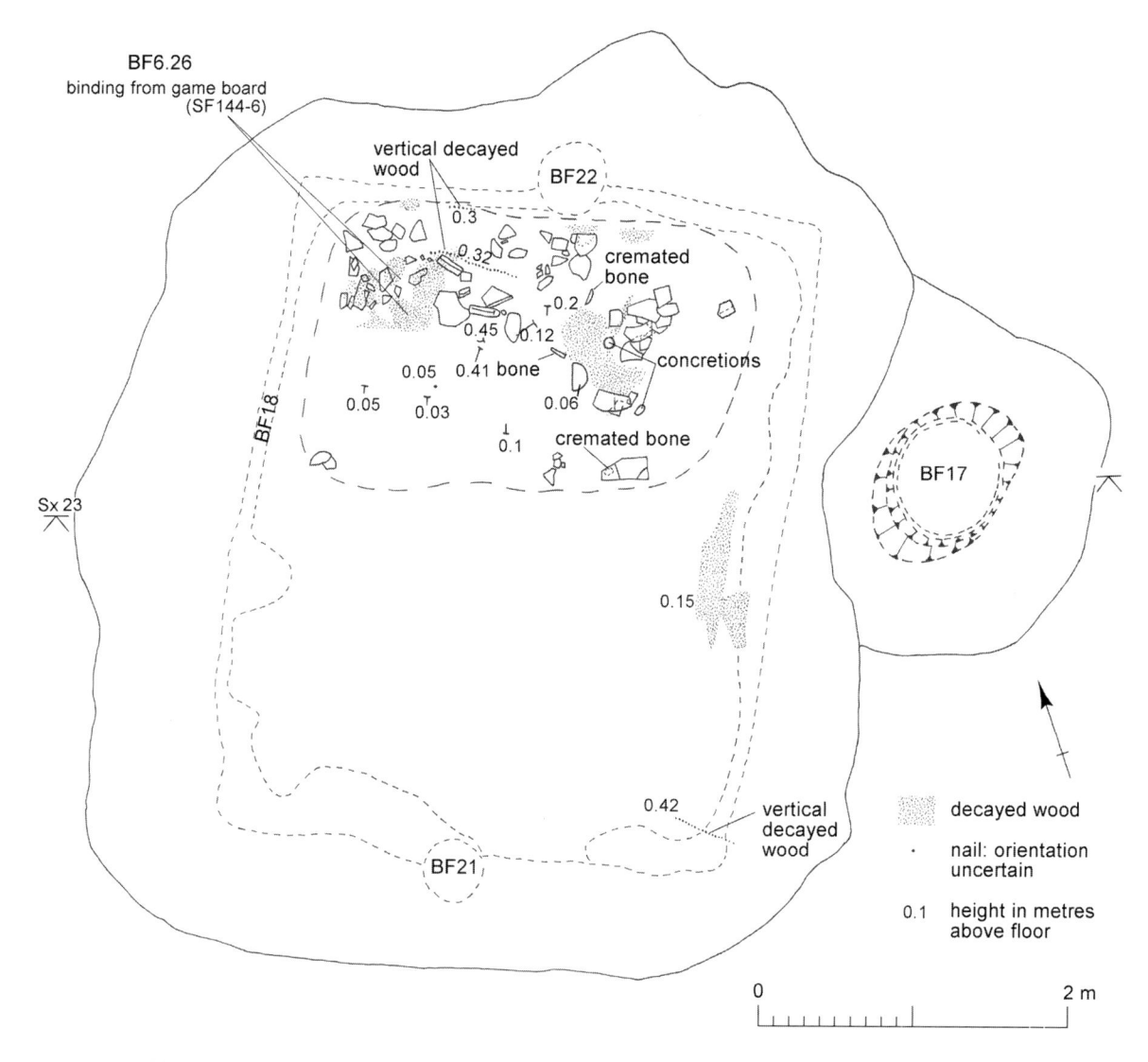

FIG. 52. Chamber BF6: plan showing location of cremated bone, decayed wood, and small finds from above the chamber floor (scale 1:45)

and sixteen Gallo-Belgic (FIG. 54, BF6.6–21). At least half were manufactured before A.D. 40, and none need have been made after that date. Therefore all could have been imported and deposited between A.D. 35–43, and by A.D. 50 at the latest. A potter's pattern mark on one of the vessels (BF6.2; pp. 294–5 and FIG. 145, Stamp 23) is paralleled in the Warrior's burial (BF64.6; pp. 294–5, Stamp 24) and can be used to support a slightly later date range of c. A.D. 40–50/5 for the chamber (p. 439). There are cursive graffiti on four vessels and patterns or scratches on three others (pp. 307–14 and FIGS 146–7).

The cremated bone lay towards the centre of the floor of the chamber (FIGS 47, 52) mainly in several small clusters (24.3 g; B92 and B157) with a scatter immediately to the south (10 g; B68, B162 and ?B208). Almost half of the largest cluster consisted of fragments of skull. Small clusters of cremated bone rested on some amphora sherds just above floor level (7.9 g; B196). Others (2.1 g; B153) were further north, 0.15 m above the floor in the dumped material. The bone belonged to an adult of indeterminate gender.

Other finds from the dumped material included fragments of copper-alloy binding and decayed wood from a game board (FIG. 52, BF6.26). These were 0.05–0.10 m above the floor immediately under some amphora sherds which, in turn, were sealed by fragments of decayed wood. Further east and still in the dumped material was a badly decayed piece of ?unburnt ?animal bone 0.25 m above the floor (FIG. 52; B128; not preserved) and eight fragments of iron nails.

There were several other pieces of decayed wood in the dumped material. Two fragments near the northern edge of it extended vertically to a height of 0.30–0.32 m above the floor (FIG. 53). The most northerly fragment was so close to the side of the chamber that it is likely to have been part of the wall. The other piece was well stratified in the dump layer and is thus likely to have been part of a wooden object such as the gaming board or a piece of furniture which had been broken up and thrown into the chamber.

The clusters of sherds and cremated bone are very significant since they indicate that the sherds and bone fragments were not already mixed with the dumped material, but were thrown into the chamber as the dumped material was being placed in it. Some of the burnt sherds from the chamber join unburnt ones, suggesting that at least some of the vessels must have been broken either before the pyre was lit or when it was burning.

Around the edges of the pit was a mixed series of layers including bands of gravelly sand and pale greyish-brown clayey deposits up to 0.4 m thick. These deposits sloped from the upper edges of the pit down to the floor, where they extended in from the sides for a distance of approximately 1.0 m. They appeared to seal the slot BF18 and the dumped material on the floor. The deposits were probably originally packing material between the sides of the pit and the wooden chamber, or simply the collapsed upper edges of the chamber pit. They would have slumped and slid forward gradually in a piecemeal fashion as the chamber decayed and collapsed.

The slumped deposits were largely devoid of finds except in the south-west corner where there were many copper-alloy fragments, the majority visibly heat-affected (FIG. 45). Identifiable objects in the slumped material include a belt-plate (BF6.29), a strap-loop (BF6.27) probably from a Roman cavalry strap-fastener, a strap-plate (BF6.28), and a short copper-alloy cylinder (BF6.32). Most of the fragments were close to the surface at or near the interface with the overlying thin dark charcoal-rich layer, although some were well within the collapsed ?packing. These finds are almost certainly residual, and belonged to the earlier adjacent pyre-site (BF1/BF16; pp. 85–90). The latter was cut through when the pit for the chamber was dug, so that some of the objects in it such as the heat-affected copper-alloy fragments ended up in the material used to fill the gap between the chamber walls and the edges of the chamber pit. The charcoal-rich layer contained a small fragment of cremated human bone (0.7 g; B103). This must similarly have derived from the adjacent pyre-site since it was near the western edge of the chamber pit.

Traces of the chamber's roof timbers were detected in a thin charcoal-rich layer 10–30 mm thick between the base of the mound and the top of the dumped material on the floor of the chamber and the slumped material along its sides. The layer was dish-shaped on account of the way the mound had collapsed into the partly empty chamber and, as a result, varied between 0.5 m and 0.05 m in height above the chamber floor (FIG. 44, Sxs 23, 25–27). The decayed planks where identifiable had a soft reddish-brown texture. The wood only appeared to have survived in a mineral-replaced form (sample B129; p. 384).

In all, sixteen east–west planks (nos 1–16) and eight north–south ones (nos 17–24) could be distinguished (FIG. 53). The most clearly defined planks were over the northern half of the pit, whereas the identification of the southernmost planks (nos 13–16) is somewhat subjective. The east–west planks extended over the eastern and central parts of the pit and were up to 2 m long and 0.2 m wide. The northernmost examples (nos 1–3) were not so well preserved as the others, and the most southerly of these (nos 10–16) appeared to have slipped slightly out of alignment. There was no convincing evidence for planks in the south-east corner of the chamber pit.

The eight north–south planks (nos 17–24) extended along the western side of the pit. These were less well defined than the others, but appeared to consist of two groups. The five northernmost planks (nos 17–21) were at least 1.75 m long and, being up to 0.15 m wide, appeared to have been narrower than the east–west ones. Towards the southern end of these planks, there was a change in slope of the underlying deposit which caused them to appear discontinuous. The southern end of plank no. 20 was especially difficult to make out because of undulations in the underlying dumped material.

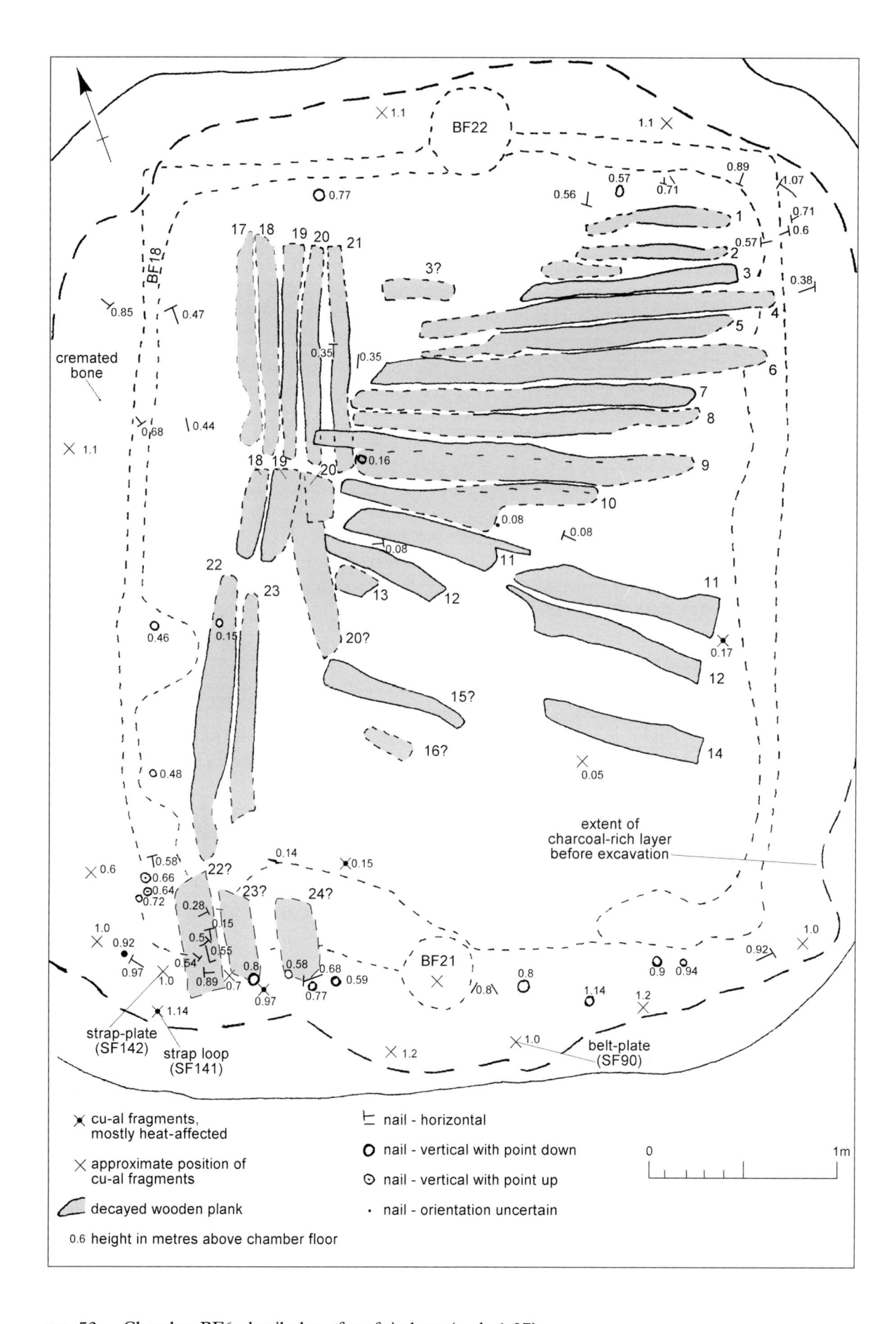

FIG. 53. Chamber BF6: detail plan of roof timbers (scale 1:27)

Further south were parts of three more north–south planks (nos 22–24). These were up to 2.2 m long and 0.2 m wide including three short poorly preserved fragments in the steeply sloping south-west corner of the pit. There were various patches of charcoal-rich areas and possible plank remains on the sloping sides of the pit, especially along the southern and western sides, but these seemed to be illusory and simply the effects of slumping.

In general the planks did not overlap each other, apart from plank no. 9 which clearly sealed north–south plank nos 20 and 21.

Over 50 iron nail fragments of different sizes (TABLE 30) were recovered from the plank remains and the charcoal-rich layer associated with them. The absence of nails well down the sides suggests that their use was confined to the upper part of the chamber. Many came from near the edges of the chamber pit where they formed lines along the western and southern sides and small clusters in the north-east and south-west corners. Several were also found at the junction of the east–west and north–south planks. While the evidence is not as clear-cut as in CF42, it seems likely that the nails at or close to the edges of the chamber pit were used to join the vertical planks forming the sides of the chamber to horizontal wooden battens. The battens were probably placed behind the upper ends of the planks to help support the roof timbers.

As in CF42, most of the nails are likely to have been lost due to later ploughing and truncation. Those that did survive did so presumably because the wood to which they were attached had slid down far enough into the chamber to escape the later processes which led to the loss of the others.

The orderly arrangement of planks was probably derived from the flat roof of the mortuary chamber which had collapsed and come to rest on the underlying dump layer. It seems as if the two sets of north–south planks laid end-to-end extended over the western third of the chamber while the east–west ones covered the eastern two-thirds (FIG. 53). The planks all appeared to be approximately 2 m long. The positions of some of the nails near the centre of the chamber suggest that the east–west planks may have been nailed over the north–south ones.

The source of the charcoal in the charcoal-rich layer is hard to explain satisfactorily if the roof timbers were not charred, as appears to have been the case. No similar layers were associated with any of the other chambers, so these are of no help in this respect. The most obvious source of the charcoal is the funeral pyre on which the body in the chamber had been burnt. The most likely site for this is BF16, a few metres to the west (pp. 85, 88). Perhaps the charcoal was spread over the chamber roof deliberately as part of the funerary rite or, far more likely, it arrived largely by virtue of the wind and trample. Another explanation is that the supposed charcoal in the layer is not charcoal at all and that the preservation of the planks was wholly due to natural processes allied to the formation of the ferromanganiferous deposits on the chamber sides.

The mound, or at least as much of it as could be seen, was made of cover loam. There was no sign in it of any structure or thin dark lines that might suggest the presence of turves, although palynological analysis of the similar mound of CF42 indicates that turves were indeed used (pp. 398–9). The mound was similar in composition to the underlying dumped material except that it did not contain any of the smashed pottery or other broken objects found in the latter. Instead finds were very sparse and included some fragments of burnt ?horse teeth (B97) 0.66 m above the chamber floor (FIG. 46), several late Iron Age or early Roman coarseware sherds (BF6.b–d), and a small fragment of burnt daub (B49) (all of which were probably residual), and faint traces of a decayed wooden object 0.15 m above the floor (FIG. 46). The teeth were probably from a single upper tooth row as if part of the cranium had been present. Within the layer were a few thin natural ferromanganiferous lenses.

The other objects in the chamber BF6 were in general badly damaged either by heat or by being deliberately broken. There is also a moderate quantity of residual material of the same type of heat-affected copper alloy as that which came from the pyre-site BF1/BF16 in the centre of Enclosure 3. Two of the objects, a spout from a copper-alloy bowl and fragments of wood and copper-alloy binding from a game board (FIG. 46, BF6.24–5), provide links to similar grave goods in CF47 and BF64 (pp. 186–90 and 217–20). There is at least one fitting, probably more, from Roman cavalry harness (FIG. 55, BF6.27–9), but in residual contexts.

The round pedestal is an imported item (FIG. 55, BF6.24). Its upper surface is quite rough from corrosion, and no scars can be seen to offer a clue as to whether a single figurine or a figure group may have been attached. At 60 mm in diameter, it is large enough to take a single standing human figure about 110 to 150 mm in height, equivalent to a Jupiter Conservator figure from Colchester (Pitts 1979, pl. 5, 3). Were an animal figure attached, it would have been smaller than the boar and bull from the Lexden Tumulus, which are 86 and 75 mm long respectively (Foster 1986, 54–9). Much grassy material, with no deliberate structure and therefore not part of a woven mat, was found beneath the pedestal, exactly paralleling that found beneath the square pedestal from the Lexden Tumulus (*ibid.*, 144). Its preservation in the latter was probably due to the copper alloy inhibiting the action of fungi and bacteria, and perhaps also to a lack of oxygen (*ibid.*, 67, 153).

The spout (FIG. 55), BF6.25 is cast, and would have been soldered on to a spun or raised sheet metal bowl about 140 to 150 mm in diameter. The bowl may have been used in conjunction with a separate strainer, or it may have been fitted with a sieve-plate, making it a strainer-bowl of similar type to that from Welwyn Garden City, and therefore allied to that from CF47 (pp. 221–4 and 323–6). It is almost certainly of continental manufacture, probably from a workshop in southern Austria or on the Danube, and belongs to the later Tiberian or early Claudian period (p. 326).

A few fragments of wood and curved copper-alloy binding (FIG. 46, BF6.26a–b) are all that remain of a game board with similar binding to that on the board in BF64 (BF64.29 g; pp. 186–90). No counters from a game were recovered from BF6.

The other objects associated with the chamber are mainly heat-affected copper-alloy fragments (FIG. 55, BF6.27–33) similar to those recovered from BF1, BF17, BL5, BL6, and BL7. Being residual, they are not directly associated with BF6. However, there is one exception. A large iron strap-slide, probably from harness (FIG. 46, BF6.30), lay on the floor of the feature and so may be a deliberate deposit rather than pyre debris in the fill. Otherwise these objects should be treated as part of the same assemblage associated with BF1 (p. 87). They include one or more cavalry harness fittings (as from BF1/BF16). One is a ?brass terminal with acorn moulding from a Roman strap-loop (FIG. 55, BF6.27). Another is a copper-alloy strap-plate (FIG. 55, BF6.28), as may be another (FIG. 55, BF6.29), also shown by analysis to be probably brass. The unillustrated pieces are listed in TABLE 29.

The chamber also produced four fragments of a narrow ?bone strip with marginal grooves (BF6.34). With so little remaining, identification can only be tentative, but it may be box veneer or inlay. This also lay on the floor of the feature.

Over hundred nails, listed in TABLE 30, were found in the chamber. Only twelve were in the dumped material or on the floor. The rest were higher up in the chamber and must have been used in its construction. All the nails are of Manning's Type 1b (1985, 134). They are incomplete unless stated otherwise in the table, although some described as complete may lack no more than 1 or 2 mm of the tip. The direction of the longitudinal grain of the wood relative to the shank is either transverse, diagonal (*i.e.* at a distinct slant), or parallel (*i.e.* the nail was hammered into end grain). Where the grain lies diagonally across the shank, the position of the head usually suggests that the nail was hammered in at an angle. The surface of several of the nails in both BF6 and the other chambers has in places the resolidified flowing appearance of tap slag, a feature also seen on some nails from pyres and cremations in the town and therefore initially considered to be evidence of scorching. However, given that some of the nails used in the construction of the chamber exhibit this characteristic, it must rather be a feature specific to the unusual burial conditions, as the first layers of surface corrosion would have developed either within the decaying wood or in the void formed by the chamber.

A range of sizes is shown by the complete nails, which fall into four groups: a) one example, 26 mm, b) two examples, 48 and 49 mm, c) three examples, 81, 84, and 86 mm, and d) three examples, 115, 116, and 124 mm. Most of the nails had at least some wood attached to the shank, and most of the wood on the shanks lies transversely, but some is diagonal and some parallel. There is little evidence as to plank thickness, but the range of nail sizes suggests that

TABLE 29: HEAT-AFFECTED COPPER ALLOY FROM BF6

Find no.	Small find no.	No. of pieces	Weight (g)	Notes
B24	81	2	3.45	one may be a loop or ring
B63	91	3	9.51	
B66	93	1	0.30	
B67	90	7	6.63	see also belt-plate/stiffener BF6.29
B93	105	2	10.07	
B152	113	3	1.04	
B158	109	15	–	
B161	107	1	9.04	
B176	135	4	1.20	
B178	122	1	7.26	includes fragment of folded sheet metal
B188	138	1	8.91	
B189	140	41	16.98	includes 5 fragments of sheet metal
B203	134	1	6.10	
B205	143	73	63.16	
B222	139	26	18.64	
B241	137	1	0.19	
B225	151	1	0.6	post-hole BF21
totals		**183**	**163.08**	

TABLE 30: IRON NAILS FROM BF6

Find no.	Nail ID	Head	Length (mm)	Wood	Grain to shank direction	Notes
B96	NA	fragment only, ?rectangular	45	y	diagonal	–
B98	NB	sub-rectangular	67	y	transverse	–
B99	NC	round	37	y	–	wood across head; clenched, giving wood thickness of 19 mm
B100	ND	–	39	y	diagonal	shank fragment
B101	north-east	sub-rectangular	51	y	transverse	–
B105	NF	round	49 (complete)	–	–	–
B106	NG	sub-rectangular	65	y	transverse	in 2 pieces
B107	NH	sub-rectangular	16	–	–	–
B108	NI	sub-rectangular	24	–	–	–
B109	NJ	–	55	y	transverse	shank fragment
B110	NK	round	81 (complete)	y	diagonal	–
B122	NL	oval	30	y	transverse	–
B136	NM	?round	36	y	?	wood structure gone
B145	NN	–	48	–	–	–
B146	NO	round	124 (complete)	–	–	in 3 pieces
B165	NP	sub-circular	51	y	parallel	in 3 pieces; wood lying over head and curving over edge to run down the shank for a short distance
B166	NQ	–	49	–	–	shank fragment
B209	NR	–	34	y	transverse	shank fragment in 2 pieces
B210	NS	–	45	–	–	shank fragment
B211	NT	round	34	y	transverse	–
B212	NU	–	28	–	–	shank fragment in 2 pieces
B217	NV	round	23	–	–	–
B228	north-west	–	72	y	transverse	shank fragment in 2 pieces
B233	NX	–	56	–	–	shank fragment
B234a	Nya	round	38	y	transverse	
B234b	Nyb	–	37	y	transverse	shank fragment in 2 pieces
B235	NZ	sub-circular	about 115	y	transverse	in 5 pieces; shank (complete) curved, giving wood thickness of about 50 mm
B237	Na	sub-rectangular	44	y	transverse	in 2 pieces; wood also across head
B238	Nb	–	78	y	?transverse	slight traces at tip only
B240	Nc	sub-circular	42	y	transverse	wood also across one edge of head
B113	SA	sub-rectangular	29	y	transverse	–

TABLE 30: (CONT'D)

Find no.	Nail ID	Head	Length (mm)	Wood	Grain to shank direction	Notes
B114	SB	–	27	y	transverse	shank fragment
B117	SC	–	46	y	transverse	shank fragment
B118	SD	round	39	y	transverse	in 2 pieces
B119	south-east	sub-circular	44	y	transverse	in 2 pieces; wood also across head
B120	SF	round	26 (complete)	y	diagonal	–
B135	SG	round	48	y	?	wood powdery, structure gone
B160	SH	round	48 (complete)	–	–	–
B167a	SIa	–	70	–	–	shank fragment in 2 pieces
B167b	SIb	–	30	y	diagonal	shank fragment
B168	SJ	–	44	–	–	shank fragment
B169	SK	–	83	–	–	shank fragment in 2 pieces
B170	SM	sub-circular	41	y	transverse	–
B171	SN	sub-circular	116 (complete)	y	transverse	in 3 pieces; traces of wood down whole length of shank
B172	SO	sub-circular	39	y	transverse	in 2 pieces
B173	SP	–	50	y	transverse	shank fragment
B181	SQ	part only, ?round	84 (complete)	y	transverse	in 2 pieces
B182	SR	–	66	y	parallel	shank fragment
B183	SS	sub-circular	37	y	transverse	–
B184a	STa	sub-circular	41	y	diagonal	–
B184b	STb	–	37	y	transverse	shank fragment, possibly part of a)
B184c	STc	–	27	y	diagonal	shank fragment, possibly part of a)
B185	SU	–	about 82	y	transverse	clenched, wood thickness of about 20 mm; wood lies on inner face of shank above bend, and all round below, suggesting it is the upper part that was bent over, not the lower
B186	SV	–	73	–	–	shank fragment in 2 pieces
B187	south-west	sub-circular	35	y	parallel	–
B191	SX	sub-rectangular	61	y	–	wood across head only; head in 2 pieces
B192a	SYa	round	51	y	transverse	in 2 pieces
B192b	SYb	–	34	y	parallel	shank fragment
B193	SZ	sub-circular	32	y	transverse	wood also across head
B54	–	sub-circular	45	y	transverse	–
B62a	–	sub-rectangular	83	y	transverse, diagonal	wood is transverse to the shank below the bend, diagonal above it; clenched, giving wood thickness above the bend of 22 mm
B62b–p	–	sub-circular	23–72	y	transverse	15 nails
B62q	–	sub-circular	28	y	diagonal	–
B62r	–	sub-circular	86 (complete)	–	–	clenched, giving wood thickness of 17 mm
B62s–t	–	sub-circular	59/64	–	–	2 nails
B62u–mm	–	–	17–78	y	transverse	19 shank fragments
B62nn–tt	–	–	36–72	y	diagonal	7 shank fragments
B62uu–fff	–	–	27–61	–	–	12 shank fragments
B62ggg	–	–	31	y	parallel	shank fragment
B95a–b	–	sub-circular	53/24	y	transverse	–
B95c	–	–	36	y	transverse	–
B102	–	round	42	y	transverse	–
B115	–	–	38	–	–	shank fragment
B174a	–	–	34	–	–	shank fragment
B174b	–	–	22	y	transverse	shank fragment
B177a–b	–	–	31/35	–	–	2 shank fragments
B177c–d	–	–	35/48	y	parallel	2 shank fragments
B177e–h	–	–	32/21/35	y	transverse	3 shank fragments, 1 in 2 pieces
B199a	–	round	9	–	–	–
B199b	–	–	39	–	–	shank fragment
B199c	–	–	29	y	transverse	shank fragment

the thickness of the planks also varied. This appears to be confirmed by what little evidence there is, with possible thicknesses being 17, 19, 20, 22, and 50 mm. A few nails had wood lying across the head. On one example, the wood curves over the head to run down the shank. These unusual characteristics probably relate to the structure of the chamber, and may arise from several planks meeting at a corner, or it may be accidental, due to plank fragments abutting in the ground as the chamber collapsed.

Pottery vessels (FIG. 54)

Samian (not illustrated)

BF6.1. B164, B157. Carinated cup: Ritterling form 5. South Gaulish. Tiberian. Probably also sherd B157. Stamp: SILVANI. Graffito on underside base: A
Condition: most of vessel present including complete base plus rim sherds.

Brenda Dickinson adds of the stamp.

Stamped SILVANI, with AN ligatured: Silvanus i of La Graufesenque. Die 11f. The form itself indicates Tiberio–Claudian date, as does the use of the stamp on a cup of Form 24 with a bevelled footring and its occurrence at Velsen, a site excavated in the 1940s. *c.* A.D. 25–50.

BF6.2. B68, B132. Carinated cup: Ritterling form 5. South Gaulish. Tib–Claudian.
Condition: half of rim circuit but no base sherds.

BF6.3. B157, B198, B150. Platter: Dragendorff form 17. South Gaulish. Tib–Claudian. Probably also sherd B150.
Condition: up to a third of base circuit.

BF6.4 B140, B214. Platter: Ritterling form 1. South Gaulish. Tib–Claudian. Graffito within footring on underside. Probably also sherd B214.
Condition: half of vessel present.

BF6.5 B148, B151, B214. Platter: Loeschcke 1a. South Gaulish. Tib–Claudian. Probably also sherds B151 and B214.
Condition: up to half of rim circuit present

Gallo-Belgic imports

BF6.6 FIG. 54. Bases: B90, B131; rims: B148, B151, B157, B161, B179, B198. Concave moulded platter Camulodunum form 7C. Fabric TR1(C). Central stamp 7: DACOVIR bordered. A.D. 15–40. Possible graffito: at least one line incised within the footring, too few sherds for certainty.
Condition: severely fragmented; complete footring restorable, non-joining rims form about half circuit, and no definite join between rims and footring circuit.

BF6.7 Not illustrated. Base: B151, B179; rim: B161, B179. Rim and outer base sherds from a concave moulded platter as BF6.6. Fabric TR1(C).

BF6.8 FIG. 45. B140, B148, B150-1; rims: B150-1, B179. Moulded platter: Camulodunum form 7/8. Fabric TR1(C). Central stamp 4: ATTISSV bordered. A.D. 25–50. Two graffiti: pattern incisions on the upper surface; six pointed star within footring.
Condition: severely fragmented, very friable, flaked and laminated; base circuit restorable, but about half rim circuit missing.

BF6.9 FIG. 54. Stamp: B112; rims: B112 (2), B198(2); base: B151.
Moulded platter: Camulodunum form 7/8. Fabric TR1(C). Central stamp 11: SMERT(UCCOS). A.D. 10–25.
Condition: bad condition due to crackling, flaking and erosion; fragmented into large sherds, but no obvious joins, possibly the result of the poor condition: two-thirds of rim and base circuit present. Segments of the applied footring missing.

BF6.10 FIG. 54. B112, B146, B157, B198. Moulded platter: Camulodunum form 7/8. Fabric TR1(C): orange matrix, red slip; worn, no finished survives. No stamp survives.
Condition: fragmented into large sherds, restores to three-quarters circuit.

BF6.11 Not illustrated. B68, B198, B214. Moulded platter: Camulodunum form 7/8. Fabric TR1(C).
Condition: only five rim sherds, about one-quarter rim circuit.

BF6.12 FIG. 45. B148, B150. Moulded platter: Camulodunum form 8. Fabric TR1(C). Central Stamp 5: CANICOS. A.D. 25–50.
Condition: the best preserved TR fabric in the assemblage, restores to complete base circuit and three-quarters rim, B148 equals half the circuit, B150 the other segment.

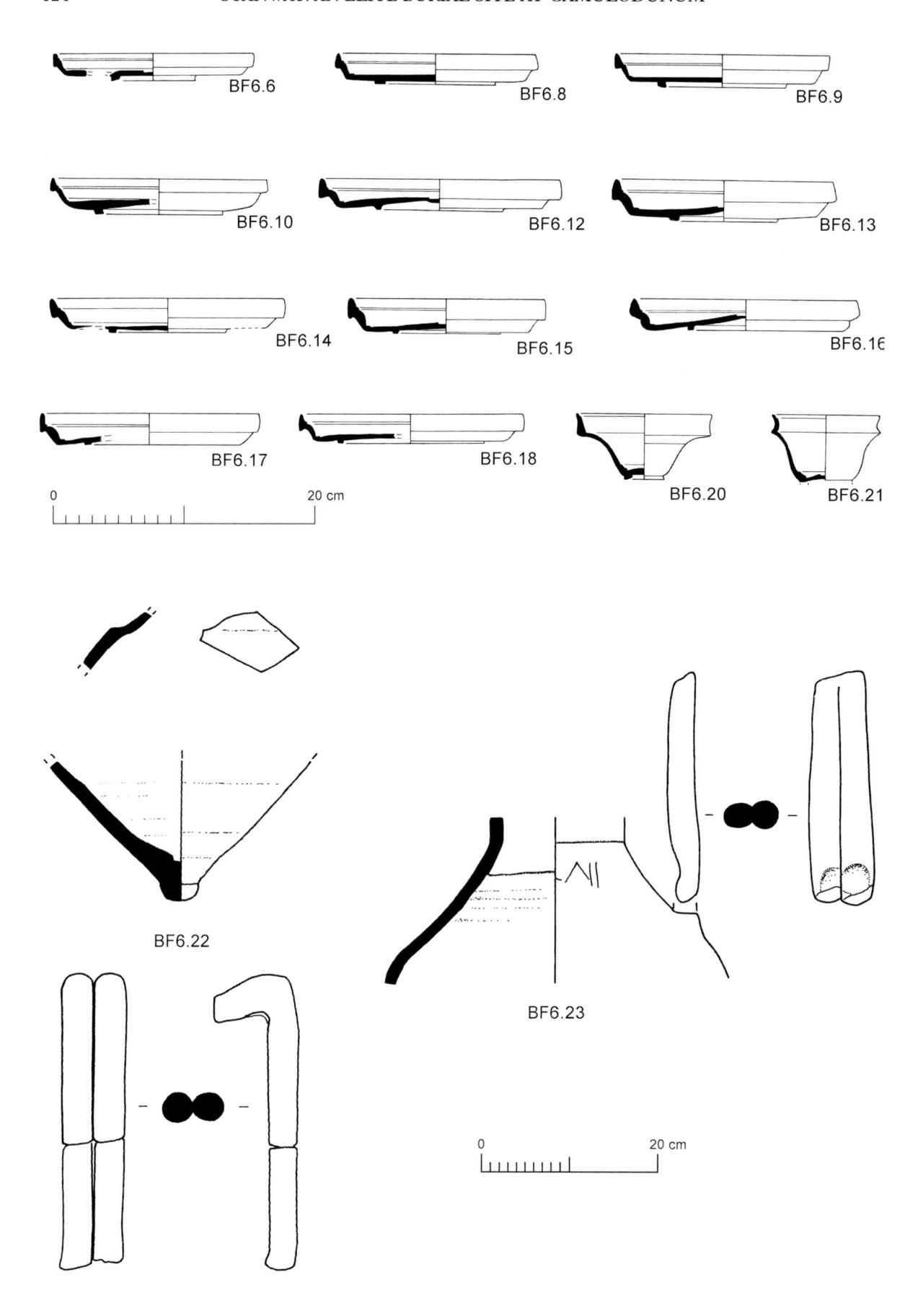

FIG. 54. Chamber BF6: pottery vessels (scale 1:4) and amphoras (scale 1:6)

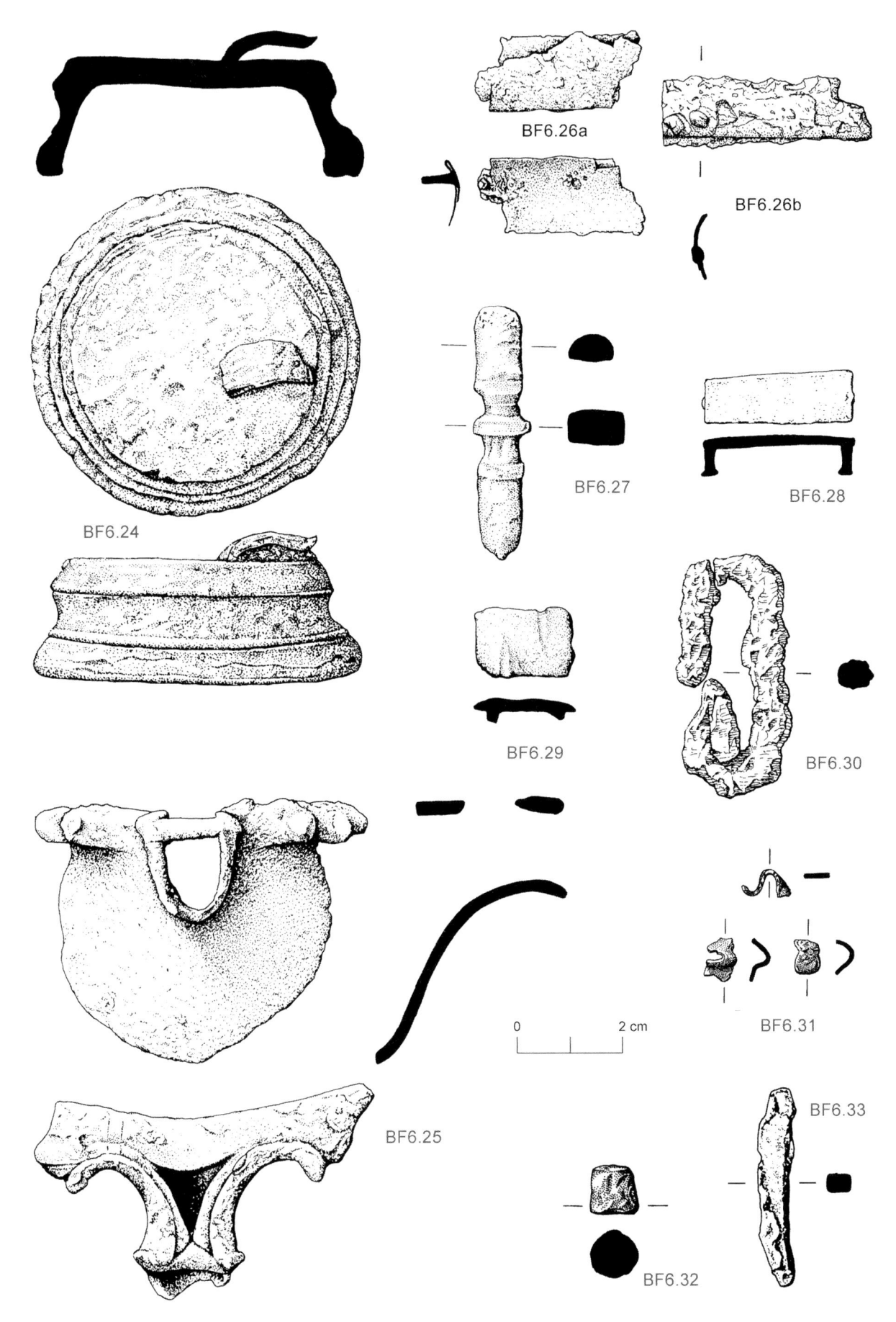

FIG. 55. Chamber BF6: objects of copper alloy (BF6.24–29 and BF6.31–33) and iron (BF6.30) (scale 1:1)

BF6.13 FIG. 54. B138, B148. Moulded platter: Camulodunum form 8. Fabric TN. Central Stamp 9: IVLIOSAV(OTIS). A.D. 25–60. Graffito on upper surface.
Condition: complete base circuit, three-quarters rim; possibly scorched by the pyre.
BF6.14 FIG. 54. Rims: B214+B150, B116(2), B150; base: B131+B151, B198, B202, B230, B242. Moulded platter: Camulodunum form 8. Fabric TN, possibly TN1(A). Central Stamp 27: VII ...] *** bordered. A.D. 25–60.
Condition: severely fragmented, all bases join to restore intermittent complete circuit; rims comprise three-quarters of circuit.
BF6.15 FIG. 54. B131, B150, B151. Moulded platter: Camulodunum form 8. Fabric TN. Central Stamp 26: chequer-board mark. A.D. 25–60. Graffito on upper surface of base.
Condition: in sherds, restorable to complete base circuit and three-quarters rim.
BF6.16 FIG. 54. B111. Moulded platter: Camulodunum form 8. Fabric TN. Central Stamp 28, broken along the edge so no impression survives. A.D. 25–60.
Condition: restores to two-thirds of circuit; possibly scorched in the pyre.
BF6.17 FIG. 54. B92, B131. Moulded platter: Camulodunum form 8. Fabric TN, possibly TN1(A); powdery white matrix, metallic blue-grey surfaces; darker-toned polished upper surface, matt lower.
Condition: two large rims.
BF6.18 FIG. 54. B131, B150, B198, B202. Moulded platter: Camulodunum form 8. Fabric TN, possibly TN1(A), powdery white matrix, metallic grey surfaces, polished upper, matt lower. Decoration: one bordered rouletted wreath.
Condition: fragmented, restores to about a half circuit, no stamp; scorched, probably near the pyre.
BF6.19 Not illustrated. B157, B219. Moulded platter: Camulodunum form 8. Fabric TN, hard white matrix, metallic grey surfaces, polished upper, matt lower. Affected by heat.
Condition at deposition: two joining sherds.
BF6.20 FIG. 54. B138, B140, B150, B151, B202. Carinated cup: Camulodunum form 56A. Fabric TR1(C). Central Stamp 14: TER bordered, uncertain reading. A.D. 15–60.
Condition: complete and standing base circuit, rim fragmented, only one sherd missing.
BF6.21 FIG. 54. B161, B131. Small carinated cup: Camulodunum form 56(C). Fabric TR1(C). Central stamp 23: mark X with four spots. A.D. 25–60.
Condition: severely fragmented and fragmentary; full profile restorable but for footring.

Amphoras
BF6.22 FIG. 45. B147 B227 shoulder, B223 handle, base, B138, B157, B179, B202, B215. Dressel 2–4 amphora (see pp. 301–3).
BF6.23 FIG. 45. B123 shoulder, B227 handle, B134, B147, B148. Dressel 2-4 amphora. Graffito: C (or G) LII *i.e.* CAE or GAII on the shoulder (see pp. 302–3).

Other finds (FIG. 55)

BF6.24. FIG. 55. SF131. B77. Round leaded bronze pedestal with moulded foot below a slight waist. Traces of lead-tin solder were found on the upper surface. A small piece of leaded ?copper sheet is attached to the surface by corrosion products. Organic material was found packed into the hollow underside of the object (pp. 110, 120). Diameter 60 mm, height 21 mm.
BF6.25. FIG. 55. SF118. B159. Leaded bronze applied spout from a bowl. A pair of volutes run from the mouth to the rim. The area between the volutes is slightly sunken and has a triangular opening with incurving sides. The mouth is corroded but the lower part appears to be worn. Height 45 mm, diameter about 140–150 mm.
BF6.26.
a FIG. 55. SF144/145. B224. Fragments of wood and copper-alloy binding from a game board. The largest fragment of the latter only is illustrated. The curvature and thickness of the binding is similar to that from CF47, but it consists of two thin layers of sheet. A tack survives at one end of the illustrated fragment. Length 31 mm, width 15 mm.
b FIG. 55. SF146. B226. Fragments of wood and ?brass binding as SF144/145 above. The largest fragment only is illustrated. It is an end piece, 39.5 mm long by 14.5 mm wide. There is part of a tack fixed in a hole close to the surviving end corner. Small amounts of tin and lead on this tack may show that solder was used to strengthen it in position. The wood could not be identified although it does not appear to have been maple, unlike the boards from BF64 and CF47. It may have been oak (p. 390).
BF6.27. FIG. 55. SF141. B194. Part of a ?brass fitting from Roman cavalry harness, with terminal in the form of an acorn, of Bishop's pre-Flavian Type 4 (Bishop 1988, 100, fig. 50, 4a–d, fig. 52, especially 4h).

Length 48 mm; weight 7.37 g. Strap-loops with similar mouldings have been found inside the Roman fortress at Colchester (*CAR* **6**, fig. 5.57, 1693, fig. 6.40, 378–9). This example has no surviving integral projections on the reverse for attachment, but is otherwise similar to a strap-fastener from Chichester, West Sussex (Down and Rule 1971, fig. 3.18, 3).

BF6.28. FIG. 55. SF142. B205. Copper-alloy strap-plate with a riveted projection for attachment at each end. Length 28 mm, width tapering slightly from 10 to 9 mm. Similar to examples from Hofheim, Germany (Ritterling 1913, Taf. 11, 50–5, 67–73) and Vindonissa, Switzerland (Unz and Deschler-Erb 1997, Taf. 69, 1978–82).

BF6.29. FIG. 55. SF90. B67.
a) ?Brass strap-plate or stiffener with two riveted projections for attachment. Length 19 mm, width 13.5 mm. b) *See* TABLE 29.

BF6.30. FIG. 55. SF136. B200. Iron strap-slide or keeper, probably from harness. Length 41 mm, width 13 mm. Weight 5.76 g.

BF6.31. FIG. 55. SF123. B164. Sixteen tiny fragments of a leaded bronze strip or strips. Some are bent, possibly heat-affected. Width 4.5 mm, length of longest (bent) 9 mm. Weight 0.86 g.

BF6.32. FIG. 55, SF121. B180. Short solid copper-alloy cylinder. Length 9 mm, diameter 9 mm. Weight 2.79 g.

BF6.33. FIG. 55. SF97. B85. Copper-alloy square-section rod or shaft, slightly curved. The surface has been heat-affected. The section and apparent absence of any taper makes this unlikely to be a brooch bow. Length 37 mm, section 4 mm square.

BF6.34. SF113. B152.
a) Four very small fragments of a tapering ?bone strip with marginal grooves, width 5 mm, largest piece 5 mm long.
b) *See* TABLE 29.

Residual pottery

BF6.a B231. Sherd from a heavily organic tempered vessel with some grog temper (5.9 g). From dump overlying chamber floor. Fabric HZ (grog-tempered)].

BF6.b B50. 2 base sherds from jar or bowl (6.7 g). Mound. Fabric GTW.

BF6.c B50. Small sherd (3.2 g). Mound. Fabric GTW.

BF6.d B231. Sherd (7.4 g) from dump overlying chamber floor. Fabric GTW.

CHAMBER BF24 (FIGS 2, 8, 56–64; TABLE 31)

Cremated bone	62.5 g	adult, sex unknown
Pottery vessels	BF24.1	Lyon-type ware raspberry cup
	BF24.2	imported *lagena*
	BF24.3	imported *lagena*
	BF24.4	local grog-tempered platter
	BF24.5	local grog-tempered platter
	BF24.6	local vesicular ware platter
	BF24.7	local vesicular ware platter
	BF24.8	local vesicular ware cup
	BF24.9	local vesicular ware cup
	BF24.10	local vesicular ware cup
	BF24.11	local vesicular ware platter
	BF24.12	local glossy burnished ware platter
	BF24.13	local glossy burnished ware platter
	BF24.14	local glossy burnished ware platter
	BF24.15	local glossy burnished ware platter
	BF24.16	local glossy burnished ware platter
	BF24.17	local glossy burnished ware platter
	BF24.18	local glossy burnished ware platter
	BF24.19	local glossy burnished ware platter
	BF24.20	local glossy burnished ware platter
	BF24.21	local micaceous sandy ware butt-beaker
	BF24.22	local micaceous sandy ware butt-beaker
Glass vessel	BF24.23	amphora-shaped unguent bottle

Other objects	BF24.24	bead necklace
	BF24.25	?brooch chain
	BF24.26	?wooden box with horn inlay
Residual finds	BF24.a–g	sherds in the mound from at least seven Late Iron Age/Roman vessels plus 58 Middle Iron Age sherds from upper fill of the chamber, loomweight fragments, burnt daub

The chamber was axially placed in Enclosure 4 so that it lay in the middle of the northern half (FIGS 2, 8). The chamber pit was approximately 3.3 m long and 2.3 m wide. The chamber itself must have been at least 1.7 m deep — perhaps as much as 2.0–2.1 m if, as seems likely, it had extended up to its contemporary ground surface. The floor of the chamber was flat. The slot (BF43), which retained the base of the planks forming the walls, was typically 200 mm wide and 100 mm deep (FIGS 56, 59).

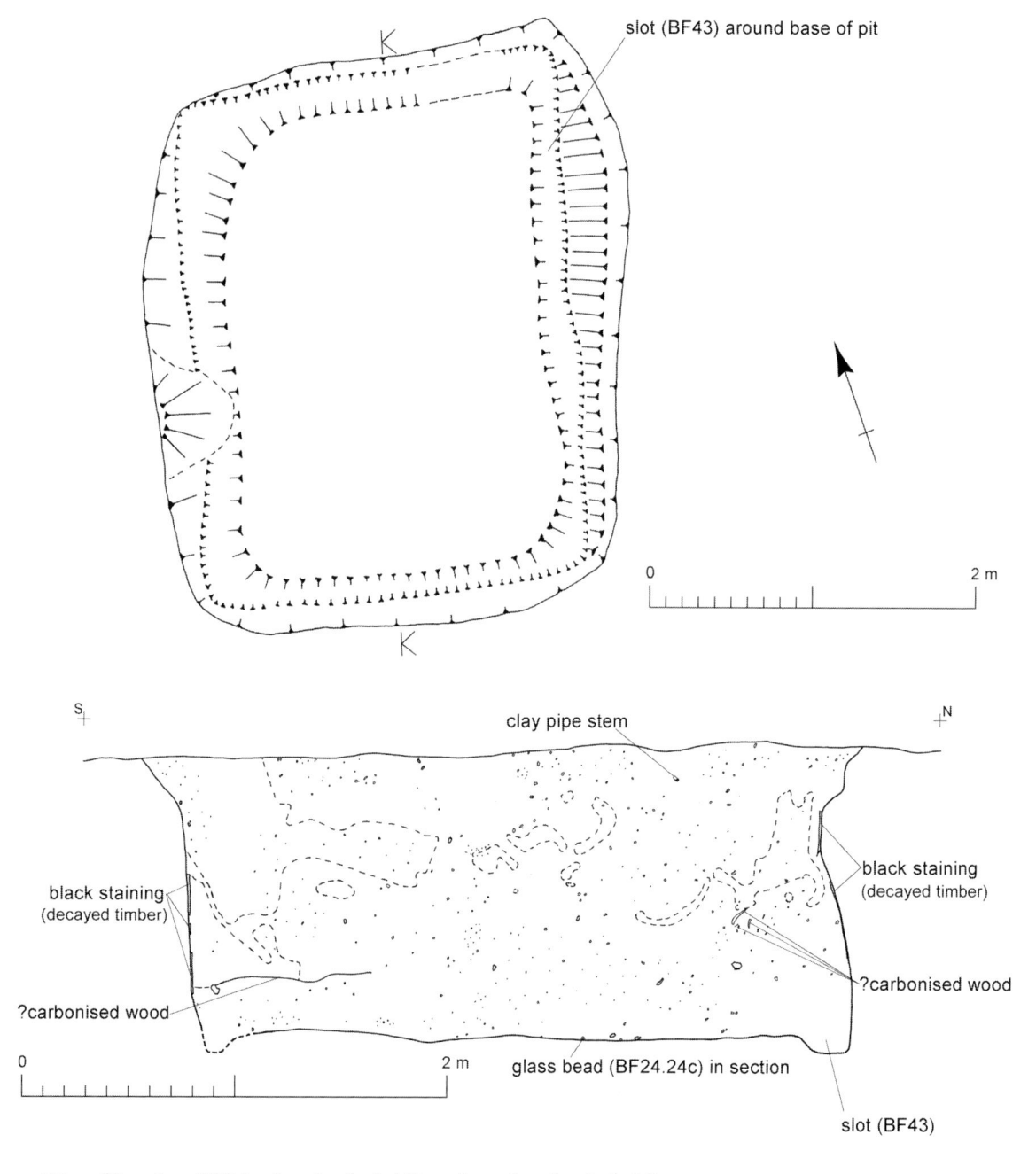

FIG. 56. Chamber BF24: plan (scale 1:40) and section (scale 1:30)

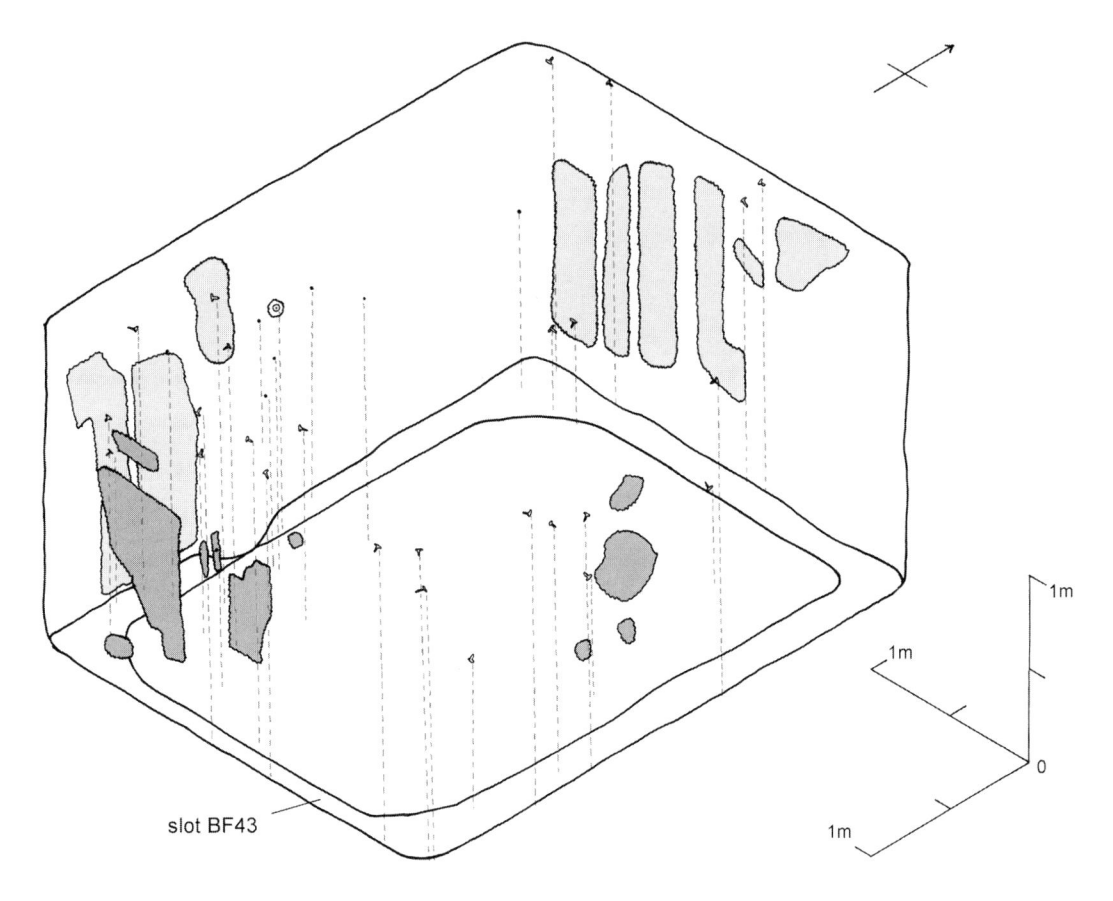

FIG. 57. Chamber BF24: isometric plan of the chamber pit with traces of wood plank lining and nails (scale 1:40)

There were indications of a plank lining against, or close to, all four sides of the chamber pit (FIG. 57). These indications took the form of very thin blackened patches, many of which had straight vertical edges. They were best preserved on the north side where six patches seem to represent five or six planks. Three more planks on the west side were almost as clearly discernible. At least two more could be identified on the south side, but on the west side there were only four small shapeless patches. There was no evidence of decayed wood in the slot at the base of the sides. Most of the vertical discoloured areas were hard up against the sides of the chamber pit showing that the plank lining had been a tight fit in the chamber pit. However, some of the planks had moved downwards and inwards as the fill slowly settled and compressed. This left three of the planks on the north side and one on the west side proud of the sides of the chamber by about 200 mm and 300 mm respectively.

There was no convincing evidence for any horizontal timbers in the walls of the chamber. On the south side, the upper parts of the blackened patches stopped along a horizontal line about one metre above the chamber floor as if there had been some horizontal timbers there, but this was not reflected in the discoloured areas on the other sides.

In the southern half of the chamber, a near-horizontal patch of very dark soil, 1 mm thick and at least 1.5 × 0.65 m in area, lay approximately 0.25 m above the floor (FIG. 56). The patch appeared to be the remains of a loose plank in the lower backfill of the chamber. This is unlikely to have been part of the collapsed top of the chamber, because there were fragments of cremated bone and pottery vessel BF24.13 above it. Small dark patches in the lowest 0.2 m of the fill might have represented other fragments of loose planking.

The fill of the chamber pit was mainly yellowish-brown sandy clay loam with brownish-yellow sandy clay loam lenses and mottles. The slot BF43 was filled with loose reddish-yellow sandy clay loam. The lowest third or so of the chamber fill differed from the overlying material in several respects. Although broadly similar to each other, the lowest part of the fill lacked the

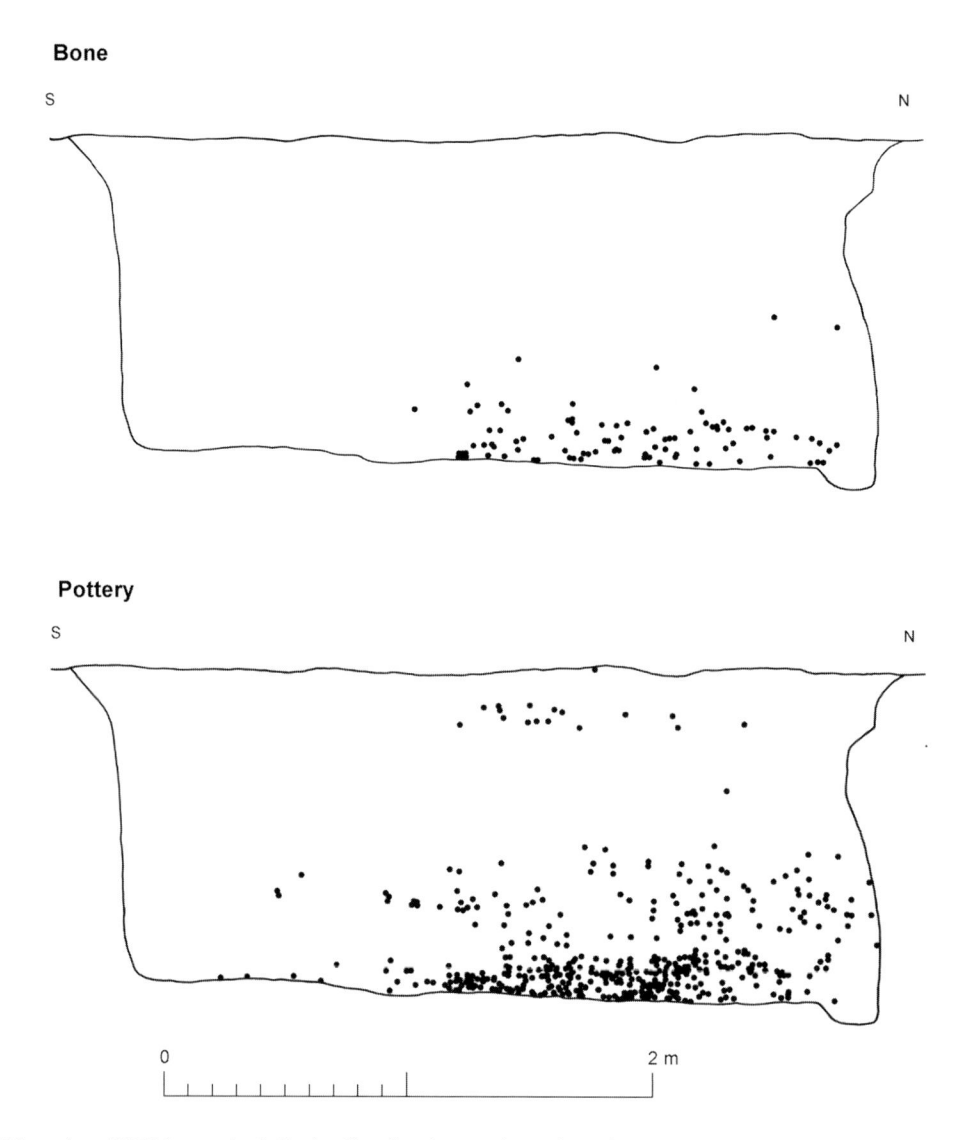

FIG. 58. Chamber BF24: vertical finds distributions plotted against section for bone and pottery (scale 1:30)

paler lenses apparent in the higher levels. It appears that, as more evident in chambers BF6 and CF42, the two deposits can be equated to dumped material below and mound above. This distinction is reinforced by the vertical distribution of finds, especially the joining sherds (FIG. 58). The bulk of the pottery and bone fragments, all the necklace beads, and the fragments of the unguent bottle lay within 0.25–0.35 m of the floor of the chamber. None of the pottery sherds in the upper fill appears to belong to any of the vessels represented in the dumped material below. This suggests that there was a dislocation between the two deposits and that the finds in the upper level are residual and presumably relate to earlier activity on the site.

The fill of the chamber resembled that of AF25 rather than those of chambers BF6 and CF42 because there was no obvious bowl-shaped deposit filling the chamber which in BF6 and CF42 represented the base of the mounds which had subsided into the part-empty chamber below. This raises the possibility that the roof had not been wholly replaced after the dumped material had been deposited in the chamber.

The cremated bone represented the remains of an adult of indeterminate gender. Most of the bone lay within the lowest 250 mm of the fill of the chamber pit, most being in the northern half of it (FIG. 58). Some also occurred higher up but with decreasing frequency. No cremated bone was found in the uppermost 0.6 m of the fill.

Twenty-two pottery vessels and one of glass were identified in the dumped material (FIG. 63). All were fragmentary and none could be completely restored because of missing pieces.

FIG. 59. Chamber BF24, fully excavated, viewed from the north

All appeared to have been broken elsewhere, and only a proportion of the sherds had been deposited in the chamber. One *lagena* (FIG. 63, BF24.3) had been cut down for reuse, but otherwise all were presumably complete when brought to the site. Sherds were common in the north and central areas, sparse in the south-west quarter and absent from the south-east corner of the chamber fill. This distribution suggests that they were deposited in the chamber from its north side. Deposition occurred between A.D. 50 and 70, most likely around A.D. 60.

Sherds 0.35 to 0.75 m above the floor were fairly evenly scattered in terms of level, but occurred only in the central and north-east part of the chamber fill (FIGS 60–3). All the remaining sherds in the part of the fill which was 0.75–1.35 m above the floor were in the uppermost 0.25 m of it, there being no sherds in the 0.75–1.1 m range. A large proportion of the sherds (from at least thirteen of the recognisable vessels) lay within 100 mm of the floor (FIG. 58). Although fragments of some of the pots were widely dispersed (*e.g.* BF24.5 and BF24.15), many of them occurred in distinct clusters (particularly BF24.10, BF24.14, and BF24.17), thereby suggesting two possibilities. One is that the pots were being broken as the dumped material was being placed in the chamber. The other is that they had been broken earlier as part of a specific process that did not lead to the dispersal of the sherds.

Despite containing a large number of pots, there are only three imports in BF24. This may have been because of limited availability or through cultural choice. Compared with the colourful displays in some of the burials and other chambers, these grave goods were drab and

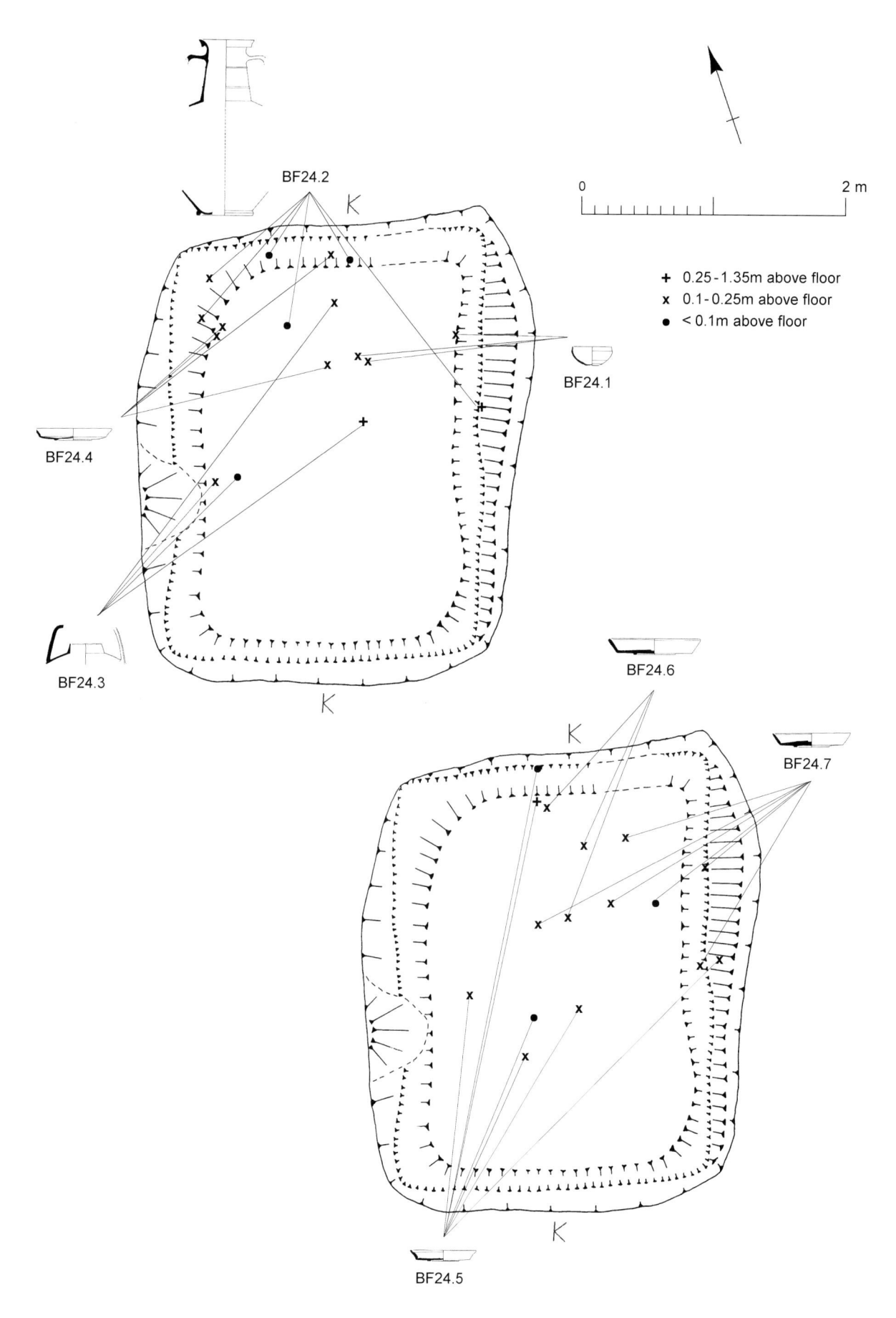

FIG. 60. Chamber BF24: plan showing location of sherds from pottery vessels BF24.1–4 and BF24.5–7 (scale 1:40)

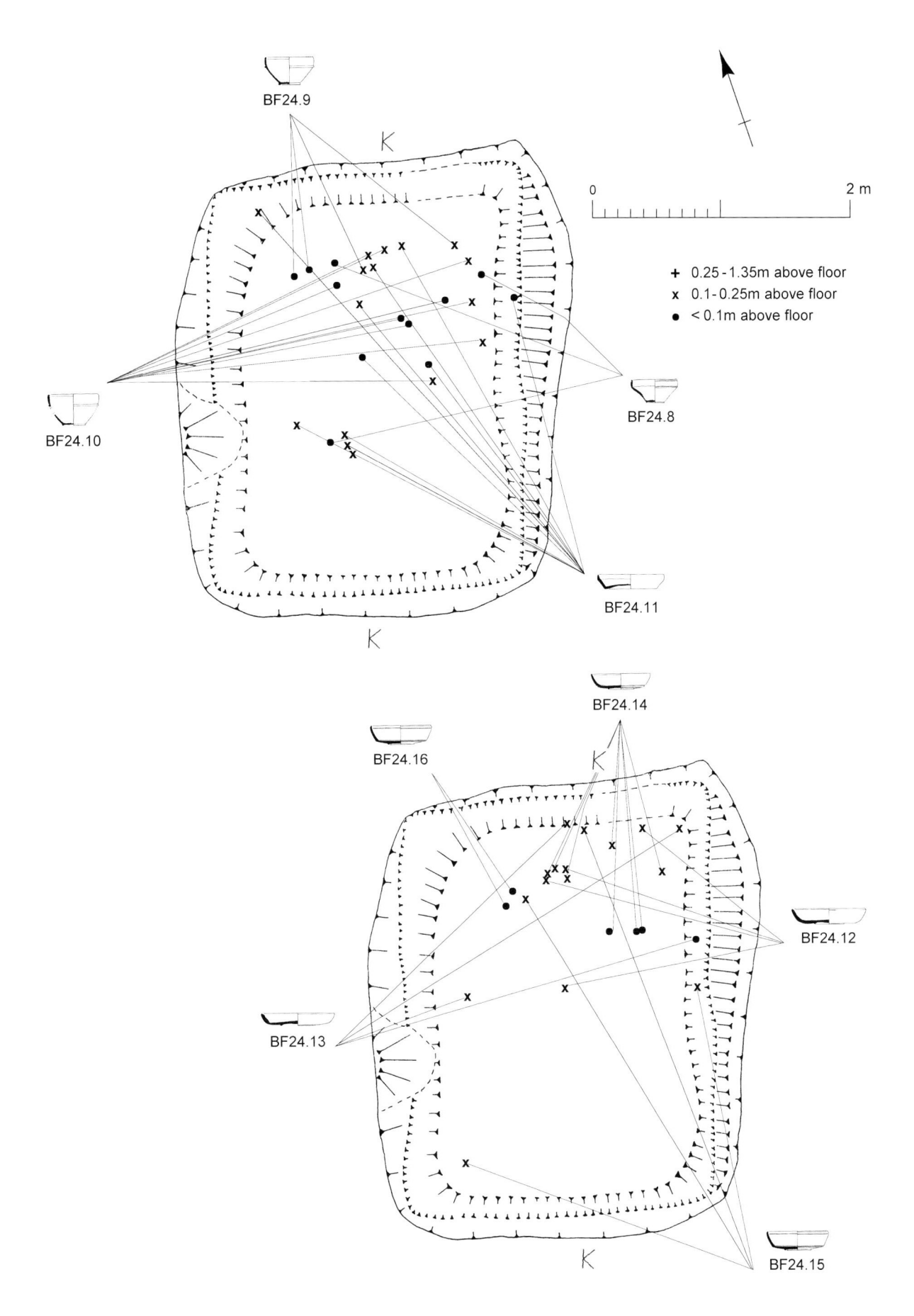

FIG. 61. Chamber BF24: plan showing location of sherds from pottery vessels BF24.8–11 and BF24.12–16 (scale 1:40)

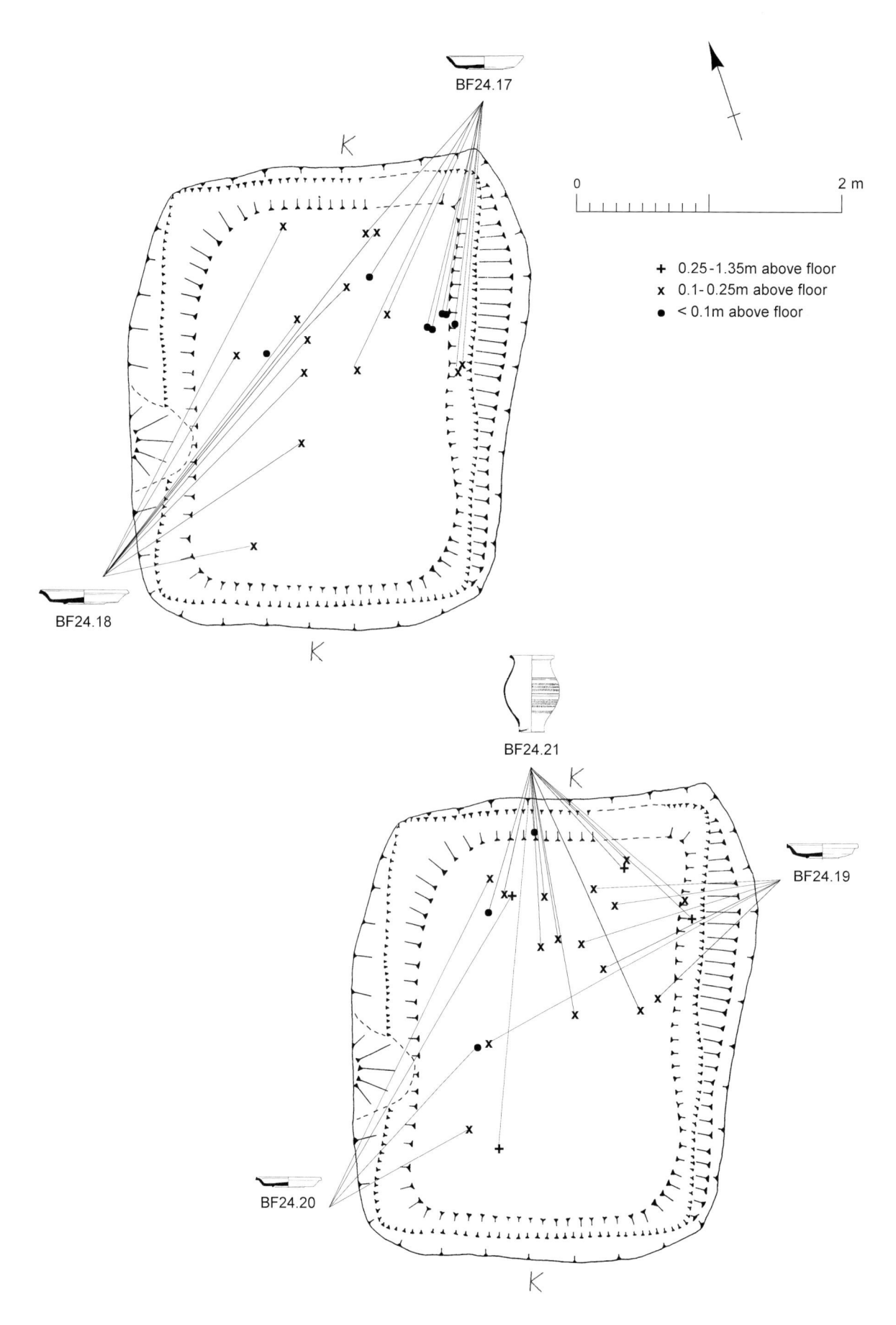

FIG. 62. Chamber BF24: plan showing location of sherds from pottery vessels BF24.17–18 and BF24.19–21 (scale 1:40)

hark back to Iron Age burials in Enclosure 1. The nineteen local products, however, give an unprecedented view of changes in ceramic technology in the period immediately after the Roman conquest, illustrating an intermediate phase while potters adjusted to the demands of the new market and assimilated new techniques.

Although fragmentary and incomplete, enough of the glass unguent bottle BF24.23 (FIG. 63) survives to show that it had been shaped in the form of a miniature amphora. An example from Wederath-Belginium, near Trier, indicates that it may have contained rouge (Goethert 1989, 276, no. e). The form is found in Tiberian to Claudian contexts on the Continent but is absent in post-conquest ones in Britain. The vessel and the case for a date of deposition for it of around or just before the conquest are described on page 344.

The other finds consisted of a few beads from a necklace (FIG. 64, BF24.24), two small silver collars or shackles probably from a brooch chain (FIG. 64, BF24.25), and four extremely thin plaques of horn, tentatively identified as box inlay or veneer (FIG. 64, BF24.26). The beads lay in the lowest 0.25 m of the fill, with the majority spread across the entire north–south length of the chamber within 100 mm of the floor. Several were found resting directly on the floor itself. All four horn plaques lay in the north-western part of the chamber. BF24.26a and BF24.26b lay next to each other within the lowest 0.5 m of fill, whereas BF24.26c and BF24.26d were recovered from the extreme north-west corner, respectively from levels approximately 0.25 m and 0.45 m above the floor. The unguent bottle (BF24.23) lay adjacent to the horn plaques BF24.26a and BF24.26b, close to the chamber floor.

The dress accessories form a striking contrast to the drabness of the ceramics in this grave. Within the pre-Boudican colony only the standard early Roman melon beads have been found, making the glass bead necklace in BF24 an elegant and extremely unusual piece both before A.D. 43 and for at least two decades later. The beads recovered are likely to be only a representative sample, rather than the complete necklace. There is a single long hexagonal-section blue-green (self-coloured) cylinder bead, five dark green barrel-shaped beads, and a maximum of 30 tiny spacer beads of pale green. That other beads were present, possibly of different shapes, is shown by shattered fragments. The beads are continental imports, with similar barrel-shaped and spacer beads being well represented among the 1st-century B.C. to mid 1st-century A.D. bead assemblage from the House of Amaranthus at Pompeii, and a spacer bead exactly similar to those from BF24 came from a necklace found there in a pre-Augustan context (Crummy forthcoming a). The hexagonal-section cylinder bead is matched by one from a woman's grave at Bessines (Poitou), France, that dates to at least as early as the last quarter of the 1st century A.D. (Bertrand 2003, 69, pl. 16, 14–15), and others have been found at Augst in 1st-century and later contexts (Riha 1990, 89).

The small silver collars are penannular, with marginal mouldings and a central cable-moulded band. They are probably the shackles from a silver chain, implying that the grave goods included a pair of silver brooches linked by a loop-in-loop chain. The use of the precious metal is an indication of both wealth and rarity. The type of brooch concerned is unknown; similar shackles or collars survive on the ends of the chain linking one of the pairs of gold brooches in the Late Iron Age Winchester hoard, dated c. 75–25 B.C (Hill et al. 2004, fig. 10), and also on the chains on 1st- and 2nd-century A.D copper-alloy brooches, for example, a Colchester derivative from Burial 5 at Baldock (Stead and Rigby 1986, fig. 27, 4–5), a Lamberton Moor brooch from York (Yorkshire Museum, H.136.2), a Backworth brooch from London (Hattatt 1987, fig. 43, 958), and an umbonate disc brooch from Richborough (Hull 1968, 88, pl. 31, 66). The basic design of the shackles, mouldings flanking a central decorated section, also occurs on the larger shackles of loose wire head-loop types such as Lamberton Moor and Backworth brooches, for example on the shackle of one of the pair of silver Backworth brooches from Chorley, Lancashire (Johns 1996, fig. 7.7).

The association of four small horn plaques in a grave with jewellery suggests that they were probably used as inlay on a box. Two have slightly rebated edges as if trimmed to accommodate another surface feature, and one is triangular, perhaps used to fill a gap at a mitred corner. The absence of peg holes implies that they were glued into position. The decoration of small wooden

TABLE 31: NAILS FROM THE CHAMBER BF24

Find no.	Nail no.	Head	Length (mm)	Wood	Grain to shank direction	Notes
B251	1	round	12	y	transverse	a) short part of shank only remains below head; b) tiny shank fragment, ?same nail as a)
B252	2	sub-circular	78	–	–	–
B253	3	–	72	–	–	shank
B254	4	round	64	y	diagonal	head slightly folded
B255	5	round	48	–	–	shank cut off cleanly
B256	6	–	19	y	transverse	shank fragment
B257	7	–	26	y	–	traces of wood only
B264	8	–	14	y	transverse	shank fragment
B265	9	sub-circular	31	–	–	–
B279	10	sub-circular	61	y	transverse	wood grain transverse below head, diagonal + diagonal (random?) about 21 mm below head; no wood on lower part of shank
B293	11	–	30	y	transverse	2 shank fragments
B295	12	–	18	y	transverse	shank fragment
B416	13	round	37	y	transverse	clenched; wood grain transverse above bend (bent) + parallel (plank thickness 27 mm approx), longitudinal below
B578	–	sub-circular	41	y	transverse	wood down whole length of shank
B608	–	–	34	y	transverse	shank fragment
B613	–	–	42	y	transverse	shank fragment
B621	–	–	26	–	–	shank fragment
B622	–	?round, small	11	y	transverse	–
B623	–	–	30/18	y	–	2 shank fragments, wood traces seem random
B624	–	–	12	y	transverse	shank fragment
B628	–	–	10	–	–	? shank fragment
B629	–	round	100	y	transverse	wood extends about 27 mm below head; some fragments also on head
B630	–	round	–	–	–	head only, scar where shank broken off
B686	–	?sub-rectangular	12	y	transverse	–
B687	–	round	94	y	transverse	the shank is bent at about 40° from the vertical (bent) halfway down its length, the wood is visible only down to the bend
B691	–	sub-circular	23	y	transverse	–
B751	–	–	34	–	–	shank fragment in 2 pieces
B764	–	round	78	y	transverse	unusually large head
B773	–	round	23	y	transverse	–
B779	–	sub-circular	42	y	–	wood traces on head only
B780	–	sub-rectangular	36	y	transverse	–
B828	–	round	33	y	transverse	wood grain lies at a slight angle rather than fully transverse; runs to about halfway down the shank, which bends at about 45° to the vertical from just below the head
B829	–	oval	25	–	–	–
B894	–	sub-circular	43	–	–	–
B1131	–	round	48	–	–	–

boxes, used to store jewellery or toilet articles, with bone or ivory veneer or inlay can be seen in Roman Italy at Pompeii (*CMNN* 1989, Ivory and Bone, no. 5), and in Roman Britain inlay or veneer fragments often occur as site finds, generally in late Roman contexts (Crummy 2001a, 100), but occasionally in the very early period (*CAR* **2**, fig. 87, 2152). The use of horn is unusual, but horn requires special burial conditions for survival, and the rarity of horn veneer can be matched to a general rarity of any items of the material. At this period, and in a native British milieu, an inlaid box for female personalia would again be a rare item.

The upper fill of the chamber BF24 contained an usually large number of sherds compared with the upper fills of the other chambers. The sherds were presumably all residual and were in the base of the mound which sealed the chamber pit. The Roman sherds are likely to belong to pots (BF24a–g) associated with earlier funerary-related activities (p. 130). Most of the sherds appeared to derive from a single cream ware flagon, although at least five other vessels may be represented in the group. The Middle Iron Age sherds are part of a background scatter of Middle Iron Age material across the whole site and, like the accompanying Roman sherds, must have been present in the topsoil which was scraped up locally to form the mound over the chamber.

Thirty-five nails were plotted three-dimensionally. None lay on the floor of the chamber and only three were noted in the lowest 0.3 m of its fill. All but eight were more or less evenly distributed at various levels around the sides of the pit extending from 0.3 m above the floor to the top of the feature. None were found in the central part of the fill. The bias of the nails towards the top and sides of the pit mirrors the distribution of nails in chambers BF6 and CF42 and supports the view that most, if not all, of them had been used to fix the roof timbers to the sides of the chambers. The differences in the heights of the nails above floor level must reflect the varying degrees to which the wood fixed by the nails had slid into the chamber as it decayed.

As with the nails from BF6, many of the nails from this chamber are incomplete (TABLE 31). All are of Manning's Type 1b (1985, 134); the longest is 100 mm (B629) and the next 94 mm (B687), and many others may also have equalled that length if complete. Most have traces of mineral-replaced wood on the shank, but it does not survive on any in sufficient quantity to provide much information about plank thickness or construction. The exception is a bent nail on which two patches of grain lie at right angles to each other and suggest a plank thickness of 27 mm (B416). The grain direction is typical of a nailed corner joint. On the longest nail, it may be no coincidence that the surviving wood grain below the head is also 27 mm long (B629). On one nail (B578), the wood grain lies in the same direction all the way down the shank, but without any indication that this represents two stacked or overlapping planks rather than one. The nail shanks are square in section unless otherwise stated, and wood remains are slight if no further comment is made. The sixth column gives the direction of the longitudinal grain of the wood relative to the shank; if transverse it lies more or less at right angles, if diagonal it lies at a distinct slant, if parallel it lies more or less along the shank, *i.e.* the nail was hammered into end grain.

Pottery vessels (FIG. 63)

Central Gaulish import

BF24.1 FIG. 63. B439, B495, B500. Raspberry cup: Camulodunum form 62, *CAR* **10** Fabric EB, Type 50. Fabric CG CC1/CC2 (Lyon ware). Even-textured fine parchment matrix, no obvious mica; traces of greenish-brown slip; inner surface ridged, no sand-rough-casting. Decoration: applied roundels ornamented with raised spots arranged concentrically; at least one row survives, probably originally two. Condition: extremely friable, severely fragmented. Few sherds survive, no rims; one-third base circuit, and three roundels.

Imports from North Gaul or the Lower Rhineland

BF24.2 FIG. 63. Rims: B261, B307, B311, B688, B801; neck: B261, B311, B354, B654, B757; bases: B267, B311, B658, B848. Cornice-rimmed *lagena*: Camulodunum form 161. Fabric WPW; typical fabric and finish.
Condition: severely fragmented; complete rim and base and one-third neck circuits, part of one handle only, sufficient sherds to restore body, but not attempted. Some scorching may have occurred.

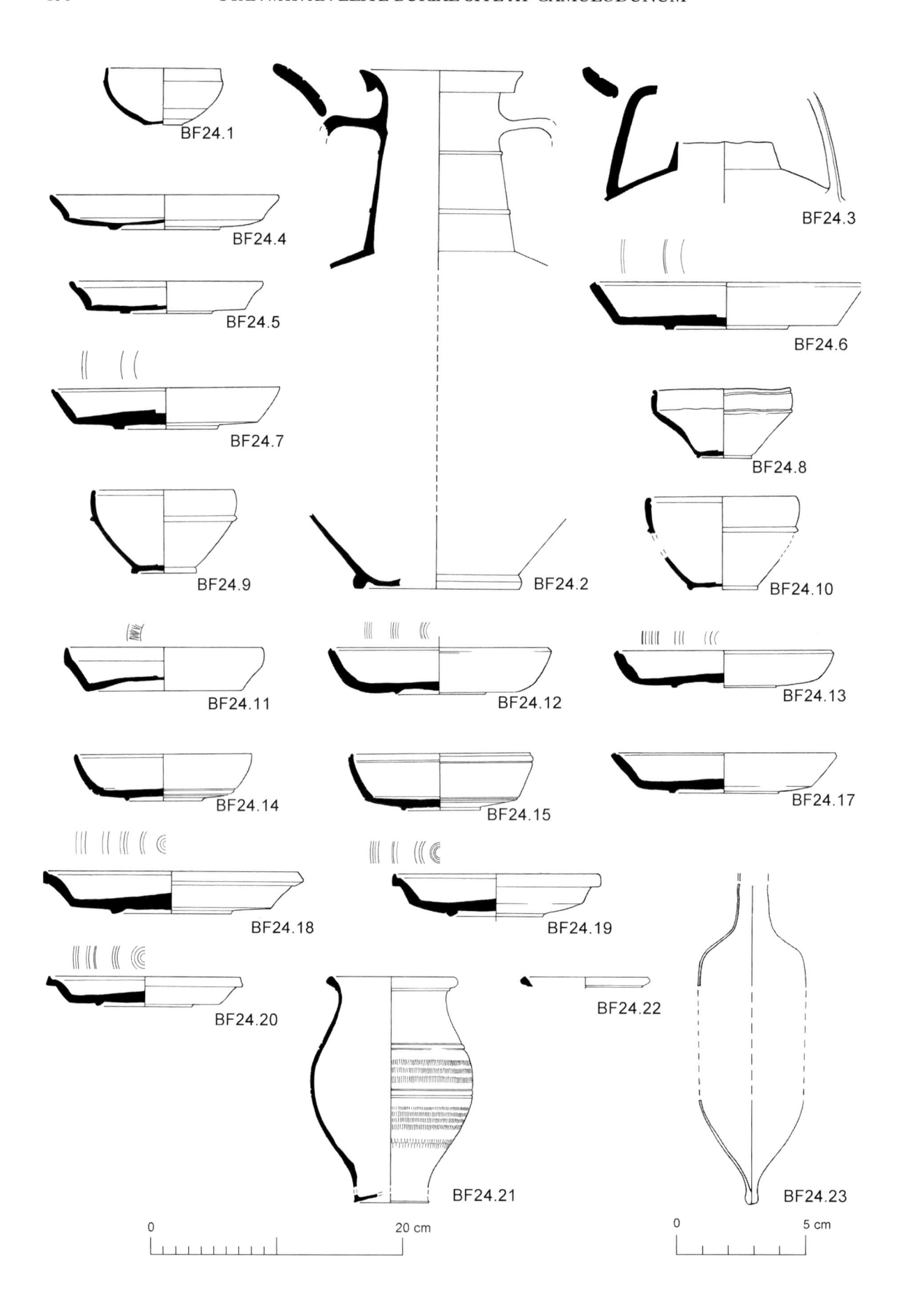

FIG. 63. Chamber BF24: pottery vessels BF24.1–22 (scale 1:4) and glass vessel BF24.23 (scale 1:2)

BF24.3 FIG. 63. B309, B610, B804, B876 + unmarked handle. Cornice-rimmed *lagena*: Camulodunum form 161. Fabric WPW; typical fabric and finish.
Condition: severely fragmented; complete lower neck circuit and two handles identified; no attempt was made to sort body sherds from the more complete example. A cut down and reused vessel. The flagon neck had been trimmed just below the neck cordon in antiquity, although substantial lengths of both handles were still apparently extant on the body but not supported by the neck.

Lagena body sherds in fabric WPW which could be parts of BF24.2, BF24.3 or flagons/*lagenae* not identified:
B261, B263, B266, B267, B268, B274, B294, B306, B311, B318, B324, B325, B326, B327, B328, B334, B358, B359, B360, B362, B365, B395, B398, B399, B400, B410, B413, B414, B419, B420, B421, B423, B425, B430, B431, B432, B446, B450, B475, B488, B489, B490, B493, B496, B501, B507, B544, B545, B566, B567, B568, B578, B591, B598, B604, B607, B652, B659, B759, B761, B768, B769, B770, B771, B784, B792, B794, B802, B803, B806, B808, B810, B812, B823, B831, B836, B837, B839, B840, B841, B842, B850, B851, B852, B853, B855, B872, B873, B875.

Local products: grog-tempered wares

BF24.4 FIG. 63. B391, B491, B661, B789, B790. Plain platter: Camulodunum form 2 copy/ Camulodunum form 21. Fabric GTW. Central stamp: totally illegible.
Condition: broken elsewhere into large sherds, further fragmentation *in situ*, just over half circuit restorable: very abraded fractures.

BF24.5 FIG. 63. B263, B317, B361, B664, B781, B817, B832. Offset platter, Camulodunum form 14 copy. Fabric GTW. Central stamp illegible.
Condition: in sherds, restorable to complete profile

Local products: mixed vesicular ware

BF24.6 FIG. 63. B273, B311, B357, B364, B503, B653, B838. Grooved platter: Camulodunum form 11, copy. Fabric MVW. Central stamp possibly reads: ABVSO, bordered.
Condition: fragmented into large sherds; complete base restorable, half rim circuit.

BF24.7 FIG. 63. B332, B366, B397, B478, B520, B796. Grooved platter, Camulodunum form 11 copy. Fabric MVW. Central stamp: totally illegible, but impression as BF24.6 ABVSO.
Condition: fragmented into large sherds restorable to complete base and two-thirds rim circuit. A smaller example but likely to be from the same source as BF24.6.

BF24.8 FIG. 63. B573, B830, B838, B847, B849. Grooved cup. Fabric MVW. Central stamp: illegible.
Condition: two non-joining half sections; with fresh breaks. Badly distorted waster.

BF24.9 FIG. 63. Base: B577; rims and sherds: B311, B510, B856, B859. Flanged cup: Camulodunum form 58 copy. Fabric MVW. Central stamp: bordered, illegible.
Condition: in sherds, half base circuit plus joining sherds and rims; new breaks, sherds missing.

BF24.10 FIG. 63. Base B339; rims B373, B452, B551, B580, B825. Flanged cup: Camulodunum form 58 copy. Fabric MVW. Central stamp: bordered; illegible.
Condition: in sherds; half base circuit plus joining sherds and rims; abraded old fracture edges.

BF24.11 FIG. 63. B315, B353, B388, B391, B443, B570, B777, B791, B798, B818, B827. Offset platter: Camulodunum form 14 copy; possibly flat-based. Fabric MVW. Central stamp: A..... or . ....V bordered.
Condition: fragmented into large sherds; restorable to complete base and three-quarters rim circuit. One joining section is very much more eroded than the rest. The whole is so severely spalled on the underside that no evidence survives of a footring. One sherd appears to have been burnt after the pot was broken.

Local products: glossy burnished ware

BF24.12 FIG. 63. Base: B308, B333; rims: B308, B311, B418, B760. Grooved convex platter. Fabric GBW. Brown matrix, brownish-black surfaces. Glossy burnished inner surface; matt unfinished outer surface. Decoration: three combed wreaths on the upper surface.
Condition: sherds; base circuit in halves with one-quarter rim circuit attached, and rims.

BF24.13 FIG. 63. Base: B262; B335; B655; B787; rims: B311; B547. Grooved convex platter. Fabric GBW. Brown matrix, brownish-black surfaces. Glossy burnished finish overall. Decoration: three combed wreaths on upper surface.
Condition: sherds; three non-joining sherds form about half base and rim circuit.

BF24.14 FIG. 63. Base: B311, B314, B336; rims: B445, B453, B480, B542, B543, B550. Double-grooved convex platter. Fabric GBW. Glossy burnished finish overall.
Condition: sherds; two-thirds base and rim circuit; some new and some abraded fracture edges.

BF24.15 FIG. 63. Base: B311, B775, B815; rims: B273, B316, B367. Deep grooved platter. Fabric GBW. Glossy burnished finish overall.
Condition: sherds; almost complete base circuit with small non-joining rims.
BF24.16 Not illustrated. B833, B846, B849, B871. Deep grooved platter. Fabric GBW. Glossy burnished finish overall.
Condition: three rims only. Possibly part of same vessel if grooving careless and uneven.
BF24.17 FIG. 63. Base: B311, B481, B352, B369, B602; rims: B262, B312, B350, B368, B372, B504, B565, B571, B574, B843. Offset platter: Camulodunum form 12, copy. Fabric GBW. Glossy burnished finish overall.
Condition: sherds; about half base and rim circuit.
BF24.18 FIG. 63. Base: B313, B783, B820, B814; rims: B311, B786, B814; ?also B260, B262, B363, B783, B793, B797, B819, B820. Lid-seated platter. Fabric GBW. Glossy burnished finish overall. Decoration: five combed wreaths on upper surface.
Condition: sherds; base circuit and three rims forming a half circuit.
BF24.19 FIG. 63. Base: B273, B441; rims: B311, B331, B389, B394, B441, B442, B826. Lid-seated platter. Fabric GBW. Glossy burnished finish overall. Decoration: four combed wreaths on upper surface; combed spiral on underside within the footring.
Condition: sherds; base and three-quarters rim circuit.
BF24.20 FIG. 63. Base: B273, B835; rims: B262, B273, B311, B824; ?also B266, B776, B816, B835. Lid-seated platter. Fabric GBW. Glossy burnished finish overall.
Condition: sherds; base circuit and two rims from opposite sides of circuit.

Local products: micaceous sandy ware (oxidised)

BF24.21 FIG. 63. Complete restored profile: B858; rims B858, B260, B267, B663; neck and shoulder B486, B807, B858; lower body B266, B267, B310, B311, B429, B822, B858. Butt-beaker copy: Camulodunum form 113 copy. Fabric FMW. A thin black coating over the exterior. Burnished finish. Decoration: rouletted zones.
Condition: severely fragmented; about a half of the vessel present, including two-thirds rim circuit.
BF24.22 FIG. 63. B267. Butt-beaker copy: Cam 113 copy. Fabric FSOW. Two rims, one lower body and a base sherd from a second example from the same source as BF24.21.

Glass vessel

BF24.23 FIG. 63. B862. Amphora-shaped unguent bottle; approximately 30 neck, shoulder, body and base fragments, rim and parts of neck and body missing. Blue/green. Cylindrical neck curving out to wide convex-curved shoulder; carination to body sloping into pointed base with terminal knob. Wall thickness 0.5–1 mm, present height (base and lower body fragments) 31 mm.

Other finds (FIG. 64)

BF24.24
a FIG. 64. SF255. B383. Long hexagonal-section cylinder bead of translucent blue-green glass. Maximum diameter 10.5 mm, length 22 mm.
b FIG. 64. SF261. B560. Long barrel-shaped bead of translucent dark green glass. Maximum diameter 6 mm, length 11 mm.
c Three other beads similar to **b** above were also found but are not illustrated: SF251, B606; SF282, B867; SF308, B408.
d FIG. 64. SF279. B549. Tiny annular spacer bead of opaque pale green glass or faience. Twenty-one others were also found as well as fragments from a maximum of nine others. Diameter varies from 2 to 4.5 mm, length 2 mm.
e The small find and context numbers of the unillustrated examples as **d** above are: SF270, B275; SF266, B305; SF147, B322; SF281, B323; SF269, B381; SF310, B474.; SF257, B498; SF277, B552; SF259, B558; SF252, B561; SF278, B563; SF264, B564; SF258, B609; SF301, B824; SF283, B865; SF284, B866.; SF286, B868; SF298, B881; SF295, B882; SF297, B883; SF256, B514, fragments; SF309, B518, fragments; SF267, B548, fragments; SF263, B555, fragment; SF275, B557, fragments; SF254, B559; fragment; SF268, B594, fragment; SF274, B562, fragments.
f SF253. B276. Green powder, possibly from a bead similar to the group above, but see also SF260 and SF307 below.
g SF260. B576. Fragments of a decayed and shattered bead of opaque green glass, probably barrel-shaped.

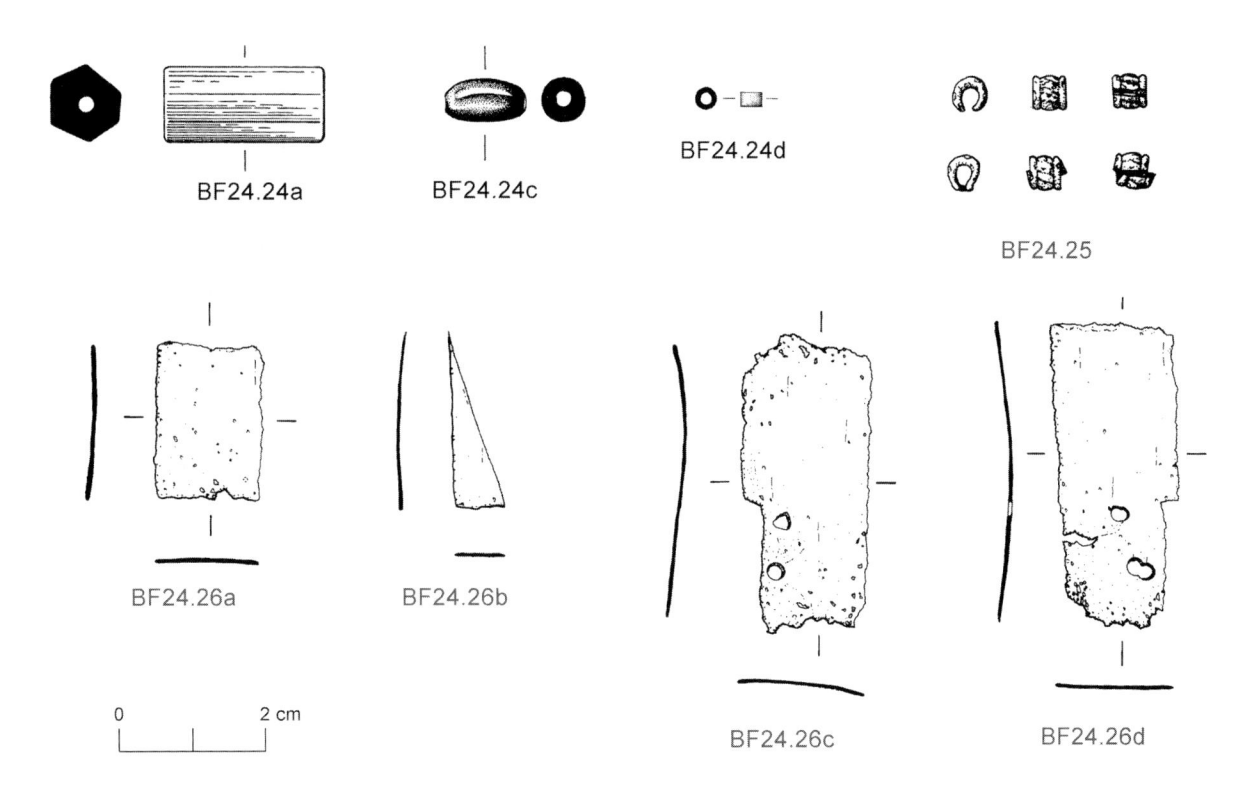

FIG. 64. Chamber BF24: glass beads (BF24.24a, BF24.24c–d), silver collars (BF24.25), and horn plaques (BF24.26a–c) (scale 1:1)

h SF307. B277. Powder from a decayed opaque green glass bead. The quantity appears too great to come from a spacer bead. It may perhaps be part of SF260 above, or from a similar bead.
BF24.25. FIG. 64. SF296. B884 BF24/SF299. B869. Two small penannular silver collars with prominent marginal mouldings and central cable-moulded band. Diameter 4.5 mm, length 4.5 mm. Weight of SF296, 0.18 g; weight of SF299, 0.19 g.
BF24.26
a FIG. 64. SF289. B863. Thin rectangular horn plaque, 21 by 14 mm, 0.4 mm thick.
b F FIG. 64. SF290. B864. Thin horn plaque cut into a right-angled triangle, sides 24 by 7 by 25 mm, 0.25 mm thick.
c FIG. 64. SF302. B778. Thin horn plaque, more or less rectangular. The ends of both short sides are damaged. One long side is slightly rebated. Close to this are two perforations, one circular, one sub-circular, which are probably natural features rather than peg holes for attachment. Maximum dimensions 41 by 18 mm, 0.25 mm thick.
d FIG. 64. SF303. B813. Thin horn plaque similar to BF24.26c, but with only the shorter of the short sides damaged. Close to the rebated edge are two overlapping circular perforations, with a third, sub-circular, close by. As on BF24.26c above, these are natural features rather than peg holes. Maximum dimensions 41 by 17 mm, 0.5 mm thick.

Residual sherds in the upper fill of the chamber
BF24.a B260. Sherd from a relatively thick-walled vessel (5.7 g). Fabric GTW.
BF24.b B458, B698, B683. 3 sherds in sandy grog-tempered fabric, possibly all from the same vessel (3.8 g). Fabric GTW.
BF24.c B683. Small thin sherd in sandy grog-tempered fabric, similar to B458/B698/B683 but much thinner, possibly a separate vessel (1.0 g). Fabric GTW.
BF24.d B627. Body sherd from a flagon in sandy yellowish-cream fabric (48.7 g). Fabric GFW.
BF24.e B294. 17 body sherds in imported fine white ware, probably a flagon, imported from North Gaul. Probably parts of BF24.2 or BF24.3 (18.0 g). Fabric WPW.
BF24.f B311. Bowl rim sherd, burnished with burnishing extending over rim (5.3 g). Fabric GTW.
BF24.g B298. Body sherd (3.4 g). Fabric GTW.
Fifty-eight? Middle Iron Age sherds (245 g).

CHAMBER CF42 (FIGS 2, 8, 65–73, TABLE 32)

Cremated bone	none	
Pottery vessels	CF42.1	TN moulded platter
	CF42.2	TN moulded platter
	CF42.3	TN moulded platter
	CF42.4	TN stepped platter
	CF42.5	TN stepped platter
	CF42.6	TR1(C) or TR2 carinated cup
	CF42.7	TR1(C) carinated cup
	CF42.8	TN flanged cup
	CF42.9	ovoid beaker
	CF42.10	Dressel 2–4 amphora
Glass vessels	CF42.11	deep cylindrical bowl
	CF42.12	unguent bottle
	CF42.13	unguent bottle
Other finds	CF42.14	single glass counter
	CF42.15	copper-alloy spoon
	CF42.16	wooden object represented by three studs or pins (a–c) each with a glass head on an iron shank and two shank fragments with missing heads (d–e)
	CF42.17	narrow iron strip
Animal bone		burnt teeth fragments (in mound) (probably horse)
Residual finds	CF42.a–f	sherds from at least six Late Iron Age/Roman vessels plus Middle Iron Age sherds in mound and backfill

The chamber was located symmetrically in the centre of the southern half of Enclosure 5 (FIGS 2, 8). The base of the pit (CF42) in which the chamber had been constructed was 1.2 m below the ground surface after stripping (FIG. 68). Its original depth must have been about 1.7 m assuming the ground-level has changed very little since the chamber was built. The uppermost surviving part of the pit was in the shape of a rectangle with rounded corners, measuring just over 4 m north to south and just under 4 m east to west. The floor of the chamber was flat, square, and 3 m across (FIGS 65–6). The sides of the chamber-pit sloped steeply inwards to a level approximately 0.5 m below the excavation ground-surface, at which depth the slope changed so that they were practically vertical. The vertical-sided part of the chamber-pit extended to a distance of 0.7 m above the floor. Around the sides of the floor was a slot (FIG. 65, CF414) which varied between 50 and 200 mm in width and 100 and 300 mm in depth. A small, curved recess (FIG. 65, CF114) had been cut just behind the middle of the slot along the south side of the chamber-pit. The base of the recess was flat and level with the floor of the pit.

The fill of the chamber consisted of two distinct deposits, both of light brown, mottled, sandy silts (FIG. 67). The lower deposit (referred to here as the 'dumped material') represents soil and debris deliberately placed in the chamber around the time of the cremation or shortly afterwards whereas the upper one was part of the base of a mound which was raised over the chamber to seal it. Neither of the deposits could have derived from the excavation of the chamber-pit, because they would have been dominated by sandy gravel. Instead both must have consisted largely of scraped-up topsoil, subsoil, and turves.

The dumped material is unlikely to have filled the chamber completely. It extended up the side of the chamber to around 750–800 mm above the chamber-floor. The deposit will have reduced in volume considerably since its deposition because of compaction and the decay of any organic material which it contained. However, to have filled the chamber completely, its volume would need to have reduced by as much 75 per cent which is conceivable but probably very unlikely.

Patches of dark-grey brownish-black deposits, approximately 10 mm thick, lay close to all four sides of the chamber-pit (FIG. 69). Traces of wood grain could be seen in some of this material. Close inspection showed that the wood had not been carbonised, but was mineral-replaced. Iron nails in close proximity to the mineral-replaced wood indicated that a large

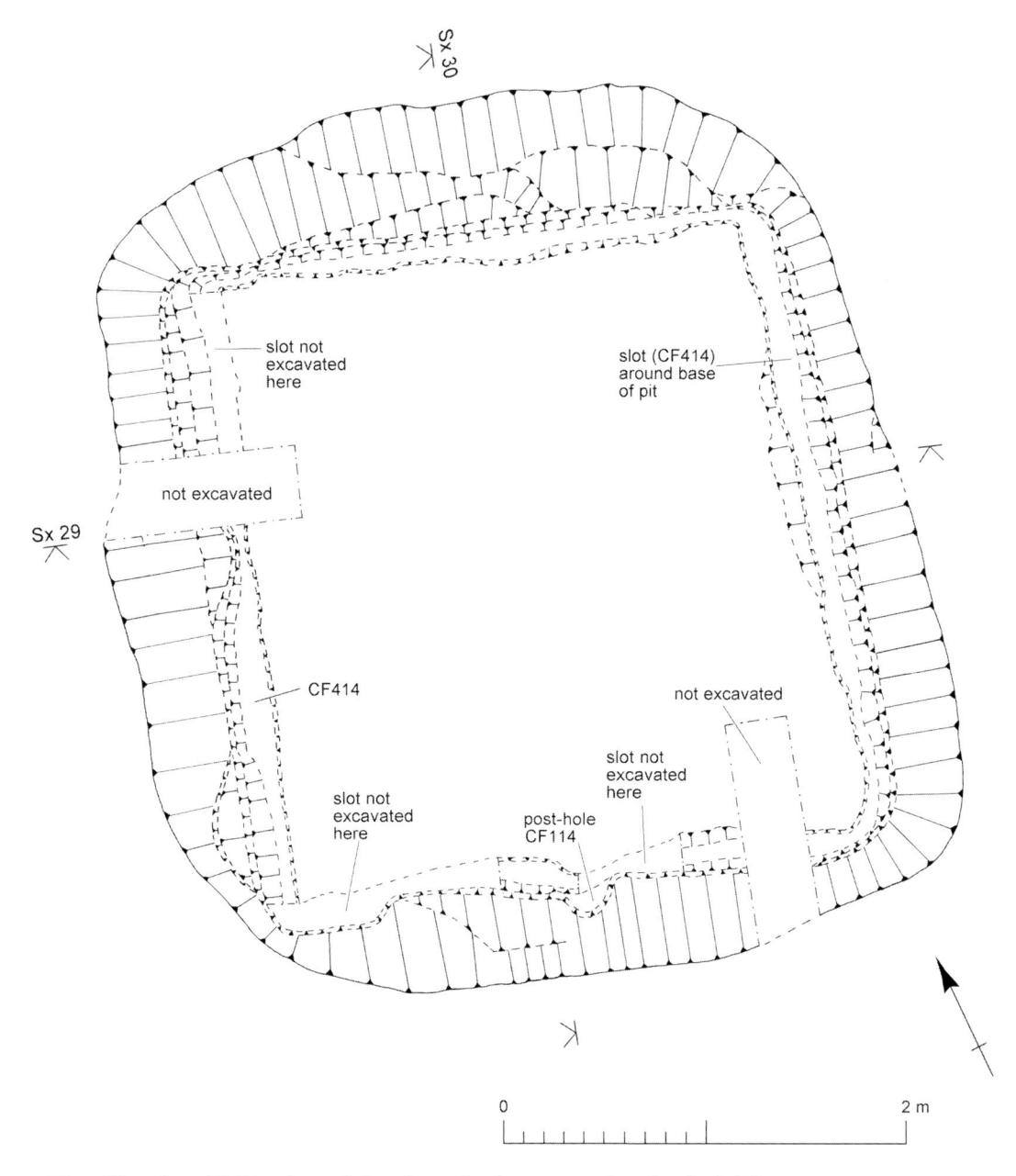

FIG. 65. Chamber CF42: plan of chamber pit after excavation (scale 1:33)

timber chamber, similar to AF25, BF6, and BF24, had been constructed inside the pit (FIG. 67). The deposits with the mineral-replaced wood covered most of the west and east sides of the chamber-pit, and overlapped each other in many places. However, they were sparse on the south edge of the pit and almost absent on the north side. The mineral-replaced wood was also present in the slot CF414, where it extended vertically downwards against the inner edge of the feature (FIG. 68).

The distribution of the nails used to make the chamber roughly corresponded with the incidence of the mineral-replaced wood. The nails were concentrated on the west side with fewer on the east and south sides, and only two or three close to the north side (FIG. 69). They were up to 120 mm in length, with most being around 50 mm. All the nail heads appeared to have been flat and round. The positions of the heads and shanks show that almost all of the nails had been driven into the timbers from the inside of the chamber, although nails 513, 622 and 748 pointed inwards.

The decayed wood along the slot CF414 appeared as an almost continuous thin dark line in which some individual upright planks were distinguishable as slight steps. The line showed that

FIG. 66. Chamber CF42, fully excavated, viewed from the south

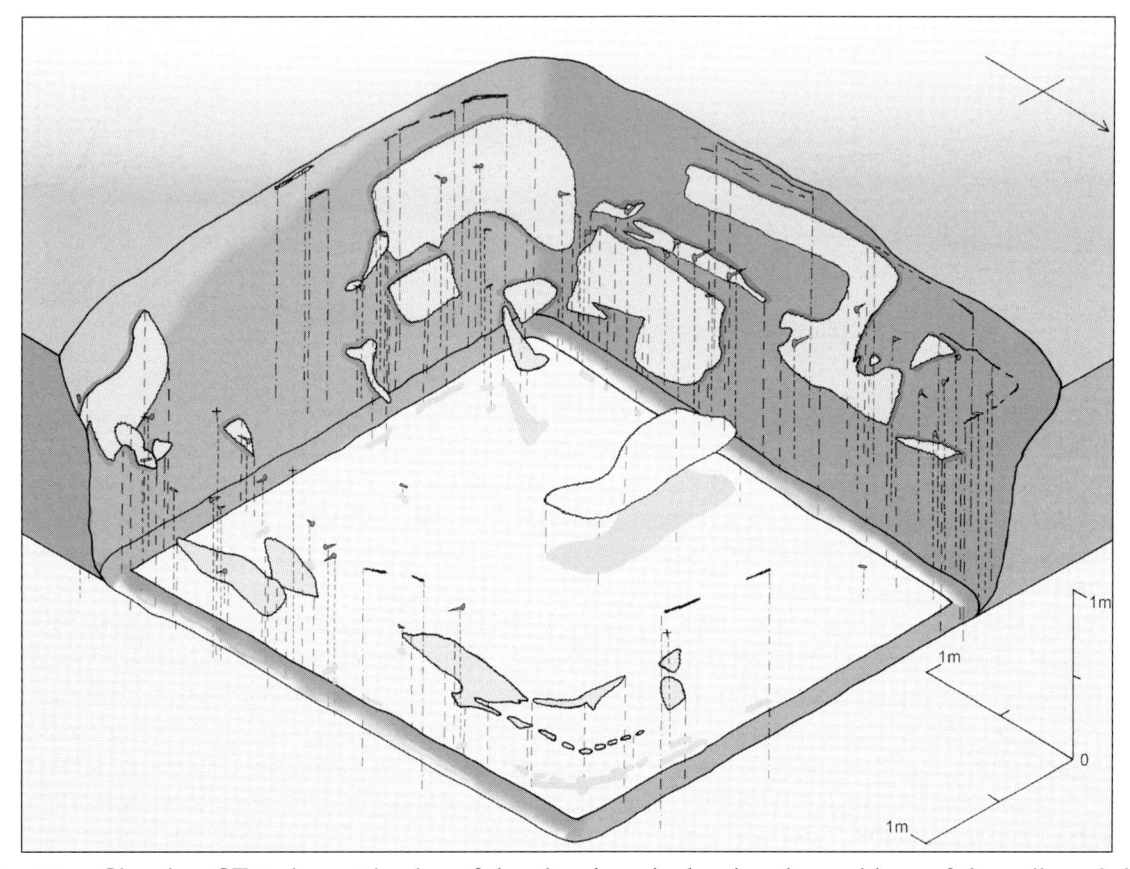

FIG. 67. Chamber CF42: isometric plan of the chamber pit showing the positions of the nails and the traces of decayed wood

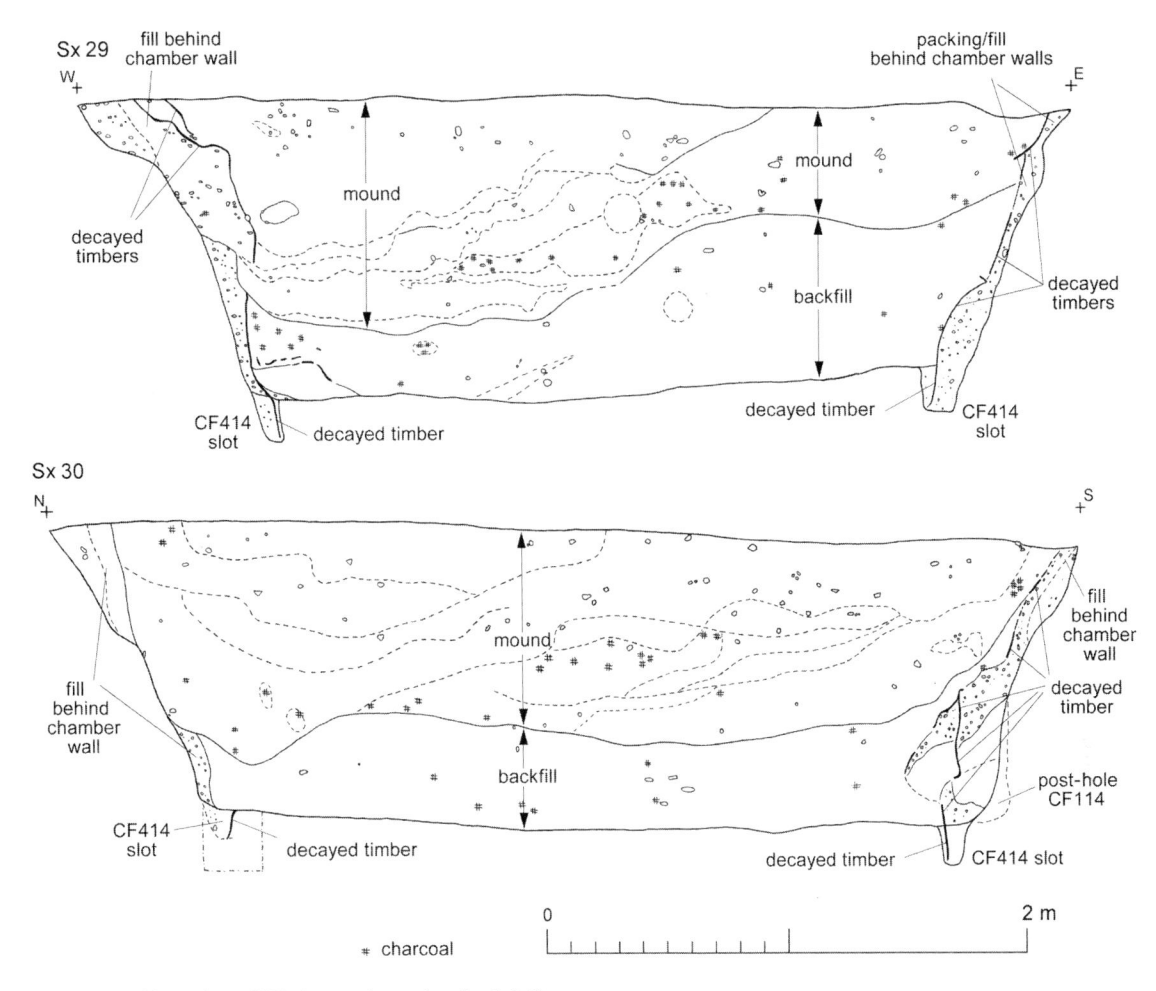

FIG. 68. Chamber CF42: sections (scale 1:30)

the chamber had been constructed of upright wooden planks placed edge to edge around the chamber-pit to form timber walls on all four sides. The steps varied in length between 50 and 150 mm. Most were around 100 mm. The existence of the steps implies that the planks had not been joined together at the base, but instead their ends had simply been dropped into the slot CF414 and held fast against its inner face by backfilling the base of the void between the planks and the sides of the chamber-pit. This explains why the decayed wood appears against the inner face of the slot in section (FIG. 68), and why there were no nails low down in the chamber. There was no trace of a wooden floor.

The curved recess cut into the centre of the south side of the chamber-pit presumably held a post (FIG. 65, CF114). Although there was no equivalent feature on the opposite side of the chamber-pit, there had probably been a similar post there so that together the two posts would have supported a timber on which would have been placed planks for the chamber roof. Faint traces of decayed wood on the top of the lower fill in the chamber in the south-west quadrant appeared to be the remains of just such a roof.

The upper fill of the chamber sealed the traces of the decayed wooden roof in the south-west area, and filled the wider, upper part of the chamber where it sealed the nails and timber stains lying against the sloping upper edges. This relationship shows that the upper fill had been placed on top of the chamber roof, and that it must have been part of the base of a mound over the chamber, so that above ground CF42 would originally have taken the form of a small earth barrow. Any void in the chamber left after it had been backfilled would have increased as the backfill proper (*i.e.* the 'dumped material') reduced in volume by compaction under its own weight and as a result of the decay of any organic material which it might have contained. As the wooden chamber roof disintegrated, the roof and sides would eventually have collapsed,

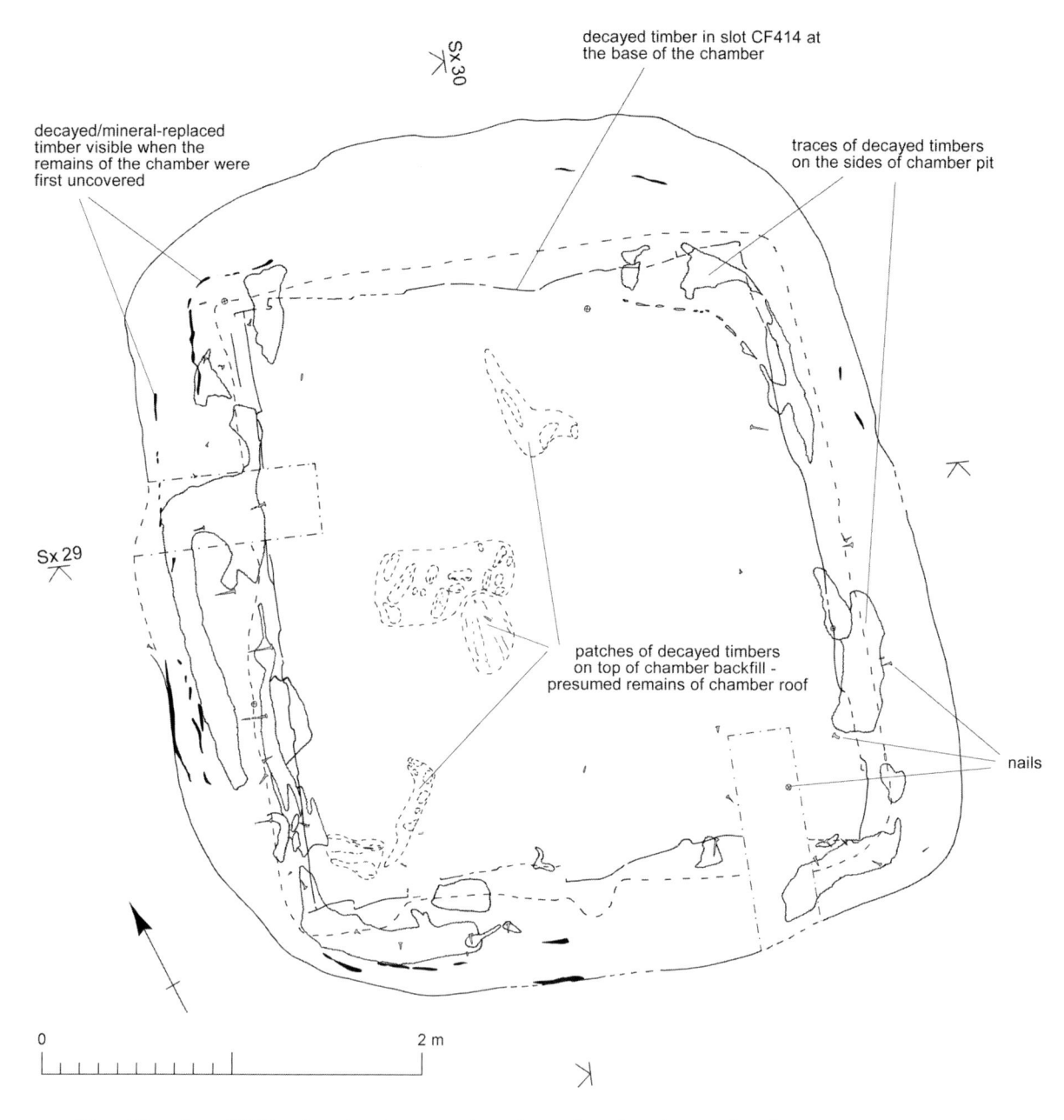

FIG. 69. Chamber CF42: plan showing remains of wooden chamber and nails (scale 1:33)

being pushed downwards into the chamber where not supported by the dumped material, and sideways into the uncompacted material filling the gap between the walls of the chamber and the sides of the chamber-pit.

The overlapping patches of decayed wood on the sides of the chamber-pit raised the possibility that the walls of the chamber had been of double thickness. However, the line of decayed wood in the slot CF414 was single, indicating that this could not have been the case. Thus the overlapping patches of decayed wood must have been a product of the process of decay whereby parts of the chamber slid downwards one over the other as the chamber gradually disintegrated after being sealed and buried under its mound. Movements of this kind would only have been possible if there had been a void in the chamber so that sections of the sides could slide or drop downwards as they decayed.

The mound contained sherds from six or so wheel-thrown local products in grog-tempered ware (p. 157, CF42.a–f). All were grog-tempered and thus different in character from the pots in the main assemblage. The forms and fabrics are well represented in other deposits and

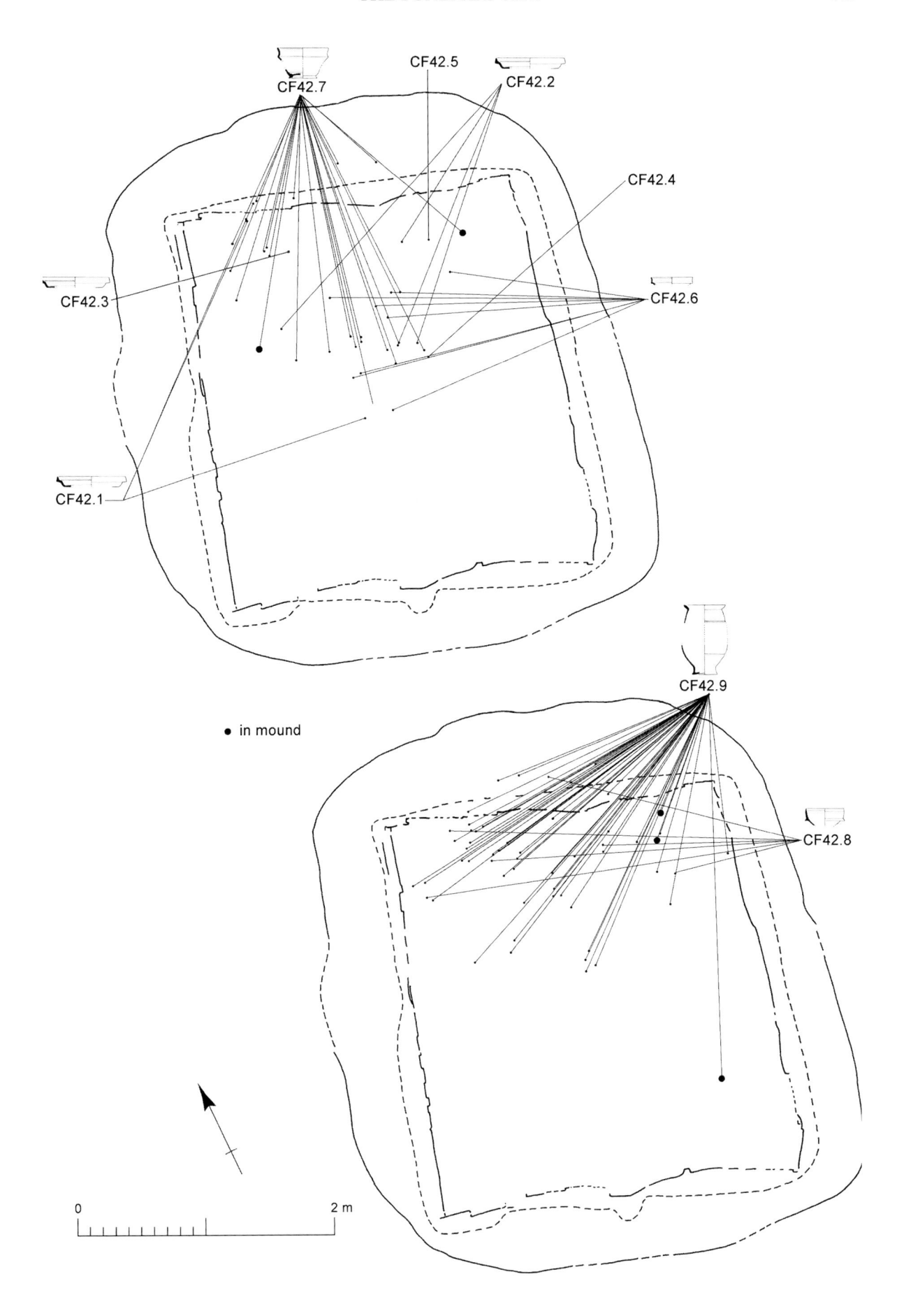

FIG. 70. CF42: plans showing location of sherds from pottery vessels CF42.1–9 (scale 1:40)

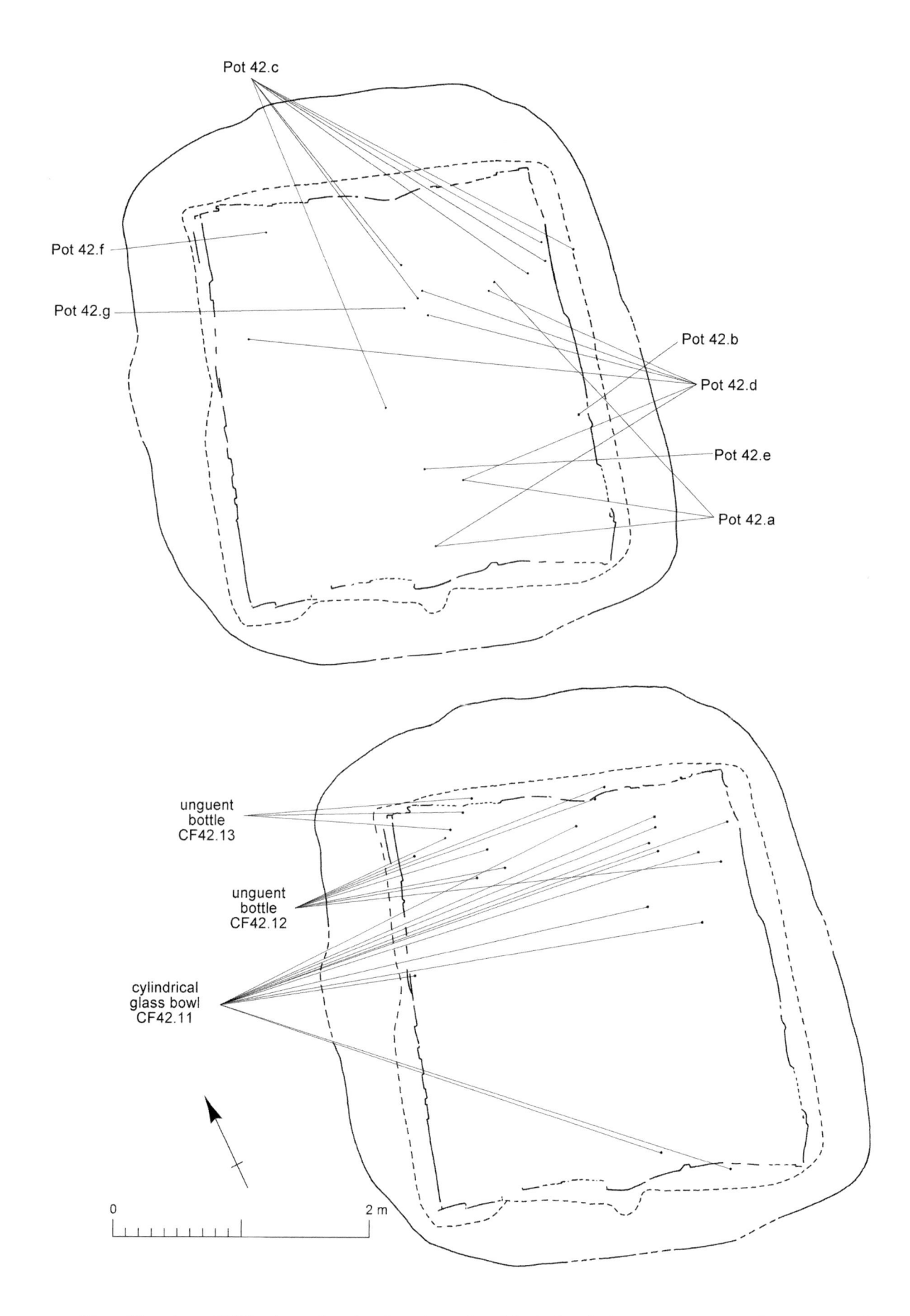

FIG. 71. Chamber CF42: plans showing location of residual sherds from pottery vessels 42.a–g and location of sherds from glass vessels CF42.11–13 (scale 1:40)

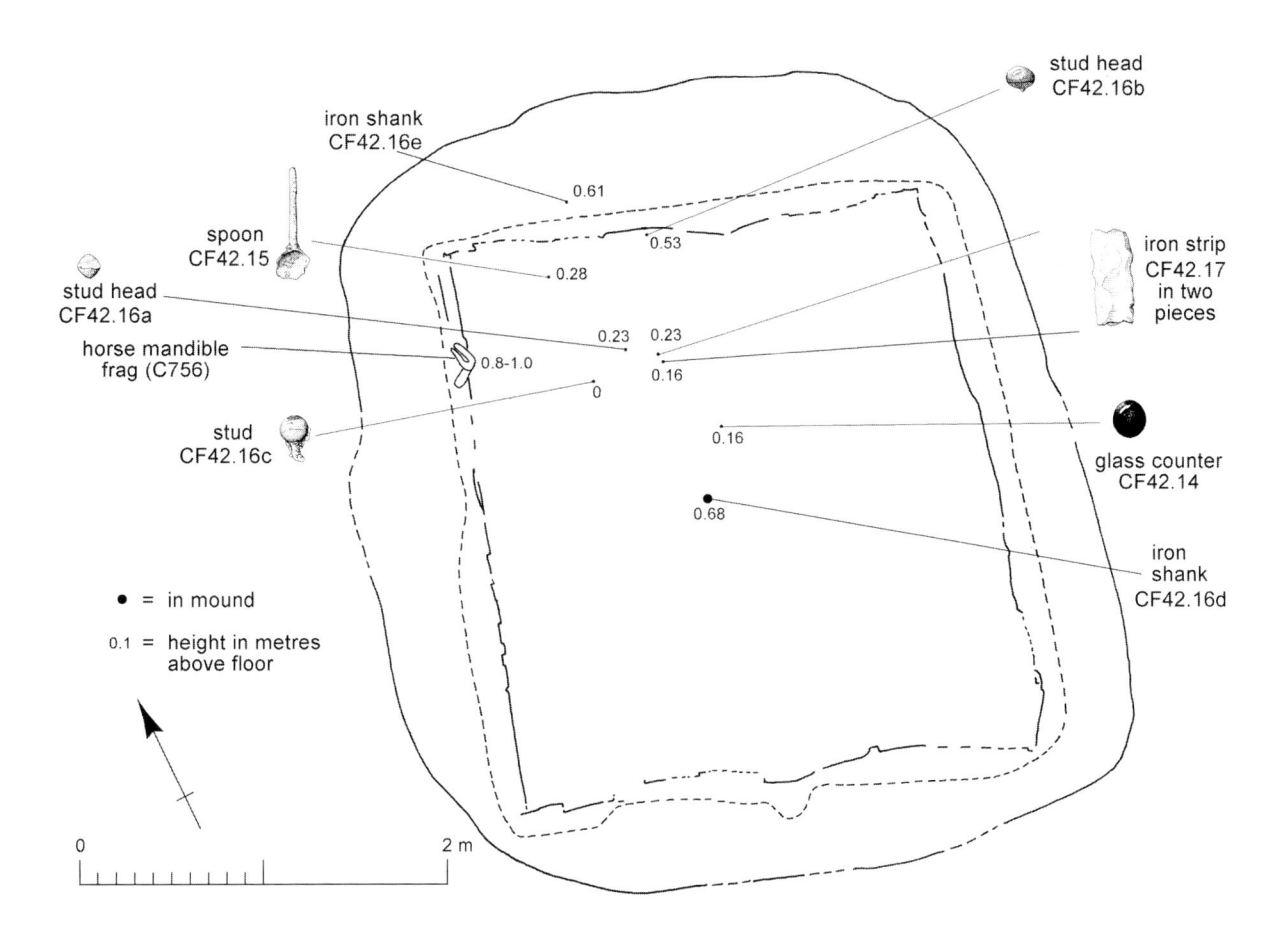

FIG. 72. Chamber CF42: plan showing location of small finds CF42.14–17 (scale 1:40)

burials at Stanway with the exception of the two large platters of Cam 5. Their likely origin is discussed elsewhere (p. 130).

Almost all the other finds from the chamber were in the dumped material. They were concentrated at the north end where this layer was at its deepest, preservation of the timber sides least in evidence, and nails absent (FIGS 70–2). As was the case in BF6, the nails were only used at the top of the chamber, presumably to fix the roof and upper ends of the wall timbers. The absence of nails in this area is very informative. If the upper part of the north side of the chamber had been nailed like the other sides, then the nails here must have been ploughed off in the relatively recent past. If true, then this shows that the top of the chamber had been within 300 mm or so of the modern ground level (*i.e.* ploughsoil depth) and that this part of the chamber could not have slipped very far, if at all, into the chamber as it decayed. The exceptional depth of the dumped material at the north end of the chamber would explain why the decaying parts of the chamber here could not move so readily. Of course, the absence of nails in this area may simply be because this part of the chamber was not nailed.

The objects in the dumped material consisted mainly of sherds of at least ten pottery and three glass vessels which had been broken prior to their deposition in the chamber (FIGS 70–1, 73). All the pottery sherds are friable and had been badly fragmented, with both old abraded fracture edges and new breaks resulting from soil conditions and the poor state of the fabrics. The minimum count using all sherds is one amphora, two large *terra nigra* platters, three small *terra nigra* platters, one small *terra rubra* cup, one large *terra rubra* cup, one small *terra nigra* cup and one *terra rubra* beaker (BF24.1–10; FIG. 73). A distinctive feature of the assemblage is the extreme degree to which the vessels had been smashed. The exceptionally small size of many of the sherds suggests that many of the vessels had not simply been broken but repeatedly pounded to reduce them to tiny fragments in a way that had not occurred elsewhere on the site.

The only bones found in CF42 were burnt teeth, which appear to have been part of a horse maxilla, in the subsided base of the mound (p. 383). The chamber did not contain any human bone, cremated or unburnt, either in the backfill or in the subsided mound. Although the fill of the chamber was not sieved, the exceptionally small size of some of the pottery fragments which were recovered shows that, had any bone been present, even as tiny fragments, then some of it would have been found.

In addition to the pottery vessels, the assemblage in the backfill included the very fragmentary remains of three glass vessels (FIG. 71). One was a cast polychrome bowl in blue, white and yellow glass (FIG. 73, CF42.11) and the other two were unguent bottles (CF42.12–13). Although fragmentary, CF42.11 appears to have been in the form of a deep hemispherical bowl. The absence of any similar rim and base fragments from pre-Boudican contexts in Colchester and elsewhere in Britain suggests that the vessel may have been a pre-conquest import (p. 343). The full profile of the unguent bottle CF42.12 (FIG. 73) cannot be reconstructed, but it may be of Isings Form 6, a globular type which occurs on the Continent in early to mid 1st-century contexts but rarely in post-conquest ones in Britain. CF42.13 is too fragmentary to reveal its shape. CF42.12 is blue-green whereas CF42.13 is an unusual yellow/brown colour which, according to Hilary Cool's suggestion (p. 345), may support a pre-conquest date.

Other finds from the chamber consisted principally of a copper-alloy spoon (FIG. 73, CF42.15), a single glass gaming counter (FIG. 73, CF42.14), and three glass-headed iron studs, possibly pins or perhaps from some kind of wooden object (FIG. 73, CF42.16a–c). The gaming counter is significant in that it suggests that the assemblage had contained a gaming board and a set of counters, as in the Doctor's burial and Warrior's burial and chamber BF6 (pp. 120, 186–90 and 217–20). The glass-headed studs are also of particular interest, not just in their own right but because a somewhat similar item in the Brooches burial (CF72.12) may point to the possibility of a link between them (pp. 254–5).

The spoon type is widespread on the Continent in both copper alloy and bone in the 1st century A.D. and into the 2nd century; two have been found in contexts of *c.* A.D. 44–60/1 at Colchester, on one of which tin plating survived (*CAR* 6, 156, no. 527, tin-plated; 215, no. 124). Their occasional close association with jewellery and toilet equipment implies that they were not only used for eating, but had some alternative function associated with the female toilette (Cool 2004, 28), and there is some evidence from the Continent and from Britain that burials containing spoons of this type are usually those of women. As many cremation cemetery reports contain little or no age and sex details based on the human bone, the following list gives only those graves with spoons (of both this type and later types; not including small toilet/medical spoons/scoops) that also contained female-specific grave goods. The list is by no means exhaustive, but it is apparent that spoons in early Roman graves are all found with females. Burials containing spoons but with no gender-related equipment have been omitted, but they are very few in number; no spoons were found with male-specific equipment. Although spoons may have been found in the graves of both men and women at Avenches, Switzerland, problems with the grave inventory meant that only those from female graves were securely provenanced, while those supposedly from male graves were seen as suspect (Amrein *et al.* 1999, 339–40).

a) Verulamium (Hertfordshire), King Harry Lane grave 325: cremation, Phase 1 (*c.* A.D. 1–40, or by Mackreth's revised dating *c.* 15 B.C–A.D. 30), spoon with mirror and two spindle-whorls (Stead and Rigby 1989, 358, fig. 157, 8, 11–13; Mackreth 1994, 288).

b) Winchester (Hampshire), Grange Road grave 2: female cremation, Flavian, spoon with melon bead necklace (Biddle 1967, fig. 9, 19, 54–61).

d) Chichester (West Sussex), St Pancras grave 171: cremation, late 1st–2nd century, spoon in jewellery box (Down and Rule 1971, 81, fig. 5.16).

e) Blicquy (Belgium), grave 240: cremation, Flavian or earlier, spoon with cosmetic palette, bead necklace and two bracelets (de Laet *et al.* 1972, 115, pl. 69).

f) Emona/Ljubljana (Slovenia), grave 341: cremation, 1st-century A.D., spoon with mirror (Plesničar-Gec 1972, pl. 90, 341/6, 10).

g) Emona, grave 567: cremation, 1st-century A.D., spoon with perfume bottle and toilet instruments (Plesničar-Gec 1972, pl. 131, 3, 8–13).
h) West Thurrock (Essex), amphora burial: cremation, 1st–2nd century?, spoon with bracelets (Hull 1963, 189; Philpott 1991, 282).
i) Emona, grave 732: cremation, 2nd century, spoon with mirrors (Plesničar-Gec 1972, pl. 169, 3–5).
j) Chichester (West Sussex), St Pancras grave 302: female cremation, later than A.D. 150, spoon with a pair of penannular brooches and a pair of bow brooches (Down and Rule 1971, 81).
k) Tournai (Belgium), la rue Perdue grave 117: female inhumation, spoon with spindle or distaff (Brulet and Coulon 1977, 100–1, pl. 23/117, 3–4).
l) Tongeren (Belgium), south-west cemetery grave 141: inhumation, 1st half of the 4th century, spoon with mirror and hairpins (Vanvinckenroye 1984, pl. 83, 3–5, 7–8).

An early cremation that probably contained spoons but is not included on this list is the unsexed adult grave 2 at Alton, Hants, because the circumstances of excavation, with some grave goods recovered in 1860 and others in 1980, make it far from certain that all these objects are from the same burial (Millett 1986, 51–8; 1987, 68). If one grave is involved, then it certainly bears links to BF64, CF42, CF72 and other funerary features at Stanway, but the profile of the large grave pit suggests that there was more than one burial, and the quality of the 19th-century excavation together with the uncertain relationships between the features in the area led to a dish of black burnished ware (BB1) originally being included in what was otherwise a Claudio–Neronian group. The grave goods found in 1860 include nine glass counters (eight white, one blue), a die, and a gold signet ring; a single glass bead was also found when the backfill of the 1860 cut was re-excavated. The items found in 1980 include two tinned or silvered copper-alloy spoons, part of a tray or game board, and a fragment of a knife. If they are all from a single grave, as the counters found in 1860 and the board found in 1980 (the remainder of which may be represented by the 'box' with metal fittings found in 1860) would seem to imply, then this may well be an example of a male grave with spoons. The grave goods are ambiguous, but the gold signet ring *may* imply that the deceased was a man; alternatively, as it dates to the second half of the 1st century B.C., it may be an heirloom whose last owner was female.

The grave that is most closely linked to that from Alton is probably that from Grange Road at Winchester (b in the list above). The sex of the person buried in the Winchester grave has been the subject of some debate, with the bones identified as those of a juvenile, probably a female, but the excavator suggesting that the drinking and writing equipment in the grave implied the dead person was male (Biddle 1967, 231, 246–8). At least three factors allow the latter suggestion to be refuted. First, the presence of the melon beads indicates that this was a female grave. Second, the 'drinking equipment' consists of cups, jugs and a single flagon rather than the wine amphorae, pans for heating wine, wine strainers, and formal hand-washing equipment of jug and handled basin often found in male graves (Poux and Feugère 2002). Third, writing equipment is by no means gender-specific. Grave 146, an adult grave at Valladas, Saint-Paul-Trois-Châteaux, Drôme, France, contained both a stylus and a mirror, and styli were found in the graves of (definitely) both men and women in the En Chaplix cemetery at Avenches, Switzerland (Bel 2002, 330–4, fig. 375, 12–13; Amrein *et al.* 1999, 334). Depictions of women holding a stylus and a writing tablet are shown in painted portraits from Pompeii, and, while the pose may be an artistic convention, it undoubtedly demonstrates that female literacy was an accepted norm in the Roman world (Ward-Perkins and Claridge 1976, no. 23; Brion 1979, fig. 9; Ciarallo and De Carolis 1999, no. 277).

That the Winchester grave is that of a female therefore also affects any interpretation of gender based on the inclusion of a game counter in CF42. The evidence for the gender of graves containing game pieces is often ambiguous or absent on the Continent (*e.g.* Amrein *et al.* 1999, 346–7; Bel 2002, 153), and where it is available for graves in Britain they are usually those of males (TABLES 55–6, taken from Cotton 2001a, 13, table A; 2001b, 27–31, esp. table 9).

TABLE 32: NAILS FROM THE CHAMBER CF42

Find	SF no.	Head	Length (mm)	Wood	Grain to shank direction	Notes
C500	214	–	44	y	diagonal	shank fragment
C504	215	–	24	y	transverse	shank fragment
C507a	218a	round	64	y	transverse	–
C507b	218b	–	54	–	–	shank fragment in 2 pieces; ?part of a) above
C512	222	–	71	y	transverse	shank fragment in 2 pieces; grain covers full length, no obvious junction between planks
C513	223	–	42	y	transverse	shank fragment in 2 pieces; grain covers full length
C514	224	–	40	y	transverse	–
C515	225	–	19	–	–	shank fragment
C517	226	?round	84	y	transverse	?plank junction 36 mm below base of head
C520	229	sub-circular	57	–	–	in 2 pieces
C521a	–	round	72	y	transverse	–
C521b	–	–	59	y	transverse	shank fragment
C522	230	round	20	y	transverse	–
C531	231	–	51	y	transverse	shank fragment
C534	233	round	101	y	transverse	wood down whole length
C539	234	–	26	y	parallel	shank fragment
C540	235	round	24	y	parallel	–
C580	242	–	44	y	transverse	shank fragment
C592a	293a	–	40	y	transverse to diagonal	shank fragment; ?same as b) below
C592b	293b	–	24	y	transverse to diagonal	shank fragment; ?same as a) above
C596	243	–	22	y	transverse	shank fragment
C599	245	–	51	y	random	shank fragment
C603	246	?round	27	y	transverse	–
C604	247	?	–	–	–	slaggy lump, probably a nail head
C605	248	oval	60	y	transverse to diagonal	–
C606	249	sub-circular	22	y	transverse	–
C618	250	–	18	y	transverse + parallel	shank tip
C624	253	–	5	–	–	small fragment, perhaps from a shank
C627	254	?sub-circular	–	y	transverse	possibly a nail head, the wood appears to run over the edge and onto the upper surface
C640	256	–	31	y	transverse	shank fragment
C641	257	round	20	y	transverse	wood lies across head
C648	259	round	57	y	parallel and twisted	at one point the wood twists from parallel to transverse
C649	–	round	66	y	transverse + parallel	head now concave; slight wood traces only
C651	261	sub-circular	51	y	transverse	–
C652	262	round	154	y	transverse	a piece of wood may curve across and below the head, as on C746 (SF283) below); only slight traces on shank
C653	–	sub-circular	90	y	transverse	–
C669	264	–	–	y	twisted	small fragments from head and top of shank only
C695	267	–	22	y	parallel	shank fragment
C700a	268a	sub-circular	40	y	transverse	–
C700b	268b	–	72	y	transverse	shank fragment; ?part of a) above
C711	269	–	79	y	parallel + random	shank fragment; very small pieces of wood (or other organic material) only
C712	270	–	95	y	transverse	shank fragment; wood down full length

TABLE 32: (CONT'D)

Find	SF no.	Head	Length (mm)	Wood	Grain to shank direction	Notes
C713	271	round	52	y	transverse	–
C714	272	round	53	y	transverse	–
C715	273	–	67	y	diagonal	shank fragment
C716	274	round	128	y	parallel to diagonal	–
C717	275	round	103	y	transverse	wood grain only clear on bottom 19 mm
C720	276	–	67	y	parallel	shank fragment; wood at lower end only
C721	277	–	56	y	transverse	shank fragment; wood down whole length
C722	278	–	60	y	transverse	shank fragment in 2 pieces
C735	280	sub-circular	38	y	random	small flecks of wood only
C737	281	sub-circular	53	y	transverse	in 4 pieces; fragment of wood also lies across head
C745	282	–	64	y	transverse	shank fragment;
C746	283	round	50	y	transverse	wood lies over head and curves to pass below it on one side; also slight traces of wood immediately below head on another side
C752	286	round	37	–	–	–
C753	287	round	53	y	transverse + parallel	transverse wood from just below head down whole length of shank; wood also across head and curving down below it to meet transverse piece
C754	288	–	41	y	parallel	shank fragment
C755	289	–	33	y	parallel	shank fragment
C760	290	–	32	y	transverse	shank fragment in 2 pieces
C761	291	round	40	–	–	–
C–	–	–	27	–	–	shank fragment

However, an important burial that confirms that female graves can include game equipment is grave 9 in the King Harry Lane cemetery at Verulamium. It held two glass counters and a mirror and is dated to Phase 3 (c. A.D. 40–60/or revised date c. A.D. 35–50/5), but was not included in Cotton's study because it did not contain a full set of counters (Stead and Rigby 1989, fig. 90, 10–11, 13; Price 1989, 109).

Three studs with globular glass heads fixed onto narrow iron shanks found in CF42 are very unusual, although there is an iron shank with a small glass bead for a head in CF72 which can be seen as a rudimentary and cheaper form of the same object type (FIG. 129, CF72.12; pp. 254–5). The style of the CF42 stud heads, with swirls and eyes of colour in a cobalt blue matrix, is La Tène, and the iron shanks suggest that they were fitted into a wooden object, perhaps an item of furniture. In support of this idea it should be noted that wood survives on the shank of CF72.12, although drawing too close a parallel between these items may be unwise in view of their technological differences. A narrow iron strip in two pieces from the chamber may belong to the same piece of furniture (CF42.17) and other shank fragments imply that more such studs originally existed (CF42.16d–e). If they do derive from a box, then, together with the one in AF48 (AF48.3) and the wooden ?trays in CF47 (CF47.25) and BF67 (BF67.4), they attest to the wide range of decorative techniques employed by skilled craftsmen in wood and metal in Late Iron Age Britain. An alternative identification is that they are hairpins or dress pins, which would suit the interpretation of CF42 as a female grave. A long iron shank fitted with a similar globular glass head with decorative trails has been found at Old Penrith, and has been identified as a dress accessory (Mould 1991, 196, fig. 99, 711). It is probably somewhat later in date than the Stanway objects, although no context details are given. Its shank is quite thick compared to those fitted into the CF42 glass heads, and would provide the correct counterbalance for the weight of the head if used as a hairpin. Functionally the same or not, technically and stylistically the CF42 and Old Penrith objects are closely matched, and their manner of fixing the glass head onto an iron shank is markedly different to that used for the Roman military copper-alloy glass-headed studs or pins found at Caerleon, Gloucester and Sheepen, and in the Lexden Tumulus, which have globules of red glass set into concave cups (Webster 1991, 132, fig. 9, 2–3; Webster 1992, 147–8; Hawkes and Hull 1947, pl. 100, 9; Foster 1986, fig. 25, 17–21).

The nails from CF42 are listed in TABLE 32. All are of Manning's Type 1b (1985, 134) apart from SF262, which just falls within the larger Type 1a. As with BF6 and BF24, a range of sizes is present, but many are quite large, *i.e.* between 90 mm and the 154 mm of SF262, and many are only shank fragments which clearly also came from large nails. Most have some mineral-replaced wood on the shank, and in general the grain runs horizontally across the metal. There are a few instances of the grain running parallel to the shank, but on none of them does both transverse and parallel grain survive sufficiently well to give an indication of plank thickness. Only on SF226 is there a suggestion of the junction of two planks, some 36 mm below the head. In some cases the wood grain is quite distorted and a few nails have wood grain on the head as well as the shank, both features that probably result from the collapse of the structure.

A small amorphous lump of vitrified clay (C607) is unlikely to be a deliberate deposit. It was presumably formed during cremation, and was probably scraped up with the soil used to backfill the chamber. It may, however, be residual from the Middle Iron Age occupation of Enclosure 2. Small flat fragments in a friable sandy fabric are probably residual pieces of structural clay and are listed in archive.

There are no individual finds from the chamber which can provide a close date for its backfilling. Collectively the pottery points to a Claudio–Neronian date for this event, although the presence of a vessel in *terra rubra* (*see* further p. 436) hints at a pre-A.D. 50 date, a conclusion supported by the two glass vessels which may be as early as pre-conquest.

All the finds listed below were found in the backfill (*i.e.* lower fill) unless otherwise indicated.

Pottery vessels (FIG. 73)

Gallo-Belgic imports

CF42.1 FIG. 73. C522, C537, C587, C654, C572, C666, C683, C688. Moulded platter: Camulodunum form 8. Fabric TN; buff fine-grained matrix, dark blue-grey surfaces. No finish survives.
Condition: four rims comprising about half rim circuit and one base sherd, none joining but almost certainly from the same vessel. No base sherds with footring identified. No evidence of burning, but surfaces crackled and abraded, and fracture edges abraded.
CF42.2 Not illustrated. Rims: C573, C575, C611, C697, C731. Moulded platter: Camulodunum form 8. Fabric TN; white powdery-grained paste, dark blue-grey surfaces. No finish survives.
Condition: six fragments from rim sherds, two joining, but all almost certainly from the same vessel. No base sherds with footring identified. No evidence of burning, but surfaces and fracture edges abraded.
CF42.3 Not illustrated. Base: C632. Moulded platter: Camulodunum form 7/8. Fabric TN; buff fine-grained matrix, dark blue-grey surfaces. Polished upper, matt lower surface.
Condition: one base sherd only. Fabric similar to CF42.1, but base step wider.
CF42.4 Not illustrated. Rim: C776. Large stepped platter: Camulodunum form 5, the variant produced by the potter Medi(illus) with a base step. Fabric TN; buff fine-grained matrix, dark blue-grey surfaces. Crackled and laminated, no finish survives.
Condition: one rim sherd only. Abraded fracture edges and burnt.
CF42.5 Not illustrated. C650, ?C656. Large stepped platter: Camulodunum form 5. Fabric TN; sandy white matrix, traces of blue-grey surfaces.
Condition: one sherd. In appalling condition due to lamination and abrasion.
No other examples of the form occur at Stanway.
CF42.6 FIG. 73. Rims: C542, C558, C577, C615, C683; C541, C557, C635, C674, C729. Carinated cup: Camulodunum form 56I small. Fabric TR1(C) or TR2, orange fine-grained matrix. Eroded surfaces, no finish survives.
Condition: small sherds join to form 1/5 of rim circuit, also two others to extend it to just over 1/4: also three carinated sherds. No base or lower body sherds.
CF42.7 FIG. 73. Rims: C551, C628, C645, C769, C773; base: C574, C578, C616, C689, C732, C762, C766; body sherds: C516, C621, C739, C757; other small TR sherds probably from CF42.7: C571,

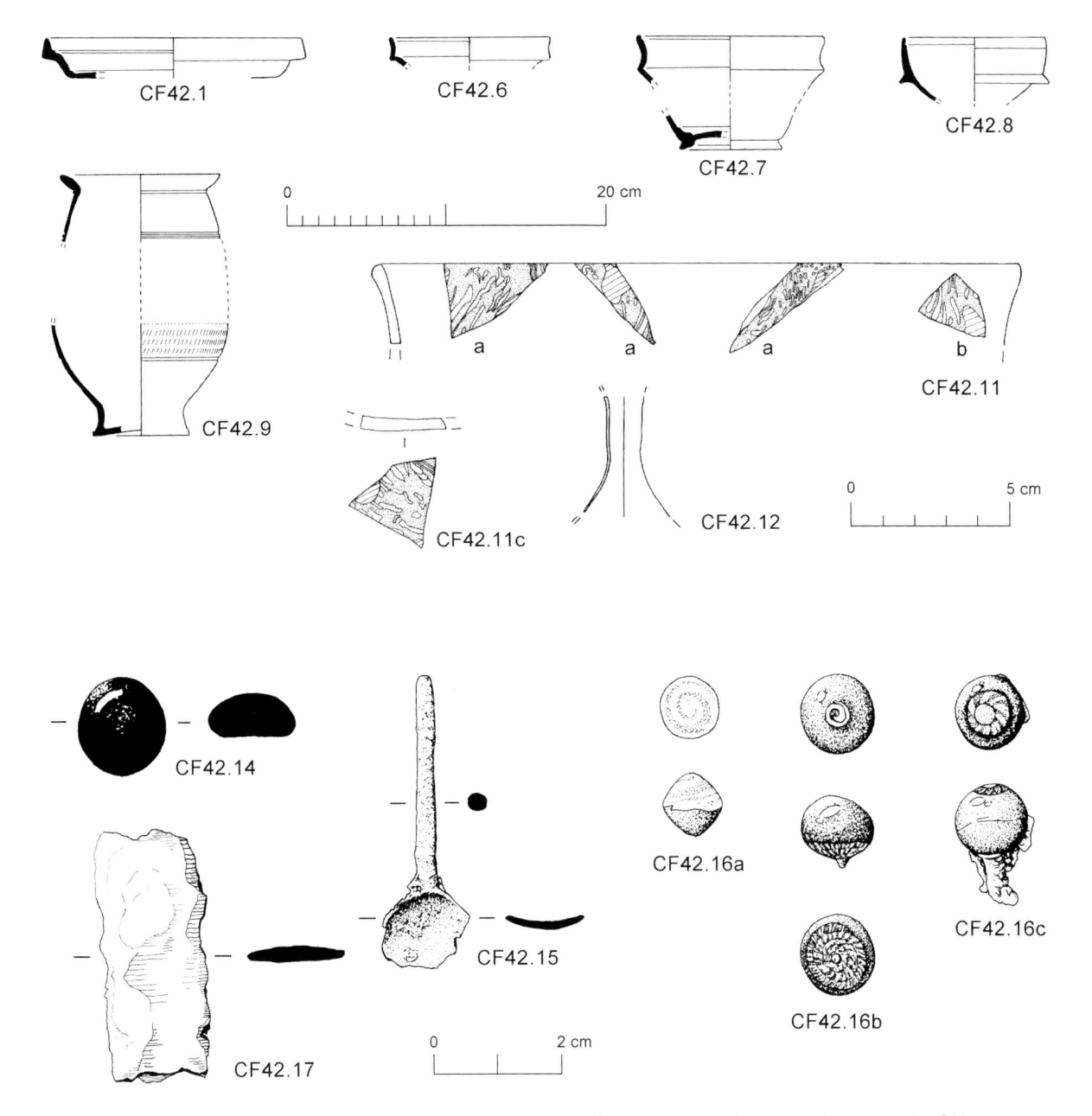

FIG. 73. Chamber CF42: pottery vessels CF42.1 and CF42.6–9 (scale 1:4), glass vessels CF42.11–12 (scale 1:2), glass gaming counter (CF42.14), copper-alloy spoon (CF42.15), studs with glass head and metal shank (CF42.16a–c), and iron object (CF42.17) (scale 1:1)

C585, C612–13, C617, C622, C629, C646, C663, C665, C707, C709–10, C727, C734, C742. Carinated cup: Camulodunum form 56I large. Fabric TR1(C); orange-red fine-grained matrix. Polished finish on the rim and interior, roughly burnished outer surface.
Condition: six rims, none large than 20 mm and none joining, with eroded fracture edges; four carinations in the same fragmented condition and one lower wall sherd; two joining footring sherds joining two bases and three cornice sherds form about almost half base circuit.
CF42.8 FIG. 73. Rims: C579, C590, C654, C684, C740; C764. Flanged cup: Camulodunum form 58. Fabric TN; fine-grained orange-buff matrix, dark blue-grey crackled and abraded surfaces. No finish survives.
Condition: two joining rims, three rims and one sherd almost certainly from the same vessel; abraded surfaces and fractured edges. No base or footring sherds identified.
CF42.9 FIG. 73. Rims: C548, C593, C625, C644, C655, C694, C724; neck and double groove: C763, C768, C573, C583, C687; lower groove: C636, C657, C677, C728, C750; base C777 joins lower body C675 and rouletting C686 and C702; also: C533, C544, C561, C562, C566, C570, C573, C582–3,

C586, C591, C598, C614, C626, C629, C633–4, C636, C638, C657, C662, C664, C668, C670, C673, C677–9, C681, C684, C687, C691–3, C696, C699, C701–5, C708, C725-6, C728, C733, C743–4, C750, C765, C771–5, C778, C1229. Ovoid beaker: Camulodunum form 112 Cb. Fabric TR3; typical fine-grained orange ware with smoked grey zones on the rim and outer surface. Polished finish over plain areas. Decoration: one broad zone of chattered rouletting defined by at the top by a double groove and at the bottom by a single groove. Identical to KHL 316, found with a miniature double-handled flagon of Camulodunum form 161, a platter in GTW, and an early silver dolphin brooch.
Condition: severely fragmented, fracture edges eroded. Six rims, none joining, making about one 1/3 circuit; four joining neck and upper body sherds with double-groove; five lower body sherds; one base joining three lower body sherds. Numerous tiny sherds, plain and rouletted. The sherds probably comprise a full profile for about 1/4 to 1/3 circuit.

Amphora

CF42.10 Not illustrated. C758. Dressel 2-4 amphora. 10 sherds/fragments (not too much attention should be paid to the sherd count because the crumbly and friable character of the vessel has led to disintegration since excavation) (15 g). Fabric soft and powdery light yellow (10YR 8/6) fabric with sparse (less than 5 per cm^2) well-sorted rounded and sub-rounded white and light grey inclusions <1mm across.

Glass vessels (FIG. 73)

CF42.11
a FIG. 73. C706, C747, C749. Deep cylindrical bowl. Cast polychrome. Canes — deep translucent blue ground with opaque yellow central dot surrounded by at least two concentric rings of opaque white spots. Three rim fragments; rounded, slightly out-bent rim, straight side possibly sloping in very slightly. Interior and exterior rotary polished. Rim diameter 150–160 mm, present height 19 mm, wall thickness 3–5.5 mm.
b FIG. 73. CL59; C589. Body fragment from CF42.11; rotary polished internally and externally. Dimensions 22.5 × 15 mm, wall thickness 3.5 mm.
c FIG. 73. CL59; C547. Base fragment from CF42.11. Flat base possibly broken at junction with side. Surfaces not polished. Dimensions 27 × 25, base thickness 3 mm.
d CL59; C554, C555, C559, C568, C576, C581, C584. Nine small chips and splinters from CF42.11.
CF42.12
a FIG.73. C767. Unguent bottle. Blue/green. Complete neck and one body fragment. Cylindrical neck curving out to missing rim; side sloping out. Neck diameter 10 mm, neck length 21 mm, wall thickness 0.5 mm.
b CL59; C535, C536, C552, C565. Four blue/green convex-curved body fragments, probably part of CF42.12.
c C685, C736, C738, C759. Six blue/green convex-curved body fragments, probably from CF42.12.
CF42.13 (Not illustrated.)
a C690. Unguent bottle. Light yellow/brown. 2 slivers from neck? fragments plus chips. Thickness 1.25 mm.
b C682. Three body fragments. Light yellow/brown. Slightly convex-curved. Probably from CF42.13. Wall thickness 0.5 mm.
c C685. Body fragment. Light yellow/brown. Slightly convex-curved. Probably from CF42.13. Wall thickness 0.5 mm.

Other finds (FIG. 73)

CF42.14. FIG. 73. SF244. C597. Counter of opaque black (very dark blue) glass. Diameter 13.5 to 15 mm, height 6.5 mm.
CF42.15. FIG. 83. SF265. C671. Part of the round bowl and the shaft of a ?brass spoon, probably originally tinned, and a separate piece of the bowl. Length 44 mm, bowl diameter approximately 16 mm.
CF42.16.
a FIG. 73. SF255. C630. Globular glass stud or pin head, the bottom half translucent cobalt blue, the top opaque white, with the spiral in which it was applied clearly visible, marvered into the blue matrix. There are faint traces of iron corrosion inside the hole for the shank. Diameter 10 mm.
b FIG. 73. SF279. C723. Globular glass stud or pin head with a short stump of the iron shank surviving. The top half is translucent cobalt blue, with a small swirl of white on the top. In the bottom half a spiral of twisted yellow and colourless glass has been marvered into the blue matrix. Diameter 12 mm.

c FIG. 73. SF285. C751. Stud or pin with narrow iron shank and large globular glass head. This is of translucent cobalt blue glass with an eye of opaque yellow inside a ring of twisted white and colourless glass on the top. The shank is incomplete. Diameter 11.5 mm, length 18 mm.
d SF227. C518 (CL60). Three tiny fragments of a narrow iron shank, probably from a stud as SFs 255, 279, and 285 above. Lengths 5, 6, and 10 mm.
e SF263. C658. Narrow iron shank fragment, polygonal in section, probably from a stud as SFs 255, 279, and 285 above. Length 13 mm.
CF42.17. FIG. 73. SF251. SF252. C619. C623. Narrow iron strip fragment, broken in two pieces. Length 67 mm, width 17 mm.
C607. Lump of vitrified clay. Weight 19 mm.

Residual pottery sherds mainly in the mound

CF42.a C530, C601, C609. Sherds of similar fabric and thickness, probably all from the same pot. Fabric GTW.
CF42.b .C642. Butt-beaker rim sherd, Cam form 113 copy, burnished with burnish extending over rim, sandy fabric with sparse fine grog temper. Fabric GTW.
CF42.c C527, C538, C550, C553, C560, C567, C698. Body sherds possibly all part of one vessel of unknown form, coarse tempered. Fabric GTW (mainly mid-lower fill).
CF42.d C523, C525, C529, C601, C609, C637. Body sherds possibly all part of one vessel of unknown form, thick walled sherds. Fabric GTW.
CF42.e C608. Base sherd from small jar, burnished externally, fabric is similar to GBW but is distinctly grog-tempered. Fabric GTW.
CF42.f C667. Rim sherd from small jar or cup (not part of CF42.e) burnished with burnish extending over rim. Fabric GTW.
CF42.g C524. Rim sherd, very small thin sherd, abraded and damaged, top of rim burnished, not part of pot CF42.f. Dark fabric ?GTW.
Middle Iron Age sherds in mound: 3 sherds (17 g).

PITS WITH PYRE DEBRIS

PIT BF17 (FIGS 2, 43–5, 74; TABLE 33)

Cremated bone	none	
Other finds	BF17.1	iron stud and sheet fragment
	BF17.2	small brass boss
	BF17.3	heat-affected iron fitting probably from a box or chest many small fragments of heat-affected copper alloy plus fragments of iron objects, including nail fragments
Residual finds	none	

A wooden barrel or tub appears to have been set upright in the ground on the east side of chamber BF6 in Enclosure 3 (FIGS 2, 8, 43–5). The vessel was placed in a pit (BF17) 0.9 m deep as measured from the excavation surface or about 1.25 m from the contemporary ground level. The backfill of the pit was mainly sand and gravel which, in places, was difficult to distinguish from the surrounding natural. This is presumably because the backfill was simply the material which had been dug out to create the pit in the first place. The backfill included thin ferromanganiferous lenses which, as in the chamber pit of BF6, had formed naturally. A little of the excavated material had been placed back in the pit so as to make a flat horizontal bedding for the barrel such that the head was 0.5 m below the modern excavation surface or about 0.85 m below the contemporary ground level.

Roman barrels were typically around 1.8–2.1 m long with a maximum girth of about 0.7–1.05 m (Marlière 2001, 194–201, table 5; Boon 1975, 54). The Stanway barrel was 0.7 m in diameter at its lowest point showing that it must have been a barrel rather than a bucket. No iron hoops were found, but far more barrels were bound with wood than metal (*see* Marlière 2001, 194–201, table 5, for bindings of hazel, beech, birch, and poplar).

The profile of the end of the barrel could be seen in the backfilled pit BF17, even although nothing of the vessel survived (FIG. 44). The sides of the pit were near vertical and the base flat and horizontal with a groove 35 mm wide and 40 mm deep around its perimeter where the staves had projected beyond the head. The clearly defined groove combined with the fact that the base of the pit was flat and horizontal show that the head had not been prized out before the barrel was set in the ground in the way that was done when barrels were reused for wells (Boon 1975, 52; Wilmot 1982, 47).

The barrel would have been only about 0.8 m long if the top of it had been flush with the ground, which is too little for a full-sized version. Thus it would seem that the barrel had been cut down in length to make a tub (one example comes from Segontium, Boon 1975, 53–4) or it had projected out of the ground to a height of perhaps as much as 1.3 m.

The lowest 0.3 m of the fill of the barrel consisted of horizontal layers of charcoal (oak and ash, *see* pp. 390–1) presumably derived from at least one pyre. These deposits were capped by a clayey layer, 0.15 m thick. No fragments of cremated bone or pottery were recovered from the charcoal-rich layers. However, there were quite a number of other finds from it, including heat-affected copper-alloy fragments, some nail and stud fragments (10.11 g; TABLE 33) and a large, heat-affected, iron plate (FIGS 45, 74). The plate and nails may have been parts of a wooden box or chest. The heat-affected copper-alloy objects were similar to the heat-affected material from the adjacent chamber BF6 and the pyre-site BF1/16, although nothing from the barrel can be related to any of the objects represented by the fragments found at the other two places. There were slight traces of burning in the backfill around the upper edges of the barrel and olive-coloured staining in the groove formed by the lower ends of the staves.

Interpretation of the fill of the barrel and its relationship to the chamber is difficult. The barrel seems to have been filled, or at least largely filled, with only charcoal and ash. Nothing else was put in the barrel when it was being used. The clayey layer over the charcoal layers seems to have been part of the mound which was raised over the chamber and barrel when they were both no longer needed. In time, the charcoal layers would undoubtedly have shrunk considerably in thickness as any unburnt organic material in them decayed and the charcoal was compressed. If, as seems likely, the original ground-level was about 500 mm above the top of the charcoal layers, then the latter must have compressed to almost one-third of their original volume if the barrel had been filled to the top with charcoal. As FIG. 44, Sx 24, clearly shows, part of the uppermost layer of the charcoal deposits had slid and stretched down into the chamber, as did part of the clayey layer (*i.e.* the mound) which sealed it. The parts of the layers which had moved downwards into the chamber were sealed by the most easterly edge of the remains of the timber roof of the chamber. But this sequence is misleading. The edge of the roof did not (in fact could not) have sealed the top of the barrel; the impression that it did was brought about by the slumping and settlement of the upper parts of the sides of the chamber-pit into the void of the chamber as its timber walls degenerated.

The charcoal layers in the bottom of the barrel were all bedded horizontally, showing that they are not the result of one backfilling episode but the product of a sequence of discrete depositions probably made over a period of time which was long enough to allow each deposit to settle and compress. This does not square with the most obvious interpretation for the charcoal layers, *i.e.* that they all derived from the pyre used to burn the body associated with the broken grave goods in chamber BF6. Maybe the sequence of layers points to the burning of more than one pyre during the life of the chamber.

It is not clear what purpose the barrel served and why sequences of pyre-related charcoal should have been placed in it. The absence of bone may indicate that the material is the sifted residue after the removal of the human remains. But then why keep the charcoal and take so much trouble over its storage? Perhaps the barrelful of charcoal is a high-status equivalent of the pits filled with pyre-related debris found elsewhere?

Finds

BF17.1 FIG. 74. SF117. B133. Iron dome-headed stud attached to a small fragment of iron sheet with traces of mineral-replaced wood on the underside. Diameter 9 mm, height 10 mm. Weight 0.93 g.

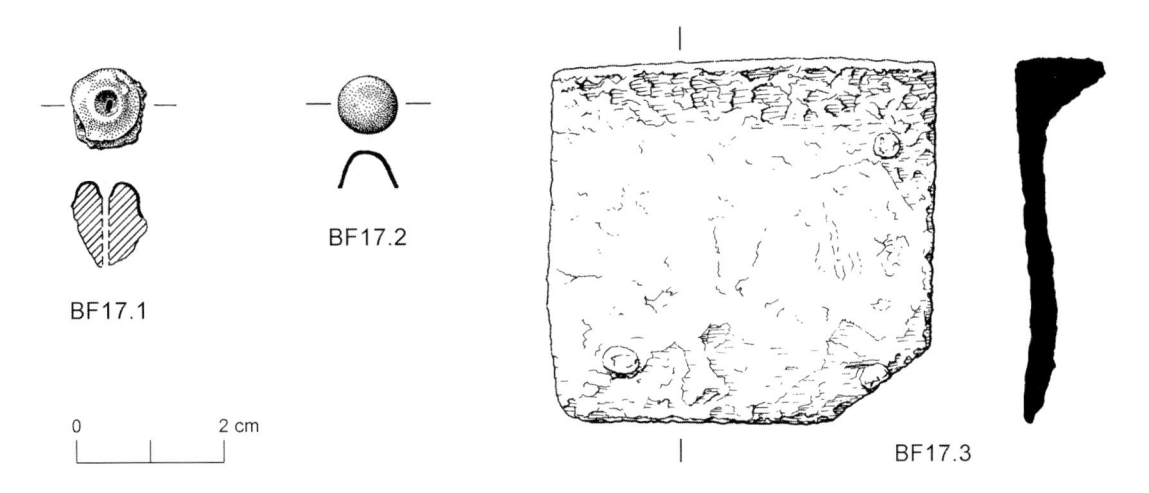

FIG. 74. Pit with pyre debris BF17: finds of iron (BF17.1 and BF17.3) and copper alloy (BF17.2) (scale 1:1).

BF17.2 FIG. 74. SF115. B155. Small ?brass dome-headed boss with iron corrosion on the underside, probably from an iron shank. Diameter 8.5 mm, height 5 mm. Weight 0.24 g. A similar stud from a grave at Emona was in association with a lock-plate and therefore identified as a box fitting (Plesničar-Gec 1972, Taf. 19, 80.8).

BF17.3 FIG. 74. SF162. B220.

a Most of a heat-affected iron fitting, originally found with burnt flint pebbles and charcoal adhering to it. It consists of a more or less square plate, with the remains of nail or rivet shanks for attachment in the corners, with a short right-angled return on one edge. No means of attachment have been located on the return. Dimensions 48.5 by 51.5 mm, return 12 mm. The section as shown at the angle is not original. This is probably a corner plaque from a box or chest.

b Not illustrated. Fragments of four iron nails, one complete, 32 mm long.

SF112. B142. Fragment of an iron nail in two pieces. The head is flat and probably originally round, the shank is square in section. Length about 31 mm.

B144. About eighty small fragments of iron, one the tip of a nail shank. Total weight 24 g.

B229. Iron nail with flat ?sub-circular head and bent shank. Length 52 mm.

TABLE 33: HEAT-AFFECTED AND RESOLIDIFIED COPPER ALLOY FROM BF17

No.	Find	Small find no.	No. of pieces	Weight (g)	Notes
	B133	116	1	0.14	
	B144	311	5	0.17	4 fragments are of sheet metal
	B154	114	4+	8.31	small fragment of iron sheet, 25 by 30 mm, with separate small pieces of at least one copper-alloy stud, including the shank; largest piece of copper alloy 22 by 14 mm, shank 13 mm long
BF17.2	B155	115	1	0.24	
	B221	159	2	1.25	copper-alloy disc (in two pieces), diameter 28 mm; resolidified pellet
	B156	110/111	–	–	specks of copper alloy with charcoal and soil
totals			13+	10.11	

PIT CF7 (FIGS 2, 75)

Cremated bone	55.8 g	adult of indeterminate age and sex
Pottery vessels	CF7.1	grog-tempered jar
Other finds	CF7.2	part of a boss-on-bow brooch (*Knotenfibel*)
	CF7.3	iron pin or needle
	CF7.4	iron fragments — remains of a ?chain
Residual finds		none

A small circular pit (CF7) containing pyre-related debris lay approximately 25 m south-east of Enclosure 5 (FIG. 2). The pit included some of the sherds from a broken Late Iron Age pottery jar (FIG. 75, CF7.1), the upper half of a Late Iron Age brooch (FIG. 75, CF7.2), an iron needle or pin (FIG. 75, CF7.3), and several fragments of iron (CF7.4), some of which may be from a chain. These, with an admixture of charcoal and a small amount of cremated human bone (adult), were found throughout the fill of the pit rather than on its floor, showing that the material was probably redeposited pyre debris rather than parts of deliberately broken grave goods. The irregular profile of the pit and the absence of a flat base support this view (FIG. 75). The jar CF7.1 is the earliest of all the pots associated with the Stanway cemetery. It is entirely pre-Roman Iron Age in typology and technique, and could have been made any time in the 1st century B.C. Although traditional potting techniques survived the Roman occupation but apparently not the Boudican revolt, so providing a conventional latest date of *c.* A.D. 65, the most likely date range for its manufacture based on typology and technology is 75–25 B.C. Allowing a couple of decades for an heirloom or kitchen cupboard factor, the latest date of deposition is likely to be *c.* 5 B.C.

The brooch (CF7.2) is of the La Tène III boss-on-bow type (*Knotenfibel*). While there are very close parallels between *Knotenfibeln* of precious metal, the details of the construction and decoration of the copper-alloy brooches varies considerably, making most brooches distinctive in some way or another. The distinguishing features of the Stanway fragment are the slightly expanded head and its narrow moulding, the lozenge-shaped section of the bow both above and below the button, and the latter with its accompanying mouldings. Many brooches of this type have expanded heads, ranging from slight, as here, to almost approaching a full trumpet shape (*e.g.* Stead 1976, fig. 1, 1–2), but the narrow moulding behind the head of the Stanway fragment is unusual. The lowest moulding on the button is unique, with its raised sides and lowered points at front and rear, the points matching the angles of the lozenge-shaped section of the lower bow. While this particular detail may be unparalleled, a related extended development of the lowest element of the button can be seen on several brooches from Deal, Folkestone, and Faversham in Kent (Stead 1976, fig. 2, 2–3, 5, fig. 3, 1), and on the most developed a small horn is set in this position (Hull and Hawkes 1987, pl. S7, 10, 14). The Stanway brooch has characteristics that suggest it may be late within the usual date range for the form: the button is set high up on the bow, and the chord is set below the spring (*i.e.* is inferior). The brooch is discussed further on pages 314–15, where a date range of *c.* 60–25/20 B.C. is proposed.

The needle or pin (CF7.3) is of a form found in the Middle and Late Iron Ages in iron, copper alloy, and bone. There are two copper-alloy examples from Maiden Castle (Sharples 1991, fig. 129, 9–10), one from the Glastonbury lake village (Bulleid and Gray 1911, pl. 42, E43), and several from Danebury, where the majority were found with pottery of ceramic phase 7, *c.* 300–100/50 B.C. (Cunliffe and Poole 1991, 359, fig. 7.31, especially 3.278–80). The fragments of iron (CF7.4) are too damaged for accurate identification. Most are narrow strips, two may be parts of chain links.

The pit CF7 clearly pre-dates Enclosure 5. The brooch provides a likely date for it of *c.* 60–25/20 B.C. with which the pot CF7.1 is in agreement although it is not so tightly datable.

Pottery vessels (FIG. 75)

CF7.1 FIG. 75. Bases: C33, C34, C36, C43 (the largest sherds), all join; intermediate sherd: C35 (joins base C36 and rim C39); rims: C31, C33, C39 (no joins). Ripple-shouldered jar; hand-shaped body, probably wheel-finished rim. Fabric GTW, with visible coarse sand and flint, also voids at the surfaces caused by the leaching of calcareous and/or organic inclusions; roughly burnished at rim and shoulder and base. Decoration: burnished lattice on deliberate matt ground.

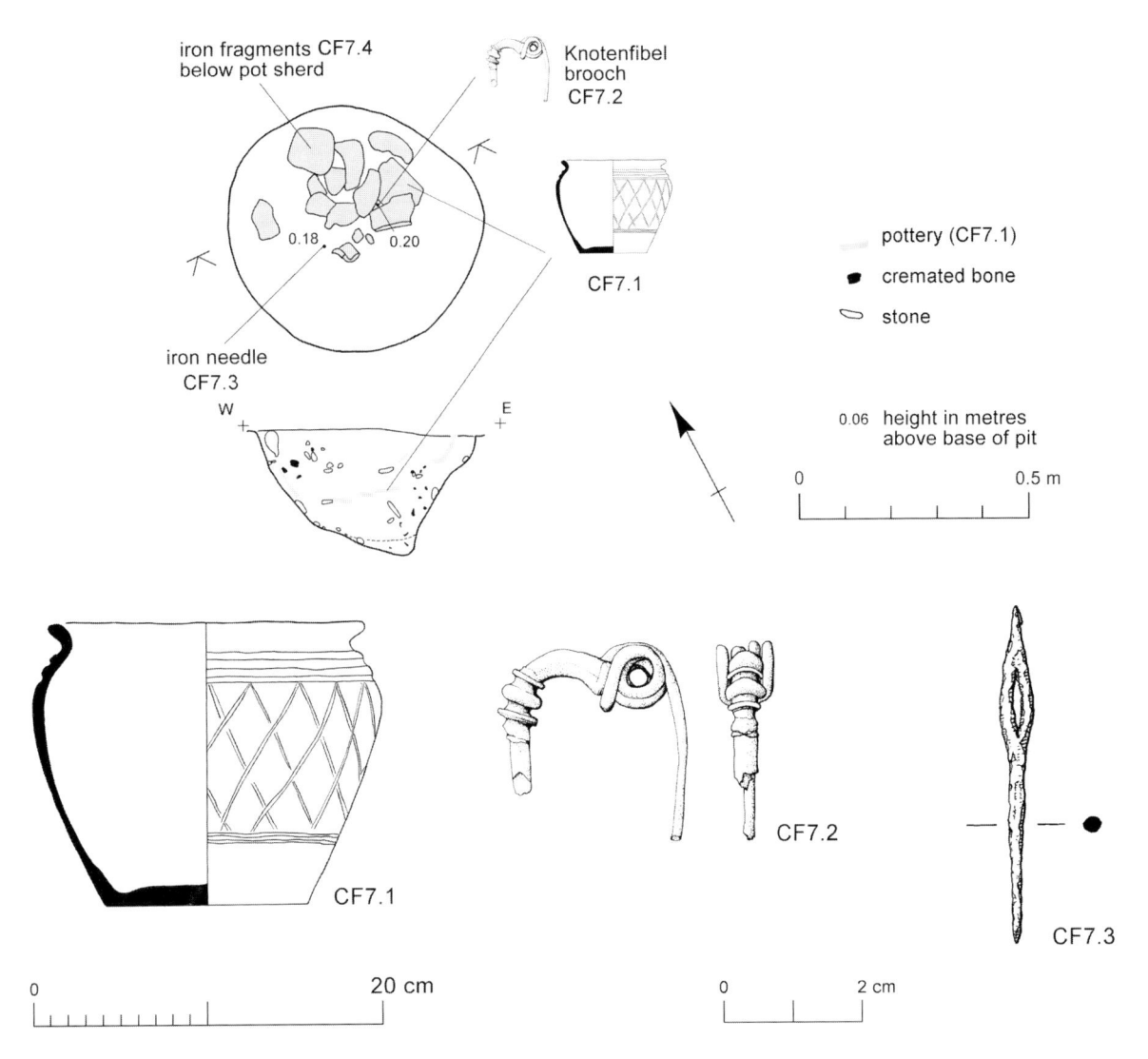

FIG. 75. Pit with pyre debris CF7: plan showing location of finds and section (scale 1:15), pottery vessel (scale 1:4), copper-alloy brooch (CF7.2), and iron needle or pin (CF7.3) (scale 1:1).

Condition: heavily burnt and discoloured after firing, probably when the pot was placed in or near the funeral pyre. Fragmented; bases join to produce complete circuit, rim and upper body sherds form less than half of the rim circuit.
Condition at deposition: The pot was fragmented before being placed in the pit. Only a selection of sherds were collected for deposition. The fragmentation seems to have occurred at or after the cremation.

Other finds (FIG. 75)

CF7.2. FIG. 75. SF198. C44. The upper part of a brass boss-on-bow brooch, with a detached part of the bow. The spring has four coils and an inferior chord. The head, more or less circular in section, is very slightly expanded and has a narrow moulding at the back next to the spring; the chord is neatly set below it. The button lies just below the curve of the bow, and there are two narrow mouldings above it. The upper moulding does not pass fully around the bow, which is of more or less circular section at this point, as are the button and the mouldings themselves. Below the button is one narrow moulding, flattened at the back, and below that, a wider one which passes all round the bow. It has lowered points at the centre front and rear of the bow, and raised sides, giving a zigzag lower edge following the contours of the bow, which is lozenge-shaped in section below it. Length (including detached piece) 33 mm.
CF7.3. FIG. 75. SF199. C45. Iron needle or pin with an elongated lozenge-shaped head and eye of a similar form. Length 48 mm.
CF7.4. SF200. C30. Eleven fragments of iron. Two are hooked and may be parts of figure-of-eight chain links, the rest are mainly narrow strips. Length of longest strip 41 mm, length of longest hooked fragment 28 mm.

PIT WITH BROKEN FUNERARY GOODS

PIT AF48 (FIGS 2, 6, 76–8)

Cremated bone	3.4 g	adult of indeterminate age and sex
Pottery vessels	AF48.1	grog-tempered jar
	AF48.2	grog-tempered bowl
Other finds	AF48.3	?wooden box bound with iron strips and a drop handle
	AF48.4	either two earrings or one finger-ring
Residual finds		Middle Iron age sherds and a flint flake

Late Iron Age pit AF48 lay between AF18 and AF25 in the northern half of Enclosure 1 (FIGS 2, 6). It was somewhat irregular in shape and up to 0.5 m deep with a slightly rounded base (FIG. 76). A small quantity of cremated human bone (3.4 g) from an adult was scattered mainly in the lower fill. A series of narrow iron and copper-alloy strips (FIG. 76, AF48.3) came from the lower fill close to the northern edge of the pit. These were mostly excavated in the museum laboratory from a soil-block lifted *in situ*, and were associated with traces of decayed wood. Other objects from the pit include a copper-alloy ?drop handle (now missing) and the remains of either a copper-alloy spiral ?finger-ring or a pair of earrings (FIG. 76, AF48.4).

Parts of at least two vessels in Late Iron Age technique were scattered mainly in the lower fill (FIG. 76; FIG. 77, AF48.2). The sherds are unburnt, and there are no joins with pottery from the other features in Enclosure 1 or elsewhere. Pot AF48.1 is paralleled by the cremation urn in burial AF18 (AF18.1) and so is presumably of the same date of manufacture within the 1st century B.C. (p. 167). The pit also contained some small, abraded residual Middle Iron Age sherds and a flint flake fragment (SF16).

The metal strips (FIG. 77, AF48.3a–d; FIG. 78) appear to be the remains of a wooden object (AF48.3) which was bound with iron strips and decorated with thin sheets of both copper alloy and iron. No hinges were found, but the presence of many solid and completely flat strips, and the absence of bucket mounts, established by real-time X-radiography before the soil-block was excavated, implies that the object is most likely to have been a box. The lost ?drop-handle would be consistent with this interpretation. No angled corner fragments survive. The ?box had apparently been deliberately damaged in antiquity. Iron and bronze strip mounts and fittings occur in a number of richly furnished burials of the late 1st century B.C. to mid 1st century A.D. Where they have not been directly associated, or recorded as directly associated, it has often been assumed that each represents a different item, the iron a large object, the copper alloy a smaller one (*e.g.* Stead 1967, table 1). In AF48, there can be no doubt of their close association, but the exact size and identification of the object they represent are not clear.

The lack of attachment nails or studs on the iron strips and copper-alloy sheet from AF48 is particularly unusual. One possible method of fixing an iron strip over a wooden object without the use of nails or studs would be to pass it around the object (be it round/oval or square/rectangular) and weld the ends of the strip firmly together at the point of junction. As the metal would have needed to be white-hot for the weld to be formed, this seems unlikely. Brazing the ends together using hard solder, a copper-zinc alloy with a low melting point, might be more suitable (Hodges 1976, 6, 86–7). Traces that may be from solder were found on iron binding strips from a Late Iron Age wooden tub in Grave 20622 at Westhampnett, West Sussex (Montague 1997, 101). The ingenuity of the craftsmen of that period should also be taken into consideration. The copper-alloy sheeting ornamenting the wooden buckets from the rich Augustan grave at Fléré-la-Rivière, Indre, France, was fixed in place by an unusual method. Rows of thin pieces of sheet copper alloy were inserted edgewise into the wood, then bands of ornamental sheet were fixed vertically to them by brazing or soldering (Ferdière and Villard 1993, 1–114).

The original object in AF48 can be assumed to be a piece of furniture consisting of flat boards. The comparative scarcity of copper-alloy to iron fragments further suggests (if not the result of differential survival) that one part of the object was more ornamented than any other. These two factors may be taken together as evidence for a box, chest, or casket, although the

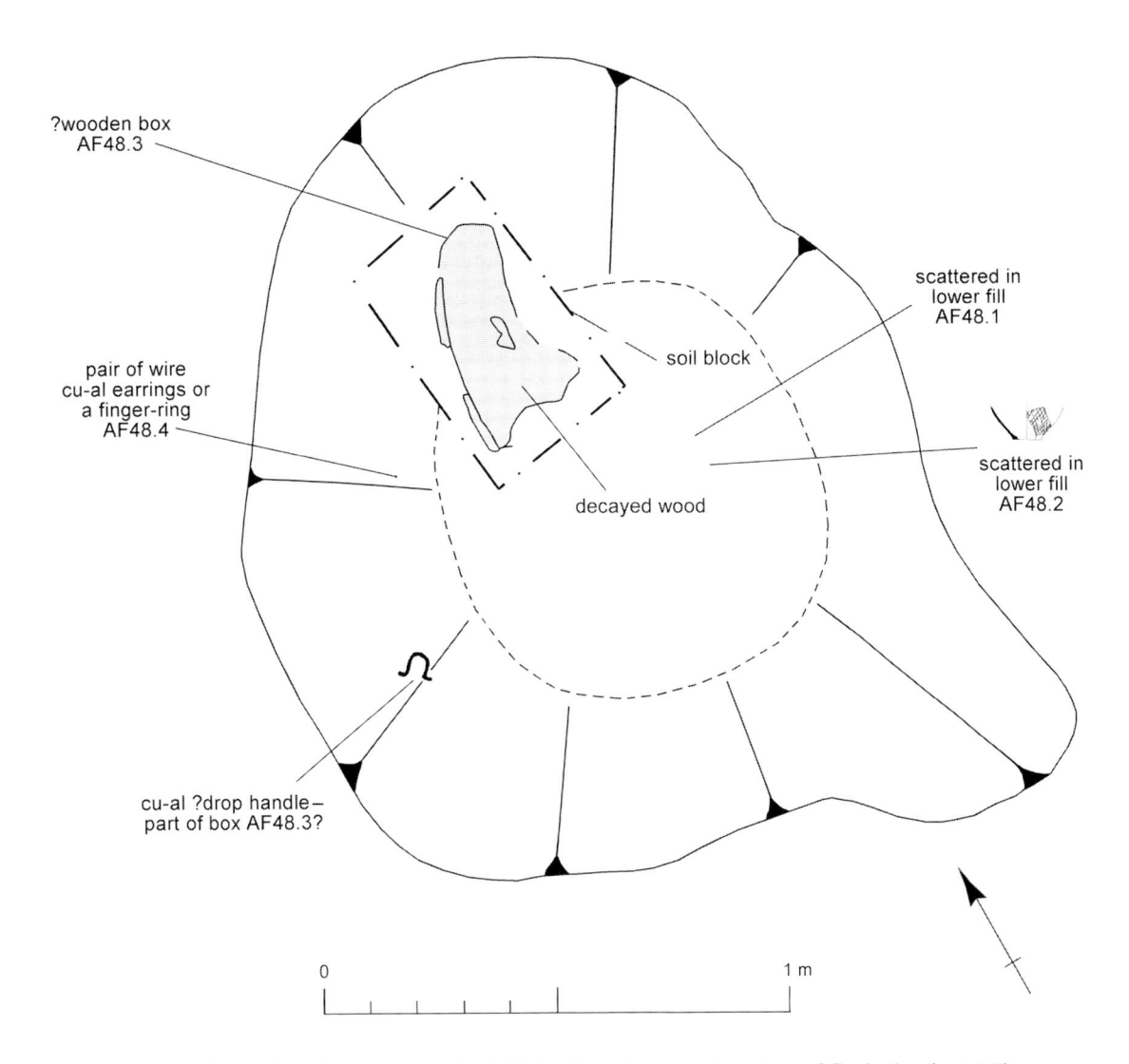

FIG. 76. Pit with broken funerary goods AF48: plan showing location of finds (scale 1:15)

possibility that the fragments derive from a more elaborate wooden object with metal fittings cannot be dismissed. In the Lexden Tumulus, fragments of iron plates overlaid with copper alloy, curved iron strips, embossed copper-alloy plates, and wood have been interpreted as together deriving from a box (Laver 1927, 249, pl. 53, fig. 1, pl. 59; Foster 1986, 95).

The repoussé decoration on the copper-alloy strips in AF48 is of typical La Tène style (FIG. 78). The fluid tendrilled scrolls with central bud detailing are similar to that on a panel from the Stanfordbury B burial, except that there the scroll is a single continuous line while here it appears to be a series of horizontal Ss (Stead 1967, 56; Jope 2000, pl. 223, g).

A second style of decoration is represented in AF48 by the small fragment, running at right angles to the main section, which shows a line of small bosses between pairs of linear mouldings (FIG. 78). This motif is also typical of the late La Tène period, occurring, for example, on a decorative sheet of a Fléré-la-Rivière bucket (Ferdière and Villard 1993, 1–113), on that of the large box in the Lexden Tumulus (Laver 1927, pl 59), on the plaque from the Stanfordbury B burial (Jope 2000, pl. 234, a–b), and on the frame of the Cadbury face-mask (Alcock 1972, pl. 12; Kilbride-Jones 1980, 26; Foster 2000, fig. 71, 14). Lines of bosses also occur on the side-plates of the Birdlip bucket (Green 1949, 189), and along the edge of a miniature votive shield of Iron Age form from Dragonby (Knowles and May 1996, fig. 11.17, 2). At Stanway they occur again on bronze sheet decorating the wooden object(s) in CF47 in Enclosure 5, and in BF67 in Enclosure 3.

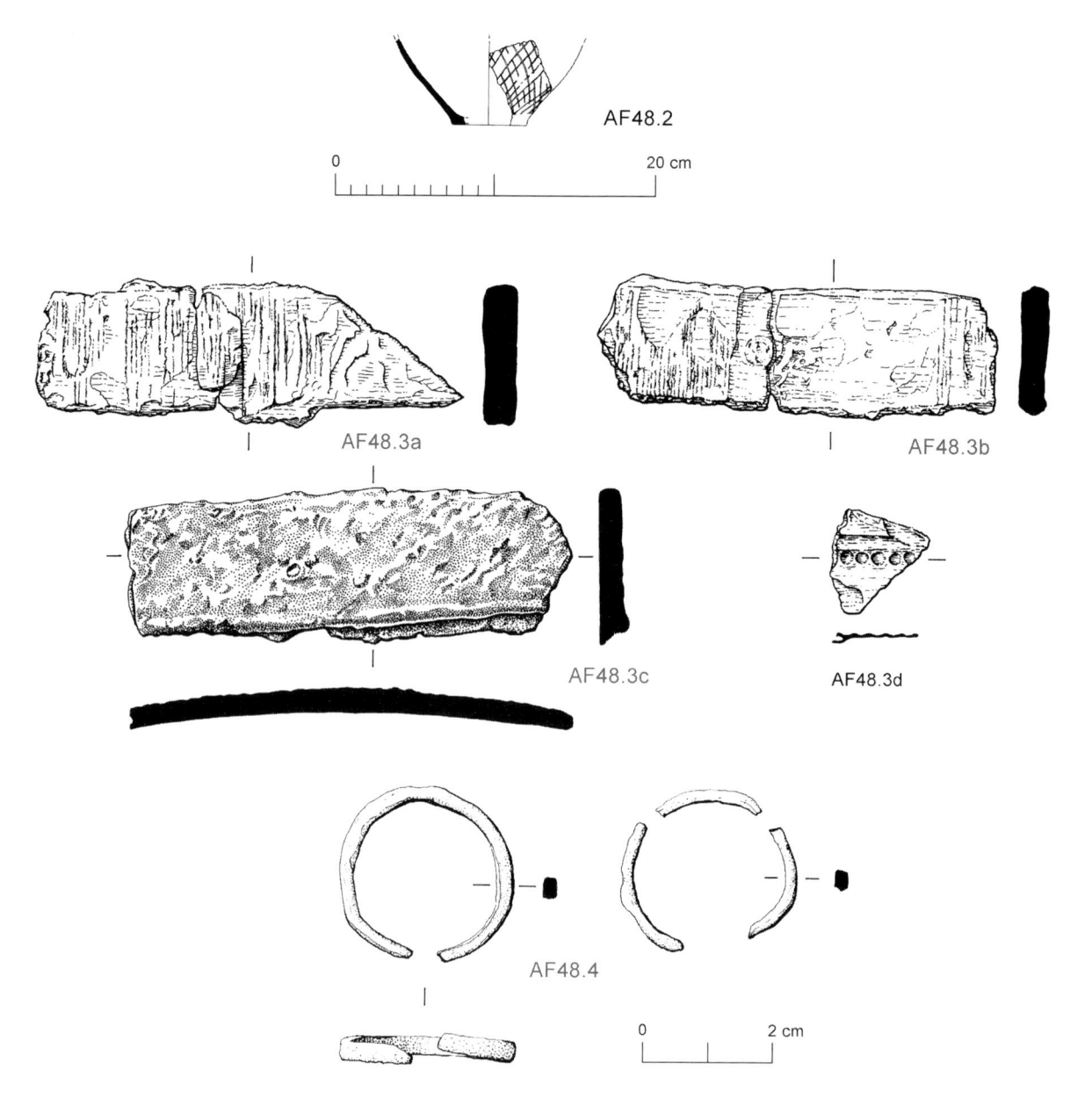

FIG. 77. Pit with broken funerary goods AF48: pottery vessel AF48.2 (scale 1:4), and objects of iron (AF48.3a–d), and copper alloy (AF48.4) (scale 1:1)

The only other metal objects from the pit fill are fragments of coiled copper-alloy wire (AF48.4), found together in the ground. They are probably a pair of wire earrings, exactly similar in size and form to a pair from Sheepen, found in a pit of Period 6 (*c*. A.D. 61–5) which had flint pebbles threaded on to the wire, and in one case also a silver bead (Hawkes and Hull 1947, fig. 61; Allason-Jones 1989, 82, nos 199–200). Alternatively, they may be part of a single finger-ring, although the very slight degree of twist on the more complete coil does not seem sufficient to justify this interpretation. Coiled finger-rings are the principal type in Late Iron Age Britain, with examples coming from, for example, Maiden Castle and Camulodunum (Wheeler 1943, fig. 86, 10–17; Sharples 1991, fig. 129, 12–14; Hawkes and Hull 1947, pl. 99, 1). A pair were found in the suite of female jewellery making up the Lamberton Moor hoard, along with two Lamberton Moor brooches and a Dragonesque brooch (Curle 1932, 363; Anderson 1905, fig. 5), but spiral finger-rings were not used exclusively by women; a gold one made of wire of similar size to the AF48 pieces, and only slightly larger at 20 mm in internal diameter, came from the male grave at Fléré-la-Rivière (Ferdière and Villard 1993, figs 1-102–3). An unsexed skeleton buried in the fill of a late 1st-century B.C. ditch at Baldock wore a copper-alloy finger-ring of this type on the left hand (Stead and Rigby 1986, 128, fig. 54, 201; Henderson 1986, 391, Burial 55). They could also be worn as toe-rings, as shown by some found on skeletons from Maiden Castle, Dorset (Wheeler 1943, 266, 278).

Pottery vessels (FIG. 77)

AF48.1 Not illustrated. A536, A537. Multi-cordoned footring jar, wheel-thrown. Fabric GTW; brown matrix; fine black inclusions; patchy dark grey and brown surfaces. Glossy burnished and burnished banded finish; glossy finish on the rim and cordons; burnished elsewhere. Very similar to that in burial AF18, but definitely a different vessel.
Condition: two joining rim sherds and a small number of largely non-conjoining body sherds; no matching base sherds identified. (Some sherds could possibly belong to a separate vessel.)
Condition at deposition: broken elsewhere, only a few sherds deposited.

AF48.2 FIG. 77. A536, A618. Wide shouldered lattice-burnished bowl with a flat base, Cam 223. Fabric GTW; brown matrix; dark grey-brown surfaces.
Condition: several conjoining body sherds and a single base sherd, no rim.
Condition at deposition: broken elsewhere, further fragmented *in situ*.

Other finds (FIGS 77–8)

AF48.3

a FIG. 77. SF39. A532. Thirty-four fragments of flat iron strips, in most cases with mineral-replaced wood on the reverse, the grain running across the width of the strips. Very few of the pieces join together. Only a few are illustrated. The strips appear to have been made by folding sheet iron two or three times. Single layer iron bands can develop hollows as they corrode, but here the layering/folding is clear on pieces that have not formed hollows.

Two widths of strip are apparent, 18–20 mm, and 23–25 mm. All are about 3.5–4 mm thick. There is also one fragment which measures 30 mm wide, and has a thinner flange on one side, similar to that on SF38 below, and equivalent to the thin flange projecting from a thicker strip shown in FIG. 78, part of SF41. No means of attachment to the wood is preserved. Similar fragments came from Grave 20185 at Westhampnett (Montague 1997, 103).

b FIG. 77. SF38. A535. Iron strip as SF39. Length 78 mm, width of main section 22 mm, width with flange 25 mm. There is a small part of a thin flange on one long side, and there may have been a similar one on the other side. No means of attachment remains. There are tiny fragments of mineral-replaced wood on the underside, the grain running across the strip.

c FIGS 77c, 78. SF41. A618. Fragmentary remains of iron strips as SFs 39 and 38 above, and of copper-alloy strips of thin decorated sheet, a few pieces of thin iron sheet, and associated wood fragments. This group was lifted as a soil block and retained in that form due to the fragile nature of the copper alloy. The block was examined using real-time X-radiography, to determine whether or not further objects lay within it, in particular pieces that might determine if it was the flattened remains of a bucket, or fragments of a box or item of furniture. No bucket fittings were found, therefore it is assumed that the pieces derive from a box or piece of furniture.

The copper-alloy sheet, and in some places also the associated thin iron sheet, is decorated with repoussé tendrilled S-scrolls with central buds. The maximum width of the copper-alloy sheet is 37 mm. The thick iron strip is 24 mm wide, or, in places where a flange projects from the side, 31 mm wide. The relationship between the iron, copper alloy, and wood in the soil block is complex. In one place (FIG. 78, Sx 2 left) a thin layer of iron, a flange projecting from a thick strip, directly overlies the copper alloy; in other places a thick strip of iron butts up against the copper alloy (FIG. 78, Sx 1 centre, Sx 2 centre); in one place a thin sheet of iron overlies, and follows the contours of, a thin sheet of repoussé-decorated copper alloy; in one place wood lies between two thin sheets of copper alloy (FIG. 78, Sx 1 left); in one place two layers of wood with different grain directions lie beneath a thick strip of iron (Sx 1 centre). Some assumptions can be made: 1) the repoussé decoration on the copper-alloy sheet must have been visible on the outside of the object; 2) the iron strips may have been either on the inside of the object, or on the outside, or both; and 3) some of the visible relationships of the metals and the wood are the result of damage, either before or during deposition, and may therefore be misleading.

It is worth noting that: 1) the wood beneath the thick iron strips always has the grain lying across the width of the metal, and this is matched on the associated fragments SFs 39 and 38; 2) both end-grain and longitudinal grain lie in close association at the same level on the soil block (FIG. 78, top left), suggesting that two boards met at that point, either jointed together or abutting and pegged; 3) the thin

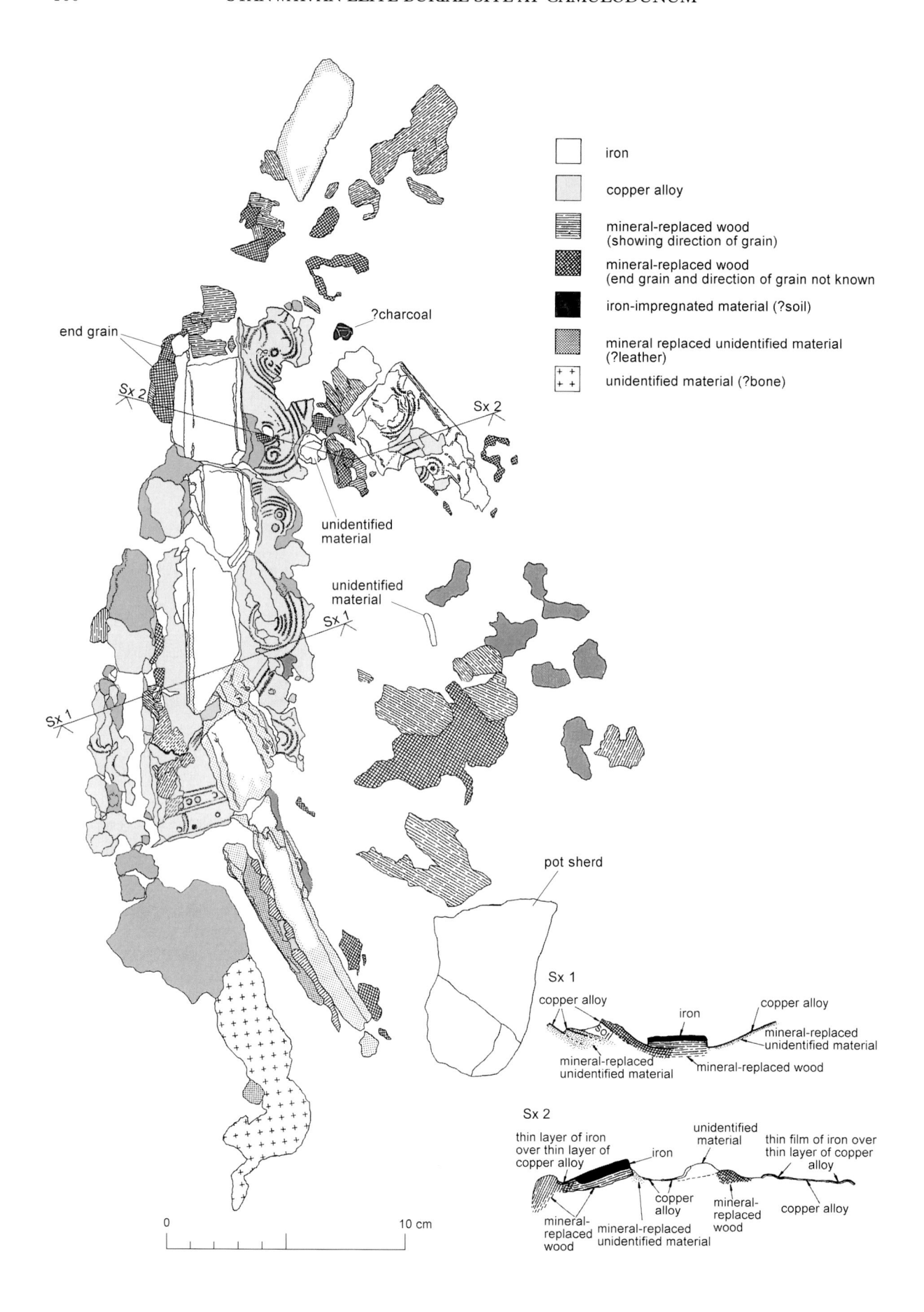

FIG. 78. Pit with broken funerary goods AF48: detail illustration of remains of ?box AF48.3 (scale 1:22)

flange on the iron strip shown on Sx 2 (left) may serve to hold the copper alloy in place; 4) most of the copper-alloy sheet abuts, and follows the line of, the main iron strip; but, 5) one piece has decoration running at a right-angle to it (to the left of the line of Sx 1); and 6) the fragment with repoussé-decorated iron over repoussé-decorated copper alloy lies at an angle to the main strips and may have been detached and deposited upside-down at the time of burial, or may have become detached and inverted as the object collapsed in the ground; 7) the iron strips are consistently flat, with no surviving angles (*see* also SF39 and 38); 8) no means for attaching the iron strips to the wood are visible (*see* also SF39 and 38).
d FIG. 77. SF42. A536. Small fragment of thin iron sheet with the negative impression of decoration of straight and curved mouldings, small dots and a large boss. The other side is rough and granular. Maximum dimensions 16 by 14 mm, 1 mm thick.
AF48.4 FIG. 77. SF36. A533. Two coils of copper-alloy wire, one in three pieces. Probably a pair of earrings or perhaps part of a coiled finger-ring. All the ends are damaged. Internal diameter of undamaged coil 17 mm, height 3 mm, thickness 2 mm.
SF37. Not illustrated. A534. Fifteen tiny fragments of copper-alloy sheet with repoussé decoration. The largest is 11 by 8 mm.

THE CREMATION BURIALS

CREMATION BURIAL AF18 (FIGS 2, 6, 79)

Cremated bone	639.7 g	adult of indeterminate age, probably female
Pottery vessel	AF18.1	grog-tempered multi-cordoned footring jar
Other find	AF18.2	small textile bag containing ?verdigris
Residual finds		none

In the northern half of Enclosure 1 an urned cremation burial was set in a small pit (AF18) 0.5 m deep (FIGS 2, 6, 79). A quantity of cremated bone (639.7 g, A247) from an adult ?female was contained within a grog-tempered ware jar (FIG. 79, AF18.1; Cam 218). Apart from a few rim sherds, the pot survived complete, although the upper part had been crushed. The vessel is typically Late Iron Age and was made between 75 B.C.–A.D. 65, but most probably in the 1st century B.C.

This burial included an extremely unusual item (FIG. 79, AF18.2), undoubtedly of considerable significance. It lay among the bone in the lower fill of the vessel. The object appears to have been burnt on the pyre and then deliberately picked out from the ashes and placed in the vessel along with the cremated bone. It consists of the contents of a small cloth bag, now solid but originally either a paste or a fine powder, as it retains the impressions of not only the gathers of the cloth but also in some places the individual threads. There is a small flattened area at one place on the side where the bag had lain on or against something hard. An attractive interpretation is that the bag was on a thong around the neck of the dead person, so that this area was flattened where it rested on the chest.

A similar shape to this can be made using a flour and water mix and a piece of muslin. The fragments may therefore either have been loose and powdery when deposited, bonding together after deposition, or, more likely, had been blended with a substance that held them together but left the mixture sufficiently pliable for it to be moulded. In both cases, the cloth of a tightly gathered bag would press into it, and a small flattened area would be formed where it rested against a solid surface, creating the present physical form of the object. The binding matrix may have been fat or oil. Only a little of either would be needed to make a powder pliable, thus minimising shrinkage, the absence of which is a major characteristic of this object.

This item is unusual, if not unique, in several ways. First, in its content, described below as possibly verdigris. Second, in its method of preservation, which is not yet fully explained. Third, in the information it supplies about the early use of verdigris as either a cosmetic or a medicine in Britain. References associating the British with face and body paint, and with tattooing, occur in a number of texts, from Caesar in the mid-1st century B.C. to Claudian in the late 4th and early 5th century (Jackson 1985, 171; Carr 2005, 288–9). Claudian's descriptions are formulaic, conforming to established poetic stereotypes of tattooed Britons and Picts, and the

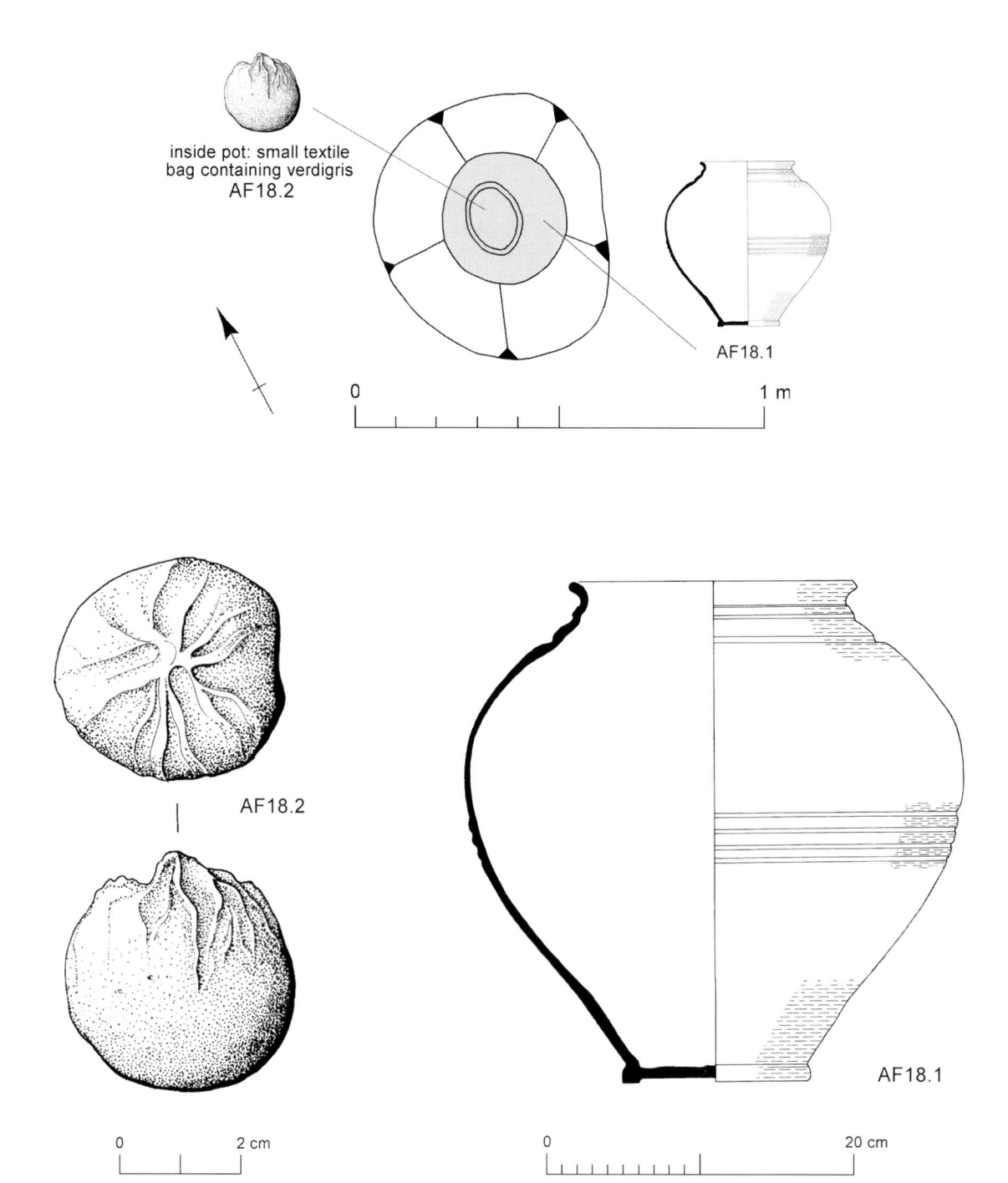

FIG. 79. Cremation burial AF18: plan showing location of finds (scale 1:15), pottery vessel (scale 1:4), and bag of ?verdigris (scale 1:1)

same may be true of many of the other references, but Caesar's description of the woad-painted British has been bolstered by Jackson's studies of the pestle-and-mortar sets used for grinding up cosmetics (1985; 1993a). These first appear in the immediately pre-conquest period and are singularly British in manufacture and distribution, reinforcing the impression that coloured cosmetics were used here in ways regarded as unconventional by the standards of Roman Italy, where the 'normal' use of a wide range of creams, lotions, foundations face-paints and other beauty aids is well documented (*e.g.* Ovid, *Ars Amatoria* III; *Medicamina Faciei Feminiae*; Pliny, *Historia Naturalis* XXVIII, 88–9, 183; Martial, *Epigrams* VI, 93; Juvenal, *Satire* VI).

This object raises two further fundamental questions: first, were similar small bags often placed among pyre goods but completely destroyed by burning at a higher temperature; and second, have such objects been found in the past in burials and, not being easily understood, omitted from the published reports? An object found in a 2nd-century burial at Weston Turville, Buckinghamshire, sounds intriguingly similar. Described as 'an apparently dried fruit nearly the size of an apple', it was found in a samian bowl together with leaves, frankincense, two brooches and some beads (Waugh 1961, 108). The object had unfortunately disappeared from Aylesbury Museum by the time that Waugh was writing, so that it cannot be directly compared with the Stanway object. The sizes of the two items seem to be much the same, but there is no hint as to the texture of the Weston Turville piece, such as hard, brittle, soft, or friable. Its association with frankincense might imply that it was valued for its scent, or, as the description suggests, it might even have been a fruit, such as an apple or pomegranate, symbolic of eternal life, and the leaves in the bowl, possibly the remains of a funerary wreath, invite such an interpretation. The female dress accessories, on the other hand, might imply that was a ball of some cosmetic substance. What is certain is that the absence of an accurate identification does not detract from the fact that it provides the only reasonably closely comparable object to AF48.2.

Pottery vessel (FIG. 79)

AF18.1 A228.
Multi-cordoned footring jar, wheel-thrown. Fabric GTW; brown matrix; fine black inclusions; patchy dark grey and brown surfaces. Glossy burnished and matt banded finish; glossy finish on the rim and cordons; burnished zone 75 mm wide at the base; matt finish between.
Condition: In sherds, but restored to complete base to two-thirds rim circuit.
Condition at deposition: complete, possibly with damaged rim.

Bag of ?verdigris (FIG. 79)

AF18.2 SF14. A248.
The contents of a small bag made of textile. The contents are inorganic, and preserved as a fine-grained, dark grey, hard, heavy, almost spherical object, with grooves of varying depth and length running up to a central point. The cloth has long since disintegrated, leaving only lines of the woven textile preserved on the object, especially in the grooves. Maximum diameter 28 mm, weight 30.41 g.

Examination of a bag of ?verdigris from AF18

By S. La Niece and C.R. Cartwright

Optical examination

The find (FIG. 79, AF18.2) was examined at low magnification and found to be composed of dark grey particulate material, in which flecks of orange, green and white are embedded. The material adheres together firmly and its spherical shape is probably the form of its original container. The form suggests a bag made of a soft fabric or leather, gathered at the neck with the folds preserved in the surface. No impressions of a woven fabric were seen but a tiny fragment of charred organic material was sampled from one of the folds. Under the optical microscope, it was identified as *Corylus avellana* (hazel) charcoal. This fragment was probably within the burial soil in which the object was found, rather than being an integral part of a container, no trace of which remains.

Analysis

Qualitative X-ray fluorescence analysis directly on the surface identified the main element present as copper, with several per cent of tin and lead, some iron and a trace of silver. X-ray diffraction analysis of particles from the surface identified them as the black copper oxide, tenorite (CuO).

The examination was entirely non-destructive so there is some uncertainty as to whether the surface is representative of the interior. However, radiography revealed no changes in density through the object, suggesting that it is composed of similar material throughout.

(BF64.21) with a glass bead (BF64.22) neatly placed centrally within it must have been close to the shield edge.

A large, tightly packed, group of amphora sherds lay in the north-west corner of the burial pit. These proved on restoration to make up all but the rim of a complete amphora (BF64.15). The rim must have been ploughed off when the site was under cultivation. Its absence and the limited spread of the sherds indicate that, rather like the amphora in the Doctor's burial (p. 212), the vessel appears to have been buried upright in the corner of the burial pit. This means that the rim of the amphora would have been 0.8–0.9 m above the floor of the burial pit. Thus the amphora must have been in pieces before the stripping of the ground prior to excavation, because only the lowest 0.4 m of the pit survived that stripping, and yet the uppermost parts (bar the rim) of the amphora were present among the sherds. The absence of the rim points to the amphora having been broken in the recent past, presumably during groundworks for the quarry.

A wooden box (BF64.30) had been placed just to the south-east of the amphora. The distribution of its metal fittings showed it to have measured 0.5 × 0.6 m (very roughly) in area. In the south-west corner of the burial pit were the fittings from a second wooden box (BF64.31) which had contained a large and exotic amber-coloured glass bowl (BF64.16). A folding gaming board (BF64.29) with copper-alloy fittings had been laid open in the south-east corner of the grave, with a set of glass gaming counters (BF64.28; eleven blue and nine white) placed in a loose group close by. (It should be noted that more counters were probably present than were recovered.) The counters, unlike those in the Doctor's burial, had not been set out on the board, but two pottery vessels, a pedestal cup (BF64.10) and a flagon (BF64.13), had been put on top of it instead. Various other vessels for serving food and drink were similarly placed around the edges of the burial pit. These consisted of three pottery vessels, *i.e.* a miniature pedestal flagon decorated with bird motifs in the form of a crane (BF64.14), a tall *terra rubra* cylindrical cup (BF64.11), and an ovoid beaker (BF64.12). There were also two small glass unguent bottles, one near the ovoid beaker (BF64.18) and the other (BF64.17) close to the wooden box BF64.31.

The arrangement of the grave goods within the burial pit is such that the smaller items, including those making up the service, occupied the central area whereas the larger pieces tended to be close to the sides (FIG. 80). This suggests that the items away from the pit edge, including the service, the shield, the gaming counters, arm-band and bead, and the cremated bone had been placed on the pit floor by somebody standing inside it. Many of the items around the sides of the pit, *i.e.* the two boxes, the spear and various of the vessels including the amphora, could have been passed or lowered into the pit by somebody standing on the pit edge.

Traces of textile have been found on the upper surfaces of the jug (BF64.25), the gaming board junction pieces (BF64.29), the shield boss (BF64.23a), and the undersides of the two brooches (BF64.19–20). J.P. Wild judges that the textile fragments very likely belonged to a single garment (BF64.36) woven in diamond twill, such as a cloak or blanket which had been spread across the grave (*see* report p. 347). The relationship of the textile to the brooches, which did not lie close together, suggests that either the brooches were placed in the burial pit after the ?cloak or they were already attached to it. If the latter, then two garments may have been present instead of one, as usually only a single brooch was needed to fasten a cloak.

Unlike the Doctor's burial, there was no surviving wood (either decayed or mineralised) to suggest that there had been a wooden cover over the burial. However, the undisturbed nature of the carefully arranged grave goods and the fact that the plates and bowls appeared to have contained food argues that such a cover must have existed to protect the vessels and their contents as the pit was backfilled. The simple rectangular burial pit would not have required an elaborate construction to cover the grave goods. At its simplest, a number of planks of the right length, with their ends wedged against the pit-sides, would have sufficed. Two iron nails (B999 and B1053) were recovered close to the pit sides near two of the corners (FIG. 80). These may have been part of a wooden cover, as were nails in the Doctor's burial (p. 207), although one of them (B1053) may have been part of the box BF64.31. Another possibility is that the garment(s) BF64.36 acted as a cover.

Using the internal evidence alone, the Warrior's burial would appear to date to *c.* A.D. 50–55. However, there may prove to be a slight disparity between the Gallo-Belgic pottery (which dates the burial to *c.* A.D. 50–60) and the glassware vessels and the Nertomarus brooches. The latter two groups together hint that the date might be slightly earlier, *c.* A.D. 40–50, because one or even both glassware vessels may be pre-conquest and the two brooches were likely to have been imported and used between *c.* A.D. 40–50/5. Date and relationships with the other funerary contexts are discussed on pages 437–9.

Pottery vessels (FIGS 81–2, BF64.1–15)

The fifteen pottery vessels were placed in the grave complete or possibly with minor damage, while at least two had been scorched possibly in the pyre. Apart from the amphora, all are functionally specialised Gaulish imports and represent the top of the market in ceramics, being the most colourful and decorative available in the immediate pre- or immediately post-conquest period. The group consists of one South Gaulish samian cup (BF64.1), four *terra nigra* platters (BF64.2–5), one *terra rubra* cup (BF64.7), three *terra nigra* cups (BF64.6 and BF64.8–9), two *terra rubra* pedestal cups (BF64.10–11), a beaker (BF64.12, a flagon (BF64.13), a miniature flagon (BF64.14) and a Dressel 2-4 amphora (BF64.15). The stamps on the Gallo-Belgic vessels are discussed on pp. 290–1, 294–5

Samian

BF64.1 FIG. 81. B1024, B1076, B1133. Conical cup: Dragendorff form 33. South Gaulish. Claudian. Possibly also includes sherds B1076 and B1133.
Central stamp: PRIMVS
Condition: fragmented, all sherds present; fractures severely eroded.
Condition at deposition: complete.
Brenda Dickinson adds of the stamp:
Primus i of La Graufesenque, Die 10a (Bémont 1976, 61, 276). There is no clear site evidence for this potter's activity, but his range of forms provided a clear indication of Tiberio–Claudian date. Die 10a was used to stamp forms 24, 25 and Ritterling 5, the first two having the bevelled footrings found on early examples. *c.* A.D. D 25–50.

Gallo-Belgic imports

BF64.2 FIG. 81. B1039. Moulded platter: Camulodunum form 7/8. Fabric TN. Central Stamp 20: ?SCVTVSII. A.D. 35–60.
Condition: complete.
BF64.3 FIG. 81. B1023, B1024, B1058. Moulded platter: Camulodunum form 7/8. Fabric TN, Central Stamp 8: IIUDO] *** bordered. A.D. 35–60.
Condition: appalling, no joining sherds but about two-thirds of rim circuit present; some evidence of scorching.
Condition at deposition: dubious; condition possibly the result of the platter being placed too near the pyre. Probably complete.
BF64.4 FIG. 81. B1040, B1090, B1091. Offset platter: Camulodunum form 14/SW Type 24. Fabric TN. Central Stamp 22: IMO (reading uncertain). A.D. 50–75.
Condition: severely fragmented and eroded, about one-quarter of circuit missing.
Condition at deposition: probably complete.
BF64.5 FIG. 81. B1055; stamp: B1038. Offset platter: Camulodunum form 14. Fabric TN.
Central Stamp 21, broken: VII.]IIS *** bordered. A.D. 50–70.
Condition: in sherds restorable to almost complete.
Condition at deposition: probably complete.
BF64.6 FIG. 81. B1038, ?B1133. Carinated cup: Camulodunum form 56C (small). Fabric TN.
Central Stamp 24: mark X with four spots. A.D. 25–60.
Condition: severely fragmented, base circuit restored to complete; about half sherds missing.
Condition at deposition: probably complete, or damaged but standing.
BF64.7 FIG. 81. B1051. Small hemispherical cup. Fabric TR1(C), darker slip over interior and exterior, excluding underside of base. Central Stamp 25: VII bordered. A.D. 40–65.
Condition: severely fragmented, no sherds missing.
Condition at deposition: complete.

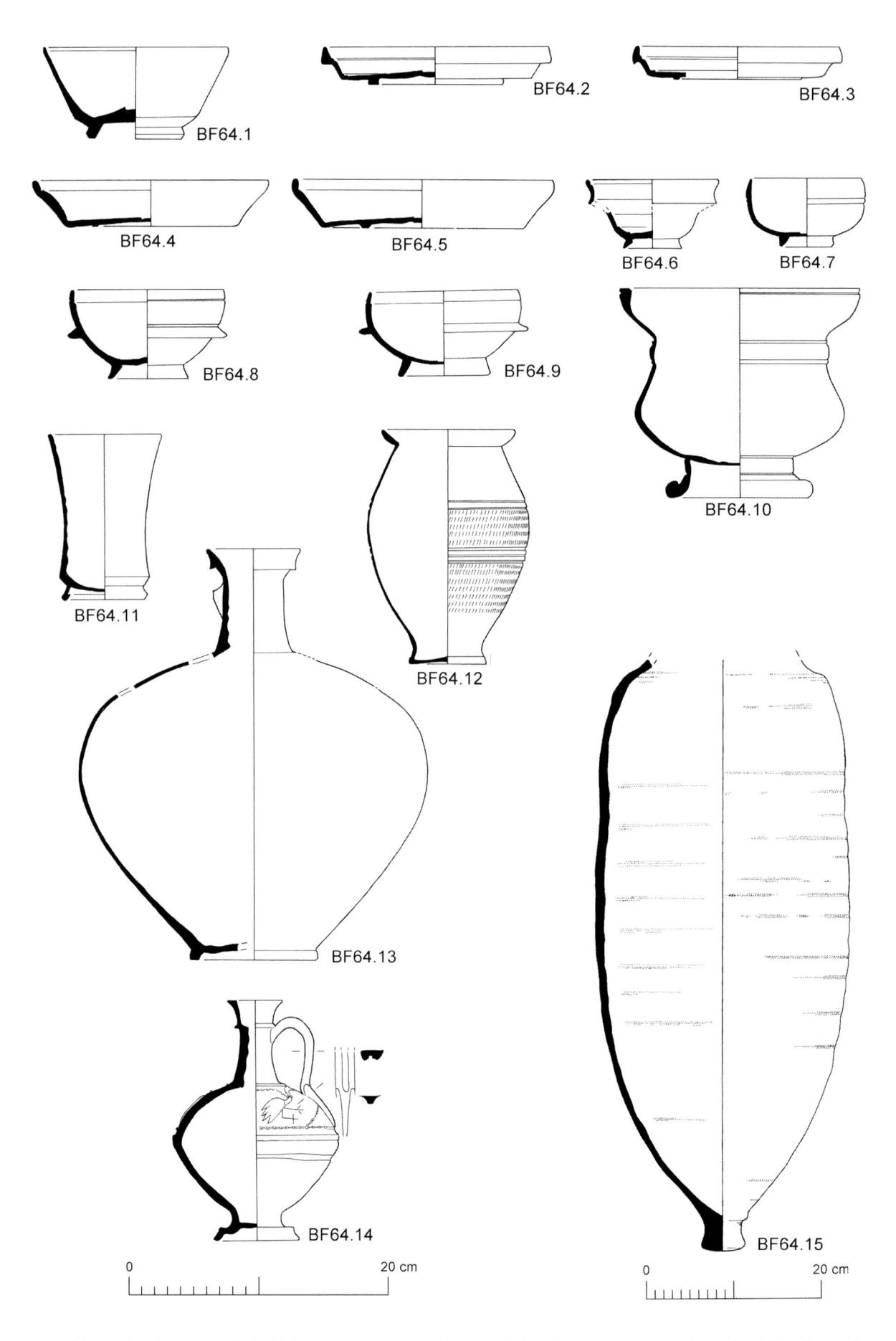

FIG. 81. Warrior's burial: BF64 pottery vessels BF64.1–14 (scale 1:4), and amphora (BF64.15) (scale 1:6)

BF64.8 FIG. 81. B1035. Flanged cup: Camulodunum form 58 (large). Fabric TN. Central Stamp 1: ACVT. A.D. 40–65.
Condition: broken, with complete and standing base circuit.
Condition at deposition: complete.
BF64.9 FIG. 81. B1091, B1051 + uncoded sherds. Flanged cup: Camulodunum form 58. Fabric TN. Central Stamp 2: ACVT].*** A.D. 40–65.
Condition: severely fragmented, about a half base circuit restorable, some rims, but about half sherds missing.
Condition at deposition: probably complete, or damaged and standing.
BF64.10 FIG. 81. B1016, B1024, B1037, B1057, B1076, B1111, B1116, B1223, B1135. Campanulate pedestal cup: Camulodunum form 76. Fabric TR1(C); orange fine-grained matrix; darker orange polished slip over the exterior visible surface; interior, unfinished.
Condition: severely fragmented, restorable to complete.
Condition at deposition: complete.
BF64.11 FIG. 81. B1017, B1036, B1037, B1076, B1081, B1082, B1116. Cylindrical pedestal cup. Fabric TR1(C); orange fine-grained ware, coral red polished slip over external visible surface; unfinished interior.
Condition: severely fragmented but restorable to complete.
Condition at deposition: complete.
This is the only recorded complete example in Britain. The example illustrated in *Camulodunum* was found in Trier (Hawkes and Hull 1947, fig. 49, no. 8). The source may have been the Sept-Saulx kilns in the Marne-Vesle potteries, near Rheims (Fromols 1938).
BF64.12 FIG. 81. B1017. Ovoid beaker: Camulodunum form 112Ca. Fabric TR3; pink smooth ware; yellowish cream outer visible surface. Decoration: uneven and asymmetrical; simple chattered rouletting in two zones separated by a double cordon.
Condition: standing, complete but for rim.
Condition at deposition: complete. Possibly a second, judging by the uneven decoration.

Northern Gaulish import
BF64.13 FIG. 81. B1016, B1037, B1079, B1111, B1135, B1169. Cornice-rimmed flagon: Cam 140. Fabric WPW, typical with greyish interior slip. Discoloration inside may be due to heating of contents.
Condition: severely fragmented, complete base and neck circuits, no handle. Traces of scorching before fracture, probably too near the pyre; handle may have been affected here.
Condition at deposition: complete but for handle.

Central Gaulish import
BF64.14 FIGS 81–2. B1081. Miniature pedestal flagon: Déchelette form 62. Fabric CNG GL1/GL2 (lead-glazed ware); buff fine-grained, even-textured micaceous matrix; traces of matt orange under-slip; traces of yellowish-green glaze. Decoration: moulded. Three repeats of the same tethered crane motif, joined by lengths of beaded chain, arranged symmetrically. The motif resembles one used on Italian samian (Oswald 1936, pl. 84, nos 2202–2203).
A thick-walled vessel. The body is two hemispheres luted together. The neck and pedestal were made separately and then luted into place. Finally the handle was added.
Condition: in sherds but restored almost to complete.
Condition at deposition: complete.

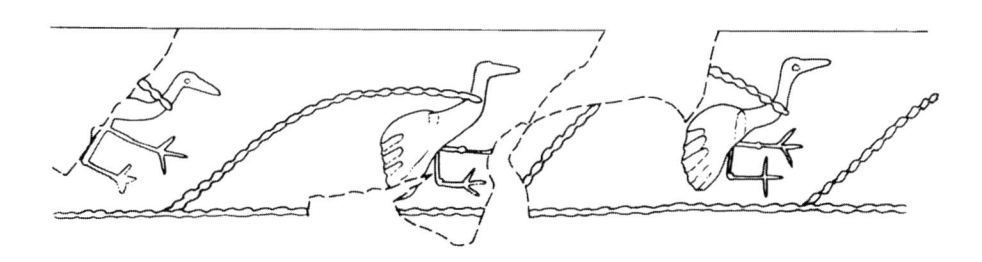

FIG. 82. Detail of crane pot BF64.14

Amphora

BF64.15 FIG. 81. B983. Dressel 2-4 (*see* pp. 300–1).

Glass vessels (FIG. 83, BF64.16–18)

The amber bowl BF64.16, which was placed in the grave inside box BF64.31, is an extraordinary vessel on account of its size. It was 252 mm wide and 125 mm deep, and thus provides an insight into the technical abilities of early glass blowers. Its diagnostic features apart from size are a rolled rim, linear wheel-cut decoration, and a base formed by a separately blown paraison. The form is not one that appears in standard typologies like Isings 1957 and Goethert-Polaschek 1977, but it has close affinities with smaller, shallower bowls made in Italy (p. 341). The form cannot be paralleled at Colchester despite the town's large pre-Boudican glass assemblage (Harden 1947; Charlesworth 1985; *CAR* 8). In the absence of a local parallel, coupled with Italian evidence for date, the bowl seems likely to have been a pre-conquest import which may have been curated for a considerable time before being buried. Hilary Cool considers the bowl in detail on pages 340–3.

BF64.17–18 are tubular unguent bottles of Isings form 8. This was the commonest form of unguent bottle in Britain in the mid 1st century A.D. (*CAR* 8, 159). They occur in Tiberian contexts on the Continent (Isings 1957, 24). BF64.18 is in the normal blue/green colour, but BF64.17 is an unusual deep blue, which Hilary Cool suggests may point to a pre-conquest date (p. 345).

BF64.16 FIG. 83. B986, B993, B1017. Bowl in many joining fragments lacking small parts of rim, upper and lower body and base ring. Light yellow/brown; occasional small bubbles. Out-curved rim, edge bent out and down to form narrow bead; concave upper body expanding out to rounded carination; slightly convex-curved lower body sloping in to slightly domed base. Separately blown foot with footring convex-curved, edge ground. Junction of two paraisons imperfect and large air bubbles trapped between leading to separation of fragments of the two. Two wheel-cut lines on upper body and one on lower body. Height 125 mm, rim diameter 252 mm, base diameter 114 mm, wall thickness 3 mm.

BF64.17 FIG. 83. B1056. Tubular unguent bottle, 2 rim, 1 neck and 5 body fragments. 1 rim and neck fragment join. Streaky deep blue with small bubbles. Rim slightly outbent and edge rolled in, cylindrical neck with tooling marks at base; straight side sloping out. Rim diameter approximately 15 mm, rim and neck length 18 mm, wall thickness 0.5–1 mm.

BF64.18 FIG. 83. B1030. Tubular unguent bottle in approximately 20 joining fragments; small parts of body, majority of neck and all of rim missing. Blue/green; occasional bubble. Cylindrical neck with slight tooling at base; straight side sloping out to convex-curved lower body and small shallowly concave base. Present height 83 mm, height of body 63 mm, maximum body diameter 32 mm, base diameter 12 mm, wall thickness 1 mm.

Dress accessories (FIGS 83–4, BF64.19–22)

The grave contained two brooches, one fragmentary (FIG. 83, BF64.19–20). Both are of Nertomarus type and were probably made in the Rhine area, perhaps among the Treveri (Behrens 1950, 5; Feugère 1985, 265, Type 14b2). They are discussed more fully on page 316, in particular the date of their import into Britain and their period of use, which can here be summarised as *c.* A.D. 40–50/5. The brooches did not lie close together in the ground and so do not appear to have been worn as a pair, implying that two cloaks had been placed in the grave.

The more complete brooch (FIG. 83, BF64.19) is stamped NERTOMA, the maker after whom the type is now named, although other makers produced the same form and also stamped their products (Behrens 1950, 3, 5). It can be assumed that the other brooch (FIG. 83, BF64.20) originally bore the same stamp. While several brooches of this form have been found in Britain, only one other stamped example has been recovered (Mackreth 1989a, 24, fig. 15, 7). It came from the gully of a Late Iron Age round-house at Piddington, Northamptonshire, and was associated with Late Iron Age fine and coarsewares. The context appears to pre-date a Roman military phase of occupation, beginning *c.* A.D. 44 (R. Friendship-Taylor, pers. comm.). Although the Piddington brooch is extremely well preserved, the stamp is not easily read. It has

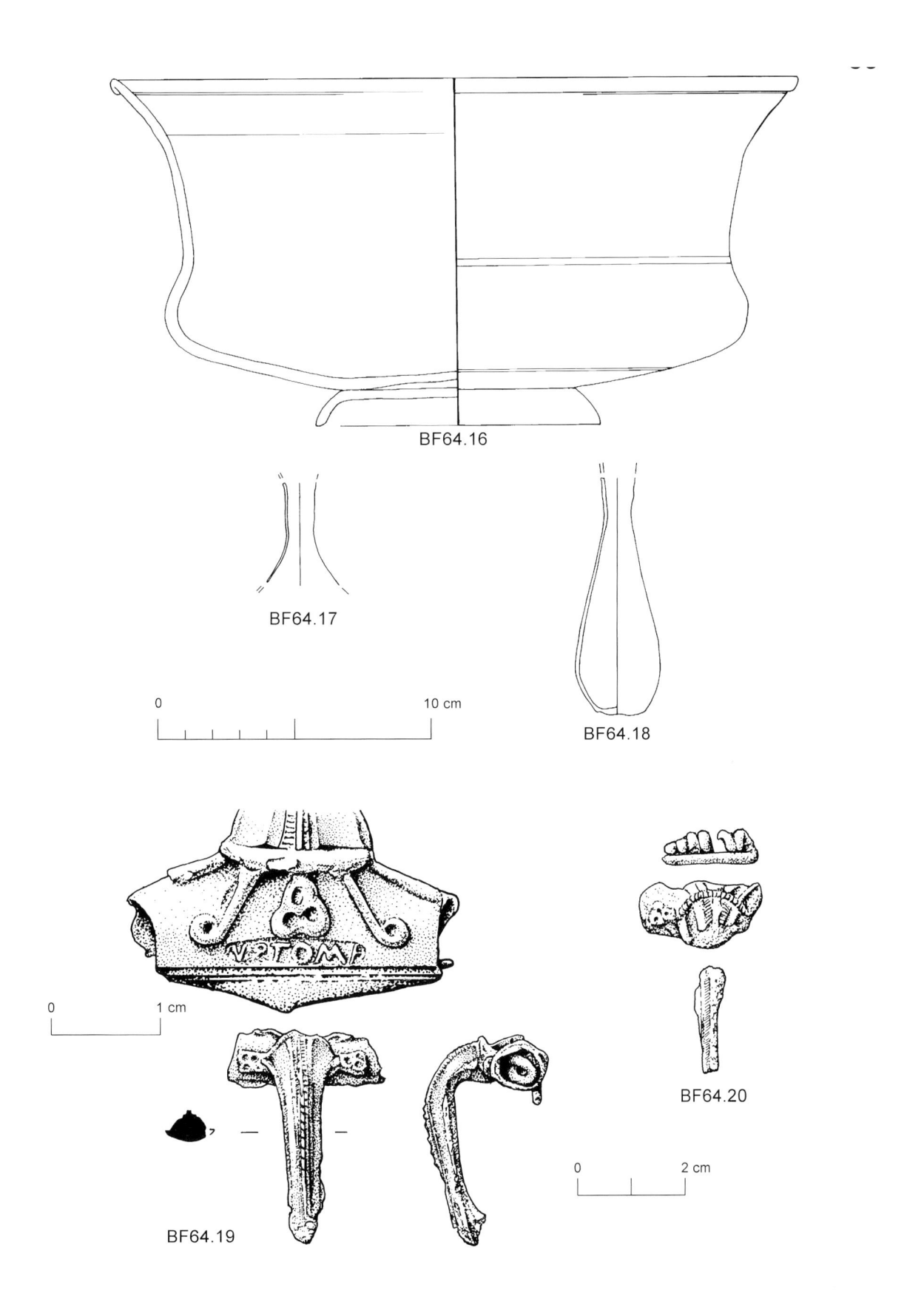

FIG. 83. Warrior's burial BF64: glass vessels BF64.16–18 (scale 1:2), copper-alloy brooches BF64.19–20 (scale 1:1), maker's name stamp on the Nertomarus brooch BF64.19 (scale 2:1)

been published as ROMV retrograde, but this was with the stamp inverted, *i.e.* viewed with the head uppermost (*RIB* 2, fasc. 3, 2421.49), which must be incorrect, as the stamps were meant to be read with the foot of the brooch pointing upwards (*e.g. RIB* 2, fasc. 3, 2421.2–2421.40; Behrens 1950, Abb. 2–4). With the brooch in the correct position, Mackreth offers another reading of BOWA (pers. comm.), although the letters are far from clear and a third alternative reading is –ER-MA, with the E reversed (and ?ligatured to R) and the MA ligatured, raising the possibility that this brooch is also a product of Nertomarus himself.

On the eastern edge of the central group of grave goods lay a large glass bead (FIG. 84, BF64.22) placed neatly within a large copper arm-ring (FIG. 84, BF64.21). The latter would have been made by wrapping a strip of sheet metal around a wooden form and then bending it, a technique linked to the manufacture of much earlier hollow torcs (Déchelette 1914, 1211–12, fig. 515, 1) and also to that of a hollow tubular armlet from a child's grave of 4th- to 7th-century date A.D. at Cannington, Somerset, which still contained the remains of a hazel branch (Rahtz *et al.* 2000, 355, fig. 239). The pliable nature of the hazel used for the Cannington armlet and the malleable copper used for the Stanway arm-ring highlight the appropriate use of materials by the smiths of antiquity that will be noted further below. The Stanway arm-ring is likely to have had a simple overlapping joint rather than more solid terminals, which would undoubtedly have survived in the ground had they existed. A smaller armlet found with the female burial at Birdlip was made into a full circle by having one end rebated and slotted into the other (Bellows 1881, 137–41, fig. 9; *BM Guide* 1925, 121). Armrings are not common finds, but there is a fragment of a hollow example from the Glastonbury lake village, with a slightly smaller hoop diameter than that from Stanway (Bulleid and Gray 1911, pl. 44, E194), while most of another hollow arm-ring, identified as a neck-ring but too small (*cf.* Macdonald 2000, 125, nos 19–20) and lacking a hinge, came from an early 1st-century context at Frocester, Gloucestershire (Price 2000, fig. 2.9, 233). An armlet was also found in the Hurstbourne Tarrant tumulus (Hawkes and Dunning 1930, fig. 31, 2), but its diameter is about 15 mm less than that of the Stanway arm-ring.

The bead (FIG. 84, BF64.22), which had been carefully placed concentrically inside the arm-ring, does not fall within Zepezauer's classification for Middle and Late Iron Age beads (Zepezauer 1993). The closest group is her Type 4.2.3, blue glass beads decorated with flecks of white glass. Although of similar size to the Stanway bead and making use of a similar decorative principle, the white flecks of Type 4.2.3 are smaller, more numerous, and, most importantly, often angular, as if made from fragments of shattered white glass added hard and cold to the blue matrix. The beads may have been rolled when soft over a scatter of solid fragments. In contrast, the smooth edges and elongated shape of the Stanway ovals show that, in this case, the white glass was either very soft when added to the matrix, or was softened for marvering. A further distinction lies in date. Most common around the area of the Manching *oppidum* in Germany, the continental Type 4.2.3 beads are almost certainly all earlier than the Stanway bead (*ibid.*, 52).

In Guido's classification of prehistoric and Roman beads from Britain, the Stanway bead falls into Group 1, a loose collection of 'large and medium annular beads with streaky or mottled design', which she notes as particular well represented in Germany but most common around Stradonice in the Czech Republic (Guido 1978, 59–60, 121, fig. 17). Only one Group 1 bead from Britain is described as blue and white, a bead from Colchester, which is of exactly the same diameter as that from BF64, but shorter (11 mm), with a smaller central hole (12 mm), and flat on each side. The white flecks in this bead are smaller and far more numerous than those in the BF64 example, and many have the angularity noted on those of Zepezauer's Type 4.2.3. They are mainly confined to the rounded outer part of the bead, but there are a few on the sides and several white streaks inside the perforation. The bead is part of Grave Group 53/18 in the Joslin Collection, dated by May to *c.* A.D. 80–120 (May 1928, 268, pl. 82), but described by Guido as A.D. 25–50 (1978, 121). May's date does not suit the bead, and Guido's does not suit the other objects, in particular a bangle-type ivory armlet of late 3rd- or 4th-century date. The Joslin Collection grave groups are not wholly reliable as he tended to separate

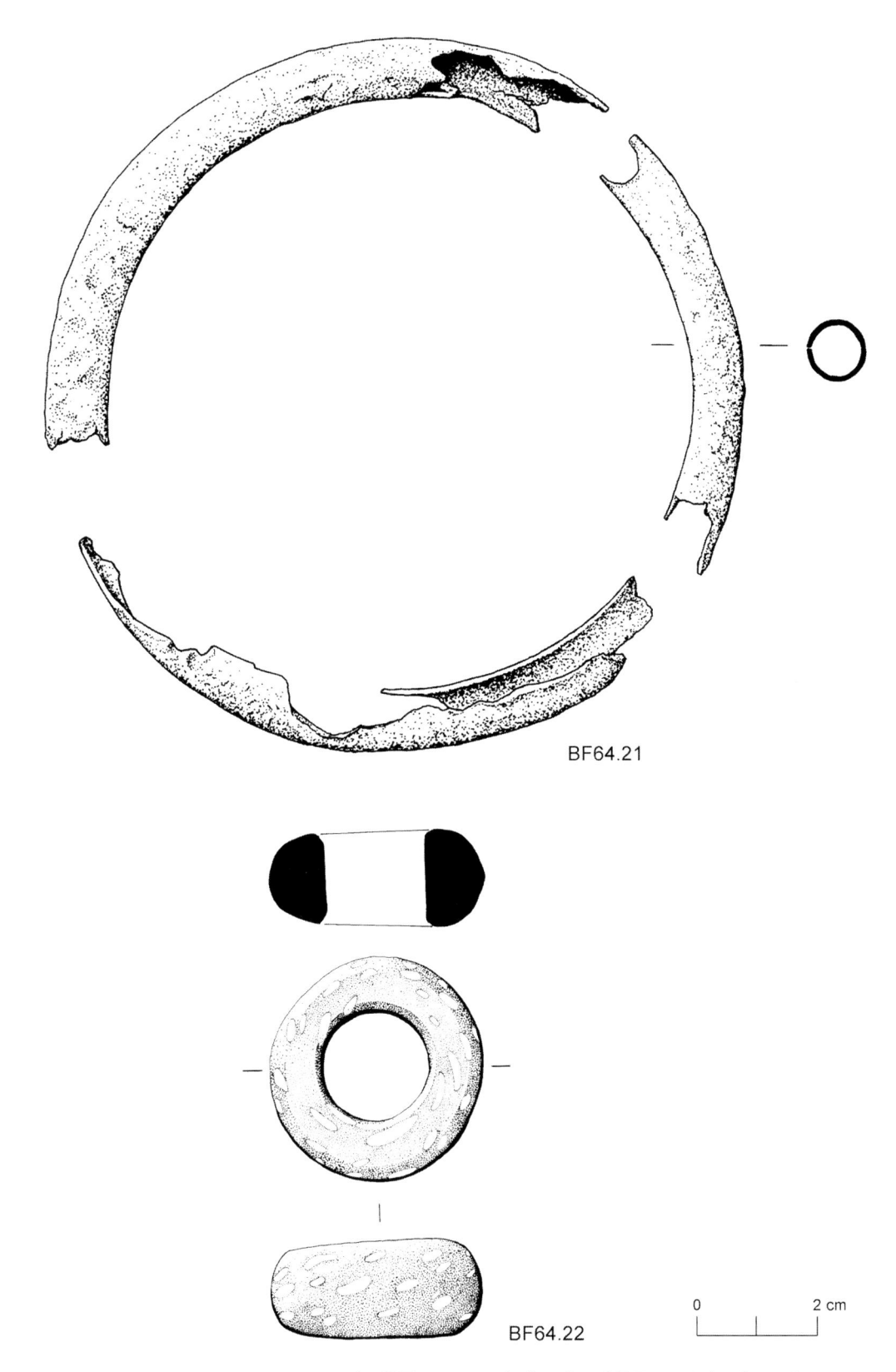

FIG. 84. Warrior's burial BF64: copper armlet BF64.21 and glass bead BF64.22 (scale 1:1)

pots from other objects, and the groups as published by May have in some cases been wrongly reassembled, as appears to be the situation here.

It may be that the Stanway bead is of British manufacture. Analysis shows it to be of slightly unusual composition. The white glass contains lead oxide, and this distinction may provide a further means of subdividing blue glass beads with white decoration. A blue and white bead from Hayling Island with a high lead content may be of British origin (*see* p. 331), and has been dated to *c.* 50 A.D. or earlier. This leaves in question whether or not its manufacture pre-dates the invasion of A.D. 43, or if it is evidence of the arrival of glass bead technology in the wake of the invasion. The same would therefore be true of the Colchester bead.

In that respect it should be noted that, like the arm-ring, this bead is of La Tène rather than Roman style. The more common related form, large cobalt blue beads with marvered trail, disappeared from this area soon after the conquest (Guido 1978, 57), a disappearance that owes much to the arrival of introduced Roman bead forms and styles of personal ornament. In the Roman world, beads were generally worn in threaded necklace groups by women (*see* BF24 in Enclosure 4), while the Stanway graves BF64, CF47 and CF72 demonstrate the La Tène custom of wearing a single large bead. That this practice was not gender specific is demonstrated by this bead from a male grave and by the bead from CF72, which is almost certainly the burial of a female. The CF47 bead is jet and was undoubtedly credited with magical and/or healing powers (p. 217). Whether or not the BF64 bead was also considered in anyway amuletic is less certain, but it seems that glass beads in Migration Period Europe were thought to have had magical properties (Meaney 1981, 192–210), and comparisons may also be made with Late Bronze Age Mesopotamia, where the various colours of stones/glass were credited with specific properties akin to beneficial magic and necklaces might have both protective and curative powers (Robson 2001, 52), and with modern Sarawak, where beads are worn for protection or to strengthen the soul of an individual or a community (H.S. Morris 1997, 103; Chin and Mashman 1991, 187).

BF64.19 FIG. 83. SF340. B1032. Nertomarus brooch, with raised decoration on the spring cover. Probably brass. The lower part of the bow with the catchplate is missing, as is the end of the pin. One side of the spring-cover and the ends of the spring are damaged, as is one side of the bow. The decoration on the head consists of three trilobate motifs separated by curling fronds. Above the central motif the brooch bears the maker's stamp, NERTOMA. The E may be ligatured with the N, or reversed and ligatured with the R. There is a raised knurled moulding on the arched head. The bow is of complex section, with a marked marginal mouldings and a prominent knurled central rib flanked by two low knurled mouldings. Length 38 mm.

BF64.20 FIG. 83. SF382a. Fragments of a second Nertomarus brooch similar to SF340, also probably brass. Only small parts of the spring, and bow remain, with a large fragment from the head and the centre of the spring-cover. Length of largest piece 13 mm.

SF388. B1084. Fragments from the narrow foot and catchplate of a brooch, probably SF382 above. Largest piece 16 mm long. Although narrow, the pieces compare with the Nertomarus brooch from Fishbourne (Hull 1971, no. 28). Also in this number are fragments of sheet iron, probably from the shield boss, which lay nearby, but possibly from the wooden box with iron fittings (BF64.31) in which the glass bowl was deposited. Largest piece 18 by 12 mm.

BF64.21 FIG. 84. SF376. B1021. Hollow round-section arm-ring of impure copper in eight fragments. It was made by rolling up a long piece of sheet metal over a solid forme, probably of wood, then removing the forme and bending the metal tube into a circle. The butt join between the long edges is set in the middle of the inside of the hoop. There is no sign of any solder. The join between the short edges has not survived. Internal diameter 87 mm, diameter of hoop 10 mm.

BF64.22 FIG. 84. SF377. B1022. Large annular bead of cobalt blue glass with white marvered oval dots. Diameter 36 mm, length 15 mm. Diameter of central hole 16.5 mm.

Shield and lance or spear (FIGS 85–6, BF64.23–24)

The shield boss (FIG. 85, BF64.23a) appears to be unique, but this is not wholly surprising as many Iron Age shield bosses are highly individual (Collis 1968, pl. IXb; 1973, especially fig. 4, 6; Stead 1985, 36–45). It is a composite piece of decorated copper alloy over an iron base, which could be an indication that it is of British origin (Stead 1985, 42; James and Rigby 1997, 60). No iron grip was found, but a fragment of cord found beneath the boss during conservation may have served as one (although J.P. Wild prefers to see this as part of textile which had been placed over many of the items in the grave). The outer areas of the boss are fragmentary and decayed, so that the form of the boss when whole is uncertain, but the edges, all of which are incomplete, must have developed into flanges that allowed the boss to be attached to the wood of the shield. The larger separate fragment (FIG. 86, BF64.23b) is probably part of the flange. An associated thin fragment with complex profile (FIG. 88, BF64.27) is unlikely to be part of the boss and may instead be from a vessel or other object not otherwise identified.

The upper part of the boss was rounded, but lower down it is clearly developing into a rectangle or perhaps a square. It does not appear to be paralleled among Late Iron Age forms, nor was it a simple hollow hemisphere with plain flange, like bosses from Lyon (Rhône), and from Karaagaè, Bulgaria, which are copper-alloy versions of the more usual iron forms (Stead 1985, 36–45; Boucher *et al.* 1980, no. 224; Karadimitrova 2002; Feugère 2002a, 87–93). A boss from a Welwyn-type burial of Claudian date at Stanfordbury may perhaps have been similar, but it has not survived (Stead 1967, 55, no. 13; 1985, 39). The three bosses from the Polden Hill hoard, although deposited at much the same date, are also much simpler in form and method of manufacture (Brailsford 1975, fig. 5).

The large decorated knob of the Stanway boss invites comparison with the knobbed copper-alloy boss from the warrior grave found at Berry-Bouy (Cher), France, but the two are again very different in shape and method of manufacture (Ferdière and Villard 1993, 135–6, figs 2-29, 2-49; Feugère 2002a, fig. 98). The Berry-Bouy boss is round and flanged, and the knob is of sheet metal reinforced by a tin-lead core (Ferdière and Villard 1993, 135–6, 2-49). A jug and handled basin found in the same grave are from a service of Nuber's Hagenow type, earlier in date than the Type E (Millingen) service found in BF64, and the grave is considered to be of Augustan date (Nuber 1972, 38–44; Ferdière and Villard 1993, 121–39).

The rocker-arm decoration on the Stanway boss is occasionally found on both Gallic and British brooches, for example Nauheims and Rosettes, on the catchplates of some Colchesters, and more frequently on some Colchester derivatives, although the latter almost certainly post-date this grave (Hawkes and Hull 1947, 311; Hattatt 1985, fig. 11, 253, fig. 12, fig. 19, 284; Feugère 1985, pl. 50). The knob has been designed so that the incised moulding of the base accurately frames the upper part with its incised triplet of circles. The use of three circles here may have some significance other than the purely decorative, perhaps religious or protective, similar to that of the three circles incised on the sides of the head of the Rearhook brooch in CF47. The knob does not seem to be fixed very securely to the base-plate, and the shield may therefore be meant for display only, not for use in battle. The knob on the boss from Berry-Bouy is also designed so that successive tiers of decoration frame that on the very top. The general, although not specific, stylistic similarities of the two knobs suggest a link between the two bosses, but whether it is one of date, which would make the Stanway shield over half a century old when buried, or of place of origin is far from clear.

Feugère (2002a, 131) has stressed the many variations in the form of lances and the lack of any convincing analysis, and the Stanway lancehead (FIG. 86, BF64.24a) is certainly idiosyncratic in its extreme length and slenderness. It may perhaps be an intentional exaggeration of the form, meant for display rather than use, as may also be the case with the shield boss. The blade is a little bent, which may be deliberate damage done at the time of the burial for ritual purposes, although given that the bend is very slight, it may just be a sign that the lance has been used. However, the lancehead may simply have distorted in the ground as it corroded (*cf.* the bends in the iron rod CF47.23a on FIG. 114). The blade is designed for deep penetration, which might be taken to be a characteristic of warfare rather than hunting, although early Roman spearheads found in Britain tend on the whole to be short and wide (Ottaway 1992, 710–11; Manning 1985, fig. 33). Of over 100 spearheads from Hod Hill, Dorset, only those of Manning's Group IVA approach the length of this example but none is of this precise form, tending to have a much more prominent midrib, which adds strength to an otherwise potentially weak form (*ibid.*, 167). A La Tène lancehead from Manching is close in length to the Stanway example, but, although narrow, does not equal it in slenderness (Sievers 1989, Abb. 2, 5). The long lances from Alésia, identified as of La Tène type, perhaps provide the best comparative material as they also have a long socket and long blade and, in some cases,

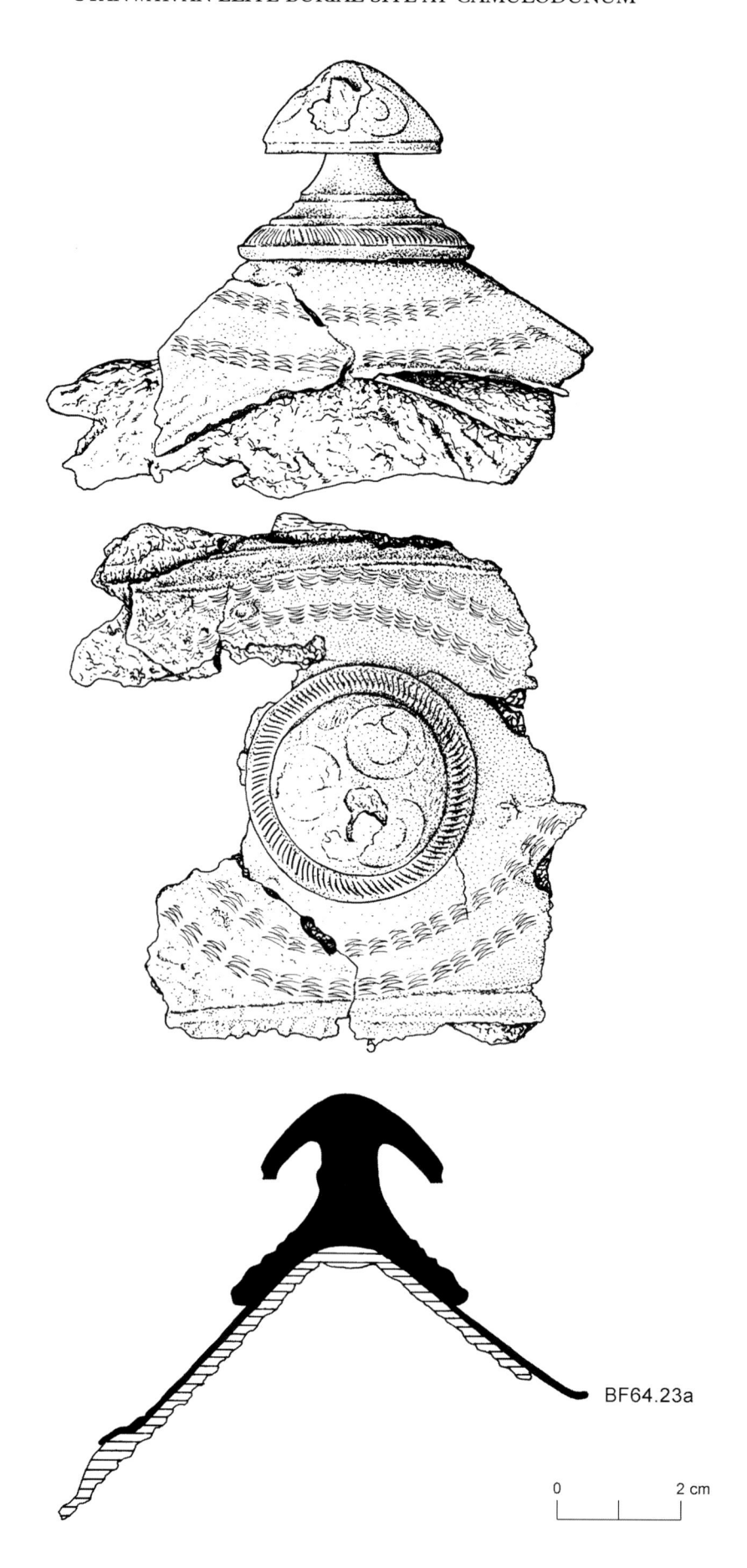

182 STANWAY: AN ÉLITE BURIAL SITE AT CAMULODUNUM

FIG. 85. Warrior's burial BF64: shield boss BF64.23a (scale 1:1)

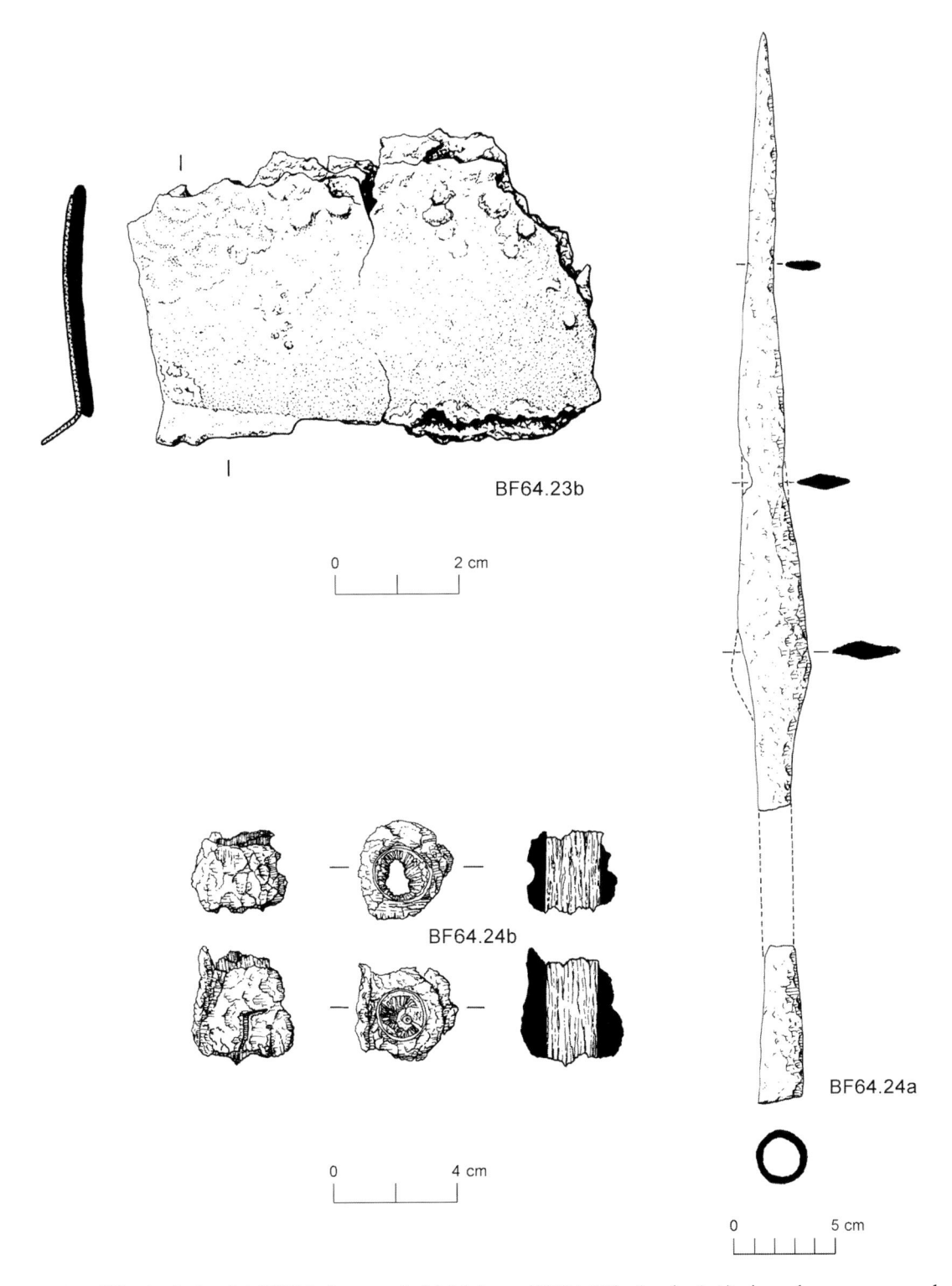

FIG. 86. Warrior's burial BF64: ?part of shield boss BF64.23b (scale 1:1), iron lance or spearhead BF64.24a (scale 1:3), and iron bands with fragments of wooden shaft BF64.24b (scale 1:2).

have shoulders set only just above the junction with the socket as does the Stanway lance, but few approach it in length (Sievers 2001, 176, pls 55–8, esp. 187, 195–6).

Two iron bands (FIG. 86, BF64.24b), with wood from a shaft surviving inside, were found in the north-west corner of the grave among a group of box fittings. They are almost certainly collar ferrules from the lance shaft and suggest that its length was not much less than that of the grave itself, *i.e.* about 1.7 to 1.8 m. Similar ferrules have been found at both Hod Hill and Alésia, presumably from British and Gallic spears respectively (Manning 1985, 141, S84–94; Sievers 2001, pl. 73, 400–6).

The absence of a sword from this grave can be seen in three ways: first, it may be a demonstration of the disarming of the native British élite in this area after A.D. 43; or second, it may show that in terms of status this burial ranks lower than graves containing a sword (and usually also either a spear and/or a shield), such as those from Great Braxted, Essex, Mill Hill, Deal, Kent, Kelvedon, Essex, and Clemency, Luxembourg, and in France those at Berry-Bouy and, in particular, Fléré-la-Rivière, which contained three swords and two spears, but equal to spear-and-shield graves such as that at Antran, France, and superior to spear-only graves such as Little Walden, Essex, and Merlsford, Fife (Stead 1985, 39; Stead 1995, 59–72; Sealey 1996, 58; Ferdière and Villard 1993; Dieudonné-Glad 1999; Hull 1963, 195; Hunter 1996, 120–2); and third, but most likely, that the lance should be seen as a general symbol of status, and not a reflection of tightly structured rank or political events.

Many more spears are known than swords in both the La Tène and Roman periods, as well as in earlier and later periods, a proportion that is no doubt affected by the different amounts of time invested in the manufacture of each weapon type, and also by their different methods of use; spears could be cast and lost and were easily damaged, swords were held in battle and could be repaired, to some extent refashioned, and may have been perceived as heirloom pieces. A parallel to Late Iron Age and early Roman graves with spears may be drawn with similar burials of the Pagan Anglo-Saxon period, when both spear- and spear-and-shield graves far outnumber sword-and-spear or sword-spear-and-shield graves (Härke 1989, tables 4.3–4.4). Härke suggests that the choice of deposited weapons at that period was not a reflection of the equipment available to the individual but was principally symbolic, driven by social and economic factors such as age, status within the family and the wider community, and wealth, and this may also have been the case in Iron Age Britain (*ibid.*, 59; James and Rigby 1997, 58). In the context of BF64 therefore, it may be said that the absence of a sword and the presence of a lance and shield need only be seen as a reflection of status/occupation, not of a specific rank, even though the manufacture, acquisition and deposition of a lance involved less real economic investment than that of a sword.

BF64.23a FIG. 85. SF347. B1006. Composite shield boss, consisting of a domed base-plate of iron capped by bronze sheet (the bronze contains a little lead), and a large decorative leaded bronze knob, separately cast and fixed, probably by solder, to the base-plate. The sides of the boss are incomplete and part of the central section is missing. The main plate is more or less rectangular in plan, with a decorative groove along the two best-preserved sides. It is decorated with lines of wide rocker-arm (zigzag; walked scorper) decoration set in rows. The knob has a wide base, hollow beneath, with concentric mouldings, the widest marked with fine incised diagonal grooves; its upper surface is mushroom-shaped and is decorated with three large incised circles with an inner circle and central dot. No inlay or plating was detected. Maximum dimensions 83 by 81 mm, 61 mm high. Given the absence of a metal strap, traces of a cord or rope found beneath the boss during conservation can perhaps be interpreted as part of the grip.

BF64.23b FIG. 86. SF373. Many other fragments of sheet iron and copper alloy from the area of the shield, together with wood from the shield board. Only the largest fragment is illustrated. The quantity of this material suggests that the boss was much larger than suggested by the main piece (BF64.23a), and this is quite possible given its unusual form and the lack of any original edge. The largest fragment (BF64.23b) is of plain sheet copper alloy over an iron plate, and probably formed part of the outer flange of the boss. The other pieces included one of sheet copper alloy only. It may be part of a shield fitting, or all that remains of a separate, unidentified, sheet-metal object (*see* BF64.27 below).

BF64.24a FIG. 86. SF357-361/363. B1028. Iron lance- or spearhead, in fragments and partly disintegrated. The shoulders form an unusual V-shape, tapering rapidly to a long and narrow blade, which has a lenticular section distorted by corrosion in places. The midrib is not prominent, disappearing completely well before the tip. Total length approximately 510 mm. Length of blade 320 mm, maximum width 37 mm. Although reconstructed from many fragments, the length of the socket shown on FIGURE 86 is considered to be accurate.

BF64.24b FIG. 86. SF381a. B1026.

1) Iron band with fragments of a wooden shaft preserved within it, and with two patches of mineral-preserved wood on the outer face. Diameter 29 mm (increased by the action of corrosion), length 19 mm

2) Similar band, but longer, and also with wood preserved inside. Diameter 23 mm, length 22 mm. These

pieces are probably from the spear shaft, and the wood on the outside of the first may be from either planks covering the grave, or from the box in the north-west corner of the grave, among the fittings from which they were found.

Copper-alloy vessels (FIGS 87–8, BF64.25–27)

The jug (FIG. 87, BF64.25) and handled basin (FIG. 87, BF64.26) form a hand-washing service of Nuber's Type E, or Millingen type, characterised by the use of plastic anthro- or zoomorphic decoration (1972, 45, Taf. 4, 1). The handled basin is of Tassinari's form H2311 at Pompeii, and the jug is form D2300 (1993, vol. 1, 40, 42, 58–9, vol. 2, 67–9, 132–7). Both forms were manufactured over a long period of time, but the use of circles to represent the shaggy hair of the ram's head on the basin handle shows this example to be an early form of the type, and of Italian manufacture (Nuber 1972, 46). The lion motif on the handle of the jug is more detailed than many other examples, with the terminals of the rim attachment bar formed into paws, the mane running well onto the crest, and a large paw on the escutcheon. This may also be indicative of an early date within the type. Textile fragments found on the jug may come from an accompanying cloth for drying the hands after washing, or it may simply have been in contact with a garment. Both vessels are further discussed on pages 321–2, 335.

There is a strong possibility that the grave contained a third copper-alloy vessel, represented by a thin fragment of sheet metal with complex profile (FIG. 88, BF64.27). The piece is seemingly necked and shouldered, and with traces of girth rings. It is not, however, regularly

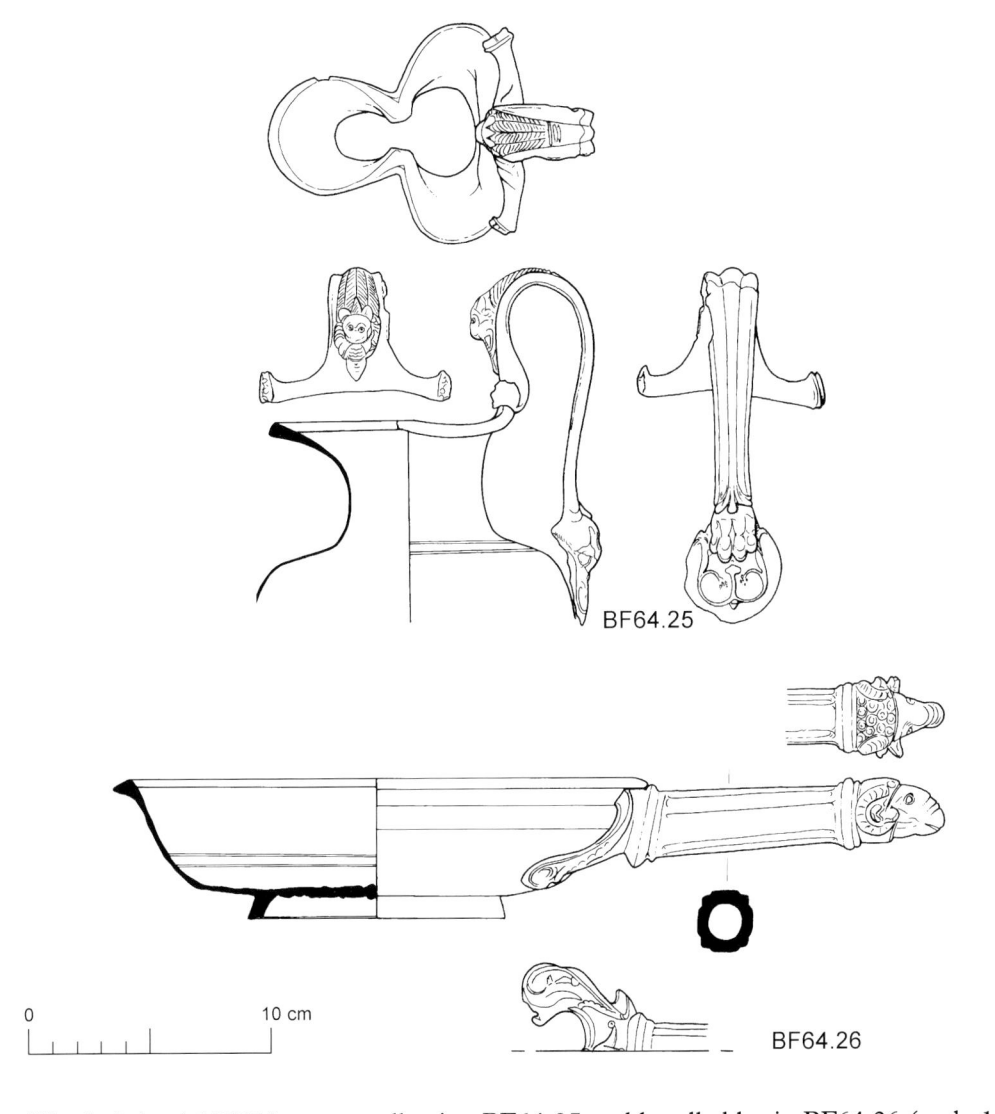

FIG. 87. Warrior's burial BF64: copper-alloy jug BF64.25 and handled basin BF64.26 (scale 1:3)

curved along its horizontal axis and cannot be attributed with certainty to a particular vessel form. The fragment was found in close association with the shield boss yet does not appear to have been part of the boss nor part of the collapsed lower section of the jug.

BF64.25 FIG. 87. SF375a. B1020. A composite copper-alloy jug, with trilobate rim and oval neck. The lower part of the vessel has been crushed and only distorted fragments remain. The handle and the upper part of the vessel were cast, the lower part spun. Both the upper and lower sections of the body are made from a bronze containing a small quantity of lead. The two were brazed together, and the join disguised by a pair of grooves. No plating was detected, but the inside of the vessel could not be analysed. The handle, which is cast in a leaded bronze, has a lion mask at the upper end, the eyes shown as circular indentations with an outer groove and inner pit. The beard is shown by half-moon punch marks and defined by incised lines. The discoid terminals of the rim attachment bar are shaped into the pads of paws. The mane runs onto the crest of the handle, where it ends in transverse mouldings. The handle has prominent marginal mouldings and a central rib below the mane. The lower end terminates in a large paw on a rounded escutcheon, with a raised peltate floral motif beneath the paw. Surviving height 150 mm. Fragments of textile found on the jug suggest it was wrapped in cloth when deposited.

BF64.26 FIG. 87. SF372. B1019. Fragmentary basin with ram's head handle. (Often called a patera or skillet, but, as it was not used for cooking, the term basin is used here.) Both the body and handle are cast in a leaded bronze, and were soldered together with a lead-tin solder. The bowl of the vessel has been restored for display, with much substitute material added, and is now asymmetrical. It is shown here as symmetrical, but the diameter and depth have both been estimated and are not necessarily wholly accurate. It has a deep footring and beaded rim. There are lathe centre marks inside both the bowl and the footring, with a number of concentric grooves set around them, and internally a moulding at the base of the wall. The escutcheon of the handle is decorated with incised marginal lines and semicircular punch marks, with a lotus bud set in the centre. The hollow cast handle has symmetrical linear mouldings. The ram's head has knurled horns, curling around the ears, and with the ends turned outwards. The hair between the horns is shown by circles with varying internal lines and dots. The facial features are well formed, even to the extent of showing the groove beneath the lower jaw. Length of handle 126 mm. Internal diameter of bowl about 202 mm, height 55 mm, probably greater originally.

BF64.27 FIG. 88. SF373. Thin copper-alloy fragment with complex profile. Possibly part of a third copper-alloy vessel.

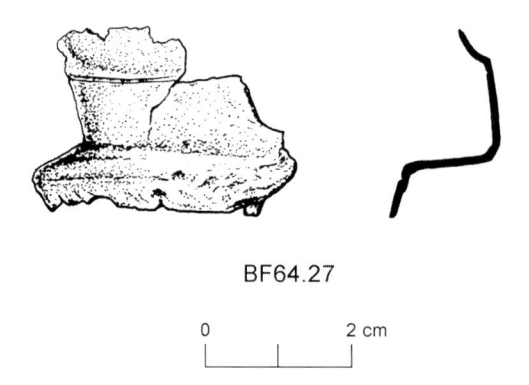

FIG. 88. Warrior's burial BF64: fragment probably from a copper-alloy vessel BF64.27 (scale 1:1)

Board game (FIGS 89–91, BF64.28–29)

A maplewood board (BF64.29) with brass fittings lay in one corner of the grave, and close by was a pile of eleven blue and nine white glass counters (FIG. 89, BF64.28). The latter are imports of standard Roman form, made by placing small 'spoonfuls' of molten glass to set on a bed of sand. All are circular, with a typical sand-roughened underside and convex top, and are between 15 and 22 mm in diameter. The majority of counters from Roman Britain are similarly monochrome dark coloured (black/blue) or white, and they contrast with the La Tène style decoration on the yellow, white, blue and green counters from the board game in the late 1st-century B.C. grave at Welwyn Garden City (Cool and Philo 1998, 190, tables 34–5; Price 1995, 129; Harden 1967, 14–16).

THE FUNERARY SITE 187

Analysis of the counters shows the lighter blue counters from BF64 to be of a different composition to the dark blue examples (p. 329), and both differ to those in CF42 and CF47 in Enclosure 5. As might be expected, all the Stanway counters differ in composition to those from the Welwyn Garden City grave (Werner and Bimson 1967, 17).

The use of brass for the drop-handles on the wooden board suggests that they were also of continental origin. The board itself was in two pieces, held together by strong junction-fittings (FIG. 91, BF64.29e–f), and had protective corner-binding (FIG. 91, BF64.29g) fixed over leather. A tinned brass drop-handle was fitted to each end by copper-alloy split-pins (FIG. 90,

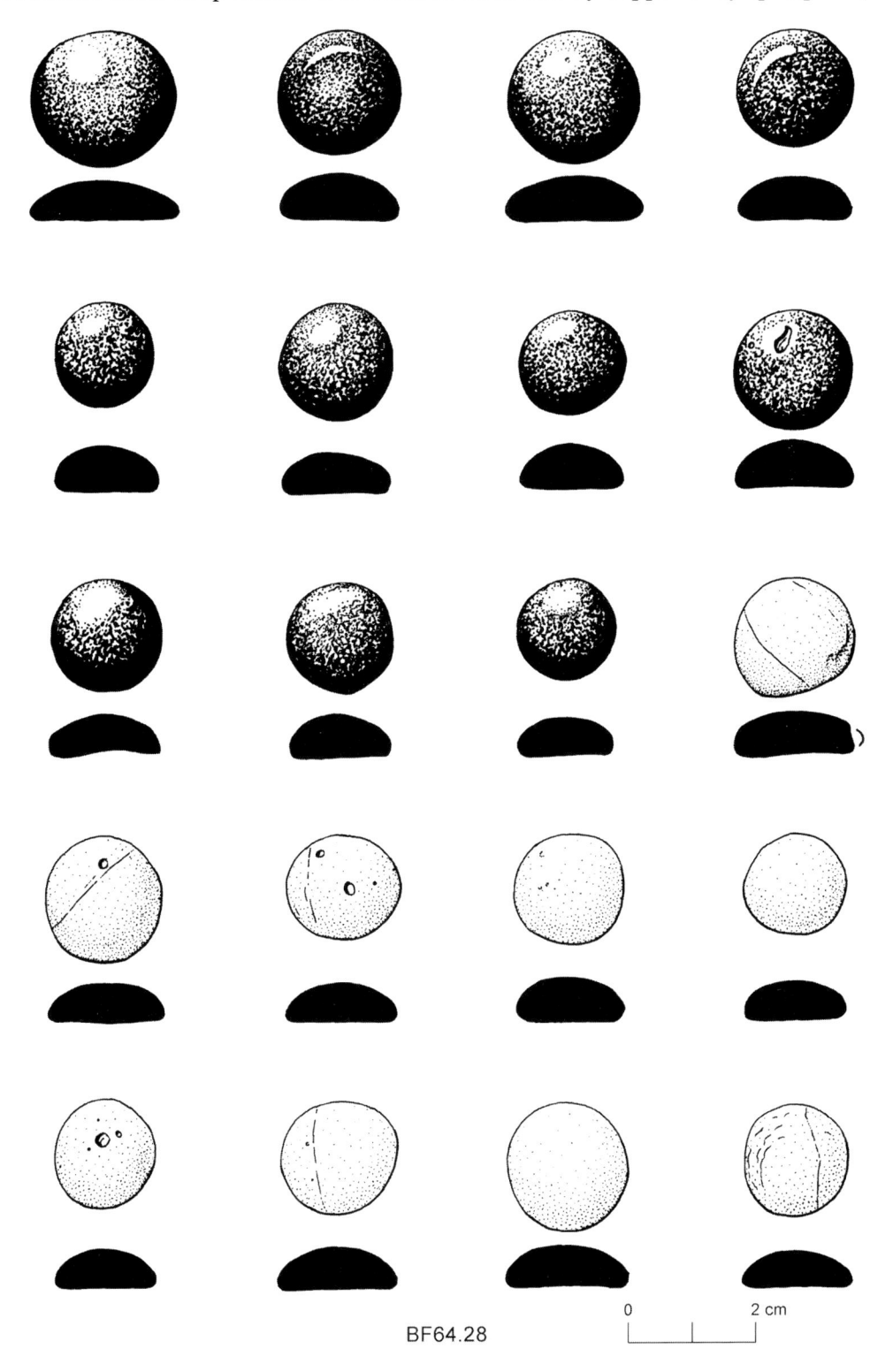

BF64.28

FIG. 89. Warrior's burial BF64: glass gaming counters BF64.28 (scale 1:1)

BF64.29.a–d). The handles are particularly well-made examples of the form, tinned, with deeply channelled grooves and crisp mouldings flanking the central bead, and well-shaped acorn terminals. Similar handles are a 1st-century form and generally interpreted as having come from boxes, although they can also be used on vessels and other domestic equipment (*e.g.* Riha 2001, 28–30; Tassinari 1993, vol. 2, 251, no. 10549; Eggers 1951, nos 75–78; Ward-Perkins and Claridge 1976, no. 159). The recovery of the pair from BF64 widens their use still further. A single drop-handle and two hinges from burial 6 at Baldock may perhaps now also be interpreted as from a game board (Stead and Rigby 1986, fig. 28, plan, 13–14, 16 and fig. 30, 13–14, 16), as may a similar group (from a leather-bound maplewood board) from grave 117 at King Harry Lane, Verulamium, although the location of the handle in this group, lying between the two sets of hinges, is odd. Yet another board, but with no handle, came from grave 309 at King Harry Lane (Stead and Rigby 1989, 109–110, figs 108, 152).

Several sets of gaming counters, in bone and pottery as well as glass have been found in burials in Britain. They have been listed by Cotton with particular reference to a set of bone counters from Ewell, Surrey (Cotton 2001a, 13, table A; 2001b, 27–31, especially table 9; and

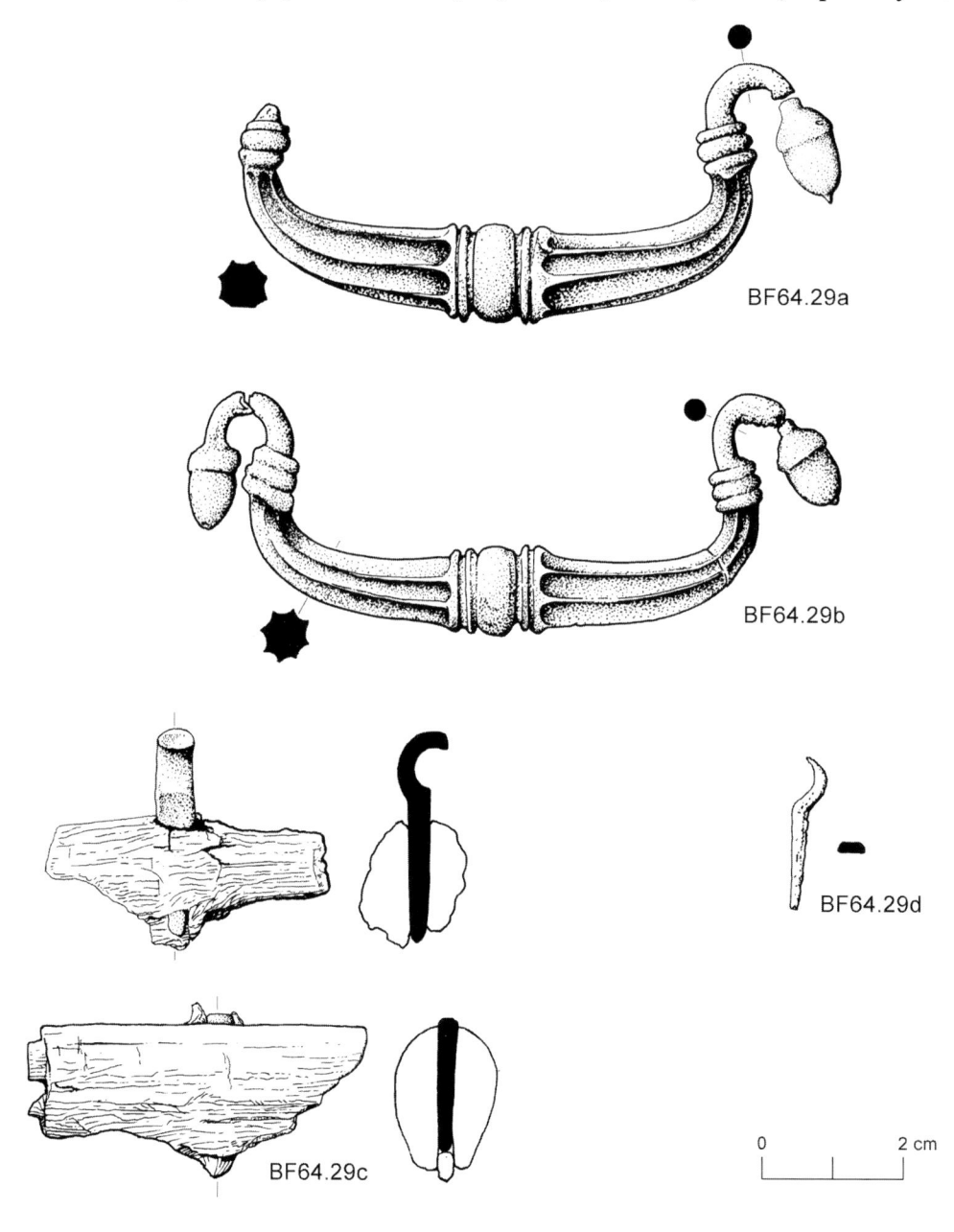

FIG. 90. Warrior's burial BF64: copper-alloy drop handles BF64.29a–b and handle attachments BF24.29c–d from the gaming board with part of the wooden board itself (scale 1:1)

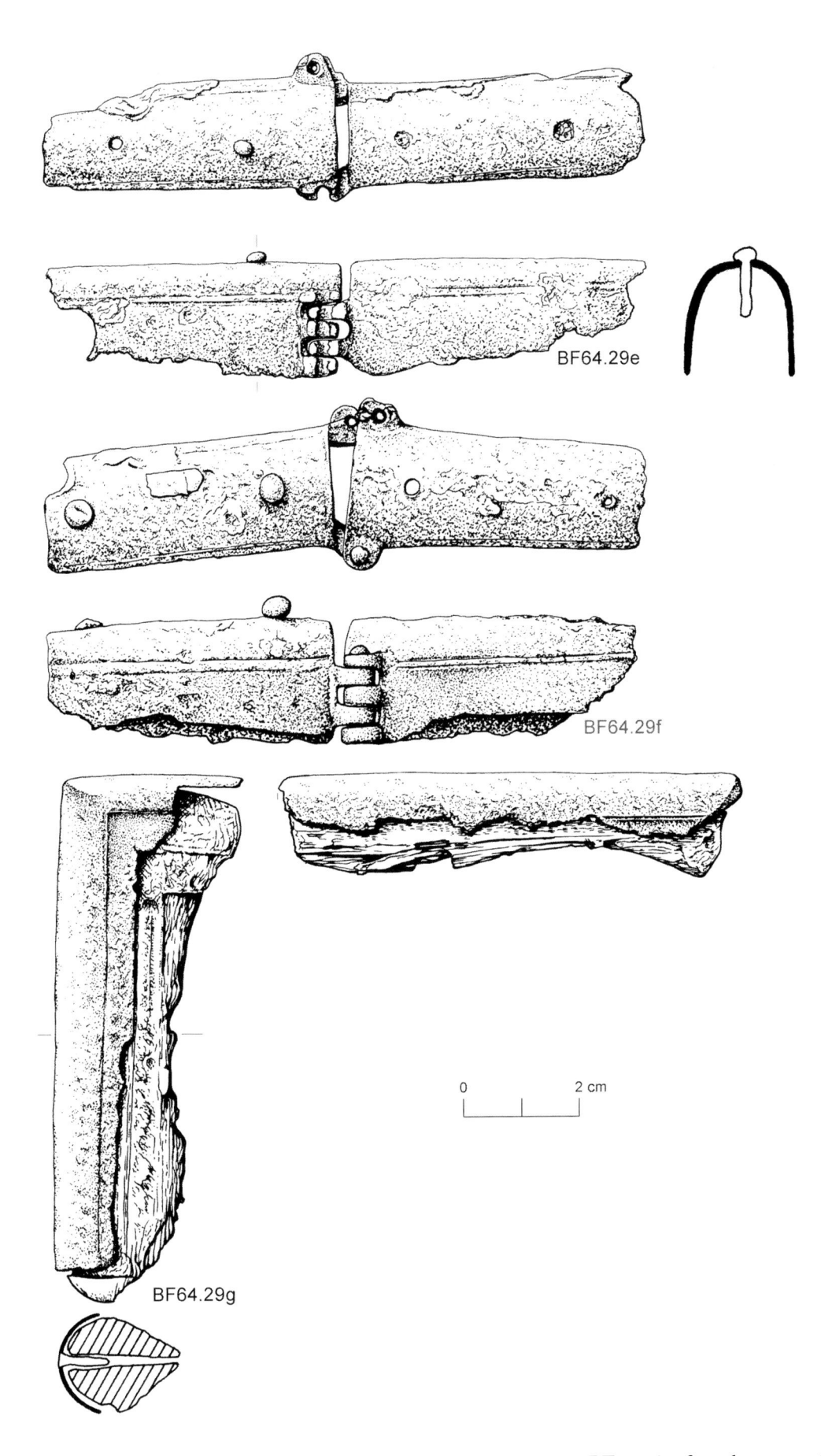

FIG. 91. Warrior's burial BF64: copper-alloy junction bidings BF64.29e–f and corner binding BF64.29g from the gaming board with part of the wooden board itself (scale 1:1).

see p. 368), and range in date from those from the Welwyn Garden City grave of *c.* 10 B.C. (Stead 1967, 14–19), to a set in a late 4th-century grave at Lankhills, Winchester (Clarke 1979, 251–4). All come from eastern or southern Britain, with the furthest west from Dorset, and the furthest north from York. They are, however, concentrated in the south-east, with eight out of twenty-three coming from Essex and Hertfordshire (including the two sets from Stanway), three from London, one each from Surrey and Suffolk, and two each from Kent and West Sussex. (A set of bone pegs from King Harry Lane is not included in this total, although it is included in Cotton's list.)

BF64.28 FIG. 89. SF313. B1015; SF397. B unstratified (from sieving of spoil from excavation of burial pit). Eleven blue and nine white glass counters. The blue counters vary from cobalt and slightly translucent through to almost black and opaque, and from round to slightly oval. SF313: Diameters 22 × 20 mm (7 mm high), 20 mm (6.5 mm high), 19 mm (7 mm high), 18 × 19 mm (7 mm high), 18 mm (7 mm high), 17 × 18 mm (6.5 mm high), 16 × 17 mm (6 mm high), 15.5 × 16 mm (6.5 mm high), 15 × 15.5 mm (6.5 mm high), 15 mm (6 mm high). SF397: Diameter 17.5 mm, height 7 mm. All have well-formed upper surfaces and slightly sand-roughened undersides. The two 6 mm high counters are the bluest. The white counters are all opaque and have slightly sand-roughened undersides. Some have pits from air bubbles on the surface, and one has a shiny swirl where the opacifier was not fully mixed into the matrix. SF313: Diameters 19 mm (6.5 mm high), 18.5 mm (6 mm high), 17.5 × 19 mm (7 mm high), 17 × 18 mm (6 mm high), 16.5 × 17 mm (7 mm high), 15.5 × 17 mm (6 mm high), 17 mm (6 mm high), 16 × 17 mm (6 mm high), 16 mm (6 mm high).

BF64.29

a FIG. 90. SF316. B1016; SF339a, B1034. Tinned brass drop-handle, one terminal missing. The handle is unusually ornate, with a central bead between transverse collar mouldings, and collar mouldings before the curve of the terminal. Stout linear mouldings run between the central and outer collars. The terminals end in well-formed acorns. Length (when complete) 88 mm.

b FIG. 90. SF317. B1080. Copper-alloy drop-handle as BF64.29a. The ends of the terminals now detached. Length (when complete) 88 mm.

c FIG. 90. SF383. Fragments of wood from the western edge of the game board, pierced by copper-alloy split-pins used for attaching one of the drop-handles. Lengths 47 and 38.5 mm. The longer fragment of wood retains a slight lip to show it was rebated to take copper-alloy binding. Small fragments of copper-alloy sheet, some curved and some of which have traces of leather adhering, are all that remain of this. They are not illustrated here.

d FIG. 90. SF382b. Fragment of a split-pin used to attach one of the handles. Length 21 mm.

e FIG. 91. SF348. B1060 ?Brass central junction binding from the northern side of the game board, with fragments of the wood. U-shaped in section, each piece has a pair of parallel grooves along the centre of each side and was fixed to the wood of the board by two small brass dome-headed tacks (one only now survives). The two pieces were joined by interlocking perforated lugs, three lugs on each side of one piece, two on the other. No axial pin or rivet remains. Length (joined) 104 mm. If a rivet or fixing pin was fitted through each set of lugs, the two pieces would have been held rigid, not hinged. If the board were intended to fold, either no pin, or a removable pin, must have been used on one side to enable the pieces to be disarticulated.

f FIG. 91. SF371. B990. Copper-alloy central junction binding from the southern side of the game board. Three of the tacks for attaching the binding to the board survive. A dome-headed pin remains in one set of lugs. The tip of the pin is blunt. Length 102 mm. The pin seems too small to remove without losing it.

g FIG. 91. SF319, B992; SF335, B1059; SF336, B991; SF339b, B1034. Four ?brass corner binding pieces, with fragments of the wooden board. SF336 is from the south-west corner, SF339 the south-east, BF64.29g (SF335) the north-east, and SF319 the north-west. Only BF64.29g (SF335) is well-preserved and illustrated here. It has one long and one short side, the inner margins defined by an incised groove. The binding is attached by two copper-alloy tacks on the long side, the heads flush with the surface of the binding. Length 83 mm. The wood has been rebated to take the binding. There are traces of leather on SF339b.

Box (north-west) (FIG. 92, BF64.30)

A group of iron fittings from the north-west corner of the grave are all that remain of a large wooden box BF64.30 (FIG. 92). The fittings consist of two L-shaped pieces, the short arm is nail-like, the long one is a strap with studs for attachment (FIG. 92, BF64.30a; BF64.30h.8);

parts of one or more loop-hinges with studs for attachment (FIG. 92, BF64.30b; BF64.30h.1); several fragments of thin iron straps, again with studs for attachment, and with one small fragment having a short return to show it came from a corner (FIG. 92, BF64.30d and BF64.30c.7; BF64.30c.4–6, BF64.30h.2–5); two split-spike loops (FIG. 92, BF64.30c.1–2); four long spikes (BF64.30i, BF64.30f, BF64.30h.6–7); a large rod (FIG. 92, BF64.30g); and fragments of studs and nail shanks or spikes (FIG. 92, BF64.30a.2; BF64.30e, BF64.30c.3, BF64.30j).

The box was clearly hinged, although only part of one loop-hinge remains. The two split-spike loops were probably replacements for the missing hinge (Manning 1985, 130). The rod, with its section different at each end, may have been a locating pin, fixed in the lid and slotting into a hole in the front board when the box was closed, but it has expanded considerably because of corrosion and this identification is far from certain. The two L-shaped fittings are unusual in the Roman period but could also act as hinges as they resemble a type of medieval pintle used for hinged items such as shutters or chest lids (Egan 1998, 46, fig. 28, 32). The long arms would have been fitted onto a surface and visible, the nail-like short arms would have been driven into the edge of a board. They would have been set so that the long arm was attached to one board with the short one driven into a board abutting at right angles. The long spikes must have been used instead of nails, and their size suggests that the boards making up the box were quite substantial, as does the size of the split-spike loops. The strap fittings, with low dome-headed studs for attachment, also occur on the box containing the glass bowl in the south-west corner of the grave.

No contents survive from this box, and so whatever it contained can be presumed to have been organic. Clothing seems to be the most likely possibility, although no mineral-replaced textile fragments were noted on the iron fittings. Thirteen graves in the cemetery of Lamadelaine at the Titelberg, Luxembourg, also contained iron fittings from wooden furniture, in some cases from large boxes or chests, and three of the graves also contained weapons (Metzler-Zens *et al.* 1999, 310–11, 386–7). It has been suggested of the Lamadelaine boxes that as well as representing the idea of the protection of property (several of the boxes were fitted with locks), they also indicated the mobility of an élite social group, and this is particularly pertinent in the context of the Stanway warrior's burial which included so many items of continental manufacture among the grave goods.

BF64.30

a FIG. 92. SF364. 1) L-shaped iron fitting, the long arm a strap, the short arm narrow for insertion into wood. The long arm is 95 mm long, 18 mm wide, tapering slightly into the corner, and 3–4 mm thick. It has two dome-headed studs or nails for attachment, head diameter 15 mm. The shafts are broken off below the strap. There is mineral-replaced wood on the underside. The short arm is 40 mm long, projecting about 25 mm beyond the inner edge of the strap, and is about 5 mm square in section. It is covered in mineral-replaced wood. 2) Iron nail with flat round head, 13 mm in diameter. Shaft length 29 mm, covered in mineral-replaced wood.

b FIG. 92. SF352. Part of an iron loop-hinge, with most of the strap but only a short length of the loop surviving. Length 111 mm, width 22 mm, tapering slightly towards the rounded end. Strap thickness 3 mm. Parts of two dome-headed nails for fixing the hinge to the wooden box remain. The heads are 15 mm in diameter, 5 mm high. Little of either shaft remains, the longest gives a minimum board thickness of 11 mm. Substantial pieces of mineral-replaced wood remain on the underside.

c FIG. 92. SF369. B1025. Two split-spike loops, a nail shaft, and 4 fragments of iron strap (one illustrated). 1) FIG. 92. Split-spike loop, the arms parallel. Length 71 mm, loop diameter 29.5 mm. There is mineral-replaced wood on both sides of the arms below the loop. 2) FIG. 92. Split-spike loop, part of one arm missing. The other is clenched. Length 47 mm to bend, 36 mm beyond it. Loop diameter 27 mm. There is mineral-replaced wood on both sides of the arms below the loop. 3) Iron nail with round flat head, diameter 10 mm. The shaft covered in mineral-replaced wood. Length (tip missing) 45 mm. 4) Fragment of an iron strap. Length 27 mm, width 34 mm, 2 mm thick. 5) Fragment of iron strap. Maximum dimensions 22 by 25 mm, 2 mm thick. 6) Fragment of iron strap. Maximum dimensions 32 by 22.5 mm, 2 mm thick. 7) FIG. 92. Fragment of iron strap with dome-headed stud. Maximum dimensions 26 by 23 mm, 2 mm thick. Stud head diameter 16 mm.

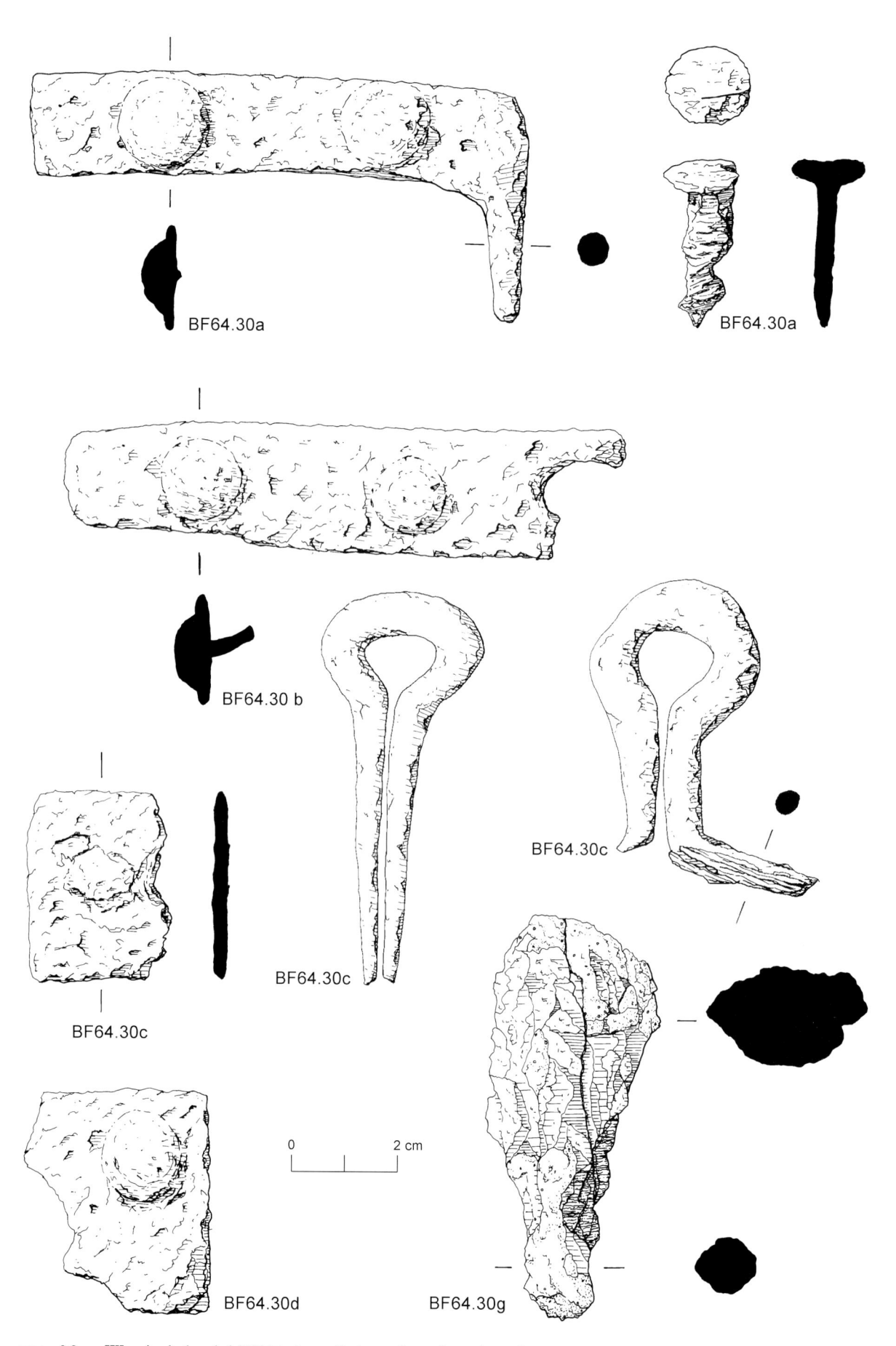

FIG. 92. Warrior's burial BF64: iron fittings from box (north-west area of burial pit) BF64.30a–d and 30g (scale 1:1)

d FIG. 92. SF367. B1025. Fragment of an iron strap, with a dome-headed stud or nail for attachment. Length 37 mm, width 35 mm, 2 mm thick. Stud head 17 mm in diameter.
e SF366. B1025. Iron stud with flat round head, now separate. Diameter 20 mm, length approximately 45 mm. There is mineral-replaced wood around the shaft and under the head.
f SF368. B1025. Iron shaft or spike, in fragments. Probably square in section and tapering towards a point, although see SF365 below. Length 76 mm, maximum diameter 20 mm.
g FIG. 92. SF351. B1029. Large iron tapering rod with mineral-replaced wood along one side. Length 69 mm. The upper end is round in section, maximum diameter 16 mm, the lower end is 10 mm square. Probably a locating pin.
h SF381b. B1026. 1) Strap fragment from a loop-hinge, as SF352, with two dome-headed studs/nails for attachment. Length 98 mm, width 18 mm, approximately 4 mm thick. Stud head diameter 15 mm, height approximately 6 mm. 2) Strap fragment with a flat-headed stud for attachment. Length 41 mm, width 30 mm, 1.5 mm thick. Stud head diameter 16 mm. 3) Strap fragment, with a stud for attachment. Only a short length of one edge remains. Maximum dimensions 42 by 28 mm, 2 mm thick. Stud head diameter 14.5 mm. 4) Strap fragment, with a stud for attachment. Length 49 mm, width (incomplete) 27 mm, 2 mm thick approx. Stud head 16 mm in diameter. 5) Small strap fragment from a corner, with part of a return at one end, and a stud for attachment set about 26 mm from the bend. The strap is very thin, only 1 mm thick, and the whole piece is distorted, no doubt caused by the collapse of the box. Surviving dimensions 39 mm by 28 mm. Stud head 17 mm in diameter. 6) Spike fragment; the top has been destroyed by large corrosion bubbles. Length 66 mm. 7) Spike fragment. Length 65 mm. 8) L-shaped fitting as SF364, in three fragments, covered with mineral-replaced wood. Length of long arm 105 mm, width 21 mm. Length of short arm 43 mm.
i SF365. BF6. Iron square-section shaft or spike, the upper end covered in mineral-replaced wood. Length 363 mm, section 10 mm square.
j SF375b. B1020. 1) Iron square-section shaft, length 36 mm, head round and flat, diameter 16 mm. The shaft and the underside of the head are covered in mineral-replaced wood. 2) Part of a stout round-section iron shaft. Length 23 mm. Possibly not a nail.

Box (south-west) (FIGS 93–4, BF64.31)

The glass bowl (FIG. 83, BF64.16) in the south-west corner of the grave had been deposited inside a large wooden box with iron fittings (FIGS 93–4, BF64.31), similar to that in the north-west corner (FIG. 92, BF64.30). The box was probably hinged using split-spike loops, although only part of one split-spike loop remains complete enough for identification (FIG. 93, BF64.31a). Apart from this piece and several nails and nail shank fragments, most of the fittings consist of straps fixed to the box by low dome-headed studs (FIGS 93–4). A large part of one of the straps can be reconstructed (FIG. 93, BF64.31b).

BF64.31
a FIG. 93. SF345. B993. The loop and a short length of the arms of an iron split-spike loop. Length 25 mm, width 23 mm. There are fragments of mineral-replaced wood on both sides.
b FIG. 93. SF353/355. B1017. Right-angled strap (in four pieces) with mineral-replaced wood on the underside. On one side the terminal is tongue-ended, on the other it is straight (FIG. 93, BF64.31b). On both sides there are two dome-headed studs for attachment. Length of tongue-ended side 100 mm, length of straight-ended side approximately 74 mm, maximum width 35 mm, 2 mm thick. Stud head diameter 16 mm, height 6 mm.
c SF353/355. B1017, five other fragments of one or more straps similar to BF64.31b, plus a nail fragment; only (1) is illustrated. 1) FIG. 94. Length 47 mm, width 34 mm, thickness 1–2 mm. Slightly curved. One stud, 16 mm diameter, 6 mm high. 2) Length 22 mm, width 35 mm, 2 mm thick. One stud, 17 mm diameter, 6 mm high. Mineral-replaced wood on underside. 3) Length 24 mm, width 34 mm, 2 mm thick. 4) Maximum dimensions 20 by 15 mm, 2 mm thick. Mineral-replaced wood on underside. 5) Maximum dimensions 22 by 16 mm, 2mm thick. One stud, 16 mm diameter, 6 mm high. Mineral-replaced wood on underside. 6) Nail shank fragment, 21 mm long.
d FIG. 94. SF392. B1092. Fragment of flat sheet iron with a dome-headed stud for attachment, as strap BF64.31b. Maximum dimensions 27 by 23 mm, 2 mm thick. Stud head diameter 16 mm, height 4.5 mm. Only a stub of the shank remains.
SF344. B994. 1) Iron nail shank with mineral-replaced wood. Length 27 mm. 2) Iron nail shank, in 3 pieces, the end apparently split and each half turned outwards like the shaft of a split-spike loop. Length

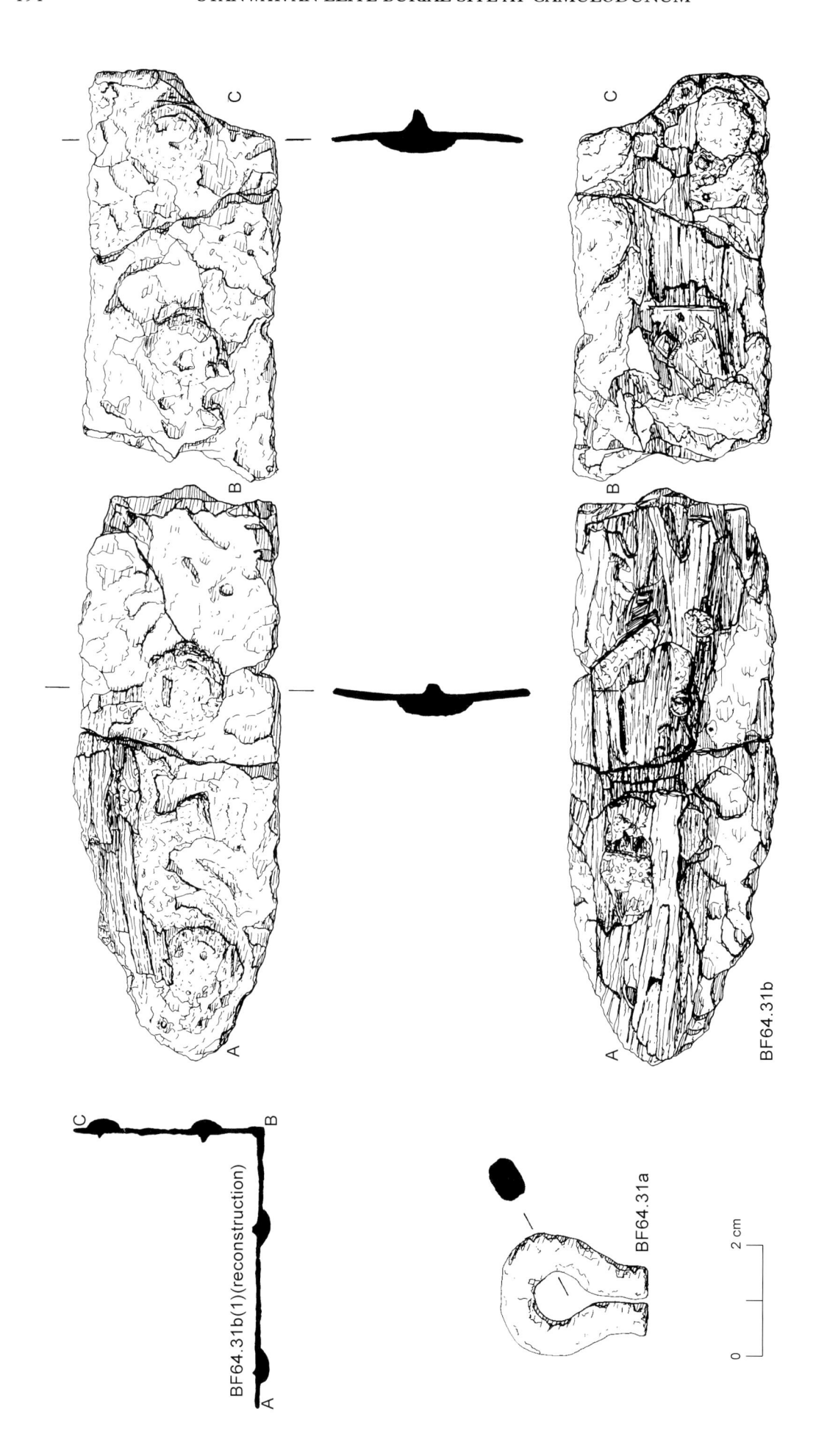

FIG. 93. Warrior's burial BF64: iron fittings from box (south-west area of burial pit) BF64.31a–b (scale 1:1)

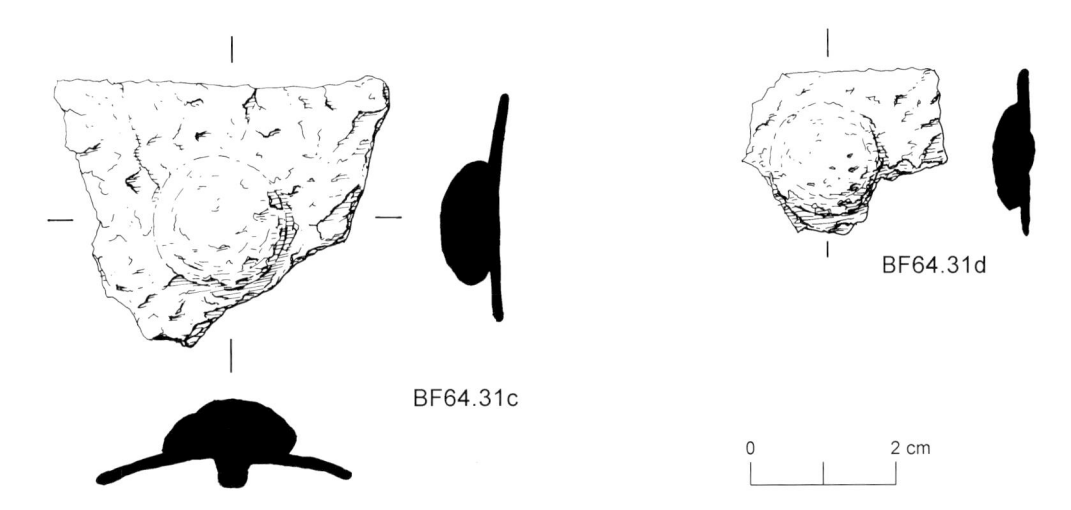

FIG. 94. Warrior's burial BF64: iron fittings from box (south-west area of burial pit) BF64.31c–d

above split 14 mm, length of longest split side 23 mm. There is mineral-replaced wood on all surfaces. 3) Nail shank fragment with mineral-replaced wood, length 14 mm. 4) Small fragment of sheet iron, 20 by 16 mm, 2 mm thick, with mineral-replaced wood on the underside.

SF415. B1140. A fragment of an iron nail and ten fragments of sheet iron, two with low dome-headed studs attached, and many with traces of mineral-replaced wood, in some cases on each face: 1) nail, flat head, probably originally round, square-section shank, 19 mm long; 2) sheet fragment with stud, 40 by 23 mm, wood each side; 3) sheet fragment with stud, 25 by 26 mm, wood on each side; 4) sheet fragment, 32 by 27 mm, wood on one side; 5) sheet fragment, 29 by 22 mm, wood on one side; 6) sheet fragment, 20 by 17 mm; 7) sheet fragment, 21 by 16 mm, wood on one side; 8) sheet fragment, 20 by 9 mm; 9) sheet fragment, 15 by 14 mm, wood on one side; 10) sheet fragment, 15 by 12 mm, wood one side; 11) sheet fragment, 13 by 11 mm.

Miscellaneous fragments (FIG. 95, BF64.32–35)

The small flat copper-alloy studs FIG. 95, BF64.33 and SF411 may be from the shield BF64.23. Many of the sheet fragments are probably from the shield boss (BF64.23a/b) or the lower part of the jug BF64.25 (which had disintegrated), or perhaps the putative third copper-alloy vessel (BF64.27) suggested by the thin fragment of copper alloy that lay close to the shield boss.

BF64.32 FIG. 95. SF386. B997. Small piece of copper-alloy sheet bent at right angles. One side is 13 mm long, the other 10 mm. Height 16 mm.
BF64.33 FIG. 95. SF390. B1086. Fragment of a flat copper-alloy stud with most of the shank. The latter appears to be cast in one with the head, not applied separately. Diameter approximately 20 mm, height 8 mm.
BF64.34 FIG. 95. SF407. B1132. Small fragment of a low convex copper-alloy boss or stud, with a moulding close to the edge. Diameter approximately 30 mm.
BF64.35 FIG. 95. SF400. B1176. 1) Iron strip fragment. Length 32.5 mm. Width tapers slightly from 16 to 14 mm. Section elliptical, maximum thickness 4 mm. 2) Not illustrated. Small irregular fragment, broken from rounded edge of plate or strip? Length 16 mm, width 3–5 mm.
SF314. B1037. Small fragment of thick copper-alloy ?sheet. No original edges survive. Maximum dimensions 10 by 5 mm.
SF387. B1083. Tiny speck of copper alloy.
SF389. B1085. Small fragments of sheet iron and sheet copper alloy, probably from the shield boss. Largest piece 16 by 12.5 mm.
SF396. B1174. Two fragments of sheet iron, the largest 17 by 18 mm. Also in this number, but intrusive in the grave, is a large (40 mm) modern lead-alloy disc with central round perforation for attachment. The sheet iron may be associated with this instead of any of the items in the grave.
SF399. B1175. Narrow copper-alloy strip, parallel-sided, angular in profile. Length 13 mm, width 4.5 mm. Possibly part of the catchplate or foot of one of the brooches.

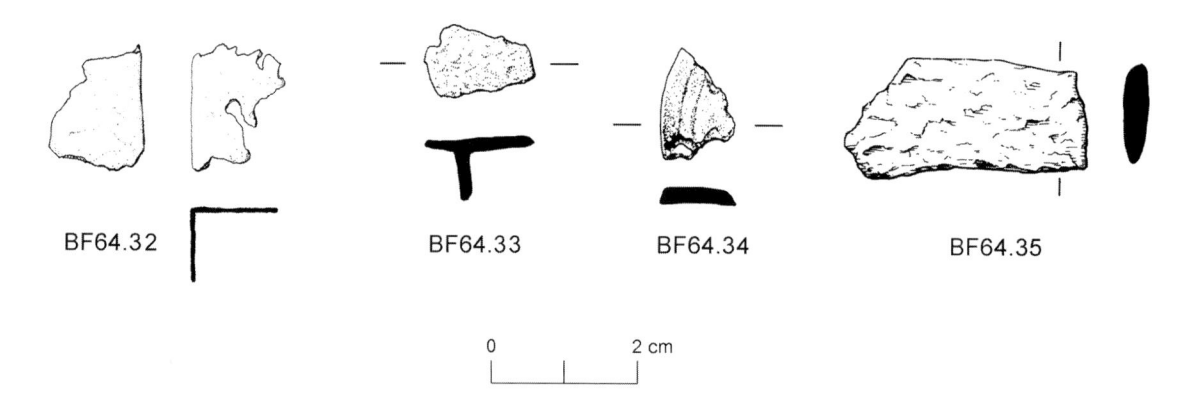

FIG. 95. Warrior's burial BF64: miscellaneous metal objects of copper alloy BF64.32–34 and iron BF64.35 (scale 1:1)

SF401. B1177. 1) Fragment of flat sheet iron with part of a curved edge remaining. Maximum dimensions 26 by 18 mm, 3.5 mm thick. If this is a disc, the diameter is approximately 50 mm. 2) Fragment, possibly from stud or nail head. Diameter 12 mm.
SF403. B1173. Fifteen small fragments of flat sheet iron, one with part of a straight edge remaining, 17.5 mm long. Largest fragment 21 by 18 mm. Laminating, thickness varies from 2–4 mm.
SF406. B1132. Fragment of flat sheet iron, as B1173. Maximum dimensions 23 by 28 mm, 2–3 mm thick, laminating.
SF411. B1108. Fragment of a copper-alloy flat-headed stud with riveted shaft. Diameter 12 mm, length 4 mm.
SF412. B1112. Unstratified. Fragment of thin sheet iron, the original edge rounded, the other two broken at right angles to each other. Possibly originally from a tongue-ended strap or part of a disc. Maximum dimensions 19 by 13 mm.
SF413. B1114. Unstratified. Two fragments of thin sheet copper alloy: a) roughly 7 mm square; b) 6 by 5 mm.
SF414. B1114. Unstratified. Circular fragment of iron with mineral-replaced wood running across one face and also partly across the other. Diameter 11 mm. Probably a nail head or rove.
SF416. B1140. Fragment of sheet copper alloy. Maximum dimensions 12 by 7 mm.
SF417. 1141. Fragment of thin sheet copper alloy, very slightly convex. Maximum dimensions 17.5 by 13.5 mm.
SF418. B1142. Three small fragments of sheet copper alloy: a) 10 by 7 mm; b) 7 by 7.5 mm; c) 6 by 4 mm.
SF419. B1143. Two fragments of thin sheet iron: a) 22 by 19 mm; b) 20 by 16 mm.
B996. Beneath BF64.16. Iron nail shank covered with mineral-replaced wood. Length 39 mm.
B1053. Iron nail shaft fragment. Length 26 mm.
B1170. Unstratified. Iron nail in two fragments. Length incomplete, 27 mm.
B1134. Unstratified. Fragment of an iron nail shank, square in section. Length 16 mm. There are traces of mineral-replaced wood around it, the grain lying transversely.

Residual pottery

BF64.a B1057. Sherd from a hand-made shouldered jar, burnished lattice on shoulder, fabric GTW, 1 (10.2 g) from bottom of pit.
Sherds recovered from spoil heaps.
B1135: 4 sherds from thin walled pot, probably all from same vessel (4.7 g). Fabric GTW.
B1135: sherd (2.2 g). Fabric GTW.
B1116: sherd (9.3 g). Fabric GTW.
B1169: rim sherd from a necked jar, Cam 266 (5.2 g). Fabric RCVW.
B1169: 2 sherds from thin-walled pot with burnished exterior surface (1.9 g). Fabric GX.
B1135: sherd/fragment (0.6 g). Fabric GX.

THE INKWELL BURIAL BF67 (FIGS 2, 8, 96–7; TABLE 34)

Cremated bone	225.6 g	adult of indeterminate age and sex
Pottery vessels	BF67.1	inkwell
	BF67.2	cornice-rimmed *lagena*
Other finds	BF67.3	copper-alloy Hod Hill variant brooch
	BF67.4	wooden tray or box with copper-alloy fittings
	BF67.5	?wooden object with up to 13 iron nails
Residual finds	BF67.a–b	two base sherds of butt-beaker, three sherds of another beaker, and perhaps up to 13 iron nails

A cremation burial (BF67) lay 16 m south-west of chamber BF6 and 3 m north-west of the Warrior's burial (BF64). It has been given the name 'Inkwell burial' from one of the two complete vessels which it contained (FIGS 2, 8). The burial pit was about 1.65 m square with a flat base up to 0.5 m below the ground-level after stripping (FIG. 96). Although no traces of decayed wood survived, its square shape may indicate that it had a wooden plank cover (*see* p. 427). A thin black ?ferromanganese deposit had formed on the bottom of the pit rather like that on the sides of the nearby chamber pit BF6. Presumably this was a natural formation. The cremated bone (225.6 g) indicated an adult, but the sex could not be determined. The bone lay in a pile on the base of the western side of the burial pit (FIG. 96). Two accompanying vessels had been placed, probably intact, on the floor of the pit. An inkwell (BF67.1) lay towards the centre of the pit and a *lagena* (BF67.2) near its northern edge. Other finds included a small Hod Hill variant brooch (BF67.3) from near the southern edge of the pit, and some decayed wood and poorly preserved copper-alloy fittings which appeared to be the remains of at least one box or wooden tray (BF67.4). The presence of the pottery inkwell but no stylus in this burial suggests that reed pens (*calami*) were originally included among the grave goods but, being organic, have not survived.

A shallow pit (BF221) immediately south-west of BF67 was probably a natural feature. A small quantity of grey ware sherds (B989 and B1014) from two separate vessels were found scattered in different parts of the pit and were probably residual.

The brooch (FIG. 97, BF67.3) is of unusual form, but can be classed as a variant combining features of both strongly profiled brooches and of the Hod Hill series. The strongly arched bow, incurving sides, and large button ally it to the former (*e.g. CAR* **2**, fig. 6, 37; *CAR* **6**, fig. 6.1, 12; Hattatt 1989, figs 184–5), but instead of being sprung the head is solid and drilled to take an iron axial bar on which to hinge the pin, in imitation of the more usual rolled head of Hod Hill types. A brooch from near Toulouse of very similar form, but larger and with a smaller button, belongs to a Hod Hill subtype dated to the Claudian period (Feugère 1985, 335, Type 23d1, pl. 144, 1804), and a similar date of *c*. A.D. 41–54 can therefore be applied to the Stanway brooch.

Fragments of a tray or box (FIG. 97, BF67.4) were found in different parts of the burial pit. It is not clear if more than one item is involved or if it was complete when deposited. Some copper-alloy studs and sheet fragments together with some decayed wood (SF378) came from the floor immediately east of the inkwell. Further copper-alloy sheet, studs and tacks together with a fragment of decayed wood (SF379), were recovered from the southern edge of the pit at a depth of 120–300 mm during metal-detecting prior to excavation. Several more small fragments of copper-alloy sheet (SF321, SF330, SF331) were found scattered in the fill. Given the difficult circumstances of the excavation, and that much of the metal survived only as a green powdery stain in the soil, the fragments are likely to represent one unbroken object. The recovery of similar copper-alloy fittings in the Doctor's burial (CF47.25) suggests that the object in BF67 should be identified as a tray or box that had been leant up against the side of the burial pit.

Up to thirteen iron nail fragments (four of which were plotted) were found mainly in the backfill over the northern half of the pit (TABLE 34). They appear too substantial for use in the construction of a small box. They may represent the remains of a grave cover or some other wooden object. Less likely, the nails may be residual in the backfill or derive from pyre debris.

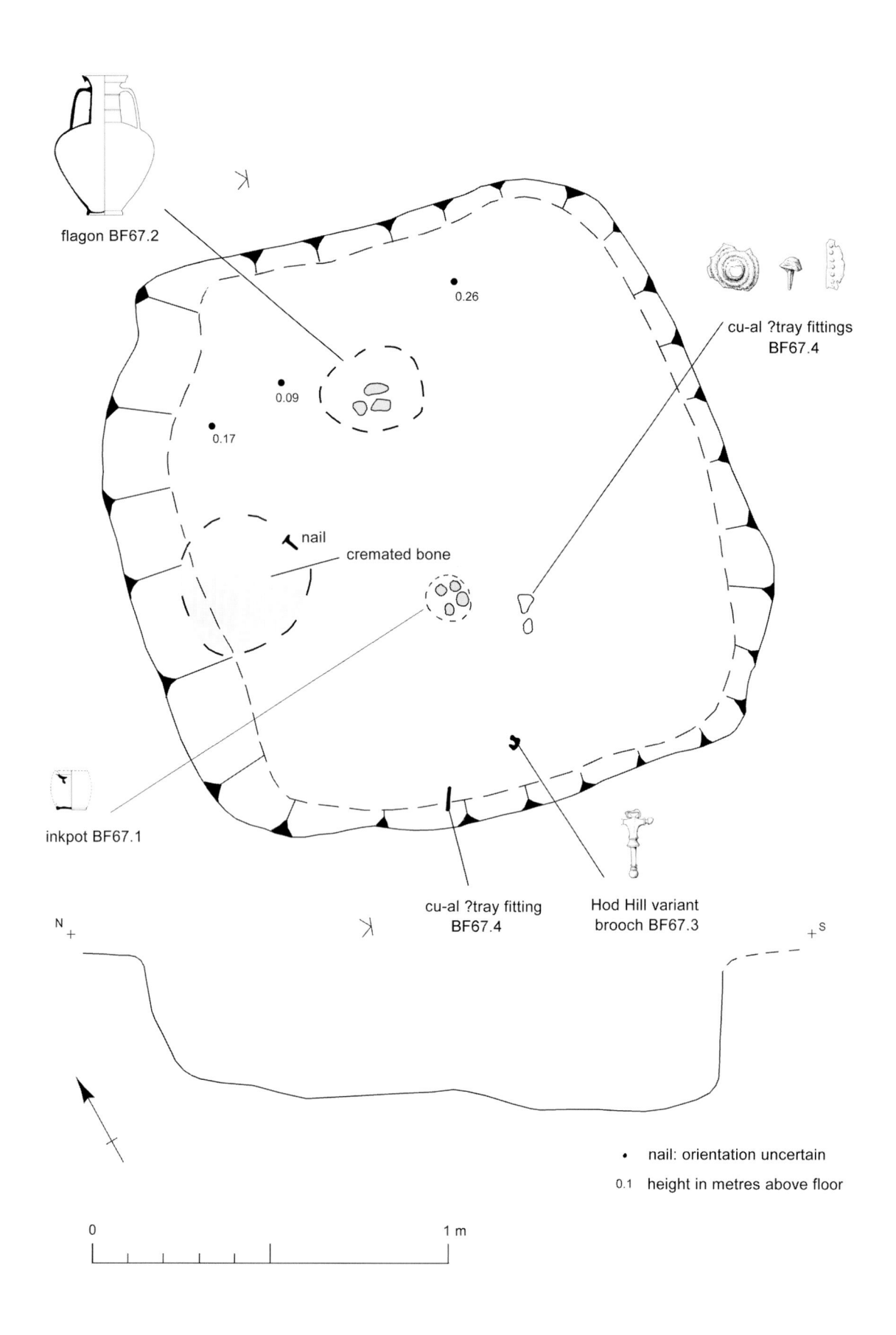

FIG. 96.   Inkwell burial BF67: plan and profile (scale 1:15)

TABLE 34: FRAGMENTS OF IRON NAILS FROM BF67

Find no.	Head	Length (mm)	Wood	Grain to shank direction	Notes
B1043	flat round	42	–	–	almost complete; lozenge-section shank
B1013	flat round	20	y	transverse	square-section shank
B1008	flat round	58	y	transverse	almost complete; square-section shank
B1008	–	48	y	transverse	wood across whole length of shank; possibly complete apart from head
B988	sub-circular	55	–	–	in 4 fragments; badly corroded
B1062	flat round	23	y	transverse	square-section shank
B1012	flat round	34	–	–	lozenge-section shank
B1065	flat round	53	–	–	complete
B1009	flat round	38	y	transverse	nearly complete; square-section shank
B1009	flat round	10	–	–	–
B1072	flat sub-circular	30	–	–	–
B1072	–	42	y	parallel	probably almost complete, missing only head and tip of shank
B1061	–	51	y	transverse	square-section shank; tip present, probably broken just below head

They are all of Manning's Type 1b with a flat round or sub-circular head (Manning 1985, 134). Two have shanks that are of lozenge-shaped section, rather than square. One is complete and is 53 mm long; three others are nearly complete at 58, 42 and 38 mm. Several have wood preserved on the shank, generally with the grain lying across it but on one it is parallel. One shank fragment, 48 mm long, has wood lying across the whole length of the shank, with no obvious sign of a junction, giving a board thickness of at least 48 mm.

The gender of the dead person in this grave is not certain. Writing equipment is not gender-specific (*see* CF42, p. 151) so there is no reason to suppose that this grave is necessarily that of a male. The single brooch suggests, but is not positive proof of, masculinity, as there was no discernible difference in the male:female pattern of brooch deposition at King Harry Lane (Stead and Rigby 1986, 102). Although the cremated bone suggests otherwise, the small brooch allows interpretation of this grave as that of a juvenile, providing a link to a pre-Flavian male adolescent grave at Litton Cheney, Dorset, that contained a set of board game counters and a stylus (Bailey 1967, 156–9; Whimster 1981, 256–7).

The two complete pots indicate a date of before A.D. 65, sherds in the backfill included local sandy wares post-dating A.D. 50, and the Hod Hill brooch suggests a date of A.D. 41–54. Collectively they point to a likely early Roman date of *c.* A.D. 50–60.

Pottery vessels (FIG. 97)

BF67.1 FIG. 97. B1041. A very fragmented inkwell; only the base and rim can now be restored. It is a small drum-shaped pot with a dished top. In the centre of the top is a small circular aperture, about 18 mm across, which has an internal non-spill moulding surrounding it. On the edge of the restored top there is a small area of damage at the join of two broken sherds forming a small indentation. One side of this damaged area appears to be part of a regularly shaped small circular hole. Small holes of this type are a common feature in the top of inkwells. The base of the vessel has a small footring around its edge.

The fabric is a pale brown-red with almost no visible inclusions, although rare small voids are present, and it is coated with a brown-red slip. The slip is now mostly matt although some exterior surface areas and internal areas protected from the surrounding soil, especially under the top of the vessel, retain a shiny, faintly metallic, gloss. Also the inner surface of the top of the vessel is rather more orange-red in colour than the exterior, although this could be the result of a thinner internal application of slip or slightly different firing conditions inside the partly closed vessel. The internal coverage of the slip appears extensive, although slightly patchy. One small area under the top of the vessel has evaded coverage by the slip, possibly also one area of the base, and a number of the body sherds also show only partial internal

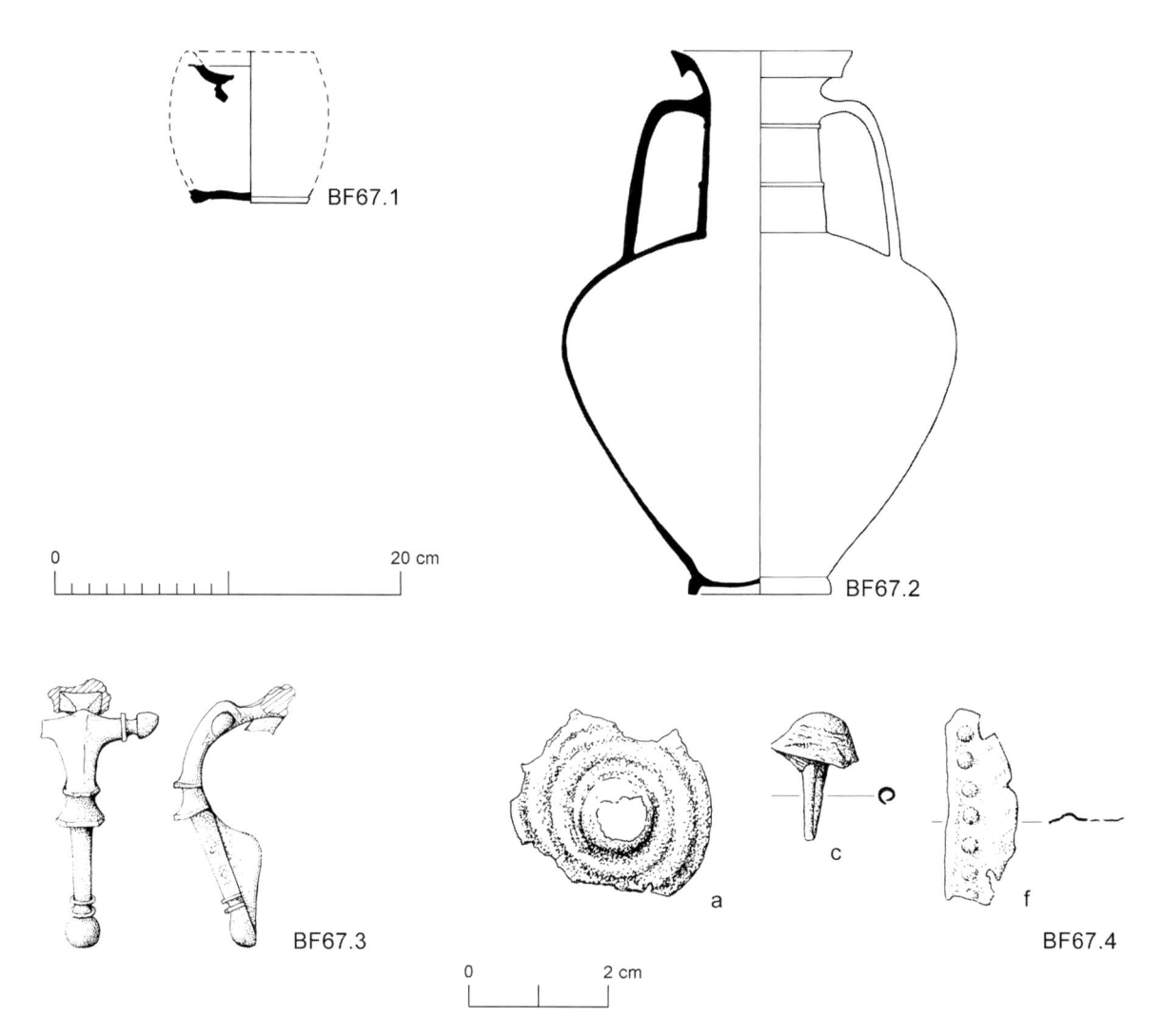

FIG. 97. Inkwell burial BF67: pottery vessels BF67.1–2 (scale 1:4), copper-alloy brooch BF67.3, and selected decorated copper-alloy studs and sheet BF67.4a, c and f (scale 1:1)

coverage. On the interior of the base are several dark patches which appear to be stains. This dark staining is also present on the interior surface of a number of the body sherds. The staining perhaps results from a former content of dark ink.

The pot has been examined by Geoff Dannell who did not believe the vessel to be samian. Philip Kenrick also considered that the pot was not of Italian origin. The vessel is unusual as most pottery inkwells are samian (Willis 2006). Pottery inkwells do occur very rarely in other fabrics, this vessel presumably being an example. The form of the vessel is also unusual as it does not closely resemble the most common samian inkwell form, Ritterling 13 (*ibid.*). However, Oswald and Pryce show a number of variants of pottery inkwells, one of which can be seen to have some similarity with the inkwell here (Oswald and Pryce 1920, pl. LXX, no. 4).
Condition: severely fragmented due to fragility of the vessel: only rim and base circuit restorable.
Condition at deposition: complete.
BF67.2 FIG. 97. B1046, B1074. Cornice-rimmed *lagena*: Camulodunum form 161. Fabric WPW.
Condition: broken but restorable to complete.
Condition at deposition: complete.

Other finds (FIG. 97)

BF67.3 FIG. 97. SF329. B1071. A small tinned brass or gunmetal Hod Hill variant brooch with most of the pin and part of the solid catchplate missing. The iron axial bar survives, fitted into a drilled hole. The bow is strongly arched and triangular in section, with the apex flattened. It has side arms at the top ending in a moulding and small knob, flat at the back. The end of the left arm is missing. The sides of the bow curve inwards, emphasising the arms. At the base of the bow there is a small button above a

larger one. Both are flat at the back. The foot is narrow and plain, with two narrow mouldings above the terminal knob. Length 36 mm.
BF67.4 FIG. 97. SF378. B1069. Fragmentary copper-alloy composite studs and decorated sheet, with small pieces of wood probably from a tray or box similar to that in CF47. Only a, c, and f are illustrated.
a Most of the head of a stud with four concentric mouldings. Diameter 28 mm, height approximately 2.5–3 mm.
b Twelve small fragments of similar studs.
c Domed centre of a stud, with a peg made from rolled sheeting fixed to it by lead-based solder. Length 17 mm, diameter of head 13 mm.
d Four similar pegs.
e Thirteen fragments of rolled sheet shanks and sixteen fragments of solder.
f Fragment of sheet with one original edge and a marginal line of small repoussé bosses. Maximum dimensions 25 by 9 mm, less then 1 mm thick.
g Two similar small fragments, decorated with small bosses, one 13 by 8 mm, the other 12 by 11 mm.
h Approximately 116 fragments of plain sheet, the largest 32 by 7 mm, most about 3 by 3 mm.
SF379. B987. 1) Seventeen fragments of plain copper-alloy sheet, the largest 11 by 9 mm; 2) Fragment of stud head with concentric mouldings, 9 by 4 mm; 3) Two fragments of rolled sheet tacks, 12 and 11 mm long; 4) Fragment of solder with part of a rolled sheet tack set into it. Also a fragment of wood.
SF330. B1001. Three tiny scraps of copper-alloy sheet. The maximum dimensions of the largest are 6 by 4 mm.
SF331. B1002. Tiny fragment of copper-alloy sheet. Maximum dimensions 2 by 2 mm.
SF328. B1003. Tiny fragment of copper-alloy sheet. Maximum dimensions 6 by 4 mm.
SF321. B1066. Traces of copper-alloy sheet in soil. Length 10 mm.

Residual pottery sherds
BF67.a B989. Base sherd and body sherd from backfill showing two grooves around body, probably part of the same vessel (9.9 g). Fabric RCW.
BF67.b B1014. Two small abraded, thin-walled sherds, patterned, butt-beaker (1.4 g) from northern half of pit. Fabric GTW.

THE DOCTOR'S BURIAL CF47 (FIGS 2, 8, 98–127; TABLES 35–6)

Cremated bone	158.1 g	of indeterminate age and sex
Pottery vessels	CF47.1	Dragendorff form 29 decorated samian bowl
	CF47.2	TR1(C) moulded platter
	CF47.3	TR1(C) moulded platter
	CF47.4	TR1(C) moulded platter
	CF47.5	TN moulded platter
	CF47.6	TN moulded platter
	CF47.7	TN offset platter
	CF47.8	TN offset platter
	CF47.9	TN carinated cup
	CF47.10	TR1(C) flanged cup
	CF47.11	TR1(C) flanged cup
	CF47.12	cornice-rimmed flagon
	CF47.13	local ware carinated cup
	CF47.14	Dressel 8 (Beltrán) amphora
Other finds	CF47.15	copper-alloy Langton Down brooch
	CF47.16	copper-alloy ring fragment
	CF47.17	copper-alloy Rearhook brooch
	CF47.18	jet bead
	CF47.19	set of 26 glass counters
	CF47.20	wooden game board plus copper-alloy fittings
	CF47.21	copper-alloy saucepan
	CF47.22	copper-alloy spouted strainer bowl
	CF47.23	set of eight rods (four iron and four brass)
	CF47.24	set of eight copper-alloy rings
	CF47.25	wooden tray(s) or box with copper-alloy fittings

CF47.26	surgical kit: iron scalpel
CF47.27	surgical kit: iron scalpel
CF47.28	surgical kit: iron saw with composite handle
CF47.29	surgical kit: combined bronze sharp and blunt hook (double-ended retractor)
CF47.30	surgical kit: combined iron sharp and blunt hook (double-ended retractor)
CF47.31	surgical kit: bronze ?retractor
CF47.32	surgical kit: smooth-jawed bronze fixation forceps
CF47.33	surgical kit: iron forceps/tweezers
CF47.34	surgical kit: iron handled needle
CF47.35	surgical kit: iron handled needle
CF47.36	surgical kit: iron handled needle
CF47.37	surgical kit: bronze scoop probe
CF47.38	surgical kit: bronze handle
CF47.39	surgical kit: iron knife
CF47.40	cloth ?garment(s)
CF47.41	oak cover over the burial
CF47.42	straw packing? under CF47.21 and over CF47.12

Residual finds   none identified

The cremation burial CF47 was located in the north-west corner of Enclosure 5 (FIGS 2, 8). It was discovered during soil-stripping when the machine clipped the top of an amphora sitting upright in the south-west corner of the burial pit. Subsequent excavation revealed another large and remarkable burial group comparable to the Warrior's burial discovered four years earlier. The group included fourteen pottery vessels (but oddly no glassware), a copper-alloy strainer bowl, a copper-alloy pan, a gaming board complete with a set of white and blue glass gaming counters, a set of surgical instruments, eight rods that may have been used for divination, eight rings also possibly used for divination, one or more wooden objects with copper-alloy fittings (a maplewood ?tray or ?trays), two brooches, and a jet bead (FIGS 98, 125). The burial takes its name from the surgical *instrumentarium* (FIGS 121–7). The vessels were all imports and, although the range is not as wide as in the Warrior's burial, the group includes some of the most colourful and decorative pots available in their day. The grave goods can be seen as three clusters: a service in the south east, vessels associated with preparing and serving food and (mainly) drink in the north east, and personalia in the west (FIGS 98, 125).

The burial pit was rectangular in plan measuring about 2.1 × 1.7 m with slightly rounded corners. The fill was mixed sands, gravels and silts. The base was flat, but was unusual because it was divided into two levels such that the western and eastern parts were respectively 0.7 m and 0.5 m below the ground-level after stripping (FIGS 99, 104). The contours of the base are likely to reflect the objects which were placed in it. The key factor that determined the depth would have been the amphora, which needed to be upright. This may also have been the indirect cause of the need to deepen the western part of the burial pit.

Eleven cups and platters (CF47.2–11, CF47.13) were spread out over the central and southern part of the eastern half of the base of the burial pit (FIG. 98). None of the vessels overlapped each other and none were nested. They had been placed face upwards as if containing food and drink.

Some of the grave goods had been stacked on top of each other near the north-east corner of the burial pit (FIGS 98–9, 101). The group consisted of the flagon (CF47.12), the copper-alloy strainer bowl (CF47.22), the copper-alloy pan (CF47.21), the samian bowl (CF47.1), and the unidentifiable maplewood object or objects (CF47.25). The lowest vessel was the flagon (CF47.12). This had been placed at the foot of the slope which separated the upper and lower levels forming the base of the burial pit. The wooden object appears to have been flat and shallow and was placed on the upper level so that it overhung the lower level and rested on the flagon below. Some straw-like material (CF47.42) was placed on top of it, followed by the pan CF47.21, the samian bowl CF47.1 and the strainer bowl CF47.22, all laid side by side.

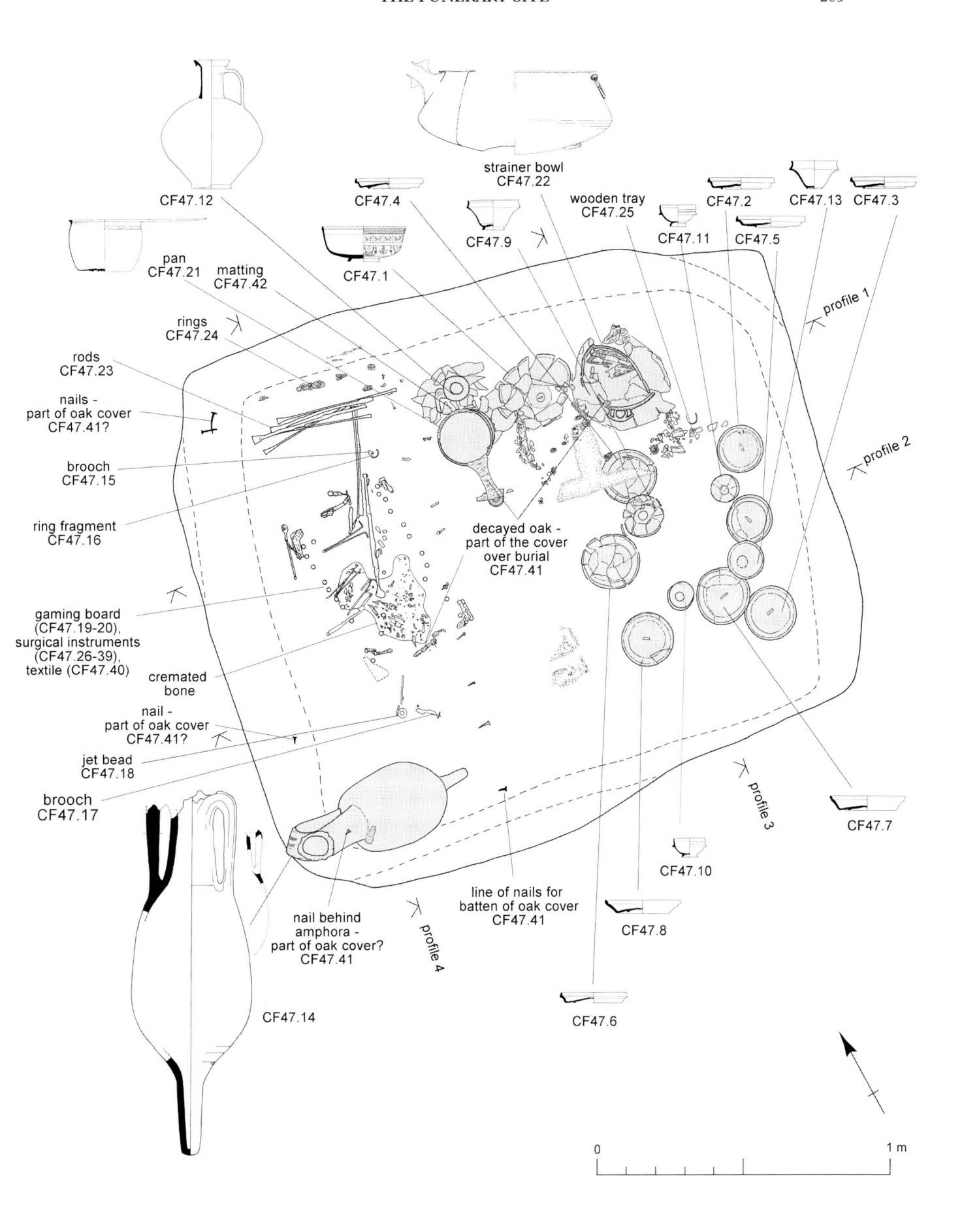

FIG. 98. Doctor's burial CF47: plan showing location of finds (scale 1:16)

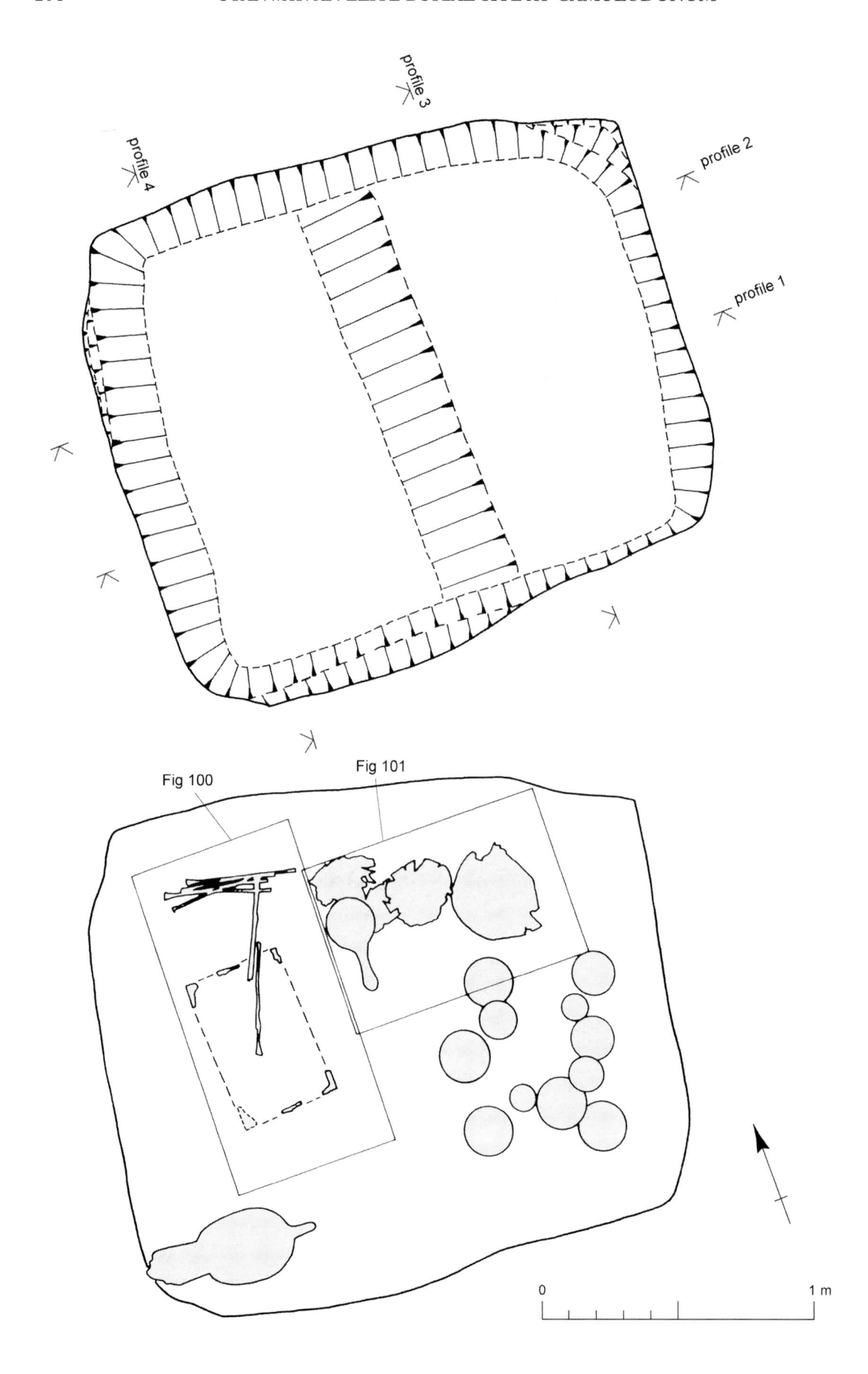

FIG. 99. Doctor's burial CF47: plan showing burial pit after excavation with location of profiles 1–4, and plan locating detail FIGS 100–1 (scale 1:20)

THE FUNERARY SITE

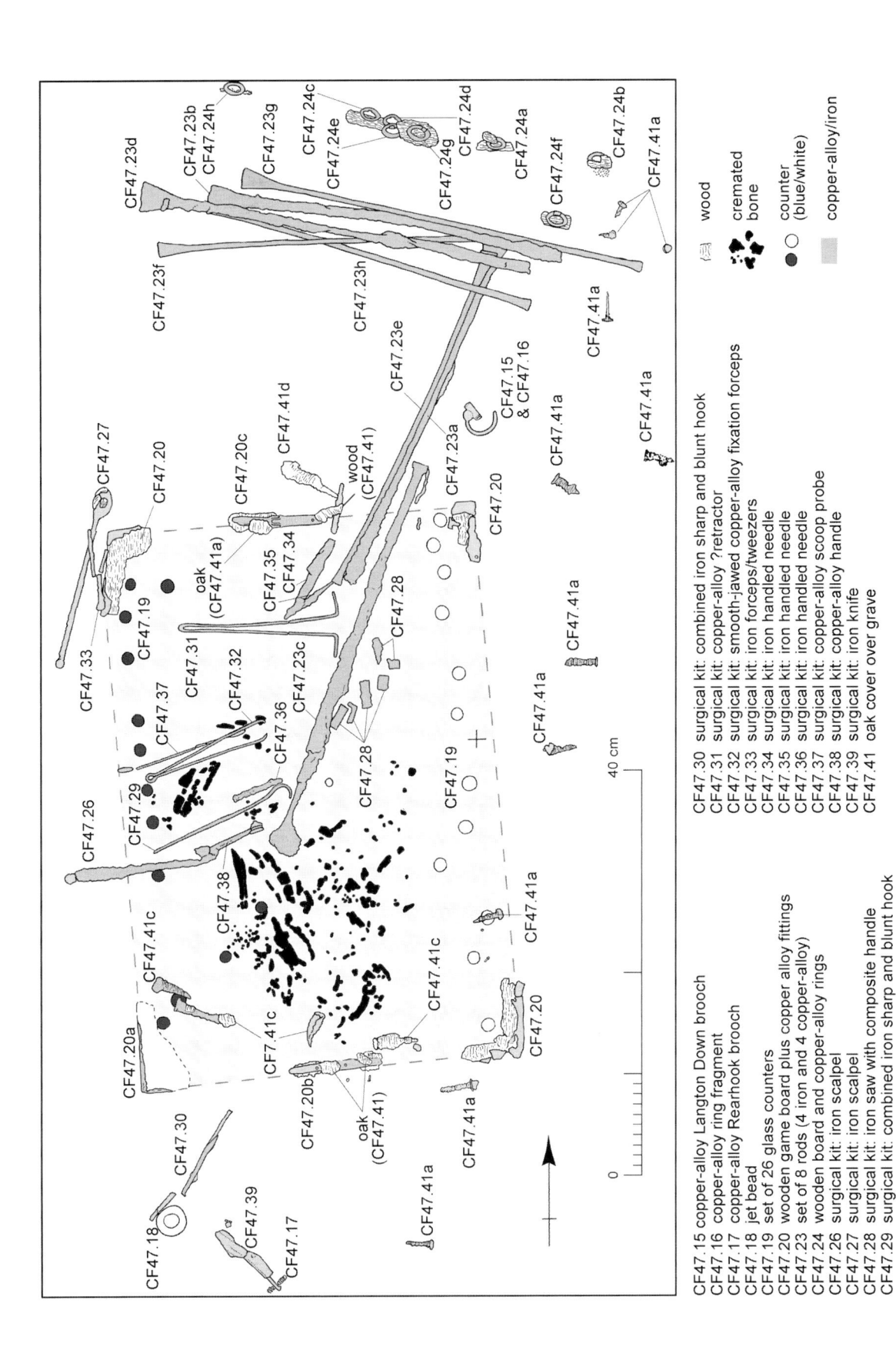

CF47.15 copper-alloy Langton Down brooch
CF47.16 copper-alloy ring fragment
CF47.17 copper-alloy Rearhook brooch
CF47.18 jet bead
CF47.19 set of 26 glass counters
CF47.20 wooden game board plus copper alloy fittings
CF47.23 set of 8 rods (4 iron and 4 copper-alloy)
CF47.24 wooden board and copper-alloy rings
CF47.26 surgical kit: iron scalpel
CF47.27 surgical kit: iron scalpel
CF47.28 surgical kit: iron saw with composite handle
CF47.29 surgical kit: combined iron sharp and blunt hook

CF47.30 surgical kit: combined iron sharp and blunt hook
CF47.31 surgical kit: copper-alloy ?retractor
CF47.32 surgical kit: smooth-jawed copper-alloy fixation forceps
CF47.33 surgical kit: iron forceps/tweezers
CF47.34 surgical kit: iron handled needle
CF47.35 surgical kit: iron handled needle
CF47.36 surgical kit: iron handled needle
CF47.37 surgical kit: copper-alloy scoop probe
CF47.38 surgical kit: copper-alloy handle
CF47.39 surgical kit: iron knife
CF47.41 oak cover over grave

FIG. 100. Doctor's burial CF47: detail of finds at west end of grave (scale 1:5.7

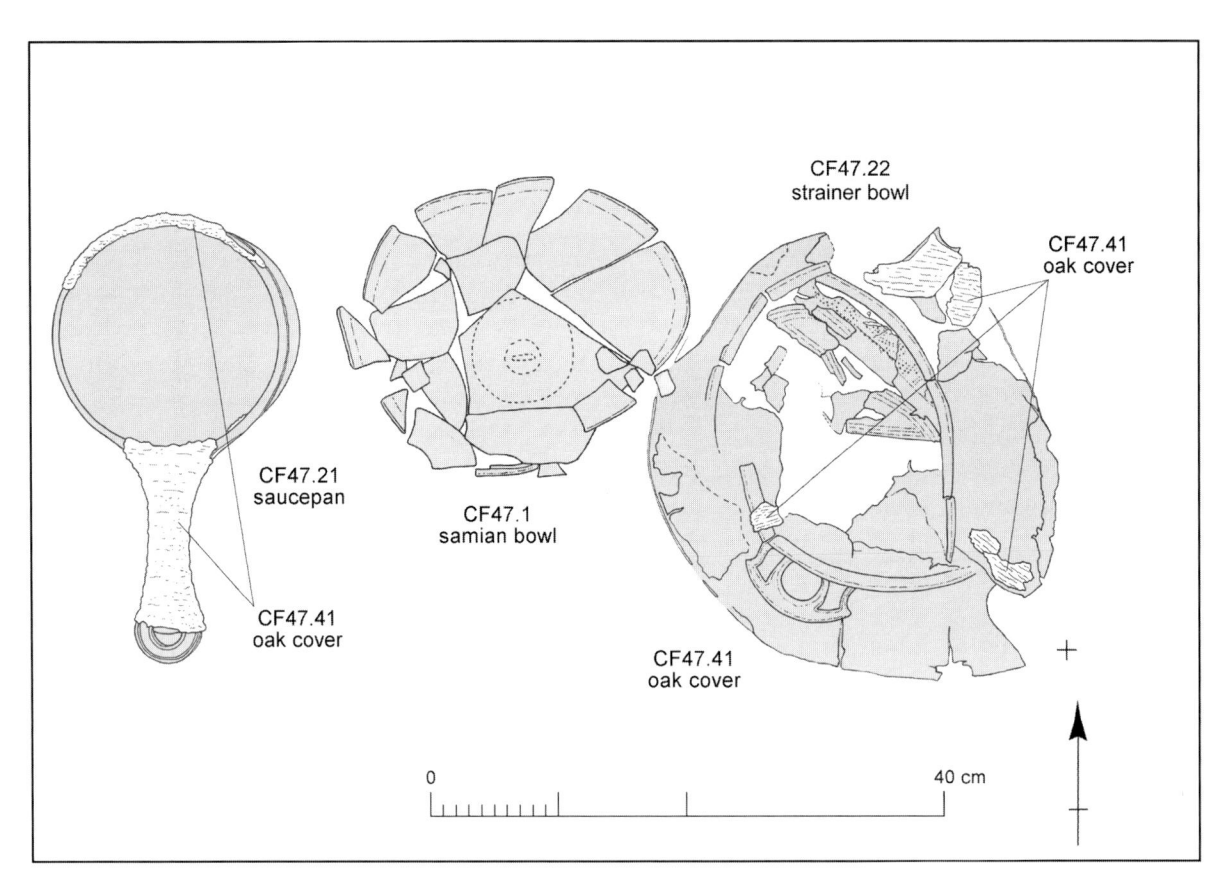

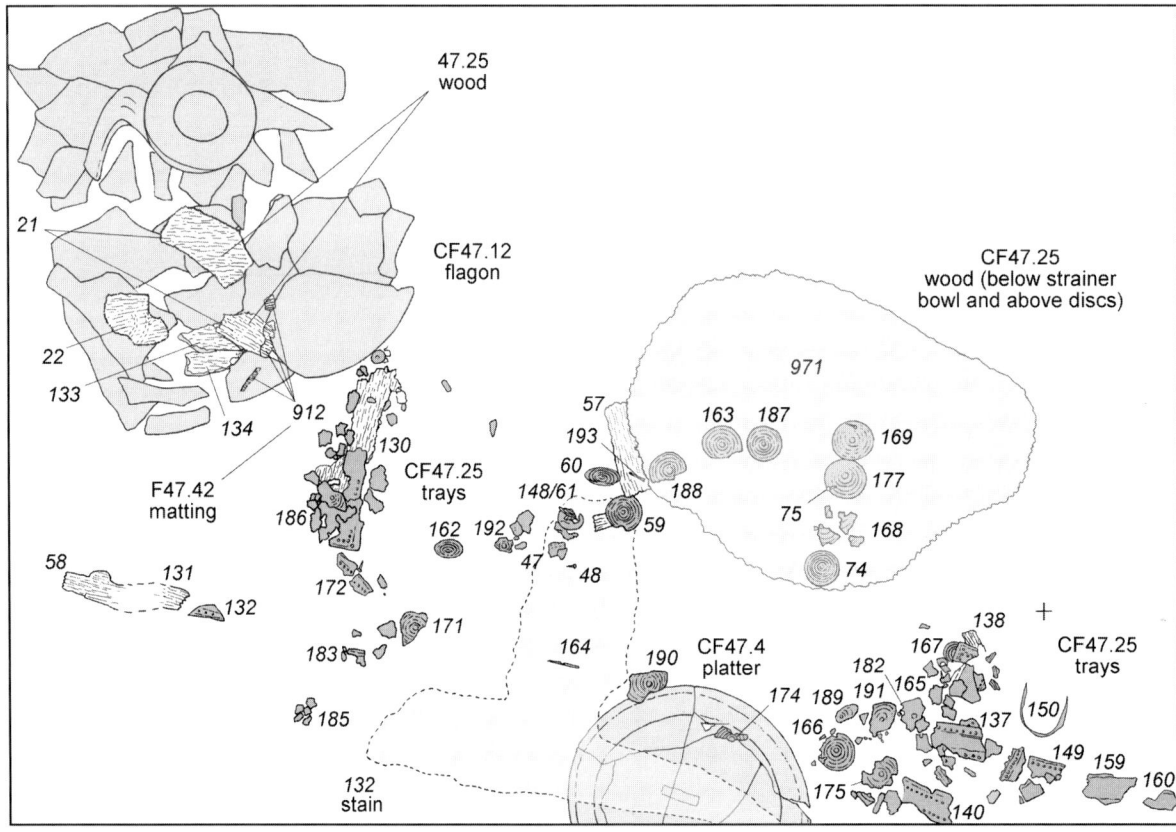

FIG. 101. Doctor's burial CF47: detail plans of objects stacked on north side of grave, copper-alloy saucepan (CF47.21), samian bowl (CF47.1) and copper-alloy strainer bowl (CF47.22), showing remains of oak cover (CF47.41) (above), and pottery flagon (CF47.12) and remains of decorated wooden ?tray (CF47.25) (below) (scale 1:5.7)

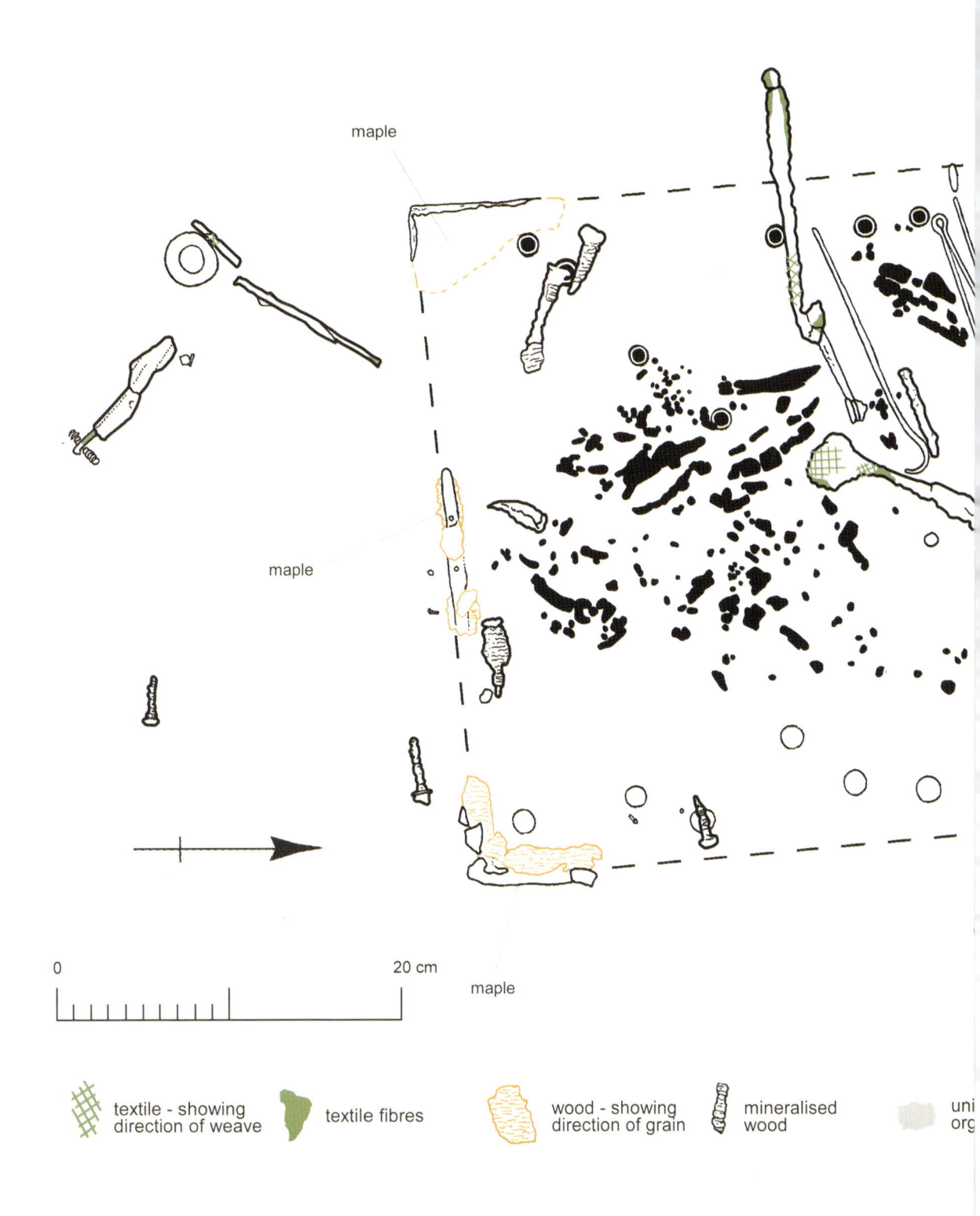

FIG. 103. Doctor's burial CF47: plan showing the locations of the organic remains on the lower surface

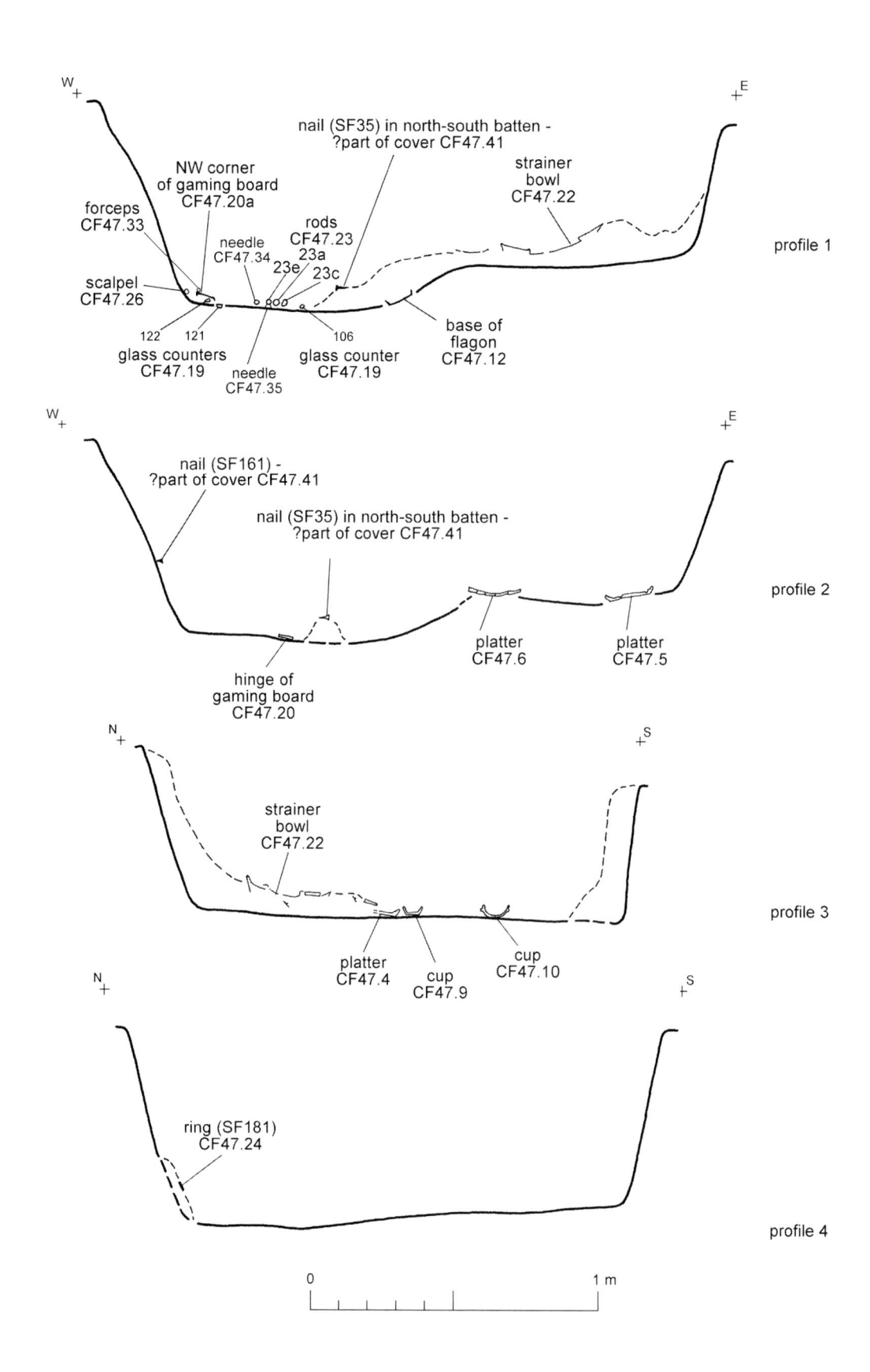

FIG. 104. Doctor's burial CF47: profiles 1–4 through grave (scale 1:20)

STAGE 3

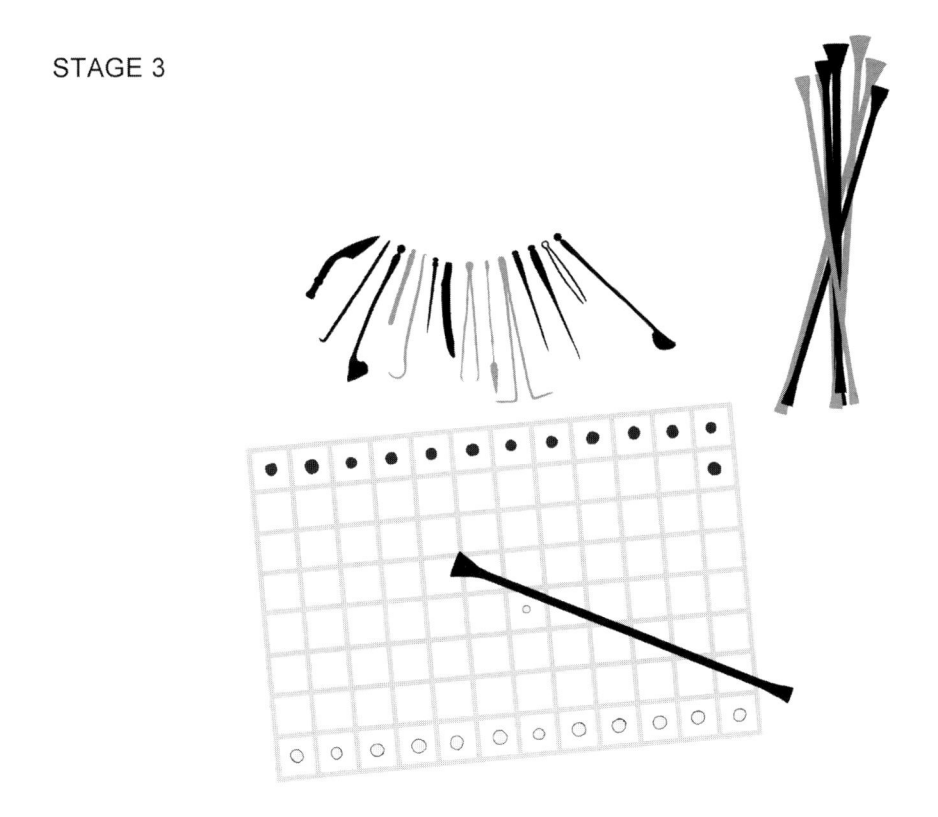

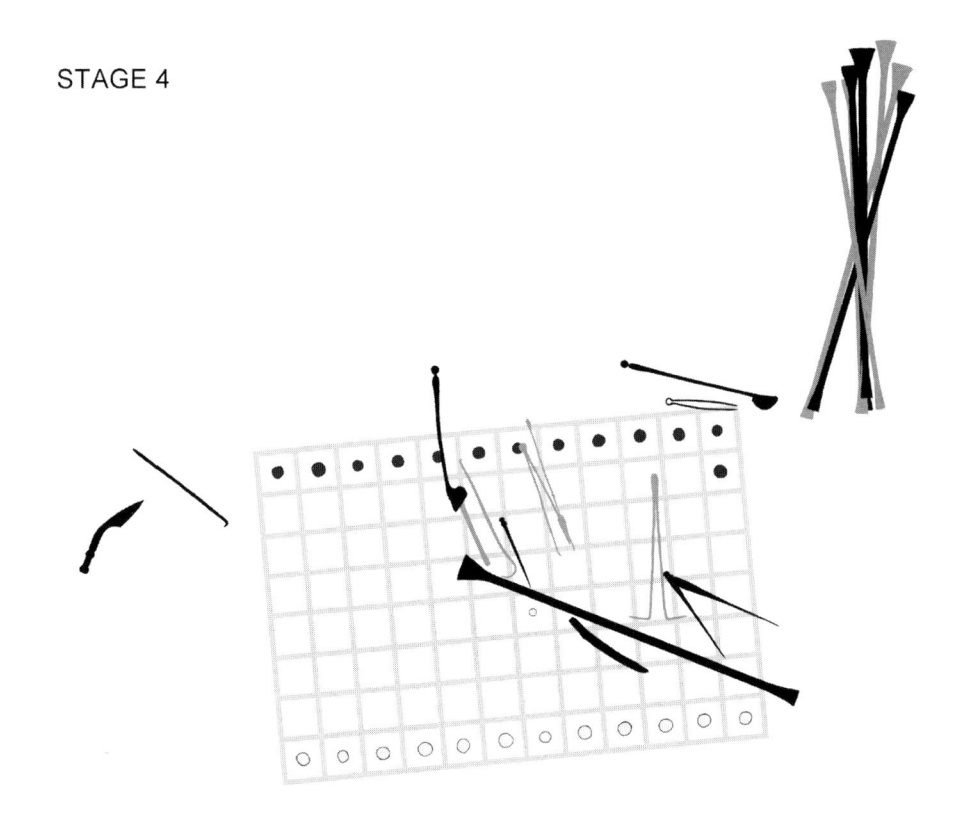

STAGE 4

FIG. 105. Doctor's burial CF47: stages 3–4 in the deposition of the medical implements and rods on and around the gaming board

STAGE 5

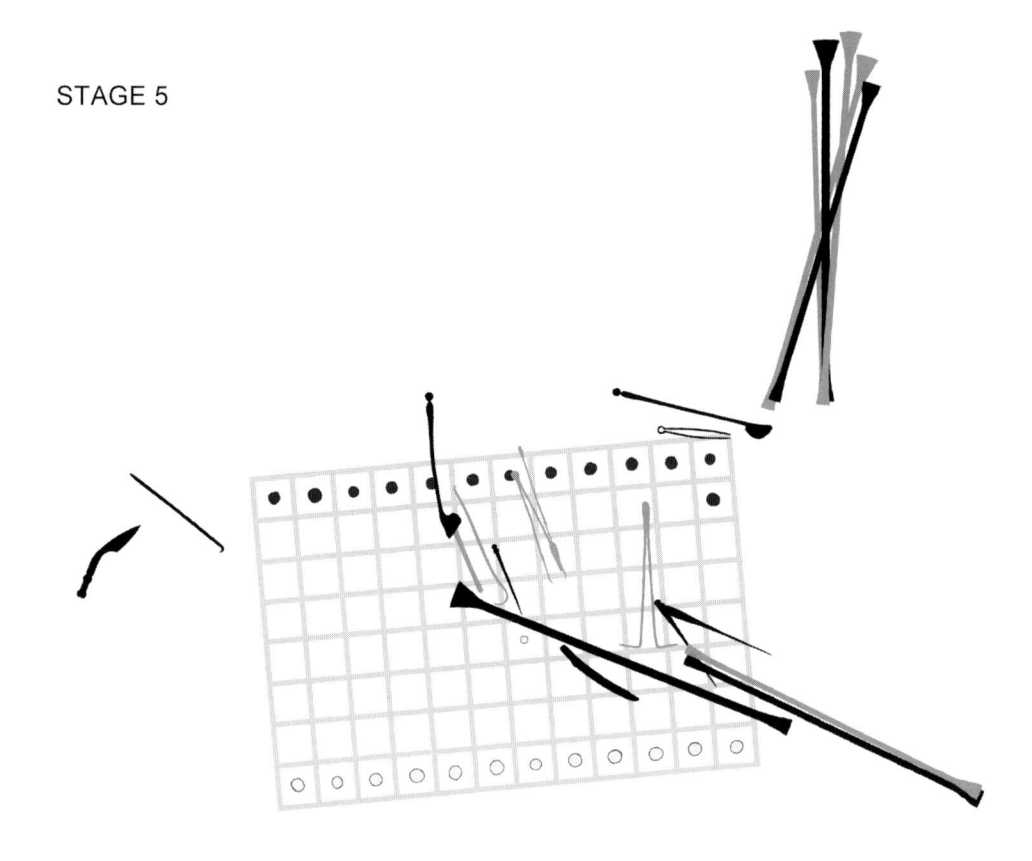

STAGE 6

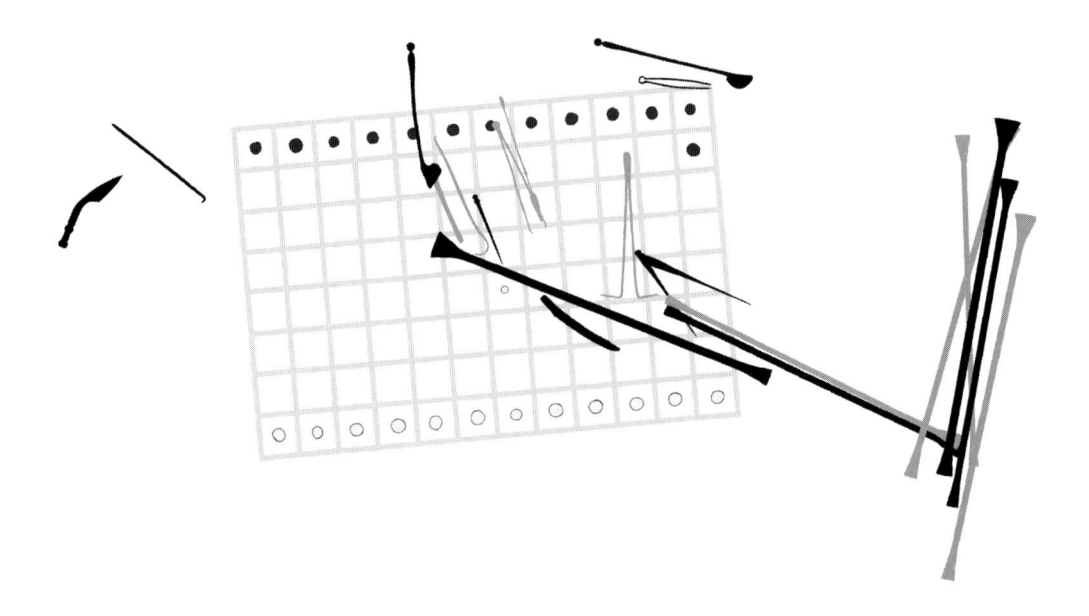

FIG. 106. Doctor's burial CF47: stages 5–6 in the deposition of the medical implements and rods on and around the gaming board

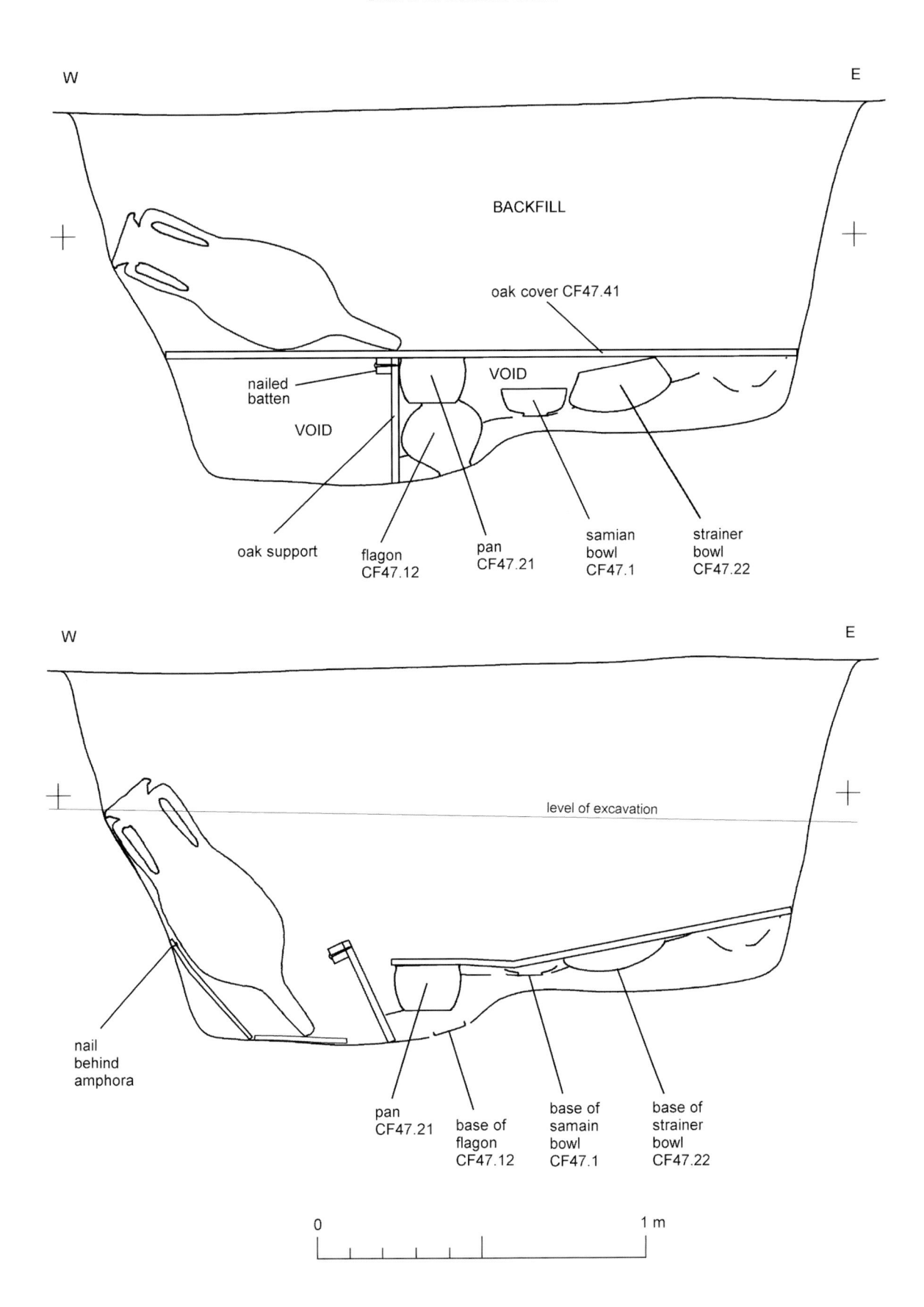

FIG. 107. Doctor's burial CF47: reconstruction of the grave and the subsequent collapse of the wooden cover and grave goods

(FIGS 98, 100, 107). The direction of the nails appears to have alternated along the partition, showing that the nails had been hammered in from alternate sides. (The second and third nails from the south are not shown this way on plan, but it was noted during excavation that they may have been accidentally moved and replaced as the work progressed.)

At the north end of this line, close to the side of the burial pit, was a group of three nails that were angled down towards the base of the pit. In the north-west corner were two larger nails and towards the south-west corner were two more (one directly behind the amphora). Collectively, these nails formed a rectangular shape filling the west end of the lower part of the burial pit (FIG. 98).

In the centre of this area were two nails (FIG. 100, CF47.41c) close to the south hinge of the game board and a further nail close to the north hinge (FIG. 100, CF47.41d). These may relate to one or more wooden objects which were laid on the gaming board or they may have attached two wooden battens to the underside of the cover so that they lay at right-angles to the partition.

The last item to be placed in the burial pit was the amphora CF47.14. It stood upright at a slight angle so as to rest against the south-west corner of the pit (FIGS 98, 125). The amphora seems to have been placed on top of the cover CF47.41, which was probably only about 0.4 m above the floor of the pit. The cover eventually rotted, allowing the amphora to drop on to the floor (FIG. 107). It had been buried complete, but the top was damaged during machine-stripping of the site.

There is also evidence for earlier post-depositional movements. The wooden cover over the burial appears to have been subjected to sufficient pressure to result in two of the vessels (the strainer bowl and the samian bowl) being squashed flat and a third (the flagon) breaking into pieces (FIGS 98, 101, 107, 114). The strainer bowl crumpled inwards under the pressure whereas the sides of the samian bowl split into many pieces and were pushed outwards. The flagon shattered, whereas the copper-alloy pan which overlay it and had been pushed into it from above was undamaged, because the flagon was the weaker of the two vessels.

The absence of any soil between the rim and base of the flattened strainer bowl shows that the damage must have occurred before the wooden cover had decayed. This means that the force which did the damage could only have been applied at the time of burial or within a few months or years afterwards. The pressure needed to crush the vessels must have been substantial. It seems highly unlikely that a force great enough to damage the three vessels in the way described could have been achieved from the surface after the burial pit had been backfilled, because the force would have spread outwards over a wide area and would have been largely dissipated because of the depth of the grave goods. The damage does not appear to have been deliberate, but it must have happened accidentally before the burial pit was backfilled or (just possibly) before it had progressed very far. We can only speculate on the precise circumstances. Perhaps somebody stood on the cover to help lower the amphora into the burial pit, and the weight of the person plus the filled amphora was enough to cause the damage (FIG. 107). Importantly, the jolt which must have occurred when the three vessels crumpled and the cover dropped slightly may also explain why the glass counters on the gaming board have moved slightly.

It had been thought that the saw CF47.28 was deliberately broken prior to burial and placed in the burial pit in pieces. This is how it appears on plan (FIG. 100). However, a careful review of the photographic record indicates that the saw had probably been buried intact and disturbed inadvertently during an early stage of the archaeological excavation.

The burial appears to date to between A.D. 40 and 50 as indicated largely by the Gallo-Belgic pottery, which is Claudio–Neronian, the samian bowl (CF47.1) dated to A.D. 40–50, a die link (Stamp 17–20) with an identical platter in the Warrior's burial (p. 294), and the two brooches, one of which (CF47.15) is pre- A.D. 50/5 in date and the other (CF47.17) A.D. 40–50 (pp. 315–17). The Doctor's burial is indistinguishable in terms of date from the Warrior's burial. The dating evidence and the likely temporal relationships between the Doctor's burial and the other funerary contexts are discussed on pages 441, 443.

Pottery vessels (FIG. 108, CF47.1–14)

The burial contained fourteen complete or only slightly damaged vessels, most of them Gaulish imports. Although perhaps slightly less distinctive in character than those in the Warrior's burial, the decorated samian bowl (CF47.1) would have been at the top of the range and highly prized at the period. The remainder of the group consists of three *terra rubra* platters (CF47.2–4), four *terra nigra* platters (CF47.5–8), one *terra nigra* and two *terra rubra* cups (CF47.9–11), a local ware cup (CF47.13), a flagon and an amphora (CF47.12, 14). All the vessels had been placed upright in the grave pit as if containing, or ready to be filled with, food and drink. The stamps on the Gallo-Belgic vessels are discussed on pages 290–5.

Decorated samian By G.B. Dannell

CF47.1 FIG. 108. C900. Decorated bowl: Dragendorff form 29. South Gaulish. Stamp: OFI·CANTI. Cantus Die 6a.
Condition: in sherds restorable to complete.
Condition at deposition: complete.
Date: *c.* A.D. 35–50, and probably from the end of that period.

Brenda Dickinson adds of the stamp:
Cantus of La Graufesenque, Die 6a (Tilhard 2001, 370, 165.14). The bulk of Cantus' output is Tiberian, but the decoration of the Stanway bowl and that of another bowl with the same stamp suggest Claudian origin. However, this stamp also appears (once) on Form 17 (not seen by the present writer), which might be Tiberian. A range of *c.* A.D. 40–50 should cover the possibilities.

Gallo-Belgic imports

CF47.2 FIG. 108. C923. Moulded platter: Camulodunum form 7/8; with straight lower facet. Fabric TR1(C). Central Stamp 17, uncertain reading, possibly: SCVTTVSI. A.D. 25–50.
Condition: complete.

CF47.3 FIG. 108. C918. Moulded platter: Camulodunum form 7/8; with straight lower facet. Fabric TR1(C). Central Stamp 18, same die as CF47.2 and CF47.4, uncertain reading, possibly: SCVTTVSI. A.D. 25–50.
Condition: complete.

CF47.4 FIG. 108. C928. Moulded platter: Camulodunum form 7/8; with straight lower facet (exact stacking pair to CF47.3). Fabric TR1(C). Central Stamp 19, same die as CF47.2 and CF47.3, uncertain reading, possibly: SCVTTVSI. A.D. 25–50.
Condition: in sherds, restored to complete.
Condition at deposition: complete.

CF47.5 FIG. 108. C921. Moulded platter: Camulodunum form 8. Fabric TN. Central Stamp 3: ACVTIOS. A.D. 30–50.
Condition: one-third circuit broken.
Condition at deposition: complete.

CF47.6 FIG. 108. C926. Moulded platter: Camulodunum form 8. Fabric TN. Central Stamp 6, light and abraded impression: CICARV *c.* A.D. 35–60.
Condition: in sherds, restorable to complete.
Condition at deposition: complete.

CF47.7 FIG. 108. C919. Offset platter: Camulodunum form 14. Fabric TN. Central Stamp 15, uncertain reading, possibly: IIIVIIOII. A.D. 50–75.
Condition: in sherds, restorable to complete.
Condition at deposition: complete.

CF47.8 FIG. 108. C925. Offset platter: Camulodunum form 14. Fabric TN. Central Stamp 16, uncertain reading, possibly: OILIILIII. A.D. 50–75. Condition: in sherds, restorable to complete.
Condition at deposition: complete.

CF47.9 FIG. 108. C927. Carinated cup: Camulodunum form 56A. Fabric TN. Central Stamp 10: NOVE/MOLL. A.D. 15–65. Condition: in sherds restorable to complete.
Condition at deposition: complete.

CF47.10 FIG. 108. C924. Flanged cup, Camulodunum form 58, small. Fabric TR1(C). Central Stamp 13, uncertain reading: HIC or AIC bordered. A.D. 50–70.
Condition: complete but for one sherd from footring.
Condition at deposition: probably complete.

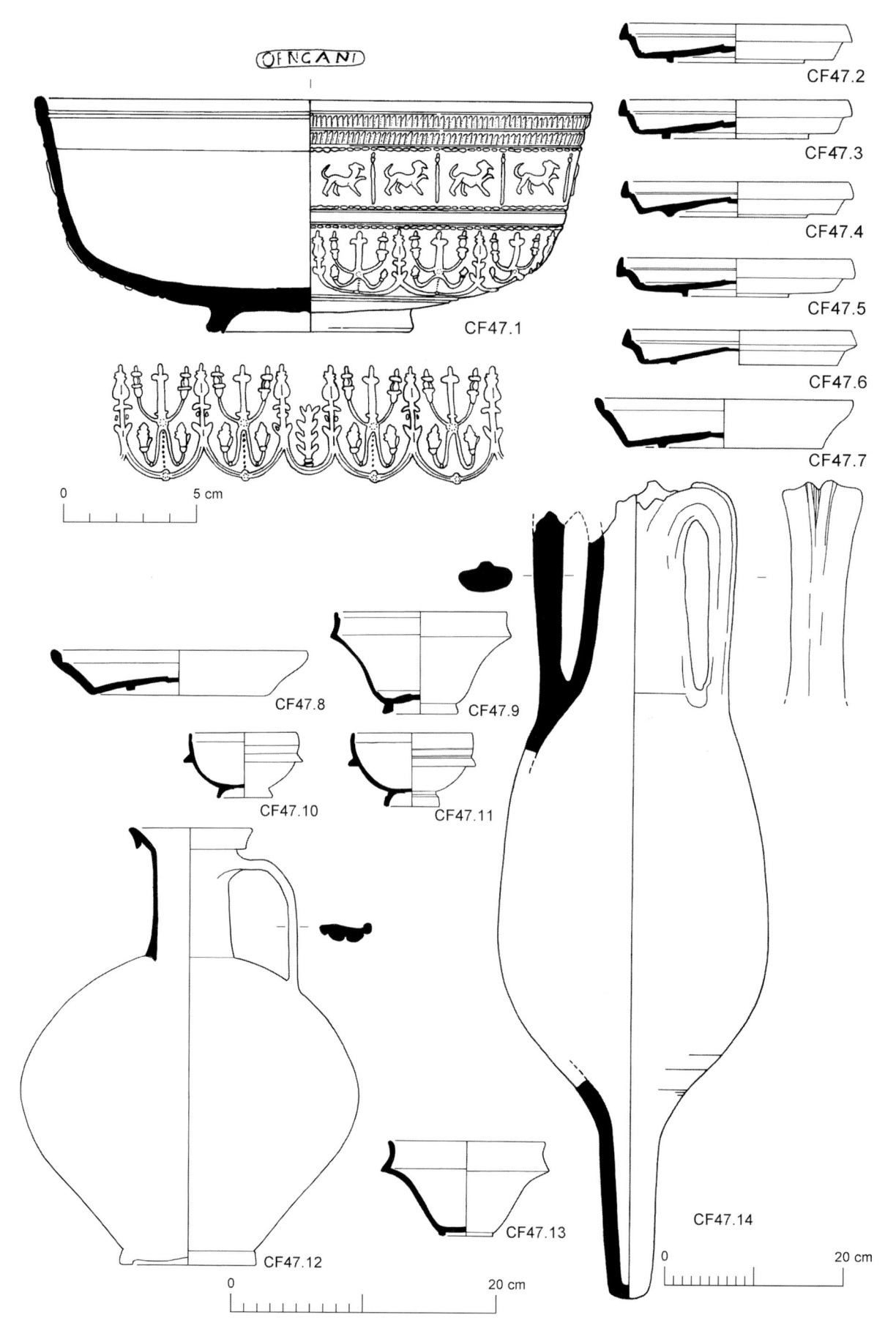

FIG. 108. Doctor's burial CF47: samian bowl CF47.1 (scale 1:2) and potter's stamp (scale 1:1), pottery vessels CF47.2–13 (scale 1:4), and amphora CF47.14 (scale 1:6)

CF47.11 FIG. 108. C922. Flanged cup, Camulodunum form 58. Fabric TR1(C). Restored, no stamp survives. A.D. 50–70. (Stamp 29.)
Condition: in sherds, restored to complete.
Condition at deposition: complete.

North Gaulish import
CF47.12 FIG. 108. C1077. Cornice-rimmed flagon, Camulodunum form 140; four-rib handle. Fabric WPW; grey slip inside.
Condition: in sherds; restorable to complete.
Condition at deposition: complete.

Local product
CF47.13 FIG. 108. C920. Carinated cup, Camulodunum form 56 copy/SW. Fabric FSW, light grey even-textured matrix; brownish-grey surfaces. Burnished finish. (Not stamped.)
Condition: complete.

Amphora
CF47.14 FIG. 108. C904. Dressel 8 (Beltrán I) *salazon* (see p. 301).

Dress accessories (FIG. 109, CF47.15–18)
Two brooches and a single bead were found in the grave. The brooches are not a pair and were not found close together. One (FIG. 109, CF47.15) is a poorly preserved Langton Down brooch of standard form, with a rounded head and a spring-cover marked only by a grooved rectangular frame. Similar brooches occur from Period 1 onwards at Sheepen, where it is Type XIIB (Hawkes and Hull 1947, 317–19), and date broadly to the first half of the 1st century A.D. The majority of spring-cover brooches went out of use by *c*. A.D. 50 (pp. 316, 318).

A fragment of a bronze ring was found attached by surface corrosion to the Langton Down brooch (FIG. 109, CF47.16). The recovery of an incomplete object, unless partially destroyed by corrosion, is unusual in this burial, but the fragment is in good condition. The lack of other miscellaneous material suggests it is unlikely to be residual. Although the grave goods were clearly all very carefully deposited, the association of brooch and ring need not pre-date the time of burial. It is nonetheless catalogued here and not with the other rings from the burial (*see* below) because of its direct contact with the brooch in the ground, the difference of its form and also its manufacture from a different alloy. Plain rings of copper alloy and lead have been found as votive offerings on sanctuary sites in Gaul and Britain, but their precise symbolism is unclear. Feugère has suggested that they may have been a substitute for coins, but it seems just as likely that they were simple solar symbols, substitutes for the more complex spoked wheel amulets also found at sanctuaries and in graves (Atkinson 1916, pl. 13, 25a–c; France and Gobel 1985, 90–5; Feugère 2002b; Fauduet 1993, 119–20; Bourgeois 1999, 99, 120–1, fig. 74, 450; Marcadal 2001, 135, fig. 122, 58; Pommeret 2001, fig. 7, 76–7, 8, 78–96). That this ring has been broken may be an indication of deliberate 'killing' before burial, but it also suggests that plain rings when halved may have been a simple method of producing a crescentic lunar symbol, in which case it may link to the circles scribed on the other brooch in this grave.

The second brooch is a well-preserved Rearhook (FIG. 109, CF47.17), a British-made form that almost certainly originated among the Iceni (Mackreth 1992, 122–3), and most, if not all, may be of Icenian manufacture. This example has two distinctive characteristics. First, it has a distinctive triplet of annulets on the thick expanded head. Their irregularity shows them to have been engraved freehand. No parallel for this style of decoration has been found on another brooch, although the use of three motifs must surely be linked to Celtic triplism, and there must be a strong possibility that these circles held the same meaning, perhaps as solar symbols, as those found on Trinovantian and Icenian coins (Allen 1980, 149; Hobbs 1996, pl. 5; Creighton 2000, 42). Second, the outer edge of the catch has a zigzag design formed of pairs of incised grooves. Decoration in this position is unusual, and appears to mark out particularly high-quality products. When found, it generally consists of zigzags or 'petals', and the main section

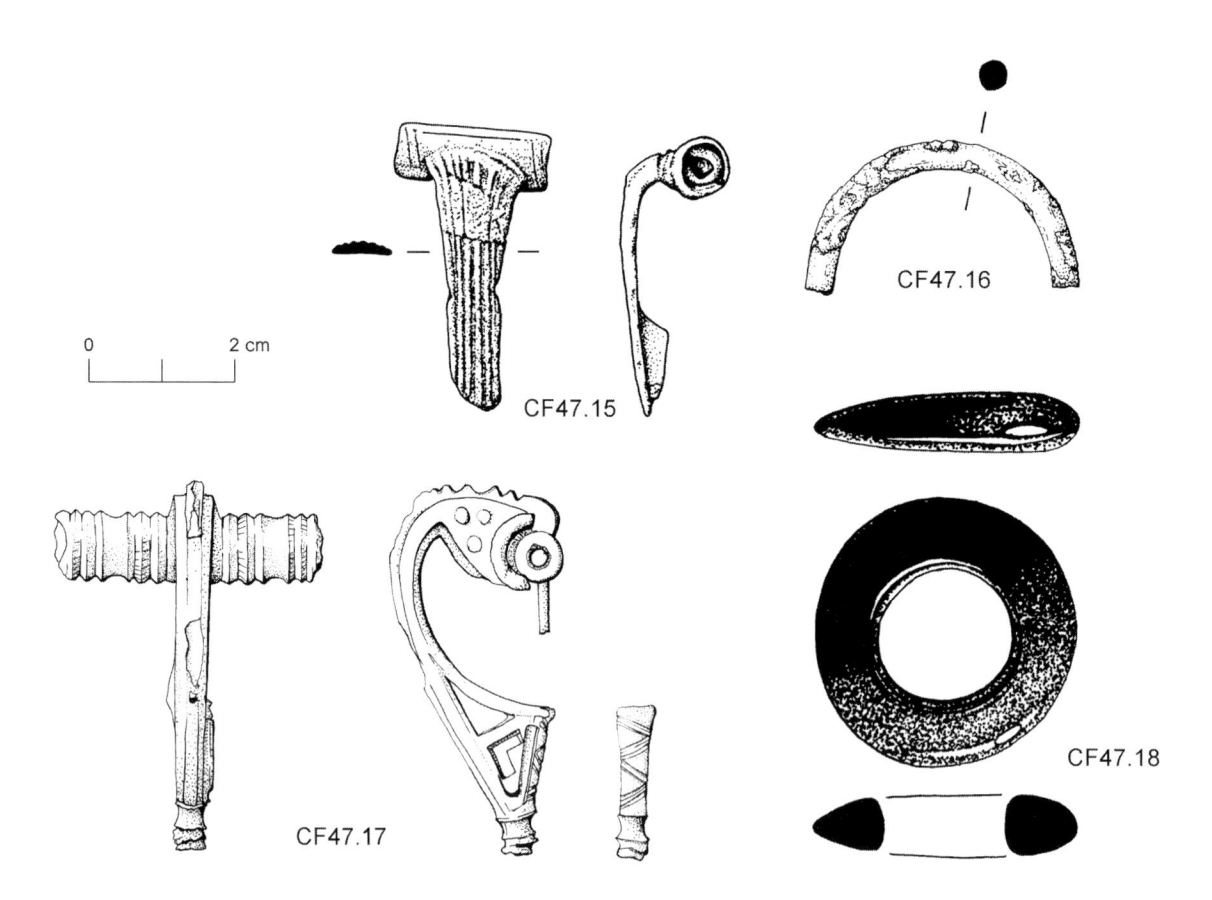

FIG. 109. Doctor's burial CF47: copper-alloy brooches CF47.15 and 17, ring fragment CF47.16, and jet bead CF47.18 (scale 1:1)

of the catchplate may also be decorated. The design on the Stanway brooch is remarkably similar to that on a pair of 1st-century B.C. silver brooches from Lauterach, Austria, on a type specimen for Almgren Type 19 (1923), and on 1st-century A.D. silver brooches from a grave group from Hoby, Denmark, but probably made in the eastern Alps (Salskov Roberts 1995, 292, fig. 11). Decoration on the catchplate edge is also found on several brooches from eastern Britain in the Colchester and Polden Hill series: for example, a Colchester brooch from Upper Deal, which also has elaborate fretwork and small ring-and-dot motifs on the catchplate (Birchall 1965, 305, fig. 12, 100); a Colchester derivative from Icklingham, Suffolk (Ashmolean Museum, 1927.234); a Colchester derivative from Baldock, Hertfordshire (Stead and Rigby 1986, fig. 27, 4); a hinged Dolphin brooch from Nottinghamshire (Hull Museum); a Polden Hill brooch from Sheepen, with decoratively pierced catchplate (Hawkes and Hull 1947, pl. 91, 43); a Polden Hill brooch from Charlton Hill, Kent, which has a pierced circular motif defined by two triangular cut-outs on the catchplate (British Museum, 1950.7-2.1); and a Polden Hill from Winchester, Hampshire, with an elaborately fretted catchplate that runs the full length of the bow right up to the head (Winchester Museum). The Icklingham brooch shares the notched crest and astragaloid mouldings on the side-wings of the Stanway Rearhook, although the catchplate is solid and there is no foot-knob.

All the brooches from eastern Britain are large examples of their types, and many have other distinctive or unusual features. With the exception of that from Upper Deal, all date to the 40s and 50s, and all are of native manufacture. Their distribution has a strong eastern bias, while the general rarity of embellishment on this part of the catchplate, together with its appearance on the La Tène silver pair from Lauterach, marks out those brooches that do bear it as being generally high-quality products.

A number of brooches from western Britain also have decoration on the catchplate edge, notably a group from Gloucester that includes Rearhook brooches but also western headloop types and Trumpet brooches (Cracknell 1990, especially fig. 1 and fig. 2, 8). All the brooch types on which it occurs are of native manufacture, and, while the catchplate edge is not visible in use, there is some possibility that the decoration had a significance beyond the purely decorative. Cracknell suggests the design is a maker's mark, although, as can be seen by its occurrence at Lauterach, its use occurs over a prolonged period, over a wide geographical area, and on many different types of brooch.

The jet bead, both by its substance and in the context of this particular grave, is unlikely to have been regarded simply as a dress accessory (FIG. 109, CF47.18). Although jet jewellery is found quite frequently in the Bronze Age in Britain, it is rare in the Iron Age and in the early Roman period. This may be largely a result of the dearth of excavated burials in the Iron Age compared to the Bronze Age, and perhaps of the use of cremation as the main funerary rite in the 1st to 3rd centuries A.D. Its rarity may thus be accidental, but the recovery of two shale beads in the rich female burial at Birdlip points to black minerals in general being regarded as of high value (Bellows 1881, 139). In addition, Pliny records that jet (and this term must here be taken to embrace all black minerals, such as shale and cannel coal) was credited with healing powers when burnt, swallowed, or applied to the skin, and also that it was used by 'wise men' in divination (*Historia Naturalis*, 36, 141–2; Allason-Jones 1996, 15). It seems unlikely that the person buried in CF47 would have been unaware of these magico-medical properties, and therefore this bead may have doubled both as ornament and as professional equipment.

CF47.15 FIG. 109. SF79a. C982. Gunmetal Langton Down brooch with rounded head. The pin, part of the spring, the foot of the bow, and part of the catchplate are missing. The pin is of impure copper. The front of the spring-cover is defined by marginal grooves. The head has a narrow moulding and groove. The bow is reeded. Length 37 mm.

CF47.16 FIG. 109. SF79b. C982. A fragment of a bronze ring of circular section. Internal diameter 27 mm, section 5 mm in diameter. This was found attached by corrosion to the Langton Down brooch SF79a.

CF47.17 FIG. 109. SF40. C942. Tinned leaded bronze Rearhook brooch, complete apart from the central section of the pin, part of the spring and chord, and the ends of the side-wings. The pin is made of brass. The spring was of sixteen coils. The side-wings have central astragaloid mouldings flanked by pairs of knurled ridges. The crest has sharp transverse ridges. The narrow bow has a central rib on a platform flanked by slight cavetto mouldings. The flat sides of the expanded head are marked by a triplet of incised circles. The catchplate has two large perforations, the upper triangular, giving the impression that the metal from the back of the bow has been pulled outwards, and the lower a thick L-shape. The edge of the catch is decorated with a pattern of incised grooves between mouldings. There is a small footknob separated from the bow by transverse mouldings. Length 47 mm.

CF47.18 FIG. 109. SF38. C940. Jet annular bead of elongated D-shaped section, slightly thinner, presumably worn, at one point. Diameter 35 mm, height 7 mm, thickness 8–9 mm. Diameter of central hole 17–18 mm.

Board game (FIGS 102, 110–11, 126; CF47.19–CF47.20)

The 26 counters, thirteen blue (CF47.19b) and thirteen white (CF47.19a), are imports of common Roman form, and their method of manufacture is described on page 186 (FIG. 110). They are of different composition to those in BF64 (BF64.28) and the single counter from CF42 (CF42.14). They appear to have been placed in position on the board as if in readiness to start a game (FIG. 126; pp. 352–75).

The wooden board (CF47.20), like that in BF64 (BF64.29), was made from two pieces of maple, joined by brass hinged fittings and reinforced at the corners by copper-alloy sheet binding fixed over leather (FIGS 102, 111). The wood had a decorative border, and traces of a red-brown pigment show that this part of the board, at least, was painted. (Elemental analysis of the paint was undertaken using a scanning electron microscope, see p. 390.) Unlike the junction bindings found on the board in BF64, the central fittings probably functioned as hinges. A reconstruction of the hinges from Burial 6 at Baldock shows that for them to work there must always have been a gap between the two pieces of the board when it was open

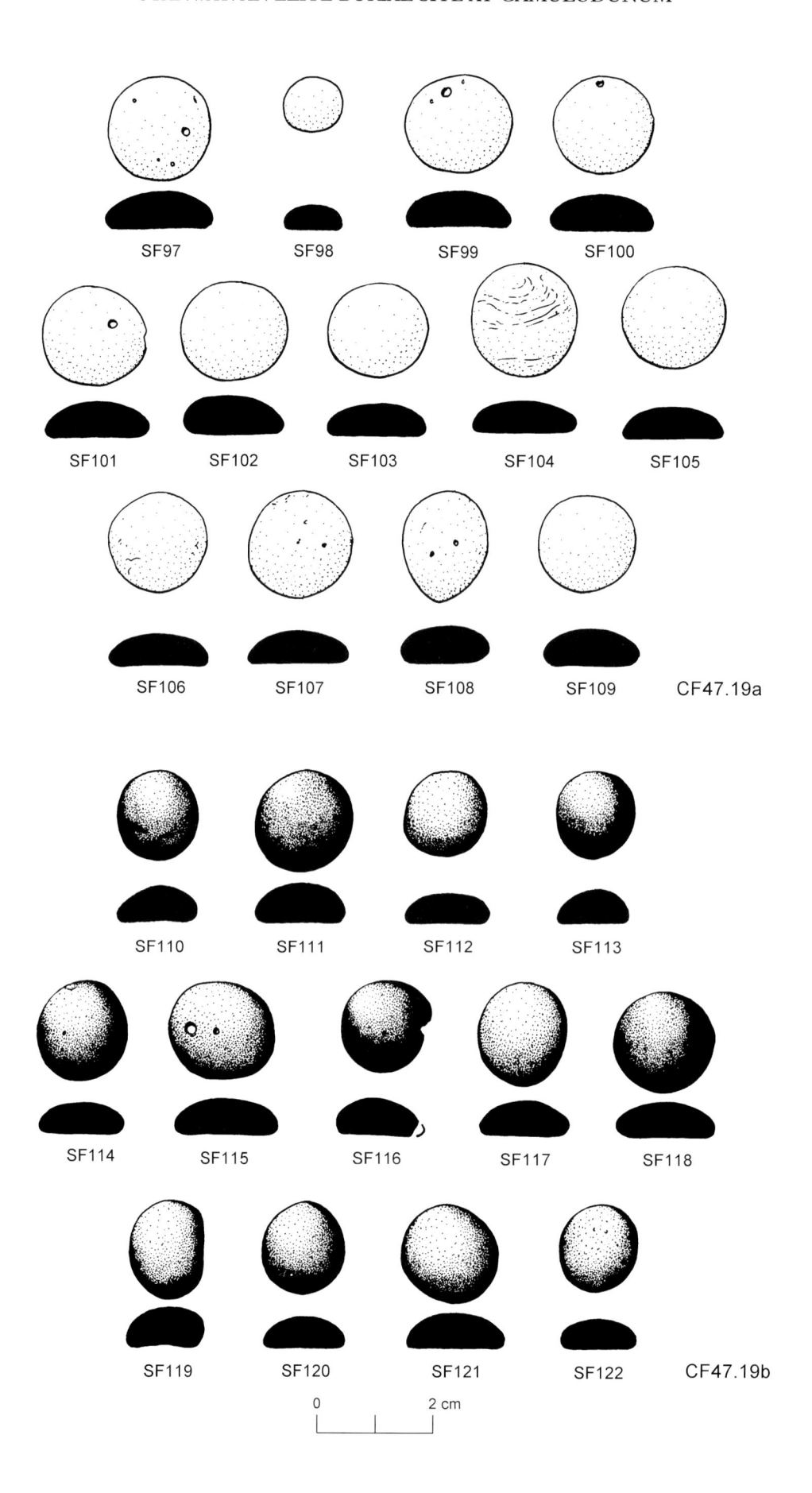

218 STANWAY: AN ÉLITE BURIAL SITE AT CAMULODUNUM

FIG. 110. Doctor's burial CF47: glass gaming counters CF47.19b (scale 1:1)

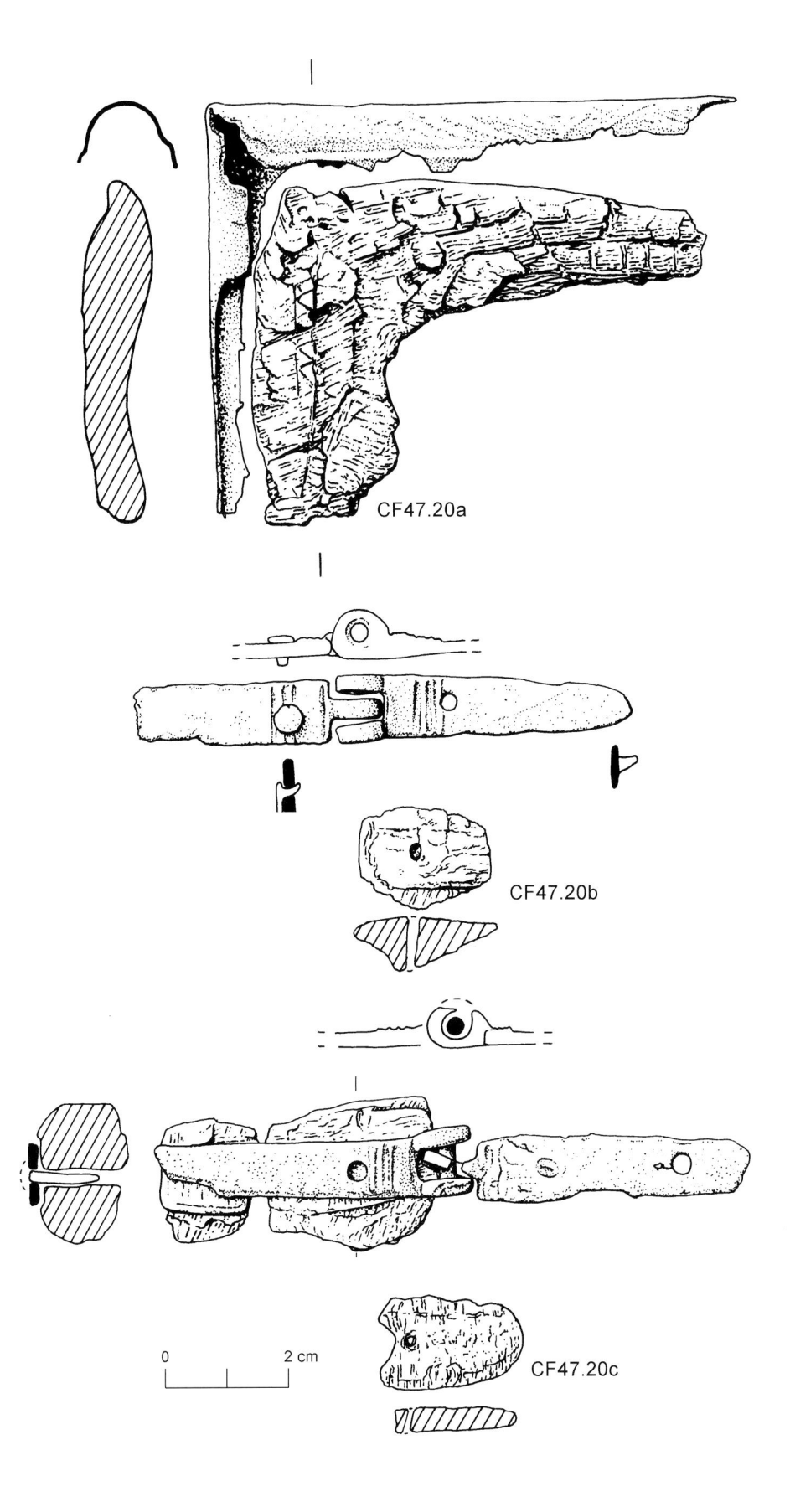

FIG. 111. Doctor's burial CF47: copper-alloy corner CF47.20a and hinges CF47.20b–c from the gaming board (scale 1:1)

(Stead and Rigby 1986, fig. 30, 13–14, and reconstruction top right). The Baldock pair are plain and wrought, with the hinge made by simply rolling the metal over the axial pin, but those from CF47 were of better quality, being cast in two pieces before being fixed together, and decorated with transverse grooves. Another similar pair are shown sitting exposed on the top of the lid of a large reconstructed box from Eckartsbrunn, Lkr. Konstanz, Germany (Riha 2001, Abb. 7).

The discovery of leather binding on the board in CF47 is rare, but leather is increasingly being found on wooden artefacts undergoing careful conservation. Grave 117 in the cemetery at King Harry Lane contained a hinged maplewood board with a drop-handle that was also leather-bound and may have been a game board (although no counters were found), and reference is made in the discussion of the Grave 117 board to a leather-bound casket from Godmanchester (*see* pp. 388, 390; Stead and Rigby 1989, 109). A box from Sheepen also retained traces of leather (Saunders 1985; Niblett 1985, 25–6), and recent excavations in Hertfordshire have uncovered a similar leather-bound box on which traces of pigment suggest the leather was brightly coloured (Network Archaeology, site CMG01, section 13, site number 13/52). Traces of leather have also been found on boxes from Augst, Switzerland (Riha 2001, 52) and at the Garrison site, Colchester (CAT Report in prep).

The board, the game, and the post-depositional movements are described and considered in detail on pages 352–75.

CF47.19

a FIG. 110. SF97–109. C1001–1013. Thirteen counters of opaque white glass, one (SF98) is markedly smaller than the others. All are well formed, round to oval, with a smooth surface occasionally marked by air bubble voids, and slightly sand-roughened underside. Two, SFs 104 and 109, have swirls of a slightly shiny off-white colour passing through them. This was also noted in a white counter from BF64, and is presumed to be the result of the opacifier being poorly mixed into the matrix. SF97: diameter 17–17.5 mm, height 6 mm. SF98: diameter 10–10.5 mm, height 5.5 mm. SF99: diameter 16–18 mm, height 6 mm. SF100: diameter 16–17 mm, height 6 mm. SF101: diameter 17–18 mm, height 6 mm. SF102: diameter 16–18.5 mm, height 6.5 mm. SF103: diameter 15.5–17 mm, height 6 mm. SF104: diameter 18–19 mm, height 6 mm. SF105: diameter 17 mm, height 6 mm. SF106: diameter 16.5–17 mm, height 6 mm. SF107: diameter 17–18 mm, height 6 mm. SF108: diameter 15–18 mm, height 6 mm. SF109: diameter 16 mm, height 6.5 mm.

b FIG. 110. SF110–122. C1014–1022. Thirteen counters of opaque blue glass, the density of the colour ranging from pale to dark. None is so dark that it appears black. As with the white counters, the undersides are slightly sand-roughened, the upper surfaces smooth apart from voids caused by air bubbles. SF110 has a ripple of slightly translucent glass in the matrix, SF111 a ripple of duller and paler glass. SF110: diameter 14–15 mm, height 6 mm. SF111: diameter 16.5–17 mm, height 6.5 mm. SF112: diameter 14–14.5 mm, height 6 mm. SF113: diameter 13–14 mm, height 6 mm. SF114: diameter 15–16 mm, height 6 mm. SF115: diameter 16.5–18 mm, height 6.5 mm. SF116: diameter 15–15.5 mm, height 6 mm. SF117: diameter 15.5–17.5 mm, height 6 mm. SF118: diameter 16.5–17 mm, height 6.5 mm. SF119: diameter 13.5–16.5 mm, height 7 mm. SF120: diameter 14–15 mm, height 6 mm. SF121: diameter 15.5–17 mm, height 6 mm. SF122: diameter 13.5–14.5mm, height 6 mm.

CF47.20

a FIG. 111. SF25/92–94. C915/996–998. Brass corner binding and wood from the board. Only SF25 is illustrated. The wood was rebated to reinforce the attachment of the metal sheet and fragments of leather remain between the two. A strip of zigzag decoration runs down at least one side of the wood, and traces of a red pigment show that it was also painted. One rivet hole survives near the end of the longest side of the binding. Length of long side 86 mm, height 17 mm.

b FIG. 111. SF96. C1000. Copper-alloy (probably brass or gunmetal, *see* CF47.20c) hinged fitting and wood from the board. Each hinge-plate is tongue-shaped and was fixed to the wood by two flat-headed tacks. The end of one plate is missing, and only parts of two tacks survive. The hinge is formed by three lugs, two on one plate, one on another. The axial riveted bar is missing. The surface of each plate close to the lugs is marked by transverse grooves. Surviving length 81 mm, maximum width 10 mm.

c FIG. 111. SF95. C999. Brass or gunmetal hinged fitting and wood as CF47.20b, with traces of leather on the wood. The axial riveted bar remains in place. Surviving length 96 mm.

Copper-alloy vessels (FIGS 112–14, CF47.21–22)

Two large vessels lay in the north-east corner of the grave, resting on a wooden object, probably a box or tray (pp. 232–6). One is a large bronze saucepan (FIG. 112, CF47.21), the bottom scarred with many wear marks, probably caused by stirring and/or scouring. The handle is decorated with a *thyrsus*, knurled grooves, mouldings, and flowing decoration made by lines of punch marks. Its end is in the shape of a disc with a lunate suspension hole. The decoration is typical of pans made in Gaul (Eggers 1951, Type 137; den Boesterd 1956, 6–7, no. 13.11; Bennett and Young 1981, 42; Tassinari 1993, Type G2100, vol. 1, 52, 55, vol. 2, 98–108).

The other vessel in CF47 is a spouted strainer bowl (FIG. 113, CF47.22), which was placed in the burial pit alongside the samian bowl and the saucepan, close to the service. The carinated bowl was spun, with the lower part bellied, the upper more or less straight. The feet, handle and spout were cast and soldered on; the spill-plate and strainer-plate wrought and soldered on (FIG. 113). The cast elements are in good condition, but the sheet-metal elements, the bowl and the two plates, are not. The bowl and spill-plate have shattered, and the collapse of the bowl then crushed the strainer-plate (FIG. 114). Some areas of the central part of the spill-plate, which is very thin, have either disintegrated completely while buried or were missing when the bowl was deposited.

Both these vessels are discussed in more detail on pages 322–6.

CF47.21 FIG. 112. SF13. C901. Bronze saucepan, probably plated with white metal internally, although the large size of the vessel made analysis impossible. The flat handle has knurled marginal grooves and mouldings. It bears a central *thyrsus* with elongated terminals and a shaft formed by a groove with a raised wavy line within it and a slightly raised rim. There may have been a contrasting inlay within the groove. The surface is further decorated with straight, curled, and wavy lines made by small punch marks, now largely obscured by corrosion. The terminal is rounded, with concentric grooves and mouldings around a small raised centre mark, and has a half-moon cut-out. The base of the pan, both internally and externally, has concentric grooves and mouldings around a lathe centre mark, those on the inside very worn, those on the outside prominent. The internal base is also scratched from stirring and/or scouring. Diameter 185 mm, height 126 mm. Length of handle 165 mm.

CF47.22 FIG. 113. SF14/67/68/70/76/91. C902/969/970/972/978/995. Copper-alloy spouted strainer bowl of carinated form with separately made spout (CF47.22a), handle (CF47.22c), three feet (CF47.22b), strainer-plate (CF47.22f) and spill-plate (CF47.22d). The spout, handle and feet are stout

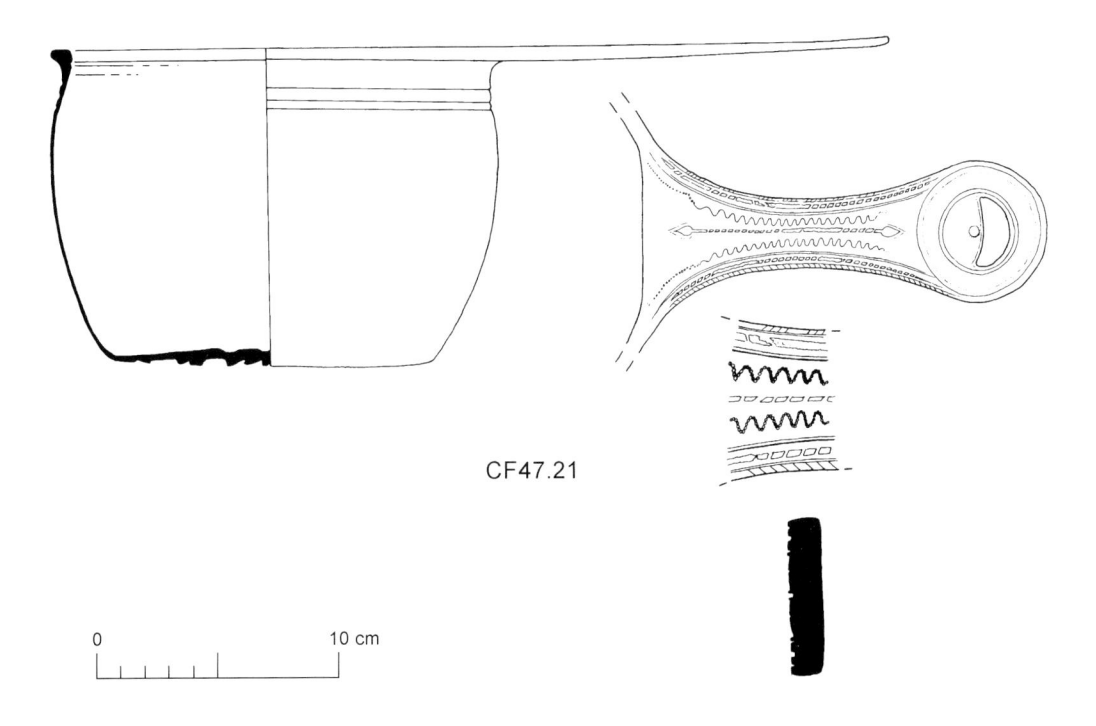

FIG. 112. Doctor's burial CF47: copper-alloy saucepan CF47.21 (scale 1:3)

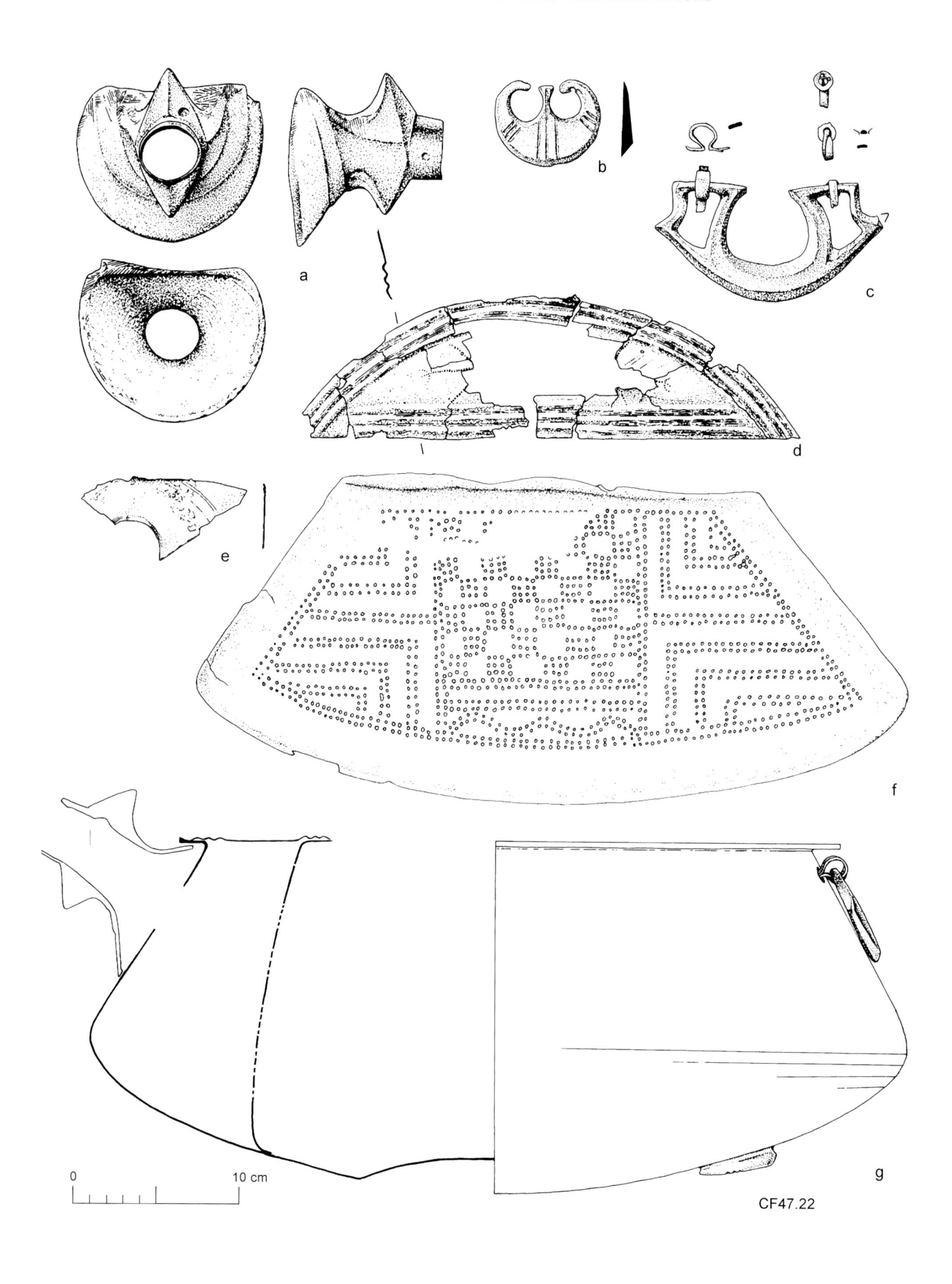

FIG. 113. Doctor's burial CF47: copper-alloy strainer bowl CF47.22 (scale 1:3)

FIG. 114. Doctor's burial CF47: the copper-alloy strainer bowl *in situ*

castings in leaded bronze and were tinned. The strainer- and spill-plates and the bowl itself are of sheet bronze, and are now in fragments. The metal of the spill-plate, which was tinned on one side, is so thin that parts have corroded away.

The internal diameter of the bowl is about 210 mm, the external diameter of the base 110 mm. The height, based on the similar bowl from Crownthorpe, Norfolk, was probably about 136 mm. The rim is flat, with a raised edge. The bowl was spun, and a slight mark from the lathe centre can be seen on the base, which is slightly raised. The outer face is highly polished. In many places, the inner face has a distinctive dull pale green patina, with tooling lines running vertically up from the base to the carination, but horizontally above it. Compass lines on a fragment of the body define the point at which the hole was cut to allow the applied spout to function (CF47.22e).

The spout has a maximum width of 72 mm, height of 58 mm, and depth of 54 mm. The whole surface is covered with file marks from finishing, in particular on the curve from the top edge to the upper point. The slightly concave top edge is quite irregularly formed and finished. The lower edge comes to a small central point. There is a low step around the base of the spout proper. This is of strong three-dimensional lozenge form, very angular. A more or less circular indentation on the upper right-hand side is probably a casting flaw, as is a similar mark on the side of the circular mouth.

The strainer-plate is made of thin sheet metal, the edges bent over and originally soldered to the wall, base, and spill-plate. It is decorated with a design of punched holes, consisting of double right-angled lines at the corner, a chequer-board in the upper part of the centre, and a double zigzag in the lower. Some of the chequers are four dots across/up, others five. The plate is crushed, but is shown straightened out in the illustration. A lump of tin-lead solder associated with this plate is probably from a repair rather than the original attachment.

The spill-plate has three angular mouldings around the margins, and fragments of a design executed in tiny punched dots on each side of the field. The centre is now missing, but need not have been solid (Stead 1967, fig. 12). Its maximum dimensions are 196 mm by 55 mm.

The handle has openwork ends, with the fittings of attachment fixed on the upper bar. Length 92 mm. These differ from side to side, clear evidence of repair. On one side is a stout brass ring-headed stud (now worn through at one point), with its ends hammered through a washer. The edges of the latter are strongly burred, suggesting that either the washer had only a very small central perforation initially, or that it was completely solid. On the other side is only a simple strip of brass formed into a clip of similar form to a split-pin.

The three cast feet (CF47.22b; SF67–8, SF70) are peltate, the backs retaining traces of the solder used to attach them to the bowl. Only SF67 is illustrated. The front of each is decorated with three groups of deep incised grooves, one placed centrally, with the inner line running up to the top of the foot, and one at the base of each arm. All are 41 mm wide, the height varying from 31 to 33 mm, and they taper in thickness from 1.5/2 mm to 5/6 mm. One (SF68) is slightly damaged, with a groove angled across the central group of three.

Rods (FIGS 115–18, CF47.23; TABLE 35)

Eight metal rods had been placed at the west end of the burial pit together with personal items such as the surgical kit and game board (FIGS 115–18). Their precise positions relative to the latter are discussed above (p. 207). Each has a spatulate end and a round end. Four are iron and four brass, and two of each metal are larger than the others. They thus form four groups of four, and four groups of two, with each rod belonging to three groups (TABLE 35). The four iron rods had been buried in contact with textile. No textile survived on the copper-alloy rods. However, given the distribution of the textile on the iron ones, the copper-alloy rods are likely to have been similarly buried with textile which does not generally appear to have survived in the burial when in contact with copper alloy (but *see* the brooch CF47.17).

The publicity that followed the excavation of CF47 brought the rods to the attention of a wide public, who put forward many ideas about their function, the majority focusing on human and animal surgery. How far this was the power of suggestive influence exerted by the set of surgical implements in the burial, and the occupation of those putting forward the suggestions, cannot be precisely established, but the effect of character, nationality, and personal experience on interpretation, in defiance of evidence, has been shown with reference to professional archaeological discussions of Migration Period spouted vessels found in female graves on the Continent (Bartel and Codreanu-Windauer 1995, 259–60; 2002, 20–1) and of an unusual form of glass flask (Cool 2002, 146). All the proposals for the function of the Stanway rods made by the general public have therefore been given serious consideration, but none can be accommodated within the considerable amount of information available about ancient surgical, and other medical, techniques. The discussion below is therefore based solely on their form and archaeological context.

To a large extent the rods resemble the form of *stylus* that has a spatulate eraser at one end and a blunt round terminal at the other end; the latter was fitted with a point, which rarely survives.

TABLE 35: TYPOLOGICAL GROUPINGS OF THE RODS IN CF47

	Four iron	*Four brass*	*Four long*	*Four short*	*Two long iron*	*Two short iron*	*Two long brass*	*Two short brass*
iron short (**CF47.23a**)	×			×		×		
iron short (**CF47.23b**)	×			×		×		
iron long (**CF47.23c**)	×		×		×			
iron long (**CF47.23d**)	×		×		×			
brass short (**CF47.23e**)		×		×				×
brass short (**CF47.23f**)		×		×				×
brass long (**CF47.23g**)		×	×				×	
brass long (**CF47.23h**)		×	×				×	

CF47.23a CF47.23b = textile CF47.23c

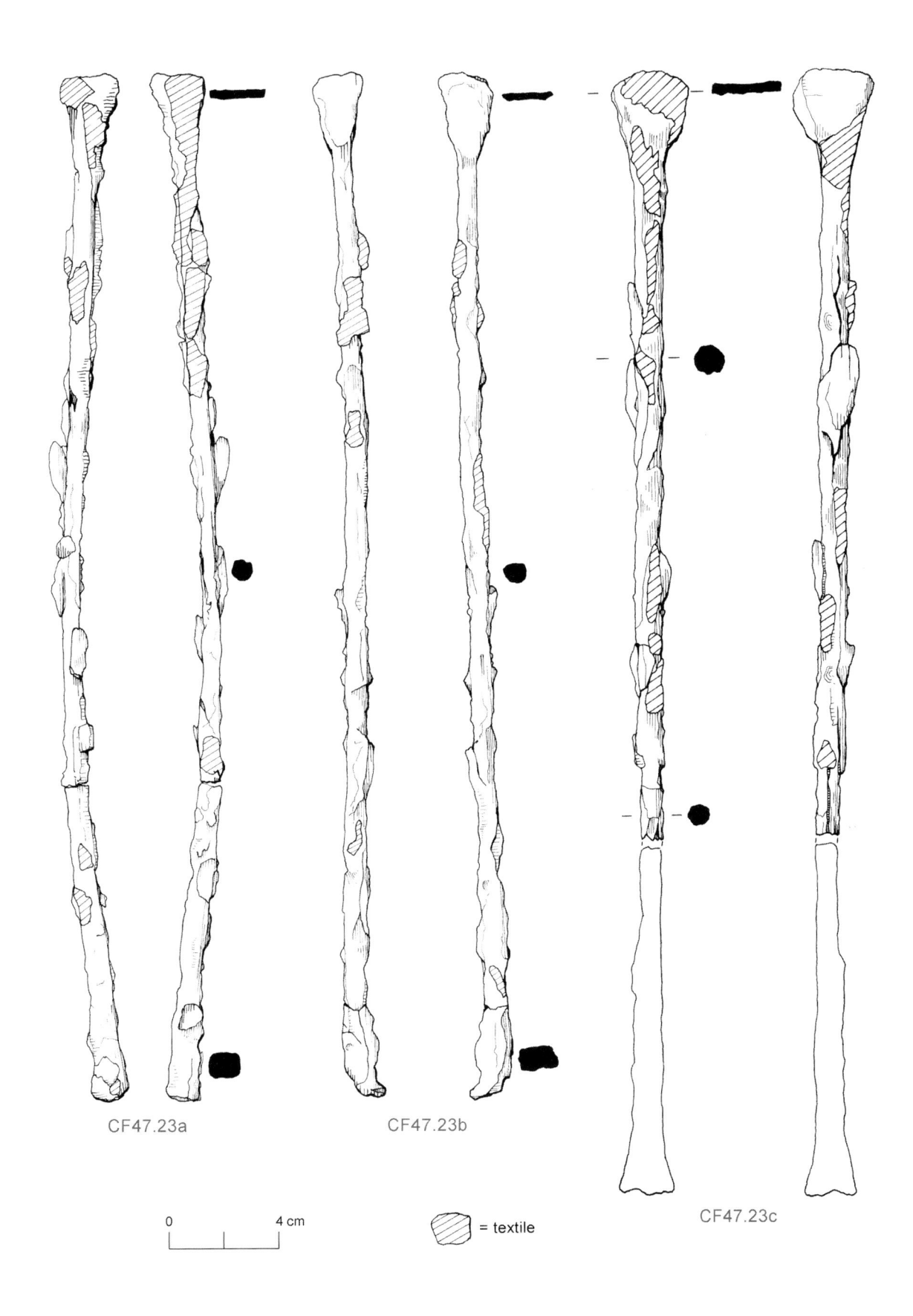

FIG. 115. Doctor's burial CF47: iron rods CF47.23a–c (scale 1:2)

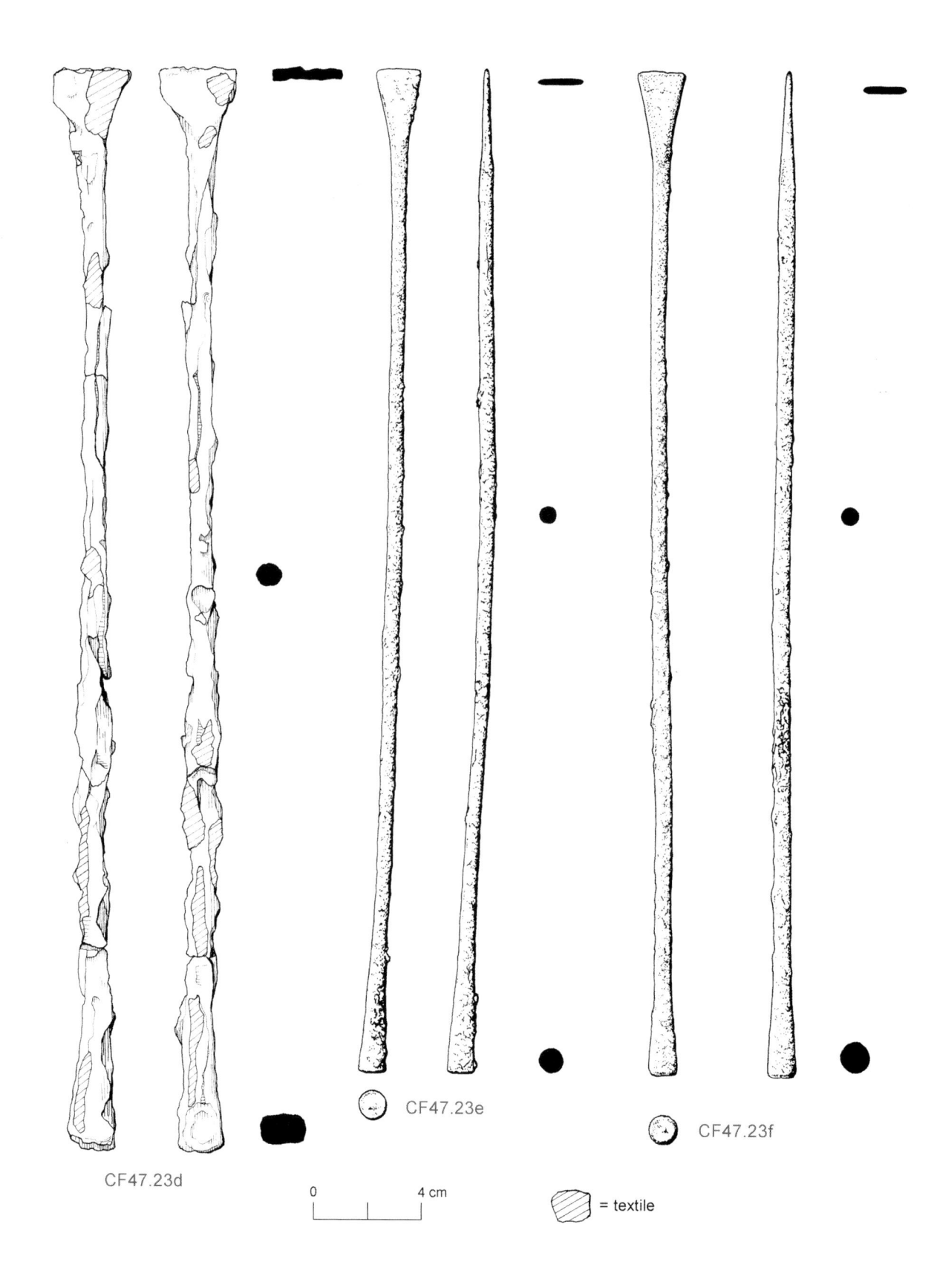

FIG. 116. Doctor's burial CF47: iron rod CF47.23d and copper-alloy rods CF47.23e–f (scale 1:2)

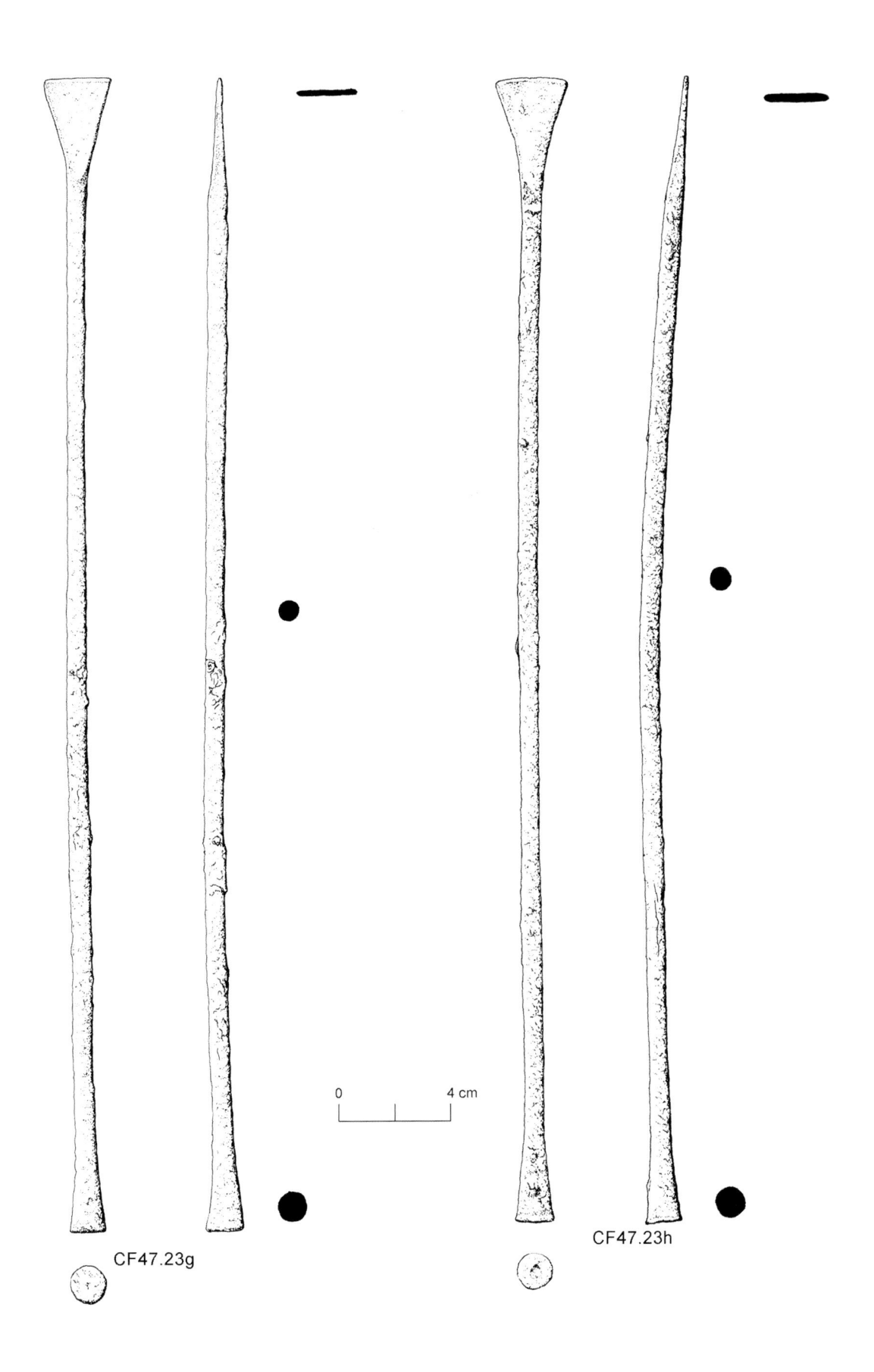

FIG. 117. Doctor's burial CF47: copper-alloy rods CF47.23g–h (scale 1:2)

FIG. 118. Doctor's burial CF47: the rods and rings *in situ*

A pair of 3rd-century copper-alloy *styli* of this form were found in a grave at the Butt Road cemetery, Colchester (*CAR* 2, fig. 107; *CAR* 9, 51). An intriguing point of similarity beyond the general form is that the small dimple in the round end of each of the Butt Road *styli* is matched by a depression on all four of the CF47 brass rods. The rods and the *styli* have been cast, and the depressions are linked to the manufacturing process (N. Nolan, pers. comm.). Despite their resemblance to *styli*, the rods are far too large to be used as such, although their size does not preclude the use of the ends in superficially related functions, *i.e.* the round ends might be used to make marks on the ground surface or a similar large area, the spatulate ends to erase them.

By far the most important characteristic of the rods is their potential for grouping, shown in TABLE 35, and therefore this can be presumed to be the major clue to their function. Placing this characteristic within the context of the medical expertise of the person buried in CF47, a pertinent and important part of treatment in the ancient world was the call for divine assistance (Jackson 1988a, 138–69). For the Romans this took various forms, such as interpretation of dreams, ritual cleansing, making sacrifices, or placing miniature votives of their diseased body parts in sanctuaries. None of these can be detected here, which, given that the deceased in CF47 was British rather than Roman (pp. 444–5), is hardly surprising; much less is known about the methods of divination used in the non-Roman world (Brunaux 1988, 132–3). However, the description by Tacitus of how the Germani practised divination, although not necessarily in the context of the healing arts, seems relevant:

> *For omens and the casting of lots they have the highest regard. Their procedure in casting lots is always the same. They cut off a branch of a nut-bearing tree and slice it into strips; these they mark with different signs and throw them completely at random onto a white cloth. Then the priest of the state, if the consultation is a public one, or the father of the family if it is private, offers a prayer to the gods, and looking up at the sky picks up three strips, one at a time, and reads their meaning from the signs previously scored on them.* (Tacitus, Germania, 10.)

Use in a similar way in divination seems to be the most likely way in which the CF47 rods were employed. It has been shown in TABLE 35 that the eight rods fall into eight groups. These groups could be described as formal and typological, but Tacitus's description serves to point out that such groupings need not necessarily be those that might be required or used in the ancient world. Random selection of rods in groups other than two or four could have been used, whether or not individual rods were marked to distinguish like pair members apart, while marking them in some way, perhaps by tying on (coloured) thread or strips of cloth, would have provided more groupings and thus more potential for interpretation.

It is possible that eight rings found in the burial were also used for divination (*see* below).

CF47.23

a FIG. 115. SF83. C987. Iron rod with one round and one spatulate end. Profile irregular along the long axis. Length 358 mm; diameter 8 mm at the centre, 13 mm at the round end; width across spatulate end 23 mm.

b FIG. 115. SF125. C1029. Iron rod with one round and one spatulate end. Curved in the centre of the long axis. Length 359 mm; diameter 8 mm at the centre, 11 mm at the round end; width across spatulate end 18 mm.

c FIG. 115. SF72. C974. Iron rod with one round and one spatulate end. In three pieces, but appears fairly straight along the long axis. Length 398 mm; diameter 10 mm at the centre, 17 mm at the round end; width across spatulate end 27 mm.

d FIG. 116. SF80. C984. Iron rod with one round and one spatulate end. Curved in profile along the long axis and also bent near round end. Length 392 mm; diameter 9–10 mm at the centre, 17 mm at the round end; width across spatulate end 27 mm.

e FIG. 116. SF82. C986. ?Brass rod with one round and one spatulate end. Curved quite markedly along the long axis. The edge of the spatulate end is slightly concave. There is a tiny sunken area, roughly triangular, in the centre of the round end. Length 357 mm; diameter 5 mm at the centre, 9 mm at the round end; width across spatulate end 16 mm.

f FIG. 116. SF126. C1030. Brass rod with one round and one spatulate end. Slightly curved along the long axis. The edge of the spatulate end is slightly concave. There is a tiny triangular sunken area in the round end, set slightly off-centre. Length 357 mm; diameter 6 mm at the centre, 9.5 mm at the round end; width across spatulate end 17 mm.

g FIG. 117. SF81. C985. ?Brass rod with one round and one spatulate end. Curved along the long axis. The edge of the spatulate end is straight. There is a tiny circular sunken area in the centre of the round end. Length 402 mm; diameter 6 mm at the centre, 13 mm at the round end; width across spatulate end 24 mm.

h FIG. 117. SF127. C1031. ?Brass rod with one round and one spatulate end. Markedly curved along the long axis. The edge of the spatulate end is slightly concave. There is a tiny sunken area, roughly square, in the centre of the round end. Length 399 mm; diameter 7 mm at the centre, 12 mm at the round end; width across spatulate end 25 mm.

Rings (FIGS 102, 118–19, CF47.24)

Eight rings of two types, plain and terret-form (FIG. 119), were found set more or less upright against one of the sides of the burial pit, in this order (right to left): plain (CF47.24h), terret-form (CF47.24c), terret-form (CF47.24d), plain (CF47.24g), terret-form (CF47.24e), terret-form (CF47.24a), plain (CF47.24f), terret-form (CF47.24b). The three plain rings may, or may not, be replacements for lost terret-form rings from an original set. The presence of the terret-shaped rings suggests that the plain ones are not votive solar symbols (*see* p. 215 for a half ring (CF47.16) from this grave that is not considered to be part of this group).

Each ring had been attached to some other object by means of a narrow leather thong, as each either had a fragment of a leather loop attached (CF47.24f–CF47.24g), or was scarred where such a loop had been. Given the absence of any metal studs, the leather must have been sewn to form the loop, and traces of yarn were indeed found on both surviving pieces of leather (*see* p. 348).

There were traces of painted wood under and on top of CF47.24a, and on top of CF47.24b, presumably all that remains of a wooden object to which the rings were attached or in which they were stored (FIGS 102–3). The paint seems to have been the same red-brown pigment

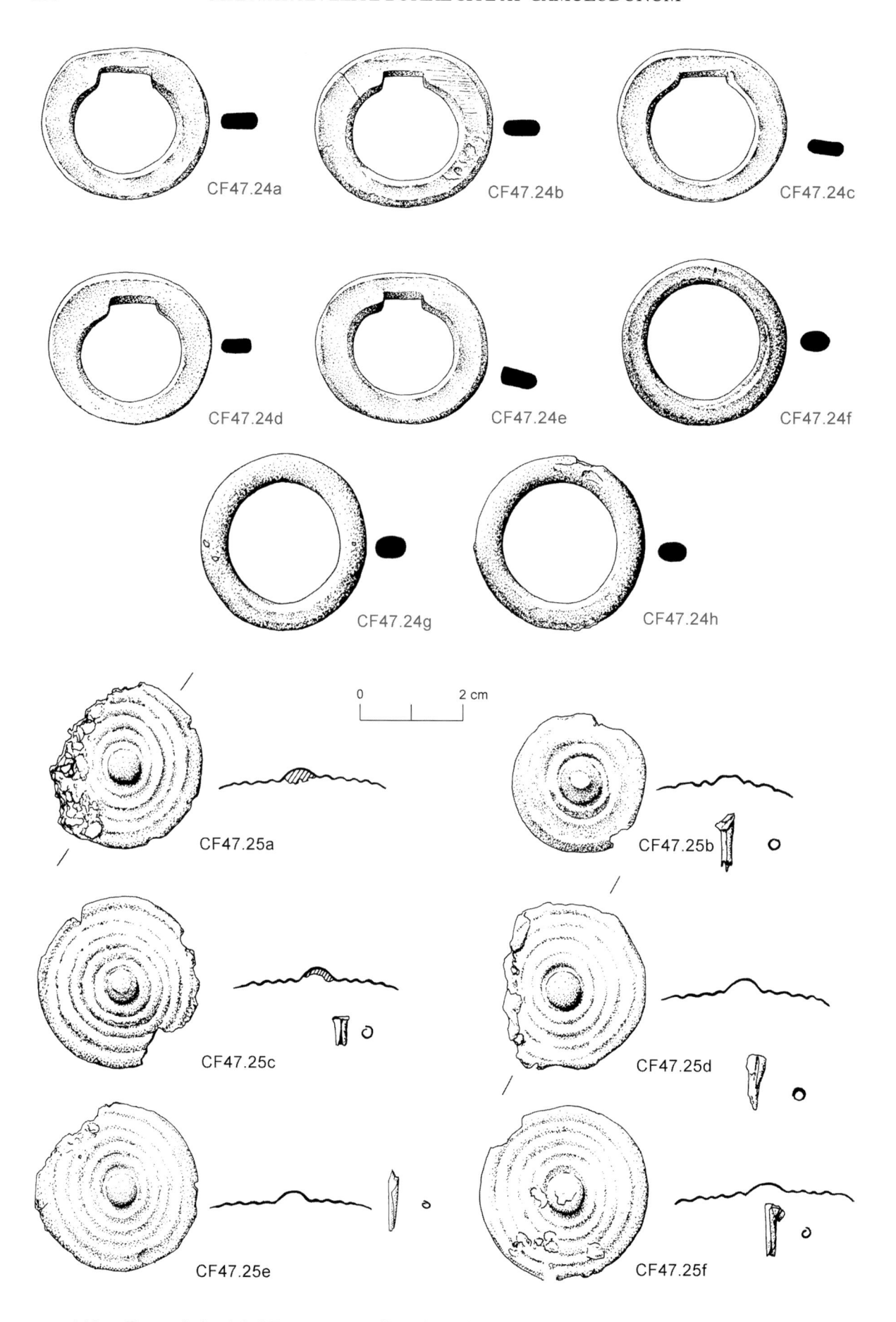

FIG. 119. Doctor's burial CF47: copper-alloy rings CF47.24a–h, and selection of decorated copper-alloy studs CF47.25a–f from the ?tray (scale 1:1)

which had been applied to part of the gaming board CF47.20 (p. 390). As it seems unlikely that rings attached to leather thongs would also be sandwiched tightly between two boards, the wood on the top of CF47.24a is presumed to have come from the collapse of this object.

Plain round rings similar to CF47.24f–CF47.24h have often been identified as harness rings (*e.g.* Jackson 1990a, nos 152–61), and three of very similar size to these examples were found on the head of a donkey skeleton at Pompeii, all that remained of a halter or head-collar; they showed a considerable amount of wear and were, like those from Stanway, scarred in places from contact with decayed leather straps (Crummy forthcoming a). An association with horse-gear could also be shown for the D-shaped terret-form rings, as in size and form they are remarkably similar to the reverse side of the miniature terrets in a 3rd-century B.C. cart-burial from Kirkburn, Yorkshire (Stead 1991, 44–7), each of which was attached to a linch-pin by means of a strap or thong passed around the rebated section.

However, despite these similarities to harness rings and terrets, the function of the rings from CF47 remains very obscure. If they were from a halter (or two), they would not have lain in a line in the burial pit. Leather straps, metal rings and wood might perhaps all be found together on a chariot pole, or perhaps on a yoke (compare the Iron Age yokes defined by five terrets set in a line from Garton Station and Kirkburn (Stead 1991, fig. 39, 40–41, fig. 40), but the comparatively short length of the line of the Stanway rings, as well as their small size, and the absence of any other gear associated with driven animals, horses or oxen, militates against this. Their resemblance to the miniature terrets from Yorkshire does, however, serve to link them to earlier Iron Age metal-working forms.

Four similar plain rings of comparable size to those from this burial were found in the rich female burial at Birdlip, Gloucestershire (Bellows 1881, figs 5–8), but their function has not been identified. They may have been from a box, perhaps used as handles or to take strapping, or even used together with split-pins as rudimentary hinges. A similar identification for the Stanway rings can be dismissed because of their concentration in the ground, and the true purpose of the rings in the Doctor's burial can perhaps only be illuminated by consideration of the group's inclusion in this highly idiosyncratic funerary assemblage. Their association with a set of surgical instruments and probable divination rods (FIG. 118) shows them to be the property of an individual whose magico-medical field of expertise is rarely visible through material culture. This serves to suggest that they formed part of an object or objects associated in some way, however obscure, with the healing arts.

The following three suggestions may be made. First, all the rings may have been attached to a single larger object intended to produce a noise, *i.e.* a 'rattle' made from leather straps onto which the rings were tied. When shaken, such an object would produce an irregular clattering. Noise was used in the ancient world to drive away evil, evidenced by amulets placed in graves, the *sistrum* used in the worship of Isis, and the *tintinnabuli* set up in Roman homes (Philpott 1991, 163; Ward-Perkins and Claridge 1976, nos 196–7, 216; Johns 1982, 67). Second, if each ring came from a separate object, then perhaps they may have served as closure rings for small cloth bags, as has been suggested for small metal rings from Anglo-Saxon graves (Dickinson 1993, 52, fig. 6.3). Small cloth bags of medicaments would be an appropriate deposit in this burial, and the survival of the contents of a cloth bag from AF18 (AF18.2) makes this interpretation seem apposite, but the absence of textile remains on the rings militates against it, and it seems almost certain, given the survival of two of the leather loops, that some fabric would have remained had the metal been in contact with cloth. Third, there may be some significance in the fact that there are eight rings and eight rods (p. 202), and, although the two sets of objects were not in direct contact, this coincidence cannot be entirely discounted. Suggestions have been made, again with reference to Anglo-Saxon finds, that groups of rings may have been regarded as amuletic, or were thrown for divination (Brodribb *et al.* 1972, 109; Malim and Hines 1998, 274).

None of these ideas, rattle, bag-ring, or divining-ring, can be substantiated either by direct contextual evidence or by direct parallels, but they serve to show that a purpose connected with the magico-medical arts may be as appropriate as a purely practical one.

CF47.24

a FIG. 119. SF142. C1085. Cast leaded bronze ring of rounded D-shape, with a straight-sided rebate on the inner edge of the upright. Maximum width 32 mm, height 28 mm, 4 mm thick. The section is more or less rectangular, with the outer edge slightly convex. Maximum internal diameter 21 mm, length of rebate 10 mm, depth 2.5 mm. There are traces of wood on at least one face.

b FIG. 119. SF147. C1098. Similar ring. Width 34.5 mm, height 19.5 mm, 4.5 mm thick. Length of rebate 8 mm. Traces of wood on both faces.

c FIG. 119. SF178. C1088. Similar ring. Width 32 mm, height 29 mm, 4 mm thick. Length of rebate 9 mm. Traces of wood on both faces.

d FIG. 119. SF179. C1089. Similar ring. Width 32 mm, height 28 mm, 4.5 mm thick. Length of rebate 9.5 mm. Traces of wood on both faces.

e FIG. 119. SF180. C1090. Similar ring. Width 33 mm, height 28.5 mm, 4 mm thick. Length of rebate 8 mm. Traces of wood on both faces.

f FIG. 119. SF143. C1086. Cast round leaded bronze ring, more or less circular in section, worn very slightly thinner at one point. Internal diameter 21 mm, external diameter 31 mm, height 5 mm, 4.5 to 5 mm thick. A loop of leather was found passed round the ring, width 5.5 mm.

g FIG. 119. SF144. C1087. Similar ring. Internal diameter 22 mm, external diameter 33 mm, height 5 mm, 5.5 mm thick. Also with a fragment of a leather loop, width 6 mm.

h FIG. 119. SF181. C1083. Similar ring. Internal diameter 22 mm, external diameter 32 mm, height 5 mm, 5 mm thick. There is a scar on the surface, 6 mm across, for a leather loop.

Tray or box (FIGS 119–20, CF47.25)

A wooden object from the north-east corner of the grave is represented by some fragments of maple, at least 26 bronze studs, and fragments of repoussé-decorated bronze sheet. The number of studs is based on the number of domed centres present and is indicated in round brackets in the list below.

All these fittings, although diverse, may have come from a single wooden board (CF47.25) with three zones of decoration, consisting of strips of decorated sheet on either side of a central area fitted with a random pattern of studs, although some studs and sheet fragments were found in close association (FIG. 101). There is some possibility, however, that three separate boards were placed side by side, as there is no straightforward physical evidence to prove that both strips and studs came from one object. Some of the studs were found upside down and these must have been fitted onto the underside of the object, but they were not located in any sort of pattern that forwarded its interpretation.

All the studs were made in two pieces, a head or boss of thin repoussé-decorated sheet and a small peg made of rolled sheet that was then soldered to the underside of the boss (FIG. 119). Twenty-five of the studs, about 31 mm in diameter, have a central dome and five concentric mouldings evenly spaced out to the edge. One stud is slightly smaller, 25.5 mm in diameter, with the centre domed but now flat-topped, probably as a result of damage sustained when it was attached to the board (FIG. 119, CF47.25b). The lack of damage to the centres of the other studs suggests that the pegs may have been set into the wood before the head was soldered on. A fragment of wood with surviving stud peg suggests that the studs were fitted over convex bosses carved into the surface of the wood (FIG. 120, CF47.25j).

The best-preserved fragment of repoussé-decorated sheet is an edge piece with rows of small bosses flanking a central plain band and marginal mouldings along the outer edge (FIG. 120, CF47.25g). The bosses were formed before the metal was fitted to the wood, but a surviving fragment shows that the marginal mouldings were made by pressing the metal into pre-cut mouldings in the wood (FIG. 120, CF47.25h). The strip was fixed into position by pegs of rolled sheet metal exactly similar to those used for the studs.

Lines of small bosses decorate many other sheet-metal objects from Late Iron Age Britain, and some examples have been given under AF48, a burial in Enclosure 1 (p. 163). The studs, with their concentric circular mouldings, probably derive from La Tène scroll/tendril decoration or from pellet-in-ring ornament. 'Mock studs' are found on an Iron Age miniature votive shield from Dragonby (Knowles and May 1996, fig. 11.7, 1), and on the sheet-metal decoration from the casket in the Lexden Tumulus (Laver 1927, pl. 59, pl. 60, fig. 1, top right; Foster 1986, fig. 26).

Both the decoration and the choice of maplewood indicate that the Stanway wooden object was a high-quality item, a much more elaborate version of the boards or trays from the unsexed Phase 1 grave 280 and Phase 3 grave 118 at King Harry Lane, Verulamium (Stead and Rigby 1989, fig. 109.118, 6–7, fig. 144, 10). Another Iron Age example of a wooden object decorated with copper-alloy sheet and/or studs is a D-shaped board set with circles and rings of copper-alloy sheet in a chariot-burial at Kirkburn, Yorkshire; it was identified as a possible lid (Stead 1991, 56–7, fig. 47). The Late Iron Age Welwyn Garden City grave appears to have been divided in two by a low wooden object set with 46 or 48 composite metal studs (Stead 1967, 27–9), although this object may perhaps more pertinently be compared to the wooden object in CF47 defined by iron nails (CF47.41).

It should be stressed that, as with the above pieces, the Stanway wooden object remains enigmatic. Its full dimensions and form are uncertain, but if rectangular it would have been about 90–100 cm long and at least 40 cm wide. It lay in the north-east corner of the burial pit, resting at the west end, where it overhung the deeper part of the pit, on the flagon CF47.12. On top of it were laid the strainer bowl, the samian bowl, and the saucepan (CF47.21, CF47.1 and CF27.22 respectively). If the wood preserved beneath the metal vessels represents a single object, then the metal sheeting appears to have defined a panel at each end, with the studs set asymmetrically in the central area. Evidence that more than one object is involved may be provided by a patch of reasonably well-preserved wood beneath the strainer bowl. This clearly overlay some of the studs, which were among those found upside down (FIG. 101). It was, however, immediately adjacent to studs that were the right way up.

It is not entirely clear if the object was two- or three-dimensional. Some of the bosses lay at an angle in slightly finer soil beneath the metal vessels (FIG. 104, profile 3), which may represent all that remains of the wood and perhaps also of the straw or hay packing. However, it was only very slightly different in texture to the rest of the fill and it was not of a consistent depth, being up to 60 mm thick in places but considerably less in others.

If the wooden object had been made from a single board, then a thickness of 60 mm, or greater if compression during its decay is considered, seems unlikely. This raises the possibility that it was three-dimensional, perhaps a shallow box or line of three boxes, the corners jointed and with a body and close-fitting lid made as two separate pieces, as no hinges or nails were recovered. The possibility that three such boxes were involved is attractive, as then the top of the one that lay largely over the flagon would have been ornamented with sheet strips, and the sharp edge defined by the mouldings on the copper-alloy fragment SF130 (FIG. 101) would represent an external edge rather than an internal element of a decorative design. Such an interpretation would also accommodate the fact that some of the bosses were upside down and others not, as they may have decorated the slumped front and side boards of a box as well as its top, and been set both inside and outside the lid. A curved piece of copper alloy to the east of the group of fittings (FIG. 101, 150), which did not survive excavation as it consisted only of green-stained soil, is more comfortably seen as some sort of box fitting, perhaps a thin drop-handle, whereas the alternative possibility, that it was an item of service such as a dipper, seems unlikely given its size and the delicacy of the metal.

There are three arguments in favour of the object being a tray or trays and against it being a box or boxes. First, only one layer of maple has been identified beneath the strainer bowl or elsewhere in this area. Second, the absence of any trace of the possible contents, as it seems likely that had any organic material existed in this particular area of CF47 at least some would have been preserved along with the wood. Third, and the strongest support for identification as a tray, is a flat wooden object with exactly similar metal fittings (embossed sheet and studs with concentric mouldings) that was found in the pre-Flavian cremation 13 at Stansted, Essex. Independently of the Stanway find, this item was interpreted by Hilary Major as a tray, although the excavators preferred the more cautious 'trencher or casket'. The Stansted burial also contained a Colchester brooch, which points to a date before *c.* AD 50, making it broadly contemporary with the Doctor's burial. A second pre-Flavian cremation burial from the same site contained a few scraps of similar embossed sheet and a Colchester derivative brooch, dated to *c.* A.D. 50–70 (Major 2004, 203–6, cremations 12 and 13).

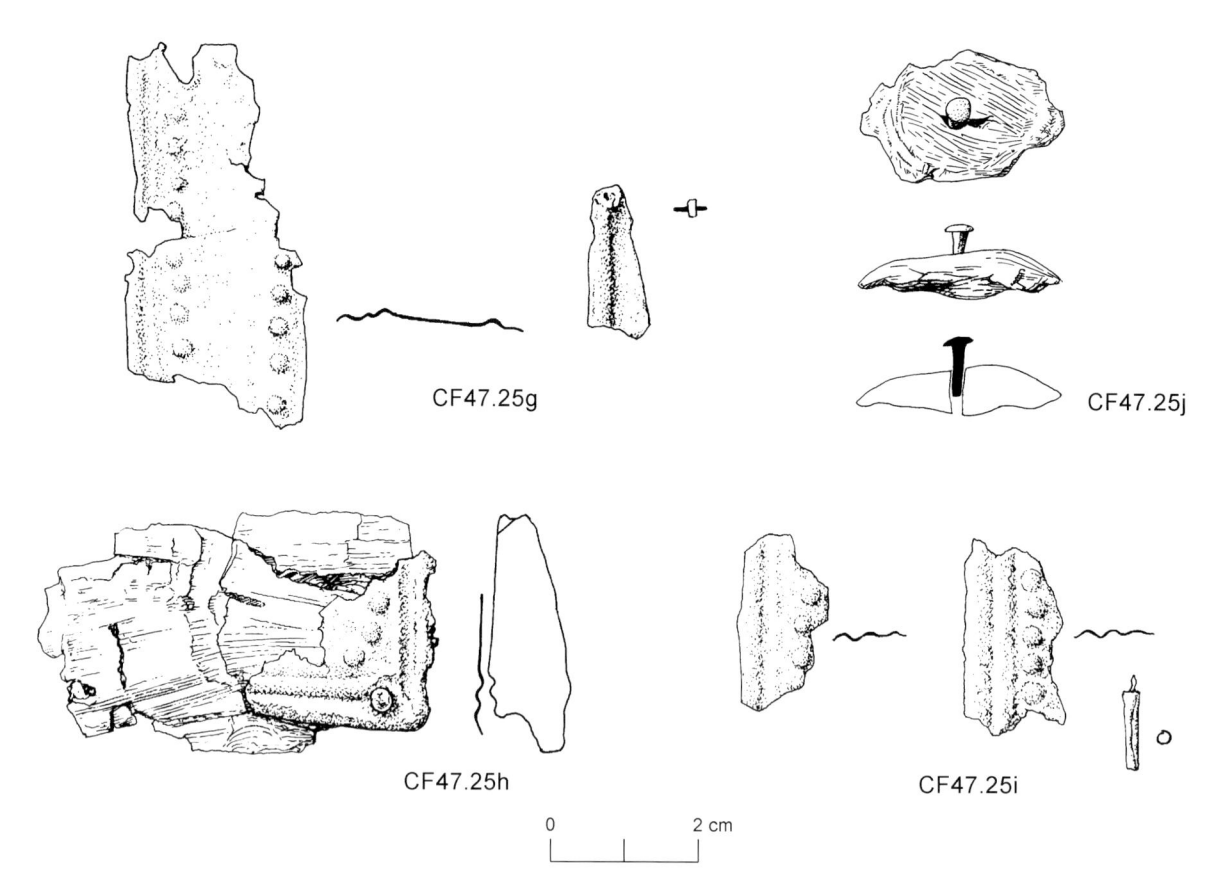

FIG. 120. Doctor's burial CF47: selection of decorated copper-alloy sheet fragments CF47.25g–i and wood fragment with peg CF47.25j from the ?tray (scale 1:1)

As with several other items in this grave, CF47.25 therefore remains quite enigmatic, with the argument in favour of a tray or trays offset by the (occasional) depth of the soil layer over much the same area as the surviving fragments of wood. Despite this ambiguity, the recovery of similar objects from the Inkwell grave BF67 and the two Stansted cremations is of considerable importance in stressing that this is almost certainly an indigenous British artefact-type, and possibly also one that may in future prove to be distinctively Catuvellaunian.

CF47.25

a FIG. 119. SF74. C976. Boss from a composite stud (7), with a lump of solder beneath the centre. Diameter 30.5 mm.

b FIG. 119. SF167. C1036. Boss from a composite stud (11). This boss is slightly different to the others, with flat-topped domed centre and only three concentric mouldings, varying in height and width. Diameter 25.5 mm, height 3 mm. The flat top of the dome may be damage caused when attaching the peg to the ?tray, rather than deliberate. The shaft is rolled; length 11 mm.

c FIG. 119. SF187. C1045. Boss from a composite stud (14), with part of a rolled shaft and a lump of solder beneath the centre. Diameter 31.5 mm.

d FIG. 119. SF163. C1046. Boss from a composite stud (15), part missing, with a rolled peg. Diameter 31 mm.

e FIG. 119. SF135. C1049. Boss from a composite stud (17) and a rolled peg, length 11 mm. Also fragments of wood and part of another rolled peg. One piece of wood has a formless fragment of copper alloy set into it, presumably part of a peg.

f FIG. 119. SF177. C1063. Boss from a composite stud (23), with a rolled peg. The top of the peg has a lump of solder attached. Diameter 31.5 mm.

g FIG. 120, SF140. C1066. One large fragment of decorated sheet and eleven small. Also small fragments of wood. Only the large fragment and a small piece with a rolled peg are illustrated. The upper end of this peg sits well above the sheeting. Only a small length of a finished edge survives on the large fragment, but it is probable that the width was not much greater. Neither end is original. Length 49 mm, width 24.5 mm.

h FIG. 120. SF130. C1061. Many fragments of wood and eight fragments of sheet, with marginal mouldings and rows of repoussé dots. One piece of wood has an attachment peg fixed into it. The two larger pieces of sheeting are illustrated, *in situ* on a piece of wood. One is a corner piece, with a peg in the corner. Maximum dimensions of the wood 55 mm by 31 mm, 17 mm thick. The underside is not original, but roughened with decay. The upper face shows clearly the grooves into which the thin metal sheeting was pressed when it was attached. Both wood and metal are bent, showing the force of compression and collapse in the grave.

i FIG. 120. SF172. C1060. Three fragments of sheet and a rolled peg. Two fragments and the peg are illustrated. Both have a surviving edge. Surviving lengths 24 and 23.5 mm, widths 13 and 11.5 mm respectively. The peg is 12 mm long.

j FIG. 120. SF24. C913. Wood with attachment peg. The peg is well preserved. Unlike the others, it is conventionally made with a square-section shaft and slightly domed sub-circular head. Length 8 mm.

SF19. C908. Wood from behind the composite studs. One fragment has a rolled peg, 8 mm long, passing through it.

SF26. C917. Boss from composite stud (1) with damaged edge.

SF47. C949. Fragment of a boss from a composite stud (2), possibly part of an incomplete one listed below, although no joins were noted.

SF59. C961. Composite stud (3), part missing, and including part of a rolled peg. Also fragments of wood.

SF60. C962. Most of a boss from a composite stud (4) in four fragments. Also two fragments from another boss (5). Also fragments of wood.

SF61. C963. Part of the boss (in two fragments) from a composite stud (6), and the rolled peg remaining fixed in a fragment of wood.

SF75. C977. Rolled peg.

SF132. C1055. Five fragments of sheet, with organic material. The two largest pieces show rows of bosses but no mouldings. Lengths 28 and 24 mm, widths 22 and 11 mm respectively. A small hole in the largest may be for an attachment peg.

SF137a. C1067. A tiny fragment of a domed centre filled with lead solder, and with a small fragment of plain copper-alloy sheet across the top. Found in association with small fragments of decorated sheet.

SF137b. C1067. Many small fragments of wood and at least 25 of copper-alloy sheet, some with marginal mouldings and at least one row of small bosses. The largest piece is 27 mm long by 15 mm wide. Also two rolled pegs. Found in association with a tiny fragment of a composite stud.

SF148. C1050. Small fragment of a boss from a composite stud, probably part of an incomplete one, although no joins were noted. Also a fragment of wood.

SF149. C1042. Fifteen fragments of sheet, mostly small and plain. The largest, in two pieces, has marginal mouldings and a row of bosses. It measures 32.5 mm long by 21 mm wide.

SF159. C1041. Fragments of sheet, including part of an edge with marginal mouldings. Length 41 mm, width 28 mm.

SF160. C1040. Fragment of sheet, length 28 mm, width 24 mm.

SF162. C1052. Boss from a composite stud (19), edge damaged, with rolled peg fragment and wood fragments.

SF164. C1053. Rolled peg.

SF165a. C1069. Four fragments of a boss from a composite stud (26). Also a fragment of flat sheet, 12 by 10 mm, with 7 mm of a straight edge surviving and broken across a hole 3 mm in diameter.

SF165b. C1069. Fragment of flat sheet, 12 by 10 mm, with 7 mm of a straight edge surviving and broken across a hole 3 mm in diameter. Found in association with a composite stud.

SF166. C1031. Many small fragments of a boss from a composite stud (8) including a domed centre and a fragment of solder.

SF168. C1064. Four fragments of a boss from a composite stud (24).

SF169. C1062. Most of the disc from a boss from a composite stud (22), and a rolled peg.

SF171. C1035. Three fragments of a boss from a composite stud (10).

SF173. C1039. Rolled peg.

SF174. C1054. Boss from a composite stud (20) with part of a rolled peg and the wood from around it. Also other fragments of wood.

SF175a C1065. Most of a boss from a composite stud (25), and a small part of another (possibly part of SF61, but not a good join). Found in association with a small fragment of plain copper-alloy sheet.

SF175b. C1065. A small fragment, 10 by 8 mm, of plain copper-alloy sheet. Found in association with two composite stud fragments.

SF176. C1072. One piece of sheet in three fragments, with marginal mouldings and a row of bosses. Length 36 mm, width 14.5 mm.

SF182. C1070. Six very small fragments of sheet, some with traces of small bosses. SF150. C1068 F47. Four small fragments with rows of small bosses. The two largest are slightly convex in section from distortion under pressure in the ground.

SF183. C1059. Seven small fragments of sheet with marginal mouldings, and part of a rolled peg, 9 mm long. The largest piece measures 14 mm long by 10 mm wide.

SF185. C1058. Four small fragments of sheet (two in two pieces), with marginal mouldings and a row of raised bosses. The two largest pieces measure 15 mm long by 9 mm wide, and 18 mm long by 10 mm wide.

SF186. C1057. Boss from a composite stud (21) in five fragments.

SF188. C1047. Boss from a composite stud (16), the edge damaged, and a rolled peg.

SF189. C1037. Three fragments of a boss from a composite stud (12).

SF190 C1034. Boss fragment from a composite stud (9), with the full diameter present but much of the disc missing.

SF191. C1038. Four fragments of a boss from a composite stud (13).

SF192. C1051. Five fragments of a boss from a composite stud (18) and two fragments of wood.

SF193. C1048. Rolled peg.

The surgical instruments (FIGS 121–7, CF47.26–39)

By Ralph Jackson

The following descriptions combine the results of detailed optical examination with information revealed by scientific analysis (X-radiography and qualitative X-ray fluorescence (XRF) analysis of the uncleaned surfaces, by Susan La Niece, British Museum, Department of Scientific Research, Project 6997). A report by Nigel Meeks and Caroline Cartwright (British Museum, Department of Scientific Research, Project 6953) on the scientific examination of the textile remains attached to instrument nos 5 and 10 is in Chapter 5, pages 350–2.

All the instruments are corroded, encrusted and brittle (FIG. 127), but their original surfaces have almost invariably been preserved, even if they are in many cases obscured by encrusted corrosion products. As is often the case with iron objects, severe corrosion has expanded the depleted metal, resulting in bursting and fissuring of the corrosion products. In consequence, it has proved very difficult, even with the use of X-radiography, to establish the precise original dimensions of certain parts of some of the objects. This applies especially to the handles and stems of the iron instruments CF47.26, CF47.27, CF47.30, and CF47.33–CF47.36. The need to provide accurate drawings and measurements for the manufacture of a set of reconstructed replicas ensured a particularly detailed and considered examination of the instruments, while the making and handling of the reconstructions gave insights into the design and manufacture of the originals.

Frequent reference is made to the *De medicina* of A. Cornelius Celsus. It is particularly appropriate to do so, partly because the work is an invaluable source of information on Greco-Roman surgery and surgical instruments, but also because its date of composition, during the reign of Tiberius, is close to the date of the CF47 interment.

The detailed catalogue of the instruments follows the more general description and discussion of their form, use and context.

Scalpels (FIG. 121, CF47.26–7)

In their precise form, these two instruments are unparalleled, yet with their distinctive blades they are clearly identifiable as scalpels (FIG. 121, CF47.26–7). Their blades, like the majority of surviving Roman examples (*see* for example Künzl 1983a, fig. 56; Jackson 1988a, pl. 28), are of a deep, bellied form, although they complement rather than duplicate one another, for one has a convex cutting edge and the other a straight leading edge. In contrast to most Roman scalpels, however, they are single-piece iron instruments. From the 1st century A.D. onwards, Roman scalpels acquired a standardised overall form comprising a copper-alloy handle, generally combining a block-like grip with a leaf-shaped blunt dissector terminal, and an iron or steel blade (Jackson 1986, 132–7; 1990b, 14, fig. 1; Krug 1993; Künzl 1996, 2447–50). The few

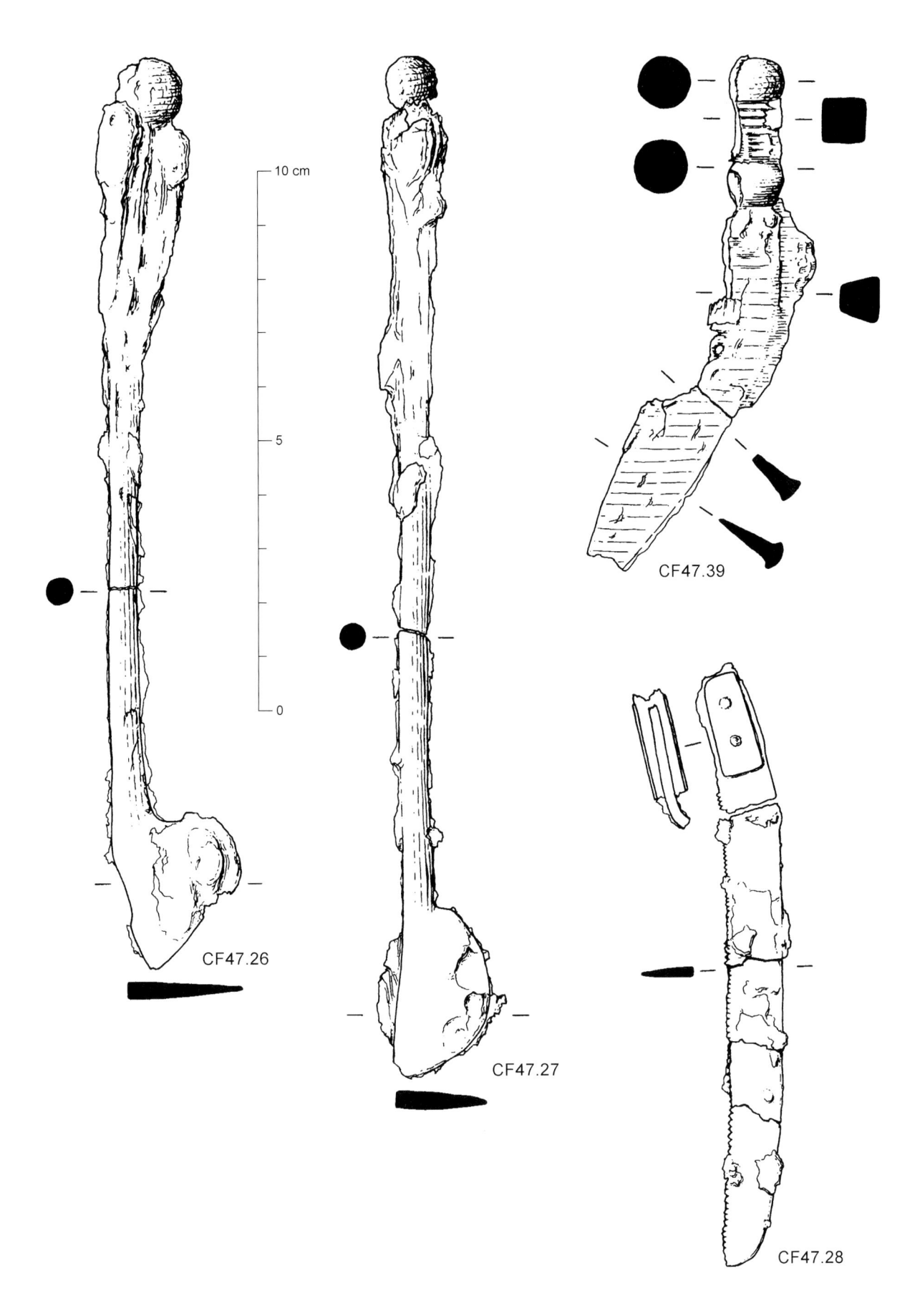

FIG. 121. Doctor's burial CF47: iron scalpels CF47.26 and 27, iron saw with composite handle CF47.28, and iron knife CF47.39 (scale 1:1)

known Roman examples of single-piece iron scalpels (*e.g.* Künzl 2002, 28–9, Taf. 18, B9–10; Krug 1985, 81, fig. 22, a2) are morphologically identical to their copper-alloy and iron counterparts, and do not resemble the form of the Stanway scalpels.

The handles of the Stanway scalpels, at approximately 135 mm and approximately 155 mm, are also longer than the Roman handles that are typically around 100 mm in length. Although this would have required (or enabled) a difference in their manipulation, the point should not be overstressed, for the Roman handles sometimes accommodated blades with an elongated stem (*e.g.* several from the Domus 'del chirurgo' find at Rimini; Ortalli 2000, 525–6), resulting in an instrument of similar overall dimensions to the Stanway scalpels. Whether their form was advantageous or simply different, the Stanway scalpels, nevertheless, would have suffered a slight disadvantage in comparison to the Roman instruments. Namely, that when their blade was broken or whetted beyond use, the whole instrument would have required re-forging, whereas the Roman operator, with his composite copper-alloy and iron instrument, needed only to remove the iron blade from its handle and replace it with another.

Virtually nothing is known of pre-Roman surgical instrumentation in Britain, and very little elsewhere. However, Ernst Künzl (1988; 1995) has consolidated the information on finds from Celtic Europe, most of which relates to trepanation. Of particular importance are three grave finds of 3rd to 2nd century B.C. date from München-Obermenzing, Bavaria (De Navarro 1955), Batina/Kis Köszeg, Croatia (Sudhoff 1913) and Galaţii Bistriţei, Romania (Bologa *et al.* 1956). Although the instruments in these graves are a couple of centuries earlier than the Stanway find, their general appearance, especially those in the Batina assemblage, is very similar to that of the Stanway scalpels, notably their manufacture as single-piece iron instruments with long, slender, gently curved stems, some with a bulbous knobbed finial (Sudhoff 1913, 596, fig. 1; Künzl 1995, 235, fig. 4), and it is possible that the maker of the Stanway iron instruments was following an established Iron Age tradition.

Saw (FIG. 121, CF47.28)

The Roman surgical saw (*serrula*) was an instrument of bone surgery (Jackson 1994, 195). However, its use was circumscribed and was not always approved by medical writers (Galen XVIII 331K; Paul of Aegina VI, xc; *P.Ryl.3* 529 (Marganne-Mélard 1987, 410)). Celsus specifies use of the *serrula* in only one operation, that for amputation of a gangrenous limb (Celsus, *De med.* VII, 33, 2), the earliest surviving account of the operation. Unfortunately he gives no description of the size or appearance of the saw. Within reason, any saw with close teeth would have sufficed, including the finer-bladed range of craftsmen's handsaws or frame-saws, which were normally made of iron and wood. However, none has yet been found in a secure context with surgical instruments, and the Stanway saw is a *unicum* (FIG. 121, CF47.28). In fact, its blade is well designed for bone surgery and bears some points of similarity with surgical and amputation saws of more recent times. With 14 teeth/cm, it is rather finer than the Larry's 'Keyhole' finger saw, included in the *c.* 1955 catalogue of the celebrated surgical instrument manufacturer Charles Thackray, which has approximately 10 teeth/cm, but the blade size and form are very similar (Thackray *c.* 1955, 464, B2489). In the same catalogue is a version of the classic amputation saw (*ibid.* 463, B2484) introduced by the disconcertingly named Dr Richard Butcher in 1851 (Bennion 1979, 23–5). This evolved from the amputation saws of Rennaissance and medieval Europe (*see*, *e.g.*, the woodcut showing a leg amputation in the *Feldtbuch der Wundtarztney* of Hans von Gerssdorff, published in Strasbourg in 1517), which were themselves an adaptation of the craftsman's bow- or frame-saw, used throughout the classical world and earlier. These are very likely the kind of saw used in Celsus' leg amputation. In size and form a relatively large frame-saw, they are very different from the rather diminutive Stanway saw, which was probably not designed for such substantial surgery. The amputation of fingers or toes may be envisaged, as also the division of slender bones like ribs, and the trimming of projecting splintered bone in complex fractures, although all these operations might alternatively be performed with bone chisels (Celsus, *De med.* VIII, 10, 7; Paul of Aegina VI, xliii, xciii; Galen II 687K). However, partly because the Stanway saw lacks a close parallel

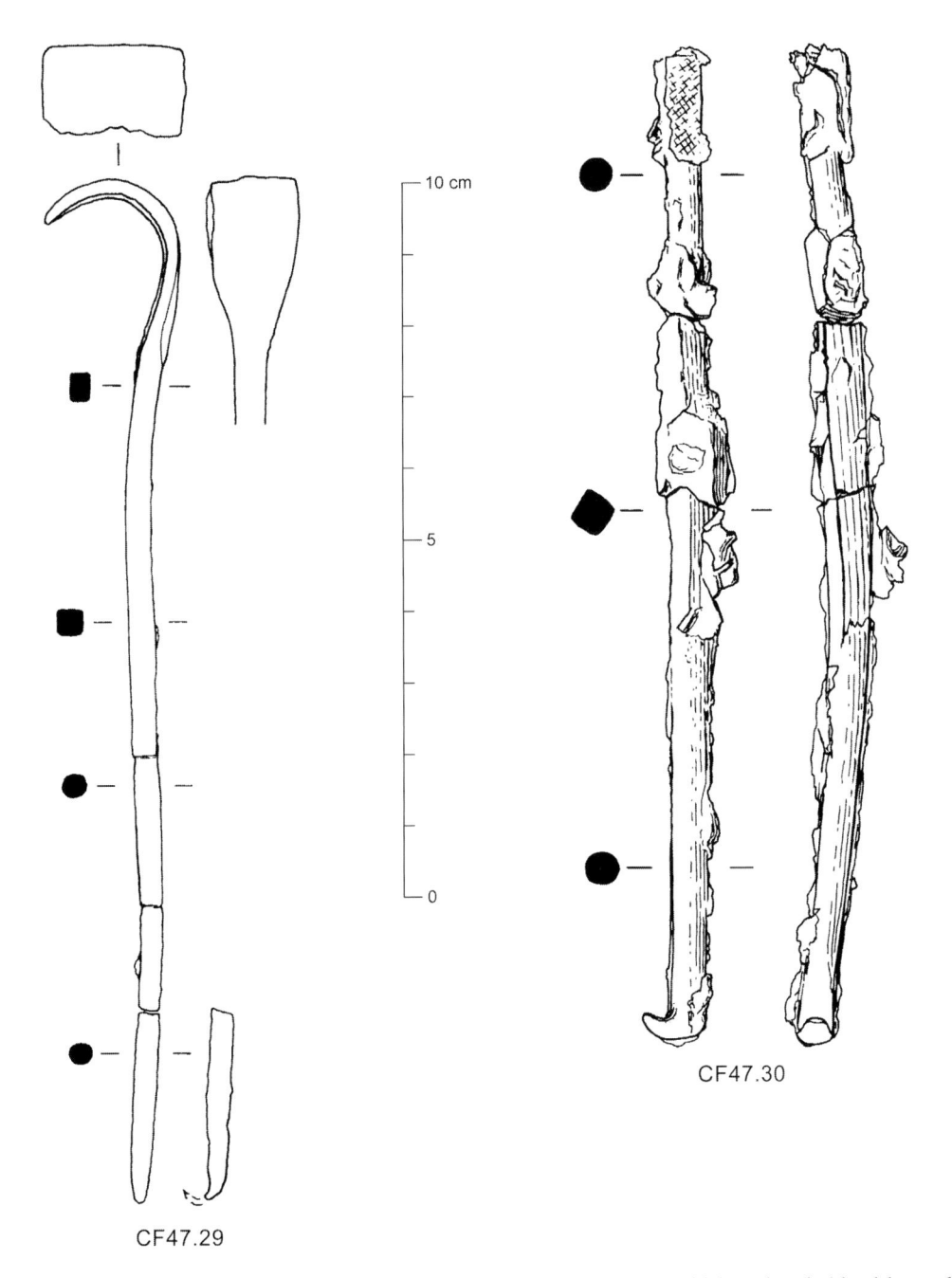

FIG. 122. Doctor's burial CF47: copper-alloy combined sharp and blunt hook (double-ended retractor) CF47.29, iron combined sharp and blunt hook (double-ended retractor) CF47.30 (scale 1:1)

and partly because the evidence implies that individual surgical instruments of the Roman period might be used for a much wider range of surgical interventions than is normal today, we should be cautious of attempting to identify too specifically any perceived function or functions for the saw. Certainly we should not exclude the possibility that it may also have been used for trepanation or other surgery of the skull. In this context, it is important to note the instrumentation in the La Tène C graves at München-Obermenzing, Batina/Kis Köszeg, and Galaţii Bistriţei. Each contains a tanged iron saw with a small blade and fine teeth, and these have been identified as trepanning saws (Brongers 1969; Künzl 1988; Künzl 1995). All differ from each other, and none is the same as the Stanway blade, which is longer than them, but all may share a common function. In overall form and size, the three Celtic finds are similar to the small-bladed Hey's saws, which became an integral part of trepanning sets, following their introduction in the early 19th century (Bennion 1979, 25–6, pls 13–14). In fact, Sir William

Hey had merely re-introduced a form of skull saw that already had a long history in medieval Europe. These saws typically had a small short blade with fine teeth on a convex or straight edge, mounted on the end of a handle, an arrangement well suited to cutting the convex surface of the skull. Although the blade of the Stanway saw is, overall, very slightly concave, it, too, seems well adapted to such use.

Hooks (FIG. 122, CF47.29–30)

Sharp hooks were an integral part of the Roman surgeon's *instrumentarium*, one of the basic tools of surgery, and they are found in most surviving ancient sets of instruments (Künzl 1983a; Jackson 1995, table 2). Blunt hooks, although not uncommon, are far less frequently found and correspondingly less frequently referred to in the ancient medical texts (Jackson 1994, 172–4). The commonest variety of sharp hook was a single hook on the end of a slender stem, which usually had a moulded handle finial to ensure a secure grip (Jackson 1990b, fig. 2, 1–3). Sometimes the hook was bifurcated to provide a broader retraction (*ibid.*, fig. 2, 4–5). Sometimes, too, as with the present examples, a dual-purpose instrument was made, combining a sharp hook with a blunt hook, one at each end of the stem (*ibid.*, fig. 2, 6). The combination of a sharp hook and a blunt hook in one instrument was a normal Roman economy, but it would also have enabled the operator to switch quickly, if the need arose, from sharp to blunt retraction. Neither of the Stanway combined hooks, however, is of normal Roman form. The bronze example (FIG. 122, CF47.29) is atypical both in the lack of decoration on its bipartite round- and rectangular-sectioned stem and in the idiosyncratic form and greater than normal breadth of its blunt hook, although the latter feature is broadly paralleled by three probable retractors from Pompeii (Jackson 1990b, fig. 2, 9; Bliquez 1994, 214–17, Ill. 228, A53–55, and Ill. 231, 53, 55). The iron example (FIG. 122, CF47.30) is unusual simply because very few identifiable instruments of iron have survived, but there is a copper-alloy blunt hook of similar size and form, from Springhead, Kent (Jackson 1990b, fig. 2, 8). With its lightly sinuous stem and its combination of round- and rectangular-sectioned grip, the Stanway iron hook resembles its bronze counterpart. Furthermore, in the provision of a variety of broad and blunt hooks, the two instruments complement one another, and it is quite conceivable that they were made together. Certainly, they combine economy of instrumentation with versatility of use.

In Celsus' *De medicina*, the applications of the sharp hook were in retracting the margins of wounds and incisions (VII, 12, 5; VII, 16, 2; VII, 31, 2), fixing margins and the underlying tissue or structure (VI, 6, 9C; VII, 20, 4 and 5), and seizing and raising tissue and small structures for excision, as for example, in tonsilectomy and delicate eye operations (VII, 7, 4B, 5 and 7C; VII, 12, 2; VII, 28, 2; VII, 30, 3B). The blunt hook was advocated for retracting the margins of a scalp incision (VII, 7, 15E), extracting a foreign body from the ear (VI, 7, 9A–B), and raising and protecting veins, arteries and sinews (VII, 5, 1C; VII, 31, 3). Celsus also gives a good description of the respective roles of the sharp and blunt hook used in combination in the operation to excise varicose veins (VII, 31, 2–3).

?Retractor (FIG. 123, CF47.31)

This distinctive object, visually the most striking instrument in the kit, is at present unparalleled in the surviving ancient *instrumentaria* (FIG. 123, CF47.31). From its mode of manufacture, it was clearly intended to be a spring instrument, with arms that could be compressed to reduce the distance between the everted tips (which are pointed but not sharp) and then released to allow the points to expand again. The replica functions in this way and permits a reduction to approximately 55 mm between the tips when the arms are fully compressed. The span returns to approximately 70 mm when the arms are released, and the pressure of the spring feels sufficient to have enabled the retraction of flesh. The instrument resembles to some extent several modern retractors (*see* for example Thackray *c.* 1955, 90, G604, G606), but identification as a wound dilator or retractor is by no means secure, for the elongated form of the everted tips is not particularly felicitous, and would have required a manipulation through 90 degrees within the wound or incision in order to achieve a retraction of the margins.

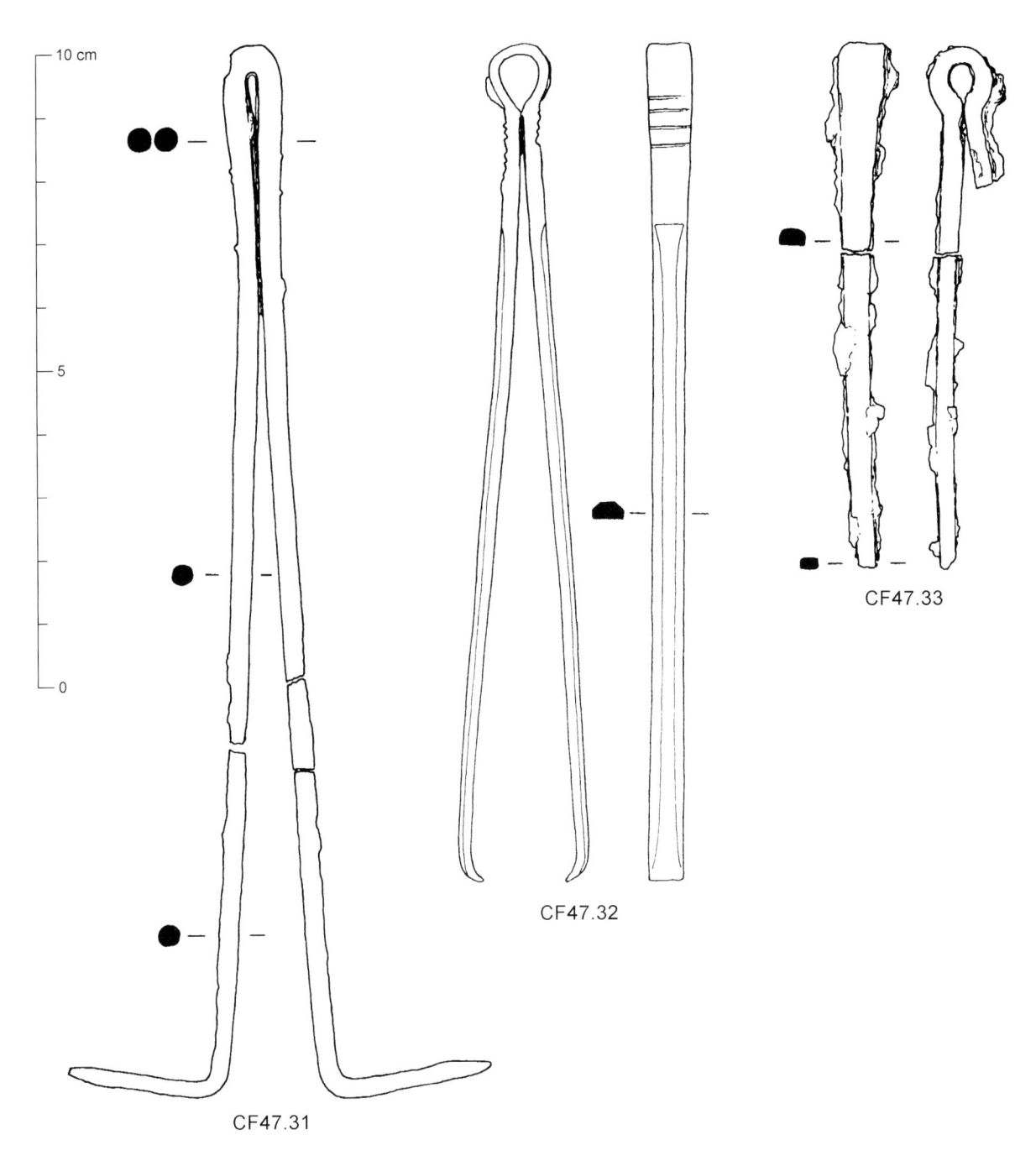

FIG. 123. Doctor's burial CF47: copper-alloy ?retractor CF47.31, copper-alloy smooth-jawed fixation forceps CF47.32, and iron forceps/tweezers CF47.33 (scale 1:1)

Forceps (FIG. 123, CF47.32–3)

In its overall length, in the form of the jaws and in the careful chamfering of the outer edges of the arms, CF47.32 (FIG. 123) closely resembles Roman examples of the smooth-jawed fixation forceps (Bliquez 1994, 172–7, nos 247–66; Jackson 1990b, fig. 3, 3). There were two principal modes of manufacture of Roman spring forceps. One, the simpler type, was formed by bending a strip of metal at its centre (*e.g.* Bliquez 1994, nos 253–5, 260, 265–9). The other type was made by cutting a bar of metal up the centre as far as the point where the decorative finial was to be worked (*e.g.* Bliquez 1994, nos 246–52, 256–7, 261–4). The second type almost invariably, and the first type often, has a distinctive angular shoulder near the top of the arms. This feature is absent on the Stanway bronze forceps (CF47.32), although the point at which it would be expected is marked by a simple light groove and by the start of the chamfering of the arms. A more fundamental difference is the presence of a looped head, which is characteristic of Roman toilet instruments, but almost never occurs on Roman surgical tools. By contrast, loops are present on a much higher proportion of the La Tène C medical instruments (Künzl 1995, figs 3–4). The impression, therefore, is of an instrument that combines features of both Roman and Iron Age origin.

Roman spring forceps, designed primarily for surgical usage, may be differentiated from tweezers, whose function was principally in toiletry: tweezers almost invariably had a loop for suspension, while forceps almost invariably did not; tweezers rarely exceed 100 mm in length, while forceps almost never measure less than that; and the jaws of tweezers are generally smooth, broad and in-turned (for epilation), while the jaw forms of forceps are much more varied. That is not to say, of course, that objects that we classify as spring forceps were not sometimes used purely in toiletry, nor that tweezers might not sometimes find medical or surgical usage (on this question of overlaps, *see* for example Jackson 1994, table 3; and Jackson 2002, esp. 89–90 and 93).

Using the above criteria, the tendency would be to identify the iron object CF47.33 (FIG. 123) as a tweezers since, when complete, it is unlikely to have exceeded 100 mm in length, and it has a looped head. However, it would appear that the jaws were originally of pointed form, suggesting a surgical function. In any case, its association with other tools of surgery implies that it, too, was a surgical tool or had surgical applications, irrespective of whether it is termed a tweezers or a forceps. Although the great majority of surviving identifiable Roman spring forceps are made of copper alloy, examples of iron have been found, as in the Rimini assemblage (inv. 184312; Jackson 2003, 317). However, like forceps CF47.32 and most other instruments in the Stanway kit, the form of CF47.33 differs from Roman examples and may instead, or in addition, be following an Iron Age tradition. Furthermore, as with the two scalpels and the two hooks, the different jaw forms of the two forceps complement one another, and their shared features of a looped head and chamfered arms indicate that they may have been made at the same time and place.

Spring forceps were general-purpose surgical tools (Jackson 1986, 137–9; 1994, 174–5), used in place of finger and thumb, and many different applications may be envisaged for the two Stanway examples. The smooth-jawed fixation forceps is the commonest Roman type, used, as the name implies, for fixation and dissection, as, for example, in surgical epilation, the operation to remove ingrowing eyelashes (Celsus, *De med.* VII, 7, 8; Paul of Aegina VI, xiii), or in the treatment of an ulcerated foreskin (Celsus, *De med.* VI, 18, 3). The addition of a sliding lock-ring, lacking from the Stanway forceps (although it may have been made of organic material), allowed secure and protracted fixation when required. Pointed-jawed forceps, like CF47.33, were similarly versatile in fine surgical work, but were often specified for the removal of bone splinters, as, for example, in fracture of the nose or in tooth extraction, and in the removal of foreign bodies from the ear (Celsus, *De med.* VII, 12, 1D; Paul of Aegina VI, xxiv).

Needles (FIG. 124, CF47.34–6)

Despite the care with which the assemblage from grave CF47 was excavated, the brittle corroded nature of the metal instruments was such that the very slender ends of CF47.34–6 could not be retrieved intact (FIG. 124). The loss of instrument tips is a quite common occurrence and very frustrating, too, since it is precisely that part that identifies the function of the tool. Quite often, however, the form of the handle and stem is sufficiently distinctive to allow a more or less certain identification of the instrument. To an extent that is true of CF47.34–6: their solid handles and tapered stems conform, generally, to the appearance of un-eyed needles in sets of Roman instruments (*cf.* Jackson 1990b, fig. 4, nos 1, 4, 5), and their pointed tip, if not their precise original length, can be restored with some confidence. Alternatives should be considered, and it is possible that CF47.35 might have terminated in a sharp hook. However, the square cross-section at the broken end of CF47.34 and the shortness of CF47.36 would seem to exclude the possibility that they were hooks, and, in view of the similarity in appearance of the three, it is preferable to regard them all as uneyed handled

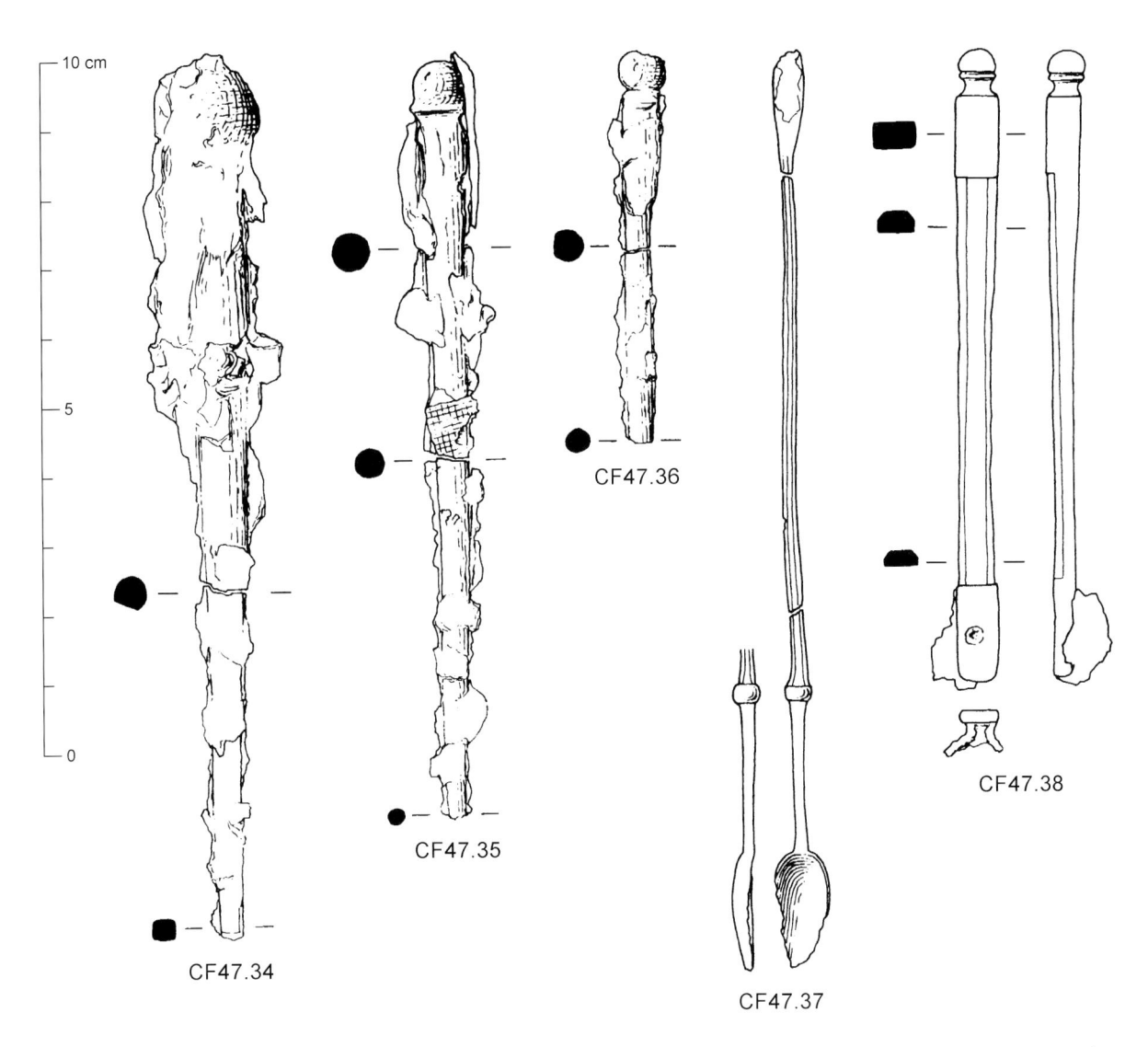

FIG. 124. Doctor's burial CF47: iron handled needles CF47.34–36, copper-alloy scoop probe CF47.37, and copper-alloy handle CF47.38 (scale 1:1)

needles. Indeed, like the scalpels, hooks and forceps, the three ?needles seem to have been carefully selected as a graded sub-set, comprising a large example with a square-sectioned tip and medium and small examples with a round-sectioned tip.

With their knobbed finials and swollen handles the ?needles are clearly related to the Stanway scalpels (FIG. 121, CF47.26–7), and they share the same general parallels cited for those, but their overall form is as yet unmatched in ancient *instrumentaria*. Roman surgical needles may be divided into two principal categories depending on whether or not they were eyed (Jackson 1994, 176–7). The eyed variety comprised both domestic needles for stitching the end of a bandage (*e.g.* Celsus, *De med.* V, 26, 24B) and surgical needles for suturing, ligating and passing a thread (*e.g. ibid.*, VII, 16, 4–5; VII, 7, 11; VII, 25, 3). Although the domestic type has been found in surgical kits (*e.g.* Künzl 1983a, fig. 11, no. 10, from Kallion, Greece; fig. 75, no. 9, from Nijmegen, Netherlands; fig. 84, from Morlungo, Italy: Bliquez 1994, pl. 26, fig. 1, from Pompeii), no certain example of an eyed surgical needle has yet been recognised, probably because they were very thin iron or steel instruments that have not survived.

The surviving needles in Roman instrument sets are generally of the second variety, namely un-eyed handled needles, and they comprise not single-piece iron examples, but single-piece copper-alloy needles or iron needle points mounted on copper-alloy handles. The former include both the distinctive instrument identified as the needle specified for couching cataract

(Feugère *et al.* 1985; 1988; Jackson 1986, 151–2), and a simpler variety of needle or needle-probe, probably used for a wider range of surgical interventions (*e.g.* Künzl 1983a, fig. 75, no. 10; Jackson 1997a, fig. 1). The latter similarly consist of a distinctive type, which has a slender copper-alloy centre grip with a socket for an iron or steel needle at one or, usually, both ends (Jackson 1986, 151–4, table 4, fig. 3, no. 24; Bliquez 1994, 165–6, Ill. 128–32, nos 221–30), and a more variable type which has a shorter, thicker copper-alloy handle with a single socket for an iron or steel needle (*e.g.* Künzl 1983a, fig. 36, no. 31, fig. 37, nos 32–9; Feugère *et al.* 1988, fig. 23).

Clearly, whatever the type of handle, it was the form of the needle that determined usage, and several of the Roman types of handled needle would appear to have been interchangeable and potentially usable in a wide variety of operations, whatever might have been their original or primary intended function. Thus, although the Stanway ?needles differ from those in use by Roman healers in their single-piece iron manufacture and in the details of the appearance of their handles, there is nevertheless no particular reason to believe that their surgical applications were fundamentally different. Those applications, as described by Roman medical authors, were principally in dissection, but also included, for example, the perforation of pustules, puncturing of skin and haemorrhoids, raising the skin of the eyelid, and transfixing small tumours on the eyeball (Celsus, *De med.* V, 28, 4D; V, 28, 19C; VI, 18, 9C; VII, 7, 8F; VII, 7, 12). In addition, needles were used as fine heated cauteries for operations on the eye and ear (*e.g. ibid.* VII, 7, 8B; VII, 7, 10; VII, 8, 3).

Scoop probe (FIG. 124, CF47.37)

An integral component of Roman *instrumentaria* was one or more probes which, by the Imperial era, were made in a range of standardised forms (Jackson 1986, 129, fig. 4, and 156–8). Often, as at Nea Paphos, Cyprus (Michaelides 1984, fig. 1, 7–13), it is evident that one of each type had been selected by the healer to cover all eventualities. The two most common varieties were the spatula probe and the scoop probe, and the Stanway scoop probe (FIG. 124, CF47.37) is widely paralleled. In fact, it is the only one of the Stanway instruments that is of standard Roman type. In the characteristic form of its long-stemmed, fragmentary scoop, it is closely related to several examples from Augst, Switzerland, Riha's Löffelsonden Variante F (Riha 1986, 70–1, 161, Taf. 46, nos 496–506), found in contexts dated from the 1st to 3rd centuries A.D., and is also closely paralleled by an example from London (Wheeler 1930, pl. 37, 7).

Most Roman probes were multi-purpose tools combining two functional ends, and they were recommended for a wide range of surgical and medical tasks, from the elevation of cartilage in a broken nose to the application of medicaments to the eyeball (*e.g.* Celsus, *De med.* VIII, 5, 11; VI, 6, 11). Like the spatula probe, the scoop probe served both as a toilet implement and a medical instrument. In medicine, they were used primarily in pharmacy, in the preparation and application of medicaments, but the scoop also had medical and surgical applications, for example as a curette, as a director, or in the removal of foreign bodies. The olivary terminal was recommended as a small cautery, as a probe for exploring large cavities, and, wrapped in wool, as a plug for occluding the nostril.

Unidentified implement (FIG. 124, CF47.38)

In the form, decor and method of manufacture, the handle of this composite bronze and iron implement (FIG. 124, CF47.38) is typically Roman, yet a parallel has proved elusive. The operative part was evidently the riveted and soldered iron component, of which such a small part survives that it is impossible to predict its original form. Other than scalpels and handled needles, one of the composite bronze and iron instruments quite frequently encountered in Roman sets of medical instruments is the bone chisel, which commonly has an iron or steel handle mounted on a copper-alloy handle. However, the slender handle of the Stanway implement and the splayed, sheet metal form of its iron component would seem to preclude such an identification. Considering the intrinsic evidence of the implement and its context within the *instrumentarium*, two possible identifications are a spoon or some kind of specialised blade.

Knife (FIG. 121, CF47.39)

This object (FIG. 121, CF47.39) was not originally regarded as part of the *instrumentarium* (it was initially so corroded that it was thought to be a nail), but its presence in the grave would seem to relate it to the other instruments, and, as a knife or razor (as opposed to a scalpel) in a surgical kit it is not without parallel (*see*, for example, Künzl 1983a, 72–3, fig. 46, no. 2; 80–5, fig. 58, no. 8; 117–18, fig. 92, no. 6). Furthermore, its knobbed and moulded handle finial is directly comparable to those of the scalpels and ?handled needles (nos 1–2 and 9–11), while its blade form complements rather than duplicates that of the two scalpels.

As with others of the Stanway instruments, the precise form of the knife is idiosyncratic and difficult to parallel. Although there is a general similarity in overall form to Manning's Type 7–9 knives, which have a down-turned blade (Manning 1985, 109, fig. 28, 111–13, esp. Type 8, pl. 54, Q25–Q28), none is a close parallel and none is as diminutive as the Stanway knife. Manning regards his Type 8 as an early Roman form, but, as Nina Crummy has pointed out (pers. comm.), the fact that all of his examples come from Hod Hill leaves open the possibility that it is a native British form.

Celsus, in a number of places, refers to a surgical knife as distinct from a scalpel (Jackson 1994, 170–1), and there is no inherent reason why this knife could not have been a purpose-made surgical knife. Alternatively, it could have been a non-surgical knife or razor incorporated into the *instrumentarium*. Again, Celsus provides an example, in the form of the razor (*novacula*) recommended for use in cases of alopecia (Celsus, *De med.* VI, 4, 3), and shaving prior to a surgical incision is likely to have been common practice, too.

Discussion

The discovery of the set of medical instruments in grave CF47 was a find of considerable importance (FIGS 125–7; Jackson 1997b; 1997c; 1998). Hitherto, no certain set had been excavated from the province of Roman Britain: the small group of instruments in the National Museum of Scotland, said to have been found at Cramond (Gilson 1983), may indeed have been a set (or part-set) that belonged together, but their British provenance is by no means secure, while the group of instruments said to have been 'uncovered south of the main east–west road at Corbridge' (Gilson 1981, 5) is unverifiable, and the published instruments lack any site context. Furthermore, *contra* Gilson (*ibid.*), the latter include only four diagnostically medical tools — three scalpel handles and one arm of a smooth-jawed fixation forceps.

The Stanway find is, therefore, the earliest known set of medical instruments from Britain. It is also one of the earliest *instrumentaria* from anywhere in the Roman world. While individual instruments have been found in 1st century B.C. and earlier contexts (Künzl 1996), it is not until the 1st century A.D. that sets of Roman instruments have been found in securely dated contexts (Künzl 1983a, 12–14, 88–90, 105, 106–7, sets from Pompeii, Cologne, Luzzi and Morlungo). That is not to say, of course, that surgery was not performed long before that time, but that some of the basic instruments used probably had not yet acquired distinctive forms, and they may therefore be hard to differentiate (if they differ at all) from the contemporaneous domestic implements and craftsmen's tools. Perhaps, too, a greater proportion of the early instruments were made of non-metallic materials which have not survived. Context is the key, as at Stanway, where the association of the instruments in a securely dated, undisturbed grave provided optimum conditions for recognition following their sensitive and painstaking excavation. Had the saw, ?handled needles, ?retractor, or iron forceps/tweezers been casually found, or even excavated as single, unassociated finds, it is most unlikely that any medical function would have been ascribed to them and, even if the suggestion had been made, it would have been incapable of proof. However, while valuing the Stanway kit for its secure context and the apparent completeness of its metal instrumentation, we should bear in mind, as ever, the choice entailed in the selection of grave goods (it may be that the whole *instrumentarium* was not included), and also the likelihood that most, if not all, ancient *instrumentaria* originally incorporated an organic component, little of which ever survives. This 'missing' list, to judge

FIG. 125. Doctor's burial CF47

from the writings of Celsus (Jackson 1994, tables 2–4), might include implements of wood, bone, leather, reed and feather, as well as an assortment of bandages, dressings, pads, plugs, ligatures, threads and sutures. The majority of the latter were made from wool or linen, and it is quite conceivable that the mineral-replaced threads and textile fragments adhering to some of the Stanway instruments are the remains of such medical paraphernalia, if not cloth wrapping for the instruments themselves (FIGS 102–3).

The Stanway *instrumentarium* is doubly significant for, not only is it the earliest find from Roman Britain and at the threshold of the discovery of such finds from the wider Roman world, but it might also be interpreted as the first pre-Roman set from Britain, since it is quite possible that some, if not all, of the instruments were made prior to the conquest of A.D. 43. These chronological and cultural implications may explain the idiosyncratic nature of the set. The majority of surviving identifiable Roman *instrumentaria* comprise predominantly metal instruments, most of which are made of copper alloy or a combination of copper alloy and iron. Copper alloy was above all the preferred metal where decoration was to be applied, primarily for grips, handles and finials. Iron was utilised especially for its strength (*e.g.* for bone levers),

FIG. 126. Doctor's burial CF47: vertical view of the gaming board and counters, with some of the surgical instruments, *in situ*

and for its ability to take a sharp edge, most notably for cutting instruments — chisel-blades and scalpel-blades — and for needles, all of which were commonly mounted on copper-alloy handles or grips. In Roman *instrumentaria*, single-piece iron instruments are the exception (see *e.g.* Künzl 1983a; Jackson 1990b), and the Stanway kit is thus remarkable for the presence of eight iron instruments: just four of the fourteen are single-piece copper-alloy tools, and only one (no. 12) is of a distinctive Roman form. Of the eight iron instruments, six have decorative finials, in three cases with adjacent mouldings. Their similarity suggests manufacture by the same artisan or in the same workshop, and that workshop is very likely to have been in Britain, probably in the Colchester region.

Parallels to the Stanway set, although presently lacking in Britain, may be found both in the Roman empire and in Celtic Europe. For the composition of the set, the best comparisons are with the Roman finds, which generally comprise a 'core' set of scalpels, hooks, forceps, needles and probes, in smaller or greater numbers, together, sometimes, with a pharmaceutical component and/or one or more 'specialised' instruments (Künzl 1983a; Jackson 1995). Typically, the core sets number from six to fifteen pieces. The composition of the fourteen-piece Stanway kit —two scalpels, two combined sharp/blunt hooks, one ?retractor, two forceps, three ?needles, one probe, one saw, one knife, one handled instrument — is, insofar as any generalisation may be made, typical of the Roman basic *instrumentaria*. In the individual form of the Stanway instruments, however, and in the preponderance of iron instruments, the Stanway kit finds parallels with Celtic surgical tools, notably the finds from the three La Tène C graves at München-Obermenzing, Bavaria (De Navarro 1955), Batina/Kis Köszeg, Croatia (Sudhoff 1913), and Galaţii Bistriţei, Romania (Bologa *et al.* 1956). In addition to the predominant use of iron, a further link between these 3rd- to 2nd-century B.C. finds and the Stanway kit is the presence of small iron saws. These are virtually absent from the surviving Roman *instrumentaria*, but are a consistent feature of the Celtic finds, in which they have been

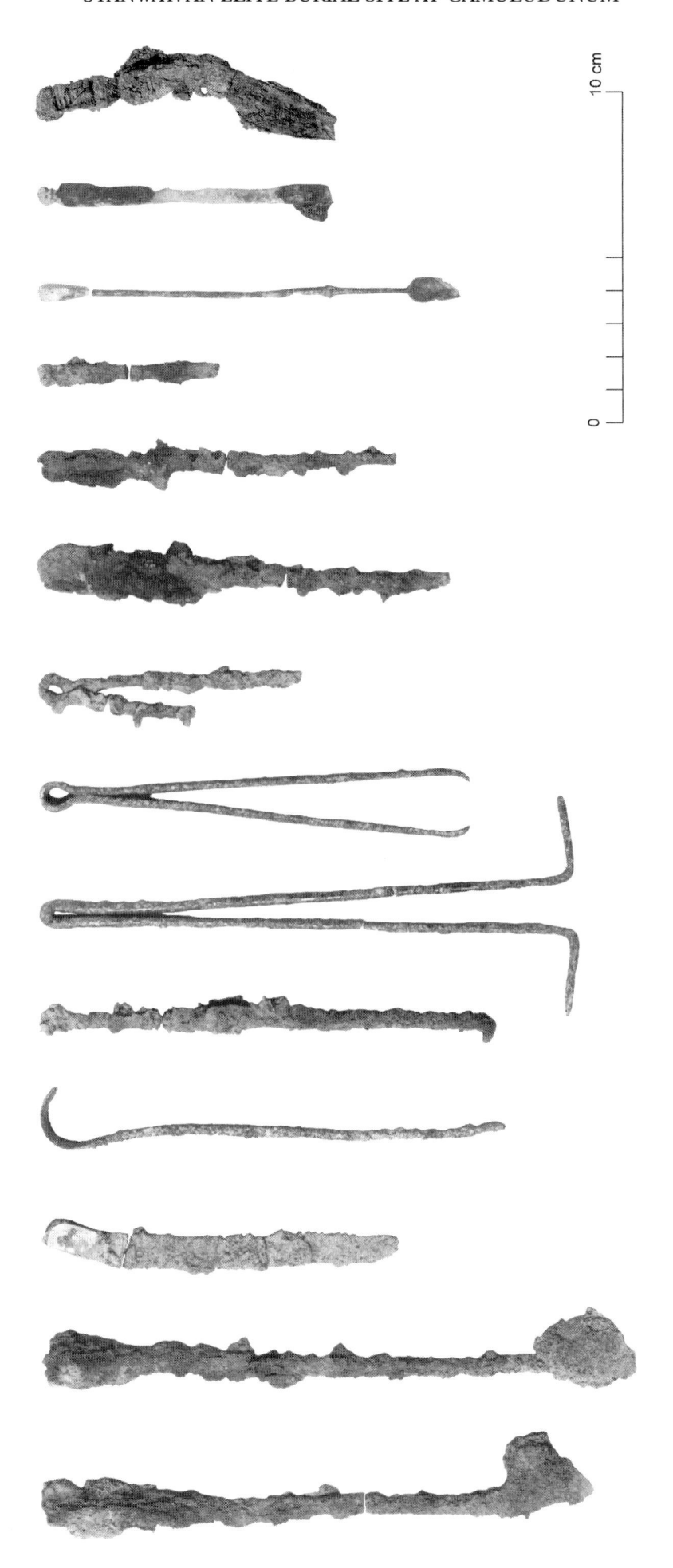

FIG. 127. Doctor's burial CF47: the surgical instruments. (Photo courtesy of British Museum.)

identified as trepanning tools. The eight iron instruments from Batina/Kis Köszeg include, as well as the saw, a scalpel, a bone lever, two hooks and two fenestrated instruments, some with solid handles or grips and some with tangs. In their general appearance, they resemble the Stanway iron instruments and they also share a number of specific characteristics: they have sinuous stems which swell and taper, they combine round and rectangular cross-sections and they have knobbed finials, occasionally with additional mouldings. Although the overall composition of the Stanway kit differs from that of Batina/Kis Köszeg, and the two finds are separated by several centuries, it is, nevertheless, possible that the maker of the Stanway instruments was following a distinctive Iron Age tradition in the manufacture of medical instruments. It is further possible that the tradition continued after Britain became a province of the Roman empire, for a number of other idiosyncratic iron instruments have been identified, including a single-piece scalpel and a combined bone lever and curette, both from Roman London (British Museum, Reg. nos P 1928.7-13.30, P 1934.12-10.46; Jackson 2005, fig. 5.2, 6). With the example of the Stanway *instrumentarium*, it is likely that more will now be recognised.

It is unfortunate that no contemporary medical writings exist to illuminate our understanding of healing in pre-Roman Britain. Nor, even, do any survive which are specific to Roman Britain (with the exception of a few tantalising references in the Vindolanda tablets: Bowman and Thomas 1994, II, 154–6 and II, 294; 2003, III, 586 and III, 591). In their absence, analogy may be made, albeit cautiously, with the contemporary medical texts from other parts of the Greek and Roman world. Such texts, above all Celsus' *De medicina*, give an impression of the range of surgical interventions undertaken and the instruments required to perform them. Some surgery was highly specialised and was carried out by a restricted number of operators using specially designed instruments, as, for example, lithotomy, the operation to cut for stone in the urinary bladder (vesical calculus) (Celsus, *De med.* VII, 26; Künzl 1983b; Jackson 1993b; 1994, 172–3, 205, fig. 2, nos 2–3; 1995). However, away from the largest cities, which might support specialists, most Roman surgery appears to have come within the ambit of 'general practitioners', who were expected to encompass the three branches into which medicine was traditionally divided, *i.e.* dietetics, drugs and surgery (Celsus, *De med.* prooemium, 9; VII, prooemium, 5; Scribonius Largus, *Compositiones* prooemium; Soranus, *Gynaecia* I, 4; Mudry 1985; Jackson 1993b). The composition of Roman medical *instrumentaria*, which often combine basic surgical tools with pharmaceutical implements and some specialised instruments, seems to support the impression given by the texts (Jackson 1995). Although the majority of the Stanway instruments fall into the category of basic surgical tools, the saw implies bone surgery, perhaps of a specialist nature, while there is the possibility that among the vessels in the grave the strainer bowl, at least, may have been used *inter alia* for the preparation of healing beverages. At all events, the *instrumentarium* would have enabled the practitioner who used it potentially to perform a wide range of surgery. For, in comparatively few instances in Celsus' *De medicina* is a specialised instrument specified — most of his surgical interventions were performed with the basic 'core' tools.

As Philip Crummy has described above, the deposition and arrangement of the grave goods in burial CF47 was, like others in the cemetery, contrived with great care and deliberation, and we may be sure they were purposefully placed. However, a full understanding of the meaning of the location of the objects is impossible to attain, not least because the poor survival conditions for organic materials have undoubtedly erased part of the evidence. Thus, we can only guess at the connections implicit in the very particular juxtaposition of the instruments with the cremated remains, board game and metal rods. Was the positioning simply or partially dictated by spatial constraints, or are we to imagine a more meaningful linkage? There is little relevant medical material with which to make comparison, either because incomplete records were kept of early excavations of burial finds, or because the deposition was of a much simpler nature, as at Wehringen, Bavaria (Künzl 1983a, 120–1, figs 95–6), where the tight grouping of six instruments and organic remains indicated that they had been held in a small leather case, or at Wederath-Belginum, Germany (Künzl 1989, fig. 1), where a similarly tight-packed arrangement of four instruments was suggestive of a former small organic box or container. The rather dispersed, uneven and non-linear arrangement of the Stanway instruments is not really consistent with burial in a container, whether a cloth pouch, wooden box or leather case. Rather the impression is of a careful placing of the instruments individually.

During the period of the Roman empire surgical and medical instruments were occasionally placed in graves (Künzl 1983a). The reason for this practice, which did not extend to the tools of other trades, is not known. Nevertheless, the presence of such instruments and implements is generally taken to indicate that the buried person in life had been a medical practitioner (although not necessarily exclusively so). In the light of such finds, it is a reasonable supposition that the *instrumentarium* in grave CF47 was owned and used by the man upon and beside whose cremated remains the instruments lay. The two accompanying copper-alloy brooches were probably made in the 40s A.D., and the pottery dating suggests that the burial took place c. A.D. 40–50/55 (p. 437). There is thus a high degree of probability that some, if not all, of the instruments were made before the Roman conquest of A.D. 43, and that the healer was practising both before and after the conquest.

What, then, was his status? The form of his burial and its furnishings, far from being those of a commoner, imply a person of some importance. He appears to have practised healing, was buried with a set of rods that were perhaps used in divination or other medico-magical rites (pp. 224–9, and was a game-player (pp. 217–20), but seemingly no warrior. In short, and notwithstanding Jane Webster's sober assessment that 'individual druids ... are unlikely to be identified archaeologically' (1999, 6), it is hard to avoid the conclusion that the Stanway healer was a druid, or at least that he belonged to the stratum of society that comprised druids, diviners and healers (Pliny, *Nat. Hist.* 30.13). Whether he was a native Briton or a newcomer, perhaps a refugee from Gaul following Roman proscriptions against druids in the early 1st century A.D. (Webster 1999, 11), it is not possible to say on the strength of the instruments alone, but see N. Crummy pp. 444–5. Whatever the case, to judge from his instrumentation, he seems to have been acquainted with both Iron Age and classical healing systems, and may well have been in contact with Roman as well as Gallo-Roman and native British personnel.

Summary catalogue

CF47.26 Scalpel. FIG. 121. SF49. C951. Length 169 mm. Weight 26.8 g. Iron, heavily corroded, in two accurately joining pieces.
A single-piece instrument comprising a long, slender, very lightly curved handle of circular cross-section, with a bulbous knobbed finial. The slightly down-turned blade has a distinctive sub-triangular form, with a lightly hollowed back and a rounded heel. Its straight cutting edge appears to extend onto the heel.

CF47.27 Scalpel. FIG. 121. SF129. C1033. Length 188 mm. Weight 25.4 g. Iron, heavily corroded, in three accurately joining pieces.
A single-piece instrument with a handle of the same form as CF47.26, but slightly longer, straighter and more slender. The small bellied blade has a convex crescentic cutting edge and a lightly concave back with an upturned bevelled tip. Mineral-replaced textile remains are preserved on the blade.

CF47.28 Saw. FIG. 121. SF63–6 and 71. C965–7, C973. Length approximately 112 mm. Weight 6.7 g. Iron blade with composite handle, the details of which were revealed very clearly by X-radiography. The blade is corroded and broken in four accurately joining pieces. The fifth piece, incorporating the handle, was bent and snapped prior to deposition. The join is secure, but not close.
A small, slender iron blade with a very lightly concave, finely toothed cutting edge (14 teeth per cm) and a lightly convex back, which slopes down at the end to form a blunt-nosed tip. The teeth are neither set nor raked, allowing the blade to cut in both directions, but probably to no great depth. The small composite block-like handle or grip (CF24.28a) comprises a short iron handle plate with flanking plates of wood or bone sandwiched between a pair of thin bronze outer plates, the whole assembly fastened by a pair of copper-alloy rivets. A short fragment of tapered iron rod of rhomboid cross-section, broken at the broader end and bent at the other (CF47.28b, SF62), was found associated with the saw fragments. It was originally assumed to be part of a tanged handle of the saw, but on examination no join could be effected with the grip, which appears to be complete, and the fragment is almost certainly the bent stem of a nail lacking its head. (There were several other nails in the vicinity.) At all events, a handle combining

a tang and handle-plate would be exceptional. In fact, although the grip is idiosyncratic, the replica saw can be held comfortably and quite securely between the thumb and the side of the second finger, with the tip of the index finger on the blade back providing sufficient pressure to cut effectively with any part of the blade, especially on a convex surface.

CF47.29 Combined sharp and blunt hook (double-ended retractor). FIG. 122. SF46. C948. Length 144 mm. Weight 10.0 g. Bronze, with crusty, flaking, green corrosion, brittle, in three joining pieces.

A single-piece instrument comprising a slender stem with a hooked terminal at each end. The broad blunt hook (width 12.1 mm) is complete, and has a rounded square end, smooth edges, and a low strengthening rib on its outer convex face. At the other end of the stem, the tip of the small sharp hook is broken, but the curved base of the hook survives. The stem has two distinct zones: that joining the blunt hook is of rectangular cross-section, while that leading to the sharp hook is of tapered circular cross-section. The lightly sinuous form of the stem was probably an intentional original feature (or a modification by the practitioner) designed to facilitate use of each hook. Surface XRF analysis of the alloy composition demonstrated that the hook is made of bronze with only traces of zinc.

CF47.30 Combined sharp and blunt hook (double-ended retractor). FIG. 122. SF42. C944. Length 140 mm. Weight 12.3 g. Iron, corroded, encrusted and fissured, in three joining pieces.

A single-piece, double-ended instrument, with a rectangular-sectioned central grip and flanking circular-sectioned (or faceted) stem, terminating at one end in a small, neatly formed blunt hook. The other terminal is damaged, but it appears to preserve the stub of a sharp hook. The stem has an even, gentle curvature, probably to facilitate usage of the instrument, and the hooks are set at a right-angle to one another. Degraded wood remains adhere to the stem adjacent to the blunt hook, and mineral-replaced textile remains adhere to the stem adjacent to the sharp hook. Examination of the latter by scanning electron microscopy revealed that the preserved fibre impressions are the remains of a woollen textile (*see* report by N.D. Meeks and C.R. Cartwright, pp. 350–2).

CF47.31 ?Retractor. FIG. 123. SF43. C945. Length 166 mm. Weight 21.2 g. Bronze, with crusty, flaking, green corrosion, brittle, in four joining pieces.

A single-piece instrument made from a slender circular-sectioned rod bent centrally to form two equal arms, each terminating in an everted, tapered point (chipped at the tip). It was initially thought that the object was a double sharp hook with a pair of projecting points that had become flattened and out-turned by breakage in the ground. However, a close inspection of the broken faces confirmed that the everted orientation of the points was an original feature. As no 4, surface XRF analysis of the alloy composition showed it to be bronze with only traces of zinc.

CF47.32 Smooth-jawed fixation forceps. FIG. 123. SF45. C947. Length 133 mm. Weight 22.3 g. Bronze, with crusty green corrosion.

A single-piece spring forceps with a looped head and in-turned jaws. Although the jaw edges are chipped it is evident that they were smooth (un-toothed). The arms have neatly chamfered outer angles and there is a simple incuse linear moulding below the loop.

CF47.33 Forceps/tweezers. FIG. 123. SF78. C980. Length 81 mm. Weight 5.7 g. Iron, corroded and encrusted, in three joining pieces, both jaws broken.

A well-made tweezers or small forceps with slender, smoothly tapered arms of rectangular cross-section with chamfered outer angles. One arm is broken short, the other is nearly complete, lacking only the jaw tip. The narrowness of the broken end of the longer surviving arm suggests the jaws were pointed.

CF47.34 Handled ?needle. FIG. 124. SF84 and 86. C988, C990. Length 127 mm. Weight 27.4 g. Iron, heavily corroded, in two joining pieces, the tip lacking.

A single-piece instrument with a knobbed finial, a stout handle, and a slender tapered stem. The handle is probably of circular cross-section, but heavy corrosion prevents certainty. The stem changes from a circular cross-section to a square cross-section as it approaches the tip. The missing tip was almost certainly a pointed, un-eyed needle. Mineral-replaced textile remains adhere to the handle and finial, and there is a small fragment of mineral-replaced wood on the stem.

CF47.35 Handled ?needle. FIG. 124. SF85. C989. Length 109 mm. Weight 9.6 g. Iron, corroded and encrusted, in two joining pieces. The tip, which is now lacking, appears to have been incorporated in the corroded head of one of the iron rods, against which the needle rested in the grave.

A solid tapered rod, of circular cross-section, with a lightly swollen handle terminating in a knobbed finial with basal double ring moulding. Like CF47.34, the tip of the slender tapered stem, now lacking, was probably a pointed, un-eyed needle. Fragmentary remains of textiles adhere to the central part of the stem and to the side of the handle and finial. Examination by scanning electron microscopy demonstrated that the remains are those of a woollen textile (see report by N.D. Meeks and C.R. Cartwright, pp. 350–2).

CF47.36 Handled ?needle. FIG. 124. SF51. C953. Length 55.4 mm. Weight 3.5 g. Iron, corroded and encrusted, in two joining pieces, the point lacking.

A slender tapered rod, of circular cross-section, with a small knobbed finial above a triple ring moulding. The broken stem probably terminated in a pointed, un-eyed needle. There is a small spot of green corrosion on the lower stem revealing a point of contact with (presumably) the adjacent bronze blunt/sharp hook CF47.29.

CF47.37 Scoop probe. FIG. 124. SF44. C946. Length 132 mm. Weight 3.7 g. Bronze, with powdery green patina, in three joining pieces, the scoop broken.

A slender example with an olivary probe and very fine incuse 'drawing' lines on the grip. A simple ring moulding divides the grip from the stemmed scoop, which is of narrow, tapered form, its end lacking.

CF47.38 Handle. FIG. 124. SF50. C952. Length 91.3 mm. Weight 7.9 g. Bronze, with powdery, pale green patina.

A small, slender, lightly tapered handle with a knobbed finial. One face of the handle, the back or underside, is plain and flat, the other neatly faceted and moulded. At the narrower end are the fragmentary remains of a thin sheet iron V-shaped or winged component that was fastened to the handle by means of an iron rivet. X-radiography revealed a small rectangular perforation in the end of the handle in which the rivet is fixed, and XRF analysis detected the remains of soft (tin-lead) solder in this region, too. Iron corrosion products at the finial end of the handle are presumably from the point of contact with the blade of scalpel CF47.26.

CF47.39 Knife. FIG. 121. SF39. C941. Length 97.7 mm. Weight 19 g. Iron, corroded and heavily encrusted, in two joining pieces, the blade tip lacking.

A small knife with a short solid handle and an acutely angled blade. The handle is finely decorated, with a knobbed finial, a zone of seven square ring-mouldings, a round vase moulding, and a further zone of square mouldings. Beyond the point where the blade turns sharply downwards there is a pronounced flanging of the blade back, a feature evidently contrived to allow the user's index finger to press down on to the blade. The blade is of elongated triangular form (its tip is missing), with a marked angle at the junction with the handle. The cutting edge is straight or very lightly convex.

Nails (TABLE 36)

The nails are listed in TABLE 36. In the majority of cases, the grain of the wood lay across the shank of the nail, but in some cases it was parallel to it. All the nails were of Manning's Type 1b, some with sub-circular and some with sub-rectangular heads. One head (SF28) is a narrow oval. The shanks are incomplete unless stated otherwise, although some described here as complete lack 1 or 2 mm of the tip. They range in length from 46 to 81 mm. The longest nail had wood grain running parallel to the shank for most of its length. Only four were clenched, giving plank thicknesses of 15–20 mm. On nails with wood grain lying across the full length of the shank for its full length, no break between planks could be seen.

TABLE 36: THE NAILS IN THE OAK GRAVE COVER (CF47.41)

Object no.	Find	SF no.	Head shape	Length (mm)	Wood	Grain to shank direction	Notes
CF47.41a	C930	28	oval	37	y	transverse	–
CF47.41a	C931	29	sub-rectangular	29	y	transverse	–
CF47.41a	C932	30	sub-rectangular	53	y	transverse	–
CF47.41a	C933	31	sub-circular	28	y	transverse	–
CF47.41a	C934	32a	sub-circular	65 (complete)	y	transverse	–
CF47.41a	C935	33	sub-rectangular	32	y	transverse	–
CF47.41a	C936	34a	sub-rectangular	47 (complete)	y	transverse	below SF34b
CF47.41a	C937	35	sub-circular	35	y	transverse	–
CF47.41a	C1078	158	sub-circular	32 (complete)	y	transverse	–
CF47.41a	C1081	170	–	21	y	transverse	–
CF47.41a	C1091	154	sub-circular	56 (complete)	y	transverse and parallel	grain transverse on upper part of shank, parallel on lower, with an upper wood thickness of about 20 mm and a lower thickness of 28 mm
CF47.41a	C1092	156	sub-circular	51 (complete)	–	–	no wood visible
CF47.41a	C1093	153	sub-circular	52 (complete)	y	parallel	wood only preserved on lower part (28 mm deep)
CF47.41b	C1079	161	sub-circular	23	y	transverse	only a small part of the head remains
CF47.41b	C1096	151	sub-circular	68	y	transverse	–
CF47.41b	C1097	152	sub–circular	81 (complete)	y	parallel	wood along most of length
CF47.41c	C954	52	sub-circular	37	y	transverse	–
CF47.41c	C955	53	sub-circular	46	y	transverse	clenched, wood thickness 16 mm
CF47.41c	C956	54	sub-circular?	53 (complete)	y	parallel	clenched, wood thickness 15 mm
CF47.41c	C957	55	sub-rectangular	46 (complete)	y	transverse	–
CF47.41c?	C1082	184	sub-circular	63 (complete)	y	parallel after bend	clenched, shank measures 42 mm above the bend, but wood is only present below the bend, running all round the shank
CF47.41a	C934	32b	–	22	y	transverse	2 shank fragments only
CF47.41d	C936	34b	sub-circular	33	y	transverse	–
CF47.41d	C991	87	sub-circular	47	y	transverse	clenched, wood thickness 20 mm
CF47.41d	C992	88	–	36	y	transverse	only a small part of the head remains

THE BROOCHES BURIAL CF72 (FIGS 2, 8, 128–31)

Cremated bone	73.7 g	adult of indeterminate age and sex
Pottery vessels	CF72.1	cornice-rimmed *lagena*
	CF72.2	grog-tempered carinated cup or bowl
	CF72.3	grog-tempered carinated cup or bowl
Glass vessel	CF72.4	*pyxis*
Other objects	CF72.5	brass Keyhole Rosette brooch
	CF72.6	copper-alloy Hod Hill brooch
	CF72.7	brass lugged circular brooch
	CF72.8	copper-alloy circular plate brooch
	CF72.9	brass lozenge-shaped brooch
	CF72.10	brass star-shaped plate brooch
	CF72.11	glass bead
	CF72.12	pin or stud with glass bead at one end
	CF72.13	iron ?knife blade
	CF72.14	a possible nail shank
	CF72.15	one or more textile garments
Residual finds		probably none

The burial lay to the west of chamber CF42 in Enclosure 5 (FIGS 2, 8, 131). The cremated remains and grave goods had been placed in a shallow pit, roughly square in shape, about 1.0 m across and about 0.2 m deep as measured from the ground surface after stripping (FIG. 128). The plan of the burial pit may have been closer to a square than appears in plan if, as seems likely, its north-west corner was disturbed by modern subsoiling. The burial is particularly noteworthy for its rare glass *pyxis* and large number of brooches.

Most of the bone was placed in a heap in the south-west part of the pit, with the rest spread out in patches on the floor of the pit to the immediate east. The grave goods then appear to have been placed in the pit, mostly directly on top of the cremated bone (FIG. 128). Four brooches (CF72.6, CF72.7, CF72.8, and CF72.10) were laid on top of the pile of bone. Two more (CF72.5 and CF72.9) were placed close by. One of these (CF72.9) was in two pieces. Its central glass setting had become detached and appeared to lie under the edge of one of the small patches of bone forming the minor spread east of the main pile. The rest of the brooch lay a short distance to the east. A pin or stud with a glass bead at one end (CF72.12) also lay on top of the main pile of cremated remains, as did the blade (probably complete) of an iron knife (CF72.13). Remains of textile on the backs of some of the brooches show that a cloth or garment probably of diamond twill (CF72.15) lay between the cremated remains and the brooches (*see* report pp. 348–9). An annular glass bead (CF72.11) lay just to the north of the main pile of bone. The glass *pyxis* (CF72.4) lay tipped over on its side partly under a pottery flagon (CF72.1). Close by the flagon and on its east side was a pottery cup (CF72.2). An almost identical vessel (CF72.3) was the only object to be found in the northern half of the burial pit (FIGS 128, 131). The only other object was a fragment of an iron shank (CF72.14), which was found close to the western edge of the burial pit, about 80 mm above the floor. Its function and context are unclear.

All the objects are likely to have been placed in the burial pit intact. A few of them look as if they might have been fragmentary at the time, but a careful consideration of the evidence reveals that this is not necessarily so and all the objects were probably complete when buried. The most obvious candidate for breakage is the plate brooch CF72.9. However, it seems likely that the object was damaged by ploughing or (more likely) a subsoiler, with the result that the central glass setting became detached from the body of the brooch and was dragged about 90 mm to the north-west (FIG. 130). Although no clear evidence of subsoiling was noted during the excavation, activity of this nature would explain the shattered state of one of the sides of the flagon CF72.1. The glass setting was found partly under a piece of cremated bone and taken at the time as evidence that its deposition preceded that of the bone. But of course this relationship would be meaningless if the area had been disturbed by subsoiling.

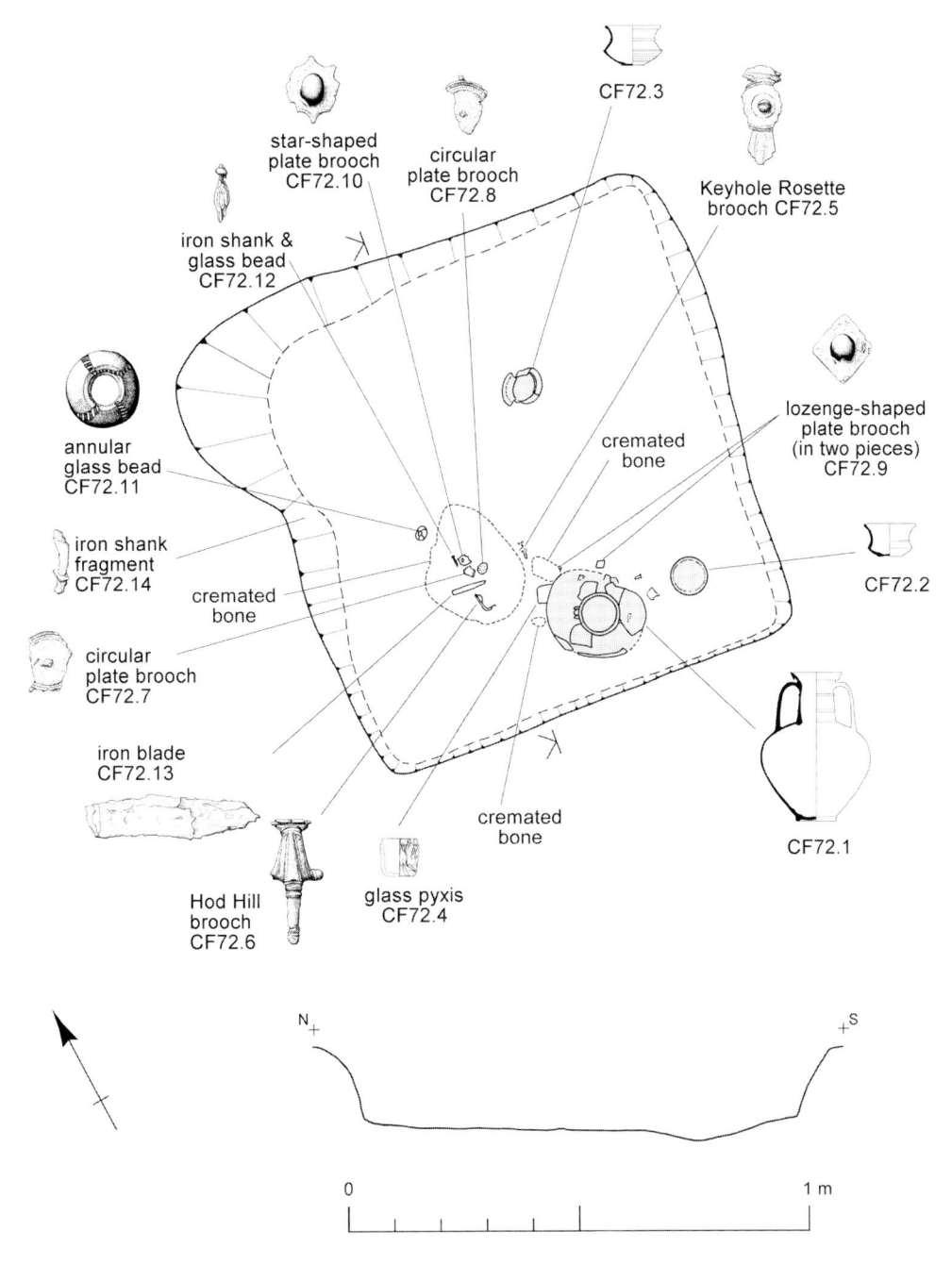

FIG. 128. Brooches burial CF72: plan and profile (scale 1:15)

Other objects which might be taken to have been fragmentary when buried are the blade CF72.13 and the shanks CF72.12 and CF72.14. However, being iron, their poor state of preservation and their delicate condition (ever deteriorating) make it hard to determine whether they were complete or not when buried. The iron blade CF72.13 looks fragmentary now (FIG. 129) but, when uncovered, did seem as if it was a complete blade and can be assumed to have been part of a knife with a wooden or bone handle that had completely decayed.

The other two objects (FIG. 129, CF72.12, CF72.14) could be the broken remains of larger pieces but, given the apparently complete state of everything else in the grave, this is unlikely to be so. The piece of wood in which was set the iron shank with the glass bead (CF72.12) appears to have been small, since the shank lay in the ground within a few millimetres of the brooch CF72.10. The lack of taper and the shank's circular section, as well as the delicate head, all suggest that it was set into a pre-drilled hole, rather than hammered into place. No parallel has been found for the object, although it can be associated in a general way with the iron pins

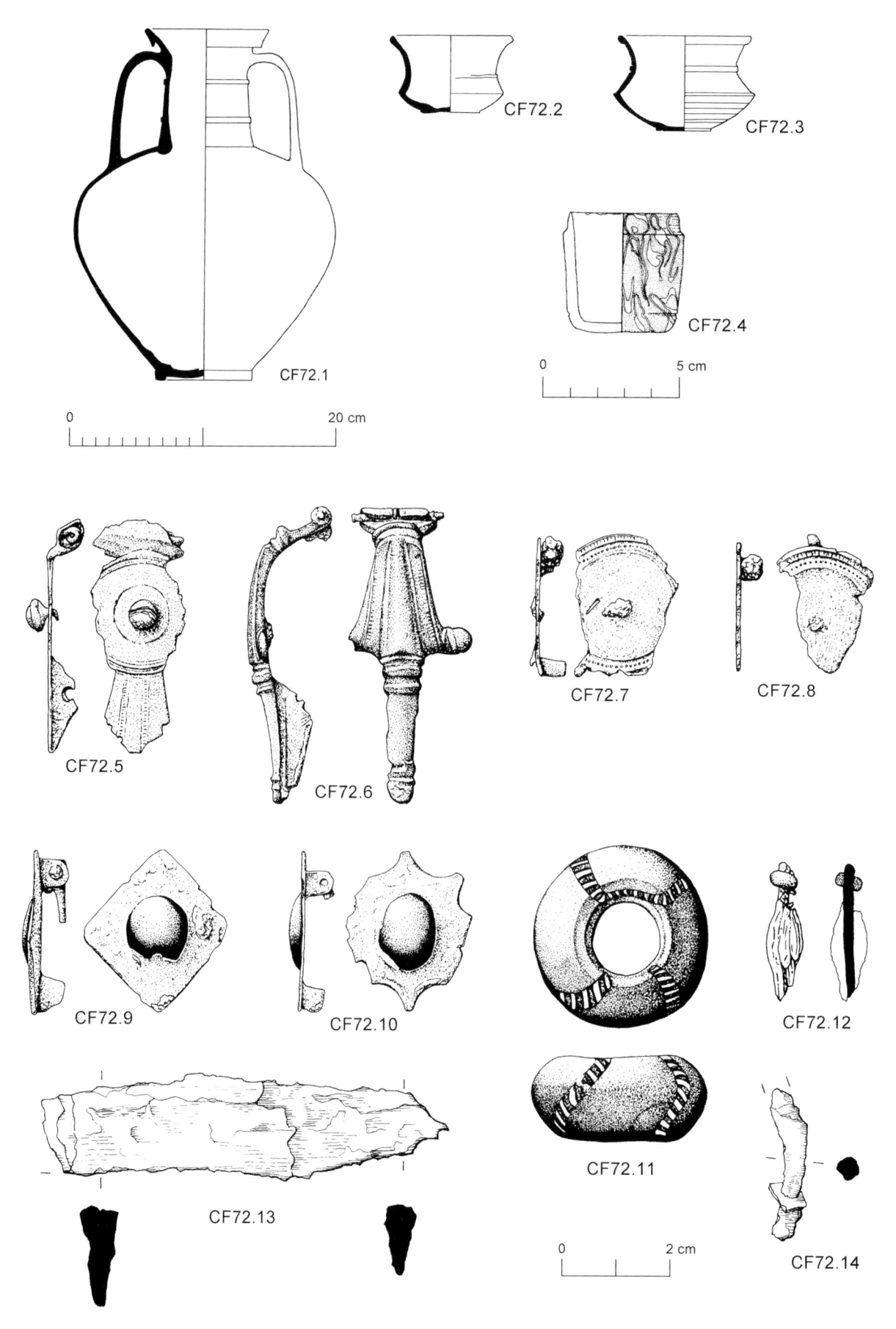

FIG. 129. Brooches burial CF72: pottery vessels CF72.1–3 (scale 1:4), glass pyxis CF72.4 (scale 1:2), copper-alloy brooches F72.5–10, glass bead CF72.11, pin or stud with iron shank with glass bead CF72.12, iron knife blade CF72.13, and iron ?nail shank CF72.14 (scale 1:1)

with globular glass heads in CF42 (FIG. 73, CF42.16a–c; pp. 150, 153–4). The burial rite in CF72 precludes identification of this pin as a token, representative of an item of furniture, as may be the case with the related studs in CF42.

The other shank (FIG. 129, CF72.14) lay well away from the other objects in the burial pit. Being close to the edge of the pit and some distance above the pit floor, its position is similar to that of some of the nails in the Doctor's burial which are taken to have been part of a wooden grave-cover (CF47.41). Alternatively the shank could have been part of one of the grave goods which, like the brooch CF72.9, had been caught and displaced by a subsoiler.

Of all the grave goods in the burial pit, the most remarkable is FIG. 129, CF72.4. The cast polychrome vessel is the body of a *pyxis* in translucent, deep blue glass with opaque white spirals. The lid is missing, but this would have fitted over the rebated rim. Glass pyxides were expensive cosmetic containers (Foy and Nenna 2001, 161), so that the presence of one in CF72 points to it being the burial place of a well-off woman. On the Continent, *pyxides* appear to have belonged to the Augustan period, thus suggesting that the Stanway example was a pre-Claudian import (pp. 343–4).

All the brooches in CF72 are Gaulish imports, but only one, a Keyhole Rosette (FIG. 129, CF72.5), is of a type that might have been imported before the conquest, the rest are forms introduced after A.D. 43. The brooches form three pairs, suggesting that they were used to fasten tube tunics at the shoulders. There are two identical circular plate brooches (FIG. 129, CF72.7–8), two composite plate brooches, one lozenge-shaped, one star-shaped, both with glass insets (CF72.9–10), and two bow brooches, a Keyhole Rosette and a Hod Hill (FIG. 129, CF72.5–6). The brooches, and particularly the dating of the Keyhole Rosette, are discussed more fully on pages 317–19.

The presence of so many pairs of brooches in what is otherwise a not particularly richly furnished grave almost certainly implies that CF72 is the grave of a female, although the evidence for gender-specific use of brooch pairs is not always clear (Croom 2003). Two similar brooches in one grave need not necessarily imply their use as a pair, which is clearly shown by the two Nertomarus bow brooches in BF64 (BF64.19–20; p. 176). That they may have been used in pairs by men is, however, shown by male graves with multiple bow brooch deposits, such as that at Hoby, Denmark, which contained two pairs of brooches and one trio (Salskov Roberts 1995, 293). This matches the evidence at King Harry Lane, where brooch use between the sexes appears to have been much the same, and where many graves contained multiple bow brooch deposits (Stead and Rigby 1989, 102, table 4). Plate brooches were not common at King Harry Lane, with only three being deposited, all singletons. Two were in graves that could be attributed to Phase 3, one a male burial, one that of an infant. The third, unphased, grave was of a young adult (*ibid.*, 96).

The single large glass bead (FIG. 129, CF72.11) is also not proof that the grave was of a woman, as there are single beads from the male burials BF64 (BF64.22) and CF47 (CF47.18). It is of Guido's Class 9, Type B, an example of which occurs at Bagendon in a context dated to *c.* A.D. 10–50 (Harden 1961, 201, fig. 42, 5). Beads of this type are not common, and the individual colours vary; they derive principally from contexts dated to the Late Iron Age or early Roman period and have a wide, although generally western, distribution (Guido 1978, 77–8, 185–6).

The knife (FIG. 129, CF72.13) is not indicative of gender or age. Knives occur in both adult and child graves at King Harry Lane (Stead and Rigby 1989, 106). Two small knives, at least one of which is probably a pen-knife as the grave also included a set of writing equipment, were in the rich Flavian burial of a young woman at Winchester (Biddle 1967, fig. 9, 20, 26A–B; Bo ič 2001, 29). Biddle lists two knives in Welwyn-type male graves, but the one from Snailwell is a large razor, and that from Stanfordbury is intrusive (Biddle 1967, table 1; Stead 1967, 55). The Welwyn-type male burial at Hertford Heath also contained a knife, but of a larger type than those found in the female graves (*ibid.*, 52, no. 20).

The burial is likely to date to the A.D. 50s. The item most diagnostic of date is the Keyhole Rosette, which suggests that the burial is no later than *c.* A.D 50/5. The other brooches simply point to the burial post-dating A.D. 43. All are generally Claudian forms. Of the three pots in the grave, all could be pre-Claudian or as late as *c.* A.D. 65.

Pottery vessels (FIG. 129)

North Gaulish import

CF72.1 FIG. 129. C412. Cornice-rimmed *lagena*: Camulodunum form 161, the small-bodied version. Fabric WPW; white matrix; slip over the exterior and partly coating interior.
Condition: restorable to complete; fragmented in the grave.

Local products

CF72.2 FIG. 129. C413. Carinated bowl. Fabric GTW; grey core; brown surfaces. Burnished exterior surface, unfinished interior.
Condition: complete.

CF72.3 FIG. 129. C400. Carinated bowl. Fabric GTW; sandwich firing, dark grey core; brown under-surface, dark brown surfaces. Unfinished interior; banded burnishing on the exterior with four burnished hoops on matt ground below the carination.
Condition: restorable to complete; fragmented in the grave.

Glass vessel (FIG. 129)

CF72.4 FIG. 129. C402. *Pyxis* (complete). Translucent deep blue glass with opaque white spirals. Rim ground to form rebate for lid seating, original smoothly ground rim present in two areas but majority of rim chipped and damaged in antiquity. Straight side sloping in very slightly, curving into flat base. Shallow ground-out channel on lower body. Interior ground; exterior of sides lightly ground, base glossy and does not appear to have been ground. Rim diameter 40 mm, body diameter 44 mm, height 45 mm, wall thickness 4 mm, base diameter 35 mm.

Other objects (FIG. 129)

CF72.5 FIG. 129. SF7. C410. Small Keyhole Rosette brooch of brass, tinned at front and back except on the disc, where it is only tinned on the perimeter. The pin (and therefore also the spring) is of impure copper. The pin, the central repoussé-plate from the disc, and most of the catchplate are missing. The spring-cover and spring, and the edges of both bow and foot, are damaged. The spring had eight to ten coils. The central disc has a pair of flat-bottomed grooves around the edge. There is another slight groove just over half-way inwards towards the centre and there are also very fine concentric ridges between the inner groove and the outer pair. These latter marks are not decorative, but from finishing. Fixed through a hole in the centre of the disc is a cupped riveted stud of impure copper containing a setting of opaque red glass. The stud would have held the missing decorative plate in position, as no solder was detected. The triangular foot has two lines of raised knurling. There is a small circular hole in the catchplate. Length 41.5 mm.

CF72.6 FIG. 129. SF6. C408. Hod Hill brooch with lugs at the base of the triangular bow. The body of the brooch is tinned leaded gunmetal, the pin is impure copper. Most of the hinged pin is missing, as is one of the lugs. The iron axial bar survives in the rolled-over head. The junction of head and bow is marked by transverse mouldings. The bow has a strong central rib which echoes its triangular shape, flanked by grooves and mouldings. The two outermost mouldings are beaded. The surviving lug has a beaded moulding and plain terminal knob. Transverse mouldings separate the bow from the plain convex foot, which ends with two transverse mouldings above a slightly thickened tip. The catchplate is solid. Length 52 mm.

CF72.7 FIG. 129. SF9. C416. Brass circular plate brooch with small round lugs set around the rim. The rim is badly damaged, and of six original lugs, only one now survives. The pin, most of which is missing, was hinged between two lugs on an iron axial bar. The small catchplate is solid. The rim of the brooch is decorated with two bands of knurling, the outermost between slight raised mouldings, the inner in a broader flat-bottomed groove. In the centre are the remains of a small riveted setting. Diameter 26 mm (excluding lugs).

CF72.8 FIG. 129. SF10. C418. Circular plate brooch as SF9 above. The rim is badly damaged and only the lug above the hinge survives. The catchplate and most of the pin are missing. There are slight traces of fibres on the undersurface. Diameter 26 mm (excluding lugs).

CF72.9 FIG. 129. SF8/11. C414/421. Brass lozenge-shaped plate brooch with blue glass setting. Part of the pin is missing. It was hinged between two lugs on an iron axial bar. The small catchplate is solid. The surface of the brooch is discoloured by lead-tin solder used to attach a repoussé-decorated plate, now missing. Length 29 mm. The central setting, a round piece of blue glass, plano-convex in section, survives but is detached (SF11). It is chipped along part of the edge. The underside is discoloured from contact with the solder, and is rough, chipped rather than sand-roughened as it would be if it had been made in

THE FUNERARY SITE 259

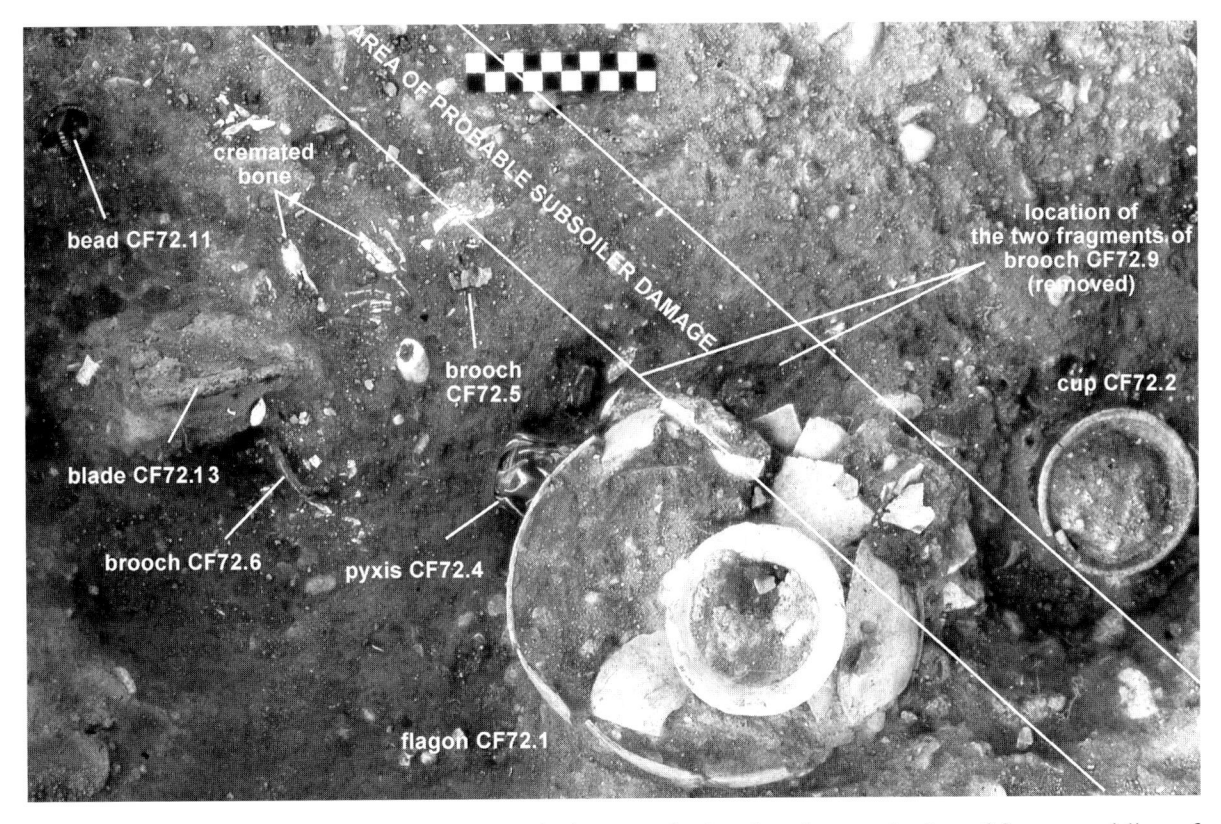

FIG. 130. Brooches burial CF72: annotated photograph showing shattered edge of flagon and line of possible subsoiler damage

FIG. 131. Brooches burial CF72

the same way as glass counters (p. 186), suggesting that it was trimmed to fit the setting. Maximum diameter of setting 11 mm.

CF72.10 FIG. 129. SF5. C406. Brass star-shaped plate brooch with blue glass setting. Part of the small solid catchplate and most of the hinged pin, held on an iron axial bar between two lugs, is missing. As with SF8/11 above, the upper surface is discoloured from lead-tin solder used to attach a missing repoussé-decorated plate. Length 28 mm. The oval blue glass central setting survives but is detached. Like the round setting from SF8/11, it is plano-convex in section. Part of one long side is straight rather than rounded. The underside is mostly covered with metal-corrosion products, but appears to be sand-roughened. Length 13 mm.

CF72.11 FIG. 129. SF2. C403. Large annular bead of cobalt blue translucent glass with four radiating spirals of twisted opaque yellow and black, marvered into the blue matrix. The spirals dip into and out of the central hole, rather than pass through it. Diameter 32.5 mm, length 15 mm. Diameter of central hole 13 mm.

CF72.12 FIG. 129. SF4. C405. Composite pin or stud, consisting of an iron circular-section shank with an annular opaque green glass bead threaded onto one end and wood fragments along most of the length of the shank below the bead. Length 24 mm. Separate small fragments of the iron shank suggest it was least a further 8 mm longer. Maximum length of wood below bead 20 mm. Diameter 5 mm, length 3 mm.

CF72.13 FIG. 129. SF3. C404. Probable iron blade fragment. Length 72 mm, maximum width 15 mm. The section is triangular, but rather wide for a knife blade, even allowing for expansion through corrosion. Both ends are broken, although one appears to be narrowing to a tang.

CF72.14 FIG. 129. SF12. C423. Small fragment of a slightly curved iron square-section shank, 25 mm long, 3 mm square. Near the bottom is what appears to be a washer threaded onto the shank, but is an integral formation, probably the result of iron corrosion spreading into a space between wooden boards or planks. A shank with similar projection came from CF115.

THE MIRROR BURIAL CF115 (FIGS 2, 8, 132)

Cremated bone	1.0 g	–
Pottery vessels	CF115.1	TN flanged cup
	CF115.2	cup-mouthed *lagena*
Glass vessel	CF115.3	unguent bottle
Other finds	CF115.4	copper-alloy mirror (fragment)
	CF115.5	iron ?decorative stud or fitting
	CF115.6	unidentified object(s) incorporating a copper-alloy strip and two iron sheet fragments
Residual finds		none could be recovered and thus uncertain if any existed

A whole pot and fragments of pottery, glass and metal were recovered in the spoil during the second phase of the machining of the enclosure. These almost certainly represent a fourth cremation burial (CF115) in Enclosure 5, close to the Brooches burial to the west of chamber CF42 (FIGS 2, 8). The grave goods included a mirror, indicating that the dead person was female. No burial pit could be located after machining and only a very small amount of cremated bone was found, although soil removed from the immediate area was sieved. The burial pit must have been relatively shallow.

The grave goods (at least those recovered) consisted of a *terra nigra* flanged cup (FIG. 132, CF115.1), a two-handled flagon (FIG. 132, CF115.2), a glass tubular unguent bottle (CF115.3), a fragment of a mirror (FIG. 132, CF115.4), and part of an iron shank (CF115.5). A copper-alloy strip and two fragments of iron sheeting (CF115.6) were also found. It is uncertain if these derived from the same object and what this object or objects might have been. The only complete item was the cup. The rest had degraded with time or had been broken during the machining. None of the objects appear to have been burnt.

The majority of Roman mirrors are made from a high-tin bronze, but there are a number which are of low-tin bronze and tinned on the surface, as appears to be the case here (Meeks 1995). After A.D. 43, continental-made mirrors were brought into the new province in considerable numbers. The distribution of the early forms shows a marked concentration in south-eastern Britain, where many were deposited in cremation burials (Lloyd-Morgan 1977, 238–9; Philpott 1991, 183). The number of mirrors recorded from Colchester in the 1970s by Lloyd-Morgan is much higher than that from London (1977, 244–8), and suggests that

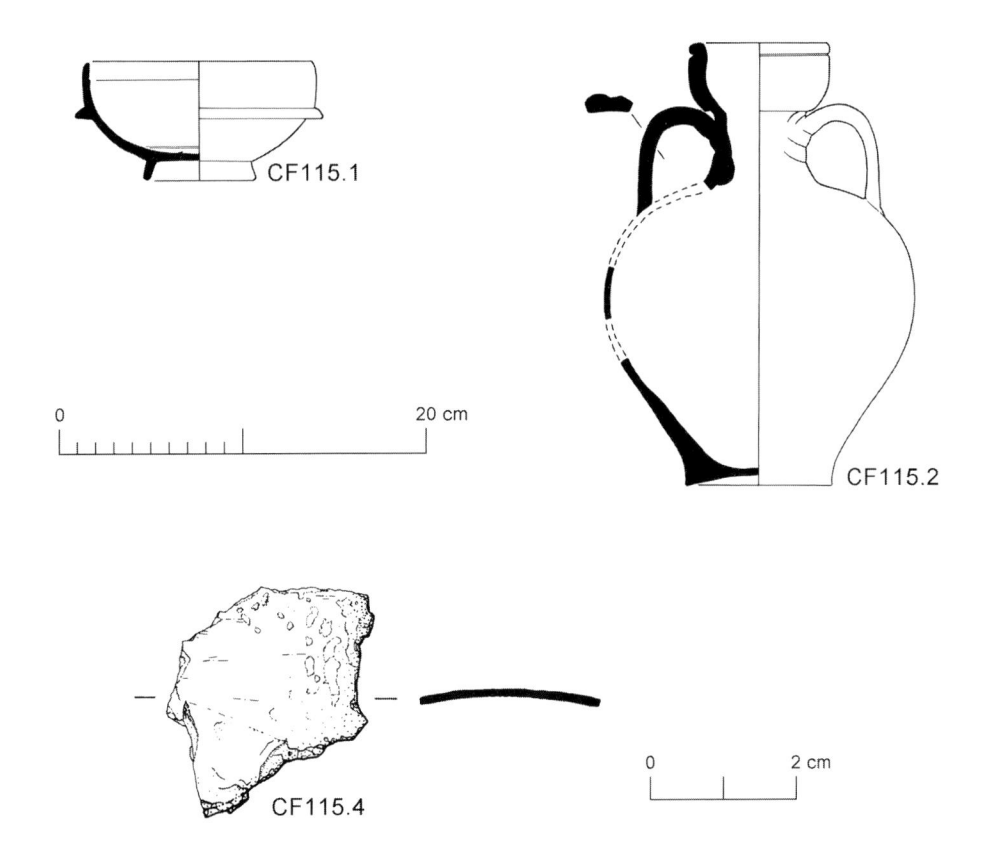

FIG. 132. Mirror burial CF115: pottery vessels CF115.1–2 (scale 1:4) and mirror fragment CF115.4 (scale 1:1)

Colchester may therefore have been the point of entry. The legionary fortress and later the *colonia* were well placed to receive cargoes from the newly established Nijmegen mirror workshops in the early years following the conquest (Lloyd-Morgan 1981, 10).

The unguent bottle CF115.3 is of Isings Form 8. This was the commonest form of unguent bottle in Britain in the mid 1st century A.D. (*CAR* **8**, 159). They are found in Tiberian contexts on the Continent (Isings 1957, 24). *See* further page 344.

The group cannot be dated closely. Its deposition should probably be placed in the period *c.* A.D. 43–75, if not *c.* A.D. 43–60, based on the cup CF115.1 (*c.* A.D. 40–75) and the mirror (probably post-conquest).

Pottery vessels (FIG. 132)

Gallo-Belgic import

CF115.1 FIG. 132. C88. Flanged cup: Camulodunum form 58. Fabric TN. Central Stamp 12, double-line: ..LOS/[FI]ICIT. A.D. 40–75. Condition: broken standing pot; quarter rim and base circuits missing. Condition at deposition: complete.

Gaulish import

CF115.2 FIG. 132. C88. Cup-mouthed *lagena*, Santrot 464–66. Fabric GFW, buff ware; paler slipped or slurried exterior surface.
Condition: complete rim and base circuits; few upper body sherds.
Condition at deposition: presumably complete.

Glass vessel

CF115.3 Not illustrated. C88. Tubular unguent bottle; blue/green; small bubbles, slightly dulled surfaces. Complete base and lower body in three joining fragments and one upper body fragment. Slightly convex-curved lower body curving into base with small central flattening. Present height 32 mm, maximum body diameter 38 mm, base diameter 8 mm.

Other finds (FIG. 132)

CF115.4 FIG. 132. SF295. L1/F115. C88. Fragment of a sheet of leaded bronze with high tin content on one side (p. 336). The fragment is slightly convex and polished on the side with the higher reading for tin. This is almost certainly all that remains of a mirror. Maximum dimensions 36 by 26 mm, 1 mm thick.

CF115.5 SF294. L1/F115. C88. Iron square-section shank with traces of mineralised wood running down its length, the grain set longitudinally. Length 48 mm. No junction between one or more boards can be seen, but about 18 mm from the bottom of the shank the metal has expanded, possibly into an air pocket in the wood. The wood above this expansion butts up against it and, in places, passes over it. A similar formation can be seen on the shank from CF72.

CF115.6

a SF295. L1/F115. C88. Copper-alloy strip in two fragments, 23 mm long by 5 mm wide, 1 mm thick. Slightly bent or curved at one end.

b SF294. L1/F115. C88. Two fragments of slightly convex iron sheet, possibly a stud or nail head. Dimensions 23 by 13 mm, 14 by 9 mm.

CREMATION BURIAL CF403 (FIGS 2, 8, 133–4)

Cremated bone	167.0 g	adult of indeterminate age and sex
Pottery vessels	CF403.1	local ware moulded platter
	CF403.2	pimply ware globular jar
Residual finds		none

Cremation burial CF403 was in Enclosure 5, approximately equidistant between cremation burials CF47 and CF72 (FIGS 2, 8). The remains had been placed in a shallow, approximately square pit which was about 0.57 m across and survived to a depth of about 0.2 m as measured from the excavation surface (FIG. 133). The cremated bone of an adult had been placed in a slightly spread heap near the centre of the pit. Two locally made grey ware vessels were then put into the pit such that one, a small jar (CF403.2), was on top of the bones and the other, a platter (CF403.1), lay between the bones and the east side of the pit. The upper part of the jar was missing, no doubt removed in recent times. The south–west half of the burial pit was devoid of any surviving finds.

The platter CF403.1 was in two parts (FIGS 133–4). The largest piece was flat on the floor of the pit and facing upwards in the usual fashion. However, the other piece was upside down and 15 mm to the north of it. It lay at a slight angle to the floor of the pit with one end resting on the base of the side of the pit. Both parts of the vessel were carefully excavated, and a critical review of the records which we have since carried out leaves no doubt about the positions and relationship of the two in the ground. On the face of it, the two pieces seem to provide incontrovertible proof that the vessel had been deliberately broken at the time of burial and placed in the pit as two separate bits. If true, this would be the only clear example of this practice in relation to the burials associated with the enclosures. And yet this explanation does not account for the fact that the smaller piece looks as if it has simply become detached from the larger piece (which did not move), flipped over 180 degrees towards the larger piece, and ended up a short distance away to the north (FIG. 133, bottom right). There does not seem to be a modern process which could explain the splitting of the vessel. It certainly did not happen during the machine-stripping of the site (this much is clear from the subsequent excavation), and it seems hard to imagine that the effect could be caused by subsoiling in the manner that left one of the brooches in the Brooches burial CF72 in two pieces (p. 254). A subsoiler could conceivably have moved and rotated the smaller part of the vessel in the way that appears to have happened but, in doing so, the subsoiler would surely have crushed the displaced piece and left it in many bits. On balance, it seems more likely that the vessel split in antiquity when there was a void in the burial pit which would allow the side of the vessel to flip over. Although there is no direct evidence for a wooden cover, the square shape of the burial pit suggests that it may have had one (p. 427). If this was the case, then there would have been a sufficiently large void for the side of the vessel to flip over and move in such a way as to leave the detached part

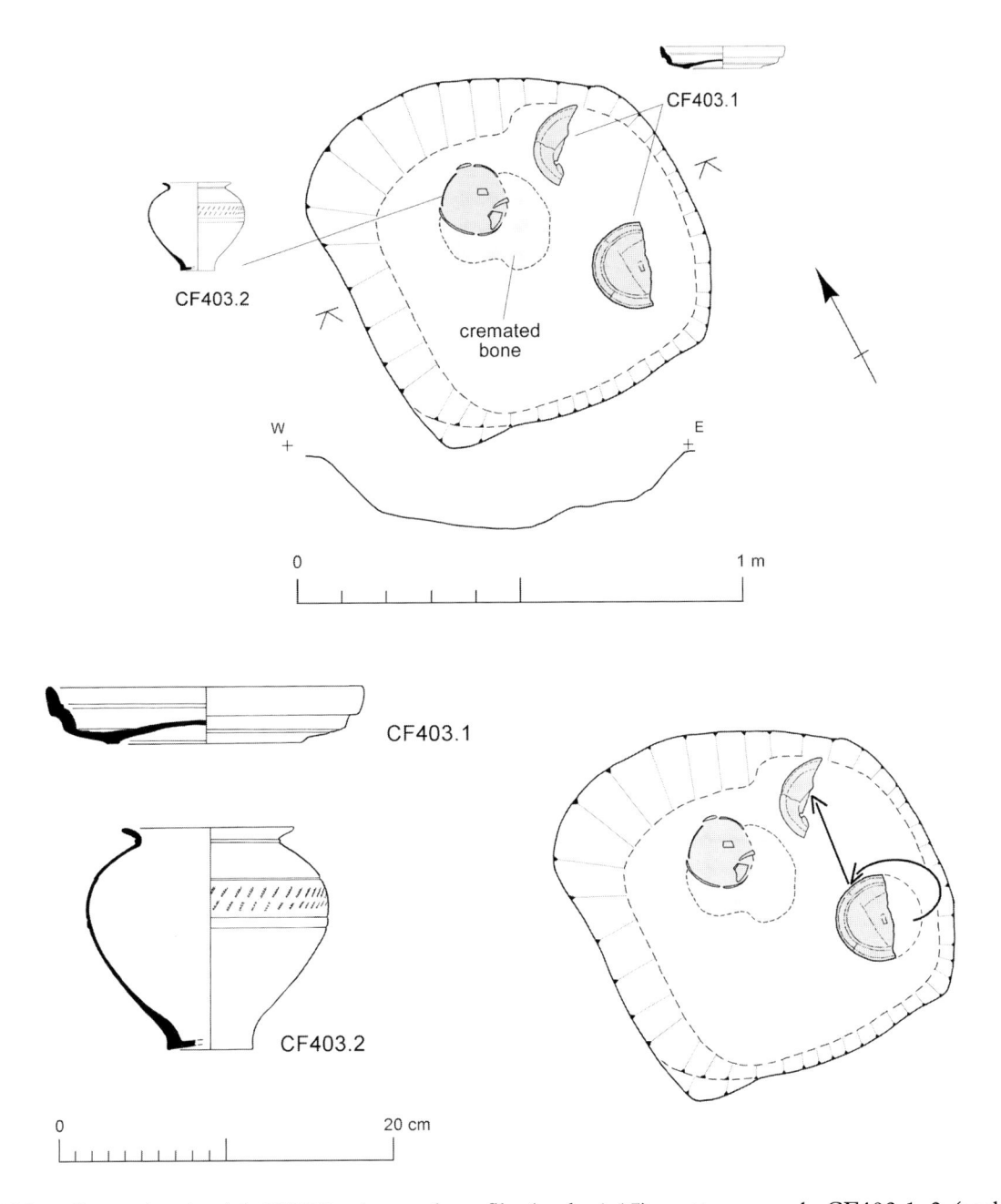

FIG. 133. Cremation burial CF403: plan and profile (scale 1:15), pottery vessels CF403.1–2 (scale 1:4), and interpretative plan showing presumed movement of a section of broken platter (scale 1:15)

in one piece. This opens up the possibility of early post-depositional movements as the explanation rather like those noted in the Doctor's burial (p. 212). But it is hard to pinpoint a likely culprit if this were the case. A burrowing animal such as a rat seems an unlikely explanation. A member of the burial party jumping or stamping on the cover prior to the backfilling of the burial pit is a more believable mechanism, but it is difficult to imagine how it would have worked. No obvious and convincing cause can thus be put forward if the vessel had indeed split in a void. However, on excavation it appeared that the smaller piece had become detached from the main body of the vessel after its deposition, which must place a question mark against the more obvious conclusion that cremation burial CF403 provides evidence of the deliberate breaking of grave goods prior to their deposition in the grave.

The jar CF403.2 is a characteristically post-conquest type of vessel which occurs commonly in 1st-century deposits in the town centre. In conjunction with the platter CF403.1, the burial can be dated broadly to *c.* A.D. 43–70, and more likely *c.* A.D. 43–60.

FIG. 134. Cremation burial CF403

Pottery vessels (FIG. 133)

Local products

CF403.1 FIG. 133. C1425. C1426. Moulded platter: Camulodunum form 8 copy. Fabric SW. Central stamp: CATV/LVSSI
Condition: fragmented, all sherds present. The sherds exhibit unequal abrasion. One of the original halves has much more abraded surfaces and fractures and the original fracture edge is so abraded the pieces do not actually join together neatly.
CF403.2 FIG. 133. C1411. C1427. Stamped globular jar: Camulodunum form 108, *CAR* **10** Fabric GX, Type 104. Fabric PW, light grey; abraded surfaces, no finish survives. Decoration: double row of sloping impressions made with simple 4-prong comb.
Condition: fragmented, quantity of sherds missing; restorable to complete base circuit to maximum girth, lacking central disc of base, diminishing upwards to one quarter-rim circuit; very abraded fractures.

THE SHAFT OR PIT CF23 (FIGS 2, 8, 135)

A deep shaft or pit (CF23) was dug into the internal angle of the south-west corner of the ditch of Enclosure 5 (FIGS 2, 8). The feature was first recognised in the top of the lower fill of the ditch, and it appeared to have been cut from the level of the top of the lower fills. However, the shaft may have been cut from higher up since its fill would have been difficult to distinguish from the upper fills of the ditch. The depth of the feature was such that a two-stage excavation was needed to allow the lower part of the feature to be shored. The shaft was roughly circular, between 800–900 mm wide (FIG. 135). Its base was just under 2 m below the level at which it was first noted. At just over 1 m down were two small circular recesses (CF166 and CF167) cut into opposing sides of the shaft wall. CF166 was at a depth of 1.1 m in the south-east wall and was 130 mm long and 60 mm wide. CF167 was at a depth of 1.15 m in the north-west wall and was 200 mm long and 80 mm wide. It seems likely that these recesses were for a horizontal wooden bar which extended across the centre of the shaft.

The upper fill was a slightly stony sandy silt with common charcoal flecks and pieces (CL34). Just back from the section near the limit of the first stage of excavation was a band of charcoal (CL51). This charcoal band extended through the north half of the shaft and appears to divide the upper and lower fill sequences. Below this (in the second stage of excavation) were further charcoal-flecked sandy silts (CL122–124) and, at about 1.4 m, there was a second band of charcoal (CL125) that extended back into a shallow hole in the north side of the feature, which probably represents an area of ancient wall collapse. The charcoal band overlay more layers of sandy silt/loam (CL127–131), and in the base was a thick deposit of gravelly sand (CL132), which probably represents material collapse from the shaft edges. There was only one sherd of

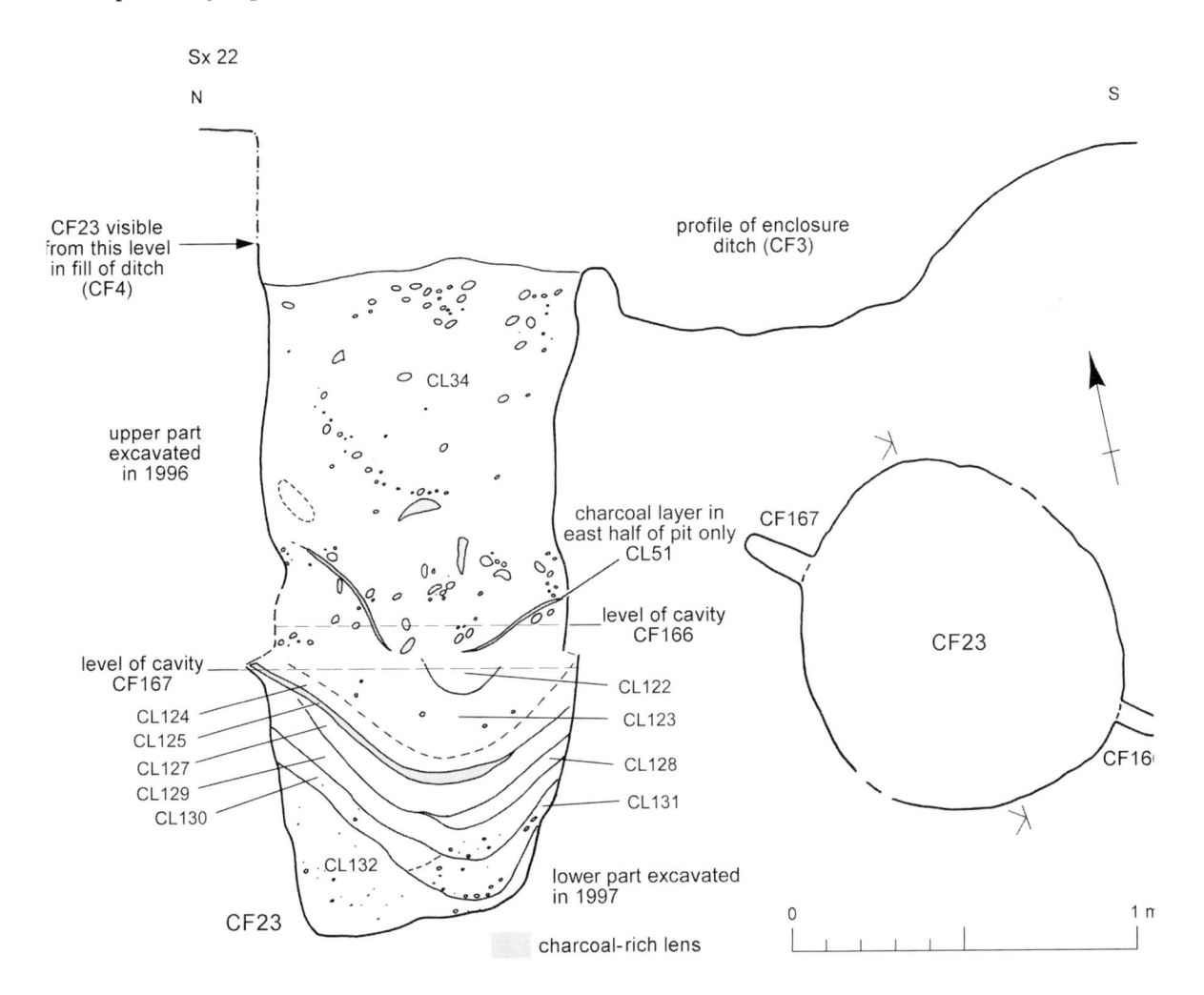

FIG. 135. Shaft or pit CF23: section and plan (scale 1:20)

pottery from this feature. This was a sherd from a large storage jar (Fabric HZ) from CL127 in the lower fill. It was badly degraded and possibly had been burnt. The upper layers (CL122–123) of the lower fill contained charred fruits and nuts from species including hawthorn, sloe, bullace and oak, which implies an episode of burning in the late summer or autumn. A similar group of material came from pit CF66, also in the enclosure ditch (pp. 8, 385).

THE SLOT OR TRENCH CF96 (FIGS 2, 8, 136–7)

Finds	CF96.1	coin of Claudius A.D. 50–60
	CF96.2	coin of Nero A.D. 64–8
		sherds of Claudian flagon
		fragments of iron nails

In Enclosure 5, approximately 6 m to the east of chamber CF42, and parallel to it, was a slot or trench (CF96) about 10 m in length (FIGS 2, 8). The slot varied in width from about 0.6 m to 1.0 m, and was between 0.1 m and 0.2 m in depth (FIGS 136–7). The central part of its eastern edge appeared to be irregular in shape, perhaps because of a small natural feature which the trench cut and could not be readily distinguished from it. The trench was filled with slightly stony, sandy silt. Its base was flat and undulating, and the sides were at about 45 degrees to the vertical. Finds were few, but included two Roman coins, one of Claudius and the other of Nero (p. 340, CF96.1–2), a very degraded top of a ring-neck flagon (FIG. 136, C169; Cam 154/155 dated Claudio–Neronian), an iron nail and some other iron fragments, possibly representing a second nail.

The coin of Nero is of considerable interest. Not only does this indicate that the slot may have been the latest feature on the site, but it provides clear proof that use of the site survived the colossal upheaval of the Boudican revolt (TABLE 79). Moreover, the coin has been heavily defaced, so that the portrait of Nero was no longer visible (FIG. 148, CF96.2).

The slot contained no charcoal, cremated bone, or other burnt material. Nor were there any signs of *in situ* scorching in its vicinity. It may therefore be that the slot was not part of a pyre-related feature, although because of the destructive effects of the ploughing, such a possibility cannot be ruled out. An alternative explanation is that it was related to an above-ground structure such as a timber temple or mausoleum which, like the temple at Gosbecks, occupied the south-east corner of the enclosure. This possibility is explored on pages 83, 447–8.

Coins (FIG. 148)

CF96.1 FIG. 148. SF197, C171: upper part of slot CF96 in Enclosure 5. Coin of Claudius A.D. 50–60 (*see* p. 340).
CF96.2 FIG. 148. SF203, C162: upper part of slot CF96 in Enclosure 5. Coin of Nero A.D. 64–8 (*see* p. 340).

Pottery sherds (FIG. 136)

FIG. 136. C169. Cam 154 ring-necked flagon. Fabric DJ(D). Part of neck rings only, very degraded and fragmented (10 sherds and fragments), Claudian.
C169. 2 sherds. Fabric HZ.

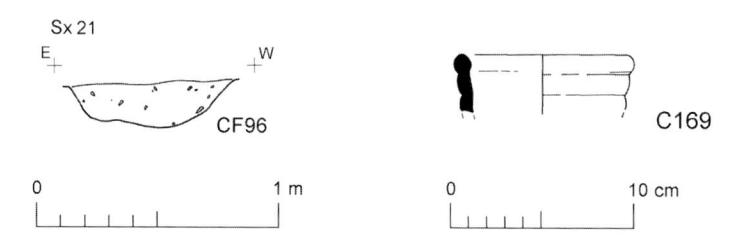

FIG. 136.   Slot or trench CF96: section (scale 1:30) and rim from pottery flagon (scale 1:4)

FIG. 137. Slot or trench CF96, viewed from the north

Other finds (not illustrated)

SF195. C167. Long slot. Iron nail with most of the shank missing. Head diameter 16 mm, length 22 mm.
SF207. C168. Fragment of iron square-section shank, 13 mm long. Also a fragment possibly from a cupped setting or nail head, maximum diameter 13 mm.

CHAPTER 5

THE SPECIALISTS' REPORTS AND DISCUSSIONS

THE LATE IRON AGE AND ROMAN POTTERY FABRICS

By Stephen Benfield

INTRODUCTION

The key accounts of the Late Iron Age and early Roman pottery from Colchester are to be found in *Camulodunum* (Hawkes and Hull 1947), *Sheepen: an early Roman industrial site at Camulodunum* (Niblett 1985), and *Colchester Archaeological Report* 10 (*CAR* 10). The first two publications deal with the large native settlement at Sheepen, whereas *CAR* 10 covers the town-centre excavations between 1971 and 1986. The Sheepen and town-centre publications each have their own pottery form and fabric type series. For the Stanway report, we have used the Sheepen form series (indicated by the usual prefix 'Cam'), but the fabrics are referenced to the series devised for *CAR* 10 and to the National Roman Fabric Reference Collection (NRFRC: Tomber and Dore 1998).

Neither of the two existing Colchester fabric series proved to be entirely suitable for recording the fabric divisions required for the Stanway coarsewares, and consequently a number of new fabric descriptions were introduced into the *CAR* 10 series for this report. The Late Iron Age pottery and early Roman coarsewares in the Camulodunum and Sheepen reports were broadly divided into groups of 'native', 'Romanising' and 'Roman' wares (Hawkes and Hull 1947, 206–7; Niblett 1985, 52, with fabric sub-codes for 'Romanising' wares). The more recent *CAR* 10 fabric series, which uses lettered codes, was based on assemblages from the Roman fortress and town and does not include 'native' Late Iron Age grog-tempered wares. Also, the 'Romanising' coarsewares of intermediate potting technique, which predominate at Stanway, could not be directly paralleled among samples from the appropriate *CAR* 10 sub-fabric groups in the fabric series archive (Colchester Museums Resource Centre). However, the pottery in the *CAR* 10 report has been quantified, and will remain the basis for much future work. In respect of this, where appropriate, *CAR* 10 fabric codes have been adopted. Although *CAR* 10 encompasses some fabrics and form-related fabric groups relevant to the Stanway assemblage, the *CAR* 10 fabric groups UR (*terra nigra*-type wares) and DZ have not been used. The *terra nigra*-type forms are divided between fabrics, although named fabrics used in *CAR* 10 under fabric group UR (*CAR* 10, 219–20) are reproduced here. Where coarseware vessels would fall into this *CAR* 10 group, this has been noted with the individual numbered pot. The description 'fine oxidising ware' (DZ) has not been used, as there are no fabric sub-divisions within this *CAR* 10 fabric group, and instead vessel fabrics were individually recorded.

It should be noted that coarsewares from the burials and features containing pyre debris, and the assemblages from the enclosure ditches, were quantified and recorded separately. At a later date, the coarseware fabrics from both assemblages were compared and rationalised into one set of fabrics. However, on comparison, there proved to be limited overlap between the pottery fabrics present in the burials and those in the enclosure ditches.

FABRIC DESCRIPTIONS

Fabric BPW/NOG WH3 Butt-beaker parchment ware/North Gaulish (Gallo-Belgic) white ware 3. Fine white fabric with cream-yellowish surfaces and commonly with grey core (NRFRC, NOG WH 3).

Fabric CAD AM Cadiz amphora. Light-coloured fabrics ranging from pale brown to pale red or orange, frequently with lighter or pale yellow to green-cream margins or self slipped surfaces. The fabric is hard with rough surfaces and an irregular fracture (NRFRC).

Fabric CAM AM 1 Campanian (Black sand) amphora 1. Pink or red to red-brown fabric, sometimes with slightly lighter internal surfaces and normally with an external slip showing as very pale pink or cream. Sherds are hard and the break is hackly with harsh surfaces (NRFRC).

Fabric CAM AM 2 (Northern) Campanian amphora 2. Fabric typically orange-brown or red-brown, occasionally with buff surfaces. The fabric is very hard with a hackly fracture and rough surfaces (NRFRC).

Fabric CAT AM Catalan amphora. Fabric is distictively red-brown to red throughout, with surfaces slightly lighter or duller in the same tones. The fabric is very hard with harsh surfaces and a hackly fracture (NRFRC).

Fabric CG CC1 CC2 Central Gaulish colour-coated wares, Lyon ware/Central Gaulish (white and cream) colour-coated wares. CG CC1: Clean white fine fabric with few inclusions, typically colour-coated or can be glazed (NRFRC, CNG CC1). CG CC2: Fabric varies from cream to buff, though occasionally pale orange, distinguished from CG CC1 by the range of inclusions and the presence of mica (NRFRC, CNG CC 2).

Fabric CNG GL1 GL2 Central Gaulish lead-glazed ware/Central Gaulish (white and cream) glazed wares 1 and 2. CNG GL1: Clean white fine fabric with few inclusions and glazed surfaces (NRFRC, CNG GL1), CNG GL2 Fabric varies from cream to buff, though occasionally pale orange, distinguished from CNG CL1 by the range of inclusions and the presence of mica (NRFRC CNG GL 2).

Fabric CSOW Coarse sandy micaceous oxidised ware. Fabric brownish-red throughout with smoothed or burnished surfaces. Fabric contains visible sand and common fine mica. The fabric appears similar to FMW and FSOW (vessels in this category could be included in *CAR* **10** under fabric group DZ – fine oxidising wares).

Fabric DJ/DJ(D) Coarse oxidised and related wares (*CAR* **10** fabric group). Predominantly local Roman oxidised wares. At Stanway the vessels are all in buff fabric with few inclusions, sub-fabric DJ(D), *CAR* **10** fabric group DJ colour code D buff/whitish buff (*CAR* **10**, 310).

Fabric FJ Brockley Hill/Verulamium region oxidised ware (*CAR* **10** fabric group). Cream or off-white hard very sandy fabric, though surfaces may vary from pink to pale orange to yellow, and often with a pale core of pink or other colour similar to the range of surface colours (NRFRC, VER WH).

Fabric FMW Fumed micaceous ware (oxidised). The fabric is closely defined with a fine-grained even textured micaceous matrix, initially fired in an oxidising atmosphere to orange and then in a final short phase of 'fuming' using 'wet' smoke to produce a thin black coating over the exterior. Being so fine-grained, a kiln structure was required to ensure that the rise in temperature was slow to prevent the pots exploding as the water of crystallisation was evaporated. The source is unknown but must be in southern Britain, possibly even at Camulodunum itself. In texture the fabric is very similar to 'silty wares', a group of more or less micaceous fine-grained fabrics (always oxidised) which were used for a range of flagons, *lagenae*, honeypots, butt-beaker copies, and lid-seated jars found in the King Harry Lane cemetery. Originally it was thought that some or all were imports, but thin-section analysis suggested that a source could be local to Verulamium and that they were the first pots made using Roman techniques of clay and temper selection, fabrication and firing in the Claudian period (Rigby and Freestone 1988). Typological research demonstrated that wherever the source, it apparently supplied a region extending at least through adjacent parts of Bedfordshire, Cambridgeshire, Essex, Hertfordshire and Northamptonshire. There are *lagenae* or flagons in cremation burials, including the Stansted Airport cemetery, Baldock, the 'Kayser Bondor Burial', Hertfordshire, and Ashton, Northamptonshire.

FSOW Fine sandy oxidised ware (micaceous). Fabric as FMW but surfaces not fumed.

Fabric FSW/EGW Fine sandy ware/early grey wares. A common, non-specific fabric group with fine-grained, even-textured matrix and fine quartz sand temper. In the hand, specimen examples vary from non-micaceous to micaceous, although the mica is not prominent. The surfaces are typically burnished and kiln-fired to grey. Micaceous sandy ware (fabric FMW, FSOW and possibly CSOW) may fall into the group. Just where and by how many potteries it was produced remains to be determined. There was a source at Much Hadham, Hertfordshire, on the main east–west road from Camulodunum, which was working from *c.* A.D. 60, and there may have been one at Camulodunum itself (*CAR* **10**, 219–20). Versions continued to be produced at Hadham in the late Roman period. It remains to be seen how significant the presence/absence of mica may be in determining the sources and dating. There is just one complete vessel at Stanway, a cup in the Doctor's grave CF47, which provides useful dating evidence for the introduction about A.D. 50 of kiln-fired, reduced, fine sandy wares (*CAR* **10**, 219).

Fabric GBW Glossy burnished ware. Surfaces burnished charcoal grey/black to dark brownish-grey. Fabric reddish-brown, though thicker sherds may have a brown-grey core. The fabric appears moderately fine and clean, sparse to occasional fragments of black burnt organic matter and grog. Typically, on platters the upper inner visible surface was finished with a smooth glossy burnish, while that on the lower outer surface varies from a smooth glossy burnish to rough and unfinished. An unusual feature is multi-pronged combed circles or spirals decorating the upper base, clearly characteristic of a concentrated group of potters if not of one workshop. The forms are post-conquest introductions, and the technology bridges Late Iron Age and Roman methods. The fabric resembles West Stow, Fabric 2, and two forms are similar to West Stow types (West 1990, 76). As the list of potters' stamps shows, some West Stow products did reach Camulodunum (*CAR* **10**, 219 — Smooth ware).

Fabric GTW Grog-tempered wares. Vessels of Late Iron Age potting tradition. Crushed fired clay was the typical Late Iron Age temper used from early in the 1st century B.C. Other inclusions like coarse sand, flint and glauconite occur in GTW depending on the type of clay selected as well as how the added temper was prepared. Fired in a bonfire, the matrix was either grey or brown with black, white and orange argillaceous inclusions depending on their origins, while the surface colours varied from light red-brown to dark brown and could be very patchy.

Fabric GX/GX(H) Other coarse wares, principally locally produced grey wares (*CAR* **10** fabric group). Various fabrics, but predominantly Roman local sandy grey wares. At Stanway all vessels appear to be in sub-fabric GX(H), very coarse sandy grey 'Colchester' fabric (*CAR* **10**, 379).

Fabric HD/HD(F) Shell-tempered and calcite-gritted wares (*CAR* **10** fabric group). Commonly vessels where the predominant temper is crushed shell. At Stanway the vessels in this fabric have been identified on form Cam 259 which only occurs in shell-tempered fabrics (*CAR* **10**, 478–9) as the shell temper has been dissolved out of the fabric leaving voids. Sub-fabric HD(F) hand-made red/brown/black fabric with sparse inclusions (*CAR* **10**, 458).

Fabric HZ Large storage jars and other vessels in heavily tempered grey wares (*CAR* **10** fabric group). Predominantly large storage jars but also other vessels where the fabric has been heavily tempered with grass, straw or other organic material which has burnt out during firing leaving an irregular pitted surface. At Stanway these vessels also commonly contain various quantities of grog temper.

Fabric MVW Mixed vesicular ware. The fine-grained smooth matrix is heavily tempered with coarse black argillaceous inclusions, possibly glauconite or grog, fragments of black burnt organic matter and white sand grains, probably flint. There are also numerous voids throughout the fabric which are most visible at the surfaces. The vesicular effect is due to the leaching of calcareous inclusions after burial or the burning out of organic inclusions during firing and/or the cremation rite. The surfaces are so eroded that it is not possible to identify the finish, but all were presumably burnished, at least on the visible surfaces. All vessels were fired to grey and blue-grey. Given the degree of tempering, no kiln structure was necessary.

Fabric PW 'Pimply' ware. Fine-grained dense matrix with coarse sand inclusions which, when the finish has been eroded, produces a rough, pimply texture to surfaces. Fired in a kiln to light grey-buff (*CAR* **10**, 219–20). A similar fabric occurred in 1st-century A.D. contexts at Baldock, Hertfordshire in a range of decorative tablewares including platters (*CAR* **10**, 220; Stead and Rigby 1986, 265, Fabric 17).

Fabric RCVW Romanising coarse vesicular ware. The fabric is grey or brown-grey in colour and is generally moderately hard. The surfaces are sometimes patchy grey to brown, but are predominantly grey in colour and often appear abraded. The surfaces are generally pitted and vesicular, with small voids from burnt-out or dissolved temper, and tiny flecks of silver mica are visible. The fabric contains dark inclusions or temper that appear to be fragments of burnt organic matter (possibly dung or sawdust) and grog. The vessels appear to be wheel-made and kiln-fired.

Fabric RCW Romanising coarse ware. The fabric colour is grey or red-brown, often with red-brown margins and a grey-brown or grey core. The fabric is generally slightly soft and sometimes has a tendency to laminate. The surfaces are dark grey-brown to dark grey, sometimes with small voids from burnt-out or dissolved temper, and tiny flecks of silver mica are visible. The surfaces are smooth, but vary from almost burnished to a coarse and 'pimply'. The fabric contains dark inclusions, or temper, that appear to be fragments of burnt organic matter (possibly dung or sawdust) and grog. The vessels appear to be wheel-made and kiln-fired.

Fabric ROW Romanising oxidised ware. Surfaces smooth or burnished and reddish-brown. Fabric generally fairly clean with reddish-brown margins and brown-grey core though with occasional dark inclusions of grog and/or possibly organic (dung) temper. (Some vessels in this category would be included in *CAR* **10** under fabric group DZ — fine oxidising wares.)

Fabric SW Sandy ware. A grouping of non-specific fabrics tempered with coarser and more visible mixed sand temper than fine sandy ware (FSW/EGW). Kiln-fired to light grey or blue-grey with a smooth burnished finish, it forms a continuum with fine sandy ware and in some cases simply reflects different production batches rather than different workshops or sources (*CAR* **10**, 219–20). There is only one certain example in the fabric, a close copy of an imported Gallo-Belgic platter in CF403, though a second sherd from BF40 (also probably part of a platter though a different vessel) may be part of this fabric group (*CAR* **10**, 220).

Fabric TN/GAB TN1(A) *Terra nigra*/Gallo-Belgic *terra nigra* 1. Grey to dark grey surfaces with a high-quality slip and fine grey fabric (NRFRC, GAB TN 1).

Fabric TR1(C)/GAB TR1(C) *Terra rubra* 1(C)/Gallo-Belgic *terra rubra* 1(C). Fabric red- to red-orange to pale orange, and surfaces with a polished slip of the same colour range but usually darker than the fabric (NRFRC GAB TR 1C).

Fabric TR3/GAB TR3 *Terra rubra* 3/Gallo-Belgic *terra rubra* 3. Fabric in variety of colours, but commonly pale red fabrics with orange surface unless the surface is fumed to darker brown (NRFRC, GBA TR 3).

Fabric WPW/NOG WH1 White pipe clay ware/North Gaulish (Gallo-Belgic) white ware 1. Fabric cream-white with slightly darker surfaces or pale pink margin (NRFRC, NOG WH 1).

THE POTS FROM FUNERARY CONTEXTS AND PYRE DEBRIS IN PITS

By Valery Rigby

Four of the five burials and ritual deposits richest in imported Gallo-Belgic pottery of the Tiberio–Neronian period in Britain have been found at Camulodunum, one in 1940 in St Clare Drive (Hull 1942) within the site of the Lexden cemetery, and three (BF64, CF47, BF6) at Stanway. They are a snapshot of what was available in the cupboard and the market place at the time of a single event and provide a useful dating tool. For sites like the Stanway cemetery, there is one basic chronological question about each burial or ritual deposit: is it pre-Caesarean, pre-conquest or pre-Boudican? — and the answer to this apparently simple question is central to any cultural interpretation illustrating either continuity or change.

Numerically, pots are the most popular surviving funerary item, with the total for the cemetery of at least 99 in thirteen deposits (*i.e.* the burials and chambers and the pits with pyre-related debris). At Stanway, averages are meaningless, for the number per context varies between a singleton and 23 pots. In addition, the numbers in individual burials/contexts with pyre-related debris differ markedly between Enclosure 1, just one and two pots, Enclosure 4 with one group of 22 pots, and Enclosures 3 and 5 where the range is from two to 23.

Richness can be measured also by whether the pots are imports or more easily obtained local products, *i.e.* made somewhere in the vicinity of Colchester. The 68 imports comprise an impressive 67 per cent, which is way ahead of the King Harry Lane (KHL) cemetery with 29 per cent. As with the total number of pots, averages per context mask the really significant numerical range. There are no imports in the Enclosure 1 contexts and only three in Enclosure 4, so the total of 63 is unevenly divided between seven deposits in Enclosures 3 and 5 where four (BF6, BF64, CF42, CF115) are entirely comprised of imports, but again the numerical range is wide; in one context, two pots out of two (CF115), in another (BF64), fifteen out of fifteen. One assemblage of fourteen pots (CF47) has a token local product apparently to make up a 'place setting' in an otherwise import-dominated burial. This is in contrast to a burial with two local pots and one import (CF72). Finally, one burial (CF403), probably the latest from the enclosures, contains just two local products.

THE CHRONOLOGY OF BURIALS, PITS WITH PYRE-RELATED DEBRIS, AND ENCLOSURES

The dating of individual burials and the enclosures is argued elsewhere and is summarised on pages 436–7. The earliest pot is from pyre-related debris filling pit CF7 which lies outside the enclosure system. It is hand-made and entirely pre-Roman Iron Age in typology and technique and could have been made any time in the 1st century B.C. Although traditional potting techniques survived Roman occupation but apparently not the Boudican revolt, so providing a conventional *terminus ante quem* of A.D. 65, the most likely date range for the manufacture of this pot, based on typology and technology, is 75–25 B.C. Thus, allowing a couple of decades for an 'heirloom' factor, the latest date of deposition would be 5 B.C.

Enclosure 1 is the earliest of the funerary enclosures. Only three pots can be identified as being funerary-related (from AF18 and the chamber AF25), but they and several incidental sherds are also pre-Roman Iron Age in typology and technique, and so a date of manufacture in the 1st century B.C. is likely. There was one imported flagon sherd in the enclosure ditch, but it is small and abraded and can be disregarded. The absence of Gallo-Belgic imports from the funerary-related contexts (AF18, AF25, AF48) supports a date of deposition before 25 B.C. If these contexts in Enclosure 1 do belong to the mid 1st century B.C., then there is a gap of at least as much as a century before Enclosures 3, 4 and 5 were laid out. This is equivalent to a gap of roughly four generations.

Using the pottery alone (and this qualification should be stressed because of the other grave goods from this feature), the earliest funerary-related context in the second stage of use could be burial CF72, for here two traditional Iron Age carinated bowls with a date range 75 B.C. to A.D. 65 are accompanied by an import with a date range A.D. 25 to 65. Theoretically, at least, the burial could be pre-Claudian and so be the earliest in Enclosure 5, despite lying in a position secondary to chamber CF42.

Using only the Gallo-Belgic stamps, the second stage sequence begins with chamber BF6 in Enclosure 3 which is the only deposit to include definitely pre-Claudian imports (13 per cent of the total) and where nothing has to date to the post-conquest period. The date of deposition should therefore lie between A.D. 35 and 50 at the latest. BF6 has numerically the largest assemblage from the site. The chamber CF42 in Enclosure 5 is later than BF6, because it contains a flanged cup Cam 58 which was standardised after A.D. 45 and continued in production until A.D. 70.

If BF6 is pre-Claudian, then Enclosure 3 spans the conquest period because the Warrior's burial (BF64) contains two Claudio–Neronian forms, two flanged cups of Cam 58 and two offset platters of Cam 14. The same two forms also feature in the Doctor's burial in Enclosure 5 (CF47), which is also post-conquest. There may be little difference between it and BF64, since the same die (Stamp 16–19) is represented in both on 'identical' platters. Enclosure 5 also contains the latest burial in the cemetery (*i.e.* CF403) deposited sometime between A.D. 50 and 70. The two pots in CF403 are local kiln-fired products which illustrates how the local ceramic production evolved in the later 1st century A.D. with the introduction of new forms as well as new techniques.

Being datable to around A.D. 60, the assemblage of pottery in BF24 in Enclosure 4 was the latest from the chambers. Although the group only contained three imports, one is a pre-Flavian Central Gaulish colour-coated cup which occurs rarely in graves. Its varied array of local products illustrates how local potters adapted to trading conditions after the Roman occupation. Three workshops producing copies of Gallo-Belgic imports have been identified.

Comparing the chronologies of the imports in the Stanway and King Harry Lane cemeteries, the latter roughly fills the gap between Enclosure 1 and Enclosures 3 and 5 suggesting that the sequence is as follows:

King Harry Lane	**Stanway**
	Stanway Enclosure 1
— a gap in both cemeteries —	
KHL Phase 1	

KHL Phase 2
KHL Phase 3 most burials

Burial CF72, Enclosure 5
central chamber BF6, Enclosure 3
Stanway Enclosures 3 and 5 (excluding Burial CF403, Enclosure 5)

KHL Phase 3 at least Burial 28, 295, 316

Stanway Enclosure 4
Stanway Enclosure 5, Burial CF403

KHL Phase 4

CHOICE OF POTS

The typological and functional range differs markedly between Enclosure 1 and Enclosures 3, 4 and 5, probably as a result of chronological differences, but possibly also due to the very small sample of just three or four vessels in the former. In Enclosure 1 (AF18, AF25, AF48), there are two closed-jar forms and one unusual straight-sided bowl or mug. They are Late Iron Age products for a Late Iron Age market showing no influence of imports in form, function or technique, although the latter must have been influenced by lathe-turned wood or shale containers. The largest jar was used as the cremation urn, the others were accessory vessels like the single pot in the isolated pyre-debris pit CF7.

In contrast, the functional range in Enclosures 3, 4 and 5 consists of so-called 'tableware', *i.e.* platters, footring cups, flagons (single- and two-handled) to decant, display and consume food and drink formally in the Roman manner, and this is regardless of whether the pots are imports or local products. Whatever happened in life, in burial there has been a complete change in manners which integrates Stanway into the customs of the wider Roman world, for while the burials in Enclosure 1 could only be found in a particular region of southern Britain, those in Enclosures 3 and 5, with the exception of burial CF72, could have been found in Gallia Belgica and Germania Inferior, that is between the Loire and lower Rhine. Given this, the inkwell in burial BF67 takes on enormous significance with the growing need for written communication.

Compared to Camulodunum, the typological range of imports, particularly the platters and cups, is limited, with few pre-Claudian products, which implies that chronology is the crucial factor. In burials BF64 and CF47, one small platter and a footring cup seem to match up into individual place settings, along with an amphora and a large flagon presumably for decanted liquid, wine, beer or water. Even the badly fragmented assemblages in the central chambers BF6 and CF42 display a probable functional symmetry occasionally present in the King Harry Lane cemetery and present in the St Clare Drive burial (Hull 1942) within the Lexden cemetery.

When choosing imports as grave goods, whether at the behest of the deceased or as their own preference, the mourners associated with the Warrior's burial and Doctor's burial demonstrated their ability to acquire these exotic objects. Just how rare they had become by A.D. 50 is questionable, but one thing is incontrovertible; the imports were the most colourful, glossy and flamboyant pots available at the time. They were in marked contrast to the earth colours of Late Iron Age techniques and the muted colours of early vessels produced using Roman techniques like those which occurred in the chamber BF24 in Enclosure 4. The most striking would have been the Warrior's burial BF64, with white, pale yellow, orange, red, blue, black and finally a glazed green miniature flagon; then there was his collection of glass and bronzes! The grave goods in the Doctor's burial too must have been almost as spectacularly colourful (CF47), and even the secondary grave BF67 with just two pots consisted of one red inkwell and a white *lagena*. The similarity in the assemblages in the two burials may indicate close family ties. Gallo-Belgic imports may predominate, but Stanway shows that increased competition from other regions of Gaul is coming on stream, particularly the samian factories of South Gaul but also the specialist workshops around Lyon in Central Gaul.

Comparison with the St Clare Drive burial (referred to above), an assemblage rich in imports, highlights two notable differences. The first and more easily explicable difference is the absence of large-diameter Gallo-Belgic platters from the Stanway burial groups, although they are present in the ?mortuary enclosure BF32 in Enclosure 4 and the chamber CF42 in Enclosure 5 which is almost certainly the result of chronology, namely the cessation by A.D. 40 to 50 of the production of large platters. The second difference is a complete surprise and not easily explained — the total absence from burials and the chamber in Enclosure 5 of buttbeakers of Cam 113 in parchment wares. This vessel was so common at the Sheepen site at Camulodunum that the excavators considered it a local product and not an import (Hawkes and Hull 1947, 238). There is one in the St Clare Drive burial and three in the Sheepen Cremation Group 3 (Niblett 1985, 25–6, fig. 15), so it was acceptable as grave goods in the specific area. There is nothing in its area of distribution or dating to account easily for the absence at Stanway of the single most common fineware type in the King Harry Lane cemetery and also in cremation burials in southern Britain generally (Parfitt 1995). The situation is rendered even more inexplicable by the occurrence of Cam 113 beakers in burials at Stanway on Site D (DF1.1 and DF28.1; pp. 402, 405) and sherds in the ditch of the ?mortuary enclosure in Enclosure 4, and in ditches of Enclosure 3, 4 and 4/5 where a minimum of eight vessels is represented, all pretty thoroughly fragmented and abraded and with almost no joins.

THE LATE IRON AGE AND ROMAN POTTERY FROM THE ENCLOSURE DITCHES AND THE DITCHES OF ?MORTUARY ENCLOSURES BF32 AND CF43–6 (FIGS 138–44; TABLES 37–42)

By Stephen Benfield

THE NATURE OF THE ASSEMBLAGE (FIGS 138–44; TABLES 37–8)

Late Iron Age and Roman pottery was recovered from all of the enclosure ditches and the ditches of the ?mortuary enclosures BF32 and CF43–6, but the amount varied greatly according to the context and circumstances of the excavation (FIG. 138; TABLE 37). The pottery assemblages from the ditches in Enclosures 3–5 proved to be different in composition to the assemblages from the burials, and the Gallo-Belgic elements in those two groups also differed.

The Late Iron Age/Roman pottery from Enclosure 2 was very small in quantity and only occurred in the main fill of the enclosure ditch. Only a small part of the enclosure ditch of Enclosure 1 was excavated, and the amount of pottery recovered from it was correspondingly limited. The much more extensive excavations of the ditches in Enclosures 3–5 provided a pottery assemblage which was not only much larger, but accounts for most of the Late Iron Age and Roman pottery that survived in those enclosures.

Much of the pottery from the ditches consisted of sherd clusters from smashed pieces of broken pots (termed here 'partial pots'). Despite the aggressive (*i.e.* acid) soil conditions which have degraded surfaces and eroded the sherd edges, it proved possible to identify sherds relating to at least 149 different pots and, in some cases, partly reconstruct them. This has provided approximate minimum numbers of broken vessels represented in the ditches (TABLE 38). Pots have been illustrated where enough of the profile can be reconstructed (FIGS 139–44).

Overall, the pottery groups from the enclosure ditches and ?mortuary enclosures represent the types and range of vessels that would be expected in domestic assemblages of the Late Iron Age and early Roman periods. The Gallo-Belgic and Gaulish imports from the ditches add status and extend the range of vessel functions to include flagons and a few cups. The approximate composition of the vessel types in the assemblage is as follows (TABLE 39): jars 34% (49), beakers 19% (28), platters 10% (15), bowls 10% (15), flagons and two-handled flagons 6% (8), cups 5% (7), amphoras 7% (10), and other 9% (13).

Apart from the Gallo-Belgic wares and a few sherds of amphoras and samian, the pottery is mostly, if not almost entirely, of local origin. Although the two shell-tempered pots (FIG. 142, Pots 104–5) may be part of the South Essex shell-tempered tradition and therefore may have originated from the south of the county, the only certain regional import is a flagon handle from the Verulamium area (Enclosure 5, Pot 134).

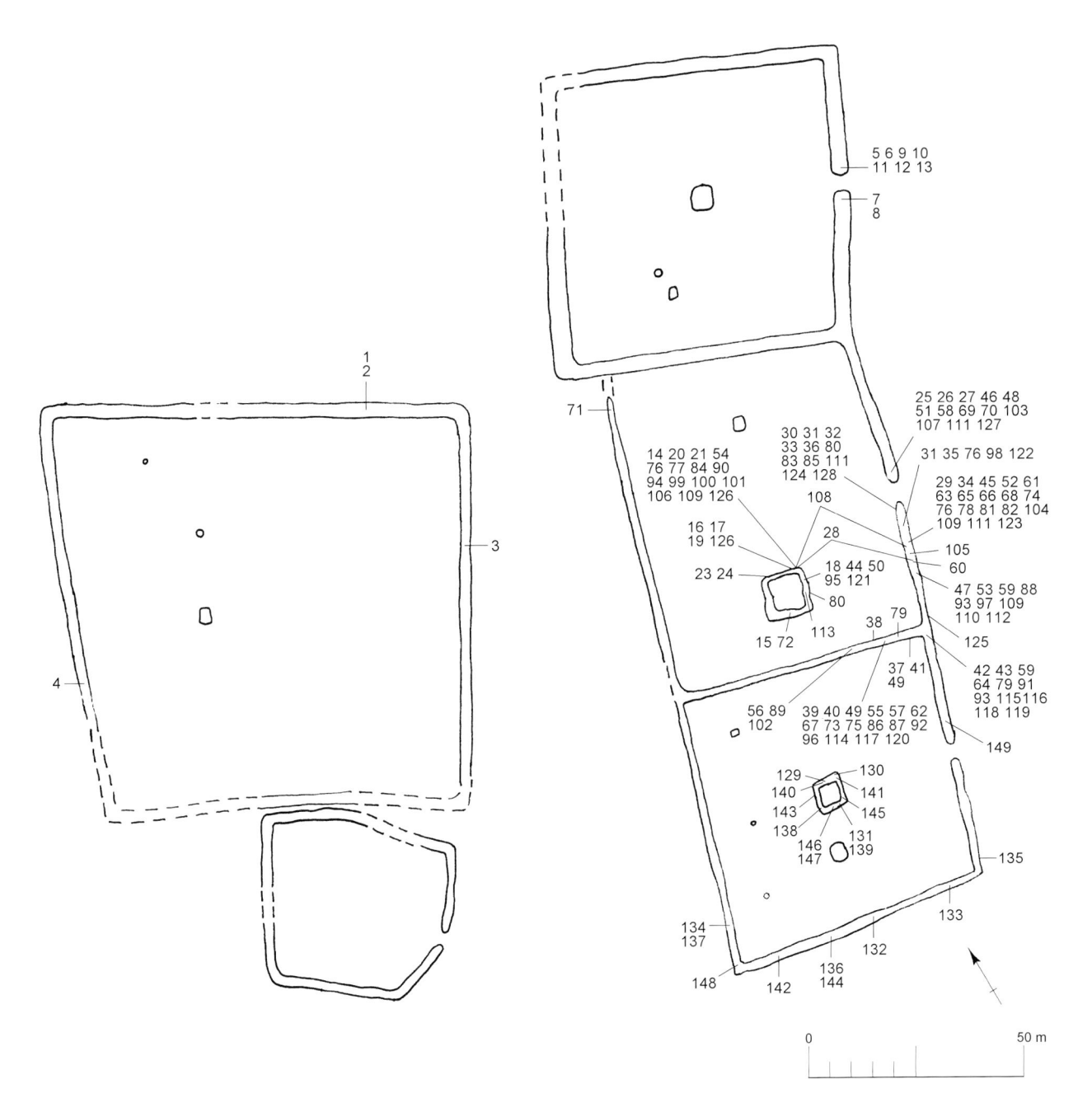

FIG. 138.   Distribution of pottery vessels in the ditches

The pottery reflects a range of vessels relating to the storage, preparation, serving and consumption of food and drink. Among the coarse wares, most of the cooking pots, together with some of the jars, show signs of use with sooting on external surfaces, and there are traces of carbonised organic matter on Pots 105 and 111. The few post-firing holes noted in bases (FIG. 141, Pots 95–6) and necks (FIG. 139, Pot 53; FIG. 141, Pot 92) of some coarseware pots are also not uncommon on occupation sites. Although not unusual among domestic assemblages, the presence of the large storage jars deserves comment. They occur as sherds in all the enclosures, but are best represented among the large assemblage associated with Enclosure 4 (FIGS 142–3). The presence on the site of so many of these vessels is somewhat surprising, considering that they were large and heavy and must have been rather awkward to move around easily.

Collectively, the enclosure ditches and ?mortuary enclosures of Enclosures 3–5 produced a different pottery assemblage from that in the burials and chambers of these enclosures. The range of forms differs, with only the two following exceptions. Two-handled flagon sherds in

TABLE 37: STANWAY POTTERY OTHER THAN AMPHORAS FROM THE ENCLOSURE DITCHES AND PYRE-SITES

Fabric	Enclosure 1 ditches Cam form	Enclosure 1 ditches fabric weight (g)	Enclosure 1 ditches fabric EVE	Enclosure 3 ditches Cam form	Enclosure 3 ditches fabric weight (g)	Enclosure 3 ditches fabric EVE	Enclosure 4 ?mortuary enclosure Cam form	Enclosure 4 ?mortuary enclosure fabric weight (g)	Enclosure 4 ?mortuary enclosure fabric EVE	Enclosure 4 ditches Cam form	Enclosure 4 ditches fabric weight (g)	Enclosure 4 ditches fabric EVE	Enclosure 5 ?mortuary enclosure Cam form	Enclosure 5 ?mortuary enclosure fabric weight (g)	Enclosure 5 ?mortuary enclosure fabric EVE	Enclosure 5 ditches Cam form	Enclosure 5 ditches fabric weight (g)	Enclosure 5 ditches fabric EVE
BPW				113	106	0.40	113 (?4+)	71	0.38	113 (?4+)	265	0.40	113	1				
CSOW					19											158	530	0.40
DJ					1			1		140D	5	0.20		11		154, 154/155	245	0.10
FJ																f	10	
FSOW	14/28	160	0.20															
GBW		2			6		?28, j, j	582	0.20	28C (2), 32, 221, 222, 230, j	1,117	1.05						
GTW	229, 263	340	0.48		29		j	87	0.13	24C, 28, 32, j, p	355	0.44	lid	98	0.18	251	895	0.82
GX		3			10			1		266	36	0.06		18		243–244/ 246, b (307?)	515	0.65
HD							258C	35	0.28	258C (2)	350	1.12						
HZ		175			5		254, 270B, ?271, 273	5,602	1.22	259, 270B (4+), ?271, 273 (3)	15,163	4.68		103		271 (?2)	411	0.10
RCVW							?218, 266 (?3)	1,446	2.14	266	496	0.85						
RFOW				114, f/l	62			48	0.28	68, ?91, bk	272	0.59						
RCW		68	0.21	266 (2)	120	0.45	24, ?30, 109, (119), 119B, 218 (2), 231/ 232, 266 (2+), j, j/bk, p	4,387	4.16	30, 44A, 92, 112, 119, 119A(4), 218 (3), 222, 228, ?230, 259, 266, (11+), j, j, j, j, j/b, p/j/b	15,205	2.93	212–17, 218 (2+), 266	502	1.84		144	0.44
RSOW				f/l	19													
SW										56, pl	56					158	530	0.40
TN							5, 7/8–8	54	0.15	8, 58, lp	149	0.39						
TR1										74 (?2)	97		(74)	3				
TR3							84, 112/91, bk	25		84, 91, 112Cb (?2+), bk	106	0.53		1	10			

Key: b – bowl, f/l – flagon/lagena, f – flagon, lp – large platter, J – jar, j/b – jar or bowl, j/bk – jar or beaker

TABLE 38: MINIMUM NUMBER OF BROKEN POTS REPRESENTED IN THE ENCLOSURE DITCHES
AND DITCHES OF THE ?MORTUARY ENCLOSURES

Enclosure	?Mortuary enclosures	Enclosure ditches	Minimum number of pots
1		4	4
3		9	9
4	27	88	115
5	11	10	21
total	**38**	**111**	**149**

TABLE 39: APPROXIMATE NUMBER OF IDENTIFIED EXAMPLES OF VESSEL TYPES FROM THE
?MORTUARY ENCLOSURES AND ENCLOSURE DITCHES AT STANWAY

Vessel type	Enclosure 1	Enclosure 3	Enclosure 4 ?mortuary enclosure	Enclosure 4 ditch	Enclosure 5 ?mortuary enclosure	Enclosure 5 ditch	Total
flagon	1	3	1	1	1	3	10
cup				5	1	1	7
beaker		2	9	20	1		32
platter	1		5	10			16
bowl	1			9	3	3	16
jar	1	2	8	30	1		42
narrow neck jar			1				1
large storage jar			1	10		1	12
lids					1		1
amphora		2	1	2	3	2	10
other			1	1			2

fabric WPW (Pots 5 and 7) from Enclosure 3 ditch terminals are probably of the same form (Cam 161) as pots BF24.2 and BF24.3 from chamber BF24, and a cup (FIG. 144, Pot 140) from the ?mortuary enclosure BF43–6 in Enclosure 5 is of the same form as the two in the cremation burial CF72 (CF72.2–3). The range of fabrics too does not overlap, apart from two platters (FIG. 139, Pots 46 and 49) in fabric GBW from the Enclosure 4 ditch which are from the same workshop as the platters from the chamber BF24.

The differences in fabric types is largely because the burials are dominated by imported products, especially Gallo-Belgic wares, which are almost absent from the ditches.

The assemblage from the ditches of Enclosure 5 is the only one of its kind to contain sherds or partial vessels which have been exposed to sufficient heat to discolour or disfigure them. Despite their modest number, these vessels are important because they would appear to provide a direct link between the breaking of the pots scattered in the ditches and the funerary ceremonies. Most of them, *i.e.* Pots 129, 130, 138 (FIG. 144; a ?waster), and 141 (FIG. 144) came from the ?mortuary enclosure CF43–CF46, so that evidence of scorching or burning is not particularly surprising in these cases. However, there were two pots (Pot 37 and the near-complete Pot 135) from the enclosure ditches that had been burnt. Pot 130 is probably the same pot as the base representing Pot 37 (from enclosure ditch BF4/CF1), and both had been burnt or scorched. Pots 135 and 138 (FIG. 144) from the ?mortuary enclosure CF43–CF46 had been badly scorched on one side, as if they had been placed on the ground close to the edge of a pyre rather than on it.

DATE (FIGS 139–44; TABLE 40)

Collectively the pottery from the ditches spans the Late Iron Age and the early Roman periods. The earliest pottery from the enclosure ditches are two grog-tempered Late Iron Age pots (FIG.

278

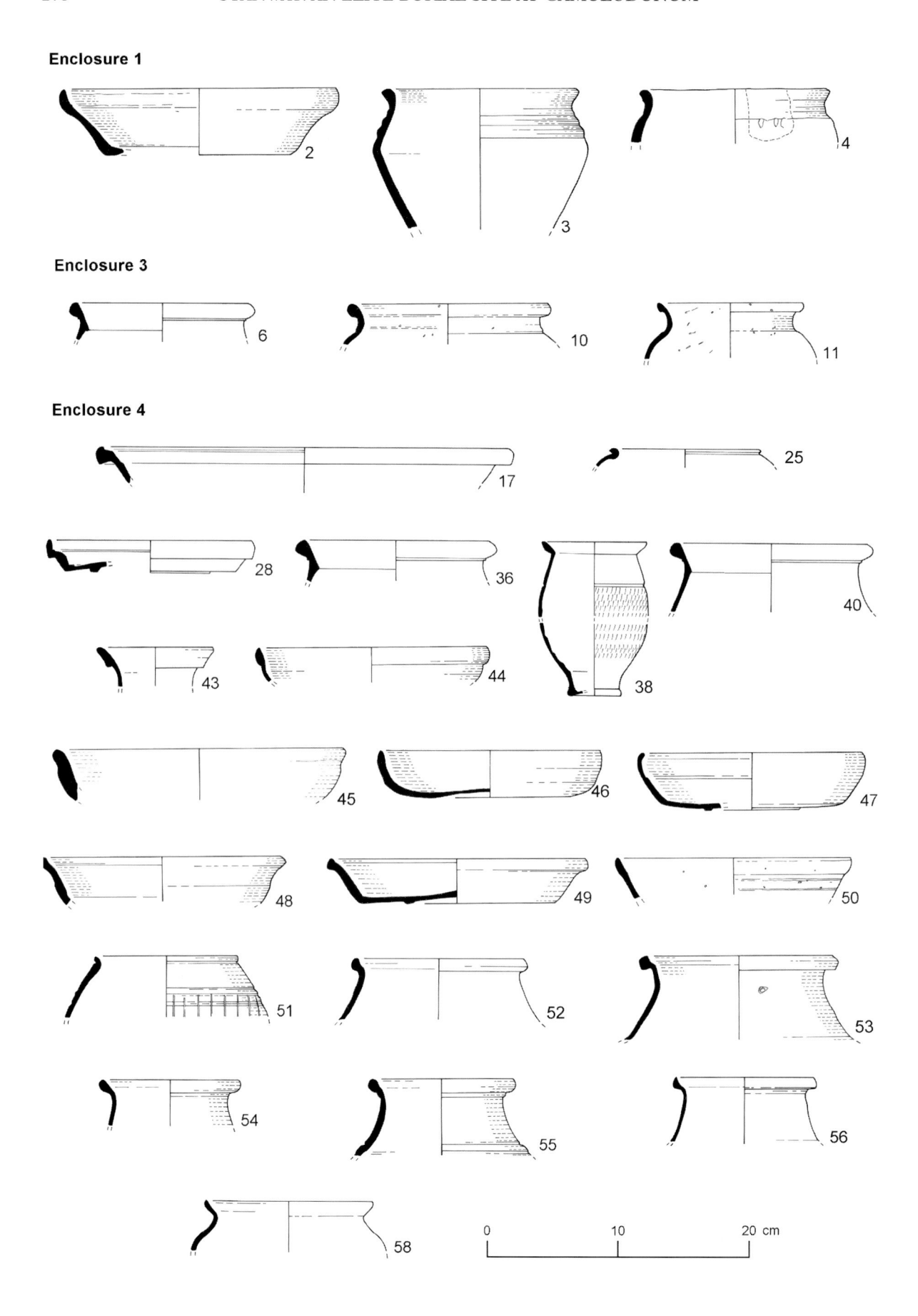

FIG. 139. Pottery vessels from the ditches of Enclosure 1 and Enclosures 3–4: Pots 2–58 (scale 1:4)

139, Pots 3–4) from the lower fill of the Enclosure 1 ditch. These can be dated to after *c.* 75–50 B.C., and have parallels at Sheepen, which is dated (not necessarily correctly) to after *c.* A.D. 5. The pottery from the ditches in Enclosures 3–5 include imported Gallo-Belgic wares, introduced *c.* 20–10 B.C. From Enclosure 5, there are Roman fabrics and pottery vessel types introduced at the conquest which remained current until the early to mid 2nd century, although there is nothing about them which need date to later than the Claudio–Neronian period.

For Enclosures 3–5, close dating of the coarsewares on their own is difficult. The pot types from the ditches are predominantly of native Late Iron Age/Gaulish background. The forms and fabrics contrast with pottery assemblages from the fortress/early *colonia*, which are of post-conquest date. The Stanway pottery is dominated by Romanising fabrics of intermediate Late Iron Age/Roman potting technique. A search of the *CAR* 10 Roman pottery fabric archive (in Colchester Museums) produced no clear parallels for the common fabric types at Stanway, although it should be borne in mind that the Stanway pottery has suffered from burial in acidic soils which makes identification of fabrics more difficult.

The presence of *terra rubra* in the ditches of Enclosures 4 and 5 may be indicative of a relatively early date for these contexts, since it is absent from stratified deposits in London where occupation is thought to date from the A.D. 50s (Davies *et al.* 1994, 166). *Terra rubra* is well represented among the Gallo-Belgic wares in Enclosures 4 and 5 with sherds from eleven pots (Pots 19, 20, 24, 25, 31–34, 37–39) from Enclosure 4 and one pot (Pot 130) from Enclosure 5.

Overall, the earliest date for at least some of the pottery associated with Enclosures 3–5 is the late 1st century B.C. There is nothing which need date to later than *c.* A.D. 70. The predominance of Romanising fabrics suggests the majority of the pottery from Enclosures 4 and 5 is of early post-conquest (Claudio–Neronian) date. The absence or low incidence of common early post-conquest fabrics and forms and the presence of *terra rubra* among the assemblages supports a Claudian date (p. 437).

The pottery assemblages from the ditches are also difficult to date by enclosure. Late Iron Age grog-tempered wares, Gallo-Belgic/Gaulish wares and early Roman fabrics and forms occur in all the enclosure ditches (except Enclosure 2). This is probably a result of the ditches being left open so that pottery sherds accumulated in them during the later life of the enclosures. Nevertheless, there are differences between the dates of each of the assemblages which can be described as follows.

Enclosure 1. Excavation of the Enclosure 1 ditches was limited, making dating difficult. However, sherds from two Late Iron Age pots came from the lower ditch fill, *i.e.* a Cam 263 (Pot 4) and a Cam 229 (Pot 3), the latter being a partial vessel (FIG. 139; TABLE 40). The pots date from *c.* 75/50 B.C. to about *c.* A.D. 5, the later date because they occur at Sheepen (Niblett 1985, 1–3, where Cam 229 is moderately well represented, but Cam 263 less so (TABLE 38). The only Gaulish import, a single sherd from a flagon (Pot 1) dated A.D. 10–60, is from the main ditch fill. There was also a small quantity of early Roman pottery from the middle of the main fill (pp. 69–70) among which was a partial pot, a Cam 14/28 platter of probable Claudio–Neronian date (FIG. 139, Pot 2). Although the pottery from the lower ditch fill is limited, the Late Iron Age pots and the absence of any imports suggest a date after *c.* 70/50 B.C. and possibly before *c.* 10 B.C. for the earliest ditch fill.

Enclosure 2. A very small quantity of grog-tempered and Late Iron Age/early Roman pottery came from the main fill of the Enclosure 2 ditch. Six sherds from the ditch terminal forming the north-east side of the entrance are all probably from one pot. They were found a short distance from the funerary feature CF415 (pp. 47–8), and the sherds could thus represent the deposition of a partial pot associated with it. The sherds demonstrate that the ditch must still have been open in the Late Iron Age and early Roman periods, and that funerary-related activities may have taken place there focused on the ditch.

TABLE 40: THE INCIDENCE OF POTTERY FORMS (OTHER THAN AMPHORA) FROM THE ?MORTUARY ENCLOSURES AND ENCLOSURE DITCHES AT STANWAY AND SHEEPEN, COLCHESTER
(after Hawkes and Hull 1947, 277–81)

Cam form	Stanway Enc. 1 ditch	Enc. 3 ditch	Enc. 4 ?mort. enclosure	Enc. 4 ditch	Enc. 5 ?mort. enclosure	Enc. 5 ditch (pyre sites & ditches)	Totals	Sheepen Cam form	Totals
5			1				1	5	376
8			1	1			2	8	393
24			1	1			2	24	54
28			?1	3			?4	28	124
14/28	1						1	14b–c	85
30			?1	1			?2	30	3
32				2			1	32	18
44A				1			1	43 & 44	7+
56				1			1	56	675
58				1			1	58	67
68				1			1	68	2
74				?2	?1		?2–3	74	38
84			1	1			2	84	275
91			?1	?2			?3	91 & 91D	57+
92				1			1	92	60
109			1				1	109	22
112			?1	?3+			?4+	112	597+
113		1	3–4+	3–4+	1		8+	113 & 113B	2750+
114		1					1	114A & B	262
119			2	5			7	119	704
140D				1			1	140D	32
154 & 154/155						1	1	154 & 155	99
158						1	1	158	6
212-217					1		1	212–17	172
218			?3	3	2		?8	218	1000+
221 & 222				3			3	221 & 222	129
228				1			1	228	2
229	1						1	229	34
230				?2			?2	230	8
231/232			1				1	231 & 232	496
243–44/246						1	1	243, 244 & 246	288
251						1	1	251	10
254			1				1	254	238
258			1	2			3	258	58
259				2			2	259	648
263	1						1	263	10
266		2	?5	13+	1		?21+	266	1000++
270A & B			1	4+			5+	270	1000++
271			?1	?1		2	?4+	271	1000++
273				1	3		4	273	37

Enclosure 3. As with Enclosure 1, the quantity of pottery recovered from the enclosure ditch is very small. Gaulish imports of flagons and butt-beakers (Pots 5–7) and sherds of Dressel 2-4 amphora (Pots 12–13) place the ditch fill after the late 1st century B.C. (TABLE 40). There is no samian, although this is probably a reflection of the small quantity of pottery recovered from the enclosure ditch. Also, there are no common post-conquest pot forms or pot forms closely associated with assemblages in the fortress/*colonia* (TABLE 42). However, there are two rims from necked jars of the Late Iron Age/early Roman form Cam 266 (Pots 10–11) from the base of the ditch fill. Overall, the pottery assemblage cannot be dated more closely than the late 1st century B.C. to the early–mid 1st century A.D.

Enclosure 4. The pottery from the enclosure ditch and the ?mortuary enclosure makes up the largest assemblage from the site. Among the coarsewares, there is a near absence of common early post-conquest forms or forms associated with assemblages in the fortress/*colonia* other than the Late Iron Age/early Roman jar form Cam 266 (TABLE 40). However, the assemblage should probably date to after the conquest. There is one collared flagon rim (FIG. 139, Pot 43) of form Cam 140 which is probably post-conquest, although this came from the ditch shared with Enclosure 5 (BF4/CF1). Given the predominance of Romanising coarsewares and the presence of South Gaulish samian, the assemblage should probably be dated to *c.* A.D. 43–50.

Enclosure 5. The pottery assemblage associated with Enclosure 5 differs from the other enclosures. Overall Gaulish imports are limited and butt-beakers are scarce, while post-conquest forms and fabrics of the type introduced and used in the fortress/*colonia* (including the Late Iron Age/early Roman jar form Cam 266) are present (TABLE 40). There are ring-neck (Cam 154; FIG. 144, Pot 133) and pinch-mouth flagons (Cam 158; FIG. 144, Pot 132), a reed-rim bowl (Cam 243–244/246; FIG. 144, Pot 137), and a second bowl in Roman grey ware (FIG. 144, Pot 136), and a sherd from the Brockley Hill/Verulamium region potteries (Pot 134). The assemblage is likely to belong to the *c.* mid A.D. 40s, and is probably not later than the Neronian period.

DEPOSITION (TABLE 41)

The manner in which the pottery was deposited in the ditches and ?mortuary enclosures at Stanway is of particular interest. Much of it was disposed of as broken-up parts of pots, forming sherd clusters and localised sherd spreads. Although some are nearly complete, all appear to represent broken 'partial pots' rather than whole vessels. For Enclosures 3–5, on average 19 per cent of each of the vessels was represented in the sherds as measured by estimated vessel equivalence (eve). This figure drops to 9.4 per cent for Enclosure 3 alone (TABLE 41).

A partial pot of Late Iron Age date (FIG. 139, Pot 3) has been identified as coming from the lower fill of the enclosure ditch of Enclosure 1. This suggests that pottery was broken and deposited in the enclosure in the same manner as occurred on a wider scale in Enclosures 3–5. An early Roman partial pot from the main ditch fill (FIG. 139, Pot 2) indicates at least one episode of this nature in the enclosure in the early Roman period. Evidence for the breaking of pots appears to be absent in Enclosure 2, although small fragments of an oxidised ware vessel (fabric RFOW) from the east terminal of the enclosure ditch could possibly indicate the deposition of a partial pot. Sherds of deliberately broken pots had clearly been deposited in the enclosure ditch of Enclosure 3, but deposition seems to have been restricted to the ditch terminals forming the entrance. It is probable that Gaulish flagon sherds (Pots 5 and 7) found on either side of the entrance are from the same pot, although there are no joining sherds to prove this supposition.

Some of the groups of sherds in Enclosure 4 were mixed and contained parts of more than one vessel, showing that some of the partial pots must already have been broken before they entered the ditches. The concentration of pottery in the south-east area of Enclosure 4 may indicate that the pots were broken and discarded in and around this area before being deposited in the ditch. Enclosure 4 is the only enclosure where parts of pottery vessels (*i.e.* Pots 28 and 108) have been positively identified in more than one feature (FIGS 139, 142). Joining sherds of

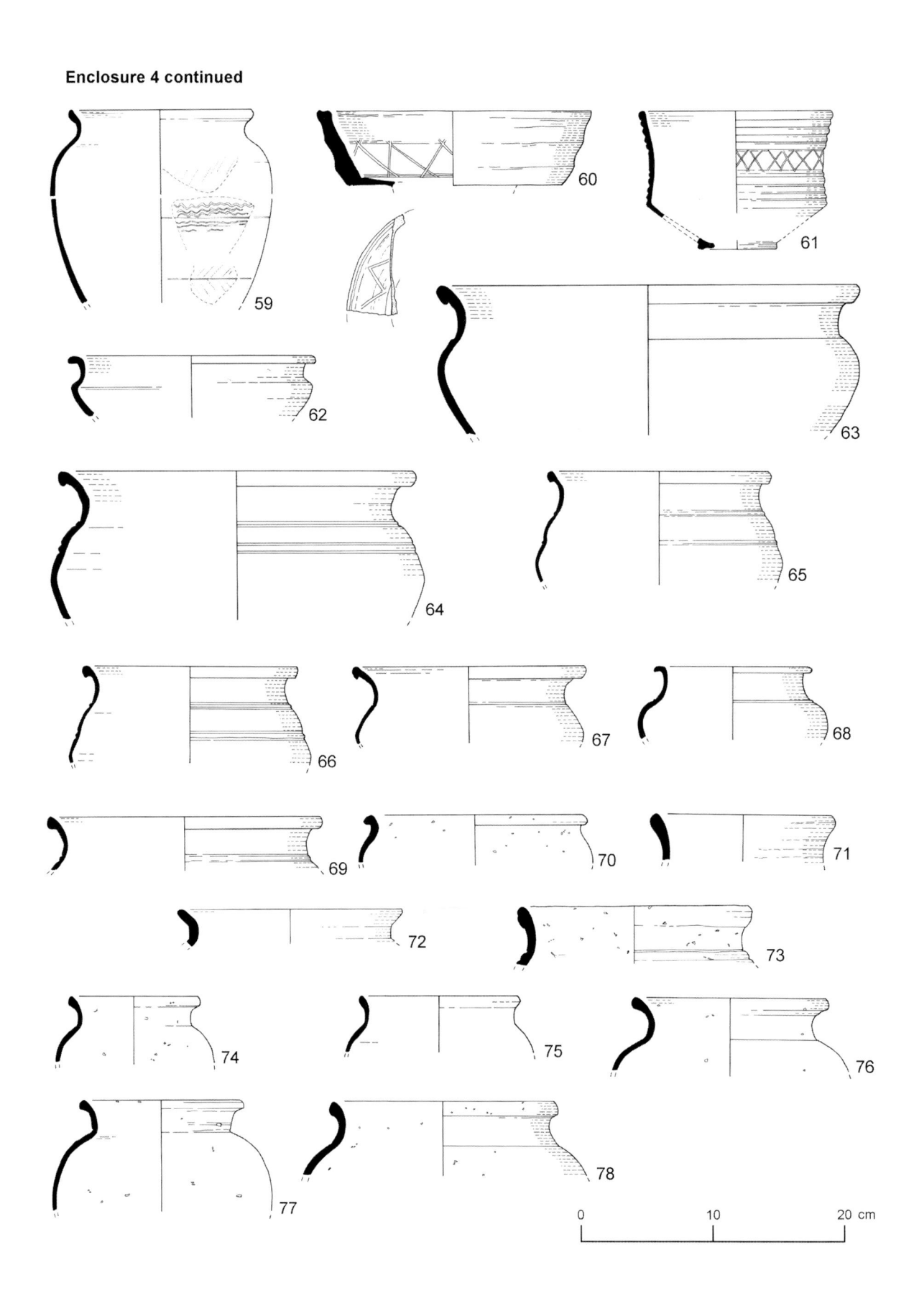

FIG. 140. Pottery vessels from the ditches of Enclosure 4: Pots 59–78 (scale 1:4)

TABLE 41: ESTIMATED VESSEL EQUIVALENCE (EVE) AS A PERCENTAGE OF IDENTIFIED VESSELS

Enclosure	Number (approx.) of identified vessels	Total eve	Eve as percentage of number of identified vessels
3	9	0.85	9.40
4	115	22.18	19.30
5	21	5.03	23.90
total/overall %	**145**	**28.06**	**19.35**

these pots were recovered from the ?mortuary enclosure BF32 and the enclosure ditch BF40/CF5. Moreover, although not joining, sherds from Pot 109 (FIG. 142) were distributed in more than one place (?mortuary enclosure BF32 and the enclosure ditch BF40/CF5), and these are sufficiently distinctive to allow them to be confidently assigned to the same vessel.

Of all the broken pots deliberately discarded in the ditch of Enclosure 5, three (FIG. 144, Pots 132, 135, 136) were almost complete. In Enclosure 5, no joining sherds were found to link the pottery from the enclosure ditches with the pottery from the ?mortuary enclosure-related CF43–6, although Pots 37 and 130 could be from the same pot, thus providing the missing connection.

Stratification of the broken pots in the ditches is interesting. The sherds in the enclosure ditches were not deposited in them when they were freshly dug, but shortly afterwards, maybe after a period of a few months or years had passed (p. 436). This was especially evident in Enclosure 5 and the ditch BF41/CF1 (which is common to Enclosures 4 and 5), where the broken pots lay at the base of the main ditch fill (as opposed to the lower, 'rapid' fill; see p. 436). Although much of the ditch of Enclosure 4 was mechanically excavated, the pottery occurred in clusters and presumably was similarly low in the ditch fill. Some of the pot sherds in the ditches of the ?mortuary enclosures were near the base of those features showing that they must have found their way into the ditches soon after they were dug.

There are some significant depositional patterns. The quantity of pottery deposited in Enclosure 4 is substantial (115 identified pots being 79 per cent of the 145 identified from Enclosures 3–5), and suggests that more pottery was used and broken in this enclosure than in all the others put together. Almost all the broken pottery was disposed of in the eastern half of the enclosures. This is in contrast to the burials, which are all located in the western halves, and may explain the near-absence of residual pottery in the backfill of the burials. The focus of pottery deposition in Enclosures 3 and 4 was at their entrances, whereas in Enclosure 5 this was clearly not the case. In Enclosure 5, the partial pots appear more discrete and isolated in their placement than in Enclosure 4, but this may simply reflect the lower numbers of pots represented there. Concentration of pottery sherds from the ?mortuary enclosures in Enclosures 4 and 5 is greatest in the ditches closest to the chamber, and thus presumably reflects the position of the chambers.

THE POTTERY ASSEMBLAGE IN RELATION TO THE CONTEMPORARY POTTERY ASSEMBLAGES FROM THE FORTRESS AND EARLY COLONIA (TABLE 42)

The rarity or absence at Stanway of common pottery forms and fabrics which appear in assemblages from the fortress/*colonia* and are introduced at the conquest requires some discussion. In pottery groups from the fortress/*colonia*, it is well-fired, often hard, fabrics which predominate (*CAR* **10** archive fabric collection, Colchester Museums). Gallo-Belgic wares/Gaulish imports, especially Cam 113 butt-beakers and Cam 161 two-handled flagons, are rare or absent. Rather than butt-beaker forms, the globular/ovoid beaker Cam 108 is common, and there are small cups (Cam 62) and beakers (Cam 94) in early fineware. The predominant flagon types are single-handled collared flagons (Cam 140) with ring-neck flagons (Cam 154). Mortaria (Cam 191–195) also form a consistent part of pottery assemblages (TABLE 42).

Enclosure 4 continued

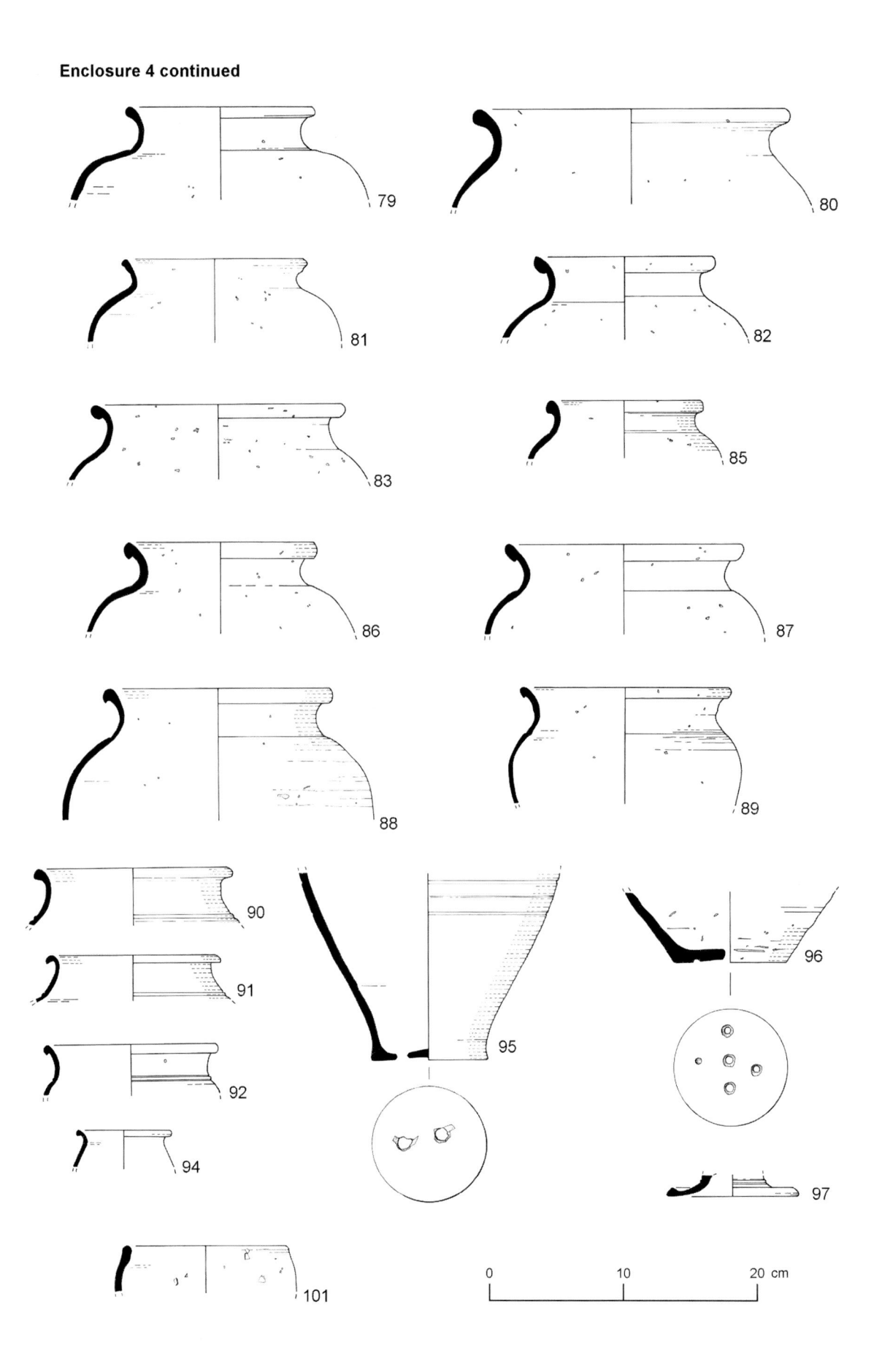

FIG. 141. Pottery vessels from the ditches of Enclosure 4: Pots 79–101 (scale 1:4)

Enclosure 4 continued

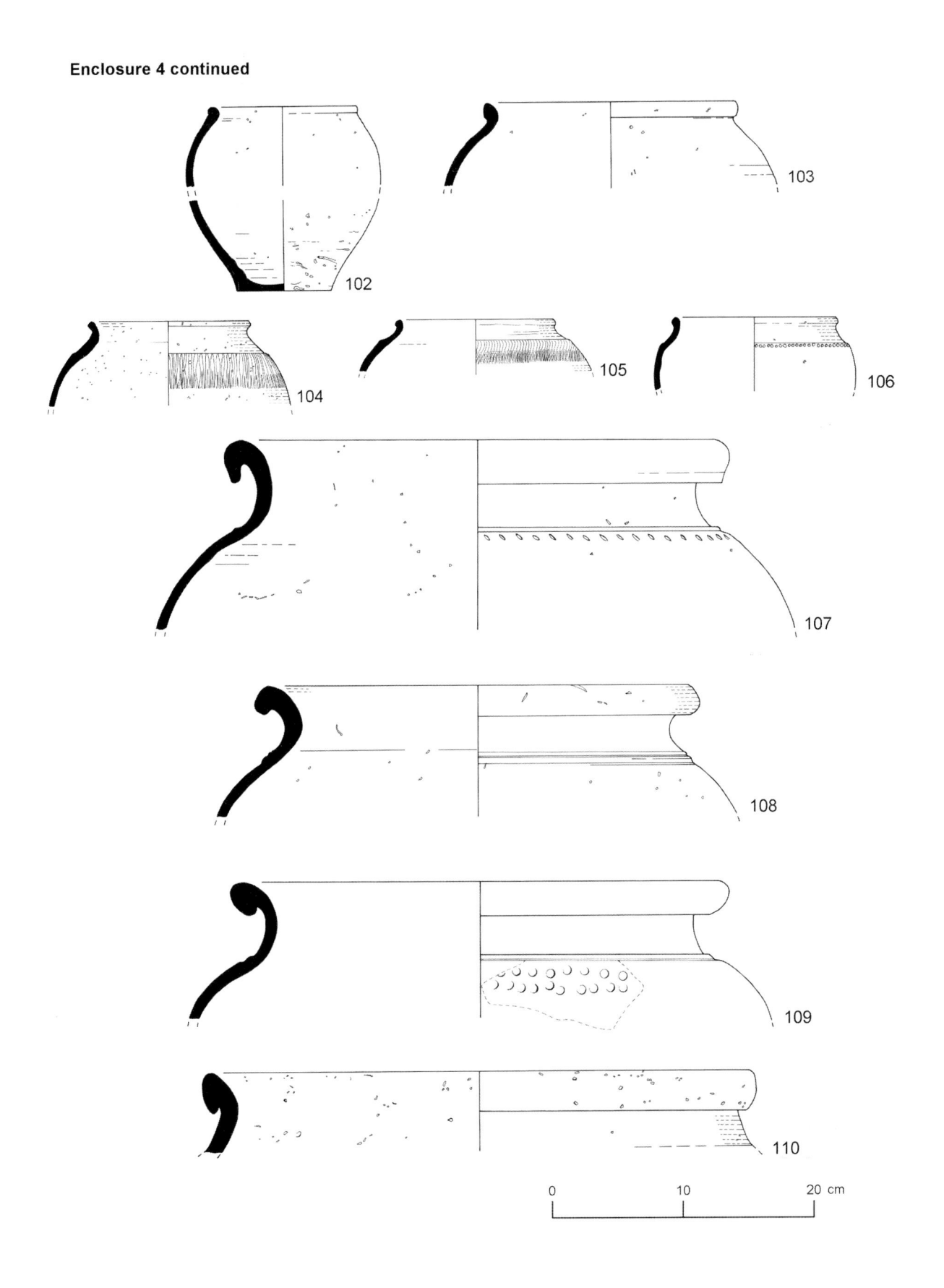

FIG. 142. Pottery vessels from the ditches of Enclosure 4: Pots 102–110 (scale 1:4)

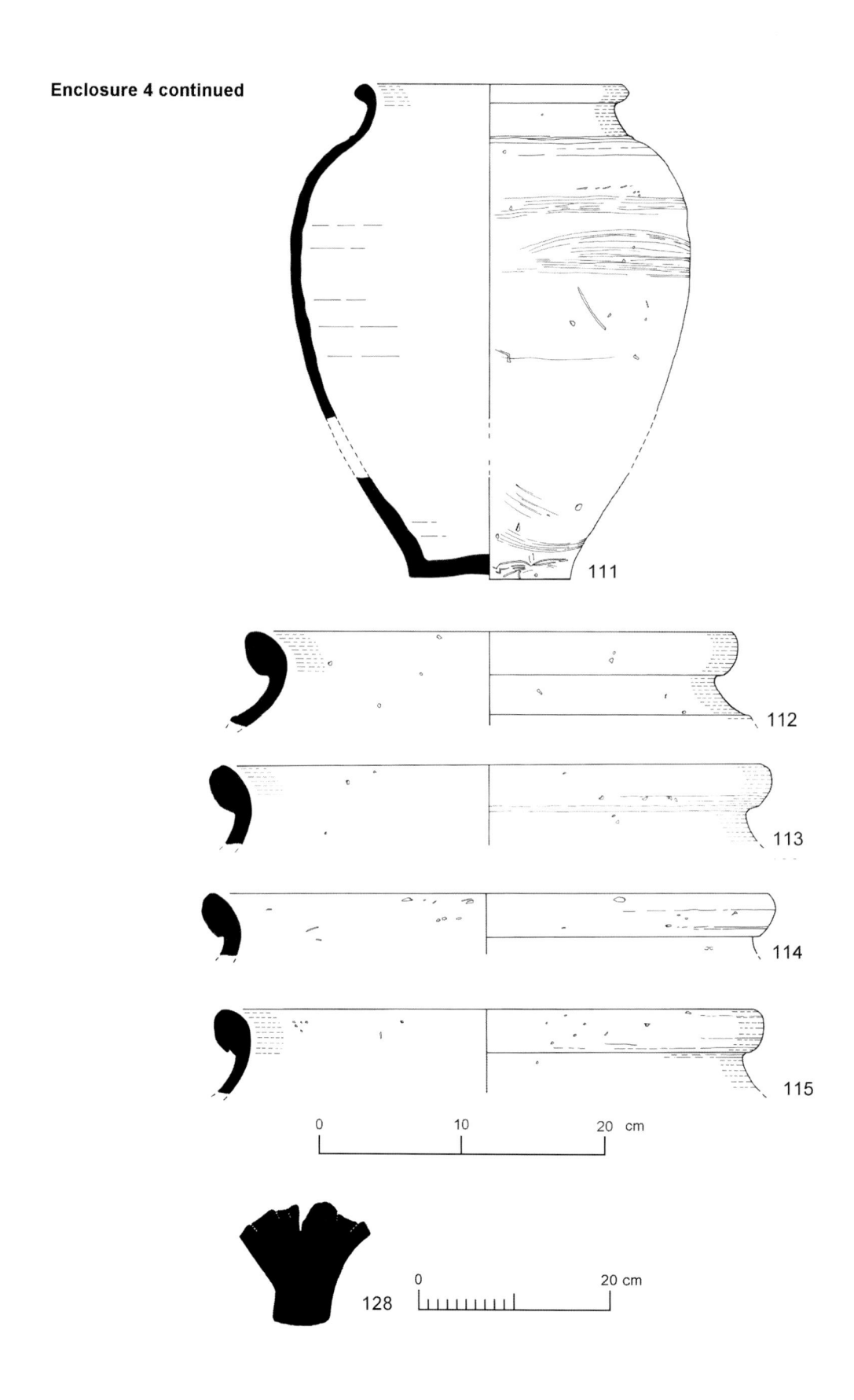

FIG. 143. Pottery vessels from the ditches of Enclosure 4: Pots 111–15 (scale 1:4) and amphora Pot 128 (scale 1:6)

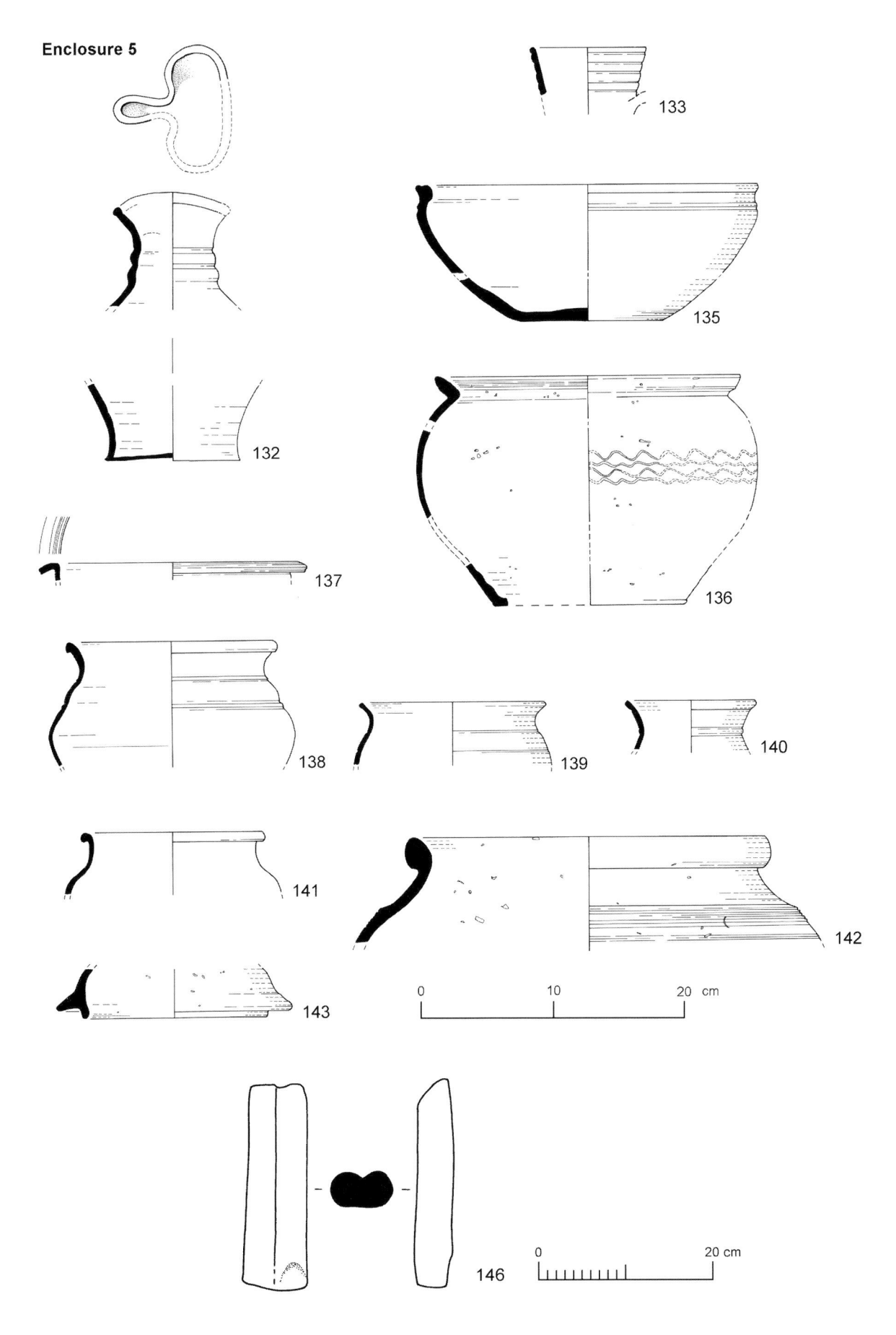

FIG. 144. Pottery vessels from the ditches of Enclosure 5: Pots 132–43 (scale 1:4) and amphora Pot 146 (scale 1:6)

TABLE 42: COMPARISON OF SELECTED POTTERY FORMS FROM STANWAY ?MORTUARY-ENCLOSURE AND DITCH ASSEMBLAGES, AND ROMAN ASSEMBLAGES FROM THE COLCHESTER FORTRESS AND THE EARLY *COLONIA*

Vessel form number	Vessel type	Numbers in ditch contexts at Stanway	Context
Forms rare or absent in Roman assemblages from Colchester			
Cam 74 (TR)	pedestal beaker	?2+	Enc. 4 (?2); Enc. 5 (1)
Cam 112	beaker	?2	Enc. 4
Cam 113	beaker	8+	Enc. 3 (1); Enc. 4 (6+); Enc. 5 (1)
Cam 114	beaker	1	Enc. 3
?Cam 161	two-handled flagon	?2+	represented by sherds in fabric WPW from Enc. 3, with single sherds from Enc. 4 and 5
Cam 212-217	carinated bowl	1	Enc. 5. (note: also two from burial CF72)
Cam 266 (LIA and 'Romanising' fabrics)	necked jar	21+	Enc. 3; Enc. 4; Enc. 5
Forms introduced at the conquest and common in early Roman assemblages at Colchester			
Cam 62	cup	absent	(note: one only from chamber BF24 in Enc. 4)
Cam 94	beaker	absent	
Cam 108	beaker	absent	(note: one only from burial CF403 in Enc. 5)
Cam 140	collared flagon	1	Enc. 4/5 (ditch CF1)
Cam 154/155	ring-neck flagon	2	Enc. 5 (ditch CF3, slot CF96)
Cam 158	pinch mouth flagon	1	Enc. 5 (ditch CF3)
Cam 241/242	carinated bowl	absent	
Cam 243/244-246	reed-rim bowl	1	Enc. 5 (ditch CF3)
Cam 266 (Roman grey ware – Fabric GX)	necked jar	absent	
Cam 191–195	mortaria	absent	

At Stanway, beaker forms in the ditches are dominated by butt-beakers (Cam 112, Cam 113 and Cam 119/119A) of Late Iron Age/Gaulish background, while the common post-conquest beaker Cam 108 is absent (TABLE 42). Smaller drinking vessels are represented by Gallo-Belgic style cups, and the early fineware cup and beaker forms Cam 62 and Cam 94 are absent. It should be noted that Cam 108 and Cam 62 appear once among the funerary assemblages (*i.e.* CF403.2 and BF24.1). Flagons are represented by Gaulish imports in Gallo-Belgic white ware (probably representing Cam 161, a form which is absent from the fortress/*colonia*). Coarseware forms and fabrics seen in the fortress/*colonia* are only associated with Enclosure 5, though mortaria as a pot type are absent from Stanway.

One form which is common at both the Roman fortress/*colonia* and Stanway is the relatively simple necked-jar form Cam 266 (Hawkes and Hull 1947, 271; *CAR* **10**, 479). Nevertheless, none of the jars described as form Cam 266 at Stanway are in Roman sandy grey ware (Fabric GX), although the majority are clear examples of the form type as previously described and illustrated (Hawkes and Hull 1947; Niblett 1985; *CAR* **10**). The presence of the jar Cam 266 in Romanising fabric is therefore not necessarily indicative of a post-conquest date.

The predominantly native character of the assemblage at Stanway in relation to the fortress/*colonia* is very striking. The differences between the two groups seem likely to be related to date, cultural background, and channels of supply. The large pottery assemblage from Enclosure 4 appears to be essentially post-conquest in date, and pottery from Enclosure 5 is certainly so. Paul Bidwell and Jane Timby have commented on aspects of the pottery assemblages of the fortress/early *colonia* in relation to imported wares. Bidwell noted the rarity of some imported Gallo-Belgic forms and that stamps on these wares are common at Sheepen but rare in the fortress/*colonia* (*CAR* 10, 488–91). Timby highlighted the lack of early imports and reliance on local military organised production among the pottery related to the fortress levels at the Head Street site (Timby 2004, 64–8). In general terms, with its Gallo-Belgic wares and butt-beakers, the Stanway pottery reflects aspects of the assemblages recovered from Sheepen rather than the fortress/*colonia*. Given an apparently post-conquest date for the majority of the pottery at Stanway, this distinctive assemblage suggests that two different supply networks operated in the immediately post-conquest period, one related to the Roman military, and the other to the native population. The character of the pottery assemblage from Enclosure 5 suggests that this situation was ending when that material was deposited.

THE POTTERS' STAMPS ON *TERRA RUBRA*, *TERRA NIGRA* AND *TERRA NIGRA*-TYPE WARES (FIG. 145)

By Valery Rigby

In all, 29 stamps survived out of a possible total of 41 platters and cups; three are too fragmentary or illegible for any identification. Had all the stamps survived, the list would have been just two short of the total in the King Harry Lane cemetery (KHL; Stead and Rigby 1989) showing just how rich in Gallo-Belgic imports the Stanway burials are in comparison.

Twenty-one different dies were recognised. One die occurs twice in burial BF64, one occurs twice in the same enclosure in burial BF64 and the central chamber BF6, while the third die occurs in different enclosures, once in burial BF64 and three times in burial CF47. They may represent specific workshop production batches which were then dispatched together to Camulodunum, the main port of import from the Late Augustan to the Neronian period.

With well over 500 stamps, the Sheepen site at Camulodunum has the longest list of Gallo-Belgic stamps of any settlement in Europe and so was clearly an important market from the late Augustan period onwards. There are die-links with most of the major settlements, early forts and cemeteries in Gallia Belgica and Germania Inferior, demonstrating just how well Camulodunum was integrated into the market of the north-west Roman provinces. While the Stanway stamp list shows a fair degree of connection with the Continent, having die links to some 16 sites, there are surprisingly few parallels with its local settlement at Sheepen. Of 21 dies, only 9 (roughly 43%) are paralleled at Sheepen, while 12 dies (over half) are new to the area. A brief comparison with the King Harry Lane cemetery at Verulamium emphasises how unexpected the Stanway results are. At King Harry Lane, 18 of 26 dies (roughly two-thirds) are also recorded at Sheepen, yet there is no overlap with the Stanway die list. Elsewhere, parallels with Stanway are comparatively few: one die in two cremations at the Stansted Airport cemetery, Essex; another in a cremation at Milton Keynes, Bucks; four in the settlement at Puckeridge–Braughing, Hertfordshire; and one each at North Ferriby, Humberside; Bagendon, Gloucestershire; and Silchester, Hampshire.

The identifiable stamps can be classified as twelve literate names, five pattern marks, and nine illiterate and cursive copies. Most of the name dies have been previously recorded, and all of the names belong to known potters: they are on forms with the late Augustan or Tiberio–Neronian date ranges. In contrast, the new dies, most of the illiterate copies and patterns, are on forms introduced in the Claudian period, the exception being Stamp 1–2, which implies a major reorganisation of supplies sometime around A.D. 50. There is a methodological problem which will exaggerate the changes. Fragmentary and abraded names are much more easily recognised and assigned to previously recorded dies than copies and patterns.

Die studies of stamps in the King Harry Lane cemetery and in pit groups at Sheepen had already suggested the idea of batch production and distribution. The Stanway and Stansted Airport cemeteries have provided more evidence.

NAME STAMPS ON *TERRA NIGRA* AND *TERRA RUBRA* WARES (FIG. 145)

Acuto/Acutios/Acutus Die 2A2

Stamp 1 FIG. 145. **BF64.8**

ACVT Central stamp: double incised circle. Flanged cup: Cam 58. TN; pale grey-buff fine smooth matrix, patchy dark blue-grey surface. Polished inner surface to flange, faceted below flange. Decoration: double incised circle.

Stamp 2 Not illustrated. **BF64.9**

A[CVT] Central stamp: double incised circle. Flanged cup: Cam 58. TN; a pair to Stamp 1.

The die is recorded four times on TN, at Silchester, Hants and Bavay, Nord, France, on the same form, and centrally on a small platter at Puckeridge–Braughing, Hertfordshire (Potter and Trow 1988, 115). The Silchester example was found in a context stated to be no later than A.D. 60 (Boon 1969, 6). In Britain, the distribution of flanged cups of Cam 58 has a marked military bias to it, and is particularly associated with forts established beyond the Fosse Way, in the north, Wales and the south-west, in the period after the Boudican revolt of A.D. 60/1 (Rigby 1977).

The ACVT A-dies are the latest related group bearing versions of the name Acuto/Acutios/Acutus, in a cursive style, which were current A.D. 40–65 (A- and B- dies, *see* also below Stamp 3). The earliest version of the name is Acutus. It occurs on TR at the late Augustan fort at Haltern, and the production centre is likely to have been in the Marne-Vesle potteries, probably Rheims. The die-cutter used the formal style of letters, with serifs, within a border and the Roman form of the name. The style is so different that more than one craftsman must have been involved. While pottery production may have continued in the Acutus family, the original die-cutter did not continue after *c*. A.D. 15 at the latest, although production of TR may have continued there into the Claudio–Neronian period. There is evidence for a workshop at Trier using Die 2B1 *c*. A.D. 40 and continuing until *c*. A.D. 65. There may have been at least one other intermediate die-cutter working in the Tiberian or Tiberio–Claudian period.

The dating evidence for four related '2A-dies', in the same style and almost certainly cut by the same hand, and the closely related '2B-dies' begins with a stamp of Die 2B1 on a TN platter found in Grave 42, in the St Matthias cemetery 1904, Trier, with an *as* of Tiberius, A.D. 23–37 (Goethert-Polaschek 1985, Taf. 5, 61). The platter is a type which occurs at the Claudio-Neronian fort of Hofheim, and on its form and fabric should be a product of Gallo-Belgic potteries in Trier: it is not found in Britain (Ritterling 1913). In addition, there are two on TR cups of Cam 56 in Cemetery E at Nijmegen and the Hunnerberg cemetery, Netherlands. Cemetery E was dated A.D. 20–40 in the publication, but the end date is too early, and a more realistic date is *c*. A.D. 50 (Holwerda 1941). The remaining finds are on TR at Rheims, Marne, France, and TN at Bavay, Nord, and Montepreux, France, and Dalheim, Luxembourg. The form range suggests that Dies 2A were in use A.D. 40–65 and the production centre could have been Rheims or Trier.

Acutios/Acuto/Acutus Die 5B6

Stamp 3 FIG. 145. **CF47.5**

ACVTIOS Central stamp: one bordered rouletted wreath. Moulded platter: Cam 8. TN; fine grey-buff matrix; black surfaces. Crackled and laminated surfaces, traces of a polished finish on upper only. Decoration: one bordered rouletted wreath.

This is the first recorded example in Britain of the die. There are four examples on similar Cam 8 platters in TR in two Claudian burials at Lebach (Gerlach 1976), while at least five on similar platters in TR and TN were found in various early Roman cemeteries at Trier, Germany (Haffner 1971; 1974; Goethert-Polaschek 1985). A related Acutios die occurs radially on large TN platters at Mainz and Frankenthal, Germany and Bavay, Nord, France. The form range suggests that Dies 5B were in use A.D. 30–50, and the production centre was at Rheims or Trier.

Attissus Die 1B2

Stamp 4 FIG. 145. **BF6.8**

ATTISSV bordered. Central stamp. Moulded platter: Cam 7/8. TR1(C); fine-grained orange matrix; traces of a darker red slip; no finish survives. Geometric graffiti incised onto the upper and lower base surfaces.

Stamps from this die are fairly common and typically occur centrally on small platters in TR as at Bagendon, Gloucestershire (Clifford 1961), and more rarely radially on large platters as at Puckeridge–Braughing, Hertfordshire (Potter and Trow 1988, 115). Similar Cam 7/8 variants occur in burials on the

Continent, four in Cemetery E, Nijmegen (Holwerda 1941, nos 702–705), one in grave 67 at Hunenknepchen à Sampont, Hachy, Belgium (Noël 1968) and one at the Titelberg (Metzler 1977). On TN there are two central stamps at Strasbourg, Alsace, and one at Bavay, Nord, France.

The closely related Die 1B1 has been recorded on four platters in TR1(C) at Sheepen, where the most useful for dating is a large platter Cam 6, a relatively rare form, in the pre-conquest pit 136 (no. 12).

A potter Attissus was working in the Marne-Vesle potteries near Rheims in the late Augustan period, before A.D. 9, using A dies. Attissus B dies, however, in a different cursive style, appear to be later, being placed in graves between A.D. 25 and 50, so it seems likely that the B dies belong to a different generation of the Attissus family. One B die on TR is recorded at the early Roman pottery at Novaesium, Germany, possibly an indication that the potter moved there.

Canicos Die 3A4

Stamp 5 FIG. 145. **BF6.12**

CANICOS Central stamp. Moulded platter: Cam 8. TR1(C); smooth orange ware with argillaceous inclusions; darker red slip; polished upper, matt lower surfaces, slightly crackled.

The potter Canicos produced cups and platters in TR and TN using at least 13 different dies, most cut by the same die-cutter in the same cursive style, and 15 stamps have already been recorded at Camulodunum where this particular die occurs radially on large TN platters Cam 2 and 5; it also occurs at Puckeridge–Braughing, Hertfordshire (Potter and Trow 1988, 115) and Bavay, Nord, France. In 1924, a small TN platter Cam 8 stamped with a related die (3A5) was found in the Lexden cemetery with three other imports. While all the British finds in this style group, with the exception of the Stanway platter, are on TN, the continental finds split almost evenly between TR and TN. The production centre is likely to have been the Marne-Vesle potteries, A.D. 25–60.

Cicarus Die 1A1

Stamp 6 FIG. 145. **CF47.6**

CICARV Central stamp; one incised circle. Moulded platter: Cam 8. TN; brown fine-grained smooth matrix; crackled grey-black surfaces. Traces of polished finish on upper surface. Decoration: one incised circle.

The die is already recorded as a central and radial stamp on a large TN platter at Camulodunum (no. 70) and also at Puckeridge-Braughing (Potter and Trow 1988, 116). It occurs on large TR platters at the Claudian forts of Hofheim, Germany, and Dalheim, Luxembourg, and on large TR platters of Cam 5 in cremations at Hofheim and Köln, the former with three Claudio–Neronian vessels (Schoppa 1958, 156). A related die was used to stamp a TR cup of Cam 56 associated with a stamped samian vessel dated A.D. 60–75 in Grave 21 at Lebach (Gerlach 1976). The production centre is likely to be the Marne-Vesle potteries, *c* A.D. 40–65.

Dacovir Die 1A1

Stamp 7 FIG. 145. **BF6.6**

DACOVIR bordered. Central stamp. Concave moulded platter: Cam 7C. TR1(C); pale orange powdery matrix; crackled coral slip, no finish survives. There are concentric incised guide-circles on the underside for the application of the footring.

This is the first record of the potter in Britain. All previous finds have been on platters chiefly in TR. A similar variant occurs in a Tiberian grave in the St Matthias cemetery, Trier, and there is a second example from Trier (Goethert-Polaschek 1985). Fifteen stamps on TR have been recorded at Luxembourg Museum (no information about provenance). There is one on a TN platter from Bavay, Nord, France. The production centre is likely to be in the Marne-Vesle potteries *c*. B.C. 10–A.D. 30.

Eudo Die 1A1

Stamp 8 FIG. 145. **BF64.3**

II[UDO] bordered. Central stamp. Moulded platter: Cam 7/8. TN; white powdery matrix; metallic blue-grey surfaces. Severely spalled and laminated, traces of a polished upper surface.

Four stamps from this die occur at Camulodunum (no. 80), all on small TN platters, one Cam 8 and one Cam 7/8, also recorded once at North Ferriby, Humberside. The fabrics are varied despite the use of a single die, which suggests batch production. One was found in a Period I context and so could be a pre-conquest import. The date range of the platter forms is A.D. 20–65, and its presence in burial BF64 reduces this to perhaps A.D. 35–60. The source is likely to be the Marne-Vesle potteries.

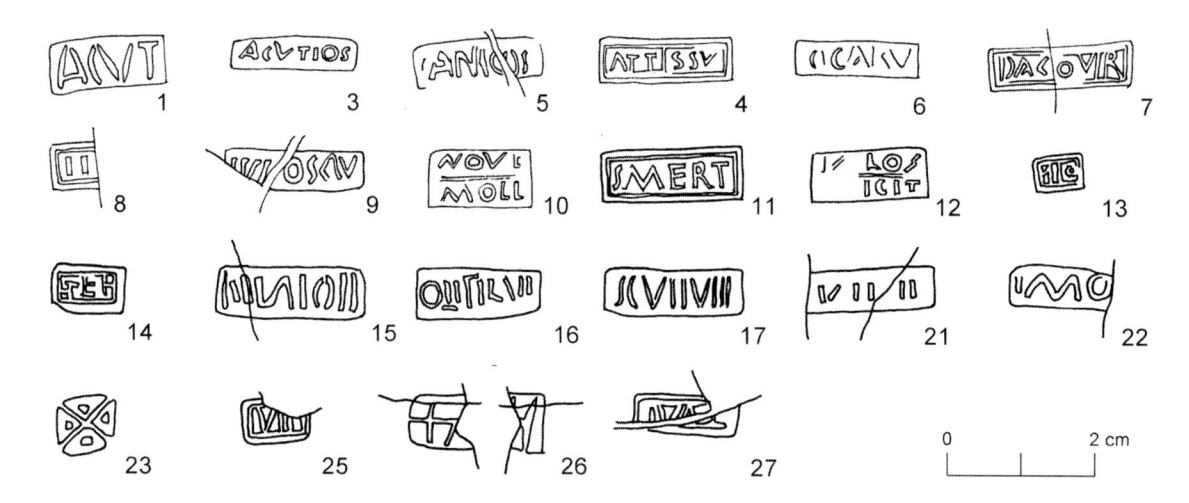

FIG. 145. Potters stamps on *terra rubra*, *terra nigra* and *terra nigra*-type wares (scale 1:1)

Jul(l)ios Die 2J1

Stamp 9 FIG. 145. **BF6.13**

IVLIOS AV(OTIS). Central stamp. Moulded platter: Cam 8. TN; buff fine-grained matrix; blue-black exterior shading to lighter blue-grey over the upper surface; traces of a polished finish overall.

The die is already recorded twice radially on large TN platters at Camulodunum, while the closely related Die 2J2 occurs three times.

Jul(l)ios is the most common name recorded on TN vessels. By 2005, no fewer than 24 dies, cut by at least 10 different die-cutters, were listed with contexts ranging from the late Augustan fort at Haltern to the Claudio-Neronian fort at Hofheim. Since then, finds from Gosbecks and Lake Farm, Dorset, have added three new double-line dies and extended the possible dating into the early Flavian period. It is unlikely that one potter survived to supply both Haltern and Hofheim. Moreover, the form range in TN includes flanged cups of Cam 58 and convex platters Cam 16 which were not common until after A.D. 50 and continued in production until *c*. A.D. 85, and in Britain are associated with Nero–Vespasianic military establishments (Rigby 1977). There are at least 46 stamps at Camulodunum/Sheepen, with at least one from the *colonia*, from a total of 59 for Britain, the find-spots including Baldock, Puckeridge-Braughing (2) and Verulamium/Prae Wood (2), Hertfordshire, Canterbury and Deal (2), Kent, Chichester, West Sussex, Cookham (2), Berkshire, Duston, Northamptonshire, and Lake Farm, Dorset. Since this is the most widely distributed name in Britain, its absence from the King Harry Lane cemetery, Verulamium, St Albans, Hertfordshire, is notable.

One die of Jul(l)ios was found at the Louvercy kiln site in the Marne-Vesle potteries, and this is the most likely source. Die 2J1 is one of the later dies, but is by no means the latest so it will have been in use between A.D. 25 and 60.

Novemollos Die 1A1

Stamp 10 FIG. 145. **CF47.9**

NOVE/MOLL two-lines. Central stamp; one in incised circle. Carinated cup Cam 56C. TN; fine-grained buff matrix; blue-black surfaces; abraded surfaces, traces of a polished finish on the inner.

A rare name recorded only on cups, at Mainz on TR (Geissner 1904, no. 322) and Bavay, Nord, France on TN. Manufactured between A.D. 50 and 75.

Smertuccos Die 4A2

Stamp 11 FIG. 145. **BF6.9**

SMERT(VCCOS) bordered. Central stamp. Moulded platter: Cam 7/8. TR1(C); fine orange ware; darker red slip, crackled and abraded so no finish survives.

Judging by the number of versions of the name, Smertuccos had a workshop producing TR on a large scale. This is a new die to add to the existing list of eight, cut in three different styles. In style, the Stanway stamp resembles two groups, dies A and C. One with the abbreviation SMERT, die 4C1, occurs only on TR platters and may have been used at the Rheims pottery (a stamp was found on the site of kilns excavated 1970–1). Stamps also occur on the concave platter, Cam 7, in Grave 5, dated Tiberian, at

Noyelles-Godault, Pas de Calais, France (Bastien and Demolon 1975), at the *oppidum* of Alésia (2), Côte d'Or, France, and in Luxembourg Museum.

Four other dies are already represented at Camulodunum. Typologically, the earliest is a full-length version of the name, a two-line stamp in formal style, die A, on a TR cup of Cam 53 which should pre-date A.D. 25, and also on a small platter found in a Period III–IV context (nos 135–6). Two at Puckeridge–Braughing, Hertfordshire, include another ligatured version of the name on a large platter in TR1(A), and therefore both should also pre-date A.D. 25. It is a rare occurrence for TR1(A) to be stamped.

The production centre is almost certainly Rheims, or the Marne-Vesle potteries, and the date of manufacture of the Stanway platter should be A.D. 10–25.

NAME FRAGMENTS (FIG. 145)

Stamp 12 FIG. 145. **CF115.1**

...LOS/[FI]ICIT or ...COS/[FI]ICIT Central stamp: double incised circle. Flanged cup: Cam 58. TN; pale grey sandy matrix; blue-black abraded surfaces; polished inner surface extending to flange.

A new die from a literate Romanised potter who used the rare FIICIT(FECIT) on the lower line rather than more colloquial AVOTIS for 'made by'. The die is likely to belong to a known potter, ILLOS, LULLOS, or the occasional misspelled version of Jul(l)ios: IVLLOS, a long-lived workshop or possibly three potters using the same name (*see* above Stamp 8). Of these, the latter is perhaps the most likely, since a similar two-line die reading IVLIO/FECIT occurs at Lake Farm, Dorset, on a Cam 58 cup in TN. Jul(l)ios is also the most common name found on TN, and clearly at least one potter of that name was still working A.D. 50–75. CANICOS is unlikely because, although his workshop made TN and production continued into the Claudian period, his dies have not been recorded on Cam 58. The form and fabric suggest that the potter could have worked in the Marne-Vesle potteries between A.D. 40 and 75.

UNCERTAIN NAMES OR COPIES (FIG. 145)

Stamp 13 FIG. 145. **CF47.10**

HIC bordered or open AIC bordered. Central stamp: one incised circle. Flanged cup: Cam 58 (small). TR1(C); orange fine-grained matrix; darker slip extends from inner surface over flange. Crackled and laminated surfaces, no finish survives. Decoration: one incised circle.

Die 1B1

A new die which may be an abbreviation. The production centre is unknown. The cup was made between A.D. 50 and 70.

Stamp 14 FIG. 145. **BF6.20**

TER bordered: uncertain reading. Carinated cup: Cam 56 (small). TR1(C): light orange powdery ware; darker red slip; abraded surfaces but traces of a polished finish on the slip, smoothed exterior. Decoration: one groove on the outside, one incised circle on the base.

Die 1A1

An unassigned die which may be an abbreviation. One impression is already recorded at Camulodunum (no. 203), also on a TR cup. The production centre is unknown, but it will have been somewhere in the Marne-Vesle potteries, and manufacture took place between A.D. 15 and 70.

Stamp 15 FIG. 145. **CF47.7**

IIIVIIOII: reading uncertain. Central stamp: two incised circles. Offset platter: Cam 14. TN; white powdery matrix; patchy blue-grey surfaces. Polished upper surface; abraded lower, no finish survives. Decoration: two incised circles.

Die 2B1

The die and potter have not been identified. The production centre is unknown, but the platter was made between A.D. 50 and 75.

Stamp 16 FIG. 145. **CF47.8**

OILIILII: reading uncertain. Central stamp: one bordered rouletted wreath. Offset platter: Cam 14. TN; hard, fine-grained white matrix; patchy metallic blue-grey surfaces. Polished upper surface, matt lower. Decoration: two burnished circles 10 mm apart.

Die 1A1

The potter's name has not been identified, but the die was used to stamp a TN cup found at Courmelois, Kiln 2, in the Marne-Vesle potteries, a likely source for the Stanway platter (Tuffreau-Libre 1988, no. 15).

Courmelois is considered one of the later locations used by potters working in the Claudio–Neronian period. The form is one of the latest to be introduced, and was only made in TN, so the platter was made between A.D. 50 and 65.

Stamp 17 FIG. 145. **CF47.2**

SCVTTVSI/SCVTIVSI: reading uncertain. Central stamp: one bordered rouletted wreath. Moulded platter: Cam 7/8. TR1(C); orange fine matrix, with some large argillaceous inclusions causing spalling; darker slip. Polished upper surface; less glossy smoothed lower, crackled. Decoration: one very fine bordered rouletted wreath.

Stamp 18 **CF47.3**

SCVTTVSI / SCVTIVSI; reading uncertain. Central stamp; two burnished circles. Moulded platter: Cam 7/8. TR1(C).

Stamp 19 **CF47.4**

SCVTTVSI / SCVTIVSI; reading uncertain. Central stamp. Moulded platter: Cam 7/8. TR1(C); orange fine matrix, with some large argillaceous inclusions; darker slip, discoloured by smoke. Spalled and laminated surfaces, no finish survives. No decoration.

Stamp 20 **BF64.2**

SCVTTVSI/SCVTIVSI; reading uncertain. Central stamp. Moulded platter: Cam 7/8. TN; bluish-white matrix, with many dark grey argillaceous impurities; metallic blue-grey surfaces. Polished upper surface, matt lower; surfaces badly spalled due to impurities in the clay.

Die 1A1

An unassigned die, possibly Scuttusi or Scutiusi. The reading is uncertain and could be interpreted as SCVTTVSII or SCUTIVSI. In Britain the die is already represented once at Camulodunum (no. 253), and on a pair of platters in a cremation at Milton Keynes, Bucks (information from the Museum of London Specialist Services); and once at the Hunnerberg cemetery, Netherlands. The same die may have been used to stamp a platter found at Courmelois, Kiln 2, in the Marne-Vesle potteries, a possible source for all four platters (Tuffreau-Libre 1981, no. 11). The form and fabric suggest manufacture between A.D. 25 and 60 in the Marne-Vesle potteries, and since three of the four stack exactly, and the fourth is very close, they should have been made by the same hand in the same batch and despatched together to Camulodunum.

Stamp 21 FIG. 145. **BF64.5**

VII[]IS bordered. Central stamp: triple incised circle. Offset platter: Cam 14. TN; white fine-grained matrix; metallic blue-grey surfaces. Polished upper surface, matt lower. Decoration: triple incised circle.

The name has not been recognised and the die cannot be paralleled. Production centre unknown. The platter was made between A.D. 50 and 70.

Stamp 22 FIG. 145. **BF64.4**

IMO: reading uncertain. Central stamp. Offset platter: Cam 14. TN; pale buff fine-grained matrix; laminated and abraded patchy blue-grey surfaces. No finish survives. Decoration: double and pair of incised circles.

The die cannot be paralleled. Production centre unknown. The platter was made between A.D. 50 and 70.

PATTERN MARKS (FIG. 145)

Stamp 23 FIG. 145. **BF6.21**

'X with four spots'. Central stamp: one incised circle. Carinated cup: Cam 56C (small). TR1(C); orange matrix, darker slip; no finish survives.
Decoration: one incised circle.

Stamp 24 **BF64.6**

'X with four spots'. Central stamp: one incised circle. Carinated cup: Cam 56C (small). TN; fine-grained pale brown ware; patchy grey-black surfaces. Polished inner, faceted outer surface.

'X with four spots' Die 1A1

The die is represented in two burials, both in Enclosure 3, once each on TR and TN. It has already been recorded four times at Camulodunum (no. 222) on small cups in TN, while three similar cups were found in two cremations in the Stansted Airport cemetery, Essex (Havis and Brooks 2004, 200, no. 19).

All must have been in the same batch imported through Camulodunum and could have been among the first to be imported after Roman occupation.

There are also two TN cups in burials at Nijmegen in Cemeteries E and OH (Holwerda 1941, 175b). Other finds include Bavay, Nord, France, and Speyer (Speyer Museum 1103). Two stamps have been found at the Courmelois kilns in the Marne-Vesle potteries, and this is the likely source area, *c.* A.D. 25–60.

Stamp 25 FIG. 145. **BF64.7**

VII bordered. Central stamp. Hemispherical cup copying Ritterling 8; double groove on the exterior. TR1(C); orange fine-grained smooth ware; traces of a darker slip over interior and exterior, excluding underside of base. Polished finish.

Die 1A1

The only impression of this die to be recorded. It may be a an illiterate mark using I and V motifs, or it could be an abbreviation reading IN(..) or NI(..) (retrograde N). A close parallel which could be from the same die is illustrated among finds from Bavay, Nord, France.

The cup is of particular interest because it is a rare form, apparently copying the early samian hemispherical cup, Ritterling 8, and no others have definitely been identified in Britain. The production centre is unknown, but the piece is likely to be contemporary with its prototype and hence was made A.D. 40–65.

Stamp 26 FIG. 145. **BF6.15**

Mark: chequerboard motif, bordered. Central stamp: one bordered rouletted wreath. Moulded platter: Cam 8. Fine-grained white powdery matrix; pale blue-grey surfaces; traces of a polished finish on upper surface, lower surface matt. Decoration: bordered rouletted wreath. Graffito on the upper base: cursive letters.

The die cannot be paralleled. Production centre unknown. The platter was made between A.D. 25 and 65.

FRAGMENTS AND ILLEGIBLE IMPRESSIONS

Stamp 27 FIG. 145. **BF6.14**

Mark: VII[...] bordered. Central stamp. Moulded platter: Cam 8. TN; possibly TN1(A) with a slip on the upper surface; powdery white matrix, metallic blue-grey surfaces; darker-toned, polished upper surface, matt lower. Decoration: two incised circles.

The impression is too fragmentary for identification. The production centre is unknown. The platter was made between A.D. 25 and 65.

Stamp 28 **BF6.16**

Stamp edge, too fragmentary for identification. Central stamp: double incised circle. Moulded platter: Cam 8. TN; pale bluish white powdery matrix; patchy blue-grey surfaces; no finish survives. Decoration: pair of incised circles.

Neither the die nor the potter can be identified. Production centre unknown. The platter was made between A.D. 25 and 65.

Stamp 29 **CF47.11**

Central stamp. Illegible impression. Flanged cup: Cam 58. TR1(C): orange fine-grained matrix; darker slip extends from inner surface over flange. Crackled and laminated surfaces, no finish survives. Potter and production centre unknown, made between A.D. 50 and 75.

POTTERS' STAMPS ON *TERRA NIGRA*-TYPE WARES

Abuso Die 1A1

MVW 1 **BF24.7**

ABVSO, an abraded impression, the reading is not certain. Central stamp. Grooved platter: Cam 11 copy. MVW; blue-grey core; leached and eroded grey surfaces; no finish survives. Decoration: two double and a single incised circle.

MVW 2 **BF24.6**

ABVSO, an illegible impression identical to MVW1. Central stamp. Grooved platter: Cam 11 copy. MVW; blue-grey core; leached and eroded grey surfaces; no finish survives. Decoration: two double and a single incised circle.

Although the platters are different sizes, they were both stamped with the same die. The name has not been previously recorded. The quality of the potting techniques, intermediate between Iron Age and Roman, suggests that the production centre should be in the vicinity of Camulodunum where a number of literate names on platters considered to be from regional or local workshops have been recorded (*CAR* **10**, 219–22).

Bordered, illegible

MVW 3 and MVW 4 **BF24.9, BF24.10**

Bordered, illegible impressions. Central stamps. Flanged cups: Cam 58 copy. MVW; grey core; leached and eroded grey-buff surfaces. No finish survives.

The bordered impressions are illegible, but were made with the same die which is not Abuso Die 1A1. The similarity of the fabric, however, suggests they are from the same source as MVW1 and 2. One is an over-fired 'second' which could indicate that it was made in the vicinity of Camulodunum.

Illegible and incomplete

MVW 5 **BF24.8**

Illegible and incomplete impression. Central stamp. Grooved cup. MVW; an over-fired and distorted 'waster'; grey core; grey-buff surfaces. No finish survives.

The cup was recovered as two non-joining half sections, with fresh breaks so the stamp is both illegible and broken, and it is not possible to see if it definitely represents a third die used for mixed vesicular ware. Since in this case it is a distorted but still functioning 'waster', the source should be at Camulodunum.

Bordered and incomplete

MVW 6 **BF24.11**

[…]V bordered, incomplete and abraded impression. Central stamp. Offset platter: Cam 14 copy. MVW; hard-fired blue-grey matrix, with rough and abrasive gritty texture; eroded and leached surfaces, no finish survives. Decoration: one bordered radially combed wreath.

The impression may be incomplete, but it is different from the three dies recorded on mixed vesicular ware. A local source is likely. It could have been manufactured any time between A.D. 50 and 200.

Catulussius Die 1A1 or 1A2

SW 1 **CF403.1**

CATVL/LVSSI central stamp. Moulded platter: Cam 8 copy. SW; blue-grey matrix; dark brown-grey surfaces. Abraded, with traces of a burnished finish on the upper surface. Decoration: one burnished circle.

The impression is too light and abraded for certain identification. Four stamps are already recorded at Camulodunum all on the same moulded platter-form although in a variety of kiln-fired sand-tempered fabrics, so it is likely that the potter worked in the vicinity (*CAR* **10**, 222, LTC4–7). The size, proportion and typological detail of the 'copies' is such that they can only have been made by a potter trained in one of the Gallo-Belgic potteries in the Tiberio–Claudian period. If the source is in Britain, the potter migrated from Gallia Belgica in the Claudian period, in the wake of the Roman army, to exploit an expanding market and save costs.

Illegible

GTW 1 **BF24.4**

Broken and illegible impression. Central stamp. Plain platter: Cam 2 copy, Cam 21. GTW; under-fired, grey core, grey-brown surfaces; severely eroded so no finish survives.

GTW 2 **BF24.5**

Broken and illegible impression. Central stamp. Offset platter: Cam 14 copy. GTW; under-fired, grey core, buff under surface, grey surfaces. Eroded but traces of a burnished finish. Decoration: double incised circle at the wall junction, pair of doubles around the stamp.

The impressions were made by different dies, and they also differ in shape and proportion from dies used on other fabric groups. It is unusual for platters in GTW to be stamped with the maker's mark. For example, only two are stamped from a total of 59 found in the King Harry Lane cemetery.

THE AMPHORAS

By Paul R. Sealey

INTRODUCTION

Amphoras reached Stanway from the eve of the Roman invasion until the aftermath of the Boudican revolt. Only two forms are present: Dressel 2-4 wine amphoras and Beltrán I *salazones*, amphoras bottled with fish-sauce or salted fish (TABLE 43). There are none of the Dressel 20 amphoras that dominate amphora assemblages in Roman Britain from the start until the 3rd century A.D. Nor is there any sign of the less common types such as Richborough 527 and Cam 189 found at the nearby legionary fortress and *colonia*. It is clear from the unusual composition of the assemblage that the Stanway amphoras are a special group from an exceptional site.

Where a given amphora fabric has already been described in *The National Roman Fabric Reference Collection* (Tomber and Dore 1998), only its alphabetic code is given here for economy of presentation. Fabrics not present in the national collection are described more fully. No petrological analysis has been undertaken.

QUANTIFICATION (TABLE 43)

Following the precedents of reports on the élite graves at Lexden (Peacock 1971, 183; Williams 1986), Folly Lane (Niblett 1999, 44; Williams 1999, 193) and Clemency (Metzler *et al.* 1991, 46, 78), the Stanway amphoras were quantified by minimum vessel number count, supplemented by sherd counts and sherd weights to the nearest gramme where appropriate. Minimum vessel count is a calculation of the lowest number of complete amphoras the extant sherds could represent, and the results for Stanway are given in TABLE 43. Two *salazones* are present and nine Dressel 2-4 wine amphoras.

One of the *salazones* is the Dressel 8 in the Doctor's grave (Pot CF47.14). A second is represented by a Beltrán I handle stub from the Enclosure 4 ditch (Pot no. 127). It is evident that this is a second *salazon* because both the handles of the amphora in the Doctor's grave are present.

The position with the nine Dressel 2-4 amphoras is less straightforward. Leaving the warrior burial and chambers until later, there were two different Italian Dressel 2-4 amphoras from the mortuary enclosure BF32 and the enclosure ditch of Enclosure 5 (Pot nos 126 and 148). Both were in the standard Campanian Fabric CAM AM 2 but the presence of two vessels is indicated by significant differences in texture. Two more Dressel 2-4 amphoras from Enclosures 4 and 5 are in fabrics that cannot be assigned to a source. One came from the enclosure ditch of Enclosure 5; sherds from the other were retrieved from the enclosure ditch of Enclosure 4 and the ?mortuary enclosure CF43–6 in Enclosure 5 (Pot nos 128 and 146 and Pot no 149). A fifth Dressel 2-4 is represented by a Catalan amphora in a cream fabric from the pyre site in Enclosure 3 (Pot BF16.1). There were two more Dressel 2-4 in Chamber BF6, one in the red

TABLE 43: AMPHORAS FROM STANWAY BY MINIMUM VESSEL NUMBER COUNT

Amphora type	Minimum number of vessels
Dressel 2-4 (Italian black sand fabric)	1
Dressel 2-4 (Italian fabric CAM AM 2)	2
Dressel 2-4 (red fabric Catalan)	1
Dressel 2-4 (cream fabric Catalan)	1
Dressel 2-4 (source unknown)	4
Dressel 8 *salazon* (part of Beltrán I)	1
Beltrán I *salazon*	1

Catalan fabric (Pot BF6.22) and another in a fine fabric of unknown origin (Pot BF6.23). The eighth Dressel 2-4 is the Italian black sand amphora from the warrior burial (Pot BF64.15) and the ninth comprises the sherds from Chamber CF42 (Pot CF42.10).

What the writer deemed to be sherds from all three amphoras in Chambers BF6 and CF42 were present in other contexts (Pot nos 12, 145 and 147). Likewise a black sand sherd (Pot no. 13) from what might be the same amphora as the Dressel 2-4 in the warrior burial was present in the enclosure ditch of Enclosure 3. It should be emphasised that there were no joins between amphora sherds from different features and that attribution to the same vessel rests only on the congruence of fabric, wall thickness or diameter. Logic dictates that the amphora sherds in question could conceivably have come from different amphoras with identical fabrics and typologies. It also has to be borne in mind that no joins could be established for any other categories of pot between these two chambers and the warrior burial on the one hand, and other features at Stanway on the other. In view of this, it would be premature to use this aspect of the amphora assemblage to make further deductions about funerary practice. Nevertheless most of the actual Dressel 2-4 vessels from Chambers BF6 and CF42 must have ended up elsewhere because so little of them was present in their chambers.

AMPHORA TYPES AT STANWAY

Dressel 2-4 wine amphoras

When production of Dressel 1 ceased *c.* 10 B.C., the major wine amphora in Italy and the West became Dressel 2-4, with a significant minor contribution from a Catalan copy of Dressel 1 called Pascual 1, until Tiberius. Dressel 2-4 was made in Italy from the time of the *c.* 75–60 B.C. Madrague de Giens shipwreck (Hesnard 1977, 159, 162, 167, fig. 4; Liou and Pomey 1985, 564, for the date of the wreck), but did not become common until towards the end of the century. In the important amphora deposit from the House of the Porch at Ostia dated *c.* 50–25 B.C., Dressel 1 amphoras outnumber Dressel 2-4 by twenty-one to two (van der Werff 1986, 119), and it would seem that Dressel 2-4 was not widely produced in Italy until the last quarter of the 1st century B.C. This is when we find the first evidence for the form in Britain, in the Lexden tumulus (Foster 1986, 124; Williams 1986) and the Dorton grave (Williams 1983; Farley 1983, 289–90).

Production of the form in Italy lasted much longer than had previously been realised. Some potteries were still making Dressel 2-4 there as late as the early 3rd century A.D. (Freed 1989). Evidence for the export of Italian Dressel 2-4 that late has emerged from the study of two large dumps of these vessels from late 2nd- to early 3rd-century A.D. warehouses at Saint-Romain-en-Gal, Rhône (Desbat *et al.* 1990). Indeed, Italian Dressel 2-4 seems to have outlasted all the other western versions of the form. But although the form had a long history, its *floruit* came in the last decades B.C. and in the 1st century A.D.

Dressel 2-4 was produced widely in Italy and the western provinces. The only provincial Dressel 2-4 identified at Stanway are the two Catalan amphoras from Tarraconensis (FIG. 54, BF6.22–3). The very few painted inscriptions that specify the wines and *acetum* bottled in these Catalan amphoras have been listed and described elsewhere (Sealey 1985, 45–6). *Acetum* was vinegar; diluted with water it gave the non-alcoholic drink *posca*. The translations of *acetum* as sour wine so common in the English-speaking world are wrong (Tchernia 1986, 9–11). We now also have a painted inscription on a Catalan Dressel 2-4 specifying Aminean wine as the contents; it was a wine named after the parent grape variety rather than the place of origin (Liou 1993, fig. 2, 135 no. 8). The fourteen shipwrecks with Catalan Dressel 2-4 reviewed by Corsi-Sciallano and Liou all fall within a half century or so of each other down to Nero and point to a vigorous but short-lived economic current, one in which Stanway participated. Elsewhere at Colchester, Catalan wine accounted for 7.36 per cent of the wine drunk at the Sheepen site between A.D. 43 and 60 (Sealey 1985, 16), but exports of wine from Catalonia were in steep decline in the second half of the 1st century A.D. (Corsi-Sciallano and Liou 1985, 171–2).

The Italian Dressel 2-4 at Stanway include a vessel (FIG. 81, BF64.15) in the familiar black sand fabric found in both Dressel 1 and Dressel 2-4, and indeed now the mid-Roman

Campanian amphoras (Williams 1994, 218). The writer has also seen the fabric in one of the Dressel 21-22 amphoras from Colchester town centre (*CAR* **10**, fig. 3.2, no. 36). A topic that can usefully be aired here is the source region for this distinctive fabric. It has been assigned to Pompeii because some of the amphoras in the fabric were stamped by L. Eumachius, a resident of the town. He also stamped tiles there (Tchernia and Zevi 1972, 37, 40). French scholars call the fabric the *Eumachi* paste. Working independently, Peacock (1977, 153) reached the same conclusion. He said that bricks in a black sand fabric were common at Pompeii and Herculaneum, but not present in other towns in the Italian volcanic tract (but my own experience of the brickwork at Pompeii and Herculaneum is that the black sand fabric is actually rare there). Doubts have occasionally been raised about the exclusive attribution of the fabric to Pompeii and Herculaneum (Peña 1990, 655). The most serious are those of a French team (Hesnard *et al.* 1989, 36–49).

Hesnard and her colleagues undertook a programme of X-ray fluorescence to clarify the chemical composition of amphoras with a black sand fabric. The results showed that they could be divided into five groups. Fabrics 1–4 are quite different to Fabric 5 (the *Eumachi* group from Pompeii), and show that the production of black sand ceramics was not confined to the region of Vesuvius. These fabrics are called *faux-Eumachi* (counterfeit *Eumachi*) and are incorporated in their Group A. Fabric 5 is their Group B, the Pompeian *Eumachi* fabric. Tiles from Pompeii with Oscan and Latin stamps in a black sand fabric were analysed, and the results showed that (with two exceptions) they belonged to Group B, the Pompeian fabric. Analyses of Dressel 2-4 amphoras stamped by L Eumachius showed they also belonged to this group, the Pompeian fabric.

A number of Graeco-Italic and Dressel 1 amphoras in a black sand fabric were examined from six sites in Gaul and Spain, ranging in date from the 3rd to the 1st centuries B.C. Only 45 per cent of the black sand amphoras were the Pompeian Fabric 5, the remainder in the Group A Fabrics 1–4 had come from elsewhere.

To begin with, the importance of the *faux-Eumachi* groups increased with the passing of time. In contexts dated *c.* 250–175 B.C. at two sites in Gaul and Spain, all the Graeco-Italic black sand fabric amphoras are Pompeian. The *faux-Eumachi* groups make their début in the second half of the 2nd century B.C. and become more common than the Pompeian black sand fabric in the 1st century B.C. They represent four different production centres; they must be Italian because Dressel 1 is an Italian form, but the precise whereabouts of any *ateliers* are unknown. Eventually the true *Eumachi* black sand fabric from the Vesuvius region came back into its own. All the black sand Dressel 2-4 from a large assemblage of late 2nd- and early 3rd-century A.D. amphoras from Saint-Romain-en-Gal (Rhône) came from the Vesuvius region, showing that viticulture was revived there after the eruption of A.D. 79 (Desbat *et al.* 1990, 206, 212).

The implications of this research are unsettling, although it has been ignored in Britain and given only summary acknowledgement in European literature (Baudoux 1996, 33). There is a real possibility that at least half the black sand fabric amphoras reaching Britain are not from the Bay of Naples but from sources elsewhere in Italy. It would seem that these other source regions lie somewhere in southern Etruria or Latium (Peña 1990, 655).

Beltrán I *salazones*

The *salazon* amphoras produced along the coast of Baetica in Roman Spain make their first appearance in the *c.* 80–60 B.C. funerary enclosure at Clemency (Luxembourg). There the rim and body sherds of a Dressel 9 (part of Beltrán I) were securely stratified with Dressel 1 amphoras in the north-east of the funerary enclosure. The excavators were understandably surprised at its presence, but the vessel was not intrusive (Metzler *et al.* 1991, fig. 61, no. 1, 78). Otherwise the most important evidence for the early export of *salazones* from Baetica is the *c.* 50 B.C. Titan shipwreck, with its cargo of Dressel 12 (Beltrán III) amphoras (Tailliez 1961, figs 1 and 4, 185, 197; Parker 1992, 424–5), and the *c.* 50–30 B.C. wreck of Cap Béar C, where the bulk of the cargo was Dressel 1, Pascual 1, and Dressel 12 amphoras (Parker 1992, 97–8). The earliest *salazones* in Britain are invariably Dressel 9 (Peacock 1981, 202), a form that disappears after Augustus (Baudoux 1996, 70). No grave in Britain has the association of a *salazon* and Dressel 1, and *salazones* do not seem to have reached here until the very end of the 1st century B.C. or the start of the 1st century A.D.

Views differ on the terminal date of Beltrán I. Panella (1973, 508) felt that Dressel forms 7-13 were too common in Flavian contexts at Ostia to be explained as residual material. A more conservative assessment comes from Martin-Kilcher (1994, 399) who was reluctant to envisage production of the form much beyond *c.* A.D. 50. My own feeling is that Beltrán I was replaced by Beltrán II in the decades A.D. 60–80, by — let us say — *c.* A.D. 75 (Sealey 1985, 84). The last definite shipwreck with the form is Ses Salines, where the form shared the hold with Dressel 20 amphoras. Stamped lead ingots show the ship sank in the reign of Vespasian (Parker 1992, 378–9).

The number of painted inscriptions with evidence for contents continues to grow and confirms the primacy of fish-sauce as the contents of the form (Ehmig 2003, 62–7). This high survival rate of inscriptions may be connected with the poorly understood surface treatment of these Baetican amphoras where they carry the inscription. An interesting new perspective on these jars has come from Masada, where research has shown that Baetican fish-sauces were kosher (because they were made from fish with scales) and so could be enjoyed by King Herod without troubling his conscience (Cotton *et al.* 1996).

The ancients had a quite different attitude to medicines than prevails today. They felt that if something was wholesome to eat or drink, then it was only natural that it should have therapeutic qualities as well. Thus the fish-sauces bottled in *salazon* amphoras were not just foodstuffs: they had medicinal uses as well. This is an important consideration at Stanway, where this particular *salazon* amphora was associated with surgical instruments: there is every likelihood that fish-sauce was used there not just in cuisine but in medicine as well.

Although *garum* and related sauces had been known in the Greek world from at least the 5th century B.C., it was not until the writings of Dioscorides in the 1st century A.D. that medical literature made reference to their uses in healing. Perhaps it was the scale of the trade in Spanish *salazones* then that led to their widespread use in medicine. *Garum* retained its medicinal uses until late antiquity and the Byzantine period. It was believed to cure conditions as diverse as headaches, diarrhoea and tuberculosis. Unhealthy states of mind such as depression and lethargy could also be treated. Gargling with *garum* was recommended for sores in the mouth. It was applied externally to treat skin conditions, bites and burns; it was also deemed useful when extracting weapons that had pierced the skin and so could have been used in conjunction with some of the surgical instruments in the Stanway grave. Occasionally *garum* made from a specific fish was held to be appropriate to a particular condition. As well as a medicine in its own right, *garum* could be added to medicinal preparations to make them more palatable and to achieve the right consistency. It also played a part in veterinary medicine (Curtis 1991, 27–37 with refs).

Apart from a Flavian Dressel 2-4 amphora found in London at Southwark that had come from Antibes in the south of France bottled with the fish-sauce *liquamen* (Hassall and Tomlin 1984, 344, no. 37, pls 27–8), Spain exercised a virtual monopoly over the supply of *salazones* to Britain in the early Roman period (Carreras Monfort 2000, 143) and dominated the markets in Gaul and the Rhineland until the 2nd century A.D. (Curtis 1991, 84).

AMPHORA CATALOGUE BY FEATURE

Warrior's burial BF64

BF64.15 FIG. 81. B983. Dressel 2-4. Italian amphora in a black sand fabric, CAM AM 1 (Tomber and Dore 1998).
What survives is the body from a short basal spike right up to a shoulder that curves steeply towards the neck. Shallow horizontal grooves about 20 mm apart on the exterior of the body give a wall 10.1 to 12.1 mm thick. Black stains on the exterior of the body were presumably caused in the same way as the stains on other amphoras from the site. Fractures at the top of the body and shoulder show no signs of abrasion after their formation. The body is restored from many joining sherds (with few gaps). We cannot tell if a complete amphora had been placed in the grave at the funeral — with the neck and rim

subsequently dislodged by plough damage or even by quarry machinery — or if only the body had originally been included in the grave (but see p. 172).

Doctor's burial CF47

CF47.14 FIG. 108. C904. Dressel 8 (Beltrán I) *salazon* (13,800 g) Fabric CAD AM (Tomber and Dore 1998). The sparse red-brown iron ore inclusions typical of this fabric group are here readily apparent in fractures, and show the vessel came from the Cadiz region. The capacity is 14.5 litres (measured with millet seed to where the uppermost part of the handle joins the neck). When complete the vessel would have held a little more, perhaps 15 litres.

Apart from the missing rim, the vessel is complete. The neck is narrower at the top than at the shoulder. The body is ovoid in section with thick walls and attains its maximum girth towards the lower end. There is a long and narrow hollow basal spike, with a rounded terminal and straight sides that widen out gently towards the body. At the top of the body, there is a short curved shoulder from which the handles rise more or less vertically. In section, the handles are oval, with a flat inner face. Along the length of the outer face, there is a low flat ridge in the centre of the handle that runs its entire length. It becomes more pronounced as it travels up the handle, and at the summit it is divided in two by a deep groove before it joins the neck. Handles of this kind are typical of Dressel 8, but are occasionally present on other *salazones* of the first half of the 1st century A.D. (Martin-Kilcher 1994, 396).

Since Zevi (1966, 229–46), it has been standard practice to amalgamate Dressel forms 7-11 as a single coherent group, linked by contents, date and origin. It used to be thought that Dressel had been more fastidious than he needed to be when he differentiated his forms 7-11. This changed with the discovery of a large group of intact amphoras dated *c*. A.D. 5 from La Longarina at Ostia. There vessels were found which corresponded exactly with Dressel forms 7-10 and 12 (Dressel 11 was not present) (Hesnard 1980, 146). Indeed, Hesnard was able to add two more closely related forms to the Dressel 7-11 family, which she called La Longarina 2 and 3. Since then, there has been an understandable move towards isolating the individual components of the Dressel 7-11 family, although this can only be done of course for more or less complete vessels like Stanway. Dressel 7-11 is included within Beltrán form I (Beltrán 1970, 388–420). Beltrán I is a useful term because it includes not just Dressel 7-11, but other related vessels that do not feature in the Dressel table of forms: Dressel 7-11 and Beltrán I are not synonyms or precise equivalents. But we still do not know why such a subtly differentiated suite of amphoras should have been thought necessary for vessels from the same region, bottled with the same contents. The Stanway vessel can be recognised as Dressel 8 on the basis of the length of its handles and spike (far greater than on Dressel forms 7 and 9-11), on the proportions of the body, and the (relatively) short and slender neck which tapers upwards towards the rim. In particular, the body reaches its maximum diameter more than half way down. This makes the Stanway amphora a classic Dressel form 8. Vessels like the Cam 186a type-specimen (Hawkes and Hull 1947, pl. 72) attain the maximum body girth midway between the shoulder and the basal spike and, although conforming to Dressel 8 in other respects, are at one remove from the vessel published by Dressel.

Thirteen painted inscriptions on Dressel 8 from Rome specify the contents as the fish-sauce *garum* (Zevi 1966, 243). Three more Dressel 8 amphoras are now known with painted inscriptions that name their contents. One was bottled with *liquamen* (a synonym for *garum*). The other two amphoras had *garum*; one of them is specified as containing the mackerel variety (Ehmig 1998, 19–20 with refs). There are painted inscriptions on two Beltrán II amphoras specifying the contents as wine, although that is no reason to predicate the same of Beltrán I. But evidence that might suggest wine was indeed a minor element in the contents of both categories of amphora has now come to light (Silvino *et al.* 2005).

Chamber BF6

BF6.22 FIG. 54. B147, B227 shoulder, B223 handle, base, B138, B157, B179, B202, B215. Dressel 2-4 amphora. 110 sherds (2,943 g, mean sherd weight 26.8 g). The fabric is the distinctive red paste with abundant white inclusions assigned to Catalonia, fabric code CAT AM (Tomber and Dore 1998).

To judge by the surviving sherds, its body had an external diameter of 370 mm; body sherds are some 12 mm thick. Three shoulder sherds are present; one has a thickening of the wall where the handle began. The handle itself is represented by two joining sherds with a figure-of-eight section made from the amalgamation of two straight rods of clay. The upper surface of the profile view is curved at the summit where it turns sharply through rather more than a right angle towards the (missing) neck. Towards the base, the handle thickens where it had been attached to the shoulder, showing that more or less the entire length is present. Another sherd comes from the base of the amphora, with a small and possibly truncated

button spike. Catalan bases on Dressel 2-4 (and more especially its predecessor, Pascual 1) are invariably long and sturdy spikes; short and slight terminals like this are rare (Miró i Canals 1988, fig. 21, nos 3 and 7, fig. 22, no. 10, 89 for some other examples). Nothing of the rim has survived. The average empty weight of the Catalan Dressel 2-4 amphoras from six of the shipwrecks catalogued by Corsi-Sciallano and Liou (1985, 19, 31, 46, 69, 77, 132) is 16.57 kg, so only about 18 per cent of the Stanway amphora found its way into the chamber. Very little survives of the white surface slip on the amphora. Surfaces are powdery and soft with hairline cracks, quite unlike the hard and smooth finish one expects of these vessels. Fractures are rounded and smooth, with no sign of the usual hackly surfaces found on a fresh break. The condition of the edges made it impossible to establish if joining sherds were present. A few sherds have jet black matter adhering to the inner and outer surfaces, and over the edges of fractures.
BF6.23 FIG. 54. B123 shoulder, B227 handle, B134, B147, B148. Dressel 2-4 amphora. 36 sherds (2,339 g, mean sherd weight 65 g). Fine light pink (5YR 7/4) fabric of untempered clay.
To judge by the surviving sherds, its body had an external diameter of 310 mm; body sherds are some 13 mm thick. There is a rounded junction where the body joins the shoulder; the shoulder rises steeply towards the neck, around the base of which there is a horizontal groove. A straight length of handle with a figure-of-eight (bifid) section is present. On the inside of the handle, there is a single thumb or finger-tip impression on each rod just below the point where the handle turns in towards the neck. Nothing of the rim and base has survived. The condition of the sherds is much like that of the Catalan amphora from the same chamber. In this case, the fabric is even more friable and powdery, and there are more hairline cracks on the surface. Many of the sherds also have a black deposit on the inner and outer surfaces that sometimes runs across the fracture. Fractures themselves are rounded and smooth. The condition of the edges made it impossible to establish if joining sherds were present. Graffito: **CΛII**, *i.e.* **GAII** (TABLE 45, FIG. 147, BF6.23), scratched on the shoulder.

Discussion of amphoras BF6.22 and BF6.23 from chamber BF6

The condition of both amphoras is very similar. Both are much altered from their original state (powdery surfaces, hairline cracks, rounded fractures and black deposits on sherd breaks and outer surfaces). Other pottery from the chamber is in the same condition. What caused this? The black deposits must have formed after the vessels had been broken because they run over sherd fractures. Similar deposits are present on amphora sherds from the *c.* 15–10 B.C. Lexden tumulus and Grave 241 at King Harry Lane (Stead and Rigby 1989, 334). At Lexden, scientific analysis showed the stains to have formed naturally in the ground after burial of the pottery (Foster 1986, 124). Bearing in mind the similar geology to Lexden, the Stanway stains presumably developed in the same way. Other aspects of the condition of the amphora sherds raised the possibility that they might be connected with trauma caused by exposure of the amphoras to the heat of a funeral pyre. But the hairline cracks and powdery surfaces of the sherds are replicated on other pottery from the site, including complete vessels from other chambers where exposure on a pyre and subsequent breakage had not taken place. Acidic soil conditions seem to be at the root of the problem. This would also account for the rounded sherd breaks, otherwise so suggestive of the abrasion that comes from a long sequence of disturbance and movement before incorporation in their final context. A similar phenomenon has been reported from the late 1st-century B.C. grave at Dorton. There it was claimed that some of the fractures on the amphoras had been smoothed by groundwater after burial (Farley 1983, 290). The writer has seen pyre-damaged amphora sherds from Iron Age contexts at the Elms Farm site at Heybridge in Essex (p. 305). At Elms Farm, the trauma was even more advanced than at Stanway. Comparison of the two groups of material leaves the writer of the opinion that the amphoras from chamber BF6 had not been exposed to a pyre and that their condition can be accounted for by hostile soil conditions.

Only a modest proportion of each amphora found its way into chamber BF6. In the case of the Catalan amphora, this was only about 18 per cent of the vessel by weight. No data on empty weights are available for the class of Dressel 2-4 amphora represented by the second vessel in the chamber, so a percentage cannot be established. It is striking that the sherd weights of both vessels are so similar: 2.943 kg for the Catalan, and 2.339 kg for its companion. When it is remembered that a complete and empty Dressel 2-4 weighs some 17 kg, this correspondence in weights might not be a coincidence. It suggests that at the funeral, it was deemed fitting to deposit more or less equal quantities of each amphora in the chamber. My wife suggested that a mourner or mourners carried the same number of handfuls of sherds from each amphora to the chamber. It follows too that although sherds of both vessels were mixed indiscriminately in the actual chamber, they had been kept apart above ground at the funeral until they were broken.

Chamber CF42

CF42.10 Not illustrated. C758. Dressel 2-4. 10 sherds (not too much attention should be paid to the sherd count because the crumbly and friable character of the vessel has led to disintegration since excavation) (15 g). Fabric soft and powdery light yellow (10YR 8/6) fabric with sparse (less than 5 per cm²) well-sorted rounded and sub-rounded white and light grey inclusions <1 mm across.

Pyre-site BF1/BF16

BF16.1 Not illustrated. B70, B79 (burnt?), B82, B88 (burnt?), B127, B204. Dressel 2-4 amphora (144 g, average sherd weight of 12 g). Cream Catalan fabric (Williams 1981, 128; 1995, 306). To judge by the body sherds present, the amphora had an external diameter of 340 mm with walls 12.6 mm thick. A neck sherd 11 mm thick has an external diameter of 120 mm. The cylindrical body and thin wall show we are dealing with Dressel 2-4, rather than with the earlier Pascual 1 form. Two sherds have the black stains present on other amphoras from the site, caused by a chemical reaction after they had been buried (p. 302). Seven of the ten sherds have black and grey scorch and burn marks. These marks continue over fractures showing that exposure to the heat source took place at the time of breakage or afterwards, not before. In many cases the colour of the sherds has turned from cream to grey (5Y 7/1), suggesting intense heat.

?Mortuary enclosure BF32

Pot 126 Not illustrated. BF31, B386, B524. Dressel 2-4 amphora. 2 body sherds (79 g, average sherd weight of 39.5 g). Brick red fabric typical of much of Latium and Campania, fabric code CAM AM 2 (Tomber and Dore 1998).

The two sherds from this Italian vessel both have external diameters of 140 mm with walls 11.5 mm thick. The tight curve shows they came from the neck .

?Mortuary enclosure CF43-6

Pot 145 Not illustrated. CF44, C112 shoulder. Dressel 2-4. 3 sherds (90 g). Fabric in the distinctive red paste with abundant white inclusions assigned to Catalonia, fabric code CAT AM (Tomber and Dore 1998).

Pot 146 FIG. 144. CF45, C185 handle. Dressel 2-4. Handle (202 g). Fabric light yellow (10YR 8/4) with common (6–10 per cm²) sub-rounded and well-sorted white and grey inclusions <1 mm across. A straight length of handle with a shallow exterior groove. The right hand half of the exterior of the handle has a thumb or finger-tip impression towards the lower end of the sherd, possibly where pressure had been applied when the handle was luted on to the shoulder.

Pot 147 Not illustrated. CF45, C185. Dressel 2-4. 30 sherds (not too much attention should be paid to the sherd counts because the crumbly and friable character of the vessel has led to disintegration since excavation) (133 g). Fabric soft and powdery light yellow (10YR 8/6) fabric with sparse (less than 5 per cm²) well-sorted rounded and sub-rounded white and light grey inclusions <1 mm across.

Enclosure ditch of Enclosure 3

Pot 12 Not illustrated. BF4, B1117. Dressel 2-4 amphora. Neck sherd (5 g). Fine light pink (5YR 7/4) fabric of untempered clay.

Pot 13 Not illustrated. BF4, B1101. Dressel 2-4 amphora. Neck sherd (12 g). Italian amphora in a black sand fabric, CAM AM 1 (Tomber and Dore 1998).

Enclosure ditch of Enclosure 4

Pot 127 Not illustrated. BF39, B932 shoulder. Beltrán I *salazon* sherd (104 g). The amphora is represented by a single sherd in the fine light yellow-green paste with powdery surfaces typical of Baetican *salazon* amphoras. Although this sherd does not have the red-brown iron ore grains of fabric code CAD AM (Tomber and Dore 1998, 87, pl. 64), it can be classified with it because the iron grains of the fabric are so sparse that even quite large sherds need not necessarily show them. The sherd has a wall 20 mm thick. The oval scar left where the handle was detached from the shoulder is plain to see. Attribution to a form is more difficult. The angle of the shoulder is not steep enough to be Beltrán II or even Dressel 11, and it is simplest to think of the vessel as Beltrán I.

Pot 128 FIG. 143. BF40, B948. Dressel 2-4. Short terminal spike (287 g). Fabric light yellow (10YR 8/4) with common (6–10 per cm²) sub-rounded and well-sorted white and grey inclusions <1 mm across.

Enclosure ditch of Enclosure 5

Pot 148 Not illustrated. CF4, C53. Italian Dressel 2-4 body sherd (51 g), with an external diameter of 380 mm and a wall thickness of 13.5 mm in fabric CAM AM 2 (Tomber and Dore 1998).

Pot 149 Not illustrated. CF2, C153. Dressel 2-4. One sherd (43 g) came from CF2, the north butt end of the ditch at the entrance. Fabric in a soft light brown fabric (7.5YR 7/6) with powdery surfaces. The inclusions are well-sorted sparse (<5 per cm²) white and dark grey grains <0.5 mm across.

DISCUSSION

There were two quite distinct ways of treating funerary amphoras at Stanway; they could be placed in the burial more or less intact, or as sherd material from a vessel smashed elsewhere.

Complete amphoras found in Late Iron Age and early Roman graves here and in north-east Gaul were put there empty: their contents had been decanted before the grave goods were arranged in the funerary pit. One says this because none has been recovered from a grave with a bung *in situ* sealing its contents. At least some bungs would have survived because some of the components of amphora stoppers were made of imperishable materials. At least one of the amphoras at Stanway had been placed in its grave intact, the Dressel 8 from the Doctor's burial (FIG. 108, CF47.14) Although the rim is missing, the fracture is recent and it had presumably been dislodged by quarry machinery. The Dressel 2-4 from the Warrior's burial is represented only by the body (FIG. 81, BF64.15); we do not know if the rest of the vessel had been placed in the grave (but see p. 172). Although the body has been restored from sherds, one feels confident it was intact at the funeral but that it had subsequently collapsed in the ground.

The condition of the amphoras from the chambers at Stanway is quite different. There the amphoras were represented by sherd material (as opposed to vessels which may have broken in the ground after burial). The vessels are amphoras BF6.22, BF6.23, and CF42.10, from chambers BF6 and CF42. All are Dressel 2-4. The quantity of amphora sherds from the single amphora in chamber CF42 was tiny. More sherds were recovered from the two amphoras in chamber BF6 but even there, only about a fifth of each vessel by weight was present (FIG. 54). Evidently the amphoras had been smashed elsewhere and only a selection of sherds cast in the chamber. The broad congruence of the sherd weights of the two amphoras shows this was not a haphazard operation. Although sherds of both pots were scattered together in the grave, the more or less equal quantities of each amphora by weight shows that the funerary ritual involved conveying much the same amount of each vessel to the grave pit. Other objects in both chambers had also been thoroughly broken.

The first Iron Age grave to be discovered with smashed amphoras was the Lexden Tumulus (Foster 1986, 124; Williams 1986), but the possibility of ancient disturbance to the grave as well as the lack of comparanda discouraged investigation of the implications at the time. Not until the King Harry Lane cemetery (Williams 1989) was it realised that amphoras could be placed in Late Iron Age graves in the form of sherd material from vessels broken elsewhere. The treatment of smashed amphoras at King Harry Lane differs from the Lexden Tumulus and Stanway chambers BF6 and CF42, and indeed Folly Lane at Verulamium (Niblett 1999, 44; Williams 1999), in that the other grave goods at King Harry Lane were hardly ever broken.

The smashed amphora sherds in chambers BF6 and CF42 resonate with the still grander funerals at the Lexden Tumulus and Folly Lane, for there too the amphoras had been broken before burial. In the present state of knowledge, the Lexden Tumulus and Folly Lane graves bear every appearance of the very pinnacle of society, with Stanway at one or two removes. A social gradient between Stanway and Folly Lane can even be seen in the wine amphoras. At Folly Lane, they are all Italian, whereas at Stanway some had been drawn from the provinces. After Nero, wine amphoras seldom feature as grave goods in Britain. When they do, it can be as little more than a convenient lid or container for the other grave goods.

We have already seen that the contents of amphoras retrieved from early graves in Britain had apparently been decanted and consumed beforehand. There is no evidence that the near complete *salazon* from the Doctor's grave or the Dressel 2-4 amphora body from the warrior burial at Stanway were old vessels that might have seen secondary use once they had been emptied. Such evidence is of necessity unavailable for the smashed amphoras from Chambers BF6 and CF42. It is theoretically possible that any of the amphoras from the Stanway graves and chambers had reached the site empty and that the consumption of their contents had taken place elsewhere. This is why the four amphoras from the enclosure ditches that could not have come from vessels found in the funerary chambers or burials are important. There is no evidence in the late Iron Age at Stanway for domestic settlement: the entire *raison d'être* of the chambers and their enclosures is funerary. Yet these four amphoras show eating and drinking taking place there, and taking place in some style with imported wines and fish-sauces. It lends weight to the suspicion that the amphoras from the graves had seen the consumption of their contents on site, and not somewhere else. Stanway provides clear evidence from late Iron Age and early Roman Britain for funeral feasts at a cemetery.

Sherds from one of the Stanway amphoras had been exposed to intense heat. The vessel in question is a Catalan wine jar from the pyre site BF16 in Enclosure 3. None of the other Stanway amphoras shows signs of trauma from combustion. The incorporation of amphoras in pyres is unusual in late Iron Age and early Roman Britain. It is only certainly attested in Iron Age contexts at the Elms Farm site at Heybridge (Essex) (Sealey forthcoming b). Amphoras that had also been exposed to a pyre are attested at Verulamium in a conquest-period context. There the fill of the *c.* A.D. 35–40/45 Grave 447 at King Harry Lane had a burnt Dressel 20 sherd, although it might conceivably have been intrusive (Williams 1989, 116). The evidence from the high-status *c.* A.D. 55 funeral at Folly Lane is unambiguous because many of the Dressel 2-4 sherds from the burial pit and mortuary chamber were burnt.

THE SAMIAN (TABLE 44)

By G.B. Dannell

The small amount of samian ware found at Stanway is in keeping with the site's date and native character but is nevertheless a remarkable collection for its period. Most vessels are South Gaulish but there is also a single piece of Italian Arretine (TABLE 44).

Three of the burials contained samian. A minimum of five plain vessels, two cups and three platters, came from chamber BF6. All are represented by fragments, and further fragments from the feature could not be allocated to one of these items and may come from other unidentified vessels. Cup BF6.1 can be dated by a stamp of Silvanus to the Tiberian period, and the other items in the chamber are Tiberio–Claudian (BF6.2–5; p. 123). The Doctor's burial contained a complete decorated serving bowl (FIG. 108, CF47.1; p. 213) that dates to the A.D. 40s, and a complete plain Claudian cup was deposited in the Warrior's burial (FIG. 81, BF64.1; p. 173).

The remainder of the plain vessels came from Enclosures 4 and 5 and may be associated with the feasting that accompanied the funerary rites. Part of an Augusto–Tiberian Arretine platter (Pot 121; p. 95) came from the east ditch BF30 of the pyre-site BF32 in Enclosure 4 and this vessel may have been an heirloom of some considerable age when deposited. A partial cup and three partial platters came from BF40/CF5, the east ditch of Enclosure 4 (Pots 122–5; p. 80), and one partial platter from CF3, the south ditch of Enclosure 5 (Pot 144; p. 84). Three of these five vessels are Claudian or probably Claudian, and the other two need not be any later.

TABLE 44: PLAIN SAMIAN

Vessel	Context nos	Context	Form	Date	Source	Comments
Enclosure 3						
BF6.1	B164/157	chamber BF6	cup: Ritt. 5 (2)	Tiberian	SG	B164 stamped Silv*ani*, with 'A' graffito under base; fragments, most of vessel present
BF6.2	B68/132	chamber BF6	cup: Ritt. 5	Tib.–Claud.	SG	fragments, large part of vessel present
BF6.3	B150/157/198	chamber BF6	platter: Drag. 17	Tib.–Claud.	SG	fragments, large part of vessel present
BF6.4	B140/214	chamber BF6	platter: Ritt. 1	Tib.–Claud.	SG	graffito under base; fragments, large part of vessel present.
BF6.5	B148/151/214	chamber BF6	platter: Loeschcke 1a	Tib.–Claud.	SG	profile as Hawkes and Hull 1947, pl 39, 2a; fragments, large part of vessel present
BF6 misc.	B98; B138; B147; B161; B179	chamber BF6	-	-	SG	no identifiable fragments
BF64.1	B1024	Warrior's burial BF64	cup: Drag. 33	Claudian	SG	stamped by Primus
Enclosure 4						
Pot 121	B586/BL38, F30	pyre-site ditch BF32	platter	Aug.–Tib.	Arezzo	
Pot 122	B950	encl. ditch BF40	cup	Pre-Flavian	SG	
Pot 123	B964	encl. ditch BF40	platter	Claudian?	SG	
Pot 124	B1196/1197	encl. ditch BF40	Drag. 15/17	Claudian	SG	two sherds probably from same vessel
Pot 125	C1380	encl. ditch CF5 (BF40)	platter: Drag. 17	Claudian?	SG	a small version
Enclosure 5						
Pot 144	C1400	encl. ditch CF3	cup: Drag. 33?	1st century	SG	

The overall picture of supply at Sheepen is complicated by the number of vessels of Tiberian date deposited in post-conquest levels, some perhaps originally owned by native Britons before the conquest, others brought to Britain among the personal effects of army officers or the household goods of the early colonists and Gaulish artisans and traders moving to Britain to take advantage of the new markets. Nevertheless, it has long been established that a quantity of Arretine and South Gaulish wares reached Camulodunum in the pre-conquest period (Hawkes and Hull 1947, 168–91; Dannell 1985), and it is from these imports that the Arretine platter and the vessels in BF6 and CF47, at the least, would have been drawn. All would have been seen as rare and desirable items of service, the decorated bowl in particular. It is quite conceivable that some products of Claudian date also reached Camulodunum before the conquest or very soon afterwards (Hawkes and Hull 1947, 177; Dannell 1985). Even in the A.D. 40s and early 50s samian ware vessels would have been seen as high-status objects in a contemporary native British milieu. After the conquest considerable numbers of vessels were in use in the fortress and early *colonia* and at Sheepen (the latter assemblage influenced by that site's close proximity to the Roman establishments), but, in strong contrast, only nine miles away at Ardleigh the earliest samian ware consisted of South Gaulish Neronian vessels (Dickinson 1999), while in the Late Iron Age and early Roman cemeteries at Stansted samian vessels only began to be deposited as grave goods in the later 1st century A.D. (Wallace 2004, 239). Compared to these two sites the Stanway samian appears both striking and unusual for its period, a reflection of early access to continental products.

Decorated samian

CF47.1 FIG. 108. C900. Dragendorff form 29. South Gaulish. **OFI/CANTI** Cantus Die 6a. Date: *c.* A.D. 35–50, and probably from the end of that period. This die was often used on Dragendorff 29. Cantus (if only one potter) is purported to have stamped ware from A.D. 20–60 (Polak 2000, 196). However, the majority of his output must stop by *c.* A.D. 50, and a *floruit* of 30 years should be seen as a maximum. He is represented among the vessels burnt in a kiln disaster at La Graufesenque, known as 'The Fosse Cirratus', although not there stamping decorated vessels. This find shows Cantus as a worker of the later Tiberian period. The current piece has Claudio–Neronian features in the panels of the upper zone. These are not present in Fosse Cirratus, but the dog, O. 1970, is on a bowl fragment there, in a medallion. The crowded lower zone retains the style of earlier pieces, but is consistent with the later date. Cantus is one of the few potters to have made Drag. 29 with ovolo decoration (Fiches 1978, fig. 4.7 from d'Ensérune). Date: *c.* A.D. 35–50, and probably from the end of that period (*see also* Dickinson on p. 213).

THE GRAFFITI FROM CHAMBER BF6 (FIGS 146–7; TABLES 45–6)

By Paul R. Sealey

INTRODUCTION (TABLE 45)

The only graffiti from Stanway are those from the funerary chamber BF6, where seven pots have marks scratched on them. The readings of the graffiti are those of M.W.C. Hassall (Tomlin and Hassall 2003, 372, nos 15–18). TABLE 45 and FIGURES 146–7 give a full listing and drawings of the graffiti. Bearing in mind the date of the chamber (*i.e. c.* A.D. 35–45/50), they represent an interesting addition to the slender corpus of early writing from Britain.

TABLE 45: THE GRAFFITI AT STANWAY BASED ON TOMLIN AND HASSALL 2003, 372, NOS 15–18. THEY ARE ALL ON SHERDS FROM CHAMBER BF6 IN ENCLOSURE 3

Pot no.	Find nos	Context	Pot type	Pot date	Comments
BF6.1	B164	chamber floor	Ritt 5 samian cup	Tiberian	The graffito A was cut after firing underneath the base within the footring.
BF6.4	B140	backfill overlying chamber floor	Ritt 1 samian platter	Tib.–Claud.	The sherd appears to carry two superimposed graffiti cut after firing underneath the base within the footring: (a) X. (b) SES, perhaps Ses(tius).
BF6.15	B150, B151	chamber floor	Cam 8 TN platter	A.D. 25–60	A graffito cut after firing on the upper surface perhaps reads: CAII, Gaii. '(Property) of Gaius'. The reading of 'A' is not certain.
BF6.23	B147	backfill overlying chamber floor	Dressel 2-4 amphora	75 B.C.–A.D. 200	A graffito probably cut after firing on a sherd from the shoulder reads: CAII, Gaii. '(Property) of Gaius'. The first letter is 'C', not 'G'.
BF6.6	B90, B131	chamber floor	Cam 7C TR platter	A.D. 15–40	A straight line, probably cut before firing underneath the base within the footring.
BF6.8	B140, B151	floor and backfill of chamber	Cam 7/8 TR platter	A.D. 25–50	A 'grid' design on the upper surface. X+V (a six-pointed star) underneath the base within the footring. Both cut after firing.
BF6.13	B138	backfill overlying chamber floor	Cam 8 TN platter	A.D. 25–60	X (cross), cut after firing on the upper surface.

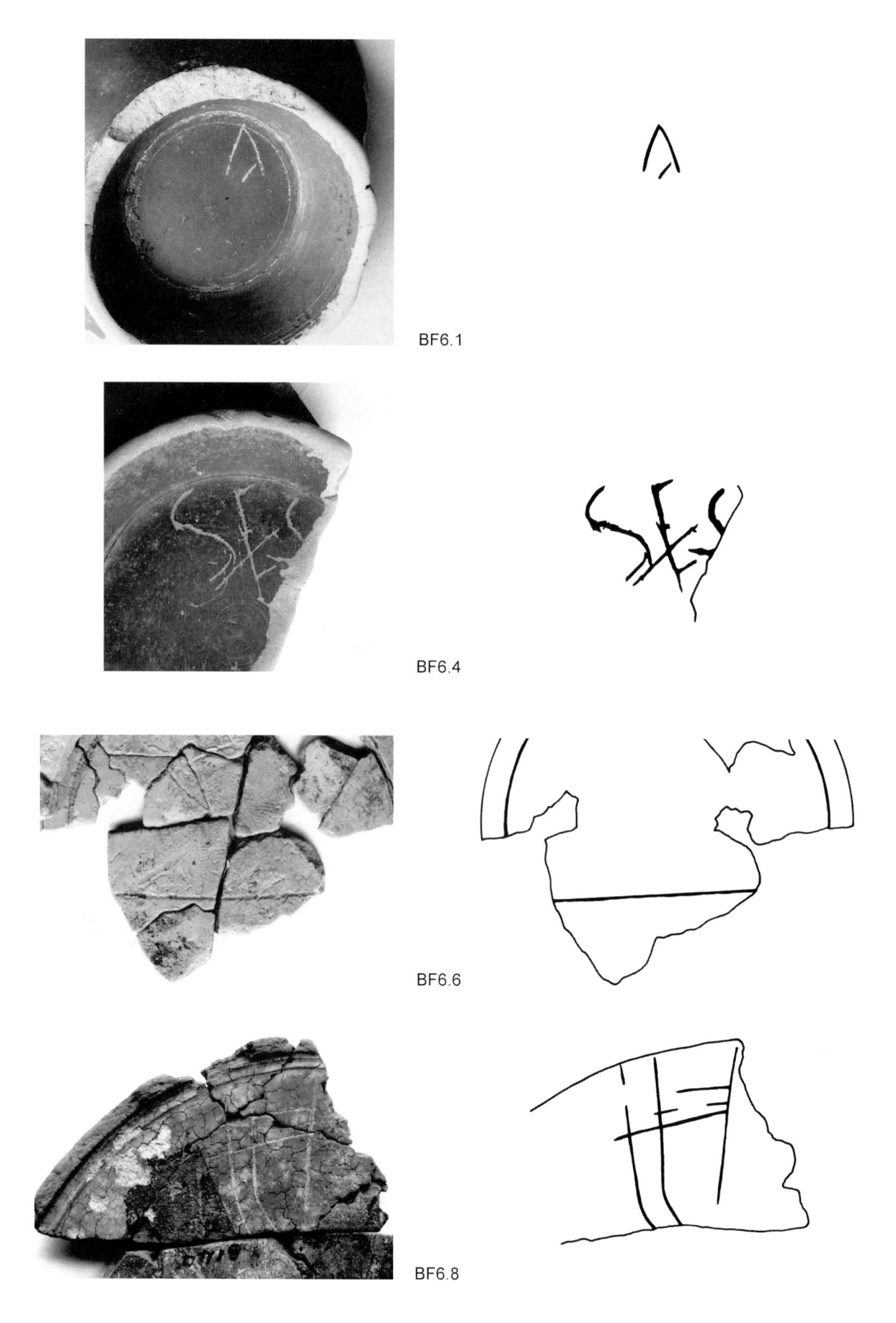

FIG. 146. Graffiti on pottery vessels from the chamber BF6: Pots BF6.1, 4, 6 and 8 (upper surface) (scale 1:1)

BF6.8

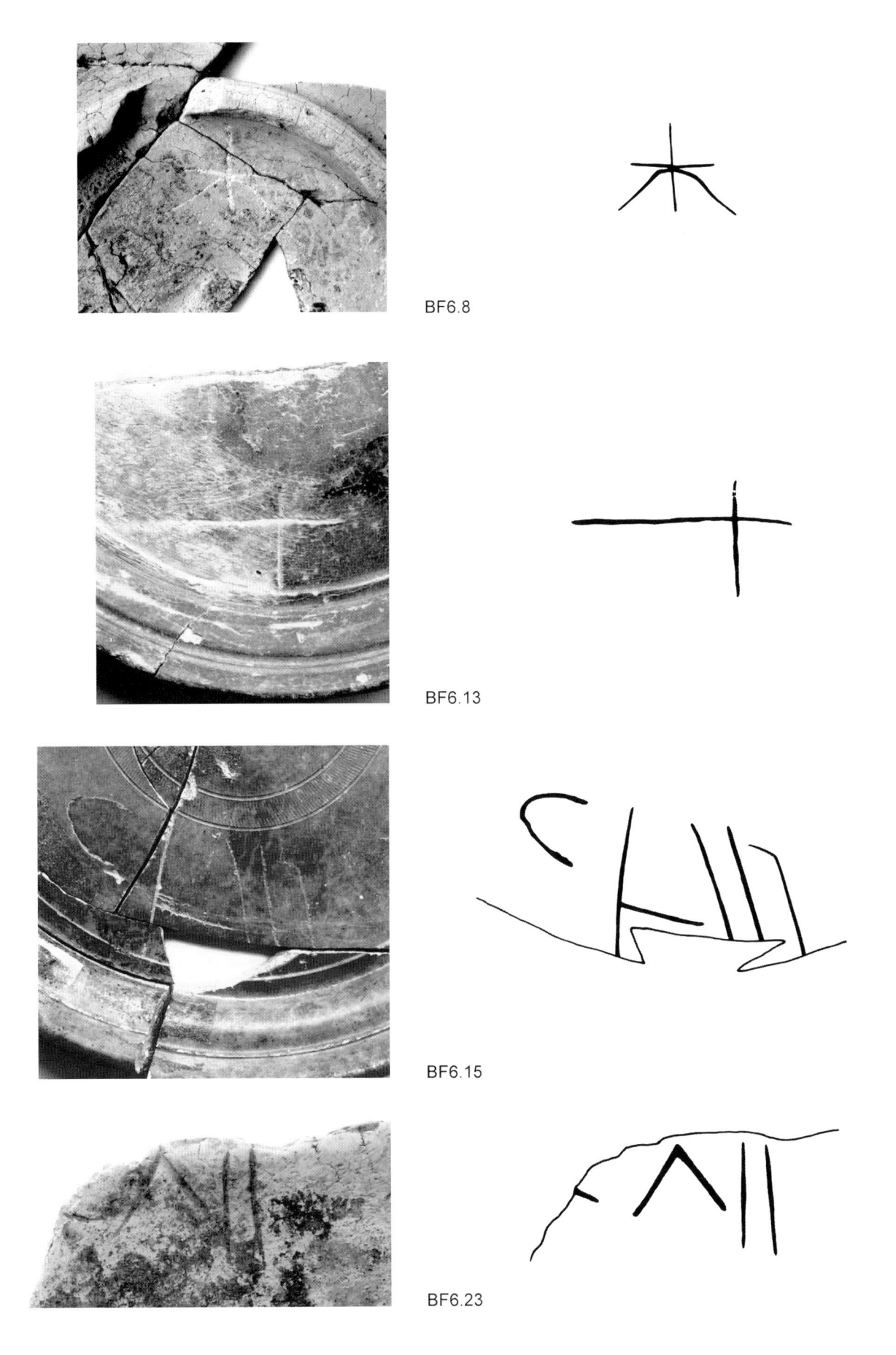

BF6.13

BF6.15

BF6.23

FIG. 147. Graffiti on pottery vessels from the chamber BF6: Pots BF6.8 (base), 13, 15 and 23 (scale 1:1)

The markings discussed here are quite distinct from the straight lines on the upper surfaces which Dr P.A. Tyers pointed out to me are cut marks from the consumption of food on the platters. Four of the graffiti are certainly letters (FIG. 146, BF6.1, BF6.4; FIG. 147, BF6.15, BF6.23). At best the other four can only be described as quasi-alphabetic; one is simply a straight line that might even have been cut before firing. The common denominator among the quasi-alphabetic graffiti is a cross; it is also present on the vessel with the SES graffito (BF6.4). Crosses are ubiquitous in the Roman period. They cannot all be the number ten or a letter of the alphabet; some are presumably ownership marks (Hassall 1982, 55). The Stanway graffiti include the earliest on an amphora from Britain and the first certain instances of the genitive case, indicating possession.

THE STANWAY GRAFFITI IN CONTEXT (TABLE 46)

Graffiti from Iron Age Britain are described in the appendix (pp. 313–14); imported pots inscribed before firing are not listed. Early graffiti from the major late Iron Age site of Elms Farm at Heybridge (Essex) have not been included because their context dates have yet to be finalised (Tomlin and Hassall 2001, 394).

Graffiti are not the earliest examples of writing generated in Britain; that honour falls to coin legends. The first are coins with single and double letters struck south of the Thames in the middle of the 1st century B.C. (Williams 2003a, 5–6). Rather later in the same part of the country, coins appear bearing the name COMMIOS from *c.* 30 B.C. (Bean 2000, 116–19). About the same time as the COMMIOS legends, we find the first graffiti north of the Thames from the Welwyn B (Hertfordshire) grave, where two Italian silver drinking cups have writing scratched on the underside of their pedestal feet. The grave itself has a Dressel 1 amphora but no imported table crockery, suggesting a date before *c.* 25 B.C. when crockery imports began (Rigby and Freestone 1997, 58). Welwyn has the only Iron Age graffiti on metalwork; all the others are on pottery. None of these other graffiti are definitely 1st-century B.C. in date, although two of the Puckeridge–Braughing examples come from contexts that span the period *c.* 15 B.C.–A.D. 20. If we take late Augustan to mean later than *c.* A.D. 1, then 24 of the 30 Iron Age graffiti listed in the appendix (80%) are 1st century A.D. in date. Evidently writing on domestic vessels began falteringly in the last decades B.C. but greatly increased in the forty years before the invasion.

Quantified details of the materials and pottery bearing Iron Age graffiti are given in TABLE 46. Nearly a quarter of the graffiti are on local vessels, including a storage jar from Puckeridge–Braughing. The rest are on imported tablewares. Half are on Arretine, and a further 16 per cent on Gallo-Belgic products. Much the same is true of Roman Britain where most ceramic graffiti are on tablewares, especially imported finewares (Evans 1988, 199, 202). The position of the graffito on the pot is not always recorded, but 12 of the 30 are on the undersides of vessels, where they would normally have been out of sight. That equates to 40 per cent and tallies exactly with the percentage of samian vessels from Roman Britain with graffiti from within the footstand (*RIB* 2, fasc. 7, 3). The only case ending certainly attested on the Iron Age graffiti is the nominative GRAECVS and MIIVS from Puckeridge–Braughing. There is no certain evidence of the genitive case, because the COMMVNIS graffito from Sandwich could be nominative or genitive. MIIVS means 'my' or 'mine' and, despite the lack of evidence for the genitive, the writing of names on these pots is best interpreted as statements of ownership. It was presumably done not so much from fear of theft but to reclaim possessions after a communal meal. Such declarations of ownership were a thoroughly Roman practice, widespread later in Roman Britain (and elsewhere of course) (*RIB* 2, fasc. 7, 5). It could not have evolved spontaneously in Iron Age Britain, and the graffiti in part at least must be the handiwork of 'Romans' resident in Iron Age Britain. This conclusion is borne out by two of the names, GRAECVS from Puckeridge–Braughing and COMMVNIS from Sandwich. Presumably these foreigners were the agents of Roman merchant houses that traded with pre-conquest Britain. GRAECVS may have been a slave or freedman of such an enterprise (*RIB* 2, fasc. 8, no. 2503.271).

TABLE 46: IRON AGE GRAFFITI BY VESSEL TYPE (STANWAY EXCLUDED)

Vessel type	Number of graffiti and site	Totals	Percentages
silver cup	Welwyn B grave (2)	2	7
Arretine	Puckeridge–Braughing (2) Colchester Sheepen (12) Fishbourne (1)	15	50
terra rubra	Puckeridge–Braughing (1) Colchester Sheepen (1)	2	7
terra nigra	Puckeridge–Braughing (1) King Harry Lane (1) Sandwich (1)	3	10
local *terra rubra* copy	Silchester (1)	1	3
other local wares	Puckeridge–Braughing (2) King Harry Lane (1) Canterbury (4)	7	23
total		**30**	

The geographical distribution of Iron Age graffiti is limited. In terms of political geography, they are confined to the Atrebates, Cantiaci, Catuvellauni and Trinovantes. Coin legends were used by outlying kingdoms such as the Corieltavi and Iceni, but there we have no graffiti to supplement the numismatic evidence for literacy. In such states, Latin should be thought of as exclusively the language of the mint, with — as yet — no hint of a wider diffusion of literacy in society. Apart from Sandwich and the Welwyn grave, Iron Age graffiti are confined to sites at the summit of the settlement hierarchy, to places with coin mints and other places invested with status.

It only remains to point out that further evidence for literacy in the Iron Age comes from finds of styli. Puckeridge–Braughing had two iron ones in Augustan contexts after *c.* 20 B.C. and three bone styli of 1st-century B.C. form from Augusto–Tiberian contexts (Jackson 1988b, 74 nos 55 and 57; Trow 1988, 159; Greep 2002). Two more iron styli were found at Iron Age Silchester in contexts dated *c.* 15 B.C.–A.D. 40/50 (Richards 2000, 360, fig. 172, 373).

THE SIGNIFICANCE OF THE DUAL NAMES AT STANWAY

Two names seem to be attested among the Stanway graffiti, Gaius and Sestius. There are no Gaulish personal names beginning with the element SES (Evans 1967), so it is possible that both names are Roman, the former a *praenomen* (forename) and the latter a *nomen* (family name). Although it is conceivable that both refer to the same individual — a Gaius Sestius — it is first worth considering the possibility that two different people are attested because of the implications for funerary practice.

The cremation grave of an adult at Baldock (Hertfordshire) dated *c.* A.D. 40–65 had pots with two different personal names. Both these graffiti are on samian; one reads MELENIO, the other, X VATILA (Stead and Rigby 1986, 71–2; Hassall 1986). The late Augustan cremation grave of an adult female in the King Harry Lane cemetery (Hertfordshire) had a local *tazza* with the graffito ANDOC, a male name (Stead and Rigby 1989, 202). Taken at face value, not all these pots can have originally belonged to the deceased. It has been suggested that such inscribed pots were not the possessions of the deceased, but donations brought to the funeral by mourners. Developing his idea that grave goods were donations by family members, Millett (1993, 266, 275–7) has argued that the decline in the number of grave goods with time at the King Harry Lane cemetery reflects the social dislocation of newcomers to the Verlamion settlement through geographical separation from their families in the decades before the Roman invasion. This overlooks the inheritance or donation of pots bearing graffiti in the lifetime of the individual eventually cremated with them: a Roman cremation pot at Colchester apparently had two successive owners (*RIB* 2, fasc. 8, no. 2503.157), and several graffiti on samian ware from Roman Britain suggest successive owners (*RIB* 2, fasc. 7, 1–2). Nor is it immediately obvious why grave goods should be confined to the family of the deceased, as opposed to friends or companions unconnected by ties of blood. The Latin of the graffiti is also at odds with the donation hypothesis. Not only are Iron Age coin legends written in the Latin alphabet, they also show some understanding of the Latin language (Creighton 2000, 171; Williams 2003a, 9; 2003b, 146–7). Were pots with graffiti donations at the funeral, the case ending of the name would be the dative, signifying 'to' or 'for' the person specified, but that case is not definitely attested in the examples cited here. Otherwise the only case ending attested on graffiti from a funerary context is the genitive (indicating possession or ownership) of the two Gaius graffiti from Stanway. In other words, the Stanway graffiti lend no support to the Millett thesis. The simplest — and indeed the preferable — explanation is that the pots naming Gaius and Sestius were acquired by the deceased of funerary chamber BF6 from people of that name in his or her lifetime.

But it is still worth considering the implications if the names on the pots were actually those of the deceased. One would have expected him or her to have had a Celtic name (taking 'Celtic' as a technical term to refer to the language spoken by Britons, without prejudice to their ethnicity). Gaius and Sestius of course are Roman names and we would need to explain how someone bearing such names was cremated at Stanway. Claudius banned *peregrini* (free adults in the empire who were not Roman citizens) from adopting a Roman family name (*nomen*) (Suetonius, *Divus Claudius*, 25.3). If the funeral took place after the invasion of A.D. 43, we might be dealing with just such a *peregrinus* before the legislation came into force. Nor did people granted citizenship by Claudius have to assume the same family name as the emperor (Hurley 2001, 174, citing Cassius Dio 60.17.7) so the deceased could have been a Sestius rather than a Claudius (had he been granted citizenship after A.D. 43). Perhaps the deceased was a Briton whose taste for things Roman led him to adopt a foreign name. That something like this could have happened in the Iron Age is suggested by the puzzling legend AGR on some rare silver issues and a gold quarter-stater of Cunobelin (de Jersey 2001, 15–16, 31–2). G. de la Bédoyère suggested the legend stands for the Roman *cognomen* Agrippa (de Jersey 2002), although it might instead be the (rare) Gaulish name Agriccos or Agrecius (Sills 2003).

Standing aside from these intricacies of nomenclature, there is no reason to think the Stanway pots with personal names were donated by mourners at the funeral. The simplest explanation is that they had been acquired by the deceased in his or her lifetime from one or two people with a Roman name. But we cannot entirely rule out the possibility that the names were those of the deceased himself, and that he was a Gaius Sestius. A Roman would hardly have been laid to rest at Stanway and there is the intriguing — if unlikely — possibility that the deceased was a Briton who had assumed the name Gaius Sestius out of enthusiasm for things Roman on the eve of the invasion or in the conquest period.

LITERACY, IDENTITY AND POWER

Stanway helps elucidate who actually scratched these early graffiti from Britain. Literacy was an exotic skill introduced here through contact with the mainland of Europe. It is clear from COMMVNIS of Sandwich and GRAECVS of Puckeridge–Braughing that some Iron Age graffiti were the work of what we might nowadays call resident aliens, quite possibly merchants — or their agents — who traded with Britain, like those attested in the graffiti from the Magdalensberg in Austria before the Roman conquest of the region (Egger 1961). Indeed it is difficult to prove that any given graffito was the work of an Iron Age Briton if it comes from a settlement site (Hawkes and Hull 1947, 285). This is why the graffiti on the silver cups from Welwyn are important because there is no reason to think the deceased was anything other than a wealthy local potentate. In other words, the first graffiti from Britain were the work of élite natives as well as guests from overseas. Stanway was a cemetery for Britons, and chamber BF6 with its graffiti was not created for a Roman merchant venturer but for a native aristocrat. Even if the Stanway graffiti with Roman names were gifts to a Briton in his or her lifetime, their inclusion in the grave implies some comprehension of literacy by a native.

The presence of at least four literate graffiti in the Stanway chamber shows that writing had been important to the individual commemorated. But why? Although literacy was not a prerequisite of statehood in temperate Europe (Woolf 1994, 94), it is clear from coin legends alone that local dynasts were prepared to use this novel skill for their own purposes. It is quite conceivable that the more advanced tribal administrations in late Iron Age Britain had a literate secretariat: the adult cremated in the Inkwell burial adjacent to chamber BF6 might have been just such a trusted functionary. It is all too easy for us nowadays to forget how miraculous writing would have appeared to communities in the past that were pre-literate, like those of Iron Age Britain (Creighton 2000, 165–6). Knowledge is power, and literacy can be a part of that equation. No doubt this was not lost on élites of the kind cremated at Stanway. One consequence of the partial adoption of literacy in Britain will have been a widening of the gulf between élites and the rank and file of the population. Indeed that may well have been some of its attraction for dynasts and their aristocratic retinues, even if it aggravated the tensions suspected between secular rulers and a Druid priesthood that would not commit its teachings to writing (Creighton 1995, 297; Webster 1999, 12). The presence of so many graffiti in the Stanway chamber makes a statement: the deceased was élite not only by virtue of wealth or birth, but also through his or her comprehension of the new skill of literacy.

APPENDIX: GRAFFITI FROM IRON AGE BRITAIN

Puckeridge–Braughing, Gatesbury Track (Hertfordshire). The graffito on the shoulder of a native storage vessel reads CIINATIN... or CINATA... It was stratified in the lowest fill of Pit F49 with local copies of a Gallo-Belgic butt-beaker (hence after *c.* 15 B.C.) and was sealed by a level with late Augustan *terra rubra* to give a date of *c.* 15 B.C.–A.D. 15 for the graffito. The graffito is a masculine or feminine version of the Celtic name Cen(n)atus (Partridge 1980, 117; *RIB* 2, fasc. 8, no. 2503.225).

Puckeridge-Braughing, Skeleton Green (Hertfordshire). Five graffiti of Iron Age date were recovered (Partridge 1982).
1. GRAECVS (the Latin adjective meaning 'Greek') on the underside of a *terra rubra* platter from a context dated *c.* A.D. 15–25. This Graecus was possibly a slave or freedman of a Roman merchant who traded with Britain (*RIB* 2, fasc. 8, no. 2503.271).
2. MIIVS on the underside of an Arretine platter from a context dated *c.* A.D. 30–40. In some forms of Latin cursive II was used for E (Allen 1980, 120), so MIIVS can be read as MEVS (the Latin adjective meaning 'my' or 'mine') (*RIB* 2, fasc. 8, no. 2504.47).
3. TE on the underside of an Arretine platter from a context dated *c.* 10 B.C.–A.D. 20 (*RIB* 2, fasc. 7, no. 2501.746).
4. SE on the underside of the base of 'a small coarseware jar' from a context dated *c.* A.D. 15–25 (*RIB* 2, fasc. 8, no. 2504.48).
5. *TE* on the underside of the base of a *terra nigra* platter from a Roman period context but deemed to be pre-conquest because of the identity of style with the other TE graffito (*RIB* 2, fasc. 8, no. 2504.49).

Canterbury, Whitehall Road (Kent). Four graffiti were recovered from Iron Age contexts dated A.D. 15-43 (Wilson 1987, fig. 79, nos 2–5, 208).
1. NVX (with reversed N) on a local jar (*RIB* 2, fasc. 8, no. 2503.566).
2. H on a local copy of a butt-beaker.
3. XXI on a local cup.
4. H on a local cup.

Colchester, Sheepen (Essex). There were twelve Arretine vessels with graffiti. Three were stratified in late Iron Age contexts, after *c.* A.D. 5. The others are unstratified or from early Roman contexts, but there can be little doubt their graffiti were cut in the Iron Age. The clearest read AR, M, SEV II, VAT, VE, SI, A and VISI (Hawkes and Hull 1947, 284–5). V.A. Rigby kindly drew my attention to another (unpublished) Iron Age graffito from the 1930–39 excavations at Sheepen on a *terra rubra* platter stamped by Attissus, and read as SA...I. It was stratified in an early Roman context, but can be added to the corpus of Iron Age graffiti because Attissus was an Augustan potter (Hawkes and Hull 1947, 209 no. 45, pl. 45 for the stamp; Timby 2000, 203 for the date).

Fishbourne Palace (West Sussex). An Arretine cup with the letters TV scratched on its base came from the old ground surface just south of a ditch with pottery dated *c* 10 B.C.–A.D. 25 in the primary fill (Manley and Rudkin 2005, 91, 94).

Silchester (Hampshire). What is apparently a local copy of a *terra rubra* beaker has a graffito in Greek letters on the base, ΧΦΑ. It was one of a group of ten pots buried in the bottom of Pit 9 in Insula XXXV 'on the eve of the Roman invasion' (St John Hope 1908, fig. 7 bottom right; May 1916, 185 no. 3, pl. 76; Boon 1969, 34 n. 6; *RIB* 2, fasc. 8, no. 2503.93).

Verlamion, King Harry Lane (Hertfordshire). Grave 123 has a late Augustan–Tiberian central Gaulish *terra nigra* platter with the graffito RX (Stead and Rigby 1989, fig. 55, 202, 303, 306). Grave 322 includes late Augustan imported pottery and a grog-tempered local *tazza* with the graffito ANDOC. The name is male but the cremated bones are female (*ibid.*, fig. 55, 202, 354, 356).

Welwyn B Grave (Hertfordshire). Two Italian silver drinking cups have graffiti on the underside of their pedestal feet, read by the writer as ACI II and ACSTIII, with the ST ligatured. It has been suggested that the inscriptions begin with the abbreviated name of the vessel (*acetabulum*) and that what follows is their capacity or weight (Wright 1964, 180, no. 15; *RIB* 2, fasc. 2, nos 2414.30–31). But the capacity and weight proposed are wrong for the cups, and in any case the Latin name for drinking cups like these was *cantharus*, not *acetabulum* (Hilgers 1969 *s.v. cantharus* and *acetabulum*) so the graffiti need not have been written before the arrival of the cups in Britain.

Sandwich, Archer's Low Farm (Kent). A late Augustan central Gaulish *terra nigra* platter from the lower fill of a ditch with immediately pre-conquest pottery bears the graffito COMMVNIS. Communis was a common Roman personal name (*cognomen*), especially in Gallia Narbonensis and Italy (Hassall and Tomlin 1993, 317, no. 9).

THE BROOCHES (TABLE 47)

By Nina Crummy

TABLE 47 shows the brooches found in the funerary contexts. One came from an isolated pit with pyre debris dating to the 1st century B.C., the rest were from mid 1st-century A.D. burials in Enclosures 3 and 5.

TABLE 47: BROOCHES FROM ENCLOSURES 1–5

Encl.	Feature	Brooch type	Context	SF	Alloy	Notes
–	CF7.2	boss-on-bow	C44	198	brass	pre-conquest import
3	BF64.19	Nertomarus	B1032	340	brass	pre-/post-conquest import
	BF64.20	Nertomarus	B–	382	brass	pre-/post-conquest import
3	BF67.3	Hod Hill variant	B1071	329	brass/gunmetal	post-conquest import
5	CF47.17	Rearhook	C942	40	leaded bronze	British, made from *c.* A.D. 40
	CF47.15	Langton Down	C982	79i	gunmetal	pre-conquest import
5	CF72.5	Keyhole Rosette	C410	7	brass	?post-conquest import
	CF72.6	Hod Hill	C408	6	leaded gunmetal	post-conquest import
	CF72.10	star-shaped plate	C406	5	brass	post-conquest import
	CF72.9	lozenge-shaped plate	C414/421	8/11	brass	post-conquest import
	CF72.7	circular lugged plate	C416	9	brass	post-conquest import
	CF72.8	circular lugged plate	C418	10	(brass)	post-conquest import

BOSS-ON-BOW BROOCH (KNOTENFIBEL)

CF7.2 FIG. 75. SF198. C44

The brooch fragment from CF7 was found in an isolated pit with pyre debris beyond the south-east corner of Enclosure 5. The brooch, with the boss set just below a downwards turn from the head (FIG. 75, CF47.2), is of a form found in Britain in burials of the Aylesford culture, both singly and in pairs, in silver, copper alloy and iron (Almgren 1923, no. 65; Feugère 1985, type 8; Birchall 1964; 1965; Stead 1971; 1976; 1984; Montague 1997, 92–3). Pairs have also been found in hoards, such as those in silver from Le Câtillon de Haut, Jersey (Fitzpatrick and Megaw 1987, pl. 17a), and in gold from near Winchester, Hampshire (Hill *et al.* 2004).

Stead (1976, 408) noted that north of the Thames the finds of *Knotenfibeln* clustered about the trade route provided by the Icknield Way, and some recent finds from, for example, Shillington, Bedfordshire (unpublished British Museum Treasure Report 2001) and Trumpington, Cambridge (Crummy 2002) bear this observation out. They are, however, far more widespread than Stead suggested. There are two iron ones further away from the Icknield Way at the King Harry Lane cemetery, Verulamium (Stead and Rigby 1989, 96, R1–2), and others from Foxholes Farm, near Hertford (Mackreth 1989b, fig. 76, 1–2). There are also several examples along the Essex and south Suffolk coast: one from Maldon Hall Farm, Maldon (Lavender 1991, fig. 4, 1), four from Elms Farm, Heybridge (Crummy forthcoming b), this brooch from Stanway, one from Colchester town centre, residual in a medieval robber trench (*CAR* 2, fig. 2, 16), two fragments from Sheepen that were not published in Hawkes and Hull 1947 because they inconveniently pre-dated the supposed start date for the site of *c.* 5 B.C. (Hull forthcoming, Type 19, nos 0248–9), and one from Burgh, Suffolk (Olivier 1988a, fig. 9, 1). The Maldon Hall Farm brooch is silver, one of the Elms Farm brooches is iron, the rest of the coastal group are copper alloy. The Colchester town centre brooch is one of the very few Iron Age objects of that date from that area, which seems to have seen little activity until the founding of the Roman fortress in *c.* A.D. 44. The retrieval of boss-on-bow brooches from sites close to the estuaries of the Colne, Blackwater and Deben points to ports of entry for the brooches, and both Camulodunum and Elms Farm received other brooch imports in the 1st century A.D. However, there is also a possibility that some of the boss-on-bow brooches, particularly those made of copper alloy or iron, may be local copies.

The Stanway and Colchester town centre brooches fall firmly into the main group of *Knotenfibeln*. The form has generally been dated to the second half of the 1st century B.C. (Stead 1976, 412; Feugère 1985, 238), but recent revisions of the overall dating of the La Tène period on the Continent have placed some examples as appearing as early as the last quarter of the 2nd century B.C. (Gebhard 1991, 94, groups 10–12), and a general start date of *c.* 100 B.C. has been proposed (Colin 1998, 39; Müller and Maute 2000, 51). At Westhampnett a date range of *c.* 90–50 B.C. was preferred, though not conclusively proven (Fitzpatrick 1997, 204), and it has been suggested that the closing date should be set at *c.* 25–20 B.C. (Fitzpatrick and Megaw 1987, 437; Colin 1998, 39). However, an iron example occurs in a Phase 3 grave at the King Harry Lane cemetery (Stead and Rigby 1989, fig. 50, 1), dated to *c.* A.D. 40–60 in the site report, but to *c.* A.D. 35–50/5 by Mackreth (1994, 288). The King Harry Lane brooch may be an heirloom, but it has an elaborately fretted catchplate, high button, inferior chord, and large expanded head, all of which could be taken as indicators of a date late in the series. It is closely similar to an iron brooch from a cremation at Hitchin (Stead 1976, fig. 3, 4).

There is no reason to suppose that the Stanway brooch was particularly old when buried, and the crispness of its moulding suggests it is not a late derivative. It compares well with the silver brooches from Great Chesterford in form and execution (Fox 1958, pl. 406; Krämer 1971, Taf. 24) and is very likely an imported piece contemporary with the main run of the type, *i.e.* dated broadly to *c.* 100–25 B.C. Mackreth (1995, 964) suggests that examples with the button set high up on the bow, as here, are later than those where it is close to the middle, and the inferior chord also places it later than those with superior chord (though the forms overlapped). The Great Chesterford and Westhampnett brooches all have a superior chord. These stylistic considerations therefore permit a date late in the range to be postulated for this brooch, probably *c.* 60–25/20 B.C., although the occurrence of similar characteristics on the King Harry Lane iron brooch may imply that a later date is not wholly improbable.

LANGTON DOWN AND NERTOMARUS BROOCHES

CF47.15 FIG. 109. SF79i. C982
BF64.19 FIG. 83. SF340. B1032
BF64.20 FIG. 83. SF382. B–

The Langton Down brooch from the Doctor's burial is of a standard form with a rounded head and a spring-cover that is plain apart from a rectangular frame defined by slight grooves (FIG.

109, CF47.15). Although the end is missing, at 37 mm long it probably falls into Camulodunum Type XIIB, which is found in Period 1 and later contexts at Sheepen (Hawkes and Hull 1947, 317–19), placing it broadly in the first half of the 1st century A.D. In Gaul it is Feugère's Type 14b1b, dated at the widest from Augustus to Nero (1985, 262–7).

No Langton Down brooches have been recovered from the area of the Roman fortress at Colchester, nor from the early colony. They are, however, well represented at Sheepen, and also occur in the Lexden cemetery (Hawkes and Hull 1947, 317–19; Bayley and Butcher 1985, nos 13–16; Hull 1942, 59–61). A brooch from the Botanic Gardens (now Castle Road and Roman Road) is from within the walled area of the town but some distance outside that of the fortress, its annexe, and the pre-Boudican colony (Wire, *Diary* 22/5/1852; *CAR* 6, fig. 2.11). At Hod Hill they only occur in pre-conquest contexts (Brailsford 1962, 8, fig. 7, C29), and they are also absent from London, which does not seem to date to much before *c.* A.D. 50. In Britain, therefore, their ownership appears to be restricted to the pre-conquest indigenous peoples, with a strong indication that their importation ceased altogether in A.D. 43, those found in post-conquest contexts being the pieces in use at that date, and most being deposited by *c.* A.D. 50.

At least one of the two brooches in the Warrior's burial is stamped by the maker Nertomarus, after whom the type is named (FIG. 83, BF64.19). It is characterised by a bow of complex section, and a pattern of trilobate and frond-like motifs on the spring-cover. The second brooch is much decayed but is the same form and may also have been a product of the same maker (FIG. 83, BF64.20). There are five brooches with Nertomarus stamps from the Continent, and eight other maker's names are known, most of Celtic origin (Behrens 1950, 3; Feugère 1985, 265). Examples of this form found on the Continent are concentrated in eastern central France and the west of Switzerland, and it may be a product of the Treveri (Behrens 1950, 5; Feugère 1985, 265). They date broadly to the first half of the 1st century A.D., with the stratified examples from Augst mainly concentrated in Claudian contexts (Riha 1979, Type 4.3.1; Riha 1994, 86; Feugère 1985, Type 14b2).

The number of Nertomarus brooches from Britain from dated contexts is very limited. Those from Sheepen and Baldock are unstratified (Hawkes and Hull 1947, pl. 95, 107; Stead and Rigby 1986, fig. 45, 86; 1989, 95, J1), and an example from Elms Farm, Heybridge, is also unstratified (Crummy forthcoming b). There is one from a late Claudian context at Bagendon (Hull 1961, fig. 32, 5), and one from Fishbourne is dated as pre-Flavian (Hull 1971, fig. 38, 28). One example from King Harry Lane comes from a Phase 3 grave (Stead and Rigby 1989, J2), dated *c.* A.D. 40–60, or *c.* 35–50/55 by Mackreth's suggested revisions (1994, 288). The only other stamped example from Britain, and the only one in a primary context with vertical stratigraphy to confirm its date of deposition, came from the gully of a Late Iron Age round-house at Piddington, Northamptonshire. The feature probably pre-dates a Roman military phase of occupation that began *c.* A.D. 44 (Mackreth 1989a, 24, fig. 15, 7; R. Friendship-Taylor, pers. comm.). Though the dating evidence thus offered is limited, the brooches from Piddington and King Harry Lane suggest that Britain may not have been receiving Nertomarus brooches until just before the invasion. This coincides with its Claudian *floruit* at Augst. A range of *c.* A.D. 40 to 50/55 is therefore suggested for the Stanway pair.

REARHOOK BROOCH

CF47.17 FIG. 109. SF40. C942

The Rearhook brooch from the Doctor's burial is a well-made and early example of this British form (FIG. 109, CF47.17). The method of attaching the spring to the main body of the brooch by a rearward-facing hook seems to have been an Icenian innovation, supported by the large number of these brooches from Norfolk (*e.g.* Brown 1986, nos 60–87; Mackreth 1992, 122–3), although they are also widespread across southern Britain. The mechanism, which is essentially weak, may have been simply strengthened by a blob of solder at the back of the left wing, where the corrosion products are slightly thicker. This method of attaching the spring to the wing and so reinforcing the rearward-facing hook has been found on a brooch from Thetford (*ibid.*, 122, fig. 112, 12).

The brooch is particularly distinctive for the zigzag decoration on the edge of the catchplate, and for three annulets incised on each side of the head. The former places it among a small number of similarly decorated brooches, generally of high quality (pp. 215–16). The annulets are unparalleled and, as they were added freehand to the brooch after casting, may be imbued with some symbolic meaning.

The catchplate suggests that this brooch belongs early in the series, *i.e.* in the A.D. 40s. It has two large perforations, the upper triangular, the lower a thick L-shape, similar to that found on catchplates with elaborately fretted or stepped cut-outs, *e.g.* those of Colchester brooches (Hawkes and Hull 1947, pl. 89, 7, pl. 90, 14).

HOD HILL AND HOD HILL VARIANT BROOCHES

BF67.3 FIG. 97. SF329. B1071
CF72.6 FIG. 129. SF6. C408

Hod Hill brooches arrived in Britain in large numbers with the Roman army in A.D. 43, and appear to have died out by *c.* A.D. 60/5. They seem to have proved popular with the native population and two Hod Hills were found in Phase 3 graves at King Harry Lane (Stead and Rigby 1989, 96). The presence of individual examples is therefore not necessarily an indicator of a Roman military presence, although in quantity, and when set against the numbers of other forms, it may be. For example, at Elms Farm, Heybridge, Essex, Hod Hills formed 14 per cent of the total assemblage of post-conquest pre-Flavian types, even though no specifically military activity was detected on the site. This compares to 30 per cent at Puckeridge–Braughing, where the high number of Hod Hill brooches was used as possible evidence for a military presence (Crummy forthcoming b; Olivier 1988b, 52). Equally, they are not necessarily an indicator of male gender, as CF72 is almost certainly the burial place of a female.

The Hod Hill variant from the Inkwell burial is of unusual form, closely similar to that of sprung strongly profiled brooches (FIG. 97, BF67.3). The Hod Hill from the Brooches burial is also of rare style, with lugs at the base of a triangular bow with strong central rib (FIG. 129, CF72.6). A practically identical brooch was found at Baldock, Hertfordshire, in an unstratified context (Stead and Rigby 1986, fig. 47, 116). Both brooches are probably Claudian (Feugère 1985, 331, 335, Type 23d1).

Both these brooches are therefore quite distinctive and unusual forms, rather than part of the general run of Hod Hills. They can almost certainly be viewed as trade goods imported some time after the conquest, rather than militaria.

KEYHOLE ROSETTE BROOCH

CF72.5 FIG. 129. SF7. C410

This variant of the Keyhole Rosette brooch is small, with two lines of knurling flanked by slight ridges down the foot, and a catchplate pierced by a single round hole (FIG. 129, CF72.5). A repoussé-decorated plate was fixed to the plain circular bow by a cup-shaped copper-alloy rivet, in which was a pellet of opaque red glass. Solder may also have been used as reinforcement where the plate and disc-bow met at the circumference.

There are a number of variants of Keyhole Rosette brooches, and, in attempting to establish a close date range for this brooch, only brooches of exactly the same form have been used. Where the plate and/or the stud are missing, the size, the foot and catchplate, and the plain circular disc-bow are generally sufficient identification. The form occurs at Augst (Riha 1979, Type 4.7.2; Riha 1994, 94).

In Britain the numbers of these brooches are small and the distribution is quite wide, but there are concentrations at Camulodunum (six with this example), and Bagendon (three). There is one definite example at King Harry Lane, and possibly two more, but the latter are unillustrated and cannot therefore be assigned with certainty to this variety.

The King Harry Lane brooch comes from a Phase 2 (*c.* A.D. 30–50/5) grave, and so may have been imported before the conquest (Stead and Rigby 1989, fig. 49, G1). If Mackreth's proposed revision of the King Harry Lane phasing is accepted, then Phase 2 dates *c.* A.D. 20–40, which would make a pre-conquest date for the type certain (Mackreth 1994, 287–8). There is one from Bancroft, Buckinghamshire, in a grave with both pre- and post-conquest pottery, and another from a pit at Dragonby, Lincolnshire, also with pre- and post-conquest pottery (Mackreth 1994, fig. 132, 17; Olivier 1996, fig. 11.6, 61). The Bancroft cremation also contained three other brooches, a Colchester, another Rosette of a more standard form, and a Langton Down (Mackreth 1994, fig. 131, 1, fig. 132, 16, fig. 133, 20), making the grave both characteristically native and unlikely to post-date A.D. 50, although not necessarily before A.D. 43.

Five brooches of this form have been found at Sheepen, all in post-conquest contexts. One is from a feature dated c. A.D. 44–48, two from a floor dated c. A.D. 49–60/1, and two from undated but post-conquest levels (Bayley and Butcher 1985, nos 22–3; Hawkes and Hull 1947, Type XI, 316, pl. 94, 80–81, and an unillustrated example). The picture is similar at Bagendon, with two from Claudian contexts and one from a context dated to late in the range c. A.D. 20/25–c. 43/45, but that also produced a Claudian plate brooch (Hull 1961, nos 29–31).

Given the association of a brooch of this variety in CF72 with five post-conquest imports, it seems possible that this particular form of Keyhole Rosette was also not imported until after A.D. 43, in which case Mackreth's suggested redating of King Harry Lane Phase 2 to c. A.D. 20–40 would be inappropriate for graves containing brooches of this style. The small size of the brooch is in itself an indication that it belongs late in the series, just as the thin metal of the circular bow indicates a mid 1st-century date, and the use of a spring-cover places it before c. A.D. 50 at the latest. Moreover, the low numbers of this type recovered from Britain compared to other Keyhole Rosette variants, such as those with repoussé-decorated plates ornamented with anthropomorphic and zoomorphic scenes (*e.g.* CAR **6**, fig. 6.1, 2), suggests that it was not long-lived. In size and quality, it is clearly linked to the hinged plate brooch Keyhole Rosettes (*e.g.* Hattatt 1987, fig. 72, 632), which have a wide spread within the province and probably replaced it.

The metal has a similar quality to that of the Claudian plate brooches in this grave, raising the possibility that this specific form of Keyhole Rosette is from the same workshop.

LOZENGE- AND STAR-SHAPED PLATE BROOCHES

CF72.9 FIG. 129. SF8/11. C414/421
CF72.10 FIG. 129. SF5. C406

These two brooches came from CF72 and may have been used as a pair. Both are post-conquest imports, and are of Claudian to early Neronian date.

The star-shaped brooch (FIG. 129, CF72.10) is the more common form of the two, occurring along the German Limes and in Pannonia (Simpson 2000, 41), and in the areas of early occupation in Britain. Some have amber glass, others blue. There are examples from Colchester (*CAR* **2**, fig. 14, 77), Richborough (Henderson 1949, pl. 25, 10), Baldock (Stead and Rigby 1986, fig. 49, 146), and Hacheston (Plouviez 2005, fig. 67, 164), and Hattatt illustrates an example found 'in Britain' (1987, 1011). The type is well represented at Augst, perhaps indicating the place of manufacture, where Riha dates it to c. A.D. 40–60 (1979, nos 1569–76; 1994, 157, Tabelle 198).

The lozenge-shaped brooch (FIG. 129, CF72.9) is rare, and from Britain the only other example is one from Canterbury, with a green glass boss (Hull forthcoming, no. 1463). A better preserved example from Augst has a top-plate decorated with a pyramid of raised dots in each angle (Riha 1994, 158, Taf. 41, 2807). A lozenge-shaped base-plate from Sheepen has one corner rolled over to form a hinge, and so is unlikely to be of this type (Hawkes and Hull 1947, pl. 98, 182).

LUGGED CIRCULAR PLATE BROOCHES

CF72.7 FIG. 129. SF9. C416
CF72.8 FIG. 129. SF10. C418

As with the star- and lozenge-shaped brooches above, these two plate brooches from the Brooches burial may have been used as a pair. They have the traces of a small riveted setting in the centre, and probably originally had six lugs around the outside, though only one now survives on one of the brooches. They belong to Feugère's Type 24a and Riha's Type 7.2.1, and have two bands of knurled decoration on the margin, rather than the more common central round knurled recess (Feugère 1985, 337; Riha 1994, 151–3). The type centres on the Claudian period, but Feugère offers a broader date range of *c.* A.D. 30/40–60/70 (Feugère 1985, 344; Riha 1994, 152, Tabelle 186).

No exact parallel to these two brooches is known from Britain, though there are a few examples with the central recess, chiefly from Colchester. There are two from Sheepen (Hawkes and Hull 1947, pl. 98, 179, and one other uncatalogued), and one from the early colony (*CAR* 2, fig. 14, 84), and one from Dragonby (Olivier 1996, fig. 11.12, 123). The illustrated Sheepen brooch came from a Period III context (*c.* 43/4–48), and that from the town centre is in post-Boudican make-up, probably residual. The Dragonby brooch and the unpublished Sheepen brooch are unstratified.

DISCUSSION

The *Knotenfibel* stands alone in this assemblage, both in its location outside any enclosure and in its early date. Inside the enclosures, no brooches were found in any of the chambers, but two were found in each richly furnished burial (BF64, CF47), one in BF67, and six in CF72. Of these brooches, only the Rearhook brooch from CF47 is British-made, the others are all continental imports. This is reflected in the alloys used to make them. The Nertomarus brooches and the plate brooches are all brass, one Hod Hill is brass or gunmetal, the other leaded gunmetal, while the Rearhook is of leaded bronze (p. 337). The Rearhook has decoration on the catchplate that defines it as of particularly high quality, and it has annular marks on the sides of the head, applied after casting, which may relate to the identity of its owner.

The imported brooches fall into two principal groups; those of types imported before the invasion of A.D. 43, and those of types introduced at or soon after that date. In the former group belong the Langton Down brooch from the Doctor's burial CF47 and the Nertomarus brooches from the Warrior's burial BF64, and in the latter group the Hod Hill from the Inkwell burial BF67 and the plate brooches from the Brooches burial CF72. It is uncertain into which group the Keyhole Rosette from CF72 should fall, but its direct association with five post-conquest brooches suggests it is of similar date. There is therefore a difference in brooch selection between the richly furnished graves and the other two less well-furnished graves. Given the contrast in the quantity and quality of the other grave goods from the Warrior's and Doctor's burials compared to those from the Inkwell and Brooches burials, it is perhaps not surprising that the latter pair might have brooches that are different in some way from those in the former. That the difference lies in their being post-conquest appears to suggest, at face value, that they are later. However, only a few years, if any, need separate the date of manufacture of the brooches in the two groups, and all could have been deposited round about the same time. Even if the importation of Langton Downs and all other spring-cover brooches ceased instantly at the conquest, those in use would have continued to be worn. Neither the Langton Down from CF47 nor the Nertomarus brooches from BF64 need therefore have been more than ten years old when buried and they might have been much less, *i.e.* they may not be much older than the post-conquest imports.

Rather than commercial availability, more complex factors associated with identity may well have been at play in the selection of brooches for deposition. The Warrior and Doctor may have been older than the people buried in the Inkwell and Brooches grave, and therefore had brooches acquired at an earlier date. Alternatively, the spring-cover brooches (the older imported technology) and the British Rearhook brooch (the indigenous, but probably not immediately local, technology) may have been more highly valued than the hinged bow and plate brooches (the new imported technology) of the post-conquest period.

The only brooch from Stanway that can be said to be a common type in this area is the Langton Down, and it has already been noted above (p. 316) that none have been found inside the fortress or early colony, which alone provides an important distinction between the Stanway brooch assemblage and that from the two Roman establishments. As the other Stanway brooch types are in general rare, or at best comparatively rare on any site, then any differences between the the two assemblages can better be defined by approaching the situation from the opposite side. Here the distinction is clear. The imported Claudio–Neronian brooch types dominating the assemblages from the fortress and early town are Hod Hills with lugged bows (as *CAR* **2**, Types 61–3), Aucissas and Nauheim Derivatives, and these brooches are all absent from Stanway (Hawkes and Hull 1947, Types VII, XVII–XVIII; Bayley and Butcher 1985).

The Sheepen brooch assemblage does provide parallels for some of the uncommon brooches found at Stanway, but it also contains large numbers of brooches of the same types as those found in the fortress/*colonia* and it was obviously strongly influenced by its proximity to the implanted Roman establishments. In contrast, the overall impression given by the Stanway assemblage is that it contains brooches of distinctive and even idiosyncratic character, and that it is unaffected by the types used in large numbers in the fortress and early town.

Another important distinction between Sheepen and Stanway, and between the early town and Stanway, is the absence of Colchester B derivative brooches from the burials at the latter (Hawkes and Hull 1947, Type IV, 36–41; *CAR* **2**, Type 92). This type probably began to be produced *c.* A.D. 50, as examples are present in the *colonia* but not the fortress. It is a two-piece form developed from the indigenous one-piece Colchester type and is common throughout the region. As these brooches varied in size and elaboration their absence could well be attributed not to a lack of style or distinction but to date, and could be taken to imply that the enclosures at Stanway had ceased to be used for burials by *c.* A.D. 50/5.

THE METAL VESSELS

By Nina Crummy

Complete copper-alloy vessels were found in the Warrior's burial BF64 and the Doctor's burial CF47, and a fragment of one came from Chamber BF6. A jug and handled basin (FIG. 87, BF64.25–26) were found in the Warrior's burial and a third vessel in this grave may be represented by fragment FIG. 88, BF64.27, a saucepan and a spouted strainer bowl came from the Doctor's burial (FIGS 112–13, CF47.21–22), and the spout from a spouted bowl (FIG. 55, BF6.25), which may perhaps also have been fitted with a strainer-plate, from BF6. The spout in BF6 is best seen in the light of the bowl from CF47 and is consequently discussed last in this section.

The current trend in theoretical archaeology is to make no assumptions about gender on the basis of grave goods, and to question any such assumptions made in the field. Were such a trend to be followed here, where the analysis of the human bone provides no evidence for sex, we would reach an unproductive stasis in interpretation. Instead, I propose here that the metal vessels from Stanway add to the evidence for determining the gender of the people with whom they were buried. The weapons in the Warrior's burial point to the grave being that of a male, and artefact deposition patterns support this view (Sealey forthcoming a). The Welwyn-type male graves of this region usually contain wine amphoras and associated serving and drinking vessels to allow feasting to continue beyond the grave (Stead 1967; Cunliffe 1991, 510), and, as it can be no coincidence that the three graves at Stanway with metal vessels also contained amphoras (pp. 300–2), it seems that the possession of metal vessels was chiefly, if not solely, the preserve of high-ranking males among this group of people in Late Iron Age and early Roman Camulodunum. (Metal vessels were also buried in the closely contemporary high-status female graves at Birdlip, Gloucestershire, and Portesham, Dorset (Bellows 1881; Fitzpatrick 1996), but this does not detract from their interpretation as male equipment at Stanway, as different practices no doubt existed between the tribes.)

That metal vessels were confined to male graves at Stanway was no doubt a factor of their use in the Roman and La Tène traditions of formal dining and feasting. The jug and handled basin in the Warrior's burial made up a set used in the formal hand-washing ceremony that preceded dining, and the saucepan in the Doctor's burial would have been used for the preparation of wine-based warm drinks to accompany formal meals. The two spouted bowls would also have been used in the preparation of similar concoctions, but, as they belong to La Tène vessel-types, the drinks need not have been wine-based.

VESSELS FROM THE WARRIOR'S BURIAL

The imported vessels found at Stanway represent not only the trade with the Continent that made them available for acquisition, if it was trade and not gift-exchange or travel abroad that led to their arrival here, but also the wider influence on manners and drinking customs exerted on south-east Britain by contact with the Gallo-Roman world, and the spread of Roman decorative art. In much the same way as the obverse and reverse images of coins conveyed propaganda for the issuer (*e.g.* Creighton 2000), these vessels introduce the idea that decoration can convey messages about both the function of the vessel and the character of the owner.

The jug in BF64 has a lion motif on the handle and the basin has a ram's head handle (FIG. 87, BF64.25–26). The iconography of the lion, a beast which can have been seen by few Britons, may have been deliberately chosen by, or given to, the man buried in BF64 both as a symbol of strength and as an exotic image. Similarly, although the ram's head handled basin is a long-lived type that occurs in considerable numbers on the Continent and is quite well represented even in Britain, in the context of this grave the ram may be seen not just as a sacrificial animal but also as a symbol of male sexual potency.

Both vessels are of composite manufacture and the choice of alloys was appropriate to the manufacturing techniques used on each section. The upper and lower parts of the body of the jug were made separately, both from a bronze containing a small quantity of lead. The pieces were then brazed together and the join disguised by a pair of grooves. The handle was cast in a leaded bronze and soldered to the body, probably with a lead-tin solder. The basin's body and handle were cast separately in a leaded bronze and then soldered together with a lead-tin solder (p. 335). The composite nature of these vessels bears upon the interpretation of the spouted bowls from BF6 and CF47 (*see* below).

Both basin and jug have parallels spread widely across the Empire, although chiefly concentrated in Italy and particularly well represented at Pompeii, where the unique circumstances of survival hint at the huge numbers that must have been manufactured for so many to have been recovered from just one town (Nuber 1972, 192, 196–7; Tassinari 1993, vol. 1, 40–42, 58–60). Both the Stanway vessels are likely to be early examples of their types and of Italian manufacture, and they are therefore yet another case of imported items on the site that pre-date the time of their burial by some years.

For Britain Nuber listed five jugs of Type E with lion handle plus lion's paw on the escutcheon from graves or hoards, from Santon, Thornborough Barrow, Shefford, Bartlow Hill 3, and Bartlow Hill 5, and five complete basins of Type E, one each from Shefford, Biggleswade and Bartlow Hill 4, and two from Welshpool (Nuber 1972, 210–11; Moore 1973, 158–9). Several ram's head handles have also been found in Britain disassociated from the body of their basin, and often in contexts much later than the period of manufacture (*e.g.* Brailsford 1962, pl. 10, A132; Waugh and Goodburn 1972, fig. 44, 148, fig. 45, 149; Moore 1973, 158–9; Cool and Philo 1998, fig. 36, 476). More have been found since Nuber was working, and the numbers of ram's head handles from Britain is now close to 40 (D. Webb, pers. comm.).

Slight variations are usual between individually cast/wrought vessels of these forms, but the Santon and Thornborough Barrow jugs are certainly close parallels to BF64.25, differing only in a few minor details (Eggers 1966, Abb. 37, b, Abb. 38, a). Similarly, the profile of the basins found in Britain can vary considerably and need not precisely parallel that of BF64.26, which is, in any case, difficult to establish precisely because of its damaged state on recovery and uneven restoration.

Textile fragments found on the jug probably came from a garment deposited in the grave (p. 347), but there is some possibility that they may derive from a cloth used for drying the hands after washing. The Bartlow Hills burials provided excellent conditions for the preservation of organic materials, and the jug in Bartlow Hill 7 had been placed in the grave standing on a basin with a handle of unusual form (Gage 1840, 3, pl. 2), with both vessels covered, either wrapped or draped, in cloth. Gage notes that a handled basin from a grave at Chatham Downs, Kent, was also found with traces of textile upon it, while flax fibres were found on one of the Welshpool basins (Boon 1961, 24). Near to the Bartlow Hill 7 service lay what were identified at the time as pieces of sponge, later exhibited to the Society of Antiquaries of London when Gage read his paper before them in 1838 (Gage 1840, 5). This provides corroboration of the ritual function identified by Nuber for these services, in which both host and guests washed their hands in clean falling water before a meal, a usage which can be dated back to at least the Homeric age:

> *A maid came with a precious golden ewer and poured water for them above its silver basin. She drew to their side a gleaming table and on it the matronly housekeeper arranged her store of bread and many prepared dishes, making an eager grace of all the hospitality.* (Homer, *Odyssey*, trans. T.E. Lawrence, 1.136–8)

Placed in this context, the textiles associated with the Stanway jug might well be considered as drying cloths. However, although they were close to each other within the burial, the jug and handled basin in BF64 were not found in direct association. The jug was placed on a *terra nigra* dish (BF64.5), and the basin stood on an oak board, possibly a tray or platter (BF64.37; TABLE 63, B1019/B1033). This might imply that although this set of vessels was a prized possession conferring status upon its owner, it was not necessarily used in the manner conventional to Roman formal dining.

VESSELS FROM THE DOCTOR'S BURIAL

While the decorative elements of the jug and handled basin in BF64 are suggestive of the character of their owner, the handle of the saucepan in CF47 (FIG. 112, CF47.21) makes a direct statement about the vessel's function. It is decorated with a *thyrsus*, the ivy-entwined, pine-cone-tipped wand carried by Bacchus, the god of wine, and saucepans of this type were used to prepare hot wine concoctions served at formal meals and feasts. The decoration is typical of pans made in Gaul (Eggers 1951, Type 137; den Boesterd 1956, 6–7, no. 13.11; Bennett and Young 1981, 42; Tassinari 1993, Type G2100, vol. 1, 52, 55, vol. 2, 98–108).

The end of the handle is in the shape of a disc with a lunate suspension hole and typological studies of saucepan handles place this form later in the series than those with swan's-head and fan-shaped handles, and earlier than those with a circular hole in the handle (Bosanquet 1936, 144; den Boesterd 1956, xxx; Bennett and Young 1981, 41–2). British finds of complete pans with lunate holes (but with less elaborate decoration) come from the Stanfordbury A burial, Bedfordshire, the bronzesmith's hoard at Glyndyfrdwy, Clwyd, and the Oulton hoard, Suffolk (Eggers 1966, Abb. 7, 29a, Abb. 20, 19b, Abb. 26, 45a; Stead 1967, 55). There is also a fragment of a similar handle from Hod Hill, Dorset (Eggers 1966, Abb. 8, 9c; Brailsford 1962, fig. 5, A134). All four differ from the Stanway bowl in having a very plain *thyrsus* or central linear motif, and three of them have a spray of radiating lines terminating in ring-and-dot 'eyes' within the circular terminal. On the Glyndyfrdwy handle the place of the spray is taken by a stamp. The plain *thyrsus* and spray design is attributed to southern Italy and is well represented in eruption levels at Pompeii, although a Flavian date for their manufacture need not necessarily be assumed as many of those vessels are likely to have been in use for some decades before the disaster (Radnóti 1938, 49; Tassinari 1975, 26; 1993, vol. 2, 98–9, 101, 103). Indeed, the Stanfordbury A burial probably dates to around the period of the conquest and also contained a pair of fire dogs and samian vessels (Stead 1967, 47, 55) and there is therefore a strong likelihood that such pans could have reached Britain in the period immediately before the conquest. The base of the Stanway pan is much scoured from cleaning and therefore saw considerable use before it was buried, which again argues for a pre-conquest date for its arrival in Britain. As there is no reason to suppose that the typological features of the handles occur later on Gaulish pans than on those of Italian manufacture, a date before A.D. 50 for the pan would also accord well with both the brooches in the burial (pp. 315–17). A closely similar vessel from Nijmegen, Holland, came from a cemetery area broadly dated to A.D. 1–70 (den Boesterd 1956, 6–7, no. 13.11).

There is, however, some possibility that CF47.21 may be later, as to a large extent the date of the Stanway vessel also depends upon the date of introduction of pans with round-holed handles, which itself depends upon the date when the Capuan bronzesmith Publius Cipius Polybius was working. Some writers argue for a Flavian date (Bosanquet 1936, 44; Radnóti 1938, 52), others perhaps for late Neronian–Flavian (Bennett and Young 1981, 43), others for very late Claudian/Neronian–Flavian (Eggers 1966, 73), and others for Claudian–Neronian (den Boesterd 1956, 8; McPeake and Moore 1978, 333). The one certainty from these various suggestions is that pans with a lunate hole in the handle pre-date the Flavian period, which is the latest possible period when round-holed handles were introduced.

There are two other factors that make dating CF47.21 difficult. First, pans themselves survived in use, or at least above ground, for a long time; the Glyndyfrdwy smith's hoard alone contains pans with three handle types: swan's head, fan-shaped, and round with lunate hole. Second, the various forms were produced over a long period; swan's head handles, for example, may have been in production from the late Augustan to Claudian periods (Bennett and Young 1981, 42). Therefore the broadest date range that can be be offered for the Stanway pan is probably later Tiberian to Neronian, but the most likely is A.D. 30–50.

The other vessel in CF47 is a spouted strainer bowl with carinated body (FIG. 113, CF47.22). Like the jug and handled basin in BF64, it is a composite object, made up of the body, a handle fixed opposite a spout, an internal vertical strainer-plate behind the spout which served to remove herbs, spices, or other solid matter from a liquid, a spill-plate fixed horizontally to the rim behind the spout and above the strainer-plate to prevent liquid splashing out when the vessel was tilted for pouring, and three cast peltate feet.

The vessel body was spun from bronze; the sides are bellied below the carination, and angled flat above it. Holes were cut into the finished body where the spout and handle were to be attached. The handle, spout and feet were cast from leaded bronze and the spill-plate and strainer-plate were wrought from bronze; all were soldered into position on the body to produce the finished article (FIG. 113; pp. 335–6). In terms of metalworking technique, this combination of using wrought metal for the vessel body, strainer- and spill-plates, but casting the stouter elements and soldering them on, parallels the method of manufacture of the jug BF64.25 and allows the most appropriate alloy to be used for each element.

The cast pieces are in good condition, but the sheet-metal elements, the bowl and the two plates, are not. The bowl and spill-plate have shattered, and the collapse of the bowl caused the strainer-plate to crumple (FIG. 125). Some areas of the central part of the spill-plate, which is very thin, have either disintegrated completely while buried or were missing when the bowl was deposited.

The latter may be possible as the vessel appears to have seen considerable use before being deposited. One of the original handle attachments has been replaced, one foot is slightly damaged, and part of the edge of the strainer-plate appears to have come loose and been soldered back into position. The wear and repairs to the vessel suggest that it was of some antiquity when buried, but instead it may simply have been quite delicate because of its manufacture from such thin metal.

The lower edge of the mouth of the spout is much thinner than the top, but, as it seems unlikely that the frequent pouring of liquid would wear down metal, this feature may be integral to the casting; if it is the result of use-wear, then hard scouring is likely to be the cause. The excavations at Sheepen in the 1930s recovered a spout of similar form, although different size, from a period VI pit (A6), c. A.D. 61–65, and fragments from a failed casting of another were found in a context belonging to periods III–IV, c. A.D. 43/4–61. (The objects were identified in the site report as helmet crest holders (Hawkes and Hull 1947, 336, pl. 102, 1).) A strainer bowl from Brandon, Suffolk, also has a similar spout (mentioned in Sealey 1999, 121, but otherwise unpublished), and it is possible to see a stylistic link, although distant, between the angular form of the Stanway spout's aperture and the gaping jaws of a fish-head spout on a strainer-bowl from Felmersham, Bedfordshire (Watson 1949, pl. 5, a–b). The Sheepen spouts therefore place the CF47 strainer bowl in the immediately pre-conquest or immediately post-conquest periods and, together with that from Brandon, point to local manufacture.

There are also two identical handles to that on CF47.22, one in eastern Britain and one in north-western France. The British find is from Baldock, but is not attached to a vessel and lacks even its means of attachment. It was found in a context dated A.D. 180–200 and is certainly residual (Stead and Rigby 1986, fig. 58, 368). The other handle is fitted to a carinated strainer bowl, very similar to that from Stanway, found at Blain, Loire-Atlantique, at the bottom of a well which was backfilled in the mid 1st century A.D. (S. Corson, pers. comm.). The Blain handle is attached by two simple clips similar to that on one side of the Stanway handle. The vessel is the only spouted and carinated strainer-bowl known from France, but its location, very close to the Loire estuary, parallels the distribution pattern of cosmetic pestle-and-mortar sets, objects peculiar to Britain of which the only example to come from France was found at Thérouanne, close to the coast in Pas de Calais (Jackson 1985; 1993a; Jackson and Thuillier 1999). In both cases they can be presumed to have been taken to Gaul by British travellers or migrants. The spout of the Blain bowl does not fit the body well, and has been attached to it by a thick application of lead-tin solder. It is not a direct parallel to that from Stanway but could be seen as of the same general type, *i.e.* angular, not zoomorphic, and very protuberant.

A third handle, from a strainer bowl found at Crownthorpe, Norfolk, is almost identical to that on CF47.22 but has a bar across the top (Norwich Castle Museum, unpublished). A fragment of sheet metal has been wrapped around this bar and passed through the rim to attach the handle to the bowl. Such poor craftsmanship conflicts with the quality of the bowl itself and must be a repair. The spout of the Crownthorpe bowl is different to that from Stanway, but is also not zoomorphic. The bowl is considered to be part of a vessel hoard.

A more elaborately shaped handle from Silchester should also be added to this group. It is generally like those from Stanway, Baldock and Blain, and is more or less contemporary with them, coming from a context phased to the period *c.* A.D. 50–80/5. It differs, however, in several details: the upper bars slope inwards, it has mouldings in the centre of the middle section, and down-curving projections on each side. The latter, and every angle of the side elements, are knobbed (Boon 2000, fig. 157, 38, fig. 158). Like that from Baldock, this handle is a loose find and lacks its means of attachment.

The spill-plates on strainer bowls all differ in details of form and decoration, although again the Crownthorpe plate is closest to that from Stanway. An interesting connection can also be drawn to two plates from one of the Birdlip burials, which mirror the way in which on the CF47.22 plate there is no attempt to interrelate the mouldings along its straight edge and those along its curved edge at the point of junction (Green 1949, pl. 25). The similarities between these items, and the use of linear mouldings and bosses to form the decoration (*see* AF48), provide yet more evidence to set the manufacture of the bowl firmly in a British La Tène tradition.

Similarly, no two strainer-plate designs are exactly the same, but again the Crownthorpe plate can be presumed to have been made by the same hand. It is extremely close to that from Stanway in design, with only some difference on the central panel.

The parallels for the various elements given above and the concentration of these carinated strainer bowls in eastern Britain argue strongly for an origin for CF47.22 in eastern Britain, and this can be narrowed down to the territory of the Catuvellauni and Trinovantes as they also occur in pottery, a rounded form CAM 322 and a carinated form CAM 323, most examples of which come from Hertfordshire and Essex. The ceramic forms occur especially frequently in and around Camulodunum, and they appear to be principally post-conquest in date (Hawkes and Hull 1947, fig. 50, 8; Niblett 1985, fig. 33, 2; Sealey 1999, 119–24). Within the last few years examples have also been found further to the west, notably one at the legionary fortress at Alchester, two in a metal vessel hoard at Kingston Deverill, Wiltshire, and one in a hoard of glass and metal vessels from Chettle, Dorset (E. Sauer, pers. comm.; Worrell 2006, 460–2). Like that from Blain, these western finds were no doubt intimately bound up with the events of the period from the conquest to the Boudican revolt, a supposition reinforced by their contexts.

In connection with a group of three, or possibly four, ceramic strainer bowls found in a pit at Ardleigh, near Colchester, Sealey gives as the precursor of the rounded CAM 322 form the rounded metal bowls from Welwyn Garden City and Felmersham, and another from Leg Piekarski, Poland, while the carinated form CAM 323 is clearly derived from the carinated metal bowls from Stanway, Brandon and Crownthorpe (*ibid.*, 121). He notes attempts by some specialists to demonstrate that the bowls themselves were of continental origin and were merely adapted for use in Britain by the addition of a spill-plate, strainer-plate, spout and handle. This idea is largely based upon the suggestion that the late 1st-century B.C. Welwyn Garden City bowl was a plain continental import adapted in Britain for use as a strainer (Stead 1967, 25; Reinert 1995, 50), making the elements added to the vessel body fully secondary in that they were intended to alter the functional use of the bowl. Based on the poor fit of the Blain spout, it too has been interpreted as a secondary addition (S. Corson, pers. comm.). Supporting evidence for secondary adaptation was seen in the occurrence of peltate feet on metal strainer bowls, as similar fittings can be found on continental vessels such as jugs, bowls, colanders and handled basins, *e.g.* Lethbridge 1953, pl VII; Tassinari 1975, pl. 28, 144–6; 1993, 128; Feugère 1981, fig. 14, 62, 68; Rérolle 1999, fig. 36; Sedlmayer 1999, Taf. 51; Le Cloirec 2001, fig. 24, 162–5.

Even if the early Welwyn vessel were itself adapted, there is little evidence to support the notion of secondary adaptation for the mid 1st-century A.D. vessels. There are no carinated bowls of exactly similar form either without or with a handle and spout among the large published collections of vessels from Pompeii, France, Britain, Holland, Pannonia, and Noricum (Tassinari 1993; 1975; Eggers 1951; 1966; den Boesterd 1956; Radnóti 1938; Sedlmayer 1999). There seems to be no reason to suppose that the metal form is anything other than Catuvellaunian/Trinovantian in origin, and the Sheepen spouts support manufacture of at least some examples in Camulodunum itself. The question of the feet can be dismissed, as the feet on the continental vessels are more extended and curvilinear, as well as generally smaller and more delicate, than those on the British bowls, which are stout and of compact form. In other words, the feet on the Stanway bowl may copy the continental practice of attaching feet to the underside of vessels, but they have a style of their own. Moreover, it has already been pointed out above that vessels are often composite items, with different sections made of different alloys and then brazed or soldered together. Just as there is no question but that the handle of the jug BF64.25 is an integral part of its design, the same is undoubtedly true of the various elements of the strainer bowls. The fittings on the Blain bowl were perceived as secondary because there is some discrepancy between the curvature of the spout and that of the bowl, and a large, perhaps excessive, amount of solder has been used to achieve a solid join, but the difference is quite minor and is not sufficient reason for such an interpretation. Similarly, the fact that a hole was cut in the body of each vessel to allow the spout to function does not mean that the spout is evidence of secondary usage. It is simply easiest to make the bowl without giving consideration to the hole, and then cut it later. Indeed, the method of attachment of the Crownthorpe handle, which certainly appears crude in contrast to the rest of the bowl, is all that suggests that it was a secondary, rather than standard, addition, but the repairs to the Stanway bowl point to the likelihood of the Crownthorpe handle also having been repaired, and neatly so, by utilising the same perforation through the rim as the original fitting, which was probably a clip like those on the Blain and Stanway handles.

The saucepan CF47.21 in the Doctor's grave can be firmly associated with the preparation of wine-based drinks, but the use of the spouted strainer bowl CF47.22 is less easily defined. From its position in the grave pit among the other household vessels, we might expect it to be classed among them, and to have been used to prepare drinks to accompany a formal meal or feast, while the strainer-plate points to the addition of solids to add flavour to the liquid (Petrovszky 1993, 135). The Welwyn Garden City strainer bowl supports this view as it was found with a silver cup, a copper-alloy serving dish, and an array of ceramic cups, plates, wine amphoras, beakers and flagons, and it is intriguing to see how the Welwyn bowl lay somewhat apart from the other vessels in the grave pit, propped on its side among the remains of a game board (Stead 1967, fig. 4). Its separation from the service reflects its unique use within the Welwyn assemblage for preparing, rather than serving or consuming, drinks, and it is similarly divorced from the liquid storage vessels, the flagons and amphoras.

Reinert suggests that the drink prepared in strainer bowls is unlikely to be wine-based (1995, 49), and the non-Roman origin of the vessels supports this, as does the presence in CF47 of the saucepan used for the preparation of hot wine concoctions, although it is fair to state that duplication of function is not impossible, only unlikely. Sealey has put forward the suggestion that strainer bowls were used for either Celtic beer or mead, or both, with herbal teas a possible third alternative (1999, 122–3). The majority of strainer bowls may have been used for one or all of these drinks at various times, but the absence of butt-beakers from the Doctor's grave militates against the use of CF47.22 for beer, although not of mead-based drinks or herbal teas, which would have been consumed in smaller quantities. It is possible that the vessel form developed not to allow a specific drink to be made, but rather to strain *any* flavoured drink or other infusion. It is therefore not inconceivable that wine-based drinks were heated in CF47.21, and then passed through CF47.22 to remove the solids used to flavour them. Whatever the use to which the Doctor's strainer bowl was put during most of its life, the analysis of a plug of solid matter recovered from CF47.22 shows that the final drink prepared in it seems to have been medicinal (pp. 397–8).

THE VESSEL SPOUT IN CHAMBER BF6

The cast spout BF6.25 (FIG. 55) is also from a bowl. Its style suggests a continental origin, and the long flanking volutes are reminiscent of those found on the nozzles of ceramic lamps of Loeschcke's Type 1 (1919, Taf 1, 1A–C). Spouts of generally similar form, but longer, open and with different detailing on the volutes, have been found at the Magdalensberg, Austria, at Prag-Bubeneč, Czech Republic, and from the Seine in France (Sedlmayer 1999, 94, Taf. 41, 1, Abb. 17; Reinert 1995, Abb. 4, 2, Abb. 5, 1). There is no equivalent on Italian bronze vessels. The spout from Prag-Bubeneč was attached to a hemispherical bowl which Reinert associates with the strainer-bowl from the Welwyn Garden City grave and with other spouted bowls, most of which lack spill- or strainer-plates. An association can also be seen with a zoomorphic spout from Grave B at Hellingen, Germany, the ears or horns of which take the place of the volutes (*ibid.*, Abb. 1–2). The Hellingen grave is dated to the mid 1st century A.D., and the spout was found in association with part of a handled bowl and a handled colander-like strainer. The Magdalensberg spout dates to the late A.D. 40s at the latest, as the settlement on the hill was abandoned when the new *municipium* of Virunum was built in the valley below it at that period.

This limited evidence suggests that the vessel to which BF6.25 belonged was a product of a workshop in southern Noricum or on the Danube in the Tiberian or early Claudian period. Used to prepare warm drinks or infusions, it may not have been fitted with a strainer-plate but instead paired with a colander to allow any solid flavourings to be removed before serving. Like so many other objects from the chambers at Stanway, the spout represents only a small part of the original whole, be that a strainer bowl or a bowl and colander set. Its parallels and likely source imply that it was used in a feasting tradition that had its roots outside the sphere of Roman influence.

CONCLUSIONS

Most of the metal vessels from the burials are imported, testifying to the very wide range of trade contacts enjoyed by Camulodunum in the late A.D. 30s and 40s. It is quite possible that all the imports are of immediately pre-conquest date, and none need post-date the late 40s. The strainer bowl in CF47 is the only local product but, most probably made at Sheepen in the A.D. 40s, it is closely contemporary with the imports.

ANALYSIS OF THE CURRENCY BARS, GRAVE GOODS AND PYRE DEBRIS
(TABLES 48–52)

By Sarah Paynter

METHODS

The two currency bars from the ditch of the Middle Iron Age enclosure and some of the copper-alloy and glass objects from the burials and other features were examined and analysed in order to characterise the materials and methods used in their construction. Metallographic examination of a sample taken from one of the currency bars enabled the iron alloy to be identified and energy dispersive spectroscopy (EDS) was used to analyse remnants of slag in the sample. A non-destructive technique, X-ray fluorescence spectrometry (XRF), was used to analyse the surface of the glass and copper-alloy objects. However, as this technique analyses only the surface of an artefact, when this is weathered or corroded the results must be interpreted with caution, as they may not be representative of the unaltered metal or glass beneath. Glass is susceptible to attack by water and the surface becomes depleted in certain oxides, particularly soda, and relatively enriched in others, particularly silica (Henderson and Warren 1981). Copper and its alloys are prone to corrosion, for example, zinc tends to be removed preferentially from brasses by 'dezincification', tin-rich corrosion crusts are often formed on high-tin bronzes, and copper ions from a corroding object can be transported and deposited elsewhere (Cronyn 1990). Also, corrosion products can incorporate elements such as chlorine or phosphorus, drawn from the surrounding environment (other elements such as carbon and hydrogen may also be present but are not detectable by XRF). Full details of the methods and standards used, and the results, are included in English Heritage Centre for Archaeology Report 72/2002 and have been deposited with the site archive.

CURRENCY BARS (TABLE 48)

The currency bars (CF6.1–2) were unusual both in terms of their easterly location in Britain and their good preservation. One (CF6.1) was complete, with a length of 542 mm including the socket and a maximum width of 52 mm. The weight of the bar (before cleaning) was 984 g. The second bar (CF6.2) was in three fragments, having broken twice at the socketed end. It was approximately 564 mm long and the maximum width was 62 mm. Although longer than the other bar, its weight was similar at 976 g. The breaks on CF6.2 allow the changing cross-section along the length to be viewed. Each bar started with a flat end, continuing into a socket formed by folding both sides of the bar up at right angles. As the socket continued, the right-angled edges of the fold become rounded so that the bar was C-shaped in cross section. The bar formed a slim, flat neck and then broadened to its maximum width before tapering at the other end. In shape the bars are similar to two recovered from Ely, categorised as plough-share bars due to their form. They had leaf-shaped blades, long U-shaped sockets and similar lengths and

TABLE 48: ANALYTICAL RESULTS FOR THE SLAG INCLUSIONS IN THE FRAGMENTED CURRENCY BAR CF6.2, AS DETERMINED BY EDS, NORMALISED WT%

Analyses	Na_2O	MgO	Al_2O_3	SiO_2	P_2O_5	SO_3	K_2O	CaO	TiO_2	MnO	FeO
	0.52	0.50	5.72	23.24	5.27	0.41	1.75	4.47	0.25	0.78	56.94
	0.62	0.89	8.25	29.95	2.34	0.18	2.26	4.19	0.30	0.95	49.90
	0.85	0.61	5.56	19.24	4.17	0.26	1.34	3.53	0.24	0.54	63.54
	0.63	0.89	8.00	30.15	3.52	0.25	2.21	4.51	0.26	1.02	48.46
	0.59	0.65	6.69	25.03	4.65	0.30	1.94	4.56	0.22	0.85	54.37
Average	0.64	0.71	6.85	25.52	3.99	0.28	1.90	4.25	0.26	0.83	54.64

widths to the Stanway bars (Crew 1994). However, the Stanway bars are heavier by 250 g and the broken Stanway bar has well-defined right angles to the sides of the socket at one point along its length.

The date, form, and use of the currency bars are discussed in detail on pages 33–6 by R. Hingley. Although the currency bars in one group or hoard often have similar weights, as do the two Stanway bars, bars of different types tend to have different weights. It is unlikely that the weight was regulated intentionally but rather that it was determined by the smelting and smithing practices of the producer. The dimensions and weights of the bars are therefore likely to be characteristic of the producer.

A small V-shaped section was taken from the broken bar, examined metallographically and found to be pure iron (also known as plain iron or ferrite). At the edge of the sample the microstructure was distorted compared to the rest of the section as a result of the bar having been 'upset'. Upsetting involved turning the bar onto its side and striking it to obtain a flat edge, correcting the rounded edges that tended to develop on the bar during smithing (C. Salter, pers. comm.). The process produced a slight lip at the edge of the bar, which, unusually, has been preserved on the Stanway examples and suggests that they were skilfully made. Elongated strings of slag were observed running across the width of the bar in the metallographic section showing that the metal had been worked considerably. Some of these slag inclusions were analysed using a scanning electron microscope with attached EDS analytical facility and the results are given in TABLE 48.

These results can be compared with analyses of the slag inclusions in bars from Danebury, Hampshire, Gretton, Northamptonshire, and Beckford, Worcestershire (Hedges and Salter 1979). The combination of raised phosphorus, sulphur and manganese in the Stanway bar distinguishes it from the previously analysed artefacts suggesting that the Stanway examples do not originate from the same source as any of these other bars. However, the uniqueness of the composition of slag inclusions in iron artefacts from different sources has yet to be established, since the dataset of published analyses available for comparison is still small. The compositional consistency of slag inclusions within bars of similar origin is also unknown. Further analysis of the inclusions in the Stanway bar, using the sample already taken but different techniques, might detect elements present in very small amounts and would characterise the bar more fully.

GLASS OBJECTS (TABLES 49–50)

Ancient glasses were produced by reacting silica, which has a high melting point, with compounds that acted as fluxes, enabling a glass to be formed and worked at accessible temperatures (about 1000° C). The alkali oxides, soda (Na_2O) and potash (K_2O), are effective fluxes and can be derived from plant ashes or mineral sources. The ratio of soda to potash, and the concentration of other compounds present, such as magnesia and lime, varies depending on whether a mineral or plant ash source of fluxes was used, and if the latter, the type and origins of the plant. Henderson (1988) and Hartmann et al. (1997) have identified glasses from c. 14th-century B.C. to 2nd-century A.D. contexts in Europe that were produced using plant ash fluxes. These glasses consequently contain varying amounts of potash, magnesia and lime in addition to soda. However, no plant ash glass was identified among the objects from Stanway. The great majority of glass from Iron Age and Roman Europe contains large amounts of soda (typically 15–20 wt%) and some lime (about 7 wt%) but little magnesia (0.5–1 wt%) or potash (about 0.5 wt%). This composition suggests that a relatively pure source of soda was used to make the glass, probably a soda-rich mineral such as the evaporitic deposit from Egypt known as natron (Freestone et al. 2000). This type of glass is known as soda-lime-silicate glass (Henderson 1988).

From about the 2nd or 1st century B.C., glass compositions are also characterised by small amounts of manganese oxide, to decolourise the glass, whereas earlier glass typically contained antimony oxide as a decolouriser (Hartmann et al. 1997; Sayre and Smith 1961; Henderson 1985). In addition, some yellow, or more rarely white, Iron Age European glass objects contain tin colourant compounds instead of the antimony colourant compounds used in glass produced within the Roman Empire (Biek and Bayley 1979).

Glass is susceptible to attack by water and the surface of archaeological material is often weathered. Some of the glass components are leached out, and the weathered surface becomes depleted in certain oxides, particularly soda, and relatively enriched in others, particularly silica. Henderson and Warren (1981) analysed a soda-lime-silicate Iron Age glass bead at different depths from the surface and found that soda was depleted, and potash was slightly enhanced, in the weathered surface layers.

Results

Recent research on glass in the Roman period has developed the model that glass was produced at a number of primary production centres and then transported to workshops where it was shaped into objects (Freestone et al. 2000). The glass used to produce the majority of Iron Age glass objects was probably produced within the Roman Empire, although glass workers outside the Empire also shaped glass objects and occasionally coloured the glass themselves. All of the glass from Stanway was found to be of the soda-lime-silicate type, typical of European Iron Age and Roman glass, containing colourants and decolourisers that were also typical.

In the glass objects from Stanway (TABLE 49) manganese oxide was used as a decolouriser and the white glass was opacified with calcium antimonate. Yellow glass from Stanway was opacified with lead antimonate; no examples of the use of lead stannate, a colourant used in regions outside the Roman Empire, were found (Henderson 1991). Traces of zinc and lead were occasionally detected and probably entered the glass as contaminants in the colourants. Dark blue glass was produced by the addition of very small amounts of the strong colourant cobalt oxide, although copper oxide (also a blue colourant) was frequently detected as well. Both the blue glass brooch settings from CF72 were lighter in colour than the game counters and also contained manganese (TABLE 50, CF72.9–10). Significant quantities of iron oxide were occasionally detected in the cobalt blue glasses, as is often the case, since the cobalt-rich minerals used as colourants also contained varying concentrations of iron, although in some instances iron oxide may also have been intentionally added. In other studies, Iron Age beads have been grouped according to the ratio of cobalt oxide to iron oxide in the glass (Henderson 1991) but none of the beads described in the literature contained such high quantities of iron oxide (in excess of 10 wt%) as detected in the surfaces of the eight dark blue counters from BF64 at Stanway (BF64.28). The two lighter blue counters in the same set proved to be of a different composition, containing much less iron oxide, and so are from a different 'batch' or maker and may be replacements (TABLE 49). The glass of the blue counters from CF47 (CF47.19b) was opacified with calcium antimonite and so differed in composition to both types of blue counter from BF64.

Of all the glass objects, the large blue and white bead from BF64 (BF64.22) had the most unusual composition. The blue glass was coloured predominantly by cobalt oxide and small amounts of manganese oxide were also detected. The white glass was opacified by calcium antimonate and decolourised by several per cent of manganese oxide, and also contained in excess of 20 wt% lead oxide. The presence of lead oxide is atypical of the majority of white glasses of this date, as demonstrated by the compositions of the other white glass objects from Stanway, including the white gaming counters and the white decoration on the stud heads, which do not contain lead. Generally white glass opacified with calcium antimonate has a soda-lime-silicate glass composition with only an increased concentration of antimony clearly distinguishing it from transparent glass.

However, the presence of lead oxide in calcium antimonate opacified white glasses is common among Roman cameo glass vessels and to a lesser extent among mosaic glass vessels and cameo glass plaques or discs. Nearly all of the Roman cameo vessels in the British Museum, including the Portland vase (possibly late 1st century B.C.) and the Auldjo jug, were found to have high concentrations of lead oxide in the white glass decoration. The white glass in some of the cameo plates and plaques, although less than half of the number analysed, also contained lead oxide (Bimson and Freestone 1983; Freestone 1990). Similar results have been obtained in studies of other collections (Mommsen et al. 1997; Mass et al. 1998). Cameo glass

TABLE 49: RESULTS SUMMARY FOR GLASS OBJECTS (see also TABLE 50 for glass brooch settings)

Enc.	Context	Feat.	Objects	Description	Results
3	B1015	BF64	BF64.28	10 blue counters (2 lighter in colour than the others)	darker blue counters contained in excess of 10 wt% iron oxide, responsible for the darker colour, about 0.11% cobalt oxide and some copper oxide; cobalt oxide was the dominant blue colourant; lighter blue counters contained much less iron oxide and a little less cobalt oxide
5	C597	CF42	CF42.14	1 dark blue translucent counter	contained a small amount of cobalt oxide (the dominant colourant), some copper oxide, and a high concentration (~4 wt%) of manganese oxide
5	C1001–13	CF47	CF47.19a	13 opaque white counters	opacified by calcium antimonate
5	C1014–26	CF47	CF47.19b	13 opaque blue counters	opacified by calcium antimonate; blue colour dominated by up to 0.1 wt% cobalt oxide, although some copper oxide also detected
3	B1022	BF64	BF64.22	large translucent blue bead with white flecks	blue glass coloured by cobalt oxide, and some manganese oxide also detected; white glass opacified by calcium antimonate, decolourised by manganese oxide, and also contained more than 20 wt% of lead oxide
4	B322	BF24	BF24.24, SF 147	pale green spacer bead	likely to be faience rather than glass; copper oxide coloured glaze; surface too weathered to determine type of flux used
4	B606	BF24	BF24.24, SF 251	dark transparent green long barrel bead	coloured by copper oxide; magnesia level slightly higher than typical; no lead detected
4	B383	BF24	BF24.24, SF 255	hexagonal transparent blue-green glass cylinder bead	manganese decolourised
5	C630	CF42	CF42.16a	translucent blue and opaque white glass stud head	blue glass contained high levels of manganese and iron, coloured predominantly by cobalt; copper and zinc also detected; magnesia content slightly higher than typical
5	C723	CF42	CF42.16b	opaque blue stud head with opaque white spiral (top) and twisted opaque yellow and colourless spiral (bottom)	blue glass contained calcium antimonate opacifier and cobalt oxide blue colourant, with some copper oxide; yellow glass coloured by lead antimonate; white glass opacified by calcium antimonate; colourless glass decolourised by manganese oxide
5	C751	CF42	CF42.16c	translucent blue glass stud head with twisted opaque white and colourless cord and opaque yellow spiral at top	blue glass coloured by cobalt oxide with somecopper and traces of zinc and lead detected; yellow glass coloured by lead antimonate; white glass opacified by calcium antimonate;colourless glass was decolourised by manganese oxide
5	C403	CF72	CF72.11	large translucent blue bead with twisted opaque yellow and transparent brown cord	blue glass coloured by cobalt oxide but also contained some copper; yellow glass coloured by lead antimonate; brownish glass coloured by manganese oxide

was made during two periods, the blue and white variety in the early empire from about 25 B.C. to A.D. 50–60 (ribbon mosaic glass is also contemporary), and a variety with a colourless background sometime between the mid 3rd and 4th centuries (Henderson 1996; Whitehouse 1991; 1997). The presence of lead oxide in the white glass reduced its melting point and hardness and so facilitated the cutting of the design.

The Stanway bead was probably formed by dabbing small blobs of heated white glass onto the blue glass bead and then marvering them into its surface; a thin strand of white glass can be seen connecting two of the white blobs. The distortion of the white decoration indicates that the glass was stretched after the white decoration had been applied, and enlarging the diameter of the bead would have produced the effect seen. The white glass blobs contain small bubbles, particularly around the edges. Marvering blobs, spirals or cords of different coloured glass into the surface of a glass object was a common method of glass decoration and was successful with typical soda-lime-silicate glasses: the large, annular, cord-decorated bead (TABLE 49, CF72.11) from Stanway is an example. Therefore the addition of lead oxide to the white glass in this large blue and white bead was not necessary to facilitate the production process.

Very few other examples of high lead, calcium antimonate opacified, white Iron Age glass have been identified. Lead was detected in a blue and white bead with cable decoration from Hayling Island, Hampshire, dated to around A.D. 50 or earlier (Bayley *et al.* forthcoming, bead 731). This was described as a baroque example, of British origin, without exact parallel. Henderson and Warren (1981) detected 20 wt% lead and some antimony oxide in the white decoration of a glass bead of Guido's class 1 (II) from an Iron Age context at Glastonbury lake village. The Stanway bead is most similar to Guido's Group 1 beads (*see* pp.178–9) but they are not widespread, rarely blue and white, and none have been analysed (Guido 1978, 59–60). Since the composition and appearance of the Stanway bead seems to be without exact known parallel, it may be a relatively local imitation, produced sometime between *c.* 25 B.C. and A.D. 50 in a workshop outside the Roman Empire, perhaps using glass derived from a Roman cameo or mosaic glass object.

COPPER-ALLOY OBJECTS (TABLES 50–2)

Copper is a soft ductile metal that can be alloyed with other metals, such as tin, zinc or lead, in order to produce an alloy with a particular colour, hardness, malleability or casting fluidity. The terms used in this report to describe different archaeological alloys are based on established definitions (Bayley and Butcher 1991). Bronze is an alloy of predominantly copper and tin. Tin levels were usually in the range of 5–12 wt% and objects containing more than about 5 wt% of tin have been described as bronze. Brass is an alloy of predominantly copper and zinc, normally with between about 10 wt% to 25% zinc. In this report, objects containing more than about 5 wt% of zinc have been described as brass. Objects from Stanway containing tin and zinc each at more than about 5 wt% have been described as gunmetal, a modern term also used to describe archaeological copper alloys with significant amounts of both tin and zinc. Lead can be added to any of these alloys and Stanway objects containing more than about 5 wt% of lead have been described as leaded. The addition of lead to alloys improved the quality of castings but was detrimental if the metal was to be worked or gilded. In this report, alloys containing less than about 5 wt% of total additions have been called impure copper. If several per cent of an element was detected, it was recorded as a 'small amount' and less than 1 wt% as a 'trace'.

There are considerable differences between the types of copper alloys used in Britain before the Late Iron Age compared to those used in Late Iron Age and Roman Britain. In the Early and Middle Iron Age bronze was the main alloy used. The lead content of Iron Age alloys was generally low, although larger, more intricate, castings occasionally contained moderate amounts of lead. However, in the Roman period many objects contained lead in low levels and some contained large amounts of up to 40 wt% (Dungworth 1996). Relatively high levels of the impurity arsenic have also been found in Iron Age copper alloys, but Roman alloys rarely contained more than 0.1 wt% arsenic.

TABLE 50: RESULTS SUMMARY OF THE METAL OBJECTS AND GLASS BROOCH SETTINGS FROM BF64, BF67, CF7, CF42, CF47, CF72 AND CF115

Enc.	Context	Feat.	Object	Description	Results
3	B1006	BF64	BF64.23	shield boss	iron base-plate, bronze sheet, leaded bronze knob
3	B1019	BF64	BF64.26	handled basin	leaded bronze, with less lead in the body, which also contained a small amount of zinc and traces of antimony and arsenic
3	B1020	BF64	BF64.25	jug	upper and lower sections both bronze; handle leaded bronze with traces of antimony
3	B1016	BF64	BF64.29, SF 316	game board handle	tinned brass
3	B992	BF64	BF64.29, SF 319	game board corner binding	likely to be brass, with small amounts of tin and lead also detected
3	B1060	BF64	BF64.29, SF 348	game board hinged fitting	likely to be brass, with small amounts of lead and tin also detected; rivet also brass
3	B1032	BF64	BF64.19	Nertomarus brooch	probably brass, with small amounts of tin and lead also detected; surface concentration of zinc may have been depleted by corrosion; no tinning found
3	B –	BF64	BF64.20	Nertomarus brooch	in very poor condition but probably brass, plus up to 5 wt% lead and with a small amount of tin; the zinc concentration on one fragment is likely to have been reduced by corrosion; spring is brass; the associated curved fragment is brass, plus a small amount of lead
3	B1021	BF64	BF64.21	arm-ring	impure copper, with a small amount of zinc and traces of lead and arsenic detected
3	B1071	BF67	BF67.3	Hod Hill variant brooch	likely to be brass or possibly gunmetal (small amounts of tin and zinc were detected but the zinc at the surface may have been reduced); pin is impure copper; large areas of the front of the brooch were tinned; the head was a solid casting drilled to take the iron axial bar
-	C44	CF7	CF7.2	boss-on-bow brooch	brass, with a small amount of tin and a trace of lead
5	C671	CF42	CF42.15	spoon	?impure copper, but lead and tin occasionally detected in high concentrations, particularly in a protrusion at the base of the handle; no silver
5	C901	CF47	CF47.21	saucepan	bronze, with tinning visible on the inner surface
5	C969	CF47	CF47.22, SF67	strainer bowl foot	leaded bronze, tinned on front, lead-tin solder on back
5	C970	CF47	CF47.22, SF68	strainer bowl foot	leaded bronze, tinned on front, lead-tin solder on back
5	C972	CF47	CF47.22, SF70	strainer bowl foot	leaded bronze, tinned on front, lead-tin solder on back
5	C978	CF47	CF47.22, SF76	strainer bowl body	bronze with trace of lead; lead-tin solder attached the spout and feet to the body
5	C902 etc.	CF47	CF47.22, SF14 etc	strainer bowl strainer-plate strainer bowl spill-plate	bronze with a trace of lead; solder around the edge was rich in lead and tin bronze, with a small amount of lead; front surface tinned; lead-tin solder present on the back

Enc.	Context	Feat.	Object	Description	Results
				spout	leaded bronze, probably tinned
				handle	leaded bronze, tinned on front; ring-headed rivet is bronze with a small amount of lead; strip rivet is brass and probably a repair
5	C998	CF47	CF47.20, SF94	game board corner binding	brass
5	C999	CF47	CF47.20, SF95	game board hinged fitting	brass or gunmetal hinge and pin, as small amounts of zinc and tin were detected but the zinc may have been depleted by corrosion (trace of lead)
5	C1049	CF47	CF47.25, SF135	stud from tray	bronze with a small amount of lead; lead-tin solder on underside
5	C1041	CF47	CF47.25, SF159	sheet from tray	bronze
5	C1030	CF47	CF47.23, SF126	short rod	brass
5	C1085	CF47	CF47.24, SF142	rebated ring	leaded bronze with a small amount of zinc; the very high levels of tin occasionally detected may be due to corrosion, since no tinning was observed; high levels of arsenic detected
5	C1086	CF47	CF47.24, SF143	plain ring	leaded bronze with a small amount of zinc; the very high levels of tin occasionally detected may be due to corrosion, since no tinning was observed
5	C982	CF47	CF47.15 + 16	Langton Down brooch, + ring fragment	gunmetal (more zinc than tin), with an impure copper pin; ring fragment bronze (plus a small amount of lead) and the level of tin detected was very high, probably due to poor preservation
5	C942	CF47	CF47.17	Rearhook brooch	leaded bronze with a small amount of zinc; stripes of tinning; pin is brass; no solder for reinforcing the spring attachment was accessible behind the side-wings
5	C410	CF72	CF72.5	Keyhole plate brooch with red glass stud	brass, although the amount of zinc detected is slightly low, probably as a result of corrosion, and it also contained a small amount of lead; tinned on the front and back, apart from the centre of the bow, which would have been covered by the missing repoussé-decorated plate; as no solder was detected in the centre of the bow, the red glass stud probably secured the plate; the pin and the cup holding the glass stud are impure copper; red glass contained over 30 wt% lead oxide, 7 wt% copper oxide and also antimony oxide, consistent with other 'sealing wax' red Iron Age and Roman enamels (Stapleton et al. 1999), coloured by small crystals of copper and/or cuprite (Cu_2O)
5	C408	CF72	CF72.6	Hod Hill brooch	leaded gunmetal, containing more zinc than tin, with parcel tinning; pin is impure copper; an iron axial bar secured the pin
5	C416	CF72	CF72.7	circular lugged plate brooch	brass with small amounts of tin and lead varyingly detected; a high concentration of tin (and some lead) was detected in the centre of the brooch front, probably the remains of solder used to secure a decorative central setting

TABLE 50: (CONT'D)

Enc.	Context	Feat.	Object	Description	Results
5	C414	CF72	CF72.9	lozenge-shaped plate brooch with blue glass setting	brass with a small amount of tin and a trace of lead; pin is impure copper; elevated levels of tin, likely to be the remains of lead-tin solder, were detected on the front of the brooch except in the centre, where the glass setting was located; there was a circular rim of thicker solder around the tin-free region; a copper alloy sheet would originally have covered the entire brooch, attached with solder, with a hole for the setting to protrude through; blue glass coloured by cobalt and copper oxides, and also contained manganese; it had a red area on the base that was compositionally similar except that more copper and lower alkali levels were detected in that area, it may be that the glass was heated on the brooch to set it in place, and the concentration of copper in the glass increased where it was in contact with the metal (as there was little oxygen available in the region between the brooch and glass the red colourant Cu_2O formed in the glass on the base of the setting)
5	CF406	CF72	CF72.10	star-shaped plate brooch with blue glass setting	brass, with some tin and a small amount of lead varyingly detected; the blue glass centre of the brooch contained manganese and was coloured mainly by cobalt with some copper; it was fixed to the brooch by lead-tin solder, as a high concentration of lead oxide was detected on the back of the glass centre and lead-tin solder covered the front of the brooch where the missing repoussé-decorated sheet was attached
5	C88	CF115	CF115.4	?mirror fragment	leaded bronze

The earliest date for the regular production of brass in the Roman Empire is 25 B.C. (Dungworth 1996). Objects made from brass began to appear in southern Britain from the early 1st century A.D. (Bayley 1988), mostly brooches of both imported and British-made types (Stead 1975; Bayley 1984; Stead and Rigby 1986, 122–3), but there is no evidence for the actual manufacture of the alloy itself in Britain until the decades following the Roman conquest, when there was a great increase in the amount of brass being used (Bayley 1990). Brass was not regularly produced prior to the Roman period because of the difficulties associated with extracting the volatile metal zinc from its ore. Roman brass was made by the cementation process, which involved heating copper, charcoal and either zinc carbonate or zinc oxide in a lidded crucible (Bayley *et al.* 2001). Gunmetal was used and may have been produced by mixing scrap bronze and brass (Dungworth 1996). However, neither leaded brass nor leaded copper were normally used in Roman times and unalloyed copper was used only in certain applications (Bayley 1988).

Results

A large number of copper-alloy objects from Stanway were analysed from burials, chambers, and ?mortuary enclosures. Unusual objects, or complex items formed from several components, are discussed individually below, followed by summaries of the results for the remaining objects.

Shield boss, BF64.23: The boss was constructed from three parts; a cast leaded bronze knob, a bronze plate (also containing a small amount of lead) and finally an iron sheet under-layer (TABLE 50).

Jug, BF64.25: The jug was constructed from three parts; the handle, the top of the jug with spout and the rounded lower body of the jug (TABLE 50). The handle was cast and was a leaded bronze with traces of antimony. The handle was probably attached using lead-tin solder, as some was visible where the handle was attached to the jug, although this area was not accessible for analysis. The top half of the jug, including the spout, was bronze and a small amount of lead was detected. This section of the jug was cast and not subsequently worked, since small dendrites (branching crystals that form as the molten metal cools) could be seen on the surface using a binocular light microscope. The metal was approximately 5 mm thick at the spout. The rounded lower body of the jug was bronze, containing only a small amount of lead, and was only 1 mm thick in places. This section of the jug was probably wrought although no uncorroded metal was visible to examine for evidence of dendrites or tool marks. No tinning or silvering was observed or detected analytically although it was not possible to analyse the internal surfaces of the item. Molten metal had been applied to the join between the top and bottom halves of the jug, in three areas on the inside. From its appearance and hardness, this metal was probably copper alloy rather than solder. No signs of the join could be discerned on the outside of the jug where it was disguised by two parallel decorative grooves. The join was probably an overlapping, rather than butt, type but since it was still intact it was not possible to establish this conclusively.

Handled basin, BF64.26: Only a few areas of the basin could be accessed for XRF analysis because of the shape and size of the object. However, examination with a binocular light microscope suggested that no surface decoration, such as tinning, silvering or inlay, was present. The basin was made from two parts; a leaded bronze handle (with a small amount of zinc) and a leaded bronze body (TABLE 50). The lead content of the body was considerably lower than that of the handle and a small amount of zinc and traces of antimony and arsenic were also detected in the former. Both the basin and handle had been cast and not subsequently worked, as characteristic, distinctively shaped dendritic crystals were visible on the surface. The two parts had been soldered together with lead-tin solder.

Saucepan, CF47.21: The remains of tinning were visible on the inside surface of the saucepan (TABLE 50). Owing to the large size it proved possible to analyse only a small fragment of the handle, which had broken from the object; this proved to be of bronze, with no lead detected. As the object was cast in one piece, the analysis of the fragment is likely to be representative of the whole. Saucepans of this type were cast in moulds using the lost wax process. The characteristic grooves on the base of this type of object were turned in the wax model around which the mould was formed, rather than being cut into the metal object once cast (Poulsen 1995).

Strainer bowl, CF47.22: The strainer bowl was a composite object constructed from several parts; three feet, a handle, a strainer-plate, a spout, a spill-plate and the strainer body itself (TABLE 50; *see* FIG. 113). The feet, spout and handle were all cast from leaded bronze and were tinned. The handle was attached to the body using two rivets: the ring-headed stud rivet was bronze and likely to be original whereas the folded strip fastening was brass and probably a repair. The bowl itself was wrought from bronze and the sheet metal was less than 1 mm thick, although the rim lip had a maximum thickness of about 2 mm. A hole was cut in the sheet metal where the spout was to be positioned and then the spout was soldered in place with lead-tin solder. The feet were also attached to the strainer body using a lead-tin solder, as elevated levels of lead and tin were detected on the base of the feet and in certain areas on the outer surface of the strainer body. The strainer-plate was wrought bronze and holes had been punched in the sheet metal to form an elaborate pattern. The spill-plate, which was attached to the bowl using lead-tin solder, was also wrought bronze and tinned on one surface. In several areas there was a grey/green patination on the outer surface of the strainer body, where elevated levels of tin were detected, but this was probably a result of corrosion rather than tinning. The strainer would have had a highly decorative appearance when complete. The spout, handle, spill-plate and feet, which would have been silver-coloured as a result of tinning, would have contrasted with the bronze-coloured bowl.

There were occasional grey areas on the inside surface of the strainer where increased concentrations of tin and/or lead were detected. However, these patches were commonly adjacent to lines of lead-tin solder and may have resulted from the corrosion of the solder rather than being evidence of tinning. Although copper-alloy vessels used for food preparation were frequently tinned to inhibit the dissolution of copper in the food (*see* the saucepan above), the strainer was unlikely to have held liquids for significant periods and therefore tinning may not have been required. Elevated levels of tin were also detected in the region of faint, silver-coloured, roughly semi-circular and circular marks on fragments of the bowl. These marks may have been the remains of soldered joints, as they had a distinct shape, but because of the severely fragmented condition of the bowl, it was not obvious whether the strainer-plate might have been attached to the fragments concerned.

No clear marks were visible on the outer surface of the strainer body but fine, parallel, annular scratches, following the circumference of the bowl, were visible on the inside of the body. These marks may have resulted from the finishing and polishing of the object, possibly using a pole lathe (Craddock and Lang 1983). In other areas with more awkward contours, also inside the strainer body, fine striations were visible running in a perpendicular direction to the annular marks previously described. These striations were present near the rim, where they continued to a depth of 50 mm into the bowl, on the base and also around the edges of the strainer-plate, and may have resulted from hand-finishing in these areas.

The strainer was crushed and fragmented when found but it was not possible to discern conclusively from examination of the strainer whether it was crushed prior to, or during, burial. The strainer body and strainer-plate were constructed from very thin, wrought bronze sheet, and so are unlikely to have been able to withstand the heavy loads that might be exerted by burial. Originally, the strainer would have collapsed by bending and folding, as was observed in one large rim fragment and the straining plate. Later, as the metal corroded post-burial, brittle fracture and fragmenting of the strainer would be anticipated, and this was observed on many fragments. Some components of the strainer showed signs of heavy wear, for example the strainer-plate was incomplete and the spout was abraded.

Rods, CF47.23: Only one of the four copper-alloy rods from CF47 was analysed as the larger rods would not fit into the XRF sample chamber (TABLE 50). It was found to be brass, and as all the rods were a similar colour it is likely that they all had a similar composition. Four iron rods were also recovered although these were not examined.

Spoon, CF42.15: The spoon is badly corroded and therefore the results are difficult to interpret; it may be of impure copper (TABLE 50). The surface was probably tinned, although no evidence for this survives. A protrusion at the base of the handle was particularly rich in lead and tin, and, as this is probably not part of the spoon (N. Crummy, pers. comm.), it may be some lead-tin alloy or corrosion product deposited from another object.

Possible mirror fragment, CF115.4: It cannot be conclusively determined without sampling whether this leaded bronze object was a mirror because of its poor condition (TABLE 50). However, the tin content on one side, which was dark and smooth, was considerably higher than on the other, and this is consistent with a type of Roman mirror made from a low-tin bronze (containing up to about 10% tin and a few per cent of lead) and tinned on one surface (Meeks 1995). Other mirrors were made from speculum, a high-tin bronze (approx 22 wt% tin).

Brooches: The analytical results for the brooches are summarised in TABLE 50. The results are all consistent with previous analyses of these brooch types (*e.g.* Bayley 1986; Bayley and

Butcher 1997; 2004). The imported brooches are brass or probably brass, apart from the Langton Down from CF47 which is of gunmetal, and the British-made Rearhook is a leaded bronze. The pins are frequently of impure copper, which is suitable for drawing out as wire and easily wound to form the spring.

Other grave deposits: A wide range of alloys is represented among the other grave goods. The arm-ring from BF64 is of impure copper, which is malleable and so suited to the method of manufacture of this object. The cast fittings from the game boards in BF64 and CF47 are of brass, as are the corner-bindings, and the drop-handle from the board in BF64 was tinned. The binding from the board fragment in the chamber BF6 is also brass (TABLE 51). Both types of ring found in CF47 were of leaded bronze, though high levels of arsenic were detected in the rebated one. The ring fragment found with the Langton Down brooch in the same grave was of bronze (TABLE 50).

TABLE 51: RESULTS SUMMARY OF THE METAL OBJECTS FROM ENCLOSURE 3 CHAMBER BF6, THE PYRE-SITE BF1/F16 AND PIT BF17

Context	Feature	Object	Description	Results
B77	BF6	BF6.24	pedestal	leaded bronze, with lead-tin solder detected on top; attached fragment appears to be leaded copper although this would be unusual
B159	BF6	BF6.25	spout	leaded bronze
B226	BF6	BF6.26, SF146	game board binding	likely to be brass, small amounts of tin and lead varyingly detected, particularly on the rivet, which may indicate that solder was used
B194	BF6	BF6.27	harness fitting	likely to be brass, with a small amount of lead
B67	BF6	BF6.29	strap-plate/stiffener and burnt fragments	?strap-plate probably brass although high levels of lead and tin in some areas may indicate the presence of solder; other analysed fragments were bronze (1) and leaded bronze (3)
B164	BF6	BF6.31	strip fragments	leaded bronze
B180	BF6	BF6.32	cylinder	lead and copper present
B158	BF6	SF109	burnt fragments	2 fragments analysed, both bronze
B75	BF1	BF1.2	fitting	likely to be brass, with zinc and lead detected; separate lump of metal is leaded bronze
B81	BF1	BF1.3	many burnt frags incl. small studs	3 analysed; leaded bronze and bronze
B87	BF1/L6	BL6.2	fitting and 2 droplets	impure copper
B83	BF16/L5	BF16.2	belt-plate/stiffener	bronze, with small amount of lead
B25	–	SF82	stud	lead and copper detected
B155	BF17	BF17.2	dome headed boss	likely to be brass, with small amount of lead

TABLE 52: RESULTS SUMMARY OF THE METAL OBJECTS FROM THE CONTEXTS ASSOCIATED WITH THE ?MORTUARY ENCLOSURE BF32 IN ENCLOSURE 4

Context	Feature	Object	Description	Results
B531	BF28	BF28.1	plaque	likely to be brass, with trace of lead
B540	BF28	SF152	dribble and fragment	copper, lead, tin and large quantities of silver
B750	BF42	BF42.1	strip	likely to be brass, with small amount of lead
B734	BL41/F42	BF42.2	fitting	likely to be brass, with small amount of lead
B646	BF42	SF 221	sheet fragments	4 analysed; all bronze with varying tin levels
B701	BF42	SF 219	fragments	impure copper
B750	BF42	SF 232	dribbles and pellets	2 analysed; one is leaded bronze; a small amount of zinc was detected in the other

Enclosure 3 chamber BF6, pyre-site BF1/BF16 and pit BF17: A number of copper-alloy objects and fragments from the chamber BF6 and the features and layers clustered in the same area were analysed and the results are summarised in TABLE 51. Several of the items are brass, or probably brass, which suits the identification of some of the pieces, such as the harness fitting from BF6, as Roman cavalry equipment (Bayley 1985; 1992).

Enclosure 4 ?mortuary enclosure BF32 and pit BF42: Several of the heat-affected objects from the ?mortuary enclosures and a charcoal-lined pit filled with burnt copper-alloy debris in Enclosure 4 also proved to be brass (TABLE 52). The fragments from B540 F28 (SF 152) were atypical as they contained large concentrations of silver (up to ~37 wt%) in addition to copper, tin and lead. It can be no coincidence that the only silver objects in the Stanway assemblage, a pair of collars probably from a brooch chain, came from BF24, the chamber in this enclosure.

CONCLUSIONS

The majority of the glass objects from the funerary enclosures were made from soda-lime-silicate glass, and a mineral source of alkali fluxes, such as natron, was probably used in the production of the glass. The glasses frequently contained significant quantities of manganese oxide and made use of antimony-based, rather than tin-based, colourants. These observations, consistent with other glass objects from Late Iron Age and Roman contexts, suggest that the glass used to produce the artefacts originated in the Roman Empire, although glass workers outside the Roman Empire may then have shaped the glass into objects. The white glass used to decorate one large blue bead was found to have a lead-rich composition typical of Roman cameo and mosaic glass.

The majority of the copper-alloy objects from the enclosures were made from bronze or leaded bronze. The exceptions were many of the brooches, assorted small fittings, game board fittings, and the rods from CF47, which were all brass. The repair on the strainer handle was also brass. The application of brass fittings to the game boards may suggest that they were imported. The dominance of bronze and leaded bronze in the assemblage is not unexpected. The occurrence of leaded bronze increased at this time (Northover 1989), as it was used for both imported and British-made items. There was also a great increase in brass objects in Britain following the conquest, but they tend to be imported military fittings and brooches (Bayley 1988). Roman vessels are normally bronze or leaded bronze; brass is only used for a few wrought vessel types.

THE IRON AGE AND ROMAN COINS (FIG. 148)

By John A. Davies

Seven coins were recovered from the Stanway excavations. They are all bronze issues. Five are Iron Age and two Roman. All can be dated within the period A.D. 10–68. Four of the Iron Age coins have been identified. One (AF17.1) comes from the ditch of Enclosure 1, three (CF5.1, BF39.2, BF39.3) from the ditch of Enclosure 4, and the last (BF30.3) from the ditch of the ?mortuary enclosure BF32 in Enclosure 4. BF30.3 is a type from Cunobelin's Middle Bronze series, dated from A.D. 10–20. All of the rest are Cunobelin's Late Bronze types, similarly dated from A.D. 20–43.

The two Roman coins came from Enclosure 5. Both are unusual types of bronze *aes*. The earlier of the two is an irregular *as* of the emperor Claudius (CF96.1). Irregular Claudian issues are not found on all Romano-British sites. They are largely found at places with a mid 1st-century military association, such as the *coloniae*, forts and routeways of this period. They can be found in profusion at military sites. The major assemblage of Claudian bronze coins from the Colchester town centre excavations between 1971–79 has been studied and published in its entirety (Kenyon 1987; 1992).

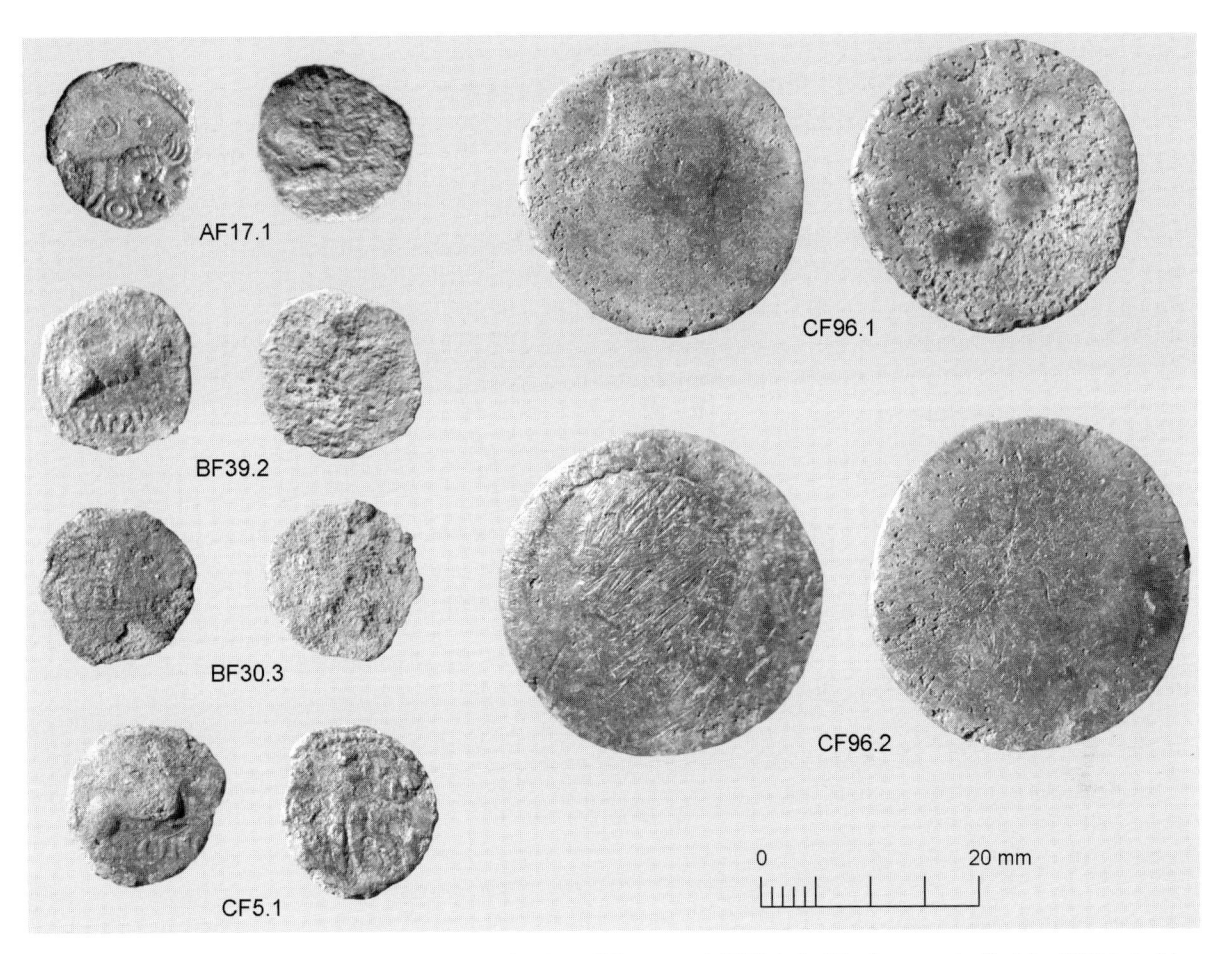

FIG. 148. Coins: AF17.1 (Enclosure 1 ditch), CF5.1 and BF39.2 (Enclosure 4 ditch), BF30.3 (the ?mortuary enclosure in Enclosure 4), CF96.1–2 (from Enclosure 5 slot or trench) (scale 1.5:1)

The other Roman coin (CF96.2) is a regular *as* of the emperor Nero. This coin is largely illegible (FIG. 148). In fact, it is the nature of the wear exhibited that makes this coin so unusual. The obverse has been heavily rubbed, with very little relief remaining. The reverse is even more heavily worn and is almost flat. This degree of wear is exceedingly unusual. It is clear from coin-hoard evidence that Roman coins of the Augustan coinage system, such as this, could stay in circulation for long periods of time. They could sometimes circulate for many decades. However, such coins do not exhibit the type of wear from normal circulation seen on this example. The very flat surfaces, especially as seen on the reverse, suggest that this coin may have been deliberately rubbed flat.

Examples of deliberately defacing the coinage of specific Roman emperors after their death have been recorded. However, in such instances, cut marks or evidence of rubbing are found on the emperors' portrait, where an attempt has been made to deface or remove his image. On the Stanway *as*, the portrait has not been specifically targeted and the reverse has suffered more than the obverse. However, Roman coins with this degree of wear are exceptionally rare. Elsewhere in East Anglia, a small group of bronze 4th-century *folles* was excavated at the temple of Sawbench, Hockwold cum Wilton, Norfolk. These had been worn almost flat on their reverse faces (unpublished, deposited with Norwich Castle Museum). It has been speculated that these coins had been deliberately rubbed smooth for an unknown purpose within the temple.

In conclusion, the Neronian *as* from Stanway does appear to have been rubbed flat for a specific purpose rather than worn smooth through normal circulation. This wear could have been the result of a functional use. Perhaps it was used as a washer between two surfaces. It is unlikely that the defacement was a deliberate comment aimed at the emperor Nero as the portrait would have been targeted. However, it is possible that the unusual wear could be associated with a ritual or symbolic practice, as yet undefined.

Catalogue

Iron Age coins (FIG. 148)

AF17.1 SF106. A589. Middle fill of northern arm of enclosure ditch of Enclosure 1. Cunobelin A.D. 20–43. AE unit. 1.09 g. 14 mm. Obv: Romanised bust right. Illegible legend: —O— . Rev: Bull butting right. Ring-and-pellet motifs above and below bull. As Van Arsdell 2095-1.

BF30.3 BF30/1. SF173, B538 BL21. Junction of northern and eastern arms of the ditch of ?mortuary enclosure BF32 in Enclosure 4. Cunobelin A.D. 10–20. AE unit. 1.18 g. 14 mm. Obv: Corroded and chipped. Writing in 2 lines, in tablet. —O— . Rev: Illegible. As Van Arsdell 1977-1.

BF39.2 SF287. B931. Middle fill of northern part of eastern arm of enclosure ditch of Enclosure 4. Cunobelin A.D. 20–43. AE unit. 1.10 g. 15 mm. Obv: Sphinx right. CVNO below. Rev: Perseus left. CAM to side. Van Arsdell 2109-1.

BF39.3 Not illustrated. SF384. B1165. Middle fill of northern part of eastern arm of enclosure ditch of Enclosure 4. Unidentified (missing).

CF5.1 SF205. C5. CF5/CL6. Upper fill of southern part of eastern arm of enclosure ditch of Enclosure 4. Cunobelin A.D. 20–43. AE unit. 1.47 g. 15 mm. Obv: Corroded. [Head of Janus.]. Rev: Sow right. CAMV in tablet below. Van Arsdell 2105-1.

Roman coins

CF96.1 SF197. C171. Upper part of slot CF96 in Enclosure 5. Claudius A.D. 50–60. Irregular *as*. 7.14 g. 25 mm. 160 degrees. Obv: [TI CLAVDIVS CA]ESAR AVG [PM TR P IMP]. Rev: S-C]; Minerva right. As RIC 1: 100.

CF96.2 SF203. C162. Upper part of slot CF96 in Enclosure 5. Nero A.D. 64–8. *As*. 9.83 g. 29 mm. Obv: Bust left. Surface heavily rubbed and relief worn away. Rev: Illegible. Surface rubbed completely flat.

THE GLASS VESSELS (FIG. 149; TABLES 53–4)

By H.E.M. Cool

INTRODUCTION

The glass vessels found at the Stanway site are an important addition to our knowledge of Roman glass in 1st-century Britain. As will be discussed below (report submitted in 2002), there are grounds for thinking that many may have been imported prior to the conquest in A.D. 43, a period when glass vessels were very rare within Britain (Price 1996). They are also important within an international context because one of them (BF64.16) appears to be an unusual survival of a large early blown bowl. As such, it has a useful contribution to make to our understanding of the capabilities of the early glass-blowers.

THE VESSEL TYPES PRESENT (FIG. 149; TABLES 53–4)

Ten vessels have been identified, which collectively represent a range of types. There is one very large blown bowl (FIG. 83, BF64.16; p. 176), a smaller cast polychrome bowl (FIG. 73, CF42.11; p. 156), a *pyxis* (FIG. 129, CF72.4; p. 258), and six unguent bottles (FIG. 83, BF64.17–18; p. 176; FIG. 63, BF24.23; p. 140; FIG. 73, CF42.12 and CF42.13 (not illustrated); p. 156; and CF115.3 (not illustrated); p. 261). There is also one fragment from a blown polychrome vessel of unknown form (FIG. 30, BF4.1; p. 73).

The amber bowl BF64.16 from the Warrior's burial is a remarkable vessel as it is unusually large, measuring a quarter of a metre in diameter and 125 mm in height (FIGS 83, 149). This is exceptional, as may be judged by comparing it to the rim diameters of the two commonest relatively deep bowl forms in use during the mid to late 1st century in Colchester (*CAR* **8**, 15–26, 94–9). The data are given in TABLE 53. As can be seen, although bowls of a comparable rim diameter have occasionally been found, they are rare and the average diameter is much smaller.

The diagnostic features of the bowl apart from its size are a rolled rim, linear wheel-cut decoration and base formed by a separately blown paraison. The form is not one that features

TABLE 53: SUMMARY OF THE RIM DIAMETERS OF PILLAR-MOULDED AND TUBULAR-RIMMED BOWLS FROM COLCHESTER (source *CAR* **8**; measurements in mm)

Bowl type	No.	Minimum	1st quartile	3rd quartile	Maximum	Mean
pillar-moulded	46	105	140	200	230	167
tubular-rimmed	29	100	140	188	270	165

in standard typologies such as those of Isings (1957) and Goethert-Polaschek (1977). Shallow bowls with similar blown paraison bases are known from contexts of the first half of the 1st century A.D. Ones with both tubular and fire-rounded rims were found buried in a room in the Atrium Publicum at Cosa, destroyed by the collapse of a wall of the Forum Basilica in *c.* A.D. 40–45 (Grose 1973, 38 nos 9–10, fig. 3). On the basis of fragments that were accumulating between 37/36 B.C. and the first decade of the 1st century A.D. in a drain in the Regia, Grose (1977, 20) has suggested that the form may have been in use by early in the 1st century A.D. at the latest. Clearly the Stanway bowl is not precisely paralleled by these Italian dishes as they are shallower, of smaller diameter, and do not appear to have been made of amber glass. They do, however, show that vertically sided open vessels with distinctive paraison bases were being used in Italy in the early to mid 1st century A.D., if not earlier.

Thanks to the Boudican uprising in A.D. 60/1, Colchester has one of the largest and best-documented collections of glass vessels belonging to the period A.D. 43–60/1 from anywhere in the Empire. It is very noticeable that neither at Sheepen (Harden 1947; Charlesworth 1985) nor at the town-centre sites (*CAR* **8**) are there any rim or base fragments that could be related to vessels similar to the Stanway bowl. The same is true in other vessel glass assemblages from good closed contexts relating to the A.D. 40s, 50s and 60s such as the Dutch fort of Valkenburg (van Lith 1978–9). Given this and the Italian evidence, it seems most likely that this was a pre-conquest import as it is difficult to see how the form could have escaped notice if it was being made in the mid 1st century. An interesting question arises, however, as to how many years prior to the conquest this particular vessel may have been made and when it arrived in Britain.

With a unique object as this vessel currently appears to be, such questions are difficult to answer, but the intriguing possibility exists that this may be an early blown vessel of a type that has puzzled glass scholarship for some time. The invention of glass-blowing is generally thought to have taken place in the mid 1st century B.C. and to have initially been concerned with blowing small flasks (*see* for example Israeli 1991; Grose 1977, 25). It was clearly a technology that spread rapidly as, within a century, blown vessels of a wide variety of forms are found throughout the Empire, and there are many different glass-blowing centres. Blown glass had many advantages, one of which was that, in comparison to the early casting techniques, the vessels could easily be transparent. This was a property that was much appreciated and it was exploited by painters decorating walls in the fantasy scenes of the Second Pompeian style, especially those of the later developments of the style which may broadly be dated mid 1st century B.C. to the early reign of Augustus (*c.* 15 B.C.) (Ling 1991, 23).

From the outset, these paintings include depictions of large transparent glass bowls, often containing fruit, a good example of this being the bowl on the east wall of Room 23 in the villa of the Poppaei at Oplontis believed to have been painted *c.* 50–40 B.C. (Ling 1991, 29, fig. 25; Naumann-Steckner 1999, 25, fig. 1). Given the size of the fruit depicted, these bowls are likely to have had a rim diameter of 200–250 mm (Naumann-Steckner 1991, 87). The archaeological record has so far not produced any evidence that large glass bowls such as these existed so soon after the invention of blowing, and the status of these depictions has been questioned. Grose (1977, 28) cautiously concludes that these vessels may indeed be depictions of blown glass bowls and that people were familiar with at least the idea of blown glass at the time. Naumann-Steckner, noting the absence of contemporary examples of the actual bowls, prefers to see them as a hybrid invention by the painters, taking the form of silver vessels but rendering them in glass to exploit the possibility of depicting transparency (Naumann-Steckner 1991, 88; 1999, 27). It is undoubtedly the case, however, that when other glass vessels are depicted they can be

FIG. 149. The amber glass bowl BF64.16 from the Warrior's burial

paralleled by actual examples (cf. Naumann-Steckner 1991, pl. 22). It may also be relevant that a study of the bronze vessels in the wall paintings has concluded that throughout the different painting styles, the vessels depicted match the contemporary forms actually in use (Riz 1990, 41).

Although the Naumann-Steckner hypothesis may be correct, the possibility that large blown bowls were in existence by the later 1st century B.C. cannot be excluded, and there is the intriguing possibility that the Stanway bowl may be an example of one. It is interesting to note that, several times, cylindrical bowls with outflaring rims not dissimilar in shape to BF64.16 are depicted in wall paintings thought to have been painted in the 20s B.C. and possibly a little later at, for example, the House of Augustus on the Palatine in Rome (Naumann-Stecker 1991, 88), in the Villa Farnesina, also in Rome (Nauman-Steckner 1999, 28, fig. 6), and in a tomb in Morlupo in Etruria (Naumann-Steckner 1991, pl. 24a; 1999, 28, fig. 7). These seem to have small ball-like feet, a most unusual feature for glass, but they are clearly transparent and are large enough to have several unguent bottles and toilet implements placed in them. Of relevance to the Stanway bowl is the fact that the best-preserved one, that from Morlupo, clearly shows two lines on the upper body and one on the lower body, possibly depicting the sort of wheel-cut lines that can be seen on BF64.16. Again, the parallel is not an exact one but might hint that the Stanway bowl could have been made in the late 1st century B.C.

An early date might also explain one of the insecurities in technique it demonstrates. Roman glass-blowers of the 1st century A.D. were probably some of the most competent that ever existed, but in this vessel the base was attached to the body rather incompetently. Large air bubbles were trapped between the two paraisons. This was such a problem that when the fragments were first excavated, it was thought that two vessels were present as some of the base paraison fragments had split away from the body along the line of the joint. It is not difficult to imagine that this sort of problem might be expected when people were experimenting with a new technology, exploring its possibilities and working at the limit of their technical capabilities.

If the hypothesis that the vessel was the product of the early Italian glass-blowing industry is correct, then it could have been half a century old when deposited. Is this feasible? The bowl certainly gives every appearance of having been carefully curated. It was found fragmented and as reconstructed is not complete, but the missing fragments are small and, given the nature of the excavation of this deposit, it seems most likely that it was deposited as a complete vessel and the missing fragments were overlooked during excavation. It was found placed within a wooden box with iron fittings which appears to have been the most substantial of any of the wooden boxes found in the cemetery. The only other pre-conquest glass bowl from a grave in southern England is the ribbed bowl from the Hertford Heath burial, and this too shows a considerable longevity. The burial is thought to belong to the first half of the 1st century B.C., probably before *c.* 20 B.C., but the bowl itself is thought to have been made prior to 70 B.C. (Price 1996).

The other bowl from Stanway is a cast polychrome bowl in blue, white and yellow (FIG. 73, CF42.11) from the chamber in Enclosure 5 (CF42). This was clearly not placed in the grave as a whole vessel since only a handful of fragments survive. These are sufficient, however, to show that, when complete, this would not have been an example of either of the standard polychrome bowl forms at Colchester, *i.e.* the pillar-moulded bowl (*CAR* **8**, 17–19, nos 1–5) and the shallow convex bowl (*ibid.*, 27–8, fig. 2.9, no. 189). In CF42.11, the side of the vessel is much more vertical and the base is flat. These features suggest that the original may have been more like what Grose has called a deep hemispherical bowl (Grose 1989, 259, figs 147–8), although the vessels tend to have slightly straighter sides than this name suggests.

Many cast polychrome vessels from Britain are represented only by small fragments and, although it is possible to distinguish between pillar-moulded bowls and the others because of the distinctive surface finish of the former, it is not always possible to identify the precise type from which the unribbed fragments came. The latter belong to Grose's Family IV of mosaic vessels for which a broad date of the late 1st century B.C. to *c.* A.D. 50 is appropriate (Grose 1989, 257). Of those from British sites that can be identified as far as form goes, most belong either to the carinated forms or to the shallow convex bowls. This perhaps suggests that the less common forms such as the deep hemispherical bowl had gone out of common use by the time of the conquest. As with BF64.16, the lack of any similar rim and base fragments in the pre-Boudican contexts at Colchester or other contemporary deposits in Britain might suggest that CF42.11 too could have been a pre-conquest import.

The other cast polychrome vessel (FIG. 129, CF72.4) also belongs to this family of vessels (Grose 1989, 259). It is the bottom part of a *pyxis* which, in its present state, is undamaged apart from a chipped rim. This chipping was perhaps the result of a long period of use as, when complete, the vessel would have had a lid which fitted over the rim and rested on the rebated edge. It was found in the Brooches burial CF72 in Enclosure 5. Such vessels were also made in monochrome glass and in gold band glass. In no colour were they ever common, and very few of those extant have any details of their provenance recorded. The discovery of this example at Stanway is therefore an important addition to the corpus.

Those with a context suggest that they were primarily in use in Italy and the Mediterranean areas of the western empire. A monochrome blue example was found in a Claudian cremation burial at Nîmes, France (Foy and Nenna 2001, 129–30, 163–11). A polychrome example with three different cane patterns set in a purple matrix is said to have been found in a tomb in the locality of Amolara in Adria, Italy (Bonomi 1996, 197, no. 447, pl. 4), and a translucent blue one is said to have been found at Cumae, Italy, with a gold band vessel, presumably in another grave (Goldstein 1979, 142, no. 293). A virtually complete purple, yellow and white marbled example is also known from Apt, France (Foy and Nenna 2001, 161, no. 225). A late 1st-century B.C. to early 1st-century A.D. date seems most likely for their manufacture. Even allowing for the fact that they are a rare form, their normal absence from mid 1st-century A.D. site assemblages suggests that most are likely to have gone out of use prior to the middle of the century. In Britain, other than the Stanway example, the only one known with certainty is represented by three body and base fragments of a gold band example from contexts of *c.* A.D. 50–75 at Fishbourne (Harden and Price 1971, 326, nos 8–10, fig. 137, pl. 25). The possibility that the Stanway example was another pre-conquest import is thus a strong one.

The closest parallel to the Stanway *pyxis* appears to be an unprovenanced yellow/brown one with opaque white marbling once in the Oppenländer collection (Von Saldern *et al.* 1974, 123, no. 330). This has a polished band below the lid seating just as the Stanway one has, and an origin in the same workshop might be suspected.

Although CF72.4 and the fragments from Fishbourne are the only examples of this form with a secure archaeological provenance in Britain, a third example is reputed to have been found at Sheepen with a small polychrome cast cup. (These were shown to the Colchester Archaeological Trust in 1978 by Mr Horace Calver, and photographs and drawings were made at the time. My comments are based on the illustrations kindly made available to me by the Trust.) This *pyxis* has white marbling in a dark purple ground, similar to the unprovenanced ones in the Corning Museum of Glass, New York State, USA (Goldstein 1979, 192, no. 518) and the Toledo Museum of Art, Ohio, USA (Grose 1989, 335, no. 587). It appears to have a polished band below the rebated rim and a shallow ground out-channel on the lower body like the Stanway example. It too was missing its lid and the rim was chipped. The small cup was hemispherical with a small base ring and possibly vertical rim. It appears to have been made with opaque white chips in a coloured ground, but it is so heavily weathered that the colour was not apparent.

From photographs, both pieces appear heavily weathered, with patches of thick iridescence noticeable on the *pyxis*. In my experience, iridescence such as this is rarely encountered on the Roman glass from either the town-centre sites in Colchester or those at Sheepen or here at Stanway. The similarity of the 'Sheepen *pyxis*' to that now recovered from Stanway does, however, suggest that the Sheepen group could well be the remains of another early to mid 1st-century grave. Given that such vessels were the expensive packaging of no doubt expensive cosmetics (Foy and Nenna 2001, 161), these two vessels cast an interesting sidelight on the both the purchasing power and the interest in cosmetics of the local élite in the first half of the 1st century A.D.

The other vessels whose form can be identified also suggest an interest in cosmetics and fragrant oils as they are all small unguent bottles. Of particular importance is FIG. 63, BF24.23 from the chamber BF24 in Enclosure 4. This is an example of an amphora-shaped unguent bottle (Isings Form 9) with a distinctive carination at the shoulder and pointed base that makes it easy to identify from the extant fragments. Isings (1957, 27) notes examples in Tiberian to Claudian contexts, and to these can be added that in the cremation burial of a juvenile of 7 to 13 years at Wederath-Belginium, near Trier (Goethert 1989, 276, e) which may be dated after A.D. 37 from a coin it contained. This does not appear to be a form present in post-conquest deposits in Britain, and so appears to have gone out of use by that time. As noted, the shoulder and base fragments are very distinctive and, had the form still been in use by the conquest, it might have been expected to have been recognised among the large numbers of unguent bottles recovered from both the town-centre sites at Colchester and in the early cremation burials.

The importance of this piece lies in the fact that it is the equivalent of cheap and cheerful packaging for its contents which, based on the deposits on the interior of the Wederath one, are thought to have been rouge. Although it is possible to imagine a cosmetics container such as the *pyxis* being curated after the contents had been used, this seems unlikely to have been the case for BF24.23. Such flasks are made of very thin glass. Rough handling or over-enthusiastic use of a toilet implement used to extract the rouge must often have resulted in breakages even before the contents were used up. The presence of such a vessel in BF24 must strongly suggest that the burial was made prior to the conquest or, at the very latest, at the time of the conquest.

The commonest unguent bottle form at Stanway is the tubular unguent bottle of Isings form 8. There are two examples (FIG. 83, BF64.17–18) from the Warrior's burial BF64 in Enclosure 3 and one (CF115.3) from the Mirror burial CF115 in Enclosure 5. This is the dominant unguent bottle type of the mid 1st century A.D. both in Britain and elsewhere in the Empire, going out of use in the Flavian period (*CAR* **8**, 159). Evidence from continental sites makes it clear they were in use as early as the reign of Tiberius (Isings 1957, 24).

Two other unguent bottles (CF42.12–13) are represented by fragments in the chamber CF42. CF42.12 (FIG. 73) would appear to have had a slightly more convex-curved body than is usual in the tubular form and may have come from a small globular example of Isings Form 6.

TABLE 54: A COMPARISON OF THE COLOURS OF THE STANWAY UNGUENT BOTTLES WITH THOSE OF TUBULAR UNGUENT BOTTLES AT VARIOUS MID 1ST-CENTURY SITES IN BRITAIN

(Sources. Stanway: this volume; Sheepen: Colchester Museums stores, including material in Harden 1947 and Charlesworth 1985 but predominantly unpublished; Colchester: *CAR* **8**, 387–8 excluding no. 1236; Kingsholm: Price and Cool 1985, 48 nos 39 and 39b, 52 nos 69–84c; Usk: Manning *et al.* 1995, 175 nos 84–91)

Colour	Stanway	Sheepen	Colchester	Kingsholm	Usk
Blue/green	4	53	32	21	35
Blue	1	1	–	–	–
Yellow/brown	1	–	–	–	–
Light green	–	1	–	–	–
Yellow/green	–	–	–	2	–

On the Continent, this is an early to mid 1st-century form, and it is not often one that is noted in post-conquest assemblages in Britain. The fragments forming CF42.13 are too small to be diagnostic and the precise shape is unknown.

Both at Sheepen and in the town-centre sites, small unguent bottles of the tubular form are very common finds as they also are in the early cemeteries around the town (May 1930, pls 76.7, 79.29, 81.48, and 52 etc.). Despite this, however, taken as a whole the group from Stanway does show some unusual features. Normally these vessels are made in blue/green glass and by far the majority from mid 1st-century Romano-British sites are that colour. Other colours do occur but are rare. At Stanway, however, one out of the three tubular examples definitely present, is coloured (BF64.17), and if all the unguent bottles are included then two out of six are. How unusual this is can be seen from TABLE 54 in which tubular unguent bottles from other mid 1st-century sites are tabulated. As well as those from Sheepen and the Colchester town-centre sites, two sites where occupation centred on the late A.D. 50s and 60s have also been included. As the data was mostly collected and/or published prior to the development of EVE measures for glass, the quantification unit is a modified fragment count, *i.e.* multiple fragments obviously from the same vessel have been counted as one. Clearly the Stanway unguent bottles are not a typical cross-section of those available after the conquest. Either special selection was being undertaken, or possibly they too may reflect a pre-conquest origin as in the case of BF24.23.

The final vessel from Stanway is represented only by a body fragment from the terminal of the ditch BF4 of Enclosure 3 (FIG. 30, BF4.1). It came from a yellow/brown vessel decorated with opaque white marvered spots. Vessels decorated in this way are not uncommon on Claudian and Neronian sites in Britain (*CAR* **8**, 59) with a few examples surviving into the Flavian period (Caruana 1992, 67, no. 5, fig. 10). On the Continent, they are clearly in use during the Tiberian period as may be seen from examples such as the amphorisk found in a grave of that date in the cemetery of Branca, Locarno, Switzerland (Simonett 1941, 115, Abb. 95). As this body fragment is so small, it is not possible to date it more closely than the Tiberian to mid Flavian period.

THE USE OF GLASS IN THE CEMETERY

Glass vessels were used in two different ways in the cemetery. They appear to have been used during the funeral ceremonies (BF64.17–18, BF24.23, CF42.12–14, CF115.3) and to have been placed entire as grave goods (BF64.16, CF72.4). They may also have featured in rituals that went on in the cemetery either at the time of the initial funeral, or perhaps later (BF4.1). One way in which they do not appear to have been used, or, to be precise, for which there is no evidence, is as pyre goods, as none of the fragments show any evidence of being distorted or shattered by heat.

Of the vessels used during the funeral ceremonies, most were presumably present merely as containers and it is their contents that are likely to have been important in the ceremonies. It does not take much imagination to envision the person whose remains were placed in the chamber BF24 being made-up with the rouge in the amphora-shaped unguent bottle BF24.23, perhaps in an attempt to banish the pallor of death while the body was being displayed prior to being placed on the pyre. It is normally assumed that the tubular unguent bottles held oil, possibly perfumed. The contents of the ones found at Stanway might have been used either to anoint the corpse to prepare it for burning, or perhaps to have been poured over the ashes when the pyre had died down. In no case was it felt important to include all of the fragments from the vessels in the burial pits, and in most cases the majority of the fragments must have been disposed of elsewhere.

The polychrome bowl CF42.14 was also present only as a small number of fragments and presumably should be seen as serving a similar purpose to the ceramic tablewares which were also possibly used during the funeral and then smashed and incorporated to a greater or lesser extent in the burial pits or chambers.

The amber bowl and the *pyxis*, by contrast, were placed entire in the grave. Given that none of the other objects in the Warrior's burial appear to have been broken when deposited in the grave, and that it was stored in a box, it seems very probable that the amber bowl was also intact when buried. It is considerably fragmented but there is no one point from which the damage radiates out, as might be expected if it had been hit to break it.

It is useful to compare the use of glass vessels at Stanway with that in other 1st-century burials at Colchester. The most obvious difference is that elsewhere glass vessels were often used as pyre goods. The early discoveries of urned cremation burials around the town frequently included fragments of melted glass which, where the form they originally took can be ascertained, were tubular unguent bottles (*see* for example May 1930, 255 Grave 9/30, no. 188–9, 260, Grave 29/47 273–4 etc.). Sometimes both melted and unmelted but complete unguent bottles were included (*see* for example May 1930, 265 Grave 44/26, nos 155–7). Other forms of glass vessel were rare and tend, where present, to be complete flasks as in the famous Child's Grave, which contained the pipeclay figurines and also unguent bottles that had been fused in the pyre (May 1930, 252, Grave 3/124, nos 1139–40 and 1142; *see* also Eckardt 1999). Only in two cremation burials at Sheepen do glass tablewares seem to feature as parts of the grave goods in two Claudio–Neronian cremation burials (Charlesworth 1985, mf. 1 A5–A8). The glass vessels do, therefore, seem to have been used in a very different way in the burials around the town and the burials at Stanway and Sheepen. Presumably this reflects differing practices between the native élites at the latter and the soldier/colonists of the town.

CONCLUSIONS

The overwhelming impression gained from the Stanway glass vessels is how very different they are to the vessels from the Colchester town-centre sites and cemeteries. Even when a type is common in both areas, as in the case of the tubular unguent bottles, the Stanway vessels show unusual features with regards to colour. To a certain extent this difference is also true when the Stanway vessels are compared to the glass from Sheepen. At the latter site, more pre-conquest glass was found than in the town centre (*see* for example Harden 1947, 293, no. 1–2, pl. 87), but, within an empire-wide perspective, the Stanway vessels are rarer forms than the ones found there. The vessels at Stanway also seem to have been used in the funeral ritual in a different way to how glass vessels are used in the cemeteries immediately around the *colonia*. Everything points to the people buried at Stanway being very different fom those living in the Roman town.

From the point of view of the glass, much of this could be explained by the burials taking place prior to the conquest, although clearly this does not accord with the other finds from many of them. Perhaps what we are looking at is a group of prestige goods entering the country prior to the conquest and becoming part of the possessions of an élite family. This interpretation should not be pressed too far, however. As already noted, long curation of some items such as the amber bowl and the *pyxis* is not difficult to imagine. When it comes to curation of vessels that are essentially packaging, such as the unguent bottle BF24.23, then that would be puzzling.

TEXTILES

By John Peter Wild

THE DATA

Warrior's burial BF64

A single textile was represented in the grave (or several identical textiles). The weave was a medium fine 2/2 diamond twill, probably of wool: the diamond could be recognised on, but not drafted from, a photograph taken in the laboratory at an early stage of conservation.

System 1, presumed warp, Z-spun, 15–20 threads per cm.
System 2, presumed weft, weaker S-spun, 15–20 threads per cm.

The surface may have had a nap and was heavily felted. The fabric was much degraded. Its yarns had been preserved because the bacteria which would normally have destroyed them were poisoned by the mineral salts leaching from the copper-alloy objects to which they now adhere.
Textile remains were recorded as follows:

a) On the copper-alloy brooch (BF64.19) traces were noted in soil attached to the head, and inside the head and bow there are two patches of about 5 × 5 mm.
b) Adhering to the body of the copper-alloy jug (BF64.25) was an area of cloth measuring approximately 30 × 15 mm, and further traces on the shoulder, on the outside of the neck, beneath (and probably over) the trefoil spout and on the outer surface of the handle (approx. 2 cm^2).
c) On the copper-alloy gaming-board junction binding (BF64.29) were two patches of 5 × 5 mm and one of 10 × 10 mm.
d) Inside the bronze-lined iron shield boss (BF64.23a) were possible traces of cloth.
e) On a second copper-alloy brooch (BF64.20), minute traces of a striped fabric containing S-spun yarns in one system can be made out.

The fragments of diamond twill probably came from a cloak (or conceivably a blanket) (BF64.36) of excellent quality which once had a soft raised nap. The position of the areas of surviving textile on the jug (BF64.25) suggests that the garment had been spread over it in the burial, but the traces of cloth on the two brooches (some 1.50 m apart) were on their undersides (*see* p. 172).

On the inner surface of the shield boss (BF64.23a) was a very short length of plied cord, about 2 mm thick. It was S-plied from two strands which themselves appear to have a Z-twist. There was a hint that the strands themselves had been made by plying, but the spin-direction of the sub-strands (if any) was obscure. The cord was associated with textile fabric, possibly even as a corded starting or finishing border in the warp. This is, however, speculation.

Doctor's burial CF47

The principal textile (CF47.40) present in the grave can be characterised as a fine 2/2 twill in wool.

System 1, presumed warp, Z-spun, 20–25 threads per cm.
System 2, presumed weft, medium S-spun, approximately 25 threads per cm.

In a very small (approximately 1 cm^2) fragment of cloth (C943), now detached, but originally associated with a copper-alloy brooch (CF47.17), the Z-spun system appeared to be 'purple' in colour, whilst the S-spun threads showed no colour. The colour contrast between the two systems was clear, especially in the best-preserved area, and was probably not just an accident of survival. It might represent the vestiges of a check or striped pattern or be a uniform decorative effect across the whole textile. Too little survived for dye analysis.

Contrasting spin-directions in warp and weft are characteristic of diamond twills in Iron Age and Roman Europe, and there is accordingly a strong probability that the textile in the Doctor's burial was also a diamond twill, although no weave reversal can now be observed. One cannot, however, completely rule out the possibility that it was a plain or even spin-patterned 2/2 twill.

Textile remains were noted on many of the metal objects within the presumed wooden chest in the western sector of the burial pit (FIGS 102–3). Fabric in contact with iron objects was mineralised, while that in contact with copper-alloy objects retained more of its original substance. In many cases, the surviving traces of textile material yielded no useful information beyond the fact that it had existed. On some items, however, the weave could be identified and measurements taken, as follows:

a) On the iron handled needle from the medical *instrumentarium* (CF47.35) there was a small patch (approx. 2 cm²) of fine 2/2 twill (Z/S, 20–25/approx 25 per cm). Scanning electron microscopy by N.D. Meeks and C.R. Cartwright (p. 350; FIG. 150) has demonstrated that the twill was of wool.

b) On the iron hook (CF47.30) about 2 cm² of the same fine twill survived as a flat sheet. That, too, proved to be of wool (p. 350).

c) On the shaft of an iron scalpel (CF47.26) there were traces of twill.

d) On the broken iron handled needle (CF47.34), about 3 cm² of twill were visible together with an approximately 10 mm length of loose Z-spun yarn.

e) On an iron scalpel (CF47.27), tiny patches (the largest approx. 2 cm²) of mineralised (replaced) twill were noted, but no detail was discernible.

f) On an iron handled needle (CF47.36), mineralised fibres were visible, but no weave structure.

g) All of the iron rods stacked near the northern corner of the burial pit showed traces of replaced textile, but the only significant remains, a patch of twill measuring 4 cm² in total, were on rod CF47.23b.

h) On the copper-alloy brooch CF47.16, a length (approx. 2 mm) of slightly Z-twisted stiff off-white yarn was preserved. It resembled flax, but was not scientifically identified.

i) On two of the copper-alloy rings (CF47.24f and CF47.24g), the leather strap passing through the rings appeared to have been secured with yarn, now heavily degraded. The fibre diameters suggest that it was wool.

The nature of the original textile and its function in life and death are hard to define. It was probably a light rectangular cloak (CF47.40) of some pretension. The precise location of the surviving remains on each object was carefully plotted by the excavators (FIGS 102–3) who noted in particular whether the textile material clung to the underside, the upper side or both sides of the artefacts as they lay in the grave. Textile-bearing objects were distributed over an area of approximately 1.20 × 0.65 m, equivalent to the entire floor area of the presumed compartment at the western end of the burial pit. On balance, it seems likely that individual items were not deliberately wrapped in pieces of cloth (although that practice is attested elsewhere, *i.e.* Burns *et al.* 1996, 109, fig. 75a, b), because, on the handled needle CF47.35 and on the iron hook CF47.30, the mineralised fabric formed a flat sheet. Rather, half of the cloak may have been spread out over the floor of the pit but after the gaming board, counters, and cremated remains had been laid out (*see* p. 207), while the other half was folded over the top. That, however, is just an hypothesis.

Brooches burial CF72

Textile remains were recorded on three brooches in the cremation burial CF72. They were also noted on a knife blade and in a sample associated with a fourth brooch. They are as follows:

a) On a brass circular plate brooch (CF72.7), traces of a fine Z/S 2/2 twill, presumably of wool, were visible on the back around the pin, that is, on the lower side of the brooch as it lay in the ground. No measurement was possible, but a thread count of at least 25 × 25 threads per cm was apparent.

b) On another brass circular plate brooch (CF72.8), there were slight remains of a ?wool fabric on the pin and of associated wool yarns attached to the back of the brooch plate. They could have belonged to the same or a similar fabric to that on brooch CF47.7 above.

c) On the brass Keyhole Rosette brooch (CF72.5), there were traces of fibrous matter on the back and fragments of ?wool fibres on the front between head and spring.

d) The faint vestiges of textile on the iron knife blade (CF72.13) were not seen by the present author, nor was the material associated with a fourth brooch (CF72.6).

The only textile (CF72.15) to be positively identified in the grave is a fine 2/2 twill with a Z-spun (?warp) and an S-spun (?weft) system and a count of about 25 × 25 threads per cm in both. It was probably, but not necessarily, diamond twill. Whether the objects were individually wrapped in cloth or simply placed on or under cloth (possibly a cloak) is not self-evident from the position of the textile remains.

DISCUSSION

The textiles in all three burials are of 2/2 twill, with one thread system (probably the warp) Z-spun, the other (probably the weft) S-spun. They are comparatively light in weight, with a relatively high thread count per cm (from 15–20/15–20 to approx. 25/approx. 25 per cm). The cloth in the Warrior's burial can be seen to be a diamond twill; the other two textiles are also likely to have been diamond twills. That in the Warrior's burial seems to have had a nap; that in the Doctor's burial had 'purple' warp coupled with apparently undyed weft. All three twills were almost certainly of wool, but only for the twill in the Doctor's burial has that been proven.

The formal date of the three burials containing textiles hovers around the year of the Claudian invasion or shortly afterwards. Whatever the date of deposition, however, it is likely that the twills were woven in Britain prior to the invasion. They illustrate the growing popularity of twill and in particular of the sophisticated, subtly decorative, diamond twill in north-west Europe during the later pre-Roman Iron Age and the early Roman period (Wild and Bender Jørgensen 1988, 80–1; Bender Jørgensen 1992, 124–5, 133–5; Wild 2002, 20).

At present, finds of Iron Age textiles are concentrated by accident of survival in the La Tène cemeteries of the Yorkshire Wolds: there are few elsewhere (Crowfoot 1991; Bender Jørgensen 1992, 19–20, 198–9). Although 2/2 twill is well represented there (including Z/S twill), too little usually survives for the weave reversals indicative of diamond twill to be recorded. One remarkable find, however, from Burton Fleming (BF20) combines a Z/S diamond twill ground weave with elaborate borders in which alternating bands of 4 Z-spun and 4 S-spun yarns succeed registers of diamond twill carrying panels of simple embroidery (Crowfoot 1991, 120, fig. 79 A–C, 125). It is reminiscent of — but at the same time distinct from — the *Prachtmanteln*, 'cloaks for display', worn by aristocratic warriors in central Europe during the later Hallstatt period (Wild and Bender Jørgensen 1988, 85 with references) and in northern Europe during the Roman Iron Age (Schlabow 1976, 63–5, Abb. 116–19, Farbtab I). Yet the latter are considerably coarser than the Stanway twills. In fact, the best parallels for the fine weaves and light weights at Stanway are to be found among the fragments of military clothing from the late Flavian–Trajanic forts at Vindolanda. A number of the published pieces are closely comparable (Wild 1977, 23 no. 46, 24 no. 47); many of equal quality from the more recent excavations there remain to be published. Clothing was supplied to the garrison by weavers working in the British Iron Age tradition; 'personal imports', material on the backs of soldiers in Batavian and Tungrian units deployed to Vindolanda, came largely from the Lower Rhineland and northern Gaul where similar early weaving traditions prevailed (Wild 1993, 65–6).

The ostensibly 'purple' thread system (?warp) in the twill from the Doctor's burial can be interpreted in various ways, already mentioned above. Worth noting for comparison's sake is the lichen-dyed purple check fabric from Vindolanda (Taylor 1983, 118 no. 10/53; Wild 1977, 7–8 no. 10). The Thorsberg *Prachtmantel* of about A.D. 200 had a check pattern achieved with woad (Schlabow 1976, 63–5).

Textiles played a significant role in late prehistoric funerary practice. In the grave chamber within the Hallstatt tumulus at Hochdorf near Stuttgart, for example, not only was the chieftain laid to rest with an exceptionally high-quality wardrobe and furnishings (including wall-hangings), but each element within the chamber was carefully wrapped in cloth for its protection (Banck-Burgess 1999, 18–32, Abb. 4). The graves of the later Iron Age aristocracy of southern Britain were more modestly furnished, but almost certainly less modestly than the meagre archaeological evidence now reveals. The initial reconstruction of the lying-in-state of the local magnate in the Folly Lane *Fürstengrab* at Verulamium (Selkirk 1992, 487) is only marginally less stark than the more colourful reconstruction published later (Niblett 1999, frontispiece). For the arguably royal burial at Lexden (*c.* 15–5 B.C.), the only sign of rich furnishings are clusters of spun-gold thread of unusual fineness which may once have belonged to a gold-and-purple textile, perhaps a soft furnishing rather than a garment (Foster 1986, 92–5, pl. 21; Wild 1970, 132 H15; Wild 2002, 18). The Stanway textiles are of a different order, but match that of the other grave goods and presumably the standing of the deceased.

A SCIENTIFIC EXAMINATION OF THE TEXTILE IMPRESSIONS IN IRON CORROSION PRODUCTS ON SURGICAL INSTRUMENTS CF47.30 AND CF47.35 (FIG. 150)

By N.D. Meeks and C.R. Cartwright, Department of Scientific Research, The British Museum

Two iron instruments, CF47.30 (double-ended retractor; FIG. 120; p. 240) and CF47.35 (handled needle; FIG. 122; p. 242), with the impressions of what appear to be textile fibres in the rust-coloured corrosion products, were submitted for examination to establish the type of fibre or textile. Because of the importance of preserving the material *in situ*, no samples were taken. Thus, the corroded objects were examined directly by scanning electron microscopy (SEM), which combines high magnification and good depth of focus for clear image recording. Areas of interest were located by observation in the SEM, first at low magnification and then at high magnification, to record in detail the physical characteristics of the fibre structures for identification.

Both objects have regions on the surface, visible at low magnification (FIG. 150a), where there is evidence of a geometric texture that has the appearance of textile within the corrosion products. Where the friable corrosion products have fractured through and some surface material has been lost, this has exposed patterns of holes that take the form of the original textile fibres (FIG. 150b). The first observation is that in many cases the original fibres have disappeared, and in their place are left almost perfect negative impressions of the outer surfaces of the fibres. In some places the fibre impressions are seen in bundles that formed original threads and, where broken through transversely, show the fibres were round in section (FIG. 150c). In other areas the thread structures are fractured longitudinally (FIG. 150d). In a few places, the threads are crossed and this indicates that they were originally woven (FIGS 150b and e), although the actual weave was never clearly seen.

At high magnification, the hollow fibre moulds have clearly defined impressions of thick scales that are characteristic of wool, and this is particularly clear where the hollow tubes have been broken longitudinally (FIGS 150f–g). The scales are similar to those of Roman period sheep's wool published by Cork *et al.* (1997). The fibres range in diameter between 20 and 40 microns with a mean around 30 microns.

Thus, the solid matrix of iron corrosion products and textile fibre impressions show that the instruments were buried in close proximity to a woollen cloth. During burial the iron corroded and impregnated the textile, no doubt accelerated by the presence of sulphur in the wool. Iron corrosion products have a much larger volume than the original metal and consequently have expanded to fully surround the textile, entombing the wool fibres in a solid matrix. This occurred before the fibres themselves had been consumed by aerobic bacterial action, which has subsequently left impressions of the wool fibres as hollow tubes, with clear impressions of the characteristic scales from the original woollen fibres.

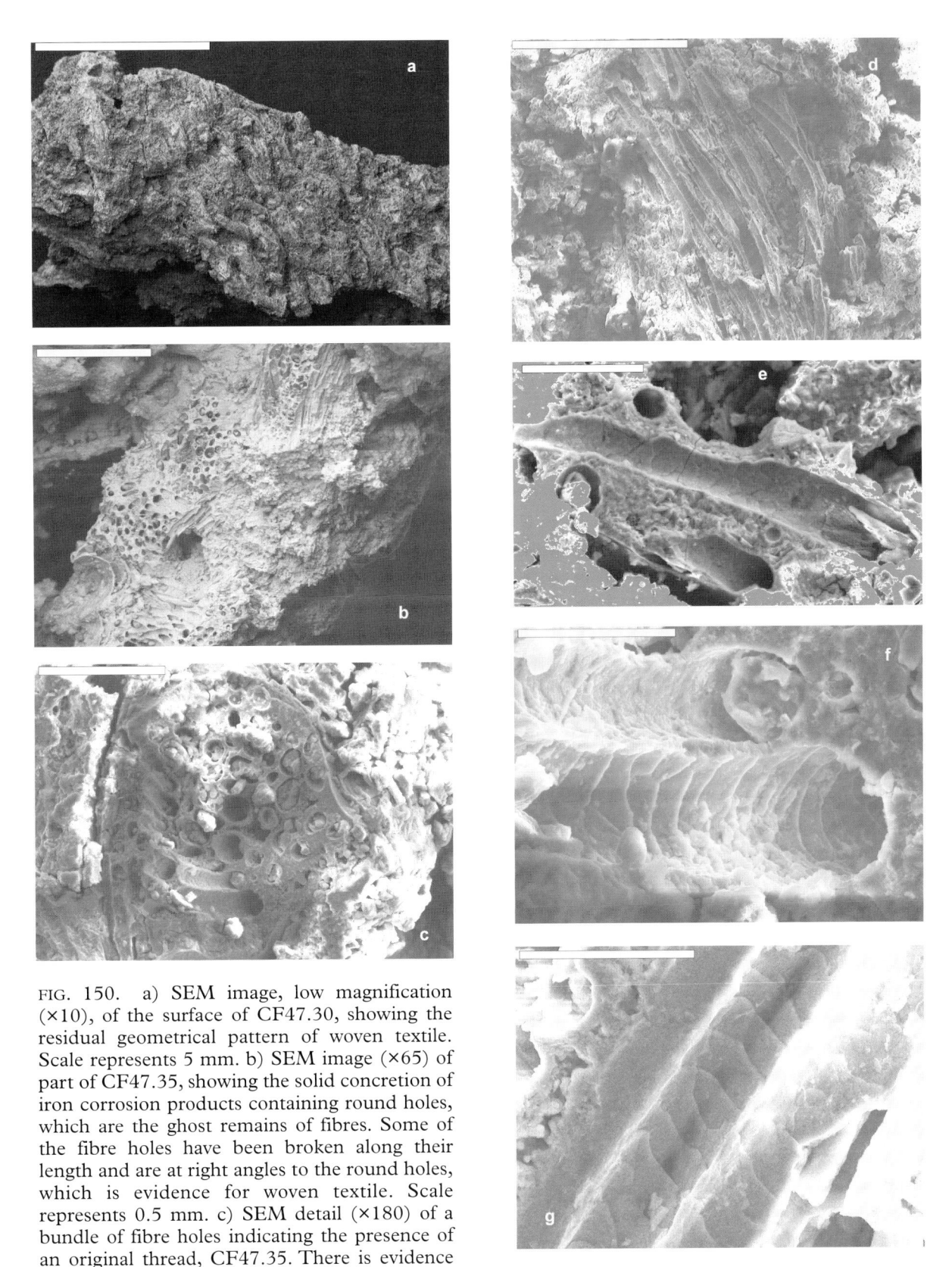

FIG. 150. a) SEM image, low magnification (×10), of the surface of CF47.30, showing the residual geometrical pattern of woven textile. Scale represents 5 mm. b) SEM image (×65) of part of CF47.35, showing the solid concretion of iron corrosion products containing round holes, which are the ghost remains of fibres. Some of the fibre holes have been broken along their length and are at right angles to the round holes, which is evidence for woven textile. Scale represents 0.5 mm. c) SEM detail (×180) of a bundle of fibre holes indicating the presence of an original thread, CF47.35. There is evidence of residual fibres in some holes. Scale represents 0.2 mm. d) SEM detail (×100) of fibre holes broken longitudinally, CF47.30. The close packing of the fibres indicates a thread. Scale represents 0.5 mm. e) SEM detail (×350) of an area where the fibres cross at right angles, indicating a woven textile. Note the wool scales moulded into the tubular wall, CF47.35. Scale represents 0.1 mm. f) SEM oblique view detail (×900) of two fibre holes broken longitudinally, showing the characteristic moulded scale marks of wool in the tube walls, CF47.35. Scale represents 0.05 mm. g) SEM detail (×1000) of wool scale marks moulded into the tubular wall of iron corrosion products, CF47.35. Scale represents 0.05 mm. Images reproduced courtesy of the Dept of Scientific Research, British Museum

The two instruments have similar concretions of iron corrosion products, which have preserved the evidence of wool fibres in the form of hollow tubes that clearly show the original surface scales of the wool. There is some evidence of a textile from the manner in which the fibres form bundles which appear to be threads, some of which lie at right angles to one another, indicating a weave. Thus, the evidence is for a woollen cloth, possibly used to wrap the instruments before burial.

THE GAMING BOARD IN CF47: THE REMAINS AS FOUND, POSSIBLE RECONSTRUCTIONS AND POST-DEPOSITIONAL MOVEMENTS
(FIGS 100, 105–6, 124, 151–4)

By Philip Crummy

The board and the gaming counters (CF47.19–20) are described here as orientated in FIGURE 151, so that the north end is referred to as 'right', the west side as 'top', and so on. The counters are referenced according to the scheme on the same figure.

AS FOUND (FIGS 105–6, 151–2)

The wood at the top left-hand corner of the board was well preserved and appears to show that, like the gaming board in the Warrior's burial, the playing surface was recessed so as to create a raised lip around the edge of the board. The lip was moulded and decorated with an incised band of chevron pattern (CF47.20a; p. 220). As will become clear, the lip is a significant feature in terms of our interpretations, since it appears to have prevented the glass gaming counters from slipping off the board after they had been set out in their 'playing' positions.

Twenty-six glass counters (CF47.19a–CF47.19b) had been placed on the board. Most of the counters lay close to the long sides of the board, with blue and white facing each other as if for a game. A few of the counters lay well away from the sides of the board, suggesting that a few preliminary moves had been made. However, these pieces may have moved for reasons which will be discussed below.

The counters lay with the curved face upwards except for one blue one (B13) which was inverted. All the counters are much the same size, except for one white counter (W13) which is markedly smaller than the others. This counter lay close to the centre of the board. A small quantity of human cremated bone had been tipped out over the left-hand side of the board. The central white counter W13 was covered by the bone, as were B4 and possibly B3, but the other counters were left clear. Three rods were then placed, partly overlapping the board. One of the large iron rods (CF47.23c) was positioned so that the flat end was near the centre and the shaft avoided any counters (FIG. 105). It looks in plan as if the rod was deliberately put to one side of the small white counter, but this is probably just a coincidence since, by this time, the counter would have been obscured by the cremated bone. The other two rods were round the other way, and seem to have been laid in the burial pit as a pair (FIG. 106). One was iron (CF47.23a) and the other copper alloy (CF47.23e). Ten of the surgical instruments were then placed on the board, and the others were spread around three of its sides (FIG. 106). Those on the board consisted of three handled needles (CF47.34, CF47.35, and CF47.36), a double hook (CF47.31), a scoop probe (CF47.37), forceps (CF47.32), a combined sharp and blunt hook (CF47.29), an unidentified instrument (CF47.38), a scalpel (CF47.26), and a saw (CF47.28) which was in pieces by this stage. The instruments around the board consisted of a scalpel (CF47.27), forceps (CF47.33), a combined sharp and blunt hook (CF47.30), and a knife (CF47.39).

DIMENSIONS AND PROPORTIONS OF THE BOARD (FIGS 151, 153)

The board measures approximately 385 by 565 mm, which is close to a ratio of 2:3. If, as the counters seem to indicate, there were twelve squares along the length of the board, then its proportions suggest that there were eight squares across its width. Interestingly, an 8 × 12 grid of squares each measuring exactly 1.75 *unciae* across seems to accord with the positions of the

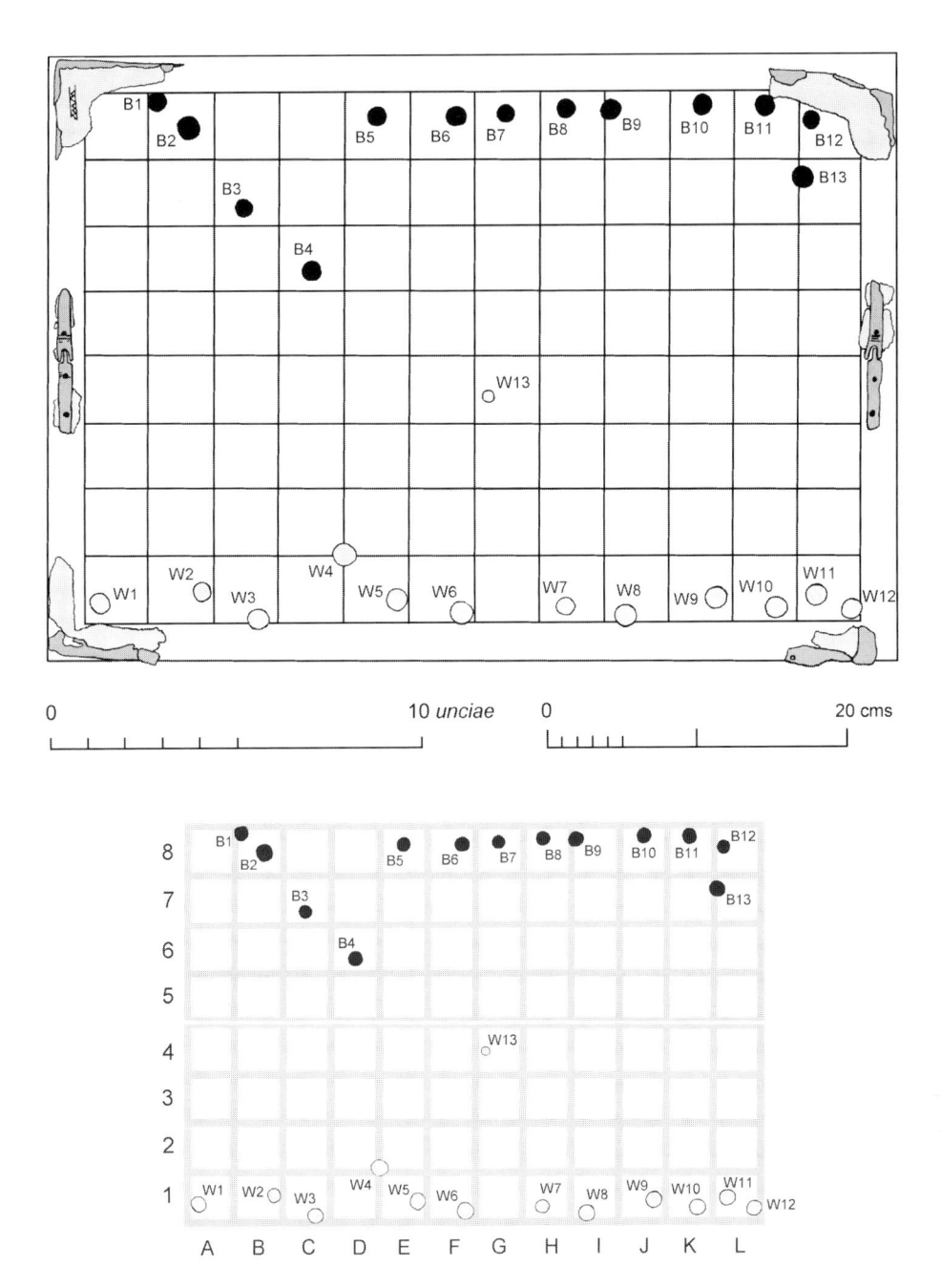

FIG. 151. Above: The counters and the remains of the gaming board in relation to a hypothetical 8 × 12 grid of 1 3/4 *unciae* squares. Below: The layout of the counters in relation to the same grid after allowing for a slight gap between the two halves of the board when folded out

pieces and corners very neatly (FIG. 151, above). (The distance in the reconstruction between the edge of the grid and the edge of the board is assumed to have been one *uncia*. This assumption seems likely in view of the position and sizes of the hinges and corner pieces, but there is no certainty.) Enough survives of the top left-hand corner of the board to suggest that the edges of such a grid as this must have been very close to, if not hard up against, the lip.

The reconstruction takes as its starting point the pins in the hinges, and assumes that they aligned with the longitudinal centre-line of the postulated grid. It looks from the reconstruction as if three or so of the white counters would have overlapped the edge of the grid suggesting that the grid needs to be moved away from them by a few millimetres. However, this would mean that the centre-line of the grid would not have aligned correctly with the hinges. Instead, it may be that there was a gap of a few millimetres between the two halves of the board when it was opened out, and this could explain the apparent imbalance (FIG. 151, below).

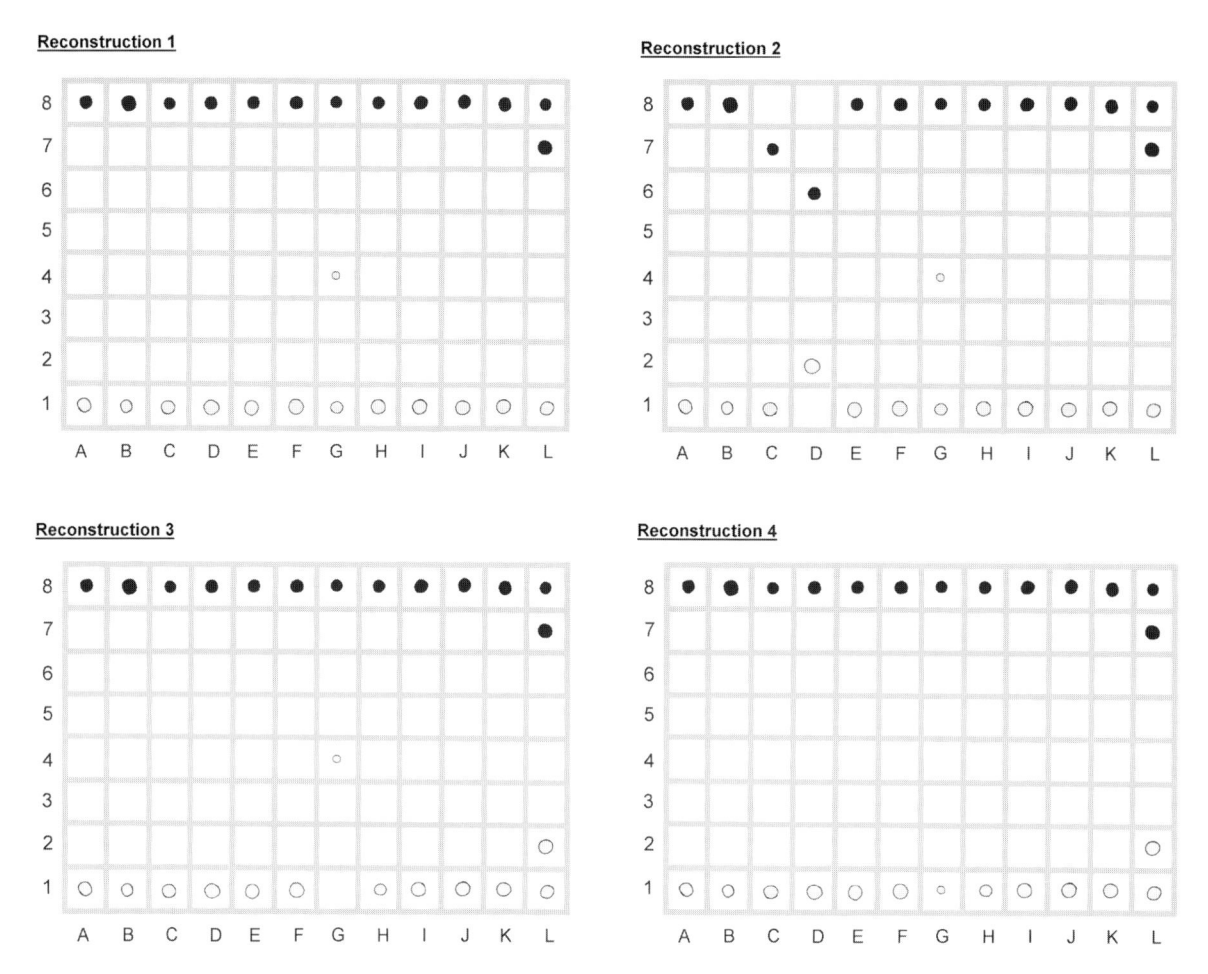

FIG. 152. Four possible arrangements of the counters on an 8 × 12 grid of squares before any post-depositional movements had taken place

Dr Schädler also believes that the inclusion of a thirteenth anomalous piece in each set of counters introduces the possibility that the playing surface had been marked with either a grid of 9 × 13 squares (despite his reservation about the existence of latticed rectangular boards) or a grid of lines providing a 9 × 13 grid of intersections. (The counters could have been placed in the middle of the squares or at the intersections of lines.) A hypothetical grid of 9 × 13 squares is shown in FIGURE 153. The length of the grid here has been taken to equal 21 *unciae* (as in the 8 × 12 grid), but the widths of the squares produced by such a grid (*i.e.* $1^{8}/_{13}$ *unciae*) would have been awkward to mark out when the board was being made unlike the much more practical $1^{3}/_{4}$ *unciae* wide squares needed for the 8 × 12 grid. A grid of 9 × 13 lines need not be so problematic, although the difficulty of having to divide up an area into thirteen equal parts still applies. A grid at intervals of $1^{5}/_{8}$ *unciae* was used to construct the grid shown on FIGURE 153 below. There is nothing about the board which suggests that the grid was laid out on this basis: it is just that a grid of this size sits fairly nicely in the space formed by the hinges and corner pieces and this would get around the problem of division into thirteen parts. However, divisions based on 13 lines or 13 squares cannot produce grids which fit the board as well as the 8 × 12 grid, and the post-depositional movement would need to have been much greater than with the 8 × 12 grid to explain the final positions of the counters. With the 9 × 13 squares (FIG. 153, above), seven or eight of the blue counters (B1, B6–B12, and ?B13) need to have moved into the adjacent square on the right, and eight of the white counters (W4–W11) need to have done the same. With the 8 × 12 grid on the other hand, the movements would have been much less with only five whites (W7–W11) and one blue (B1) needing to jump squares. Greater post-depositional movement required by a 9 × 13 grid does not in itself rule out such an arrangement, but it does add weight to the view that the 8 × 12 grid is the most likely layout.

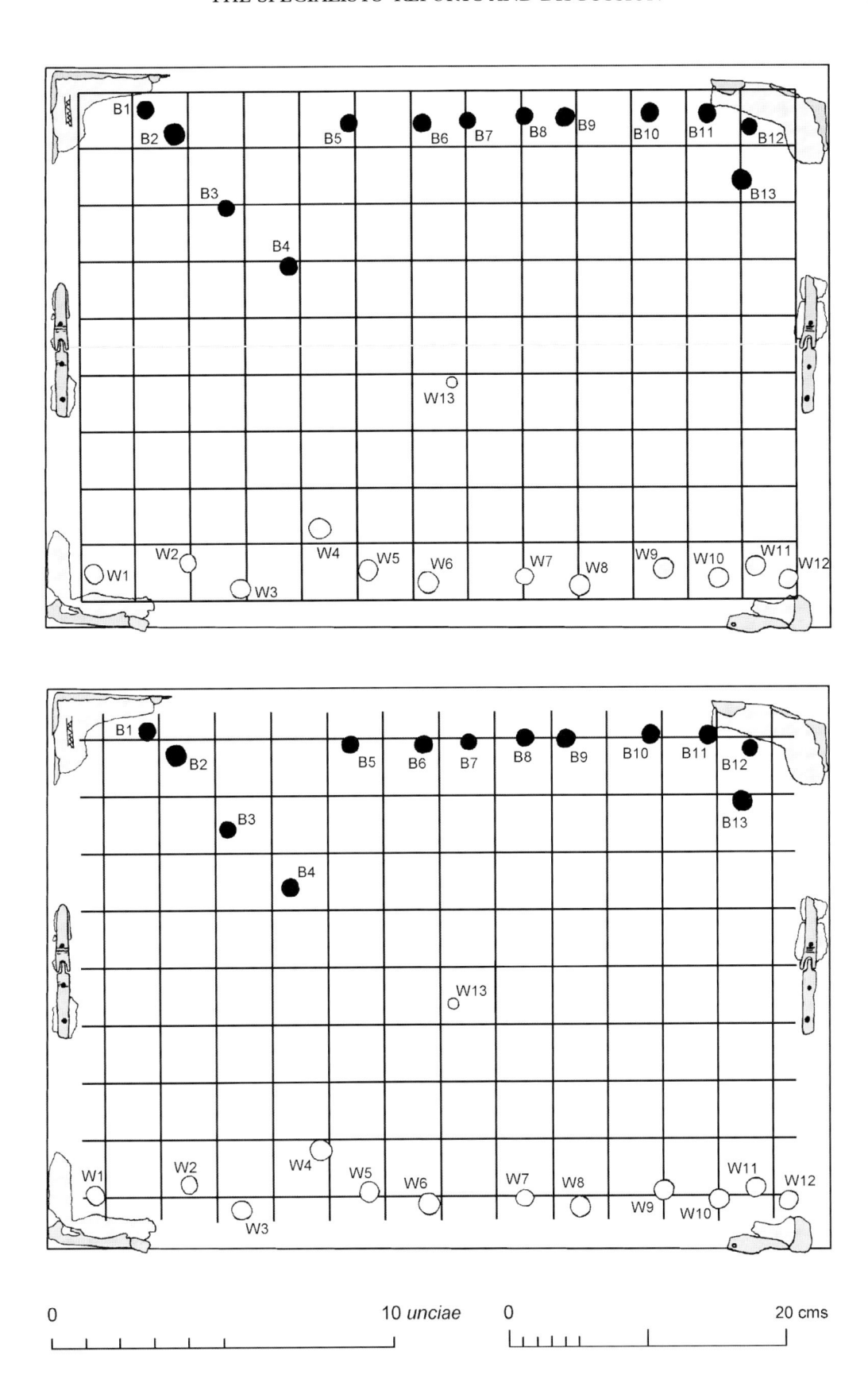

FIG. 153. Above: The counters and the remains of the gaming board in relation to a hypothetical 9 × 13 grid of squares whose width (left to right) is equal to the width of the hypothetical 8 × 12 grid shown in FIG. 151. Below: The remains of the gaming board as found in relation to a hypothetical 9 × 13 grid of lines exactly 15/8 *unciae* apart

POST-DEPOSITIONAL MOVEMENTS OF BOARD AND PIECES (FIGS 100, 124, 151)

The distribution of the counters and their relationships to the putative grid suggest that there was significant movement of the pieces after they were set out on the board and any moves made. If we are to reconstruct the original layout of the counters, we need to identify and discuss the ways in which the counters might have subsequently moved. In these considerations, it is important to bear in mind the sequence in which the items were laid on the board. The spatial relationships between the rods and the surgical instruments show that the rods must have been placed on the board before the instruments, and the placing of the instruments and rods must post-date the deposit of cremated bone because some of them lay on top of fragments of bone. In short, the order of deposition on the board was as follows: the counters, the cremated bone, the three rods, and the surgical instruments. (The sequence is discussed further on p. 207.)

The post-depositional movements are most apparent in the positions of the white counters (FIG. 151). These pieces are bunched to the right of the board, with W2, W3, W4, W5, W6, W9, W10 and W12 all seeming to have moved to the right. The blue counters fit the grid much better and show much less evidence of displacement. Only one (B1) can be said to have clearly moved. Two others (B9 and B12) may also have shifted a little, although they still might be in their original positions if the pieces were not carefully centred on their squares when they were set out. The relatively limited movement of the blue counters may be because something was placed on top of them, such as clothing, which reduced the chances of subsequent lateral movement. Conceivably, all but B1 of the blue counters could have been covered in this way.

Four possible mechanisms can be postulated to explain the movements. They are described in order of likelihood, starting with the greatest.

a) movements when the grave goods and cremated bone were being deposited
The board could have been accidentally jolted as other items were being laid on it. This seems a likely explanation for the bunching of the white pieces. A sharp knock horizontally at the bottom right-hand side of the board could have made the white pieces slide sideways towards the right. (In reality, the board would have moved to the left, but the counters would tend to stay still.) Also some of the counters could have been moved accidentally as items were being laid on the board. The advanced positions of B3 and B4 might in reality be a consequence of the two counters being dragged across the board when the cremated bone was being deposited on it.

b) movements when the burial pit was being backfilled
The crushed vessels at the other end of the grave seem to show that the burial rite involved stamping or jumping on the burial cover at a very early stage in the backfilling process, if not immediately before it started (p. 212). Vibration caused by these actions could have caused the counters to move. Also, the throwing of soil on top of the burial cover during the early stage of the backfilling might have had the same effect, particularly if the gaming board was in a void.

c) vertical movements as the board decayed
All the counters must have moved vertically downwards as the wooden board decayed to nothing. The floor of the burial pit would not have been flat. It would have been irregular with many little depressions and bumps because of the high gravel content in the natural. The vertical distance dropped by each of the counters would have been equal to the thickness of the board plus the depth of any depression immediately underneath it. The movement must have been very slow, maybe lasting several centuries.

The gaming board is likely to have been buried in a void which was created by a wooden cover over the burial (p. 207). If the void survived long enough, then there may also have been some lateral movement of the counters and fittings as the rotting wood cracked, shrank, curled and distorted. If there was no void, then sideways movement caused by the decaying board would have been minimal, because the material above the counters and board would have dropped as the counters dropped and so continued to hold them in place.

d) movements when the grave was being archaeologically excavated

We need to consider if some or parts of the apparent movements are not real, but a product of the process of excavation and recording. The gaming board and everything on it was uncovered very carefully over a period of a few weeks. The white counters could be confused with pieces of gravel as they were being uncovered, so the excavation had to proceed slowly, and care was taken not to disturb any of the counters so that an accurate and reliable record could be made of their positions in the ground. Lisa Hepi, helped by David Burnand, managed to complete the task with great skill and patience. The recorded positions of the counters and the metal fittings of the board have since been carefully checked against the sequence of photographs taken throughout their excavation, and no significant variations have been found. We are therefore confident that FIGURE 151 represents a reliable record of the relative positions of the counters and fittings.

The only problem is the top left-hand corner of the board. This was the first corner to be uncovered, and it was removed for conservation almost as soon as it was found. Had this not happened, then we probably would not have known about the band of chevron pattern on the lip of the board. However, its removal introduced an uncertainty about the precise position of the corner in relation to everything else. On a few occasions, the corner was put back in the grave for photography, but it was difficult to do this accurately, as a careful comparison of FIGURES 100 and 126 shows.

THE INVERTED COUNTER B13

The counter B13 was the only one which lay upside down. It was carefully and slowly uncovered with a small brush, and we are certain that the counter was not accidentally turned over during the excavation. Thus in antiquity either the counter had been deliberately placed upside down on the board or, somehow, it flipped over by chance. The former explanation seems the more likely by far. The counter is unlikely to have turned upside down as the board rotted. The process of decay would have been too gradual and even to allow a sufficiently deep cavity to develop under the counter to the extent that the counter could have tipped down and flipped over. If the counter ended up inverted by chance, then it probably rolled off and under the board when the objects were being laid on it. Perhaps the jolt which moved the white counters to the right was violent enough to send B13 off the board or flip it upside down on the board. The same jolt could also have moved B1 to the right, but, as mentioned above, the other blue counters were hardly affected by such a jolt because they were held in place by something organic laid on top of them.

Curiously, B13 was the last counter to be found, but this fact cannot be taken to imply that it had been under the board. Presumably, having its curved side downwards, the counter settled neatly into a depression in the floor directly under it after the board had rotted away completely, which is why it seemed to be the lowest of the counters.

LAYOUT OF THE GAME BASED ON AN 8 × 12 GRID OF SQUARES (FIGS 106, 152)

Broadly, four reconstructions of the positions of the counters prior to any post-depositional movements can be offered on the basis that the board had been marked out with an 8 × 12 grid of squares (FIG. 152). For these four reconstructions, each player is taken to have had twelve standard pieces plus one of different rank. White's thirteenth piece (W13) is differentiated by its size, whereas Blue's thirteenth piece (B13), being the same size as the others, had to be inverted.

In Reconstructions 1 and 2, it is assumed that each player laid out twelve pieces along their starting ranks, and each chose where to place their thirteenth piece, *i.e.* W13 on G4 and B13 on L7. Reconstruction 2 is a development of Reconstruction 1 in that a few opening moves in a game are supposed, *i.e.* B4 to D6, W4 to D2, and B3 to C7. (The first and last moves are interchangeable.) Reconstruction 3 is like Reconstruction 1, except that it has the virtue of needing less post-depositional movement to account for the bunching of the white counters.

Reconstruction 4 supposes that W13 was accidentally moved from G1 to G4, presumably when other objects were being deposited in the grave but before or during the deposition of the cremated bone. Such an exceptionally large movement might be possible, because W13 is the lightest of the counters, and any accidental movement which involved a knock could have resulted in this counter moving farther than any of the others. Nevertheless, Reconstruction 4 does not seem likely, because i) the magnitude of the assumed post-depositional movement of W13 seems to be too great when compared with the others, ii) the direction of the movement is not shared by others, and iii) it seems too much of a coincidence that the post-depositional movement of W13 turned out to be along File G.

Reconstructions 1, 3 and 4 all require B3 and B4 to have moved accidentally. Since these counters are unlikely to have moved much horizontally after the deposition of the bone, then the most likely occasion for the movement was when the bone was deposited.

The final position of W11 militates against Reconstructions 3 and 4, and favours Reconstructions 1 and 2 instead. This is because the counter does not seem to be far enough into the board, but is on a level with W9.

It is noticeable how the ends of three of the instruments (*i.e.* the combined sharp and blunt hook CF47.29, the copper-alloy forceps CF47.32, and the scoop probe CF47.37) lie between blue counters without making contact with them (FIG. 106). This seems to suggest that the board was not knocked hard after the instruments were placed on top of it.

In conclusion, it is clear that the counters were arranged in an order on the board which was not random, but post-depositional movements have obscured the layout to such a degree that it can now be only tentatively reconstructed and to a limited extent. Assuming an 8 × 12 grid, the most likely reconstructions seem to be Reconstructions 1 and 2, with Reconstruction 1 having the edge on 2, but it must be allowed that other reconstructions are possible of which Reconstructions 3 and 4 are perhaps the two most obvious. The nature and time of the post-depositional movements are obscure and the evidence is ambivalent. However, it would appear that most of the largest of them took place before or during the deposition of the cremated bone.

LAYOUT OF THE GAME BASED ON A 9 × 13 GRID OF SQUARES OR LINES (FIG. 154)

Two alternative layouts are presented in FIGURE 154 for a grid of 9 × 13 squares. These seem to be the simplest and most likely, but other permutations are possible involving B3, B4, and W13. (The diagram only shows squares but the pattern of counters on the intersections of a 9 × 13 grid of lines would of course be the same.) As already explained, a layout based on a 9 × 13 grid does not seem very likely. This is because a grid of this nature does not lend itself easily to the size and shape of the board as indicated by the positions of the hinges and corner pieces, and it would imply greater post-depositional movements than with an 8 × 12 grid. However, Dr Schädler makes the case that a 9 × 13 grid would be a realistic possibility when the evidence is viewed from the perspective of the current knowledge and understanding of ancient games especially in western Europe and the Roman world (pp. 361–2).

IDENTIFICATION OF THE GAME

On pages 365–75, Ulrich Schädler considers the possible identification of the game which could have been played on the board and concludes that the most likely answer is not *ludus latrunculorum* or any other Roman import but an early form of the game which appears later in Ireland as *fidchcheall* and in Wales as *gwyddbwyll*. He highlights the rectangular shape of the board, the relatively low number of counters in relation to its size, and the inclusion in each side of a thirteenth piece apparently of different rank as features combining to present problems with the identification of the game or games which could be played on it. Dr Schädler contends that rectangular gaming boards of the Roman period appear more likely to have been for the game of *XII scripta* than for *ludus latrunculorum*. Unlike *XII scripta*, *ludus latrunculorum* needed a grid of squares, but the boards were generally square in shape or at least close to it, and the ratio of counters to squares was much higher than appears to have been the case with the Stanway board (assuming it to have been latticed).

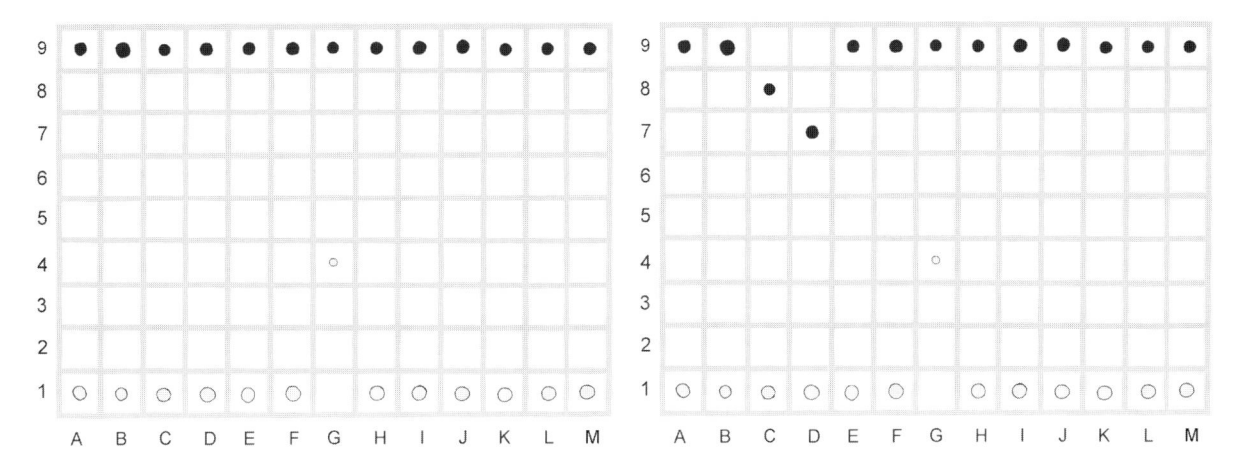

FIG. 154. Two possible arrangements of the counters on an 9 × 13 grid of squares before any post-depositional movements had taken place

Dr Schädler also makes the point that, as far as can be gauged, rectangular boards like the one in the Doctor's burial, with its width to length ratio of about 2:3 or more, were not latticed. However, all three boards which he cites from Britain as having measurable dimensions (*i.e.* the Doctor's burial at Stanway, Grave 117 at King Harry Lane (Stead and Rigby 1989, 109) and Burial 6 at Baldock (Stead and Rigby 1986, 68–9)) are likely to have been broadly of the same type and may even be from the same workshop, thereby opening up the possibility that they represent a type of board and game not recognised before. Although these boards were not identical (they did not all have metal corner pieces and handles), various features bind them together as a group, *i.e.* a) all three were hinged, b) at least two (Stanway and Baldock) were made of maple, the wood of the third being unidentified, c) Baldock and Stanway were very similar in size and shape, and King Harry Lane could have been the same (same length as the other two but of indeterminate width), and d) leather traces were found on the boards at Stanway and King Harry Lane. All three were found in the territory of the Catuvellauni (and we include Camulodunum in this), although this relatively tight distribution might simply be the result of chance. Thus the three boards, plus those in the Warrior's burial and in Chamber BF6 (pp. 126, 186–90) and the possible board in Grave 309 at King Harry Lane (Stead and Rigby 1989, 109–10, figs 108, 152), could have been part of a distinctive British body of artefacts linked to a specific game popular among a group of Britons in the south-east of the country with strong connections with the nearby Romanised Continent. The case for *fidhcheall* needs to be balanced against the fact that Roman counters and boards in the possession of Romanised Britons provides strong evidence in favour of the playing of a Roman game of some sort.

THE DOCTOR'S GAME — NEW LIGHT ON THE HISTORY OF ANCIENT BOARD GAMES (TABLES 55–6)

By Ulrich Schädler

THE BOARD

To judge from the position of the metal corners and hinges, the game board found in the Doctor's burial was a rectangular wooden board of approximately 385 × 565 mm, which was to be folded thanks to the hinges in the middle of the short sides. In contrast to some other gaming boards, it had no handle.

Gaming boards with metal fittings, sometimes provided with a handle, have come to light at Stanway itself as well as at various other places, as follows.

1) The Warrior's burial in Enclosure 3 produced counters and the remains of another gaming board. The board consisted of two parts, but, in contrast to the Doctor's board, the Warrior's

one was not to be folded (at least no metal hinges were found) and had two identical copper-alloy handles (BF64.29a and BF64.29b). The handles are characterised by grooves, a bead between discs in the centre, and recurved terminals each capped by a boss (for comparisons, *see* Allason-Jones 1988, 167, fig. 79, 78; Allason-Jones and Miket 1984, 164, cat. 3.413; Bushe-Fox 1928, pl. 21, fig. 1, 45; Hawkes and Hull 1947, pl. 100, 3; Riha 2001, pl. 8, no. 99, 28–30 with footnote 57).

2) At Baldock, the late Flavian burial no. 6 produced two metal hinges, which were found open lying parallel to each other at a distance of 520 mm. A bronze drop-handle was found near the centre of the presumed third edge of the wooden board to which the hinges once belonged (Stead and Rigby 1986, 63ff, no. 13, 14, 16, figs 28, 30). From the position of the handle relative to the presumed centre of the board given by the hinges, it can be inferred that the board had rectangular proportions with a width of about 400 mm, whereas the length must have been slightly more than 560 mm (distance of the hinges plus their width of 20 mm and 14 mm respectively). These proportions are very close if not identical to those of the game-board in the Doctor's burial at Stanway measuring approximately 385 × 565 mm. Although joints of meat covered what was once the wooden board at Baldock, it is unlikely that the board was used as a tray as suggested by the excavators, since hinges to fold a board and only one handle would not make much sense for a tray. Presumably the metal fittings belonged to a game-board.

3) Bronze corner fittings are also known from Heiligenhafen, Germany (Krüger 1982, 242, fig. 47.3–5). Remains of the corner fittings of a wooden board, 58 white and black glass gaming counters, all upside down, and one die were found placed on the legs of the deceased.

4) In a rich Germanic 'Fürstengrab' of the 3rd century A.D. at Gommern (Elbe), Germany, 24 dark glass counters, metal corners, and the handle of a game-board came to light (Fröhlich 2001, 158s). Unfortunately, they were irregularly dispersed over a limited area.

5) At Neudorf-Bornstein, Germany, several wooden boards in graves dating to the 3rd and 4th centuries have been detected. In grave no. 4 (Schäfer 1968, 49 with fig.), three boards lay one above the other. One board was easily recognisable from the wooden remains with four metal corners still in position showing that the board was rectangular and measured approximately 440 × 760 mm. (Information kindly provided by Ingo Gabriel, Schleswig.) Of a second board, only two metal corner fittings at a distance of approximately 600 mm were found. Between the limits of this board and the former, there were 24 black and 18 white glass counters. Their arrangement suggests that they were not disposed on one of the two boards mentioned, but on a third. A few counters lay in a row, while most of them were scattered irregularly over the ground. It therefore seems that the pieces had been disturbed later. A small bronze handle belonged to one of the boards.

6) The remains of a board with pieces were also found in grave 7 (Schäfer 1968, 57, fig. 12). The rectangular board measured 360 × 440 mm. (Information kindly provided by Ingo Gabriel, Schleswig.) It had bronze corners and a bronze handle. Twenty-six glass counters (18 blue, 3 green, 2 brown and 3 white) were lying on the board in somewhat irregular rows.

7) At Lullingstone, a wooden board with bronze angle pieces dated to the 4th century appears to have been 470 mm square (Meates 1979, 129–30, pl. 24).

8) At the Viking-age site of Birka, Sweden, the iron fittings of three boards survived (Arbmann 1940, grave 58B, 205, no. 624, 886). The board in grave no. 886 (*hnefatafl*) had a raised rim (*ibid.*, pl. 146, 1a), similar to the game board for *XII scripta/alea* found at Qustul (Schädler 1995, 80).

9) A game-board with two handles — one at each of the long sides — is also known from Ephesus, where a *XII scripta/alea*-board measuring 390 × 490 mm (without handles) was carved into a marble table plate from one of the 'Hanghäuser'. The gaming table represents the only game-board ever found in a Roman house. It dates to before the middle of the 3rd century, when the roof of the building collapsed. The engraving suggests a wooden board with the two omega-shaped metal handles fixed by two nails to the outer sides of the board. The gaming table is kept in the museum at Selçuk.

THE BOARD — 8 BY 12 SQUARES?

The general proportions of the board as indicated by the metal fittings and the position of the counters in more or less regular rows along the long edges of the board suggested a preliminary reconstruction of the playing surface as one with 8 by 12 squares (pp. 352–3). But much too easily, one may be caught in the trap of a circular argument. Neither is the position of the pieces an *a priori* indication for the design of the board, since we do not know if they were placed in any position relative to the board or game. As an example for a purely decorative positioning of the counters, compare the find from Leuna (*see* below). Nor can the fact that one white counter is much smaller than the others and one blue counter turned upside down *a priori* be taken as an argument for 12 squares, since the assumption that these two counters are extra pieces is not established beyond doubt and depends on presumed rules of the unknown game.

First of all, we do not know if the board did have an orthogonal grid at all. During the Doctor's lifetime, *i.e.* the first half of the 1st century A.D., different designs of game-boards existed in the ancient world. It may suffice to draw attention to the Roman *XII scripta/alea*-boards (Schädler 1995), the Greek 5-lines-boards consisting of parallel lines (Schädler 1999), or the presumed Roman game-board from Augst (Schädler 2002a) with a totally different layout.

A fairly large number of ancient gaming boards with orthogonal grids has come to light all over the Graeco-Roman world, many of which are from Roman Britain. Without listing all the known boards of this type, it can be observed that complete ones normally have 7 × 7, 7 × 8, 9 × 9, or 9 × 10 squares, and very often 8 × 8 squares (Schädler 1994, 50). A board with 11 × 12 squares incised into the surface of a former architectural marble block can be seen in the sanctuary of Hera on the island of Samos, and a further board with 8 × 8 squares of unknown date has been uncovered in the northern cryptoportico of the agora at ancient Smyrna (Izmir). Depictions of real game-boards may be added. A terracotta group dating to the 1st century in the National Museum at Athens shows two persons playing a game on a board with 6 × 7 squares (Bursian 1855, 55–6; Michaelis 1863; Richter 1887, 100–3, figs 48–9; Schädler 1994, 51 with fig. on p. 53). A terracotta model of a similar board with 6 × 7 squares and 17 pieces in two colours was found by Flinders Petrie in a grave dating to the Roman period in the Egyptian Fayyum (Petrie 1927, 55 pl. 48, no. 177; Schädler 2002b, 98, fig. 1).

With these last objects having been found in the Greek east, the game depicted was presumably the game πόλ(ε)ιζ ('city' or 'cities') mentioned by Pollux (*Onomastikon* IX 98) in the 2nd century A.D., a game with the same interception method of capture as the Roman *ludus latrunculorum* and therefore supposedly more or less identical with this last (Schädler 2002b, 99). The finds clearly demonstrate that the counters were placed in the squares and not on the points of intersection of the lines. This is also indicated by Pollux, who says that the game πόλ(ε)ιζ 'has fields bounded by lines', as well as by Varro (*De lingua latina*, 10, 12) who compares a declination table (with six columns for singular and plural in all the three genders and six lines for the cases) to a gaming board for *ludus latrunculorum*. We can therefore conclude that at least those two ancient board games were played on the squares.

Having said this, the first observation to be made is that the proportions of latticed game-boards are usually square or close to square, *i.e.* n:n or n:n+1 where n is the number of squares in rank and file. On the other hand, a 1:1 ratio of squares does not automatically imply that the proportions of the board itself were square too. A board with 8 × 8 squares from Chedworth, for example, measures 254 × 178 mm (*Trans. Bristol Glos. Arch. Soc.* 45, 1923, 285). Many game-boards, especially those carved into pavements or roof tiles, exhibit decidedly rectangular 'squares'. However, it seems that with gaming-boards of finer workmanship, such as the marble board formerly at Zurich (May 1991, 175, fig. 169), care was taken to create square fields. Therefore the assumption that, if there was an orthogonal grid of lines on the Doctor's board, these lines created squares of equal length and width is plausible, although not as obvious as it seems at first sight. On the other hand the assumption of square fields would lead to an unusual and hitherto unique ratio of the game-board of 2n:3n or n:n+4 squares in rank and file.

The general proportions of the Doctor's board measuring approximately 385 × 565 mm, giving a ratio of width to length of 0.68, are more consistent with Roman *XII scripta/alea*-boards, composed of three parallel rows of two groups of six spaces. Gaming boards of this type are normally rectangular, usually with a ratio of width to length of about 2:3. Two examples among many others may be quoted relating to boards from Damous-al-Kharita (Tunisia), measuring 490 × 720 mm and 470 × 660 mm respectively, thus giving proportions of 0.68 and 0.71 respectively (Delattre 1911, 12). A board in the Roman catacombs of St Tecla measures 460 × 620 mm (Ferrua 1964, 3, n. 133), and therefore has a ratio of 0.74. At Ephesus, a board carefully incised into a marble block measures approximately 550 × 815 mm including the raised rim, giving a ratio of 0.67 (Börker and Merkelbach 1979, 226, n. 536). The famous board from Trier (Horn 1989, 154) measures 420 × 700 mm with a ratio of 0.6. And a board scratched into the pavement of the Tower of the Winds at Athens (Schädler 1995) measures approximately 370 × 600 mm, *i.e.* a ratio of 0.61. The well-known board for beginners from Ostia (*CIL* XIV 5317) measures roughly 180 × 290 mm, and has therefore a proportion of 0.62. There are also some boards which are close to square, such as the board from Holt, Denbighshire (Austin 1938, 250), measuring 432 × 486 mm (0.88), and a few others with even more elongated proportions, such as the board from Porta Portese in the British Museum measuring 370 × 820 mm (Austin 1938, 250; May 1991, 178, fig. 175).

What might argue against a reconstruction of the Doctor's board as a board for *XII scripta/alea* is the number of pieces, since that game was played with 15 black and 15 white counters. Moreover it was played with dice, which have not been found in the Doctor's burial. And finally the position of the pieces on the board does not correspond to the layout of the game, since we have pieces in the middle of both long sides, exactly where the *XII scripta/alea* boards have an ornament dividing the twelve spaces of each row into groups of six. However, all the three arguments are not convincing enough to discard the possibility completely: the number of gaming counters might not represent a complete set. As a matter of fact, complete sets of counters have been found only in rare and exceptional cases (*see* below concerning the problem of complete sets). At Leuna for example, 59 counters have been found together with a board bearing a grid of lines on one side and a *XII scripta/alea*-pattern on the other – nearly twice the number of counters needed to play *XII scripta/alea*, and nonetheless obviously incomplete. Dice, normally made of bone and often very small, may have decayed. Also, the pieces may have been placed just along the edges of the board and not on regular fields.

Secondly, a closer look at the position of the counters demonstrates that they do not lie as orderly as it may seem at a first glance. In fact, there must have been considerable movement of the pieces after their initial laying out on the board (*see* above). It is the number and position of the counters in particular which may make the reconstruction of a game played with twice 13 pieces on 8 × 12 squares questionable. There are definitely 13 pieces on both sides of the board. With only 12 squares in one direction and an assumed starting position of 12 pieces in a row, one piece would have to be placed in front of the others. But since 12 is an even number, there would not be a natural place for it, such as a central column. The 13th piece would always come to be placed on an undefined field. The difference between 12 and 13 places in a row is not just quantitative. An odd number of places would create a central column, which is absent on even-numbered boards. On the other hand, the small white counter was placed centrally such that it was flanked by six white pieces, which makes it possible if not likely that the board had 13 spaces in longitudinal direction. Therefore we should take the possibility into account that, if the board did have an orthogonal grid of lines, the counters were placed either on squares formed by a grid of 9 × 13 (FIG. 153, above) rather than 8 × 12 lines or on the intersections of a 9 × 13 grid of lines (FIG. 153, below). Yet another possible explanation would of course be that the counters did not belong to the game-board on the side of the board they were placed upon, but perhaps to a game depicted on the reverse side. Game-boards with two different games on both sides are known from various written sources as well as from archaeological finds.

THE POSITION OF THE COUNTERS — A STARTING POSITION?

The more or less orderly alignment of almost all the counters along the opposite edges of the game-board with only very few exceptions raises the question whether or not the position of the pieces represents the start of a game with only a few moves being already made (Parlett 1999, 236). However, we must be careful in interpreting the layout of the pieces on the board. The interpretation of the position of the counters as a starting position requires some previous assumptions: one has to assume that the person who set out the counters on the board had a particular game in mind when doing so, that he knew that game, and that the number of pieces represents a complete set of counters necessary for it. We have no clues to answer any of these questions. The intention of placing the counters in rows could have been simply to create an orderly arrangement instead of throwing all the counters randomly on to the surface. In grave III/1926 at Leuna, Germany, for example, the pieces were laid out in an ornamental pattern completely independent from the game-board. To judge from one square still preserved at the time of excavation, it could be concluded that the upper side of the board had an orthogonal grid with 13 squares in one direction. Twenty-six out of 30 white and 29 dark stones had been set out in alternate groups of three black or white pieces along one edge and the two adjacent corners of the board to make 18 in a row (Schulz 1953, 22, fig. 37, 28ff). The position of the counters may thus have no relation at all to the game proper.

Several counters on the Doctor's game-board do not stand in line with the others. This may be either because they have been moved or the result of a hard push against the board or by the deposition of the cremated bone or other grave goods. If they were placed like this on purpose, one would raise the question why more than one move has been executed. Assuming that the rook's move was applied, Black would have moved twice (with B3 and B4). If the pieces moved only one square at a time, Black would have had three moves (B3 from C8 to C7, B4 from D8 to D7, and from D7 to D6), and White according to the reconstruction preferred three (FIG. 152: Reconstructions 1 and 3) or even four times (FIG. 152: Reconstruction 2).

Finally, as a more general reflection it can be observed that the experience with chess and draughts sometimes leads to the premature assumption that a board game would naturally require a starting position. This is not the case. According to our knowledge, the board games known in antiquity only rarely had a starting position. The literary sources never describe any such arrangement. Only the ancient Greek board game conventionally called *'pente grammai'* ('five lines'), according to depictions on Greek vases, Etruscan mirrors and a terracotta model at Copenhagen, seems to have had one, in that all the pieces were placed on the opposite ends of the parallel lines (Schädler 1998, 16–17; Schädler 1999, 42). No such initial position is known from Roman board games. It has often been taken for granted that *ludus latrunculorum* had a starting position in opposite lines, but especially in the light of *Laus Pisonis*, the most detailed description of the game dating to the 1st century A.D., this assumption can be ruled out with a fair degree of plausibility (cf. Schädler 1994, 52). The author of *Laus Pisonis* describes the beginning of the game with the following words: '*callidiore modo tabula variatur aperta calculus...*', translated by Roland Austin (1935, 30) as 'cunningly the pieces are disposed on the open board'. All six words in this short phrase strongly speak against a fixed initial arrangement and in favour of the possibility for the players to choose where to place the pieces: '*callidiore modo*', '*variatur calculus*' and '*tabula aperta*'. A standard position of counters with equal strength does certainly not offer the possibility to place the pieces in an 'intelligent way' (*callidiore modo*). Moreover the term '*variatur*' clearly means 'distribute' and not 'arrange pieces in a straight line or order'. And finally the 'open board' (*tabula aperta*) does not refer to a folding board opened, but indicates that the playing area was empty at the start. To understand better the meaning of the phrase quoted above, we have to follow yet another line of argument, *i.e.* that the aim of the author is to show Piso's qualities and that the purpose of the passage dealing with the board game is to emphasise Piso's ability as a military leader. This is the reason why the game is described in terms of military terminology, comparing the game to a real battle. According to the literary sources dealing with strategy in ancient Greek and Roman times, the first phase of a battle consisted of arranging the troops. The general was free to arrange his troops according to the circumstances in which he found himself (the enemy's weapons, the strength and position of the enemy's army, the topography of the battle site, the weather, etc.). The arrangement of the phalanxes, legions, cavalry, or auxiliary units before the battle started was a constant and most important part of Greek and Roman warfare, and is therefore always mentioned in the ancient texts such as Arrian's report about Alexander's campaigns, Caesar's *de Bello Gallico*, and Frontinus' *Strategemata*. It was by the clever positioning of the troops that the general was able to demonstrate his strategic skills, and often the sources underline the fact that the initial arrangement of the army proved decisive in the battle. The readers of *Laus Pisonis* found the expected description of this initial formation in the phrase '*callidiore modo tabula variatur aperta calculus...*' quoted above. Therefore it seems obvious that in the *latrunculi* game the players had the choice of placing their pieces deliberately on the open board, without any obligation to arrange them in opposite lines. Such a starting position in rows would anyway lead to a boring initial phase of the game, where the pieces move towards each other without anything of interest happening. Moreover, capture by enclosing an enemy piece from two sides would hardly work this way. Hence it is likely that the game proper started when all the pieces had been placed, just as supposed by R.C. Bell (1979, 82) in analogy to the North African game of Seega or Kharbga.

From a historical point of view, the introduction of starting positions in ancient board games was a development which seems to be connected with a desire to accelerate games. This tendency can be observed not only in ancient Rome where, for example, the number of dice used in *XII scripta* was raised from two to three between the 3rd and 5th centuries (Schädler 1995). Most successful was the reduction of the number of rows from three to two and the introduction of the starting position still applied in modern backgammon. According to literary sources, it was invented in Persia about the same time, reducing the length of the track compared to the Roman game, where all the pieces had to be entered on the board first. The desire for more dynamic board games is still omnipresent in the book of games commissioned by the Spanish king Alfonso from 1283 (Schädler and Calvo 2006), where dice are explicitly introduced into chess to make it faster, before the new queen's and bishop's moves were invented with the same effect shortly before 1500. A second motivation for the introduction of a starting position into board games may have been the invention of a special piece, such as the king in the *tafl*-games (*see* below), which rather automatically leads to the question where to put it if not in the centre.

B13 AND W13 — TWO EXTRA COUNTERS?

All the counters are relatively equal in size. Therefore the smaller white piece (W13) standing close to the centre of the board is striking. It is possible that it was a replacement for a counter of normal size which had been lost. On the other hand, one blue counter (B13) has been found turned upside down, which raises the question if this was deliberately done in order to compensate for the absence of a similarly smaller blue counter. After a thorough re-examination of the excavation process and the documentation, it can be excluded with a fair degree of plausibility that the counter flipped over during excavation or as a consequence of the deterioration of the wooden surface it was placed on. But nevertheless it remains a possibility that the person who placed the counters on the board turned over this one blue piece intending to create a blue equivalent to the small white piece, in the absence of a blue counter of different size or shape. Based on this assumption, the question arises whether or not these two pieces might have played a special role in the game.

There are several arguments against this hypothesis. First of all, the position of the blue counter B13 as found seems somewhat accidental. It has been found at the corner of the board, whereas the small white counter W13 was placed exactly in the centre of the white side. Therefore one cannot ascribe a special function to that inverted blue counter without making assumptions about the way the game was played, by inventing a rule that the players could choose where to place the special piece after having set out the other pieces on to the first row of squares.

Secondly, ancient Greek or Roman board games with an extra piece are not known. Several authors assumed that the terms *latrones*, *bellatores*, *milites* or *latrunculi* used by Roman poets to designate the counters of *ludus latrunculorum* indicated gaming stones of different function (Becq de Fouquières 1869, 429s, 435; Marquardt and Mau 1886, 856; Decker 1972, 19; May 1991, 174), an assumption already convincingly rejected (Blümner 1911, 415; Lamer 1927, col. 1928; Owen 1967, 255). The differentiation in terminology is due to the poetic character of the sources, with the poets aiming at avoiding a repetition of words (Schädler 2003). A good comparison in this respect may be Seneca's *Apocolocyntosis* (15, 1), where the author uses *alea*, *talus* (*i.e.* the knucklebone) and *tessera* as synonyms for the cubic die in one and the same short poem of eight verses about the emperor Claudius playing at dice in the underworld.

These observations would lead to three possible conclusions.

1) Neither piece had a special function in the game, *i.e.* the blue counter was inverted by chance and the small white one is a reserve piece.
2) Both pieces had a special function; if so, the game is probably not a Roman game, but was to be played with Roman material, which would explain the absence of especially designed extra pieces and the *ad hoc* improvisation.
3) Only the small white counter served as a special piece, so that we are dealing with an asymmetrical board game: 13 blue counters against 12 + 1 white counters. If so, the game is probably not a Roman game since, with the only possible exception of a presumed gaming board at Augst (Schädler 2002a), no asymmetrical board games are known from the ancient Roman world.

THE GAME — PRELIMINARY CONCLUSIONS (TABLES 55–6)

'*Owing to the meagre and vague character of the evidence, the student who would elucidate the nature of the various board games ... must tread warily. Not only is the evidence slight and ambiguous but it is sometimes contradictory. However some possibilities and probabilities can be shown, and a few impossibilities likewise.*' This statement by Eóin MacWhite (1946, 25) with regard to ancient Irish board games also holds true for the study of ancient board games in general. Taking into account that there are no certainties, and the lack of detailed information and unambiguous evidence prevents us from getting in touch with the object of our research and keeps us at a certain distance, I would like to present the following reflections.

The overall proportions of the Doctor's board correspond fairly well with ancient Roman *XII scripta/alea* boards. With these boards having three parallel rows of 12 spaces, it would be difficult to imagine any particular relationship between the 13 counters on each side – *i.e.* two counters less than necessary to play the game – and the layout of the board. As regards the white counters, one might imagine that they have been placed on regular spaces with the small white piece on the central ornament that such boards usually have. On the other hand, the position of the pieces and their more or less uniform distances relative to each other seem to speak in favour of an orthogonal grid of lines, assuming the counters were set out on regular places of the game-board. If so, the number and distances of the counters in relation to the overall proportions of the board and the fact that the latter was a work of craftsmanship and not just a game spontaneously scratched into a flat surface, suggest a grid of 8 × 12 or 9 × 13 squares of equal length and width. This ratio of squares does not find any parallels among ancient Roman game boards, with only one possible exception: the board from Leuna obviously had 13 squares in one direction and, given the *XII scripta/alea* board on the reverse side and the usual rectangular proportion of these boards, perhaps 9, 10 or 11 in the other. Assuming the counters represent a complete set, their number (13 on both sides) suggests that the game was played on the intersections of the 9 × 13 lines of a board with 8 × 12 squares or on a board with 9 × 13 squares, although we cannot definitely ascertain if the counters were placed on the cells or on the points of intersection. It is the fact that on both the blue and the white sides, there are two pieces bunched in the corner (W11 and W12, B12 and B13) which suggests that by some means the board moved slightly to the left during the burial rite, and consequently the pieces on it moved to the right, where the

TABLE 55: SETS OF GAMING COUNTERS ASSOCIATED WITH CREMATION AND INHUMATION BURIALS IN BRITAIN (after Cotton 2001a–b). Grave type: crem. cremation, inhum. inhumation, (m) male (f) female

Site	No. of counters	Mat.	Grave	Date	Main reference
Welwyn Garden City, Herts	24 (4 × 6)	glass	crem. (m)	c. 10 B.C.	Stead 1967, 14–19
King Harry Lane, Verulamium, Herts	21 (10 decorated, 11 plain)	bone	crem.	A.D. 1–40	Stead and Rigby 1989, 108, fig. 137
Stanway, Colchester, Essex ('Warrior's burial')	20	glass	crem. (m)	c. A.D. 43–50	pp. 186–90
Stanway, Colchester, Essex ('Doctor's burial')	26 (2 × 13)	glass	crem. (?m)	c. A.D. 43–50	pp. 217–20
Alton, Hants	19	glass	crem. (?m)	A.D. 45–65	Millett 1986, 43, 53–6
Litton Cheney, Dorset	20 (2 × 10)	chalk/pottery	inhum. (m)	mid 1st	Bailey 1967, 156–9
St Martin's-le-Grand, London	?	bone	crem.	?mid 1st	RCHM 1928, 154
King Harry Lane, Verulamium, Herts	22	glass	crem. (m)	A.D. 80–90	Niblett 1990, 412–13
Grange Road, Winchester, Hants	18 (2 blue, 4 black, 12 white)	glass	crem. (?f)	A.D. 85–95	Biddle 1967, 243
The Looe, Ewell, Surrey	10	bone/pottery	crem. (m)	late 1st–early 2nd	Cotton 2001b
Old Kent Road, London	26	bone	crem.	late 1st–early 2nd	R. Jackson, pers. comm.
Mansell Street, London	24	glass	inhum.	late 1st–early 2nd	A. Wardle, pers. comm.
Old Newton, Suffolk	10	glass	crem.	late 1st–early 2nd	Philpott 1991, 185
Colchester, Essex	24 + 3 cubic dice	glass	crem.	early–mid 2nd	May 1930, 275, Joslin Grave group 81 a–b/94
Elsenham, Essex	19	glass/bone	crem.	mid 2nd	C. Johns, pers. comm.
Victoria Road, Winchester. Hants	29	bone	crem.	mid–late 2nd	Rees et al. forthcoming
Ospringe, Kent	24 (12 white, 4 black, 4 yellow, 1 blue, 1 green + 2 dice)	glass/bone	crem.	late 2nd	Whiting 1925, 95
Trentholme Drive, York	46 (12 with graffiti)	bone	crem. (m)	late 2nd	Wenham 1968, 97 no. 46
St Pancras, Chichester, W Sussex	25/6	bone	crem.	A.D. 150–200	Down and Rule 1971, 83, fig. 5.15
Elms Farm, Heybridge. Essex	14	bone	crem. (child)	2nd	Atkinson and Preston 1998, 28
St Pancras, Chichester, W Sussex	23	bone	crem.	3rd	Down and Rule 1971, 83, fig. 5.15
Holgate Bridge, York	20 +	bone	inhum. (child)	?3rd–4th	RCHM 1962, 101
Lullingstone, Kent	30 (15 white, 15 brown)	glass	inhum. (m)	late 3rd–4th	Meates 1987, 123–5, 139–42 no. 391
Lankhills, Winchester, Hants	26	glass	inhum.	late 4th	Clarke 1979, 251–4

TABLE 56: SETS/GROUPS OF GAMING COUNTERS FROM NON-FUNERARY CONTEXTS
(after Cotton 2001a–b)

Site	No.	Material	Context	Date	Main reference
Skeleton Green, Herts	4 pegs	bone	well	*c.* 10 B.C.–A.D. 20	Partridge 1981, 61, fig. 26
Tooley Street, Southwark, London	12	bone	floor	late 1st–early 2nd	Sheldon 1974, 100, fig. 47
Caerleon, Gwent	28	bone/glass	drain	late 1st–early 2nd	Zienkiewicz 1986, 155–6, 202–7
Castleford, Yorks	18	bone/glass	floor	late 1st–early 2nd	Cool and Philo 1998, 362
Brecon Gaer, Powys	8	bone	drain	early 2nd	Wheeler 1926, 120
Corbridge, Northumberland	54	glass	box	early 2nd	Allason-Jones and Bishop 1988, 82
Caerleon, Gwent	40	bone/glass	drain	late 2nd–early 3rd	Zienkiewicz 1986, 155–6, 202–7
Ravenglass, Cumbria	126	bone/glass	floor	late 2nd–early 3rd	Potter 1979, 75–87
Church Street, York	45	bone/glass/pottery	sewer	late 2nd–early 3rd	MacGregor 1976, 2–4, 21–2
Corbridge, Northumberland	20	bone	road	?	RIB 2, fasc. 3, no. 2440
Balkerne Lane, Colchester, Essex	12	bone	pit	1st–4th	*CAR* 2, 91, fig. 94

rim of the board prevented the pieces close to the right-hand corner of the board falling off it. A reconstruction of a grid of 9 × 13 squares fits more closely with this scenario, since all the pieces appear to have moved to the right, whereas on a grid of 8 × 12 squares most of the white counters but only a few of the blue appear to have shifted. What argues against a grid of 9 × 13 squares is the fact that the two halves of the folding board would meet in the middle of the central row of squares, which does not seem very practical.

Concerning a presumed particular function of the small white and the inverted blue counter, no definite conclusion can be reached. The assumption that the small white counter served as an extra piece seems plausible. Although in asymmetrical board games the number of pieces on one side usually exceeds by far the number of pieces on the other, its position in the centre of the white counters argues in favour of this hypothesis. A remarkable find from the King Harry Lane site at Verulamium may further strengthen this suggestion. In burial no. 249, dating to the first half of the 1st century and therefore contemporary with the Doctor's lifetime, 21 gaming pieces in the shape of pegs were found, 11 of which were plain while 10 had decorated heads. Moreover, one of the decorated pieces is further distinguished by a dot in a circle (Stead and Rigby 1989, 108, 339, fig. 137). The excavators assumed that one piece of the decorated group is missing from a complete set of twice eleven counters. The find suggests that the pegs belonged to an asymmetrical board game with 9 + 1 or 10 + 1 pieces on one side and 11 on the other, played on a board with holes, similar to the Viking-age game boards from Ballinderry (Hencken 1933; Hencken 1937; Sterckx 1970, 604, with bibliography and fig. 1) and Knockanboy (Simpson 1972).

However, neither of the other possibilities for the small white and the inverted blue counters can be discarded with certainty (*i.e.* that both counters served as an extra piece, or that neither of the counters served as an extra piece, with the former being less likely). The question as to whether or not counters B13 and/or W13 served a special function in the game seems to be linked to the interpretation of the position of the pieces as a starting position. From what has been said above, it seems that the introduction of an extra piece rather automatically leads to a starting position (as attested for the *tafl*-games), whereas a game with undifferentiated counters such as *ludus latrunculorum* would not necessarily require an initial arrangement.

Other finds of gaming counters from graves of Roman Britain provide no help (TABLES 55–6 generously provided by Jon Cotton of the Museum of London; Cotton 2001a–b): the numbers of counters and the distribution of colours differ enormously. The difference in numbers may result from the fact that distinguishing between glass gaming counters and pieces of stone during excavation may sometimes be difficult, so that not all the counters may have been identified. Another reason may be that it was not the intention of the people who arranged the grave goods to lay down 'complete' sets of counters, but just the counters possessed by the buried person. One has to consider the everyday culture of play at the time. With so many game-boards being scratched into the pavements of public places, it is obvious that anyone wanting to play had to bring his own dice and counters, which had to be sufficient in number to play different games. With three counters one could play three men's morris, with fifteen a game of *XII scripta* was possible and seventeen counters, for example, made sure that there were still enough in case a counter got lost, or stuck between two slabs of the pavement. The expectation of finding complete sets of counters seems to be strongly influenced by the modern market in boxed games. A set of counters can only be complete with regard to the standard of one particular game.

It may, on the contrary, have even been the intention to lay down incomplete sets of counters. As has been observed with the much later finds of gaming counters in Germanic graves, there are reasons to believe that here the pieces have been deliberately reduced in number: in several instances there are one or two counters fewer on one side. To quote a few examples: in grave III/1926 at Leuna, Germany, 30 white and 29 dark stones have been found (Schulz 1953, 22, fig. 37, 28ff). Fragments of 26 or 27 white counters and between 25 and 27 multicoloured ones have been uncovered in a male grave at Emersleben, Germany (Schulz 1952, 108, 131). In a female burial (grave I) at Sackrau (Zakrzów), Poland, 19 white and 20 black counters came to light (Kosinna 1922, 125; compare Schulz 1953, 64: 18 and 19 counters), while in another grave at the same site (grave III) 14 greenish-white and 15 black counters have been excavated (Schulz 1952, 132). And among the grave goods of a burial at Vallöby, Sweden, there were 31 black and 29 white counters (Schulz 1952, 132; Schulz 1953, 64).

A possible explanation for these unequal sets of counters could, of course, be that the counters belonged to an asymmetric game such as the *tafl*-games, with one player having an extra piece. But the finds quoted above did not contain specially designed extra pieces (such as the king in the *tafl*-games). Moreover, as will be shown below, not one of the numerous sets for the game of *hnefatafl* found in the Viking-age graves at Birka seems to be complete according to the rules given by the literary sources. It is therefore possible that the number of counters has been reduced on purpose to remove the games from secular use, in the same way other grave goods were often deliberately destroyed.

A SUGGESTION FOR A SCENARIO AND THE GAME

With regard to the possible identification of the board game in the Doctor's burial, attention has focused on the *ludus latrunculorum*. However, this is simply because it is the only Roman board game known that was played with counters on a latticed board. Nevertheless, a closer look at the evidence comparing the archaeological evidence from Stanway with what literary and archaeological sources tell us about the *ludus latrunculorum* shows that this assumption can be ruled out with a fair degree of confidence. Since we cannot definitely be sure either about the special function of the small white and the inverted blue counters or the starting position, there are two major arguments:

1) The *ludus latrunculorum* was played on a more or less square board with a ratio of squares of n:n or n:n+1. The proportions of the board in the Doctor's burial suggest a more rectangular gaming area of n:n+4 squares.
2) The interception method of capture applied in the *ludus latrunculorum* requires more pieces than twice 12 or 13 on a board with at least 96 (8 × 12), if not 117 (9 × 13) squares. Even on the small terracotta models of games in course of play (*i.e.* with less than the complete number of counters on the board) quoted above, there are relatively more pieces per square

left on the board: one calculates 2.47 squares/counter on the model in the Petrie Museum, 3.5 squares per counter on the little board in Athens, whereas the Stanway board would have 3.69 squares/counter with a board of 8 × 12 and even 4.5 with a board of 9 × 13. The Malayan game of *sodok-apit*, where the same interception method of capture as in the *ludus latrunculorum* is applied, is played on a draughts board with 16 pieces on both sides (Samusah 1932, 130), *i.e.* 2.00 squares/counter. Therefore it seems rather unlikely that the Doctor played at the Roman *ludus latrunculorum*.

Philip Crummy described in detail how the counters must have moved significantly on the board after their initial set up. A possible explanation for this would be a hard knock against the right-hand side of the board during the deposition of the grave goods (pp. 356–7). If a grid of 8 × 12 squares is assumed, the white pieces appear to have shifted while the blue counters remained more or less in position, a fact that requires explanation. Reconstructing 13 squares on the long sides of the board would provide a more consistent picture, with nearly all the pieces having shifted slightly to the right. On the right-hand side of the corner, the raised rim of the board stopped the counters from slipping off the board, which would explain the clustering of the pieces in both the corners. Is it possible that B13 was pushed against the raised lip of the board and turned around? As the photograph reveals (FIG. 124), the counters which seem to have been moved intentionally as in a game towards the centre of the board are in the same area where the cremated bone was subsequently deposited. It may, therefore, have been during the deposition of the cremated bone that these pieces were dragged across the board. This does not seem to hold true for the small white counter, W13. Despite its small size, it seems rather unlikely that the counter could have been shifted so far. Its position close to the centre of the board suggests instead that it was placed on the central space of a 9 × 13 board right from the beginning. This position, with six white counters on either side, compared to the rather accidental position of the inverted blue counter B13 on the one hand and the remarkable find from Verulamium on the other would argue for the assumption that the piece served as an extra piece of the white party and placed in the centre of the board, and that the game was to be played by 12 + 1 white counters against 13 blue pieces.

A game like this is not known from Roman sources, nor is — as already observed — a rectangular game-board with 8 × 12 or 9 × 13 lines or squares. One may raise the question therefore whether we are facing not a Roman but a Celtic board game. Given the typically Roman glass counters, the possible Roman system of measurements used in the design of the board, and finally the degree to which the members of the local upper class were already Romanised in the early years of Roman presence in Britain, one would perhaps expect the game to be Roman. Nonetheless, a closer look at what we know about board games in Iron Age Britain may be fruitful.

ANCIENT CELTIC BOARD GAMES

Our knowledge of ancient Celtic board games is even more limited than that concerning Roman games. That there was an indigenous tradition of board games is strongly suggested by the exceptional find from Welwyn Garden City. In a rich grave dating to the last quarter of the 1st century B.C., four groups of six glass counters in four different colours as well as six fragments of glass beads and bracelets with worn edges, which apparently were used as dice in the game, came to light (Stead 1967, 14–18, fig. 10; Harden *et al.* 1968, 35, n. 42). The counters do strikingly resemble much older Celtic military helmets (*see* Feugère 1994, 23). If this is a complete set of counters, it would suggest a game for four players. This would be the oldest four-handed board game in Europe, since all other ancient board games are for two players only. One exception might be the 'game of twice the 20-squares' found in ancient Egypt, which consists of two boards of the game of 20 squares (Pusch 1977), and therefore might perhaps have been played by four players.

More can be said about another group of board games known from archaeological as well as literary Scandinavian and British sources, *i.e.* the so-called *tafl*-games. By combining a description by Carl von Linnée in 1732 of the game *tablut* played by the Saami of Lapland with various literary sources, it has been possible to establish that the games variously called *tafl*, *hnefatafl*, *tawl-bwrdd*, *brandubh*, and *tablut* all belonged to one family of asymmetrical board games popular during the Viking period and the early middle ages in Scandinavia and Britain (Murray 1913, 445–6; 1952, 55; Articus 1983; Sterckx 1970; Parlett 1999, 196ff; Helmfrid 2000). These games were played on latticed boards with an odd number of places in both directions (*i.e.* 7 × 7, 11 × 11, 13 × 13, 15 × 15 or 19 × 19 cells or lines). The two players had unequal forces at their disposition: one large group of attackers tried to capture the king-piece, initially placed on the central square or intersection of the board. The king's defenders are outnumbered by the attackers 2:1. As in the *ludus latrunculorum*, a piece was captured when enclosed from two sides. As to the use of dice in the game, never mentioned in the sources, the term *tawl-bwrdd* has created some confusion, since it has been suggested that the term, which can be translated as 'throw-board', is connected with the throwing of dice (D.P.F. 1860, appendix E, li; Bell 1979, 2, 44). A closer look at the meanings of the noun *tawl* and the verb *tawlu* (Owen 1803) though reveals that the 'throwing' is unlikely to refer to the rolling of dice but to the counters thrown off, taken off, and put aside from the board when captured. It is a board for a game where captured pieces are thrown off, so that *tawl-bwrdd* may be more adequately translated as 'throw-off-board'.

Among the most important archaeological evidence connected with the *tafl*-games, wooden and stone gaming boards as well as counters may be mentioned. A gaming board from the Gokstad ship dating to the 9th century has a nine men's morris on one side of the board, while the other side has an orthogonal grid of probably 13 × 13 squares, of which 13 squares in one direction, but only 4 in the other are preserved. Two wooden gaming boards with holes for counters in the shape of pegs (Hencken 1937, 158, fig. 26b, 165) have been found at Ballinderry in Ireland. While one of the boards is only partly preserved (Hencken 1937, 149), the other one is broken but complete. It shows 7 × 7 holes, the central hole and the holes in the four corners marked by a circle and quarter-circles respectively (Hencken 1933, pl. 1; 1937, 135, 175ff, pl. 25; Murray 1952, 59, fig. 23), a feature to be compared to an engraving of a gaming board on a rune stone from Ockelbo, Sweden. Probably dating to the later 10th century (Hencken 1933, 93), it is now kept in the National Museum of Ireland in Dublin. Most significant is a find from Knowth, Ireland (Eogan 1974, 68–70, 76–80), from a double inhumation grave dated 'perhaps not later than the middle of the millennium', *i.e.* about A.D. 500. Here 13 bone pegs for a game board with holes such as the Ballinderry board and three long dice numbered 3-5-4-6 came to light. The type of long dice is, according to Krüger, typical for the Celtic *oppida* on the Continent and Germanic sites (Krüger 1982, 187), thus demonstrating that the British Isles were 'ludographically' connected with the Iron Age Continent. Also from Ireland comes a similar board found at Knockanboy, which is perhaps even earlier in date than the board from Ballinderry, but appears to be lost (Simpson 1972, 63–4). The drawing by J. Bleakly dated 25/26 March 1838 shows 7 × 8 peg-holes, but this may be due to the sketchy character of the drawing. Comparable boards with 7 × 7 lines and the central intersection marked by a circle have been found carved in stone at the 9th-century Viking settlement of Buckquoy on the Orkney Islands (Sterckx 1973, 675–89). One of the boards (*ibid.*, figs 1–2, pl. 3) apparently was used as a teaching board where, by drawing circles on the intersections and retracing the lines, somebody tried to explain that the pieces had to be placed on the intersections and not on the squares. A fragment of a wooden board of 15 × 15 squares dating to the 10th century has come to light at Coppergate, York (Hall 1984, 114). Toftanes Eysturoy, Faroes, produced a board with 13 × 13 squares, which is also dated to the 10th century and kept in the Foroya Fornminnissavn at Torshavn (Roesdahl and Wilson 1992, 311). At Trondheim, Norway, more than one half of a board dated to the 12th century was discovered (McLees 1990, 80–1, pl. 11; Roesdahl and Wilson 1992, 378), which is kept in the Vitenskapsmuseet; it has 11 × 11 squares, of which the central square and the 2nd and 3rd squares from the edges in the 6th column and line were marked by a cross. The reverse side bears a nine-men's morris. Also from Trondheim comes a wooden fragment with three incomplete rows of at least ten squares (McLees 1990, 81, pl. 12). From late Viking-age Norway comes a board with 13 × 13 squares found at Bergen, Tyskebryggen, with the 4th, the 7th (centre), and the 10th squares of the central row marked by a cross (Articus 1983, 95, fig. 11). A set of gaming pieces made of walrus bone and ivory, including a king piece made of bronze, has been found in a rich grave at Oldenburg, Germany, dating to the middle of the 10th century (Gabriel 1985, 207–15). Many of the 10th-century graves at the important Viking-age settlement on the island of Björkö, Sweden, produced a considerable amount of gaming equipment. Among the sets of counters which, to judge from the existence of a distinctive piece and two different groups of counters, most clearly belonged to *tafl*, those from the following graves may be mentioned: grave no. 523 contained a king piece and 5 and 14 men all made of glass, which were originally deposited in a leather bag (Arbmann 1940/43, 157–60 pl. 148.1). The king-piece found in grave no. 524 is distinguished by crossed grooves imitating a helmet (*ibid.*, 160, pl. 149.1), while the king in grave no. 624 has a hat of gilded bronze (*ibid.*, 205–7 pl. 149.3, 150.6). The extraordinarily rich burial no. 581 of a man with two horses produced an Arabic coin struck under caliph al Muktadir (301–20 H = A.D. 913–33) and a set consisting of a king-piece, six defenders, and 20 assailants, together with three cubic dice (*ibid.*, 188–90, fig. 143, pl. 147.3). The set found in grave no. 750 consisted of 17 pieces of light-blue-green glass and eight of opaque dark green glass plus a dark green larger piece fashioned like a man with a head (*ibid.*, 147, 271). In grave no 986, a pawn-shaped king with six decorated and ten undecorated men were found (*ibid.*, 412, pl. 150.2, 6). The gaming equipment found in a chamber grave (no. 644) with a double inhumation of a woman and a man is unusual, and roughly dated by a Samanid coin struck for Nasr ibn Ahmad in the year 308 H, *i.e.* A.D. 920–1 (*ibid.*, 221–6, figs 182, 183, pl. 148.2). Apart from three long dice, the set consisted of two nearly identical king-pieces with 20 glass counters of the same manufacture as the pieces in grave no. 523. Numerous other finds of single gaming stones, king pieces or incomplete sets shed no more light on the nature and history of the game.

Among the most important literary sources (*see* Murray 1952, 61; Sterckx 1970) is a document dating to the 10th century in Oxford, conventionally called *alea evangelii*, containing in particular a drawing of a board of 19 × 19 intersections (Bell 1979, 80, fig. 68, and pl. 5), where 48 black stones attacked 24 white ones and the *primarius vir*. *Tawl-bwrdd* is frequently mentioned in the 'Ancient Laws of Wales' ascribed to the king Howell Dda (10th century) although, according to Murray, not older than the middle of the 13th century. It demonstrates that 8 men defended the king against 16 white attackers. A description of *tawl-bwrdd* and a drawing of a board with 11 × 11 squares can also be found in a Welsh manuscript by Robert ap Ifan from 1587 (Welsh National Library, Peniarth ms 158, p. 4) — the latest reference to the game in Britain. It may be interesting to note that none of the sets of *tafl*-counters found in the Birka graves correspond with the number of pieces mentioned in these literary sources, nor are there twice the number of attackers in relation to the number of pieces on the king's side. The variability of the numbers of counters at Birka would lead to two possible explanations: either the number of pieces varied depending on convention or nearly all the sets are incomplete. The presence in some of the burials of dice, not mentioned in the literary sources, does not indicate that the *tafl*-game was played with dice but that, in addition to the counters for the *tafl*-game, dice to play dice-games were themselves offered to the dead.

The family of *tafl*-games has hitherto mostly been connected with the Scandinavian peoples, who would have introduced it to Britain during the Viking age. When and where this group of games originated is unknown. Archaeological evidence to corroborate Murray's statement, that the *tafl*-games were 'already played by the Scandinavian peoples before A.D. 400' (Murray 1952, 56), *i.e.* in the Roman Iron Age, is rare. To judge from their exceptional size and shape, some of the glass counters found at Lundeborg, Denmark, may have been used as king pieces in *hnefatafl* (Michaelsen 1992, 46–8; 2002, 73), but they date no earlier than the 3rd century. It is of note that none of the Germanic sites which provided game-boards, dice, and counters, studied by Krüger, has produced any evidence for counters with a special function required for the *tafl*-games (Krüger 1982, 161). Kosinna's interpretation as a gaming piece of a cone-shaped bronze object from Kommerau (Komorow, Poland) dating to the 3rd century (Kosinna 1922, 122, 127, figs 15, 15a) has been rejected by Krüger (1982, 139, 224, fig. 29.8).

On the other hand, an earlier date for the game is suggested by its affinities to Roman games, in particular to the *ludus latrunculorum*. The capturing method of enclosure common to both games seems to indicate that the latter exhibited a certain influence on the *tafl*-games. Moreover the name *tafl* derives from the Latin *tabula* meaning '(gaming)board' or 'counter'. Finally, the fact that the boards from Vimose (*c.* A.D. 400) (Engelhardt 1869, 11, pl. 3.9–11; Schulz 1953, 64, fig. 75.1–3; Krüger 1982, 222, fig. 10.7–10; Michaelsen 2002, figs 3, 14) and from Leuna (3rd century A.D.) bear a *XII scripta/alea* on one side (Schulz 1953, 65, fig. 76; Krüger 1982, 233, fig. 38.10–11) clearly demonstrates a close connection between the Germanic and the Roman world of board games. In fact, the central ornament of the outer row of the board from Leuna, consisting of one half of a six-petalled rosette inscribed in a semi-circle with its ends scrolled to the inside (Schulz 1953, 29, fig. 56), finds close parallels in several game-boards from all over the Roman empire. For the semi-circle, compare boards from Damous al-Karita (Delattre 1909, 375; 1911, 12ff, fig. on p. 13; Schädler 1995, 88, fig. 7b) and Rome (Ferrua 1964, 17, fig. 7m; 1948, pl. 4.7). For the three-leaves motif in a semicircle, *see* for example a game-board found near Porta Portese in Rome now kept in the British Museum (Austin 1938, 251, figs 2 and 3; May 1991, 178, n. 283, fig. 175), a board in the Roman catacombs (Ferrua 1964, 17, fig. 7n) and a carefully executed gaming-table at Aphrodisias (Roueché 1989, 110, pl. 16, n. 69). The indication of the houses through circles divided into two groups by a larger semi-circle, as executed on one of the boards from Vimose, was very popular, especially in the eastern part of the Roman empire. No less than nine such game-boards can be seen on the steps of the stadium at Aphrodisias. Their exact location is as follows:

1 northern part of east curve, 1st segment after curve
2 eastern part of north side, 3rd step from above
3 western part of north side, 5th segment from west, 2nd step from above
4 western part of north side, 5th segment from west, 2nd step from above (another one)
5 north side, 4th segment from west
6 north side, 3rd segment from west, 2nd step from above
7 north side, 2nd segment from west, 4th step from above
8 south side, 5th segment from east, uppermost step
9 south side, 2nd segment from east, uppermost step.

Three other gaming boards of the type can be seen at Ephesus, two on a threshold in the street between the theatre and the stadium, and another one in the street of the *curetes*, close to the *nymphaeum* of Trajan.

There are several parallels for the houses marked by semi-circles, as on the second board from Vimose: a board found at Avenches, Switzerland (May 1991, 181, no. 284, fig. 177), and a board from the theatre at Leptis Magna, Libya (Caputo 1987, 121, no. 4, 122, no. B, pl. 94.4). The triangular ornament in the semi-circle finds a close analogy on a late antique gaming-board in the portico of the agora at Perge, Turkey (Mansel 1975, 79 and fig. 43 on p. 81).

Thus there are good reasons to believe that the *XII scripta/alea*-boards as well as the latticed boards from Vimose are imported boards of Roman manufacture.

Although the latticed board from Vimose is often quoted by authors dealing with the *tafl*-games, it is not clear which game was played on the board. In particular, only one side of the board is preserved completely, showing that there were 19 lines or 18 squares in one direction. Some authors have questioned the figure of 18 squares, but with the diagonally cut joints of the frame being preserved on both sides of the fragment, there can be no doubt that the preserved edge represents the first complete row of 18 squares. Since the outermost lines appear to be too close to the rim, it seems that the board should be regarded as consisting of squares rather than a grid of lines. With 18 squares in one direction, the board cannot have been used for a game of the *tafl*-type, which required an odd number of cells or lines. On the other hand, grids of 18 squares in one direction are hitherto without parallel in the Roman world, which makes it rather unlikely that the board was used for *ludus latrunculorum*. Moreover, the usual assumption, that the board consisted of 19 × 19 lines or 18 × 18 squares, ignores the possibility that the fragment shows the reverse side of one of the *XII scripta/alea*-boards. With these boards usually being rectangular, a square shape for the orthogonal grid of lines or squares could definitely be ruled out. The same holds true for Leuna, where, although the board has an odd number of squares (13) in one direction, the fact that its reverse side was prepared for *XII scripta/alea* makes a square grid of lines or squares unlikely. Moreover, no special piece was found among the uniform white and dark glass counters. Nor have Roman *latrunculi*-boards with 13 squares in one direction hitherto come to light. So we have to reckon with yet another board game played in Roman times with uniform counters on a rectangular grid of (an odd number of?) lines or squares. The fact that the *XII scripta/alea* on one side is a Roman game does not automatically imply that the game on the reverse side was a Roman game as well. Given the prestige as status symbols of board games (*see* below) on the one hand and Roman imports on the other, there are reasons to believe that such 'Roman' gaming boards may have been manufactured especially for Germanic (or Celtic) clients, and may therefore have been equipped with a Roman game on one side and an indigenous game on the other. The same may, *mutatis mutandis*, hold true for the Doctor's game board.

A possible candidate for the game we are looking for would be an ancient board game called *fidhcheall* or *ficheall* in Ireland and *gwyddbwyll* (*gwyzbwyll*) in Wales (MacWhite 1946, 25–35; Murray 1952, 34; Nuti 2001). According to the literary sources, it was played on a rectangular board by two players with equal forces of undifferentiated counters, and may therefore be regarded as a closer relative of the Roman *ludus latrunculorum*. Most interesting in the context of the present discussion is the statement in Cormac's Glossary (O'Donovan and Stokes 1868) that 'it is a different person who wins every other time', a statement confirmed by other sources as well (Nuti 2001, 25, 27). While MacWhite (1946, 33) expressed his irritation concerning this piece of evidence which appeared to him to be incompatible with the statement that the forces were equal, Sterckx (1970, 600) was led to infer that one side obviously had a certain advantage. Recently Nuti observed that the game is often mentioned in tales and episodes about a king being challenged by another person, and argued that '*anche un eventuale medesimo numero di pedine per entrambi i giocatori non implica necessariamente che in un gioco non vi sia una pedina che svolga un ruolo centrale; specificamente, un pezzo accostabile alla figura del re*' ('also a possible equal number of pawns for both players does not necessarily imply that in a game one pawn does not play a central role; specifically, a piece approximating to the figure of the king') (Nuti 2001, 27).

It seems to me that in the light of the finds from King Harry Lane and Stanway, those seemingly contradictory statements in the literary sources make sense, inasmuch as they describe an asymmetrical board game, where one of the otherwise equal forces was distinguished by a special piece.

CONCLUSIONS

The evidence from the Doctor's burial at Stanway is not as self-evident as it might seem at first glance. In fact it is difficult to interpret the remains of the game board and the number and position of the blue and white counters on it without making assumptions on games and their rules and of people, their knowledge of games and the intentions they had when they placed the game into the grave. To judge from the rectangular form of the wooden board alone, which seems to be of Roman manufacture, one would expect the game to be a *XII scripta*. No Roman board game played on a rectangular latticed board is known to have existed in the 1st century A.D., neither from archaeological nor literary sources. If so, the twice 13 pieces would neither represent a complete set of counters for this game nor would their position on the board have a closer connection with the game, nor would the small white counter and the inverted blue one have had a special function. This would not at all contradict the interpretation, since these assumptions are absolutely consistent with what has been observed in numerous other places.

But since our knowledge of ancient board games is rather limited, and the findspot is located in an area of cross-cultural interchange, the possibility exists that the game was a Celto-Roman hybrid. In fact, in Britain an independent tradition of board games existed long before the Roman presence. And from contemporary archaeological as well as later literary sources, we learn of an asymmetrical board game with a special piece on one side, called *fidhcheall* or *gwyddbwyll* in later Irish and Welsh sources. It was played on a latticed board with an odd number of spaces. This game seems to be similar to or a kind of predecessor of the Scandinavian *hnefatafl*. In the light of the asymmetrical sets of gaming pegs including one special piece found at Verulamium, it seems not impossible that, also in the Doctor's game at Stanway, the white party of 13 counters was distinguished by such a special piece. Moreover, the more or less regular arrangement of the counters seems to speak in favour of a board with an orthogonal grid of lines and squares. Therefore it may not be completely absurd to say that the Doctor's game possibly testifies to such an asymmetrical 'special piece game' as early as the Augustan age in Britain. Both suggestions — the *XII scripta* and the latticed gaming surfaces – need not necessarily exclude each other. In fact double-sided gaming boards existed at the time, and the board from Leuna with a *XII scripta* on one and a latticed board of 13 × 9, 10, or 11 squares on the reverse side, would offer an excellent yet much later parallel.

It is a world-wide phenomenon that in ancient civilisations board games were used not only as symbols of wealth and fortune, but apparently also of virtue. Gaming boards, dice, and counters often belong to the repertoire of grave goods in burials, especially of members of the upper classes. In direct relation to the wealth of the burial, these games often appear as luxury goods, elaborate and artistic products of skilled craftsmanship, often made of prestigious materials. Examples may be quoted of the Royal game of Ur (Woolley 1934), the well-known gaming tables in the grave of Tut'Ankhamun (Tait 1982), the fine wooden board game from the graves of the kings of Meroë in Qustul (Emery and Kirwan 1938, 345ff, fig. 111, pl. 87; Emery 1948, 46, pl. 8, 32; Horn 1989, 152, figs 16–18), as well as the games found in rich burials in ancient China such as the *Liubo* in the grave of emperor Zhao Mo from 122 B.C. (Prüch 1998; Röllicke 1999, 26, no. 9). In the Viking-age burials at Birka (Sweden), glass gaming stones mainly belonged to those who were distinguished members of the society, as evidenced by far-reaching contacts documented by Arabic coins. Board games were also found in Germanic *Fürstengräbern* such as those at Gommern (Fröhlich 2001, 158) and Leuna. Generally speaking these games can be explained in that they symbolise a peaceful and carefree (after)life not only of the wealthy but also of the brave. Already in Greek archaic vase paintings depicting the heroes Ajax and Achilleus playing *pente grammai* (Schädler 1999, 40ff), the idea seems to be inherent that bravery and play belong together. Particularly in ancient Rome, the focus obviously lies on the virtues of the players. Several hexagrams of Roman game boards for *XII scripta/alea* demonstrate that bravery in warfare was looked on as the prerequisite for peace and public wealth and consequently the possibility of playing with neither fear nor sorrow (Schädler 1995, 80; 1996, 72): VIRTVS IMPERI HOSTES VINCTI LVDANT ROMANI (Ihm 1890, 238, no. 49; Huelsen 1904, 143, n. 1), HOSTES VICTOS ITALIA GAVDET [LVDI]TE ROMANI (Huelsen 1904, 143, no. 2; Ferrua 1948, 33, no. 79), PARTHI OCCISI BR[I]TT[O] VICTVS LVDIT[E R]OMANI (Huelsen 1904, 142; Ferrua 1948, 33, no. 80) and ... ... [GENTES] PACATE [LVDIT]E ROMANI (Ihm 1890; 238, no. 50; Huelsen 1904, 143, no. 3). On a pyrgus dating to the 4th century from Froitzheim (Germany), one reads PICTOS VICTOS HOSTIS DELETA LVDITE SECVRI (Horn 1989, 139ff esp. 146). Finally, a hitherto unpublished *XII scripta/alea*-board incised into the pavement of the palaestra of the Petronii in the summer baths at Thuburbo Maius (Tunisia) may be mentioned, reading: PATRIA SANCTA FACIAS UTMEOS SALVOS VIDEAM. These mottoes allude to the bravery of the members of the society and the virtues of the political system they were part of, which guaranteed peace and wealth as a pre-condition for people passing their time by playing games instead of struggling for daily survival. Although this interpretation refers to Roman board games, especially of the 3rd and 4th centuries, it may also hold true for neighbouring peoples. It is certainly not coincidence that *XII scripta/alea*-boards in particular have been found in Germanic contexts (Vimose, Leuna).

However, later British sources such as the Ancient Laws of Wales demonstrate that, in Britain, board games had a prominent role in the installation in office of dignitaries, inasmuch as they were used as insignia (Forbes 1860). When admitted to his office, a chancellor in Wales received a gold ring, a harp and a game from the king, which he was expected to preserve for the rest of his life. A judge of court received playing pieces made of sea-animal bone from the king and a gold ring from the queen, which he likewise was expected never to sell or give away (Forbes 1860). Possibly the feature from Welwyn Garden City must be seen in the same context. Apart from the extraordinary glass gaming pieces in the burial which, to judge from the presence of imported Roman silver and bronze vessels, belonged to a high-ranking personage, iron fittings were found which probably had served for a carefully executed repair of a wooden gaming board (Stead 1967, 31–6, figs 20, 21). This would be an early archaeological reference for the particular role of board games as status symbols in Iron Age and Roman Britain.

THE SALT BRIQUETAGE (FIGS 35–6; TABLES 57–8)

By Nina Crummy

DESCRIPTION (TABLES 57–8)

The ditches of the ?mortuary enclosures in Enclosures 4 and 5 produced several sherds of briquetage from rectangular troughs used in the Late Iron Age and early Roman periods in the production of sea-salt at 'red hill' sites on the Essex coast. Further fragments came from the southern arm of the main eastern ditch of Enclosure 4. The contextual information of the briquetage is summarised in TABLE 57, together with the sherd count and total weight per context. The following two fragments are illustrated.

BF30.2 FIG. 35. BL21 B283. ?Mortuary enclosure ditch, Enclosure 4. Rim sherd from the corner of a rectangular vessel. The knife-trimmed rim has sagged downwards from the corner. Surviving height 76 mm, maximum thickness 31 mm. Weight 223 g.
CF44.1 FIG. 36. C140. ?Mortuary enclosure ditch, Enclosure 5. Large wall sherd. Surviving height 115 mm, 23 mm thick. Weight 223 g.

The fabric of all but one of these sherds is typical of the Type A briquetage found in north-east Essex, usually about 19 mm thick, sometimes much greater, and with much vegetable tempering (Rodwell 1979, 149–53; Fawn *et al.* 1990, 11). The surfaces are in general oxidised, but several have some reduction on one face and in the core. Surviving rims have been knife-trimmed, and one has been thumb-pressed. One sherd is only 11.5 mm thick and has rather less vegetable tempering. It has fired to a regular brown colour throughout. This piece belongs to Type B, production of which centres on the red hills to the south of the county, around Canvey Island. It is rarely found in north-east Essex.

The 29 recovered sherds had a total weight of 1343 g. Few of the sherds were abraded, and only one markedly so. As deposited (several pieces are friable and have broken at excavation or later), the average sherd weight is 46.3 g, which is substantially greater than that recorded at some other Essex sites (TABLE 58), although individual sherds from elsewhere in the county have equalled the largest here (Sealey 1995, 66, fig. 2) and both weight and sherd count are rarely given in the majority of reports. The low level of abrasion and the high average sherd weight together suggest that the majority of the vessels from which these pieces derive were broken not long before being deposited in the ditches.

DISCUSSION

Made from coastal alluvium mixed with much chopped vegetable matter, large quantities of vessel briquetage are found at the Essex salt-production sites, red hills, together with settling tanks, hearths, and hearth furniture such as firebars and pedestals (Fawn *et al.* 1990, 69). The

TABLE 57: THE SALT BRIQUETAGE — SUMMARY OF THE EVIDENCE

Context	Context description and date	Sherds	Total wt (g)	Comments
Ditch of Enclosure 4				
B964 BF40	east ditch, LIA/ER	8	315	1 corner sherd (?2), 1 small piece abraded
B970 BF40	east ditch, LIA/ER	2	142	
?Mortuary enclosure BF32				
B283 BF30 (BL23)	east ditch, Enclosure 4, LIA/ER	1	223	BF30.2 fig. 35; rim and corner of rectangular trough, possibly the same vessel as B1130
B501 BF30 (BL21)	east ditch, Enclosure 4, LIA/ER	6	64	knife-trimmed and thumb-pressed rim sherd; also corner sherd
B586 BF30 (BL38)	east ditch, Enclosure 4, LIA/ER	2	42	one very abraded, one rim/corner
B385 BF31, BL31	north ditch, Enclosure 4, LIA/ER	1	12	thin Type B sherd
B1130 BF31	north ditch, Enclosure 4, LIA/ER	1	143	knife-trimmed rim of thick-walled vessel; possibly the same as B283
?Mortuary enclosure CF43-6				
C112 CF44, Sx 1	east ditch, Enclosure 5, LIA/ER	3	96	slightly abraded
C140 CF44, Sx 3	east ditch, Enclosure 5, LIA/ER	1	223	CF44.1 fig. 36
C141, CF45, Sx 2	south ditch, Enclosure 5, LIA/ER	1	71	slightly abraded; weight includes some charcoal adhering to inner surface
C182 CF45, Sx 3	south ditch, Enclosure 5, LIA/ER	1	8	
C183 CF43	south ditch, Enclosure 5, LIA/ER	2	4	

TABLE 58: AVERAGE SHERD WEIGHT OF SALT BRIQUETAGE FROM SOME ESSEX SITES

Site	No. of sherds	Total weight (g)	Average weight (g)	Reference
Stanway	29	1,343.0	46.3	–
Ardleigh	281	5,891.0	21.0	Major 1999, 157
Burnham-on-Crouch (1991)	20	421.5	21.0	Sealey 1995, 65
Burnham-on-Crouch (1992)	8	250.0	31.0	Sealey 1995, 65

peak period of salt-making activity on these sites is generally Late Iron Age to early Roman, and it has been argued that the *oppidum* of Camulodunum owed some of its pre-eminence to trade in this valuable commodity (Rodwell 1979, 159–60). The river Colne was probably tidal as far as Sheepen, and the recovery there of briquetage vessels and hearth furniture has led to suggestions that salt production took place not only along the coast but also within the *oppidum* itself (Hawkes and Hull 1947, 346–7; Niblett 1985, 23). However, fragments of both vessels and hearth furniture are increasingly being recognised on inland sites, making the Sheepen material less likely to be evidence of production. The inland finds have long been the subject of study, and the find spot most distant from the coast may be Baldock, Hertfordshire (Rodwell 1979; Rigby and Foster 1986, 188; Barford 1990, 79–80; Sealey 1995).

Rodwell suggested two possible methods for the material to travel inland: first, that salt was traded in the vessels in which it was made, and second, that salt production may have been a seasonal occupation, providing a link between inland and coastal sites and a means whereby hearth furniture might travel as well as vessels (Rodwell 1979, 159–60, 172). In discussing briquetage from Kelvedon, Eddy added that raw salt-cakes might be acquired at the coast to be refined inland (Eddy 1982, 26).

Suggestions have also been made, to some extent based on the rural nature of many of the inland find-spots and the dearth of briquetage from inside the *colonia* at Colchester, that broken briquetage was traded in its own right, perhaps to be used as salt-licks for livestock (Barford 1990, 79). These ideas have been refuted by Sealey (1995, 68–9), and are certainly unlikely to explain the presence of this material at Stanway, where there is no evidence for either domestic occupation or animal husbandry contemporary with the funerary use of the site.

The concentration of the briquetage sherds at Stanway in the ditches of the ?mortuary enclosure in Enclosures 4 and 5, and the adjacent east ditch of Enclosure 4, suggests that the most likely source for the fragments is the activity that took place in both ?mortuary enclosures. If the burial rite associated with the chambers included a prolonged period when the body was exposed, the preserving qualities of salt may have been a useful aid in absorbing body fluids and minimising putrefaction. Alternatively, briquetage fragments may be interpreted as evidence for feasting in the enclosures. The availability of salt may have been an important feature of a high-status meal, and it is also possible that briquetage vessels were used as containers for fish preserved in salt, a likely secondary product of the red hills (Hawkes and Hull 1947, 347; Fawn *et al.* 1990, 33), which could have been included in the food taken to a funerary feast. The wider potential for domestic reuse of the vessels once emptied of their original contents should also be considered. The presence of the south Essex Type B sherd may imply the import of fish from the Thames to Camulodunum, or perhaps a gift of salt for the funeral feast. Finally, and most speculatively, salt may also have been related to some other part of the burial rite. In the Roman world, sacrificial animals were sprinkled with wine and *mola salsa*, a bread of flour and salt made specifically for that purpose (Sandys 1910, 157–8), and a similar ritual is not inconceivable in the Late Iron Age/early Roman transition period in Camulodunum.

THE ENVIRONMENTAL AND FAUNAL REMAINS

THE CREMATED HUMAN REMAINS

By S.A. Mays

Of the contexts yielding cremated human bone, seven were *in situ* cremation burials (AF18, BF64, BF67, CF47, CF72, CF403, and presumably CF115). In addition, cremated remains were recovered from two pyre-sites (BF16 and BF32), there were two pits containing redeposited cremation debris (AF48 and CF7), scatters of cremated human bone in three of the chambers (AF25, BF6 and BF24), and small clusters or scatters of bone in places in the enclosure ditches of Enclosure 2 (CF6, CF415) and Enclosure 3 (BF46). None of these contexts produced evidence for the cremation of more than a single body. Ten of the groups appeared to be adult, the rest being indeterminate. In only one instance could sex be inferred, *i.e.* the probable female in AF18. The Warrior's burial (BF64) yielded an unburnt fragment of what appears to be a human juvenile long-bone. The fragment lay about 0.5 m from the burnt bone burial and thus must presumably be residual.

Burnt animal bone was found in close association with cremated human bone in one of the chambers (AF25) and at the pyre-site BF16.

Cremation of an adult corpse yields about 2 kg of bone (studies cited in Wahl 1982). Using this as a guide, it is clear that all the cremation burials from Stanway are substantially incomplete, the greatest weight of bone (639.7 g) coming from AF18, and the least (3.4 g) from AF48. Damage to the cremations by later activities is clearly an important factor contributing to the loss of bone but, above all, the nature of the context and the funerary rite itself are likely to have determined how much of the cremated material ended up in its place of burial (p. 433). Inevitable losses of bone during recovery, and destruction of bone during its long sojourn in the soil, should also not be forgotten.

All the cremated bone is predominantly neutral white in colour. Shipman *et al.* (1984) demonstrate that bone colour may be used as a very approximate guide to firing temperature; the appearance of the Stanway remains suggests thorough, even firing with temperatures in excess of 940°C. The uniformity of the colouration of the bone fragments from most burials may indicate uniformity of firing, although the possibility that less well-fired fragments may have failed to survive the aggressive Stanway soils should not be forgotten. In a few instances fragments were found with white outer surfaces but with black broken and internal surfaces. This suggests that in these cases firing was of insufficient duration for the full heat of the pyre to penetrate the bone completely.

Context **AF18** (A247), Late Iron Age urned cremation burial in Enclosure 1; A247 consists of the lower fill of the urn.
Recovery The fill of the pot was wet-sieved through a 1 mm mesh and the bone recovered from the residue by hand.
Material

	weight (g)	fragment size (mm) mean	maximum	approximate fragment count
Skull	29.5	10	30	40
Post-cranial and unidentified	610.2	4	60	10,000
Total	639.7			10,040

Included in identified elements. Fragments of skull vault, mandible (including genial tubercles), the head of a rib, fibula, acetabulum and indeterminate long-bones.
Colour   Mainly neutral white, some grey (for example endocranial surfaces of many skull vault fragments).
Sex   Probably female (based on robusticity of cranial and post-cranial bones).
Age   Adult.
Notes   Also recovered was 17.1 g of sieved residue containing fine gravels and very small fragments of cremated bone.

Context. **AF22** (A388, A461), Middle Iron Age pit in Enclosure 2.
Recovery The fill was wet-sieved through a 1 mm mesh and the bone recovered from the residue by hand.
Material

weight (g)	fragment size (mm) mean	maximum	approximate fragment count
1.1	5	10	40

Colours White.
Sex   Unknown.
Age   Unknown.

Context. **AF25** (A463, A509, A512, A528), Late Iron Age chamber in Enclosure 1.
Recovery Hand-recovered on site.
Material

weight (g)	fragment size (mm) mean	maximum	approximate fragment count
11.8	18	32	38

Included in identified elements. Fragments of indeterminate long-bones.
Colours Neutral white.
Sex   Unknown.
Age   Unknown.
Notes   A522, also from AF25, included three fragments of unburnt bone (0.1 g). Although the skeletal elements present could not be identified, this bone is probably human. A512 also included 5.4 g of burnt animal bone (cattle/horse teeth) and A528 similarly contained a little burnt animal bone including a pig molar. Firmly adhering soil precluded weighing this material. (*See* animal bone report, pp. 382–3.)

Context **AF48** (A536), Late Iron Age pit with cremation-related debris in Enclosure 1.
Recovery Hand-recovered on site.
Material

weight (g)	fragment size (mm) mean	maximum	approximate fragment count
3.4	12	32	6

Colours Neutral white.
Sex   Unknown.
Age   Adult.

Context **BF6** (B68, B92, B97, B103, B153, B157, B162, B196, B208), Late Iron Age/early Roman chamber in Enclosure 3.
Recovery Hand-recovered on site, although contexts B157, B162 and B196 were also dry-sieved through a 10 mm mesh on site.
Material

	weight (g)	fragment size (mm) mean	maximum	approximate fragment count
Skull	5.5	16	25	8
Post-cranial and unidentified	39.5	14	43	122
Total	45.0			130

Included in identified elements. Fragments of skull vault and indeterminate long-bones.
Colours Neutral white.
Sex Unknown.
Age Adult.

Context **BF24**, Early Roman burial chamber in Enclosure 4.
Recovery Hand-recovered on site.
Material

	weight (g)	fragment size (mm) mean	maximum	approximate fragment count
Skull	12.3	12	32	12
Post-cranial and unidentified	50.2	12	47	148
Total	62.5			160

Included in identified elements. Fragments of skull vault and indeterminate long-bones.
Colours Neutral white.
Sex Unknown.
Age Adult.

Context **BF30** (B522), eastern ditch of Late Iron Age/early Roman pyre-site BF32 in Enclosure 4.
Recovery Hand-recovered on site.
Material

weight (g)	fragment size (mm) mean	maximum	approximate fragment count
0.1	5	14	10

Colours Neutral white.
Sex Unknown.
Age Unknown.

Context **BF64** (B1052, B1077, B1078, B1090), 'Warrior's burial' in Enclosure 3.
Recovery Hand-recovered on site.
Material

	weight (g)	fragment size (mm) mean	maximum	approximate fragment count
Skull	2.4	4	5	10
Post-cranial and unidentified	135.1	8	28	790
Total	137.5			800

Colours Neutral white.
Sex Unknown.
Age Adult.
Notes Also from BF64 but not included in the above figures are the following four fragments: B1040, a fragment of unburnt bone, 0.4 g, probably from a juvenile long-bone; B1171, three fragments of burnt human bone, 0.5 g, recovered from spoil heap associated with BF64.

Context **BF67** (B1004, B1010, B1042, B1045, B1047, B1067, B1068), early Roman 'Inkwell burial' in Enclosure 3.
Recovery Hand-recovered on site.

Material

	weight (g)	fragment size (mm) mean	maximum	approximate fragment count
Skull	3.8	5	10	10
Post-cranial and unidentified	221.8	4	40	990
Total	225.6			1000

Colours Mainly, neutral white, some fragments have black endosteal and broken surfaces.
Sex Unknown.
Age Adult.

Context **BF16** (BL5: B72, B73, B88), upper fill of Late Iron Age/early Roman pyre-site BF16, adjacent to chamber BF6 in Enclosure 3.
Recovery Hand-recovered on site, although contexts B72 and B73 were also dry-sieved through a 10 mm mesh on site.
Material

weight (g)	fragment size (mm) mean	maximum	approximate fragment count
13.4	8	23	162

Included in identified elements. Fragments of fibula.
Colours Neutral white, grey.
Sex Unknown.
Age Unknown.
Notes Some of these fragments seem to be (unidentifiable) animal bone.

Context **BF16** (BL7: B69, B204), lower fill of Late Iron Age/early Roman pyre-site BF16, adjacent to chamber BF6 in Enclosure 3.
Recovery Hand-recovered on site and the contexts were then dry-sieved through a 10 mm mesh on site.
Material

	weight (g)	fragment size (mm) mean	maximum	approximate fragment count
Skull		-		
Post-cranial and unidentified	1.2	-	23	2
Total	1.2			2

Colours Neutral white.
Sex Unknown.
Age Unknown.
Related contexts **B30** (3.1 g) and **B38** (0.5 g): unstratified material found when cleaning between BF6 and BF16 in Enclosure 3. Probably from BF16.

Context **CF7** (CL14: C28; CL14: C49), Late Iron Age pyre-related pit, outside Enclosure 5.
Recovery Hand-recovered on site.
Material

	weight (g)	fragment size (mm) mean	maximum	approximate fragment count
Skull	7.3	20	30	10
Post-cranial and unidentified	48.5	6	45	500
Total	55.8			510

Colours Neutral white.
Sex Unknown.
Age Adult.

Context **CF47** (C916, C983), Late Iron Age/early Roman 'Doctor's burial' in Enclosure 5.
Recovery Hand-recovered on site.
Material

weight (g)	fragment size (mm) mean	maximum	approximate fragment count
158.1	3	40	300

Colours Mainly neutral white, some grey.

Sex Unknown.
Age Unknown.
Notes Also recovered was 154.4 g of sieved residue containing fine gravel and many very small fragments of cremated bone.

Context **CF72** (C407, C419, C420, C422), early Roman 'Brooches burial' in Enclosure 5.
Recovery Hand-recovered on site.
Material

	weight (g)	fragment size (mm) mean	maximum	approximate fragment count
Skull	0.7	4	6	2
Post-cranial and unidentified	73.0	4	40	158
Total	73.7			160

Colours Neutral white, some grey, some broken surfaces black.
Sex Unknown.
Age Adult.
Notes Also recovered was 220.3 g of sieved residue containing fine gravel and many very small fragments of cremated bone.

Context **CF403** (C1412, C1427, C1428), early Roman unurned cremation burial in Enclosure 5.
Recovery Hand-recovered on site.
Material

	weight (g)	fragment size (mm) mean	maximum	approximate fragment count
Skull	8.4	10	28	3
Post-cranial and unidentified	158.6	4	30	522
Total	167.0			525

Colours Neutral white.
Sex Unknown.
Age Adult.
Notes Also recovered was 216.6 g of sieved residue containing fine gravel and many very small fragments of cremated bone.

Context. **CF415** (CL178: C1474), small ?Late Iron Age pit cut into the fill of the ditch of Enclosure 2 (CF6).
Recovery Hand-recovered on site.
Material

	weight (g)	fragment size (mm) mean	maximum	approximate fragment count
Skull	9.1	10	15	10
Post-cranial and unidentified	21.8	4	27	40
Total	30.9			50

Colours Neutral white.
Sex Unknown.
Age Adult.

In addition to the above, a few fragments of burnt bone were recovered from each of the following contexts.

AF30: undated pit in Enclosure 1 but probably Early Iron Age or earlier: <0.1 g (could be human or animal).
BF42: a small pit which appears to have been part of the ?mortuary enclosure BF32 in Enclosure 4: <0.1 g (probably or certainly human).
BF46: a small charcoal-filled scoop (BF46) cutting the upper fill of the ditch of Enclosure 3 (BF5): 0.1 g (could be human or animal).
CF6: upper fill of the ditch of Enclosure 2): 3.3 g (probably human).
CF115: early Roman disturbed cremation burial in Enclosure 5: 1.0 g (could be human or animal although the context suggests the former).
CF169: Middle Iron Age pit in Enclosure 2: 0.6 g (could be human or animal).

THE FAUNAL REMAINS (TABLE 59)

By Alec Wade

The excavations produced a small, highly fragmented assemblage of animal bone consisting of over 484 pieces weighing a total of approximately 0.5 kg (TABLE 59). The remains were recovered from a variety of features including enclosure ditches, pits and burials. These dated from the Middle Iron Age, Late Iron Age and early Roman periods. Survival conditions were extremely poor and fragments from teeth, generally the most enduring of skeletal elements, dominated much of the assemblage. Many pieces had been burnt.

Tooth fragments (perhaps cattle) were recovered from the Enclosure 1 ditch AF31 of Late Iron Age date. Chambers AF25, BF6, and CF42, of Late Iron Age to early Roman date, also produced fragments of tooth. Chamber AF25 yielded burnt tooth fragments of a pig and a large mammal. Two very small amorphous bone fragments also from this feature were of a texture and density suggestive of human bone (though reliability for this is very low). Chamber BF6 contained elements of at least three teeth, probably horse molars, which may have been subject to burning. These may have been upper teeth, suggesting that at least part of the maxilla or skull was also originally present. Chamber CF42 produced dozens of small fragments from at least five or six horse upper molars. These fragments were in extremely poor condition and may also have been burnt. Several lumps of very degraded bone were recovered in association with the tooth fragments, suggesting that at least part of the maxilla, skull or lower jaw was also originally present (as in chamber BF6). Middle Iron Age pit CF250 also produced tooth fragments, perhaps from cattle.

Other features that contained animal bone included Enclosure 2 ditch CF6, pyre-site BF1/BF16 and the Warrior's burial BF64. Middle Iron Age ditch CF6 produced a quantity of tooth fragments, probably sheep or goat. A small quantity of burnt animal bone including a ?sheep carpal and a fragment of canid mandible was recovered from the pyre-site BF1/BF16. As well as some unidentifiable mammal bone, the Warrior's burial BF64 produced part of a sheep or goat molar and fragments of cattle tooth.

Near complete rabbit skeletons were recovered from Enclosure 4 ditch BF40 and from a natural feature BF192 nearby. The good condition of the bone supports the conclusion that these were relatively recent animals that had burrowed into earlier deposits.

A NOTE ON TEETH AND MANDIBLE FRAGMENTS

By Anthony J. Legge

The material is poorly preserved and has suffered a great deal of post-depositional erosion. Most of the specimens are teeth or fragments of teeth and these consist of little more than a shell of enamel from which all of the dentine has been removed by the action of soil acids. There need be no significance in the fact that the fragments are mostly horse teeth; the skeleton of this animal is notably robust and it may simply have survived the best.

Chamber BF6, B97

Upper left molars of an equid, probably from the horse, *Equus caballus*. Two more complete specimens are from the middle of the tooth row (probably P^3 and P^4). The size of these teeth is indicative of an animal of moderate size which would be described now as a 'pony'. There are numerous fragments of the enamel from other horse teeth, very likely to have been a tooth row from one animal, but probably not an entire horse skull. From the height of the enamel part remaining, it can be said that the equid was neither young nor old.

Pyre-site BF1/BF16, BL7, B204

Fragment of right canid mandible, edentate, broken through socket of canine and premolar 3. Has the sockets of premolars 1 and 2. The bone is white and calcined from burning. This is probably a fragment of dog mandible from an animal of quite small size (bigger than a lap dog, smaller than a labrador). Rather close-spaced tooth sockets suggest a fairly short-faced animal.

Chamber CF42, C756

Many fragments of equid molar, probably horse. These include four upper right premolars or molars. The remaining fragments represent at least one and probably two further teeth, likely to be from the same tooth row, so that this was probably whole when discarded.

TABLE 59: FAUNAL REMAINS

Feature	Context	Finds number	Weight (g)	Description
AF25	Chamber	A512	4	4 fragments of tooth enamel in poor condition, large mammal, probably burnt, and 2 unidentified fragments.
AF25	Chamber	A522	1	3 amorphous bone fragments. Very light weight and texture suggestive of human bone but reliability is low.
AF25	Chamber	A528	4	A fragment of pig molar, burnt.
AF31	Enclosure ditch	A445	1	14 fragments of tooth enamel in very poor condition (cattle?), probably burnt.
BF1	Pyre-site	B79, BL6	1	A few fragments of burnt animal bone, including a ?sheep carpal.
BF6	Chamber	B97	102	64+ tooth fragments, probably horse. Mostly enamel flakes in very poor condition but including parts of at least 3 upper molars, probably burnt (see separate note)
BF16	Pyre-site	B204, BL7	0.6	Fragment of right canid mandible, burnt (see separate note)
BF40	Enclosure ditch	B1157	27.3	Approximately 70 pieces of rabbit bone from a single individual. Material is in poor condition and presumably intrusive in the LIA/ERB context.
BF64	Warrior's burial	B1132	6	2 fragments of large mammal bone (unidentifiable) and a fragment of a lower sheep or goat molar. From spoil heap.
BF64	Warrior's burial	B1172	1	2 fragments of tooth, probably cattle. From spoil heap.
BF192	Pit	B1182	90	100+ pieces of bone from at least 2 mature rabbits. Mainly skull, mandible and limb bones.
CF4	Enclosure ditch	C1424	1	Damaged small mammal (rabbit-sized) vertebra. Probably intrusive.
CF6	Enclosure ditch	C55, CL29	4	Approximately 33 fragments and flakes of tooth enamel, large mammal.
CF6	Enclosure ditch	C1295,	8	Approximately 14 larger fragments of tooth enamel, probably sheep or goat, in CL126 very poor condition plus many smaller flakes. May have been burned.
CF42	Chamber	C756	178	Approximately 150+ fragments and enamel flakes from 5 or 6 horse teeth, mostly upper molars, in very poor condition and probably burnt (see separate note). Very degraded pieces of maxilla/mandible may also be present (246g of degraded material).
CF250	Pit	C1391, CL175	4	Approximately 17 fragments of tooth enamel in very poor condition, large mammal.
U/S	U/S	A15	1	A fragment of a large-sized bird coracoid (immature).
U/S	U/S	A45	4	A fragment of large mammal rib which has been chopped or sawn through.

THE PLANT MACROFOSSILS (TABLES 60–1)

By Peter Murphy and Val Fryer

Excavation and sampling were intermittent (related to phases of commercial gravel extraction), and there was no overall defined sampling strategy for the site. However, the majority of feature fills consisted of very clean sandy gravel, and sampling was therefore focused on deposits that appeared to contain concentrations of charred plant material. Subsequent sample treatment reflects changing practice in the 1990s: the samples collected before 1992 were fully quantified despite the low densities of material, whereas those examined later were assessed, but were not thought to merit quantification. A report on thirteen bulk samples collected up to 1992 was prepared by one of us (Murphy 1992). Later, 33 further bulk samples were rapidly appraised by Val Fryer, who subsequently assessed fourteen of them in detail (Fryer, unpublished). This report presents a synthesis of the two reports.

Charred plant material was separated by water flotation, using 0.5 mm collecting meshes throughout. Up until 1992, machine flotation was employed; thereafter manual flotation. The non-floating residues were wet-sieved on a 0.5 mm mesh, and small artefacts and cremated bone fragments >2 mm were separated. The dried flots were examined under a binocular microscope at magnifications of up to ×16. Nomenclature follows Stace 1997. The results are given in TABLES 60–1.

Samples from pits certainly or possibly dated to the Late Neolithic or Early Iron Age (TABLE 60) included charcoal, charred nutshell fragments of hazel (*Corylus avellana*), and fruitstones of hawthorn (*Crataegus monogyna*) and sloe (*Prunus spinosa*). There were no charred remains of cereals or arable weeds.

Bulk samples from Middle Iron Age pits, mainly in Enclosure 2 (TABLE 61), included low densities of charred cereal grains and chaff, of emmer (*Triticum dicoccum*), spelt (*Triticum spelta*), and barley (including six-row barley, *Hordeum vulgare*). Remains of oats (*Avena*) were also present, but the material did not show features that would have permitted identification to a wild or cultivated species. Fruits and seeds of arable weeds, particularly fat hen (*Chenopodium album*) and brome grass (*Bromus* sp.) were associated. There were a few remains of wetland plants, with hazel nutshell fragments. Charcoal occurred in variable quantities, together with other indeterminate charred plant macrofossils, and charred and vitrified material thought to be mainly of plant origin. Unburnt bone had not survived, but small scraps of burnt/cremated bone were noted. The material from these samples is thought to indicate settlement activity. The small coal fragments present are likely to be intrusive, relating to 19th-/20th-century steam ploughing.

The remaining samples were from contexts associated with burials or their enclosures (TABLE 61). Within Enclosure 3, the pyre deposit BF16/BL5 (B72) included wood charcoal with charred fragments of indeterminate tubers, rhizomes and monocotyledonous stem fragments, moss stem fragments and fruits and seeds of heath grass (*Danthonia decumbens*) and the herb blinks (*Montia fontana*). This points to damp, partly flushed, acid grassland, presumably growing locally on leached gravel-based soils. Assemblages of grassland plants and rhizomatous material commonly occur in Bronze Age cremation deposits (*e.g.* Murphy 1990a), but have also been reported from another Late Iron Age 'pyre-pit' at Baldock, Hertfordshire (Murphy 1990b). Possible interpretations are that the charred plant material represents plants uprooted for kindling or vegetation charred *in situ* beneath a pyre. Additionally, Dr Allan Hall (pers. comm.) raised the possibility that the material might represent charred residues from burnt turves. Turf as a component of grave fills is evidenced at Stanway and Folly Lane, Verulamium (Wiltshire 1999). It seems to have been commonly associated with high-status burials of this period. It might also have been used as a material for pyre construction. A somewhat similar assemblage of charcoal with rhizomatous material came from the ?cremation pit CF415 (CL178) cutting the enclosure ditch of Enclosure 2, although there were no identifiable seeds nor stem fragments in this sample (TABLE 61).

A sample from chamber BF6 (B129) in Enclosure 3 was from planking in the chamber (p. 117). It included some small charcoal fragments, but most of the material recovered by flotation comprised black to reddish-brown wood fragments preserved by ferrimanganiferous replacement. This material was not charred. Charcoal fragments were present, but at a density which represents the 'background scatter' of charcoal to be expected in any archaeological context. Preservation was mainly due to impregnation with minerals leached down through the gravel fill of the chamber pit.

Samples from Enclosure 5 were from the shaft CF23 (CL122 and CL123) and the pit CF66 (CL74/5) which cut into the fill of the enclosure ditch of Enclosure 5 (TABLE 61). Charred cereal and crop plant remains were present, but at exceedingly low densities. Reliable interpretation is impossible. The consistent presence of charred fruits and nuts of trees and shrubs is unusual. These include hawthorn (*Crataegus monogyna*), sloe (*Prunus spinosa*), bullace (*Prunus domestica* subsp. *insititia*) and oak (*Quercus* sp.). Charred indeterminate buds were also present, together with wood charcoal. The remains of trees and shrubs were not abundant, yet it is rare to find charred remains of such plants at all in samples from Late Iron Age and Roman settlements. A simple functional interpretation might be that this material represents charred residues from bonfires after hedge trimming. However, given the nature of the site, and also that only three samples were examined from Enclosure 5, yet all three included fruits and nuts of trees and shrubs, some special significance might reasonably be attached to this material.

TABLE 60: PLANT MACROFOSSILS AND OTHER REMAINS FROM LATE NEOLITHIC AND ?EARLY IRON AGE CONTEXTS
(× = 1–10 specimens; ×× = 11–100 specimens; ××× = 100+ specimens)

	Late Neolithic		**?Early Iron Age**	
Feature no.	AF16	AF16	AF30	AF30
Find no.	A113	A208	A432	A460
Context type	pit		pit	
Enclosure	n of E1	n E1	1	1
Trees and shrubs				
Corylus avellana L.				3(d)
Crataegus monogyna Jacq.				3
P. spinosa L.				1
Charcoal	×××	××	×	×××
Heathland plants				
Indeterminate seeds etc.				1
Other material				
Cremated/burnt bone			×	
Sample volume (litres)	10.5	9.5	13	7.5
% flot sorted	25	50	100	25

TABLE 61: CHARRED PLANT MACROFOSSILS AND OTHER REMAINS FROM MIDDLE IRON AGE TO LATE

	Middle Iron Age								
Feature no.	AF22	AF22	AF27	AF38	AF56	CF21	CF21	CF168	CF169
Layer no.						CL28	CL28		
Find no.	A388	A461	A419	A508	A577				
Context type	pit		pit	pit	pit	pit	pit	pit	pit
Enclosure	2	2	1	2	1	2	2	2	2
Cereals									
Triticum dicoccum Schubl. (gb)	2			1		×	×	×	
Triticum dicoccum Schubl. (spf)	1								
Triticum spelta L (gb)	3			1				×	
Triticum spelta L (spf)								×	
Triticum spp. (ca)	19			3	6	××	×	×	×
Triticum spp. (gb)	17					××		×	×
Triticum spp. (spb)	11							×	
Hordeum vulgare L. (ca)					4(a)				
Hordeum spp. (ca)	3			2		×	×		cf
Hordeum/Secale (rn)						×	×	××	
Cereal indet. (ca. fr.)	×	×		×	×	×	×	×	×
Cereal indet. (ca)	28			6	6	×	×	××	×
Cereal/large Poaceae (cn)		1			1	×			
Dryland herbs (weeds/grassland)									
Asteraceae indet.									
Atriplex sp.						×			
Avena sp. (a. fr)	×					××		×	
Avena sp. (ca)	13			4	1	××	×	×	
Avena sp. (fb)						××	××		
Avena/Bromus	6			4	1				
Brassicaceae indet.						×			
Bromus mollis/secalinus	18	1		5		××	××	××	×
Chenopodiaceae indet.	13			5		×	×	×	
Chenopodium album L.	44(b)	1		27(b)	2	×	×	×	
Fabaceae indet.				3					
Fallopia convolvulus (L.) A. Love	3	1				×	×	×	
Galium aparine L.									
Medicago/Trifolium/Lotus-type						×	×		
Persicaria sp.	3					×	×	×	
Plantago lanceolata L.				2		×	×	×	
Poaceae indet.	2			2		×	×	×	
Polygonaceae indet.						×	×		
Polygonum aviculare L.					1	×			
cf. *Potentilla* sp.							×		
Rumex acetosella L.		1		1		×		×	×
Rumex spp.	1			1		×	×	x	
Stellaria graminea L.									
Vicia/Lathyrus sp.				1		×	×		
Wetland plants									
Carex sp.	1					×	×	×	
Eleocharis sp.								x	
Montia fontana subsp. *minor* Hayw.				1		×	×		
Trees and shrubs									
Corylus avellana L.					1(d)	×		××	
Crataegus monogyna Jacq.									
Prunus sp.									
P. domestica subsp. *Insititia* L.									
P. spinosa L.									
Quercus sp. (cupule frag.)									
Quercus sp. (immature acorn)									
Sambucus nigra L.									
Charcoal	××	×	×××	×	××	×××	×××	×××	×××
Heathland plants									
Danthonia decumbens (L.) DC									
Ericaceae indet. (flo.)									
Other plant macrofossils									
Moss stem fragments									
Root/stem/rhizome						×	×	×	
Tuber fragment						×			
Buds									
Indeterminate fruitstone frags.									
Indeterminate inflorescence fragments						×	×		
Indeterminate seeds etc.	3	1		1	1	×	×	×	
Mineral replaced wood									
Other material									
Black porous 'cokey' material						××	××	×	××
Black tarry material						×	×		×
Siliceous globules						×	×		
Vitrified material						×	×		
Small coal fragments						×	×	×	××
Cremated/burnt bone	×	×			×				×
Sample volume (litres)	12	7	3	11.5	6	26	20.5	36	26
% flot sorted	100	100	25	100	100	50	100	100	50

IRON AGE/EARLY ROMAN CONTEXTS (× = 1–10 specimens; ×× = 11–100 specimens; ××× = 100+ specimens)

					?MIA	*LIA*	*LIA/early Roman*					
CF170	CF171	CF173	CF250	CF250	AF44	CF415	BF6	BF16	BF17	CF23	CF23	CF66
CL158	CL169	CL175/6	CL176		CL178		BL5		CL123	CL122	CL74/5
					A498		B129	B72	B144	C1418	C1416	
pit	*pit*	*pit*	*pit*		*pit*	*pit*	*chamber*	*pyre site*	*pit*	*shaft*		*pit*
2	2	2	2	2	2	2	3	3	3	5	5	5

	×		×	×								
				×								
	×	×	×	×		×						
			×									
			×									
		×	×			×						
×	×		×	×								
×	×		×	×		×					×	
				×								
	×											
		×										
			×									
×												
		×	×	×								
		×		×								
×		×	×	×								
		×								×		×
										×		
		×	×									
		×		×								
	×	×									×	
			×									
			×									
			×									
			×									
								1				
			×									×
										×	×	×
										×		
										×	×	×
										×		
×××	× ×××	× ××	×××	×××	×××	×××	×	×××	×××	×××	×××	×××
								6				
						×						
								×				
×	×	××	×	×		×××		×		×	×	×
×						×××		2		××	×	×
						×				×		
×	×	×				×		4	1			×
						×						
×	×	×	×			×				×		×
×						×						
	×					×						
	×					×						
×	×	×	×			×		×				
				×								
25	24.5	13	11	20.5	2.5	25	20	14	16.5	20	2	4
50	100	100	100	100	25	25	100	25	3.125	50	100	100

THE WOOD AND LEATHER REMAINS (TABLES 62–7)

By Anne-Maria Bojko and Nina Crummy, incorporating information from Ashok Roy

INTRODUCTION *(AMB)*

Despite the aggressive soil conditions, the preservation of organic material at Stanway was especially rich for this district. The following categories of material were identified: wood, textile, leather, and plant remains, including moss and grasses. Only the wood and leather are described here, the other materials have been discussed by the relevant specialists elsewhere in the volume. While some of the organic matter has been preserved due to mineralisation by iron salts, most has survived in an unmineralised state owing to its proximity to copper-alloy objects.

The wood divides into three groups: artefacts, structural remains, and charcoal. The latter forms the bulk of the assemblage, and has been recovered from the Middle Iron Age enclosure (Enclosure 2) and from all the funerary enclosures, although most comes from Enclosure 5, the ditches and other features that were the most intensively excavated. There is a distinct difference between the assemblages from Enclosures 2 and 5, with hazel the most commonly occurring species at the former, ash at the latter.

PRESERVATION *(AMB)*

Wood was recovered in the three following states: unaltered, mineralised, and charcoal. A distinction can be made between wood that has been deliberately worked in order to make an artefact or structure and wood that has been used in an unaltered state, *i.e.* for fuel in the funeral pyres. The vast majority of charcoal specimens examined were twig or branch wood.

Unaltered wood is invariably preserved only where it has been in direct contact with copper-alloy artefacts in burial contexts, doubtless due to the biocidal effect of copper alloy, and several features have produced both fragments of oak planking and of a maple game board in this state. While the wood is compressed and desiccated by the burial conditions, it is generally well enough preserved to allow identification.

Mineralised wood was preserved because of its proximity to iron and is mainly found on the nails from the graves and chambers. Positive identification has not been undertaken on this category of material. Unmineralised wood was also found in close proximity to nails and it may be assumed that it forms part of the same structure.

Charcoal was principally found in the enclosure ditches, and some was also recovered from burials and other features inside the enclosures. The state of preservation of the charcoal varies considerably, from very good to poor. It is possible that some of the poorly preserved specimens are wood which was quite degraded prior to burning. This is probably true of some of the specimens of oak, which appear very flattened and distorted.

Leather was found only in CF47, in contact with both the copper-alloy fittings on the game board (CF47.20a and CF47.20c) and two of the copper-alloy rings (CF47.24f and CF47.24g).

METHOD OF EXAMINATION *(AMB)*

Samples of unaltered wood were sectioned with a razor blade to provide thin sections of transverse, tangential longitudinal and radial longitudinal planes. Charcoal was fractured along these planes. The structures were examined using transmitted light for the thin sections and incident light for the charcoal.

RESULTS *(NC from identifications by AMB)*

Enclosure 2 (TABLE 62)

Only charcoal fragments, mostly twigs, were recovered from the Middle Iron Age enclosure. Most came from the enclosure ditches, but a few pits also produced fragments (TABLE 62). They may be debris from hedge fires or the discarded remnants of fuel cleared from hearths, ovens or furnaces.

TABLE 62: CHARCOAL FROM ENCLOSURE 2

Find	Feature	Context description	Species	Common name
C13	CF6	enclosure ditch	*Hedera helix*	ivy
C13	CF6	enclosure ditch	*Fraxinus excelsior*	ash
C20	CF6 Sx 1	enclosure ditch	*Corylus avellana*	hazel
C20	CF6 Sx 1	enclosure ditch	*Betula* sp.	birch
C20	CF6 Sx 1	enclosure ditch	*Quercus* sp.	oak
C25	CF6 Sx 1	enclosure ditch	*Corylus avellana*	hazel
C26	CF6 Sx 1	enclosure ditch	*Corylus avellana*	hazel
C47	CF6 Sx 1	enclosure ditch	probably *Acer* sp.	maple
C55	CF6 Sx 2	enclosure ditch	*Ulmus* sp.	elm
C59	CF6 Sx 1	enclosure ditch	*Betula* sp.	birch
C61	CF6 Sx 1	enclosure ditch	*Betula* sp.	birch
C61	CF6 Sx 1	enclosure ditch	*Corylus avellana*	hazel
C61	CF6 Sx 1	enclosure ditch	?bark	–
C62	CF6 Sx 1	enclosure ditch	*Betula* sp.	birch
C75	CF6 Sx 1	enclosure ditch	*Corylus avellana*	hazel
C1228	CF6	enclosure ditch	*Quercus* sp.	oak
C1253	CF6	enclosure ditch	*Corylus avellana*	hazel
C1259	CF6 Sx 9	enclosure ditch	*Quercus* sp.	oak
C1459	CF6	enclosure ditch	*Corylus avellana*	hazel
C1459	CF6	enclosure ditch	*Fraxinus excelsior*	ash
C1459	CF6	enclosure ditch	*Quercus* sp.	oak
C1469	CF6	enclosure ditch	*Fraxinus excelsior*	ash
C1469	CF6	enclosure ditch	*Ulmus* sp.	elm
C1469	CF6	enclosure ditch	*Corylus avellana*	hazel
C1469	CF6	enclosure ditch	*Quercus* sp.	oak
C1480	CF6	enclosure ditch	Maloideae or *Acer*	fruitwoods or maple
C1446	CF21	pit	*Acer* sp.	maple
C1446	CF21	pit	*Quercus* sp.	oak
C1455	CF21	pit	*Quercus* sp.	oak
C1460	CF21	pit	*Quercus* sp.	oak
C–	CF21	pit	*Quercus* sp.	oak
C1264	CF168	pit	*Quercus* sp.	oak
C1429	CF168	pit	*Quercus* sp.	oak
C1329	CF171	pit	*Quercus* sp.	oak
C1431	CF173	pit	*Quercus* sp.	oak

Six or seven tree species are represented by the charcoal in the ditch, all native. Of 24 identified fragments, eight were of hazel (33 per cent), five of oak (21 per cent), four of birch (17 per cent), three of ash (13 per cent), two of elm (8 per cent), and there was also one piece of maple and another of either a fruitwood or maple. One fragment of ivy was also found. This group could come from a mixed species hedge, but the absence of large fragments suggests it may be the result of random collection of brushwood for fuel, and the preponderance of hazel and oak may be caused by the burning of offcuts of coppiced wood used for hurdles, fences, or wattle-and-daub structures. The absence of species preferring wet conditions such as alder, willow and poplar suggests that most of the wood came from trees in the immediate vicinity of the site, which lies on a plateau above the damp soils of the Roman River valley and its small tributary streams.

In contrast to the range of species present in the enclosure ditch, all the charcoal from the pits is of oak except for a single fragment of maple. The latter and four of the oak fragments (out of eight) came from CF21, a pit that also produced a considerable quantity of burnt or scorched structural clay (pp. 36–8). These pieces may therefore be all that remains of wattles from the same structure. The three other pits, CF168, CF171 and CF173, also produced fragments of structural clay. Although slight, this deposition pattern may indicate a preference for the use of coppiced oak for wattles (Gale 1996, 262; Straker 2000, 513).

Enclosure 1 (TABLE 64)

Only two fragments of charcoal came from Enclosure 1, both from the section across the north ditch AF17 (TABLE 64). One piece is ash and the other oak.

Enclosure 3 (TABLES 63–4)

Wood associated with the very fragmentary copper-alloy game board fittings in BF6 could not be positively identified (TABLE 63). However, it appears to be ring porous, and the rays are uniseriate and homogeneous, which suggests that it is oak (*Quercus* sp.). It is certainly not maple, which was used for the game boards in BF64 and CF47.

The wood preserved in the copper-alloy fittings from the game board in BF64 is maple (*Acer* sp.). If this is the native field maple, then it is a tree that flourishes today in the Stanway area and wider region. The wood works well and is particularly good for turning. Large field maples are rarely found in England today, but the fact that maple was the wood of choice for all the identifiable wooden artefacts found at Stanway suggests that there was no shortage of good-sized boards from large trees in the mid 1st century A.D. Alternatively, the game board may have been worked from imported timber, or was imported ready-made.

Fragments of wood found beneath the handled basin in BF64 are of oak (*Quercus* sp.), and might be the remains of a wooden platter or tray.

Two fragments of charcoal came from the ditches of Enclosure 3, both of hazel, and two fragments of oak and one of ash came from BF17, a feature that also produced heat-affected metalwork (TABLE 64). The latter group can be assumed to be pyre debris, the former may be either from pyres or from fires associated with funerary feasts.

Charcoal, again probably pyre debris but not found with the cremated bone, also came from two of the burials in this enclosure, BF64 and BF67 (TABLE 63). All the pieces recovered are of oak.

Enclosure 4 (TABLE 64)

Four fragments of charcoal came from the southern half of the east ditch of Enclosure 4, two of oak and one each of elm and ash. The ditches of the ?mortuary enclosure produced a fragment of ash and a fragment of oak (TABLE 64).

Enclosure 5 (TABLES 63, 65–7)

The well-furnished burial CF47 produced several unaltered wood samples (TABLE 63), some from grave goods, others from the funerary structure. Fragments of a game board of maple (*Acer* sp.) were preserved in association with its copper-alloy fittings, and other organic materials were also found in association with the board. On the underside were traces of a straw-like material covering the outer surface of the copper-alloy fittings and extending onto the board itself. When the wood was removed from the metal, a dark smooth substance was observed on the surface of the wood. This has no obvious structure when viewed under low-power magnification and is probably leather. Similar fragments were associated with the hinge. Also observed on the wood of the board were small patches of a powdery red pigment (C939, SF37). This was analysed by Ashok Roy of the National Gallery and found to be a definite paint layer of natural earth pigment (report in archive).

Maple was also used for a wooden board or tray decorated with copper-alloy studs and sheet. Some of the wood from this object was also preserved beneath the strainer bowl in the grave.

Fragments of oak planks (*Quercus* sp.) were found covering the strainer bowl, on the handle of the saucepan, and over the game board, and also behind the rings that lay against the wall of the grave. Traces of the same red pigment found on the wood of the game board coated both sides of the oak fragments associated with the rings. Small fragments of leather loops were found surviving in contact with two of the rings.

TABLE 63: WOOD FROM BURIALS AND CHAMBERS IN ENCLOSURES 3 AND 5

Enclosure	Find	Feature	Location in burial	Condition	Species	Common name
3	B226	BF6	board of game board (with game board fittings BF6.24b)	unaltered	possibly *Quercus* sp.	oak
3	B–/1059–60	BF64	board with game board (with game board fittings BF64.29e)	unaltered	*Acer* sp.	maple
3	B1019	BF64	beneath the handled basin BF64.26	unaltered	*Quercus* sp.	oak
3	B1135	BF64	spoil heap	charcoal	*Quercus* sp.	oak
3	B1144	BF67/BF64	spoil heap	charcoal	*Quercus* sp.	oak
3	B1005	BF67	fill	charcoal	*Quercus* sp.	oak
5	C524	CL49/BF42	upper fill	charcoal	*Quercus* sp.	oak
5	C901–2/906–7	CF47	remains of ?grave cover CF47.41 (fragments on top of strainer bowl CF47.22)	unaltered	*Quercus* sp.	oak
5	C905	CF47	remains of ?grave cover CF47.41 (on top of handle of saucepan CF47.21)	unaltered	*Quercus* sp.	oak
5	C908/913/971/979	CF47	tray CF47.25 (with studs CF47.25 and sheet CF47.25 and beneath strainer bowl CF47.22)	unaltered	*Acer* sp.	maple
5	C915/996–999	CF47	board of game (with fittings CF47.20a)	unaltered	*Acer* sp.	maple
5	C938–9	CF47	with rings CF47.24	unaltered	*Quercus* sp.	oak

TABLE 64: CHARCOAL FROM ENCLOSURES 1, 3 AND 4

Enclosure	Find	Feature	Context description	Species	Common name
1	A592	AF17	north enclosure ditch	*Fraxinus excelsior*	ash
1	A592	AF17	north enclosure ditch	*Quercus* sp.	oak
3	B1102	BF4	east enclosure ditch	*Corylus avellana*	hazel
3	B1103	BF4	east enclosure ditch	*Corylus avellana*	hazel
3	B124	BF17	pit	*Quercus* sp.	oak
3	B142	BF17	pit	*Quercus* sp.	oak
3	B154	BF17	pit	*Fraxinus excelsior*	ash
4	B942	BF40	east enclosure ditch	possibly *Ulmus* sp.	elm
4	B970	BF40	east enclosure ditch	*Quercus* sp.	oak
4	B970	BF40	east enclosure ditch	*Fraxinus excelsior*	ash
4	C9	CF5	east enclosure ditch (south end)	probably *Quercus* sp.	oak
4	B586	BF30	east ditch of ?mortuary encl	*Fraxinus excelsior*	ash
4	B524	BF30/31	north/east ditch of ?mortuary encl.	*Quercus* sp.	oak
4	B1159	BF180	?natural feature	probably *Quercus* sp.	oak

A large number of charcoal fragments, presumably debris from pyre fuel or from funerary feasting, were recovered from the north ditch of Enclosure 5, with a few also from a patch of burning in the west ditch and two from the south ditch (TABLE 65). The north ditch was shared with Enclosure 4 and is close to the ?mortuary enclosure BF32, and therefore these fragments may relate to the funerary rites in either enclosure. The north and south ditches produced charcoal from four native species: ash (42%), oak (27%), hazel (12%), and elm (12%), and one fragment each of one or two others, *Prunus sp.* and either hazel or alder. In contrast, the charcoal in the west ditch was only of oak, but also included a ?plant stem and a piece of bark.

TABLE 65: CHARCOAL FROM THE DITCHES OF ENCLOSURE 5

Find	Feature	Context description	Species	Common name
C6	CF1	north enclosure ditch	*Fraxinus excelsior*	ash
C7	CF1 Sx 1	north enclosure ditch	*Quercus* sp.	oak
C7	CF1 Sx 1	north enclosure ditch	*Fraxinus excelsior*	ash
C8	CF1 Sx 1	north enclosure ditch	*Fraxinus excelsior*	ash
C10	CF1 Sx 1	north enclosure ditch	*Fraxinus excelsior*	ash
C11	CF1 Sx 1	north enclosure ditch	*Fraxinus excelsior*	ash
C11	CF1 Sx 1	north enclosure ditch	*Quercus* sp.	oak
C12	CF1 Sx 1	north enclosure ditch	*Corylus avellana*	hazel
C18	CF1 Sx 1	north enclosure ditch	*Fraxinus excelsior*	ash
C71	CF1 Sx 4	north enclosure ditch	*Quercus* sp.	oak
C139	CF1 Sx 6	north enclosure ditch	*Quercus* sp.	oak
C139	CF1 Sx 6	north enclosure ditch	*Ulmus* sp.	elm
C139	CF1 Sx 6	north enclosure ditch	*Fraxinus excelsior*	ash
C146	CF1 Sx 6	north enclosure ditch	*Quercus* sp.	oak
C147	CF1 Sx 7	north enclosure ditch	*Quercus* sp.	oak
C147	CF1 Sx 7	north enclosure ditch	*Fraxinus excelsior*	ash
C158	CF1	north enclosure ditch	*Fraxinus excelsior*	ash
C158	CF1	north enclosure ditch	?folded bark	–
C158	CF1	north enclosure ditch	*Corylus avellana*	hazel
C158	CF1	north enclosure ditch	*Ulmus* sp.	elm
C158	CF1	north enclosure ditch	probably *Prunus* sp.	plum *etc*
C1364	CF1	north enclosure ditch	*Fraxinus excelsior*	ash
C1365	CF1	north enclosure ditch	*Ulmus* sp.	elm
C1377	CF1	north enclosure ditch	*Quercus* sp.	oak
C1383	CF1 Sx 11	north enclosure ditch	*Fraxinus excelsior*	ash
C50	CF3	south enclosure ditch	*Corylus avellana*	hazel
C1397	CF3 Sx 11	south enclosure ditch	*Corylus* or *Alnus*	hazel or alder
C111	CF66	burning in west enclosure ditch	*Quercus* sp.	oak
C111	CF66	burning in west enclosure ditch	?plant stem	–
C116	CF66	burning in west enclosure ditch	*Quercus* sp.	oak
C116	CF66	burning in west enclosure ditch	?bark fragment	–
C173	CF66	burning in west enclosure ditch	*Quercus* sp.	oak

All the ditches of the ?mortuary enclosure CF43–6 in Enclosure 5 also contained many charcoal fragments; most were found on the east side, perhaps the result of the prevailing west wind (TABLE 66). Five native species are present, with ash and oak occurring in exactly the same proportions as in the main enclosure ditches, 42% and 27% respectively, followed by small quantities of birch, alder and hazel. The similarity between the principal components of the two assemblages may show not only the local species available for fuel collection, but also deliberate proportional selection of various woods for a well-managed fire. The high, and seemingly consistent, proportions of ash and oak, which are both good fuel woods (Gale 1996, 262), may therefore be deliberate. The charcoal fragments from the burial pit at Folly Lane, Verulamium, also contained much ash and oak, as well as a similar amount of hazel and a quantity of blackthorn (Gale 1999, 393).

In the other features in Enclosure 5, many of them probably natural, the charcoal is predominantly oak. A pit or hearth near the ?mortuary enclosure, CF64, produced a single fragment of birch, also a good fuel wood (TABLE 67).

TABLE 66: CHARCOAL FROM THE ?MORTUARY ENCLOSURE CF43–6 IN ENCLOSURE 5

Find	Feature	Context description	Species	Common name
C178	F43 Sx 4	north ditch	*Fraxinus excelsior*	ash
C180	F43 Sx 4	north ditch	*Fraxinus excelsior*	ash
C180	F43 Sx 4	north ditch	*Quercus* sp.	oak
C130	F44 Sx 2	east ditch	*Fraxinus excelsior*	ash
C130	F44 Sx 2	east ditch	*Quercus* sp.	oak
C134	F44 Sx 3	east ditch	*Quercus* sp.	oak
C134	F44 Sx 3	east ditch	*Fraxinus excelsior*	ash
C145	F44 Sx 3	east ditch	*Quercus* sp.	oak
C145	F44 Sx 3	east ditch	*Alnus* sp.	alder
C145	F44 Sx 3	east ditch	*Fraxinus excelsior*	ash
C143	F44 Sx 4	east ditch	*Quercus* sp.	oak
C143	F44 Sx 4	east ditch	*Fraxinus excelsior*	ash
C143	F44 Sx 4	east ditch	*Alnus* sp.	alder
C179	F44 Sx 6	east ditch	*Fraxinus excelsior*	ash
C179	F44 Sx 6	east ditch	*Quercus* sp.	oak
C181	F44 Sx 6	east ditch	*Fraxinus excelsior*	ash
C181	F44 Sx 6	east ditch	*Quercus* sp.	oak
C190	F44 Sx 7	east ditch	*Betula* sp.	birch
C142	F45 Sx 2	south ditch	*Fraxinus excelsior*	ash
C191	F45 Sx 6	south ditch	*Betula* sp.	birch
C191	F45 Sx 6	south ditch	*Fraxinus excelsior*	ash
C192	F45 Sx 6	south ditch	*Betula* sp.	birch
C136	F46 Sx 4	west ditch	probably *Fraxinus*	ash
C170	F46 Sx 5	west ditch	possibly *Alnus* or *Betula*	alder or birch
C170	F46 Sx 5	west ditch	*Corylus avellana*	hazel
C170	F46 Sx 5	west ditch	*Quercus* sp.	oak
C170	F46 Sx 5	west ditch	*Hedera helix*	ivy

TABLE 67: CHARCOAL FROM OTHER FEATURES IN ENCLOSURE 5

Find	Feature	Context description	Species	Common name
C54	CF22 Sx 1	linear feature, probably natural	*Quercus* sp.	oak
C78	CF23	shaft/post-pit	*Quercus* sp.	oak
C80	CF23	shaft/post-pit	possibly *Corylus*	hazel
C104	CF23	shaft/post-pit	*Quercus* sp.	oak
C118	CF64	pit/hearth near ?mortuary encl	*Betula* sp.	birch
C128	CF77	pit	*Corylus avellana*	hazel
C172	CF96 Sx 13	slot	*Prunus* sp.	plum etc.
C195	CF96	slot	probably *Quercus*	oak
C51	CF13	?natural feature	*Quercus* sp.	oak
C52	CF14	?natural feature	*Quercus* sp.	oak
C1374	CF211	?natural feature	*Quercus* sp.	oak
C1374	CF211	?natural feature	*Fraxinus excelsior*	ash
C1401	CF360	?natural feature, probable tree hollow	2 pieces *Quercus* sp.	oak

PALYNOLOGICAL ANALYSIS OF THE ORGANIC MATERIAL LODGED IN THE SPOUT OF THE STRAINER BOWL (FIGS 155–6; TABLES 68–70)

By Patricia E.J. Wiltshire

The plug of organic debris retrieved from the spout of this container (CF47.22) was initially examined by Peter Murphy using scanning electron microscopy, but it appeared to consist of an amorphous mass of organic material. To maximise the information, it was decided to sacrifice a proportion of the plug in order to carry out palynological analysis of the matrix.

Standard preparation procedures were used to process the sample (Dimbleby 1985). It was acetolysed and treated with hydrofluoric acid, and then lightly stained with 0.5% safranine and mounted in glycerol jelly. Pollen counting was carried out with a Zeiss phase contrast microscope at ×400 and ×1000 magnification. Counts for pollen and plant spores exceeded 500. Pollen and plant spores were expressed as percentages of total land pollen and spores (tlp/s). Palynological nomenclature follows that of Bennett *et al.* 1994 and Moore *et al.* 1991. Cereal-type pollen refers to all Poaceae grains >40 μm with annulus diameters >8 μm (Anderson 1979; Edwards 1989). Botanical nomenclature follows that of Stace (1997).

The results are shown in TABLES 68–70, and FIGURES 155–6. TABLE 68 shows the percentage of total land pollen and spores (tlp/s) of all the palynological taxa found in the plug. These have been arranged according to plant family and probable taphonomic status. TABLE 69 shows the proportions of the various taxa represented in the plug, excluding artemisia. TABLE 70 gives a list of chemical compounds extracted from *Artemisia absinthium* and *A. vulgaris*. FIGURE 155 is a pie chart showing the proportions of artemisia to 'bee flower' pollen and that of probable adventive pollen. FIGURE 156 is a pie chart illustrating the proportions of pollen from various 'bee flowers'.

The data shown in TABLE 68 are quite startling in their degree of bias towards a limited range of palynological taxa. They demonstrate quite clearly that the plug of organic material represents the collection of a specific range of plant material by one or more agencies. The assemblage of taxa could not, in any way, represent the natural pollen rain. In the first place, very few plant families were represented, the major ones being Asteraceae (daisy family), Fabaceae (clover, pea, and bean family), Lamiaceae (white deadnettle family), and Rosaceae (rose family). Secondly, the assemblage was overwhelmingly dominated by artemisia (mugwort

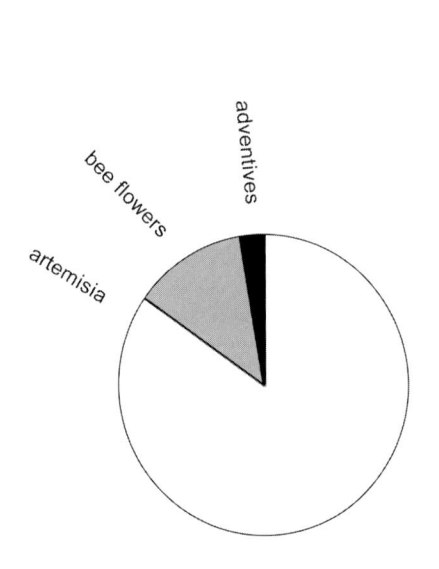

FIG. 155. Doctor's burial CF47 strainer bowl: the proportions of artemisia to 'bee flower' pollen and that of probable adventive pollen from the plug of organic debris

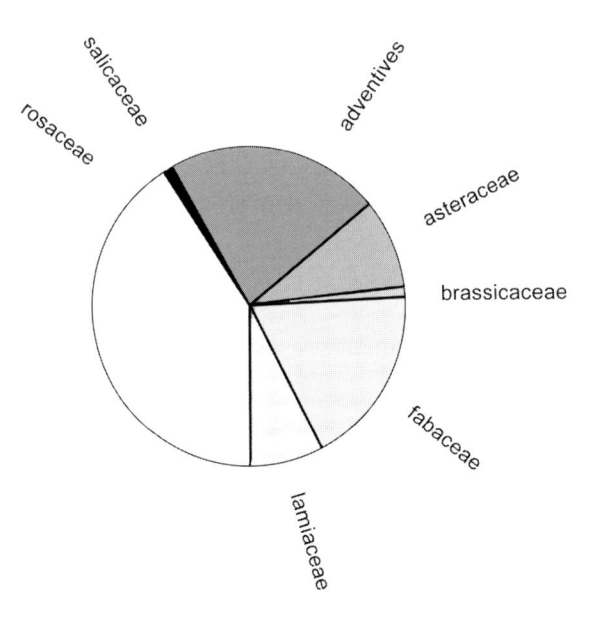

FIG. 156. Doctor's burial CF47 strainer bowl: the proportions of various bee flower pollen from the plug of organic debris

TABLE 68: THE PERCENTAGES OF TOTAL LAND POLLEN AND SPORES (TLP/S) OF ALL THE PALYNOLOGICAL TAXA FOUND IN THE PLUG

Pollen taxa	Possible/probable plant taxa	% total pollen
Medicinal plant		
Artemisia	mugwort/wormwood	84.7
Bee plants		
Aster-type	daisy/ragwort/coltsfoot/fleabane	0.8
Asteracaea (fenestrate)	dandelion-like plants	0.6
Sinapis type	bitter cresses/lady's smock/hedge mustard	+
Ononis (cf.)	rest harrow	0.8
Trifolium type	clovers/medicks	+
Vicia type	vetches	1.4
Fabaceae indet.	pea/bean/clover/broom	+
Lamium (cf.)	white and red dead nettles	0.6
Stachys type	woundworts	+
Crataegus (cf.)	hawthorn	+
Rubus (cf.)	bramble	5.8
Sorbus (cf.)	rowan/white beam	+
Salix	willow	+
Adventives		
Quercus	oak	+
Cereal type	cereal	+
Plantago lanceolata	ribwort plantain	0.8
Poaceae	grasses	2.0

or wormwood) while most of the rest of the assemblage were from plants that are characteristically pollinated by insects, particularly bees.

Insect-pollinated plants rarely dominate pollen assemblages in samples from natural habitats, or from archaeological features where sediments have accumulated over periods of time. Their pollen production is characteristically low, and dispersal is poor (Faegri and Iversen 1989). In very many instances, the plant may be represented in the pollen record only if its tissues have been incorporated into a deposit, or if it has been introduced artificially (personal observation).

Artemisia is considered to be wind-pollinated, but its representation in the air is generally as low as that for many insect-pollinated plants, and it is restricted to a short period between late July and August (Proctor *et al.* 1996). Of the other taxa represented, the only taxa usually well represented in the pollen rain are those listed as adventives. Even here, however, cereal pollen does not travel far from the plant.

ARTEMISIA

There are four species of artemisia native to Britain, the most common and widespread being *A. vulgaris* (mugwort) and *A. absinthium* (wormwood) (Stace 1997). In Britain, both have their centres of distribution in the south but, today, mugwort is much more widespread than wormwood. Nevertheless, both species of artemisia are freely available in Essex and, presumably, would have been so in the past. Unfortunately, the two species cannot be differentiated through pollen morphology (certainly not by light microscopy), so it is not possible to say which artemisia is present in the copper-alloy vessel. Indeed, the organic plug might have contained a mixture of both.

The large concentration of mugwort/wormwood pollen suggests that considerable amounts of the plant (leaves and/or flowers) had been placed into the vessel. The archaeological evidence (surgical instruments) from the grave indicates that it was of a medical practitioner. It is likely, therefore, that herbal remedies were being administered as well as surgical treatments.

TABLE 69: THE PROPORTIONS OF THE VARIOUS TAXA REPRESENTED IN THE PLUG, EXCLUDING ARTEMISIA

Plant family	% sum minus Artemisia
Asteraceae	9.2
Brassicaceae	1.2
Fabaceae	18.4
Lamiaceae	7.8
Rosaceae	0.8
Salicaceae	1.3
Adventives	22.4

TABLE 70: THE CHEMICAL COMPOUNDS EXTRACTED FROM *ARTEMISIA ABSINTHIUM* AND *A. VULGARIS*

Compound	Class of compound	Activity/comments	Artemisia species
Vulgarin	Sesquiterpene lactone	Cytotoxic and anti-tumour	*A. vulgaris* (& many spp.)
Santamarin	Sesquiterpene lactone	Cytotoxic and anti-tumour	Many species
Desacetoxymatricarin	Sesquiterpene lactone	Cytotoxic and anti-tumour	Many species
Canin	Sesquiterpene lactone	Cytotoxic and anti-tumour	Many species
Alpha-Santonin	Sesquiterpene lactone	Anti-helminthic, ascaricidal, insect-deterrent, cytotoxic and anti-tumour	Many species
Beta-Santonin	Sesquiterpene lactone	Anti-helminthic but highly toxic	Many species
Absinthin	Sesquiterpene lactone	Main bitter principle (causes nervousness, convulsions, death)	*A. absinthium*
Artabsin	Sesquiterpene lactone	Converted to chamazulene on steam distillation (*see below*)	*A. absinthium*
Achillin	Sesquiterpene lactone	Converted to chamazulene on steam distillation (*see below*)	Several species
Chamazulene	Sesquiterpenoid	Anti-inflammatory, anti-pyretic	*A. absinthium*
Thujone	Monoterpenoid	Anti-helminthic (may cause convulsions)	*A. absinthium*
Camphor	Monoterpenoid	Rubefacient, mild analgesic, topical anti-pruritic, affects central nervous system (toxic to humans)	Many species
Naringen	Flavonone	Anti-bacterial, anti-fungal, anti-hepatotoxic, anti-spasmodic, anti-ulcer, inhibits serotonin, inhibits platelet aggregation	Many species
Axillarin	Flavonol	Anti-viral	Many species
Isochlorogenic acid b	Phenylpropanoid	Inhibits lipid peroxidation in mitochondria and microsomes of liver	Many species

Both species of artemisia have a long history in herbal medicine and have had uses as diuretics and treatments for, among other things, fevers, hysteria, problems associated with childbirth, epilepsy, jaundice, oedema, throat infections, bruising, gravel, and flatulence. They have also been used to counteract the effects of opiates, and as an antidote to poisoning by hemlock and toadstools. They have also been used as strewing herbs (to discourage fleas, moths, and other pests), as well as components of love potions. One of the most important and widespread uses of both species was for treating intestinal worm infestations, particularly those caused by nematodes such as roundworm, threadworm, and pinworm. A medicine was made by infusing the plant in hot water, the liquid filtered, and the filtrate administered orally to the patient. However, it has been noted that a 'spirit' infusion (probably in some alcoholic drink) was more effective (Grieve 1992, 556–8, 858–60).

This genus has been of considerable interest to modern biochemists and many active principles have been characterised. A list of known bioactive compounds that have been extracted from the aerial parts of artemisia is given in TABLE 70 (Harborne et al. 1999). It is of interest that many of the symptoms thought by herbalists to have been alleviated by application of the plant extracts, are actually caused by some of these active principles. When given in excess some are lethal, so ancient medical practitioners are likely to have been skilled in assessing appropriate dosage when medication involved oral administration.

All artemisia species are very bitter but *A. absinthium* is the bitterest herb known (Grieve 1992). It is not surprising, therefore, to find a significant percentage of the total pollen sum to be represented by bee-pollinated plants. The addition of honey to the mugwort/wormwood medicine would make it more palatable.

BEE FLOWERS

TABLES 68 and 69 show the range of pollen taxa other than artemisia in the plug from the spout of the copper vessel. Most of the plants represented in the assemblage are insect-pollinated and many produce typical 'bee flowers', particularly the Asteraceae, Fabaceae, and Lamiaceae. These families have evolved flowers where the rewards of pollen and/or nectar are hidden in the corolla of the flower so that only insects with specific tongue lengths can gain access to them (Proctor et al. 1996). However, excluding artemisia, the most frequent taxon represented in the plug was Rosaceae (rose family) with cf. *Rubus* (bramble) being the most abundant (38.2% of total pollen excluding artemisia). Rosaceous flowers are accessible to a wide range of insects and are frequently visited by bees, as are most of the flowers represented in TABLES 68 and 69.

ADVENTIVES

The plants included in this category are commonly found in the pollen rain, and their pollen is known to settle on many surfaces, including those of other plants. They may, therefore, be considered as 'contaminants' in this particular assemblage. Leaves, flowers, and stems can filter pollen out of the air, and a plant can often be coated with pollen from other species. It would be very difficult, therefore, to exclude them when collecting plant material for a specific purpose such as making medicine. It is not surprising to find the pollen of *Quercus* (oak), *Plantago lanceolata* (ribwort plantain), and Poaceae (grasses) because all are wind-pollinated and are high pollen producers. Cereals, on the other hand, have poor production and dispersal and their presence might indicate the proximity of cereal fields to the collected material.

INTERPRETATION

It seems highly likely that the owner of the copper-alloy vessel had collected artemisia plants and was in the practice of making infusions for some medical purpose. Considering the proven efficacy of many of the compounds produced by both mugwort and wormwood, it is reasonable to suggest that either or both of these plants were being used as treatment. Texts of herbalism such as that by Nicholas Culpeper (17th century) and M. Grieve (1992; first published 1931 and revised in 1973) list a wide range of ailments treated by artemisia species. For example, it is perfectly reasonable to suggest that the Stanway doctor was treating his patients for complaints such as intestinal worms. Archaeological features regularly yield *Trichuris* (whipworm) and *Ascaris* (roundworm) eggs (personal observation), and this suggests that people in the past were troubled by nematode worm infections. Certainly, in temperate regions today, infestation by nematodes such as pinworm (*Enterobius vermicularis*) is very common, especially in children (Smyth 1962).

As shown in TABLE 70, many bioactive compounds have been identified in artemisia species, and there is scientific evidence for their effectiveness in treating a range of ailments. All artemisia species contain bitter principles that would render any infusion highly unpalatable. The very high representation of 'bee flower' plants in the assemblage is indicative of honey having been added in an attempt to sweeten the medicine. The adventive pollen in the assemblage probably represents grains accumulated by the aerial parts of the collected plants.

Mugwort (the common name of *Artemisia vulgaris*) is thought to derive from the fact that the plant was used to flavour drinks. It was certainly added to beer for flavouring before the introduction of hops (Grieve 1992, 556). There are also records of artemisia having been used to flavour wine in ancient times (Pliny, *Historia Naturalis* 14, 109). However, if the copper-alloy vessel had contained wine, at least a trace of *Vitis vinifera* (grapevine) might have been expected in the pollen profile from the plug. Grapevine pollen was certainly found in wine containers excavated from a high-status Roman burial in Wheathampstead, Hertfordshire (Wiltshire, unpublished report: Verulamium Museum). If mugwort had been added to some form of ale or beer, relatively large amounts of cereal pollen might have been present.

No *Vitis* was found, and cereal pollen was present merely as a trace. The evidence suggests, therefore, that even if the vessel had started out life straining alcoholic drinks, it later functioned as a container for the preparation of some bitter medicine.

THE PALYNOLOGICAL ANALYSIS OF THE PALAEOTURF FORMING THE COLLAPSED MOUND IN THE CHAMBER CF42 (FIG. 157; TABLE 71)

By Patricia E.J. Wiltshire

The methods used in the analysis of the turf were the same as those for the plug of debris in the strainer bowl (p. 394). TABLE 71 shows the percentage values for the palynological assemblage in a single horizon of one of the turf layers in the subsided mound filling most of the chamber pit, while FIGURE 157 shows the proportions of various palynological taxa present in the turf soil.

Palynological analysis of buried turves has shown that they can yield important information on the nature of ancient landscapes (Wiltshire 1997; 1999). It proved possible to locate the horizon within a turf that represented a buried land surface at Stanway. Although only a single turf was analysed, it gave important information regarding the Late Iron Age countryside from which it was collected.

There is little doubt that the turf was collected from a very open environment. The only trees represented were *Betula* (birch), *Fraxinus* (ash), and *Quercus* (oak). Oak had the highest percentage (2.3%), but this must be considered to be a low value. It is likely that either trees were very heavily managed by coppicing and pollarding so that they had little opportunity to flower, or that the landscape in the environs of the turf collection was virtually treeless. There might have been isolated individual trees scattered locally.

The values for cereal-type pollen (6.2%) must be considered high and it is likely that the turf was collected in the vicinity of arable fields or near cereal-processing sites. Some of the

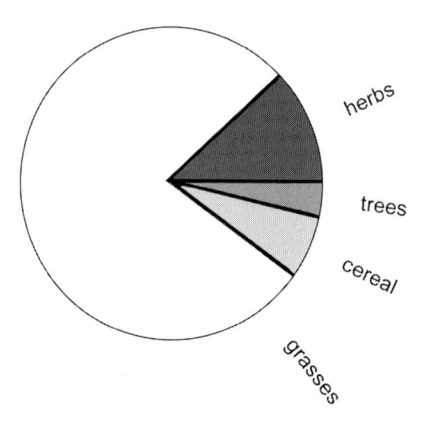

FIG. 157. Chamber CF42: proportions of various palynological taxa present in the turf (turf 1) from the mound

TABLE 71: PERCENTAGE VALUES FOR TAXA FOUND IN THE TURF IN CHAMBER CF42

Trees and shrubs	English name	Turf (CF42) % tlp/s
Betula	birch	0.6
Fraxinus	ash	0.8
Quercus	oak	2.3
Crops		
Cereal type	cereals	6.2
Herbs		
Artemisia	mugwort, wormwood	2.0
Aster type	e.g. daisy	+
Capsella type	e.g. shepherd's purse	+
Centaurea nigra type	e.g. knapweed	0.8
Lactuceae	dandelion-like plants	3.1
Papaver	poppy	+
Plantago lanceolata	ribwort plantain	2.4
Poaceae	grasses	78.4
Ranunculus type	e.g. buttercup	0.6
Reseda luteola	dyer's rocket	+
Sinapis type	e.g. charlock	0.9
Spergula type	e.g. corn spurrey	+
Urtica	nettle	+
Ferns		
Polypodium	polypody fern	+
Pteridium	bracken	1.6

herbaceous taxa such as *Capsella* type (shepherd's purse and others), *Papaver* (poppy), *Ranunculus* type (buttercups), *Reseda luteola* (weld or dyer's rocket), and *Spergula* type (corn spurrey and others) could represent weeds of the cornfield, although some of them could also be growing in a grass sward. The area certainly seems to have been dominated by weedy grassland, and the high value for Poaceae (grass) pollen might suggest that the local grassland was not over-grazed. Percentages of grass pollen can be very low indeed in the centre of a small, mown lawn (personal observation). A similar picture is often seen for Lactuceae (dandelion-like plants) and *Plantago lanceolata* (ribwort plantain) where constant grazing drastically reduces flowering. It is possible, therefore, that the immediate vicinity in the area of turf collection had escaped intense grazing or cutting.

Many of the weeds could also have been growing as ruderals, and it is very difficult to define accurately the mosaic of micro-habitats in a place so pressurised by human activity.

THE LANDSCAPE OF THE SITE OF TURF COLLECTION

The area from which the turf was collected was very open with few trees. In fact, the landscape probably had fewer trees than the landscape around Stanway today. It appears to have been an area dominated by herb-rich grassland and broken soils. It was also close to cereal fields or a place where cereal-processing took place. If the turf were collected from pasture, it would seem that the stocking density of animals was low. *Artemisia* (p. 395) was certainly growing in the catchment and would have been available for the doctor to give appropriate treatment to his patients.

CHAPTER 6

EXCAVATIONS ON SITE D IN 2002–3

INTRODUCTION (FIGS 1–2, 158)

Excavation took place in 2002–3 in advance of an extension of the quarry to the south-east of Enclosures 1–5, which had been excavated between 1987 and 1997. The site (Site D, TL 9570 2240) lay on a south-facing incline, and was bounded by Maldon Road to the south and by Gryme's Dyke South to the east (FIGS 1–2). It measured up to 188 m east–west by 134 m north–south. The Colchester Museums accession number for Site D is 2002.247. The small finds numbers are a continuation of the series used on Site C.

Some charcoal-rich features were discovered in November 2002 when the topsoil over the site was mechanically stripped in readiness for quarrying. A brief archaeological excavation followed in December 2002 when several of the features were investigated and more were discovered (FIG. 158). The features were located between 72 m and 206 m south of Enclosure 5. A geophysical survey took place on the site in March–April 2003 (Black and Black 2003), and excavation of the features resumed in December of that year. Delicately controlled machine-clearance of the surface was also carried out to check for any additional features. This was done in alternating north–south strips, mostly about 4 m in width, so as to cover just over 50 per cent of the site. The fills of the cremation burials and the more convincing pits with pyre-related material were all retained in their entirety to recover finds and obtain samples for environmental analysis. Many of the remaining features were bulk sampled for environmental analysis.

Archaeological monitoring also took place during machine-stripping of topsoil in August 2004 to the south-west of the enclosures. This area (Site E) lay immediately to the west of Site D, 100 m south-west of Enclosure 5, and measured approximately 230 m east–west by up to 117 m north–south. Little of archaeological significance was recorded in this area, although the edges of the silt-filled palaeochannel located on Site C (CF52) were traced over the eastern part of the site.

THE EXCAVATION (FIG. 158)

Five unstratified worked flints were recovered from Site D, including an early Mesolithic obliquely blunted microlith (SF403, FIG. 168; p. 422). There were no definite man-made prehistoric features pre-dating the Late Iron Age. A few probable natural features were excavated. These are recorded in the archive.

The archaeological features (FIG. 158) are described below in terms of the following four groups:

a) cremation burials (three examples)
b) pits with pyre-related debris (four, possibly five examples)
c) pits with charcoal-rich fill and no cremated bone or pottery or other artefacts (fourteen, possibly fifteen examples)
d) other features (a boundary ditch, a sand-and-gravel pit, and seven other pits).

Many of the features on the site had been truncated, and presumably an unknown number of shallow ones completely destroyed, both by long-term ploughing and by the machine-stripping of the topsoil in advance of quarrying operations. Any lost features are likely to have belonged to the third of the groups listed above, which, as suggested below, are likely to be of modern origin.

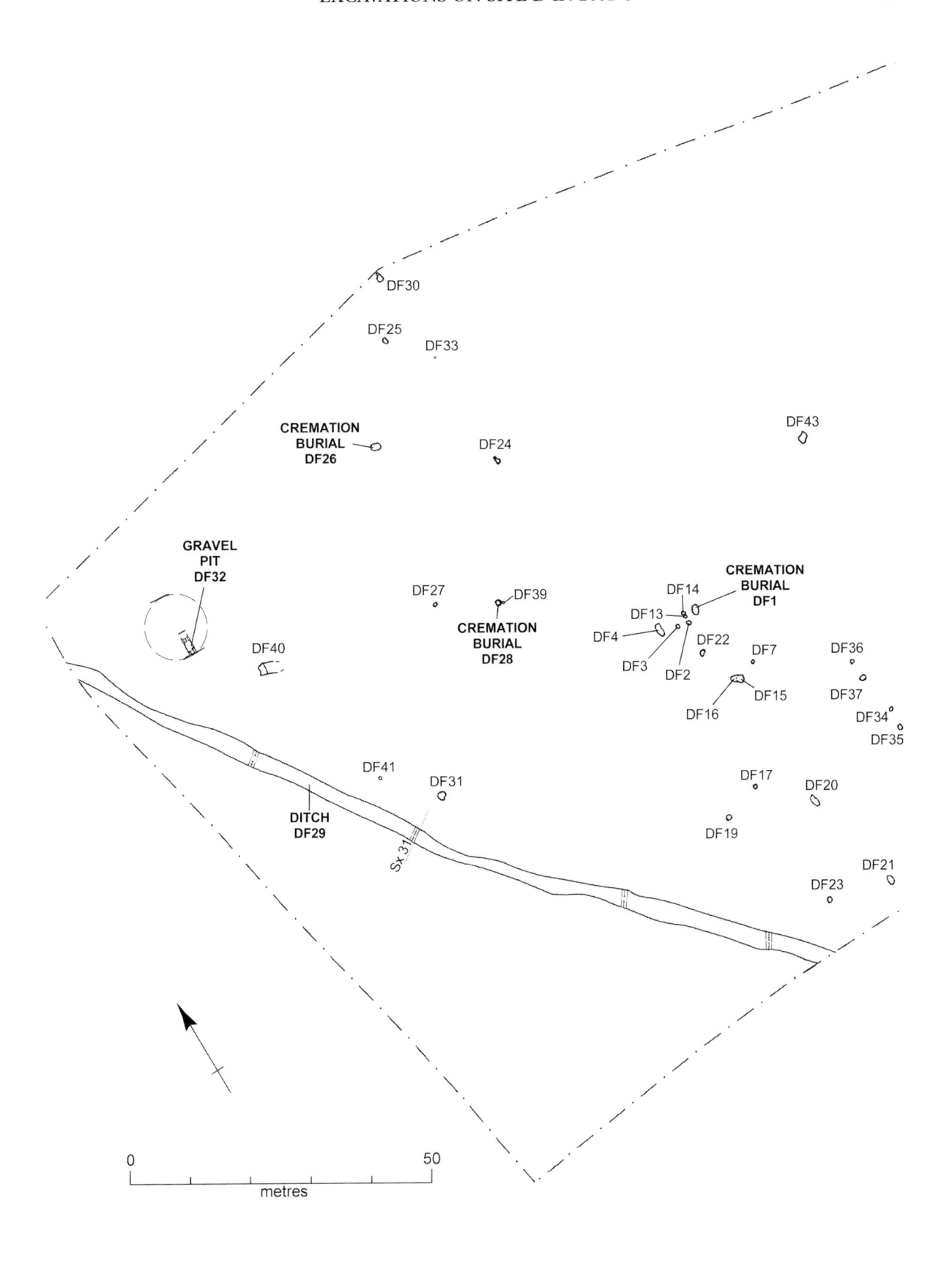

FIG. 158. Site D: plan

THE CREMATION BURIALS

Of the three definite cremation burials, two were inurned (DF1 and DF26) and one unurned (DF28). This small sample therefore contrasts with the broadly contemporary burials in Enclosures 3, 4 and 5 which were probably all unurned. In one of the inurned burials (DF1), the cremated bone was inside an imported butt-beaker, placed off-centre in the burial pit. In the other (DF26), the bone had been put in a lidded bowl placed centrally in the pit. The unurned burial (DF28) was the most well furnished. In addition to the flagon, it had a butt-beaker, two cups or small carinated bowls, and three brooches, as well as copper-alloy sheet fragments and hobnails. The inclusion of the flagon and the carinated cups, perhaps as a drinking set, is paralleled in other burials, such as the Brooches grave (CF72) in Enclosure 5, which also produced plate brooches. The provision and number of the grave-goods in DF28 may imply a significant element of social differentiation compared to the inurned cremation burials.

Two of the cremation burials (DF1 and DF26) showed no evidence for the breaking or burning of objects prior to burial. However, prior to burial in DF28, one of the pots (DF28.1) was in pieces, another (DF28.4) may have been scorched, and all three brooches (DF28.5-7) seem to have been broken. In addition, there were some heat-affected copper-alloy fragments (SF398 and SF399) in DF28 presumably belonging to the remains of a ?box which must have been destroyed on the pyre.

Of the three cremation burials, the earliest is probably DF26 (pre-conquest) and the latest is DF28 (probably Claudio–Neronian or later, depending on the date of the plate brooch DF28.5).

CREMATION BURIAL DF1 (FIG. 159)

Cremated bone	338.5 g	adult, sex unknown
Pottery	DF1.1	imported butt-beaker
Other objects		several iron nail fragments
Residual finds		none

DF1 was a circular pit which was approximately 1.1 m in diameter and 0.16 m deep (FIG. 159). The upper fill of the pit was a charcoal-rich layer, up to 0.08 m thick, and was probably derived from the pyre. This sealed a lower fill of sand and sandy silt loam, up to 0.1 m thick, which was presumably redeposited natural. A butt-beaker (FIG. 159, DF1.1) had been placed upright in a depression 0.23 m deep on the western side of the pit. The beaker contained most of the cremated bone and a few iron nail fragments. A small quantity of cremated bone (6.6 g) was also recovered from the upper and lower fills of the pit. The rim of the beaker was missing, opening up the possibility that bone may have been dragged from inside the beaker during modern ploughing. Samples of the fills and the contents of the beaker provided limited evidence for charred seeds of grasses and grassland plants as well as other plant macrofossils (p. 420). A few fragments of iron nails and chips of iron (probably also from nails) were recovered from an environmental sample (TABLE 72). While the burial and the circular pit appeared to be contemporary, it is possible that the pit was an unconnected pyre-related feature that cut the burial.

The butt-beaker is of form Cam 113. The type was common at Sheepen but rare in the Colchester Roman fortress and early *colonia*. The burial thus probably dates to *c.* A.D. 10–43, although it may be as late as *c.* A.D. 60.

DF1.1 FIG. 159. D1. Butt-beaker Cam 113 in fabric BPW. The vessel is almost complete, although the rim is missing and the upper part of the vessel is more fragmented. Approximately 100 sherds and fragments. Condition at deposition: presumed complete.

DF1. From an environmental sample. a) Six iron nail shank fragments. Lengths 9, 11, 15, 15 (clenched), 16 and 21 mm. b) Four small iron fragments. Lengths 6, 9, 9 and 9 mm.

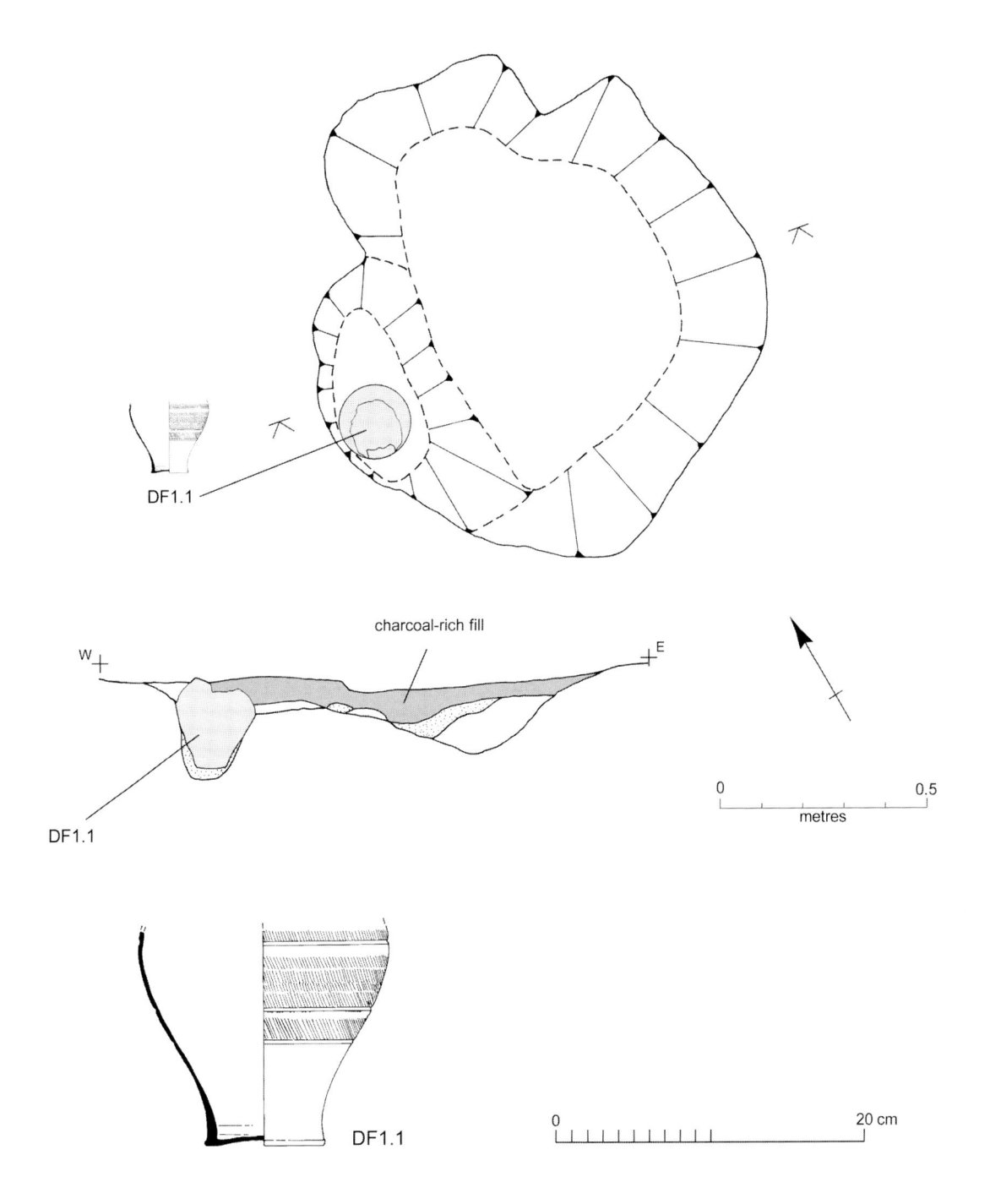

FIG. 159. Cremation burial DF1: plan and section (scale 1:15) and pottery vessel DF1.1 (scale 1:4)

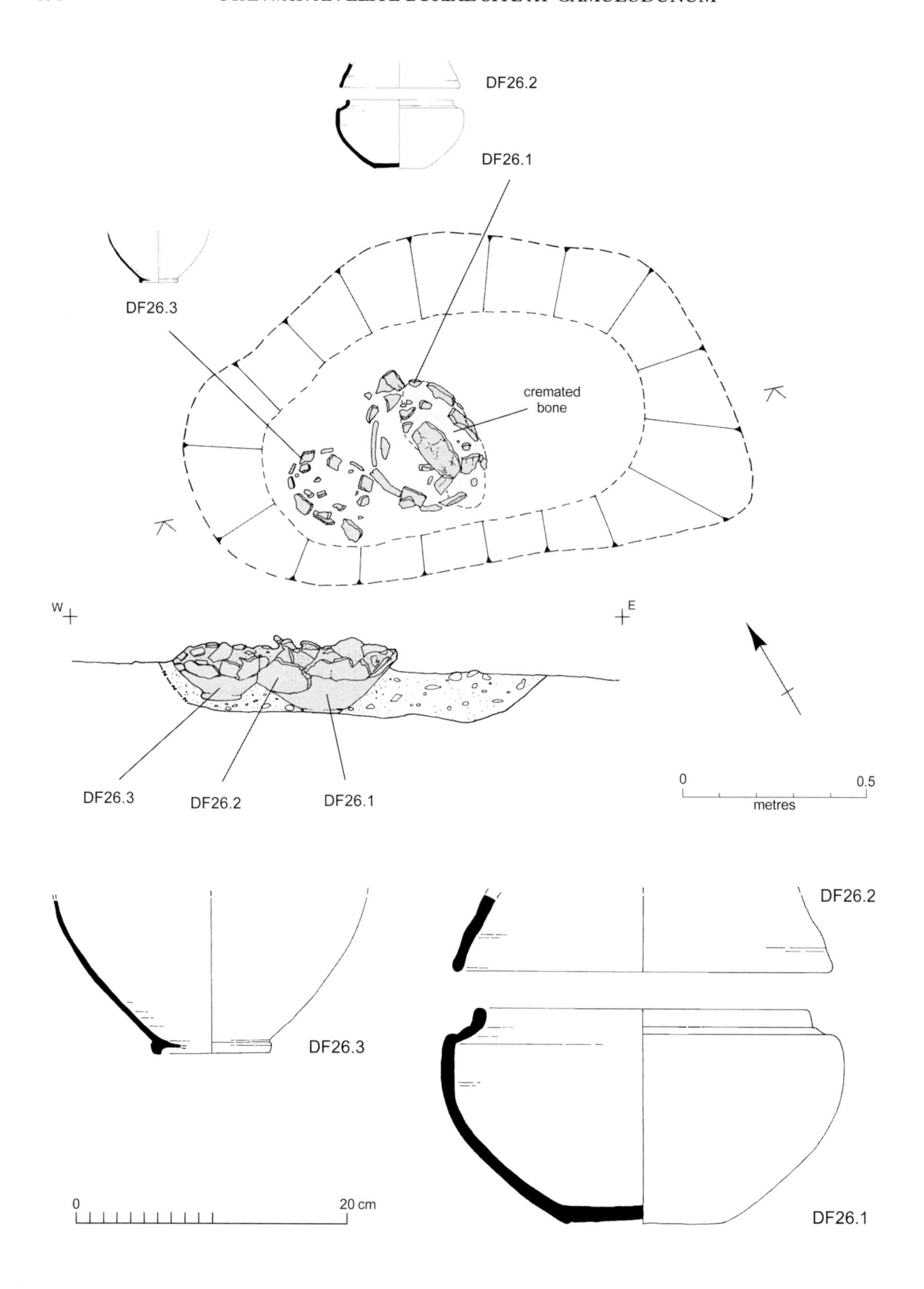

FIG. 160. Cremation burial DF26: plan and section (scale 1:15) and pottery vessels DF26.1–3 (scale 1:4).

CREMATION BURIAL DF26 (FIG. 160)

Cremated bone	38.1 g	age and sex unknown
Pottery	DF26.1	local grog-tempered bowl
	DF26.2	local grog-tempered lid
	DF26.3	imported flagon
Other objects		none
Residual finds		none

The fill of the pit, which survived up to 0.2 m deep, consisted of sand and gravel and did not contain significant amounts of charcoal. The cremated bone was contained in a lidded bowl (DF26.1 and DF26.2) which had been placed upright towards the centre of an oval-shaped pit (FIG. 160). The lid and the rim of the bowl had been very badly damaged by later ploughing and/or machining. The quantity of cremated bone found in the bowl was small, but unaffected by later disturbances. The lid is tall and matches the bowl in shape and fabric (grog-tempered ware). An imported North Gaulish flagon (FIG. 160, DF26.3) had been placed upright adjacent to the bowl on the western side of the pit. The upper part of this vessel had also been badly affected by ploughing and/or machining.

The bowl is of form Cam 253 and has a number of parallels from Sheepen (Hawkes and Hull 1947, 281). The imported flagon is also almost certainly of pre-conquest date. The two vessels thus indicate that the burial probably belonged to the earlier 1st century A.D.

DF26.1 and **DF26.2** FIG. 160. D41, also a few sherds from D43; DF26.2: D43, and a few sherds from D41. Deep lid-seated bowl with in-bent rim flattened for tall bead-rimmed lid. Cam 253 bowl (DF26.1) and lid (DF26.2) in fabric GTW. Most of bowl including all of base and probably all of body, although only about 50% of bowl shoulder/rim identified. Much of lower part of lid (rim approximately 60–70% identified). Upper part of lid missing. Bowl approximately 40 sherds and 60 small sherds. Lid approximately 40 sherds and small sherds. Condition at deposition: presumed complete.

DF26.3 FIG. 160. D42. Flagon in fabric WPW. All of base and some body sherds. Upper part of vessel missing. Approximately 100 sherds including base and body sherds with some fragments. Condition at deposition: presumed complete.

CREMATION BURIAL DF28 (FIGS 161–3)

Cremated bone	61.1 g	age and sex unknown
Pottery	DF28.1	imported butt-beaker
	DF28.2	buff ware flagon, possibly imported
	DF28.3	small local carinated bowl
	DF28.4	small local carinated bowl
Other objects	DF28.5	copper-alloy plate brooch
	DF28.6	copper-alloy penannular brooch
	DF28.7	copper-alloy penannular brooch
	DF28.8	copper-alloy sheet fragments and fragments of mineralised oak (?box)
	DF28.9	single fragment of a glass vessel (not an unguent bottle)
	DF28.10	3 hobnails from a pair of sandals or shoes, plus a copper-alloy shank and two iron nail fragments (parts of **DF28.8**?)
Residual finds		small bowl sherd/fragment of ?shale

The cremated bone lay mostly in a small cluster on the floor in the south-western part of the pit (FIG. 161). A few fragments were also found to the south of the cluster, scattered in an extensive charcoal-rich lens which covered much of the floor of the pit. The bone was closely associated with rim and body sherds from a Cam 113 butt-beaker (FIG. 163, DF28.1) which had been broken in antiquity. A few of these sherds appeared to seal the bone. The base and more body sherds from the beaker lay fragmented on the floor to the north of the bone.

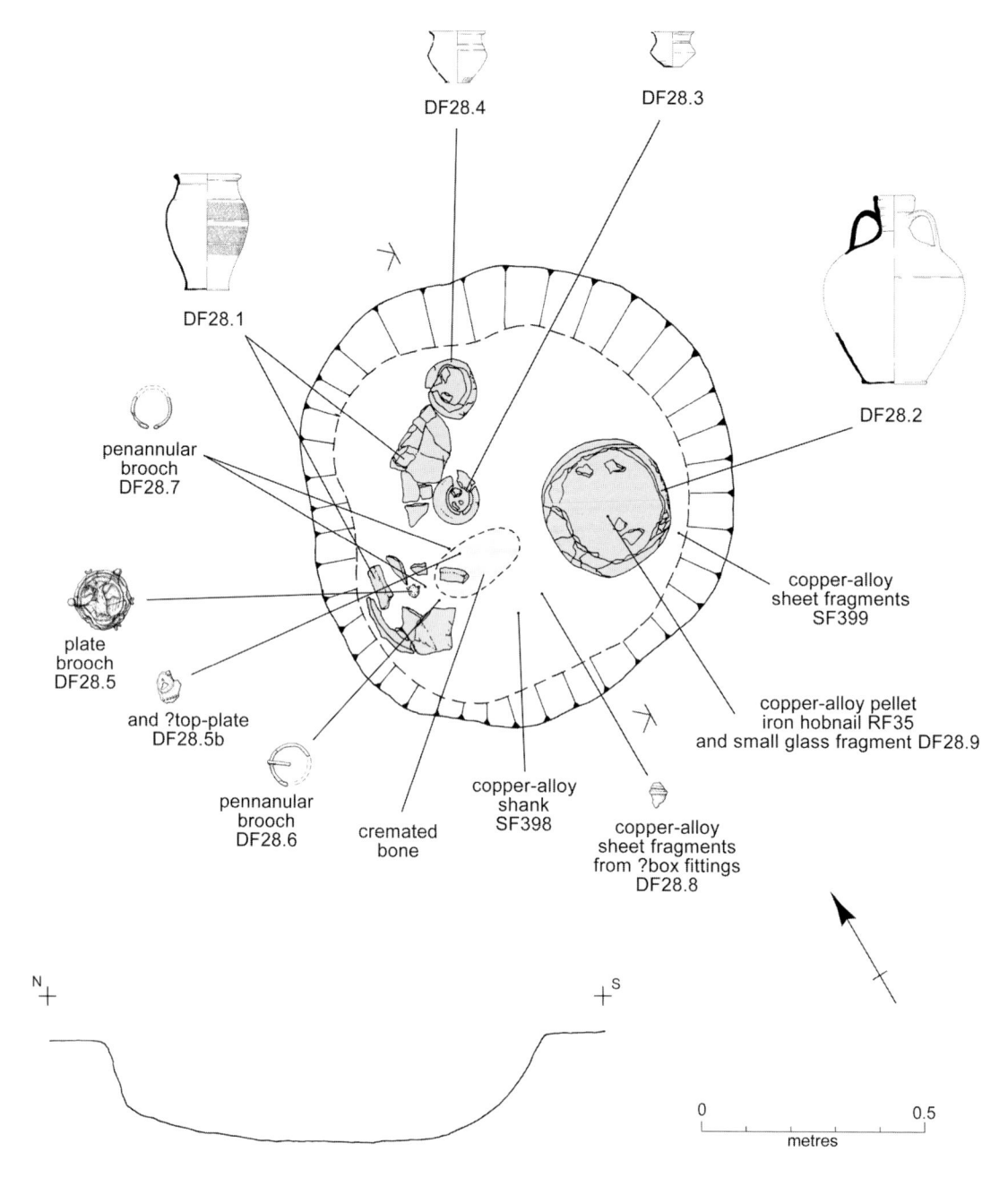

FIG. 161. Cremation burial DF28: plan and profile (scale 1:15)

A two-handled flagon (FIG. 163, DF28.2) of form Cam 170 (variant) lay in the south-east corner of the pit, tipped slightly on its side. It had probably been complete when put in the pit, but the upper part had been damaged by ploughing and/or machining. Two small carinated bowls of form Cam 212-217 had been placed upright and probably intact in the pit. One (FIG. 163, DF28.3) lay slightly north-west of centre, and the other (FIG. 163, DF28.4) was 0.11 m away, close to the northern edge of the pit; DF28.4 may have been burnt. Both bowls sealed sherds from the beaker.

The burial pit was roughly circular, up to 1 m in diameter and 0.25 m deep. The thin dark charcoal-rich layer on the bottom of the feature was probably derived from the pyre. It appeared to seal or envelop most of the objects on the floor of the pit, with the possible exception of the flagon (FIGS 161–2).

Among the broken butt-beaker sherds close to the cremated bone in the south-west corner of the pit were a copper-alloy plate brooch (FIG. 163, DF28.5) and two copper-alloy penannular brooches (FIG. 163, DF28.6–7). A small fragment of copper-alloy sheet with a rivet (FIG. 163,

FIG. 162.   Cremation burial DF28

DF28.5b) from the same area was probably part of the top-plate of the brooch DF28.5. All three brooches appear to have been broken or damaged in antiquity, but were unburnt. A ?bowl fragment possibly of shale also lay among the butt-beaker sherds. Being only a single, very small sherd, it must be residual or intrusive.

A small fragment of heat-affected copper-alloy (SF402), an iron hobnail (RF35), and a small piece of a colourless glass vessel (but not an unguent bottle) (DF28.9) were recovered from the soil filling the remains of the flagon. They are not likely to have been deliberately buried in the pot, but were in the soil when it fell into it.

Several fragments of copper-alloy sheet (one only illustrated, FIG. 163, DF28.8), probably from box fittings, were recovered from the pit-fill to the west of the flagon. These were associated with some small fragments of mineralised oak. Also from this area were another small heat-affected copper-alloy fragment (SF398) and an iron nail fragment (SF397b). Another iron nail fragment (D55) was found near DF28.4 at the northern end of the pit. Two heat-affected copper-alloy sheet fragments (SF399) came from the edge of the pit adjacent to the flagon. All this material may belong to the same ?box.

Two, possibly three, iron hobnails (DF28.10) were recovered from environmental samples. One of the hobnails (RF35) was in the fill of the flagon DF28.2 (as already mentioned), another (RF29) was in the charcoal-rich lower fill of the pit, and a third (a ?hobnail: RF31) was in the vicinity of the sherds of the broken butt-beaker DF28.1. They parallel the hobnails excavated at the Handford House site in Colchester in 2003, where their presence in a large proportion

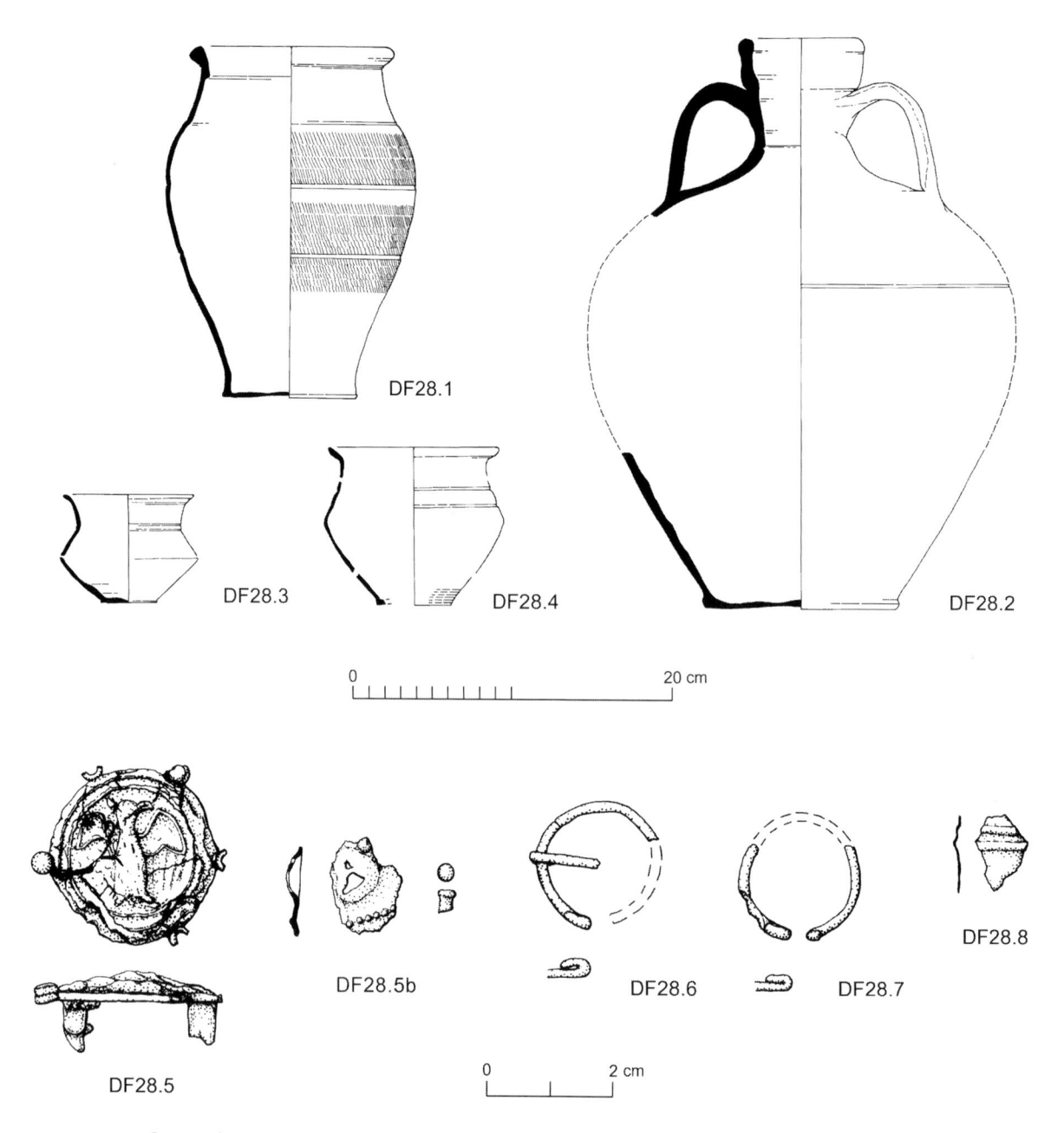

FIG. 163. Cremation burial DF28: pottery vessels DF28.1–4 (scale 1:4), copper-alloy brooches DF28.5–7, and moulded sheet DF28.8 (scale 1:1)

of the burials and pyre-sites suggests that most of the dead were wearing nailed shoes or sandals when cremated (Orr 2006).

The plate brooch (FIG. 163, DF28.5) is unusual; the technique of manufacture is similar to that used on pre-conquest spring-cover brooches, although on those the solder is much more thinly applied (*e.g.* Feugère 1985, 293, Type 20c). Almost certainly an import, the method of manufacture allies it to the group with a top-plate bearing designs based on triskeles, human faces, animals, and copies of Hadrianic coin reverse types (Hattatt and Webster 1985), although none of these have peripheral lugs. Although many of these brooches are 2nd century in date, a few belong to the 1st century, notably one with a ?griffin design from Santon (Fox 1958, pl. 37b). The repoussé-decorated top-plate of the Stanway brooch is missing, but the design, an eagle with outstretched wings, is visible in the solder. A small fragment of the top-plate, showing part of a beaded frame, was recovered from an environmental sample.

The penannular brooches (FIG. 163, DF28.6–7) are small copper-alloy examples of Fowler's Type D2 (1960, 152), with the terminal turned back on top of the ring and constricted at the midpoint. The form is British and occurs in contexts dated from the 1st to 4th centuries. Examples from pre-conquest or immediately post-conquest contexts have been found at Sheepen, Maiden Castle, Bagendon, Hod Hill, and, in iron, at Dragonby (Hawkes and Hull 1947, 327, nos 6–8; Wheeler 1943, fig. 86, 8; Hull 1961, 184, nos 63–9; Brailsford 1962, nos E11–16; Olivier 1996, fig. 11.13, 152). There are no examples from the King Harry Lane cemetery.

Although most of the vessels are primarily associated with the Late Iron Age, the flagon, possibly an import, is probably post-conquest and dates the burial to the early post-conquest Claudio–Neronian period. A post-conquest date is also indicated by the inclusion of hobnails. The presence of the unusual plate brooch and particularly the small glass fragment could suggest a slightly later date.

DF28.1 FIG. 163. D49, also D55, D59. Butt-beaker Cam 113 in fabric BPW. All of rim, most or all of main body, approximately 60% of base identified. Slightly degraded surfaces and edges. Approximately 114+ medium to small sherds and crumbs. Condition at deposition: broken in antiquity, possibly complete.

DF28.2 FIG. 163. D48, also D49, D64. *Lagena* Cam 170 variant in a fabric which is a coarse version of North Gaulish Flagon ware (NOG WH) and possibly an import. Almost all of the vessel, all of the base present, although only part of the rim identified. Approximately 200 sherds varying from medium to large fragments. Condition at deposition: presumed complete.

DF28.3 FIG. 163. D54, also D67. Small carinated bowl Cam 212–217 in fabric RCW. Part (55%) of the rim (in small pieces). All of the base, and probably all or most of body. Burnished. Some degraded surfaces and sherd edges. 36 sherds and 28 fragments. Condition at deposition: presumed complete.

DF28.4 FIG. 163 D55, also D4. Small carinated bowl Cam 212–217 in fabric RCW. Much of the vessel present but only part of the rim (approximately 30%) and base (approximately 20%). Burnished. Some sherds are disoloured brownish-red with outer surfaces degraded: they may have been burnt. 30 sherds and approximately 42 fragments (179 g). Condition at deposition: presumed complete.

DF28.5 FIG. 163. SF396. D47. Discoid plate brooch; only the top of the pin remains, hinged on an iron rivet between close-set lugs. The body of the brooch consisted of a copper-alloy back-plate with a repoussé-decorated top-plate attached by a thick layer of lead-/tin-based solder. The top-plate is now missing, but parts may have been recovered elsewhere (*see* DF28.5b and DF28.8). The solder retains the image of an eagle with outstretched wings. Six lugs were originally spaced equidistantly around the circumference, but only one now survives intact; it has a bone cap. Diameter (excluding peripheral lugs) 26 mm.

DF28.5b FIG. 163. SF409. D59. From an environmental sample. 1) Thin copper-alloy repoussé-decorated sheet fragment, part of the top-plate of brooch DF28.5. Maximum dimensions 15 by 12 mm. 2) Tiny dome-headed rivet or stud, end of shank missing. Diameter 3 mm, length 4 mm.

DF28.6 FIG. 163. SF400. D58. Fragment, in two pieces, of a small copper-alloy penannular brooch of Fowler's Type D2, one of a pair with DF28.7. The surviving terminal is turned up and back to lie along the top of the hoop and has a slight central constriction. The hoop is of round section and plain. Part of the pin remains, also round in section. Internal diameter 14 mm; hoop diameter 2 mm.

DF28.7 FIG. 163. SF401/408. D62/59. From an environmental sample. Two terminal fragments from a small copper-alloy penannular brooch of Fowler's Type D2, one of a pair with DF28.6. The hoop is of round section and plain; the central section is missing, as is the pin. On SF401 (D62) the terminal has a central constriction that gives it a zoomorphic appearance. The end of the terminal of SF408 (D59) is missing. Internal diameter 14 mm; hoop diameter 2 mm.

DF28.8 FIG. 163. SF397. D50. ?Box
a) Several fragments of thin copper-alloy sheet, the largest measuring 15 by 11 mm. Only one is illustrated. It has two parallel narrow mouldings while the rest are plain. Most are probably from box fittings, but some may be part of the top-plate of brooch DF28.5.
Other parts of DF28.8?
b) Iron nail shank fragment. Length 23 mm.
c) SF398. D51. Fragment of a heat-affected copper-alloy ?shank. Length 16 mm.
d) SF399. D56. Two fragments of heat-affected copper-alloy sheet. Weight 0.2 g.
e) SF402. D65. Pellet of heat-affected copper alloy, with associated pieces of charcoal. Weight 0.3 g.
f) D55. Iron nail. Length 43 mm.

DF28.9 Not illustrated. D64. From an environmental sample of the fill of flagon. A chip from a glass body fragment retaining no original surfaces. It probably derived from a decolourised vessel. Decolourised vessels start appearing in the 60s although they do not become at all common until the end of the century (*CAR* **8**, table 1.4). It will not have come from an unguent bottle. Colourless glass was used for high-quality tablewares at this period. Dimensions 9 × 6 mm, wall thickness 0.5–1 mm.

DF28.10 Not illustrated.

a) RF29. D45. From an environmental sample. Iron hobnail. Length 14 mm, incomplete.

b) RF35. D64. From an environmental sample. Iron hobnail. Length 16 mm.

c) RF31. D59. From an environmental sample. Thin iron nail shank fragment, probably from a hobnail. Length 7 mm.

PITS WITH PYRE-RELATED DEBRIS (FIGS 158, 164, 166)

The five features identified as being pits with pyre-related debris (FIGS 158, 164 and 166, DF2, DF3, DF7, DF13/DF14 and DF25) all had charcoal-rich fills and contained fragments of cremated bone. Two of them included broken and/or heat-affected objects, thus securely identifying them as good examples of pyre-related features like those found further north on the main Stanway site (particularly CF7). These are DF7 which contained a heat-affected brooch and DF3 which included a flagon that had been broken and subjected to intense heat before burial. The cremated bone fragments from DF3 may have derived from at least two individuals (p. 419), a fact which would appear to support its interpretation as a pit with pyre-related debris rather than a cremation burial. Two of the remaining pits are regarded as being pyre-related on the basis of their fill and the presence of artefacts: pit DF13/14 included hobnails from a pair of shoes or sandals, and pit DF2 a coin of Vespasian. The fifth pit (DF25) has little to place it in this category other than its charcoal-rich fill and the presence of a very small amount of cremated bone. It could conceivably belong to our next group, *i.e.* 'pits with charcoal-rich fill and no cremated bone or pottery or other artefacts', if the bone was residual or not human. (The bone is described as 'probably human' in the osteology report; p. 419.)

The integrity of the category of 'pits with pyre-related debris' is supported by the distribution of its members. All occur in the vicinity of the cremation burial DF1 apart from DF25, which, as already explained, may not belong to the group in the first place.

Of the four pits which can be dated, all are interpreted as being post-conquest. DF2 was no earlier than early Flavian, DF3 was no earlier than Claudio–Neronian, and DF7 was not before the early Flavian period.

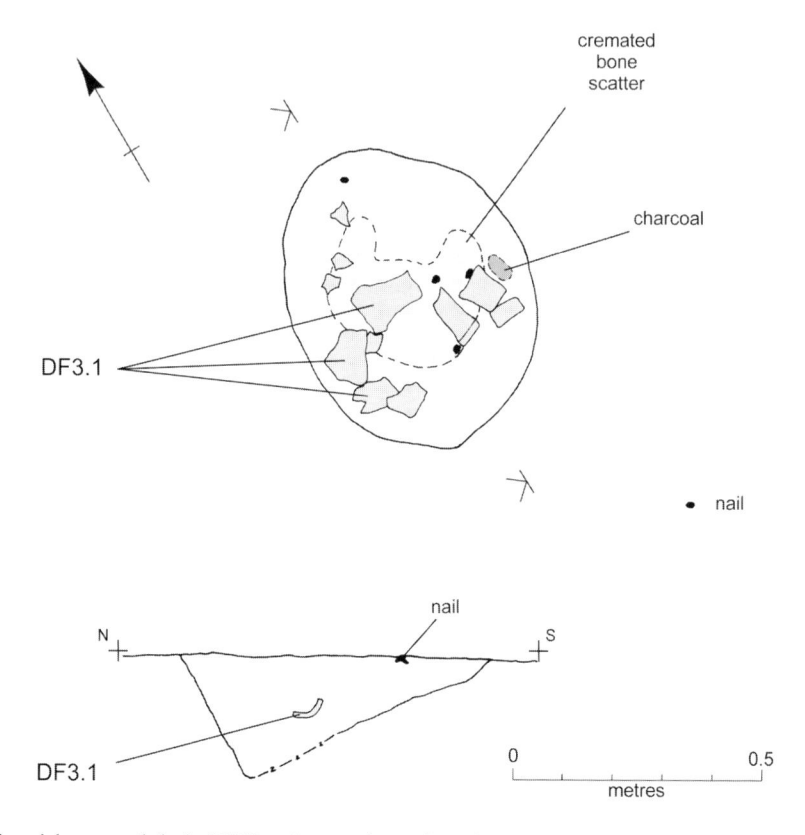

FIG. 164.   Pit with pyre debris DF3: plan and section (scale 1:15)

DF2 (FIGS 158, 166)

Cremated bone	7.1 g	age and sex unknown
Pottery	none	
Other objects	DF2.1	copper-alloy coin of Vespasian, plus several iron nail fragments and a small piece of burnt daub
Residual finds	none	

Pit DF2 was a shallow feature, 1.2 m north–south by up to 0.8 m east–west, with a small oval depression, 0.65 m east–west by 0.45 m north–south and 0.17 m deep, at its southern end (FIGS 158, 166). The cremated bone was scattered in the charcoal-rich upper fill, mainly towards the southern end. A coin of Vespasian (DF2.1) also came from this layer at the southern end at a depth of 0.05 m (FIG. 166). Several iron nail fragments were scattered throughout the fill. The sandy lower fill is likely to have been redeposited natural. Undulations in the bottom of the feature were probably due to animal and/or root disturbance. The coin is clear evidence for the funerary use of the site as late as the early Flavian period.

DF2.1 SF394. D6. Worn copper-alloy *as* of Vespasian, reverse eagle on globe; RIC 747. Diameter 28 mm, weight 8.92 g. Date: A.D. 69–79.
D8. Two nails with most of the shank missing, and three nail shank fragments. Lengths 18, 30, 28, 29 and 30 mm.
D16. From environmental sample. Small fragment of burnt daub. Weight 0.2 g.

DF3 (FIGS 158, 164)

Cremated bone	151.1 g	possibly a minimum of two individuals, one adult and one juvenile
Pottery	DF3.1	local ring-necked flagon
Other objects		several iron nail fragments and small pieces of heat-affected copper alloy
Residual finds		small pot sherd in soft brown sandy fabric
Animal bone		one unidentified fragment

The cremated bone was scattered in the charcoal-rich fill of a small oval pit (FIGS 158, 164), along with the fragmentary, partial remains of a ring-necked flagon (DF3.1) which had been broken elsewhere in antiquity. The bone is of particular interest because, unusually, it possibly represents the remains of at least two individuals (p. 419). The flagon is of form Cam 154/155 and is Claudio–Neronian in date. Some of the sherds had been burnt, presumably on or near the pyre. Also recovered were several iron nail fragments, two small dribbles of resolidified copper alloy (RF8c and RF13), a pellet of heat-affected copper alloy (SF410), and a small residual pot sherd.

DF3.1 Not illustrated. D4, also sherds from D15, D18. Ring-neck flagon Cam 154/155 in buff fabric, fabric DJ(D). Four-rib handle and probably four-ring neck. Vessel fragmented. All parts of pot represented including all of rim, but only part of base, and probably much of body missing. A few sherds discoloured grey on exterior, probably burnt. Approximately 100 sherds and fragments (304 g).
Condition at deposition: broken, partial.
SF410. D15. From environmental sample. Pellet of resolidified copper alloy. Weight 0.01 g.
RF5. D15. From environmental sample. Eight iron nail shank fragments. Lengths 9, 12, 13, 14, 14, 16, 17 and 18 mm.
RF8. D18. From environmental sample. a) Two incomplete iron nails, a detached nail head, and seven nail shank fragments. Lengths 17, 28, 10, 10, 16, 17, 18, 22 and 25 mm. b) Many tiny iron fragments and flecks. c) Small dribble of copper alloy. Weight 0.2 g.
RF13. D23. From environmental sample. Thin iron nail or pin shank with a dribble of copper alloy attached. Length 15 mm.
RF41. D2. From environmental sample. Iron nail shank fragment. Length 22 mm.
D18. Four incomplete iron nails, and three nail shank fragments. Lengths 12, 15, 17, 18, 26, 30 and 32 mm.

DF7 (FIGS 158, 165–6)

Cremated bone	197.9 g	age and sex unknown
Pottery		none
Other objects	DF7.1	copper-alloy trumpet brooch, plus several iron nail fragments and a small piece of pale green glass
Residual finds		none

The pit DF7 was small and circular, and measured 0.56 m across and 0.14 m in depth. The cremated bone was scattered in the charcoal-rich fill, mainly in compact lenses of charcoal which occurred within it (FIGS 158, 166). A copper-alloy trumpet brooch (FIG. 165, DF7.1) lay at a depth of 0.1 m towards the centre of the pit. It had been slightly deformed by heat. Also scattered in the fill were several incomplete nail fragments and a small piece of pale green glass. The glass fragment was not affected by heat and therefore is unlikely to have been part of a vessel which was placed on the pyre. Several undulations in the bottom of the feature were probably due to animal and/or root disturbance.

The brooch is a small and distinctive example of the type, which is of British origin. The calyx-like mouldings are unusual. The vegetal mouldings on the majority of trumpet brooches are based on the acanthus and point in towards the button, rather than upwards to the bow and downwards to the foot, as here. There are a few brooches with similar mouldings from military sites such as Chester, Caerleon, Holt, Caerwent and Caernarvon (Hull forthcoming, Type 154). None are, however, a close parallel to this brooch, being in general much larger and having a plain foot. A brooch from Wanborough and two from London are perhaps the closest in size and the form of the mouldings, but all lack a headloop and the buttons, footknobs and feet are all plain (Hattatt 1985, fig. 45, 435, 437; Butcher 2001, fig. 24, 110).

The brooch provides the best indication of date for the pit. Trumpet brooches are not common in this region, being mainly found in the west and the north. A brooch with mouldings of this quality is likely to be either pre-Flavian or early Flavian in date.

DF7.1 FIG. 165. SF393. D5. Copper-alloy trumpet brooch, in two pieces. Most of the pin is missing and the headloop and the edge of the catchplate are damaged. The whole brooch, particularly at the back, is slightly deformed by heat. The spring is fitted into the hollow behind the trumpet head. The headloop has dropped to point forward over the top of the bow, but would originally have stood upright; it would have held a chain linking this brooch to a second one. The bow is short and plain and rises from a calyx-like moulding above the button, which is prominent and ribbed. The foot issues from a second calyx moulding below the button. It has a central rib flanked by recessed triangles that would have held niello or enamel. There is a rounded vegetal moulding above the footknob, which is ribbed to match the button. Length 41 mm.
RF4. D14. From environmental sample. a) Iron nail, incomplete, and nail shank fragment. Lengths 18 and 14 mm. b) Small iron fragment, possibly from a nail head. Length 10 mm.

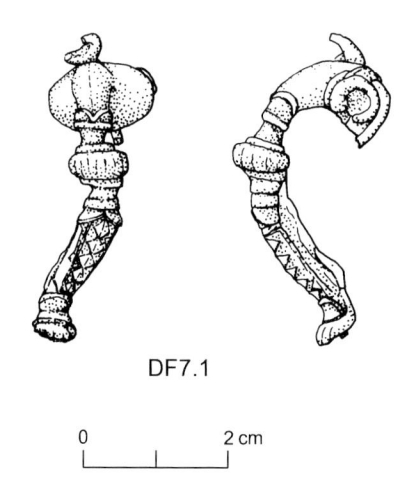

FIG. 165. Pit with pyre debris DF7: copper-alloy brooch DF7.1 (scale 1:1)

RF7. D17. From environmental sample. Two iron nails, both incomplete, and five nail shank fragments, one with an amorphous mass of corrosion attached. Lengths 11, 21, 7, 9, 14, 26 and 28 mm.
D17. From environmental sample. Small glass body fragment. Pale green. It does not appear to be obviously heat affected, so was probably not placed on the pyre. It is too small to say what it came from, but this colour was used for unguent bottles occasionally. It is not a colour that is chronologically sensitive like the colourless piece from DF28. Dimensions 7 × 4 mm, wall thickness 1 mm.

DF13 AND DF14 (FIGS 158, 166)

DF13

Cremated bone	30.4 g	juvenile, sex unknown
Pottery		none
Other objects	DF13.1	ten iron hobnails representing a pair of sandals or shoes
		a small piece of burnt daub
Residual finds		none

DF14

Cremated bone	1.4 g	age and sex unknown
Pottery		none
Other objects		none
Residual finds		none

Pits DF13 and DF14 had evidence of animal and/or root disturbance. They were only 0.3 m apart and were probably the truncated remains of a single larger pyre-related feature (FIGS 158, 166). Pit DF13 was a shallow scoop, 0.3 m across and 0.06 m deep, with a reddish-brown, charcoal-rich fill. Throughout its fill the pit contained fragments of cremated bone, at least ten iron hobnails, a small piece of burnt daub, and some burnt stones. Pit DF14 was 0.5 m across and 0.16 m deep. It had a reddish-brown fill, which contained lenses of charcoal, fragments of cremated bone, and burnt stones.

The hobnails from DF13 are the remains of at least one pair of shoes or sandals (DF13.1) that were burnt on the pyre. They suggest a post-conquest date for the feature.

DF13.1 RF17. D28. From environmental sample. Ten iron hobnails, some represented by the head only. Length of best preserved 14 mm.
D28. DF13. From environmental sample. Small fragment of burnt daub. Weight 0.3 g.

DF25 (FIGS 158, 166)

Cremated bone	2.2 g	age and sex unknown
Pottery		none
Other objects		none
Residual finds		none

DF25 was a small, oval-shaped pit, 0.55 m across and 0.29 m deep. It contained a small quantity of cremated bone, and had a dark reddish-brown, charcoal-rich fill with burnt stones.

PITS WITH CHARCOAL-RICH FILL BUT NO CREMATED BONE, POTTERY OR OTHER ARTEFACTS (FIGS 158, 166)

Fourteen features across the site are categorised as pits with fills rich in reddish-brown burnt material and charcoal but where no cremated bone was recovered and unequivocal pyre-related debris, such as broken or burnt sherds or fragments of other artefacts, was absent. They were mostly small, circular or oval features (FIG. 158). Charred plant macrofossils were identified in a few of them (pp. 420–2), but there were no finds apart from a small fragment of undatable iron nail in DF22. Two of the group (DF17 and DF20) had burnt sides indicating that fires had been lit in them. None can be dated. If they really had been pits with pyre-related debris, then

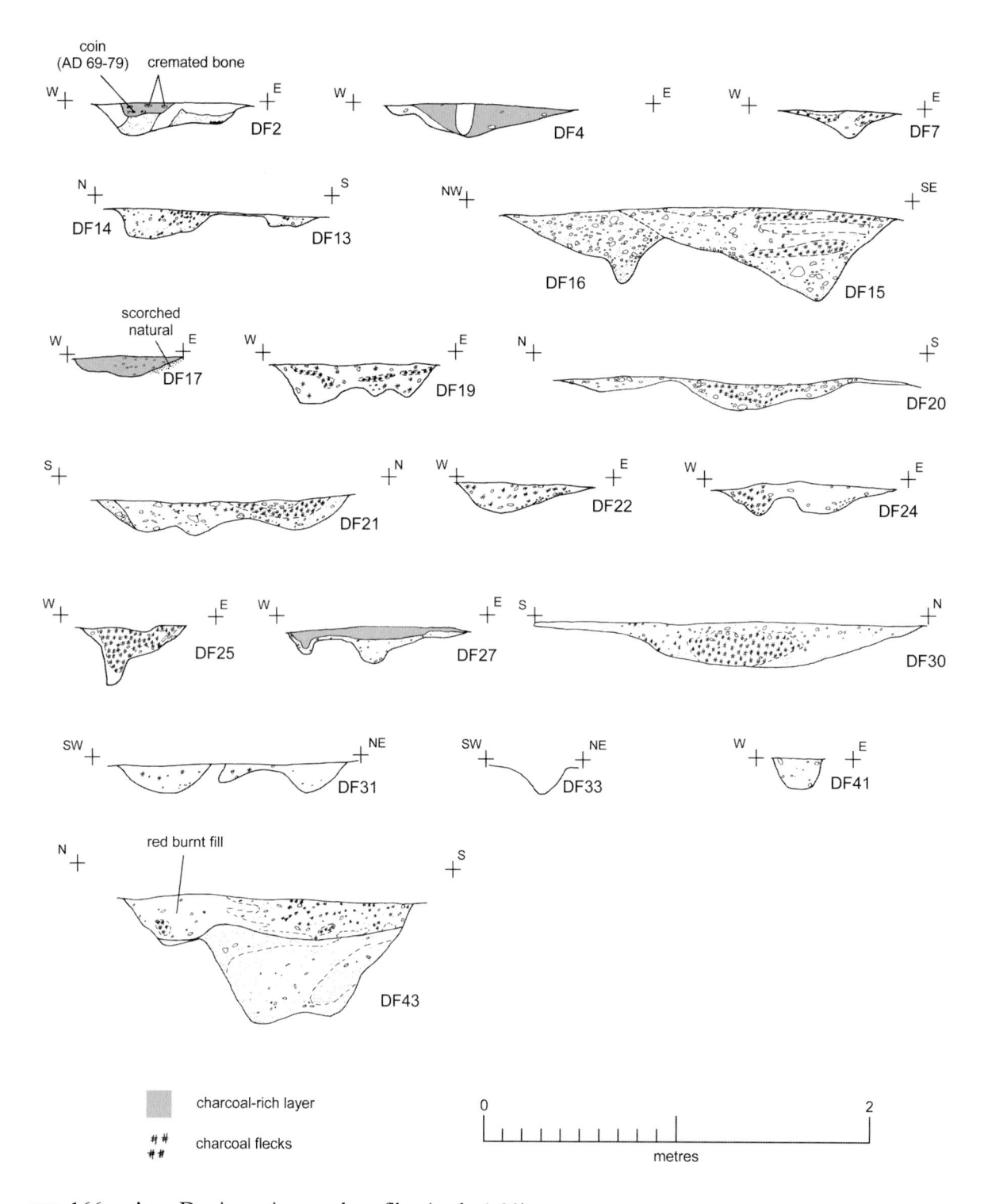

FIG. 166. Area D: pit sections and profiles (scale 1:30)

it seems odd there were so many of them compared to the number of cremation burials recognised in the area. A preferable explanation for the pits in this group is that they represent the remains of shallow-rooted trees which were pulled over in relatively recent times and their roots burnt *in situ*.

The pit DF22 is problematic. It was the only feature in the group to produce a find (a nail fragment), and the amount of charcoal in its fill was relatively low compared with the others, so that it may belong to the group of pits with pyre-related debris. This is perhaps reinforced by its location, close to cremation burial DF1 and other pits with pyre-related debris. (Similarly, DF4 and DF15/16 may also belong to this group.)

DF4

The pit DF4 was roughly rectangular in shape and was 2.2 m long, 1.0 m wide and 0.2 m deep (FIGS 158, 166). The main fill was rich in charcoal, although no cremated bone or other finds were recovered from it. A series of small undulations in the sides and bottom of the feature were probably the result of animal and/or root activity. Immediately to the north and west of the pit were several thin spreads of charcoal, which were probably redeposited from the feature during machine-stripping.

DF15/16

DF15/16 was an oval-shaped feature, 2 m long and up to 0.46 m deep, with a burnt, reddish-brown fill (FIGS 158, 166). It contained lenses of charcoal, particularly in the southern part of the fill (DF15). Burnt stones were also present, but no other finds. Two scoops in the bottom of the feature and slight differences in the fill possibly indicate that it had two phases whereby DF15 cut DF16.

DF17

DF17 was a small pit, 0.55 m across and 0.12 m deep (FIGS 158, 166). It had a black charcoal-rich fill, but no finds. The natural sand and gravel on the bottom of the feature was scorched.

DF19

DF19 was a small pit, 0.8 m across and 0.2 m deep (FIGS 158, 166). It had a reddish-brown fill with some burnt stones. There were lenses of charcoal towards the bottom of the feature, which in places appeared to be lightly scorched. Undulations at the bottom of the feature were probably due to animal and/or root disturbance.

DF20

DF20 was a shallow pit, 1.8 m long and 0.14 m deep (FIGS 158, 166). It had a reddish-brown fill with lenses of charcoal and some burnt stones. The natural sand and gravel on the bottom of the feature was scorched.

DF21

DF21 was an oval-shaped pit, 1.35 m long and 0.15 m deep (FIGS 158, 166). It had a reddish-brown fill with charcoal-rich lenses and some burnt gravels.

DF22

DF22 was a small pit, 1 m long by 0.7 m wide and 0.15 m deep (FIGS 158, 166). It had a reddish-brown fill with charcoal flecks, and contained an iron nail fragment.

RF23. D36. From environmental sample. Iron nail shank fragment, bent double at one end. Length 16 mm.

DF24

DF24 was an irregularly shaped feature, 1.5 m long by 0.8 m wide and 0.17 m deep (FIGS 158, 166). It consisted of several shallow north–south linear scoops. The fill was reddish-brown and contained lenses of charcoal, especially along the western side, as well as burnt stones. No other finds were recovered, but it was possibly a pyre-site and the scoops were perhaps under-pyre flues.

DF27

DF27 was a small oval-shaped pit which was 0.9 m long and up to 0.2 m deep (FIGS 158, 166). It had a black charcoal-rich fill with burnt stones. Undulations at the bottom of the feature were probably due to animal and/or root disturbance.

DF30

DF30 was a shallow, oval pit at the northern edge of the site (FIG. 158). It had been badly disturbed by machining and ploughing. The pit was 1.5 m long and 0.23 m deep, and had a dark brown fill with burnt stones and abundant charcoal flecks (FIG. 166).

DF31

DF31 was an irregularly shaped feature, 1.2 m across and 0.15 m deep (FIGS 158, 166). It had a dark reddish-brown fill with abundant charcoal flecks. A curved scoop formed the western side of the feature and suggested DF31 may have been a pyre-site. Some undulations at the bottom of the feature were probably due to animal and/or root disturbance.

DF33

DF33 was a small pit, 0.3 m across and 0.13 m deep, with a dark charcoal-rich fill (FIGS 158, 166).

DF41

DF41 was a small pit, 0.3 m across and 0.15 m deep, with a dark brown charcoal-rich fill (FIGS 158, 166).

DF43

Pit DF43 was 1.5 m across and 0.65 m deep (FIGS 158, 166). The lower fill was yellowish-brown sand. The upper fill was 0.25 m thick and consisted of burnt material. The latter was mainly reddish-brown in colour with patches of charcoal and burnt stones, but by the northern edge it was red. The upper fill was either a recut or (more likely) pyre-related material dumped in the top of a sand-filled pit.

OTHER FEATURES (FIGS 158, 167)

An undated ditch (DF29) extended for 135 m from north-west to south-east across the western side of the site (FIG. 158). It was sectioned in four places and was up to 3 m wide and 0.7 m deep (FIG. 167). Only two small undiagnostic fragments of burnt daub (6.4 g) were recovered from its fill. The ditch was traced on aerial photographs for at least another 250 m to the north-west. There appeared to be a possible entrance 100 m north-west of the site.

In the north-west corner of the site, there was a large undated pit (FIG. 167, DF32), some 10 m east of the ditch DF29. The pit measured about 10.5 m north–south, although the position of the eastern and western edges was not established by excavation. Where sectioned, it was 1.1 m deep and had a ledge along the southern side. The pit was probably dug for the extraction of sand and gravel. This and several other possible quarry pits further to the west (plan in archive) are visible on aerial photographs.

Approximately 10 m to the south of BF32 was a large undated pit (FIG. 167, DF40), 1.9 m north–south and 0.52 m deep, with several charcoal-enriched lenses in the fill. It measured at least 3.0 m east–west, although the position of the eastern edge of the feature was not established.

The remaining undated features consist of: a small pit (FIG. 167, DF23), 0.22 m deep, at the southern end of the site; a north–south line of four small pits or post-holes (FIG. 167, DF34–37), 0.13–0.25 m deep, in the south-eastern part of the site; and a small pit or post-hole (FIG. 167, DF39), 0.15 m deep, immediately to the south-east of DF28.

Two small, unstratified fragments of Roman tile, including a probable piece of box-flue tile, were found in the north-east corner of the site, but there were no other indications of a building.

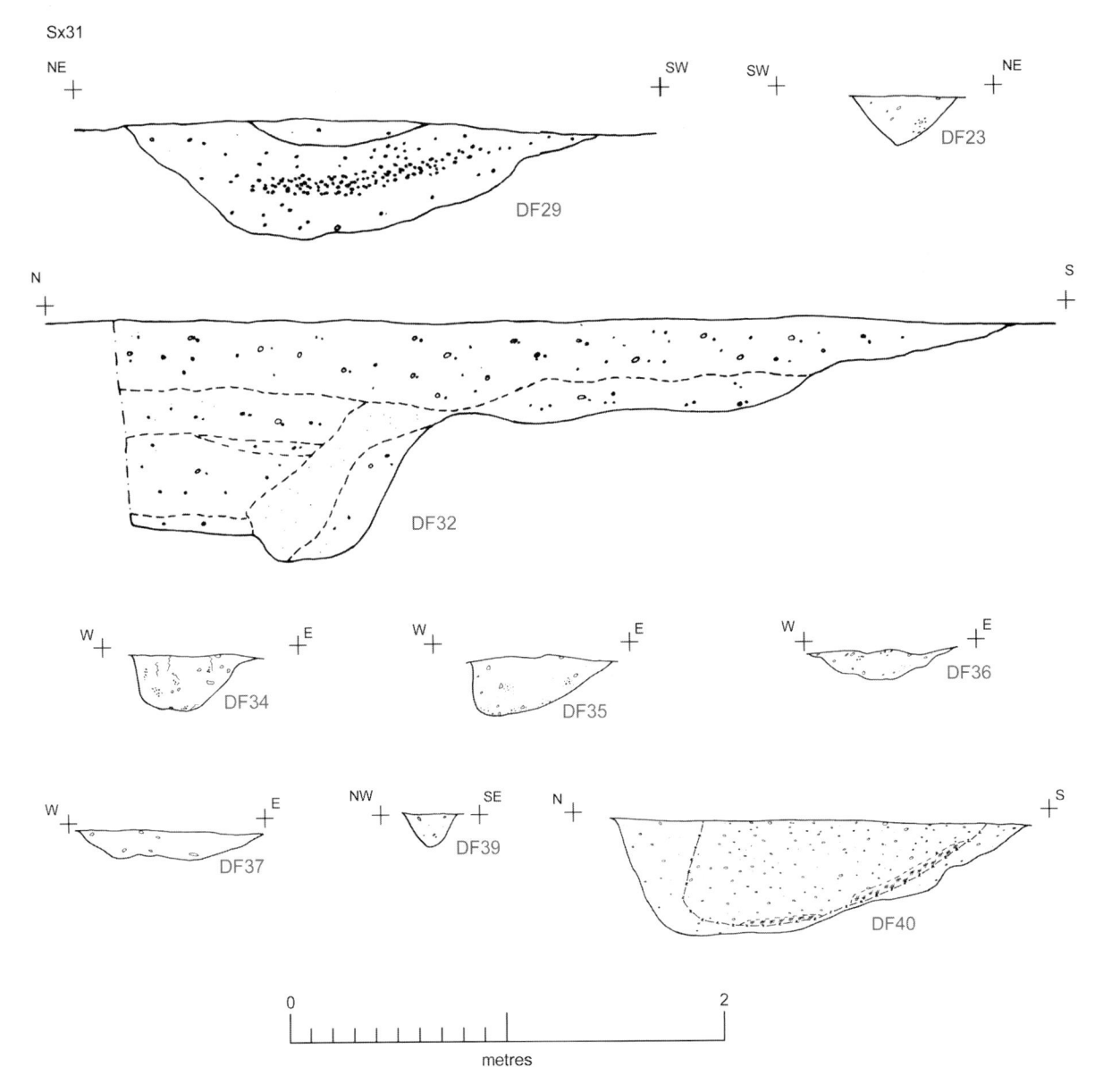

FIG. 167. Site D: ditch DF29 section and pit sections and profiles (scale 1:30)

SPECIALISTS' REPORTS

DISCUSSION OF THE LATE IRON AGE AND ROMAN POTTERY FROM SITE D

By Stephen Benfield and Valery Rigby

The eight pots from three cremation burials and one pit with pyre-related material on Site D can be dated generally to the Late Iron Age and early Roman (pre-Flavian) period. One burial (DF26) is probably of Late Iron Age date, and one possibly so (DF1). DF26 contained a Late Iron Age lidded bowl (Cam 253; FIG. 160, DF26.1–2) and a North Gaulish flagon of unknown form (fabric WPW) which is probably a pre-conquest import (FIG. 160, DF26.3), while DF1 contained a single Cam 113 butt-beaker (FIG. 159, DF1.1). However, the other burial (DF28) and the pit (DF3) are certainly post-conquest as they contain flagon forms of Claudian date or later (FIG. 163, DF28.2; not illustrated, DF3.1).

Imported North Gaulish wares are well represented with three, possibly four, pots. As well as one flagon (FIG. 160, DF26.3), there are two Cam 113 butt-beakers (FIG. 159, DF1.1 and FIG. 163, DF28.1) in fabric BPW, and possibly a two-handled flagon (FIG. 163, DF28.2) is also an import. The form Cam 113 is common at Sheepen but rare in assemblages from the fortress/early *colonia* (*CAR* 10, 472). The inclusion of the form Cam 113 among these burials is striking as it is completely absent from the burials and chambers within the enclosures. However, it does occur among the assemblages from the enclosure ditches and pyre-sites (p. 288). There are also other links with the pottery from the enclosure ditches (rather than the burials) both in the presence of the flagon form Cam 154/155 and the fabric RCW.

It can also be noted that, overall, the selection of grave goods among the Site D burials is predominantly associated with the consumption or provision of liquids (wine/beer) rather than food. This is represented by flagons and beakers, with flagons or beakers occurring in all three of the definite cremation burials, whereas there are no platters. Moreover, the two bowls in DF28 (FIG. 163, DF28.3–4) are small and were probably used as cups.

The choice of ceramics included with the cremation burials from Site D is typical of the cremation rite of the Late Iron Age and early Romano-British period in southern Britain, while the high number of imports in the burials in the enclosures make them appear similar to vessel grave groups found in northern France, Holland and Germany. This is not intended to imply that the enclosure burials are those of incomers, but rather that social considerations place them apart from the general south-east British population, of whom those buried on Site D are a typical group.

THE CREMATED BONE FROM SITE D

By S. A. Mays

The cremated bone from Site D comprises material from three cremation burials and six pits containing pyre debris. All bone was highly comminuted, limiting the information which could be gained from it. In many cases, no fragments could be identified to specific elements, although all contexts contained bone which was definitely or probably human.

Each of the burials contained very much less bone than would be obtained from cremation of an adult corpse (2 kg). In all instances, recovered bone was neutral white in colour, suggesting thorough firing at temperatures in excess of about 940°C (Shipman *et al.* 1984).

The colour of the bone from the pits resembled that from the three burials. This may suggest similar firing for remains from all contexts or that more incompletely burnt fragments may not have survived under the soil conditions at Stanway. It was tentatively suggested that material from one of the pits (DF3) may have derived from at least two individuals.

Context **DF1** (D1, D3, D11, D12, D19). Urned cremation burial.
Material

weight (g)	fragment size (mm)		approximate fragment count
	mean	maximum	
338.5	9	45	2100

Included in identified elements. Fragments of skull, tibia and radius.
All fragments certainly or probably human.
Colour Neutral white
Sex Unknown
Age Adult

Context **DF2** (D7, D16). Pit with pyre-related material. 7.1 g of burnt bone. Some fragments certainly human, the rest probably human.

Context **DF3** (D2, D4, D15, D18, D23). Pit with pyre-related material.
Material

weight (g)	fragment size (mm)		approximate fragment count
	mean	maximum	
151.1	6	25	650

Included in identified elements. Fragments of skull.
Some fragments certainly human, most of the rest are probably human except for one fragment which appears to be animal bone.
Colour Neutral white
Sex Unknown
Age On the basis of variations in the thickness of cranial vault fragments, there may be a minimum of two individuals, one adult and one juvenile.

Context **DF7** (D4, D17). Pit with pyre-related material.
Material

weight (g)	fragment size (mm)		approximate fragment count
	mean	maximum	
197.9	8	35	650

Included in identified elements. Fragments of skull and pelvic bones.
Some fragments certainly human, the rest probably human.
Colour Neutral white
Sex Unknown
Age Unknown

Context **DF13**. Pit with pyre-related debris.
Material

weight (g)	fragment size (mm)		approximate fragment count
	mean	maximum	
30.4	6	20	350

Some fragments certainly human, the rest probably human.
Sex Unknown.
Age Some skull fragments from a juvenile individual were identifiable.

Context **DF14**. Pit with pyre-related material. 1.4 g burnt bone. All fragments probably human.

Context **DF25**. Pit with pyre-related material. 2.2 g burnt bone. All fragments probably human.

Context **DF26** (D41, D63). Urned cremation burial.
Material

weight (g)	fragment size (mm)		approximate fragment count
	mean	maximum	
38.1	4	15	500

Included in identified elements. Fragments of skull.
All fragments probably human.

Colour Neutral white
Sex Unknown
Age Unknown

Context **DF28** (D55, D59). Unurned cremation burial.
Material.

weight (g)	fragment size (mm)		approximate fragment count
	mean	maximum	
61.1	9	30	550

All fragments probably human
Colour Neutral white
Sex Unknown
Age Unknown

THE CHARRED PLANT MACROFOSSILS AND OTHER REMAINS FROM SITE D (TABLES 72–3)

By Val Fryer

Forty-four samples from 21 pits excavated on Site D were submitted for the extraction of the plant macrofossil assemblages. The samples (or sub-samples thereof in the case of those over 50 litres in size) were processed by manual water flotation/washover, collecting the flots in a 500-micron mesh sieve. The dried flots were scanned under a binocular microscope at magnifications up to ×16, and the plant macrofossils and other remains noted are listed in TABLES 72–3 and in the archive. Identifications were made by comparison with modern reference specimens, and the material is categorised as follows: herbs, tree/shrub macrofossils, other plant macrofossils, and other materials. Nomenclature within the tables follows Stace (1997). All plant remains were charred. Insufficient macrofossils were recovered for quantitative analysis. The density of material within the assemblages is expressed in the tables as follows: × = 1–10 specimens, ×× = 10–100 specimens, and ××× = 100+ specimens. Modern contaminants including fibrous roots and seeds were recorded throughout. The non-floating residues were collected in a 1 mm-mesh sieve and sorted when dry. Fragments of burnt bone and other artefacts/ecofacts were retained for further specialist analysis.

Although charcoal fragments and pieces of charred root/stem were abundant throughout, other plant macrofossils were exceedingly rare. The few seeds recovered were all very poorly preserved, with most being puffed, distorted and fragmented.

Seeds of grasses and grassland plants were recorded as single specimens from only six samples (2, 5, 9, 30, 38, and 40). Taxa noted included medick/clover/trefoil (*Medicago/Trifolium/Lotus* sp.), ribwort plantain (*Plantago lanceolata*) and vetch/vetchling (*Vicia/Lathyrus* sp.). Small fragments of hazel (*Corylus avellana*) nutshell were noted in Samples 5, 25 and 33. Other plant macrofossils included indeterminate culm nodes, fruit stone fragments, seeds and tubers.

The majority of the black porous and tarry residues are probably derived from either the cremation processes or the combustion of organic materials at very high temperatures. However, some pieces had a more industrial appearance and, along with the coal fragments,* these may be waste products from the use of steam implements on the land in recent times. Other materials included small fragments of burnt bone, burnt stone and globules of vitrified material.

CONCLUSIONS (TABLES 72–3)

Of the 44 samples processed, 29 contain only charcoal, pieces of charred root/stem and occasional other remains. These have not been tabulated but are listed in the site archive.

Although charcoal fragments are abundant in all sixteen samples taken from the cremation burial deposits, only eight assemblages contain rare additional plant remains, the most notable of which are the charred tuber fragments. These, along with the pieces of charred root/stem and grassland herb seeds, are almost certainly derived from either dried plant material used as

TABLE 72: PLANT MACROFOSSILS FROM CREMATION BURIALS DF1, DF26 AND DF28.
(b burnt, cf. compare)

Sample no.	1	2	9	10	11	40	39	38
Feature no.	DF1	DF1	DF1	DF1	DF1	DF1	DF26	DF28
Finds no.	D11	D12	D19	D20	D21	D1	D69	D68
Herbs								
Medicago/Trifolium/Lotus sp.			×cf			×cf		
Vicia/Lathyrus sp.		×						
Plantago lanceolata L.								×
Other plant macrofossils								
Charcoal <2mm	×××	×××	×××	×××	××	××	×	××
Charcoal >2mm	×	×		×				×××
Charred root/rhizome/stem	××	××	××	××	×	××		×
Indet. culm nodes							×	
Indet. seeds							×	
Indet. tuber	×	××	××	×	×	×		
Other materials								
Black porous 'cokey' material	×	×	××	×	×	×		
Black tarry material	×	××	×		×	×	×	
Bone	×b		×b	×b		××b		
Burnt/fired clay	×	×	×					×
Burnt stone				×				
?Metallic residue	×							
Small coal fragments	×	×	×	×			×	
Vitrified material	×	×	×	×				
Sample volume (litres)	20	20	36	16	20	2	8	1
Volume of flot (litres)	0.1	<0.1	0.1	<0.1	<0.1	<0.1	<0.1	0.1
% flot sorted	100%	100%	100%	100%	100%	100%	100%	100%

TABLE 73: PLANT MACROFOSSILS FROM PITS DF3, DF7, DF20, DF21, DF30 AND DF41
(b burnt)

Sample no.	5	13	4	25	26	30	33
Feature no.	DF3	DF3	DF7	DF21	DF20	DF30	DF41
Finds no.	D15	D23	D14	D38	D39	D57	D61
Herbs							
Fabaceae indet.	×						
Poaceae indet.						×	
Tree/shrub macrofossils							
Corylus avellana L.	×			×			×
Other plant macrofossils							
Charcoal <2mm	×××	×××	××	×	×××	×××	×××
Charcoal >2mm		×				×	×
Charred root/rhizome/stem	××	×	×			××	
Indet. fruit stone fragment					×		
Indet. seeds	×		×			×	
Indet. tuber	×	×				×	
Other materials							
Black porous 'cokey' material			××	×	×	××	×
Black tarry material	×	×	×	×	×		×
Bone	×b	×b	×b	×b			
Burnt/fired clay				×	×		×
Burnt stone				×			
Small coal frags.	×		×		×	×	×
Vitrified material	×						
Sample volume (litres)	10	10	16	8	8	8	10
Volume of flot (litres)	0.2	<0.1	<0.1	<0.1	<0.1	0.1	<0.1
% flot sorted	50%	100%	100%	100%	100%	100%	100%

kindling or fuel for the cremations, or from material burnt *in situ* beneath the pyres. The assemblages from the pits DF3, DF7 and DF30 were sufficiently similar to the cremation burial deposits to suggest a common source. Individual seeds, pieces of nutshell, fruit-stone fragments or culm nodes are also present in a further four samples (TABLES 72–3), but the assemblages in which they occur are too small to be conclusively interpreted.

In summary, wood and/or charcoal appear to have been the principal fuels used for the Stanway cremations. However, the poor condition of the few surviving macrofossils may indicate that combustion occurred at a sufficiently high temperature to destroy a high proportion of any additional materials which may have originally been incorporated within the pyres. It would appear that dried grasses and grassland herbs, some of which were pulled up by the roots, might have been used as either kindling or a supplementary fuel source.

*Editor's note. Fragments of coal were also found in environmental samples from the Middle Iron Age pits at Stanway (p. 384). No fragments were noted on site in any of the archaeological contexts. This absence indicates that the coal which does occur in those contexts must all be in tiny pieces and must have been washed down from above through channels left in the soil by worms and decayed roots.

THE WORKED FLINT FROM SITE D (FIG. 168; TABLE 74)

By Hazel Martingell

Five worked flints were recovered from the Site D excavations. They were all from unstratified contexts, but are probably not far from their original sites. They consist of an obliquely blunted microlith (FIG. 168; TABLE 74), a retouched blade, a core-scraper, and two flakes.

The most interesting piece is the obliquely blunted microlith (Jacobi Class 1B, fig. 11). These artefacts are type fossils for the early Mesolithic. They are projectile points and not common in Essex. Only seven locations in Essex with early Mesolithic microliths were known of in 1996 (Jacobi 1996): Hullbridge; Dawes Heath, Thundersley; Chelmsford site V; White Colne; High Beech, Epping; Pledgdon; and Little Clacton. It is possible that the retouched blade could also be Mesolithic. The core-scraper is a much rougher piece and is most likely to be later prehistoric in date. The two flakes are waste pieces and not datable.

The recovery of the early Mesolithic microlith is of special interest. It suggests the presence of hunter-gatherers in the Roman river valley some time during the 8th millennium B.C., and is a significant addition to the evidence.

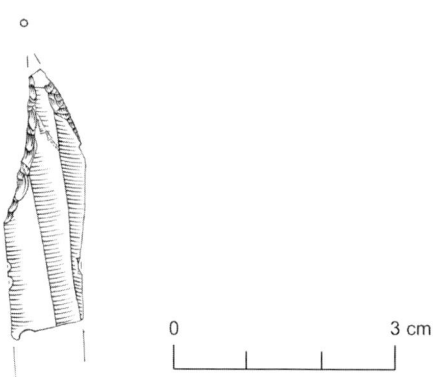

FIG. 168. Site D: early Mesolithic microlith (scale 1:1)

TABLE 74: THE WORKED FLINT FROM SITE D

SF403	D26	Unstratified	1 microlith. Early Mesolithic type, obliquely blunted long blade.
SF404	D26	Unstratified	1 flake, tertiary.
SF405	D26	Unstratified	1 flake, secondary, slight patination, hinged termination.
SF406	D26	Unstratified	1 retouched blade, secondary, retouch on left edge, slightly patinated.
SF407	D26	Unstratified	1 core scraper, secondary, thick section.

CHAPTER 7

ASPECTS OF THE STANWAY CEMETERY

By Philip Crummy

INTRODUCTION

Stanway is an interesting and important funerary site for many reasons. Some are obvious and derive from some of the unusual objects and features which it contained, especially the medical instruments, the gaming boards, and the mortuary chambers. Others are relatively esoteric and are linked to personal and communal power. They relate to location, date, and a ruling élite known to us through histories and coin studies. In some ways the site conforms to its type, but in others it does not. Teasing out what was normal and what was not is part of the challenge in understanding the site and seeing what it can offer in terms of our understanding not just of funerary practice in south-eastern Britain around the time of the Roman invasion, but also of the political and military developments of its time.

The site lies on the periphery of Camulodunum. Part of the funerary sequence (Enclosures 3 to 5) belongs to that critical period when Cunobelin had just died and Claudius captured Camulodunum as the first stage in the Roman conquest of much of Britain. The people whose remains were buried at Stanway in Enclosures 3 to 5 were of high status. The character of the site and the objects buried there show that this was so. Those people must not merely have witnessed events which were to have such a profound effect on the country in the next few centuries to come, they must have been a part of them. As will be argued below, the Stanway site provides clues about who the inhabitants of Camulodunum were and their relationships with the Roman world across the English Channel.

The funerary aspect of the Stanway site is characterised by the following components: large funerary enclosures, timber mortuary chambers, cremation burials, pyre-sites, small ditched areas perhaps for pyres or structures for the display of the dead (our so-called '?mortuary enclosures'), pits with pyre debris, a single pit with broken funerary goods (but not pyre debris) and smashed pots in the ditches. These have been described in turn earlier in this report on a context by context basis. Most can be related to the seven-stage process of disposing of the dead defined by Pearce (1998, table 1). The various steps and the features associated with them can be summarised in a slightly extended form as follows:

1) preliminaries involving the construction of structures such as the enclosures, chambers, ?mortuary enclosures, and shaft/barrels,
2) the display or storage of the deceased and their grave goods in the chambers or perhaps in some cases above ground in the ?mortuary enclosures,
3) the act of cremation on the pyres with the consequent production of pyre debris,
4) pyre-side rituals involving the collection of burnt bones and pyre debris, the deposition of pyre debris in the shaft/barrels, the deliberate breaking of funerary goods away from the pyre, and perhaps the deliberate breaking of the goods on the pyre,
5) the collection from the pyre, and from the places where funerary goods were broken, of cremated bone, pyre debris, and burnt and/or broken funerary goods,
6) the interment and deposition in pits, chambers and shafts/barrels of intact cremated bone, grave goods, deliberately broken funerary goods, and pyre debris,
7) the marking of the chambers with mounds, and finally

8) commemorative feasting and the deliberate deposition of broken pots in the enclosure ditches and ?mortuary enclosures, and perhaps the construction of the structure in Enclosure 5 implied by the slot CF96.

Theoretical approaches would define the whole process thus: digging an enclosure and placing a body in a chamber or in a ?mortuary enclosure represents the initial rite of separating the dead from the living by placing them in a liminal situation, while the stages from the pyre to either burial or the ?scattering of ashes mark the transit of the dead person into an altered state, an 'other' world; the construction of a mound, the consumption of a funeral feast and the smashing of the pots used during the meal are symbolic of the dead person's final departure and disappearance from life (Pearce 1998, 105; Parker Pearson 2003, 50, 147). Theory aside, what is certain is that the burial rites practised at Stanway were highly structured, and they appear to have been graded to some degree in accordance with the status of each deceased person.

The following section is a review and discussion of the stratigraphic and finds evidence according to specific topics not already covered in the previous sections. In particular, some generalised conclusions are drawn about various categories of funerary context, especially the nature and structure of the chambers and the physical appearance and contents of the cremation burials. The evidence for dating and phasing is also reviewed at length and various inherent difficulties and limitations are highlighted. Finally, consideration is given to the (possibly contentious) question as to whether anything can be deduced about the likely identity of the people represented at Stanway as indicated by their funerary practices.

ASPECTS OF THE PHYSICAL REMAINS (FIG. 169; TABLES 75–8)

SYMMETRY AND ORGANISATION OF THE FUNERARY ENCLOSURES

The layout of the funerary enclosures and the features and finds from them all display a degree of organisation which can hardly have been random and must reflect the burial and other rites which took place inside them, as does the awareness of the points of the compass which is evident in many places. Aspects of the site which reveal or hint at an all-embracing symmetry and order can be summarised as follows. The chamber BF6 was centrally placed in its enclosure, the other three being axial. The pyre was central in Enclosure 3 as was the ?mortuary enclosure in Enclosure 5. The ?mortuary enclosure in Enclosure 4 was axial. No evidence of a pyre was found in Enclosure 1, but the position of the chamber there hints that it had been in the middle. All the cremation burials lay in the western halves of their enclosures. Those in Enclosure 5 were all about the same distance from the enclosure ditch (*i.e.* 8–10 m). The bulk of the partial pots not only in the ditches but also in the ditched pyre-sites BF32 and CF43–6 were in the eastern halves of their enclosures. The burial pits and the chambers were all aligned with their enclosures apart from AF18 which, not being rectilinear or square, could not be aligned with anything. The entrances of the enclosures were on their east sides (leaving aside Enclosure 1 where the location of the entrance cannot be determined).

CHAMBERS: STRUCTURE, MOUNDS AND BROKEN GRAVE GOODS (FIG. 169)

Of the four chambers, three were nailed. The earliest one (AF25) had been constructed without nails. The sides of the nailed chambers were made of vertical planks held in place in the base by a slot and nailed in place at the top. None of them appears to have had plank floors. BF6 seems to have had straw or hay spread over the floor. BF6 and CF42 were the largest and most complicated. Both incorporated a horizontal timber suspended along the length of the chamber to support the roof (FIG. 169). The ends of these timbers were carried on vertical posts placed in the centre of the north and south sides. Chamber AF25 was different in that the planks forming its walls appear to have been set horizontally. Support for this conclusion was provided by the absence of the slot around all four sides of the floor, which was a feature of the nailed chambers. The horizontal placement of the planks is likely to be related to the way the chamber

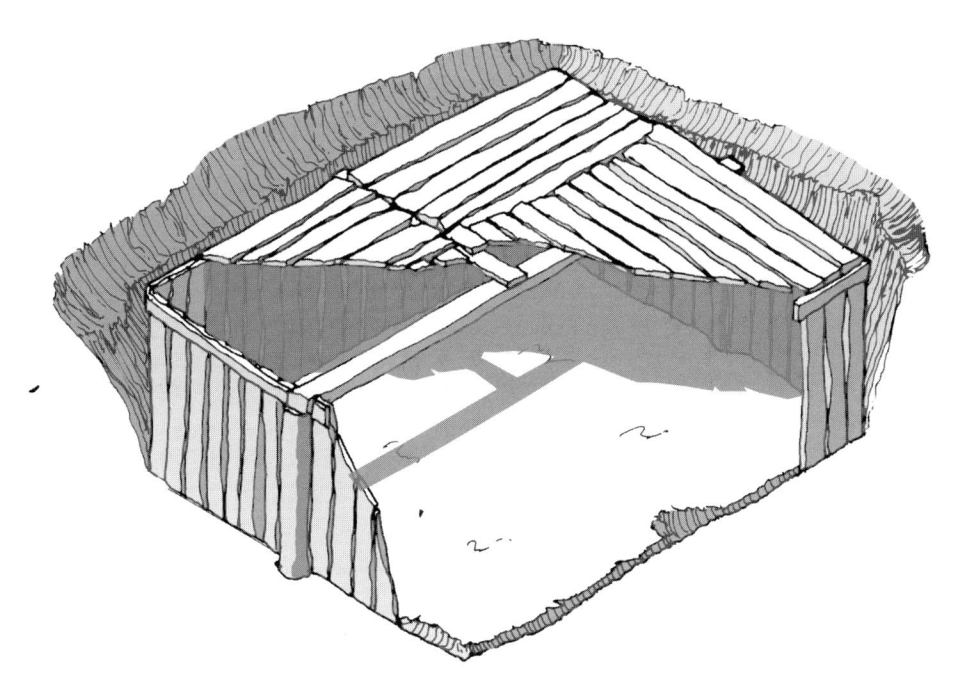

FIG. 169. Conjectural reconstruction of chamber BF6, viewed from the south-east (J. Chittenden)

was made, and suggests that it was constructed like some wooden wells, such as those found at Sheepen where the sides consisted of a series of horizontally laid frames. Here the use of nails was avoided by shoulder-jointing the planks to make the frames which were then stacked one above the other to form the walls (Hawkes and Hull 1947, 126–8, figs 38 and 40).

In all three nailed chambers, the distribution of the surviving nails indicates that many others around the edges must have been ploughed off, and thus implies that the roofs of the chambers had been close to the surface, if not at ground-level (FIG. 169). The proximity of the uppermost parts of those three chambers to the contemporary ground-level meant that it would have been impossible to cover them over without a mound of some sort. The bases of mounds which once stood over chambers BF6 and CF42 were very clear in section as 'sagging', dish-shaped deposits making up most of the fill of those chambers. The layers constituting the upper fills of AF25 and BF24 were not dish-shaped, but were bedded horizontally and gave the appearance of being simple backfill. The previous existence of a mound over AF25 is therefore uncertain but, as shown in BF24, its horizontally bedded upper fill does not rule out this possibility.

The mounds are likely to have been low since there were no surviving earthworks. Presumably they were destroyed by later ploughing and other agricultural activities. Nor were the mounds likely to have been very extensive, to judge by the proximity of other features. The maximum possible width for a mound over CF42 would have been 16 m, so as to leave clear the slot CF96 and the ?mortuary enclosure CF43–6. The alignments of both CF96 and CF43–6 and their proximity to the chamber raises the possibility of square mounds. A mound over BF24 could have been no bigger than 23 m across to keep clear of the enclosure ditch BF5. A mound over BF6 is not likely to have been wider than 38 m to allow for the Inkwell burial; presumably it was a lot less. There was nothing to indicate the likely area of a mound over AF25, if indeed one ever existed.

Burial rites must also lie behind not only the deposition pattern of the broken funerary goods and the cremated bone in the chambers (at least the material in Enclosures 3 to 5) but in the selection of their content. The debris (*i.e.* the lower fill of the chambers) must have been regarded as being of some significance since, in BF6, BF24 and CF42, it had been placed into the chamber from the north side. This is very clear from the distribution of the broken grave goods in all three chambers, where there were obvious concentrations of them at the north ends of their chambers. There is evidence too of selection in the material that was dumped on the floor of the chambers. The human bone in the chambers appears to have been added deliberately after it had been picked out of the ashes of the pyre. This was clearest in BF6 where the burnt human bone seemed to lie in small scatters on or close to the floor, as if thrown into the chamber a handful at a time. There is also similar evidence in the distribution of the other material in the dumped deposits on the floors of the chambers. Although the broken pots and other items were scattered throughout the deposits, there were hints of some clustering of fragments from the same vessels in chamber CF42 which might show deliberate selection. And in BF6 and BF24, some of the other items, such as the spout BF6.25, the pedestal BF6.24 and some of the beads BF24.24, lay on or close to the floor as if they had been deliberately selected for early deposition in the dumping process. However, it is unlikely that individual sherds were picked out for redeposition in the chamber, but rather that the debris containing the broken items was picked over and parts with suitable concentrations of sherds were scraped up and redeposited in the chamber *en masse*.

Not only were the broken grave goods concentrated towards the north ends of the chambers, but they also occurred in greater numbers on or just above the chamber floors. These concentrations show that the broken material was deposited in the chambers from the north ends, with some selection early on in the depositional process when the pieces were relatively plentiful in the dumped material. Moreover, although the bits of broken pots lay scattered throughout most of the debris in a jumbled way, there were hints of limited clustering. The amphoras in BF6 had the most distinctive distribution, with a clear concentration near the north end of the chamber.

Interestingly, a similar concentration of broken objects was found in the Lexden Tumulus during the excavations of 1924 (Foster 1986, 166–9), in which the smashed artefacts were found throughout the lower fill of the grave but apparently with distinct concentrations on or near the floor. The similarities between Stanway and the Lexden Tumulus may also extend to the amphoras. Remains of at least 17 smashed vessels of this type lay near the centre of the north end of the grave (*ibid.*, 131). These were thought to have been broken by later 'robbers' (Laver 1927; Foster 1986, 163–4), but in the light of the evidence from Stanway, especially BF6, it is more likely that the vessels had been smashed at the same time as the other objects there and the resulting debris deposited in the grave from the north side just as at Stanway.

PYRES AND PITS WITH PYRE DEBRIS

At least two pyres had been lit in the centre of Enclosure 3, where vents in the shape of long pits showed where they had been sited. Elsewhere the locations of the pyres were difficult to determine, but the two ?mortuary enclosures BF32 and CF43–6 are plausible candidates. Both were in the form of clusters of small pits or post-holes within a squared ditched enclosure, but identification of these sites as the locations of pyres can only be tentative and, as is discussed below, there is the possibility that they represent the remains of structures, subsequently burnt, used for the display of corpses or their excarnation. Other pyre-sites must have existed in other places but, being largely surface features, they would be hard to detect without the deep vents, post-holes, and ditches present in the ones that we have found.

Pits with pyre-related debris are now widely recognised as a specific type of feature that occurs on cemeteries of the Late Iron Age and Roman periods. They are characterised by the inclusion of charcoal, fragments of burnt and broken funerary goods, and sometimes cremated bone. Difficulties on some sites in distinguishing between pits with pyre debris and unurned cremation burials mean that it is often impossible to determine reliable numbers. In the main Stanway site (as opposed to Site D), there were only two pits which contained pyre debris (BF17 and CF7). At Site D there were proportionally more, with four or five pits with pyre-related debris as opposed to only three cremation burials. However, there are so many factors governing the numbers, or at least the apparent numbers, of pyre-related features on sites that any ratios are not likely to be of much value. In Colchester, the cemeteries on the Abbey Field to the south of the town (excavated in 2000) and Turner Rise to the north (excavated 1996–97) produced around one pit with pyre-related debris to every four or five cremation burials (Crossan 2001 and Shimmin forthcoming resp.). Further afield at Westhampnett in West Sussex, the ratio was similar (Fitzpatrick 1997, 18), whereas at King Harry Lane in Verulamium, at one to twenty, it was considerably lower (Niblett 1999, 402). Moreover, in London thick layers of pyre debris show that this material may simply have been spread out over a wide area (maybe in wide scoops) rather than buried in pits (Barber and Bowsher 2000, 63).

Pits with pyre debris are hard to explain as a phenomenon, but generally they are felt to represent the deliberate burial of debris which had some special significance to those who buried it (Polfer 2000, 32; Fitzpatrick 1997, 231, 233–4). Although the dumped material in the bottoms of the chambers does not seem to have contained pyre debris, these deposits must have had a similar significance since they contained fragments of broken funerary goods and in the cases of BF6 and BF24 handfuls of cremated human bone, which appear to have been added as the material was being deposited.

?MORTUARY ENCLOSURES

The purpose of the two square ditched areas which we have termed '?mortuary enclosures' (*i.e.* BF32 and CF43–6) is unclear. BF32 had the appearance of a pyre-site because it incorporated a patch of scorched natural and included a few pieces of cremated bone, much charcoal, and a considerable amount of heat-affected metalwork, that is, the same sort of material that was associated with pyre-site BF1/BF16. Presumably the pits enclosed by BF32's ditch must have held posts which strengthened the pyre. However, CF43–6 was similar in plan to BF32 but there was little else about it to suggest that it too had been a pyre-site apart from a single, tiny scrap of heat-affected copper alloy. Had they both been pyre-sites, then their ditches perhaps should have contained much more debris from the pyres than they did.

A possibility that cannot be discounted is that each ?mortuary enclosure enclosed an above-ground type of structure used for excarnation (Carr and Knüsel 1997) or, perhaps more likely, the display of the body prior to cremation such as suggested for Acy-Romance in the French Ardennes (Lambot *et al.* 1994). Both ?mortuary enclosures appear to have been relatively short-lived, so that excarnation is probably the least likely of the two possibilities. Perhaps the explanation is more complicated; for example, they may have enclosed above-ground structures that were subsequently burnt *in situ* as part of a pyre. The enclosures would certainly make sense as places for structures used to display the dead since they would then have served as the above-ground equivalent of the wooden mortuary chamber. But Enclosure 4 contained both a chamber and a ?mortuary enclosure. Why have both, especially if, as appears to have been the case, there were no burials in the enclosure? On balance, they seem best seen as pyre sites in view of the burnt material and the scorched area in BF32, but this interpretation remains problematic.

CREMATION BURIALS: COVERS, DEPTHS, CHARACTER AND PRESENCE OR ABSENCE OF A SERVICE (TABLE 75)

All the cremation burials were rectangular or square in plan (with the exception of AF18 and possibly CF403, the shape of which is unknown). The reason for their shape is that their contents were probably protected by a cover made of wooden planks. The remains of plank covers have been recognised in circular graves at Stansted and King Harry Lane, but the absence there of nails suggests that the planks were simply laid loose in the burial pit. Thus nailed wooden covers may prove more likely in rectangular or square burial pits. Other than shape, the evidence for covers at Stanway is limited. Wood from a fairly complicated cover survived in the Doctor's burial, as did many nails which seem to have been part of it (CF47.41). Nails in the Inkwell burial might also have been part of a cover (BF67.5). No wood or nails were found in the Warrior's burial that could be interpreted as having belonged to a cover, although it is possible that a cover was not thought necessary since the open vessels seem to have been protected by a cloak or blanket (BF64.36).

The height of the amphoras in the Doctor's burial and the Warrior's burial determined the depth of their burial pits because they had been placed upright or nearly so. This meant that both burial pits were much deeper than the others.

TABLE 75: TYPES OF CREMATION BURIALS

Inurned	Unurned and with a service	Unurned and without a service
AF18	BF64 (Warrior's burial)	BF67 (Inkwell burial)
	CF47 (Doctor's burial)	CF72 (Brooches burial)
	CF115 (Mirror burial)	
	CF403	

The seven burials from the enclosures can be grouped according to content, *i.e.* inurned cremation burials, unurned cremation burials with a service, and unurned cremation burials without a service (TABLE 75). As mentioned above, the difference in the quantity of bone between the inurned burial and the others is probably the result of a slightly different rite for each of the two categories, and the distinction between burials which were inurned and those which were not is probably a meaningful one in terms of funerary practice. The inclusion or absence of a service clearly made a big difference to the size and appearance of a group of grave goods, but it is less certain how significant that might have been in terms of rite or status of the dead person. This much is made clear from the Brooches burial which, despite not containing a service, could be seen as relatively well endowed since it contained six brooches and an expensive cosmetic container in the form of a rare glass *pyxis*. Six brooches in one burial is a high number: out of 472 burials at King Harry Lane, the largest number in any one grave was four (Stead and Rigby 1989, appendix 6). In Colchester, a grave at Lexden provides an example of a pre-conquest example of a rich burial without a service but again with six brooches (Hull 1942). We can only speculate as to why burial groups with such high-quality grave goods should have excluded a service. It was not a matter of gender, since services could occur with both males (*e.g.* BF64) and females (chamber BF24).

GRAVE GOODS: SOCIAL STATUS AND FUNCTION (TABLE 76)

In Britain, there is a growing belief that the number and quality of grave goods should not be taken as an indicator of the status which the dead person enjoyed in life (Biddulph 2005, 38; Fitzpatrick 2000, 17; Parker Pearson 2003, 78–80). Certainly at the macro level, *i.e.* individuals within a specific cemetery, it would be too simplistic to suppose that, for example, a person interred with six grave goods had been a more important person than one with, say, three. The Brooches burial is a good illustration of this point. The burial contained relatively few objects compared with the Doctor's burial or the Warrior's burial, yet the glass *pyxis* and the high number of brooches show that this was probably the burial place of a relatively well-off person whose social standing and economic circumstances are now indistinguishable from the other two. Nevertheless, it does seem an inescapable conclusion that collectively the people interred in Enclosures 3 to 5 at Stanway were of a different social status than, say, those whose remains were buried on Site D. This is evident not just from the grave goods but also from the manner of burial in the first group, *i.e.* the presence of chambers, the existence and the scale of the funerary enclosures, and the very low density of burials within them. The difference can be presumed to be a consequence of Enclosures 3–5 and Site D being the burial places of two different social groups, separated not only by status but also by different ties of close kinship. Put in more general terms, the grave goods in a particular cemetery viewed as a group (communal burial grounds apart) ought to reveal something about the status and wealth of the dead buried within it, because the grave goods are likely to reflect the collective status and wealth of the family concerned. Martin Millett (1993, 275) made much the same point but preferred the less specific, wider construct of 'social network'.

The largest services at Stanway (in BF64, CF47, BF6, CF42 and BF24) give the impression of having comprised settings for two people (TABLE 76). Although they do not necessarily seem to split into two identical halves, there is nevertheless an impression in the range of sizes and forms of two roughly similar sets of bowls, plates and cups. A two-way division is most evident

TABLE 76: VESSELS RELATED TO FOOD AND DRINK

| | **Drink** | | | | **Food** | | |
	Storage Amphoras	Presentation/serving Lagenae/flagons	Beakers*	Others?	Drinking Cups	Eating Shallow bowls and/or platters	Presentation? Jars/deep bowls
Cremation burials							
AF18	–	–	–	–	–	–	–
BF64	1	2	?1	hand-washing set	2 small 2 large	2 platters 2 bowls	1 samian cup
BF67	–	1	–	–	–	–	–
CF47	1 (**)	1	–	bronze saucepan, copper-alloy strainer bowl (***)	2 small 2 large	7 platters	1 samian bowl
CF72	–	1	–	–	1 small 1 large	–	–
CF115	–	1	–	–	1	–	–
CF403	–	–	–	–	–	1 platter	1 jar
Chambers (probably incomplete groups)							
AF25	–	–	–	–	–	–	2
BF6	2	–	–	copper-alloy strainer bowl	2 small 2 large	17	–
BF24	–	2	2	–	2 small (different types) 2 large	14	–
CF42	1	–	1	–	2 small 1 large	5	1 glass bowl

* Beakers may have been used for presentation.
** May have contained *garum*, a condiment rather than a drink.
*** May have contained a tea-like medicinal drink made from artemisia.

in the cups, particularly in the Doctor's burial and, to a lesser extent, the Warrior's burial where the vessels seem to be paired according to size and shape. A similar split can occasionally be seen in some burials from elsewhere, *e.g.* the pair of silver cups from Welwyn (Stead 1967, 58). Powerful support for the idea that some of the groups made provision for two people is given by the gaming board in the Doctor's burial which, of course, was laid out as if in readiness for two people to play a game. This begs the question of who that second person might have been. One unlikely possibility is that burials with two settings (if that indeed is what they are) contained the cremated remains of two people. It is true that the cremated bone provided no indication of more than one person, but then little of the bone survives and, being cremated, it would be difficult to tell if the remains of more than a single person were present unless one had been an adult and the other a child. It is worth noting in this regard that the Lexden Tumulus may have contained the remains of more than one person (Foster 1986, 138–9).

As is invariably the case with burials of the Late Iron Age and Roman periods, the vessels were laid out face upwards in the graves with almost no nesting of one within another. The amphoras in the Doctor's burial and the Warrior's burial were placed upright against a corner of the burial pit. Although there was no evidence to indicate otherwise, the arrangements strongly point to the vessels having contained food and drink. Amphoras can be taken to have included wine (but see below). Flagons, *lagenae* (two-handled flagons), and beakers would have been for the presentation and serving of drink, presumably wine or beer, although beakers may have been used for communal drinking (Pitts 2005, 148). Bowls and jars are likely to have been used for the presentation of food, cups were for drinking and platters and shallow bowls for eating as well as serving (TABLE 76; Biddulph 2005; Pitts 2005). The upright position of the amphoras also suggests that they had been opened before burial because their contents might have spilled or leaked out if they had been laid on their sides. (For a contrary point of view, see p. 304.)

The simplest combination of grave goods was found in CF115 where a small flagon had been deposited with a single cup. Unless food had been provided on wooden platters, it would appear that the dead person was sent off into the other world with nothing more than a relatively modest drink. CF403, on the other hand, seemed only to have been provided with something to eat, and, if the grave goods are to be taken at face value, the much earlier AF18 in Enclosure 1 apparently had nothing at all. It is, of course, not possible to tell what is missing. Wooden and leather items would have decayed completely without trace, and food and liquids could have been placed or poured either into the burial pit or on to the surface after it had been backfilled.

Chamber BF6 contained parts of two wine amphoras, chamber CF42 parts of another. The Doctor's burial and the Warrior's burial both contained a single amphora. The amphora in the Doctor's burial is a Beltrán I which, coming from Baetica, is universally regarded by amphora specialists as a container for *garum* rather than wine. Given that *garum* was a condiment, we have to wonder why it was considered necessary to provide the deceased with so much of it. The question applies equally if the *garum* was included for its medicinal properties (p. 300). Certainly it would make more sense if the Doctor's amphora had contained wine, given that a feature of Welwyn-type burials is the inclusion of one or more wine amphoras (Stead 1967, 44, 49; Cunliffe 1991, 510) and that the grave contained a saucepan for preparing heated wine-based drinks (p. 322).

Of the nine burial groups represented in Enclosures 3 to 5, four included gaming equipment. The Doctor's burial and the Warrior's burial each contained the remains of a board and a set of gaming pieces. The fragmentary remains in chambers BF6 and CF42 indicated that they had been similarly equipped, since the former included the corner of a board and the latter a single glass gaming piece. Out of 472 burials from the Iron Age cemetery at King Harry Lane, only two (graves 117 and 309, Stead and Rigby 1989, 109–10) appear to have included gaming boards, which is in marked contrast to the higher-status burial ground at Stanway. In the La Tène world, gaming was a pastime associated with the élite (p. 374). Two stories from the later literature stress the connection between board games and high-status protagonists. *The Wooing of Etain* from the Irish literature mentions games of fidchell (*fidhcheall*) played between Echu Airem, king of Temuir, and Mider of Brí Léith, in which the stakes were fifty superb grey horses and their enamelled bridles, fifty boars, a vat large enough to hold the boars, fifty gold-hilted swords, fifty white cows and fifty white calves, fifty wethers, fifty ivory-hilted swords, and fifty colourful cloaks (Gantz 1981, 52–3). *The Dream of Rhonabwy*, a medieval Welsh story attached to *The Mabinogion*, deliberately looks back to an earlier heroic age and its action centres around a series of games of *gwyddbwyll* played between Arthur and Owain, son of Urien (Jones and Jones 1970, 145–50). In both these cases the game boards are described as silver and the pieces as gold, no doubt chiefly as a poetic device designed to reinforce the high status of the players and to enhance the sense of awe and distance that the telling of the stories would raise in the hearers. Nevertheless, the two examples serve to paint a picture of a warrior society where board games formed part of the normal activities of the court and could be played for high stakes.

BROKEN FUNERARY GOODS AS INDICATORS OF RITUAL (TABLE 77)

Three different types of context contained parts of broken funerary goods, namely chambers, ditches, and pyres/pyre debris. The proportion of burnt material present in each of those types of contexts was different, as are the likely explanations for the condition of the damaged objects which they contained. The site at Alton in Hampshire (Millett 1986) is of particular relevance to Stanway since it provides useful contextual information about funerary rituals and the deliberate breaking of pots which is not so clearly visible at Stanway.

All four chambers at Stanway contained broken pots but no clearly identifiable pyre-debris (as indicated above all by charcoal). The absence of this material in the chambers shows that the parts of the broken objects they contained came from pots and other items broken sufficiently far away from the pyre to be unaffected by it. This rite accounts for the incomplete metal objects in BF6 (*e.g.* the bronze pedestal BF6.24, the fragment of a bronze vessel BF6.25, and the parts of a gaming board BF6.26), and is clearly recognisable as similar to the Lexden Tumulus and Folly Lane where the funerary goods were broken or cut up but not burnt.

Like the funerary pots in the chambers, collectively the broken pot fragments from the enclosure ditches and ?mortuary enclosures at Stanway exhibit little evidence that they had been placed on a pyre. Those that do appear to have been heat-affected are so few in number (TABLE 77) that they are just as likely to have been wasters or seconds. The most obvious explanation for their presence on the site is that they were connected with feasting at the time of the funerals or (less likely) later during commemorative events in the cemetery. The range of pots represented in the ditches is different from that evident in the funerary goods in terms of fabric and type (p. 274). The funerary goods in the burial pits and chambers consist mainly of vessels for drinking, eating and serving, most of which are imported finewares. On the other hand, the pottery from the ditches consists predominantly of jars and beakers largely made in local wares. The composition of the group seems similar to the Sheepen assemblage taken as a whole (TABLE 40; p. 289), where the commonest vessels were jars and bowls (especially CAM 218 and 266) closely followed by butt beakers (mainly CAM 113) and where platters (mostly CAM 28), cups (CAM 56 and 58), and amphoras were relatively rare. In both places, the assemblages were dominated by jars, bowls, and butt beakers. The difference between the two

TABLE 77: POTS AND SHERDS ALMOST CERTAINLY BURNT OR SCORCHED POST-FIRING

Context	Pot or sherd no.	When scorched or burnt	Total no. of pots from context	No. of scorched/ burnt pots
Enclosure 1				
Chamber AF25	AF25.2	not clear, but possibly after or during breakage	2	1
Enclosure 2				
Enclosure ditch CF6	C1473	Late Iron Age grog-tempered sherd; not clear when burnt, but possibly after or during breakage	?2	1
Enclosure 3				
Chamber BF6	BF6.13	if scorched, then before breakage	23	?4
	BF6.16	if scorched, then before breakage		
	BF6.18	if scorched, then before breakage		
	BF6.19	if scorched, then before breakage		
Pyre site BF1/BF16	BF16.1	not clear if burnt, but if so, then before or after breakage	1	1
Burial BF64	BF64.13	if scorched then on one side of the pot and before breakage	15	?1
Enclosure 4				
Enclosure ditches BF40 and CF1	Pot 37*	not clear when	88	1
Enclosure 5				
Chamber CF42	CF42.4	possibly scorched on exterior, but unclear if this happened before or after breakage	7	1
Pyre site CF43–6	Pot 129	not clear, possibly after breakage	11	4
	Pot 130*	not clear when		
	Pot 138	scorched before breakage on one side of pot		
	Pot 141	not clear when		
Enclosure ditches CF2	Pot 135	scorched before breakage as sherds show differential scorching across surfaces	10	1
Outside enclosures				
Pyre debris pit CF7	CF7.1	scorched after or during breakage as there are differences in degrees of scorching between joining sherds	1	1

groups seems to show different eating and drinking habits. The funerary goods at Stanway reflect formal Roman-style dining whereas the material in the ditches appears in keeping with what was evidently everyday British-style eating practice, whereby beer was drunk from butt beakers and food eaten from deep bowls and jars rather than from platters.

Broken pots represented in pyres and pyre debris are limited in number to the extent that in the enclosures there are only about a dozen burnt sherds of this kind. These were found in the pyre-site BF1/BF16 and they are all amphora sherds, apparently from the same vessel (BF16.1). Given that amphora sherds form a relatively small component of the broken material from the site as a whole, the pieces in this pyre-site suggest that amphoras rather than any other kind of vessel were more likely to have ended up next to or on top of a funeral pyre. Indications of the same close association between amphoras and pyres are evident at other similar funerary sites. For example at Folly Lane, although no pottery was found on the pyre site itself, the pyre debris in the burial pit near the chamber contained almost 1.5 kg of burnt amphora sherds as opposed to only four small pieces of other pottery (Niblett 1999, 47–8, 51). And at Clemency, with its 'pavement' of hundreds of amphora sherds and its 'principal pyre site' containing 293 amphora sherds, the connection was even more marked. In each place at Clemency, the proportion of amphora sherds that were burnt was 41 per cent and the number of other kinds of vessels represented in those groups was tiny (Metzler *et al.* 1991, 38–40). It is not possible to determine if the amphora BF16.1 at Stanway was in pieces because it had been deliberately broken or if it had simply disintegrated in the heat of the fire, although the small size of the surviving sherds and the presence of so many deliberately broken pots elsewhere on the site point to premeditated destruction. Nor is it possible to know if the amphora had been empty when it was placed on the pyre (but *see* p. 430 for a discussion of this point).

Apart from amphora sherds, the only other objects found on the pyre-site BF1/BF16 were fragments of heat-affected copper-alloy items and ironwork. This is typical of pyre-sites generally. The copper-alloy pieces are presumably the remains of personal items worn on the body or placed by it in the pyre. The ironwork may indicate that broken-up wooden items of various sorts had been used as fuel, as suggested for Westhampnett (Fitzpatrick 1997, 106, 109). They might also derive from a bier or other item on which the body was burnt.

At Folly Lane, the main deposit of burnt funerary goods was found in the burial pit, not the chamber. Of all the broken pottery in the latter, only three sherds showed signs of having been burnt and these were in the backfilling not the primary deposit (Niblett 1999, 44). There was no obvious equivalent feature at Stanway to the burial pit at Folly Lane (unless it was the ?barrel BF17 in Enclosure 3).

Three of the burials in the cemetery at Alton in Hampshire (Millett 1986) are of particular relevance to Stanway. A very large assemblage of funerary goods had been placed intact on the floor of Grave 5. The group was made up of the usual range of dining and serving vessels. However, in the backfill of the burial pit was the remains of a collection of twelve broken identifiable vessels, consisting of jars and wide bowls just as in the ditches at Stanway. Two other burials from the same cemetery showed a similar pattern but with fewer pots present. The Alton pots are important to Stanway for three reasons. Firstly, they provide an example of the dichotomy which is apparent at Stanway: the vessels on the floors of the graves were appropriate for a formal Roman world whereas those in the grave backfills were more suited to everyday consumption in a local manner. Secondly, the Alton pots show with a precision not possible at Stanway that the deliberate breaking of pots of the sorts found in the Stanway ditches (*i.e.* for the 'informal' consumption of food and drink) could have occurred during the interment of funerary goods and thus could have been an integral part of that process. At Stanway, this means that we can be more confident that the breaking of the pots in the ditches occurred during the funerals rather than at later commemorative events. The stratification of the broken sherds in the ditch fills at Stanway suggests that this was likely to be so (p. 436), but the evidence is not as conclusive as at Alton. Thirdly, the Alton site shows that any of the cremations at Stanway, not just those associated with the chambers, could have been accompanied by the breaking of pots for the 'informal' consumption of food and drink.

WEIGHTS OF THE CREMATED HUMAN BONE (TABLE 78)

The weights of the recovered cremated human bone point to ritual practices at play, since the amounts fall far short of the 2 kg or so that might have been left in the ashes of the funerary pyre after the cremation of each adult (p. 377; Mays and Steele 1999, 108). The shortfalls not only from the chambers and heaped cremation burials but even from the inurned AF18, where a substantial amount of bone might be expected (TABLE 78), suggest that as full a recovery as possible of the burnt bone from the pyre was not considered important, or that the funerary rites at Stanway involved the disposal of most of the cremated bone in a way or ways that did not involve burial on the site, such as scattering in the open air (cf. Parker Pearson 2003, 49). The context with the most bone was the inurned cremation burial AF18 in Enclosure 1 (the only inurned cremation within the funerary enclosures) where the total quantity in the cremation urn was 640 g, representing about a third to a quarter of the bone produced by the average adult. The lower end of the estimated range can be as low as 1,000 g (McKinley 1993), which could make the amount recovered from AF18 closer to a half or two-thirds of the possible total, but it would still not represent full recovery of the bone from the pyre.

The bone in the other six cremation burials had been placed in one or more heaps on the floors of their burial pits or, in the case of the Doctor's burial, on top of a gaming board. The average weight of bone in these instances was around 150 g which is about a quarter the weight of the bone in AF18. This difference is unlikely to be simply a result of chance because the weights of the bone in the 'heaped' burials are fairly consistent. They show that the bone deposited in those places was probably only a small part of what was collected or could have been collected after the bodies had been burnt. The chambers cannot be considered to constitute burial places, at least in any material sense. This is clear from the chamber CF42 which contained no cremated bone whatsoever.

The under-representation of cremated bone is a familiar feature of Late Iron Age cemeteries both in Britain (McKinley 2000) and in Belgic Gaul, for example at Lamadelaine, where these deposits are seen more as tokens (Metzler-Zens *et al.* 1999, 252–7). The amount deposited does not appear to have mattered, even to the point that 'empty' graves such as CF42 at Stanway could have been regarded as cenotaphs (Boulestin *et al.* 2002; Fitzpatrick 1997, 236; McKinley 1997, 57, 71–2).

TABLE 78: WEIGHTS OF CREMATED HUMAN BONE IN THE CHAMBERS, PITS WITH PYRE DEBRIS, CREMATION BURIALS, ?MORTUARY ENCLOSURES, AND SHAFT/BARRELS IN ENCLOSURES 3–5

	Context	*Weight (g)*
Chambers	AF25	11.8
	BF6	45.0
	BF24	62.5
	CF42	0
Pits with pyre debris or broken funerary goods	AF48	3.4
	CF7	55.8
Cremation burials	AF18 (urned)	639.7
	BF64 (in a pile)	137.5
	BF67 (in a pile)	225.6
	CF47 (in a pile)	158.1
	CF72 (in a pile)	73.7
	CF115 (in a pile)	1.0
	CF403 (in a pile)	167.0
?Mortuary enclosures	BF32	0.1
	CF43-6	0
Shafts/barrels	BF17	0
	CF23	0

CREMATED ANIMAL BONE: HORSE AND OTHER REMAINS

The burnt head of a probable horse, or at least a part of it, lay in the mound of CF42. This is indicated by some burnt upper molars and premolars of a large equid, judged by A. Legge and A. Wade to be probably of horse (pp. 382–3). The teeth were poorly preserved, but they lay in a row showing that they had not been loose but were part of a cranium that had almost completely decayed as a result of the hostile soil conditions. A very similar find was made in the mound of BF6 (pp. 382–3). Considering how little was found in the two mounds, the presence of the burnt teeth in both strongly suggests that the deposition of a horse head or part of it in the mounds of CF42 and BF6 was part of the funerary rite.

The soil is too acidic for unburnt bone to survive, but burnt material is clearly a different matter, as the cremated human bone shows. It is, therefore, curious that more of the bone did not survive if the teeth had indeed been burnt. Perhaps the mounds were even more acidic than the fills of most of the pits and burials on the site, or perhaps the teeth were not burnt at all but just look as if they had been because of their heavily decayed state.

On balance, it seems likely that each of these deposits was limited to a fragment of a burnt cranium. However, it is impossible to judge how much of the horse had been deposited in the mound. Could it have been the whole cranium? Was the mandible included so that it was the whole head? Or could the whole carcass have been placed in the mound? Teeth are the most resistant of the bones to decay so that the presence of teeth alone need not preclude much more of the animal originally being present. However, we should also wonder why so few teeth survived. Was only a fragment of horse cranium placed in the mound, or could it be that the horse head had only been partly burnt?

No animal bone was found in the mounds of the other two chambers. The only other remains of this kind to survive in the chambers — or indeed any of the burials or pits with pyre debris — were teeth fragments in chamber AF25 (pig and an unidentified mammal) and the Warrior's burial (sheep/goat, cattle, and an unidentified mammal — all unstratified). The pig tooth in chamber AF25 lay very close to the floor and, like the horse remains in the mounds of BF6 and CF42, was probably all that survived of an animal or parts of an animal that had been burnt on the funeral pyre.

The pyre-site BF1/BF16 contained a ?sheep carpal and ?dog mandible, the latter again suggesting that the head only had been burnt. The presence of both horse and dog carcasses on a funerary site with élite graves can be taken to imply that they were slaughtered because they were animals associated with the élite pastime of hunting (Méniel 2002), but may alternatively be evidence for their chthonic aspects as the guides and guardians of the soul on its journey between life and death (Jenkins 1957, 65; Black 1983; Merrifield 1987, 46–7, 66–7; Green 1997, 178, 186). The dog motif on the samian bowl in the Doctor's burial (CF47.1) may also have been selected for deposition because of the animal's funerary associations, although it was also linked with healing deities and may have been chosen by or for the deceased for that reason.

RESIDUAL POTTERY: INDICATOR OF EARLY EPISODES OF POT-BREAKING?

Residual pottery can be identified in the backfills of the cremation burials and the mounds of the chambers. The material consists of discarded sherds of pottery that had lain in soil scraped or dug up to create the mounds covering the chambers or to backfill the burials and make any mounds that covered them. The residual sherds are very limited in number but they are of interest because they seem to reveal past funerary activities that are otherwise invisible. There will have been residual pottery in the ditch fills too, but distinguishing these sherds from the remains of deliberately placed partial pots is problematic. Residual material of various kinds was also evident in the pyre-sites BF1 and BF16 and the packing material behind the sides of BF6. It was relatively easy to identify, and this proved helpful in determining relationships between those three features.

The minimum number of vessels represented by the residual pottery from the chamber mounds and the cremation burials can be summarised in terms of fabrics and forms as follows:

chamber mounds
BF6: GTW jar or bowl × 1, GTW × 2, HZ (which is also GTW) × 1
BF24: GTW bowl × 1, GTW x 4, GFW flagon × 2
CF42: GTW butt beaker × 1, GTW jar × 1, GTW × 3
backfill of cremation burials
BF64: GTW × 4, RCVW jar × 1, GX × 2
BF67: RCW × 1, GTW butt-beaker × 1

We have already highlighted the differences in fabrics and forms between the pottery assemblages from the enclosure ditches as opposed to those from the chambers and burials (p. 431). The residual pottery from the chambers and burials, with its mixture of flagons, beakers and jars, is closer in terms of forms to the pottery assemblages from the ditches than those forming the grave goods in the chambers and burials. However, the dominance of grog-tempered wares (GTW) in the residual material shows that the two groups were nevertheless quite different, at least in broad terms. What, then, might be the origin of the residual material? Its high proportion of grog-tempered ware is reminiscent of the earliest material in Enclosure 1. The mix of beakers, flagons and jars/bowls, combined with the domination of the group by grog-tempered wares, suggests that the sherds may be the scrappy remains of pots that had been broken some time before Enclosures 3–5 were constructed. These few sherds may therefore be all that survives of cremation ceremonies which took place in that area during the long gap between chamber AF25 and burial AF18 and the first of the cremations in Enclosure 3. Such activities help give a context to the pit CF7 which would otherwise have been in complete isolation.

Of course, it should be asked, where are the cremation burials that would have accompanied this earlier phase of pot-breaking? The pit CF7 is hardly enough on its own. One possibility is that the burial of cremated bone was a rite which was only accorded to a few people and that most corpses, perhaps even the overwhelming majority of them, were subject to a process that did not involve the digging of pits, such as excarnation. Certainly, although we have suggested that the burials in Enclosures 3 to 5 were of people who were related to each other, it does seem as if only a few of them were buried there. It is true that, even where we find buried cremated bone, it only represents a small sample of the amount of bone that should have been left after the body had been burnt. Either the collection process was very inefficient or most of the bone was disposed of in a way that did not involve some kind of excavation. Moreover the number of burials even in Enclosures 3 to 5 seems small compared to the numbers that a wide kinship group might be expected to encompass. It is also striking that there are no children present, although their burial may have required a different rite. The enigmatic ?mortuary enclosures in Enclosures 4 and 5 may represent a later, more substantial expression of such a funerary process.

SEQUENCE AND CHRONOLOGY (FIG. 170; TABLES 79–80)

THE MIDDLE IRON AGE FARMSTEAD

The uppermost fill of the enclosure ditch of Enclosure 2 contained a small amount of grog-tempered and Roman pottery, whereas the features inside the enclosure itself contained only Middle Iron Age material. This distribution shows that the farmstead ceased to exist by or during the 1st century B.C. and that its enclosure ditch continued to survive as an earthwork. Grog-tempered pottery first appears around the middle of the 1st century B.C. (p. 56). The date when the farmstead was founded is a good deal more problematic, but there is no good reason to suppose that it pre-dates the Middle Iron Age. The currency bars appear, from their relationship with the sides of the enclosure ditch, to have been placed in position early in the life of the farmstead (p. 26), so that they should help date its foundation. However, as Richard Hingley explains, currency bars cannot be closely dated. In general, they seem to have belonged to the Middle Iron Age, although there is some evidence for their deposition as late as the Roman period (p. 33). The loomweights are also of limited help with dating since the triangular form, of which there were many fragments associated with the farmstead (p. 38), is reckoned, rather like the currency bars, to have been current throughout the Middle Iron Age to just after the Roman conquest (p. 43).

The dating of the pottery assemblage has its problems too. Over much of southern Britain from the Late Bronze Age to the Middle Iron Age there was a trend from flint- to sand-tempered pottery which is so marked that the relative proportions of the two materials can be taken as a crude indicator of date (p. 50). Paul Sealey believes that the temper in the pots from the farmstead at Stanway contained much more flint than the pots from the nearby contemporary sites at Abbotstone (Pooley and Benfield 2005) and Ypres Road (Garrison Area 2: Brooks and Masefield 2005). A divergence such as this is at odds with the 'flint-to-sand' model and is surprising since, as Paul Sealey says, the sites were within easy walking distance of each other (p. 58). (Abbotstone is only 1.4 km west of Stanway and Ypres Road 3.9 km to the east.) One possible explanation for this divergence is that a substantial proportion of the sherds with flint tempering are residual and derive from an earlier phase of occupation which left behind no features apart from one or two pits (AF46 and possibly AF28) that we have elsewhere described as Early Iron Age (p. 16). The recognition of a significant Early Iron Age component on the site would be helpful since it would provide a less controversial context for the flints, which Hazel Martingell otherwise hesitates to date as late as the Middle Iron Age (p. 21).

THE FUNERARY ENCLOSURES AND ASSOCIATED CONTEXTS

The key dating evidence and probable dates for the funerary enclosures and the features and deposits in them are summarised below. However, it should be noted that there is no useful dating material from the lower fills of the enclosure ditches that can be used to indicate when they were dug. We must rely on the deposition of the partial pots to provide a *terminus ante quem* for this event. They were found at the top of the lower fill and the base of the main fill. A measure of how long it might have taken for the lower fill to have accumulated was found in 1996 when the base of the enclosure ditch CF6 was re-sectioned a year after it had been excavated in order to consider this very point. Around 100–200 mm of sand and gravel was found to have accumulated in the bottom of it, which more or less corresponds to the depth of the original lower fill. Too much should not be made of this agreement, given the range of different factors that are likely to have affected the rate at which the ditch would have begun to fill up; nevertheless, the investigation in 1996 suggests that the partial pots were likely to have been deposited in the enclosure ditches within weeks or months of their being dug rather than years.

The dumped material (lower fill) in the chambers

AF25 The pots in AF25 in Enclosure 1 are grog-tempered and wheel-thrown and thus should not pre-date c. 75–50 B.C. The terminal date for the two pots is more difficult to fix but should be set well into the 1st century A.D. Probable date range given the absence of Gallo-Belgic wares: second half of the 1st century B.C.

BF6 Five South Gaulish samian vessels are represented, all of which are of Tiberio–Claudian date. These include a stamped cup dated c. A.D. 25–50. Of the ten stamps on the Gallo-Belgic imports, the date ranges collectively point to a date of c. A.D. 25 to 50/60. A potter's pattern mark on one of the vessels (BF6.21) appears on a vessel in the Warrior's burial (BF64.6) and provides a link with it. Probable date range: c. A.D. 35–50.

BF24 The group is dominated by local copies of Gallo-Belgic forms which are difficult to assign a close date other than probably Claudio–Neronian. The assemblage includes a pre-Flavian Lyon-type ware cup and a glass unguent bottle which is Tiberio–Claudian but possibly not post-conquest in date. Probable date range: c. A.D. 40–60.

CF42 The pottery indicates a broad Claudio–Neronian date. There are no stamps, but the inclusion of a *terra rubra* vessel may indicate that the group pre-dates c. A.D. 50. The two glass vessels may be pre-conquest. Probable date range: c. A.D 40–50/60.

Cremation burials

AF18 The only vessel in the cremation burial is typically Late Iron Age in character. It is wheel-thrown and grog-tempered. The pot dates to between c. 75 B.C. and A.D. 65, but most probably belongs to the 1st century B.C. Probable date: late 1st century B.C.

BF64 The Gallo-Belgic pottery points to a date of *c.* A.D. 50–60. Other closely datable finds hint that the group may be slightly earlier. The South Gaulish samian cup is Tiberio–Claudian and stamped Primus, which places it *c.* A.D. 25–50. The Nertomarus brooches are likely to belong to the period *c.* A.D. 40–50/55 and one, possibly both, of the glass vessels may be pre-conquest. The same die on platters in BF64 (BF64.2) and the Doctor's burial (CF47.3) and the same pattern mark on vessels in BF64 (BF64.6) and BF6 (BF6.21) raise the possibility that those pots were purchased from the same consignments of goods from the manufacturers (p. 295). Probable date range: *c.* A.D. 40–50/55.

BF67 The pots indicate a date before A.D. 65 and the brooch probably dates to the 40s. Probable date range: *c.* A.D. 40–60.

CF47 The Gallo-Belgic pottery is Claudio–Neronian (*c.* A.D. 30–70 as indicated by the ten stamps). The stamped South Gaulish samian bowl is dated A.D. 40–50. Of the two brooches, one pre-dates A.D. 50/5, the other belongs to the period A.D. 40–50. There is also a die link with a platter in BF64. Probable date range: *c.* A.D. 40–50/55.

CF72 All six brooches are of forms that in Britain belong to the Claudian period. Five show the burial to be post-conquest; the Keyhole Rosette brooch could be pre-conquest but points to a date no later than *c.* A.D. 50/55. The glass *pyxis* is pre-conquest, probably Augustan. Probable date range: *c.* A.D. 40–50/55.

CF115 The group cannot be dated closely. The *terra nigra* cup is datable to *c.* A.D. 40–75 and the mirror is probably post-conquest. Probable date range: *c.* A.D. 40–60/75.

CF403 The jar is the only CAM 108 from the site. It is a common form in the Roman town and suggests that CF403 may be the latest of the cremation burials from the enclosures. The burial can thus be dated to *c.* A.D. 43–70 and more likely *c.* A.D. 43–60.

Pyre site

BF1 and BF16 No closely datable finds.

Pits with pyre debris

BF17 No datable finds.

CF7 The *Knotenfibel* brooch dates to *c.* 60–20/25 B.C. The pot is wheel-thrown and grog-tempered and thus dates to *c.* 75/50 B.C.–*c.* A.D. 65. Probable date range: *c.* 60–1 B.C.

Pit with broken funerary goods but no pyre debris

AF48 Parts of two grog-tempered vessels, one of which is very similar to the vessel in AF18. Probable date: late 1st century B.C.

Partial pots in the ?mortuary enclosures

BF32 The pottery assemblage consists of fragments of at least 28 vessels but contains few diagnostic pieces. Three *terra rubra* vessels, a sherd of Augustan–Tiberian Arretine, and a coin of Cunobelin combine to indicate a pre-A.D. 50 if not pre-conquest date. However, the predominance of Romanising coarsewares favours a date range of *c.* A.D. 40–50. Probable date range: *c.* A.D. 40–45/50.

CF43–6 The assemblage represents at least eleven vessels. It includes one *terra rubra* vessel plus some relatively late forms and fabrics not found elsewhere within the enclosures apart from the enclosure ditch of Enclosure 5. Probable date range: *c.* A.D. 40–55.

The enclosure ditches

Enclosure 1 A single Late Iron Age grog-tempered vessel datable to between *c.* 75–50 B.C. and the mid 1st century A.D. A coin of Cunobelin, A.D. 20–43.

Enclosure 3 Nine vessels which cannot be dated more closely than the late 1st century B.C. to the mid 1st century A.D., although the absence of some of the forms and fabrics which characterise the assemblages of the fortress and early *colonia* suggests that the group is pre-conquest. Probable date range: *c.* 10 B.C.–*c.* A.D. 50.

Enclosure 4 Eighty-nine vessels of which twelve are *terra rubra* and three are Claudian or ?Claudian samian. Stamped *terra nigra* points to a date of *c.* A.D. 45/50–65. Also two coins of Cunobelin and one other Late Iron Age coin. Probable date range: *c.* A.D. 40–50.

Enclosure 5 Ten vessels, including types commonly found in the legionary fortress/early town, *i.e.* a Drag. 33 (1st century), a reeded-rim bowl, a wide-mouth bowl, and a sherd of a flagon from the Brockley Hill/Verulamium region potteries. There is no *terra rubra*, although the number of vessels is too low for its absence to be meaningful. Probable date range: *c.* A.D. 40/45–55.

REFINED SEQUENCE AND DATING FOR ENCLOSURES 3, 4 AND 5
(FIG 170; TABLES 79–80)

The dates given above derive from a consideration of the items in each context in isolation from the others (TABLE 79). These dates can be refined by taking into account the temporal relationships between the various features and the breaking of the pots as far as they can be judged (TABLE 80). The stratigraphic and other relationships between the features in Enclosures 3–5 which indicate evidence of sequence are limited and are as follows.

a) The plan of all three enclosures suggests that Enclosures 4 and 5 were laid out as one and that both post-dated the creation of Enclosure 3. Such a chronology is broadly supported by the finds since the partial pots and the pyre debris in Enclosures 4 and 5 seem later than the equivalent material in Enclosure 3.

b) The chamber BF6 cut the pyre-site BF1 and therefore post-dated it. This indicates that each chamber and its enclosure were not necessarily laid out as one, despite the presence of a single chamber in each of the enclosures giving the impression that they might have been. Had each chamber been contemporary with the laying out of its enclosure, then it would follow that the chambers in Enclosures 4 and 5 were for two people who died around the same time. Of course such an event is not impossible.

c) Joining sherds linking the enclosure ditch in Enclosure 4 and the ?mortuary enclosure in the same enclosure suggest that the partial pots in both contexts were deposited at the same time as part of the same event. Most, if not all, of the partial pots in the enclosure ditch and the ditch of the ?mortuary enclosure in Enclosure 4 had been deposited near the top of the lower fills, showing that a period of weeks or months must have elapsed between the digging of those ditches and the deposition of the pot fragments in them. Although the stratigraphic evidence is not so clear, the same relationship between the broken pots in the ?mortuary enclosure and those in the enclosure ditch of Enclosure 4 probably applies equally to those of Enclosure 5. However, the situation in Enclosure 3 is different. In contrast to Enclosures 4 and 5, the partial pots in the enclosure ditch of Enclosure 3 lay on the base of the ditch, indicating that the event which produced those broken pots occurred immediately or very soon after the enclosure ditch was laid out.

A simplistic interpretation of the broken pots in the ditches and the chambers is that they were all the product of just one pot-breaking event in each of the enclosures. In other words, there were four events, one for each enclosure, when all the pots represented in the chambers and ditches in each of those enclosures had been deliberately broken. Such a conclusion is an obvious and reasonable one to make because the act of pot-breaking was clearly associated with the chambers. Indeed, it is clear from the small size of many of the sherds in chamber CF42 that the act of breaking pots was of importance in its own right, because some of the pots found there had not simply been broken but had been repeatedly pounded. However, we can make no certain connection between the breaking of the pots in the ditches and the breaking of the pots represented in the chambers. We only assume that this was so on the grounds that the rite was well represented in both places. In fact, there is evidence that links cremation burials with the breaking of pots, despite there being no deliberately broken pots in them. Firstly, the partial pots in Enclosure 3 lay at the base of the enclosure ditch. Thus, in view of the relationship between the chamber BF6 and the pyre-site BF1, it seems likely that the partial pots in the enclosure ditch were associated with BF1 rather than the chamber BF6 unless, of course, BF6 followed BF1 very quickly (which is possible). Secondly, the residual pottery in the backfill of the burials and the mounds of the chambers suggests that there were early occasions when pots were broken, which, as far as can be judged, must have pre-dated the chambers. Both pieces of evidence suggest that not only could pot-breaking events have taken place more than once in any of the funerary enclosures, but that pot-breaking episodes could have occurred during cremation ceremonies which were not associated with chambers. And of course, we can draw exactly the same conclusion in a more convincing manner from the cemetery at Alton in

Hampshire (p. 432). On balance, then, we may suspect that any pots deliberately broken during the interment of cremations are not likely to stand out in the ditch fills because they were swamped by larger numbers of partial pots produced by pot-smashing events linked to the chambers.

Taking into account the various relationships between the features in Enclosures 3 to 5 and the partial pots found in them, the chronology can be refined as shown in TABLE 80. This probably represents the best and most conservative scheme for this part of the site. It is noticeable how the dates are all very close to one another and all fall within a period of probably less than twenty years, *i.e.* A.D. 35–55, if not one decade, *i.e.* A.D. 40–50. The narrowness of these date ranges emphasises the fact that Enclosures 3 to 5 together represent the burial place of a single family.

There is one fact which may significantly affect our estimate of dates, and that is the presence of arms in the Warrior's burial. Dio Cassius (LX, 21) specifically records that Claudius disarmed 'the Britons'. That being so, the inclusion of a spear and shield in the grave could well point to the warrior having been buried before the invasion. It is true that the spear in the grave may have been better suited to hunting than warfare (p. 181), which may have allowed it to be excluded from any rigidly applied law of disarmament, and it is also true that the effectiveness and sustainability of total disarmament (as opposed to the *lex Julia*'s ruling about bearing arms in public) is questionable simply in practical terms, especially as in the provinces it only appears to have been used to control specific disaffected groups (Brunt 1975; 1990). Nevertheless, support for a pre-conquest date for the Warrior's burial comes from the other warrior graves known in Britain. There are less than fifteen of them, all believed to belong the last 200–300 years of the Iron Age (Whimster 1981, 139–42; Collis 1973, 129) and, of those, warriors with the full spear, sword and shield are late and are attributable to the 1st century B.C. and the opening decades of the 1st century A.D. (Sealey forthcoming a). Recently studied is the Kelvedon Warrior burial which, having been found only 9.5 km from Stanway, is particularly pertinent. He died *c.* 75–25 B.C. (*ibid.*), and again fits the pattern where all of the warrior graves pre-date the conquest by Rome. Our preferred date ranges as set out in TABLE 79 do indeed allow for a pre-conquest date for the Warrior's burial, even if it is only a marginal one. If we assume that he died on the eve of the conquest, then it is possible to refine the dates even further. This is done in Table 80, where not only is it assumed that the warrior died in or shortly before A.D. 43, but also certain of the other connections described above are taken into account, such as the presumed relationship between chamber BF6 and the pyre-site BF1.

Although TABLE 80 is an expression of our most refined date ranges for the various elements, it does not show at all clearly how these might have sequenced. Instead this is presented visually in FIGURE 170. Attributing close dates is a process fraught with uncertainty, but determining the likely sequence is even more problematic. FIGURE 170 is very hypothetical and takes some of the evidence further than can be rigorously justified. The idea is a fanciful one that pottery and other finds such as brooches and even coins can be used to date 2,000-year-old archaeological features to within a five-year period or even less. However, although the chances are remote that FIGURE 170 is correct in every detail, it is a useful exercise in trying to understand how the cemetery might have developed and how its constituent parts might have fitted together. The figure should be regarded as two statements that are independent of each other to a degree but rolled into one, *i.e.* our preferred sequence and our preferred dates.

The sequence begins with the construction of Enclosure 3 and the cremation of a body in the middle of it, in pyre-site BF1. In FIGURE 170, it is suggested that the body was that of our warrior, whose remains were then interred in the south-west quarter of the enclosure. At first sight, it seems odd to think that the first cremation was that of the warrior and was not connected to the chamber. However, the connection between BF1 and BF64 is a plausible one. The pyre-site BF1 included fragments of cavalry fittings, and our warrior could have been a mounted one in life. Then followed the construction of the chamber BF6 before any appreciable silt had accumulated in the ditch. The deceased and the grave goods were placed in the chamber for a short period of time. A wooden barrel was set into the ground near the

TABLE 79: REFINED CHRONOLOGIES FOR ENCLOSURES 3–5

(No links assumed)

Context	Date range	Assumptions
Enclosure 3		
digging of the enclosure ditch of Enclosure 3	c. A.D. ?25–50	could be as early as c. 10 B.C. but unlikely
pyre-site BF1	c. A.D. ?25–50	cut by BF6
shaft BF17	c. A.D. 25–50	is no later than BF6 but could pre-date it
chamber BF6	c. A.D. 35–50	post-dates BF1
deposition of many broken pots in the enclosure ditch	c. A.D. ?25–50	low proportion of GTW brings earliest possible date forward, well into 1st century A.D.
pyre-site BF16	c. A.D. 35–50	
Warrior's burial BF64	c. A.D. 40–50/55	
Inkwell burial BF67	c. A.D. 40–55	
Enclosure 4		
digging of the enclosure ditch of Enclosure 4	c. A.D. 40–45/50	
pyre-site BF32	c. A.D. 40–45/50	
chamber BF24	c. A.D. 40–45/50	
deposition of many broken pots in the enclosure ditch	c. A.D. 40–45/50	occurred after a period of weeks or months after the digging of the enclosure ditch
deposition of many broken pots in BF32 after the digging of the enclosure ditch	c. A.D. 40–45/50	occurred after a period of weeks or months
Enclosure 5		
digging of the enclosure ditch of Enclosure 5	c. A.D. 40–50/55	
pyre-site CF43–6	c. A.D. 40–50/55	
chamber CF42	c. A.D. 40–50/60	
Doctor's burial CF47	c. A.D. 40–50/55	
deposition of many broken pots in the enclosure ditch	c. A.D. 40/45–55	occurred after a period of weeks or months after the digging of the enclosure ditch
deposition of many broken pots in CF43–6	c. A.D. 40/45–55	occurred after a period of weeks or months after the digging of the enclosure ditch
Brooches burial CF72	c. A.D. 40–50/55	
Mirror burial CF115	c. A.D. 40–60/75	
cremation burial CF403	c. A.D. 45–60	
shaft CF23	c. A.D. 40–60	
slot CF96	c. A.D. 65–75	

middle of the enclosure to make a wood-lined shaft. (It is possible that the barrel was already in the ground and that it was related to the first pyre-site BF1.) The body was then taken out of the chamber and burnt on a pyre a short distance to the west on the pyre-site BF16. The grave goods were also removed from the chamber and deliberately smashed close to or on the pyre as part of the funerary rite. At the same time, mourners ate a funerary meal and then, in the eastern half of the enclosure, they broke the pots in which they had brought their food and drink to the cemetery, and deposited bits of them in the enclosure ditch, especially around the entrance. All this was done before any silt had accumulated in the ditch. When the pyre had cooled, debris from it was placed into the chamber from the north side, along with a few handfuls of cremated bone hand-picked from the ashes and some of the smashed grave goods, a few of which had been close enough to the pyre to be burnt. The roof of the chamber was fully replaced, and soil and turf scraped and/or dug up from somewhere in the vicinity was heaped up to cover the chamber and barrel/shaft and form a low mound.

Perhaps around this time there was another cremation which was to result in our Inkwell burial (BF67). But let us not forget the problem of the cremated remains of the people in the chambers. Were they dispersed in some way or were they buried on site? Could BF67 be the place where the rest of the bone from the body from the chamber was buried? On the face of

TABLE 80: THE MOST REFINED CHRONOLOGY WITH MANY LINKS ASSUMED AND THE WARRIOR'S BURIAL TAKEN TO BE NO LATER THAN A.D. 43

Context	Date range	Assumptions
Enclosure 3		
digging of the enclosure ditch of Enclosure 3	c. A.D. 35–43	the first pyre in the enclosure was on BF1
pyre-site BF1	c. A.D. 35–43	some of the pyre debris from BF1 was redeposited in chamber BF6
shaft BF17	c. A.D. 35–50	
chamber BF6	c. A.D. 35–50	the body in the chamber was burnt on pyre-site BF1
deposition of many broken pots in the enclosure ditch	c. A.D. 35–50	
pyre-site BF16	c. A.D. 35–50	
Warrior's burial BF64	c. A.D. 40–43	the inclusion of arms means that the burial dated to A.D. 43 at the latest
Inkwell burial BF67	c. A.D. 40–55	
Enclosure 4		
digging of the enclosure ditch of Enclosure 4	c. A.D. 40–45	
pyre-site BF32	c. A.D. 40–45/50	
chamber BF24	c. A.D. 40–45/50	
deposition of many broken pots in the enclosure ditch	c. A.D. 40–45/50	occurred after a period of weeks or months after the digging of the enclosure ditch
deposition of many broken pots in BF32	c. A.D. 40–45/50	occurred after a period of weeks or months after the digging of the enclosure ditch
Enclosure 5		
digging of the enclosure ditch of Enclosure 5	c. A.D. 40–45	
pyre-site CF43-6	c. A.D. 40–45	
chamber CF42	c. A.D. 40–50	
Doctor's burial CF47	c. A.D. 40–45	the Doctor's burial is broadly contemporary with the Warrior's burial
deposition of many broken pots in the enclosure ditch	c. A.D. 40–50	occurred after a period of weeks or months after the digging of the enclosure ditch
deposition of many broken pots in CF43–6	c. A.D. 40–50	occurred after a period of weeks or months after the digging of the enclosure ditch
Brooches burial CF72	c. A.D. 40–50	
Mirror burial CF115	c. A.D. 40–60	
cremation burial CF403	c. A.D. 45–60	
shaft CF23	c. A.D. 40–60	
slot CF96	c. A.D. 65–75	

it, the Inkwell burial seems far too modest considering the quantity of grave goods evident in the debris in the chamber, but such an unlikely equation is a neat one and ought not to be entirely dismissed. There were only two burials in the enclosure (at least as far as we know), and there are two pyre-sites. If the warrior was burnt on one of them, then maybe the person in the Inkwell burial was burnt on the other, in which case that person is one we are equating with the chamber. Moreover, the presence of an inkwell suggests that the dead person had been literate. A connection with the chamber seems an attractive one, not only because some of the pot fragments from the chamber had graffiti scratched on them, but also because this was the only place on the site where graffiti were found.

At about the same time Enclosures 4 and 5 were added as one unit to the south side of Enclosure 3, perhaps because two of our kinship group had just died, *i.e.* the 'Doctor' and the woman represented in chamber BF24. The Doctor's body was burnt on a pyre placed in the

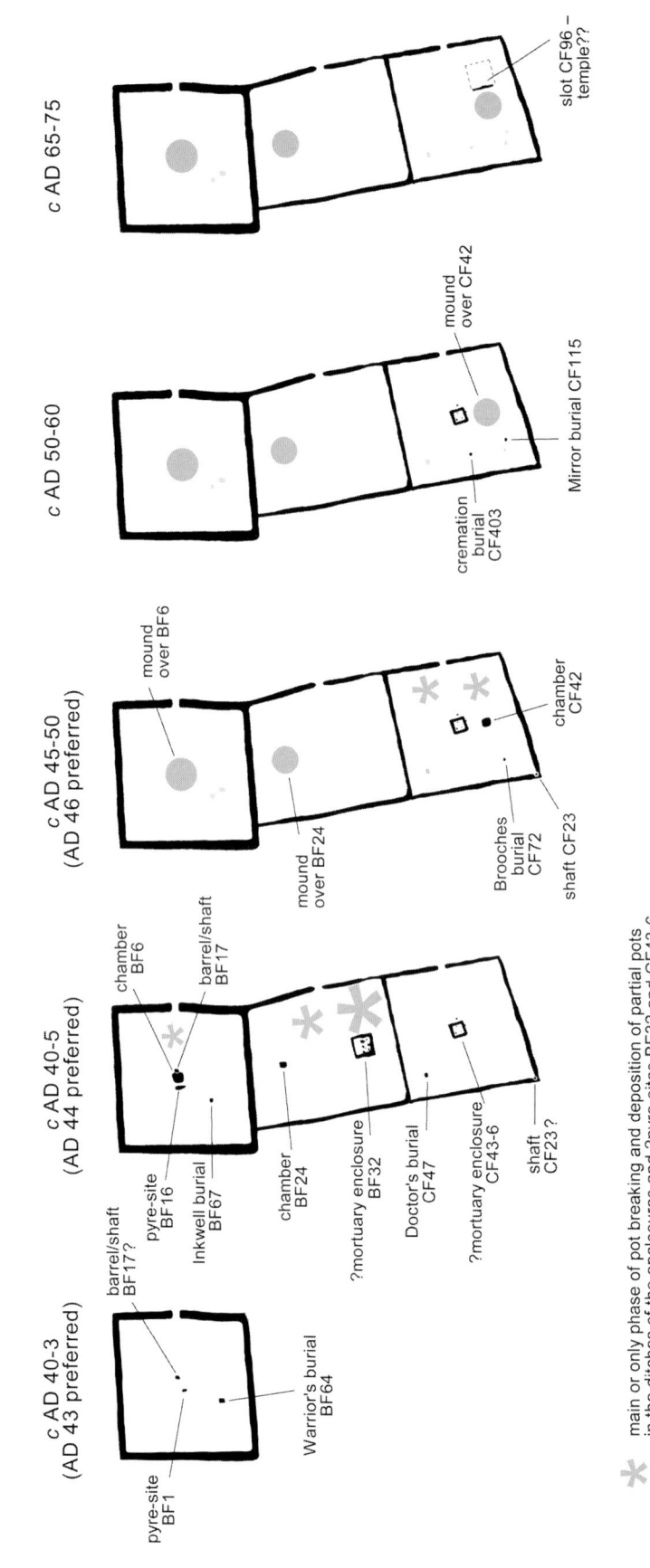

FIG. 170. Speculative sequence and dates for the development of Enclosures 3–5

centre of Enclosure 5 and his remains were buried in a pit symmetrically set in the north-west corner of the enclosure. A chamber (BF24) was constructed in the centre of the northern half of Enclosure 4 at around the same time and the body of the woman was laid to rest there for some weeks or months along with the customary service, food, drink and personal possessions. Her funeral pyre was constructed in the middle of the southern half of the enclosure, probably when the chamber was built and before any silt had begun to accumulate in the bottom of the enclosure ditch. Just as with chamber BF6, her body was subsequently burnt on the pyre during a grand pot-breaking rite involving mourners who ate a funerary meal and deposited parts of their food vessels in the ditch of the east side of the enclosure and all around the ?mortuary enclosure BF32. Again, debris from the pyre, including cremated bone, and broken grave goods were placed in the redundant chamber from the north side before it was buried under an earth and turf mound. A shallow vertical shaft probably lined with wooden barrels was dug in the extreme south-west corner of Enclosure 5, maybe as a replacement for the one which had just been buried under the mound over BF6.

By this stage, the focus of attention was now in Enclosure 5, and the central pyre-site was used at least three more times. First was the body that had been kept for a short while in a chamber (CF42) constructed in the middle of the southern half of the enclosure. The ceremony during which the body was cremated involved the usual breaking of pots at the end of a pyre-side funerary meal. The deposition of the pot sherds and debris from the pyre followed the same pattern evident in Enclosures 3 and 4, with the debris being placed in the chamber from its north side and the pot sherds being concentrated on the east side of the enclosure. Perhaps around this time another funeral took place, this one producing the Brooches burial which was sited neatly in the south-west corner of the enclosure so as to balance the earlier Doctor's burial. Then followed the cremation burial CF403 which, maintaining the symmetry of the Doctor's burial and Brooches burial, was placed neatly between the two so as to lie immediately west of the pyre-site. Finally came the Mirror burial which, like the Brooches burial before it, was placed in the south-west corner of the enclosure.

Iron shanks with glass heads in both the Brooches burial and the nearby chamber CF42, although not closely comparable as the example in the former is a simple version (or weak imitation) of those in the latter, hint at a link of some sort between the two and, just as with the Inkwell burial and chamber BF6, this raises the question again about the fate of the cremated remains of the bodies kept in the chambers. Could the cremated remains of the body which had been laid to rest for a while in the chamber have been buried in the Brooches burial? But like the Inkwell burial and the chamber BF6, there is a mismatch in the quality of the objects in both of them which suggests otherwise. Although the glass *pyxis* was indeed an exceptional object, it was chipped and incomplete when buried (the lid was missing) and, being old, its original (expensive) contents had no doubt long since been used up.

If it were true that the bodies in the chambers BF6 and CF42 ended up in the Inkwell burial and the Brooches burial respectively, then we need to consider where the cremated remains from BF24 might have been buried. The apparent absence of a burial in Enclosure 4 suggests that either one was missed during the excavation or the cremated remains were buried elsewhere. The interiors of Enclosures 3 and 5 were thoroughly checked (pp. 6–7), so it is very unlikely that any were missed there. However, Enclosure 4 had to be examined in a piecemeal way, and if a burial had been missed anywhere in that enclosure (although still unlikely), it would have been in the north-west corner, which was covered during much of the excavation by part of a large earth bank. This seems a likely spot since it is due west of the chamber BF24. Otherwise there is no obvious candidate anywhere else. The Mirror burial CF115 in Enclosure 5 was female (as in BF24) and might be a suitable candidate, although there is nothing to link the chamber and burial together.

On balance, it seems most likely that the bodies that had presumably been kept temporarily in the chambers were treated differently to the bodies represented in the cremation burials and that their cremated remains were not interred, at least in this cemetery.

STANWAY IN LOCAL AND WIDER CONTEXTS (FIGS 171–176; TABLE 81)

FAMILIAL RELATIONSHIPS BETWEEN THE DEAD

The spatial and physical relationships between all five enclosures and their enclosure ditches at Stanway help reveal a chronological sequence in the construction of the enclosures which has already been discussed. The whole group of five enclosures also shows a degree of cohesion, which suggests that there were factors at work which bound its members together despite the functional differences between Enclosure 2 and the rest. The intimate relationship between Enclosures 3, 4 and 5 points to an even closer bond between them than must have existed between them and the earlier Enclosure 1 (the other funerary enclosure). There can be little doubt that we can see in Enclosures 3–5 the funerary arrangements for at least a few of the members of a relatively high-status family unit, and it is from this group of enclosures that we can speculate that Enclosure 1 would have been the burial place of their ancestors. But those people died 50 or even as much as 75 years earlier, so that at least one subsequent generation must be missing from the cemetery. A characteristic of the Stanway site is the low number of burials it contained, especially in relation to the size of the enclosures. Perhaps the site was always a place where only a select few members of the family were buried and there was nobody in the missing generation or generations who qualified. Certainly the apparent absence of sub-adults in the cremated remains shows that a degree of selectivity did apply to who was interred there and who was not.

It is interesting to speculate on the possible relationships between the individuals represented in Enclosures 3–5. The important individuals seem to have been those who had their own chamber. This is supported by the fact that the grave goods in the chambers were the most extensive and the chambers occupied either a central or axial position in its enclosure. Of the assemblages from the chambers, BF6 appears to have been male, whereas certainly BF24 and probably CF42 were female. On this basis, we can speculate that BF6 was for a high-ranking man and that BF24 and CF42 were for his wife and a daughter, or perhaps a second wife or sister. The other burials would therefore have been for close relatives or servants. The warrior in the Warrior's burial may have been a brother of the man in BF6 or perhaps his armour-bearer. Even if unconnected by blood ties, he could be of high status, as evidenced by Vellocatus, the armour-bearer of the Brigantian Venutius and his replacement as the husband of Queen Cartimandua (Tacitus, *Annals*, XII, 40; *Histories*, III, 45). In a similar vein, the Inkwell burial might represent the clerk or even tutor of BF6 (assuming of course that they were not one and the same person (pp. 440–3)) just as, for example, Seneca was tutor and then advisor to the young Nero. The rest of the burials seem to have been of females with the exception of the Doctor (p. 445). He may have been another brother of the man represented in BF6 who had developed special skills in medicine and divination, or he might have been somebody who had a special duty of care towards the person in CF42.

The nature of the relationship between Enclosure 2 and the other enclosures poses a difficult problem of interpretation. Although clearly Enclosure 2 must have survived as a visible landscape feature when Enclosure 1 was laid out, it is debatable whether the people who built it were ancestors of those who followed. This point will be explored further below (p. 456).

THE IDENTITIES OF THE 'DOCTOR' AND THE 'WARRIOR'

By Nina Crummy

While acknowledging that current thinking tends to stress the diversity and mutability of cultural identity (p. 320), it is fair to state that there can be no doubt but that the 'Doctor's burial' was the resting place of a Briton. Of the two brooches present one is a Rearhook, probably of Icenian manufacture. The other is a Langton Down, an imported form well represented in Camulodunum but not occurring in the Roman fortress or *colonia* (p. 316). Ralph Jackson considers some of the tools in the medical kit to be insular interpretations of Roman forms (p. 247). The carinated strainer bowl is a vessel-type found in both metal and pottery principally in eastern England, especially in and around Camulodunum, and a failed casting of a spout of the same form as that on the bowl in CF47 is paralleled at Sheepen.

The practice of medicine in the ancient world went hand in hand with the practice of magic, as invocations to the gods formed an essential part of treatment. Other than the medical kit, there are several items within the grave that may be postulated as belonging to the magico-medical rôle of the dead individual, and all were found at the end of the grave containing the kit and other personalia such as the game board and counters. A large jet bead was almost certainly as much a piece of professional medical equipment as a dress accessory; the healing properties of the black mineral are described by Pliny, who also mentions that it was used in divination (*Historia Naturalis*, 36, 141–2). Eight enigmatic rods of iron and copper alloy were probably also used in divination, as may have been eight equally enigmatic rings. A reference to medicine may also be seen in the choice of a samian bowl decorated with a dog motif, as the animal is associated with healing deities, among them Apollo and Aesculapius from the Graeco-Roman world, and Nodens from Britain (Green 1997, 70, 155, 175–6).

To describe the individual buried in CF47 as a druid, as Ralph Jackson has done (p. 250), may be too specific and overly interpretative of the grave goods, given that druids acted not only as priests but also as lawgivers and natural and moral philosophers, activities that have no material artefacts essential to their practice and so are undetectable in the context of a grave, and that Caesar omits all mention of medicine in his description of the duties of druids (*de Bello Gallico*, VI, 13–14). Nevertheless, even if it cannot be proven, such an interpretation is not inconsistent with the evidence.

The sex of the Doctor may remain a matter for speculation, but some evidence that the grave is that of a male is supplied by the saucepan for preparing wine-based drinks to accompany a formal Roman-style meal or a feast (p. 322), and by the two brooches, which were found some distance apart and must therefore have been pinned to two cloaks, or at opposite corners of one very large cloak, rather than to the shoulders of a woman's tube dress. Indeed, the dress accessories mirror those in the Warrior's burial BF64: two brooches, and a single large bead, which points to a parallel style of dress and therefore a parallel gender. It is only fair to point out, however, that wearing a single bead is not necessarily a gender-specific practice, as shown by the bead in CF72, which is almost certainly the grave of a female.

The Warrior's burial is assumed to be that of a male and was so named because of the presence among the deposited objects of a shield and lance (Cunliffe 1991, 510). As well as these pieces, several other items call for attention as indicators of the buried individual's character, rank and sex, some with explicit iconography, some by virtue of their rarity. The choice of animal imagery appears to be deliberate. The colour-coat jug (BF64.14) is decorated with cranes, perhaps referring to the major Celtic deity, Esus, who can be connected with both Mercury and Mars, the latter in not only his military but also his fertility aspects, although the figure type may derive from samian ware (p. 175; Lucan, *Pharsalia*, 499; de Vries 1961, 97–8; Ross 1967, 279–81; Thevenot 1968, 142–4; Green 1997, 187). The basin with a ram's head handle (BF64.26) and the jug with lion decoration (BF64.25) are common enough items in the Roman Empire (there are large numbers from Pompeii alone), but it is worth noting that the image of the ram is one of male sexual potency. The lion design speaks both of royalty and of male aggression, here made exotic and dramatic as only Britons who had travelled abroad might have seen a live lion, although the animal does occur on a coin-type of Cunobelin, the image having been copied from a Roman *denarius* (van Arsdell 1989, no. 2107-1; Creighton 2000, 121).

The two brooches in the Warrior's burial (BF64.19–BF64.20) are of a form made in a workshop in central eastern France or western Switzerland that is not well represented in Britain; at least one is stamped with its Gaulish maker's name (BF64.19), which may well have increased its value, whether real or perceived. A large arm-ring (BF64.21) and bead (BF64.22) are also unusual. Both are of La Tène style and were probably made in Britain. The bead, when seen in the context of the jet bead from the Doctor's burial, may have been credited with amuletic powers.

The shield boss (BF64.23) is similarly distinctive, although idiosyncracy is a major characteristic of La Tène bosses, and the lancehead (BF64.24a) is exceptionally long and slender. Three incised circles on the top of the boss repeat a motif also found on a brooch in CF47 (CF47.17), and may perhaps be perceived as protective, probably solar, symbols. The drop-handles (BF64.29a and b) from the game board (BF64.29) are particularly well-made examples of their type and lack very close parallels, although drop-handles are common enough as general site finds. The beautiful and unusual large amber glass bowl (BF64.16) had been deposited within a large wooden box with iron strap-fittings (BF64.31), and another large box (BF64.30), with iron fittings of a different type, lay in the north-west corner of the burial pit. Whatever it held has not survived, and can be presumed to have been organic, most likely clothing, although nothing remains in the corrosion on the iron fittings to assist identification. What is certain is that the contents of this box would have matched the quality of the metal, glass, and ceramic grave goods. However, as neither box in BF64 has decorative copper-alloy fittings, they do not seem to have been intended for display. The box containing the amber bowl can be presumed to have been used specifically to store it and may even be the original 'packaging' in which it was imported. The other may have been simply used for storage, but could also have been used to transport personal belongings when travelling (Metzler-Zens et al. 1999, 387). If the person buried in BF64 *did* travel, then the continental-made grave goods need not have been imported into Britain and then acquired, but may represent a personal collection formed abroad. All these objects can be variously defined as statements of individuality, of strength, of display, perhaps even of what might be termed connoisseurship, and together they attest to a much more complex character than that simply conveyed by the term 'Warrior'.

It remains to be considered whether this is the burial place of an auxiliary in the service of Rome, as has been suggested for the Folly Lane burial, Verulamium, and for many Gallic warrior burials, usually those containing swords (Foster 1999, 176; Metzler 1984, 99; Metzler et al. 1999, 174; Ferdière and Villard 1993, 281–2; Dieudonné-Glad 1999, 56). The similarities between the grave goods in BF64 and those in some of the rich continental graves are striking, but while the weapons in the latter graves can be paralleled by Roman or Germanic military equipment, the shield boss in BF64 is not recognisably a 1st-century A.D. continental type, nor are the brooches in the grave common Roman military types, while the lancehead, arm-ring and bead are of La Tène style. The lance need not be a weapon of warfare, but could well have been used for hunting, which was an aristocratic pursuit (Méniel 2002; Struck 2000, 88).

Many auxiliaries were not mounted, and there is no horse harness from BF64, nor in the burials at Fléré-la-Rivière, Berry-Bouy, and Antran. The Folly Lane horsegear is associated with a nave hoop from a wheeled vehicle and at least one other fitting associated with driving harness; all the fittings may therefore potentially have come from a driven rather than ridden animal (*pace* Foster 1999, who suggests that the bit was best suited for riding). It should perhaps be borne in mind that some Roman military horse equipment came from BF6 in Enclosure 3, but it may pre-date the burial in BF64. However, the possibility that the warrior was cremated on the pyre-site BF1 (p. 439) means that he might be able to claim as his own the military horse equipment not only from BF1 but also from the pyre site BF16 and the chamber BF6. Whichever burial the harness fittings at Stanway were originally associated with, they may have been acquired through other means, such as inheritance, purchase, gift-exchange, or even plunder. A parallel can be drawn here with the chain mail in Colchester's Lexden Tumulus, dated to *c*. 15–10 B.C. (Foster 1986, 178), which might have been acquired during service in the auxiliaries, but is surely just as likely to have been purchased or received as a gift, as are the other continental-made items among the deposits in that grave.

On balance, therefore, although auxiliary troops used their native weapons and fought in their own style (Feugère 2002a, 42), the idiosyncratic weapons in the Stanway warrior grave place it in the tradition of Late Iron Age British weapon burials, and there is no reason to assume that it is the burial of someone who has served as a Roman auxiliary when no Roman military equipment is directly associated with it. Indeed, any such notion rests on the assumption that interpretations of other warrior burials as those of auxiliaries are correct, and ignores the line of similar richly furnished burials of warriors and weapon-bearing princes that pre-dates the use of auxiliaries by the Roman army, a line that stretches back in Europe to the Early Iron Age and earlier still, making it unnecessary to invoke a connection with the Roman army or empire to explain the presence of weaponry among the other grave goods (*e.g.* Kimmig and Rest 1954; Kimmig 1981; Biel 1985; Brun 1987, 57–8; Cunliffe 1997, 57–62, 93–105).

SIMILAR FUNERARY SITES (FIGS 171–6; TABLE 81)

The closest parallel to the Stanway enclosures in Britain is the single, rectangular-shaped enclosure at Folly Lane, St Albans (FIG. 171; Niblett 1999), but no doubt there were others, although given that the known sites are of high status, they are likely to prove rare in Britain.

The Folly Lane enclosure has much in common with Stanway. The date is very similar to Enclosures 3–5 at Stanway, and it has a pyre site and a wooden chamber containing fragments of funerary goods broken at the time of the cremation ceremony. But there are significant differences too. Folly Lane seems largely to have been concerned with one person — somebody who was a king, whose chamber was much larger than the largest of those at Stanway and whose funerary goods were far more numerous, varied and rich. His greater importance is reflected in the size of his enclosure and presumably the later construction within it of a temple. Folly Lane in many ways is more akin to the Lexden Tumulus than to Stanway.

The square ditched temple enclosure at Gosbecks may be another comparable site, since it looks as if it might, in physical terms, represent a cross between Stanway and Folly Lane. Like

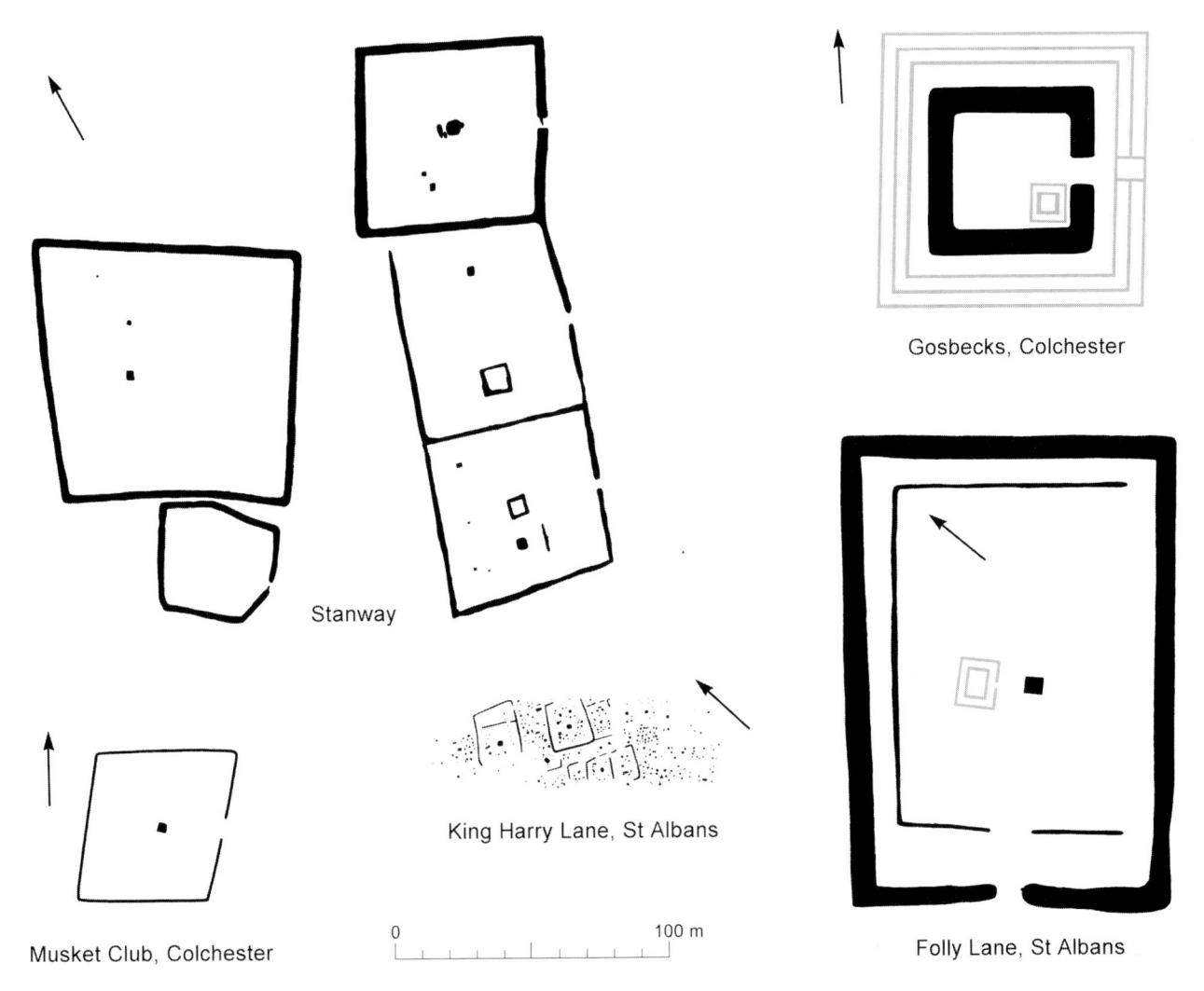

FIG. 171. The funerary enclosures at Stanway in comparison with sites in Colchester and Verulamium, St Albans

the latter, Gosbecks features a Romano-Celtic temple inside a large enclosure demarcated by a very substantial ditch (FIG. 171). The most obvious conclusion to draw from the location of the site and its monumental nature is that it was a funerary enclosure in the Folly Lane/Stanway tradition where Cunobelin was cremated. The other possibility is that the Gosbecks site was a religious one which should be compared with a major temple site such as Hayling Island rather than Folly Lane (King and Soffe 2001; Creighton 2006, 130–5).

A limited programme of archaeological excavation and geophysical survey was undertaken on the site of the Gosbecks temple between 1995 and 1999 (report in preparation) for Colchester Borough Council who had just acquired the site. Two trenches were excavated across the temple, a single section was cut through the enclosure ditch, and a series of small trenches were placed at strategic places to fix the position and determine the exact dimensions of the surrounding portico. The trench across the enclosure ditch showed it to have been dug around the middle of the 1st century A.D. and to contain near the bottom some fragments of a few mid 1st-century pots reminiscent of the broken vessels in the enclosure ditches at Stanway. The excavations were accompanied by an exhaustive programme of geophysical survey of the interior of the ditched enclosure (first by Peter Cott and then by Tim Dennis of the University of Essex, aided by Aline and David Black). The techniques employed were ground-penetrating radar, magnetometry, and resistivity. All proved to be effective in their own particular ways and various anomalies were identified that were of particular interest in terms of Stanway.

The central area of the enclosure proved to have been occupied by a major feature which measures 14 × 16 m and has an approximate square-within-a-square plan (FIG. 172). On the east side of the feature is a large irregularly shaped anomaly that is probably a pit of some kind, and further east there appears to be a rectangular pit about 3.5 × 3.0 m in area. The feature in the centre of the enclosure might be the remains of a temple that pre-dated the one in the south-east corner of the enclosure or it could be a very large example of a pyre/excarnation site of the sort seen in Enclosures 4 and 5 at Stanway. The larger (outer) square looks at first sight as if it is made up of many small pits or post-holes, especially along the south side. But this is probably illusory, and these apparent post-holes merely represent parts of a single slot or trench which continues around all four sides to make up the outer square. Either way, the results of the geophysical survey suggest that there was no chamber or other large excavated feature in the centre of the enclosure. The rectangular-shaped pit to the east lies on the central east–west axis of the enclosure, opposite what was later to be the site of the doorway in the north side of the temple. The most obvious interpretation for this anomaly is that it represents the remains of a burial chamber, since its shape would fit such an explanation, and its position in relation to the enclosure and temple corresponds closely to that of the chamber at Folly Lane. However, if this is indeed what it is, then the chamber seems to have been around the size of BF6 at Stanway (TABLE 81) which seems far too modest to have been associated with Cunobelin. Thus, in summary, the geophysical surveys have helpfully revealed very interesting features at the Gosbecks temple site, but unfortunately only excavation can show what they represent. A funerary enclosure like the one at Folly Lane and those at Stanway seems a plausible explanation at the moment, although a multi-period temple site is another possibility.

TABLE 81: DIMENSIONS OF THE CHAMBERS AT STANWAY AND FOLLY LANE AND POSSIBLE CHAMBERS ELSEWHERE

		Length (m)	Width (m)
Stanway	BF6	4.2/4.3	3.4/3.6
Stanway	CF42	3.0	3.0
Stanway	AF25	3.3	2.5
Stanway	BF24	3.3	2.3
Folly Lane		6.8/7.1	6.6/7.1
?Lexden Tumulus		?4.0 (very approx.)	?4.0 (very approx.)
?Gosbecks		3.5	3.0

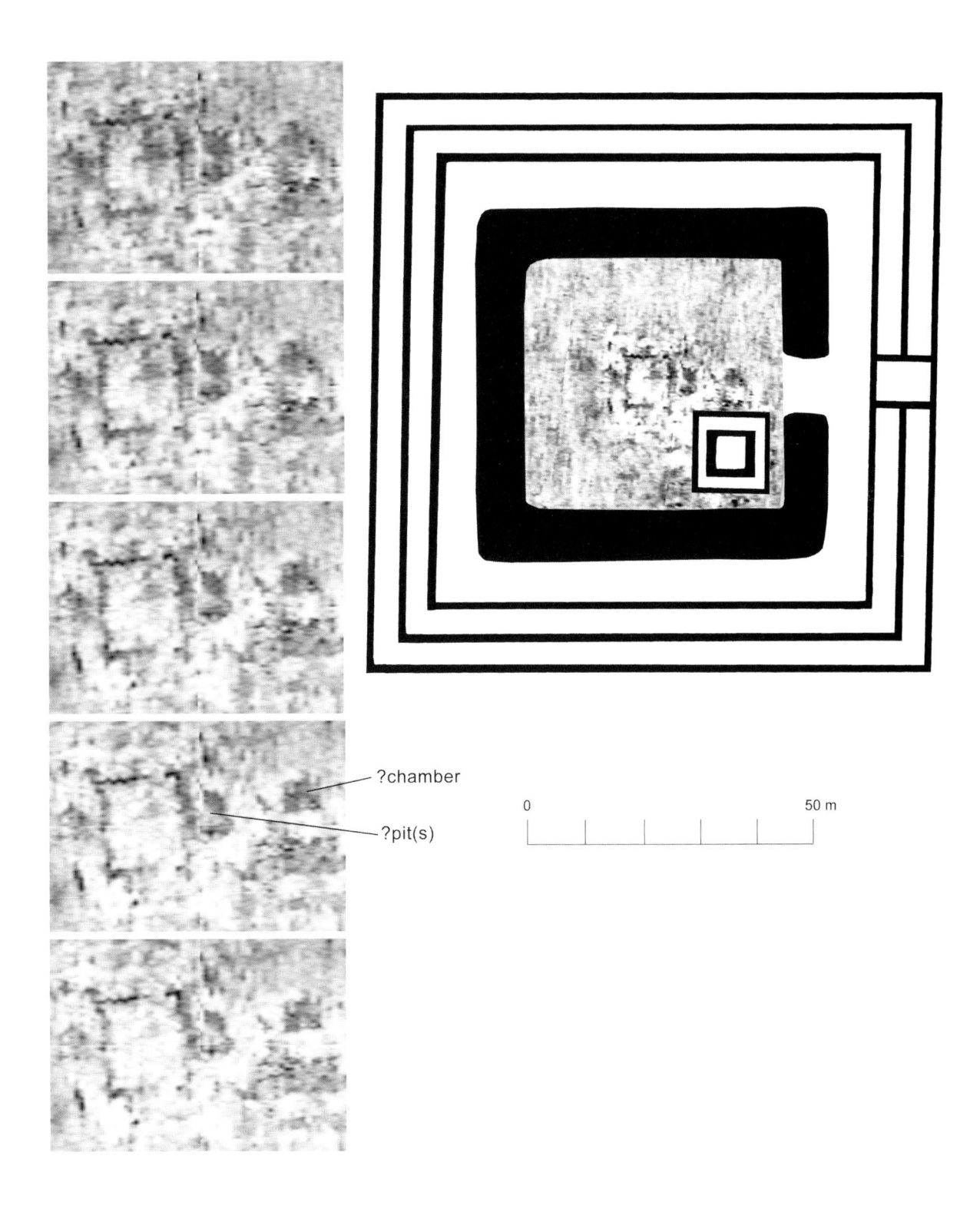

FIG. 172. The Gosbecks temple site. The ground radar survey was undertaken by Peter Cott, Dr Aline Black and David Black. Dr Tim Dennis of the University of Essex carried out the signal processing

Another possible example of a Folly Lane/Stanway type funerary site in Colchester is known as the 'Musket Club enclosure' (FIG. 171). It was spotted and photographed from the air as a cropmark many years ago. The enclosure has all the characteristics of those at Stanway, being rectangular in shape and aligned north–south with a similarly aligned rectangular chamber-like pit in the centre and an entrance in the middle of the east side. At 54 × 52 m, its size is also comparable. Six sections were dug across the enclosure ditch in 2004–2005 with no positive outcome since the investigation produced almost no finds except for a few sherds of Early and Middle Iron Age pottery, and the central feature could not be explored (Brooks 2005). The site lies about 1.6 km due east of the temple enclosure at Gosbecks. Presumably coincidentally, a straight line on an east–west alignment can be drawn exactly through the centres of the Gosbecks and Musket Club enclosures and Enclosure 5 at Stanway.

Yet another possible example has been suggested at Birch, 2.8 km from the Stanway site, where a complex of two large enclosures and two small ones has been recognised from aerial photography (Bennet 1995, 233, fig. 7). The two largest enclosures bear a striking resemblance to Enclosures 1 and 2 at Stanway. The largest of the Birch enclosures is rectilinear and about 85 m across. It has two small rectilinear pits in the interior, although neither of them is in a coaxial position, which might be expected had the enclosure been funerary in function.

There is a hierarchy evident in the arrangement of the burials and chambers within Enclosures 3 and 5 which is reminiscent of the hierarchical and distinctive clustering of burials at the King Harry Lane site at St Albans, Hertfordshire (Stead and Rigby 1989). Indeed, a careful comparison of these sites suggests, surprisingly, that in many ways Stanway was closer to King Harry Lane than to Folly Lane. At King Harry Lane, the burial area was divided up into small rectilinear plots (FIG. 171). The burials form distinct clusters, many of which have as their focus a central larger burial. These clusters and enclosures are each seen as the burial place of individual families with the central burial being the resting place of the dominant person in that group (Stead and Rigby 1989, 80–3, but see Fitzpatrick 1991 for a contrary view). All this is mirrored at Stanway, but on a much larger scale. In a few of the King Harry Lane enclosures the burials show a degree of internal organisation, especially in the two enclosures with graves 41 and 241 at their centres as in Stanway's Enclosure 3. The enclosure focused on grave 41 has an internal division to form what in effect were two conjoined enclosures, rather like Enclosures 4 and 5 at Stanway. The burials in the ditched enclosures look as if they have been deliberately set back from the edges of the ditches and kept clear of the central burials. Earthworks could explain the patterning, *i.e.* a bank along the inside edges of the ditches and a mound over each of the central burials. Whatever the explanation, the four burials inside Enclosure 5 at Stanway appear to bear similar relationships to their enclosures.

But the similarities between the two sites go further. Rosalind Niblett (1999, 401–2), following observations by Martin Millett about pyre debris (Millett 1993, 226), noted that, although there was not much pyre debris at King Harry Lane, what there was of it showed a distribution biased towards the central features in its enclosures (FIG. 173). Moreover, although in general there was no clear evidence for the deliberate breaking of pottery vessels, two of the six amphoras were represented in their graves only by token sherds (Stead and Rigby 1989, 202–3). One of these (grave 241) was in a central grave. Also the central burial grave 41 (FIG. 173) included two pots. One was complete but the other had been broken before deposition, and only part of it placed in the burial pit. Cremated bone lay in a pile near the centre of the floor. A pit cutting into the burial pit gave the impression that it had been robbed. However, were it not for this secondary pit, the burial and its contents would have recalled the chambers at Stanway, especially AF25.

All in all then, there are elements in King Harry Lane that resonate with Stanway. The rites practised at both sites had much in common with each other except that there were differences in scale and numbers of funerary goods which are explicable in terms of social standing. King Harry Lane was arguably the burial ground of a series of families, each with their own plot. The common burial practices and the spatial relationships between these plots show the families to have been parts of the same close-knit community. At least eight different family units can be

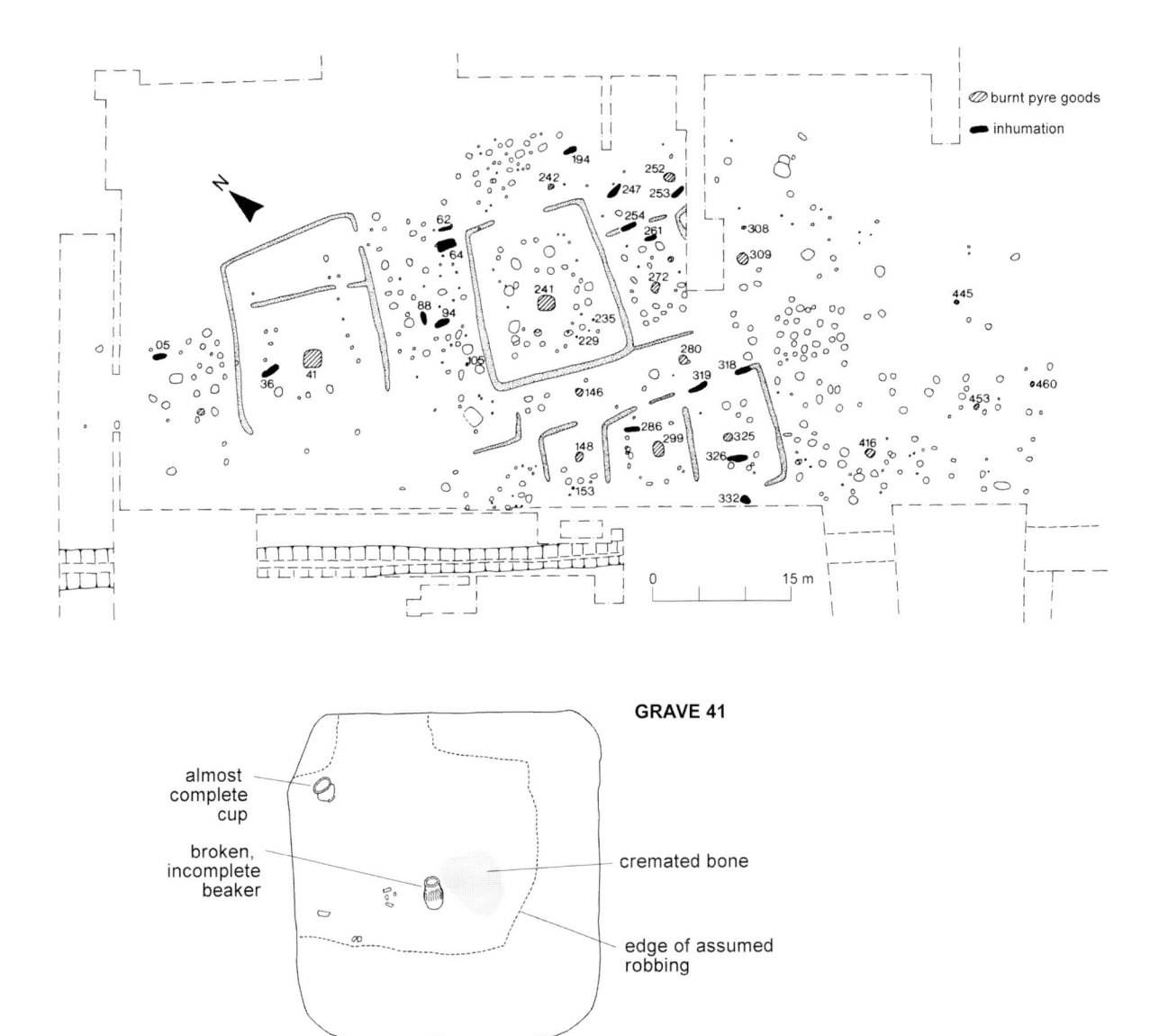

FIG. 173. King Harry Lane cemetery. Above: plan (adapted from Niblett 1999, fig. 114 which is after Stead and Rigby 1989, fig. 182). Below: detailed plan of grave 41 from the same cemetery (after Stead and Rigby 1989, fig. 95)

postulated in the burial clusters and enclosures there. Collectively they seem likely to have represented the ordinary members of one of the clans which formed the Catuvellauni. Stanway, on the other hand, represents the burial place of a high-ranking kinship group at Camulodunum, whose standing in the community was such that they were not buried with ordinary clansmen. Indeed, the numbers of graves seem so low in the Stanway enclosures that some degree of selection must have been in play when it came to deciding who was to be buried there and who was not. It would be the same mechanism that would explain why, when it came to somebody at the top of the social scale as at Folly Lane, the dead person did not have to share his funerary space with anyone else.

There can be little doubt that the inspiration for the burial practices such as are evident at Stanway, Folly Lane, and King Harry Lane lay in the part of north-west Europe closest to the coast of Britain (FIG. 174). There are plenty of parallels in that part of the world for the rich burials termed 'Welwyn graves' (Stead 1967), of which the Stanway Doctor's and Warrior's burial are good examples, and there is also evidence for the use of wooden mortuary chambers

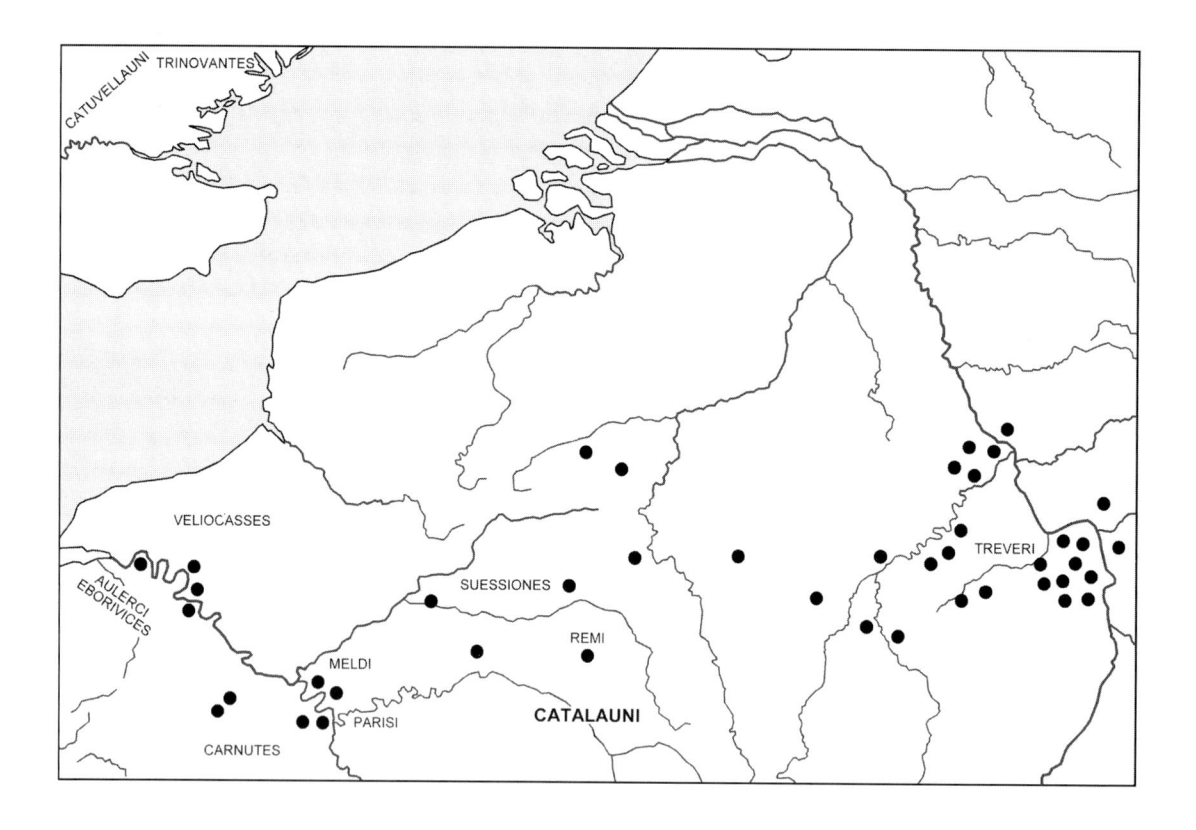

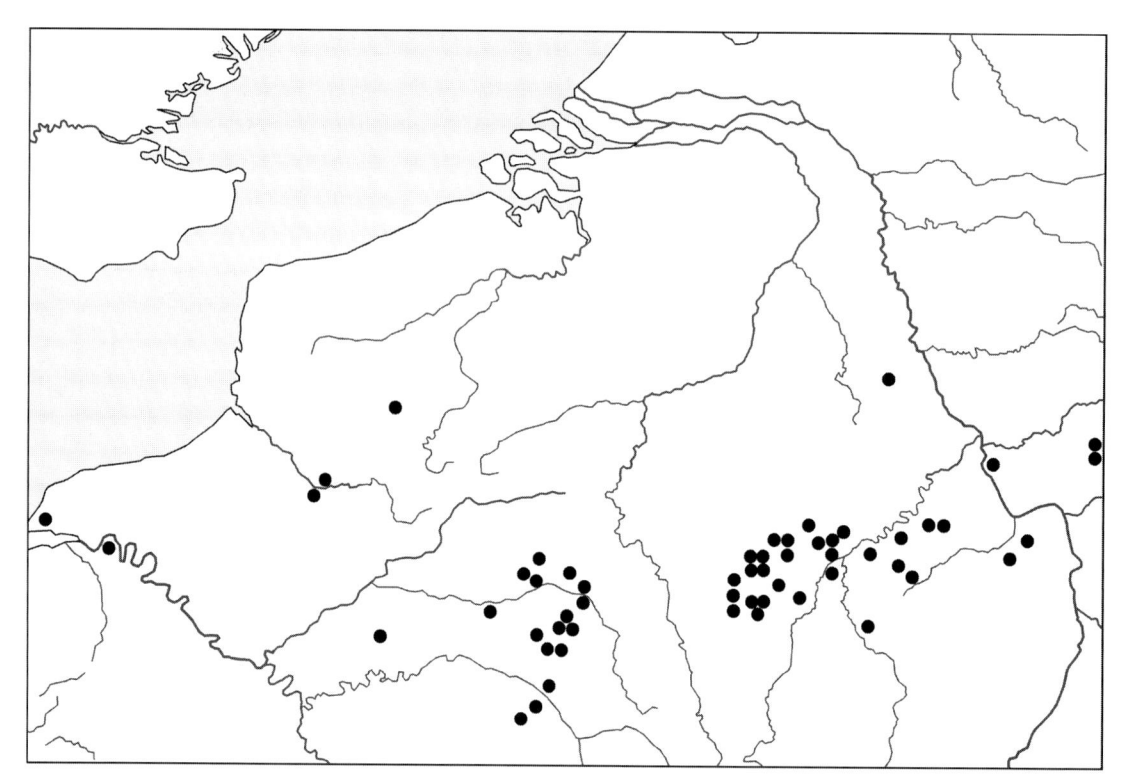

FIG. 174. Above: distribution of the Middle and Late La Tène chariot burials in northern Gaul (based on Metzler *et al.* 1991, fig. 113 which in turn is based on Haffner-Joachim 1985 and Duval 1985). Below: distribution of Late La Tène burials in northern Gaul which contained Italian imports (based on Metzler *et al.* 1991, fig. 114)

in the late La Tène, notably at Clemency in Luxembourg (Metzler *et al.* 1991), Goeblange-Nospelt in Luxembourg (Thill 1966; Waringo 1991, 112–16; Metzler 2002, 182), and Wederath in Germany (Haffner 1971; 1974; 1978; Waringo 1991, 132–4).

In this part of the world there are also aristocratic cemeteries similar in appearance to Stanway. These take the form of square or circular enclosures, sometimes of a considerable size and set out in rows, containing centrally placed rectangular chambers with secondary burials around. Two examples (Avaux and Avançon) are shown here in FIG. 175, out of 37 examples illustrated by Bernard Lambot in his study of the northern part of the Champagne region of northern France (Lambot 1993, 132–5, figs 11 and 13). Of particular importance to Stanway is the cemetery at Vieux-les-Asfeld (*ibid.*, 124–7; 2002, 91–3), which, coincidentally, is very close to the sites at Avaux and Avançon. Here three wooden chambers have been excavated (Graves 1, 3, and 5), which have much in common with those at Stanway, not only in plan and in section (FIG. 176), but also because they contained only the remains of broken funerary goods. Each of the chambers lay in the centre of three circular ditched enclosures which were *c.* 20 m in diameter and strung out in a line (Lambot 1993, 133, fig. 11, no. 8). All three chambers dated to the 1st century B.C. They were comparable in size to those at Stanway, being smaller than BF6 and CF42 but larger than AF25 and BF24. Grave 3 included eight posts around the perimeter of the pit in a manner reminiscent of chambers BF6 and CF42. The timber planking around the sides of Graves 1 and 5 was supported in a slot around the edge of the floor just as in BF6 and BF24 at Stanway except that, being 0.3 m deep, the slots at Vieux-les-Asfeld were much more substantial.

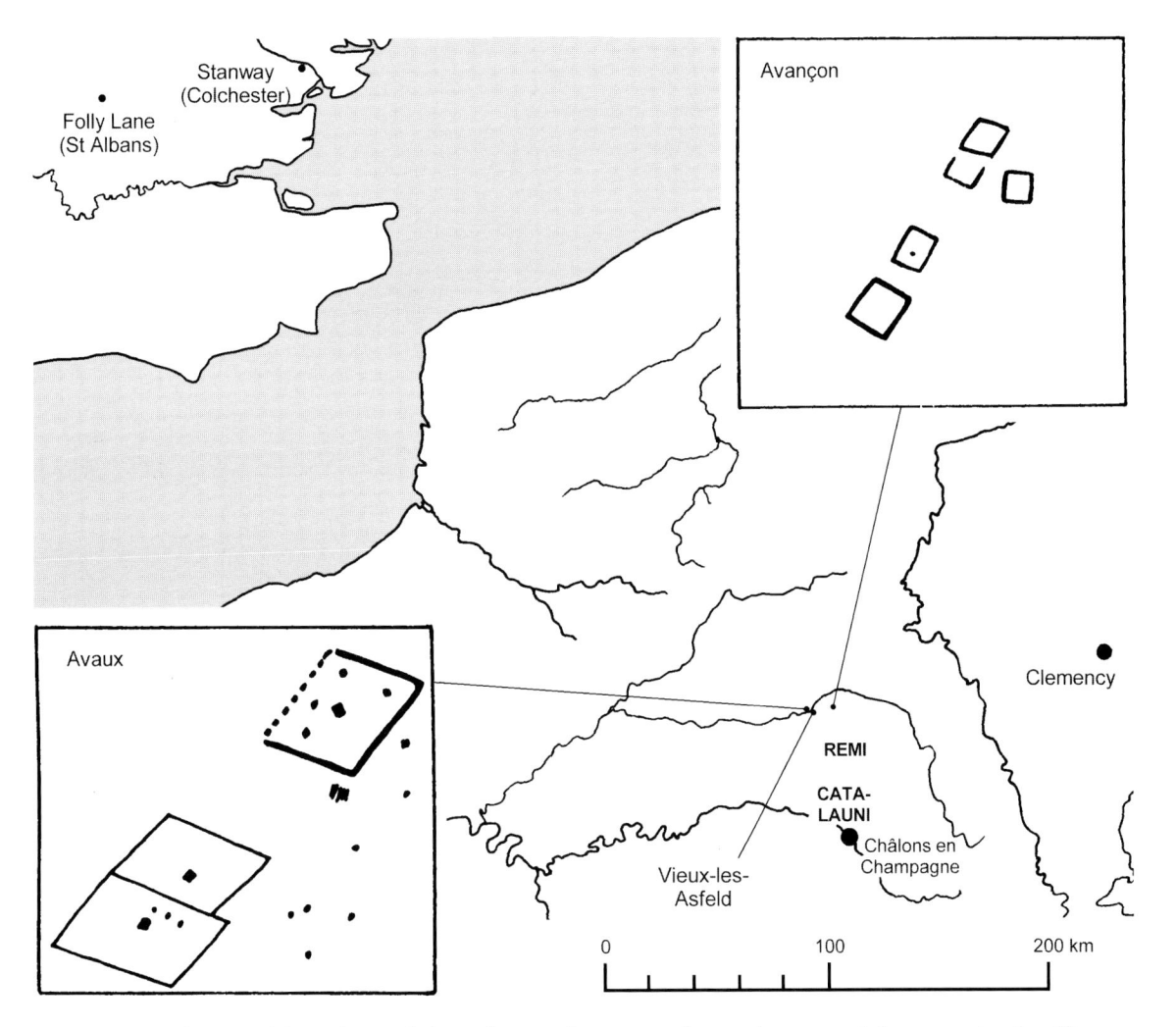

FIG. 175. Plans and locations of the aristocratic cemeteries at Avaux and Avançon in the Champagne region of France. The plans of Avaux and Avançon (Lambot 1993, fig. 11, no. 6 and fig. 13, no. 2) are reproduced with the kind permission of Bernard Lambot

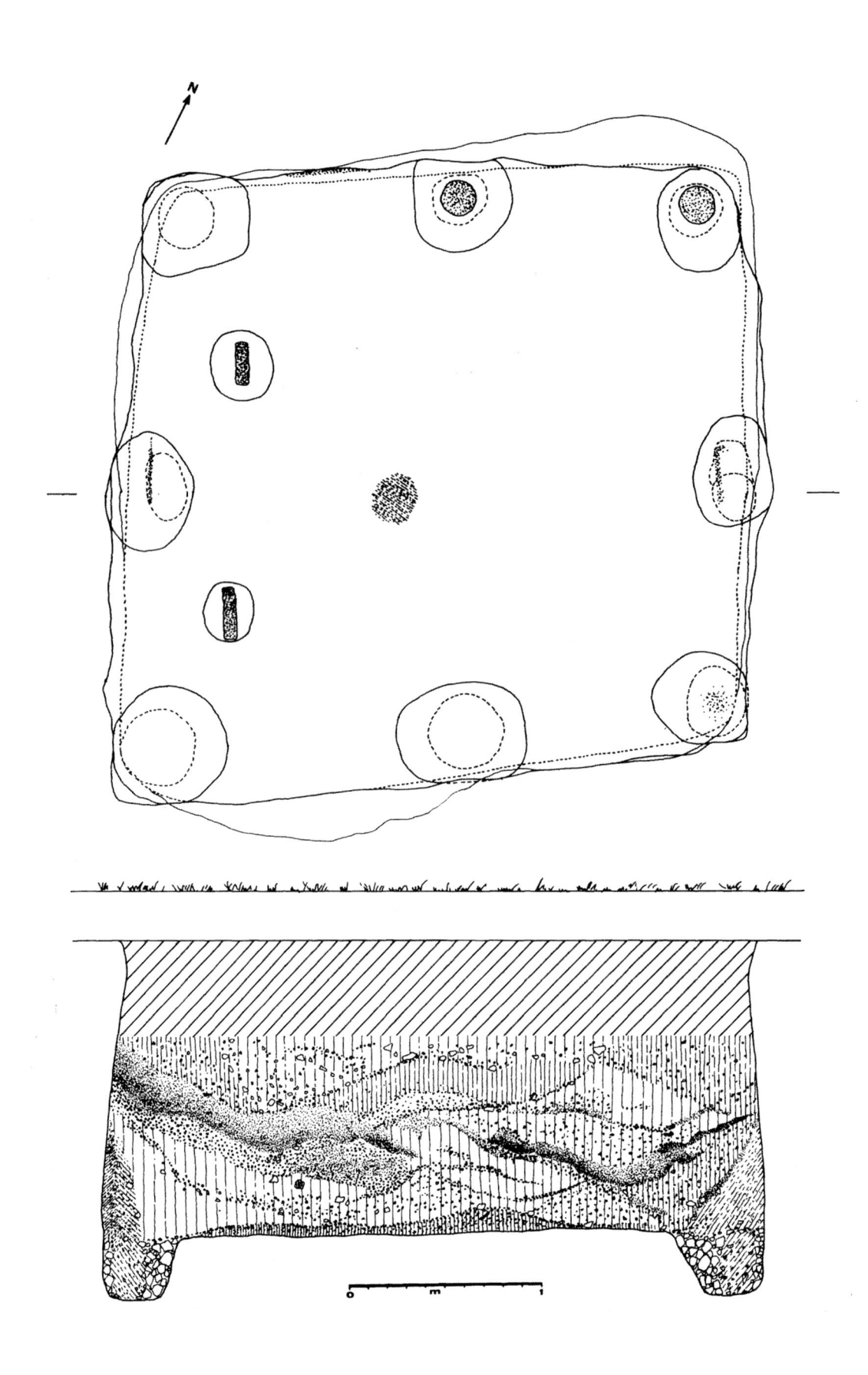

FIG. 176. Grave 3 at Vieux-les-Asfeld in the Champagne region of France. The illustration (Lambot 1993, fig. 4) is reproduced with the kind permission of Bernard Lambot

In northern Gaul and Germany, especially in and around the territory of the Treveri (FIG. 174), the inclusion in rich graves of fragments of chariots is a recurrent pattern regarded as an example of the rite of *pars pro toto* (Metzler 2002, 176–81). These vehicles were burnt on the pyre, and the deliberate breaking of funerary goods away from the pyre as a separate step in the funerary process is something which seems harder to find and recognise in the archaeological record both in Britain and on the Continent. At Clemency the remains of six bowls lay in a way that suggested to the excavators that they had been thrown or placed in pieces on the roof of the chamber (Metzler *et al.* 1991, 33, fig. 25). The rite is otherwise absent at Clemency. Broken amphoras in one corner of the chamber there are interpreted as evidence for Augustan-period looting (Metzler *et al.* 1991, 33, fig. 25). A similar explanation is put forward to explain the broken pottery scattered in the fills of the three excavated chambers at Vieux-les-Asfeld. Bernard Lambot, the excavator, has no doubt that the tombs had been pillaged, an important piece of the evidence for this conclusion being what appears to be an intrusive sherd of a Drag. 33 vessel in the fill of Grave 5 (Lambot 1993, 93). However, there is no denying the striking stratigraphic similarities between the chambers at Stanway and Vieux-les-Asfeld (*e.g.* cf. FIGS 42, 56, 67 and 176), similarities so marked that it is hard to imagine that the chambers at one place were pillaged and the chambers at the other were not. Rosalind Niblett came to the same conclusion when considering Vieux-les-Asfeld in relation to Folly Lane (Niblett 1999, 397). If the chambers at Stanway had been looted, then they must have been broken into before the roofs collapsed through decay. This is quite plausible, but we would need to accept that at least one of the grave robbers' purposes was to remove or break whatever they found there and take away much of the resulting debris from the chamber. Moreover, we would have to conceive of a process of withdrawal by the grave robbers that would result in the broken debris left behind in the chambers being mixed with lots of soil and in the careful replacement of the roof. None of this is entirely inconceivable, but given the presence of the broken pots in the ditches at Stanway, which can hardly have been the result of looting or later deliberate destruction, it is hard to explain the presence of broken pottery and other damaged items in the chambers as a product of robbing or even desecration.

CONTINUITY AND THE CATUVELLAUNI

Stanway provides some useful evidence in relation to the difficult issue of the origin of Camulodunum. Until the 1990s, the earliest date attributable to Camulodunum was *c.* 25 B.C. (*CAR* 11, 174–8). The date is very approximate and takes into account the following three factors: CAM on an early coin of Tasciovanus dated to the mid to late 1st century B.C. (Hobbs 1996, 19), the Lexden Tumulus dated to *c.* 15/10 B.C. (*CAR* 11, 85–94), and a small cemetery near the tumulus dated to *c.* 50 B.C.–15/10 B.C. (*ibid.*, 164–70). Stanway conforms to this supposition since Enclosure 1 and the nearby pit CF7 together point to a date somewhere in the range *c.* 60–1 B.C. for the earliest of the funerary activities there. Of course, this still does not mean that Camulodunum necessarily existed any earlier than *c.* 25 B.C., but it reinforces the possibility that it might have done. Significantly, Stanway thus lends support to the possibility that Camulodunum was in existence when Julius Caesar invaded Britain in 55 and 54 B.C.

As we have explained, it would seem reasonable to suppose that all four enclosures at Stanway represented the burial places of a closely related group of people living in or close to Camulodunum over a period of at least fifty years, given the similarities between Enclosures 3–5 and Enclosure 1. The burial practices employed in Enclosure 1 look too much like those evident in Enclosures 3–5 fifty or more years later to suggest anything other than continuity of habitation in the vicinity. They suggest that the people living and dying in Camulodunum around the time of the Claudian invasion were the descendants of the people living and dying in the settlement at least half a century earlier, if not long before. Since Cunobelin was Catuvellaunian, then it follows that Camulodunum is likely to have been a Catuvellaunian stronghold quite probably from at least the late 1st century B.C., if not from its origin, whenever that might have been.

The continental burial rite that is so well expressed at Clemency in Luxembourg, with its wooden chamber, mound, and square ditched enclosure (Metzler *et al.* 1991) and so closely paralleled in certain details at Vieux-les-Asfeld, seems so similar to that used at Stanway and Folly Lane that we must wonder if all this can simply be put down to close contact through trade and exchange.

It seems an odd coincidence that the two places where mortuary chambers have been discovered in Britain were the main Catuvellaunian centres. Others may be found elsewhere in due course, but we need to wonder if their distribution will turn out to be limited to high-status sites. Perhaps we should recall the debate about migrations of the Belgae long since down-graded in favour of continuous continental contact and acculturation (*e.g.* Birchall 1964; 1965; Collis 2003, 180–2; Cunliffe 1991, 108–10; Hawkes 1968; 1980; Hawkes and Dunning 1930; James and Rigby 1997, 14; Stead 1976, 402). The character of the Stanway and Folly Lane sites appears to provide support for the view that there had indeed been significant emigration of Belgae from northern Gaul into Britain, but the numbers need only have been small and led by members of the ruling élite. Certainly the distributions of the coins of Epaticcus (self-proclaimed descendant of Tasciovanus), Cara (?Caratacus, son of Cunobelin), and Amminus (?Adminius, son of Cunobelin) south of the Thames (Hobbs 1996, 20–22; Van Arsdell 1989, 109–10, 183, 476) can be taken as evidence that the Catuvellauni (or at least some of their leading members) were mobile. Camulodunum can be viewed as an earlier example of these movements whereby a group of Catuvellauni settled in an area that had presumably been Trinovantian. An intrusion such as this in the mid 1st century B.C. could neatly explain the serious problems between Cassivellaunus and the Trinovantes, which Caesar touches on in his *de Bello Gallico* (V, 20). (This of course assumes that Cassivellaunus had indeed been Catuvellaunian which, to judge by the location of his territory as evident in Caesar, must surely have been the case.)

Thus the distinctive Folly Lane/Stanway burial rite can be seen as being a direct expression of what it was to be Catuvellaunian, rather than something acquired through social contact and material exchange. Arguably the groups who practised these rites in Camulodunum and Verulamium seem more likely to have been the descendants of immigrants from northern Gaul rather than any indigenous British (represented earlier at Stanway by Enclosure 2). As Christopher Hawkes and others wondered many years ago (Hawkes and Dunning 1930, 245–6; Hawkes 1968, 9), the obvious candidates are the Catalauni from the southern part of the Champagne region in France. Perhaps significantly, the Catalauni were clients of the Remi, the neighbouring tribe in whose territory lay the cemeteries at Vieux-les-Asfeld, Avaux, and Avançon. Certainly, enduring political and cultural ties between ruling élites on either side of the English Channel in this early period are implicit in that often-quoted passage in Caesar to the effect that the authority of Diviciacus, king of the Suessiones, extended to Britain (*de Bello Gallico*, II, 4). The appearance on coinage in southern Britain of the name Commios, if equatable with Caesar's Commius or one of his descendants (*ibid.*, IV, 27; Hobbs 1996, 17; Collis 2003, 114), appears to provide not only an example of how a member of the Belgic ruling élite could migrate, settle and dominate, but also more evidence of the existence of strong connections between the upper classes of northern Gaul and Britain. The Romanisation of the Catuvellauni at Verulamium and Camulodunum in the century or so leading up to the Claudian invasion of Britain was thus likely to have owed as much to contact with their kinsfolk in northern Gaul who, under Augustus and Tiberius, were fast becoming good Roman Gauls, as to other mechanisms such as trade or the enforced education in a Roman environment of the offspring of the ruling élite (Creighton 2000). Once settled in Britain, the Catuvellauni and immigrant groups like them are likely themselves to have played a significant rôle in the process of Roman acculturation among the pre-existing population.

BIBLIOGRAPHY

ABBREVIATIONS

BAR	British Archaeological Reports
BM Guide 1925	*A Guide to the Iron Age Antiquities in the British Museum*
CAR 2	N. Crummy, *The Roman Small Finds from Excavations in Colchester 1971–9*, Colchester Archaeological Report 2 (Colchester; 1983, reprinted 1995)
CAR 4	N. Crummy (ed.), *The Coins from Excavations in Colchester 1971–9*, Colchester Archaeological Report 4 (Colchester; 1987)
CAR 6	P. Crummy, *Excavations at Culver Street, the Gilberd School, and other sites in Colchester 1971–85*, Colchester Archaeological Report 6 (Colchester; 1992)
CAR 8	H.E.M. Cool and J. Price, *Roman Vessel Glass from Excavations in Colchester, 1971–85*, Colchester Archaeological Report 8 (Colchester; 1995)
CAR 9	N. Crummy, P. Crummy and C. Crossan, *Excavations of Roman and Later Cemeteries, Churches and Monastic Sites in Colchester, 1971–88*, Colchester Archaeological Report 9 (Colchester; 1993)
CAR 10	R.P. Symonds and S. Wade, *Roman Pottery from Excavations in Colchester, 1971–86*, edited by P. Bidwell and A. Croom, Colchester Archaeological Report 10 (Colchester; 1999)
CAR 11	C.F.C. Hawkes and P. Crummy, *Camulodunum 2*, Colchester Archaeological Report 11 (Colchester; 1995)
CAT	Colchester Archaeological Trust
CBA	Council for British Archaeology
CIL	*Corpus Inscriptionum Latinarum*
CMG	*Corpus medicorum Graecorum*
CMNN 1989	*Le collezioni del Museo Nazionale di Napoli*, I.1 (Naples)
Col. Archaeol.	*The Colchester Archaeologist*
DPF 1860	'Chess among the Welsh', in D. Forbes, *The History of Chess* (London), xlvii–lii, appendix E
EH	English Heritage
Galen	C.G. Kuhn, *Claudii Galeni Opera Omnia*, 20 vols in 22 (Leipzig; 1821–33. Reproduced Hildesheim; 1964–5)
KHL	see Stead and Rigby 1989
NRFRC	see Tomber and Dore 1998
O	Felix Oswald, *Index of Figure Types on Terra Sigillata ('Samian Ware')*, Supp. Ann. Arch. Anth., University of Liverpool, 1937
Paul of Aegina	J.L. Heiberg, *Paulus Aegineta*, 2 vols *CMG* 9, 1, 2 (Leipzig/Berlin; 1921, 1924). Also Adams, F. *The seven books of Paulus Aegineta*, English translation, 3 vols (London; 1844, 1846, 1847)
P. Ryl.	*Catalogue of the Greek and Latin papyri in the John Rylands Library, Manchester* (Manchester; 1911–1952)
RCHM 1928	*Roman London*, Royal Commission on Historical Monuments, An Inventory of the Historical Monuments in London III (London)
RCHM 1962	*Eburacum, Roman York*, Royal Commission on Historical Monuments (London)

RIB   The Roman Inscriptions of Britain, by R.G. Collingwood and R.P. Wright
                 1, edited R.S.O. Tomlin: Inscriptions on stone (Stroud; 1995)
                 2, edited by S.S. Frere and R.S.O. Tomlin, Instrumentum Domesticum
                 fasc. 2: Weights, vessels, spoons (Stroud; 1991)
                 fasc. 3: Brooches, rings, gems (Stroud; 1991)
                 fasc. 7: Graffiti on samian ware (Stroud; 1995)
                 fasc. 8: Graffiti on coarse pottery (Stroud; 1995)
RIC   Mattingley, H., Sydenham, E.A., Sutherland, C.H.V. and Carson, R.A., *Roman Imperial Coinage* (10 vols) (London, 1923–84)
Scribonius Largus S. Sconocchia, *Scribonii Largi Compositiones* (Leipzig; 1983)
Soranus   J. Ilberg, *Sorani Gynaeciorum Libri IV, De Signis Fracturarum, De Fasciis, Vita Hippocratis secundum Soranum*, CMG 4 (Leipzig/Berlin; 1927). Also O. Temkin, *Soranus' Gynecology*, English translation (Baltimore; 1956)
Van Arsdell   see Van Arsdell 1989

BIBLIOGRAPHY

Alcock, L. 1972: *'By South Cadbury is that Camelot...': excavations at Cadbury Castle, 1966–70* (London)

Allason-Jones, L. 1988: 'The small finds', in M.C. Bishop and J.N. Dore, *Corbridge. Excavations at the Roman Fort and Town 1947–80*, EH Archaeol. Rep. 8 (London)

— 1989: *Ear-rings in Roman Britain*, BAR British Series 201 (Oxford)

— 1996: *Roman Jet in the Yorkshire Museum* (York)

— and Bishop, M. C. 1988: *Excavations at Roman Corbridge: The Hoard*, EH Archaeol. Rep. 7 (London)

— and Miket, R. 1984: *The Catalogue of the Small Finds from South Shields Roman Fort*, Soc. Antiq. Newcastle upon Tyne Monograph 2 (Newcastle upon Tyne)

Allen, D. 1967: 'Iron currency bars in Britain', *Proc. Prehist. Soc.* 33, 307–35

— 1980: *The Coins of the Ancient Celts*, edited by D. Nash (Edinburgh)

Almgren, O. 1923: *Studien über nord-europäische Fibelformen*, Mannus-Bibliothek 32, 2 edn

Amrein, H., Cottier, M., Duvauchelle, A. and Rez-Vodoz, V. 1999: 'Le petit mobilier', in D. Castella, C. Martin Pruvot, H. Amrein, A. Duvauchelle and F.E. Kœnig, *La nécropole gallo-romaine d'Avenches 'En Chaplix', fouilles 1987–1992 2: l'étude du mobilier*, Cahiers d'Archéologie Romande 78 (Lausanne)

Anderson, J. 1905: 'Notes on a Romano-British hoard of bronze vessels and personal ornaments found in a moss on Lamberton Moor, Berwickshire', *Proc. Soc. Antiq. Scot.* 39, 367–76

Anderson, S. Th. 1979: 'Identification of wild grasses and cereal pollen', *Danmarks Geologiske Undersogelse Arbog 1978*, 69–92

Arbmann, H. 1940/1943: *Birka. I Die Gräber, Uppsala. Teil I Tafeln* (Uppsala; 1940), *Teil II Text* (Uppsala; 1943)

Arnold, D.E. 1985: *Ceramic Theory and Cultural Process* (Cambridge)

Articus, R. 1983: 'Vom Brettspiel der Wikinger', in *Duisburg und die Wikinger*, cat. of the Exhibition Duisburg 1983 (Duisburg), 91–6

Atkinson, D. 1916 *The Romano-British Site on Lowbury Hill in Berkshire* (Reading)

Atkinson, M. and Preston, S.J. 1998: 'The Late Iron Age and Roman settlement at Heybridge, Essex, excavations 1993–5: an interim report', *Britannia* 29, 85–110

Austin, R.G. 1935: 'Roman board games, II', *Greece and Rome* 4.11, 76-82

— 1938: 'A Roman game-board from Holt, Denbighshire', *Archaeol. Cambrensis* 93, 250

Bailey, C.J. 1967: 'An Early Iron Age/Romano-British site at Pins Knoll, Litton Cheney: final report', *Proc. Dorset Nat. Hist. Archaeol. Soc.* 89, 147–59

Banck-Burgess, J. 1999: *Hochdorf IV: Die Textilfunde aus dem späthallstattzeitlichen Fürstengrab von Eberdingen-Hochdorf (Kreis Ludwigsburg) und weitere Grabtextilien aus hallstatt- und latènezeitlichen Kulturgruppen* (Stuttgart)

Barber, B. and Bowsher, D. 2000: *The Eastern Cemetery of Roman London: excavations 1983–1990*, Museum of London Archaeol. Service Monograph 4 (London)

Barber, J. and Ashmore, F. 1990: 'Organic residues in archaeology', *Scottish Archaeol Review* 7, 139–45

Barclay, K. 2001: *Scientific Analysis of Archaeological Ceramics: a handbook of resources* (Oxford)

Barford, P.M. 1990: 'Briquetage finds from inland sites', in Fawn *et al.* 1990, 79–80

— 2002: *Excavations at Little Oakley, Essex, 1951–78: Roman Villa and Saxon Settlement*, East Anglian Archaeol. Rep. 98 (Chelmsford)

Barnett, S.M. 2000: 'Luminescence dating of pottery from later prehistoric Britain', *Archaeometry* 42, 431–57

Barrett, J.C. 1978: 'The EPRIA prehistoric pottery', in J. Hedges and D.G. Buckley, 'Excavations at a Neolithic causewayed enclosure, Orsett, Essex, 1975', *Proc. Prehist. Soc.* 44, 268–88

Bartel, A. and Codreanu-Windauer, S. 1995: 'Spindel, Wirtel, Topf; ein besonderer Beigabenkomplex aus Pfakofen, Lkr Regensburg', *Bayerische Vorgeschichtsblätter* 60, 252–72

— 2002: 'Spindle, whorl, pot – a remarkable group of grave goods from Pfakofen, Lkr Regensburg, Bavaria', *Lucerna* 23, 17–27

Barton, K.J. 1962: 'Settlements of the Iron Age and pagan Saxon periods at Linford, Essex', *Trans. Essex Archaeol. Soc.* 1, 57–104

Bastien, J.M. and Demolon, P. 1975: 'Villa et cimetière du 1er siècle après J-C. à Noyelles-Godault (Pas de Calais)', *Septentrion* 5, 1–36

Bates, P.J. and Winham, R.P. 1985: 'Loomweights', in P.J. Fasham, *The Prehistoric Settlement at Winnall Down, Winchester*, Hampshire Field Club Monograph 2

Baudoux, J. 1996: *Les Amphores du Nord-est de la Gaule* (Paris)

Bayley, J. 1984: 'Roman brass-making in Britain', *Historical Metallurgy* 18(1), 42–3

— 1985: 'The analysis of copper-alloy objects', in Niblett 1985, 115

— 1986: 'Brooches', in Stead and Rigby 1986, 381–4

— 1988: 'Non-ferrous metal-working: continuity and change' in E.A. Slater and J.O. Tate (eds), *Science and Archaeology Glasgow 1987, Proceedings of a conference on the application of scientific techniques to archaeology*, BAR British Series 196 (Oxford), 193–207.

— 1990: 'The production of brass in Antiquity with particular reference to Roman Britain', in P.T. Craddock (ed.), *2000 Years of Zinc and Brass*, British Museum Occasional Paper 50 (London), 7–26

— 1992: Note on the alloys used for military equipment, in *CAR* 6, 233

— and Butcher, S. 1985: 'The brooches – descriptive catalogue', in Niblett 1985, microfiche 3, C3–C9

— 1991: 'Romano-British plate brooches: composition and decoration', *Jewellery Studies* 3, 25–32

— 1997: 'The composition and decoration of Roman brooches' in A. Sinclair, E. Slater and J. Gowlett (eds), *Archaeological Sciences 1995*, Oxbow Monograph 64 (Oxford), 101–6

— 2004: *Roman Brooches in Britain: a technological and typological study based on the Richborough collection* (London)

Bayley, J., Dungworth D. and Paynter S. 2001: *Centre for Archaeology Guidelines: archaeometallurgy* (London)

Bayley, J., Biek L., Guido, M. and Henderson, J. forthcoming: *The Glass Beads from Hayling Island, Hants*, Centre for Archaeology Report

Bean, S.C. 2000: *The Coinage of the Atrebates and Regni*, Studies in Celtic Coinage 4/Oxford Univ. School Archaeol. Monograph 50 (Oxford)

Bedwin, O.R. 1991: 'Asheldam Camp – an early Iron Age hill fort: the 1985 excavations', *Essex Archaeol. Hist.* 22, 13–37

Bedwin, O. (ed.) 1996: *The Archaeology of Essex: proceedings of the Writtle conference* (Chelmsford)

Becq de Fouquières, L. 1869: *Les Jeux des Anciens* (Paris)

Behrens, G. 1950: 'Römische Fibeln mit Inschrift', in G. Behrens and J. Werner (eds), *Festschrift zum 75. Geburtstag von Paul Reinecke am 25. September 1947* (Mainz), 1–12

Bel, V. 2002: *Pratiques funéraires du Haut-Empire dans le Midi de la Gaule: la nécropole gallo-romaine du Valladas à Saint-Paul-Trois Châteaux (Drôme)*, Monographies d'Archéologie Méditerranéenne 11 (Lattes)

Bell, R.C. 1979: *Board and Table Games from Many Civilizations*, revised edn (New York)

Bellows, J. 1881: 'On some bronze and other articles found near Birdlip', *Trans. Bristol Gloucestershire Archaeol. Soc.* 5 (1880–1), 137–41

Beltrán Lloris, M. 1970: *Las Anforas Romanas en Espana*, Monografias Arqueológicas, Anejos de Caesaraugusta 8 (Zaragoza)

Bémont, C. 1976: *Recherches méthodologiques sur la céramique sigilée: les vases estampillés de Glanum*, Bibliothèque des Écoles francaises d'Athènes et de Rome: fasc. 227 (Paris)

Bender Jørgensen, L. 1992: *North European Textiles until AD 1000* (Aarhus)

Benfield, S.F. and Brooks, H. 1999: 'Prehistoric and Roman enclosures at Abbotstone quarry, Colchester', *Tarmac Papers* (Archives and history initiative of Tarmac plc) 3, 3–9

Bennet, A. (ed.) 1995: 'Work of the Archaeological Section 1994', *Essex Arch. Hist.* 26, 222–37

Bennet, K.D., Whittington, G. and Edwards, K.J. 1994: 'Recent plant nomenclatural changes and pollen morphology in the British Isles', *Quaternary Newsletter* 73, 1–6

Bennett, J. and Young, R. 1981: 'Some new and some forgotten stamped skillets and the date of P. Cipius Polybius', *Britannia* 12, 37–44

Bennion, E. 1979: *Antique Medical Instruments* (London)

Bertrand, I. 2003: *Objects de parure et de soins du corps d'époque romaine dans l'Est picton (Deux-Sèvres, Vienne)*, Mémoire de l'Association des Publications Chauvinoises XXIII (Chauvigny)

Biddle, M. 1967: 'Two Flavian burials from Grange Road, Winchester', *Antiq. J.* 47 (1967), 224–50

Biddulph, E. 2005: 'Last orders: choosing pottery for funerals in Roman Essex', *Oxford J. Archaeol.* 24, 23–45

Biek, L. and Bayley, J. 1979: 'Glass and other vitreous materials', *World Archaeol.* 11(1), 1–25

Biel, J. 1985: *Der Keltenfürst von Hochdorf* (Stuttgart)

Bimson, M. and Freestone I.C. 1983: 'An analytical study of the relationship between the Portland Vase and other Roman cameo glasses', *J. Glass Studies* 25, 55–64

Birchall, A. 1964: 'The Belgic problem: Aylesford revisited', *Brit. Mus. Quart.* 28, 21–9

— 1965: 'The Aylesford-Swarling Culture – the problem of the Belgae reconsidered', *Proc. Prehist. Soc.* 31, 241–367

Bishop, M.C. 1988: 'Cavalry equipment of the Roman army in the 1st century AD', in J.C. Coulston (ed.), *Military Equipment and the Identity of Roman Soldiers*, Proceedings of the Fourth Roman Military Equipment Conference, BAR International Series 394 (Oxford), 67–195

Black, A. and Black, D. 2003: *Geophysical Survey at Tarmac Sand and Gravel Extraction Site (OS 595222)*, unpublished report for CAT

Black, E. 1983: 'Ritual dog burials from Roman sites', *Kent Archaeological Review* 71, 20–2

Bliquez, L.J. 1994: *Roman Surgical Instruments and other Minor Objects in the Archaeological Museum of Naples. With a catalogue of the surgical instruments in the 'Antiquarium' at Pompeii by Ralph Jackson* (Mainz)

Blümner, H. 1911: *Die römischen Privataltertümer*, 3rd edn (Munich)

den Boesterd, M.H.P. 1956: *Description of the Collections of the Rijksmuseum G M Kam at Nijmegen 5: the bronze vessels* (Nijmegen)

Bologa, V.L., Danila, S. and Ghitan, T. 1956: 'Sägeartiges Instrument aus einem keltischen Brandgrab, gefunden bei Galaţii Bistriţei/Nord-Rumänien/wahrscheinlich Trepanationssäge', *Actos del XV congreso internacional de historia de la medicina* 2 (Madrid), 65–70

Bonomi, S. 1996: *Vetri antichi del Museo Archeologico Nazionale di Adria*, Corpus delle collezioni Archeologiche del Vetro nel Veneto 2 (Venice)

Boon, G.C. 1961: 'Roman antiquities at Welshpool', *Antiq. J.* 41, 13–31

— 1969: 'Belgic and Roman Silchester: the excavations of 1954–8 with an excursus on the early history of Calleva', *Archaeologia* 102, 1–81

— 1975: 'Segontium 50 years on: 1, a Roman stave of larchwood and other unpublished finds mainly of organic materials, together with a note on late barracks', *Archaeol. Cambrensis* 124, 52–67

— 2000:	'The other objects of copper alloy', in Fulford and Timby 2000, 338–57
Börker, Ch. and Merkelbach, R. 1979:	*Die Inschriften von Ephesos II* (Bonn)
Bosanquet, R.C. 1936:	'A Roman skillet from South Shields' (ed. A. Richmond), *Archaeologia Aeliana* 4th ser 13, 139–51
Boucher, S., Perdu, G. and Feugère, M. 1980:	*Bronze antiques du Musée de la civilisation gallo-romaine à Lyon II: instrumentum, Aegyptica* (Lyon)
Boulestin, B., Buisson, J-F. and Gomez de Soto, J. 2002:	'"Tombes" sans défunt laténiennes et du Haut-Empire en Gaule: pour une relecture hérétique', in Guichard and Perrin 2002, 189–97
Bourgeois, L. (ed.) 1999:	*Le sanctuaire rural de Bennecourt (Yvelines)*, Documents d'Archéologie Francaise 77 (Paris)
Bowden, M. and McOmish, D. 1987:	'The required barrier', *Scottish Archaeol. Review* 4, 76–84
Bowman, A.K. and Thomas, J.D. 1994:	*The Vindolanda Writing-tablets. Tabulae Vindolandenses II* (London)
— 2003:	*The Vindolanda Writing-tablets. Tabulae Vindolandenses III* (London)
Bowman, S.G.E. 1990:	*Radiocarbon Dating* (London)
Božič, D. 2001:	'Über den Verwendungszweck einiger römischer Messerchen', *Bulletin Instrumentum* 13, 28–9
Brailsford, J.W. 1962:	*Hod Hill 1: antiquities in the Durden Collection* (London)
— 1975:	'The Polden Hill hoard', *Proc. Prehist. Soc.* 41, 222–34
Bretz-Mahler, D. 1971:	*La Civilisation de La Tène I en Champagne: Le Faciès Marnien*, Gallia Supplement 23 (Paris)
Brion, M. 1979:	*Pompeii and Herculaneum, the Glory and the Grief* (London)
Brodribb, A.C.C., Hands, A.R. and Walker, D. 1972:	*Excavations at Shakenoak Farm, near Wilcote, Oxfordshire 3* (Oxford)
Brongers, J.A. 1969:	'Ancient old-world trepanning instruments', *Berichten van de Rijksdienst voor het Oudheidkundig Bodemonderzoek* 19, 7–16
Brooks, H. 2005:	*An Archaeological Excavation and Watching Brief at the Musket Club, Homefield Road, Colchester, Essex, December 2004–February 2005*, CAT Archive Rep. 311 (Colchester)
Brooks, H. and Masefield, R. 2005:	*The Colchester Garrison PFI project, Colchester, Essex: a report on the 2003 excavation of Areas 2, 6, 10 August–November 2003*, CAT Archive Rep. 292 (Colchester)
Brown, N.R. 1987:	'The prehistoric pottery', in Wickenden 1987, 31–3
— 1988:	'A late Bronze Age enclosure at Lofts Farm, Essex', *Proc. Prehist. Soc.* 54, 249–302
— 1991:	'Middle Iron Age decorated pottery around the Thames estuary', *Essex Archaeol. Hist.* 22, 165–6
— 1992:	'Prehistoric pottery', in O.R. Bedwin, 'Early Iron Age settlement at Maldon and the Maldon *burh*: excavations at Beacon Green 1987', *Essex Archaeol. Hist.* 23, 15–18
— 1993:	'Prehistoric pottery', in W.J. Rodwell, *The Origins and Early Development of Witham, Essex: A Study in Settlement and Fortification, Prehistoric to Medieval*, Oxbow Monograph 26 (Oxford), 107–110
— 1995:	'Later Bronze Age and early to middle Iron Age pottery', in Wymer and Brown 1995, 77–88
— 1996:	'The archaeology of Essex c. 1500–500 BC', in Bedwin 1996, 26–37
— 1998a:	'Prehistoric pottery', in Wallis and Waughman 1998, 132–41
— 1998b:	'Earlier Iron Age pottery', in Carter 1998, 88–9
— 1999:	'The prehistoric pottery', in N.J. Lavender, 'Bronze Age and medieval sites at Springfield, Chelmsford: excavations near the A12 Boreham interchange, 1993', *Essex Archaeol. Hist.* 30, 12–16
— 2001:	'The prehistoric pottery', in Buckley *et al.* 2001, 123–34
— 2003:	'Prehistoric pottery', in M. Germany, *Excavations at Great Holts Farm, Boreham, Essex, 1992–94*, East Anglian Archaeol. 105, 93–6
— 2004:	'Late Bronze Age, early and middle Iron Age pottery', in Havis and Brooks 2004, 39–54

Brown, R.A. 1986: 'The Iron Age and Romano-British settlement at Woodcock Hall, Saham Toney, Norfolk', *Britannia* 17, 1–58
Brulet, R. and Coulon, G. 1977: *La nécropole gallo-romaine de la rue Perdue à Tournai* (Louvain)
Brun, P. 1987: *Princes et princesses de la celtique, le premier Age du Fer* (Paris)
Brunaux, J. 1988: *The Celtic Gauls: Gods, Rites and Sanctuaries*, translated by D. Nash (London)
Brunt, P.A. 1975: 'Did imperial Rome disarm her subjects?', *Phoenix* 29, 260–70
— 1990: *Roman Imperial Themes* (Oxford)
Buckley, D.G. and Major, H. 1983: 'Quernstones', in *CAR 2*, 73–6
Buckley, D.G., Hedges, J.D. and Priddy, D.A. 1987: *Excavations at Woodham Walter and an Assessment of Essex Enclosures*, East Anglian Archaeol. 33 (Chelmsford)
Buckley, D.G., Hedges, J.D. and Brown, N.R., 2001: 'Excavations at a Neolithic cursus, Springfield, Essex, 1979–85', *Proc. Prehist. Soc.* 67, 101–62
Bulleid, A. and Gray, H. St George 1911: *The Glastonbury Lake Village 1* (Glastonbury)
Burns, B., Cunliffe, B. and Sebire, H. 1996: *Guernsey: an island community of the Atlantic Iron Age*, Oxford University Committee for Archaeol. Monograph 43 (Oxford)
Bursian, C. 1855: 'Museographisches. 1. Aus Athen', *Archäologische Zeitung* 13, 53–8
Burstow, G.P. and Holleyman, G.A. 1957: 'Late Bronze Age settlement on Itford Hill, Sussex', *Proc. Prehist. Soc.* 23, 167–212
Bushe-Fox, J.P. 1928: *Second Report on the Excavations of the Roman Fort at Richborough, Kent* (London)
Butcher, S. 2001: 'The brooches', in A.S. Anderson, J.S. Wacher and A.P. Fitzpatrick, *The Romano-British 'small town' at Wanborough, Wiltshire*, Britannia Monograph 19, 41–69

Caputo, G. 1987: *Il teatro Augusteo di Leptis Magna. Scavo e Restauro (1937–1951)* (Roma)
Carr, G. 2005: 'Woad, tattooing and identity in later Iron Age and early Roman Britain', *Oxford J. Archaeol.* 24, 273–92
— and Knüsel, C. 1997: 'The ritual framework of excarnation by exposure as the mortuary practice of the Early and Middle Iron Ages of central southern Britain', in Gwilt and Haselgrove 1997, 167–73
Carreras Monfort, C. 2000: *Economía de la Britannia romana: la importación de alimentos* (Barcelona)
Carter, G.A. 1998: *Excavations at the Orsett 'Cock' enclosure, Essex, 1976*, East Anglian Archaeol. 86 (Chelmsford)
Caruana, I. 1992: 'Carlisle: excavation of a section of the annexe ditch of the first Flavian fort, 1990', *Britannia* 23, 45–109
Celsus, A. Cornelius: *De medicina*, Loeb Classical Library, vols 1–3, with English translation by W.G. Spencer (London/Cambridge, Mass.; 1935, 1938)
Charlesworth, D. 1985: 'The glass', in Niblett 1985, microfiche 1:A6–A9, 3:F1–F11
Chin, L. and Mashman, V. 1991: *Sarawak, Cultural Legacy, a Living Tradition* (Kuching)
Ciarallo, A. and De Carolis, E. (eds) 1999: *Pompeii, Life in a Roman Town* (Milan)
Clarke, G. 1979: *The Roman Cemetery at Lankhills*, Winchester Studies 3 (Oxford)
Clifford, E.M. 1961: *Bagendon: a Belgic Oppidum* (London)
Colin, A. 1998: *Chronologie des oppida de la Gaule non méditerranéene*, Documents d'Archéologie Française 71 (Paris)
Collis, J.R. 1968: 'Excavations at Owlesbury, Hants: an interim report', *Antiq. J.* 48, 18–31
— 1973: 'Burials with weapons in Iron Age Britain', *Germania* 51, 121–33
— 2003: *The Celts: Origins, Myths, Inventions* (Stroud)
Cool, H.E.M. 2002: 'Bottles for Bacchus?', in M. Aldhouse-Green and P. Webster, *Artefacts and Archaeology, Aspects of the Celtic and Roman World*, (Cardiff), 132–51
— 2004: 'Some notes on spoons and mortaria', in B. Croxford, H. Eckardt, J. Meade and J. Weekes (eds), *TRAC. 2003, Proceedings of the 13th Annual Theoretical Roman Archaeology Conference, Leicester 2003* (Oxford), 28–35

— and Philo, C. 1998: *Roman Castleford, Excavations 1974–85 1: the small finds*, Yorkshire Archaeol. 4 (Wakefield)

Cork, C.R., Wild, J.P., Cooke, W.D. and Fang-Lu, L. 1997: 'Analysis and evaluation of a group of early Roman textiles from Vindolanda, Northumberland', *J. Archaeol. Science* 24, 19–32

Corsi-Sciallano, M. and Liou, B. 1985: *Les épaves de Tarraconaise à chargement d'amphores Dressel 2-4*, Archaeonautica 5 (Paris)

Cotton, H., Lernau, O. and Goren, Y. 1996: 'Fish sauces from Herodian Masada', *J. Roman Archaeol.* 9, 223–8

Cotton, J. 2001a: 'Bibliography of sets of gaming counters', *Lucerna (Roman Finds Group Newsletter)* 22, 12–13

— 2001b: 'Prehistoric and Roman settlement in Reigate Road, Ewell: fieldwork conducted by T.K. Walls, 1946–52', *Surrey Archaeological Collections* 88, 1–42

Couchman, C. 1977: 'Work of Essex County Council Archaeology Section 1977', *Essex Archaeol. Hist.* 9, 60–94

Cra'ster, M.D. 1965: 'Aldwick, Barley: recent work at the Iron Age site', *Proc. Cambridge Antiq. Soc.* 58, 1–11

Cracknell, P.M. 1990: 'A group of marked brooches from Gloucester', *Britannia* 21, 197–206

Craddock, P.T. and Lang J. 1983: 'Spinning, turning and polishing', *Historical Metallurgy* 17(2), 79–81

Creighton, J.D. 1995: 'Visions of power: imagery and symbols in late Iron Age Britain', *Britannia* 26, 285–30

— 2000: *Coins and Power in Late Iron Age Britain* (Cambridge)

— 2006: *Britannia: the Creation of a Roman Province* (London/New York)

Crew, P. 1991: 'The experimental production of prehistoric bar iron', *Historical Metallurgy* 25.1, 21–36

— 1994: 'Currency bars in Great Britain', in M. Mangin (ed.), *La sidérurgie ancienne de l'Est de la France dans son contexte européen: archéologie et archéométrie*, Actes du Colloque de Besançon, 10–13 novembre 1993, Annales littéraires de l'Université de Besançon 536 (Paris), 345–50

— 1995a: 'Aspects of the iron supply', in B.W. Cunliffe, *Danebury, an Iron Age Hillfort in Hampshire 6: a hillfort community in perspective*, CBA Res. Rep. 102 (London), 276–84

— 1995b: 'Currency bars and other forms of trade iron', *Historical Metallurgy Soc. Archaeol. Datasheet* 8

Cronyn, J.M. 1990: *The Elements of Archaeological Conservation* (London)

Croom, A. 2003 'Sexing brooches', *Lucerna, Roman Finds Group Newsletter* 26, 16–19

Crossan, C. 2001: *Archaeological Excavations at the Garrison Sports Pitch, Circular Road North, Colchester, Essex* (Abbey Field), CAT Rep. 138

Crowfoot, E. 1991: 'The textiles', in Stead 1991, 119–25

Crowther, D.R. 1985: 'The other finds', in F. Pryor and C. French, *Archaeology and Environment in the Lower Welland Valley 1*, East Anglian Archaeol. 27 (Cambridge), 163–95

Crummy, N. 2001a: 'Bone-working in Roman Britain: a model for itinerant craftsmen?' in M. Polfer (ed.), *L'artisanat romain: évolutions, continuités et ruptures (Italie et provinces occidentales)*, Monographies Instrumentum 20 (Montagnac), 97–109

— 2001b: 'Nail-cleaners: regionality at the clean edge of Empire', *Lucerna (Roman Finds Group Newsletter)*, 22, 2–6

— 2002: Assessment of the metalwork from the Plant Breeding Institute site, Trumpington, Cambridge, for Cambridgeshire County Council Archaeol. Field Unit

— 2005: 'Small finds, briquetage and daub', in Pooley and Benfield 2005, 52–61

— forthcoming a: 'Small finds', in report on the excavations in Pompeii, Regio I Insula 9, Houses 11–12, by the University of Reading and the British School at Rome

— forthcoming b: 'The brooches', Elms Farm, Heybridge, report for Essex County Council Field Archaeol. Unit

— and Eckardt, H. 2004:	'Regional identities and technologies of the self: nail-cleaners in Roman Britain', *Archaeol. J.* 160 (for 2003), 44–69
Culpeper, N. 1652:	*Culpeper's Complete Herbal* (London/New York; many editions)
Cunliffe, B.W. 1968:	'Early pre-Roman Iron Age communities in eastern England', *Antiq J.* 48, 175–91
— 1971:	*Excavations at Fishbourne 1961–9, 2: the finds* (London)
— 1978:	*Iron Age Communities in Britain*, 2nd edn (London)
— 1987:	*Hengistbury Head, Dorset, 1: the prehistoric and Roman settlement, 3500 BC–AD 500*, Oxford Univ. Comm. Archaeol. Monograph 13 (Oxford)
— 1991:	*Iron Age Communities in Britain*, 3rd edn (London)
— 1992:	'Pits, preconceptions and propitiation in the British Iron Age', *Oxford J. Archaeol.* 11, 69–83
— 1995:	*Danebury: an Iron Age Hillfort in Hampshire, 6: a hillfort community in perspective*, CBA Res. Rep. 102 (York)
— 1997:	*The Ancient Celts* (Oxford/New York)
— and Poole, C. 1991:	*Danebury: an Iron Age Hillfort in Hampshire, 5: The excavations 1979–88: the finds*, CBA Res. Rep. 73 (London)
Curle, J. 1932:	'An inventory of objects of Roman and provincial Roman origin found on sites in Scotland not definitely associated with Roman constructions', *Proc. Soc. Antiq. Scot.* 66, 277–397
Curtis, R.I. 1991:	*Garum and Salsamenta: production and commerce in Materia Medica*, Studies in Ancient Medicine 3 (New York)
Dannell, G. 1985:	'The samian ware – discussion and conclusions', in Niblett 1985, 83
Davies, J.A. and Williamson, T.M. (eds) 1999:	*Land of the Iceni: the Iron Age in Northern East Anglia*, Studies in East Anglian History 4 (Norwich)
Davies, B.J., Richardson, B. and Tomber, R.S. 1994:	*A Dated Corpus of Early Roman Pottery from the City of London*, The Archaeology of Roman London V/CBA Res. Rep. 98 (York)
Déchelette, J. 1914:	*Manuel d'archéologie: second âge du fer* (Paris)
Decker, K.V. 1972:	*Römisches Spielbrett und Spielgerät im Mittelrheinischen Landesmuseum Mainz*, Bonner Hefte zur Vorgeschichte 3, Festschrift O. Kleemann 1 (Bonn)
de Laet, S.J., van Doorselaer, A., Spitaels, P. and Thoen, H. 1972:	*La nécropole gallo-romaine de Blicquy (Hainault-Belgique)* (Bruges)
Delattre, A-L. 1909:	'Tabula lusoria trouvée à Carthage', *Bull. Soc. Nationale Antiquaires France* (1909), 374–9
— 1911:	'Deux tables de jeu trouvé à Carthage', *Revue Tunisienne* 18, 12–19
Desbat, A., Savay-Guerraz, H. and Picon, M. 1990:	'Note sur la découverte d'amphores Dressel 2/4 italiques, tardives, à Saint-Romain-en-Gal (Rhône)', *Gallia* 47, 203–13
de Vries, J. 1961:	*Keltische Religion* (Stuttgart)
Dickinson, B. 1999:	'The samian', in N.R. Brown, *The Archaeology of Ardleigh, Essex: excavations 1955–1980*, East Anglian Archaeol. 90 (Chelmsford), 125
Dickinson, T. 1993:	'An Anglo-Saxon "cunning woman" from Bidford-on-Avon', in M. Carver (ed.), *In Search of Cult: archaeological investigations in honour of Philip Rahtz* (Woodbridge)
Dieudonné-Glad, N. 1999:	'Les objects en fer', in J.-P. Pautreau (ed.), *Antran, un ensemble aristocratique du premier siècle* (Poitiers), 53–6
Dimbleby, G.W. 1985:	*The Palynology of Archaeological Sites* (London)
Doswald, C. 1994:	'Les lingots de fer protohistoriques en Europe occidentale: problématique générale', in M. Mangin (ed.), *La sidérurgie ancienne de l'Est de la France dans son contexte européen: archéologie et archéométrie*, Actes du Colloque de Besançon, 10–13 novembre 1993, Annales littéraires de l'Université de Besançon, 536, (Paris), 333–45
Down, A. and Rule, M. 1971:	*Chichester Excavations 1* (Chichester)
Drury, P.J. 1978:	*Excavations at Little Waltham 1970–71*, Chelmsford Arch. Trust Rep. 1/CBA Res. Rep. 26 (London)
Drury, P.J. and Wickenden, N.P. 1982:	'An early Saxon settlement within the Romano-British small town at Heybridge, Essex', *Med. Archaeol.* 26, 1–40

Dungworth, D. 1996: 'The production of copper alloys in Iron Age Britain', *Proc. Prehist. Soc.* 62, 399–421
Duval, A. 1985: 'Les tombes de l'aristocratie gaulois', *Histoire et archéologie* 98, 36–41
Dyer, D.F. 1976: 'Ravensburgh Castle, Hertfordshire', in D.W. Harding (ed.), *Hillforts: later prehistoric earthworks in Britain and Ireland* (London), 153–9, 421–3

Eckardt, H. 1999: 'The Colchester "child's grave"', *Britannia* 30, 57–89
Eddy, M. 1982: *Kelvedon: the origins and development of a Roman small town*, Essex County Council Occasional Paper 3 (Chelmsford)
Edwards, K.J. 1989: 'The cereal pollen record and early agriculture', in A. Milles, D. Williams and N. Gardner (eds), *The Beginnings of Agriculture*, Symposia of the Association for Environmental Archaeology 8/BAR International Series 496 (Oxford), 113–35
Egan, G. 1998: *The Medieval Household*, Medieval Finds from Excavations in London 6 (London)
Egger, R. 1961: *Die Stadt auf dem Magdalensberg: ein Grosshandelsplatz* (Vienna)
Eggers, H.-J. 1951: *Der romische Import im freien Germanien*, Atlas der Urgeschichte 1 (Hamburg)
— 1966: 'Römische Bronzegefässe in Britannien', *Jahrbuch Römisch-Germanischen Zentralmuseums Mainz* 13, 67–164
Ehmig, U. 1998: 'M – eine Amphore sucht ihren Inhalt', *Carnuntum Jahrbuch* (for 1997), 9–21
— 2003: *Die römischen Amphoren aus Mainz*, Frankfurter Archäologische Schriften 4 (Möhnesee)
Elsdon, S.M. 1975: *Stamped Iron Age Pottery*, BAR British Series 10 (Oxford)
— 1979 'Baked clay objects: Iron Age', in H, Wheeler, 'Excavation at Willington, Derbyshire, 1970–72', *Derbyshire Archaeological Journal* 99, 58–220
— 1992: 'East Midlands scored ware', *Trans. Leics. Archaeol. Hist. Soc.* 66, 83–91
Emery, W.B. 1948: *Nubian Treasure; an account of the discoveries at Ballana and Qustul* (London)
— and Kirwan, L.P. 1938: *The Royal Tombs of Ballana and Qustul* (Cairo)
Engelhardt, C. 1869: *Vimose Fundet. Fynske Mosefund* II (Copenhagen)
Eogan, G. 1974: 'Report on the excavations of some passage graves, unprotected inhumation burials and a settlement site at Knowth, Co. Meath', *Proc. Royal Irish Acad.* 74C, 11–112
Erith, F.H. and Holbert, P.R. 1970: 'The Iron Age "A" farmstead at Vinces Farm, Ardleigh', *Colchester Archaeol. Group Quarterly Bulletin* 13, 1–26
Evans, D.E. 1967: *Gaulish Personal Names: a Study of Some Continental Formations* (Oxford)
Evans, J. 1978: 'Examination of charred "food" residue on a potsherd', in Drury 1978, 118
— 1987a: 'Carbonized residue analysis', in Buckley *et al.* 1987, 41
— 1987b: 'Crucible analysis', in Buckley *et al.* 1987, 39–40
— 1988: 'Graffiti and the evidence of literacy and pottery use in Roman Britain', *Archaeol. J.* 144 (for 1987), 191–204

Faegri, K. and Iversen, J. 1989: *Textbook of Pollen Analysis*, 4th edn, edited by K. Faegri, P.E. Kalande and K. Krzyywinski (Chichester)
Farley, M.E. 1983: 'A mirror burial from Dorton, Buckinghamshire', *Proc. Prehist. Soc.* 49, 269–302
Farrar, R.A.H., Hull, M.R. and Pullinger, J. 2000: 'The Iron Age pottery', in J.A. Alexander and J. Pullinger, 'Roman Cambridge: excavations on Castle Hill 1956–1988', *Proc. Cambridge Antiq. Soc.* 88 (for 1999), 117–30
Fauduet, I. 1993: *Les temples de tradition celtique* (Paris)
Fawn, A.J., Evans, K.A., McMaster, I. and Davies, G.M.R. 1990: *The Red Hills of Essex* (Colchester)
Ferdière, A. and Villard, A. 1993: *La tombe augustéene de Fléré-la-Rivière (Indre)*, Mémoire 2 du Musée d'Argentomarus, Revue Archéologique du Centre, Supplément 7 (Saint-Marcel)
Ferrua, A. 1948: *Tavole lusorie scritte*, Epigraphica 10

— 1964: *Nuove tabulae lusoriae iscritte*, Epigraphica 26
Feugère, M. 1981: 'Decouvertes au quartier de Villeneuve, Fréjus (Var): le mobilier métallique et la parure', *Documents d'Archéologie Meridionale* 4, 137–68
— 1985: *Les fibules en Gaule Méridionale*, Revue Archéologique de Narbonnaise 12 (Paris)
— 1994: *Casques antiques. Les visages de la guerre de Mycènes à l'Antiquité tardive* (Paris)
— 2000: 'Un nouveau dépôt de lingots de fer de La Tène finale: Bretteville-sur-Odon', *Bulletin Instrumentum* 11, 15
— 2002a: *Weapons of the Romans* (Stroud)
— 2002b: 'Le mobilier votif d'un sanctuaire salyen', *Bulletin Instrumentum* 16, 16–17
—, Künzl, E. and Weisser, U. 1985: 'Die Starnadeln von Montbellet (Saône-et-Loire). Ein Beitrag zur antiken und islamischen Augenheilkunde', *Jahrbuch des Römisch-Germanischen Zentralmuseums Mainz* 32, 436–508
—, Künzl, E. and Weisser, U. 1988: *Les aiguilles à cataracte de Montbellet (Saône-et-Loire). Contribution à l'étude de l'ophtalmologie antique et islamique*, Société des Amis des Arts et des Sciences de Tournus 87
Fiches, J-L. 1978: 'Les coupes Drag. 29 en Languedoc-Roussillon', *Figlina* 3, Publications de la S.F.E.C.A.G. (Lyon), 43–70
Fitzpatrick, A.P. 1991: 'Death in a material world: the Late Iron Age and Romano-British cemetery at King Harry Lane, St Albans, Hertfordshire', *Britannia* 22, 323–7
— 1996: '1st-century AD 'Durotrigian' inhumation burial with a decorated Iron Age mirror from Portesham, Dorset', *Proc. Dorset Nat. Hist. Archaeol. Soc.* 118, 51–70
— 1997: *Archaeological Excavations on the Route of the A27 Westhampnett Bypass, West Sussex, 1992, 2: the late Iron Age, Romano-British, and Anglo-Saxon cemeteries*, Wessex Archaeol. Rep. 12 (Salisbury)
— 2000: 'Ritual, sequence and structure in Late Iron Age mortuary practices in North-West Europe', in Pearce *et al.* 2000, 15–29
— and Megaw, J.V.S. 1987: 'Further finds from the Le Catillon hoard', *Proc. Prehist. Soc.* 53, 433–44
Forbes, D.P. 1860: 'Chess among the Welsh', in D. Forbes, *History of Chess* (London), Appendix E
Foster, J. 1986: *The Lexden Tumulus: a re-appraisal of an Iron Age burial from Colchester, Essex*, BAR British Series 156 (Oxford)
— 1999: 'The funerary finds – general discussion', in Niblett 1999, 175–6
— 2000: 'Copper-alloy objects (excluding brooches)', in J.C. Barrett, P.W.M. Freeman and A. Woodward, *Cadbury Castle, Somerset, the Later Prehistoric and Early Historic Archaeology*, EH Archaeol. Rep. 20 (London), 143–7
Fowler, E. 1960: 'The origins and development of the penannular brooch in Europe', *Proc. Prehist. Soc.* 26, 149–77
Fowler, P.J. 1981: 'Later prehistory', in S. Piggott (ed.), *The Agrarian History of England and Wales. Vol. 1.1. Prehistory* (Cambridge), 63–298
— 2002: *Farming in the First Millennium AD: British agriculture between Julius Caesar and William the Conqueror* (Cambridge)
Fox, C. 1958: *Pattern and Purpose: a survey of early Celtic art in Britain* (Cardiff)
Foy, D. and Nenna, M-D. 2001: *Tout feu, tout sable* (Marseilles)
France, N.E. and Gobel, B.M. 1985: *The Romano-British temple at Harlow* (Gloucester)
Freed, J. 1989: 'Late stamped Dressel 2/4 amphoras from a deposit dated post 200 A.D. at villa site 10 on the Via Gabina', in M. Lenoir, D. Manacorda and C. Panella (eds), *Amphores romaines et histoire économique: dix ans de recherche*, Collection de l'École Française de Rome 114 (Rome), 616–17
Freestone, I.C. 1990: 'Studies of the Portland Vase', *J. Glass Studies* 32, 103–107
—, Gorin-Rosen, Y. and Hughes, M.J. 2000: 'Primary glass from Israel and the production of glass in antiquity and the early Islamic period' in M.D. Nenna (ed.), *La route du verre*, Travaux de la Maison de l'Orient Méditerranéen (Lyon), 65–83

Fröhlich, S. (ed.) 2001:	*Gold für die Ewigkeit. Das germanische Fürstengrab von Gommern*, Begleitband zur Sonderausstellung vom 18.10.2000 bis 28.02.2001 im Landesmuseum für Vorgeschichte Halle (Saale), 2nd edn (Halle/Saale)
Fromols, J. 1938:	'L'atelier céramique de Sept-Saulx (Marne)', *Bull. Soc. Archéol. Champenoise* 32, 49–98
Fryer, V. 2003:	'Charred plant macrofossils and other remains', in M. Hinman, *A Late Iron Age Farmstead and Romano-British Site at Haddon, Peterborough*, BAR British Series 358/Cambridgeshire County Council Archaeol. Field Unit Monograph 2 (Oxford), 133–5
Fulford, M. and Timby, J. 2000:	*Late Iron Age and Roman Silchester*, Britannia Monograph 15 (London)
Gabriel, I. 1985:	'Brettspiel in Oldenburg vor tausend Jahren', in K. Ehlers (ed), *750 Jahre Stadtrecht Oldenburg in Holstein* (Oldenburg), 207–220
Gaffney, V. and Tingle, M. 1989:	*The Maddle Farm Project*, BAR British Series 200 (Oxford)
Gage, J. 1840:	'An account of further discoveries of Roman sepulchral relics at the Bartlow Hills', *Archaeologia* 28, 1–6
Gale, R. 1996:	'Wood identification' in R.J. Williams, P.J. Hart and A.T.L. Williams, *Wavendon Gate, a late Iron Age and Roman settlement in Milton Keynes*, Buckinghamshire Archaeol. Soc. Monograph 10 (Aylesbury), 260–6
Gale, R. 1999:	'Report on charcoal samples from the burial pit and funerary shaft', in Niblett 1999, 388–93
Gantz, J. 1981:	*Early Irish Myths and Sagas*, trans. J. Gantz (London)
Gebhard, R. 1991:	*Die Fibeln aus dem oppidum von Manching*, Die Ausgrabungen in Manching 14 (Stuttgart)
Geissner, V. 1904:	*Die im Mainzer Museum befindlichen Sigillata-Gefässe der nachaugusteischen Zeit und ihrer Stempel* (Mainz)
Gerlach, G. 1976:	*Das Graberfeld 'Die Motte' bei Lebach*, Saarbrucker Beitrage zur Altertumskunde 16 (Bonn)
Gibson, A. 1995:	'First impressions: a review of Peterborough Ware in Wales', in I. Kinnes, and G. Varndell (eds), *'Unbaked Urns of Rudely Shape', Essays on British and Irish Pottery for Ian Longworth*, Oxbow Monograph 55 (Oxford), 23–40
— and Kinnes, I. 1997:	'On the urns of a dilemma: radiocarbon and the Peterborough problem', *Oxford J. Archaeol.* 16, 65–72
Gilson, A.G. 1981:	'A group of Roman surgical and medical instruments from Corbridge', *Saalburg Jahrbuch* 37, 5–9
— 1983:	'A group of Roman surgical and medical instruments from Cramond, Scotland', *Medizinhistorisches J.* 18, 384–93
Goethert, K. 1989:	'Zur Körper- und Schönheitspflege in frührömischer Zeit', in A. Haffner, *Gräbe – Spiegel des Lebens*, Schriftenreihe des Rheinischen Landesmuseums Trier 2 (Mainz am Rhein), 275–88
Goethert-Polaschek, K. 1977:	*Katalog der Römischen Gläser des Rheinischen Landesmuseums Trier* (Mainz am Rhein)
— 1985:	*Katalog der romischen Lampen des Rheinischen Landesmuseums Trier*, Trierer Grabungen und Forschungen 15 (Mainz)
Goldstein, S.M. 1979:	*Pre-Roman and early Roman glass in the Corning Museum of Glass* (Corning, New York State).
Green, C. 1949:	'The Birdlip early Iron Age burials: a review', *Proc. Prehist. Soc.* 15, 188–90
Green, M. 1997:	*Celtic Goddesses* (London)
Greep, S.J. 2002:	'Bone styli', *Lucerna (Roman Finds Group Newsletter)* 24, 11–12
Gregory, A.K. 1992:	*Excavations in Thetford, 1980–82, Fison Way 1*, East Anglian Archaeol. 53 (Dereham)
— 1995:	'The Iron Age pottery', in R. Rickett, *The Anglo-Saxon cemetery at Spong Hill, North Elmham; Part VII: the Iron Age, Roman and early Saxon settlement*, East Anglian Archaeol. Rep. 73 (Dereham), 90–4
Grieve, M. 1992:	*A Modern Herbal*, edited and introduced by C.F. Leyel (London; first published 1931, revised 1973)

Grose, D.F., 1973:	'Roman glass of the first century AD. A dated deposit of glassware from Cosa, Italy', *Annales du 6e Congrès de l'Association Internationale pour l'Histoire du Verre* 31–52
— 1977:	'Early blown glass: the western evidence', *J. Glass Studies* 19, 9–29
— 1989:	*The Toledo Museum of Art: early ancient glass* (New York)
Guichard, V. and Perrin, F. (eds) 2002:	*L'aristocratie celte à la fin de l'âge du Fer, (du IIe siècle avant J.-C. au Ier siècle après J.-C.)*, Collection Bibracte 5 (Glux-en-Glenne)
Guido, M. 1978:	*The Glass Beads of the Prehistoric and Roman Periods in Britain and Ireland* (London)
Gwilt, A. and Haselgrove, C.C. (eds) 1997:	*Reconstructing Iron Age Societies: new approaches to the British Iron Age*, Oxbow Monograph 71 (Oxford)
Haffner, A. 1971, 1974, 1978:	*Das Keltische-Römische Gräberfeld von Wederath-Belginum*, 1 (1971), 2 (1974), 3 (1978), Trierer Grabungen und Forschungen 6 (Mainz)
— and Joachim, H. E. 1985:	'Die keltischen Wagengräber der Mittelrheingruppe', *Keltski Voz*, 71–87
Hall, R.A. 1984:	*The Viking Dig* (London)
Hamilton, S. 1998:	'Using elderly databases: Iron Age pit deposits at the Caburn, East Sussex, and related sites', *Sussex Archaeol. Collections* 136, 23–39
Hamilton, S.D. 1988:	'Fabric analysis of selected first millennium BC pottery types. Earlier first millennium BC pottery from Rectory Road and Baker Street', in Wilkinson 1988, 75–80
Hancocks, A. 2003:	'Little Paxton pottery', in A.M. Gibson (ed.), *Prehistoric pottery: people, pattern and purpose*, BAR International Series 1156/Prehistoric Ceramics Research Group Occasional Publication 4 (Oxford), 71–110
Harborne, J.B., Baxter, H. and Moss, G.P. (eds) 1999:	*Phytochemical Dictionary: a handbook of bioactive compounds from plants* (London)
Harden, D.B. 1947:	'The glass', in Hawkes and Hull 1947, 287–307
— 1961:	'Glass', in Clifford 1961, 199–201
— 1967:	Report on the gaming-pieces, in Stead 1967, 14–16
— and Price, J. 1971:	'The glass', in Cunliffe 1971, 317–68
—, Painter, K.S., Pinder-Wilson, R.H. and Tait, H. 1968:	*Masterpieces of Glass* (London)
Härke, H. 1989:	'Early Anglo-Saxon weapon burials: frequencies, distributions and weapon combinations', in S.C. Hawkes (ed.), *Weapons and Warfare in Anglo-Saxon England*, Oxford Univ. Comm. Archaeol. Monograph 21 (Oxford), 49–61
Hartmann, G., Kappel, I.,G Grote, K. and Arndt, B. 1997:	'Chemistry and technology of prehistoric glass from Lower Saxony and Hesse', *J. Archaeol. Science* 24, 547–59
Haselgrove, C.C. 1997:	'Iron Age brooch deposition and chronology', in Gwilt and Haselgrove 1997, 51–72
—, Armit, I., Champion, T.C., Creighton, J.D., Gwilt, A., Hill, J.D., Hunter, F. and Woodward, A.B. 2001:	*Understanding the British Iron Age: an agenda for action* (Salisbury)
Hassall, M.W.C. 1982:	'Inscriptions and graffiti', in G.C. Boon and M.W.C. Hassall, *Report on the Excavations at Usk 1965–1976, 3. The coins, inscriptions and graffiti* (Cardiff), 47–58
— 1986:	'Graffiti', in Stead and Rigby 1986, 189–90
Hassall, M.W.C. and Tomlin, R.S.O. 1984:	'Roman Britain in 1983. II. Inscriptions', *Britannia* 15, 333–56
— 1993:	'Roman Britain in 1992. II. Inscriptions', *Britannia* 24, 310–22
Hatt, J-J. and Roualet, P. 1977:	'La chronologie de La Tène en Champagne', *Revue Archéologique de l'Est et Centre-Est* 28, 7–36
Hattatt, R.A. 1985:	*Iron Age and Roman Brooches* (Oxford)
— 1987:	*Brooches of Antiquity* (Oxford)
— 1989:	*Ancient Brooches and other Artefacts* (Oxford)
— and Webster, G. 1985:	'New light on "Adlocutio" repoussé disc brooches', *Antiq. J.* 65, 434–7

Havis, R. and Brooks, H. 2004: *Excavations at Stansted Airport, 1986–91, 1: Prehistoric and Romano-British*, East Anglian Archaeol. 107 (Chelmsford)

Hawkes, C.F.C. 1962: 'Early Iron Age pottery from Linford, Essex: notes on the forms and ornament', in Barton 1962, 83–7

— 1968: 'New thoughts on the Belgae', *Antiquity* 42, 6–16

— 1980: 'From Caesar, and the century before him, to the Essex of Claudius', in D.G. Buckley (ed.), *Archaeology in Essex to AD 1500*, CBA Res. Rep. 34, 55–8

— and Dunning, G.C. 1930: 'The Belgae of Gaul and Britain', *Archaeol. J.* 87, 150–335

— and Hull, M. R. 1947: *Camulodunum*, Soc. Antiq. London Res. Rep. 14 (London)

Hedges, J.D. 1977: 'Broom Wood, Stock', in C.R. Couchman, 'Work of Essex County Council Archaeology Section 1977', *Essex Archaeol. Hist.* 9 (1977), 75–7

Hedges, R.E.M. and Salter, C.J. 1979: 'Source determination of iron currency bars', *Archaeometry* 21(2), 161–75

Helmfrid, S. 2000: *Hnefatafl – the Strategic Board Game of the Vikings. An overview of rules and variations of the game, version 2*, May 1, 2000, http://hem.bredband.net/b512479

Hencken, H. O'Neill 1933: 'A gaming board of the Viking age', *Acta Archaeol.* 4, 85–104

— 1937: 'Ballinderry Crannog No. 1', *Proc. Royal Irish Acad.* 43C, 103–240

Henderson, A.M. 1949: 'Small objects in metal, bone, glass etc.', in J.P. Bushe-Fox, *Fourth Report on the Excavations of the Roman fort at Richborough, Kent* (London), 106–60

Henderson, Janet 1986: 'The human bones', in Stead and Rigby 1986, Appendix IV, 390–6

Henderson, Julian 1985: 'The raw materials of early glass production', *Oxford J Archaeol.* 4, 267–91

— 1988: 'Electron probe microanalysis of mixed-alkali glasses', *Archaeometry* 30(1), 77–91

— 1991: 'Industrial specialization in Late Iron Age Britain and Europe', *Archaeol. J.* 148, 104–48

— 1996: 'Analysis of ancient glasses part 2: luxury Roman and early medieval glasses, *J. Materials* 48(2), 62–4

— and Warren, S. 1981: 'X-Ray Fluorescence analyses of Iron Age glass: Beads from Meare and Glastonbury Lake Villages', *Archaeometry* 23(1), 83–94

Hesnard, A. 1977: 'Note sur un atelier d'amphores Dr.1 et Dr.2-4 près de Terracine', *Mélanges de l'Ecole Française de Rome (Antiquité)* 89, 157–68

— 1980: 'Un dépôt augustéen d'amphores à La Longarina, Ostie', in J.H. D'Arms and E.C. Kopff (eds), *The Seaborne Commerce of Ancient Rome: studies in archaeology and history*, Memoirs of the American Academy in Rome 36 (Rome), 141–56

—, Ricq, M., Arthur, P.R., Picon, M. and Tchernia, A. 1989: 'Aires de production des gréco-italiques et des Dr. 1', in M. Lenoir, D. Manacorda and C. Panella (eds), *Amphores romaines et histoire économique: dix ans de recherche*, Collection de l'École Française de Rome 114 (Rome), 21–65

Hilgers, W. 1969: *Lateinische Gefäßnamen*, Beihefte der Bonner Jahrbücher 31 (Düsseldorf)

Hill, J. D. 1995: *Ritual and rubbish in the Iron Age of Wessex: a study on the formation of a specific archaeological record*, BAR British Series 242 (Oxford)

— 1999a: 'Later prehistoric pottery', in C. Evans, 'The Lingwood wells: waterlogged remains from a first millennium BC settlement at Cottenham, Cambridgeshire', *Proc. Cambridge Antiq. Soc.* 87 (for 1998), 23–6

— 1999b: 'Settlement, landscape and regionality: Norfolk and Suffolk in the pre-Roman Iron Age of Britain and beyond', in Davies and Williamson 1999, 185–207

— 2002: 'Just about the potter's wheel? Using, making and depositing middle and later Iron Age pots in East Anglia', in Woodward and Hill 2002, 143–60

— and Horne, L. 2003: 'Iron Age and early Roman pottery', in C. Evans, *Power and Island Communities: excavations at the Wardy Hill Ringwork, Coveney, Ely*, East Anglian Archaeology Report 103 (Cambridge), 145–84

—, Evans, C. and Alexander, M. 1999: 'The Hinxton rings – a late Iron Age cemetery at Hinxton, Cambridgeshire, with a reconsideration of northern Aylesford-Swarling distributions', *Proc. Prehist. Soc.* 65, 243–73

—, Spence, A.J., La Niece, S., and Worrall, S. 2004: 'The Winchester Hoard: a find of unique Iron Age gold jewellery from southern England', *Antiq. J.* 84, 1–22

Hingley, R. 1990: 'Iron Age "currency bars": The archaeological and social context', *Archaeol. J.* 147, 91–117

— 1997: 'Iron, ironworking and regeneration: a study of the symbolic meaning of metalworking in Iron Age Britain', in Gwilt and Haselgrove 1997, 9–18

— 2005: 'Iron Age currency bars: items of exchange in a ritual context?', in C. Haselgrove and D. Wigg (eds), *Ritual and Iron Age Coinage. Studien zu Fundmunzen der Antike* (Mainz), 183–205

Hinman, M. 2003: *Bob's Wood: the story so far; an introduction to the Hinchingbrooke excavations*, Cambridgeshire County Council Archaeological Field Unit report

Hobbs, R. 1996: *British Iron Age Coins in the British Museum* (London)

Hodges, H. 1976: *Artifacts: an introduction to early materials and technology* (London)

Hodson, F.R. 1962: 'Some pottery from Eastbourne, the "Marnians" and the pre-Roman Iron Age in southern England', *Proc. Prehist. Soc.* 28, 140–55

Holwerda, J.H. 1941: *Die Belgische Waar in Nijmegen* (Nijmegen)

Horn, H.G. 1989: 'Se per mi misit, nil nisi feret. Ein römischer Spielturm aus Froitzheim', *Bonner Jahrbücher* 189, 139–60

Huelsen, C. 1904: 'Neue Inschriften', *Röm. Mitteilungen* 19, 142–53

Hull, M.R. 1942: 'Note on an early Claudian burial found at Colchester', *Antiq. J.* 22, 59–65

— 1958: *Roman Colchester*, Soc. Antiq. London. Res. Rep. 20 (London)

— 1961: 'The brooches at Bagendon', in Clifford 1961, 167–85

— 1963: 'Roman gazetteer', in W.R. Powell (ed.), *The Victoria History of the Counties of England: A history of Essex III* (London), 35–204

— 1968: 'The brooches', in B. Cunliffe, *Fifth Report on the Excavations of the Roman Fort at Richborough, Kent* (London), 74–93

— 1971: 'The brooches', in Cunliffe 1971, 100–7

— forthcoming: *Brooches in pre-Roman and Roman Britain*, edited by G.M. Simpson, N. Crummy and B. Blance

— and Hawkes, C.F.C. 1987: *Corpus of Ancient Brooches in Britain: pre-Roman bow brooches*, BAR British Series 168 (Oxford)

Hunter, F. 1996: 'Recent Roman Iron Age metalwork finds from Fife and Tayside', *Tayside and Fife Archaeological Journal* 2, 113–25

Hurley, D.W. 2001: *Suetonius: Divus Claudius* (Cambridge)

Ihm, M. 1890: 'Römische Spieltafeln', *Bonner Studien: Aufsatze aus der Altertumswissenschaft Reinhard Kekulé* (Berlin), 223–39

Isings, C., 1957: *Roman Glass from Dated Finds* (Groningen)

Israeli, Y. 1991: 'The invention of blowing', in Newby and Painter 1991, 46–55

Jackson, R. 1985: 'Cosmetic sets from Late Iron Age and Roman Britain', *Britannia* 16, 165–192

— 1986: 'A set of Roman medical instruments from Italy', *Britannia* 17, 119–67

— 1988a: *Doctors and Diseases in the Roman Empire* (London)

— 1988b: 'Ironwork', in Potter and Trow 1988, 70–8

— 1990a: *Camerton: the late Iron Age and early Roman Metalwork* (London)

— 1990b: 'Roman doctors and their instruments: recent research into ancient practice', *J. Roman Archaeol.* 3, 5–27

— 1993a: 'The function and manufacture of Romano-British cosmetic grinders: two important new finds from London', *Antiq. J.* 73, 165–9

— 1993b: 'Roman medicine: the practitioners and their practices', in W. Haase (ed.), *Aufstieg und Niedergang der römischen Welt (ANRW)*, II, 37, 1, 79–101 (Berlin/New York)

— 1994: 'The surgical instruments, appliances and equipment in Celsus' *De medicina*' in G. Sabbah and P. Mudry (eds), *La médecine de Celse: Aspects historiques, scientifiques et littéraires*, Mémoires XIII (Saint-Étienne), 167–209

— 1995: 'The composition of Roman medical *instrumentaria* as an indicator of medical practice: a provisional assessment', in P.J. van der Eijk, H.F.J.

	Horstmanshoff and P.H. Schrijvers (eds), *Ancient Medicine in its Sociocultural Context*, Clio Medica 27/28 (Leiden), 189–207
— 1997a:	'Medical instruments in the Roman World', *Medicina nei Secoli –Arte e Scienza* 9/2, 223–48
— 1997b:	'An ancient British medical kit from Stanway, Essex', *The Lancet* 350, 1471–3
— 1997c:	'Ancient British medical kit found', *Minerva* 8 (5), 3–5
— 1998:	'Early surgical kit from Stanway', *Colchester Archaeol.* 11, 8–10
— 2002:	'Roman surgery: the evidence of the instruments', in R. Arnott (ed.), *The Archaeology of Medicine*, BAR International Series 1046 (Oxford), 87–94
— 2003:	'The domus "del chirugo" at Rimini: an interim account of the medical assemblage', *J. Roman Archaeol.* 16, 312–21
— 2005:	'Holding on to health? Bone surgery and instrumentation in the Roman Empire', in H. King (ed.), *Health in Antiquity* (London), 97–119
— and Thuillier, F. 1999:	'A British cosmetic set (nécessaire à fard) from Thérouanne (Pas de Calais, France)', *Bulletin Instrumentum* 9, 23–4
Jacobi, R.M. 1996:	'Late Upper Paleolithic and Mesolithic in Essex', in Bedwin 1996, 10–14
James, S. and Rigby, V. 1997:	*Britain and the Celtic Iron Age* (London)
Jenkins, F. 1957:	'The rôle of the dog in Romano-Gaulish religion', *Latomus* 16, 60–76
de Jersey, P. 2001:	'Cunobelin's silver', *Britannia* 32, 1–44
— 2002:	'AGR, and life after Cunobelin', *Chris Rudd Celtic Coins Sales Catalogue* 64, 5–8
Johns, C., 1982	*Sex or Symbol* (London)
— 1996:	*The Jewellery of Roman Britain, Celtic and Classical Traditions* (London)
Jones, G. and Jones, T. 1970:	*The Mabinogion*, trans. G. Jones and T. Jones (London/New York)
Jones, M.U. and Jones, W.T. 1973:	'The Mucking excavations 1972', *J. Thurrock Local Hist. Soc.* 16, 32–8
Jope, E.M. 2000:	*Early Celtic Art in the British Isles* (Oxford)
Jordan, D., Haddon-Reece, D. and Bayliss, A. 1994:	*Radiocarbon Dates from Samples funded by English Heritage and dated before 1981* (London)
Karadimitrova, K. 2002:	'Schildbuckel mit eingepunzten Inschriften von Karaaga? (Bulgarien)', *Bulletin Instrumentum* 15, 22
Kenyon, R. 1987:	'The Claudian coinage', in *CAR* 4, 24–41
— 1992:	'The Claudian coins from Culver Street Phase 2 and the Gilberd School', in *CAR* 6, 295–307
Kilbride-Jones, H.E. 1980:	*Celtic Craftsmanship in Bronze* (London)
Kimmig, W. 1981:	'Ein Grabfund der jüngeren Urnenfelderzeit mit Eisenschwert von Singen am Hohentwiel', *Festschrift Hartwig Zürn. Fundberichte aus Baden-Württemberg* 6, 91–119
— and Rest, W. 1954:	'Ein Fürstengrab der späten Hallstattzeit von Kappel am Rhein', *Jahrbuch des Römisch-Germanischen Zentralmuseums* 1, 179–216
King, A. and Soffe, G. 2001:	'Internal organisation and deposition at the Iron Age temple on Hayling Island, Hampshire', in J. Collis (ed.), *Society and Settlement in Iron Age Europe* (Sheffield), 111–24.
Knowles, M. and May, J. 1996:	'Catalogue of silver and copper-alloy artefacts', in May 1996, 270–85
Kosinna, G. 1922:	*Das Reitergrab von Kommerau in Westpreussen*, Mannus 14
Krämer, W. 1971:	'Silberne Fibelpaare aus dem letztem vorchristlichen Jahrhundert', *Germania* 49, 111–32
Krug, A. 1985:	*Heilkunst und Heilkult: Medizin in der Antike* (Munich)
— 1993:	'Römische Skalpelle. Herstellungstechnische Anmerkungen', *Medizinhistorisches J.* 28, 93–100
Krüger, T. 1982:	'Das Brett- und Würfelspiel der Spätlatènezeit und römischen Kaiserzeit im freien Germanien', *Neue Ausgrabungen und Forschungen in Niedersachsen* 15, 135–324
Künzl, E. 1983a:	*Medizinische Instrumente aus Sepulkralfunden der römischen Kaiserzeit*. Unter Mitarbeit von Franz Josef Hassel und Susanna Künzl. Kunst und Altertum am Rhein 115 (Cologne/Bonn)

— 1983b:	'Eine Spezialität römischer Chirurgen: die Lithotomie', *Archäol. Korrespondenzblatt* 13, 487–93
— 1988:	'Archäologische Beiträge zur Medizingeschichte: Methoden-Ergebnisse-Ziele', *Études de médecine romaine. Mémoires VIII* (Saint-Étienne), 61–79
— 1989:	'Die Zahnarztgräber 1600 und 1539' in A. Haffner, *Gräber – Spiegel des Lebens*, Schriftenreihe des Rheinischen Landesmuseums Trier 2 ((Mainz), 289–98
— 1995:	'Medizin der Kelten. Ein Archäologischer Forschungsbericht', in R. Bedon and P. M. Martin (eds), *Mélanges Raymond Chevallier, 2: Histoire et archéologie* (Tours), 221–39
— 1996	'Forschungsbericht zu den antiken medizinischen instrumenten', in W. Haase and H. Temporini (eds), *Aufstieg und Niedergang der römischen Welt (ANRW)*, II 37.3 (Berlin/New York), 2433–639
— 2002:	*Medizinische Instrumente der römischen Kaiserzeit im Römisch-Germanischen Zentralmuseum*, Kataloge vor- und frühgeschichtlicher Altertümer 28 (Mainz/Bonn)
Lambot, B. 1993:	'Habitats, nécropoles et organisation du territoire à La Tène finale en Champagne septentrionale', in A. Ferdière (ed.), *Monde des morts, monde des vivants en Gaule rurale* (Tours), 121–51
— 2002:	'Noblesse, aristocratie et signes extérieurs de richesse à La Tène finale en Champagne', in Guichard and Perrin 2002, 87–108
—, Friboulet, M. and Méniel, P. 1994:	*Le site protohistorique d'Acy-Romance (Ardennes) – II. Les nécropoles dans leur contexte régional (Thugney-Trugny et tombes aristocratiques) 1986–1988–1989*, Mémoire de la Soc. Archéol. Champenoise 8 (Reims)
Lambrick, G. 1984:	'Pitfalls and possibilities in Iron Age pottery studies – experiences in the Upper Thames Valley', in B.W. Cunliffe and D. Miles (eds), *Aspects of the Iron Age in Central Southern Britain*, University of Oxford Comm. for Archaeol. Monograph 2 (Oxford), 162–77
— and Robinson, M. 1979:	*Iron Age and Roman Riverside Settlements at Farmoor, Oxfordshire*, Oxfordshire Archaeol. Unit Rep. 2, CBA Res. Rep. 32 (London)
Lamer, H. 1927:	'Lucaria tabula' in Pauly-Wissowa, *Realencyklopädie des classischen Altertums* XIII.2 (Stuttgart), 1900ff
Lavender, N. 1991:	'A Late Iron Age burial enclosure from Maldon Hall Farm, Essex: excavations 1989', *Proc. Prehist. Soc.* 57, 203–9
Laver, P.G. 1927:	'The excavation of a tumulus at Lexden, Colchester', *Archaeologia* 76, 241–54
Le Cloirec, G. 2001:	*Les bronzes antiques de Corseul (Côtes-d'Armor)*, Monographies Instrumentum 18 (Montagnac)
Legge, A., Payne, S. and Rowley-Conwy, P. 1998:	'The study of food remains in prehistoric Britain', in J. Bayley (ed.), *Science in Archaeology: an agenda for the future* (London), 89–94
Lethbridge, T.C. 1953:	'Burial of an Iron Age warrior at Snailwell', *Proc. Cambridge Antiq. Soc.* 47, 25–37
Ling, R. 1991:	*Roman Painting* (Cambridge)
Liou, B. 1993:	'Inscriptions peintes sur amphores de Narbonne (Port-la-Nautique)', *Archaeonautica* 11, 131–48
— and Pomey, P. 1985:	'Direction des recherches archéologiques sous-marines', *Gallia* 43, 547–76
van Lith, S.M.E., 1978–79:	'Römisches Glas aus Valkenburg Z.H.', *Oudeidkundige mededelingen uit het Rijksmuseum van Oudheden te Leiden* 59–60, 1–150
Lloyd-Morgan, G. 1977:	'Mirrors in Roman Britain', in J. Munby and M. Henig (eds), *Roman Life and Art in Britain*, BAR British Series 41 (Oxford), 231–52
— 1981:	*Description of the Collections in the Rijksmuseum G.M. Kam at Nijmegen, IX: the mirrors* (Nijmegen)
Loeschcke, S. 1919:	*Lampen aus Vindonissa* (Zurich)
Lucan (M. Annaeus Lucanus)	*Pharsalia*, translated by S.H. Braund (Oxford; 1992)
Lyons, A. and Percival, S. 2000:	'Pottery', in S. Bates, 'Excavations at Quidney Farm, Saham Toney, Norfolk 1995', *Britannia* 31, 211–22

Macdonald, P. 2000:	'The ironwork', in J.C. Barrett, P.W.M. Freeman and A. Woodward, *Cadbury Castle, Somerset, the later Prehistoric and early Historic Archaeology*, EH Archaeol. Rep. 20 (London), 122–32
MacGregor, A. 1976:	*Finds from a Roman Sewer System and an Adjacent Building in Church Street*, The Archaeology of York AY 17/1 (London)
Mackreth, D. 1989a:	'Selection of first century brooches from Piddington', in R.M. Friendship-Taylor and D.E. Friendship-Taylor, *Iron Age and Roman Piddington*, Upper Nene Valley Archaeol. Soc. Fascicule I (Piddington), 24–6
— 1989b:	'The brooches', in Partridge 1989, 129–34
— 1992:	'Brooches of copper alloy and of iron', in Gregory 1992, 120–9
— 1994:	'The brooches', in R.J. Williams and R.J. Zeepvat, *Bancroft, a late Bronze Age/Iron Age Settlement, Roman Villa, and Temple Mausoleum*, Bucks Archaeol. Soc. Monograph 7 (Aylesbury), 285–303
— 1995:	'Pre-Roman and Roman brooches', in K. Blockley, M. Blockley, P. Blockley, S.S. Frere and S. Stow, *Excavations in the Marlowe Car Park and Surrounding Areas*, The Archaeology of Canterbury 5 (Canterbury), 955–82
MacWhite, E. 1946:	'Early Irish Board Games', *Eigse: A Journal of Irish Studies* V, 25–35
Major, H. 1983:	'Iron Age triangular clay loomweights', in D. Priddy, 'Work of the Essex County Council Archaeology Section, 1981' in *Essex Archaeol. Hist.* 14 (for 1982), 117–22
— 1987:	'Fired clay', in Buckley *et al.* 1987, 39
— 1988:	'Baked and fired clay objects' in Wilkinson 1988, 94–7
— 1994:	'Small finds reports', in M. Medlycott, 'Iron Age and Roman material from Birchanger, near Bishops Stortford; excavations at Woodside Industrial park, 1992' *Essex Archaeol. Hist.* 25, 42–3
— 1998a:	'Objects of baked clay', in Wallis and Waughman 1998, 160–3
— 1998b:	'Fired clay', in Carter 1998, 106–10
— 1998c:	'Metalwork', in Carter 1998, 78–83
— 1999:	'Fired clay', in N.R. Brown, *The Archaeology of Ardleigh, Essex: excavations 1955–80*, East Anglian Archaeol. 90 (Chelmsford), 157
— 2004:	'Metalwork', in Havis and Brooks 2004, *passim*
Malim, T. and Hines, J. 1998:	*The Anglo-Saxon Cemetery at Edix Hill (Barrington A)*, Cambridgeshire, CBA Res. Rep. 112 (York)
Manley, J. and Rudkin, D.J. 2005:	'A pre-AD 43 ditch at Fishbourne Roman palace, Chichester', *Britannia* 36, 55–99
Manning, W.H. 1985:	*Catalogue of the Romano-British Iron Tools, Fittings and Weapons in the British Museum* (London)
Manning, W.H., with Price, J. and Webster, J. 1995:	*The Roman Small Finds*, Report on the excavations at Usk 1965–1976, 7 (Cardiff)
Mansel, A.M. 1975:	*Bericht über die Ausgrabungen und Untersuchungen in Pamphylien in den Jahren 1957-1972*, Archäol. Anzeiger 90
Marcadal, Y. 2001:	*Un complex cultuel dédié à Jupiter, 1er-IIIe siècle après J.-C., Calès-Mézin* (Lot-et-Garonne)
Marganne-Mélard, M-H. 1987:	'Les instruments chirurgicaux de l'Égypte gréco-romaine', in *Archéologie et médecine: Actes du colloque 23–24–25 octobre 1986*, CNRS, Mus. Arch. d'Antibes (Juan-les-Pins), 403–12
Marlière, É. 2001:	'Le tonneau en Gaul romaine', *Gallia* 58, 181–201
— 2002:	*L'outre et le tonneau dans l'Occident romain*, Monographies Instrumentum 22 (Montagnac)
Marquardt, J. and Mau, A. 1886:	*Das Privatleben der Römer* 2, 2nd edn (Leipzig; reprinted 1975, Darmstadt)
Martin, E.A. 1988:	*Burgh: the Iron Age and Roman Enclosure*, East Anglian Archaeol. 40 (Ipswich)
— 1993:	*Settlements on Hill-tops: seven prehistoric sites in Suffolk*, East Anglian Archaeol. Rep. 65 (Ipswich)
— 1999:	'Suffolk in the Iron Age', in Davies and Williamson 1999, 44–99
Martin, Th. and Ruffat, H. 1998:	'Un dépôt de lingots de fer du début de La Tène III à Montans (Tarn)', in M. Feugère and V. Serneels (eds), *Recherches sur l'économie du fer en*

	Méditerranée nord-occidentale, Monographies Instrumentum 4 (Montagnac), 110–15
Martin-Kilcher, S. 1994:	*Die Römischen Amphoren aus Augst und Kaiseraugst. 2: Die Amphoren für Win, Fischsauce, Südfrüchte (Gruppen 2–24) und Gesamtauswertung* (Augst)
Mass, J.L., Stone, R.E. and Wypyski, M.T. 1998:	'The mineralogical and metallurgical origins of Roman opaque colored glasses', in P. McCray (ed.), *The Prehistory and History of Glassmaking Technology III*, Ceramics and Civilisation 8, 121–44
May, J. 1996:	*Dragonby: report on excavations at an Iron Age and Romano-British settlement in North Lincolnshire*, Oxbow Monograph 61 (Oxford)
May, R. 1991:	*Jouer dans l'Antiquité*, Catalogue of the exhibition, Marseille 1991/92 (Marseille)
May, T. 1916:	*The Pottery Found at Silchester* (Reading)
— 1928 (and 1930):	*Catalogue of the Roman Pottery in the Colchester and Essex Museum* (Cambridge)
Mays, S.A. and Steele, J. 1999:	'The human bone', in Niblett 1999, 307–23
McKinley, J.I. 1993:	'Bone fragment size and weights of bone from modern British cremations and the implications for the interpretation of archaeological cremations', *International J. Osteoarchaeol.* 3, 283–7
— 1997:	'The cremated human bone from burial and cremation-related contexts', in Fitzpatrick 1997, 55–73
— 2000:	'Phoenix rising: aspects of cremation in Roman Britain', in Pearce *et al.* 2000, 38–44
McLees, C. 1990:	*Games People Played. Gaming-pieces, boards and dice from excavations in the medieval town of Trondheim, Norway*, Meddelelser 24
McPeake, J.C. and Moore, C.N. 1978:	'A bronze skillet handle from Chester and other vessels from the British Isles', *Britannia* 9, 331–4
Meaney, A.L. 1981:	*Anglo-Saxon Amulets and Curing Stones*, BAR British Series 96 (Oxford)
Meates, G.W. 1979:	*The Roman Villa at Lullingstone, Kent* I (Ashford/London)
— 1987:	*The Roman Villa at Lullingstone, Kent, II: the wall paintings and finds* (Maidstone)
Meeks, N. 1995:	'A technical study of Roman bronze mirrors', *Acta of the 12th international congress on ancient bronzes, Nijmegen* (Nijmegen), 179–93
Méniel, P. 2002:	'La chasse en Gaule, une activité aristocratique?', in Guichard and Perrin 2002, 223–30
Merrifield, R. 1987:	*The Archaeology of Ritual and Magic* (London)
Metzler, J. 1977:	'Beiträge zur Archäologie des Titelberges', *Publications de la Section Historique de l'Institut G.-D. de Luxembourg* 91 (Luxembourg), 13–116
— 1984:	'Treverische Reitergräber von Goeblingen-Nospelt', in *Trier Augustusstadt der Treverer*, Rheinisches Landesmuseum Trier exhibition catalogue (Mayence), 87–99
— 2002:	'Réflexions sur les sépultures aristocratiques en pays trévire', in Guichard and Perrin 2002, 175–86
—, Waringo, R., Bis, R. and Metzler-Zens, N. 1991:	*Clemency et les tombes de l'aristocratie en Gaule Belgique*, Dossiers d'Archéologie du Musée National d'Histoire et d'Art 1 (Luxembourg)
Metzler-Zens, N., Metzler-Zens, J. and Méniel, P. 1999:	*Lamadelaine, une necropole de l'oppidum du Titelberg* (Luxembourg)
Michaelides, D. 1984:	'A Roman surgeon's tomb from Nea Paphos', *Report of the Department of Antiquities Cyprus* (Nicosia), 315–32
Michaelis, A. 1863:	'Terracottagruppe aus Athen', *Archäologische Zeitung* 21, 37–43
Michaelsen, K.K. 1992:	*Braet og Brik. Spil i jernalderen* (Højbjerg)
— 2002:	'Games and gaming pieces in Iron Age Denmark', in J. Retschitzki and R. Haddad-Zubel (eds.) *Step by Step. Proceedings of the 4th Colloquium on Board Games in Academia, Fribourg 2001* (Fribourg), 65–76
Millett, M. 1986:	'An early Roman cemetery at Alton, Hampshire', *Proc. Hampshire Field Club Archaeol. Soc.* 42, 43–87
— 1987:	'An early Roman burial tradition in central southern England', *Oxford J. Archaeol.* 6, 63–8

— 1993: 'A cemetery in an age of transition: King Harry Lane reconsidered', in M. Struck (ed.) *Römerzeitliche Gräber als Quellen zu Religion, Bevölkerungsstruktur und Sozialgeschichte*, Archäologische Schriften des Institut für Vor- und Frühgeschichte der Johannes Gutenberg-Universität Mainz 3 (Mainz), 255–82

Miró i Canals, J. 1988: *La Producción de Ánforas Romanas en Catalunya*, BAR International Series 473 (Oxford)

Miron, A. 1989: 'Toilettebestecke mit Scharnierkonstruktion', *Archaeologia Mosellana* 1, 41–65

Mommsen, H., Brüning, A., Dittmann, H., Hein, A., Rosenberg, A. and Sarrazin, G. 1997: *Recent Investigations of Early Cameo Glass II: induced by synchotron radiation (SYXRF)*, http://www.iskp.uni-bonn.de/gruppen/mommsen/publ/cameo/cam_hp.html, Institut für Strahlen-und Kernphysik, University of Bonn, Germany

Montague, R. 1997: 'Metalwork', in Fitzpatrick 1997, 89–109

Moore, C.N. 1973 'Two examples of late Celtic and early Roman metalwork from South Lincolnshire', *Britannia* 4, 153–9

Moore, P.D., Webb J.A. and Collinson M.E. 1991: *Pollen Analysis*, 2nd edn (Oxford)

Moorhouse, S. 1986: 'Non-dating uses of medieval pottery', *Medieval Ceramics* 10, 85–123

Morris, E.L. 1995: 'Pottery production and resource locations: an examination of the Danebury collection', in Cunliffe 1995, 239–45

— 1997: 'Where is the Danebury ware?', in Gwilt and Haselgrove 1997, 36–9

— and Champion, T.C. 2001: 'Seven thousand collections – on the web', *Antiquity* 75, 253–4

Morris, H.S. 1997: *The Oya Melanau: traditional ritual and belief* (ed. B. Clayre), The Sarawak Museum Journal Special Monograph 7 (vol. 52, no. 73, new series)

Mould, Q. 1991: 'Metalwork', in P.S. Austen, *Bewcastle and Old Penrith: a Roman outpost fort and a frontier vicus*, Cumberland Westmorland Antiq. Archaeol. Soc. Res. Series 6 (Kendal), 185–212

Mudry, P. 1985: 'Médecins et spécialistes: le problème de l'unité de la médecine à Rome au premier siècle ap. J-C.', *Gesnerus* 42, 329–36

Muller, F. 1990: *Der Massenfund von der Tiefenau bei Bern: zur Deutung latènezeitlicter Sammelfunde mit Waffen* (Basel)

Müller, R. and Maute, M. 2000: 'Latènezeit', in H. Beck, H. Steuer, D. Timpe and R. Wenskus (eds), *Fibel und Fibeltracht*, Reallexikon der Germanischen Altertumskunde 8 (Berlin), 46–57

Murphy, P. 1990a: *Moverons Farm, Brightlingsea, Essex: carbonised plant remains from a Bronze Age cremation cemetery*, Ancient Monuments Laboratory Report Series, 126/90, English Heritage (London)

— 1990b: *Baldock, Hertfordshire: land molluscs, carbonised cereals and crop weeds, charcoal, avian eggshell and coprolites from prehistoric and Roman contexts*, Ancient Monuments Laboratory Report Series, 123/90, English Heritage (London)

— 1992: *Stanway, Essex; plant remains from Late Neolithic/Early Bronze Age and Middle Iron Age pits and Late Iron Age burials*, Ancient Monuments Laboratory Report Series, 29/92, English Heritage (London)

Murray, H.J.R. 1913: *A History of Chess* (Oxford)

— 1952: *A History of Board Games other than Chess* (Oxford)

Naumann-Steckner, F. 1991: 'Depictions of glass in Roman wall paintings', in Newby and Painter 1991, 86–98

— 1999: 'Glasgefässe in der römischen Wandmalerei', in M.J. Klein (ed.), *Römische Glaskunst und Wandmalerei*m (Mainz am Rhein), 25–33

De Navarro, J.M. 1955: 'A doctor's grave of the middle La Tène period from Bavaria', *Proc. Prehist. Soc.* 21, 231–48

Needham, S.P. 1996a: 'The late Bronze Age pottery: style, fabric and finish', in S.P. Needham and A. Spence, *Refuse and Disposal at Area 16 East, Runnymede*, Runnymede Bridge Research Excavations 2 (London), 106–60

— 1996b: 'Post Deverel-Rimbury pottery', in R.P.J. Jackson and T.W. Potter, *Excavations at Stonea, Cambridgeshire, 1980–85* (London), 245–57

Newby, M. and Painter, K. 1991: *Roman Glass: Two centuries of Art and Invention*, Soc. Antiq. London Occasional Paper 13 (London)

Niblett, R. 1985: *Sheepen: an early Roman industrial site at Camulodunum*, CBA Res. Rep. 57 (London)

— 1990: 'Verulamium', *Current Archaeol* 120, 410–17

— 1999: *The Excavation of a Ceremonial Site at Folly Lane, Verulamium*, Britannia Monograph 14 (London)

— 2000: 'Funerary rites in Verulamium during the early Roman period', in Pearce *et al.* 2000, 97–104

Noël, J. 1968: *La nécropole gallo-romaine de Hunenknepchen à Sampont (commune de Hachy)*, Archaeol. Belgica 106 (Brussels)

Northover, P. 1989: 'Non-ferrous metallurgy in archaeology', in J. Henderson (ed.), *Scientific Analysis in Archaeology*, Oxford Univ. Comm. Archaeol. Monograph 19 (Oxford), 213–36

Nuber, H.U. 1972: 'Kanne und Griffschale. Ihr Gebrauch im täglichen Leben und die Beigabe in Gräbern der römischen Kaiserzeit', *Bericht Römisch-Germanischen Kommission* 53, 1–232

Nuti, A. 2001: 'Il gioco del fidchell nella letteratura celtica medievale', *Ludica* 7, 18–33

O'Donovan, J. and Stokes, W. 1868: *Cormac's Glossary*, translated and annotated by J. O'Donovan, ed. W. Stokes (Calcutta)

Olivier, A.C.H. 1988a: 'Brooches, 1975 excavation', in E. Martin, *Burgh: the Iron Age and Roman enclosure*, East Anglian Archaeol. 40 (Ipswich), 16–19

— 1988b: 'The brooches', in Potter and Trow 1988, 35–53

— 1996: 'Brooches of silver, copper alloy and iron from Dragonby', in May 1996, 231–64

Orr, K. 2006: *An Archaeological Excavation at Handford House, 1 Queens Road (now Handford Place), Colchester, Essex: February 2003–April 2004*, CAT Rep. 323

Ortalli, J. 2000: 'Rimini: La domus 'del chirurgo'', in M. Marini Calvani (ed.), *Aemilia. La cultura romana in Emilia Romagna dal III secolo a. C. all'età costantiniana* (Venice), 512–26

Oswald, F. 1936: *Index of Figure Types on Terra Sigillata ('samian ware')* (Liverpool; reprinted London, 1964)

— and Pryce, T.D. 1920: *An Introduction to the Study of Terra Sigillata* (London)

Ottaway, P. 1992: *Anglo-Scandinavian Ironwork from Coppergate*, The Archaeology of York AY 17/6 (York)

Owen, S.G. 1967: *P. Ovidius Nasonis Tristium Liber Secundus* (Amsterdam)

Owen, W. 1803: *A Dictionary of the Welsh language, explained in English*, 2 vols. (London)

Ozanne, P.C. 1961: 'The pottery', in M.D. Cra'ster, 'The Aldwick Iron Age settlement, Barley, Hertfordshire', *Proc. Cambridge Antiq. Soc.* 54 (for 1960), 36–45

Panella, C. 1973: 'Appunti su un gruppo di anfore della prima, media e tarda età imperiale', in A. Carandini and C. Panella (eds), *Ostia III. Parte Seconda*, Studi Miscellanei 21 (Rome), 460–633

Parfitt, K. 1995: *Iron Age Burials from Mill Hill, Deal* (London)

Parker, A.J. 1992: *Ancient Shipwrecks of the Mediterranean and the Roman Provinces*, BAR International Series 580 (Oxford)

Parker Pearson, M. 2003: *The Archaeology of Death and Burial* (Stroud)

Parlett, D. 1999: *The Oxford History of Board Games* (Oxford)

Partridge, C.R. 1980: 'Excavations at Puckeridge and Braughing 1975–79', *Hertfordshire Archaeol.* 7 (for 1979), 28–132

— 1981: *Skeleton Green: a late Iron Age and Romano-British site*, Britannia Monograph 2 (London)

— 1982: 'Graffiti from Skeleton Green', *Britannia* 13, 325–6

— 1989: *Foxholes Farm: A Multi-Period Gravel Site*, Hertfordshire Archaeological Trust Monograph (Hertford)

Partridge, J.J. 1993: 'The investigation of cropmarks at Church Lane, Stanway, Colchester', *Essex Archaeol. Hist.* 24, 214–18

Payne, S. 1973:	'Kill off patterns in sheep and goats: the mandibles from Asvan Kale', *Anatolian Studies* 23, 281–303
Peacock, D.P.S. 1971:	'Roman amphorae in pre-Roman Britain', in D. Hill and M. Jesson (eds), *The Iron Age and its Hill-forts: papers presented to Sir Mortimer Wheeler* (Southampton), 161–88
— 1977:	'Pompeian red ware', in D.P.S. Peacock (ed.), *Pottery and Early Commerce: Characterization and Trade in Roman and Later Ceramics* (London), 147–62
— 1981:	'The amphorae', in Partridge 1981, 199–204
Pearce, J. 1998:	'From death to deposition: the sequence of ritual in cremation burials of the Roman period', in C. Forcey, J. Hawthorne and R. Witcher, *TRAC 97. Proceedings of the 7th Annual Theoretical Roman Archaeology Conference* (Oxford), 99–111
Pearce, J., Millett M. and Struck, M. (eds) 2000:	*Burial, Society and Context in the Roman World* (Oxford)
Peña, J.T. 1990:	'Internal red-slip cookware (Pompeian Red Ware) from Cetamura del Chianti, Italy: mineralogical composition and provenience', *American J. Archaeol.* 94, 647–61
Percival, S. 1999:	'Iron Age pottery in Norfolk', in Davies and Williamson 1999, 173–84
— 2000:	'Pottery', in T. Ashwin and S. Bates, *Norwich Southern Bypass, Part I: excavations at Bixley, Caistor St Edmund, Trowse, Cringleford and Little Melton*, East Anglian Archaeol. Rep. 91 (Dereham), 108–14, 170–9
Petrie, W.M. Flinders, Sir 1927:	*Objects of Daily Use: with over 1800 figures from University College, London* (London; reproduced 1974)
Petrovszky, R. 1993:	*Studien zu römischen Bronzegefässen mit Meisterstempeln*, Kölner Studien zur Archäologie der Römischen Provinzen 1 (Cologne)
Philpott, R. 1991:	*Burial Practices in Roman Britain*, BAR British Series 219 (Oxford)
Pitts, L.F. 1979:	*Roman Bronze Figurines of the Catuvellauni and Trinovantes*, BAR British Series 60 (Oxford)
Pitts, M. 2005:	'Pots and pits: drinking and deposition in Late Iron Age south-east Britain, *Oxford J. Archaeol.* 24, 143–61
Plesničar-Gec, L. 1972:	*The Northern Necropolis of Emona* (Ljubljana)
Pliny (Gaius Plinius Secundus)	*Historia Naturalis*, Loeb Classical Library, volumes variously transled by H. Rackham, W.H.S. Jones and D.E. Eichholz (London/Cambridge, Mass.; 1944–62)
Plouviez, J. 2005:	'Brooches', in T. Blagg, J. Plouviez and A. Tester, *Excavations at a large Romano-British Settlement at Hacheston, Suffolk in 1973-4*, East Anglian Archaeol. 106 (Ipswich), 87–108
Polak, M. 2000:	*South Gaulish Terra Sigillata with Potters' Stamps from Vechten*, Rei Cretariae Romanae Fautorum Acta, Supplementum 9 (Nijmegen)
Polfer, M. 2000:	'Reconstructing funerary rituals: the evidence of *ustrina* and related archaeological structures', in Pearce *et al.* 2000, 30–7
Pollard, R.J. 1988:	*The Roman Pottery of Kent*, Kent Archaeol. Soc. Monograph 5 (Maidstone)
Pommeret, C. 2001:	*Le sanctuaire antique des Bolards à Nuits-Saint-Georges (Côte d'Or)* (Dijon)
Poole, C. 1995:	'Pits and propitiation', in Cunliffe 1995, 249–75
Pooley, L. and Benfield, S. 2005:	*Excavations at Abbotstone Field, Bellhouse Pit, Tarmac Colchester Quarry, Warren Lane, Stanway, Colchester, Essex 1999–2001*, CAT Rep. 312
Potter, T.W. 1979:	*Romans in North-west England: excavations at the Roman forts of Ravenglass, Watercrook and Bowness on Solway*, Cumberland Westmorland Antiq. Archaeol. Soc. Research Series v.1 (Cumberland)
— and Trow, S.D. 1988:	*Puckeridge-Braughing, Herts: the Ermine Street Excavations 1971–72*, Herts Archaeology 10 (Hertford)
Poulsen, E. 1995:	'Remarks on Roman bronze skillets with deep grooves under the base', *Acta of the 12th International Congress on Ancient Bronzes, Nijmegen* (Nijmegen), 59–67
Poux, M. and Feugère, M. 2002:	'Le festin, miroir privilégié des élites celtiques de Gaule indépendante', in Guichard and Perrin 2002, 199–22
Price, E. 2000:	*Frocester, a Romano-British settlement, its antecedents and successors* (Stonehouse)

Price, J. 1989: 'Glass objects', in Stead and Rigby 1989, 108–9
— 1995: 'Glass counters and gaming pieces', in Manning *et al* 1995, 129–34
— 1996: 'A ribbed bowl from a late Iron Age burial at Hertford Heath, Hertfordshire', *Annales du 13e Congrès de l'Association Internationale pour l'Histoire du Verre*, 47–54
— and Cool, H.E.M., 1985: 'Glass (including glass from 72 Dean's Way)', in H.R. Hurst, *Kingsholm*, Gloucester Archaeol. Rep. 1 (Cambridge), 41–54.
Proctor, M., Yeo P. and Lack A. 1996: *The Natural History of Pollination* (London)
Prüch, M. 1998: *Schätze für Zhao Mo. Das Grab von Nan Yue* (Heidelberg)
Pusch, E. 1977: 'Eine unbeachtete Brettspielart', *Studien zur altägyptischen Kultur* 5, 199–212

Radnóti, A. 1938: *Die römischen Bronzegefässe von Pannonien*, Dissertationes Pannonicae ser 2, 6 (Budapest)
Rahtz, P.A., Hirst, S. and Wright, S.M. 2000: *Cannington Cemetery. Excavations 1962–3 of Prehistoric, Roman, Post-Roman and Later Features at Cannington Park Quarry, near Bridgwater, Somerset*, Britannia Monograph 17 (London)
Ratcliffe-Densham, H.B.A. and Ratcliffe-Densham, M.M. 1961: 'An anomalous earthwork of the Late Bronze Age on Cock Hill', *Sussex Archaeol. Collections* 99, 78–101
Rees, H., Crummy, N. and Ottaway, P. forthcoming: *Artefacts and Society in Roman and Medieval Winchester: small finds from the suburbs and city defences*, Winchester City Museums publication 6
Reinert, F. 1995: 'Tierkopfförmige Ausgüsse und Sieb-Becken am Übergang der Spätlatènezeit zur frühen römischen Kaiserzeit', in W. Czysz, C.-M. Hüssen, H.-P. Kuhnen, C. Sebastian Sommer and G. Weber (eds), *Provinzialrömiche Forschungen, Festschrift für Günter Ulbert zum 65 Geburtstag* (Munich), 41–50
Rérolle, M. 1999: 'Les objets de bronze', in J.-P. Pautreau, *Antran. Un ensemble aristocratique du premier siècle* (Poitiers), 31–52
Rhodes, P.P. 1952: 'The Celtic field-systems on the Berkshire downs', *Oxoniensia* 15 (for 1950), 1–28
Richards, D. 2000: 'The ironwork', in Fulford and Timby 2000, 360–79
Richter, W. 1887: *Die Spiele der Griechen und Römer* (Leipzig)
Rigby, V.A. 1977: 'The Gallo-Belgic Wares from Cirencester', in J. Dore and K. Greene, *Roman Pottery Studies in Britain and Beyond: papers presented to John Gillam, July 1977*, BAR Supp. Ser. 30 (Oxford), 37–45
— 1986: 'The stratified groups of Iron Age and Roman pottery', in Stead and Rigby 1986, 257–379
— 1988: 'The late prehistoric, Roman and later wares', in I.H. Longworth, A.B. Ellison and V.A. Rigby, *Excavations at Grimes Graves, Norfolk, 1972–1976, 2: the Neolithic, Bronze Age and later pottery* (London), 100–10
— and Foster, J. 1986: 'Building materials', in Stead and Rigby 1986, 183–8
— and Freestone, I. C. 1988: 'The introduction of Roman styles and techniques into Roman Britain: a case study from the King Harry Lane cemetery, St Albans', in E.V. Sayre, P. Vandiver, J. Druzik and C. Stevenson (eds), *Materials Issues in Art and Archaeology*, Materials Research Society Symposium Proceedings 123 (Pittsburgh), 109–15
— and Freestone, I.C. 1997: 'Ceramic changes in late Iron Age Britain', in I.C. Freestone and D.R.M. Gaimster (eds), *Pottery in the Making: World Ceramic Traditions* (London), 56–61
Riha, E. 1979: *Die römischen Fibeln aus Augst und Kaiseraugst*, Forschungen in Augst 3 (Augst)
— 1986: *Römisches Toilettgerät und medizinische Instrumente aus Augst und Kaiseraugst*, Forschungen in Augst 6 (Augst)
— 1990: *Der römische Schmuck aus Augst und Kaiseraugst*, Forschungen in Augst 10 (Augst)
— 1994: *Die römischen Fibeln aus Augst und Kaiseraugst: Die Neufunde seit 1975*, Forschungen in Augst 18 (Augst)

— 2001:	*Kästchen, Truhen, Tische – Möbelteile aus Augusta Raurica*, Forschungen in Augst 31 (Augst)
Ritterling, E. 1913:	*Das frührömische Lager bei Hofheim in Taunus* (Wiesbaden)
Riz, A.E. 1990:	*Bronzegefässe in der römisch-pompejanischen Wandmalerei*, Deutsches Archäologisches Institut Rom Sonderschriften 7 (Mainz am Rhein)
Robson, E. 2001:	'Technology in society: three textual case studies from Late Bronze Age Mesopotamia', in A.J. Shortland (ed), *The Social Context of Technological Change, Egypt and the Near East, 1650–1550 BC* (Oxford), 39–57
Rodwell, W.J. 1979:	'Iron Age and Roman salt-winning on the Essex coast', in B.C. Burnham and H.B. Johnson (eds), *Invasion and Response*, BAR British Series 73 (Oxford), 133–75
— 1983:	'The production and distribution of pottery and tiles in the territory of the Trinovantes', *Essex Archaeol. Hist.* 14 (for 1982), 15–76
— 1987:	'The pottery and its implications', in Buckley *et al.* 1987, 20–39
— 1993:	*The Origins and Early Development of Witham, Essex: a study in settlement and fortification, prehistoric to medieval*, Oxbow Monograph 26 (Oxford)
Roesdahl, E. and Wilson, D.M. 1992:	*From Viking to Crusader* (New York)
Röllicke, H-J. 1999:	'Von 'Winkelwegen', 'Eulen' und 'Fischziehern' – liubo: ein altchinesisches Brettspiel für Geister und Menschen', *Board Game Studies* 2, 24–41
Ross, A. 1967:	*Pagan Celtic Britain* (London)
Roueché, Ch. 1989:	*Aphrodisias in Late Antiquity: the late Roman and Byzantine inscriptions including texts from the excavations at Aphrodisias conducted by Kenan T. Erim* (London)
St John Hope, W.H. 1908:	'Excavations on the site of the Roman city at Silchester, Hants, in 1907', *Archaeologia* 61, 199–218
Von Saldern, A., Nolte, B., LaBaume, P. and Haevernick, T.E. 1974:	*Gläser der Antike* (Mainz)
Salskov Roberts, H. 1995:	'Imports into Denmark from pre-Roman and Roman Italy', in J. Swaddling, S. Walker and P. Roberts (eds), *Italy in Europe: economic relations 700 BC–AD 50*, British Museum Occasional Paper 97 (London), 291–304
Salter, C. and Ehrenreich, R. 1984:	'Iron Age metallurgy in Central Southern England', in B. Cunliffe and D. Miles (eds), *Aspects of the Iron Age in Central Southern Britain* (Oxford), 146–61
Samusah, R. 1932:	'The Malay Game of Apit', *Journal of the Malayan Branch of the Royal Asiatic Society* X, 130–40
Sandys, J.E. 1910:	*A Companion to Latin Studies* (Cambridge)
Saunders, C. 1985:	'The burial casket', in Niblett 1985, microfiche I:A9–13
Sayre, E.V. and Smith, R.W. 1961:	'Compositional categories of ancient glass', *Science* 133, 1824–26
Schädler, U. 1994:	'Latrunculi - ein verlorenes strategisches Brettspiel der Römer', *Homo Ludens. Der spielende Mensch* IV, 47–67
— 1995:	'XII Scripta, Alea, Tabula - new evidence for the Roman history of "Backgammon"', in A.J. de Voogt (ed.), *New Approaches to Board Games Research* (Leiden), 73–98
— 1996:	'Spielen mit Astragalen', *Archäologischer Anzeiger* 1, 61–73
— 1998:	'Mancala in Roman Asia Minor?', *Board Games Studies* 1, 10–25
— 1999:	'Damnosa alea – Würfelspiel in Griechenland und Rom', in *5000 Jahre Würfelspiel. Catalogue of the exhibition. Homo Ludens Supplement* (Salzburg), 39–58
— 2002a:	'Bärenjagd in Augusta Raurica?' *Gazette Augusta Raurica* 2002.1, 8–11
— 2002b:	'The Talmud, Firdausi, and the Greek game "City"', in J. Retschitzki and Rosita Haddad-Zubel (eds), *Step by Step. Proceedings of the 4th Colloquium on Board Games in Academia, Fribourg 2001* (Fribourg), 91–10
— 2003:	'Von Heydebrands Studie über die griechischen und römischen Brettspiele' in V. Fiala and S. Sierpowski, *Proceedings of the International Conference of Chess Historians – Kórnick 2002* (Kórnik), 235–44

— and Calvo, R. 2006:	*Alfons der Weise. Das Buch der Spiele* (Möhnesee)
Schäfer, G. 1968:	'Bericht über die Auffindung und Untersuchung von Fürstengräbern der jüngeren römischen Kaiserzeit bei Bornstein, Kreis Eckernförde', *Jahrbuch Eckernförde* 26, 41–59
Schlabow, K. 1976:	*Textilfunde der Eisenzeit in Norddeutschland*, Göttinger Schriften zur Vor- und Frühgeschichte 15 (Neumünster)
Schoppa, H. 1958:	'Ein frührömisches Brandgrab in Hofheim, Maintaunuskreis', *Germania* 36, 154–6
Schulz, W. 1952:	'Die Grabfunde des 4. Jahrhunderts von Emersleben bei Halberstadt', *Jahresschrift für mitteldeutsche Vorgeschichte* 36, 102–39
— 1953:	*Leuna, ein germanischer Bestattungsplatz der spätrömischen Kaiserzeit* (Berlin)
Scott, D. 2002:	*Copper and Bronze in Art: corrosion, colorants, conservation* (Los Angeles)
Sealey, P.R. 1985:	*Amphoras from the 1970 Excavations at Colchester Sheepen*, BAR British Series 142 (Oxford)
— 1995:	'New light on the salt industry and Red Hills of prehistoric and Roman Essex', *Essex Archaeol. Hist.* 26, 65–81
— 1996:	'The Iron Age of Essex', in Bedwin 1996, 46–68
— 1999:	'Finds from the cauldron pit', in N.R. Brown, *The Archaeology of Ardleigh, Essex: excavations 1955–1980*, East Anglian Archaeol. 90 (Chelmsford), 117–24
— 2005:	'The pre-Belgic pottery', in Pooley and Benfield 2005, 18–30
— forthcoming a:	*A Late Iron Age Warrior Burial from Kelvedon, Essex*, East Anglian Archaeol.
— forthcoming b:	'Amphoras', Elms Farm, Heybridge, report for Essex County Council Field Archaeol. Unit
Sedlmayer, H. 1999:	*Die römischen Bronzegefässe in Noricum*, Monographies Instrumentum 10 (Montagnac)
Selkirk, A. 1992:	'A royal burial at St Albans', *Current Archaeology* 132, 484–8
Sellwood, L. 1984:	'Objects of iron', in B. Cunliffe, *Danebury, an Iron Age Hillfort in Hampshire 2, the excavations 1969–78: the finds*, CBA Res. Rep. 52 (London), 346–71
Serneels, V. 1998:	'La chaîne opératoire de la sidérurgie ancienne', in M. Feugère and V. Serneels (eds), *Recherches sur l'économie du fer en Méditerranée nord-occidentale*, Monographies Instrumentum 4 (Montagnac), 7–44
Sharples, N.M. 1990:	'Late Iron Age society and continental trade in Dorset', in I. Duval, J. Le Bihan and Y. Menez (eds.). *Les Gaulois d'Armorique: la fin de l'Age du Fer en Europe tempérée*, Revue Archéologique de l'Ouest, supplément 3 (Rennes), 99–304
— 1991:	*Maiden Castle, Excavations and Field Survey 1985–6*, HBMCE Archaeol. Rep. 19 (London)
Sheldon, H. 1974:	'Excavations at Toppings and Sun Wharves, Southwark, 1970–1972', *Trans. London Middx Archaeol. Soc.* 25, 1–116
Shimmin, D. forthcoming:	*Archaeological Excavations at Turner Rise, Colchester, Essex, 1996–1999*, CAT Rep.
Shipman, P., Forster, G. and Schoeninger, M. 1984:	'Burnt bones and teeth; an experimental study of colour, morphology, crystal structure, and shrinkage', *J. Archaeol. Science* 11, 307–25
Sievers, S. 1989:	'Die Waffen von Manching unter Berücksichtigung des Übergangs von LT C zu LT D: ein zwischenbericht', *Germania* 67.1, 97–120
— 2001:	'Catalogue des armes' and 'Les armes d'Alésia', in M. Reddé and S. von Schnurbein (eds), *Alésia, fouilles et recherches franco-allemandes sur les travaux militaires romains autour du Mont-Auxois (1991–1997), 2: le matériel*, Memoires de l'Academie des Inscriptions et Belles-Lettres (Paris), 121–292
Sills, J. 2003:	'Celtic or Roman ? AGR and ESVPRASTO', in *Chris Rudd Celtic Coins Sales Catalogue*, 70, 2–4
Silvino, T., Poux, M. and Garnier, N. 2005:	'Où est passé le vin de Bétique? Nouvelles données sur le contenu des amphores dites "à sauces de poisson et à saumures" de types Dressel 7/11, Pompéi VII, Beltrán II (1er s. av.J.-C.-2e s. apr. J.-C).', in L. Rivet (ed.), *Société Française d'Étude de la Céramique Antique en Gaule: Actes du Congrès de Blois* (Marseilles), 501–14

Simonett, C., 1941: *Tessiner Gräberfelder*, Monographien zur Ur -und Frühgeschichte der Schweiz III (Basel)

Simpson, G. 2000: *Roman Weapons, Tools, Bronze Equipment and Brooches from Neuss – Novaesium Excavations 1955–1972*, BAR International Series 862 (Oxford)

Simpson, W.G. 1972: 'A gaming-board of Ballinderry-type from Knockanboy, Derrykeighan, Co. Antrim', *Ulster Journal of Archaeology* 35, 63–4

Smith, R. 1905: 'The ancient British iron currency', *Proc. Soc. Antiq. London* 20, 179–95

Smyth, J.D. 1962: *Animal Parasitology* (London)

Stace, C. 1997: *A new Flora of the British Isles*, 2nd edn (Cambridge)

Stapleton, C., Freestone, I. and Bowman, S. 1999: 'Composition and origin of early medieval opaque red enamels from Britain and Ireland', *J. Archaeol. Science* 26(8), 913–922

Stead, I.M. 1967: 'A La Tène III burial at Welwyn Garden City', *Archaeologia* 101, 1–62

— 1971: 'The reconstruction of Iron Age buckets from Aylesford and Baldock', *Brit. Mus. Quarterly* 35, 250–82

— 1975: 'A Roman brooch blank from Baldock, Herts', *Antiq. J.* 55(2), 397

— 1976: 'The earliest burials of the Aylesford culture' in G. de G. Sieveking, I.H. Longworth and K.E. Wilson (eds), *Problems in Economic and Social Archaeology* (London), 401–16

— 1979: *The Arras Culture* (York)

— 1984: 'Some notes in imported metalwork in Iron Age Britain', in S. Macready and F.H. Thompson (eds), *Cross-Channel Trade between Gaul and Britain in the Pre-Roman Iron Age*, Soc. Antiq. London Occasional Paper 4 (London), 43–66

— 1985: *The Battersea Shield* (London)

— 1991: *Iron Age Cemeteries in East Yorkshire*, HBMCE Archaeol. Rep. 22 (London)

— 1995: 'The metalwork', in K. Parfitt, *Iron Age Burials from Mill Hill, Deal* (London), 59–111

— and Rigby, V. 1986: *Baldock, the Excavation of a Roman and pre-Roman settlement, 1968–72*, Britannia Monograph 7 (London)

— and Rigby, V. 1989: *Verulamium: the King Harry Lane site*, HBMCE Archaeol. Rep.12 (London)

Sterckx, C. 1970: 'Les jeux de damiers celtiques', *Annales de Bretagne* 77.4, 597–609

— 1973: 'Les trois damiers de Buckquoy (Orcades)', *Annales de Bretagne* 80.3/4, 675–89

Straker, V. 2000: 'Charcoal', in Fulford and Timby 2000, 512–23

Struck, M. 2000: 'High status burials in Roman Britain (first–third century) – potential interpretation', in Pearce *et al.* 2000, 85–96

Sudhoff, K. 1913: 'Chirurgische Instrumente aus Ungarn', *Prähistorische Zeitschrift* 5, 595–7

Swan, V.G. and Bidwell, P.T. 1998: 'Camelon and Flavian troop-movements in southern Britain: some ceramic evidence', in J. Bird (ed.), *Form and Fabric: Studies in Rome's Material Past in Honour of B.R. Hartley*, Oxbow Monograph 80 (Oxford), 21–30

Tacitus, Cornelius *Annals*, Loeb Classical Library, translation by J. Jackson (London/Cambridge, Mass.; 1931)

Tacitus, Cornelius *Germania*, Penguin Classics, translation by H. Mattingly, revised by S.A. Handford (London; 1970)

Tacitus, Cornelius *Histories*, Loeb Classical Library, translation by C.H. Moore (London/Cambridge, Mass.; 1925)

Tailliez, P. 1961: 'Travaux de l'été 1958 sur l'épave du "Titan" à l'ile du Levant (Toulon)' in *Atti del II Congresso Internazionale di Archeologia Sottomarina, Albenga 1958* (Bordighera), 175–98

Tait, W.J. 1982: *Game-Boxes and Accessories from the Tomb of Tut'Ankhamun*, Tut'Ankhamun's Tomb Series 7 (Oxford)

Tassinari, S. 1975: *La vaiselle de bronze, romaine et provinciale, au Musée des Antiquités Nationales*, Gallia Supplément 29 (Paris)

— 1993: *Il vassellame bronzeo di Pompei* (Rome)

Taylor, C. C. 1975: *Fields in the English Landscape* (London)

Taylor, G.W. 1983: 'Detection and identification of dyes on pre-Hadrianic textiles from Vindolanda', *Textile History* 14(2), 115–24

Tchernia, A. 1986:	*Le Vin de l'Italie Romaine: Essai d'Histoire Économique d'après les Amphores* (Rome)
— and Zevi, F. 1972:	'Amphores vinaires de Campanie et de Tarraconaise à Ostia', in P. Baldacci, G. Kapitän, N. Lamboglia, C. Panella, E. Rodriguez Almeida, B. Sciarra, A. Tchernia and F. Zevi, *Recherches sur les amphores romaines*, Collection de L'École Française de Rome 10 (Rome), 35–67
Thackray, C.F., c. 1955:	*A Catalogue of Surgical Instruments and Surgical Sundries* (Leeds/London)
Thevenot, É. 1968:	*Divinités et sanctuaires de la Gaule* (Paris)
Thill, G. 1966:	'Ausgrabungen in Goeblingen-Nospelt. Vier spätlatenezeitliche Bandgräber auf "Scheirheck"', *Hémecht* 18, 483–91
Thompson, I.M. 1982:	*Grog tempered 'Belgic' Pottery of South-eastern England*, BAR British Series 108 (Oxford)
— 1988:	'Late Iron Age pottery from Ardale Area B' in Wilkinson 1988, 86–8
— 1995:	'Belgic', in Wymer and Brown 1995, 88–92
Tilhard, J-L. 2001:	*La céramique sigilée à Poitiers (estampilles et décors moulés)*, doctoral thesis, Université de Poitiers (Poitiers)
Timby, J.R. 2000:	'The pottery', in Fulford and Timby 2000, 180–287
— 2004:	'The prehistoric and Roman pottery', in H. Brooks, *Archaeological Excavation at 29–39 Head Street, Colchester, Essex, May–September 2000*, CAT Rep. 268
Tomber, R. and Dore, J. 1998:	*The National Roman Fabric Reference Collection: a Handbook*, MOLAS Monograph 2 (London)
Tomlin, R.S.O. and Hassall, M.W.C. 2001:	'Roman Britain in 2000. II. Inscriptions', *Britannia* 32, 387–400
— 2003:	'Roman Britain in 2002. II. Inscriptions', *Britannia* 34, 361–82
Trow, S.D. 1988:	'Braughing-Puckeridge in the late pre-Roman Iron Age', in Potter and Trow 1988, 156–9
Tuffreau-Libre, M. 1981:	'L'industrie de la céramique gallo-belge dans la vallée de la Vesle (Marne)', *Bull. Soc. Archéol. Champenoise* 2, 81–93
— 1988:	'Les faciès régionaux de la céramique gallo-romaine du Nord de la France et du Bassin parisien', *Hélinium* 28, 81–112
Turner-Walker, C. and Wallace, C.R. 1999:	'The Iron Age and Roman pottery', in B.R.G. Turner, *Excavations of an Iron Age Settlement and Roman Religious Complex at Ivy Chimneys, Witham, Essex 1978–83*, East Anglian Archaeol. Rep. 88 (Chelmsford), 123–79
Unz, C. and Deschler-Erb, E. 1997:	*Katalog der Militaria aus Vindonissa: militärische Funde, Pferdegeschirr und Jochteile bis 1976*, Veröffentlichungen der Gesellschaft pro Vindonissa 14 (Brugg)
van Arsdell, R.D. 1989:	*Celtic Coinage in Britain* (London)
Vanvinckenroye, W. 1984:	*De Romeinse Zuidwest-begraafplaats van Tongeren* (Tongeren)
Wahl, J. 1982:	'Leichenbranduntersuchungen. Ein Überblick über die Bearbeitungs- und Aussagemöglichkeiten von Brandgräbern', *Praehistorische Zeitschrift* 57, 1–125
Wainwright, G.J. 1979:	*Gussage All Saints: an Iron Age settlement in Dorset*, DoE Archaeol. Rep. 10 (London)
Wallace, C. 2004:	'Pottery from DFS and DCS cremations', in Havis and Brooks 2004, 238–42
Wallis, S.P. 1998:	'Excavations at Slough House Farm', in Wallis and Waughman 1998, 5–58
— and Waughman, M. 1998:	*Archaeology and the Landscape in the Lower Blackwater Valley*, East Anglian Archaeol. 82 (Chelmsford)
Ward-Perkins, J. and Claridge, A. 1976:	*Pompeii AD 79* (Bristol)
Waringo, R. 1991:	'Inventaire des tombes à amphores républicaines de la partie occidentale du pays trévire', in Metzler *et al.* 1991, 112–36
Watson, W. 1949:	'Belgic bronzes and pottery found at Felmersham-on-Ouse, Bedfordshire', *Antiq. J.* 29, 37–61

Waugh, H. 1961:	'The Romano-British burial at Weston Turville, Bucks', *Records of Buckinghamshire* 17, 107–14
— and Goodburn, R. 1972:	'The non-ferrous metal objects', in S.S. Frere, *Verulamium Excavations* 1 (London), 114–62
Webster, Jane 1999:	'At the end of the world: druidic and other revitalization movements in post-conquest Gaul and Britain', *Britannia* 30, 1–20
Webster, Janet 1991:	'Objects of copper-alloy', in E.M. Evans, 'Excavations at "Sandygate", Cold Bath Road, Caerleon, Gwent', *Britannia* 22, 103–36
Webster, J. 1992:	'Objects of bronze', in D.R. Evans and V.M. Metcalf, *Roman Gates, Caerleon*, Oxbow Monograph 15 (Oxford), 103–63
Wenham, L.P. 1968:	*The Romano-British Cemetery at Trentholme Drive, York* (London)
van der Werff, J.H. 1986:	'The amphora wall in the House of the Porch, Ostia', in J. Boersma, D. Yntema and J. van der Werff, 'Excavations in the House of the Porch (V.ii.4–5) at Ostia', *Babesch* 61, 96–137
Werner, A.E. and Bimson, M. 1967:	Technical report on the glass gaming-pieces, in Stead 1967, 16–17
Weser, U. 1987:	'Biochemical basis of the use of copper in ancient Egyptian and Roman medicine', in J. Black (ed.), *Recent Advances in the Conservation and Analysis of Artefacts* (London)
West, S. 1985:	*West Stow, the Anglo-Saxon village*, East Anglian Archaeol. 24 (Ipswich)
— 1990:	*West Stow: the Prehistoric and Romano-British Occupation*, East Anglian Archaeol. 48 (Ipswich)
Wheeler, R.E.M. 1926:	'The Roman Fort near Brecon', *Y Cymmrodor* 37 (London)
— 1930:	*London in Roman Times* (London)
— 1943:	*Maiden Castle, Dorset* (London)
Whimster, R. 1981:	*Burial Practices in Iron Age Britain*, BAR British Series 90 (Oxford)
White, K.D. 1970:	*Roman Farming* (London)
Whitehouse, D. 1991:	'Cameo glass', in Newby and Painter 1991, 19–32
— 1997:	*Roman Glass in the Corning Museum of Glass* (New York)
Whiting, W. 1925:	'The Roman cemetery at Ospringe', *Archaeol. Cantiana* 37, 83–96
Wickenden, N. P. 1987:	'Prehistoric settlement and the Romano-British small town at Heybridge, Essex', *Essex Archaeol. Hist.* 17 (for 1986), 7–68
Wild, J.P. 1970:	*Textile Manufacture in the Northern Roman Provinces* (Cambridge)
— 1977:	*The Textiles from Vindolanda 1973–1975*, Vindolanda III (Bardon Mill)
— 1993:	'Vindolanda 1985–1988: the textiles', in R.E. Birley, *The Early Wooden Forts*, Vindolanda Research Reports NS III (Bardon Mill), 76–86
— 2002:	'The textile industries of Roman Britain', *Britannia* 33, 1–42
— and Bender Jørgensen, L. 1988:	'Clothes from the Roman Empire: Barbarians and Romans', in L. Bender Jørgensen, B. Magnus and E. Munksgaard (eds), *Archaeological Textiles: report from the second NESAT symposium 1–4 V 1984*, Arkaeologiske Skrifter 2 (Copenhagen), 65–98
Wilhelmi, K. 1977:	'Zur Funktion und Verbreitung Dreieckiger Tongewichte der Eisenzeit', *Germania* 55, 180–4
Wilkinson, T.J. 1988:	*Archaeology and Environment in South Essex: rescue archaeology along the Grays by-pass, 1979/80*, East Anglian Archaeol. 42 (Chelmsford), 94–7
Williams, D.F. 1981:	'The Roman amphora trade with late Iron Age Britain', in H. Howard and E.L. Morris (eds), *Production and Distribution: a Ceramic Viewpoint*, BAR International Series 120 (Oxford), 123–32
— 1983:	'Report on the amphorae', in Farley 1983, 291
— 1986:	'The amphorae', in Foster 1986, 124–32
— 1989:	'Amphorae', in Stead and Rigby 1989, 115–16
— 1994:	'Campanian amphorae', in P.T. Bidwell and S. Speak, *Excavations at South Shields Roman Fort I*, Soc. Antiq. Newcastle upon Tyne Monograph 4 (Newcastle upon Tyne), 217–19
— 1995:	'A petrological note on amphora fabrics from the survey and along the eastern Spanish coast', in J.-M. Carreté, S.J. Keay and M.J. Millett, *A Roman Provincial Capital and its Hinterland: the survey of the territory of Tarragona, Spain, 1985–1990*, J. Roman Archaeol. Supplementary Series 15 (Ann Arbor), 304–11

— 1999: 'The amphorae', in Niblett 1999, 193–4
Williams, J.H.C. 2003a: 'Coin inscriptions and the origin of writing in pre-Roman Britain', *Brit. Numis. J.* 71 (for 2001), 1–17
— 2003b: 'Pottery stamps, coin designs, and writing in late Iron Age Britain', in A.E. Cooley (ed.), *Becoming Roman, Writing Latin ? Literacy and epigraphy in the Roman West*, J. Roman Archaeol. Supplementary Series 48 (Portsmouth), 135–49
Willis, S.H. 2002: 'A date with the past: late Bronze Age and Iron Age pottery and chronology', in Woodward and Hill 2002, 4–21
— 2006: 'The context of writing and written records in ink: the archaeology of samian inkwells in Roman Britain', *Archaeol. J.* 162, 96–45
Wilmott, A. 1982: 'Excavations at Queen Street, City of London, 1953 and 1960, and Roman timber-lined wells in London', *Trans. London Middx Archaeol. Soc.* 33, 1–78
Wilson, M.G. 1987: 'The pottery', in S.S. Frere, P. Bennett, J. Rady and S. Stow, *Canterbury Excavations: Intra- and Extra-mural sites, 1949–55 and 1980-84*, The Archaeology of Canterbury 8 (Maidstone), 195–208
Wiltshire, P.E.J. 1997: 'The pre-Roman environment', in T. Wilmott, *Birdoswald: excavations of a Roman fort on Hadrian's Wall and its successor settlements: 1987–1992*, EH Archaeol. Rep. 14, 25–40
— 1999: 'Palynological analysis of filling in the funerary shaft', in Niblett 1999, 346–4
Winbolt, S.E. 1925: 'The pre-Roman finds at Folkestone', *Antiq. J.* 5, 63–7
Wire, W. n.d: *Diary*, unpublished mss in Essex Record Office
Woodward, A.B. and Hill, J.D. (eds) 2002: *Prehistoric Britain: the ceramic basis*, Prehistoric Ceramics Research Group Occasional Publication 3 (Oxford)
Woolf, G.D. 1994: 'Power and the spread of writing in the West', in A.K. Bowman and G.D. Woolf (eds), *Literacy and Power in the Ancient World* (Cambridge), 84–98
Woolley, C.L. 1934: *Ur Excavations Vol. II. The Royal Cemetery: a report on the Predynastic and Sargonid graves excavated between 1926 and 1931* (Philadelphia)
Worrell, S. 2006: 'Roman Britain in 2005. II. Finds reported under the Portable Antiquities Scheme', *Britannia* 37, 429–66
Woudhuysen, M. 1998: 'Pottery', in T. Malim, 'Prehistoric and Roman remains at Edix Hill, Barrington, Cambridgeshire', *Proc. Cambridge Antiq. Soc.* 86 (for 1997), 33–8, 50–3
Wright, R.P. 1964: 'Roman Britain in 1963. II. Inscriptions', *J. Roman Studies* 54, 177–85
Wymer, J.J. and Brown, N.R. 1995: *North Shoebury: settlement and economy in South-east Essex*, East Anglian Archaeol. 75 (Chelmsford)
Young, R. and Humphrey, J. 1999: 'Flint use in England after the Bronze Age: time for a re-evaluation?', *Proc. Prehist. Soc.* 65, 231–42
Zepezauer, M.A. 1993: *Glasperlen der vorrömischen Eisenzeit III: mittel- und spätlatènezeitliche Perlen*, Marburger Studien zur Vor und Frühgeschichte 15 (Marburg)
Zevi, F. 1966: 'Appunti sulle anfore romane', *Archeologia Classica* 18, 208–47
Zienkiewicz, J.D. 1986: *The Legionary Fortress Baths at Caerleon* (Cardiff)

STANWAY INDEX

Compiled by Nina Crummy

Figures and tables are not individually distinguished in the index. Terms that occur frequently throughout the text, such as burial, enclosure, pyre debris, pit and ditch have not been indexed. The sections of the text describing the principal features of the site are shown in **bold**.

Abbey Field, Colchester 426
Abbotstone, Colchester 58–9, 62, 76, 436
acetum 298
Acy-Romance, France 427
Adria, Italy 343
aerial photographs 1, 5, 30, 69, 416, 450
Aesculapius 445
Airport Catering Site, *see* Stansted
Alchester, Oxon 324
alea evangelii 371
Alésia, France 181, 183, 293
Alexander 364
Alfonso of Spain 364
All Saints' church, Stanway 13
Alton, Hants 151, 366, 430, 432, 438–9
Amminus/Adminius 456
Amolara, *see* Adria
amphoras 14, 72–3, 75, 80–1, 84–5, 90–1, 95, 98, 100, 104, 110, 115–16, 124, 126, 142, 149, 151, 156, 170, 172–4, 176, 201–4, 211–15, 246, 269, 273–4, 277, 281, 286–7, 297–305, 307, 310, 320, 326, 426–7, 429–32, 450, 455
amulets, *see* symbol
Antibes, France 300
Antran, France 184, 446
Aphrodisias, Turkey 372
Apt, France 343
Ardale, Essex 43
Ardleigh, Essex 43, 61–2, 306–7, 325, 376
arm-ring 171–2, 178–80, 332, 337, 445–6
arms, *see* weapons, *see also* disarmament
Arrian 364
artemisia 207, 394–9, 429

Arthur 430
artillery bolt 67
Asheldam Camp, Essex 56
Ashton, Northants 269
Athens, Greece 362, 369
Atrebates 311
Augst, Switzerland 135, 220, 244, 316–18, 361, 365
Auldjo jug 329
auxiliaries, Roman 446–7
Avançon, France 453, 456
Avaux, France 453, 456
Avenches, Switzerland 150–1, 372
axe 33
Aylesford culture 314

Baetica 299, 430
bags 167–70, 231, 250
Bagendon, Glos 257, 289–90, 316–18, 409
Baldock, Herts 56, 59, 61, 135, 164–5, 188, 216–17, 220, 269–70, 292, 311, 316–18, 324, 359–60, 376, 384
Ballinderry, Ireland 367, 370
Bancroft, Bucks 318
banks 8, 26, 33, 52, 69, 71, 443, 450
Barley, Herts 61–2
barrels 104, 157–8, 423, 432–3, 439–40, 442–3
Barrington, Cambs 34
Bartlow Hills, Cambs 321–2
basins 151, 171, 181, 185–6, 320–3, 332, 335, 390, 445
Batina/Kis Köszeg, Croatia 238–9, 247–8
battens 208, 211–12
Bavay, France 290–2, 295
beads 128, 130, 135, 140–1, 150–1, 164, 169, 171–2, 178–80, 201–3, 205, 215–17, 254–7, 259, 329–31, 426, 445–6
beakers 72–3, 75–8, 92–3, 100, 127, 134, 138, 140, 142, 147, 149, 155–7, 170, 172–5, 197, 201, 268, 274, 276–7, 281, 283, 288–9, 313–14, 326, 402–3, 405–9, 418, 429, 431–2, 435, 451

485

Beckford, Worcs 328
Bedfordshire 269
bees 394–5, 397
beer 273, 326, 398, 418, 429, 432
Belgae 456
Belgium 33
belt-plates, see strap-fittings
Bergen, Norway 371
Berry-Bouy, France 181, 184, 446
Bessines, France 135
Biggleswade, Beds 321
Birch, Essex 450
Birchanger, Essex 38
bird 383, see also cranes
Birdlip, Glos 163, 178, 217, 231, 320, 324
Birka, Sweden 360, 368, 371, 374
Björkö, Sweden 371
Black, A. 7, 448–9
Black, D. 7, 448–9
Blain, France 324–5
blanket, see cloak
Blicquy, Belgium 150
board games, see games
boars 430
bone, see also cremated bone
  animal 43, 85, 90, 101–4, 116, 142, 149–50, 171, 377, 382–3, 433
  human 13, 26, 47, 85, 101–4, 150, 159–60, 162, 167, 170–1, 179, 197, 246, 254, 262, 377–83, 410, 426, 428, 433–4, see also cremated bone
  objects 104, 110–11, 120, 127, 137, see also horn
Boreham, Essex 59
Borough Hill, Northants 88
Botanic Gardens, Colchester 316
Boudican revolt 1, 160, 266, 290, 297, 325, 341
bowls 50, 55–7, 59, 61–2, 69–70, 78, 81, 84, 97, 100–3, 110, 119, 127, 141–2, 148, 150, 155–6, 162, 164–5, 169–70, 172, 176–7, 180, 191, 193, 201–4, 206, 211–13, 221, 233, 246, 254, 258, 273–4, 276–7, 281, 288, 305–7, 326, 340–3, 346, 402, 404–6, 408–9, 418, 428–9, 431–2, 434–5, 445–6, 455, see also spouts, strainer bowls
boxes 10, 13, 120, 127–8, 135, 137, 150–1, 153, 157–9, 162–7, 171–2, 176, 180, 190–5, 197, 201–2, 221, 231–3, 250, 343, 346, 402, 405–7, 409, 446
bracelets 150–1, 178, see also arm-ring
Branca, see Locarno
Brandon, Suffolk 323–5
brandubh 370
Brecon Gaer, Powys 367
Brigantes 444
briquetage 90, 93, 96–100, 375–7
Britons 167–8, 228, 306, 312, 359, 439, 444–5, 456

brooches 10, 45, 55–6, 70–1, 81–2, 84, 127–8, 135, 151, 156, 160–1, 164, 169, 171–3, 176–8, 181, 195, 197–203, 205, 212, 215–17, 224, 233, 250, 254–60, 314–20, 329, 332–4, 336–8, 347–9, 402, 405–10, 412, 437, 439, 444–6
Brooches burial CF72 7, 11, 13, 83–4, 90, 150–1, 153, 180, **254–60**, 262, 272–3, 277, 314, 317–19, 329–30, 332–4, 343, 348–9, 377, 381, 428–9, 433, 440–3, 445
buckets 162–3
Buckquoy, Orkney 370
Burgh, Suffolk 43, 62, 315
burial rite see funerary rite
Burnham-on-Crouch, Essex 44, 376
Burton Fleming, Yorks 349
butt-beaker, see beaker
Butt Road, Colchester 228

Caburn, the, East Sussex 44
Cadbury Castle, Somerset 88, 163
Cadiz, Spain 301
Caerleon, Gwent 154, 367, 412
Caernarvon, Gwynedd 158, 412
Caerwent, Gwent 412
Caesar, Gaius Julius 167–8, 364, 445, 455–6
Caistor St Edmund, Norfolk 62
calami, see pens
Calver, H. 344
Cambridgeshire 50, 56, 59, 62, 269
cameo glass 329, 331, 338
Camerton, Somerset 33
Campania, Italy 95, 303
Camulodunum 1, 14, 31, 164, 268–9, 271, 273–4, 289, 291–6, 306, 315, 317, 320, 324–6, 359, 376–7, 423, 444–5, 451, 455–6, see also Gosbecks, Lexden, St Clare Drive, Sheepen
Cannington, Somerset 178
Canterbury, Kent 292, 311, 313, 318
Cantiaci 311
Canvey Island, Essex 375
Cara/Caratacus 456
Cartimandua 444
Cassivellaunus 456
Castleford, Yorks 367
Catalauni 452–3, 456
Catalonia 298, 303
cattle 171, 382–3, 430, 434
Catuvellauni 234, 311, 324–5, 359, 451, 455–6
Celsus 170, 236, 238, 240, 245–6, 249
cereal 384–7, 394–5, 397–9, see also grain
Chadwell, Essex 62
chain 127, 135, 141, 160–1, 338
chain-mail 6, 446
Châlons en Champagne, France 453
chambers
  AF25 6, 9–10, 13, 22–3, 38, 40, 48, 52–4, 69,

71, **101–3**, 130, 143, 272, 377–9, 382–3, 424–5, 429, 431, 433–6, 450, 453
BF6 6, 11, 13, 71, 73, 85, 87–8, **104–27**, 130, 143, 149–50, 157–8, 197, 207, 272–3, 289–95, 297–8, 301–13, 320–1, 337–8, 359, 377–8, 382–3, 390–1, 424–7, 429–31, 433–44, 446, 448, 453
BF24 6, 11, 13, 20, 38, 40, 54, 57, 66, 75, 81, 91–2, **127–41**, 143, 272–3, 277, 283, 330, 344–6, 377–8, 424–7, 429, 433, 435–6, 440–4, 453
CF42 7, 11, 13, 24, 83–4, 98, 119, 130, **142–57**, 199, 254, 257, 260, 266, 272–4, 283, 298, 303–5, 330, 332, 343–5, 382–3, 398–9, 424–6, 429–31, 433–6, 440–4, 453
Champagne, France 453–4, 456
charcoal 7, 15–16, 26, 30–2, 56, 73, 82–6, 88, 90–1, 98, 104, 111, 117, 119, 158–60, 169, 266, 384–93, 400, 402, 405–7, 409–13, 415–16, 420–2, 426–7, 430
chariot burials 231, 233, 452, 455
Charlton Hill, Kent 216
Chatham Downs, Kent 322
Chedworth, Glos 361
Chelmsford, Essex 422
chess 364
chest 157–9, 348, *see also* boxes
Chester, Cheshire 412
Chettle, Dorset 324
Chichester, West Sussex 127, 150–1, 292, 366
Child's Grave, Colchester 346
China 374
Chorley, Lancs 135
chronology
  of burials, from pottery alone 272–3
  of Early–Middle Iron Age pottery 55–6
  site, detailed 438–43
  site, simplified 7–14
Church Lane, Stanway, Essex 62
Claudian 167–8
Claudius 266, 312, 338, 340, 365, 423, 439
clay sources 58–9
Clemency, Luxembourg 184, 297, 299, 432, 453, 455–6
cloaks 171–2, 176, 347–9, 356, 427, 430, 445, *see also* textile
cloth/clothing, *see* bags, cloaks, textile
coal 384–7, 420–1
Cock Hill, Sussex 44
coins 12–13, 69–70, 74, 76, 80–1, 90, 97, 215, 266, 290, 310–13, 321, 338–40, 344, 371, 374, 408, 410–11, 414, 423, 437, 439, 445, 455–6
Colchester Quarry 1
Colchester town centre, see *colonia*
Colne, river 2, 315, 376
Cologne, Germany 245, 291
colonia, Colchester 2, 76, 88, 135, 150, 176, 260–1, 263, 268, 279, 281, 283, 288–9, 292, 297, 299, 306, 315–16, 318–20, 338, 340–1, 343–6, 366–7, 376, 402, 418, 437, 444
colony, *see colonia*
Commios/Commius 310, 456
condiments 429–30
conquest, Roman, *see* invasion
Cookham, Berks 292
Copenhagen, Denmark 363
copper alloy
  analysis of 170, 331–8
  heat-affected 85–98, 104, 109–10, 117, 119–21, 125, 127, 157–9, 337–8, 390, 402, 407, 409, 411, 427, 432
Corbridge, Northumberland 245, 367
cord 180, 184, 347
Corieltavi 311
Cosa, Italy 341
cosmetics 135, 167–70, 257, 344–6
cosmetic palette 150
cosmetic sets 168, 324
Cott, P. 448–9
Cotton, J. 188, 366–8
counters 74, 76, 80, 120, 142, 149–51, 153, 155–6, 171–2, 186–8, 190, 199, 201–2, 205, 207–8, 212, 217–18, 220, 260, 329–30, 348, 352–75, 430, 445
Courmelois, France 293–5
covers, wooden 172, 197, 202–3, 205–8, 211–12, 257, 262–3, 356, 427
Cramond, Lothian Region 245
cranes 171, 174–5, 445
cremated bone 13, 15, 26, 47, 85, 88, 90–1, 97, 101–4, 111, 116–17, 127, 129–30, 142, 157–8, 160, 162, 167, 170–2, 197, 199, 201–3, 205, 207, 249–50, 254, 259, 262–3, 266, 314, 348, 352, 356, 369, 377–81, 384–7, 390, 400, 402, 404–6, 410–15, 418–20, 423, 425–7, 429, 433–5, 440, 443, 450–1
cremation burials 5, 7, 9–10, 13–14, 69, 71, 83–4, 120, 150–1, 162, **167–264**, 260, 269, 275, 311, 346–8, 366, 377–81, 384, 388, 400–10, 414, 418, 422–4, 426–30, 433–43, 450
Crew, P. 33–4
cropmarks 1–2, 30, 69, 450
Crownthorpe, Norfolk 223, 324–5
Cumae, Italy 343
Cunobelin 69–70, 74, 76, 80–1, 90, 97, 312, 338, 340, 423, 437, 445, 448, 455–6
cups 76–7, 80, 100, 104, 111, 113, 123–4, 126, 132–3, 137–9, 142, 147, 149, 151, 154–5, 157, 170–5, 201–4, 208, 213–15, 254–6, 258–61, 270, 272–4, 277, 283, 288–90, 292–6, 305–7, 310, 312–14, 325, 344, 402, 418, 428–31, 436, 451
currency bars 7–9, 26, 33–6, 45–7, 65, 327–8, 435

Dalheim, Luxembourg 290–1
Damous-al-Kharita, Tunisia 362, 372
Danebury, Hants 43, 61, 88, 160, 328
Danube, river 120, 326
Darmsden, Suffolk 61
dating *see* chronology
daub 31–2, 37, 69, 71, 74, 81, 90, 101, 103–4, 119, 128, 413, 416, *see also* structural clay
Dawes Heath, Thundersley, Essex 422
Deal, Kent 82, 184, 160, 216, 292
Dennis, T. 448–9
d'Ensérune, France 307
dice 151, 362, 364–5, 368, 370, 371, 374
Dio Cassius 439
Dioscorides 300
disarmament 184, 439
disc 30, 46–7
display of corpses 13, 426–7
distaff 151
Diviciacus 456
divination 202, 217, 228–9, 231, 250, 444–5
Doctor's burial CF47 5, 7, 11–13, 83–4, 102, 119–20, 150, 163, 172, 180, 197, **201–53**, 257, 262–3, 270, 272–3, 289–95, 297, 301, 304–5, 307, 314–17, 319, 320–6, 329–30, 332–3, 335–7, 347–9, 352–75, 377, 379–80, 388, 390–1, 394–8, 399, 427–30, 433–4, 437, 440–6, 451
dog 85, 90, 307, 382–3, 434, 445
donkey 231
Dorset 35, 190
Dorton, Bucks 298, 302
Dragonby, Lincs 163, 232, 318–19, 409
Dream of Rhonabwy, The 430
drinks 151, 171–2, 202, 213, 273, 275, 305, 322, 325–6, 418, 429–30, 440, 443, 445, *see also* beer, mead, medicine, tea, wine
droveways 2, 30–1, 50
druids 250, 313, 445
duodecim scripta, see XII scripta
Duston, Northants 292
dye 347, 349
dykes 1–2

earrings 10, 162–4, 167,
East Anglia 13, 34, 48, 56–7, 59–62, 339, 445
Echu Airem of Temuir 430
Eckartsbrunn, Germany 220
Egypt 328, 361, 369
Elms Farm, Essex, *see* Heybridge
Elsenham, Essex 366
Ely, Cambs 34, 327
Emersleben, Germany 368
Emona (Ljubljana), Slovenia 150–1, 159
enamel 333, 430
Enclosure 1 5–6, 8, 10, 13, 16, 18, 20, 22–3, 31–3, 36, 38, 40, 45, 48–53, 63, **69–71**, 135, 162, 167, 232, 271–81, 338–40, 378, 381–2, 388, 390–1, 400, 424, 431, 435–7, 444, 450, 455
Enclosure 2 5–10, 13, 16–17, 20–1, 23, **26–67**, 69, 154, 274, 327, 377–8, 381–90, 400, 431, 435–6, 442, 444, 450, 456
Enclosure 3 5–6, 11–13, 20, 23, 31, 54, **71–3**, 81, 85, 104, 106, 119, 157, 163, 171, 271–81, 283, 297–8, 303, 314, 337–8, 344–5, 377–9, 381, 384–8, 390–1, 400, 423–5, 428, 431, 435, 438–44, 447, 450, 455
Enclosure 4 5–6, 11–13, 20, 54, 57, 66, **74–81**, 91, 128, 271–86, 288, 297, 303–6, 314, 337–40, 344, 359, 375–8, 381–3, 388, 390–1, 400, 423, 425, 427–8, 431–2, 435, 437–44, 447–8, 450, 455
Enclosure 5 5–7, 10–13, 16, 20, 23–4, 38, 40, 54, 75, **81–4**, 97, 142, 160, 163, 202, 254, 260, 262, 265–6, 271–7, 279–81, 283, 287–8, 297, 304–6, 314, 339–40, 343–4, 375–7, 379–81, 385–8, 390–3, 400, 423–5, 427–8, 431–2, 435, 437–44, 447–8, 450, 455
English Heritage 1, 6
entrances 6, 26, 30, 45–6, 69, 71, 74, 76, 81, 424, 440, 450
Epaticcus 456
Ephesus, Turkey 360, 362, ,372
Essex 13, 17, 43, 48, 50–2, 55–7, 59–63, 190, 269, 274, 315, 324, 375, 395, 422
Essex County Council 6
Essex History Fair 6
Esus 445
Etruria 299
Eumachius 299
Ewell, Surrey 188, 366
excarnation 11–12, 426–7, 435, 448

family 184, 273, 428, 444, 450–1, 455, *see also* kinship
farmstead 1, 8–9, 13, 26, 38, 69, 435
Faversham, Kent 160
Fayyum, the, Egypt 361
feasting 305, 320, 322, 325–6, 377, 390–1, 424, 431–2, 445, *see also* funerary rites
Felmersham, Beds 324–5
ferns 399
fibre 43
fidchell, *fidhcheall* 358–9, 373–4, 430
figurines 120, 346, *see also* pedestal
finger-rings 10, 151, 162–5, 167
fish 297, 377, *see also* fish-sauce
Fishbourne, West Sussex 88, 180, 311, 313, 316, 343–4
fish-sauce 297, 300, 305, *see also garum, liquamen*
flagons 70, 72–3, 75, 77, 81, 84, 93, 100, 127, 131, 137–9, 141, 151, 170, 172–5, 197–8, 200–4, 206, 208, 211–15, 233, 254–6,

258–61, 266, 269, 272–7, 279, 281, 283, 288, 326, 402, 404–11, 418, 429–30, 435, 437
Fléré-la-Rivière, France 162–4, 184, 446
flints, worked 7, 9, 16, 21–5, 32, 103, 162, 400, 422, 436
floors 101–4, 109–11, 116–17, 119–20, 127–9, 131, 135, 137, 142, 145, 424, 426
Folkestone, Kent 160
Folly Lane, Verulamium, Herts 5–6, 109, 297, 304–5, 350, 384, 392, 431–2, 446–8, 450–1, 453, 455–6
food 171–2, 202, 213, 273, 275, 300, 305, 310, 360, 377, 418, 429–30, 432, 440, 443
footwear 407–8, 410, 413, *see also* hobnails
forceps 202, 205, 208, 241–3, 245, 247, 251, 352, 358
Fordham, Cambs 55
fortress, Colchester 76, 261, 268, 279, 281, 283, 288–9, 297, 306, 315–16, 319–20, 346, 402, 418, 437, 444
Fosse Way 290
Foxholes Farm, Herts 56, 315
France 33, 316, 324–5, 418, 445, 453–4, 456, *see also* Gaul
Frankenthal, Germany 290
frankincense 169
Frocester, Glos 178
Frontinus 364
fruit 82, 169, 266, 384–7, 420–2
fuel 85, 388, 391–2, 420–2, 432
funerary goods, *see also* grave goods
  broken 162–7, 402, 425–7, 430–2, 447, 453, 455
  burnt 168, 402, 423, 426
funerary rite 12, 36, 38, 53, 137, 257, 277, 279, 297, 302–3, 305, 312, 345–6, 350, 356, 377, 385, 391, 423–8, 430–5, 440, 443, 450, 456
furniture, *see* boxes, wooden objects

Gage, J. 322
Galaţii Bistriţei, Romania 238–9, 247
games/gaming 151, 153, 352–75, 429–30, *see also* counters
  game boards 104, 116–17, 119–20, 125–6, 150–1, 171–2, 186–90, 201–5, 207–10, 212, 217–20, 224, 231, 249–50, 326, 332–3, 337–8, 347–8, 352–75, 388, 390, 423, 429–31, 433, 445–6
Garrison site, Colchester 30, 61, 220, 436
Garton Station, Yorks 231
garum 300–1, 429–30, *see also liquamen*
Gaul, 55, 215, 221, 250, 273, 289, 296, 299–300, 304, 314, 316, 322, 324, 349, 452, 455–6, *see also* France
geophysics 7, 400, 448
Germani 228
Germany 33, 273, 289, 318, 418, 455

glass objects, *see* beads, brooches, cameo glass, counters, glassware, Portland vase, shanks with glass head
  analysis of 179, 187, 328–31, 338
glassware 71, 73, 127, 130, 135, 138, 140, 142, 148–51, 155–6, 170, 172–3, 176–7, 180, 191, 193, 202, 224, 254–8, 260–1, 324, 340–6, 405, 407, 409, 412–13, 428–9, 436–7, 443, 446
  smashed 343–4, 346
Glastonbury, Somerset 160, 178, 331
Gloucester, Glos 154, 216–17
Glyndyfrdwy, Clwyd 322–3
goat 43, 171, 382–3, 434
Godmanchester, Cambs 220
Goeblange-Nospelt, Luxembourg 453
Gokstad, Norway 370
gold 151, 164, 350, 375, 430
Gommern, Germany 360, 374
Gosbecks 1–3, 31, 266, 292, 447–50
graffiti 116, 123, 126, 290, 295, 302, 307–14, 441
grain 32, 50, 56, *see also* cereals
grass 110, 120, 384–8, 394, 397–9, 420–2
grave goods, broken 10–11, 14, 111, 119, 130–1, 149, 158, 160, 162, 171, 260, 262–3, 410, 423, 425–6, 440, 443, *see also* pottery/broken/smashed
grazing 399
Great Braxted, Essex 184
Great Chesterford, Essex 315
Gretton, Northants 328
gruel 60
Gryme's Dyke 1–2, 400
Gussage All Saints, Dorset 43
gwyddbwyll (gwyzbwyll) 358, 373–4, 430

Hacheston, Suffolk 318
Haltern, Germany 290, 292
Handford House, Colchester 407–8
hand-washing sets 151, 171, 181, 185–6, 320–2, 429, *see also* basin, jug
harness *see* horsegear
harp 375
hay *see* grass, straw
Hayling Island, Hants 180, 331, 448
Head Street, Colchester 289
healing, *see* medicine
Heiligenhafen, Germany 360
Hellingen, Germany 326
Hengistbury Head, Dorset 88
herb 323, 326, 384–7, 395–6, 398–9, 420–2
Herculaneum, Italy 299
Herod 300
Hertford Heath, Herts 257, 343
Hertfordshire 62, 190, 220, 269, 324
Hey, Sir William 239–40
Heybridge, Essex 56, 59–62, 302, 305, 310,

315–17, 366
High Beech, Epping, Essex 422
hillfort 36, 61
Hinchingbrooke Park Road, Cambs 36
Hitchin, Herts 315
hnefatafl 360, 368, 370, 374, see also *tafl*
hoards 9, 33, 35–6, 65, 67, 135, 164, 181, 314, 322–4
hobnails 71, 73, 402, 405–10, 413
Hoby, Denmark 216, 257
Hochdorf, Stuttgart, Germany 350
Hockwold cum Wilton, Norfolk 339
Hod Hill, Dorset 88, 181, 183, 245, 316, 322, 409
Hofheim, Germany 126, 290–2
holdfast 76, 85, 88–90
Holland, see Netherlands
Holt, Denbighs 362, 412
honey 207, 397
hooks 202, 205, 239–40, 242–3, 247–9, 251, 348, 352, 358
horn objects 128, 135, 137, 141
horses 104, 109, 119, 149–50, 231, 382–3, 430, 434
horsegear 6, 87, 104, 108, 110–11, 117, 119–20, 126–7, 231, 337–8, 430, 446
Howell Dda 371
Howell's Farm, Essex 62
Hullbridge, Essex 422
Hunenknepchen à Sampont, Belgium 291
Hunnerberg, Netherlands 290, 294
hunting 181, 434, 439, 446
Hurstborne Tarrant, Hants 178

Iceni 215, 311, 316
Icklingham, Suffolk 216
Icknield Way 315
identity 424, 444–7
ingot 300
inkwell 12, 197–200, 273, 441
Inkwell burial BF67 6, 11–13, 71, 73, 163, **197–201**, 234, 273, 313–14, 317, 319, 332, 377–8, 390–1, 425, 427–9, 433, 435, 437, 440–4
inlay 120, 128, 135, 137, see also bone objects, horn objects
inscription, painted 298, 300–1
instrumentarium, see surgical instruments
invasion, Roman 48, 56, 67, 76, 297, 314, 319, 349, 423, 436, 439, 455–6
Ireland 358, 370, 373
ironwork, heat-affected 432
iron-working 45
Italy 168, 176, 298, 314, 321–2, 326, 341, 343
Itford Hill, Sussex 44
ivory 178, 430
Ivy Chimneys, Witham, Essex 51, 57, 62
Izmir, see Smyrna

jars 49–50, 56–7, 61–2, 70, 72–3, 75–6, 78–80, 84, 93, 95, 97, 100, 127, 157, 160, 162, 165, 167–9, 196, 262–4, 266, 270, 273–7, 281, 288, 313, 429, 431–2, 435, 437
jet objects 180, 201–3, 205, 215–17
jugs 151, 171–2, 181, 185–6, 195, 320–3, 329, 332, 335, 347, 445

Kallion, Greece 243
Karaagaè, Bulgaria 181
Kayser Bondor burial, Herts 269
Kelvedon, Essex 376
Kelvedon Warrior burial 184, 439
Kent 56, 62, 190
Kharbga 364
kiln, see oven
King Harry Lane, Verulamium, Herts 150, 153, 156, 188, 190, 199, 220, 233, 257, 269, 271–4, 289, 292, 296, 302, 304–5, 311, 314–18, 359, 366–7, 373, 409, 427, 430, 447, 450–1
Kingsholm, Glos 345
Kingston Deverill, Wilts 324
kinship 428, 435, 441, 444, 451, see also families
Kirkburn, Yorks 231, 233
knives 151, 202, 205, 237, 245, 247–8, 252, 254–7, 259–60, 348–9, 352
Knockanboy, Ireland 367, 370
Knowth, Ireland 370
Kommerau (Komorow), Poland 372

lagenae, see flagons
Lake Farm, Dorset 292–3
Lamadelaine, Luxembourg 191, 433
Lamberton Moor, Berwicks 164
Lambot, B. 453–5
lamps 326
lance 171, 180–1, 183–5, 445–6, see also spears
landscape 398–9
Langwood Ridge, Cambs 59
Lapland 370
Latium 95, 299, 303
Laus Pisonis 363–4
Lauterach, Austria 216–17
lead objects 66–8, 300
leather objects 169, 188, 207, 217, 220, 229, 231–2, 246, 249, 348, 371, 388, 390, 430
Lebach, Germany 290–1
Le Câtillon de Haut, Jersey 314
Leg Piekarski, Poland 325
Leptis Magna, Libya 372
Leuna, Germany 361–3, 365, 368, 372–4
Lexden, Colchester 1, 271, 273, 291, 297, 302, 316, 350, 428, see also St Clare Drive, Lexden Tumulus
Lexden Tumulus 1, 109, 120, 154, 163, 232, 297–8, 302, 304–5, 350, 426, 429, 431, 446–8, 455

lex Julia 439
lids 76, 100, 257, 277, 304, 343–4, 404–5, 418
Linford, Essex 50
lion 185–6, 321, 445
liquamen 300, *see also* garum
literacy 12, 151, 273, 310, 312–13, 441
Little Clacton, Essex 422
Little Oakley, Essex 62
Little Paxton, Cambs 62
Little Walden, Essex 184
Little Waltham, Essex 37, 51, 55–6, 60, 62
Litton Cheney, Dorset 199, 366
Liubo 374
Locarno, Switzerland 345
Lofts Farm, Essex 50, 55
London 88, 135, 190, 244, 249, 260, 279, 300, 316, 366–7, 412, 427
looms 43–4
loomweights 8, 13, 37–45, 69, 90, 101, 103, 128, 435–6
Louvercy, France 292
ludus latrunculorum 358, 361, 363, 365, 367–70, 372–3
Lullingstone, Kent 360, 366
luminescence dates 55
Lundeborg, Denmark 371
Luxembourg 291, 293, 453, 456
Luzzi, Italy 245
Lyon, France 181

Mabinogion, The 430
macrofossils 384–7, 402, 413, 420–2
Magdalensberg, the, Austria 312, 326
magic 180, 217, 231, 250, 445, *see also* divination
Maiden Castle, Dorset 160, 164–5, 409
Maidstone, Kent 62
Mainz, Germany 290, 292
Maldon, Essex 50, 315
Manching, Germany 178, 181
Marne, France 55, 290
Marne-Vesle potteries 175, 290–5
Masada, Israel 300
mausoleum 266
Maxey, Cambs 43
mead 326
medical kit, *see* surgical instruments
medicine/medicinal drinks 167, 170, 180, 207, 217, 236–52, 224, 228, 231, 250, 300, 326, 395–8, 429, 434, 444–5, *see also* surgical instruments
Merslford, Fife 184
Mesopotamia 180
Mider of Brí Léith 430
military equipment 85, 117, 119–20, 126–7, 317, 337–8, 349, 446, *see also* horsegear
Mill Hill, *see* Deal
Milton Keynes, Bucks 289, 294

miniature vessels 57, 60–1, 66
mirrors 150–1, 153, 260–2, 334, 336, 437
Mirror burial CF115 11, 13, 83–4, **260–2**, 293, 336, 344, 377, 381, 428, 430, 433, 437, 440–3
Montepreux, France 290
Morlungo, Italy 243, 245
Morlupo, Italy 342
mortaria 283, 288
?mortuary enclosures 6–7, 11, 13–14, 38, 40, 54, 66, 75–6, 81, 83–4, 90–100, 274–7, 280–1, 283, 288, 297, 303, 305–6, 334, 337–40, 375–8, 381, 390–3, 423–7, 431, 433, 437–8, 440–3, 448, *see also* pyres
mounds 88, 101–4, 107, 109, 117, 119, 127, 130, 137, 142, 145–6, 150, 157, 398, 423–5, 434–5, 438, 440, 443, 456
Mount Farm, Oxon 60
Much Hadham, Herts 269
Mucking, Essex 50, 56, 62
mug 101–3, 273
mugwort, *see* artemisia
München-Obermenzig, Germany 238–9, 247
Musket Club, Colchester 447, 450

nail-cleaner 81–4, *see also* toilet implements
nails 45, 47, 70–1, 73–6, 81–2, 85, 88, 90, 92–3, 95, 97–8, 110, 116, 118–23, 129, 136–7, 142–4, 149, 152–4, 157–9, 162, 172, 191–3, 195–9, 203, 205, 207–8, 211–12, 233, 245, 250, 252–5, 257, 260, 262, 266–7, 388, 402, 405, 407, 409, 411–15, 424–5, 427
Nea Paphos, Cyprus 244
necklaces 128, 130, 135, 150, 180, *see also* beads
needles 160–1, 202, 205, 208, 242–5, 247–8, 251–2, 348, 350–2
Nero 266, 298, 305, 316, 339–40
Netherlands 325, 418
Neudorf-Bornstein, Germany 360
Nijmegen, Netherlands 243, 261, 290–1, 295, 323
Nîmes, France 343
nine men's morris 370
Norfolk 50, 56, 62, 316
Noricum 325–6
Northamptonshire 269
North Ferriby, Humberside 289, 291
North Shoebury, Essex 43, 50, 55
Nottinghamshire 216
Novaesium, Germany 291
Noyelles–Godault, France 292–3
nuts 82, 228, 266, 384–7, 420–2

Ockelbo, Sweden 370
Oldenburg, Germany 371
Old Newton, Suffolk 366

Old Penrith, Cumbria 153–4
oil, perfumed 344, 346
Oplontis, Italy 341
Oppenländer collection 344
Orsett, Essex 31, 43, 51, 55, 67
Ospringe, Kent 366
Ostia, Italy 298, 300–1, 362
Oulton, Suffolk 322
oven 32, 36–8, 388–9
Owain, son of Urien 430
oxen 231
Oxford, Oxon 371

paint, see pigment
painting, wall 341–2
palaeochannel 7–8, 26, 66–8, 400
Pannonia 318, 325
pars pro toto, see tokenism
partial pots 14, 69–81, 84, 90–3, 97–8, 100, 274–5, 277–9, 281–3, 424, 434, 436–9, 443, see also broken/smashed pottery
pattern mark, potters' 116, 289, 436–7
pedestal, from figurine 104, 110–11, 120, 125–6, 207, 337, 426, 431
pens 197
pente grammai 363, 374
Perge, Turkey 372
Persia 364
phasing see chronology
Picts 167–8
Piddington, Northants 176, 178, 316
pig 101–2, 382–3, 434
pigment 170, 207, 217, 220, 229, 231, 390, see also cosmetics
pins 150–1, 153–4, 160–1, 255, 257, 260, see also shanks with glass heads
pit
  earlier prehistoric 7, 16–21, 48, 51, 436
  Middle Iron Age 20, 26, 30–3, 36, 38, 44–5, 52
  with broken funerary goods 6, 10, 13, 23, 69, 71, 153, **162–7**, 377–8, 423, 433, 437
  with pyre debris 6–7, 10, 13–14, 20, 23, **157–61**, 268, 271–2, 314, 377, 379, 400, 410–14, 418, 423, 426–7, 431, 433, 437
planks 101, 107–10, 117–20, 123, 128–9, 137, 142–6, 154, 172, 185, 197, 260, 384–5, 388, 424, 427
plant remains 17, 75, 85, 167, 384–99, 402, 413, 420–2
plates/platters 69–70, 76–7, 80, 93, 95, 104, 111–14, 123–4, 126–7, 132–4, 138–40, 142, 147, 149, 154–6, 170–4, 201–4, 206, 208, 212–14, 262–4, 270–4, 276–7, 279, 289–96, 305–7, 313–14, 322, 325, 390, 418, 428–32
Pledgdon, Essex 422
Pliny the Elder 170, 445
Polden Hill, Somerset 181

πόλ(ε)ις 361
pollen 394–9
Pollux 361
Pompeii, Italy 135, 137, 151, 185, 231, 240, 243, 245, 299, 321–2, 325, 445
Porta Portese, see Rome
Portesham, Dorset 320
porticos 1, 448
Portland vase 329
posca 298
post-Roman features 13
posts 26, 30, 91, 110, 145, 424, 427, 453
pot-boilers, see Stones burnt
pottery, see also amphoras, beakers, bowls, cups, flagons, jars, lids, mortaria, mug, pattern marks, plates, serving dish, stamps, *tazza*
  Arretine 305–6, 310, 313, 437
  Aylesford–Swarling 56–7
  Belgic 33, 52, 56
  Brockley Hill/Verulamium 269, 281, 437
  broken/smashed 5–6, 11–12, 69–73, 75, 81, 98, 102–3, 111–15, 117, 119, 130–4, 137–40, 149, 154, 274, 277, 281, 283, 302, 304, 346, 402, 410–11, 413, 423–4, 426, 430–2, 434–5, 438–41, 443, 450–1, 455, see also partial pots
  Bronze Age 16–17, 44, 55, 59
  burnt 11, 49, 85, 88, 90, 98, 100, 102–3, 111, 117, 137, 139, 154, 160, 277, 303, 305, 410–11, 413, 431
  burnt residues on 18, 59–60, 63, 65
  Chinnor–Wandlebury 55, 59
  Darmsden–Linton 50, 55, 61
  Early Iron Age 16–17, 69, 71, 48–51, 53, 55–9, 61–2, 74, 81, 450
  East Midlands scored ware 62
  fabric descriptions 14–15, 17, 48–9, 268–71
  Gallo-Belgic wares 14, 75, 81, 91–2, 98, 103–4, 116, 123–4, 126, 142, 147, 149, 154–6, 170–1, 173–5, 201–2, 212–13, 261, 268–9, 271–4, 277, 279, 283, 288–96, 310, 313–14, 436–7
  Gaulish 14, 80–1, 84, 111, 127, 137, 173–5, 213, 258, 261, 268–9, 271–4, 279, 281, 283, 288, 305–7, 405, 409, 418, 436–7, 445, see also Gallo–Belgic
  Glastonbury ware 59
  grog-tempered 47–8, 52, 56–7, 60, 66, 69, 101–4, 127, 139, 141, 146, 148–9, 157, 160–1, 167–9, 171, 268, 270, 277, 279, 314, 405, 435–7
  Middle Iron Age 8, 13, 30–3, 48–66, 69, 71, 73–4, 76, 81, 85, 90, 101, 103, 128, 137, 141–2, 157, 162, 436, 450
    placed deposits 30, 61
    traded wares 59
  Late Iron Age 13, 26, 52–4, 57, 60, 101–3, 160–1, 167–9, 436

Late Iron Age/early Roman 14–15, 47–8, 52, 56–7, 66–7, 69–70, 73, 75–81, 84, 89–92, 95–6, 98, 100–4, 111–17, 119, 123–4, 126–8, 130, 137–42, 146–9, 151, 154–6, 170, 173–6, 197–201, 213–15, 254–6, 258, 260–1, 262–6, 268–314, 405, 418, 435–7
Neolithic 16–18, 51
samian 14, 75, 80, 84, 95, 104, 111, 123, 169–70, 173, 175, 200–4, 206, 211–13, 221, 233, 246, 273–4, 281, 305–7, 310–12, 322, 434, 436–7, 445, 455
Prae Wood, Verulamium, Herts 292
Prag Bubenenič, Czech Republic 326
Publius Cipius Polybius 323
Puckeridge–Braughing, Herts 289–93, 310–13, 317
pyre debris, definition 15
pyres 6, 10–11, 13, 20, 54, 71, 73, 75, 84–92, 98, 102, 104, 106–9, 111, 117, 119–20, 158, 160, 167–8, 170, 173, 197, 266, 297, 302–3, 305–6, 337–8, 345–6, 377–80, 382–8, 390–1, 406, 412–13, 415–16, 422–4, 426–7, 430–4, 437–43, 446–8, 455, *see also* mortuary enclosures
pyxis 254–9, 340, 343–4, 346, 428, 443

Queen's Barrow, Arras, Yorks 82
quern 74, 76, 81
Qustul, Sudan 360, 374

rabbits 382–3
radiocarbon dates 55, 60
ram 185–6, 321, 445
Ravenglass, Cumbria 367
Ravensburgh, Herts 55
recording system 14
red hills 375–7
Remi 452–3, 456
retractor 202, 205, 240–2, 245, 247–8, 251, 350–2, *see also* hooks
Rheims, France 175, 290–3
Rhineland 176, 300, 349
Richborough, Kent 135, 318
Rimini, Italy 238, 242
rings 47, 81–4, 90, 96–7, 100, 165, 201–3, 205, 207–8, 215–16, 228–32, 333, 337, 348, 375, 388, 390, 445, *see also* finger-ring, earring
ritual/ritual deposition 9, 18, 35, 44–5, 61, 67, *see also* funerary rites
Robert ap Ifan 371
robbing 450–1, 455
rods 181, 201–5, 207–10, 224–9, 231, 246, 249–50, 332, 336, 338, 348, 352, 356, 445
Roman river, Essex 59, 389
Rome, Italy 342, 362, 364, 372, 374
roofs 85, 88, 104, 110, 117–19, 130, 137, 145, 149, 158, 424–5, 440, 455
rouge, *see* cosmetics

Roy, A. 390
round-houses 8, 26, 30, 61, 176
Runnymede Bridge, Surrey 50

Saami 370
Sackrau (Zakrzów), Poland 368
St Clare Drive, Colchester 271, 273–4, *see also* Lexden
Saint-Romain-en-Gal, France 298–9
Saint-Paul-Trois-Châteaux, France 151
St Tecla catacombs, *see* Rome
salt 60, 375–7, *see also* briquetage
Samos, Greece 361
sanctuaries, *see* temples
Sandwich, Kent 310–11, 314
Santon, Norfolk 321, 408
Sarawak 180
saucepans 151, 201–2, 204, 206–7, 211–12, 221, 233, 246, 320–3, 325–6, 332, 335, 390, 430, 445
Sawbench, *see* Hockwold cum Wilton
saws 30, 45–7, 202, 205, 237–40, 245, 247–51, 212, 352
scalpels 202, 205, 208, 236–8, 242–3, 245, 247–50, 348, 352
Scandinavia 370–1
scoop probe 202, 243–4, 247–8, 252, 352, 358
seeds 85, 384–7, 420–2
Seega 364
Segontium, *see* Caernarvon
Seine, river, France 326
selection 425–6, 451
Seneca 365, 444
Sept-Saulx, France 175
services 172, 202, 221, 233, 246, 326, 427–8, 443
serving dish 325
shafts 7, 11–13, 24, 82, 84, 265–6, 385–7, 393, 423, 433, 440–3, *see also* barrels
shale objects 217, 273, 405, 407
shanks, iron, with glass heads 90, 142, 149–50, 153–7, 254–6, 260, 330, 443
sheep 43, 85, 90, 171, 350, 382–3, 430, 434
Sheepen, Colchester 1, 154, 164, 215–16, 220, 268, 274, 279–80, 288–9, 291–2, 298, 306, 311, 313, 315–16, 318–20, 323–5, 341, 344–6, 376, 402, 405, 409, 418, 425, 431, 445, *see also* Camulodunum
sheet metal 47, 85, 89–90, 94–5, 121, 159, 184, 195–8, 200–1, 217, 232–6, 260, 262, 337, 390, 402, 405–9
Shefford, Beds 321
Shepton Mallett, Somerset 59
shield 12, 171–2, 180–4, 195, 232, 332, 335, 347, 439, 445–6
Shillington, Beds 315
shipwrecks 298–300, 302
shrubs 399

Silchester, Hants 289–90, 311, 314, 324
silver 135, 141, 156, 164, 310, 312, 314–15, 325, 337–8, 375, 430
Site A 4–6
Site B 4–6
Site C 4–5, 7
Site D 4–5, 7, 13, 274, 400–22, 426, 428
Site E 4–5, 7, 400
Skeleton Green, Herts 367
slag 45–7, 70, 73, 327–8
slot CF96 7, 11–13, 83–4, 339–40, **266–7**, 393, 424–5, 440–1
Slough House Farm, Essex 43, 61–2
Smyrna (Izmir), Turkey 361
Snailwell, Cambs 257
sodok-apit 369
Spain 299–300
spears 7–9, 12, 66–8, 171–2, 180–1, 183–5, 439
Speyer, Germany 295
spices 323
spindle 151
spindlewhorls 150
Spong Hill, Norfolk 62
sponge 322
spoons 142, 150–1, 155–6, 332, 336
Springfield, Essex 17–18
Springhead, Kent 240
spouts 104, 110–11, 119–20, 125–6, 224, 320–1, 323–6, 337, 445, *see also* strainer bowls
stamps, brooch-makers' 176–8, 180
stamps, potter's 14, 123, 126, 173, 175, 212–15, 261, 264, 269, 272, 288–96, 305–7, 436–7
Stanfordbury, Beds 163, 181, 257, 322
Stansted, Essex 31, 50, 55, 57, 61, 233–4, 269, 289, 294, 306–7, 427
Stanway Hall, Colchester 13
status 1, 82, 184, 191, 304–6, 312–13, 320, 344, 346, 348, 350, 374–5, 377, 384, 423–4, 428, 430, 434, 444–6, 450, 456
Stock, Essex 60
stone object 30, 45–7
stones, burnt 16–21, 31–2, 51, 413, 415–16, 420–1
Stradonice, Czech Republic 178
strainer bowl 120, 201–4, 206–8, 211–12, 221–4, 233, 246, 320–1, 323–6, 332, 335–6, 338, 390, 394–8, 398, 444–5, *see also* spouts
strap-fittings 74, 76, 80, 85–90, 93, 96–7, 104, 117, 120–1, 125, 127, 337
Strasbourg, France 291
straw 202–3, 207, 233, 390, 424
structural clay 36–8, 154, 389–90, *see also* daub
studs 85–6, 88–90, 93–4, 96–7, 100, 142, 150, 153–9, 162, 190–8, 200–1, 206, 229–30, 232–6, 260, 333, 337, 390
styli 151, 197, 199, 224, 228, 311

Suessiones 452, 456
Suffolk 50, 56, 62–3, 190, 315
surgical instruments 12, 202–5, 207–10, 224, 231, 236–52, 300, 348, 350–2, 356, 358, 423, 444–5, *see also* forceps, hooks, knives, needles, retractor, saws, scalpels, scoop probe
Surrey 190
Sussex 61, 190
Switzerland 33, 316, 445
swords 184, 430, 439, 446
symbol 18, 35–6, 45, 169, 180–1, 215, 229, 231, 317, 339, 445–6, *see also* ritual, funerary rites

tablut 369–70
Tacitus 228–9
tafl 364, 367–72, *see also* brandubh, hnefatafl, tablut, tawl-bwrdd
Tarmac 1, 6–7
Tarraconensis (Spain) 298
Tasciovanus 455–6
tawl-bwrdd 370–1
tazza 311, 314
teas, herbal 207, 326, 396–8, 429
temples 1, 12, 83, 215, 228, 266, 339, 447–9
tenorite 169–70
terrets 231
textiles 167, 169, 172, 180, 185, 191, 202, 207, 224–6, 228–9, 231, 236, 246, 251, 254, 258, 321–2, 347–52, 388
theatre 1
Thérouanne, France 324
Thetford, Norfolk 43, 316
Thornborough, Bucks 321
Thorsberg, Germany 349
three men's morris 368
Thuburbo Maius, Tunisia 374
thyrsus 221, 322
Tiberius 236, 290, 344, 456
tile 299, 361, 416
timber(s) 37, 85, 88, 110, 118, 129, 137, 142, 145–6, 149, 158, 424, *see also* planks, wood
Titelberg, the, Luxembourg 191, 291
toe-rings 165
Toftanes Eysturoy, Faroes 370
toilet implements 150–1, 342, 344, *see also* cosmetic sets, mirrors, nail–cleaner, spoons
tokenism 254, 433, 450, 455
Tongeren, Belgium 151
Toulouse, France 197
Tournai, Belgium 151
trays 151, 153, 171, 197–8, 201–3, 206, 221, 230, 232–6, 322, 333, 360, 390
trees 85, 385–93, 395, 397–9, 421
Treveri 176, 316, 452, 455
Trier, Germany 135, 175, 290–1, 344, 362
Trinovantes 215, 311, 324–5, 456

Trondheim, Norway 370–1
Trowse, Norfolk 50, 59
Trumpington, Cambridgeshire 315
tubs 158, 162
tubers 384–7, 420–1
turf 119, 142, 384, 398–9, 440, 443
Turner Rise, Colchester 426
tweezers, *see* forceps

unguent bottles 127, 130, 135, 138, 140, 142, 148, 150–1, 155–6, 170, 172, 176–7, 260–1, 340, 342, 344–6, 405, 409, 436
Usk, Gwent 345

Valkenburg, Netherlands 341
Valladas, *see* Saint-Paul-Trois-Châteaux
Vallöby, Sweden 368
Varro 361
vat 430
vehicle 446, *see also* chariot burials
Vellocatus 444
veneer, *see* inlay
Venutius 444
verdigris 167
Verlamion, *see* Verulamium
Verulamium, St Albans, Herts 2, 5, 269, 274, 305, 311, 369, 374, 456, *see also* Folly Lane, King Harry Lane, pottery/Brockley Hill, Prae Wood, Wheathampstead
vessels, *see* basins, beakers, bowls, cups, flagons, glassware, jars, jugs, miniature vessels, mortaria, mug, plates/platters, pottery, *pyxis*, saucepan, services, serving dish, strainer bowls, unguent bottles
Vieux-les-Asfeld, France 453–6
Villeneuve, France 80
Vimose, Denmark 372, 374
Vindolanda, Northumberland 249, 349
Vindonissa, Switzerland 127
Virunum, Austria 326

Wales 290, 358, 371, 373, 375
walls 425
Wanborough, Wiltshire 412
Wandlebury, Cambridgeshire 59
Wardy Hill, Cambridgeshire 60, 62
warfare 181, 439
Warrior's burial BF64 5–6, 11–13, 71, 73, 116, 119–20, 150–1, **170–96**, 197, 202, 212–13, 217, 257, 272–3, 289–91, 294–5, 297–8, 300–1, 304–6, 314–16, 319–22, 329–32, 335, 337, 340–4, 346–7, 349, 359–60, 366, 377–8, 382–3, 390–1, 427–31, 433–7, 439–42, 444–7, 451
warrior graves, general 439, *see also* Kelvedon Warrior burial
water 273
wealth 428

weapons 171, 191, 439, *see also* artillery bolt, lance, spears, shields, swords
Wederath-Belginum, Germany 135, 249–50, 344, 453
weeds 384 399
Wehringen, Germany 249
wells 425
Welshpool, Powys 321–2
Welwyn, Welwyn Garden City, Hertfordshire 82, 120, 181, 186–7, 190, 233, 310–12, 314, 325–6, 366, 369, 375, 429
Welwyn-type burials 257, 320, 430, 451, *see also* Doctor's burial, Warrior's burial
Wessex 35, 61
Western Isles, Scotland 60
Westhampnett, West Sussex 56, 85, 88, 162, 165, 315, 427, 432
West Midlands 35
Weston Turville, Buckinghamshire 169
West Stow, Suffolk 43–4, 62, 270
West Sussex, *see* Sussex
West Thurrock, Essex 151
Wheathampstead, Herts 398
White Colne, Essex 422
Willington, Derbyshire 38
Winchester, Hants 135, 150–1, 190, 216, 257, 314, 366
wine 151, 273, 297–8, 301, 304, 320–2, 325–6, 398, 418, 429–30
Winnall Down, Hampshire 43–4
Witham, Essex 51, 62, *see also* Ivy Chimneys
writing, *see* graffiti, literacy, writing equipment
writing equipment 151, 199, 257
wood 101–2, 109–10, 116–22, 128–9, 136, 142–6, 152–3, 158, 162–3, 165–7, 172, 178, 184–5, 190, 197, 199, 202, 206–7, 217, 219–21, 229, 232–4, 252–3, 255, 260, 262, 321, 352, 384–5, 388, 407, 422, 427, *see also* charcoal, planks, timber, wooden objects, woodworking
wooden objects 69, 76, 82, 104, 107–8, 110, 117, 119–20, 126, 128, 142, 150, 153, 157, 163, 171, 180, 197, 201–12, 217–20, 229, 230–6, 246, 257, 262, 265–6, 273, 322, 352–75, 430, 432, *see also* barrels, boxes, chest, game boards
Woodham Walter, Essex 37, 61
woodworking 45
Wooing of Etain, The 430
wool 43, 251, 347–52

XII scripta/alea 358, 360–2, 364–5, 368, 372–4

York, Yorks 135, 190, 366–7, 370
Yorkshire 349
Ypres Road, Colchester 61, 436

Zurich, Switzerland 361